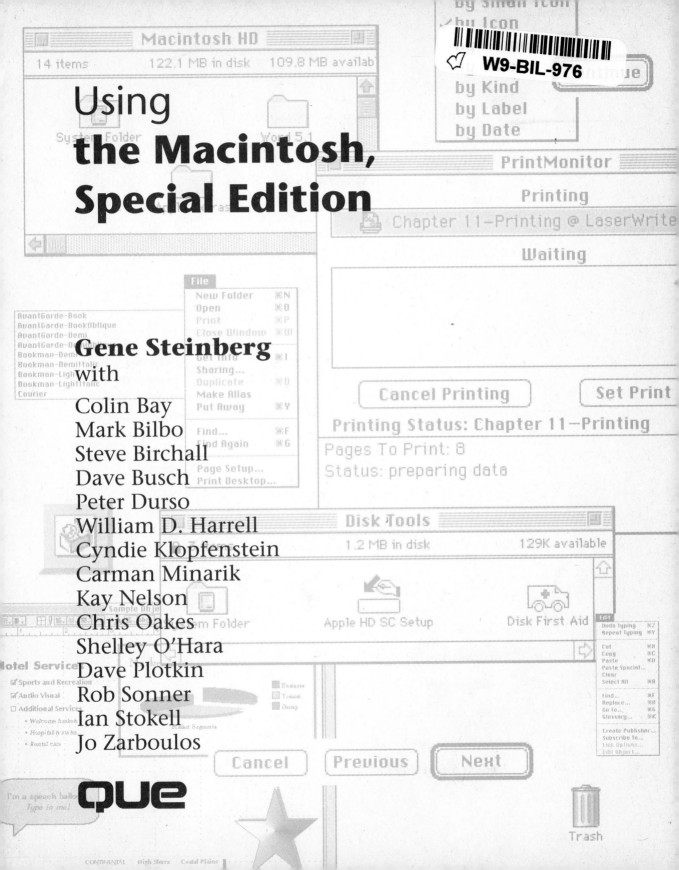

Using the Macintosh, Special Edition

Gene Steinberg

with

Colin Bay
Mark Bilbo
Steve Birchall
Dave Busch
Peter Durso
William D. Harrell
Cyndie Klopfenstein
Carman Minarik
Kay Nelson
Chris Oakes
Shelley O'Hara
Dave Plotkin
Rob Sonner
Ian Stokell
Jo Zarboulos

que

Using the Macintosh

Copyright © 1994 by Que® Corporation

Library of Congress Catalog No.: 94-67039

ISBN: 1-56529-826-8

97   96   95   94   6   5   4   3   2   1

Interpretation of the printing code: the rightmost double-digit number is the year of the book's printing; the rightmost single-digit number, the number of the book's printing. For example, a printing code of 94-1 shows that the first printing of the book occurred in 1994.

Screen reproductions in this book were created using Capture from Mainstay, Camarillo, CA.

Publisher: David P. Ewing

Associate Publisher: Corinne Walls

Publishing Director: Brad R. Koch

Managing Editor: Anne Owen

Product Marketing Manager: Greg Wiegand

Credits

Publishing Manager
Thomas H. Bennett

Acquisitions Editor
Nancy Stevenson

Product Director
Stephanie Gould

Production Editor
Colleen Rainsberger

Editors
Elsa Bethanis
Danielle Bird
Kelli Brooks
Noelle Gasco
Mitzi Gianakos
Patrick Kanouse
Mike La Bonne
Chris Nelson
Maureen Schneeberger
Linda Seifert

Technical Editors
Todd Knowlton
Beth Kohn Keister
Donna Minarik
Michael Watson

Figure Specialist
Cari Ohm

Book Designer
Amy Peppler-Adams

Editorial Assistant
Theresa Mathias

Acquistions Assistant
Ruth Slates

Production Team
Steve Adams
Angela D. Bannan
Cameron Booker
Cheryl Cameron
Amy Cornwell
Stephanie Davis
Karen Dodson
Chad Dressler
Terri Edwards
DiMonique Ford
Bob LaRoche
Beth Lewis
Steph Mineart
Wendy Ott
G. Alan Palmore
Nanci Sears Perry
Kaylene Rieman
Caroline Roop
Clair Schweinler
Michael Thomas
Suzanne Tully

Indexer
Bront Davis

Composed in *Stone Serif* and *MCPdigital* by Que Corporation

Acknowledgments

It would have been impossible for me to have written my modest contribution to this book without the help and ready advice from scores of industry professionals and experienced Mac users. I am especially grateful to Ric Ralston of APS Technologies (the hard drive manufacturer) for putting up with my incessant questions about the ins and outs of hard drive lore and SCSI hookups.

I also wish to thank the following who went out of their way to provide the help and counsel I needed in writing my sections of *Using the Macintosh*: Rich Blanchard and Patricia J. Pane of Adobe Systems, Inc.; Leonard Rosenthol of Aladdin Systems Inc.; Hans Gomez, Steve McAdoo, and Abbo Peterson of Aldus Corporation; Tim Barwick, David Liberman, and Craig Mayo of America Online, Inc.; Amy Bonetti, Kristin Brownstone, Mary Devincenzi, Jeffrey Robbin, Noah Price, and Eric Slosser of Apple Computer, Inc.; John Catalano of Casa Blanca Works, Inc.; Greg Cornelison of Claris Corporation; David Jones of Delrina (Canada) Corporation; Martin Doettling of Frame Technology Corporation; Jeff Dripps of The Freesoft Company; Amy Bayersdorfer of Global Village Communication, Inc.; Pieter Paulson, the Mac guru at Nike, Inc.; Edwina Riblet of Nisus Software, Inc.; Tom Appleton-DeMoulin, Kevin Dormeyer, Elizabeth Jones, and John Maggiora of Quark, Inc.; Bill Evans of Manhattan Graphics; Paul Celestin of Software Ventures Corporation; Steve Meyers of STF Technologies; and Mike Tippets of WordPerfect Corporation.

Finally, a grateful thank you to Tom Bennett, Patty Brooks, Stephanie D. Gould, and Nancy Stevenson of Que Corporation and our top-notch technical editors, Todd Knowlton, Beth Kohn Keister, Donna Minarik, and Michael Watson for allowing me free reign to do it my way. And, of course, much love always to my nuclear family, Barbara and Grayson, for letting me do my thing without complaint.

Gene Steinberg

Scottsdale, Arizona

Trademarks

About the Authors

Gene Steinberg first studied broadcasting in school and then worked for a number of years as a disc jockey and newscaster. Gene is now a full-time writer and Macintosh software and systems consultant. His published work includes feature articles and product reviews for *Macworld*.

Colin Bay is a technical communicator and user advocate who has worked with several major software developers and publishers. He and his family live happily in Portland, Oregon.

Mark Bilbo has in turn been a technical support representative, a programmer, a consultant/support person, nearly everything else for a television show, and a full-time freelance writer. Chased by smog, gridlock, and traffic jams, he fled Los Angeles to return to his home in East Texas and even now plans for the day that he and his Mac will live deep in the woods where only the birds can find them.

Steve Birchall has divided his time between music and technology throughout his life. He studied composition with Burrill Phillips, Jeno Takacs, and John Cage and taught music at several small colleges. He has written two symphonies, concertos for various instruments, and much chamber music. After completing a Doctor of Musical Arts degree in composition at the University of Cincinnati (with previous study at the Eastman School of Music and DePauw University), he became active in analog electronic music and multimedia productions. In the mid-1970s, before sampling and hard disk-based recording, he wrote a series of compositions (*Frogdreams*, *Souvenirs from Spain*, and *Postcards from Nova Scotia*) using recorded sounds altered electronically and mixed with purely electronic sounds. Later, he worked in audio retailing and management. After that, he turned to magazine publishing and editing, serving as Assistant Editor at *The Audio Amateur* and *Speaker Builder*, Technical Editor of *SoftSide* and Editor-in-Chief of *Digital Audio*. As a founding partner of Hottwitz & Associates, he works extensively in the Macintosh industry and was involved in the launch of *MacUser* and the *MacWarehouse Catalog*. He served as Secretary of the Boston Section of the Audio Engineering Society for four years and was Chairman during 1993–1994.

Dave Busch was the first person to win "Best Book" honors twice from the Computer Press Association. A no-nonsense approach (tempered with light humor) in his 43 books have helped to translate confusing computer concepts into simple yet in-depth descriptions for the average computer user.

Peter Durso has been writing about mainframe and personal computers for users since 1983. He worked for a major telecommunications company in the Northeast for 22 years, until late 1993. A Mac maven, a DOS/Windows capable artist/techie, he now resides with his wife and two daughters in Wilmington, North Carolina, where he plays great electric blues guitar whenever he can.

William D. Harrell is a writer and desktop publisher. He has written nine computer books, including co-authoring *Using QuarkXpress 3.3,* Special Edition. He has also written numerous magazine articles for computer publications including *Publish*, *PC World*, and *Windows Magazine*.

Cyndie Klopfenstin has a 20-year background in the printing and pre-press industries. She has worked for the past eight years as a corporate trainer for companies that are converting to electronic pre-press. She also produces a series of videos and other books geared toward the electronic graphics community.

Carman Minarik manages the computer services and training department for an Intelligent Electronics reseller in Midland, Michigan whose clients range from Fortune 100 companies to small businesses to individual users. He has written and presented training materials for most major operating systems and software packages for more than 7 years and is a member of the American Society for Training and Development. Helping computer users become more productive is a commitment Carman takes very seriously. His motto is "They're smart enough if I'm good enough."

Carman lives is Midland with his wife, son, and cat. His off-line time is spent enjoying his family, camping (where there are no computers), and listening to music.

Chris Oakes is a freelance writer trapped in Mill Valley, California. Formerly the managing editor of *Computer Currents* magazine, he now writes the magazine's "Creative Mac" and "Macintosh Way" columns. He also writes for *Morph's Outpost*, *Home Office Computing*, and *Information Week* magazines, as well as the ZiffNet/Mac Online service. His Mac beat includes Power Macintosh, telecommunications, the Internet, music MIDI, and multimedia.

Shelley O'Hara owns her own technical writing and training company in Indianapolis, Indiana. She has written over 25 computer books, including the best-selling Que books—*Easy Windows, Easy DOS, Easy 1-2-3,* and *Easy WordPerfect*. O'Hara has a B.A. in English from the University of South Carolina and an M.A. in English from the University of Maryland.

Dave Plotkin is a Business Area Analyst with Integral Systems in Walnut Creek, California. He has extensive experience in designing and implementing databases, both at the desktop and on Client Server systems. He writes extensively for various computer periodicals, and his favorite editor is his wife, Marisa.

Rob Sonner is an expert in computer imaging and is currently employed by HSC Software in Santa Monica, California, working in Product Development and Support. He also works for America Online as a Forum Assistant for the Macintosh Multimedia Forum. In prior lives, Rob has worked for Apple Computer, Inc., Viking Office Products, and World Media, Inc., as well as writing for the *Los Angeles Times* and the *LA Weekly*.

Ian Stokell is a freelance writer and editor living in the Sierra Foothills of northern California with his wife and three children. He is also the Managing Editor of *Newsbytes News Network*, an international daily newswire covering the computer and telecommunications industries. His writing career began with a 1981 article published in the UK's *New Statesman* and has since encompassed over 1,300 articles in a variety of computing and non-computing publications. He has also written on assignment for such magazines as *PC World*. He is currently seeking representation for two completed novels and a screenplay.

Jo Zarboulas has lived in several places—from California to Washington D.C., Ghana to Greece—and had several occupations—from elementary school teacher to proofreader to textbook editor. She is now settled both geographically—she lives in Austin, Texas—and occupationally—she's a technical writer. In 1987, Jo first put her hands on a computer, her son's Macintosh 512K. As he explained to her the difference between the desktop and an application, Jo couldn't imagine that just three years later, her two sons would form a company to write and sell software for the Mac, and that she would write the company's first software manual. Or that she would go on to write about software for a living!

Contents at a Glance

Troubleshooting/Maintenance

Appendixes

Contents

II System 7 Essentials 53

4 What's New in System 7.5 55

5 Understanding the Desktop and Finder 67

6 Using System 7 for the Performa and At Ease 87

7 Organizing Your Files, Folders, and Disks   109

8 All about Fonts   143

III Customizing Your Macintosh   241

11 Changing the Look of Your Desktop   243

12 Creating and Modifying Icons   267

13 Music and Sound   279

IV Macintosh Software 357

16 Word Processing 359

18 Spreadsheets 461

19 Databases 511

24 Using CD-ROM Drives and Software   685

25 Utilities   711

26 Personal and Business Management 733

27 Games and Education 757

28 Shareware and Other Cool Stuff   795

31 Using eWorld 887

32 Connecting to the Internet 911

VI The Mac at Work   935

33 Networking   937

34 Data Exchange   977

35 On The Road 995

38 Preventive Maintenance   **1103**

Introduction

Has it been a decade?

In January 1984, millions of viewers watched the Super Bowl. Among the usual run of forgettable automobile and soft drink commercials, one commercial stood out from the pack. In fact, it changed the world of personal computing as we know it today.

The commercial was shown only one time. It featured a woman wearing a Macintosh T-shirt who proceeded to smash an image that was meant to depict the enemy, an IBM PC. Thus began the advertising campaign that introduced the Mac to an unsuspecting world. (It is ironic that Apple today works hand-in-hand with IBM on the PowerPC and other development projects. How things have changed!)

The original product described in that commercial, the Macintosh 128K, seemed an unlikely product to start a worldwide revolution in the personal computer industry. It housed the computer and a small black-and-white screen in a single small case. On the surface it didn't look terribly impressive. It had a single 3-1/2 inch disk drive, and no expansion slots of any kind—not for additional memory, a hard drive, or an additional monitor. At a suggested list price of $2500, some people thought it was too expensive for what it offered. Besides, aside from the software that was bundled with it, there wasn't very much else available.

Many people were skeptical about the prospects for success of this odd little product. Not only did it look different, but it worked differently.

Until the Macintosh, experienced computer users did their work by entering commands in text form on their computer's keyboard. The task of learning how to use such a computer was truly daunting to beginners. You had to take special courses, or plough through long, thick, complex manuals containing obscure terminology to figure out how to make your computer do what you wanted it to do.

Compared to these other computers, using the Macintosh was like traveling to another universe. Its interface was presented to you in images. You did your work on a desktop, and the software and files you worked with were represented by icons, featuring fancy artwork that identified the kind of file you were using. Instead of entering commands on your keyboard, you used a little plastic pointing device called a mouse to transport a cursor across the screen, and you clicked on one of the icons to activate a particular function, such as opening up a program. When you wanted to organize your files, you put them in a folder, and when you wanted to get rid of the file, you transported (dragged) it to the icon of a trash can on your screen.

Instead of having to seek out listings of the commands needed to operate your software, you clicked a white bar at the top of your screen to select the label identifying the type of function you wanted to activate. A pull-down menu displayed a list of commands to choose from.

To simplify matters, the manufacturer of this product, Apple Computer, issued strong guidelines to software developers so that their products would look and feel the same. That way, a novice user, having mastered the essentials of pointing and clicking, could learn new software easily and become productive in a shorter period of time.

Additionally, Apple offered a host of opportunities for you to customize the look of your desktop work area to your personal taste. For example, you could choose to use icons or to display a directory of titles. This near-infinite level of opportunities to customize your work environment gave the computer a warm, friendly feel, and offered folks who feared technology an easy path to learning this technological marvel.

The Early Days

It has been written elsewhere (and it's become akin to a modern folklore) how Apple's engineers in 1979 visited Xerox's Palo Alto Research Center and had a gander at a computer interface called Smalltalk, which was being used on a prototype of a never-released product called the Alto. Smalltalk used pop-up menus to activate command functions. You used that little plastic device, called the *mouse*, to drag files across the screen.

Like all true creative artists, the folks at Apple picked up many ideas from this unique new computer interface, incorporated changes and additions of their own and, after a five year period of gestation, introduced the first Macintosh computer.

The Macintosh revolution was slow in coming, and the computer didn't ring up stratospheric sales overnight.

It took a few years for "the little computer that could" to grow up. More memory options were added, hard drives to store additional files became available. Like the manufacturers of the rival DOS computers, Apple introduced modular Macintosh models with expansion slots. You could now add video display adapters, network communication boards, and other options. Color was part of the bargain, too. As software development mushroomed, all sorts of categories of products became available on the Mac.

The Word Spreads

One of the first fields to embrace the Macintosh was the typesetting industry. Up through the mid-1980s, a typesetting studio would produce their work on mini computers costing tens of thousands of dollars. In order to make the computers work, you had to enter long chains of complex commands on a keyboard and then check the results of your labors on a television screen that consisted solely of text and text-based commands. While a skilled typographer could usually visualize the outcome of all these command line decisions, the true results of these labors were not known until the job was printed with a photo imaging device. And sometimes things didn't look quite the way they were supposed to look.

The Macintosh brought typesetting to the desktop. Instead of requiring specially trained technicians to work on those high cost, hard-to-use mini computers, you could do work of similar quality on a personal computer. The Mac's screen would display the exact properties of the printed page before you printed a document, thus introducing the concept of what-you-see-is-what-you-get (or *WYSIWYG,* for short).

Slowly but surely, that strange looking desktop computer began to replace those older expensive composition computers.

Yes, the Macintosh had truly arrived.

The Sincerest Form of Flattery

It didn't take long for the folks on the DOS side of the world to take notice. Windows and other graphical user interfaces (sometimes called GUI for short) proliferated, thus legitimizing the Macintosh approach to personal computing as the right one.

In fact, most personal computers you buy today, even though they are not made by Apple Computer, use some sort of graphical interface and are equipped with a mouse or pointing device of some sort. Many of the software products you buy are offered in versions that will work on a Mac or on a PC running Windows.

The Macintosh has another important feature that has yet to be matched on the PC side of the universe—the concept of plug and play. With a Mac, you attach a printer, and it's recognized by the computer immediately. If you want to add memory or storage devices, it can be done within minutes, with little fuss, and with little need to configure anything to get it all to work the next time you switch everything on.

A More Complicated World

Long gone are the days when the number of software products you could buy could be counted on the fingers of one hand, and where the variety of Macintosh models offered could be accounted for in the same fashion.

Today, thousands of software options and many hundreds of hardware add-ons are available, allowing the Macintosh to perform a wide variety of tasks, such as digital audio and video (including motion picture special effects); billing, record-keeping, and scheduling at a doctor's office; and generating the pages for many of the most popular books, magazines, and newspapers.

Whenever you want to buy a new computer, add a printer, or simply upgrade the equipment you have, you are presented with a bewildering array of choices—and you don't just choose the software and hardware add-ons.

Apple Computer has advanced from introducing one or two models a year, to as many as half a dozen or more every two or three months. You have a choice of all-in-one Macs geared for the consumer and educational markets, modular (expandable) Macs providing performance that rivals high-priced computer workstations, and a line of portable models that you can pack in a small bag and take with you on the road.

You can buy a new Macintosh at a computer reseller, a business supply supermarket, a consumer electronics store and even from a mail-order catalog.

So many decisions to make!

Using the Macintosh, Special Edition, is designed to help you cope with this vastly more complicated world of personal computing. Que Publishing has assembled a group of writers with the collective experience of many decades in Mac computing to help you learn how to use your Macintosh more efficiently, select the right software with which to do the work you want to do, and to make the right choices when it comes time to purchase your new computer, printer, a hard drive and other accessories.

In order to keep you abreast of the newest developments in Macintosh computing, both from the hardware and software standpoint, we've had the chance to take a first-hand, behind-the-scenes look at the newest developments from Apple Computer and the major software publishers.

We've also provided special coverage about Apple's newest line of PowerPC computers, and we've even compared them with the fastest PC computers that use Intel's Pentium chip. There's a preview of the newest version of the Macintosh operating system, System 7.5, and a complete profile of some of the newest versions of your favorite software products in the pages that follow.

Who Can Use This Book?

Using the Macintosh is designed for both the beginning Macintosh owner and the experienced user.

This book helps you purchase the right hardware and the right software to assemble a Macintosh system to do the work you want to do. When it comes time to customize the look and feel of your Mac to your own personal taste, *Using the Macintosh* teaches you how. For any problems you encounter along the way, this book contains scores of tips and tricks and helpful shortcuts to help you get over the rough spots.

If you're already experienced at Mac computing, you'll find a wealth of new information that goes far beyond what you'll find in product brochures and instruction manuals, information that will help make your computing experience more effective, more fun, and as trouble-free as possible.

How This Book Is Organized

We want this book to be easy and fun for you to read, so we've organized *Using The Macintosh* into seven parts, each of which deals with a specific area of Mac computing. You may want to read this book from cover to cover. Or you may want to look up specific topics you want to learn more about. This book makes it easy for you to seek out those topics.

Part I, "About the Macintosh," discusses the Macintosh line, beginning with the original 128K back in 1984, and working up through the present Power Macintosh models. In addition, this part of the book gives you a few hints about what sort of models Apple is expected to introduce in the years to come. An entire chapter is devoted to the interface that gives the Mac its unique personality and easy-to-use quality.

Part II, "System 7 Essentials," provides a comprehensive look at the Macintosh operating system, the software that directs everything you do on your computer. First, Chapter 4 reviews System 7.5, Apple's newest system version, and later chapters explain the ins and outs of the Desktop and Finder. This part of the book explains the simplified system software that ships with Apple's consumer-oriented computer line, the Performa, and you get advice on how to organize your files and disks. The other chapters cover the most effective way to acquire and use fonts and explain how to share data with other applications. These chapters probe deep into the Macintosh's unique printing architecture and tell you what Apple has up its sleeve for the future.

Part III, "Customizing Your Macintosh," tells you how to change the look of your Mac's Desktop (for now, consider the Macintosh Desktop a blackboard that you can write on and customize precisely to your taste). The chapters in this part provide easy-to-master techniques for creating and customizing file icons. The Mac's multimedia capabilities, which allow you to easily work with music and sound on your computer, are also discussed.

If you're a fan of the various *Star Trek* TV shows and motion pictures, no doubt you're familiar with their ubiquitous talking computers that respond to spoken commands. Well, Apple Computer has begun to add similar capabilities to some Macintosh models. Part III tells you how you can talk to your Mac and have it talk back to you (after a fashion). And finally, all those handy keyboard shortcuts that you can use to traverse your Mac's desktop without ever touching your mouse are listed. You also learn a little about how to use macros, which allow you to record a series of steps and then play them back with keyboard commands.

Your Macintosh can't get any work done without software, so Part IV contains a comprehensive review of hundreds of Mac software products. This part of the chapter covers word processing, business graphics, spreadsheets, databases, integrated software, desktop publishing, drawing and painting, digital photography and desktop video, CD-ROM software, utilities, personal and business management, games and education, and the very interesting software gems that are available as shareware. The chapters contain profiles of the most popular Mac software products as well as our recommendations as to which ones are best for you.

After you master your Mac and its software, you'll want to consider joining the information superhighway. In Part V, "Reaching Out," you learn how to buy and set up a modem (a device that helps you telecommunicate with a remote computer or online service). The most popular communications software is described. You tour the major online services—America Online, CompuServe, and eWorld. You also take a brief tour of the largest online service in the world, the Internet.

When you use your Macintosh in the workplace, you usually do not work in isolation. You need to network your computer to other Macs, printers, and computers running DOS and Windows. Part VI, "The Mac at Work," tells you the most efficient ways to hook up your Macs to a network. This part of the book explains such networking schemes as LocalTalk and Ethernet. After you're networked, you'll often need to exchange data with DOS and Windows computers, too. This part tells you how. When it comes time to take your work on the road, you'll want to consider one of Apple's award-winning PowerBook computers, which is described model by model. The chapters in this part also offer techniques for staying in touch when you're on the road. And if you are doing all or part of your work at home, you'll want to read the suggestions for setting up your home office.

The Mac is essentially a trouble-free computer, but with so many installation possibilities and thousands of software products from which to choose, sometimes things just don't work as they should. Part VII, "Troubleshooting and Preventive Maintenance," provides advice on how to solve common Mac problems. You also get many tips on preventive maintenance so that you can take steps to help prevent things from going wrong.

Technobabble?

It's inevitable that users of a personal computer will use words and phrases that may seem strange to the novice. We've tried as much as possible to avoid using terms that are difficult to understand. Where we must use these terms to describe a particular function of your Mac, or the software it uses, we try to define the terms. The end of this book contains a comprehensive glossary so that you can quickly learn the meaning of the words that may not seem familiar to you.

This book is written in a casual, conversational manner. We don't want you to feel you are in a classroom environment when you read this book; we want you to feel as if we are sitting across the room talking to you while you explore the many nooks and crannies of Macintosh computing. We are, all of us, Mac users just like you. We've learned lots of new things about our computers in researching and writing this book, and we hope that *Using the Macintosh* will be a source for you to learn more about your Mac. We want you to learn how to make your Mac run most efficiently and use this knowledge as a jumping point to explore the tremendous creative potential of the product that literally changed the world of computing.

Gene Steinberg

Scottsdale, Arizona
June, 1994

Part I

About the Macintosh

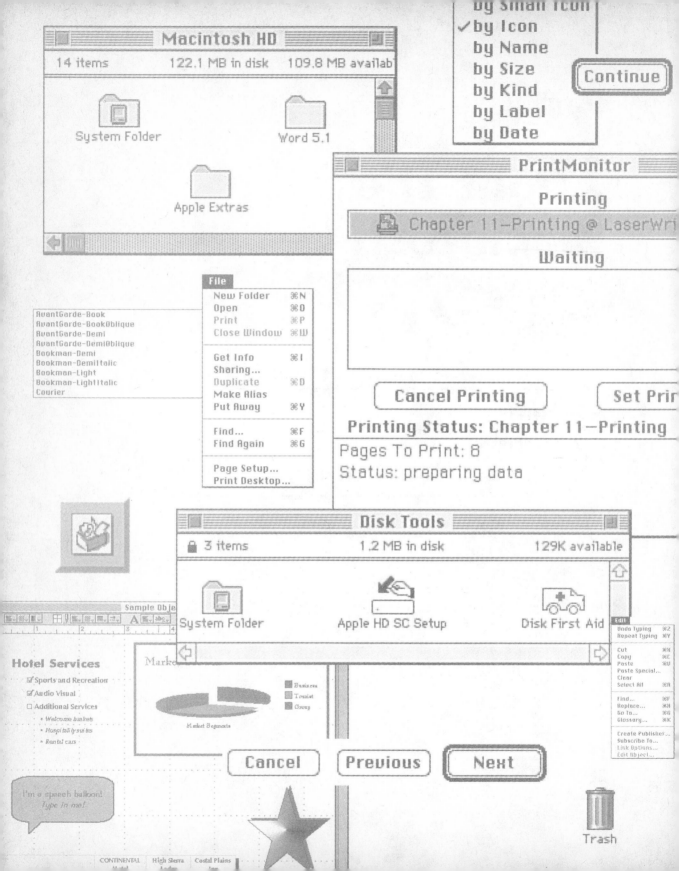

Chapter 1

Macs of the Past

by William D. Harrell

This chapter examines the innovations and pitfalls of Apple's rise to greatness through the development and manufacturing of the Mac. The chapter discusses the following topics:

- The pre-Macintosh Lisa, a bold experiment that set the stage for Macintosh

- The first Mac, an all-in-one unit intended to meet the needs of all users

- Developments by other companies that influenced decisions at Apple

- The desktop publishing explosion

- The influence of the Mac PowerBook on the world of notebook computing

A Decade of Trend Setting

The Mac—the "computer with the smiling face"—began ten years ago as a self-contained, all-in-one machine. Since then, the Mac has changed the personal computing world as well as the personality of computers.

Apple's two-pronged approach to computing—the self-contained unit (keyboard and monitor built-in) and fun, easy-to-use computers—contradicted all conventional wisdom.

The Mac's graphical interface revolutionized the way we use our desktop. In fact, it was the Macintosh's use of the desktop metaphor that inspired the Windows revolution in the IBM-compatible world. Because of the cute little box Apple called *Macintosh,* more people use computers, and we all have more fun and endure less tedium doing so.

Life Before the Mac

What set the Mac apart from other computers was the concept of a human-centered computer, a machine that works the way people do. The Mac did away with esoteric commands and dark screens. The hardware and software behind the technology were not new, however.

As early as 30 years before the Mac's debut, many computer companies experimented with graphical interfaces. Perhaps the most significant forerunners were pre-personal computers experiments at Xerox's Palo Alto Research Center. In fact, several accounts of Apple Computer's history and biographies of Steve Jobs, one of the company founders, place him at the Palo Alto Research Center on more than one occasion before the development of the Macintosh.

Apple's first attempt at the human-centered graphical interface was in 1983, an all-in-one machine the company called *Lisa*. The Lisa was a grand experiment, but at $10,000 per unit, it had little chance to succeed.

The Lisa computer, shown in figure 1.1, introduced virtually every feature of the Mac interface: the graphical user interface (GUI), use of the mouse, the desktop metaphor, pull-down menus, graphical dialog boxes and more. But not many Lisas were sold. Depending on your point of view, it was either an expensive bomb or a bold experiment. Either way, Apple learned some hard lessons from creating and manufacturing Lisa, and they used this knowledge to develop the Macintosh.

Fig. 1.1
The Lisa computer introduced virtually every feature of the Mac interface.

The Original Mac

The original Mac had 128K of memory. Compared to the IBM-PC's 512K, this was small indeed. But remember that most of the Mac's operating system burned into the system's ROM, which meant that a good portion of the 128K was not available for programs to use. Even by 1984's standards, however, 128K doesn't provide much room for program code to stretch out. Quickly following the 128K came the 512K and, a bit later, the 512Ke. Figure 1.2 shows the first Mac.

Fig. 1.2
The first Mac had
128K of memory.

The memory problem solved, the Mac—billed by Apple as the computer for the rest of us—was ready to conquer the world. Still, Mac sales were dismal. Apple soon discovered several other obstacles to overcome. For example, the first Mac could not boot from a hard disk and lacked a port for connecting to a hard drive. Apple expected users to connect hard drives through a modem and start their Macs from a floppy.

Although the Mac made advancements, software vendors had not yet shown a great deal of interest in the new platform. Few Macintosh programs were available. To perform meaningful tasks with a computer, you need software, right? You can't do much without it. Hence another reason Mac sales were so bad. Without software, the Macintosh was little more than a cute, smiling nightlight.

In the Meantime: 1983-1986

Today's Macintosh is unique, but it did not (and does not) exist in a vacuum. As Apple developed and improved the Mac, IBM, Microsoft, NEC, and thousands of other companies were developing and introducing technology that influenced the entire computer industry, including the development of the Macintosh. The following list describes some of the significant events between 1983 and 1986:

- *1983:* IBM had sold over 1 million PCs. DOS machines were on the fast track to becoming the desktop standard. Then Big Blue released the PCJr, a bomb that proved to be the first loose thread in IBM's unraveling.

- *1983:* Microsoft announced a graphical user interface called Windows that was supposed to revolutionize the PC, making it easy for everybody to use. Windows didn't ship for another three years, however, and its reception was tepid. Bugs and a sluggish interface made Windows 1.0 almost unusable.

- *1984:* Microsoft announced and released several programs for the Mac, including Word, Multiplan, File, Chart, Basic, and many others. Vendors began selling Macintosh software. In 1985, Microsoft released Excel for the Mac, finally rounding out the platform's business application selection. Desktop publishing came of age that same year when Aldus released PageMaker for the Mac.

- *1984:* IBM released the PC AT, and Hewlett-Packard shipped the HP LaserJet. Both products went on to become the IBM-compatible desktop standard.

- *1984:* Philips announced a CD-ROM for PCs costing less than $1,000. Few people knew it at the time, but several years later CD-ROM drives would revolutionize desktop publishing and multimedia.

■ *1984/1985:* Drive makers developed and released the 3.5-inch floppy disk drive, which Apple quickly adapted. Shortly thereafter, Sony introduced the 1.4MB disk drive, and about the same time, NEC brought out the first multisyncing monitor—all of which would greatly increase productivity and enhance desktop publishing capabilities.

■ *1986:* Steve Jobs left Apple, and the Mac Plus with SCSI was introduced. Compaq shipped the first 386 PC, virtually halting IBM's role as PC technology leader. Aldus and other companies announced the Tagged Image File Format (TIFF), which went on to become the standard in bitmapped and photograph graphics.

Up from the Ruins

By 1986, Apple had stockpiled a year's supply of Macintoshes. Sales were dead and the future looked bleak. But fate and a series of ongoing, lifesaving events brought the Mac out of mothballs. First, several major software developers, including Lotus and Software Publishing, announced commitments to write programs for the Macintosh, legitimizing the platform and finally providing business-oriented applications. Second, Apple released the Macintosh Plus, with expandable memory and the SCSI bus, greatly increasing power and peripheral expansion capabilities. Third, desktop publishing debuted with the release of PageMaker, the LaserWriter, and other budding technologies.

Finally, the business world had a few good reasons to invest in Macs.

Desktop Publishing with the Macintosh

More than any other technology, desktop publishing defined and legitimized the Macintosh.

During the Mac's formative years, IBM-compatible PCs were selling like mad. These serious, arcane, dark-screened monsters were ideal for databases, spreadsheets, and other unexciting applications. In order to survive, the Mac had to find a niche.

Many of the major contributing factors making Mac the platform of choice for page layout and graphics artist were developments by other companies, such as Aldus and Adobe. But the Apple Macintosh provided the key ingredient: a *WYSIWYG* (what-you-see-is-what-you-get) graphical environment.

Typography and PostScript

What set the Mac apart from other desktop machines was its graphical user interface. Its screen rendered fonts much as they would appear when printed. WYSIWYG had arrived. All that was needed now was a way to get what displayed on-screen onto paper.

The answer came a year after the Mac's debut, in the form of Apple's LaserWriter printer. Utilizing a new printer language developed by Adobe, called *PostScript*, the LaserWriter was the first relatively inexpensive ($6,995) output device to provide a wide variety of typefaces and have the capability to print a full page of graphics—at a rate of a whopping 300 dots per inch.

The LaserWriter was also the first printer introduced with built-in RAM. The first LaserWriter shipped with 1.5MB of RAM and 512K of ROM containing PostScript. This large chunk of memory enabled the printer to process not only pages containing the few fonts built into the printer but also to accept softfont outlines sent from the computer. Outline fonts allowed for font rendering in virtually any point size. The DOS standard (the LaserJet), on the other hand, used *bitmapped* fonts, which could render fonts only in fixed sizes.

PostScript revolutionized publishing. New high-end typesetting equipment, such as the Linotronic imagesetter, adopted PostScript, as did most color printers and 35mm slide recorders. As a result of the Macintosh-PostScript revolution, the way we get mass-produced printed material has completely changed, and a whole new industry—*prepress*, or preparing documents for the printing press—has sprung up. Service bureaus, high-tech shops full of fancy output devices (such as imagesetters, high-resolution lasers, thermal wax color printers, dye-sublimation proofing printers, and slide recorders), support desktop publishers and designers around the world.

DTP for Everybody

The desktop publishing revolution was spurred on primarily by powerful, easy-to-use page layout programs, particularly Aldus PageMaker. In those days, desktop publishing consisted mostly of typesetting. You still couldn't import images into your layout, except by using the most rudimentary clip art, but the storage capacity of the Mac could not have accommodated large graphics and photograph files anyway. PageMaker 1.0 was designed to run on the first 512K Mac with two floppy drives—one for the program and one for your document.

Since then, PageMaker and other DTP programs (primarily QuarkXPress) have provided page layout to the masses. Today you can accomplish layout designs unheard of just a few years ago. Low-cost laser printers have enabled people in all walks of life to produce professional-looking documents on their desktops. And the degree of sophistication is ever-increasing. Type and graphics manipulation continually reach new heights, all the while becoming increasingly easier to master.

Beyond Words

In the early days of DTP, computers primarily set type. When graphics were necessary, the designer left spaces in the layout and the print shop stripped the images in. Scanners were not capable of high quality reproductions—only 16 levels of gray and no color. Besides, the first Macs could not save and store the images, and the first Mac was too slow to render them. Then, in 1987, the Mac II debuted, changing the face of desktop publishing.

The new Macs enabled users to view up to 256 levels of gray on the monitor, and they supported larger hard drives, providing storage for large files. The new Macs were also capable of displaying color. Before long, grayscale image-editing software began to emerge, as did scanners capable of discerning up to 256 levels of gray. For a few thousand dollars—the price of a Mac, a laser printer, and a copy of PageMaker—anybody could turn out grayscale, black-and-white, or spot-color flyers, newsletters, and brochures from their desktop.

In Living Color

About the only area of publishing still in a critical maturing stage is the use of photo-realistic color. Getting the colors you see on your monitor to reproduce on a printing press is a tricky business. The technology has come a long way but is expensive, and the process requires a great deal of skill and knowledge. It works reasonably well in the hands of experts but is still not ready for prime time.

While the Mac II was capable of displaying color, it could handle only 8-bit color, or 256 colors. Some companies, such as RasterOps, developed 24-bit graphics NuBus cards, but they were incredibly slow. Photo-realistic color wasn't really viable on the Mac until Apple developed 32-bit QuickDraw in 1989, which allowed graphics card makers to establish a 24-bit color standard for displaying 16.7 million colors with reasonable speed. (*QuickDraw* is the technology Macs use to render images for display on a monitor.) The 32-bit QuickDraw standard opened the door to a flood of sophisticated graphics and image editing software, as well as many QuickDraw accelerator NuBus cards.

As mentioned previously, the primary problem in color publishing today is getting monitor colors to match printed output. Companies such as Apple, Electronics for Imaging, and Kodak have attempted to solve these discrepancies by introducing color management systems. Another key ingredient for color processing is hardware calibration products, such as Kodak's Color-Sense. These technologies are still expensive and sophisticated. The day when practically anybody can produce full-color documents on his or her desktop is on the near horizon, however.

Other Significant Developments

With the release of the LaserWriter came the birth of AppleTalk, the Macintosh personal network. Not only did AppleTalk connect Macs to print-ers, but it also connected Macs to other Macs, allowing companies with more than one Macintosh to share files easily, however slowly. In the same year, AppleLink (Apple's electronic information service for Macs with modems) went on-line, providing Macintosh users with an easy way to exchange files, use e-mail, and get support from Apple Computers.

During the developing years of the Macintosh, Apple entered the modern corporate world—the era of managers. The remaining cofounder, Steve Jobs, was replaced as CEO by John Sculley, a former president of Pepsi-Co. Jobs, who was slowly but surely edged out of the company altogether, went on to form Next, Inc. Next made an attempt at marketing expensive Mac-like com-puters but has met with limited success and acceptance.

It was also in 1987 when Apple introduced the Mac Plus, the first Mac to utilize the SCSI expansion interface mentioned earlier. SCSI made adding disk drives, removeables, and other input devices, such as scanners, easier. In fact, SCSI was a revolutionary way to add devices to computers. All users had to do was connect, or "chain," one device to another and, in some cases, install an INIT in the System folder. SCSI supports up to seven devices, which is much more than most users would ever need. This technology was not fully devel-oped, however, and complete expansion options were not realized until the next generation of Macs.

Macintosh Comes of Age

Originally, the Mac was supposed to come standard with all anybody ever needed to use it. This idea—that the Mac should be an all-in-one appliance—came from the top at Apple and was made into dogma by cofounder Steve Jobs. By 1987, however, it was obvious that different applications required specific hardware. Because creating a computer that had all the hardware every application required would render the machine too expensive, Apple went the way of the DOS-based PC and opened up the architecture to allow memory upgrades, expansion slots, and hard drives.

The First Open Macs

The first open Macs were the Mac II and the SE. Both models had 800K floppy drives. (Subsequent models would sport the Mac SuperDrive, which, with the right software, can read both Mac and PC disks.) The first SE was built around the 68000 processor, and the Mac II had the 68020. Both models were quickly upgraded to the 68030 processor. (The higher the processor number, the faster the CPU.)

The SE became the SE/30 and had only one expansion slot. It was also the first Mac to be released with 68882 math coprocessor for math-intensive applications, which made the SE about four times faster than the original SE. The subsequent Mac IIs later came out in several additional models, including the IIx and IIcx. The IIx was identical to the II, except for the faster processor, and the IIcx came in a smaller case that had only three expansion slots. Figure 1.3 shows the Mac IIcx.

Fig. 1.3
The Mac IIcx had only three expansion slots.

Before the Mac IIs, Apple discouraged third-party expansion of Macs. One of the more innovative features of the Mac II was the addition of NuBus technology, which, unlike DOS PCs, required no user configuration of jumpers or switches. To add a video card or other expansion device, all you did was plug and play. With its new offering, Apple reversed its position, sanctioning expansion. Finally, the company recognized its different kinds of customers (corporate, small business, home, and so on). This commitment to versatility and expansion continued into the '90s with the introduction of the LC and the Mac Classic. Figure 1.4 shows the Mac LC.

Fig. 1.4
The Mac LC was
versatile and
expandable.

The Fast Track

During period spanning 1990 to 1993, the pace of Macintosh technology remained slow. Several application-specific models, such as the Macintosh Portable, Macintosh IIci, and the first PowerBooks, were released, but most models, such as the IIci, had long life spans—up to three years. PCs, on the other hand, were constantly being upgraded, with new processors and faster clock speeds being introduced all the time. In 1993, Apple jumped on the bandwagon, releasing seven different computers based on the 68040 processor.

To accomplish this fast-track approach, Apple had to change its design approach. No longer could the Mac sport the cute, unique, hand-crafted appearance that Jobs had insisted on. In 1992 Apple began reusing one basic design for several models. The Centris 650, Quadra 800, and Quadra 650, for example, are quite similar in design, as are the LC III, LC 520, Performa 475 and 550, and Quadra 605.

It was also during this period when Apple began to rely on other companies to design and manufacture products and components. Sony, for example, developed and manufactured the PowerBook 100; Sharp developed the Newton, and Logitech manufactures the PowerBook's built-in trackballs. This new approach enabled Apple to deliver products to market in a more timely fashion.

Over the years, Apple has produced many Macs in various configurations. Table 1.1 provides an exhaustive list of some of these models.

Table 1.1   Mac Models through December 1993

Model	Processor	Clock Speed	Maximum RAM	PDS/ NuBus Slots
128K	68000	8	128K	0/0
512K	68000	8	512K	0/0
512Ke	68000	8	512K	0/0
Plus	68000	8	4MB	0/0
SE	68000	8	4MB	1/0
Portable	68000	16	10MB	1/0
Classic	68000	8	5MB	0/0
Mac II	68020	16	8MB[1]	0/6
LC	68020	16	10MB	1/0
SE/30	68030	16	128MB	1/0
IIx	68030	16	128MB	0/6
IIcx	68030	16	128MB	0/3
IIci/IIcx	68030	25/16	128MB	1/3
IIvi/IIvx	68030	16/32	16MB	0/3
IIfx	68030	40	128MB	1/6
IIsi	68030	20	20MB	1 or 1
Classic II	68030	10	18MB	0
LC II	68030	10	12MB	1/0
Color Classic	68030	16	12MB	1/0
LC III	68030	25	36MB	1/0
LC 475	68LC040	25	36MB	1/0
LC 520	68030	25	36MB	1 or 1

(continues)

Table 1.1 Continued

Model	Processor	Clock Speed	Maximum RAM	PDS/NuBus Slots
Centris 610	68040	20	68MB	1 or 1
Centris	68040	25	68MB	1 or 1
Quadra 605	68040	25	68MB	1/0
Quadra 610	68040	25	72MB	1/1[2]
Quadra 650	68040	33	128MB	1/3
Quadra 700	68040	25	64MB	1/2
Quadra 800	68040	33	128MB	1/3
Quadra 840AV[3]	68040	40	128MB	0/3
Quadra 900	68040	25	256MB	1/5
Quadra 950	68040	33	256MB	1/5
Performa 200	68030	16	8MB	0/0
Performa 400, 405, 410, 430	68030	16	10MB	1/0
Performa 450	60830	25	32MB	1/0
Performa 460, 466, 467	68030	33	32MB	1/0
Performa 475, 476	68040	25	32MB	1/0
Performa 550	68030	33	32MB	1/0
Performa 600, 600CD	68030	33	16MB	1/3

1. Mac II can be upgraded to SuperDrive, which also includes upgrade to 512K ROM, allowing you to use 4MB SIMMS, for a total of 68MB RAM.

2. Requires adapter. You can use only one or the other type slot. The Quadra 610 only has room for a 7 PDS or 1 NuBus card.

3. Contains DSP chip for accelerated sound and video. The AV comes ready to input and output TV signals and full-motion video.

The Mac Interface

In many ways, the Mac interface hasn't changed much. Unlike Windows, the Mac system software still looks and feels about the same as it did on the Lisa. By 1986, before the release of the Mac II, no sound was available and the display was still black and white. Also missing were HyperCard, MultiFinder and the use of hierarchical menus, 32-bit QuickDraw for fast screen redraws, and QuickTime for running full-motion video. While most of these components were available by System 6, it wasn't until System 7 that the Mac reached its current level of maturity with the final addition of QuickTime.

As you read this book, Apple probably has already released System 7.5 and is working on System 8. Be sure to read Chapter 2 for an overview of the Macintosh of the future.

In the Meantime: 1987-1993

In six short years, the Macintosh went from innovation leader to performance lagger. Advances in Intel's 80X86 technology had taken system performance far beyond that of the cute, smiling computer. Macintoshes were relegated to niche applications, such as high-end publishing, music composition, and film editing. Windows-based PCs began to take over business desktops, replacing the DOS-prompt, which is what Apple had hoped the Mac would do. Mac still had a loyal following, but speed advances, low prices, and graphical user interfaces in the IBM-compatible world caused many Macintosh loyalists to jump ship. The following events shaped Apple and the rest of the computer world:

- *1987:* Radius introduced the first full-page monitor—desktop publishing got easier.

- *1987:* The first active matrix LCD screens for portable computers were introduced.

- *1987:* Forethought released PowerPoint, a powerful, easy-to-use presentation program. PowerPoint has subsequently been taken over by Microsoft and remains a leader in presentation software for Windows and the Mac.

- *1987:* Aldus released PageMaker for Windows, creating the first chink in the Mac's cornered DTP market.

- *1988:* Adobe and Aldus shipped the first viable drawing programs: Illustrator and FreeHand. The Mac became the first electronic graphics designer tool.

- *1988:* Novell shipped the first version of NetWare for the Mac, making it possible to network PC and Macintoshes, and provide faster data transfers among Macs than possible through LocalTalk.

(continues)

(continued)

- *1989:* The first 486 PC notebooks shipped, enabling users to take Windows on the road. Windows was still a buggy, unstable mess that most PC users continued to avoid, however.

- *1989:* Adobe released font secrets, opening up Type 1 font technology. Microsoft and Apple already developed TrueType technology, however, which they released in 1990, both subsequently incorporated as system fonts in Windows 3.1 and System 7.

- *1989:* Adobe released Adobe Type Manager (ATM), providing easy, nearly foolproof Type 1 font handling for both the Mac and Windows.

- *1990:* The other shoe dropped. Microsoft released Windows 3.0. The first viable challenge to the Macintosh quality standard was unleashed, and a PC software phenomenon was born.

- *1990:* Adobe released Photoshop for Mac. The Macintosh became the industry standard for editing and processing photographs.

- *1991:* Apple and IBM entered into an agreement to develop and adopt IBM's PowerPC CPU and other significant new technologies, such as Apple's OpenDoc. The future was at hand.

- *1991:* Microsoft released Windows 3.1. An explosion of PCs running Windows occurred, and vendors began porting all their once-proprietary applications from the Macintosh to Windows.

- *1992:* Intel introduced the PCI local bus, a 64-bit I/O system. Most major computer manufacturers, including Apple, agreed to support it.

- *1992:* Apple, IBM, Compaq, and other vendors began a major push to provide value-oriented systems to consumers through department stores, discount warehouses, and other nonconventional outlets. Apple's response was the low-cost Performas.

- *1993:* The first portable document software—Common Ground, Acrobat, and Replica—were released.

- *1993:* The first Pentiums were released. Intel reinforced its hold on performance and slashed chip prices in anticipation of the 1994 release of the PowerPC.

Taking Mac on the Road

As people became dependent on computers, the need to take their data on the road arose. As early as 1989, PC users had true notebook computers, complete with large screens and hard drives, available. But not Macintosh users.

Apple's approach was the Macintosh Portable—a small, supposedly lightweight unit with a small monitor (see fig. 1.5). By miniaturization and portability standards, however, the Portable was large, heavy, and cumbersome. The Macintosh Portable was a dismal failure.

Fig. 1.5
The Macintosh Portable was large, heavy, and cumbersome.

In the meantime, IBM-compatible color notebook sales soared. In October 1991, Apple released the first PowerBook, and Mac users were finally able to take their work on the road (see fig. 1.6). The PowerBook was a trendsetter. It was lightweight, had a built-in trackball, wrist rests for ergonomic advantages, and backlit screens capable of displaying the graphical interface. The PowerBook also sported the sophisticated power management feature that debuted in the Portable. Also important was the PowerBook's built-in support of AppleTalk, which meant that users could easily connect their notebooks to their home office units or to their office networks.

The PowerBook had a tremendous effect on the PC notebook market. Intel soon released the 386SL and 486SL CPUs, which incorporated power management, and Microsoft began to include power management tools in DOS and Windows. Vendors began to build trackballs into their units. Apple was now not only competing for the desktop but also the laptop. By 1992, the PowerBook led all other notebooks in sales, even the popular IBM ThinkPad.

Notebook makers kept releasing new innovations. They released color displays, docking stations, subnotebooks, and several other enhancements. Apple kept up, but failed to lead the innovations. Today's PowerBook is similar to other notebooks, but it runs System 7. In 1993, IBM released the new

ThinkPad with a radical new pointing device that wooed buyers away from the PowerBook, and it looks as if Apple doesn't really have anything new planned until the release of the Power PC PowerBooks in late 1994. As of this writing, the company is not disclosing any of the PowerPC PowerBook's special features.

Fig. 1.6
With the Powerbook 140, users could easily take their Mac on the road.

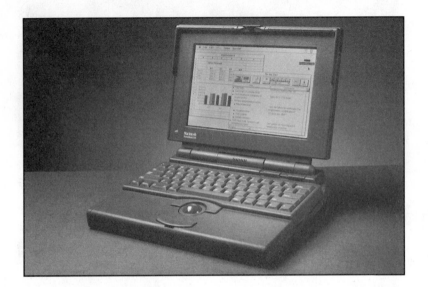

Since introduction of the PowerBook, Apple has released several varieties of PowerBooks, described in table 1.2.

Table 1.2 Macintosh PowerBooks as of December 1993					
Model	**Processor**	**Clock Speed**	**Maximum RAM**	**Screen Type**	**Weight**
100	68000	16	8MB	10" backlit supertwist	5.1 lb.
140	68030	16	6MB	10" backlit supertwist	6.8 lb.
145	68030	25	6MB	10" backlit supertwist	6.8 lb.
145B	68030	25	8MB	10" backlit supertwist	6.8 lb.
160	68030	25	14MB	10" backlit supertwist	6.8 lb.

Model	Processor	Clock Speed	Maximum RAM	Screen Type	Weight
165	68030	33	14MB	10" backlit supertwist	6.8 lb.
165c	68030	25	14MB	9" backlit color passive matrix	7.0 lb.
170	68030	25	8MB	10" backlit active-matrix	6.8 lb.
180	68030	33	14MB	10" backlit active-matrix	6.8 lb.
180c	68030	33	14MB	8.5" backlit color active-matrix	7.1 lb.

From Here...

From here you may want to consider the next chapter covering the present and future of the Mac, and the chapters on software. Chapters 16 through 28 cover different categories of software and discuss the leading products in each to help you get better acquainted with various applications.

■ Chapters 3, 4, and 5 cover the Mac's system software, including the philosophy behind the Interface, System 7.5, and using the Finder. Chapter 5 also shows you how to manage folders and files.

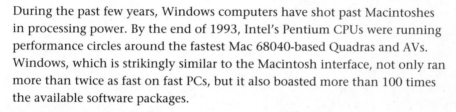

Chapter 2

MacPresent and MacFuture

by William D. Harrell

During the past few years, Windows computers have shot past Macintoshes in processing power. By the end of 1993, Intel's Pentium CPUs were running performance circles around the fastest Mac 68040-based Quadras and AVs. Windows, which is strikingly similar to the Macintosh interface, not only ran more than twice as fast on fast PCs, but it also boasted more than 100 times the available software packages.

To compete, Apple had to break the speed barrier imposed by the Motorola CISC (complex instruction set computers) 68000-processors used in conventional Macintoshes. No matter what Motorola could have done to improve the chip, the 68000's death knell had become loud and clear. In an attempt to counterbalance the Microsoft Windows on-slaught, Apple teamed up with IBM to adapt the latter's RISC (reduced instruction set computer) processor, which has resulted in the Power Macintosh.

The Power Mac is a powerful new computer that promises to out-run anything based on Intel's 80X86 or Pentium CISC-based machines including the Macintosh PowerPC. As I write this, Power Macs have started to show up in computer stores. Not only do these new Macs have the potential to run much faster than the Pentium, but they also run Windows and DOS software and allow you to exchange data between the two platforms. As this book goes to press, Apple, committed to the Power Mac, is systematically phasing out Macs as we know them. By the end of 1994, you may not be able to find a new Macintosh based on the Motorola 680X0 processor. But take heart—it will still run almost all your current Mac software, although, depending on your current system, a little slowly.

RISC versus CISC CPUs

During the past ten years of personal computing, desktop computers were powered by complex instruction set computer (CISC) chips, Macs by the Motorola 680X0, and DOS machines by Intel's 80X86/Pentium. A few years ago, Apple realized that the CISC technology would reach a performance plateau. In 1991, the company teamed up with IBM and Motorola to develop the PowerPC family of reduced instruction set computer (RISC) chips. The idea was that PowerPC performance would start somewhere near the same rate as the fastest CISC processors and then, through the development of successive RISC generations, shoot through the roof. Power Mac promises this tremendous power surge, while allowing you to continue using existing Macintosh software.

RISC: Simply Faster

PowerPC RISC CPUs achieve better performance by processing instructions faster than CISC CPUs. RISC processors use smaller, more uniform instruction sets that expedite instruction fetching. In other words, the processor never has to pause to retrieve additional information to complete a pending instruction. The reduced set of instructions allows the CPU to process commands more quickly. There's simply not as much code to read. RISC processors also address memory quickly and do not include complex calculations and multiple memory references required in CISC-based processing. And these obvious improvements only scratch the surface—PowerPC CPUs contain all kinds of advanced processing power, such as the capability to process several sets of instructions concurrently in one clock cycle.

PowerPC versus Pentium

What does all this technical mumbo-jumbo mean in terms of performance of one platform versus another? Frankly, the Intel Pentium is a screamer and is by no means dead yet. In fact, it even sports several processing technologies found in the PowerPC. However, it also contains circuitry to keep it compatible with the 80X86 line of Intel CPUs. What that means is that you don't have to switch software. The PowerPC, on the other hand, is not completely backwards compatible. Conventional Mac System 7 programs run in emulation mode, making them run more slowly than they would on the fastest 68000-based Macs. To get the full performance boost from a Power Mac, you must upgrade your software to native Power Mac versions.

RISC processors require fewer transistors and less power—and they can be produced significantly cheaper than Pentium chips. Unless Intel finds a way to make the Pentium more efficient, Apple and other PowerPC manufacturers (such as IBM) have a significant pricing advantage. Despite the lukewarm growth of the Macintosh installed user base over the years, the PowerPC does seem to have a better long-term advantage. Again, although the Pentium does incorporate some RISC technology to gain speed, it gets bogged down by maintaining its backwards-compatibility with the earlier 80X86 line. The PowerPC RISC CPU is in its first generation and provides Motorola and Apple with an excellent platform to build on.

The First Power Macs

If it looks like a Mac and acts like a Mac, it must be a Mac, right? Well, almost. On March 14, 1994, Apple released its first line of Power Macs—the 6100, 7100 and 8100. For all practical purposes, these machines are Power Mac equivalents to the Quadra 610, 650, and 800 (see fig. 2.1). In addition to the PowerPC 601 processor, however, some significant differences among the models exist. All Power Macs so far have built-in Ethernet networking circuitry and AV configurations through an expansion card. Even the non-AV configurations support telephony, speech, and stereo capabilities. All models also support multisync monitors and on-the-fly resolution switching. And all except the non-AV 6100 have two video ports.

The new Macs also utilize the on-board video better, via PDS cards. Non-AV 7100s have cards with 1MB VRAM, expandable to 2MB, which means that you can get HiColor on 21-inch monitors, and up to 16.7 million colors on smaller, 16- and 17-inch monitors. The non-AV 8100s come with cards containing 2MB VRAM, expandable to 4MB. With 4MB, the 8100s allow true-color, 16.7 million colors on a 21-inch monitor (and smaller). Several benchmarks in Macintosh trade publications have placed the new video cards at two to three times faster than the on-board video on standard Macs, but only when running native Power Mac software, discussed in the next section, "Power Mac Software."

Until the release of the Power Mac, Mac model names were confusing. For example, do you have trouble remembering how the CPU speed of a Centris 650 differs from a Quadra 650? With the debut of the Power Mac, Apple developed a new naming scheme. The Power Macs include the CPU speeds in their names. The Power Mac 6100/60 has 60Mhz CPU, the 7100/66 a 66Mhz processor and the 8100/80 is 80Mhz. If the company were to introduce an 80Mhz 7100, it would be called a 7100/80.

Fig. 2.1

The 6100, 7100, and 8100 are virtually PowerPC equivalents to the Quadra 610, 650, and 800.

Fig. 2.1
Continued

You will also notice a subtle difference when you start a new Power Mac. Instead of the chime you're used to hearing when pressing the power button, the Power Mac gives you a guitar cord strummed by jazz artist, Stanley Jordan. If there's a problem during bootup, a car crash sounds—cute indeed, but the best news is that you don't have to go broke buying a new Power Mac. Power Macs are currently selling for about the same price as their original Macintosh equivalents.

Power Mac Software

Frankly, most software, such as word processors and spreadsheets, already runs fast enough on existing Macs, especially the later models built around the 68040 processor. However, speed and performance are critical issues in applications where graphics, sound, and video are used, primarily desktop publishing and multimedia presentations. Photoshop users, for example, can use all the power they get, as can the creators of sophisticated multimedia presentations that feature large sound clips and QuickTime full-motion video. Here's where the Power Mac comes in.

When running software written to conventional System 7 Macintoshes, however, the Power Mac must emulate the Mac operating system, which slows down processing substantially. Performance degradation is so extreme that some programs even run slower on the Power Mac than on higher-end conventional Macs, such as Quadras. The bottom line: in order to reap the performance benefits of the PowerPC processor, you must run software written specifically for that platform.

This isn't as bad as it sounds. If you are worried about learning a new operating system, have no fear. Power Macs run a version of System 7 written especially for the PowerPC chip. In addition, almost all companies writing software for the Macintosh, including Microsoft, Aldus, Quark, and Adobe, have committed to developing for the Power Mac. Power Mac versions of PageMaker and QuarkXPress are currently going to market—and boy, are they ever fast.

Running Windows on a Mac

▶ See "Using Aldus PageMaker," p. 562

▶ See "Using QuarkXPress," p. 585

One of the disadvantages of using a Mac in a world dominated by IBM-compatible PCs is a lack of compatibility with 85 to 90 percent of the information age. Apple and other companies have made great strides in closing the compatibility gaps between the two platforms. Perhaps the most significant step in this direction was the introduction of the SuperDrive on the Mac, which allowed Macintosh users to use PC-formatted disks. Aldus, Quark, Frame Technologies, and several other companies have made significant advancements in writing software that creates documents almost completely compatible across both platforms. None of these solutions are seamless, however.

Power Mac closes the compatibility chasm—almost. Finally, with the PowerPC chip, a processor fast enough to run Windows emulation software at a reasonable clip is available. In a nutshell, emulation software bridges the differences in the way PowerPC and Intel CISC chips process data. As of this writing, the only Apple-endorsed Windows emulation solution is Insignia's SoftWindows.

At present, SoftWindows is by no means a perfect solution. It has several limitations—the most severe being that it can only run in Standard, or 286, mode. One of the major benefits of Windows is its capability to multitask, which requires the operating environment to run in 386 Enhanced mode. Multitasking allows the computer to perform several operations at once, such as print in the background or download a file while you work in your word processor. You can open two or more applications at once in Standard mode, but you cannot multitask.

Some applications, such as WordPerfect for Windows (and several others), require that Windows run in 386 Enhanced mode; otherwise, the program won't boot. Another serious limitation is the amount of RAM required to run SoftWindows. To use the software at all, your system must have at least 16MB RAM, as compared to the 4MB required on a PC. This is a minimum configuration. Some Windows applications, like their Mac counterparts, require additional RAM to run, and many of those that don't require more RAM still need it to perform well.

The first Power Macs built around PowerPC 601 chip can run Windows software at a speed comparable to a 486SX, or an entry-level DOS machine. To Mac users, this performance level is probably about the same as one of the slower Quadras, such as the 610. The difference between 486SX performance and that of a 486DX4 or a Pentium is dramatic—even unacceptable—to Windows power users.

Running Windows applications on the Mac has two advantages, however. First, despite its drawbacks, the SoftWindows solution does enable you to exchange data, such as text and graphics, between the two platforms through the Clipboard. Second, thousands of Windows applications are currently unavailable to Macintosh users, and vice versa. The ability to run Windows on a Mac opens a vast library of applications.

Still, given the current situation, most dedicated Windows users will not find the Power Mac Windows implementation powerful enough to justify switching. Instead, the Power Mac is a better solution for Mac users who want to run occasional Windows sessions. But as the RISC chip gets faster and the emulation software improves, who knows what might happen?

Upgrading to Power Macintosh

In the recent history (the past 10 years or so) of the desktop computer, the PowerPC-based Power Mac is the first to make a complete platform shift—in other words, to discontinue total backward compatibility at the processor level. (Remember that by itself, the PowerPC cannot run Macintosh software. Apple has built System 7 emulation into the Power Macintosh.) If the Power Mac takes off, software developers may stop writing versions for the conventional Macintosh system software, even though Apple is commited to continue upgrading operating systems as they develop newer versions for Power Macs (see fig. 2.2).

▶ See "Hard Disk
Problems,"
p. 1072

Rest assured that the company has not left most Mac owners in the cold.
Most of today's Macs can be upgraded to PowerPCs. Apple has already
planned motherboard upgrades for the most recent Macs, including most
Quadras, Centrises, and Performas. You'll even be able to use existing drives
and peripherals (although some may require driver upgrades), but if you have
an old, small, slow hard disk, you should also change it. It makes little sense
to soup up your Mac and then leave it to limp along with a slow hard disk
bottleneck.

Fig. 2.2
The PowerPC.

Initially, Apple has set the motherboard upgrade prices to range from about
$1,000 to $2,000, with 8100 AV upgrades being the most expensive. For all
practical purposes, these upgrades turn your existing system into a Power
Mac with the same specs as those listed previously in the section "The First
Power Mac's." In case the Logic Board upgrade price is too stiff, however,
Apple offers another, less expensive option by way of a PDS card that fits into
one of your Macs expansion slots. For about $600 to $700, you can turn your
Mac into a totally compatible 60Mhz Power Mac. In some cases, this method
is a little bit less powerful a solution (the card interfaces with the logic board
at 32 bits, instead of the PowerPC's 64 bits), but it allows you to easily switch
back between Power Mac and conventional Mac, which is a great way to
avoid the emulation performance lag while developers upgrade their software.

End of an Era

A primary difference between the Macintosh and DOS PCs is that for 10 years now, Apple Computer has been the only company to manufacture Macs. DOS machines, on the other hand, have been manufactured and distributed by several vendors. Apple has been quite successful at keeping tight reins on its technology—which is good and bad. Being a proprietary platform has left Apple free of competition. On the PC side, there has been great competition, which has spurred performance boosts, innovations and lower prices. Undoubtedly, one reason Macs fell behind in performance was that Apple didn't have to contend with other companies in its marketplace. And until about one year ago, Macintoshes were much more expensive than comparably equipped DOS PCs.

The advantage of having the same company manufacture all the computers on a given platform is superior compatibility. Macintosh users do not have to contend with some of the software and hardware mismatch nightmares that Windows users pull hair and lose sleep over. Guess what? All that's about to change.

Competition and Apple's quest for survival has spurred the end of this proprietary trend. Recently, Apple announced a program to license its system software to third-party developers. In the near future, you may be able to buy a Power Mac made by a company other than Apple Computers. It will be strange indeed to see Macintosh software running on a computer without a bright-colored apple on the front. Life goes on.

As we move into the PowerPC era, at least one company, DayStar, has already taken Apple up on its licensing offer. DayStar has released its own version of the PDS Power Mac upgrade for Quadras and Centrises. The company said that they will soon re-lease cards to upgrade other Macs. This new trend, third-party Macintoshes, will probably be a double-edged sword. As in the DOS PC world, competition will spawn advancements. A diversity of developers will probably create some compatibility headaches.

The MacFuture

The conventional Mac as we know it is on its way out. By the time you read this book, you may not be able to buy a new Centris, Quadra, or Performa. This is not to say, however, that the existing machines will not be around for a while and that you won't be able to buy software for them. As it stands right now, most software vendors, including the key players, such as Aldus, Adobe, Quark, and others, have announced commitments to continue developing products for non-PowerPC Macs. How quickly the installed Macintosh base switches to PowerPC will undoubtedly determine how long this continues.

Although the conventional Mac platform is still a contender, over the next few years, the emphasis will probably switch to the PowerPC. Apple has outlined the future development of the Power Macintosh and other product strategies, covered briefly in the following sections.

Future PowerPC CPUs

▶ See "PowerBooks and Duos," p. 995

The PowerPC 601 chip is just the first of several PowerPC chips planned by Motorola. The next version is the 603. This chip has several advantages over the 601. First, the 603 is faster—perhaps two or three times faster. It can process up to three instruction sets per wait state, for example, instead of the 601's one instruction set per wait state. But the real advantage is that it consumes much less power by shutting down parts of the chip not in use—without the software knowing about the change. This and other power management features make it ideal for battery-operated computers. Apple plans PowerPC PowerBooks based on the 603 by the end of 1994.

Another advantage of the 603 is that the chip is smaller and should be less expensive to manufacture. We'll probably also see this CPU in home and entry-level Macs. In 1995, we should see a significantly more powerful CPU, the 604. Expect to see the 604 replace the 601 in midrange and high-end desktop Macs sometime in 1995. The 603 and 604 should remain in use for several years. Another chip, the 620, is being designed for workstations. Look for a few extremely high-end Macintosh workstations and servers based on this chip in the future.

Also planned is the implementation of technology designed to process data faster, such as the Peripheral Component Interconnect currently used on IBM-compatibles, which transfers video and other data along a 64-bit path. To enhance network performance, Apple plans to turn to a new technology called QuickRing, which will transmit and receive data at a whopping 200MB per second.

The MacFuture looks exciting, indeed.

The MacFuture of Software

Although the outlook for the next year or two of PowerPC CPUs seems clear, the future of Mac software is not as certain. As the Windows and Mac platforms converge, it's difficult to predict which standards will survive. While experts don't know which standards will live on, they do seem to agree on the general direction computer software will take. As demonstrated by the application suites, such as Microsoft Office, a group of programs consisting of e-mail, word processing, spreadsheet, database, and presentation software, the indication is that the future of software is modular.

In other words, instead of buying a full-featured word processor in the future, you'll buy modules that plug into an open document system. Documents will exist primarily at or one step above the system level, and you'll use modules, or plug-ins, to enhance them. Suppose that you need to create indexes for your documents. Rather than purchasing a full-featured word processor, you'll simply get a simple indexing module. To edit and import graphics, you'll use a graphics editing plug-in.

Apple's proposed approach to this system is OpenDoc, a system close to that described above. The snag in the OpenDoc approach is that currently it is based on the Macintosh data-sharing convention of Publish and Subscribe. To become cross-platform compatible, Open Document must also support Windows' Object Linking and Embedding (OLE) technology. If not, many cross-platform applications, such as, say, PageMaker or QuarkXPress, will not be able to transfer documents seamlessly.

Also in question is whether it makes sense to create a standard that includes two distinctly different modes of data linking—Publish and Subscribe and OLE. It seems to make little sense, and many experts agree that OLE is by far a superior standard.

In addition to OpenDoc, Apple seems to be banking on PlainTalk speech recognition, Audio/Video processing, and making the Mac more capable of running Windows while also offering the benefits unique to the Macintosh. Look for an upgrade to the Mac system software sometime in 1995, to System 8.0. However, Apple is remaining tight-lipped about upgrades past 7.5. You should look for a move toward OpenDoc in System 8.0 software and perhaps an implementation of OLE. For more information on System 7.5, see Chapter 4, "What's New in System 7.5."

From Here...

The decision whether to buy or upgrade to a Power Macintosh may seem difficult, but it isn't, really. If you're happy with your current Mac's performance, hold onto your money for a while. If current trends continue (and there's no reason to believe they won't), computer prices will continue to drop. If you're in a graphics or DTP environment and can afford it, go on and take the plunge. You won't regret it; the performance boost is substantial.

From here you may want to consider Part II of the book and the chapters on System software. Chapters 3 through 10 cover the Mac interface and how to use it. In addition, you should consider the following chapters:

- Chapters 16, 17, 18, 19, and the others in Part IV cover using software applications. You'll find a wealth of tips on and information on being more productive with your Mac.

- Chapters 33, 34, 35, and 36 can also help. Networking, data exchange, and being on the road are all issues related to being more productive with your computer.

Chapter 3

The Macintosh Interface Philosophy

by Chris Oakes

As you saw in the first two chapters, Macintosh hardware has experienced major generational changes over the years. Throughout the Mac's history, however, the graphical Macintosh user interface—the figurative levers and pedals that control this remarkable machine—has remained constant. And along with this unchanging look and feel, common tasks can be performed in new Macintosh applications the same way as in old Macintosh applications. The way you copy and paste text in a Macintosh word processor, for example, is no different in 1994 than it was in 1984. Procedures are also consistent across applications. You copy text, for example, the exact same way in the word processor Microsoft Word as you do in Claris MacWrite, another Macintosh word processor. This consistency among applications and common tasks is what keeps the Mac easy to use.

This chapter explains the following Macintosh interface concepts:

- Macintosh interface philosophy

- What consistency among Macintosh tasks looks like and how it helps you work better

- Consistency in Macintosh menus

- Consistency in Macintosh menu commands

- Consistency in Macintosh windows

The Familiar Steering Wheel

The steering wheel is a simple control common to all automobiles. The steering wheel also illustrates why such common controls should be consistently positioned and used among different machines. To turn a car to the left or right, every driver knows to use the steering wheel. Turning the wheel to the left always turns a car to the left, and vice versa. It doesn't matter whether you're in a Ford or Toyota, a sports car or truck—you know where this important control is located, and you know just how to use it. This standard implementation of common controls and the tasks they perform is what interface consistency refers to. Used in car design, it lets you hop into even the most sophisticated of sports cars and cruise out onto the open highway—without having ever driven that car before. This standardization is also what consistency among Macintosh applications is all about.

Even slight deviation from an interface standard can be disconcerting. In most countries, for example, cars are driven on the right side of the road. But if you have ever driven in Britain, where cars travel on the left side of the road, you know how this little variation can throw you off. Instead of operating as you normally do, you must relearn the task at hand. That means extra time and effort spent on training. Consistency among these common tasks reduces that.

The designers of the Macintosh wanted people to be as comfortable with the Mac interface as they were with the steering wheels of their cars. To do that, they decided that the various elements of the interface—such as menus, windows, and common menu commands—should remain constant throughout the Finder and all Macintosh applications. Mac users, therefore, would have familiar tools to use no matter what they were doing.

Apple's Interface Guidelines

At the outset, an Apple document called "Human Interface Guidelines" expressed this ideal of interface consistency. To make sure that Macintosh applications feature similar procedures and characteristics, Apple encourages all software companies to follow these guidelines. In his book about the creation of the Macintosh, *Insanely Great,* Steven Levy notes that these guidelines came to be known, sometimes derisively, as the *Macintosh Religion*. But these guidelines are responsible for making the Macintosh famous for two important assets: ease of learning and ease of use. Levy underscores the effect of the Human Interface Guidelines on Macintosh software in *Insanely Great*:

The entire software base of Macintosh became a coherently created world in itself, one with an immediate familiarity to anyone who had mastered the elemental skills of using the machine.... You could launch a strange application, and accomplish something instantly, without even touching the manual. After some painless exploration, and perhaps a glance or two at the documentation, you could probably get serious work done. It was an ambitious plan, and, amazingly, it worked.

In a moment, we'll take a look at these universal interface features and the tasks they accomplish. After a while, you will become familiar with these features, the steering wheels and gas pedals of the Macintosh interface, and you will be ready to jump into any Mac application and take it for a spin. The following sections examine what happens when such consistency is missing.

Computing without Consistency

Perhaps the best way to see the virtue of universal interface features is to consider working in their absence. The IBM PC world has long bemoaned such an absence. Before the Microsoft Windows operating system, DOS-based programs (programs based on text commands—an interface where users issue instructions by typing lines of text) hardly even tried to have consistency among applications. The way you performed tasks differed greatly from one program to the next. At best, common methods might be found in two software programs from the same company. There was little hope that by learning one program you were on the road to learning others. More often, learning a new program meant learning from scratch.

Microsoft Windows

When Microsoft Windows 3.0 exploded onto the PC scene in 1990, part of its mission was to bring Mac-like consistency to PC software. It certainly helped the situation, but several conditions prevented it from matching the Mac completely. For one, Windows was only a shell around DOS, which was still the underlying operating system that saddled the computer and made it run. Windows was still bound to many of DOS's unintuitive and difficult-to-grasp characteristics, such as cryptic file names and confusing file directories.

Second, although it brought a set of common graphical features, many of the methods for carrying out frequently used commands in Windows still varied from application to application. The commands to open and close files, copy text, and other typical functions were not uniform across the board. These inconsistencies remained largely because developers of Windows software weren't dealing with a set of interface guidelines like those for the Mac. Like Windows, Windows software had its roots in DOS.

To this day, new versions of Windows strive to remedy this situation. Meanwhile, the Mac world, though not immune to confusion, has a much stronger footing in the all-important area of interface consistency. The next section shows you the features of Macintosh interface consistency.

> **Note**
>
> A new version of Windows, code-named Chicago, makes the strongest effort yet to escape the problems of DOS. This version works as a full-fledged operating system, not as a shell around DOS. Consequently, DOS is no longer necessary.

The Familiar Features of Macintosh

Figure 3.1 shows a typical scene in the Finder, the first thing you see after your Macintosh finishes its startup process. Now take a look at figure 3.2. This figure shows what you see after you launch the word processing application Microsoft Word. Notice that the two scenes are pretty similar. Becoming familiar with one of them brings natural familiarity with the other.

Fig. 3.1
The Macintosh
Finder.

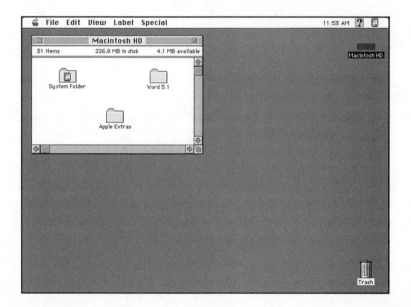

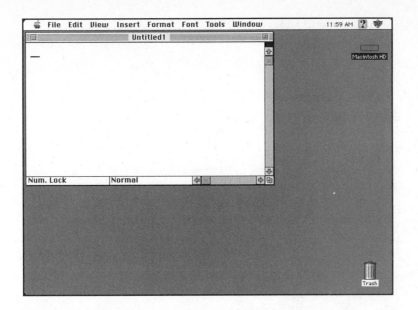

Fig. 3.2
Microsoft Word.

Which features are common to both figures? First, both screens feature the Macintosh menu bar along the top edge. And both screens feature *windows* (the empty white box in figure 3.2 and the similar, though not empty, box in figure 3.1).

Note

Both figures 3.1 and 3.2 feature the Macintosh HD and Trash icons, but these icons belong only to the Finder. Why are they visible in the Microsoft Word screen shot? Because although Word is in the foreground, the Finder waits idly by in the background. The Finder is still visible and accessible *underneath* Microsoft Word. It is possible to hide the Finder with the Performa series of computers or with System 7.5. This option was added by Apple for novice users who are apt to click the desktop accidentally and thus exit their active document window.

▶ See "Using the Performa Control Panel," p. 99

Although the applications don't exactly have a boatload of similarities, these few common characteristics make a world of difference when you learn and use the Macintosh. Chapter 5, "Understanding the Desktop and Finder," burrows into the specifics of using these interface elements. In this chapter, the building blocks of Macintosh consistency—the commandments of the Macintosh Religion—are summarized to show how they make computing simpler.

Issuing Commands with the Macintosh Menu

Every user needs to talk to his or her computer. Because you can't just speak to your computer, however, computer designers had to concoct an alternate method of telling the machine to do something. *To do something* in computer lingo is to *carry out a command.* As discussed in the preceding section, the Macintosh brought its unique graphical style to these commands—a radical improvement on the conventional method of typing out text in order to *do something.*

> **Note**
>
> Some Macintoshes recognize a limited set of speech commands. This feature is found on Power Macintoshes and "AV" models, which are discussed in Chapter 14.

This common need to issue commands was the perfect place to start applying Macintosh consistency. And so the Macintosh menu bar was created. Recognizable in all Macintosh applications, the menu bar contains *menus.* Menus are indicated by words such as File, Edit, and View. Figure 3.3 shows the File menu, as seen in the Finder's menu bar.

Every menu offers a visible list of commands, such as Open, Close, and Print. To view these commands, click a menu with your mouse, hold the mouse button down and *presto!*—the list of commands appears. To choose a command, move your mouse over the command and then release the mouse button. You issue commands this way not only in the Finder but in every application written for the Macintosh. Just by reading this brief section, you've gained an understanding of how to issue commands in hundreds of Macintosh applications. That's the power of consistency.

Fig. 3.3
The File menu as
seen in the Finder.

The language of menus is more like the English language than a computer language. In some cases, by mentally combining a menu's name—File or Edit, for example—with one of the items in that menu, you can assemble a logical English command. Open File, for example. Or Print File. Or View By Icon, available in the Finder's View menu (see fig. 3.4). In some menus, such as the Finder's Edit menu (see fig. 3.5), the commands stand alone. You certainly don't have to construct literal English phrases out of menu commands—but their familiar, English-like syntax is a helpful touch. In the next section, menu commands are used in the Finder and Microsoft Word. A simple copy-and-paste example illustrates how consistency among menu commands can keep your work simple.

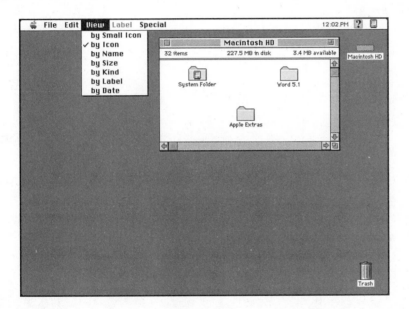

Fig. 3.4
The Finder's View Menu.

Fig. 3.5
The Finder's Edit Menu.

Copying and Pasting: Consistency in Action

Suppose that while working in the Finder, you want to copy the name of a particular file for use in a memo. In the Finder, you select the file's name.

To copy the file name, choose Copy from the Edit menu (fig. 3.5). (Chapter 5 discusses these procedures in detail.)

Now you need to paste the file's name into a Microsoft Word document, where you're crafting your memo. In Microsoft Word, you find the same menu you used in the Finder—the Edit menu, shown in figure 3.6. When you open the menu, you find the Cut, Copy, and Paste commands. Notice that the commands are located in the same place as they were in the Finder.

Fig. 3.6

The Edit menu in Microsoft Word.

The Cut, Copy, and Clear commands are visible but gray. Because you just made a copy in the Finder, the Mac knows that next you need to Paste. (You learn more about this capability in Chapter 5.) Other commands that are exclusive to Microsoft Word also appear in the menu, but the *common* commands are all under the same menu bar. This would be the case in any Macintosh application that allows you to copy and paste objects.

> **Note**
>
> Although menus offer a nice, visual way to issue commands, sometimes you may want to use the *keyboard shortcut*. Keyboard shortcuts are frequently listed in menus right next to the command. As you get more familiar with Macintosh, you may find that typing the key combination (such as ⌘-C for the Copy command) is a nice shortcut. And just like the menu commands, these keyboard shortcuts are usually consistent throughout all Macintosh applications.

In this section, you witnessed consistent element #1, the Macintosh menu, in action. In the next sections, you learn about an even simpler consistent element—the Macintosh window.

The Macintosh Window

As you've seen in the previous sections, menus perform actions. They can act upon any of a number of Macintosh objects—a piece of text, a photograph, a drawing, or even a frame of video. In all cases, these editable contents are kept in containers known as *files*. You create and edit files with *applications*. For example, you might use a word processor such as Microsoft Word to create and edit a text file. When you open a file on a Macintosh, the file's contents are displayed in a Macintosh window—and no matter what application you're using, a window looks and acts basically the same way.

> **Note**
>
> Entire windows and files themselves can be on the receiving end of a command. An entire file, for example, might be "exported" for use in another application.

Previously, you saw some windows in the Finder and Microsoft Word. In this section, you examine a FileMaker Pro window. Figure 3.7 shows an open FileMaker Pro file that contains a database of name and address. (Chapter 20 discusses FileMaker Pro, a database application from Claris Corporation, in detail.)

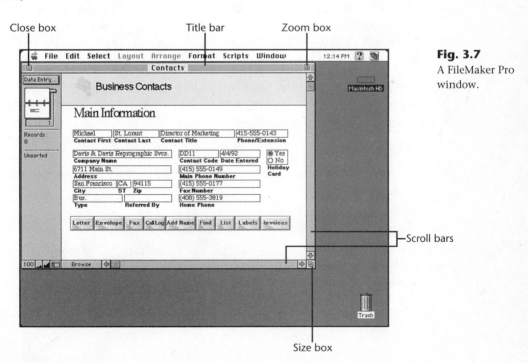

Fig. 3.7
A FileMaker Pro window.

You probably recognize some common interface elements in this screen shot. Although you are dealing with an entirely different application, the menu bar is still visible at the top, as are those two common menus, File and Edit. Notice that the Finder's Trash and disk icons are visible in the background, just as they were in previous figures. Finally, notice the window, that distinctive rectangle prominent in previous figures as well. The file name, Contacts, appears at the top of the window, and the file's contents appear inside the window. To copy any of the text displayed in this window, you would use the familiar Copy command located in the Edit menu.

Examine the window in figure 3.7. The bar along the top of the window is called the *title bar*; it contains the window's title (again, Contacts in this case). In the window's upper left corner, there is a small box for closing the window, which puts the file away for the time being. This box is called the *close box*. In the window's upper left corner is a box for maximizing the size of the window, called the *zoom box*. One click on the zoom box maximizes the window's size, a second restores it to its original size. The double box in the lower right corner of the window enables you to stretch and shrink the window to any size you want. It is therefore called the *size box*.

Finally, the window contains two gray bars—one along the full length of the window's right side and one along most of the window's bottom. Those bars—with arrows at each end and the box in between—are the *scroll bars*. Like a television camera moving left and right or up and down, the scroll bars let you bring hidden window areas into view.

That's the gist of consistent element #2, the Macintosh window. Again, all of its features are the same no matter what application you're using. As omnipresent as the menu bar, you will see a window around every file you ever open on your Macintosh. You will therefore recognize and know how to use this tool in every Macintosh application. In fact, you already know a little about it. You may want to take a moment to fiddle with some menus and windows on your Mac right now.

> **Note**
>
> Many Macintosh programs allow you to open multiple windows. This feature is convenient because it enables you to easily transfer text and other data among files. You can copy text in one window, for example, and paste it into another one. To move to another window you just click it.

More Power Than Meets the Eye

This chapter covered only two features—menus and windows. But quite a few common capabilities are contained within them. Table 3.1 lists the many commands contained in just the File and Edit menus. If you multiply these commands by the number of applications you'll use on your Macintosh, you'll find that you have quite an arsenal of software knowledge.

Table 3.1 Common Macintosh Commands		
Menu	**Command**	**Action**
File	New	Creates a new file or folder
	Open	Opens an existing file or folder
	Close	Closes an open file or folder
	Save	Saves changes to a file
	Save As	Saves a file as a new, separate file
	Print	Prints the contents of a file
	Quit	Quits an application
Edit	Undo	Takes back ("Un-does") your most recent action
	Cut	Cuts out a selection (of text, graphic, and so on)
	Copy	Copies a selection
	Paste	Pastes a selection in a new place
	Clear	Deletes a selection
	Select All	Selects all the contents of a file or folder

Now that you understand these common Macintosh features, you will understand other common features more easily. When you read other chapters in this book, you will witness the Mac's wide use of many consistent features. In the Finder, you'll see that every file is represented by an icon, no matter what's in the file. You'll see that you move, delete, and copy all icons in the same way. Fonts, which are covered in Chapter 8, are often displayed in a Font menu. A common menu called Style changes font characteristics. You'll see that *dialog boxes* change every file's settings—and that they all use a variety of similar-looking buttons. And you'll see that printing files follows a similar routine in every Macintosh program as well.

Consider: A few simple, recognizable menus contain all the commands listed in table 3.1. Imagine if you had to memorize typed commands for each one.

▶ See "Icons: Representing Files, Folders, and Disks," p. 74

▶ See "Putting Files into a Folder," p. 117

▶ See "Printing a Document—from A–Z," p. 206

Then every time you wanted to copy something, you would have to use an awkward combination of keystrokes. Or worse, you might have to remember different commands for the same action, depending on which program you were using. Although the Mac allows you to issue keystroke commands, I'm sure you'll agree that it's much easier to learn and use these commands by using a set of familiar menus.

From Here...

In this chapter, you learned about the design philosophy behind the Macintosh interface. Upcoming chapters delve into the specifics of this interface. The following chapters focus on special interface features and how to use them in your work on the Macintosh.

- Chapter 5, "Understanding the Desktop and Finder," specific Macintosh features such as folders, icons, windows, and menus—and how they work together to create that special workspace known as the Finder.

- Chapter 7, "Organizing Your Files, Folders, and Disks," shows you how to carry out common Finder tasks and how to use these tasks to organize your files, folders, and disks.

- Chapter 11, "Changing the Look of Your Desktop," shows you how you can make modifications to your Macintosh's interface so that it better suits your working style.

Part II

System 7 Essentials

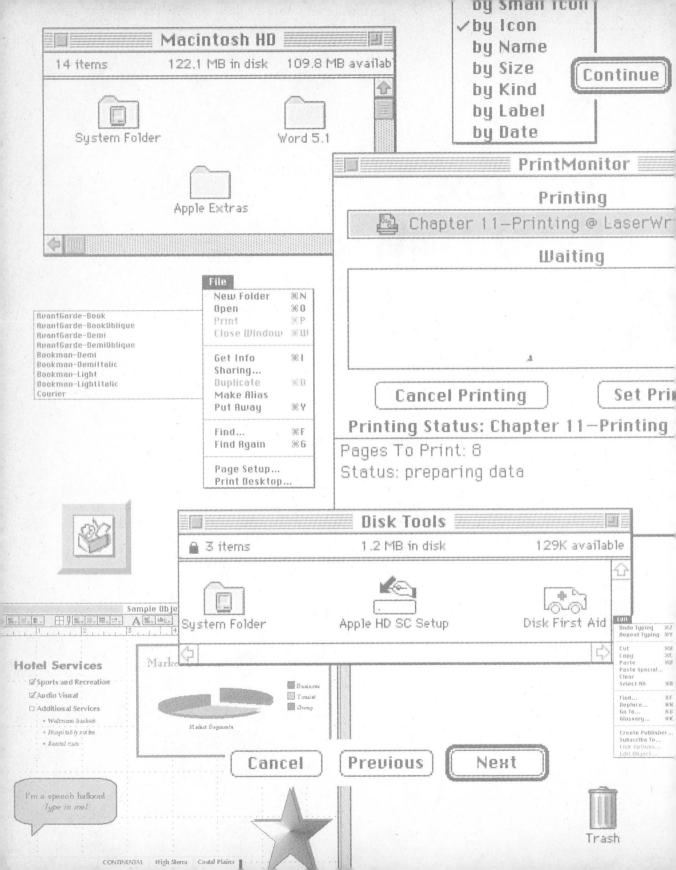

by Small Icon
✓ by Icon
by Name
by Size
by Kind
by Label
by Date

Continue

Macintosh HD

14 items   122.1 MB in disk   109.8 MB availab

System Folder   Word 5.1

Apple Extras

PrintMonitor

Printing

Chapter 11—Printing @ LaserWr

Waiting

Cancel Printing   Set Pri

Printing Status: Chapter 11—Printing

Pages To Print: 8
Status: preparing data

File

New Folder	⌘N
Open	⌘O
Print	⌘P
Close Window	⌘W
Get Info	⌘I
Sharing...	
Duplicate	⌘D
Make Alias	
Put Away	⌘Y
Find...	⌘F
Find Again	⌘G
Page Setup...	
Print Desktop...	

AvantGarde-Book
AvantGarde-BookOblique
AvantGarde-Demi
AvantGarde-DemiOblique
Bookman-Demi
Bookman-DemiItalic
Bookman-Light
Bookman-LightItalic
Courier

Disk Tools

🔒 3 items   1.2 MB in disk   129K available

System Folder   Apple HD SC Setup   Disk First Aid

Sample Obje

A

1   2   3   4

Hotel Services

☑ Sports and Recreation
☑ Audio Visual
☐ Additional Services
  • Welcome baskets
  • Hospitality suites
  • Rental cars

Marke

Business
Tourist
Group

Market Segments

Edit

Undo Typing	⌘Z
Repeat Typing	⌘Y
Cut	⌘H
Copy	⌘C
Paste	⌘U
Paste Special...	
Clear	
Select All	⌘B
Find...	⌘F
Replace...	⌘N
Go To...	⌘G
Glossary...	⌘K
Create Publisher...	
Subscribe To...	
Link Options...	
Edit Object...	

Cancel   Previous   Next

I'm a speech balloon!
Type in me!

Trash

CONTINENTAL   High Sierra   Costal Plains

Chapter 4

What's New in System 7.5

by Gene Steinberg

When System 7.0 first appeared in May of 1991, it took the Macintosh world by storm. It offered enhanced Finder capabilities, 32-bit memory addressing (the 8MB barrier could be exceeded at long last), and features such as File Sharing, and Publish and Subscribe. System 7.0 also caused a few headaches along the way as users had to buy software upgrades and update their hard drives to avoid strange and mysterious crashes.

A year and a half later, System 7.1 gave us WorldScript, for quick adaptation of the operating system for foreign language use, and System Enablers—the ability to quickly configure the operating system for use with new hardware simply by dropping a file into the System Folder.

Apple gave us desktop electronic mail capability with System 7.1.1, better known as System 7 Pro, which added a few cute Finder tricks too, such as placing a shaded rectangle around the directory window to which you're copying a file.

System 7.5 rolls all the features of previous System 7 versions into one huge package, cleans up some long-standing bugs here and there, and provides a number of new features to whet your appetite. In all, Apple promises over 50 enhancements for System 7.5.

The next few pages highlight the salient features of System 7.5. Then I give you a few helpful hints you'll want to know before you install it on your Macintosh.

Who Can Install System 7.5?

System 7.5, all by itself, requires a Mac Plus or later running at least 4MB of RAM. If you opt to add some of the frills, such as QuickDraw GX and PowerTalk, you want 8MB RAM available on your Mac. And it doesn't seem so long ago when a 1MB Macintosh could do it all.

System 7.5 Overview

As described in the pages that follow, Apple has assembled many System-related enhancements that you once had to buy separately and rolled them all together into System 7.5. Some of the handy utilities that you may have used to display a menu bar clock, provide submenus from your Apple menu, and offer other enhancements are now included as well.

In addition to offering new features, System 7.5 reportedly provides improved performance. Apple states that Finder-related functions (such as copying files, launching applications, switching among applications, and accessing items from the menu bar) will be noticeably faster. These are the areas that System 6 users long touted as superior to System 7. In addition, all of those bug fixes and enhancements from the System 7 Tune-Up and the various System Software Update packages will be rolled into System 7.5.

The next sections discuss some of the major features of System 7.5.

New Features

On the surface, System 7.5 looks much like previous System 7 versions. But as you begin to work with the new system software, you'll find some obvious and not-so-obvious changes. The following sections describe some of the highlights.

Apple Guide

System 7's hokey Balloon Help is here, but Apple has found a better way to guide you through your tasks. It's called Apple Guide, and it's almost good enough to replace some of the manuals that come with your new Macintosh.

If you are familiar with the context-sensitive help features of some programs, Apple Guide won't seem so strange to you, although it goes much further in terms of flexibility. Apple Guide offers step-by-step assistance to help you accomplish a particular function, and the initial help package is available at the Finder desktop, right from the Balloon Help menu. In addition to providing clearly-written text screens, on-screen objects are highlighted, or windows are opened and brought to the front, so you can see exactly what's being described in the text. Figure 4.1 shows the Macintosh Guide, the first Apple Guide module.

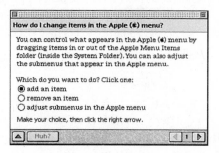

Fig. 4.1
Apple Guide
is a convenient,
interactive, online
manual for your
Macintosh.

Apple Guide is extensible. That means that software developers can include hooks to it in their software so that the same easy-to-understand learning environment can be transplanted to your word processing software, your publishing software, and other software products.

Macintosh Drag and Drop
The clunky cut-and-paste routine to transfer files between documents or from one part of a document to another may soon be a thing of the past. Macintosh Drag and Drop lets you literally drag a text or graphic object from one document and move it to another—without having to use the clipboard as an intermediary. You'll already find some drag-and-drop capability implemented in Microsoft Word, Nisus Writer, QuarkXPress, and WordPerfect. When software publishers fully support Macintosh Drag and Drop, you'll even be able to move information from one document to another without losing formatting. In addition, you'll be able to drag graphics and text right onto the Macintosh desktop and save it as a "Clippings" file. This file can later be dropped into another document or simply into another location in the document you were already working on.

Scriptable Finder
Using AppleScript, you'll be able to automate Finder operations and "play" them back with a simple keyboard command. As with macro programs such as QuicKeys and Tempo II Plus, you can record the operations you perform and then have AppleScript repeat the steps at your command.

II

System 7 Essentials

Enhanced Apple Menus

Here's one of those utilities that you used to have to buy as a separate product or download from a BBS as shareware. Enhanced Apple Menus is a Control Panel based on Microseeds HAM (Hierarchical Apple Menu). It generates submenus of up to five levels deep from your Apple menu. In addition, it sets aside folders that you can access to launch recently used applications, documents, or file server hookups.

WindowShade

WindowShade represents another Apple execution of a utility that's popular on the shareware circuit. After you install this utility, you can click the title bar of any window to collapse (reduce) it to the size of the title bar itself, as shown in figure 4.2. Clicking the title bar again (you have the choice of single-clicking, double-clicking, or triple-clicking in the WindowShade Control Panel) restores the window to its regular size. This feature will be a boon to people whose Mac desktop gets as cluttered as mine does.

Fig. 4.2
Apple's
WindowShade
allows you to
click away your
cluttered Mac
desktop and leave
just the title bars
in its place.

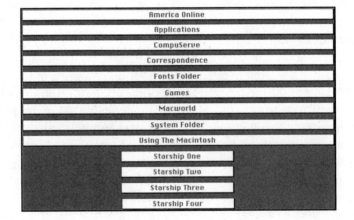

Desktop Hiding

Apple first introduced this feature (and some of those to follow) in its lower-cost Performa line. When you are working in an application, the Finder can be hidden automatically. That way you can't click out of your document and return to the Finder by mistake. You can still switch applications from the Finder's application menu, a number of handy third-party programs, and the one discussed next.

Launcher

Launcher is another feature of the Performa line. Like some popular commercial and shareware programs, Launcher puts up a floating palette with icon buttons representing applications, documents, and folders. It's a handy tool for quickly opening frequently used files.

Document Folder

The Performa-borne Document Folder sets aside a default location to store your document files. That relieves you of the task of hunting for files that are buried in a mass of folders and subfolders. This feature already exists in programs such as Now Software's Super Boomerang (part of Now Utilities) and in shareware favorites such as Default Folder.

Electronic "Sticky" Notes

If your working area, like mine, is cluttered with little notes reminding you to do one thing or another, you'll appreciate Apple's Electronic Notes feature. It allows you to create little notes on-screen and format them in different colors and type styles. And with Macintosh Drag and Drop installed, you can drag one note file to another.

New Scrapbook

Apple has at last taken a step towards making the Scrapbook more usable as a storage place for graphic and text items. The new Scrapbook will be sizeable. You'll be able to drag pictures right from your document to the Scrapbook and store them there. And you'll be able to drag items from the Scrapbook and place them in another document. Of course, some of this will require programs that support Macintosh Drag and Drop—and you won't see too many of those for a while.

New Notepad

In addition to Electronic Notes, Apple has made its Notepad a useful repository of text items. Instead of just cutting and pasting your notes into your documents, you'll be able to print directly from the Notepad desk accessory. You'll also be able to search out text items, as shown in figure 4.3, and place those items right into your document by using Macintosh Drag and Drop. The program in which you're working must support Drag and Drop for this feature to work.

Fig. 4.3
Searching for a
specific word in
a specific note
made easy with
Apple's new
Notepad desk
accessory.

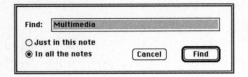

Time and Date Displayed in Menu Bar

In the past, a lot of Mac users have said that Apple programmer Steve
Christenson's popular freeware utility, SuperClock, should become part of
Apple's system software. SuperClock was one of the first menu bar clock utilities. You can customize the information you want on the clock and even
have it chime (with your chosen sounds) at 15-minute intervals. Well, Apple
has gotten the message, and you'll find all of SuperClock's functionality incorporated in System 7.5's Date and Time Control Panel (see fig. 4.4).

Fig. 4.4
Apple's enhanced
Date and Time
Control Panel
incorporates the
functions of
SuperClock.

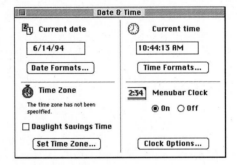

System and Application Folder Locking

Here is another Performa-bred feature. You can click checkboxes in the enhanced General Control Panel (shown in fig. 4.5) and prevent changes from
being made to the System Folder or any application folder. So if your Mac is
being used by a child or novice user, you have a slight measure of protection
against unexpected changes.

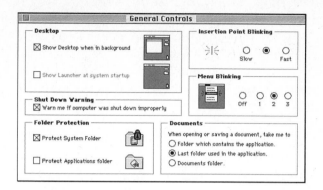

Fig. 4.5
Apple's new
General Control
Panel offers a new
repertoire of
options, many
borrowed from the
Performa line.

More Colorful Desktop Patterns

Apple has created a new program, called Desktop Patterns, that allows you to choose from up to 50 fancy desktop patterns. Figure 4.6 shows one of the selections.

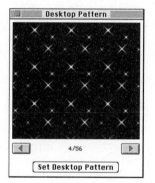

Fig. 4.6
One of the fancy
new patterns you
can create on your
Mac's desktop
under System 7.5.

The new repertoire of desktop patterns doesn't quite replace the wide range of choices you have in programs such as Now Fun, UnderWare, or Wallpaper, but many users will consider it more than satisfactory.

PC Compatibility

The awkward-to-use Apple File Exchange program is history. In its place, Apple is including two programs in System 7.5 that used to be available separately. First is Macintosh PC Exchange, which enables you to mount DOS/Windows disks on your desktop and copy the files to your Mac. If you have a Mac equivalent of a DOS or Windows program (such as Microsoft Word and WordPerfect), you'll be able to open those documents on your Mac and retain much of the document formatting.

The second program is Macintosh Easy Open, which enables you to attach a specific document file type to one of the applications you have. This helps to eliminate the dreaded message about an application being unavailable. Apple bundles file format translators with some of their products that will also provide almost seamless translation from a variety of DOS or Windows documents (even if you don't have a Mac equivalent to these programs).

PowerTalk

Apple's desktop electronic mail system will be included as part of System 7.5. You won't have to buy a separate product, as you did with System 7 Pro. As the number of PowerTalk-savvy programs grows, you'll be able to include e-mail from a mail server, online service, the Internet, fax, pagers, or voice mail in a single universal mailbox.

Performance Enhancements

The new features of System 7.5 discussed so far are largely window dressing. Many of the important parts of the new operating system lie beneath the surface. The following sections describe some of these features.

Four Gigabyte Volume Support

The Mac is being used more and more for multimedia production, both audio and video, and these files can positively eat up disk space with abandon. Multi-gigabyte hard drives are common, but the Mac operating system has only supported a two gigabyte volume until now. If you had a hard drive with greater capacity, you just partitioned it to divide it into smaller volumes. System 7.5 modifies the file system to accept single volumes of larger capacity. Remember that the minimum file size increases in direct proportion to the size of the drive, however—so even a small text file can grow as a result. Keep this in mind if you want to take advantage of this new feature.

Universal Enabler

Apple devised System Enablers so that they didn't have to produce a new system software version every time a new piece of hardware hit the streets. Unfortunately, System Enablers have been a curse to many of us. They are labeled with numbers instead of names, so it's hard to know which file goes with which machine (such as 088, 040, and so on). With System 7.5, Apple is going to support all existing Mac models without the need to have those pesky little Enablers running loose in the System Folder (there will be lots of other new things, though). Of course, relief is only temporary. When the next new Macintosh rolls down the pike, the Enablers will be back.

Apple Threads Manager

This feature requires a little explanation. The Mac operating system has what's called *cooperative multitasking*. That means that your active programs share CPU time, with the foreground program (the one you're working on) getting the lion's share of the attention. This sort of thing works most times, but when your Mac is working on things in the background (such as transferring files via modem or printing), you'll experience sluggish performance sometimes. Mouse movement will become imprecise. You'll enter text into a document and find that the display cannot keep up with your typing, just to cover a couple of examples.

Preemptive multitasking gives a program the authority to take over CPU cycles entirely, if needed. In theory, this creates a more stable working environment. A side effect is that if a program crashes for any reason, the other programs you're working on won't necessary be subject to crashing too, so you can continue working without restarting.

In practice, applications will have to be updated to support the Threads Manager, which is a first step towards preemptive multitasking, something Apple plans to offer in future operating systems beginning in 1995 and beyond.

QuickDraw GX

Chapter 10, "The Printing Chapter," discusses many of QuickDraw GX's enhancements to the Mac's printing architecture. The following list highlights some of the features:

- *Desktop Printers.* When you install QuickDraw GX, your printers will appear as desktop icons. You will be able to monitor the progress of a print job by double-clicking the icon, drag documents from one printer to another, and cancel a print job by dragging the icon representing that job to the trash. You also will be able to print a document by dragging the document icon to the printer icon.

- *New Print Dialog.* When you use a GX-savvy program, you'll be able to select the printer you want to process the job from a pop-up list—without having to go to the Chooser.

- *Electronic Documents.* QuickDraw GX's Portable Digital Document feature will allow you to create documents that can be viewed and printed on any Mac—even if the source program and fonts are not available.

- *Built-in Adobe Type Manager.* ATM is included with the GX package, providing clear display of your Type 1 fonts and good print quality with non-PostScript printers.

■ *WYSIWYG Color.* QuickDraw GX includes Apple's ColorSync technology, which allows precise color matching from the screen to the printer.

■ *Advanced Typography.* Additional character sets and foreign language keyboards will be supported by QuickDraw GX. Fancy typographic effects, such as ligatures, fractions, hanging punctuation, and optical alignment will be available when you use fonts and programs that are GX-savvy.

■ *New Clipboard Format.* The drudgery of converting pictures to formats such as EPS, PICT, or TIFF will be a thing of the past once GX-aware applications are available. You'll be able to cut and paste seamlessly. Macintosh Drag and Drop will provide an added convenience in moving files from one document to another.

■ *Multiple Page Formats.* This feature is, in part, already available in FrameMaker, the high-end document creation program from Frame Technologies—at least the ability to use both horizontal and vertical pages within a single document. QuickDraw GX adds the capability to use multiple page sizes as well.

System 7.5 Installation Strategies

Chapter 37, "Troubleshooting," explains how to perform a full, clean, system software installation. If you run into trouble with your System 7.5 installation, try following the steps presented in that chapter. For most System 7.5 installations, however, the following steps should result in an easy transition to the new Mac operating system:

1. Restart your Mac by using the System 7.5 Disk Tools floppy disk.

2. Run Apple's Disk First Aid on all your available hard drives.

3. If your Mac has an Apple hard drive, use Apple's HD SC Setup to update your hard drive.

> **Note**
>
> If you have non-Apple hard drives—or your hard drives are formatted with a non-Apple program—use that program to update your hard drives. Be sure that the formatting program is System 7 compatible.

4. Go to the System Folder on your startup disk (usually your internal hard drive) and remove the System file. Place it in the Preferences folder

or, if you don't want to retrieve any fonts or sounds from it, move it directly to the trash. Rename your startup disks System Folder to **Storage**.

5. Restart with your System 7.5 InstallMeFirst floppy disk. The Installer launches automatically.

6. Select the Easy Install option or, if you want to add or remove System 7.5 features, use the Customize option.

7. After installation has finished, pressing the Quit button on the Installer application window gives you the option to Restart or Shut Down your Macintosh. Choose Restart.

> **Note**
>
> Apple has updated the Macintosh file system to allow it to support a larger hard disk volume size. As a result, the desktop files on all of your hard drives are rebuilt automatically when you restart. This is a normal process.

8. After you've restarted your Mac, take a little time to adjust Control Panel settings and to launch a few of your favorite programs to make sure everything is working okay.

9. If your Mac is running normally, go to the Storage folder and drag over special application folders, such as the Aldus or Claris folders, to your newly created System Folder.

> **Caution**
>
> Before you reinstall any of your original Control Panels and Extensions, check Apple's ReadMe that comes with your System 7.5 upgrade package for late-breaking information on configuring the new operating system and compatibility with existing software.

10. Restore your non-Apple Extensions to the new System Folder in groups of two or three, restarting each time to make sure they are working properly before you restore the next batch.

11. If you have any problems using System 7.5, please read Chapter 37, "Troubleshooting," for further help.

> **Note**
>
> System 7.5 will also be available on a CD-ROM. If your Mac will boot from a CD-ROM, you can follow the steps we've outlined above in essentially the same way, except that your Disk Tools diagnostics will be done right from the CD-ROM, and you will have to double-click on the Apple Installer program icon to launch it. If your Mac cannot boot from a CD-ROM drive, you'll need to change your installation strategy somewhat. In this situation, we suggest you remove or disable all non-Apple Extensions in your System Folder (other than those you need to run your CD-ROM drive), reboot your Mac, and insert your System 7.5 CD-ROM disk. Then launch the System 7.5 installer and proceed with your system installation. If you have any difficulties in getting your new installation to work successfully, make a set of floppy disks from the disk image files on your CD-ROM disk, using the Apple Disk Copy program provided, and install from them, following the steps we've outlined above.

From Here...

This chapter only covered the basics of System 7.5. Throughout this book, a System 7.5 icon is placed in the margin next to paragraphs containing features that apply to Apple's new operating system.

What makes System 7.5 special is that almost everything will look and feel very close to what you're used to with previous System 7 versions, only it will work faster and smoother. You should be able to make the transition easily and with few software difficulties.

■ If you run into any problems installing System 7.5, read Chapter 37, "Troubleshooting." This chapter will help you get over any rough spots you might encounter.

Chapter 5

Understanding the Desktop and Finder

by Chris Oakes

The Finder appears on-screen each time you turn on your Macintosh. Its main purpose is to make it easy for you to manage the files you create with your applications (such as a word processor or a spreadsheet program).

This chapter explains the major elements of the Finder. These elements—windows, icons, menus, and folders—are simple to understand, and quite powerful in helping you manage your work. By the end of the chapter, you'll understand the following concepts and procedures:

- Where the Finder fits into your Macintosh work

- The difference between applications and documents

- What Icons represent

- Folders and Files

- The parts of the Macintosh window

- Pointing, clicking and dragging with the mouse

- How to use a menu

- How to use Macintosh Guide and Balloon Help

Once you understand these fundamentals of the Finder and the desktop, you'll be ready to learn how to organize your files, folders, and disks—the topic of Chapter 7, "Organizing Your Files, Folders, and Disks."

To help you better understand the Finder's workings, watch a demonstration of a basic Finder task: opening a document. This procedure involves many commonly used Finder elements and provides a context for the specific features covered later in the chapter. Before the demonstration of using the Finder to open a document, you should become familiar with one concept: the differences between applications, documents, and files.

Applications, Documents, and Files

An *application* is a software program, such as a word processor or financial spreadsheet, that applies the capabilities of the computer to a specific function. Sometimes, applications are referred to as *programs,* or *software.* The word processing application Microsoft Word was discussed in Chapter 4. When you use an application to create and edit text, sound, pictures or other types of information, you create and edit a *document,* which serves as a container for the information. Collectively, documents and applications are often referred to as *files.* "File" is also often used to refer to a document (see note).

> **Note**
>
> *Files,* in the plural form, is often used to refer to a group of Macintosh items. A group may consist of both documents and applications, as well as other types of files that may reside on a Macintosh disk. *File* and *document* are often used interchangeably. In Chapter 4, the term *file* was used throughout to keep the concepts simple, but the more specific term for a file created by an application is *document.*

Demonstration: Opening a Document

The document in this demonstration was created by the application TeachText. The name of the document is Read Me. It resides inside a folder on the hard disk called Macintosh HD. The hard disk appears in the upper right corner of figure 5.1.

Note

The names of items in this demonstration, including the names of folders, the document, and the name of the hard disk, are just examples. They do not necessarily match the names of items on your own hard disk. Nonetheless, the procedures used in the demonstration apply to all documents, folders, and disks, regardless of their actual names.

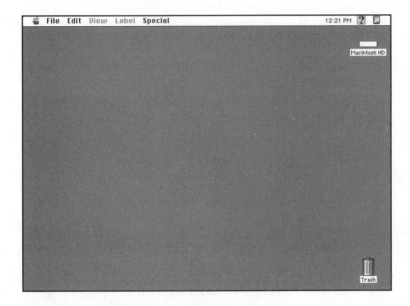

Fig. 5.1
The Macintosh Finder. The Macintosh hard disk is represented by Macintosh HD, displayed in the upper right corner.

To access the folder that contains the document, you need to open the hard disk by selecting the hard drive and choosing the Open command. The same procedure is used to open the folder—and finally, the document. The folder containing Read Me is called Apple Files. The following steps outline the procedure.

1. Using the mouse, click on the hard drive to select it. When the hard drive has been selected, the hard disk becomes darkened. In Macintosh terms, the object is said to be *highlighted,* as shown in figure 5.2. (Over the hard disk icon, you see the arrow cursor used to select it. You learn more about the cursor and the mouse later in this chapter.)

II

System 7 Essentials

Fig. 5.2
Once selected,
Macintosh HD
becomes high-
lighted.

2. From the File menu, choose the Open command. The hard drive window opens (the box entitled Macintosh HD in fig. 5.3). The open window contains a folder named Apple Files. Because the document you
   want to open is inside this folder, you need to open Apple Files next,
   just as you opened the hard drive.

3. Select the Apple Files folder and then choose Open from the File menu,
   as shown on the left side of figure 5.3. The Apple Files window opens.
   This window contains the document Read Me, which is the one you
   want to open.

Fig. 5.3
The Macintosh HD
window and the
Open command,
selected from the
File menu.

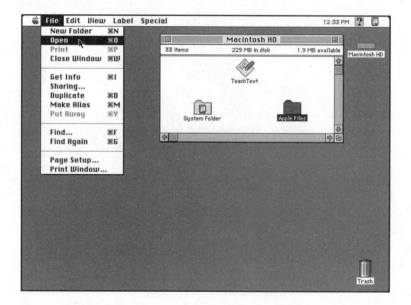

4. Using the mouse, select the document Read Me. The document is highlighted.

5. From the File menu, choose the Open command. Figure 5.4 shows the
   document selected in the Apple Files window. A pause occurs while the
   application that created the document launches—TeachText, in this
   case. After TeachText launches, the document's contents appear in a
   TeachText window (see fig. 5.5).

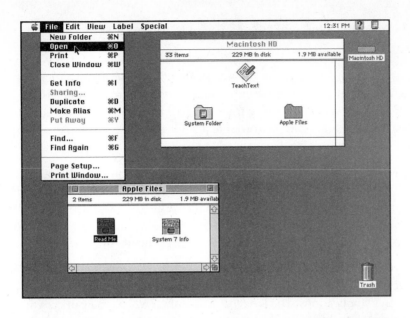

Fig. 5.4
"Read Me" is selected, and the Open command is chosen.

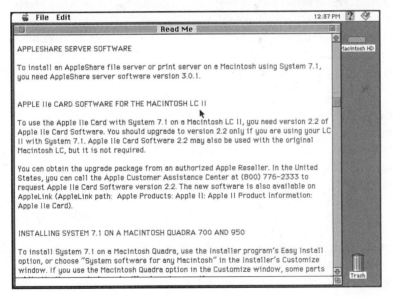

Fig. 5.5
The contents of the Read Me document, as seen in a window in the application TeachText.

System 7 Essentials

By carrying out this simple action, you have witnessed many of the Finder's features in action. A disk and folder were selected and opened, displaying windows. A menu command was chosen. Objects were selected with the mouse. In the rest of the chapter, you learn what these things are and how to manipulate them by using the mouse.

The Finder and Its Contents

The preceding procedure may have seemed natural enough, but if you think about it a little, you might wonder where it all took place. Until the final step, you weren't in any application, such as a word processor or a database program. You weren't choosing from a simple list of files or responding to a blinking command prompt. You were just in that "place" first pictured in figure 5.1.

One of the advantages of the Macintosh is that you don't have to be in a specific application to be "somewhere." The designers of the Macintosh didn't want you to turn on your computer only to be faced with a blank screen that waited for you to type a command. They made sure that you were somewhere right away. That somewhere is the Macintosh Finder.

Technically, the Finder is an application. This particular application serves as a place for you to organize and control your Macintosh disks, documents, and other applications. The Finder is also a place where you can get your bearings. You can visually perceive the things that reside on your Macintosh and then decide what you want to do with them. This visual orientation of the Finder is central to the Macintosh's famous graphical user interface. For the first time, the Macintosh Finder gave the personal computer user a recognizable, visual environment with which to start working.

Working on the Mac really is not much different than sitting down and working with the things on the top of a desk. That's why the gray area below the menu bar is called the *desktop*. It's also why organizing and manipulating the disks, folders, and files that reside on the desktop is known as *desktop management*. This familiar scene greets you every time you turn on your Macintosh.

Not only do you find your documents, applications, and disks in the Finder, but you also find a sense of comfort in knowing where you are and what is on your Macintosh. In this way, the Finder is like your Macintosh home. As you learn and use your Macintosh, you'll become comfortable and reassured by the Finder, just as you are by your real home.

What the Finder Is For

The Finder's main function is to provide a location for you to manage your desktop: where you organize and control your disks and the assorted documents and applications you have on them. This process is commonly referred to as *file management*. The following are tasks you can accomplish with files and disks in the Finder:

▶ See "The Finder as File Cabinet," p. 110

- View which files are on your hard disk and floppy disks

- Copy files from one disk to another

- Create new places to keep files (called *folders*)

- Move files to different places on the disk

- Erase files from disks

- Erase entire disks and *reformat* them, which enables you to use them all over again

- Assign special labels to files, indicating such properties as priority and purpose

- Obtain special information about files, such as their size, when they were created, and when they were last modified. You can also see which application created a document file.

- Search for files

Those tasks are the primary file management features of the Finder. You also can perform the following tasks, which don't fall under the file management category:

- Launch applications and open documents, as shown in the demonstration at the beginning of this chapter

- Access special Macintosh applications and features contained in the Apple menu, which is indicated by the little apple picture in the upper left of the menu bar.

II

System 7 Essentials

Although these lists tell you what the Finder does, you still may not be familiar with some of the terms. The following sections examine the elements of the Finder in detail.

System 6 Differences

All new Macintoshes run on System 7.0 (or later versions), but some older Macs run on a version of System 6.0, such as 6.0.4 or System 6.0.8. Many differences exist between System 7 and System 6, but in keeping with Macintosh interface consistency, they appear and behave in much the same way.

One difference in the System 6 Finder is the absence of the Label menu. Also, color Macs running System 6 might show a Color menu to the right of the Special menu. This menu enables you to change the color of a selected object.

Another difference is a less visual one. In System 7, when you deposit files in the Trash can, they are still there the next time you turn on your Macintosh. In System 6, these files are regularly deleted by the Macintosh—such as when you launch an application or shut down your Macintosh.

Icons: Representing Files, Folders, and Disks

When you first turn on your Macintosh, you usually see only two objects on the desktop: the hard disk and the Trash can. These objects are the two objects visible in figure 5.1. But what are these objects? The little picture called the hard disk, for example, is not the physical hard disk that contains your files. The actual hard disk is located inside your Macintosh case. And the Trash can is not really a trash can but just a picture of a trash can.

You have seen that these objects are more than just images. To be fair, they have plenty of substance to them. You have opened the hard disk and worked with its files. These files had real contents in them. As you may have guessed, the images *represent* actual objects. When you do something to the images, it happens to the objects they represent. The official name for these images is *icons*, and they are as important to the graphical Macintosh interface as windows and menus. They are another way for you to see, and thereby easily manipulate, the objects that reside on your Macintosh. Figure 5.6 shows and table 5.1 describes common Finder icons and the objects they represent.

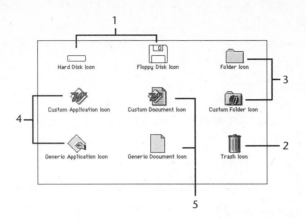

Fig. 5.6
Typical Finder
icons.

Table 5.1	Icons and Their Meanings
Icon	**What It Represents**
Disk icon (1)	An entire hard disk or floppy disk.
Trash icon (2)	File deletion. Files in the Trash will be "thrown away" or deleted.
Folder icon (3)	A container, like a real cardboard folder, for other folders and files.
Application icon (4)	A Macintosh application, such as a word processor.
Document icon (5)	A Macintosh document, such as a letter. It can also represent special files that make the Macintosh system work. Document icons often have the markings of the application that created them.

Folders and Files

Chances are, you are already familiar with folders. Just like manila folders, Macintosh folders can contain artwork and photographic documents. Any type of Macintosh file, including applications, can reside in a folder. Just as a file is a container of text and pictures, a folder is a container for Macintosh files. And like a file, a folder can be opened and closed.

You can create and name a folder and put it anywhere in the Finder. Macintosh *folders* commonly contain documents. For example, you can keep your letters home in a folder called Home Letters. You can keep monthly sales-related documents in a folder called January Sales Documents. And better yet, you can put that folder inside *another* folder called 1994 Sales Documents. As you can see, a folder in the Macintosh Finder is not much different from the manila folders you keep in your file cabinet.

▶ See "Creating a New Folder," p. 114

II

System 7 Essentials

The Window

So far, you have learned about several elements of the Finder—icons, files, and folders. This section discusses the Finder window.

If you have read all of Part II so far (Chapter 4 and the first part of this chapter), you have already had quite a bit of exposure to Macintosh windows. As you learned in Chapter 4, windows are one of the key ingredients in the Macintosh's interface consistency.

▶ See "Viewing Files and Folders," p. 122

In an application, a window displays the contents of a file. In the Finder, a window displays the contents of a disk or folder.

There are several parts of the window that let you control its size, position, and other characteristics. Figure 5.7 identifies these parts and the following list describes them:

- *Title bar.* The bar along the top of the window is called the title bar because it contains the window's title. To move a window, you click anywhere on the title bar and then drag the image to a new location.

- *Close box.* The small box at the left end of the title bar is the close box. Clicking in the close box closes the window, making it disappear from the desktop until you reopen it.

- *Zoom box.* At the other end of the title bar is a box with a smaller box in its corner. This box is called the zoom box and is used to maximize and reduce the size of the window on the desktop.

- *Size box.* The double box in the lower-right-hand corner of the window is the size box. It enables you to stretch and shrink the window to any size you want.

- *Scroll bars.* The shaded bars along the right and bottom edge of the window are the scroll bars. If you click the arrows at each end of the scroll bars, the currently invisible areas of the window come into view, while visible areas move out of view. Alternatively, the box inside the scroll bar (called the *scroll box*) can be moved to scroll left or right, up or down. (In the Finder and most applications, if an entire window's contents are already visible, the scroll bars are made inactive. Inactive scroll bars do not show the gray shading and scroll boxes that appear in active scroll bars.)

In order to manipulate (select, move, copy, and delete) the objects in the Finder, you need to know how to use the mouse. After you learn how to use the mouse, you will use it to manipulate the final element of the Macintosh Finder: the menu.

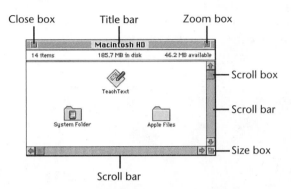

Fig. 5.7
The parts of a Macintosh window.

The Mouse: Your Virtual Hand

Imagine that the Macintosh desktop were an actual desktop. To move an object, you would just reach out your hand, grab the object, and move it. Use a "virtual hand" to manipulate objects on the desktop—the mouse controls the arrow pointer on-screen.

You move the *mouse,* the small rolling unit with a cord like a mouse tail, around your actual desktop. Its position and movement are matched on the Macintosh screen by the small black arrow pointer. When you move the mouse, the arrow moves to reflect the movement. Move the mouse left, and the arrow moves left. Move the mouse straight away from you and the cursor moves upward on the screen. Any direction you move the mouse is matched by the movement of the arrow. If you're unfamiliar with these motions, a few minutes of fiddling will make you comfortable with mouse movements.

Pointing, Clicking, and Dragging

Positioning the arrow over a desired object is called *pointing* at the object. Suppose that you point to an object in the Finder, such as the hard disk, and want to manipulate it. As you saw in the demonstration, to manipulate an object on-screen, you first must *select* it. After you point at the object, you press the mouse button to select it. The mouse button is located on the top of the mouse, at the end where the cord is connected. To select an object with the mouse then, point at the object, and then press mouse button once. This is called *clicking* on the object.

II

System 7 Essentials

As on a real desktop, you can move objects on the Finder's desktop. You may want to move an object into the Trash, for example.

Figure 5.8 shows the Trash can after it has been moved from its home in the lower right corner to the middle of the desktop.

To *drag* an object, use the mouse to click the object, and then hold the mouse button down. When you move the mouse around, an outline of the object stays with the cursor (as if it's "in your hand"). When you release the mouse button, the object appears at the new place on the desktop.

Fig. 5.8

The Finder's Trash can has been *dragged* to the middle of the desktop.

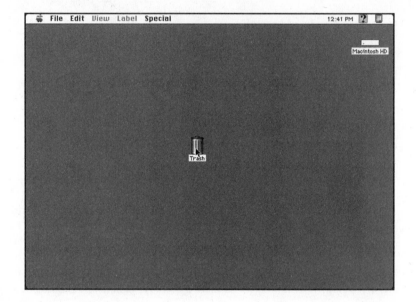

There is an interesting variation on the ubiquitous mouse-click. It is the *double-click*. A double-click consists of clicking on an icon two times quickly. This unique action has the same effect as selecting the icon of any disk, folder, document or application and choosing the Open command from the File menu. Many people find double-clicking a nice shortcut for the Open command, because it reduces several steps to one. Try it—you just might like it!

> **Note**
>
> Double-clicking is used as a shortcut in Macintosh applications, as well. It's used in dialog boxes, for example, such as the Open and Save As dialog boxes accessed within applications. Double-clicking a file or folder in an Open dialog box has the same effect as in the Finder—it opens the item in one easy step. In fact, double-clicking is often incorporated into certain features of applications. A lot can be discovered in some applications by "double-clicking your way around." Tool palettes and icon bars are often good candidates for double-clicking short-cuts. If in doubt, double-click—you just might learn something new! (Use caution to make sure your actions won't affect any important document data.)

Tip
If you have any problems double-clicking, you may need to adjust the speed. Simply open the Apple menu, choose Control panels and Mouse. Select one of the three speed options available. The space between the arrows corresponds to the time between clicks.

As you can see, the mouse is a crucial part of using the Macintosh. Before long, it will feel like a natural extension of your own hand. Some practice will get you comfortable with this virtual hand in no time. Having learned the simple ways of the Macintosh mouse, you're now ready to see how it's used to choose a menu command.

Choosing a Menu Command

In both Chapter 4 and in the demonstration at the beginning of this chapter, menu commands were used to manipulate objects—to open documents, launch applications, and copy and paste text. In all cases, the mouse was used to issue these commands. We'll now look at the exact procedure for choosing commands.

To use a menu command, you select it with the mouse. But first you need to click the menu. When you do so, the menu will appear, but disappear again as soon as you release the mouse button. To keep the menu visible, therefore, you simply hold the mouse button down.

Suppose that you want to select the Open command from the File menu, the left-most word on the menu bar. You would follow these steps:

1. Point and click anywhere on the word File in the menu bar, holding the mouse button down after you click. As seen in figure 5.9, a list of commands appears.

II

System 7 Essentials

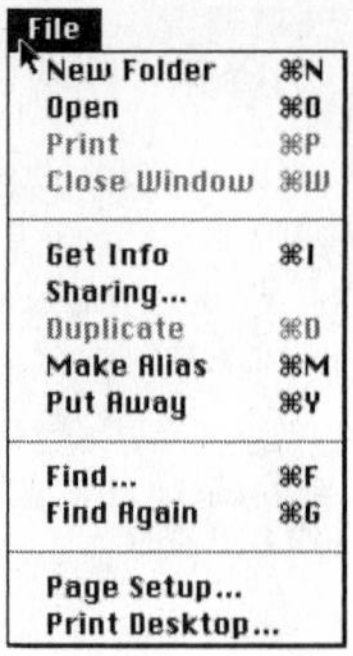

Fig. 5.9

The Finder's File menu, after it has been selected with the mouse.

2. Move the cursor down the menu. When you pass over the available commands, they are highlighted (the command turns white, and the background turns black). The Open command is shown highlighted in figure 5.10.

Fig. 5.10

The File menu's Open command has been high-lighted.

3. To select the Open command, release the mouse button when the command is highlighted. The menu blinks, and the selected object opens.

This procedure is applied to any menu selection. After a little practice, choosing menu commands is easy. If you get confused about how to use the mouse while reading on in the book, just come back and review these simple procedures.

Table 5.2 Elements of the Finder

Finder Element	What It Does
Icon	Represents a Macintosh application, document, folder, or disk
Disk	A container for Macintosh files; like a file cabinet
Folder	A categorized container for Macintosh files; Like a manila folder
Application	A Macintosh program, such as a word processor
Document	A file created with an application; may contain text, pictures, sound, or video
Window	Displays the contents of a disk or folder
Menu	Displays a list of selectable commands
Trash Can	Holds files you want to throw away

Using Macintosh Guide and Balloon Help

This chapter's introduction to the Finder and the desktop helps you gain a general understanding of the Finder and its various features. The Macintosh itself can help you take this understanding further with a remarkable new feature included in System 7.5. This feature helps both novice and intermediate users learn specific techniques and concepts relating to the Finder and the Macintosh in general. It's called Macintosh Guide.

While System 7.0's built-in help system, Balloon Help, helps you identify simple Finder features such as icons, menus, and parts of a Macintosh window, Macintosh Guide goes much further by actually *showing* you how to accomplish specific Finder tasks.

> **Note**
>
> To use System 7.0's and 7.1's Balloon Help, from the Help menu (indicated by the question mark icon at the right end of the menu bar), choose Show Balloons. Then, by simply pointing at various items in the Finder, such as icons and menus, you see informational text contained in small speech balloons (see fig. 5.11). Some Macintosh applications support Balloon Help, too. You turn Balloon Help on in an application the same way as in the Finder. With Balloon Help active, you can continue to use your Macintosh as usual—balloons will appear and disappear without getting in your way. The balloons provide basic information about what each particular Finder element is for and how to use it. To turn off Balloon help, from the Help menu, choose Hide Balloons.

Fig. 5.11
Balloon Help appears when you point at Finder items such as the Trash can.

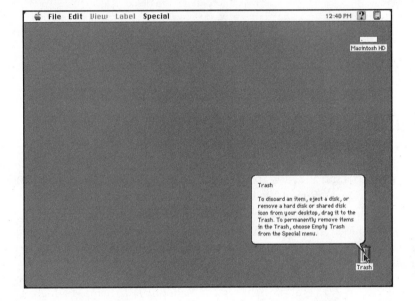

Macintosh Guide tells you how to perform a task, and then actually helps you complete the task by guiding you to the menus, icons, and other elements that the task might involve. The Macintosh circles these elements much like you'd circle items on a piece of paper using a highlighting marker. (Refer to figure 5.12.) It also guides you by underlining key menu items. If you have a color monitor, it will also make these menu items appear in red. The Guide waits patiently by while you perform each step of a particular task, and then guides you on to the next step.

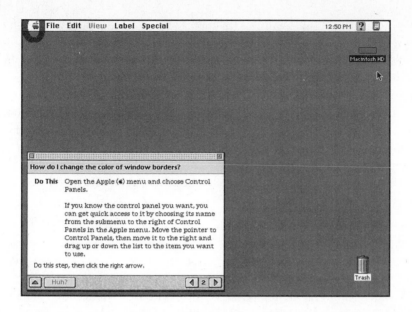

Fig. 5.12
Macintosh Guide indicates menus and other items involved in a task by actually marking the item with a thick circle. The Apple menu icon is circled here.

You access Macintosh Guide using the same menu used to access Balloon Help in early versions of System 7 (see note), although this menu's icon is now yellow and red in color. In fact, Balloon Help remains available in the same menu.

To access Macintosh Guide, from the Help menu (indicated by the question mark icon on the right end of the menu bar), choose Macintosh Guide. The Macintosh Guide window then appears on your screen (see fig. 5.13) You can view help information by Topic, by Index subjects, or by having Macintosh Guide look for the information for you. A button for each of these options appears at the top of the Macintosh Guide window, as seen in figure 5.13. Click once on one of these buttons to make your choice.

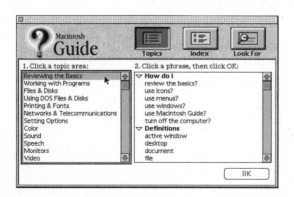

Fig. 5.13
Information viewed by Topic in Macintosh Guide's open window.

Viewing by topic is like perusing the table of contents in a book. The main topic headings appear in the list on the left, while subheadings for each topic appear on the right. To bring up a topic and its associated subheadings, simply click once on the topic's name in the list on the left. The subheadings will appear in the list on the right. (There may be a short pause before the subheadings appear.) To have Macintosh Guide show you the steps involved in one of these subheadings, click on the subheading once and then click the button marked "OK," which appears in the lower-right of the Macintosh Guide window. Alternatively, you can simply double-click on the subheading in the list. To view any additional items in either list, use the scroll arrows in the scroll bar to the right of the list.

If you know the specific topic you want information about, such as "active window," "copying," or "desktop," click the "Index" button. It causes an alphabetical list to appear on the left, much like a book's alphabetical index. Click one of the items in the list to see its associated subheadings, which appear in a list on the right (see fig. 5.14). To choose a subheading, once again you click on the subheading and click the "OK" button—or simply double-click the subheading. The horizontal bar with the letters of the alphabet at the top of the index list on the left will let you quickly change the alphabetical letter of the topics that are listed (see fig. 5.14). To quickly move to topics beginning with the letter "G" simply click on "G" in the slider bar. If the letter you want doesn't appear on the bar, click on the last letter on the right (or left) and drag your mouse to the right (or left) while holding the mouse button down. More letters of the alphabet will come into view.

Fig. 5.14
Macintosh Guide subjects as seen after clicking the Index button.

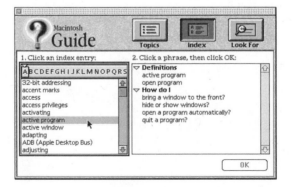

If you want Macintosh Guide to look for a specific topic, such as "window," click the "Look For" button. After you click this button, a small space is provided where you can type the name of the topic to look for (see fig. 5.15). Once you've done so, click the "Search" button. After a short wait, a list of subheadings appears in a list on the right. To choose one of them, click on the subheading and click the "OK" button, or just double-click on the subheading.

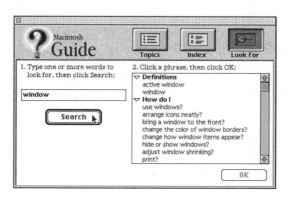

Fig. 5.15
Macintosh Guide's "Look For" window allows you to search for topics by keywords, such as "window."

Once you've chosen the desired subheading using any of these methods, Macintosh Guide will lead the way from there. Simply read the definitions or step-by-step instructions provided in each informational window. You'll find Macintosh Guide very easy to use and learn.

Note

If you're still unclear about how to use Macintosh Guide, you can have Macintosh Guide itself provide you with more tips on how to use it. Simply use the "Look For" button to search for the subject "Guide," Macintosh Guide will appear in the list on the right. Double-click on it and Macintosh Guide will soon be telling you a little bit more about itself. (Talk about self-help!)

II

System 7 Essentials

From Here...

In this chapter, you learned about the main elements of the Macintosh Finder and desktop. Upcoming chapters contain more Finder information. See the following chapters to learn how to manipulate and organize the Finder's files and to learn about special versions of the Finder, System 7, and System 7.5.

- Chapter 4, "What's New in System 7.5," highlights some of the special new features of the Finder and the Macintosh in general with the introduction of System 7.5.

- Chapter 6, "Using System 7 for the Performa and At Ease," shows you the special features contained in System 7 on Performa Macintosh models. It also covers the special file management utility, "At Ease."

- Chapter 7, "Organizing Your Files, Folders, and Disks," shows you how to carry out common Finder tasks, and how to use these tasks to organize your files, folders, and disks.

Chapter 6

Using System 7 for the Performa and At Ease

by Kay Nelson

You may be using a special kind of Macintosh called a Performa. Performas are sold in retail stores such as Sears and Circuit City instead of at Apple dealers. A Performa has the same hardware as a regular Macintosh; the difference between it and other Macs is that it uses a slightly modified operating system called System 7.P that makes it easier for new users to find their way around. A Performa usually comes with several different programs already installed on the machine so that new users don't have to worry about installing software.

This chapter helps you understand the differences between the Performa and other Macs. You learn the following:

- How to launch programs on a Performa
- How to save documents
- How to switch between programs
- How to back up the software that came with your Performa
- How to set up and use At Ease

There are two major differences in the ways you use the Performa's operating system and the standard System 7:

- You normally launch programs from a special window called the Launcher that appears when you start your Performa.
- You save documents in a special Documents folder, which makes it easy to locate all your documents.

One other difference that experienced Mac users will note is that the Performa shows you only one program at a time, even if you have several running. This makes it easy for new users to switch from one running program to another.

This chapter assumes that you know the basics of how to get around on a Macintosh, such as double-clicking, choosing items from menus, and opening and closing windows.

Using the Launcher

When you first start your Performa, you'll see a special window called the Launcher on your desktop (see fig. 6.1). The icons in it represent programs that were already installed on your Performa, so the ones you see in figure 6.1 may not match what you see on-screen, depending on which programs you have. You can add programs to the Launcher or remove them from it, as you'll see later.

Fig. 6.1
The Launcher appears when you start a Performa.

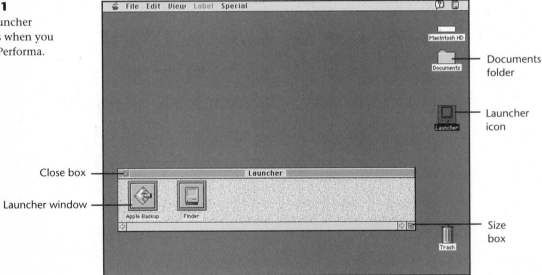

To start a program, all you have to do is click its icon in the Launcher window. You'll hear a click, and then the program will start. If the Launcher window isn't active (with stripes in its title bar), you have to click in its window twice—once to activate the Launcher window and then again to start the program you're launching. Here's how to work in the Launcher:

- *Scrolling in the Launcher*. If there are more programs stored on your Performa than the Launcher window can display, you can scroll with the scroll arrows or scroll box to see the other programs.

- *Resizing the Launcher*. You can also resize the Launcher window. Drag the size box in the lower right corner inward to make the window smaller or outward to make it larger.

- *Closing the Launcher*. If you want to close the Launcher window to get it out of your way, click its Close box or press ⌘-W when that window is active.

> ### Note
>
> You'll also see icons for the Launcher and for a Documents folder on your desktop. If you close the Launcher window and need to open it again, double-click that Launcher icon on the desktop.

- *Arranging the Launcher Window*. You can move the Launcher window around on your desktop by dragging it by its title bar. If you'd rather always have it stacked on one side of the desktop when you start your Performa, select Vertical from the View menu.

Adding and Deleting Programs

When you work with your computer system, you'll want to add and delete programs. With the Launcher, adding and deleting programs is easy.

Adding a Program

You need to add any new programs you buy to the Launcher. You can make an alias (see Chapter 5) of the program so that the original program icon stays in its original folder. Follow these steps:

1. Install the program according to the manufacturer's instructions. Normally, you'll double-click an Installer icon that's on the disk the program comes on. Then follow the instructions on-screen.

2. When the program has been installed, locate its icon on your hard disk. It will probably be in a folder that has the same name as the program. If you install ClarisWorks, for example, look for a foldername Claris-Works, followed by a version number. You can use the Find command on the Finder's File menu to find the folder; ⌘-F is the shortcut.

3. Click the program icon to select the folder. From the File menu, choose Make Alias. Drag the alias to the desktop and then to the Launcher Items folder in the System Folder (see fig. 6.2).

Now your program appears in the Launcher when you start the Performa.

Fig. 6.2
Make an alias of any new programs you get and drag it to the Launcher Items folder inside the System Folder.

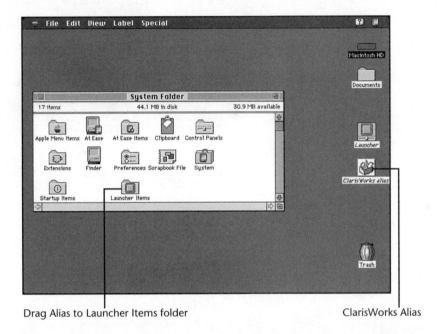

Drag Alias to Launcher Items folder   ClarisWorks Alias

Note

You can't drag icons to the Launcher window. The buttons in the Launcher window represent the programs that are in the Launcher Items folder in your System Folder. You could drag the original icon of a program to the Launcher Items folder if you wanted, but using aliases enables you to keep the original icon of the program in the folder with its other program files.

Deleting a Program

To delete a program from the Launcher, drag its icon out of the Launcher Items folder in the System Folder. If you're deleting an alias (its name will be in italics), you can drag it to the Trash and get rid of it. If you're deleting an original program icon, drag it to the desktop and use the Put Away command (⌘-Y) on it to put it back where it came from.

Working with Documents

The Documents folder on a Performa normally holds all the documents you create. Whenever you save a document, the Performa automatically opens the Documents folder for you to save it in. That way, beginners can easily find all the documents they create without looking through a series of folders for them. There may be other documents that are stored in folders that come with programs when you install them, so each and every one of your documents may not be in that Documents folder. All the documents you save will be stored there, unless you take extra steps to store them elsewhere. You'll see how to do that soon.

Opening Documents

You can open documents in the following two ways:

■ By double-clicking a document's icon in the Documents folder

■ By opening a program's File menu and choosing the Open command (⌘-O)

If you use the Open command in a program, you'll be taken to the Documents folder. Just double-click the name of the document you want (see fig. 6.3). The dialog box you see may be slightly different from the one in figure 6.3, depending on the program you're using. This dialog box is for ClarisWorks.

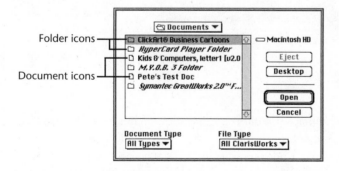

Fig. 6.3
Document icons look like small pages with one corner turned down.

II

System 7 Essentials

If the document you want isn't in the Documents folder, you may need to look for the folder that it is in. You can click any folder icons in the list to open them. Click the Desktop button to the right of the list to go to the desktop. Then double-click the name of your hard disk to open it and see the folders that are stored on it. You can keep opening folders until you find the document for which you're looking.

> **Note**
>
> Click the Documents folder name at the top of the dialog box. You'll see `Desktop` listed at the bottom of the hierarchy of folders that lead to the folder you're in. Drag to `Desktop` and release the mouse button to go to the desktop. You can also click the tiny icon next to the name of your hard disk, just to the right of the list in an Open dialog box, to go to the desktop.

Saving Documents

On a Performa, whenever you use a program's File menu's Save As command, you are taken to the Documents folder to save your document (see fig. 6.4). (When you choose Save, the document is saved in whichever folder it was previously saved in.)

Fig. 6.4
Other programs' Save As dialog boxes may look a little different from this one from ClarisWorks, but they all work basically the same.

> **Note**
>
> The first time you save a document, no matter whether you use the Save (⌘-S) or Save As command, you are taken to the Save As dialog box because the document doesn't have a name yet.

Just start typing to replace the name Untitled; then click Save or press the Return key. If a document with the same name is already in the Documents folder, you are asked whether you want to replace it with the document you're saving now. Be sure to give each document you save a unique name so that you don't mistakenly replace something you want to keep with something else.

Saving into a Different Folder

You may not always want to save documents into the Documents folder, but it's a good idea to do that if you're a beginner. You can save a document into a folder other than the Documents folder in the following ways:

- Double-click any folder listed in the Documents folder to open it, and then save the document in it.

- Click the Desktop button to go to the desktop, where you can double-click the name of your hard disk (Macintosh HD in the list in figure 6.5) and then open any folder on your hard disk and save the document in it.

Fig. 6.5
Double-click the
name of your hard
disk to open it and
save documents
on it.

You can also save a document onto a floppy disk, as discussed later in this chapter.

Note

When you become accustomed to your Performa and get more experienced, you may not want to save all your documents in the Documents folder any more. All you need to do is change the option in the Performa control panel (see the "Using the Performa Control Panel" section later in this chapter) or rename the Documents folder, and the Performa's operating system won't automatically take you there any more.

Saving a Document under Another Name

To save another version of a document you've already saved, or save the same document under another name so that you have two copies of it, choose Save As from the File menu and give the document a different name.

Note

You can use the Finder's Duplicate command (⌘-D) to make a copy of a file. Using this command is often faster than using the Save As command and renaming the document. The Finder will automatically add copy to the end of the document's name so that you know exactly what it's a copy of, instead of trying to remember which names you gave it and its copy.

Saving onto a Floppy Disk

Sometimes you may want to save a document onto a floppy disk so that you can take it with you, keep a backup copy of it, or give it to somebody else. To save a document onto a floppy disk instead of onto your hard disk, if you're running a program, follow these steps:

1. Insert the floppy disk in your disk drive.

2. From the program's File menu, choose Save As.

3. When you see the Save As dialog box, click the Desktop button. Notice in figure 6.6 that the floppy disk that's in the drive is listed: `New Disk`.

Fig. 6.6
A floppy disk that's been inserted in the drive (*New Disk* in this figure) is listed in the desktop.

4. Double-click the name of the floppy disk to open it.

5. Save your document.

If you're at the desktop, instead of running a program, you can simply drag the icon of a document to the icon of the floppy disk to make a copy of it on that disk.

Creating a New Document

If you're running a program on a Performa, you create a completely new document just as you do on a regular Macintosh: from the File menu, choose New or press ⌘-N for the keyboard shortcut. The Open command is for documents that have already been saved.

Note

In some programs, like TeachText, you may need to close the window you were working in before you create a new document because you can only have one document at a time open. If you try to choose New from the File menu, that command will be dimmed. Just click the window's close box or press ⌘-W to close the window.

Switching between Programs on a Performa

Another way a Performa's operating system is different from that of a standard Macintosh is that you see only one program running at a time, although you may have launched several programs. On a standard Macintosh, it's easy for your screen to become cluttered with windows from several different programs. To move from one program to another, all you have to do is click in a window of that program. This can confuse beginners, so a Performa shows you only one program at a time (the one that's active), although that program may have several windows open.

The icon at the upper right corner of your screen, on the far right of the menu bar, represents the active program. It changes, depending on which application is active. This icon is called the Application menu (see fig. 6.7).

To switch between programs that are running, click the Application menu icon.

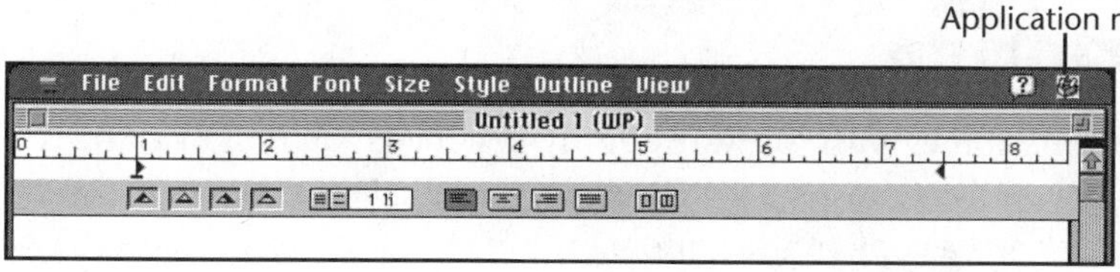

Application menu

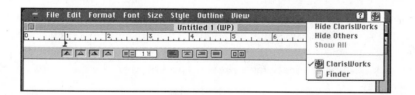

Fig. 6.7
The active program's icon appears in the Application menu.

All the programs that are running are listed there (see fig. 6.8). To select a different program, drag to highlight the program's name; then release the mouse button when the program's name is highlighted.

Fig. 6.8
The check mark indicates which program is active.

Caution

Windows can sometimes cover up other windows. You can resize windows or drag them by their title bars to see what's underneath.

Starting Programs When Other Programs Are Running

If you're working in one program, you may sometimes want to start another program and then switch to it. To do that on a Performa, follow these steps:

1. Choose Finder from the Application menu.

2. The Launcher window should appear. If it doesn't, double-click the Launcher alias on your desktop.

3. Click the program's icon to start it.

If the program you want to start running isn't in the Launcher, locate its icon in the Finder and double-click it, or double-click an icon of a document that the program created.

Backing Up the Programs on Your Performa

A Performa comes with software already installed; you don't get the programs on floppy disks because they've been pre-installed on your hard disk for you. You may need a copy of these programs on floppy disks if something goes wrong with your computer. The Performa also comes with a built-in Backup utility program, so you should use it right away to back up the contents of your hard disk.

You'll need at least 20 high-density floppy disks to back up what's on your Performa as it comes from the factory. If you installed new programs on your computer after unpacking it, you'll need more than 20 disks. To start the backup process, click the Apple Backup icon in the Launcher. Then follow the directions on-screen (see fig. 6.9). You'll be told when to insert a new disk as each disk fills up. Be sure to label the disks according to the directions on-screen.

> **Note**
>
> Lock each disk as soon as it's full so that you don't use it for something else by mistake. Open the tab on the disk so that you can see through the hole. When the hole is open, the disk is locked, and its contents can't be changed.

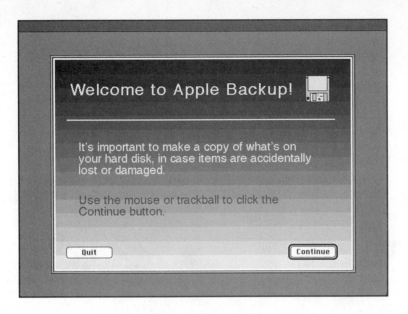

Fig 6.9
Use Apple Backup
to start backing up
your hard disk.

Backing Up the System Folder

You can just back up your System Folder instead of backing up everything on your Performa. If you don't have enough disks on hand for a full backup, back up just the System Folder; you'll need only five disks to do that. If something happens to your Performa later and you can't get it started, you'll be able to restore the System Folder and perhaps get started again. When you have enough disks, back up the whole Performa so that you can restore all of its programs and files if necessary.

Caution
It is extremely important to make a backup of the System as some Performa models are sold with only a full copy of the System software on the hard drive.

Restoring Your Programs

If something happens and you need to restore your System Folder, the programs you've backed up, or both, to your Performa's hard disk, turn your Performa off. Then locate the backup disks that you made, and follow these steps:

1. Put the Utilities disk that came with the Performa in the disk drive and turn on the computer.

2. Double-click the Apple Restore icon on the Utilities disk.

3. Follow the instructions on the screen to restore your System Folder or all of your files.

4. Restart the Performa.

Startup Tricks for Advanced Users

If you're already experienced on a Macintosh, you may find returning to the Launcher to start programs a little cumbersome. Try these tricks to speed up starting programs on a Performa:

■ Start programs by double-clicking their icons outside the Launcher. Your programs are normally stored in an Applications folder on your hard disk, and you can double-click their icons or names to start them from that folder.

■ Make aliases of programs and put them anywhere on your desktop. If there are programs you use frequently, make aliases of them and store the aliases out on the desktop or put them in the Apple Menu Items folder in your System Folder so that they appear on the Apple menu.

■ Put any program you always want to start up inside your Startup Items folder. Drag a program's icon (or an alias of its icon) into the Startup Items folder inside your System Folder. When your Performa starts, all you have to do is click in the program's window to go to it.

■ Start a program running by double-clicking a document that was created in the program.

Documents are stored in a special folder, as you'll see in the section "Working with Documents" later in this chapter.

Removing the Launcher

As you get accustomed to your Performa, you may decide that you want to do away with the Launcher so your computer operates more like a regular Macintosh. To remove the Launcher, follow these steps:

1. Open the Apple menu and choose Control Panels.

2. Select the Launcher icon and drag it out of the Control Panels folder.

Don't put it in your System Folder. You can drag it to the icon of your hard disk to store it there.

3. Close the Control Panels window.

4. Open your System Folder (you can use the Find command, ⌘-F, to locate it quickly).

5. Open the Startup Items folder in the System Folder.

6. Drag the icon of the Launcher alias out of the Startup Items folder. You can throw it away in the Trash because you can always make a new alias from the original Launcher icon later.

7. Drag the icon of the Launcher alias on the desktop to the trash.

8. Empty the Trash.

To make the Launcher appear again when you start up, drag its alias back into the Startup Items folder and drag its original icon back into the Control Panels folder. Then restart your Performa, and the Launcher window will automatically appear on startup again.

Using the Performa Control Panel

Rather than remove the Launcher, you may just want to turn some of the special features on or off. You can customize the Launcher in the Performa control panel (which is found in the Control Panels folder inside the System Folder). These features, such as hiding the Finder and establishing a default folder for your documents, are what separates the Performa system software from the standard versions of System 7.

Following is a description of the capabilities provided in the Performa control panel. The following four features are active if there's an X in the check box. Simply click the check box to turn the features off.

- *Finder Hiding.* When you work in an application, all items on your desktop are hidden when this option is checked, except for the desktop pattern you've selected. If you want to switch to the Finder or another program, you select it from the application menu at the upper right side of the menu bar.

- *Launcher Open at Startup.* When this feature is checked, the Launcher window opens automatically when you boot your Performa.

■ *System Folder Protection.* When this feature is checked, you cannot delete or rename files in the System Folder.

■ *Applications Folder.* When this feature is checked, you cannot delete or rename files in the Applications folder.

There are three more selections offered in the Performa control panel. They are used to specify a default location for all the new documents that you save for the first time, using the Save As dialog box. These selections help simplify the task of finding a document if you want to work on it at a later time. It also helps prevent your documents from being saved in unpredictable locations. Here are the choices that are available:

■ *Default to Folder with Application.* Each program you use on your Performa has its own folder that contains the application and some of its support files. When you choose this option, all new files you save are placed in that folder.

■ *Default to Documents Folder.* When you choose this option, all new files you save are placed in the Documents folder.

■ *Default to Last Folder Used.* When you choose this option, your new document is saved to the last folder used, no matter what it is.

> ### Note
>
> In System 7.5, all of the features of the Performa control panel (except the automatic opening of Launcher at startup) become a part of the General Control Panel and are available to all Macintosh users.

Setting Up At Ease

At Ease 2.0 is a special program that comes with the Performa. It makes the computer much simpler to use than System 7 or 7.P, but what you can do is also more restricted. With At Ease on, Applications are in an Applications folder, documents are represented by buttons in a Documents folder, and there's no Trash, so nothing can be deleted by mistake. If password protection is on, there's no way to get to the desktop unless you know the password. As the "owner," or system administrator—even though your "system" may be a third-grade class, a few part-time office workers, or a couple of young children in the home—you choose which programs and documents each user can have access to, whether to display full or restricted menus, and how users can open and save documents.

If you're setting up At Ease for others to use, you'll need to read this section. Later in this chapter, the section "Using At Ease" provides more information on At Ease.

If At Ease is on, you'll see a screen similar to the one in figure 6.10 when you start your Performa.

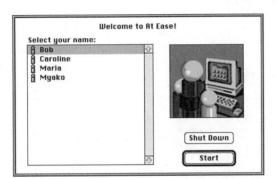

Fig. 6.10
The At Ease startup screen.

Note

At Ease can be installed on any Macintosh, not just on a Performa. If you're an experienced user, you may want to purchase this program and install it on any Macintosh that allows access to small children or the general public or in any other situation in which users have unrestricted access to a Macintosh.

Turning On At Ease

On a Performa just out of the box, At Ease has been installed but not turned on yet. If you don't see the screen in figure 6.10 or a similar screen when you start your computer, you'll need to turn At Ease on.

1. Locate the At Ease Setup icon stored on your hard disk.

2. Start At Ease Setup by double-clicking its icon.

3. Click the On button.

4. Choose Quit from the File menu.

If you can't locate the At Ease Setup icon, At Ease hasn't been installed on your computer. If you don't have the At Ease setup disks, you need to purchase them and double-click the Installer icon that comes with At Ease to install the program. At Ease is normally supplied pre-installed on a Performa but is a separate purchase for a regular Macintosh.

After you turn At Ease on, restart your computer so that At Ease will take effect.

Setting the Administrator Password

The first step in setting up At Ease is to assign an administrator password for yourself. Only the users to which you give this password will be able to change At Ease's setup. Choose Go To At Ease Setup from the Special menu. Then, from the Options menu, choose Administrator Password. You'll see the dialog box in figure 6.11, where you can type as many as 15 characters for the password and up to 63 characters for the clue that helps you remember it. The clue will appear each time At Ease asks for the password.

Fig. 6.11
Assign a clue that only you can figure out.

```
┌─────────────────────────────────────────────┐
│ Administrator Password                    🖰 │
│                                              │
│   Enter new password:    [•••••        ]     │
│                                              │
│   Reenter new password:  [•••••        ]     │
│                                              │
│   Clue: │Miss Smith's cat              │     │
│         │                              │     │
│         │                              │     │
│         └──────────────────────────────┘     │
│                                              │
│                       ( Cancel )  ╔══ OK ══╗  │
└─────────────────────────────────────────────┘
```

Note

If you forget your password, you can just set another one.

Start the computer with the Utilities disk, if you have a Performa, or the Disk Tools disk, if you have a regular Macintosh. Then open the System Folder and the At Ease Items folder inside it. Drag the At Ease Preferences file to the Trash and empty the Trash. From the Special menu, choose Restart. When the computer restarts, double-click the At Ease Setup icon and set a new password.

You can also choose User Greeting (⌘-G) from the Special menu and type a personalized greeting for your users to see on startup.

Setting Up Users

In the At Ease Setup window, click New to set up the configuration for each user who has access to your computer. You can give each user a different password if you like, or assign all your users the same password. Unlike the system administrator password, users can change their passwords whenever they like.

Click Stay in At Ease if you want the user you're setting up to have access only to the programs and documents you choose, or click Switch to Finder if you want the user to have unlimited access to everything on the computer (see fig. 6.12).

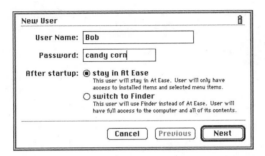

Fig. 6.12
You can set the level of access and assign a password for each person who will use At Ease.

Assigning Programs and Documents

If you allowed this user unrestricted access to the computer, you don't have any more setting up to do—click Done. Otherwise, click Next to assign which applications and documents to which you want users to have access (see fig. 6.13).

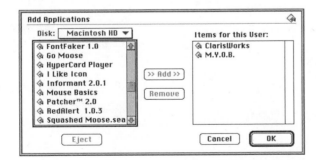

Fig. 6.13
Add all the programs to which you want the user to have access.

1. Click Add Applications and then select the programs you want the user to use. You can Shift-click to select several programs at once.

2. When you've selected all the programs you want, click Add.

3. To give the user access to documents, click Find Items and enter the name of the document for which you want to search (see fig. 6.14).

Tip
If you set up At Ease for a group, set up a user named Guest. Tell the group to choose Guest on the At Ease startup screen.

System 7 Essentials

II

Click Find to start the search. When the search is done, select the document's name in the Items Found on Disk list and click OK to add it to the Items for This User list.

4. When you finish adding items, click OK.

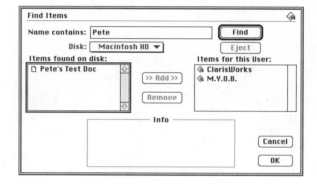

Deciding Which Menus Appear

Next, you'll decide which At Ease menus your user will see. In the next dialog box, choose Minimal to limit the menus to the most basic commands like Close and Quit, or choose All to give access to all At Ease menu commands, which will allow the user to copy, rename, and delete files (see fig. 6.15).

Fig. 6.15
You choose which menus your user will see, either full menus or minimal menus.

Tip
If you click Speak Button Names, the computer will "speak" the name of a button when you point to a button with the mouse pointer.

Setting Up How Users Save with At Ease

At Ease also allows you to be in charge of how users can save their documents. After you set up which menus appear and then click Next for the next screen, you can decide whether this user can save files anywhere on the hard disk, only in their folder (which will be inside the Documents folder on the computer), or only on a floppy disk (see fig. 6.16). Choose Only on Floppy Disk if you don't want the user to be able to save anything without inserting a floppy disk first. This keeps the computer from filling up with first-time users' documents, which can proliferate.

Fig. 6.16
You also decide
how users will save
their documents.

You can also mark the Allow Access to Finder check box if you want this user to have full, unrestricted access to everything on the computer.

Tip
To change a
user's access
privileges,
select his or
her name in
the At Ease
Setup window
and click
Open. Follow
the same se-
quence as
described here
to change the
user's privi-
leges.

> **Caution**
>
> Marking the Allow Access to Finder check box is the same as checking the switch to Finder button when you first started setting up this user. If there was a good reason you didn't choose unlimited access for that user, the same reason is probably valid now.

After you fill out this screen, you're through setting up this user. Click Done. Now you can add another user, or from the File menu, choose Quit (⌘-Q) to leave At Ease Setup.

Attaching Sounds to Buttons

If you're the system administrator, you can attach sounds to buttons so that when the user clicks a button, the sound plays. Recording instructions by using your Macintosh's microphone and attaching them to buttons is a good way to give new users additional information about using the computer.

To do this, start the At Ease Setup program. From the File menu, select Attach Sounds. Click the item you want to attach a sound to; then click Import Sound to attach a sound file that you've already stored on your hard disk or Record Sound if you're recording a sound with your Macintosh's micro-phone. If you're importing a sound, select a sound file; if you're recording a sound, you'll see a screen resembling the controls on a tape deck that allows you to record a sound.

Turning Off and Removing At Ease

To turn At Ease off, double-click the At Ease Setup icon on your hard disk. You have to be an administrator to turn it off because it will ask you for the administrator password. Then simply click the Off button. At Ease will be off the next time the computer starts.

II

System 7 Essentials

To remove At Ease from the computer, turn At Ease off. Then take the following steps:

1. Insert the At Ease Install disk 1 and double-click the Installer icon.

2. Click Customize and select At Ease.

3. Press the Option key, and you'll see the Install button change to Remove. Click Remove.

Using At Ease

When your users start the computer with At Ease installed, they'll see a welcome screen with their names listed. After clicking their name, they are asked for a password, if you assigned one to them. After providing the password, they'll see their folders (see fig. 6.17). All they have to do is click a button to start a program or open a document. Documents they've saved (if you've allowed them to save without using a floppy disk) are represented by buttons on their user panel, the one labeled with their name.

Fig. 6.17
The At Ease
desktop.

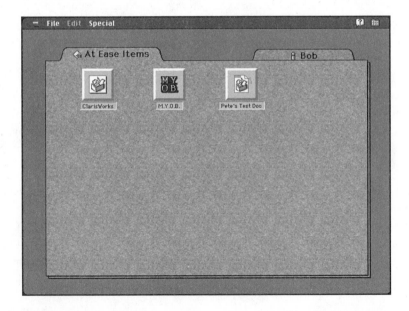

To switch between folders (also called *panels*), a user clicks the tab at the top. If there are are more items than can fit on one folder, a dog-eared tab appears in the lower right corner of the folder on which to click. A user can also click in the folder's tab and hold the mouse button down to see a list of all available folders and can go directly to a folder by choosing it from that list.

To close a folder, the user clicks the folder's Close button on the tab. Option-clicking closes all the folders.

> **Note**
>
> At Ease has hidden keyboard shortcuts that experienced users may want to know about. Pressing Tab switches you between the At Ease Items folder and the user folder. Pressing the left-arrow key and right-arrow key take you forward or back one page (if you have more than one page), and ⌘-left arrow and ⌘-right arrow take you to the first and last page in the At Ease folders. You can also type the first few characters of a button's name to move directly to it.

The At Ease Menus

When At Ease is running, the menus your users see depend on whether you allowed them access to full menus or minimal menus when you set up At Ease. For example, with minimal menus, the File menu contains only two commands: Close and Quit. With full menus, a user has commands for creating new folders, opening programs, and documents (the Open Other command), renaming, deleting, and finding files, getting information about files and folders, closing windows, copying files to and from floppy disks, and quitting. The Edit menu is the same, whether users have full or minimal access. The View menu does not appear with minimal access. The Special menu consists of Turn Sound Off, Eject Disk, Go To At Ease Setup, Restart, and Shut Down if the user has minimal access; with full access the Go To Finder command is also available.

Switching between Programs with At Ease

Users can have several programs running under At Ease if they've clicked different Application buttons, but only one program normally shows at a time. The Application menu at the far-right corner of the screen lists all the programs that are running. Users can switch to a different program by choosing it from that menu, just as in System 7 or 7.P. They can also switch back to At Ease to start a new program by choosing At Ease from that list.

From Here...

For additional information relating directly to using your system software on a Macintosh, you may want to review the following chapters of this book:

- Chapter 5, "Understanding the Desktop and Finder," discusses aspects of the system software common to all Macintoshes, including Performas.

- Chapter 7, "Organizing Your Files, Folders, and Disks," shows additional details of how to work with files, folders, and disks if you decide to bypass using System 7.P or At Ease.

- Chapter 10, "The Printing Chapter," illustrates how to print documents on any Macintosh.

- Chapter 13, "Adding Sounds," discusses recording and working with sound on your Macintosh.

Chapter 7

Organizing Your Files, Folders, and Disks

by Chris Oakes

At any workspace—be it a desk, a workbench, or a corral—you do more than work on specific tasks. You also sort out and organize the various items used in getting those tasks done. You store tools in drawers, file things away, gather new materials, and more to prepare for and carry out your work. The Macintosh is a workspace too, and is no different in this respect. It is not only where you get things done, but also where you organize and manage the things you do.

These two halves of your daily work on the Macintosh are handled by the Macintosh application and the Macintosh Finder. The application is where you work on specific tasks, and as you saw in Chapter 5, the Finder is where you manage them. In more concrete terms: You write a letter in a word processing application; you categorize, rename, or move the letter from one place to another in the Finder.

In this chapter, you learn the following:

- How to create, name, move, and trash folders and files

- Ways to view files and file information

- How to clean up and sort files

- How to use labels, stationery, and aliases

The Finder as File Cabinet

Many Macintosh applications have a recognizable, real-world counterpart. A word processor is like a typewriter, for example, and an address database can be compared to a Rolodex file. But is there any real-world object to which the Finder can be compared?

In fact, there is. The Finder can be compared to the common and familiar storage device known as the file cabinet. The file cabinet, just like the Macintosh Finder, is meant for the storage and management of files. Macintosh designers purposefully chose the file cabinet as a model because it is recognized as a familiar and easy-to-use tool of our everyday world.

Accordingly, the storage, retrieval, and organization of your Macintosh files are very much like the storage, retrieval, and organization of the files in a file cabinet. Indeed, as you well know by now, the things you shuffle around in a file cabinet—files and folders—even have the same names on the Macintosh: files and folders. As with so many other Macintosh concepts, before you've even started, you know a great deal about the Finder—simply by knowing what a file cabinet is.

The basic parts of the file cabinet have corresponding parts in the Macintosh Finder. Table 7.1 shows how these parts correspond.

Table 7.1 The Components of the File Cabinet and Their Finder Equivalents	
File Cabinet	**Finder Equivalent**
File (document, photo, and so on)	File
Folder	Folder
File Drawer	Disk

As you can see, a pretty direct relationship exists between the Finder and the file cabinet. With the exception of the file drawer, the two systems consist of identical components. In fact, if you named your hard disk File Drawer (which is easy to do), the comparison would be even more obvious.

Now that you've seen the relationship between the file cabinet and the Finder, look at how their individual parts relate to one another. With the file cabinet, there is a structured order to the file, the folder, and the file drawer.

This order stipulates that certain items are put inside other items, resulting in a *three-level hierarchy*. A file (level 1), such as a photograph or document, is put inside a folder (level 2). And the folder is put inside a file drawer (level 3). As you know, you can also put one folder inside another folder, adding another level to the hierarchy.

In the Finder, the hierarchy is the same: a file goes inside a folder, and a folder goes inside—or, more correctly, *on*—a disk. And just as you can put a file cabinet folder inside another one, you can do the same thing in the Finder.

But the Finder one-ups the file cabinet by letting you put as many folders as you like inside other folders. This is part of the Macintosh's multilevel, hierarchical file system. As shown in figure 7.1, this capability enables you to get much more sophisticated in the management of your Macintosh files.

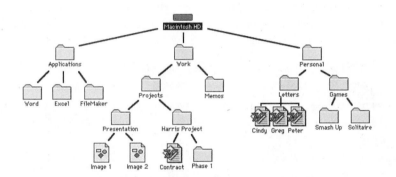

Fig. 7.1
The Finder's hierarchical file system allows for sophisticated file organization.

Putting folders and files inside other folders on the Macintosh is called *nesting* folders. One folder is nested inside another, which is nested inside another—and so on. The *deepness* of a file or folder refers to how many folders that file or folder is nested in, or how deep within the file hierarchy it sits.

In a file cabinet, you're limited to the amount of nesting you can practically do. On the Macintosh, the maximum number of nested folders is 64. While this may appear to be more confusing at first glance, it actually helps avoid confusion by letting you structure your files better. The result is that you can easily arrange your Macintosh files according to how you work with them.

> **Note**
>
> You can put a file inside a file drawer without any folder, and you can do the same thing with a Macintosh file. In other words, a file can simply reside on a disk without being inside any folder—carefree and folderless, so to speak. Any file—or folder, for that matter—that resides on a disk like this is said to be at the *top level* of the disk because it resides at the top of the file hierarchy. (This is also sometimes referred to as the *root* level of the disk, confusing though it is.) As you can imagine, however, if too many files and folders are kept at the top level, it becomes more difficult to keep track of them. Therefore, the fewer folders and files at this level the better.

Organizing Your Hard Disk

The three items dealt with so far in this chapter—files, folders, and disks—make up the simple building blocks of Macintosh file management. With just these three simple elements, you can be very organized.

This section examines how you might go about developing an organizational strategy for your hard disk, the main disk you'll be working with.

> **Note**
>
> This chapter focuses on the organization of the hard disk because most Macintoshes now have a hard disk on which most of its files are kept. The organizational principles discussed here, however, apply to the organization of floppy disks (or any other disk for that matter).

When you first turned on your Macintosh, you probably encountered just a few folders and files on your hard disk. You probably found the System Folder (containing essential software used to run the Macintosh), the application TeachText (or perhaps SimpleText, the updated version of TeachText for System 7.5), and a document called Read Me. That's a pretty small number of items, all residing at the top level (or root level) of the disk. It doesn't require much effort to keep these files organized.

But as you start writing letters, creating spreadsheets, and keeping databases of information, the number of files on your disk starts to, well, explode—to put it mildly. This ever-growing load of personal files, and the applications used to create them, call for a more sophisticated system of organization.

That may sound a little scary, but all it really means is keeping your files in appropriate groups. And the very simple, familiar tool of grouping on the Mac is, of course, the folder.

The next step in this chapter is to show you how you can easily create your own organizational system. After that, you'll learn the various procedures used in creating, moving, and viewing your Macintosh files so that you can start setting that system up right away.

File Hierarchy in Action

As you've seen in most of the figures so far in this chapter, the hierarchical file system gives you the freedom to arrange and group things in any order you like.

When you start a new business project, for example, you can easily create a new folder for the project in an existing Business folder. Or if you've decided to abandon your poetry career, you can easily drag the Poetry folder to the trash. Whatever the change, make sure the current order of your hard disk reflects the current order of your daily work. This keeps your Macintosh work more orderly and efficient.

> **Note**
>
> Planning your disk organization is a good idea, but you need to be loose enough to accommodate changes as you go. It's similar to a garden, in which you plant flowers and plants in an orderly way, but allow for changes as the garden grows. Nothing dictates a better organizational system than actual patterns of use. So keep an eye on your habits as you go, and when a clear pattern emerges, make the necessary changes to accommodate it.

> **Note**
>
> New versions of the Macintosh operating system to appear throughout 1995 and 1996 will add more built-in file management features. Some of the features of the latest upgrade, System 7.5, are covered in this chapter and throughout the book.

The strategy of organization that you design is, of course, entirely up to you. Different people have different styles of organization. Some are rigid, some are loose—and some apocalyptic. Witness the file cabinet again. The order of people's file cabinets varies from one person to another. Some might keep all their files alphabetically, while others might divide them by topic. To give you an idea of some common Macintosh ordering strategies, look at table 7.2 for a sampling of these strategies and what they mean.

Table 7.2 Some File Organization Strategies	
Strategy	**What It Means**
Application-oriented	Grouping documents with the applications that created them.
Computer-oriented	Grouping documents by computer task: word processing, desktop publishing, illustrations, databases, and so on.
Work/Project-oriented	Grouping documents according to work: business, personal, computer, correspondence, and so on.

Of course, no one strategy must be used to the exclusion of others. Many users like to keep all their applications grouped together, for example, and then group documents by project. Meanwhile, they might keep their Macintosh *utility files,* meant for the maintenance of the Macintosh, in their own group. Again, after you set up one or more of these strategies, you can always modify them as you go.

Before you learn about the basic organizational tools of the Finder, you should understand where the desktop fits into the Finder hierarchy. You can drag any file or folder—from its location anywhere on a disk—out onto the open desktop. (The *desktop* is the large, usually gray area that fills most of your Finder's screen.) To the Macintosh, files on the desktop reside in the *desktop folder.* Files in this folder reside, like the desktop, at the root level of a disk's hierarchy. For more information, see "The Hierarchy of Files, Folders, and Disks," previously in this chapter.

> **Note**
>
> In Open and Save As Dialog boxes, click the Desktop button to navigate to an item that's on the desktop. Alternatively, you can use the dialog box's pop-up menu. The desktop level appears at the bottom of this menu.

Creating a New Folder

To arrange your files into a sensible order, you need to know how to create the all-important folder. Fortunately, this task couldn't be easier.

Before you learn this one-step procedure, you should be aware of where a new folder will appear after you create it. If no windows in the Finder are open, a new folder appears on the desktop, usually just below your disk icon(s). Otherwise, the new folder appears in the active window.

> **Note**
>
> The active window can be identified by its *title bar,* the bar along the top edge of the window. When a window is active, its close box and the horizontal stripes on either side of the window's title are visible. Inactive windows only display their title—these other features aren't visible. In figure 7.2, the window named Macintosh HD is active.

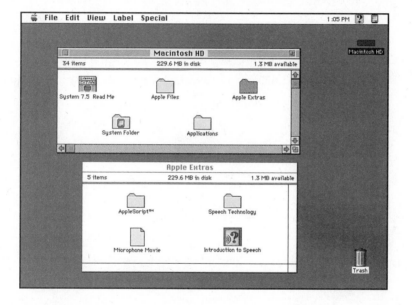

Fig. 7.2
An active window can be identified by its distinctive title bar. In this case, the window named Macintosh HD is active.

To make a window active, you just click anywhere on the window. When you open any disk or folder, its window automatically becomes the active window.

To create and name a new folder that will appear on the desktop or in the active window, follow these simple steps.

1. Choose New Folder from the File menu. A new folder called Untitled Folder will appear on the desktop or in the active window.

2. The name Untitled Folder is automatically highlighted. Type a new name for the folder and press Return.

> **Note**
>
> Why doesn't this section cover creating a file, the other member of the disk-folder-file hierarchy? Because you create files with applications themselves, not in the Finder. But in almost all applications, the command is very similar to creating a folder—you choose New from the application's File menu. Individual applications are covered in the chapters of Part IV of this book. Note, however, that you can rename files as well as folders in the Finder. Naming these items is covered in the next section.

Naming Folders and Files

If you need to change the name of a file or folder, simply follow the steps below.

1. Select the folder's or file's name by clicking once anywhere on the existing name (which is Untitled Folder on newly created folders). After a brief pause, the name becomes highlighted. Figure 7.3 shows a folder with its name highlighted.

Fig. 7.3
The folder's name has been highlighted.

2. Type a new name for the folder. The name will replace the existing name of the folder.

3. Press the Return or Enter key. Alternatively, you can click anywhere outside of the disk's icon with the mouse.

You now know how to create and name a new folder. Now you can put any file or other folder inside your new folder. How to do that is explained in the next section.

Tip
To highlight an item's name without enduring the short rename delay, click once on the file icon itself, and then press the Return key. The icon's name will be selected immediately.

> **Note**
>
> You can, if you wish, simply modify the existing name of any folder or file, instead of replacing the whole thing. After the existing name has been highlighted, use the cursor to select the part of the name you want to change. As with any Macintosh text, the characters you want to replace are highlighted as you drag the cursor over them. You can use the arrow keys on your keyboard to move the cursor. The Delete key also is handy in renaming items.

Putting Files into a Folder

Now that you have a folder, you're ready to put files—or other folders—inside it. To do that, you simply select the item and drag it over the folder's icon. Alternatively, you can open the folder and drag the item into the folder's window.

The following steps are involved in putting an item (a file or folder) into a folder. The item's original position may be on the desktop or in another folder.

1. Select the item.

2. Drag it over the icon of the folder. When the item is positioned correctly, the folder icon becomes highlighted. Figure 7.4 shows an item ready for dropping into a highlighted folder.

3. Drop the item by letting go of the mouse button.

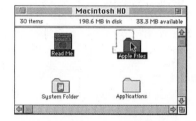

Fig. 7.4
Drop an item on to the destination folder after it has become highlighted, as seen here.

Note

You learned how to drag items in the demonstration in Chapter 5. To recap, you simply hold the mouse button down after selecting the item. Then, when you move your mouse around, an outline of the item moves as your mouse moves. When you're ready to drop the item in the new location, let go of the mouse button.

This procedure causes the item to appear in the folder's window. As indicated previously, the item can also be dragged directly into the folder's open window.

II

System 7 Essentials

Note

For the most part you, the user, create the folders that appear on your disks. But under System 7.5, the Macintosh will create one special folder automatically: the default documents folder. This folder, named Documents, is created on the desktop as a default place to save documents when working in applications. Its purpose is to make it easier for new users to keep track of documents. Without this folder, it's possible for a novice to not be able to find a saved document. Now such users need only open the Documents folder, which sits clearly visible on the desktop. You should regularly relocate files in this folder, however, to an appropriately categorized folder. To activate or deactivate the Documents folder in the General Controls control panel, select the Documents folder option in the control panel's lower-right section. (The section is entitled "Documents.")

Selecting and Moving a Group of Files

When organizing your files, you may want to move several items to a new folder. You could move them one at a time, but it's much quicker to move them as a group. You can do this by selecting them all simultaneously and then treating the group as you would any individual item.

To select multiple items, they must all be in the same window (or on the desktop). Follow the steps below once you've picked the group of files you want to work with:

1. Select the first item.

2. Holding down the Shift key, select the next item. The first item remains highlighted along with the new item.

3. Repeat step 2 until all items are selected.

To move the group of items after they've been selected, click one of the items and drag it to the new location. It doesn't matter which item you click—all of the items will move with that item. Just make sure you deposit the item you click into the proper folder—the rest will follow. Here is a quicker, alternative method for selecting a group of files that are close to each other. It works best when items are in icon view, although it works with list views as well.

1. Click the window (or desktop) just outside one corner of the group of items. *Note:* Do not click one of the items; click in the white space of the window. (If the files are on the desktop, you'd click the desktop itself.)

2. Holding the mouse button down, drag the cursor to the opposite corner of the group of items. A dotted line rectangle is formed as you drag the mouse. Items within the rectangle are selected as you drag. (Refer to figure 7.5.) If you drag too far, back up. Any selected items will be de-selected as you do so.

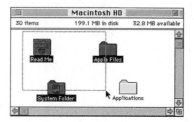

Fig. 7.5
When the dotted rectangle moves over an item, it is selected.

3. Let go of the mouse button when all the items are highlighted. Other items can also be added to this group by clicking on them while holding down the Shift key.

Note also that all the items on the desktop or in a window can be selected by choosing the Select All command from the Edit menu. (⌘-A achieves the same result.)

Caution

It's not probable, but it is possible to accidentally highlight the name of a folder or file while selecting items. If you do this unknowingly, you risk changing or deleting the name. If this happens and you notice it immediately, just choose the Undo command from the Edit menu (or press ⌘-Z). This will undo the change. Otherwise, you'll have to rename the file or folder. If the file is a document and you can't remember the name, open the file to reveal its contents, then rename it accordingly.

Trashing Files and Folders

Creating files and folders is a central part of organizing your disk. But so is eliminating them. And this is just what the Finder's Trash can is for. Just as you should keep your important files in good order, you should also trash the ones you no longer need. To do so, you simply drag the folder or file to the Trash icon.

When the Trash contains items ready for the digital dump, its icon bulges. (Much like the trash bag under your sink. See figure 7.6.)

Fig. 7.6
A bulging Trash
icon indicates that
there are files
inside.

You can drag any item—a single file, a whole folder, or an entire group of
folders and files—to the trash at once. Unlike a real trash can, it has no limit.

Digital reality continues to parallel physical reality with the Trash can. I'm
sure you've noticed that the trash can under your sink requires that you
empty it. And so does the Finder's Trash. (If you use System 6, refer to the
note following figure 7.7.) When you want to empty the Trash, which will
delete these files for good, you simply choose Empty Trash from the Special
menu. A warning dialog will appear telling you how many items are to be
trashed, along with the size of this particular heap of trash. When you click
OK, the deed is done. To temporarily avoid this dialog, press the Option key
while choosing the Empty Trash command.

Note

The Trash warning, while important to new users, can become a nuisance if you have
to empty the Trash frequently. Fortunately, there is an easy way to keep it from
appearing. Select the Trash icon, then choose Get Info from the File menu. At the
bottom of the Info window, there is a check box option: Warn before emptying. (See
figure 7.7.) Uncheck this option and the dialog will stop warning you—but be careful
that you don't accidentally trash important files.

Fig. 7.7
Unchecking the
Warn before
emptying option
will avoid
warning dialogs
when you empty
the Trash.

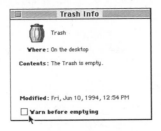

> **Note**
>
> System 7 users have the luxury of emptying the Trash at their leisure. That way, you
> know that something isn't really gone until you issue the Empty Trash command. But
> under System 6, the Trash will be taken out without you saying or doing anything.
> While this may be desirable in real life, it's not always desired on the Mac. System 6's
> Finder will empty the Trash when you launch an application, shut down or restart the
> computer. System 7, on the other hand, will hold your Trash until you intentionally
> empty it. Thus, you have the opportunity to retrieve an accidentally trashed file.

Un-Trashing Files

As mentioned above, once a file is in the Trash, you have the opportunity to
take it back out—as long as the Trash hasn't been emptied. To do so, simply
select the Trash icon and choose Open from the File menu. You may find it
easier to open the trash by double-clicking on its icon. Either way, the Trash's
window opens up to display its contents just like any other window. Select
the desired item and drag it to the desktop (or anywhere else you'd like to put
it).

Moving Files to the Desktop and Putting Them Away

It's often handy to move files from a folder to the desktop. You may want to
gather a group of files there to copy them to a floppy disk for example. The
method for doing this is one you know—you simply drag the items from the
folder's window to the desktop. While it's often convenient to store them
there temporarily, putting them away later—especially if it's a large group—is
anything but convenient.

To put them away by hand, you'd have to open all the original folders (if you
can remember them) and redeposit the files. Fortunately, however, the
Macintosh will take of this ugly task for you. All you need to do is select the
items to put away and choose the Put Away command, located in the File
menu.

> **Note**
>
> If the file or folder was originally created on the desktop, the Put Away command will
> have no effect—the file is already put away.

> **Note**
>
> As mentioned, the desktop can be a convenient place to put files temporarily. If you're saving a file in an application and it doesn't have an appropriate folder yet, the desktop serves as a temporary holding place where you won't lose or forget about the file. But be sure you promptly give the file a home somewhere in your organizational system. Overusing the desktop as a holding place can turn its pretty graphical interface into graphical chaos.

Viewing Files and Folders

In order to organize your files, you need to look at them, of course. In Chapter 5, "Understanding the Desktop and Finder," you already saw how you can easily open disks and folders to look at and work with files that may be nested a few folders deep. The disk and folders containing the desired document were selected and opened until the document was visible.

> **Note**
>
> If a file is nested very deep, this can create a large number of opened windows on the desktop, cluttering your view of things. Thus, it is a good idea to close windows as soon as you've opened the target folder contained within the window. The Finder will do this for you automatically if you hold down the Option key as you open new windows.

Tip

If you choose one of higher-level folders in a window's pop-up menu while holding the Option key (along with the command key), the higher-level folder will open and the currently active window will close.

Once you get to your target document or folder, you may need to know which higher-level folders contained it. (They are higher-level folders because they are higher in the file hierarchy.) Or you may want to reopen one of those folders. The pop-up menu available at the top of every window serves this very purpose. To access this menu, simply click on the window's name in the title bar while holding down the command key. A list showing the names of higher-level folders (if there are any) and the disk containing them will pop down. Dragging the mouse down to highlight one will open the window for that folder or disk.

Note

System 7.5 includes a control panel called WindowShade. Designed to help reduce desktop clutter, it reduces a window to only its title bar when not in use. To reduce a window like this, you simply double-click on its title bar. You will hear a short sound and all but the title bar will disappear. (If you don't hear the sound and want to, check the Make sounds... option in the WindowShade control panel.) To view the window in its entirety again, you just double-click on the title bar once more. This feature can make a crowded desktop much more manageable.

Icon and List Views

When you have the window of your target folder or disk open, what exactly do you see? If the window is displayed in an icon view, you see documents and folders, which appear as icons with their names below them. No other file information (other than the name) is provided in this view. Most figures so far in this chapter and others have shown the icon view.

But files can also be viewed in a more informative (though less appealing) list format. The default format for this kind of view shows a very small icon next to the item's name. To the right of the item's name appears its size, kind, label, and the date the item was last modified. (Refer to figure 7.8.) In System 7, a small right-pointing triangle also appears to the left of the folder. This triangle is discussed later in this section.)

	To Be Sorted			
Name	Size	Kind	Label	Last Modified
☐ List Of Oscar Winners	4K	MacCIM™, ZiffNet...	–	Tue, Mar 22, 1994, 1:13 PM
▷ ☐ Mac Generator	–	folder	–	Mon, Jan 31, 1994, 5:16 PM
▷ ☐ Mac Mania	–	folder	–	Mon, Jan 31, 1994, 1:47 PM
☐ Mom's News	120K	document	–	Mon, Jan 31, 1994, 4:45 PM
▷ ☐ More Downloads	–	folder	–	Fri, Jun 10, 1994, 2:00 PM
☐ New Chip Products Anno...	4K	MacCIM™, ZiffNet...	–	Mon, Mar 7, 1994, 6:57 PM
☐ Pause & Play /NRBQ	8K	MacCIM™, ZiffNet...	–	Tue, May 17, 1994, 9:44 PM

Fig. 7.8
Viewed in list form, windows display file information to the right of the file.

To change the type of view for any window, you use the View menu. While the window is active, choose the desired view from the menu.

II

System 7 Essentials

See table 7.3 for an explanation of what you'll see with each of the seven view types. The first two views (Small Icon and Icon) are graphical views, while the others show files and folders in a text-intensive list, sorted according to the criterion of that particular view. You can use the sorting ability of the list views to quickly identify and group large items, items with certain labels (discussed in detail later in this chapter), items of a certain kind, and so on. This is very helpful when you are organizing or reorganizing groups of files. (The section, "Using the Find Command To Round Up Files," later in this chapter further explains the Finder's ability to help you group and sort files.)

Table 7.3 Types of Window Views	
View	**What It Shows**
Small Icon	Shows folders and files as small icons; a reduced icon size allows more items to fit into a window.
Icon	Shows items as normal-sized icons.
Name	Shows items in a list, sorted alphabetically by name.
Size	Lists items, sorted by their size, from bigger to smaller. (Folders, which don't normally show a size, are listed last in alphabetical order.)
Kind	Lists items, sorted by the kind of file (application, document, control panel, and so on).
Label	Lists items, sorted by label (hot, cool, and so on).
Date	Lists items, sorted by the date they were last modified; more recent items at top.

In addition to changing the type of view in the View menu, you can also change the way information is presented in each view. The control panel called Views allows you to make these changes (refer to fig. 7.9). Table 7.4 explains the effect the various settings have on a window's view.

Table 7.4 The Options of the Views Control Panel	
Option	**Purpose**
Font for Views	The two pop-down menus let you change the typeface and size of the font for all disk, folder, and file names.
Icon Views	Affecting the two icon views, these options determine whether icons are in straight or staggered rows when the

Option	Purpose
	Clean Up command is used on a window (discussed later in this chapter).
Always snap to grid	When you put an item into a new window, this automatically aligns it with the existing items.
List Views	Will display larger icons next to file names in list views. The various Show… options determine which file information is included in list views.
Calculate folder sizes	Includes folder sizes in list views. Note: this may cause windows to take longer to open.
Show disk info in header	In list views, displays disk info such as the amount of free space on disk, which is normally shown only in icon views.

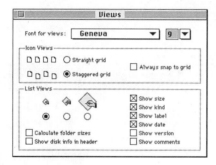

Fig. 7.9
The Views control panel.

Getting More File Information

As you've seen, windows in list view show a good deal of information about each file. Sometimes you might want even more information, however. The Get Info command, located in the File menu, is the way to get it. (This is also the only way to get file information in icon views.) Simply select the item(s) you want more information for, then choose the Get Info command. An information window will appear for each item you've selected, displaying a variety of file data. Figure 7.10 shows the window and its information.

The version information in the Info window of figure 7.10 shows *n/a*, or not applicable. That's because version information only applies to applications. If you have Microsoft Word version 4.0, for example, the exact version number, 4.0, would appear here in its Info window.

Fig. 7.10

A file Info window, accessed via the File menu's Get Info command.

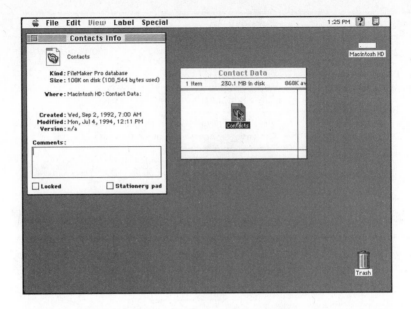

Note

The box labeled Comments in the Info window is intended as a place for you to type quick notes about a file. Rebuilding the Desktop will erase these comments, so it's not a good idea to keep important information here. As a result, most users never use the Comments box. However, there are shareware programs available that will restore the Finder comments if you want this option.

Locking Files in the Info Window

You may have occasion to create a file that you want to remain unchanged. It is easy to prevent such a file from being modified (or edited). Just use the Locked option in the Info window. Check the Locked box, located near the bottom of the Info window. The result is that the file can be opened and viewed in applications, but it cannot be modified in any way. The Stationery option is a variation on the Locked option, and is discussed later in this chapter.

Using Folder Triangles to View Folder Contents

You've probably noticed the little right-pointing triangles next to folder names in list views. (Figure 7.11 shows several.) What are they for? When navigating through folders, it helps to minimize the number of windows you have to open. This reduces the clutter on your desktop.

Clicking on this triangle once causes the triangle to point downward and the folder's contents to appear in list format beneath it. Thus, that folder's contents can be seen without opening a new window.

To differentiate the folder's contents from the rest of the window's contents, the list of its files appears indented from the rest. (Refer to figure 7.11.) To hide the folder's contents, click on the triangle again.

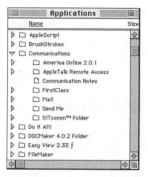

Fig. 7.11
When folder triangles are used, a folder's contents appear indented below the folder.

Cleaning Up Your Files

When you view a window in a list view, such as view by name, the icons are always in a straight, orderly list. But in icon views, things are not always so orderly. Icons might be overlapping one another and instead of neat rows, you might see something that represents abstract art with icons as the medium. To neaten things up, of course, you can shuffle them around with the mouse. But the Finder has a handy little command to take care of the bulk of the work for you. This is the Clean Up command, located in the Special menu.

When chosen, it will straighten up some or all of the icons on the desktop, or the icons in a window. To clean up the icons on the desktop, click on one of the desktop icons, then choose the Clean Up command from the Special menu. To clean up the icons in a window, choose the Clean Up command while the window is active. For different types of clean ups, there are several ways of choosing the command from the menu. Table 7.5 outlines these methods. The result of the action in the left column is shown in the right column.

Table 7.5 Clean Up Command Variations	
Clean Up Action	**Result**
Pressing Shift while choosing Clean Up	Selected icons are straightened.
Pressing Option while choosing Clean Up	Icons are cleaned up alphabetically by name or by size (whichever view was most recently chosen in the View menu).
Pressing Option while performing desktop clean ups	Aligns icons along right edge of the desktop.

Special File Organization Tools

The Finder features some special tools designed expressly for easing the task of file management. Namely, they are Labels, Aliases, Stationery, and the Find command. This section shows you how to use them.

Using Labels

While the Finder attaches all kinds of its own information to a file—its name, size, and so on—you may want to attach some of your own. More specifically, you may want to indicate that a certain file pertains to a certain project or deadline. This is just what the Label menu of System 7 lets you do. It lets you label files, just as you would label a folder or document with a stick-on color tab.

Tip

If you don't like the default label names, you can change them using the Labels control panel. Click the color or name of the label in the control panel to change the label's characteristics.

There are seven labels available in the Label menu. Each has a color associated with it. Items with a particular label will appear in that color in any window view (on color monitors only, of course). Each label also has a default name: Essential, Hot, In Progress, Cool, Personal Project 1, and Project 2. The label name will appear to the right of the file name in list views if you so choose. To assign one of these labels to a file or folder, follow this simple procedure:

1. Select the item

2. From the Label menu, choose the appropriate label.

> **Note**
>
> On color systems running System 6, you are able to assign colors to files with the Color menu. While this is not as advanced as System 7's labeling feature, it can be used for similar purposes. A red item could be considered urgent, green ones low priority, and so on.

By assigning labels to your files and folders, you are able to make them part of a group of items—even though those items may not be located in the same folder. You'll be able to exploit this grouping power using the Find command discussed later in this section. The Find command will conduct a search for all files that share the same label, easily locating a scattered group of associated files.

Using Aliases

There is a special kind of Macintosh file that doesn't have an obvious counterpart in our everyday world. This is the Macintosh alias, a feature added to the Macintosh Finder with System 7. To understand what an alias is, consider the following file cabinet scenario.

Say you keep a folder for your taxes in your file cabinet, called, of course, Taxes. Inside, there is an invoice for one of your freelance projects. While this document pertains to the Taxes folder, it also pertains to a folder you keep called Freelance Income.

It would be helpful to have the document in both of these folders. This way, you wouldn't overlook the document when you open the Freelance Income folder. Used for many dual-category files, this would let you much more easily locate and use important files.

To have a file appear in two folders, you could make a complete copy of the document and keep it in both folders. But if it happened to be a document with many pages, or a photograph, making and keeping a copy could be quite awkward. Besides, you don't want to waste precious space (or paper) in your file drawer.

There is a more convenient alternative. Instead of keeping a full copy of the document in the second folder, you could make a short note about it on a small piece of paper. This note would indicate the name of the document and the folder it is actually located in. You could keep such a note in every folder whose topic relates to the document.

Thus, while the document would actually exist in only one place, it would *virtually* exist in every folder that contains the note about it. Instead of having a bunch of space- and paper-wasting copies, you would have these small, convenient notes referring to—and pointing the way to—the actual document. Macintosh aliases are just like these notes.

> **Note**
>
> Although there is such a thing as an alias in the real world, its purpose does not exactly parallel the purpose of a Macintosh alias.

Macintosh aliases, however, bear much more power than sheer reference notes. Not only can you put them anywhere and everywhere on your hard disk, but each alias you make behaves as if it is the file itself. That means that you can open the actual file using any of its aliases. An alias will also let you gain quick access to the actual document.

Finally, while the example of a document was used in the explanation above, aliases can be created for any type of Macintosh file—be it an application, control panel, document, folder—or even an entire hard disk. An unlimited number of aliases can be created for each of these Macintosh file types. The result is convenient access to any type of Macintosh file from anywhere on a disk.

The Alias File

What does a Macintosh alias look like? When you create an alias on your Macintosh, it looks just like any other Macintosh file with just one visible difference: the name appears in italic text. Figure 7.12 shows you the difference between a regular Macintosh file and its alias. The original file is called Important Document and the alias is called Important Document alias.

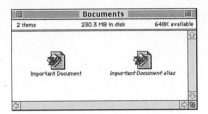

Fig. 7.12
A regular file (left)
and its alias
(right).

As you can see, the icons for both the file and the alias are identical. But the text that indicates the name, being italic, slants to the right.

Beyond their appearance, the two icons are similar in behavior. That means that double-clicking on, or choosing the Open command for either one has the same effect: it opens the original file. But there is an important difference between the two as well. The alias takes up much less disk space. Like any other Macintosh file it has a size, but no matter how big the original file, the alias is very small. Therefore, you can freely spread the icons around your hard disk without worrying about occupying large chunks of valuable space.

Creating an Alias

Making an alias for a file is as easy as issuing any other Finder command. You simply select the item you want an alias for. Then, from the File menu, choose the Make Alias command. The alias immediately appears in the same window, with the same name. (As discussed, the letters are in italic text and the word alias is attached to the end of the file name.)

Once it's created, you can put an alias in any location you like. After it's been relocated, you may want to rename it. The alias will still be able to open the original file, no matter what its name. For your own sake, it's a good idea to use a name that indicates what the original file is. Most users just give it the same name as the original, simply by deleting the word alias.

> **Note**
>
> If you are going to delete *alias* from the alias's name, you have to wait until after you've moved it. The Finder won't let you keep two items with the same name in the same folder.

Places to Keep Aliases

You can, of course, keep an alias anywhere you like. A logical approach is to keep them in related folders and locations that you access most frequently.

Tip
An easy way to find an original file is to open the Info window for the alias (with the Get Info command discussed earlier) and click the button named Find Original.

II

System 7 Essentials

One of these is the desktop itself. Some users like to line up aliases of their favorite applications or documents along one edge of the desktop, as seen in figure 7.13. Thus, these items are always a mouse-click away. Use caution, however, not to clutter the desktop with too many aliases. Otherwise, the purpose of easily locating items is defeated.

Fig. 7.13
Application and document aliases arranged on the desktop for easy access.

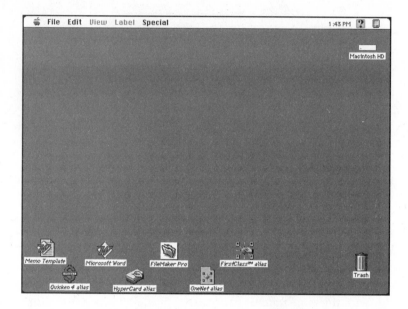

One of the most favored places for aliases is in the Apple menu. Just as this menu gives you quick access to popular tools like a calculator and a clock, it can give you quick access to any file or folder you like. To make your frequently used items part of this menu, follow this procedure:

1. Make and name an alias for the item. (See "Creating an Alias.")

2. Open the System Folder (located on your hard disk).

3. In the System Folder, open the folder called Apple Menu Items.

4. Drag the alias into its window. (Alternatively, you can skip step 3 and drag the alias right to the Apple Menu Items folder icon.)

After completing these steps, the item will appear in the Apple menu, according to its alphabetical order. Choose the item just as you would choose any other item in the Apple menu.

System 7.5 makes its own special additions to the Apple menu. You can easily open recently used applications and documents by selecting the Recent Applications or Recent Documents items that appear in the Apple menu. If you hold the mouse button down while these items are selected, a submenu appears to the right. The Recent Applications submenu displays a list of recently used applications. Selecting one of them launches that application. Selecting items in the Recent Documents submenu will open any recently opened document. This is much more convenient than navigating through multiple windows to access frequently used files. For more details on these special Apple menu items, see "Easily Opening Recent Applications and Documents" later.

Using Stationery

There is one more special kind of Macintosh file useful in organizing and using documents. This is the stationery file. A stationery file is like a template of a document. It holds contents you regularly include in new documents. Each time you open a stationery file, you open a copy instead of the original.

It's easier to understand if you compare it to normal office stationery, which also acts a template. It may contain preprinted text and graphics that appear on every letter or memo you write. Usually the preprinted material would include a company logo and its address and phone number. You can create a similar file with a word processing or graphics application with a stationery file. To make any file a stationery file, check the stationery option in its Info window (see "Getting More File Information," earlier in this chapter.)

After a file is turned into stationery, you'll be asked to name and save a new copy of the file whenever you open it in the Finder. (Refer to figure 7.14.) The appropriate application then launches to open the copied file. Applications that recognize stationery files, however, will immediately open a new copy in an untitled window. You then save the new document as you usually would, using the Save command. You can edit this new file, adding the text of your letter and so on to the existing company logo and address.

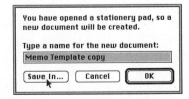

Fig. 7.14
This dialog is displayed when you open a stationery file in the Finder. It lets you name the stationery's copy file and save it where you like.

Whenever you want to edit the original stationery file again, you'll need to uncheck the stationery option in the Info window.

Caution

Most new applications recognize stationery files, so you are able to open them from within the application. The application will open a copy of the file, usually in an untitled window. If the application doesn't recognize the stationery, you'll get a warning that you are about to open (and possibly alter) a stationery file. The safest way to open a stationery file, therefore, is in the Finder.

Using the Find Command to Round Up Files

As discussed at the outset of this chapter, the growing number of files on your disk can become unwieldy without an organizational plan. Even with such a plan, however, you may have difficulty tracking down items on your disk. Thankfully, you can put your Macintosh on the job of finding lost files. Even if they're not lost, the Mac can help you avoid opening folder after folder to get to a file. To do this in System 7.1, you use the Find command, located in the File menu. The dialog displayed in figure 7.15 will appear. Note that this Find command is also available in System 7.5. But System 7.5 adds an improved file-finding utility, called Find File and accessed in the Apple menu, which is discussed at the end of this section.

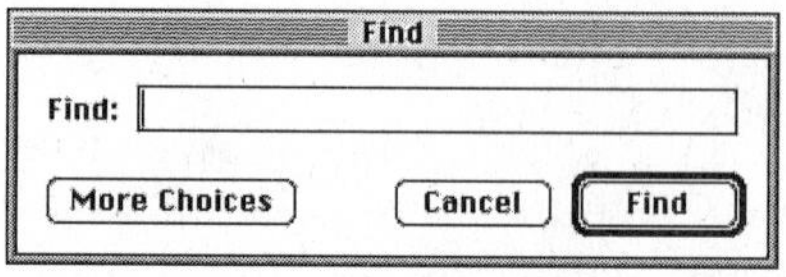

Fig. 7.15
The dialog displayed when the Find command is used.

Tip
The more completely you type the file's name in the Find dialog, the fewer guesses the Finder will have to make in locating a matching file.

When you type some or all in the file's name into the empty field and click the Find button, the Finder starts its search. When it finds a file or folder with those letters in its name the Finder displays the window containing that item. You can then proceed as usual.

If the item it finds for you is not the one you're after, you can have it continue to search. To do this, simply choose the Find Again command in the File menu. It will display the next file whose name contains those letters. You can continue this way until you reach the file you want.

You may have noticed the Find dialog's More Choices button. (Refer to fig. 7.15.) If you click this button, you are given a broader range of criteria to search for, as displayed in figure 7.16.

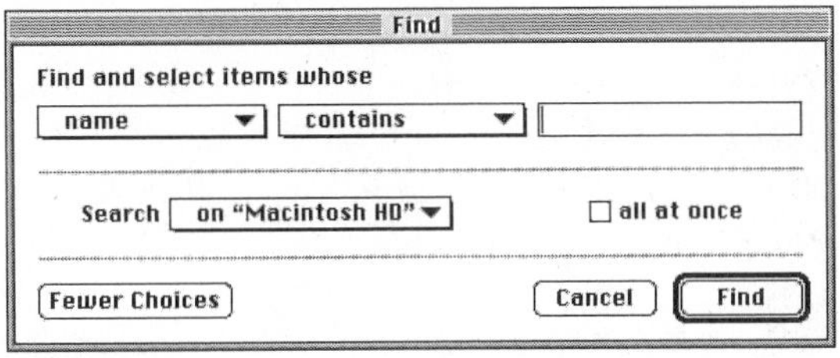

(Refer to fig. 7.15.)

Find

Find and select items whose

| name ▼ | contains ▼ | |

Search [on "Macintosh HD" ▼]   ☐ all at once

[Fewer Choices]   [Cancel]   [Find]

Fig. 7.16
The Find dialog after the More Choices button is clicked.

When periodically sorting out and gathering files for organization, this dialog can be a great help. Because you can use this feature to search for files by size, kind, label, date created or modified, version, comments, and locked status.

You may want to search for all your files over 1M in size, for example, to delete the ones you don't need. Or you may want to search for all items with a Hot label. As mentioned in the section "Using Labels to Tie Items Together," searching by label gives you easy access to all items associated with a particular file. Also, to search for all items you modified on a particular date, you can search by the date modified criterion. In these ways, the Find command can be a very powerful file management tool.

If you want to see a set of found files at once, check the all at once option. This option causes all found items to appear at once in a window in list view. The Finder indicates found items by selecting them.

Note

To search by more than one criterion, conduct a search by the first criterion with the all at once option checked. Found items will be shown selected in a window. Next, choose Selected Items from the Search pop-up menu. Search again by the second criterion. Repeat the last two steps for all your criteria. The items that meet all the criteria will be selected in a window when you're done.

To limit the search to a particular disk, folder, or group of folders, use the Search pop-up menu in the middle of the dialog.

II

System 7 Essentials

The standard Find command described previously is also available in System 7.5, but a much improved file finding utility is added as well. To access it, from the Apple menu, choose Find File. With this new utility, all finding criteria are immediately available for any search. In the initial dialog, you can choose a criterion from the pop-up menu and then enter any text, date, and so on. in the empty field. Each time you click the More Choices button, an identical search dialog (with pop-up menu and text field) is added below the first one. Thus, additional criteria can be easily entered. Refer to figure 7.17 to see how a multiple-criteria search looks.

Fig. 7.17
System 7.5's new Find command produces this improved dialog. Additional search criteria are easily added to a search by clicking the More Choices button.

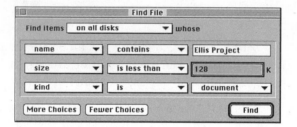

When items are found, they are now displayed all at once in an easy to view list (refer to fig. 7.18). This list can be viewed by name, size, kind, or date. To open one of the items, choose the Open command from the File menu or simply double-click on the item. To view an item in its own window, choose the Open Enclosing Folder command from the File menu.

Fig. 7.18
System 7.5 displays found files in an easy-to-view list.

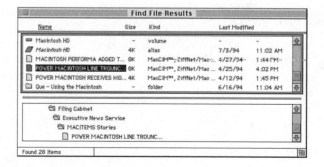

Easily Opening Recent Applications and Documents

With the introduction System 7.5, there is now a convenient way to access frequently used applications and documents. A memo or a recent sales report are examples of documents you might be working with frequently over a period of days or weeks. It's handy to have quick access to these items each time you go back to work, without having to open up a series of nested folders. To provide you with this quick access, System 7.5 *automatically* does the following:

- Creates aliases of recently used applications and documents

- Keeps these aliases in two special folders: Recent Applications and Recent Documents

- Makes both of these folders available through the Apple menu

To access a recently used document, you simply select Recent Documents in the Apple menu. This opens the Recent Documents folder, which displays aliases of your most recently used documents. The same procedure is followed for recent applications by selecting Recent Applications in the Apple menu.

There is an even quicker way to access these recently used items, however, with another new capability of System 7.5. The Apple menu can now display submenus for folders contained in the menu such as the control panels and the Recent Applications and Documents folders. These submenus display the items contained in each folder.

> **Note**
>
> If your Apple menu is not displaying submenus under System 7.5, use the Apple Menu Options control panel to turn this feature on. In the section of the control panel entitled Submenus, click the On option. You can also set how many files should be shown in the various submenus.

In the case of the Recent Applications and Documents folders, the items displayed in the submenus are the aliases of the recent items. Choosing one of these items in the submenus opens that particular application or document. (Refer to figure 7.19.)

Tip
System 7.5's Find window displays a list of an item's enclosing folders (or its *file path*) just below the list of found items. Clicking on one of these folders (or the enclosing disk) opens that folder's window.

II

System 7 Essentials

Fig. 7.19
A recently used application being selected in the Apple menu's Recent Applications submenu.

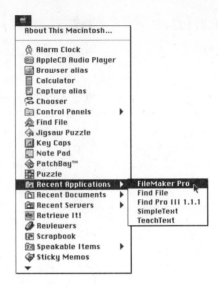

To change the number of recently used items that are displayed in the submenus, use the Apple Menu Options control panel. In the section entitled Recent Items, change any of the default numbers for each folder to the number of your choice. Once you experience the convenience of this new feature, you may find opening applications and documents this way easier than opening up several folders at a time.

> **Note**
>
> The alias of any folder or disk can be placed in the Apple menu to have its contents displayed in submenus. This gives you instant Apple menu access to disk and folder contents up to five folders deep without opening any folders. The contents of any nested folders appear in a submenu attached to the first submenu—and so on until the contents of up to five nested folders are displayed. Try placing an alias of your hard disk in the Apple Menu Items folder (located inside your System Folder) to see how this works.

> **Note**
>
> Another Recent folder appears below the Recent Applications and Recent Documents folders in the Apple menu: the Recent Servers folder. This lets you access any servers that may have been recently mounted over a network just as easily as you can access recent documents. For more on servers and networks in general, refer to Chapter 33, "Networking."

Using the Launcher

Just as you can add items to the Apple menu, you can now add items to a special window added to the Finder in System 7.5. This window is called Launcher. Adding items to the Launcher is just like adding items to the Apple menu. You simply make an alias of the item (application, document, or any other file) and put it in the Launcher Items folder, which is located inside the System Folder. These items appear in the Launcher window in the Finder, as seen in figure 7.20. Each item gets its own big button. Clicking once on the button opens that particular item.

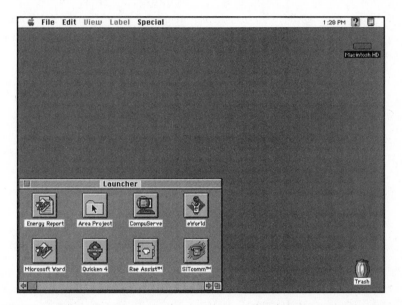

Fig. 7.20
The Launcher provides quick access to applications and documents in the Finder.

II

System 7 Essentials

> **Note**
>
> If the Launcher window does not appear in your Finder, you can make it do so by opening the Launcher control panel. Doing so immediately causes the Launcher to appear. To hide the Launcher window, simply click its close box.

Useful AppleScripts

Since AppleScript is now part of standard system software with System 7.5, more users have access to its handy automation features. A few such features are provided with the system software as well, in the form of ready-made scripts for performing some common file management tasks. These scripts are kept, along with an excellent explanation of AppleScript called AppleScript Guide, inside a folder called Apple Extras. The Apple system software installer locates this folder at the top level of your hard disk. It's easier to locate the folder, however, by using the Apple menu, where the installer also leaves an alias of the Useful Scripts folder. With the submenus option turned on (see note in "Opening Recent Applications and Documents" previously), you can instantly access the scripts contained within the folder.

AppleScripts will automatically perform tasks such as making an alias for the Apple menu, finding an alias's original file, and so on. To use the scripts in the Useful Scripts folder, you don't really need to know that much about AppleScript, just how to properly use the scripts themselves. Following are descriptions of the scripts for file management and how they are used.

- Add Alias to Apple Menu. This script automatically creates aliases of any file or folder and places it in the Apple Menu Items folder, which causes it to appear in the apple menu. Simply select any item(s) you want in the Apple menu, then choose this script in the Useful Scripts submenu. Alternatively, you can open the Useful Scripts folder and drag and drop the items directly onto the script's icon.

- Close Finder Windows. Select this script in the menu to automatically close all open windows in the Finder. (Personally, I prefer to close one of the windows with the Option key held down, which accomplishes the same thing.)

- Eject All. Select this script to eject any floppy disks, compact discs, and Syquest or Bernoulli cartridges that may be mounted on your Macintosh. If file sharing is active for any of these disks, the script turns off file sharing, ejects the disks and then restarts file sharing. (Use caution to ensure no users are sharing files on any of the disks before running this script.)

- Find Original. If you select one or more aliases in the Finder and then select this script, it will find all the original files for each of the aliases.

- Hide/Show Folder Sizes. If folder sizes are currently displayed in list views, selecting this script will hide them, and vice versa. (This is an easier alternative to turning this option on and off via the Views control panel.)

■ Sync Folders. Selecting this script will match up—or *synchronize*—the contents of two folders. You may want to make sure a backup folder you keep on a floppy disk, for example, is synchronized with the original folder on your hard disk. If one folder contains a document that the other one doesn't, this script copies the document to the other folder. For documents with the same name, the script copies the one with the more recent modification date to the other folder. To use the script, select it and it will prompt you to show it which two folders to synchronize.

From Here...

In this chapter, you learned how to use the Finder's main file management features. Of course, you won't have much to manage until you start using applications to create new files. Many such applications are covered in Part IV, "Macintosh Software." You'll also find a great deal more Finder information in Part III, "Customizing Your Macintosh" and Part VII, "Troubleshooting and Preventive Maintenance."

■ Chapter 11, "Changing the Look of Your Desktop" shows you how to use Apple and other companies' control panels and extensions to modify the Finder and the desktop to better suit your working style.

■ Chapter 12, "Creating and Modifying Icons," plunges into customizing that most common feature of the Finder, the icon. You'll learn how to make any icon look just right for the job.

■ Chapter 38, "Preventive Maintenance," should not be skipped. In covering good Mac habits, it will show you what habits should be part of your regular Finder work. The section on essential utilities will also show you some key maintenance utilities for keeping your files and disks in tip-top shape.

Chapter 8

All about Fonts

In the days when typefaces were cast from lead, a font consisted of a set of letters, both upper- and lowercase (except for all caps styles), numbers, and additional characters—all in a single size. Through time, that definition has become blurred, beginning with the advent of phototypesetting systems in the 1960s when all of these letterforms were stored on film negatives and reproduced on photosensitive paper or film. Although some of these early typesetting machines kept with tradition and had a single set of negatives for each size, others used a lens assembly to enlarge the image to produce size changes.

The 1970s brought the digital type revolution, as the contents of these fonts were reduced to a set of ones and zeros, and contained on floppy disks or hard drives. Imaging was done with a cathode ray tube assembly that imaged the letters onto the same photosensitive media used in the earlier generations of typesetting machines.

When the Macintosh came on the scene in the 1980s, several key developments occurred, sparking the desktop publishing revolution. One was the invention of PostScript by Adobe Systems, and another was the introduction of the original Apple LaserWriter, which contained a computer that read PostScript code. A third event was the arrival of several desktop publishing software applications that enabled users to view the pages of their documents WYSIWYG style (what-you-see-is-what-you-get) on-screen. Chapter 21, "Desktop Publishing," discusses the latest versions of those programs in more detail.

In this chapter, you learn the following:

- ■ What Macintosh fonts consist of

- ■ How to choose the correct font for your document

- How to cope with bitmap, PostScript, and TrueType fonts

- How to effectively manage your font library

The fonts you buy today for your Macintosh are often derived from the very same designs that were available to typographers years ago. The wider market for fonts has also encouraged a new generation of artists to design fonts based on traditional designs or to create their own designs from scratch. You can choose from thousands of fonts, ranging in price from less than a dollar, to fancy packages on CD-ROM costing thousands of dollars.

There is also a confusing dichotomy in font formats. Installing and working with fonts on your Macintosh isn't always a simple process. Sometimes it's fraught with pitfalls. The following sections concentrate less on showing you some of the available fonts and more on how to install and use them more effectively on your Mac.

Serif Fonts

Fonts are generally divided into two broad categories, although some fancier designs have characteristics of both categories. The first category, a *serif font*, contains little hooks or stems that extend outward from the top or sides of the character, as shown in figure 8.1.

Fig. 8.1
Times Roman, a typical serif font.

How razorback jumping frogs

Although serif fonts look fine for headlines, they are typically used most effectively for setting body text. As with all artistic considerations, your taste is what counts.

Sans Serif Fonts

A *sans serif font* simply means the font was designed without those little hooks or stems, as shown in figure 8.2.

A sans serif typeface is commonly used for headlines or large text, although it can be used in some body text applications.

How razorback jumping frogs

Fig. 8.2
Helvetica, a
popular typeface
used for both text
and headlines.

More Font Lingo

When you begin to use fonts, you will encounter some specialized terms that aren't a normal part of the English language. Following are some commonly used terms:

- *Point size.* A font is measured by figuring the distance between the bottom part of a character, such as the letter *g,* known as the *descender,* to the top of the character, known as the *ascender.* A point is roughly a 72nd of an inch. I say roughly because in traditional typesetting there were 72.27 points to the inch, but this measurement has been rounded off for the desktop publishing world.

- *Leading (pronounced* ledding*).* Sometimes known as line spacing, leading is the distance from one line of type to the next.

- *Monospace font.* These are fonts that match the ones you use on a normal typewriter. All the characters in the font occupy the same space. Monospace fonts include Courier and Monaco. Figure 8.3 shows a sample of a monospace font.

```
How razorback jumping frogs
```

Fig. 8.3
Courier, a common
monospace font.

- *Proportional font.* These are the fonts used most often for your desktop publishing or word processing chores. Each character in the font gets its own custom increment of space. The letter *i,* for example, occupies less space than the letter *m.* Figure 8.4 shows a popular proportional font with wide spacing differences between the narrowest and widest letters.

- *Em-space.* This is a common measure of space, usually used to indent text at the beginning of a paragraph. It usually refers to the width of the capital letter M, which is generally the widest letter of the alphabet in a proportional font.

System 7 Essentials

Fig. 8.4
Adobe's Stone
Informal, used
widely for writing
letters and as body
text in newsletters
to provide a
friendly (or
informal) feel.

How razorback jumping frogs

■ *En-space.* Sometimes an en-space is defined as the width of a numeral, but actually it refers to the width of the lowercase *n*, which is about half the width of the em-space.

■ *Em-dash.* This character is a long dash, which looks like — on the printed page (an em dash is represented by two hyphens on a type-writer, such as —). It is generally used to indicate a change in thought in the middle of a sentence—like this.

■ *En-dash.* This is a middle-sized dash, which usually is used to represent a range of numbers, such as *from 9:30–10:30 PM.*

■ *Ligatures.* This is a typesetting tradition that's fallen into disuse to a large degree. It involves a single character consisting of two or more letters run together, which provides an improved appearance. Ligatures are commonly used with serif typefaces in high quality books and advertising. The most common use is for such combinations as *fi* or _ or *fl* and _. The other most commonly used ligature, *ffl,* is not found on most Macintosh fonts, except for the Adobe Expert Collection.

> **Caution**
>
> If you set your text with ligatures, you are apt to foul up most spelling checkers, which will almost always flag the unusual letter combination and slow down the spelling checking process. Other than QuarkXPress, which automatically recognizes the programs automatic ligature feature, you are best advised to add ligatures after you spell check your document. Just do a standard search-and-replace routine.

■ *Smart Quotes.* When the keyboards in personal computers were designed, they kept some relics of old-fashioned typewriters, such as those awkward stickup quotes, which use a single character to represent an open or closed quote, rather than a separate character. But the typical

Macintosh font does have those characters, called "curly" or "smart" quotes. You just have to hunt for them. For a true open quote, just like the ones used in this book, press ⌘-[. For a closed quote, press ⌘-Shift-[. A single open quote is produced with ⌘-], and a single closed quote or apostrophe is produced by pressing ⌘-Shift-].

> **Note**
>
> Thankfully, most desktop publishing and word processing software has a smart quotes option, which enables you to type a regular stickup quote and get a curly quote instead. If your software doesn't have this option, you can use programs such as the freeware SmartKeys (available on local BBS and the regular online services) or a commercial product, Thunder 7, an interactive spelling checker from Baseline Publishing, to provide automatic curly quotes.

■ *French spacing.* With a normal typewriter, with all characters in a font having the same amount of space, you put two spaces between sentences to make your material more readable. In typesetting, you space just once between sentences. It's something experienced typists must get used to when learning the basics of desktop publishing. But there are times that designers will ask for *French spacing,* which simply means that you revert to that old forgotten skill you learned in typing class, and type two spaces between sentences.

Font Formats

Macintosh fonts come in three flavors: bitmap, Postscript, and TrueType.

Bitmap Fonts

Originally, there were bitmap or fixed size fonts, which reduced the letters and numbers in a font to little dots, based on a 72-dots-per-inch (dpi) resolution. These fonts were also known as fixed size fonts, and you needed a separate font for every size. If you didn't have a font in a particular size, your Macintosh would use its QuickDraw imaging model to build a font from the sizes you did have, often resulting in a jagged or brick-like aspect to the fonts. Figure 8.5 shows what a bitmapped font looks like when set in its actual size, and figure 8.6 shows what happens when you deviate from that size.

Fig. 8.5
An 18-point
bitmapped font.

How razorback jumping frogs

Fig. 8.6
The same bit-
mapped font set
in 72 point.

How razorback jumping frogs

In the days when Apple's ImageWriter or a similar impact printer were the only ones you could buy, a bitmapped font was all you had. And considering the 144-dpi limitations in printer resolution, it was sufficient. But when desktop publishing came to the Macintosh in 1985, you needed something more.

> **Note**
>
> You can tell a bitmapped font simply by looking at its name and icon, as shown in figure 8.7. The bitmapped font comes in a suitcase, and the file itself has a name that includes its size.

Fig. 8.7
A typical bit-
mapped font icon.

1Stone Serif 12

Enter PostScript Fonts

The folks at Adobe Systems invented a page description language, called *PostScript*, that described the contents of a page in mathematical terms. By so doing, they made the file independent of the output resolution of the printer that was used—the words Adobe used were *device independence*. So if you output your job on a standard 300-dpi laser printer, you would get 300-dpi output. If you took the same file and ran it on an imagesetter capable of 3600-dpi, the result would be correspondingly sharper.

PostScript fonts use the same technology to describe the outlines of a font. The printer fills in the spaces between the outlines and creates a bitmap consisting of the image of the page, fonts and all. A PostScript font is often called a *scalable* font because it will print sharp and clear at whatever size you set, whether 2 point or 720 point or more.

Type 1 and Type 3

When Adobe created the PostScript font format, it released a Type 3 version, which was freely available to other font vendors, and a Type 1 specification, which was tightly controlled and had to be licensed. Type 1 fonts, of course, printed more efficiently; it also had hints, or little programming tricks, that made it look sharper when printed on a low resolution printer in smaller sizes.

When TrueType fonts, another second scalable font format, was announced by Apple and Microsoft, Adobe did two things. First, it released Adobe Type Manager, a truly marvelous little program described later in this chapter. Second, it made the Type 1 font format freely available, so all font developers could produce as many Type 1 fonts as they wished without writing a check with the name *Adobe* on it.

The outcome was that Type 1 fonts flourished, and Type 3 fonts languished. Although Type 3 fonts are generally not as useful as Type 1 fonts, they have the advantage of supporting complex fills and shadings that are not feasible with Type 1 fonts. You are still apt to find a Type 3 font here and there containing a truly decorative logo of some sort.

Screen Fonts

The most confusing aspect of Type 1 fonts is that you need to install two files to use them. The first file is known as the printer or outline font. Their icons vary from developer to developer. Figure 8.8 shows two samples.

StoneSer   BCCenNor

Fig. 8.8
The icons of Type 1 PostScript fonts from Adobe (left) and Font Company (right).

The second file is a fixed size bitmap font, or screen font, that contains the metric (size and width information) of the font, including the preset character kerning pairs (and we'll get to kerning shortly). In order to use your PostScript font, you need both a printer *and* screen font for each face. Having either just won't cut it. If you just have the outline font, that face won't even show up on your font menu. If the screen font is installed, and the printer font is missing, you'll see the font listed among your available fonts, but the quality of reproduction will be poor, the same as if you used those old-fashioned bitmap fonts described in the preceding section.

Enter TrueType Fonts

The third member of our font trio is a font format first announced by Apple under the name *Royal,* which was designed to be a part of System 7.0 when it was released in May of 1991. Like PostScript fonts, TrueType was a scalable font format. The font could be set in any size you wanted. But it had two big advantages over PostScript fonts. The first was that you didn't need to install two font files. The bitmap and outline font were combined. True, sometimes a set of screen fonts would be supplied with TrueType, to provide slightly faster, sharper screen display, but you did not have to install them if you wanted to save a little disk space.

The second advantage was that the *rasterizer,* or font processing software, for TrueType fonts was a part of Apple's System 7. You didn't have to have a PostScript printer, and you didn't need to install another Extension, Adobe Type Manager (or ATM), to make your fonts look good on-screen and print clearly on a QuickDraw printer.

> **Note**
>
> To use TrueType fonts under System 6, you need to install Apple's TrueType init, which is part of the TrueType disks available on the major online services, such as America Online, CompuServe, and eWorld, or from a local user group. This init, along with Font/DA Mover 4.1, is all System 6 users need to use TrueType fonts. The init is supported by Apple for System 6.0.7 or 6.0.8, but is reported to work with System 6.0.5 as well.

To the eye, the icon of a TrueType font looks the same as the bitmap font, with two differences, as shown in figure 8.9.

Fig. 8.9
A TrueType
font icon.

AppleGaramond Bd

The first difference is the design showing three A's, each progressively larger than the other. This indicates this is a scalable font. The second difference is the lack of a size in the font's name.

Font Use Priorities

Although it only affects you in a marginal way, your Mac running System 7.0 has built-in font priorities that it uses in bringing images to your screen. If you have a bitmap font installed, it is used. If you have a TrueType version and not the bitmap font, it gets next priority, and if the bitmap is generated by using Adobe Type Manager (covered shortly), it gets next priority. If you're using a size for which there's no bitmap equivalent, no TrueType font, and ATM is not installed, the Mac will generate a screen image based on its best (and it's none too good) efforts.

Your PostScript printer has different priorities. If a PostScript font is installed in the printer's ROM (a *resident font*), that's what is printed, regardless of whether there's a TrueType version installed on your Mac. If there's no PostScript printer font available, the TrueType font gets called. When none of these options are handy, the bitmapped font is used to generate a 72-dpi image of the text you see on-screen (definitely not recommended).

The priorities are changed with a QuickDraw or non-PostScript printer. If a TrueType font is available, it's called upon to do its thing first. The PostScript font, if available, gets called next in order. And finally, when these two are unavailable, the bitmapped font is used.

PostScript or TrueType—Which Is Best?

When TrueType fonts first came on the scene, there were heated arguments as to which font format would reign supreme. The furor soon died down. TrueType fonts failed to attract large design studios and service bureaus with an investment of tens of thousands of dollars in PostScript fonts and high resolution printers, but they managed to get a new lease on life when Microsoft decided that Windows 3.1 would emphasize TrueType.

Today both fonts coexist, with more TrueType fonts available in lower-cost packages, but PostScript fonts are getting cheaper as well (more about that later in this chapter).

In theory, TrueType fonts are capable of more sophisticated hinting. But since font developers usually produce their PostScript and TrueType fonts from the same set of artwork, the printed quality is pretty much the same. TrueType fonts have a disadvantage at service bureaus, where older image-setters and high resolution laser printers may need hardware updates to support this font format. Chapter 11 covers printing-related issues.

Mixing and Matching

The choice of which font format to use is yours, and you will get satisfactory results with either PostScript or TrueType. You can install fonts in both formats on your Mac, *as long as you don't install the same font in both versions*.

II

System 7 Essentials

If you have, say, a PostScript version and a TrueType version of Helvetica, you are apt to have a font conflict, with incorrect or missing characters appearing on-screen or on the printed page.

Which Is Faster?

If you use Adobe Type Manager, the fonts display more quickly on the screen than a TrueType font—if you don't have a screen font available in the size you pick. The reason for this is that ATM stores its screen font bitmaps in a RAM cache, while System 7 builds a TrueType screen font dynamically as needed and doesn't store it. (Adobe Type Manager is covered later in this chapter.)

▶ See "What is *PostScript Compatible?*" p. 211

As for printing, a PostScript printer generally processes a PostScript font faster, unless it has a built-in TrueType rasterizer on hand, which will more or less place performance on roughly equal terms. The manual for your printer will explain whether it does or not. As far as a non-PostScript printer is concerned, don't expect much of a performance advantage one way or the other.

How Not to Use Fonts

The watchword in selecting fonts for your document is *restraint*. Too many styles, too many sizes, and you'll end up making your document difficult to read. The simplest way to design your document is to use a serif typeface for text and a sans serif face for headlines, as shown in figure 8.10.

Fig. 8.10
A simple headline and a paragraph of body text, using two popular serif and sans serif fonts.

Math
By clicking on the Math Button within the Table Bar, simple math functions (add, subtract, multiply, divide, sum, and average) are offered within tables. Using the Math Bar, you can quickly sum a selected row or column of numbers with the click of a button. You can also create formulas involving multiple rows or columns and check them for syntax errors.

Remember that you want your document to be easy to read, and you don't want the design to get in the way of clarity and readability. Using a type design for body text that is difficult to read or meant strictly for headline use will only make your document less attractive and less apt to be read carefully by the end user. Figure 8.11 shows you what happens when you pick a typeface for body text that looks fancy but requires extra effort to read.

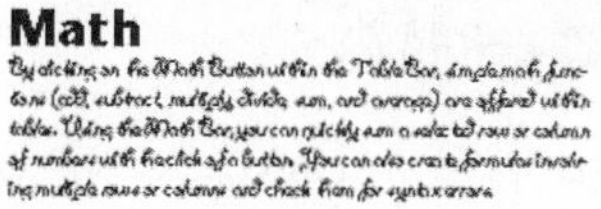

Math

By clicking on the Math Button within the Table Bar, simple math functions (add, subtract, multiply, divide, sum, and average) are offered within tables. Using the Math Bar, you can quickly sum a selected rows or column of numbers with the click of a button. You can also create formulas involving multiple rows or columns and check them for syntax errors.

Fig. 8.11
Can you read this
text easily—or at
all?

The Mac's Confusing Type Styles

Just about every Macintosh program has a font style menu that displays the
same choices—Roman, Bold, Italic—as shown in figure 8.12. If you select
both Bold and Italic, you get Bold Italic. Fonts produced by the major developers carry a family relationship, so if you select the italic variation, that's
what you get on-screen and on the printed page.

Fig. 8.12
A typical
program's style
menu.

The problem occurs when the font has more than four styles—and many do.
You may find variations such as demi-bold, demi-bold italic, extrabold,
extrabold condensed—you get the picture. These additional styles aren't
available from your Style menu, so you are left with choosing them from
your regular Font menu.

> **Note**
>
> One notable exception exists to this four-style rule: FrameMaker's sophisticated
> Paragraph Designer and Character Designer features (which are described fully in
> Chapter 21, "Desktop Publishing") offer all of the variations available in a typeface
> family, whether six, eight, twelve, or more.

> **Caution**
>
> If you don't have the actual styled variation of a font installed, and you choose that
> version from the Style menu, your Mac will try to generate it on-screen, but your
> PostScript printer will give you the regular or Roman version—or at worst, you'll get
> a doubled image. A QuickDraw printer uses your Mac to process documents and
> will usually try to simulate the missing style, but not necessarily with great precision.
> If you aren't certain that the correct style is installed, choose it directly from the Font
> menu.

Font Menu Modifiers

Normally, your typical Mac program shows each typeface style separately in your Font menu. This can get confusing with some of the older Adobe fonts, which use oddly labeled styles such as *B Times Bold* or *I Times Italic*. They don't show up in alphabetical order on your font menu, so picking the right face sometimes becomes a chore (see fig. 8.13).

Fig. 8.13
Some Mac fonts have confusing names and don't appear in alphabetical order.

Thankfully, most newer fonts use names that are properly alphabetized. But even then, your font menu may grow long, especially if you have a smaller screen or a large number of fonts at your beck and call. There are several handy programs that keep your font menus organized. One is Adobe Type Reunion, which places all styles in a given font family in a sub-menu. Both Menu Fonts from Dubl-Click Software and WYSIWYG Menus, part of Now Utilities from Now Software, not only group fonts by family, but show them in their actual typeface as well (see fig. 8.14).

Fig. 8.14
WYSIWYG Menus from Now Software shows fonts in their true styles.

Menu Fonts and WYSIWYG Menus have an added convenience. When you're using a font with all symbols, or a fancy script font whose name may not show clearly on a font menu, you can have those fonts display in a generic font or another typeface.

Kerning

As you increase the size of your type, the space between letters increases as well. Most publishing software give you tools to reduce the space between those letters. It's called *tracking,* and sometimes *range kerning,* because it refers to reducing white space over more than two characters. The larger the size, the more you need to reduce character spacing. Figures 8.15 and 8.16 show you what a difference a little space can make.

It is very logical

Fig. 8.15
Forty-eight point type, with normal letterspacing.

It is very logical

Fig. 8.16
Forty-eight point type, with letter-spacing reduced to give a good character fit.

Each letter gets its own increment of space; how much depends on the width of the character. With certain letter combinations, such as the capital T and the lower case *o,* you may see a wide gulf between the two characters, which you'll want to reduce for a better appearance, especially as the sizes get larger. The process of reducing the space between just two letters, to tuck one into the other, as it were, is called *kerning,* or *pair kerning.* Most modern-day fonts contain built-in kerning pairs that are specified by the font designers, but they never seem to be enough to meet the exacting needs of many users. Most desktop publishing and some word processing software will recognize those kerning pairs and usually provide the tools to refine kerning still further.

Figures 8.17 and 8.18 show the effect kerning can have on a document.

Where to start kerning is a matter of personal taste. Most publishing software set a kerning threshold of 10 point or 12 point, but some designers want *everything* kerned, however small it is. I have worked in typography studios where exact kerning was required in text as small as two points. In one case, I used a magnifying glass to enlarge it so that I could read it.

Fig. 8.17
Not kerned.

To be or not to be

Fig. 8.18
Kerned.

To be or not to be

The Lowdown on Low-Cost Fonts

Developing a new font is an exacting job. It can take a designer months or years to perfect each character of each style of a particular typeface family. Not only must the letterforms be rendered correctly, but the exact letterspacing from character to character must be tested and refined. It stands to reason that original font designs can be expensive to produce, and expensive to buy. Prices of from $100 to $400 for a single family of typefaces is not at all uncommon.

In recent years, a number of fonts have hit the market at prices of a dollar or less each, with the promise of quality to match the high-priced spread.

How do they do it?

These low-cost fonts aren't necessarily inferior in quality to their brand name counterparts. They are simply taking advantage of the limitations of the U.S. copyright laws to produce their products at lower prices. It seems you can copyright the name of a typeface, such as Helvetica or Times, and the software that contains the typeface, but you cannot copyright the actual character shapes. For example, you could produce a version of Helvetica named Spock, use different software, but copy the characters exactly and not be in violation of copyright and trademark laws.

We'll skirt the issue of whether marketing a copy of a typeface without paying royalties to the original designer or foundry is a good thing to do. We can only state that you can find bargains among such font collections, but you should ask the following questions before you buy:

- Do the fonts have complete character sets? Some low-cost fonts contain the letters of the alphabet and numbers, but are missing foreign accents and extended characters.

- If PostScript fonts, are they Type 1 fonts or Type 3? The older Type 3 format is not compatible with Adobe Type Manager, and thus won't work with QuickDraw printers or produce screen images that are free of jaggies in sizes for which screen fonts aren't available.

■ Are they shareware fonts? While some shareware fonts are produced by budding type designers with exceptional abilities, some are poor imitations of a traditional design.

■ Finally, even if the fonts all have complete character sets and meet all the other criteria, they may be poorly rendered. You might find rough edges around curves, erratic character spacing, and other artifacts of a product produced with poor quality control.

Using Adobe Type Manager

When you get used to this nifty little program, it's hard to imagine how one used to get work done without it. When Adobe Type Manager, or ATM, first appeared on the scene in October of 1989, it took the desktop publishing world by storm. Back then TrueType didn't exist, and the most popular scalable font format was Type 1 fonts.

Before ATM, your PostScript screen (or bitmap) font was used to generate the characters you saw on your Mac's screen. You had a separate screen font for each size. Normally font packages would ship with the most popular sizes, from 9 point to 18 point, and maybe a few larger sizes thrown in. If you chose another type size, your Mac would scale a QuickDraw image from your screen font, and the results would vary in quality depending on how far removed in size it was from the original. If you scaled it large enough, it would take on the aspect of a set of bricks, as shown in figure 8.19.

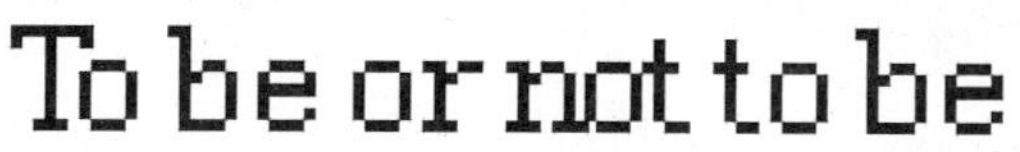

To be or not to be

Fig. 8.19
Your text result when ATM and a bitmap font aren't available in the size you choose.

ATM is, in effect, a small PostScript rasterizer. When you select a point size for which there's no screen font, ATM intercepts the call and creates a bitmap font, using the information from your PostScript printer font. The result is clear, sharp type on-screen as well as on your printer (see fig. 8.20).

If you don't have a PostScript printer on hand, you have the added bonus of having ATM around to process your Type 1 fonts, so they'll print clearly, up to the maximum resolution of your printer. Even the venerable ImageWriter benefits from ATM.

Tip
To save disk space with ATM installed, discard all screen fonts other than the basic 10 and 12 point text sizes.

II

System 7 Essentials

Fig. 8.20
The combination of ATM and Type 1 PostScript fonts clear up the jaggies on your Mac's screen.

To be or not to be

ATM builds screen fonts on the fly and stores them in a little bit of RAM it sets aside for that purpose. It takes roughly 50K of RAM to store each bitmap. By default, the latest versions of ATM are set up for 256K RAM, roughly enough to build five different screen fonts at one time. If your document has a lot of fonts on a single page, you can speed up ATM by giving it more RAM in the ATM Control Panel, as shown in figure 8.21.

Fig. 8.21
Set ATM's cache in the handy Control Panel.

Installing Fonts

If you have a library consisting of your basic Macintosh fonts, or even the ones that come with most PostScript laser printers, you won't have to worry too much about where to put those fonts. System 7's Finder was intelligently designed to know what kind of fonts you are trying to install and where to put them.

But to avoid the confusing nature of all of the font formats that are available, we wanted to tell you where they go, because it depends on which system version you have and what type of fonts you're using.

System 6 Font Installation

- Bitmap fonts are installed in the System file using Font/DA Mover.

- PostScript printer fonts are left loose in the System Folder.

- TrueType fonts are installed in the System file using Font/DA Mover.

> **Caution**
>
> TrueType fonts can only be used on System 6.0.5 or later, if you have Apple's TrueType init installed (TrueTypes answer to ATM).

System 7.0 and 7.0.1 Font Installation

- Bitmap fonts are installed in the System file when you drag them to the closed System Folder icon.

- PostScript printer fonts are installed in the Extensions Folder (inside the System Folder) when you drag them to the closed System Folder icon.

- TrueType fonts are installed in the System file when you drag them to the closed System Folder icon.

System 7.1- 7.5 Font Installation

- All fonts—bitmap, PostScript, and TrueType—go into the Fonts Folder when you drag them to the closed System Folder icon.

> **Note**
>
> Although you can install fonts in their proper locations manually in System 7.1 or later, letting the Finder do it for you has the added advantage of having them checked automatically for font numbering conflicts. Because some older Mac applications use font identification numbers to recognize fonts, using the Finder can help you avoid a font conflict which may result in erratic spacing, displaying, or printing of the wrong font, or other problems when you try to view or print a document.

Font Folder Limitations

In order to allow for optimum performance, Apple's software engineers decreed that the new Fonts folder, first introduced in System 7.1, would store 128 font resources. A font resource, by their definition, is a bitmap font or a TrueType font—PostScript fonts don't count.

> **Note**
>
> Contrary to popular belief, fonts do not use up much RAM unless they are actually being used. The only RAM they use otherwise is minimal, amounting simply to a reference to the fonts' availability to the System.

Tip
You can get around the Font folder's 128 resource limitation by dragging one font suitcase on top of another so that more fonts can be installed.

Font Resource Managers

If you have less than 50 or 100 fonts at hand, you don't have to read this section. Storing your fonts in the usual ways described in the preceding sections will provide satisfactory performance on your Mac.

But if you make a living from graphic design— or like me, you are simply a type junkie who likes to collect new and fancy styles—no doubt your font library will soon become unmanageable. Even if you sidestep System 7.1's Fonts folder limitations described in the preceding section, you will probably find some applications opening much more slowly when a great deal of fonts are installed. Font menus will become unbearably large, and selecting just a single font will take longer than it should.

You can move fonts in and out of the System Folder under System 7 as needed, but this process is slow, and you still have to quit open applications and relaunch them for the font menus to be updated.

There are other ways to manage your fonts, and these techniques are used by large design studios and service bureaus that maintain libraries of literally thousands of fonts. It involves placing your fonts in locations other than your System Folder— even on another hard drive or network server—and using programs that manage resources to load and unload fonts as needed. The following section discusses these programs. But first, you need to know a few ground rules to organize your font library so that these programs can do their magic.

Caution

The following tips require installation of either MasterJuggler or Suitcase. They will not work without a program such as these, which are described in the following pages.

Following are a few font organization tips that I've learned while managing huge font libraries for service bureaus (we're talking of anywhere from a few hundred to a few thousand fonts here):

- It's a good idea to leave just your standard Macintosh System display fonts in the proper locations in your System Folder. These include Chicago, Geneva, Monaco, and New York. You may want to add to that list some of the fonts you use very often, such as Helvetica, Times, or other commonly used faces.

> **Caution**
>
> When you install your System software, such faces as Chicago, Geneva, Monaco, and New York are automatically installed. These fonts are all used to display directories and other information on your Mac's screen. Most Mac software uses these fonts for screen display as well—so don't remove them.

■ All other fonts should be placed in another folder, which I'll call Resource Folder (you can call it whatever you want). This Resource Folder can be placed on your startup disk. You don't have to place it in the System Folder, however—it can also be placed on another drive, or even on a networked disk.

■ When you are using PostScript fonts, or TrueType fonts with extra screen fonts, place all the font resources for a particular typeface in the same folder, not separated by another folder. Otherwise ATM won't work, and the fonts will not download properly to your printer.

■ To keep your Resource Folder from being too large, you can subdivide your Resource Folder, by creating a separate folder for each typeface family. An example would be separate folders for each of the following: Avant Garde, Bookman, Helvetica, Times, and so on.

■ Some programs, such as Aldus PageMaker and QuarkXPress, will update font menus dynamically when you open and close font resources with a font resource manager. This is especially convenient if you open a document, realize you don't have the right font installed, and rush to install that font using one of the two programs described in the following sections. Installing fonts the regular way—with the Fonts folder in System 7.1 and later—requires that you close an application and relaunch it for the font changes to take effect.

Using Suitcase

Steve Brecher's Suitcase, now published by Symantec, was first on the market with a resource management program in 1988. Even though the Fonts folder in System 7.1 and later system revisions have made the issue of dealing with a font library simpler, Suitcase still has its place, because it makes it possible to open and close fonts when you need them. It also frees you from reliance on your System Folder to handle your font library.

In effect, what Suitcase does is fool the System into thinking that fonts and other resources are really installed in their correct locations in the System Folder, without affecting performance in any way (except for that occasional conflict that may occur when Apple does a major System upgrade).

Suitcase is a System Extension that loads from the Extensions Folder in the various versions of System 7, and lies loose in the System Folder under System 6. The latest versions display your fonts, DAs, Fkeys, and sounds in two windows, and group your resources in sets for easy organization, as shown in the Sets and Suitcases window in figure 8.22.

Fig. 8.22
Sets & Suitcases open with Symantec's Suitcase.

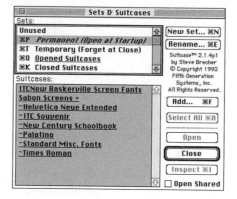

The program is handy in managing fonts, but you have to take a little time working with the program to appreciate its flexibility. Consider the concept of a Set, for example, which is simply a group of font resources. Each font resource shown in figure 8.22 represents a single suitcase. That suitcase can contain one font, one font family, or several different font families.

You can build a font suitcase under System 7 simply by dragging one suitcase and dropping it on another, or by double-clicking the suitcase to display the list of available fonts, and then moving them to another suitcase, as shown in figure 8.23.

> **Note**
>
> Under System 6, you need to use Font/DA Mover to add to or remove fonts from a font suitcase.

A single suitcase can contain all the fonts you need for a particular job, and you can even label it by an appropriate title, such as one for your newsletter, another for your business cards, and a third for form letters. Suitcase enables you to create a set consisting of several suitcases and then give it a name appropriate for the job. To create a new set, click the New Set button, or type ⌘-N, which opens the dialog box shown in figure 8.24.

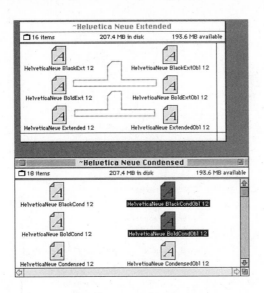

Fig. 8.23
Moving fonts from one suitcase to another.

Fig. 8.24
Creating a new set in Suitcase.

After you name your set, you can fill it with font resources by clicking the Add button or typing ⌘-F in the main Suitcase Sets & Suitcases window, which opens a regular Open dialog box (see fig. 8.25). You can add fonts to any existing set by first clicking that set's name on the list.

You can Add one font suitcase in the list or just Add All, which you should use cautiously if your folder is filled with many font suitcases. I've seen literally hundreds of fonts added by mistake this way. When you're done, click the Cancel button.

The Permanent set, which is italicized, shows the list of fonts that will always open automatically when you boot your Mac. You can Close any font suitcase individually, or in a batch by Shift-clicking the names. Each time you close a font, you receive a warning notice (see fig. 8.26).

II

System 7 Essentials

Fig. 8.25
Adding fonts
to Suitcase.

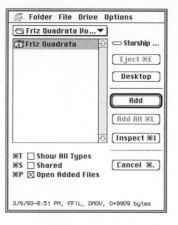

Fig. 8.26
Suitcase presents a
warning whenever
you close a font
suitcase.

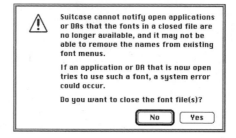

When a font resource is closed, it will no longer be underlined in the list. At this point, if it's in a Permanent (italicized) set, it'll just be opened again next time you restart your Mac. To remove the font suitcase, select it and then choose Cut from the File menu. You can use this technique to cut and paste fonts from one set to another.

Caution

Suitcase Sets that are not made permanent will close automatically next time you boot your Mac. This is convenient if you only intend to use the fonts for that work session, but not so convenient if your Mac crashes for any reason.

Note

You can make a Suitcase Set permanent simply by double-clicking the Set's name, which changes the listing to italics. Double-clicking the Set's name again changes it back to normal. The default Sets, which have keyboard shortcuts listed for them, cannot be changed in this manner.

The second window in Suitcase, the Resources window, is used to display all available resources, whether opened through Suitcase or by virtue of being installed in the proper places in the System Folder (see fig. 8.27). Clicking a font's name, by the way, opens a three-letter display showing what the font looks like.

Fig. 8.27
Suitcase's Resources window shows available fonts, DAs, sounds, and Fkeys.

Using MasterJuggler

Alsoft's MasterJuggler is the second of the two commercial programs that can fool the System into thinking that resources such as fonts and sounds are located in their proper places in the System Folder. While many users favor Suitcase, others appreciate some of the additional features available in MasterJuggler, such as its convenient pop-up menus.

MasterJuggler is an Extension that installs in System 7's Extensions Folder or System 6's System Folder, and is accessed from your Apple Menu, or by using a keyboard shortcut you can set in the program's preferences. When you bring up the main MasterJuggler window you'll be able to easily open your font and sound resources (see fig. 8.28).

To open a font resource, simply select it from the list at the top half of the window, which shows available files, and then click the Open button. The file will then be added to the bottom list, which displays open files. To remove the font resource, select it from the list of open files and click the Close button.

> **Note**
>
> Font resource managers do not work with fonts already installed in their proper places in your System Folder. They only work with fonts installed elsewhere, using the techniques previously described.

II

System 7 Essentials

Fig. 8.28
MasterJuggler's
main window.

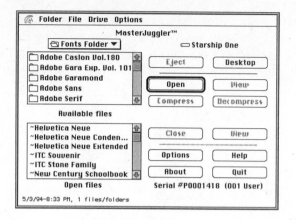

In addition to opening font resource and sounds, MasterJuggler can open DAs, Fkeys, and sounds. It also can display several varieties of pop-up menus, including one listing fonts in their actual typeface and even a list of available applications. You can configure the program still further by clicking the Options button on the main MasterJuggler window, which opens the window shown in figure 8.29.

Fig. 8.29
MasterJuggler
Options window
lets you customize
the program.

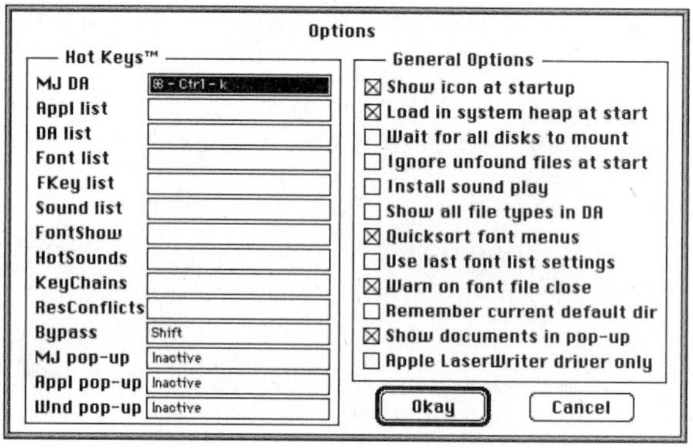

The most useful options are the convenient hot keys you can set up to activate the various MasterJuggler lists and windows. Among General Options, the most important one, which is usually off by default, is *Wait for all disks to mount.* As explained previously, you don't have to have your available fonts installed on your startup disk. You can have them available on external drives or even a networked server. If you check this option, MasterJuggler will wait for those disks to mount before searching for open font resources.

Which One Is for You?

Both Suitcase and MasterJuggler patch the System to provide their magic. When Apple makes a major change to its operating system, it's not unusual to find a revision to either of these programs coming along shortly thereafter. Suitcase's author is also a frequent visitor to the online services and provides friendly support and free software update patches whenever it is necessary to fix bugs that users might find in the program. Alsoft has also actively updated MasterJuggler as new hardware and system updates require programming changes.

In its present form, Suitcase is a better tool to manage your font library, because of the immense flexibility in the way you can set it up, once you get the hang of it. MasterJuggler has the advantage of costing less than Suitcase, and if you're choosing a program strictly on price alone, you may prefer it, even though MasterJuggler's font loading capabilities are nowhere near as fluid as its competition.

The Future of Fonts

A new variation has been added to the font universe—QuickDraw GX. Apple's major upgrade to its native imaging technology places many of the fancier font tricks on a system level, such as ligatures and character kerning and spectacular graphic effects with both type and illustrations.

In the next few years, we'll see just how the advent of QuickDraw GX will change font technology. Having new tools to handle fonts may encourage developers to produce a whole new generation of GXsavvy fonts, containing additional characters and doing stuff behind the scenes, on the system level, that will greatly enhance the look of your documents.

In the meantime, your existing font investment will be protected. Your TrueType fonts will work just fine when you install QuickDraw GX on your Macintosh, and Adobe is supplying a special font converter with the QuickDraw GX software that will allow you to continue to use your existing PostScript fonts.

From Here...

This chapter provided the basics of what a Macintosh font is and explained how to use them most effectively in your document. The chapter even gave you some helpful hints on using ATM and a font resource manager to help you get control of your font library.

- Chapter 10, "The Printing Chapter," provides some helpful hints on printing the documents you create with all those fancy new fonts.

- In case you run into trouble, read chapters 37 and 38, where the steps you need to take to troubleshoot common problems with your Mac are described, as well as how you can solve them before they become serious.

Chapter 9

Sharing Data between Applications

by Jo Zarboulos

No Mac is an island. Not any more, that is. A few short years ago, legions of individual users happily computed away on an individual Mac in an individual space. MacPaint or MacWrite were likely to be their only applications, the ImageWriter their only connection, and the Clipboard their only method of sharing data. Copying and pasting seemed a major miracle.

Now just a few years but several Mac generations later, we want our files and applications to share with each other, so we can place an image retouched in Photoshop inside a newsletter laid out in PageMaker, incorporate an Excel spreadsheet into a report written in Microsoft Word, import clip art into our HyperCard stacks, merge an Excel mailing list we purchased with a resident FileMaker mailing list, and open a colleague's WordPerfect file from our Microsoft Word application.

All this sharing may be good for our psyches and our bottom lines, but it can create problems. When we e-mail a file half-way around the world, the recipients may not have the application to read it. We may not know how to edit our Photoshop image when we place it in PageMaker. The Excel mailing list may lose its text formatting when we merge it with the FileMaker mailing list. Our colleague's WordPerfect file may crash when we try to open it from Word.

The aim of this chapter is to help you understand the various methods of sharing files between applications so you can choose the methods that work best in your work situation. The chapter discusses the following topics:

- Understanding file formats

- Copying and pasting via the Clipboard and the Scrapbook

- Importing and exporting

- Publishing and subscribing

- Linking and embedding

Understanding File Formats

When you want to share data between applications (or share data between *computers* as discussed in Chapter 35), you often have to contend in some way or other with the differences between file formats. It helps to begin by knowing what a file format is.

A *file format* is a set of conventions that determines how information is stored—something like the conventions that determine how human languages are written. A basic convention of English, for example, is that characters are written from left to right. We couldn't read English text if it were written in a foreign convention—unless we could figure out how to translate it. If you can read the following words—siht daer ot yrt—you are translating a foreign convention into your native convention.

Similarly, every application creates, saves, and manipulates data in its own *native file format*. When you transfer data in from a different application, the first application needs to be able to read or translate the *foreign file format*.

You might ask, "Why can't there be just one standard file format, in keeping with the Macintosh philosophy of standardization, consistency, and ease of use discussed in Chapter 3?"

One reason is that different types of applications store different types of information. A word processor, for example, needs to store such things as fonts, sizes, styles, margins, and spacing, as well as the data. A graphics application using bit-maps needs to store such things as line width, color, and fill, as well as coordinates for each pixel. A spreadsheet application needs to store the widths of columns and rows, as well as numbers and formulas. And so on.

When exchanging data, you can deal with different file formats in many ways. With some methods (embedding in particular), the applications take care of translating file formats for you. In other methods (importing and exporting in particular), you generally have to be more involved in the translation of file formats. In this chapter, information about specific file formats is given where it is most needed, in the section "Importing and Exporting." Information on Clipboard formats is given in "Using the Clipboard."

Transferring Static Data

When you want to transfer some information from one application to another, and you don't plan to update the information or share it over the network, you can choose one of the following methods discussed in this section:

■ Copying and pasting by using the Clipboard

■ Copying and pasting by using the Scrapbook

■ Importing (and exporting first if necessary)

Using the Clipboard

Using the Clipboard is so easy and so basic to the operation of the Macintosh, that even experienced users tend to forget how useful it can be. They may struggle with more difficult ways to transfer data between applications when a simple copy and paste would do.

Consider the Clipboard a temporary storage area where graphic and text items can be held until you decide where to put then. It's also volatile, meaning that if you restart or shut down your Mac, the data in your Clipboard is gone.

There are three basic steps you'll always follow in using the Clipboard. You'll find them in the Edit menu (or you can use the handy keyboard shortcuts I've listed). Some software products offer additional options for Clipboard use that are mentioned in the program's manuals, but the steps I'm about to describe apply to virtually all Mac programs:

1. Cut (or Command-X): This function removes the selected item from your document and places it in the Clipboard.

2. Copy (or Command-C): This function copies (but does not remove) the selected item from your document and places it in the Clipboard.

3. Paste (or Command-V): This function places the material from the keyboard into your document.

II

System 7 Essentials

As a rule of thumb, when you want to do a one-time transfer of graphics or text (or even sound and QuickTime movies) and you're not concerned that the data will change, try the Clipboard first.

Understanding Clipboard Formatting

When you cut text from one application and paste it into another, the pasted copy usually retains the formatting style of the source. But sometimes it doesn't work as expected—the font or its size or style are changed, or you can't edit what you've pasted. To make the results more predictable, it helps to understand how the Clipboard works.

Most applications store the data you cut or copy to the Clipboard in several versions, each version in a different format (though only one version is visible in the Clipboard window).

These formats are similar to file formats, but designed especially for the Clipboard. Generally, each application stores one version of the information in its own native Clipboard format. If you paste within the same application, the information will usually retain its exact formatting.

Other versions of the information can be stored in one of the following standard Clipboard formats:

- *The PICT format.* This format stores data, whether a graphic or text, as a picture (either object-oriented or bit-mapped). Text stored in PICT format is not editable.

- *The TEXT format.* This format stores data as text only. Text stored in this format loses its font and style information.

- *The STYL format.* This format stores data as text, complete with font and formatting information.

- *The MOOV format.* If you have Apple's QuickTime extension installed, this format is used to store QuickTime movies.

- *The SND format.* This format stores sounds—either those supplied with the system software or those you record yourself—for transferring between applications that support sounds.

Applications store multiple versions of Clipboard data in order to give applications on the paste side a good chance of finding a format they understand, and thus preserve as much of the original formatting instructions as possible.

Suppose that you are copying cells from an Excel spreadsheet and pasting them into a Word 5 document. One of the formats Excel uses in the Clipboard is RTF (for Rich-Text Format), an interchange format that Word 5 understands as well. Word chooses the copy with that format and is able to paste it with the original formatting.

Some programs, on the other hand, don't understand RTF. Thus if you paste the same Excel spreadsheet cells into a document created by a non-Microsoft program, that application may choose the TEXT format—and the pasted copy will lose its font formatting.

> **Note**
>
> In addition to using the standard Apple Clipboard, Microsoft Word maintains its own private Clipboard. If you are unable to get Word to recognize something you've copied to the Clipboard from another program, simply switch out of Word to another program or to the Finder, then back to Word. That is usually sufficient to force Word to update its Clipboard properly.

To get out of the Clipboard what you put into it, the destination application must either understand the source application's native Clipboard format, or both applications must have another format in common.

You can determine the Clipboard formats an application uses in the following manner. Select some data from a file within the application and then choose Copy. Open the Scrapbook from the Apple menu and then choose Paste. The selection appears in the Scrapbook's window. (I'll tell you more about the Scrapbook later in this chapter.) The Clipboard formats are displayed at the bottom right of the window.

◄ See "New Features," p. 56

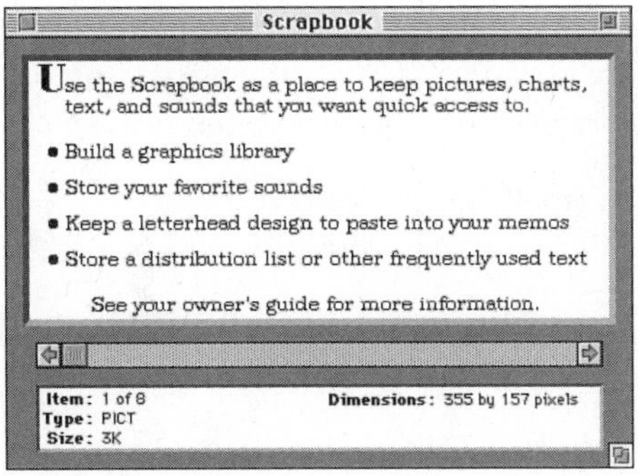

Fig. 9.1
The Scrapbook, referred to later in this chapter, can be used as a library for frequently used material.

The data is displayed in the Scrapbook in only one format, although the data is probably stored in others you don't see. Therefore the data may *look* as if it's incorrectly formatted. But if the application you paste into can find a format it can read, it will restore the original formatting (or as much of the formatting as the application can read).

Some applications have a Paste Special command (under the Edit menu) that allows you to choose among the available Clipboard formats. For information about the specific choices in the dialog box, see the application's documentation.

If you are still not satisfied with the results when you transfer data by using the Clipboard, you may want to try importing. Importing and exporting is covered in detail later in this chapter.

Did You Know?: Clipboard Tips and Tricks

Many people don't know as much as they think they do about the Clipboard. See whether you know all these tips and tricks:

- You can transfer entire files via the Clipboard, even large ones. If the data exceeds what can be held in memory, many applications will save it to disk. In that case, the size of information you can copy to the Clipboard is limited only by the space available on your hard disk.

- You can copy the current time and date from the Alarm Clock desk accessory and paste it at the beginning of a file.

- You can copy the results of a calculation made with the Calculator desk accessory, and then paste it into a file.

- You can go the other direction and paste a numerical problem, including common math symbols, from a file to the Calculator. The Calculator's keys flash to reflect what you have pasted, and the answer appears. Then you can paste the answer back into your file. (The Calculator beeps for each symbol it doesn't recognize.)

- You can copy a small amount of text into a file's Get Info box (available from the Finder) to remind yourself what's in the file.

- If you have the equipment to record sound, you can Copy and Paste sounds between applications that support them.

- You can transfer QuickTime movie frames by using the Clipboard.

- Sometimes the Clipboard comes up empty when you try to paste between applications. This may be because the receiving application understands only its own Clipboard. If this happens, use the Scrapbook instead.

- If you cut or copy something, and then realize you want what was previously held on the Clipboard, you can press ⌘-Z to undo, or return the Clipboard to its previous state.

- You can keep what is currently on the Clipboard by using the Delete key to remove unwanted items in your document instead of the Cut command to delete.

- When you want to transfer data from a PostScript application like Illustrator or Freehand to an application that doesn't understand PostScript data, you can transfer through the Clipboard by holding down the Option key while you choose Copy from the Edit menu.

- MultiClip by Olduvai (Miami, FL) is a utility that gives you multiple clipboards, which you can view, edit, or move to the Scrapbook for more permanent storage.

Using the Scrapbook

The Scrapbook, located under the Apple menu, is often overlooked as a means of transferring data. Unlike the Clipboard, what you store in the Scrapbook is saved to disk and thus doesn't go away when you paste something else, quit an application, or turn off the computer. You can paste as many items as you want—text or graphics.

The Scrapbook consists of two files. First is the desk accessory (or application under System 7.5) that is available from the Apple menu. The second is the Scrapbook file itself (located in your System Folder). Consider the Scrapbook as a library in which you can store frequently-used text or graphic items.

When you first use the Scrapbook, its behavior may seem strange at first because it follows a different set of rules than the rest of the Macintosh. Following are the rules á la Scrapbook:

- You don't select something from the Scrapbook to cut or copy. You simply choose Cut or Copy from the Edit menu while the page you want to cut or copy is displayed and the Scrapbook window is active.

- Each time you paste, you create a new page of the Scrapbook. You can't paste over an existing page. What you paste affects the page before or the page after the one displayed.

■ The number of the current page is displayed at the bottom left of the screen, along with the total number of pages in the Scrapbook. You use the scroll bar to display different pages.

■ When you paste a large selection, you can't scroll to see it all, nor can you resize the window. You just have to have faith that it's all there. (The size of data you paste into the Scrapbook is limited only by the size you can copy to the Clipboard, in order to transfer it.)

■ As explained in the section on the Clipboard, pasted data is often saved in multiple formats. The name of the format or formats appears at the bottom of the Scrapbook screen. (But you can only see one of those formats in the Scrapbook window.)

Did You Know? Scrapbook Tips and Tricks

Following are some tips and tricks concerning the Scrapbook:

■ What you store in the Scrapbook file is kept in the startup volume's System folder under the name *Scrapbook File*. You can transfer that file from one disk or volume to another.

■ You can create and store multiple Scrapbooks and name them according to contents. For example, you might have Scrpbk.dogs and Scrpbk.cats. You then can use one of these files by renaming it *Scrapbook File* and moving it into the System folder.

■ ClickPaste by Mainstay (Camarillo, CA) is a utility that allows you to store Scrapbook pages in hierarchical folders. In Version 2, you can store sounds and play them back before you paste them.

■ SmartScrap by Portfolio Systems (Cupertino, CA) lets you store multiple scrapbooks which you can access without renaming them. You can select any portion of a stored image for copying, name each page of each scrapbook, search through the contents by name, and build a table of contents with thumbnail views of each page. To open a page, you click on its thumbnail image.

Table 9.1 shows you some ideas for using the Scrapbook.

Table 9.1 Ideas for Pages to Store in the Scrapbook

Example	Description
SoftwareProductName	Long words (especially interCapped words) or passages of text you type repeatedly.
® ™ © π á à â é è ¢ ≠ Æ	Symbols you use often, but not often enough to remember the key combinations.
Jo Zarboulas	Your signature, to personalize documents you relay via the network, fax, or modem.
	Your company's logo, to use in marketing and official documents.
	Your business card, to uniquely personalize your faxes and letters.
	Your letterhead, to create instant stationery you can never run out of.
	A happy face and a sad face you draw in a graphics program, to convey your feelings. (Or if you have a camera and a scanner, how about happy and sad portraits of yourself?)

Importing brings data created in one application into another application. If your application is not able to accept another application's data, you need to save it in another file format first, a process called *exporting*.

Generally speaking, you import an entire file, rather than selected data, though database applications like FileMaker Pro allow you to select the fields you want to import. (If you want to use importing to bring in selected data, you can do so in a roundabout way: import the whole file, and then cut the data you don't want.)

Tip
To write smoothly with a graphics program, write very large and then reduce the results.

Depending on your applications, you import a file in one of the following ways:

■ From application A, you import application B's file directly, using the Import, Open, or Place command from the File menu. Application A must have the built-in ability to read B's file format.

■ From application A, you import application B's file, using the Import, Open, or Place command. Application A must have an installed plug-in filter to convert B's format to A's native format.

■ From application B, you export the file to an intermediate format, using the Export, or Save As command. Then from application A you import the resulting file. Application A converts the file to its native format.

Importing Files Directly

Most applications have built-in file conversion capabilities that allow them to read files in certain foreign file formats directly. Often these are applications that work with a similar type of data, and therefore have similar file formats. For example, Excel and Lotus 1-2-3 can open and save each other's files directly, and so can Word and WordPerfect.

But this does not always work perfectly. Certain features of an application may get lost in the translation, causing unwanted formatting changes, or even crashes. For example, some programs have difficulty opening or importing a Word file that has been saved with Word's fast-save feature. (If you encounter any difficulty, you can resave the Word file with the fast-save feature disabled.)

> **Note**
>
> The kind of formatting information that's recognized when you import a file from another application into your document may vary from program to program. It is a good idea to check your manuals for information about file conversions. Both Word and WordPerfect include special text files that explain how well files are translated from one format to another.

Another problem is that a file you are attempting to open may contain portions of text or a graphic that cannot be read by the application trying to open it. In such cases, you may want to use a program called Can Opener by Abbott Systems (of Pleasantville, NY), which can extract any portion of a file that is in a commonly used text, graphics, or sound format.

You can tell if an application can open another's files by starting the application and choosing the Open, Place, or Import command. In the dialog box that appears, you can navigate through your folders to the files created in that application. Often you can narrow down the search by selecting the type of file you're looking for. For example, in the Microsoft Word Open dialog box shown in figure 9.2, you can select Graphics Files to see only graphics files, or you can narrow the search further to see only those graphics files saved in PICT format.

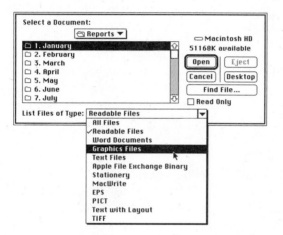

Fig. 9.2
Use Word's Open dialog box to select the kind of files you wish to see listed in the directory.

In most applications, when you import (or open) a file in a foreign file format, it appears in a new, untitled window. When you save this new file, you will probably prefer to choose a new name for it, rather than replace the original file. You'll probably also want to save the file in the native format of your current application. You might want to add a few letters to the end of the file name to indicate that it's been saved in a different application, such as Status Report.W for a file saved in Word and Status Report.WP for one saved in WordPerfect.

If you want to incorporate all of the new file, or any portion of it, in another file of this application, you can cut (or copy) it and paste it into the other file.

In page layout applications such as PageMaker and QuarkXPress and some drawing programs, you place text or graphics directly in the active window of the application, rather than a separate window. Usually you use the Place command to do this. In QuarkXPress you choose either the Get Text or the Get Picture command.

Using Plug-In Filters

Many applications include small programs with their software, called *filters* or *converters* or *translators* (wouldn't it be nice if they could standardize the term!). Each filter enables the application to open files written in a specific file format. These filters are more extensive than built-in file conversion capabilities, and therefore cause fewer problems.

Filters are modular, so you can install only the ones you need for applications you use. And you can add new ones as they become available. Many developers make filters available for downloading from on-line services like America Online and CompuServe.

One type of filter, developed by Claris, but owned by Apple and used by many other major developers, establishes a standard design for filters, called *XTND*. The standard allows new filters to be designed for translating any other application that supports XTND. A company called DataViz (located in Trumbull, CT) sells packages of filters, called *MacLink Plus Translators*, that work with any XTND application.

Exporting Files to Other File Formats

When two applications can't read each other's files, you may be able to find an intermediate format that both applications understand (sort of like an Italian and a Spaniard using English as an intermediate language to communicate with each other). You export the file in the intermediate format, then open the resulting file from the other application, which converts it into its own format. Formats designed especially to be intermediate formats are called *interchange formats*.

To export a file to an interchange format and then open it in another application, follow these steps:

1. Open the file in question in its own application. If you make any changes, be sure to use the Save command to save the file in its native format, in case you need it later.

2. Choose the Export command if it exists. Otherwise, choose Save As.

   The dialog box for either of these commands should contain a list of formats to choose from. Figure 9.3 shows the Save As dialog box from Word.

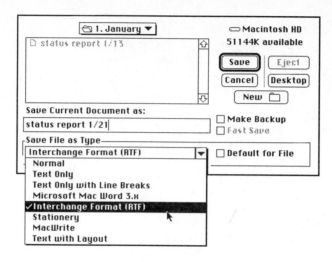

Fig. 9.3
Word's Save As dialog box gives you a choice of file formats in which you can save your document.

3. Choose a format the receiving application will understand. Some common formats for different types of applications are described a bit later in this chapter.

4. Choose a name for the new file, preferably the same name but with a file extension to indicate the format. For example, you could name a January report saved in RTF January.RTF.

5. Close the file. If there's not enough memory to launch another application, quit the program.

6. Launch the other application.

7. Choose the Open, Import, Place, Get Text, or Get Picture command. In the dialog box that appears, you may need to select the file format or type of file you used to save or export the other file.

8. Double-click the file you want to open.

   You will probably see a message telling you the application is converting the file to the application's native file format.

The most common interchange formats for text, graphics, and spreadsheets

Text Formats:

■ ASCII (American Standard Code for Information Interchange) or Text Only. The most basic of formats, the one you can almost always use when all else fails. ASCII (pronounced ASK-key) is a standard set of 256 codes, each

(continues)

II

System 7 Essentials

(continued)

standing for a letter, number, special character, or rudimentary formatting instruction, such as a tab or carriage return. All other formatting information is stripped away. Most applications that read text understand ASCII, as do all computers. Many e-mail systems, on-line services, and bulletin boards use ASCII (Text Only) files.

- *RTF (Rich-Text Format)*. A good choice for word processing files, since RTF retains most text formatting and graphics formatting as well. Developed by Microsoft, it is supported by Word, WordPerfect, WriteNow, PageMaker, and others.

- *MacWrite*. Though this format is the MacWrite word processor's native file format, it is so widely supported that it can serve as an interchange format.

Graphics Formats:

- *TIFF (Tagged Image File Format)*. A standard high-resolution format for bit-mapped graphics, TIFF is used by many scanning and image manipulating applications, such as Photoshop. Files can be large and take a long time to open.

- *PTNG*. This is MacPaint's native format, but it is so common it can be used as an intermediate format. However, PTNG is severely limited. It stores bit-mapped, monochrome images only, which must have a resolution of 72 dots per inch, and be no larger than 8" x 10", with a vertical orientation.

- *PICT* and *PICT2*. These are standard, widely used formats for either object-oriented or bit-mapped graphics. PICT supports only eight colors and thus is most useful for black and white graphics. PICT2 supports as many colors as your monitor allows.

- *MacPaint*. Because MacPaint was bundled with the first Macintosh computers and was the first graphics file format, nearly every Macintosh graphics, layout, or word processor program can read this format. Files in this format contain only low resolution black and white information and have a fixed size of 576 by 720 pixels.

- *EPS (Encapsulated PostScript)*. EPS is recommended for graphics to be printed on a PostScript printer. If you use such a printer, this format will best preserve the attributes of complex graphics, especially if in color. Most important, an EPS file is device independent, which means that you can scale an EPS graphic to any size and still have it reproduce at your printer's maximum resolution. EPS is supported by major graphics and desktop publishing applications like Aldus Freehand, Adobe Illustrator, Aldus PageMaker, FrameMaker and QuarkXPress, as well as many word processors.

Spreadsheet and Database Formats:

- *DIF (Data Interchange Format).* DIF transfers spreadsheet data but not the formulas used to calculate the data. Cell formatting and widths are not retained. The main purpose of this format is to transfer data so that it can be graphed in a presentation or charting application.

- *SYLK (Symbolic Link).* SYLK transfers spreadsheet data and the formulas used to calculate. It retains some formatting information, including commas, column widths, and cell alignment, but loses font, size, and style.

- *ASCII (American Standard Code for Information Interchange)* or *Text Only*. As described under the Text Formats section of this list, ASCII or Text Only files lose text formatting. If you must save in ASCII for lack of another common format when exchanging a spreadsheet or a database, use Tab-Separated Text or Comma-Separated Text.

- *Tab-Separated Text* or *Comma-Separated Text*. These are ASCII formats with the addition of delimiters—carriage returns, and tabs or commas—to tell the importing application where the rows and columns of the spreadsheet or the records of the database begin and end.

Transferring Live Data

As useful as copying and pasting can be, it has one major limitation: once information is transferred, it's disconnected from its source. If the original information changes, you have to go back and recopy, and then repaste. If the information changes frequently, or if you need to paste it into multiple files, this can be a tedious process. And it can be unreliable, because you might not remember all the places where the information has been pasted.

Three other methods of exchanging data address these problems in different ways: publish and subscribe, linking, and embedding. All three methods keep information connected to its source in some way, and so can be considered live.

Deciding on a Method

To help you decide which method of transferring live data to use in a particular situation, find the category of information you are dealing with in the following list and read about the recommended method(s). You might also want to see table 9.3 for a comparison of the advantages and limitations of the three methods.

II

System 7 Essentials

■ Information Subject to Change

You may create files containing information that is subject to change, such as financial data, product descriptions, and project schedules. To keep the files up-to-date when the original information changes, you can use *linking* or *publish and subscribe*. Linking is easier, but it works only with a single Macintosh, and requires that all source applications be available. If the information is to appear over the network, use *publish and subscribe*.

■ Information From Other People on the Network

If you want to create a file that includes information created by different people, such as a flyer with contributions from various writers and graphic artists, use *publish and subscribe*.

■ Information to Be Used by Other People on the Network

If you want to create or maintain information to be used by others over the network, such as a corporate logo, a mission statement or slogan, and legal disclaimers, use *publish and subscribe*.

■ Cross-References

You can use *linking* to update cross-references automatically so that when figures, chapters, or sections are renumbered or renamed, the references to them change accordingly.

■ Information for a Specific Document

You may want to create information especially for a document, using another application. For example, within a sales report, you may want to include a chart you create in Excel. Use *embedding* to create the information from within the sales report document.

■ Information for Transporting by Floppy Disk

If you plan to transfer a document by using a floppy disk, and the document has information from other sources, use embedding, which requires storing all the information in only one file. If the recipient does not need to edit the embedded information, then they do not need the application(s) used for the source information. But they will need to be able to open the base document, either by having the application that created it or by having another application that understands its file format.

Using Publish and Subscribe

Publish and subscribe is probably System 7's most underutilized feature. Introduced as a "sophisticated Copy and Paste," many users seem to think it's *too* sophisticated—that is, difficult to understand and use.

It *is* a little more complicated than other methods, and its clumsy, non-intuitive terminology doesn't help. But it can be well worth using, particularly if you work with information that is subject to change or information that appears in various documents throughout an organization.

Comparing publish and subscribe to copy and paste may help explain how it works. Publish and subscribe is often called a "live copy and paste." Instead of copying the source information, you *publish* it. Instead of going to the Clipboard, and thus being held in memory, the published information goes to a special file called an *Edition,* which is saved on disk. Instead of pasting the information, you then *subscribe to* the Edition, causing it to appear in your document. Table 9.2 shows the similarities between the two methods up to this point.

Table 9.2 Publish and Subscribe in Analogy to Copy and Paste				
Source		**Holding Area**		**Destination**
Copy	↔	Clipboard, (in memory)	↔	Paste
Publish	⇒	Edition, (on disk)	⇒	Subscribe to

After the information you published has been subscribed to, the similarity to copy and paste ends. When you paste a file into your document from the Clipboard, there is no link to the original file. With publish and subscribe, the items you publish remain linked via the Edition file. When the original published information changes, those same changes appear in the Edition, either automatically or on command. In fact, subscribing files can be updated even when they are not open. You can also subscribe to the same Edition from as many documents and applications as you want. If you share the Edition over the network, other users can subscribe to it as well.

What Can You Do with Publish and Subscribe?

Clearly, the more places a piece of information appears, or the more times it changes, the more useful—essential, even—the publish and subscribe method becomes. Over a network, it can save the time of many people, and ensure that everyone is working with the latest information.

If you find it difficult to envision how you can benefit by using publish and subscribe, the following list of possible uses may help you think of some. It is not meant to be an exhaustive list, or even a logical one. Categories and items overlap a good deal, but are designed only to spur ideas.

Publish and Subscribe—What to Use It For

Information subject to regular or frequent updating:

- Spreadsheet data (sales figures, expenses, price lists, and so on)

- Product descriptions, product identification numbers, graphics or photographs of products

- Customer databases

- Employee databases

- Employee sketches and resumes

- Corporate or organizational mission statements, slogans, blurbs,   legal disclaimers, copyright notice

- Templates for brochures, manuals, memos, status reports, invoices, and so on

- Meeting minutes

- Proposals

- Contracts

- Schedules, calendars, project tracking

- Employee worksheets, contract invoices

- Flow charts

- Error reports, customer questions and complaints

Work being created at one source but used (or edited) in other locations:

- Logos, icons

- Product presentations, internal presentations

- Screenshots or photographs, descriptions of software or other products under development

Composite work pulled in from several sources:

- Flyers, newsletters, brochures

- Data sheets

- Presentations

Information created in one application but used in another:

- Spreadsheet data used in word processors or page layout applictions

- Database data used in word processors or presentation programs

- Graphics used in spreadsheets or databases

- Data in specialized applications concerned with flow charts, meetings, decisions, presentations, etc. used in another specialized application or a word processor

Master repositories or catalogs of information subscribed to by multiple users:

- "Boiler plate" blurbs or phrases, such as product descriptions

- Scanned photographs or slides

- QuickTime movie clips

- Recorded messages

Home use:

- Graphic designs you use in multiple places, perhaps as you work to improve them over time

- Financial totals and other data updated from one spreadsheet or accounting application to another, such as from Quicken to MacInTax

- Updates from employers or clients over the modem via Apple Remote Access

Note

Create a graphic or scanned photo, and then subscribe to it any number of times on the same page. When you edit the original, you get a new design. Do a Save As and repeat to create different designs. In addition to editing or replacing the published graphic, you can rearrange the subscribers on the page for a variety of effects.

A Publish and Subscribe Scenario

Suppose you are in charge of producing an internal monthly sales report. Every month you must gather from other staff the latest graph of sales figures, a scanned photograph of the current "employee of the month," and a column about that person.

II

System 7 Essentials

Fig 9.4
A sales report for
the first month.

Each contributor to the report publishes his or her information, thus creating Editions you subscribe to from the layout you created in PageMaker. A copy of each Edition file is placed in your PageMaker document. You can resize the information if you want.

In May, your report might look like the one shown in Figure 9.4.

After the report is distributed, your PageMaker document will receive updates (manually or automatically) made by your contributors for the June issue. After you have received your updates, your report might look like the one shown in figure 9.5.

If you want, you can edit the published information by selecting Open Publisher, an option that launches the other application and file directly from your PageMaker document. Or you can leave the editing to your contributors, receiving their updates.

Fig. 9.5
The sales report automatically updated through publish and subscribe.

Applications That Support Publish and Subscribe

Publish and subscribe is only a *potential* capability built into System 7. It doesn't work if the capability is not implemented by the applications on both sides of the transaction.

Some applications implement only the Publish feature, and others only the Subscribe feature. For example, PageMaker 5 can subscribe but not publish. QuarkXPress can only subscribe to graphic items (although an extra-cost QuarkXTension will let you subscribe to text too). (A utility called Publishist, by Addison-Wesley of Reading, MA, enables users to publish and subscribe between two programs when only one of them has the feature built-in.)

To learn what kind of support for publish and subscribe an application has, look in the manual or under the menus (usually the Edit menu) while running the application for the terms *publish*, *subscribe*, or *edition*.

Procedure for Publishing Data

When you publish information, a copy of it is sent to an Edition file, to which you and others with the relevant access privileges can subscribe.

When the publisher (the information you publish) changes, the Edition and all documents subscribing to it change accordingly.

Most applications that support publish and subscribe allow you to copy an entire file or any portion of it. You may want to check your application's manual to see if you can do both.

The procedures for publishing may differ slightly in the application you are using, but you should have no trouble following the steps given here.

To publish data, follow these steps:

1. In your document, select the information you want to publish.

2. Within the same application, choose Create Publisher. Usually the command is under the Edit menu. (In FileMaker Pro it is under the File menu's Import/Export submenu.) A dialog box like the one in figure 9.6 appears.

Fig. 9.6
A typical Create Publisher dialog box.

3. Select a name and location for the Edition file.

The Edition is the intermediary file where the data you publish is kept.

> **Note**
>
> To help you keep track of your Editions, leave the word *Edition* in the title of the file. You may want to create a new folder to hold all your Editions. Alternatively, you may want to keep your Editions in the same folders as the published information. Consistency is important.

4. Choose Publish.

> **Caution**
>
> After an Edition file is created, you can rename it and move it to another location on the same volume if you wish. However, if you move an Edition to a different volume, the System will not be able to find it.

Now you or anyone else can subscribe to the Edition you just created. You may want to choose when changes made to the published information (called the *publisher*) are sent—when you save the document automatically (the default) or manually. (Be sure to save the document that contains publisher, in case you want to changed the published information in the future.) The following section provides more information.

Choosing Publisher Options

Most applications have publisher options to enable you to choose when to send changes to subscribers, and to enable you to cancel all links to the publisher.

To make changes to publisher options, follow these steps:

1. In the document where it was created, put your cursor within the publisher.

> **Note**
>
> To help you find published information in a document, many applications surround publishers with gray borders. In some applications, there is an option to Show/Hide Borders in the Edit menu. In others, borders are controlled by the command that shows and hides other markers, such as paragraph markers.

2. Choose Publisher Options, usually from the Edit menu. A dialog box resembling the one in figure 9.7 appears.

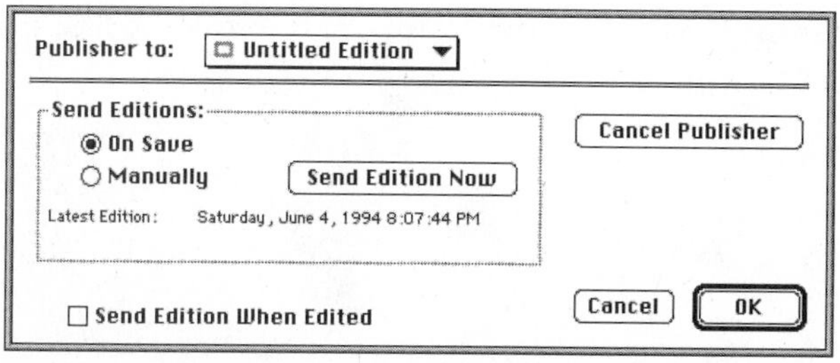

Fig. 9.7
Here are some of the typica Publisher Options that are available.

> **Note**
>
> The options in your application may differ slightly from those pictured here, which are from Word.

3. Select the option or options you want.

   The following options are fairly standard:

   ■ *Send Editions/On Save/Manually*. If you choose to send On Save, up-dates will be sent to all subscribers as soon as changes are saved.

   If you choose to send updates Manually, click that button. Then whenever you want, you can send the changes by clicking the Send Edition Now button.

   > **Note**
   >
   > Sending updates to the Edition is not necessarily the same as having each subscriber receive them. Final control of when the changes are actually made is up to each subscriber through the Subscriber Options dialog box.

   ■ *Send Edition Now*. This button allows you to send editions whenever you want. If the Manually radio button is selected, this button is the only way to send updates. If the On Save button is selected, you can use this button to send an update between saves.

   ■ *Cancel Publisher*. This button breaks links from this published data to all current subscribers. The contents of the publisher remain in your document, and the Edition remains on disk, but changes are no longer sent to the Edition or to subscribers. If you don't want users to subscribe to the disconnected Edition as it currently stands, delete it from the Finder. If you click this button, you will be asked to confirm that you want to break the link to the Edition file.

4. Choose OK.

Editing Published Information

You can edit published information just as you edit any other information in a document. (But remember, your changes will also be made in any other locations where the same published information is subscribed to.)

To edit the publisher, open the document that contains it, find the publisher, and make any changes you want. The changes are sent according to the selection in the Publisher Options dialog box (usually either On Save or Manually). See the section "Choosing Publisher Options" for more information.

If you have difficulty finding the publisher in order to make changes, see whether the application has a Show Brackets command, or whether brackets show when you select a command that shows other markers, such as Show Paragraphs.

If you are looking at a subscriber and decide you want to edit its publisher, there is an easier way to find it. (If the publisher is on another network volume, you must have access to it to use this method.) Put your cursor in the subscriber, and select Subscriber Options, usually from the Edit menu. In the dialog box that appears, choose the Open Publisher button. The publisher appears on-screen, allowing you to make changes.

Procedure for Subscribing to Data

If you have previously created an Edition by publishing some information, or if you have access to an Edition created by someone else, you can insert a copy of the published information in your document by subscribing to the Edition.

To subscribe to published data, follow these steps:

1. If the Edition is on another Macintosh, connect to that Macintosh. (See Chapter 34 for information on file sharing.)

2. Position your cursor in your document where you want a copy of the Edition to appear.

3. Choose Subscribe To, usually from the Edit menu. A dialog box resembling the one in figure 9.8 appears.

Fig. 9.8

A typical Subscribe To dialog box (usually available from the Edit menu).

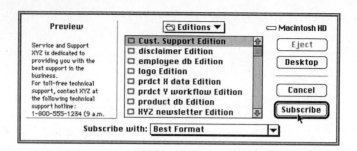

4. Navigate through the folders until you find the Edition you want. If the Edition is located on another hard disk or another Macintosh, choose the Desktop button first.

   Many applications help you find the Edition you want by displaying the first part of any Edition you select in a small Preview box.

   Select the Edition you want.

5. If there is a choice of file formats, choose the one you want.

   The TEXT and PICT formats, similar to those used in the Clipboard, are usually available, in addition to private formats. (See "Understanding File Formats" for information on formats.) Don't worry if you don't know which format to choose. You can easily resubscribe if the data is not displayed properly. You can also change the format from the Subscriber Options dialog box.

6. Choose Subscribe.

Now that you have subscribed to an Edition, you may want to choose when changes sent from the publisher will be made in your document—automatically or whenever you choose to send them manually. See the following section for more information.

Choosing Subscriber Options

After you have subscribed to a copy of published data, you can select several subscriber options: how changes from the subscriber are made (automatically or manually), the file format to be used in the subscriber, and whether formatting changes made in the subscriber are to be kept when the information is updated. You can also open the publisher to edit it, and you can cancel the subscriber so no more updates will be sent.

To select subscriber options, follow these steps:

1. In the file that subscribes to published data, select that data.

    Note that the data is selected as a block, so that you cannot edit it, except for cosmetic font changes, or changes to the size and shape of a graphic.

2. Select Subscriber Options from the Edit menu. A dialog box resembling the one in figure 9.9 appears.

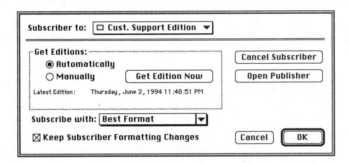

Fig. 9.9
A typical Subscriber Options dialog box (usually available from the Edit menu).

3. Select the option or options you want.

    Options like the following are included by most applications:

    ■ *Get Editions/Automatically/Manually*. If you choose Automatically, changes will be made as soon as they are sent from the publisher.

    If you choose Manually, you must access this dialog box again whenever you are ready for an update, and click the Get Edition Now button. The latest changes will then appear in your document, if any updates have been sent by the publisher.

    > **Note**
    >
    > Choosing when you get Editions only affects when you receive changes that have been sent by the publisher. Publisher Options determines when changes are sent. For more information, see "Choosing Publisher Options" earlier in this chapter.

    ■ *Get Edition Now*. Whether you have chosen the Automatically or the Manually button, pressing Get Edition Now immediately brings in changes that have been sent from the publisher.

II

System 7 Essentials

■ *Cancel Subscriber.* If you click this button, this particular subscriber will no longer receive changes from the publisher. The information will remain in your document and you will be able to edit it normally. You will be asked to confirm.

■ *Open Publisher.* Clicking this button takes you directly to the published data, even if it is in another application. This allows you to edit the source data if you want.

> **Caution**
>
> When collaborating with other people on a network, be certain that the editing you do to the publisher is desired by all subscribers.

■ *Subscribe with.* The TEXT and PICT formats used in the Clipboard are usually available, in addition to private formats. See "Understanding File Formats" for more information on formats.

The following option appears in Word and a few other applications:

■ *Keep Subscriber Formatting Changes.* This option keeps formatting changes you make to this instance of the published data, such as font changes, or changes to the size and shape of a graphic, when the data content is updated. (Such cosmetic formatting changes are usually allowed only to the whole block of information, not to parts of it.)

4. Choose OK.

> **Note**
>
> You can cut, copy, and paste subscribed data at will, without losing the connection to the published data.

Editing Subscriber Information

Many applications allow you to do limited cosmetic editing to subscribers, that is, changes to form but not content. Microsoft Word, for example, allows you to change fonts and font characteristics in the subscriber. Generally, the changes must be to the entire block of information. For example, you may be able to make the entire block of subscriber information appear in boldface type, but you probably cannot make a single word appear in boldface type.

Changes you make in the subscriber are usually overridden when the subscriber is updated, unless you select a publisher option to maintain the changes.

To change the content of a subscriber, such as deleting a word from a word processing application, a line from a graphics application, or a number from a spreadsheet, you must edit the publisher. See "Editing Published Information" earlier in this chapter for more information.

Troubleshooting

I have trouble keeping track of Editions—where they are located, who has subscribed to each one, and which subscribers have been updated and which haven't.

If you can get hold of a utility called Traffic Controller, most recently marketed by Olduvai (Miami, FL), you can display an audit trail of Editions and their subscribers. Unfortunately, the product is no longer being marketed.

Applications compatible with OpenDoc (described in the "The Future of Document Exchange" section at the end of this chapter) will solve tracking problems by creating and naming Editions automatically whenever information is published. The Editions are to be stored in the folder where the published information is located.

If you don't have System 7.5 or OpenDoc applications, what can you do to manage the use of publish and subscribe, short of writing a tracking utility yourself?

Use a consistent system for what to name and where to store Editions, and be sure everyone understands the system. You might want to write a set of rules, such as the following:

- Whenever anyone publishes information, they are to send an e-mail message to the entire group of potential subscribers describing what they published, where its Edition is located, how it will be updated, and in what documents it should appear. The same rules apply when someone changes published information.

- (If it fits your situation, the following rule ensures consistency.) Anyone publishing information is to choose the option Send Editions Automatically. Anyone subscribing to information is to choose the Get Editions Automatically button.

- Editions should not be moved or renamed unless there is a good reason to do so, and everyone is informed of the changes.

The updated information my document receives doesn't always match the publisher exactly.

(continues)

(continued)

There may be two versions of the publisher. This can happen in two ways:

1. You or someone on the network may have done a Save As to save the document with the publisher under a different name. Changes may then be made from both documents to the same Edition.

2. You or someone else may have copied and pasted information containing a publisher. Changes may then be made from both instances of the publisher to the same Edition.

The publisher may be set to send changes manually, or the subscriber may be set to receive changes manually. Though changes have been made to the publisher, they either have not been sent from the publisher or received at the subscriber. To send the latest changes, put your cursor in the publisher and select the Send Editions Now button from Publisher Options. To receive the latest changes, put your cursor in the subscriber and select the Get Editions Now button in the Subscriber Options dialog box.

Linking and Embedding (OLE)

With certain applications, you can use another system of live data exchange called OLE for *object linking and embedding*. As the name indicates, OLE (pronounced *oh-LAY*) is actually two related technologies, object linking and object embedding. In both linking and embedding, you add objects (text or graphics) to a document and associate them with the applications with which they were created.

Developed and owned by Microsoft, OLE is used in some of the most popular programs for the Mac, namely Microsoft Word, Microsoft, Excel and Aldus PageMaker 5.0.

Linking

Linking resembles publish and subscribe, described previously in this chapter, in that it updates one or more copies of data when the original data changes. It resembles copying and pasting even more, and is almost as easy to implement.

With linking, you copy information from a *source* by using the usual Copy command. Then you paste the information at a *destination* by holding down the Shift key as you give the Paste command. The linked information appears to the right of your cursor. Alternatively, you can use the Paste Special command, which allows you to choose a file format before pasting the linked information, as shown in figure 9.10.

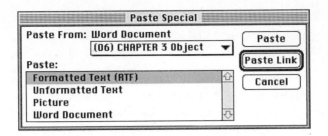

Fig. 9.10
Use Paste Special to
select a file format.

Linking is particularly useful when you want to place a single copy of information within the same document or group of documents as its source. You can link an entire file or any portion of it that you can copy to the Clipboard.

Cross-references are probably the best example. By linking figure and table numbers to references to them in text, such as "see figure 3.3," the references will remain correct if the figures are rearranged and renumbered. Similarly, linking references to titles or chapter headings ensures accuracy if the titles or chapter headings change.

Linking can also be useful to link two files created by different applications on the same machine, but your machine must have enough memory to run both applications simultaneously. For example, to link between a Word document and an Excel document, you need at least 4 megabytes (MB) of memory. If you machine doesn't have enough memory, or if you want to link to or from information on another machine, you can accomplish the same task with the publish and subscribe method. See "Using Publish and Subscribe" earlier in this chapter for more information.

You can choose to update links automatically or manually—but you can also choose to never update. (That's intended as a *temporary* never.) Other link options, which are chosen on the destination side of the link, let you cancel the link, open the source, edit the link, and select a file format.

To help you decide whether linking is the most suitable method of data exchange for your needs, see table 9.3, which compares publish and subscribe, linking, and embedding.

For specific instructions for using linking, look in the manual that came with your OLE-compatible software.

Embedding

Embedding is the second half of Microsoft's Object Linking and Embedding technology. Embedding allows you to add to a document information created in a different application. The information becomes an embedded object, and all the information used to create it, including its file format, and information about how to display and edit it, is included in the document. The classic example is embedding an Excel worksheet in a Word document.

You can embed an existing object by pasting it into your document with the Paste Object command, which appears in the Edit menu when you hold down the Shift key. Or you can create a new object for the document by using the Insert Object command. You can embed an entire file or any portion of it that you can copy to the Clipboard.

Embedded objects contain not only the information you create, but the code from the foreign application that lets you display and edit the information. This allows you to edit in place, without having to leave your current application to launch the other application.

In an Excel worksheet embedded in a Word document, for example, you double-click the worksheet to edit it in an object window. All the Excel editing tools are available in the window, enabling you to edit just as you would in Excel itself. When you're finished editing, you save and close the window. The embedded object is displayed in your Word document with the changes you just made.

Embedding is a convenient method when you want to include information created especially for a specific document. If you are writing a presentation, for example, you can create and embed an Excel chart on the spot to illustrate your point. Unlike publish and subscribe, the original document that created the embedded object is unaffected by changes made to the embedded object since it is no longer linked to it in any way.

If you plan to transfer your document on a floppy disk, embedding is probably the most convenient method of exchanging data because it requires only one file, as opposed to the two files needed for linking, and three for publish and subscribe. Moreover, the receiving person or machine does not need the application(s) used for embedded information unless the recipient wants to edit it. (However, the recipient will need to be able to open the base document, either by having the application that created it or by having another application that understands its file format.)

As with linking, embedding requires that your Mac have enough memory to have both applications open simultaneously. To embed information between Excel and a Word document or vice versa, for example, you need at least 4 MB of memory. Embedding can also increase the size of your document considerably.

Embedding is not a good choice if you want to make more than one copy of the same information in a document, because you cannot update embedded objects simultaneously. Each instance of an embedded object has to be edited individually.

To help you decide whether embedding is the most suitable method of data exchange for your needs, see table 9.3, which compares publish and subscribe, linking and embedding.

Table 9.3 Comparison of Methods of Live Data Exchange		
Publish & Subscribe	**Linking (OLE 1.0)**	**Embedding (OLE 1.0)**
Especially suitable for information that occurs frequently or changes frequently, or for networked information	Especially suitable for cross-references and other information within the same document or group of documents	Especially suitable for including information created in another application, or for documents to be transported by floppy
Works over the network	Doesn't work over the network	Doesn't work over the network
Multiple files can be updated simultaneously	Multiple files can be updated simultaneously	Each file containing embedded data must be updated individually
File sizes virtually unaffected	File sizes virtually unaffected	File containing embedded data can become very large
Requires three files, making transport difficult	Requires two files, making transport difficult	Requires one self-contained file, fully transportable
Data updated on save or manually	Data updated automatically or manually	Data updated automatically
Multiple copies can be updated simultaneously	Multiple copies can be updated simultaneously	Each copy must be updated individually
Source applications not needed	All source applications needed	All source applications needed
Renaming or moving source file or Edition files OK on same hard disk	Renaming or moving source file can disturb the link	Renaming or moving source file OK anywhere
Memory to run two applications simultaneously not required	Memory to run two applications simultaneously required	Memory to run two applications simultaneously required

The Future of Document Exchange

System 7.5 will add a new wrinkle to the process of transferring files from one document to another. It's called Drag and Drop, and it allows you to select and drag a text or graphic item and drop it into another document window (even into a document created in a different program). You'll also be able to place the item you drag from one document and leave it on your desktop (as a "clipping"), in case the receiving document window is not yet open. Of course all this requires software developers to support this neat new feature in their programs.

You can get a brief idea of how drag and drop works (at least for text in a single document) in some current Macintosh software, such as Microsoft Word, Nisus Writer, WordPerfect and QuarkXPress.

Another development on the horizon is OpenDoc, which, in effect, frees the document from its association with a single program. With OpenDoc, when it hits the marketplace of course, you'll be able to use one mini application to create the text in your document, then use another mini application (perhaps by a different software publisher) to create a drawing or a spreadsheet in the very same document. You can get a glimmer on how this sort of thing works with some of the integrated software packages, such as ClarisWorks or Microsoft Works, all of which offer application modules for such functions as drawing, spreadsheets and word processing. But with these programs you are still locked into using the modules provided by a single software publisher to create your document.

From Here...

Now that you have worked with exchanging data between applications, you will probably want to learn about other forms of exchanging data. You may want to read the following chapters:

- Chapter 20, "Integrated Software," covers three integrated applications, including how data is exchanged between their component mini-applications.

- Chapter 34, "Data Exchange," gives more information on text and graphics file formats, and includes exchanging files with PCs as well as working with cross-platform applications.

- Chapter 35, "On the Road," covers PowerBooks, faxing, e-mail, wireless communication, giving presentations, and so on.

Chapter 10

The Printing Chapter

by Gene Steinberg

When you finish working with your document file (or want to see how it looks while it's in progress) you simply open the File menu and select the Print command, or press ⌘-P. In the Print dialog box, click the Print button. That simple action activates the Mac's Print function, beginning a complex chain of events that ends with your document coming out of your printer.

This chapter shows you the following:

- How your Mac processes a document for printing

- The differences between QuickDraw printers and PostScript printers

- What Level 2 PostScript means to you

- How to solve common printing problems

- How Apple's new QuickDraw GX imaging technology affects you

How the Printing Process Works

When you activate the Print function, several things can happen, depending on whether you activate background printing (the process allowing your Mac to print a document while you continue your work). If you select background printing in the Chooser, the data required to print your document is written by a program called a printer driver to a special print file (called a spool file) that is placed in your PrintMonitor documents folder under System 7.

After the document has been created by the printer driver, the data is fed directly to your printer. This process can take anywhere from a few seconds for a simple document to many minutes for a complex document containing many pages and illustrations. When the page is fully processed, the printed page is fed out of your printer.

Background Printing or Not

Under System 6, you could work in two modes. First was finder mode, under which you could run one application plus, of course, the Finder. The second mode (which is in effect by default under System 7) was MultiFinder, which allowed you to run more than one application at a time (if you had enough memory installed on your Mac).

In System 7 and System 6, MultiFinder gives you the option to activate background printing. Background printing allows your Mac to process a document for printing while you are working on something else. The process has its limitations. Background printing can make your Mac seem slower and result in occasionally sluggish mouse movement. That's because the Mac's CPU is dividing its time between two or more tasks.

Note

If you are using System 6 and cannot turn on background printing, even when MultiFinder is active, open your System Folder and look for a file named Backgrounder. This file provides the background printing capability. If that file is missing, you must reinstall it from your system disks.

The other limitation is memory. Background printing requires an application, PrintMonitor (discussed in the next section of this chapter), which uses a small amount of memory to do its stuff. The Mac operating system is also grabbing additional memory at this time—so it's possible your Mac will put up a message that there's not enough memory to print (if you don't have a great deal of installed RAM to begin with).

To turn off background printing, open the Chooser and click on the Off button on the right side of the Chooser window. Under System 7, if not enough memory is available to print a document, you are offered the option of turning off background printing just for that particular job.

Note

With some printers, such as Apple's ImageWriter, the option to activate background printing may not be available. You can get background printing capability using a program such as the now-discontinued SuperLaserSpool by Symantec (you may still find a copy on some dealer's display racks). Another alternative is one of the PowerPrint products from GDT Softworks, which includes a print spooling utility.

PrintMonitor

Your Mac's system software contains a bare bones print spooling utility, called *PrintMonitor*. Although you seldom see this program, you activate it whenever you print a document with background printing turned on. The program is launched when your Mac finishes creating a *spool file* (a file on your hard disk that represents the contents of a document). The program quits when all your documents have been processed.

PrintMonitor feeds the print file of your document to the printer, which then prints your document. A few options are available. You can cancel a print job or remove it from the list of queued documents (the documents ready to be printed), as shown in figure 10.1. Or you can postpone a print job to a later time (or indefinitely).

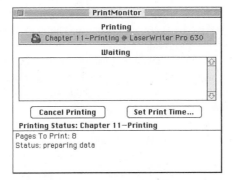

Fig. 10.1
Click the Cancel button to remove your job from the print queue.

While printing is in progress, the PrintMonitor window isn't visible unless you select it from the Application menu, which under System 7 is located at the right of the menu bar. If you select Preferences from the File menu while the PrintMonitor window is active, you have some more options. The one I always recommend is the option to keep the PrintMonitor window open all the time (see fig.10.2). I recommend this choice because it enables you to easily monitor the progress of your job while working on another document—and to know right away if printing trouble is afoot.

Although PrintMonitor has served basic Mac printing needs for several years, its days may be numbered when Apple's new QuickDraw GX technology goes into general circulation. The major upgrade of Apple's imaging model is discussed later in this chapter.

Fig. 10.2
PrintMonitor's Preferences window enables you to configure the settings of Apple's printing spooling program.

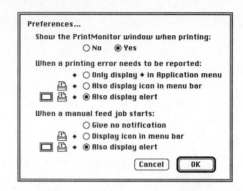

Tip
If you receive warnings of a printing problem on your Mac's screen while printing a document, open the PrintMonitor window right away. Even if the message isn't terribly descriptive, a dialog box that gives you the chance to try printing again will appear.

▶ See "Trouble-shooting," p. 1051

Caution

When you use background printing, make sure that your boot drive has enough room to contain the print file. A large document with complex graphics can occupy several megabytes or more of disk space. If drive space is tight and you receive a disk full message, turn off background printing. This fix won't work with the new PostScript Level 2 driver (known as PSPrinter or LaserWriter8) because that driver uses a two-pass processing scheme, in which a spool file (PrintMonitor document file) is always created even if background printing is turned off. We discuss the new printer driver later in this chapter.

Printing a Document—From A to Z

After you choose the Print function, the next action you take depends on whether background printing is selected. If background printing is selected, you'll be able to observe some of the following steps in the PrintMonitor window:

1. The application with which you're working displays a status box showing that printing has begun (see fig. 10.3). While this status box is displayed, the contents of your document are converted by the printer driver into a file that can be interpreted by your printer, such as a PostScript file for a PostScript laser printer.

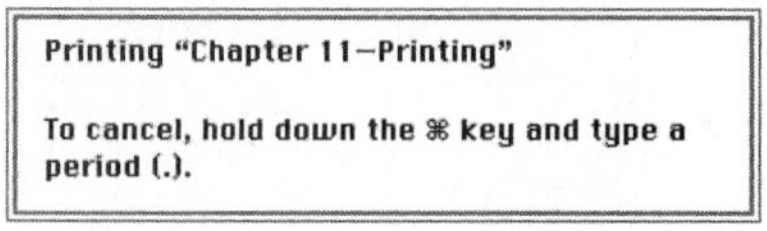

Fig. 10.3
The printing process has begun.

> Printing "Chapter 11—Printing"
>
> To cancel, hold down the ⌘ key and type a period (.).

2. In a few minutes, when the status box disappears, your Mac is again available for you to resume working.

3. Within seconds, PrintMonitor is launched, and the printer driver sends a query across your network to locate your selected laser printer (see fig. 10.4).

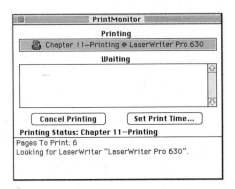

Fig. 10.4
Looking for your selected laser printer.

4. If the printer has not been used for processing a file since you turned it on, the Initializing Printer message appears. When the Mac initializes the printer, a laser prep file that contains instructions necessary for it to process your document is transmitted to the printer.

5. Now that job really starts. Figure 10.5 shows the message displayed in the PrintMonitor window.

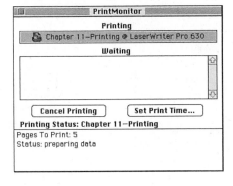

Fig. 10.5
When background printing is turned off, a status window below the menu bar displays the processing steps.

6. The next message displayed is processing job, which simply means that the Mac is now downloading to the printer the information needed to print the document. When the processing stage is complete, the PrintMonitor window disappears. It may take a while longer for the document to emerge from the printer, however.

II

System 7 Essentials

If you turn off background printing to speed up the printing process or to work with a complex document that you cant print normally, PrintMonitor is deactivated. The messages described in the preceding paragraphs will appear in a status window below the menu bar, as shown in figure 10.6.

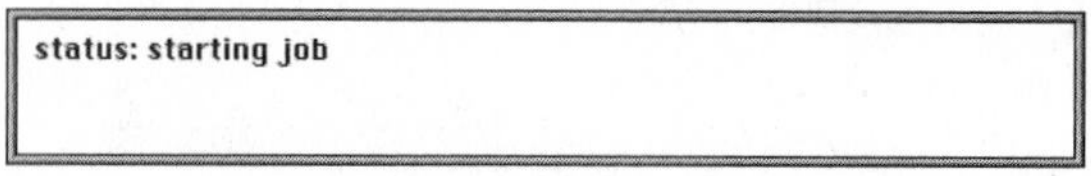

Fig. 10.6
After the printer is found and the laser prep file is downloaded (if necessary), printing really begins.

status: starting job

QuickDraw versus PostScript

The biggest difference between a QuickDraw printer and a PostScript printer, aside from the price, is that a PostScript printer (with the exception of some very expensive color-proofing devices) has its own onboard computer. A PostScript printer therefore doesn't need the Mac to process a document when a file is sent to the printer, or *spooled*. A PostScript printer is also faster because the time it takes to print doesn't depend so much on the computer crunching data.

> **Note**
>
> If you get an Initializing Printer message each time you send a new job to your printer, it probably indicates that different versions of the printer driver may be used by various Macs on your network (such as the System 6 and System 7 versions). If you are using both System 6 and System 7 on your Mac network, you can safely install System 7 printing software on all of your Macs to avoid the repeated initializing messages and improve printer performance. You can generally mix versions of System 7 printer drivers without a problem.

A QuickDraw printer, such as an ImageWriter, a DeskWriter, or a StyleWriter, uses the Mac's native imaging model and the Mac's CPU to process documents. The speed with which your document is handled depends on how fast your Mac crunches data and how many fonts and graphics are contained in the graphic.

The QuickDraw printer has other limitations besides speed. It cannot handle PostScript fonts without a program to process (*rasterize*) those fonts to convert them into bitmaps that the printer can image. Adobe Type Manager or a PostScript emulator program such as Freedom of Press is required for this purpose.

You also will suffer the limitations of QuickDraw technology when you attempt to rotate text and graphics. Although some drawing programs, such as Canvas, are optimized to offer quality printing on a QuickDraw printer, other software will only reward you with jagged edges on picture elements. If a document includes linked EPS graphics, the printout will represent the low resolution 72 dpi PICT image that you see on your Mac's screen.

PostScript technology was first introduced by Adobe Systems in 1985, and it revolutionized the switch from traditional typesetting to desktop publishing. Briefly, PostScript printer drivers reduce the content of your document to a mathematically-based description of what the page looks like, which is why PostScript is called a *page description* language. The description of the page is independent of the resolution of your printer. You can get 300 dpi printing on your 300 dpi laser printer. If you take the very same document and image it on a 2400 dpi imagesetter, you have a 2400 dpi printout.

The PostScript printer's controller board contains an onboard CPU that rasterizes or converts the description of a page into a bitmap that is then imaged onto paper or film. Because the printer does the processing, the slowdown you experience while the Mac is in background printing mode is reduced. The speed it takes to print your document depends on the printer's processor and imaging engine.

Dot Matrix Printers

The dot matrix printer, typified by the Apple ImageWriter series, is the closest approximation in the Mac computing world to an electronic typewriter. The dot matrix printer uses a printer head that strikes a moving ribbon of some sort—much like a typewriter's ribbon. Each character is made up of little dots (hence the name *dot matrix*). Printers commonly offer 9-pin and 24-pin capability. Printers with 24-pin capability provide a sharper printout, but the output quality, even in letter-quality setting, seldom exceeds that of your garden variety typewriter.

Apple's ImageWriter

Apple's first printer, the ImageWriter, and its various descendants (such as the ImageWriter II), are still in regular use by thousands of users. In fact, for certain forms to work, requiring multi-part copies, an impact printer may be your only choice.

When run in its "best" setting, the ImageWriter is capable of a resolution of 160 dots per inch horizontal, 144 dpi vertical. Although this setting is fine for text, it does odd things to graphics, which are based on the Mac's 72 dpi

II

System 7 Essentials

Tip
If you must use the Tall Adjusted option, you might consider horizontally scaling your text (which can be done in most publishing programs) to compensate, or to print text on a separate page.

metaphor. In order to make a circle (and not an oval), for example, you have to print using the Tall Adjusted option. This fixes your graphics, but has the disadvantage of reducing the width of your document by approximately 11%. You end up with properly proportioned graphics, but skinny text.

Inkjet Printers

The new family of inkjet printers has pretty much replaced dot matrix printers for many Mac owners. With prices starting at less than three hundred dollars, an inkjet printer can provide 300 dpi output or better. These printers use little ink-laden cartridges that travel back and forth, spraying letters and graphics across the printed page as it moves through the printer.

Output quality isn't quite up to laser printer standards, however. The ink has a tendency to smear and spread on the page. Type and graphics aren't as sharp as laser printer output. And inkjet printers can be slow. Speeds of up to two pages per minute are advertised for products from Apple and Hewlett-Packard, but these models can bog down on complex jobs and take many minutes to image a single page. Since they are QuickDraw devices, the limits in text and graphics handling described above apply here, too. Some PostScript software for these printers is hitting the marketplace, which will improve the quality of your output but not the speed with which it's processed.

Laser Printers

Even though the products themselves may bear such names as Apple, Hewlett-Packard, NEC, or QMS, laser printer engines are often made by the same manufacturers as copy machines, such as Canon and Toshiba, and they share many components. A laser printer actually uses a low-power laser device that shines a light beam onto a metal drum. Toner particles are attracted to the drum by an electrostatic process and are then transferred to the paper by a set of heated or fusing rollers.

The toner is often contained in a cartridge that also contains the drum. That makes the process of toner replacement fast and clean. Maintenance costs are kept down because the drum is regularly replaced. Some models include separate toner and drum cartridges, others supply toner in powder form.

Some printers use a special fine grain toner, made up of very small particles, as a means to offer higher quality output. But the phenomenon of the toner spreading slightly as its fused onto the printed page will make laser printer output suffer somewhat in comparison to an imagesetter (discussed later in this chapter).

When PostScript laser printers first came out, they often cost as much as a high-end Macintosh. But as technology has improved, and the price of PostScript interpreters was reduced, the price of a new printer has fallen below a thousand dollars in some models. Although laser printers are still available as QuickDraw devices, which process documents in the same manner as a dot matrix or ink jet printer, price reductions of PostScript models—and their higher processing speed and quality—make them the better buy.

Resident Fonts

PostScript laser printers usually come with a small library of fonts stored in the printers ROM chips (see fig. 10.7). These are known as *resident fonts* and usually contain a basic set of 35 fonts (although some printers offer less). They range from such commonly used styles as Helvetica, Palatino, and Times, to decorative styles such as Avant Garde, Bookman, and Zapf Chancery.

Fig. 10.7
This display, from the LaserWriter Utility program, shows some standard laser printer fonts.

Some models also supply additional fonts on an attached SCSI drive, or on separate disks. Because these fonts might cost hundreds of dollars if bought separately, buying a printer with extra fonts might be a good idea. The basic laser printer fonts are overused and abused, and a little variety is bound to spruce up your documents.

What is *PostScript Compatible?*

A number of laser printers are advertised as "PostScript Compatible." This phrase indicates that the printer is not using a PostScript interpreter licensed from Adobe. Instead, the printer is using an imaging technology that emulates PostScript. Sometimes these are known as *clone printers.* In the past, a manufacturer would often be able to offer such products at lower cost because they didn't have to pay formerly high royalties to Adobe to license the right to use the real thing.

The word PostScript *clone* or *compatible* used to put up danger signals in the eyes of the would-be purchaser. The emulator programs used by these printers would often choke on TrueType fonts, Adobe's Multiple Master fonts, or even on complex illustrations. Sometimes the hinting used by font manufacturers to make their type faces look better in small point sizes at low resolution weren't supported. Printouts of small text were often blurred or chunky, with fine details of serif characters being filled in.

Over time, the quality of the imitation PostScript printer has come close to the real thing. To the naked eye, you cannot tell the difference. But the price of a true Adobe PostScript printer has decreased to the point where there is little, if any, price differential. Your choice in a printer should probably be based on price, output quality, and the features that are meaningful to you.

Resolving the Question of Resolution

The very first laser printers offered 300 dpi resolution. Compared to a typewriter or dot matrix output, the printouts were sharp, crisp, and clean, quite close to what you'd see in some printed material. But when using high quality graphics, the limitations of 300 dpi are obvious. At best such a printer is useful for text documents, letters, or inter-office memos.

Improvements in printer engine technology have now brought about a whole new line of 600 dpi laser printers, costing less than $1500 in some models. To get a clear picture of what 600 dpi means to you, consider that printer resolution is the number of dots that fill a square inch (the total of the horizontal and vertical specs). A 300 dpi printer puts 90,000 dots on a single square inch of a printed page. A 600 dpi printer (600 dpi horizontal, 600 dpi vertical) puts 360,000 dots on the same square inch—thus you get four times the resolution.

Some printers offer odd resolution capabilities, such as 400 dpi, or even 600 x 300 dpi (600 dpi horizontal, 300 dpi vertical), which isn't quite as good. When in doubt, look at a printed sample as a means of comparison.

Some laser printers advertise near-imagesetter quality, with resolution of 1200 dpi or greater, for not much more than a few hundred dollars over the cost of the 600 dpi version. What's the secret?

Most of these printers use the very same 300 to 600 dpi printing engines as their lower-resolution counterparts. But the printer's controller board uses software to vary the size of the dots that make up the image, or even controlling the way the drum turns as it processes a page. The combination of such techniques results in 1200 dpi interpolated output. While the printed copy is often sharper than a 600 dpi page, toner particle residue and the limitations of plain paper often conspire to minimize the differences.

If you compare the output to that of even a 1200 dpi imagesetter (which uses an imaging engine designed from the ground up for high resolution and photographic paper or film), the differences even to the naked eye are still quite noticeable.

Using Hard Disks for Font Storage

A number of laser printers offer you the option of attaching a SCSI drive for font storage. Some expensive models are already equipped with a hard drive. This option does have its advantages. You get faster printing speeds with documents that contain a large number of fonts, since the fonts no longer have to be downloaded from your Mac.

There are downsides, however. The process of downloading your fonts to the printer's disk is time-consuming. It can take up to 30 seconds or more per font, and with a huge font library, installation can take hours or days to complete. Also, traditional hard drive backup and repair tools will not support your printer's hard drive. Should the drive crash, you are left with no recourse other than to reformat the drive and download your fonts all over again.

Another shortcoming affects users of TrueType fonts, or PostScript fonts with Adobe Type Manager. In order for you to retain that crisp, sharp screen display of your type, you must keep the very same copies of your fonts on your Mac's hard drive. Apple's TrueType rasterizer and ATM are not able to retrieve font outline information from your printer or its SCSI drive. Whatever conveniences it offers, saving disk space is not one of them.

Caution

Apple's LaserWriter Utility and some printers are finicky about the kind of hard drives they will support. Before deciding to convert or purchase a drive to attach to your printer, consult the manual or contact the manufacturer as to whether the drive you want to buy is compatible.

II

System 7 Essentials

LaserWriter Utilities and Font Downloaders

Apple and many other font and printer vendors offer free software that lets you download fonts to your printer or your printer's hard drive, format the drive, print font lists, download print to disk files, and even activate custom features from your printer.

This section describes Apple's LaserWriter Utility because it ships with the system software disks and is also supplied with the installation disks for Apple's laser printers. But these features are often available in non-Apple utilities as well. Your printer's manual, or a simple exploration of the software, will yield some surprising features. They are described in order here, but bear in mind that not every printer will support all of these features.

When you run LaserWriter Utility, it probes your printer first to record information about make and model and special features. If an item in the menu is grayed, that item is not supported by your printer.

Caution

If you are presently printing a document, don't launch LaserWriter Utility. Its modal (non-movable) dialog box will prevent you from working on your Mac until the operation is cancelled or all documents have been printed.

■ *Download Fonts*. This feature allows you to send fonts to your printer's RAM or to a hard drive installed on your printer. The font downloading process is simple, as shown in figure 10.8. Follow these steps:

Fig. 10.8
Adding fonts to
your laser
printer's memory
or disk.

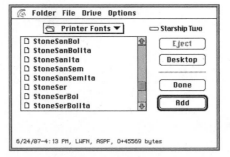

1. First you launch the LaserWriter Utility and wait for a few seconds for it to get information about your printer. You then open the Download Fonts dialog box, and click the Add button.

2. A standard dialog box appears, and you select the fonts you want to add.

3. After you select the fonts, you return to the main Download Fonts window (see fig. 10.9).

4. Select the destination for your fonts. If your printer has a SCSI drive attached to it, the Printers disk(s) option will be available.

5. Click the Download button. Be prepared to wait several minutes for the download process to run its course.

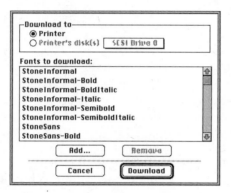

Fig. 10.9
A list of fonts ready to be downloaded to your printer.

Caution

If you download a font to your printer's RAM, turning off or restarting that printer causes the font information to be flushed from its memory. Downloading too many fonts simply overwhelms the printer's memory bank or provides less RAM in which to process a complex document.

- *Display Available Fonts.* This is a fast way to see just what fonts are stored on your printer.

- *Initialize Printers Disk.* When you install a hard drive on your printer's SCSI port, you need to format the drive especially for storage of printer font files.

- *Print Font Catalog.* Here's a fast and dirty method of providing a catalog of the fonts stored on your printer. Fonts that are only available on your Mac's hard drive are not included in this printout.

- *Print Font Samples.* This is a font style sheet, complete with a single sentence set in each typeface stored on the printer or printer's disk.

■ *Name Printer.* If LaserWriter Pro 630 or a similar dry description doesn't appeal to you, here's where you can exercise your creativity, as shown in figure 10.10.

Fig. 10.10
Personalizing your
laser printer.

■ *Set Startup Page.* Turning off the startup page that spews forth from your printer when you first turn it on is a way to preserve our natural resources. The downside is that the startup page is a useful tool to determine whether the printer is working properly, or if toner is spent. Consider that before shutting off this feature.

■ *Get Page Count.* If you turn off the startup page, you should check this selection on occasion if your printer's running up a lot of mileage, to see whether an overhaul is needed.

■ *Imaging Options.* This selection allows you to turn off special resolution enhancement features or to switch printer resolution. You can also change some of these settings in the Print dialog box, under Options, if you're using the Level 2 PostScript printer.

■ *Calibrate Printer.* On some models, such as Apple's LaserWriter IIf and IIg, you can print sample pages and adjust gray scale reproduction.

■ *Configure Communication.* Some printers allow you to adjust which ports support which printer emulation in this manner.

■ *Print Configuration Page.* This option allows you to print a page showing the settings that are active on your printer.

■ *Download PostScript File.* If you have a print-to-disk file, this option allows you to send it on to your printer for output. Just follow these steps:

1. Select the Download option in the LaserWriter Utility.

2. A standard dialog box opens, and you can choose the file you want to download to your printer in the same way as you would open any other file.

3. After the file is selected, you are offered the chance to create a log describing the print process, as shown in figure 10.11.

4. No background printing is in effect when you download a file to your printer this way (see fig. 10.12). You just have to wait until the process is finished.

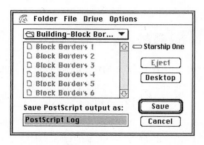

Fig. 10.11
Creating a log of your PostScript file's printing process.

Fig. 10.12
A status report showing the PostScript file being downloaded to your printer.

■ *Remove TrueType.* This option, supported by some models, enables you to remove support for TrueType fonts.

■ *Restart Printer.* This option is basically the equivalent of pressing the power switch off and on again. The printer goes through its normal startup routine, and, if enabled, prints a startup page.

■ *Change Zone.* This feature is supported by some models of networked printers used in multiple zone setups.

■ *Print Density.* Some printer's offer a slider or dial wheel with which to adjust printer density. Others do it with software.

■ *Paper Handling.* You can set the printer's default paper tray and other special features with this option, as shown in figure 10.13.

■ *Power Saving.* Some new printers are Energy Star compliant; that is, they will automatically power down into an *idle* mode when inactive for a certain period of time. When a document is sent to the printer, it will automatically power up again. Since the startup process can take a minute or two, if you are sending a great deal of work to the printer, you may decide to turn this feature off.

Fig. 10.13
Changing the
default paper size
on a LaserWriter
Pro 630's Multi-
purpose tray.

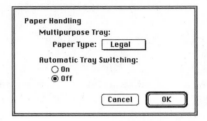

Having a Dialog with Your Printer

Depending on the kind of printer you're using, you'll have a number of choices to make each time you print your document, if you're not just okaying the standard page setup. The dialog boxes described in the following sections will change, often considerably, from program to program. So if what you see when you invoke the Page Setup command doesn't quite jibe with our description, consult your software manual or Help menu for further assistance.

ImageWriter Setup Options

You don't have too many choices here (see fig. 10.14). You can select paper size and orientation (portrait or landscape). The important options are Tall Adjusted, which allows illustrations to print in their proper proportions, and 50% Reduction, which offers sharper output for your illustration.

Fig. 10.14
An ImageWriter's
limited Page Setup
options.

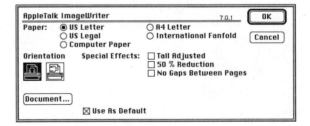

StyleWriter Setup Options

The standard Apple StyleWriter setup (other inkjet printers are similar) enables you to select paper size and orientation (see fig. 10.15). You have the added capability of scaling your document to a particular size. This is useful, especially if your publication needs to be reduced in size to fit on regular letter or legal-sized paper.

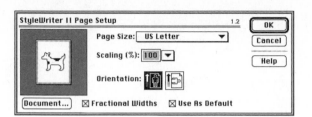

Fig. 10.15
Your Page Setup options with a StyleWriter II.

LaserWriter Setup Options

Setting up your document when you're using a laser printer confronts you with a number of different choices that are summarized in this section, as shown in figure 10.16.

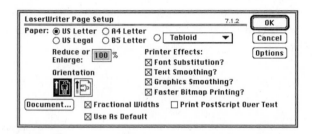

Fig. 10.16
A larger number of Page Setup options are available to you if you're using a laser printer.

II

System 7 Essentials

> **Caution**
>
> If you are using the Level 2 PostScript driver, the printing choices described in the following paragraphs are available only by clicking the Options button.

Some of the printer options described in the following list are turned on by default, but you can switch them off if the features are of no value to you. In fact, when you have a problem printing a document, unchecking a few of these items (which are sometimes called *printer effects*) may improve printing speed somewhat. You should select the following printer options:

- First you want to choose the correct paper size and orientation.

- Document scaling should be selected next, if other than the standard 100%.

- *Font Substitution.* This setting is a relic of the early days of the Macintosh. Apple system software typically installs such screen display fonts as Chicago, Geneva, Monaco, and New York, but until System 7 came along, there were no printer font equivalents. You checked font

Tip
If your documents print in a size different from what you expect, check your Page Setup box and see whether the document reduction or enlargement setting is correct.

substitution to allow Helvetica to substitute for Monaco, for example, and Times to substitute for New York.

■ *Font Smoothing.* In theory, bitmapped fonts will print sharper on a laser printer with this option selected. Since low-cost PostScript and TrueType fonts are readily available, bitmapped fonts have quickly gone out of fashion.

■ *Graphics Smoothing.* This option supposedly does for bitmapped graphics what Font Smoothing does for bitmapped fonts; it makes them print cleaner and crisper. But for most users, this choice has little or no effect.

■ *Faster Bitmap Printing.* Here's another theory that doesn't always translate into a practical benefit. The intention is to optimize bitmap graphics before they are fed to your printer to speed up the printing process. The reality is that the reverse often happens. If you are using the Level 2 printer driver, you will not have this option.

With the standard LaserWriter printer drivers, the following choices are available only when you click the Options button (see fig. 10.17):

Fig. 10.17
Optional settings for your laser printer.

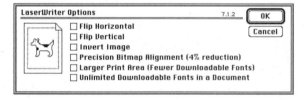

■ *Flip Horizontal/Flip Vertical.* When you prepare a document for film output on an imagesetter, you will often hear requests such as *emulsion side* down. *Flip Horizontal* is the selection you want to make. As for *Flip Vertical,* that's an option I cannot imagine ever choosing.

■ *Invert Image.* This selection changes your positive image to a negative, useful for some printing requirements, especially when outputting to a film master.

■ *Precision Bitmap Alignment.* This feature is useful when printing bitmapped graphics on a laser printer. Since these graphics are typically 72 dpi (or a multiple thereof), they won't look very clear when printed on a 300 dpi laser printer. Scaling them down four percent (which affects your text, too) will offer crisper printouts.

If your printer offers a resolution other than 300 dpi, this feature can be worthless.

> **Note**
>
> The latest versions of Level 2 PostScript driver don't show the 4% reduction option, because the driver will automatically scale a document to the correct size even if the target printer is 400 dpi, 600 dpi, or greater.

- *Larger Print Area.* In order to conserve memory and allow it to be used for additional fonts, some laser printers have a preset limit in page width. It's typically one half to one full inch. If your document's print area exceeds that margin (and part of the printout is cut off as a result), you need to select this option.

> **Caution**
>
> Some printers may require a RAM upgrade to image legal-size pages to the full printing area. Other models, like Apple's original LaserWriter or LaserWriter Plus, may not be able to print documents with this selection at all.

Tip

If you are using the Level 2 PostScript driver, the Larger Print Area option may be grayed, because the standard print area is the largest available for the selected printer.

- *Unlimited Downloadable Fonts.* This is a time when one choice doesn't override another, and it should. If you select this option *and* Larger Print Area at the same time, you will probably find your documents won't print at all. This is a selection you want only as a last resort, when your printer doesn't have enough RAM to process all of the fonts you are using in your document.

This option allows the printer driver to download a batch of fonts into RAM and then remove or flush them, and download the next batch. This keeps the printer's memory bank from getting overwhelmed with font information. It also slows down the printing process, but when nothing else works, this may be the only choice you have.

> **Caution**
>
> If you suffer from Courier font substitution on a document with linked EPS graphics, turn off Unlimited Downloadable Fonts. Font information from your EPS graphic may not be downloaded correctly. If you must use this printer effect, try to convert the font in your EPS graphic to outlines, if your software offers that choice. If not, use the font itself somewhere in the text area of your document (even if the text is set to white so it is not reproduced). This little workaround will often allow the font to be used correctly in your document.

II

System 7 Essentials

Okaying the Print Process

The options you have in printing your document depend on the printer you're using, and the program from which you're going to print. The dialog box shown in figure 10.18 applies if you're using the Level 2 driver with Microsoft Word.

Fig. 10.18
When you click the Print button, it only represents the start of the print process.

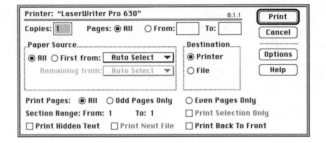

Across the top of the dialog box, you can select the number of pages you want to print and whether all the pages, or just a range of pages, will be printed. Some printers give you the option of selecting a paper source, such as a multipurpose or alternate paper tray. Under System 7 you can choose the destination for your document, whether it is the printer or a PostScript (print-to-disk) file. The options beneath these allow you to choose odd or even pages. (I left out the selections at the very bottom of the dialog box, which are specific to Microsoft Word only.)

> **Note**
>
> The selection of individual pages varies from program to program. Aldus PageMaker 5.0, for example, allows you to choose a non-contiguous range, mixing even and odd pages from different parts of your document.

The Lowdown on Level 2 PostScript

In 1991, new printers arrived on the scene with the buzzword Level 2 PostScript. Rather than just reflecting some advertising copywriter's idea of how to sell a few more products, Level 2 PostScript represented a major up-grade to printing technology.

The printers themselves used a new line of PostScript interpreters that were designed to process and image documents more efficiently, with some neat new capabilities (described shortly).

If you were one of the first purchasers into the new technology, it really didn't offer any real advantage at first. It took another two years for Adobe and Apple to release printer drivers to support the new technology. The following list discusses what—if anything—Level 2 means to you:

- *More efficient printing.* Even if your printer did not support Level 2, the new printer driver creates more efficient PostScript code that results in somewhat faster printing, and a fewer number of aggravating reports of PostScript errors. On a Level 2-equipped printer, the speedup would normally be from 10% to 30%, depending on the complexity of the document.

- *Compression and decompression.* In order to speed transfer of data across the network to your printer, some programs will actually compress the data. The Level 2 printer can decompress this data when it reaches the printer's controller.

- *Memory Management.* Running out of memory is an all-too-common occurrence with PostScript printers. Up until now, your printer's RAM was split up in little blocks, each performing a specific function, such as handling text or graphics. A Level 2 printer can tap whatever available memory it needs in order to process a document.

- *Higher Quality Halftones.* Halftone reproduction can be a problem, even on an imagesetter. The Level 2 driver has an improved halftone processing routine that results in improved quality output, free of moire patterns and other untoward side-effects.

- *PostScript Printer Descriptions.* The newest model laser printers sport multiple paper trays, special resolution enhancement techniques, and resolution adjustments. The Level 2 drivers come with a set of PPD files (which are installed in a special folder inside System 7's Extensions folder called Printer Descriptions) that allow you to tap your printer's unique features. With the correct PPD file installed, you can redirect the job to a different paper tray or change a printer's default settings right from your Print dialog box.

- *Forms and pattern caching.* The Level 2 driver is capable of storing frequently used forms, such as invoices or patterns. Although early releases of the Level 2 driver didn't support these features, it allowed you to speedily print monthly statements and documents containing special illustrations that are used over and over again.

Tip
If your printer's PPD file didn't come with the Level 2 driver or a software package, call the manufacturer for a copy.

II

System 7 Essentials

> **Caution**
>
> Turning off background printing with the Level 2 driver will probably not speed up the printing process. The early releases of the Level 2 driver use a two-pass processing technique that is designed to optimize PostScript code. The downside is that a printer spool file is created whether background printing is on or off.

Installing the Level 2 Driver

Adobe and Apple's Level 2 driver comes in several flavors. Usually it's named PSPrinter (the Adobe edition) or LaserWriter 8 (from Apple). You can get a copy of the Apple version with a brand new Apple laser printer, or from online services such as America Online, CompuServe, or eWorld. The new driver is bundled with such software products as Aldus FreeHand, Aldus PageMaker, and Frame Technology's FrameMaker.

The driver is also packaged with a small manual and is available for a modest price from either Adobe or Apple. It is also shipping with System 7.5.

Installation is simple. An Installer application on the installation disks deposits the correct files in your System Folder (see fig. 10.19). Under System 7, the Level 2 driver and a folder named Printer Descriptions are in your Extensions folder. They are loose in the System Folder under System 6.

Fig. 10.19
Installing the new Level 2 printer drive is a snap.

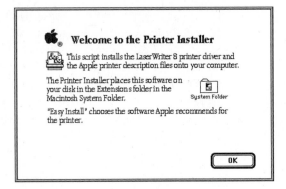

Level 2 Printer RAM Requirements

Before you install the Level 2 driver, be sure your Mac has enough RAM and the correct system software version. For System 6 users, you need to be running System 6.0.7 or 6.0.8 and have at least 2MB of installed RAM. For

System 7, RAM requirements are 4MB. (If you have less than 4MB available, you should probably not be using System 7 in the first place.)

Printer Setup

The Level 2 driver comes with a selection of PPD (PostScript Printer Description) files for many popular printers. Apple's LaserWriter 8 ships strictly with Apple PPD files. You will find additional selections in some of the software packages that have bundled the driver. If your printer's PPD is not included, check the installation disks that came with your model. Sometimes you'll find a copy there. Or call the manufacturer of your printer. In the meantime, you can often get by with the driver's internal General PPD. You will probably get satisfactory printing results, but you will miss out on using your printer's special features through the print dialog box, such as multiple paper trays and resolution switching.

To set up the driver to support your printers, follow these simple steps:

1. Open the Apple menu and select the Chooser. In the Chooser dialog box, select LaserWriter 8 (or PSPrinter), as shown in figure 10.20.

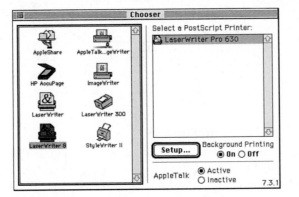

Fig. 10.20
Select the Level 2 driver from the Chooser desk accessory.

2. Click the Setup button in the lower right corner of the Chooser window.

3. Choose Auto Setup, as shown in figure 10.21. The driver will probe your Printer Descriptions folder and choose the correct PPD file. If one is not available, you'll be offered the option of selecting an alternate PPD file.

II

System 7 Essentials

Fig. 10.21

For most printers, the Auto Setup option is enough to get you up and running with the Level 2 driver.

4. If Auto Setup won't work for you, click the More Choices button, which will allow you to examine your printers RAM setup, PostScript version, and other juicy details. You'll also have the option of manually selecting a PPD file that may be usable if the automatic option doesn't work.

   If all else fails, consult the Help feature for more advice, as shown in figure 10.22.

Fig. 10.22

If you run into trouble setting up the Level 2 driver, click the Help button for more advice.

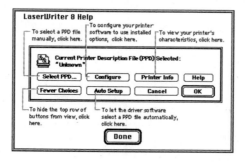

Exclusive Level 2 Options

The Level 2 driver makes printing a PostScript file a snap. It also gives you some new options that are useful if you want to create an EPS graphic from a program, say an older paint application, that doesn't offer an EPS option. Because many desktop publishing programs and laser printers choke on a diet of PICT graphics, this choice may mean the difference between getting the job done or having to deal with a procession of printer error messages.

To see how easy it is to make your own EPS files with the Level 2 driver, follow these steps:

1. To create a print-to-disk or EPS file, open the File menu and choose Print.

2. You have a choice of two Destinations for your print job. You'll want to select File, as shown in figure 10.23.

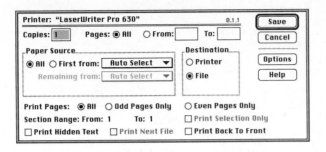

Fig. 10.23
Preparing to send a document to a PostScript or EPS file rather than a printer.

3. You can use the file name selected by the driver or pick one of your own, along with the destination of the new file.

4. Open the Format menu to select the kind of file you want, as shown in figure 10.24. To create an EPS file, you should choose EPS Mac Standard Preview or EPS Mac Enhanced Preview. The second choice will make a larger file, but a better screen display when you import or place the EPS graphic into your document.

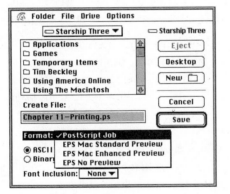

Fig. 10.24
Choosing the file format for your EPS file.

5. If you are going to create a print-to-disk file for a printer non-Level 2 printer, you only need to change the file format settings; otherwise you can ignore those selections.

6. The Font inclusion pull-down menu allows you to decide whether your EPS file will contain fonts, as shown in figure 10.25. The usual setting is None, which keeps your EPS file down to a more manageable size.

You can opt to include All fonts, which may be useful if you need to select the Unlimited Downloadable Fonts option in your printer's Page Setup box. That ought to minimize font substitution problems. If your EPS file contains the basic 13 fonts, such as Helvetica and Times, select the final font option.

II

System 7 Essentials

Fig. 10.25
Deciding whether
your EPS file will
include font
information.

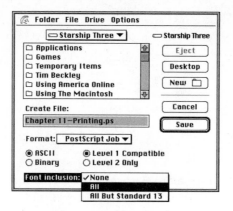

Some Hard-Won Tips on Buying a Printer

Not too many years ago, a PostScript laser printer was an item that only a large business or service bureau could afford to buy. The rest of us were content with a dot matrix printer or a QuickDraw laser printer.

But just as powerful Macintosh computers are now available at prices beginning at less than a grand, the same holds true for a laser printer. If you opt for the small inkjet or bubble jet model, you can get by with a model for less than three hundred dollars. The following sections offer a few helpful hints on what to look for when you go printer shopping.

How Many Real Pages Per Minute?

In big, bold letters, the ads for many popular laser printers will state their speed in pages per minute, usually four, eight, sometimes up to 20. And it is true that the imaging engine of your printer is, in theory at least, capable of performance at that level.

That is, if your are printing a simple all text document with resident (ROM) fonts, or multiple copies of the same document.

Your real speed limitation is not the maximum speed of the printer's engine but of its controller board, the assemblage of components, RAM, ROM, and a CPU that actually processes your print job. When you compare speed of a printer, you want to know how long it takes to tackle your document from the time you okay the print process on your Mac, until the printed page slides out of your printer.

Printers using the same engine can take different amounts of time to actually print something; it all depends on the capabilities of its controller board in being able to process data.

Image Enhancement

There are a number of techniques used to spruce up the quality of laser printed text and graphics. They have such names as FinePrint or PhotoGrade (from Apple), RET (Resolution Enhancement Technology) from Hewlett-Packard, or Turbo Gray from LaserMaster. They are all designed to sharpen text or provide spiffy halftones by increasing the number of steps of gray.

When shopping for a new printer, try to look at a sample printout with and without these enhancement technologies, and see whether you can actually see the difference. Some of these features may require a RAM upgrade or slow down printing performance to some degree because the print files take longer to process. Be sure to read the fine print.

Networking

Your standard laser printer should network to a regular LocalTalk network, but most newer Macintosh models support Ethernet connections as well. Some printers offer Ethernet standard, others offer an Ethernet option. Chapter 33, "Networking," describes many of the possibilities for you in much more detail.

Very briefly, you can yield a noticeable performance boost if you take the Ethernet route. When using background printing, your Mac will not suffer as great a performance drag while a document is being processed. The increased bandwidth of Ethernet will also keep your network from bogging down when a number of jobs are being fed to several workgroup printers.

Because cross-platform networks are very common, its also necessary these days for printers to speak both Macintosh and Windows language. Some printers offer multiple active ports, meaning that Macs and PCs can queue jobs to the printer without having to push dip switches or make a new software setting.

Plain Paper Imagesetters

Previously in this chapter, I described the resolution boosting techniques used by printer manufacturers. The long and short of it is that the quality of the text on one of these devices may look quite sharp and clean to the naked eye, especially when you use a high quality grade of laser printer paper, but it doesn't quite compare to the output that emerges from one of the regular imagesetters. There may even be a wider gap between the quality of halftones and other graphics. But for many applications outside of a slick magazine or book, the level of reproduction from one of these laser printers may be more than sufficient for you.

Paper Size

The standard laser printer can handle traditional letter size (8-1/2 x 11) and legal size paper (8-1/2 x 14). Some models accept tabloid (or ledger) size paper (11 x 17) as well, and a few models can handle 13 x 19 or similar large sizes, which allows them to support a two-page printer's spread of a letter-sized page, complete with crop marks. These larger printers carry much higher price tags, and toner cartridge replacement is apt to be more costly as well. If you don't intend to use a larger paper size, you don't need to consider such a model.

Printer's RAM

Most laser printers are shipped with enough memory to support the largest paper size that the model can handle. Some products, however, require a RAM upgrade to provide the maximum possible width on a larger paper size or to support some image enhancement features. Check the manufacturer's literature or manuals for the specifics.

Beyond enhancing basic features, a RAM upgrade allows your printer to store a larger number of downloadable fonts (which only yields a slight performance improvement), or even process a very complex document that may not image properly with a standard RAM configuration. But printer RAM upgrades—on models where they are available—may be more costly than the RAM upgrades you buy for your Mac. If you have no trouble printing complex pages with your stock setup—and you don't need extra RAM to support special printer features—a RAM upgrade may not really be necessary.

QuickDraw GX

 Fonts, graphics, and printing are overhauled with Apple's new QuickDraw GX technology. The new imaging model will be included with System 7.5, and will likely be offered separately by Mac publishers to allow you to take advantage of special features of their software.

The biggest change you are likely to see when you install QuickDraw GX will be the absence of the familiar PrintMonitor window if you use background printing on your jobs, and the addition of some neat new ways to organize the printing of your documents. You'll see the change the first time you print a document. After printers are configured in the Chooser, you are offered a popup menu of available printers in your standard Print dialog box (see fig. 10.26). You don't have to go through a wearisome process revisiting the Chooser and adjusting Page Setups each time you select a different printer to process documents.

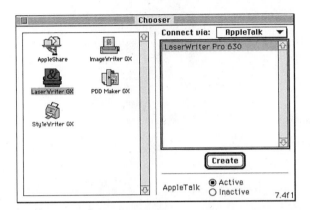

Fig. 10.26
Once you've selected all your printers in the Chooser, you can switch them on the fly in your print dialog box.

The following sections provide a few of QuickDraw GXs improvements to print technology.

Color Printing

QuickGraw GX ships with an updated version of Apple's ColorSync Control Panel, which allows you to calibrate the color image from your monitor, your scanner, and your color printers. This program allows you to get consistent color results throughout the production chain. A basic set of color profiles for Apple products is supplied. It will be up to non-Apple manufacturers to make available profiles for their own products.

Desktop Printer Icons

When you first select the QuickDraw GX driver and your printer in the Chooser, you have the option to Create a printer queue icon. This icon will then appear on the right side of your Mac's desktop below the disk icons (see fig. 10.27). You can create a separate icon for each printer on your network.

You can print a document simply by dragging its file icon to the the desktop icon representing your printer.

II

System 7 Essentials

Fig. 10.27
Your chosen printers appear as icons on your Macs desktop.

Tracking the Printer Queue

To check the progress of your print job, double-click the Printer icon, which will open a window that reports the status of your job (see fig. 10.28). If a printer's queue is backed up with waiting jobs, you can drag the job to another printer's icon or simply reorder the queue to have a job image faster.

Fig. 10.28
QuickDraw GX's answer to PrintMonitor, a printer status window.

Type 1 Font Enabler

If you have a library of Type 1 PostScript fonts, you need to convert them for use with QuickDraw GX. Adobe Systems has developed a handy utility, Type 1 Font Enabler, that generates a QuickDraw GX-ready copy of your Type 1 fonts without changing the original font, which you can still use for regular printing applications with your original printer drivers (see fig. 10.29).

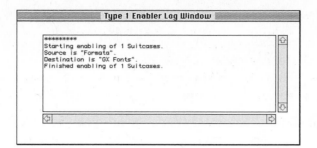

Fig. 10.29
Adobe's Type 1
Font Enabler.

Electronic Paper

QuickDraw GX will have its own counterpart to such portable document creation tools as Adobe's Acrobat or No Hands Common Ground. Its called a *Portable Digital Document,* or PDD for short. You'll be able to create a document that can be viewed and printed on any Mac that has QuickDraw GX installed, even if you don't have the fonts or the application that was used when that document was created. This development is apt to be a boon for service bureaus, freeing them of the need to have huge libraries of obscure fonts and software.

What It Means to You

QuickDraw GX will be demanding of memory (using an additional 1MB of system RAM) and somewhat demanding of hard drive space. But it promises to revolutionize the way you print your jobs, and its font and graphics handling capabilities will make for smaller, more efficient software, once software publishers get into the act.

Preserving the Environment

In addition to offering energy saving features on some models, Apple, Hewlett-Packard, and other printer manufacturers offer free mailing tickets so that you can send your spent toner cartridges off to their recycling plant. Some local business supply stores will even give you a few bucks if you turn in your used toner cartridges (though not all models are supported by these refund programs).

If you really want to preserve natural resources, and maybe save some money too, you can buy a recycled toner cartridge. You can find recycling firms in your local yellow pages, or in the back pages of such magazines as *MacUser* and *Macworld.* Some of these products are even available at regular retail channels.

Tip
You can stretch
the life of a toner
cartridge by turn-
ing down the
printer's density
setting for rough
proofs. Just re-
member to turn it
back up again for
final copy.

Following are a few things to consider before you go the recycled cartridge route:

- Recycled toner can vary in quality. When selecting a vendor for recycled cartridges, ask to see a printed sample to compare output against what a new cartridge may provide.

- If you cannot get a printed sample, be sure your purchase is covered by a money-back or exchange warranty if you are not satisfied with the quality.

- If your laser printer is used only as a proofing device, output quality may not matter. But service and cartridge longevity are important. If you aren't satisfied with one supplier, don't hesitate to shop around.

- The toner recycling process isn't always perfect. If output quality is paramount, and your finished documents will be used as master copy by your printer, you may wish to stick with a brand new cartridge. That will ensure your documents have consistent quality. Sending your used toner cartridges in for recycling is still an excellent idea.

Your typical inkjet cartridge costs $20 or more and lasts for several hundred copies. Sometimes it's possible to stretch the life of these cartridges by giving them an ink transplant. You can buy kits from JetFill and other manufacturers for roughly half the cost of a new cartridge. Refilling involves using an ink-filled syringe to inoculate the cartridge with a new ink supply. It's a process best done with care and many paper towels, so as to avoid dirtying a home or office floor.

Some folks have developed a low-cost home brew technique with water soluble ink and a syringe from a medical supply store. The same warnings about the potential mess the process creates apply here too. But if your inkjet printer gets a heavy workaround, it might be worth trying a cartridge refill, at least once or twice, to see whether you can get the hang of it.

Some No-Nonsense Service Bureau Advice

There are times when the output of a high resolution laser printer isn't sufficient for your needs. Laser printer quality is very high. The newest generation of 600 dpi (and greater) printers provide output quality that is every bit as good as that of one of those large, noisy traditional typesetting machines of 15 or 20 years ago. And for many uses, even when used as master copy for a printing press, you will be quite satisfied with the quality.

If you need high quality color separations, or require superior reproduction of halftones and illustrations, there is no substitute for an imagesetter and a visit to your local service bureau.

Caution

Where possible, do not use PICT files in your document. Although PICT is your native Macintosh format for screen display, laser printers and imagesetters do not take well to processing documents with PICT graphics. To save aggravation later on (and a panic-stricken phone call from your service bureau), stick with EPS and TIFF.

Imagesetter Background

The modern-day imagesetter is a huge box that doesn't look dissimilar to those typesetting machines of old. Rather than paper output, the imagesetter accepts rolls or individual sheets of photographic paper or film. The material, called *media,* moves through the imagesetter and is exposed by its image generating mechanism (usually a laser beam source, just like your regular laser printer).

The media is usually spooled into a large plastic cassette and the service bureau technician takes that cassette to a light-tight developing machine that is closely related to the processing device used by doctors to develop x-rays.

The media is transported through baths of chemicals through an assembly of racks and rollers. The paper first reaches a bath of a developing chemical that displays the image on the paper. The image is then stabilized or *fixed,* just like it's done with regular photos, so that the image is preserved. The media moves through a bath of water to clean the chemical residue off and then usually through a drying mechanism.

It usually takes from two to three minutes for the first pages to begin to appear at the other side of the developing machine.

Imagesetter Printer Drivers

Despite the difference in the cost and material used by the imagesetter, you will find the process of actually printing to an imagesetter to be very much like that involved in using a regular laser printer (described previously in this chapter).

Most imagesetters use the very same printer drivers that you use with your regular laser printer. Settings such as Page Setup and the various printer effects settings are quite the same. The only differences you may encounter result from having a different set of paper size options. If you are setting up a document for service bureau output, contact the service bureau about proper printer and page selections.

Preparing Your Job for Imagesetting

Tip
Since service bureaus will often output work at night, leave a home telephone number on your job request form in case a technician needs to telephone you about a problem with your job.

Many service bureaus have information sheets or booklets with helpful hints and advice on preparing your work for imagesetter output. I've distilled some of those hints for this chapter. The important thing to realize is that a service bureau isn't responsible for your mistakes, so if you provide work that isn't properly organized, and is missing fonts or graphics, or has mistakes in it, you have to pay for fixing those mistakes.

Following is my advice, based on hard-won experience working for and sending jobs to service bureaus:

- As you are working on your job, call your service bureau and ask them about their requirements for setting up work for output.

- Be sure the service bureau has the same fonts from the same vendors as you have. While most of these firms will have a good selection of fonts from the Adobe library, fonts from other vendors, such as Agfa, Bitstream, Font Company, Image Club, Linotype, Monotype, and some of the discount font suppliers, may not be as readily available. Many vendors will offer fonts with the same names, such as Futura. But if the service bureau uses a different Futura than you do, you may be in for a rude shock when your work is output. Line endings may be different, and the actual size of the type characters themselves may vary, too.

- Before using TrueType fonts, ask your service bureau whether their imagesetters can support this font format. Some output devices require expensive hardware upgrades to support TrueType, and not all service bureaus are willing to make the plunge. PostScript fonts are still the standard for high-end output devices.

- Most service bureaus will have the latest versions of Aldus PageMaker or QuarkXPress at hand. If you are using a program that is not as ubiquitous, such as FrameMaker, Publish-It Easy, or Ready,Set,Go, make sure that the service bureau has the same programs you do. If you are using an older version of your publishing software, be sure to inform the service bureau of that fact. Quite often the newer version of such a program will alter the appearance of a document created in an older version, or in some cases, not be able to read the document at all.

■ If you have a printer, be sure to send the service bureau a clear, crisp copy of your documents. The service bureau will be able to use that copy to compare to their imagesetter output for glitches or other problems.

■ If you have difficulty outputting that job to your laser printer, expect it to be all the more difficult on an imagesetter, which has to process much more information in order to image a page. Consider that a single 1200 dpi page has 16 times as many dots per square inch as your 300 dpi page (1,440,000, as compared to 90,000). A service bureau will typically tack on a huge hourly fee for work that takes a long time to process. It is best to solve your printing problems before the job leaves your home or office.

■ Collect all of the files needed to output your job in a single folder. In addition to the actual document, you will need to provide a copy of linked or placed graphics, such as EPS and TIFF files. A missing graphic file may result in poor quality, bitmapped output. Since the service bureau is not responsible if you fail to send all the files needed to image the document, you may risk a missed deadline or having to pay to run the job again to get it right.

If you cannot fit all of the files on a single disk, consider other options, such as compression or providing the work on several clearly labeled floppy disks.

If your work contains large graphic files, such as color photographs, it may be a good idea to buy a removable drive of some sort, such as a Bernoulli, optical, or SyQuest. Before you make such a purchasing decision, contact your local service bureaus and ask what sort of devices they use. The issue of compatibility may be more important than the reliability of a particular removable format. Besides, all of these products are engineered to provide years of trouble-free service, so long as you don't abuse the removable media.

■ If your job uses process or spot color, ask your service bureau and printer about their requirements for such work. Such features as trapping are present in the popular desktop publishing software packages, but complex work requires skilled hands to do right. A mistake may not show up on a laser print, or even a composite imagesetter print. You may find it more convenient to pay extra to have someone else take the color-preparation chores off your hands.

II

System 7 Essentials

PostScript Files

Some service bureaus find it convenient to have their customers send their work as a print-to-disk file. Both System 7 and the Level 2 LaserWriter driver offer the option of printing to a file rather than to a printer, making the job simple. Because the service bureau doesn't have to go through a page setup process on each job, sending a PostScript file can sometimes save you some cash, but it has some drawbacks, outlined in the following list:

■ Consider a PostScript file to be etched in stone. Making even a simple change may require the service bureau to pour through thousands of characters of PostScript code, if it can be done at all—and they charge you by the hour.

■ Ask your service bureau for the correct printer setup information before you print your PostScript file. If the job is setup for the wrong printer, it will print incorrectly.

■ Because your Mac's screen may not capture the fine details of character kerning, and the look and feel of illustrations, be sure you review a paper print of your job for any mistakes before making your printer file.

■ PostScript files can be huge. Even what seems to be a relatively simple document may fill several megabytes of space. Review step seven in the instructions on preparing work for the service bureau, about compression and removable drive options for storing your work.

Filling In The Job Ticket

Tip
If you are using LaserWriter 8, you can reduce the size of your PostScript files but not including the font information. Just make sure that your service bureau has the correct fonts available.

Most service bureaus offer a job ticket or information form for you to fill out. When preparing your work for output, be sure that all the requested information is filled in accurately. Even if the questions aren't asked, you ought to provide the following information to keep problems from happening later on.

■ List the actual file name of the document you want printed.

■ List the names of the fonts used in that document. Also name the vendor or manufacturer of the font (such as Adobe, Agfa, Bitstream, Font Company Image Club, Linotype, or Monotype). Many font developers will have fonts with the same names in their product line. But a Futura, for example, from one vendor, will look quite different from that of a different vendor.

■ List the names of all linked or placed graphics (EPS, TIFF, etc.) used in your document.

- Identify the software you used to create your document and the version number.

- List the kind of prints you want, paper or film.

- List the output resolution you want. 1200 dpi output and 2400 dpi output are priced differently. You can save a few bucks and not suffer much in terms of quality if you opt for lower resolution. But when color separations, halftones, and shaded elements are required, order the best quality output you can.

- State the finished size of the document, especially if it's other than your standard letter-sized page.

- If the output is to be printed at other than the standard 100% setting, be sure that fact is clearly noted.

From Here...

This chapter described how the Mac's printing features work, outlined some of the new advances in printing technology, and described a few things you might consider when you are ready to buy a new printer.

- Chapter 8, "All about Fonts," gave you valuable information about fonts and how to use them.

- For additional advice on setting up a printer on your network, read Chapter 33, "Networking."

- Chapters 37 and 38 expand upon the steps you need to take to trouble-shoot common problems with your Mac and explain how you can solve them before they become serious.

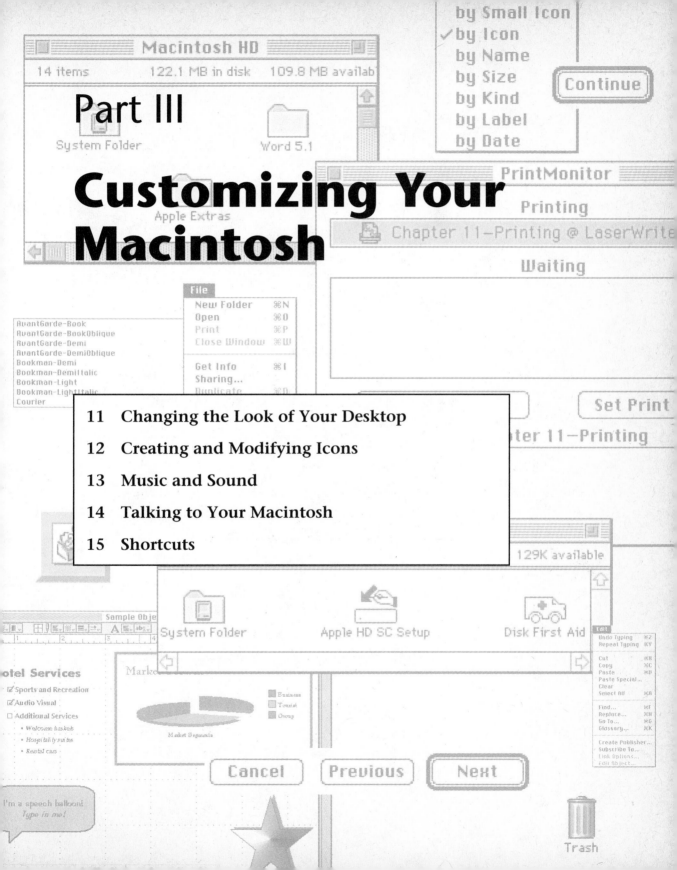

Part III

Customizing Your Macintosh

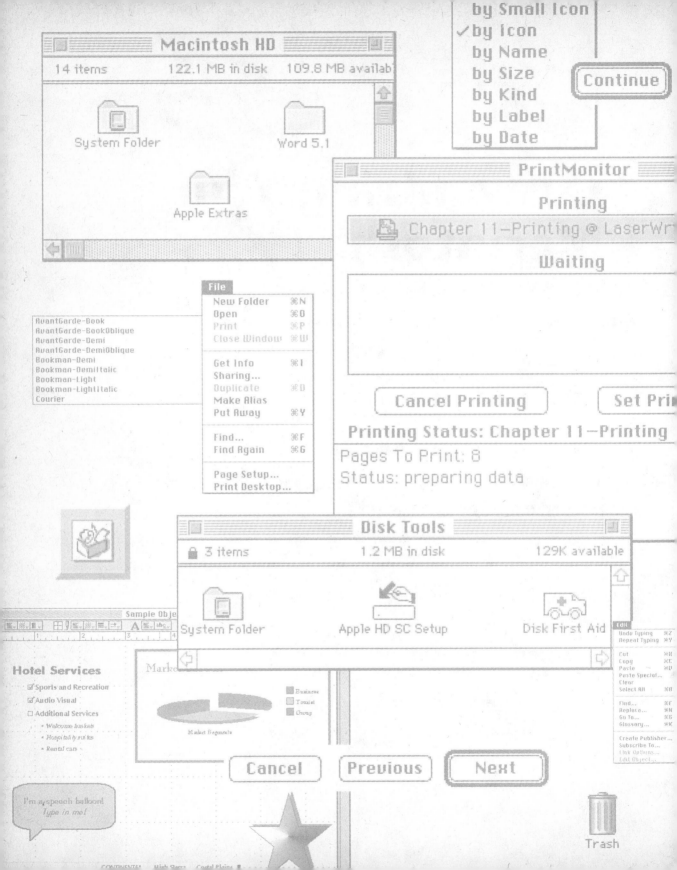

Chapter 11

Changing the Look of Your Desktop

by Carman Minarik

The Macintosh operating system allows almost complete control over the appearance and functionality of the desktop. Everything from the color and pattern of the desktop background to the speed at which the mouse pointer travels across the screen can be changed to suit your needs and preferences.

In this chapter, you learn how to do the following:

- ■ Modify your desktop colors and patterns

- ■ Alter the fonts, icons, and colors used in Finder windows

- ■ Change the appearance of dates, times, and numbers

- ■ Control the functionality of the keyboard and mouse

- ■ Create and use customized screen backgrounds, menus, window controls, and other Finder elements

Control Panels Included with the Macintosh Operating System

Control Panels are special applications that extend the functionality of the Macintosh operating system. On Macintoshes running System 7.0 or later, Control Panels are found in the Control Panels folder inside the System folder.

Caution

Control Panel files must load along with the other system files at startup time. The Control Panel files must be located in the Control Panels folder inside the System folder in order to be activated upon startup. If a Control Panel has been moved from the Control Panels folder, access to the Control Panel will not be available. To regain access, move the Control Panel file into the Control Panels folder and restart the Macintosh.

The Macintosh operating system provides several Control Panels that enable you to customize your system. In System 7.5, if you open the Apple menu and choose Control Panels, you'll be able to select a specific Control Panel from a sub-menu. In earlier versions of System 7, Control Panels can be accessed by opening the Control Panels folder inside the System folder or by selecting the Apple menu choice Control Panels. In earlier versions of System 7, a window similar to the one shown in figure 11.1 opens.

Fig. 11.1
This window, viewed by icon, shows the Control Panels available for use.

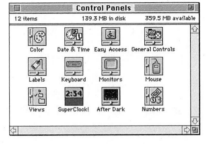

As with any other application, you launch individual Control Panels by double-clicking the desired Control Panel's icon.

Note

Under operating systems prior to System 7.0, Control Panels are not stored as individual applications. Instead, they are stored as a special type of startup file called a CDEV, short for Control Device. The CDEVs are stored in the System folder and launch as additions to the System file at startup time.

The following sections of this chapter describe the Control Panels that are supplied by Apple as part of the Macintosh operating system.

General Controls

The General Controls Control Panel is used to change desktop settings. Double-click the General Controls icon, and a window similar to the one shown in figure 11.2 appears.

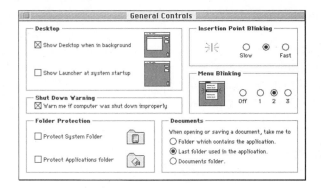

Fig. 11.2
Use the General Controls window to change the desktop display, menu blinking, and insertion point blinking.

Desktop

If the check box labeled "Show Desktop when in background" is activated, the Macintosh desktop, including open Finder windows and disk icons, will be visible behind any open application windows. If this box is not activated, desktop items will not be visible when a software application is active.

Activate the check box labeled "Show Launcher at system startup" to run an application called Launcher whenever the Macintosh is started. Launcher represents an alternative method to launch frequently used applications and documents.

◀ See "The Finder and Its Contents," p. 72

Insertion Point Blinking

Any time you are working with text in any Macintosh software, an insertion point is visible on-screen. This insertion point indicates where text will appear when you start typing. To increase its visibility, the insertion point is designed to blink on the screen.

◀ See "New Features," p. 56

You can control how fast the insertion point will blink in the General Controls dialog box. Three options for Insertion Point Blinking are available: slow, medium, and fast. Click the radio button for the rate you want. The sample insertion point changes its blinking rate to reflect the new setting. The insertion point in most software will use the rate set in this Control Panel.

III

Customizing Your Mac

Menu Blinking

◀ See "Organizing Your Hard Disk," p. 112

Whenever you make a menu choice in any Macintosh software, the menu option chosen blinks in confirmation of your selection. Options on the General Controls screen enable you to change the number of times the menu blinks. Choose 1, 2, or 3 blinks by clicking the appropriate button. Choose Off to disable menu blinking.

Other General Controls

Other options in the General Controls window allow you to protect the contents of your System and applications folder, require the Macintosh to inform you if it was not shut down properly, and control the initial file locations displayed in Open and Save dialog boxes.

Desktop Patterns

Apple provides several predefined desktop patterns from which to choose. Open the Desktop Patterns Control Panel to select a new desktop pattern from the predefined list. A window will open (see fig. 11.3).

Fig. 11.3
The Desktop Patterns window allows you to select from a variety of screen backgrounds.

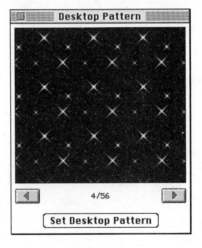

Follow these steps to choose a new pattern:

1. Click the right/left arrow of the Pattern Selection bar to browse forward through the predefined patterns.

2. Click in the left side of the Pattern Selection bar to browse backward through the predefined patterns.

3. When you have found the pattern you want to use, click in the Set Desktop Pattern box to activate the displayed desktop pattern, or double-click in the Pattern Area of the dialog box.

The Macintosh will retain the new pattern settings, as well as all other Control Panel settings, from one session to the next.

Color

The Color Control Panel allows you to change the accent colors for your windows and the color used to highlight text. Double-click the Color icon, and a window similar to the one shown in figure 11.4 appears.

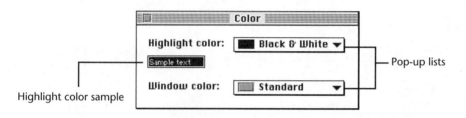

Fig. 11.4
In the Color window, you can choose text highlight and window colors.

Select the desired text highlight and window accent colors from the pop-up lists.

Choosing Other from the highlight color list will open the color dialog box containing either a color wheel or color bars.

An example of the color dialog box is shown in figure 11.5.

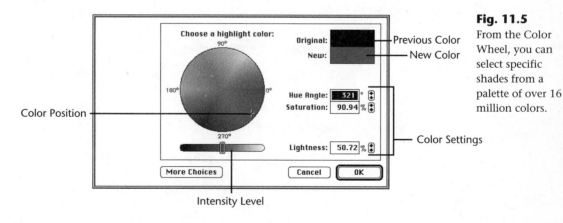

Fig. 11.5
From the Color Wheel, you can select specific shades from a palette of over 16 million colors.

To select a desired color in the color dialog box, follow these steps:

1. Use the intensity level scroll bar beneath the Color Wheel to set the overall brightness of the colors.

2. Position the mouse pointer over the area on the color wheel that displays the desired color and click.

   A sample of the newly selected color is displayed directly above the original color in the upper-left area of the Color Wheel window.

3. If you know the exact color setting numbers for the desired color, you can enter them in the color setting boxes.

4. Click OK.

> **Note**
>
> The color dialog box provides two methods to set desired colors—the HLS (Hue, Lightness, and Saturation) method and the RGB (Red, Green, and Blue) method. The More Choices button at the bottom of the color dialog box allows you to choose the method you want to use. The preceding section has described the HLS controls. The dialog box displays red, green, and blue color bars if the RBG option is selected.

◀ See "Icon and List Views," p. 123

Views

Use the Views Control Panel to alter the way Finder information is presented in icon and list views. Double-click the Views icon to access a window, as shown in figure 11.6.

Fig. 11.6
The Views window provides controls for view fonts, icon sizes, and other aspects of Finder information display.

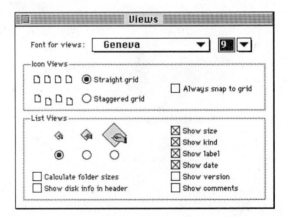

The Views window provides control over several options, all of which impact the appearance of information in Finder windows.

Fonts

You can choose any font installed in your system for display in Finder windows. Choose the desired font and point size from the pop-up lists at the top of the Views window. (Chapter 8, "All about Fonts," provides detailed information about different types of fonts and their uses.)

> **Note**
>
> Though you can select any installed font and point size, choose a font and size for which a bit-mapped screen font was installed. Bit-mapped fonts produce more clearly defined on-screen characters, especially at smaller point sizes.

For more details on fonts and font types, see Chapter 8, "All about Fonts."

Icon Views

The Special menu choice Clean Up Window automatically arranges the icons in a window according to a grid pattern. The Views control panel enables you to choose either a straight or a staggered grid pattern.

Choose the desired grid pattern by clicking the associated button.

Activate the Always snap to grid check box if you want any icon moved into a window to be arranged to the grid pattern automatically.

List Views

File and folder icons in list views are normally presented as small pictures without much detail. By choosing the radio buttons for medium or large icons in the Views window, you can increase the size and detail level for the icons in list views. The large icon option will produce icons which look the same as those presented in a normal icon view.

The check boxes to the right of the Views window allow you to select the columns of file and folder information which will appear in list views. Activate the items you want to display by clicking in the appropriate check boxes.

Activate the Show disk info in header check box if you want to display disk size and available space information at the top of list view windows.

Activate the Calculate folder sizes check box if you want the total size of all files contained in a folder to be shown as the folder's size in a list view.

Tip

If many of your file and folder names are long, a staggered grid allows closer placement of icons in a window without overlapping the file or folder names.

III

Customizing Your Mac

> **Note**
>
> If scrolling speed through a list window is slow, deactivate the Calculate folder sizes check box. Calculating folder sizes requires more effort when displaying a list view, particularly when the folders contain many files or nested folders.

Labels

◀ See "Using
Labels,"
p. 128

The Labels capability in System 7 allows you to assign text labels and associated colors to files and folders in Finder windows. You can use these labels to organize your desktop more efficiently or to add interest to your screens with additional colors.

To assign labels to Finder items, follow these steps:

1. Select the item or items you want to label.

2. Open the Label menu.

3. Select the desired label and associated color. The selected files or folders change color, and the label text is shown for the selected files and folders in list views.

4. To remove labels from selected files or folders, open the Labels menu and choose None.

You may want to change the label text or the colors associated with the labels. Using the Labels Control Panel, you can change the text and the colors for each label on the Label menu.

 Double-click the Labels icon in the Control Panels folder, and a screen similar to the one shown in figure 11.7 appears.

Fig. 11.7
The Labels Control Panel allows you to change label text and colors.

- To change label text, drag across the text to be changed and type the new text.

- To change label colors, double-click the color box you want to change. The color dialog box opens. Use this screen as described previously in this chapter.

- Changes made to a label's text and color automatically update any items which have that label assigned.

> **Note**
>
> In operating system versions prior to System 7.0, the Labels menu and Labels Control Panel do not exist. The equivalent function is found on the Color menu—you can change colors for Finder items, but label text is not supported.

Date and Time

Use the Date and Time Control Panel to alter the appearance of date and time information in Finder windows. Changes made in the Date and Time Control Panel will impact many Macintosh software packages, as well.

Double-click the Date and Time icon in the Control Panels folder to open the window shown in figure 11.8.

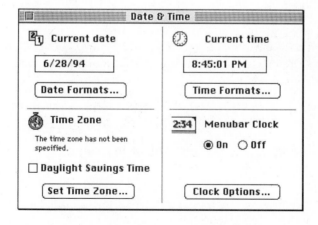

Fig. 11.8
The Date and Time window allows you to change date and time formats.

On this screen, you can change the date and time settings for the Macintosh system clock.

Customized Dates

Click the Date Format button in the Date and Time window, and a screen like the one shown in figure 11.9 opens.

Fig. 11.9
Use the Date Format screen to modify the appearance of dates in Finder windows.

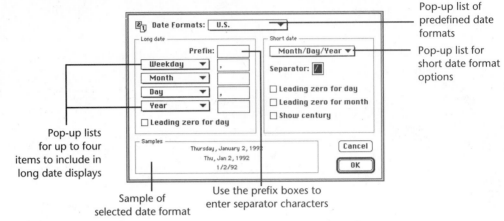

Pop-up list of predefined date formats

Pop-up list for short date format options

Pop-up lists for up to four items to include in long date displays

Sample of selected date format

Use the prefix boxes to enter separator characters

At the top of the Date Format screen, you will see a pop-up list of predefined date formats. This list contains predefined date formatting for several different countries. Choose one of the countries on this list to automatically set your date formatting for that country.

Custom date formats can also be created. You see a sample of the selected date formatting options at the bottom of the Date Format screen. The samples reflect the current date format options in effect.

The rest of the Date Format screen is divided into two main sections—long date formatting options and short date formatting options. The following list describes these options:

■ *Long Date Formatting* is used when date information is displayed partly in words. Follow these steps for long date formatting:

   1. Choose the desired option for up to four items to be included in your long date format from the corresponding pop-up lists. Each list contains options for Weekday, Month, Day, Year, and None. By choosing different options in different positions, you can create any type of date format you need.

   2. You can type separator characters in the prefix boxes which correspond to each pop-up list. Characters entered in the prefix boxes will be displayed between the items selected in the drop-down boxes. Using the formatting shown in figure 11.10, for example, a comma will be displayed between the Weekday and the Month, and another comma will be displayed between the Day and the Year.

3. Activate the Leading zero for day check box if you want to display a leading zero for single-digit day numbers.

■ *Short Date Formatting* is used when date information is displayed entirely in numbers. To format short dates, follow these steps:

1. Select the desired short date formatting from the pop-up list.

2. Type the separator character you want in the separator box.

3. Activate the check boxes labeled "Leading zero for day" and "Leading zero" for month if you want to display single-digit days or months with leading zeros.

4. Activate the Show century check box to display all 4 digits of the year.

Customized Times

Click the Time Formats button in the Date and Time window. The screen illustrated in figure 11.10 appears.

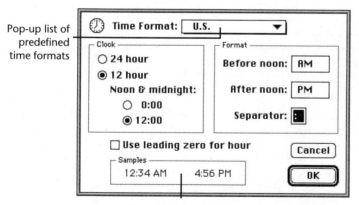

Pop-up list of predefined time formats

Sample of selected time formats

Fig. 11.10
Use this screen to modify time formats.

To modify the time formatting in use, follow these steps:

1. The pop-up list of predefined time formats functions in the same manner as the list of date formats described previously.

III

2. Select the button for 12-hour or 24-hour time display. If you select 12-hour display, you may also choose whether to display noon and midnight as 12:00 or 0:00.

3. Enter the before noon and after noon identifying text to be displayed as part of the time format.

4. Enter the separator character to be displayed between elements of the time format.

5. Activate the Use leading zeros for hour check box if you want single-digit hours to be displayed with leading zeros.

Time Zone

Click the Set Time Zone button to open a list of cities from many countries around the world. Choose a city in your area to set the current time zone.

Activate the Daylight Savings Time check box if daylight savings time is in effect in your time zone.

Menubar Clock

Turn on the Menubar Clock option to place the current time on the Menu Bar in all applications.

When you click the Clock Options button, a screen like the one in figure 11.11 appears.

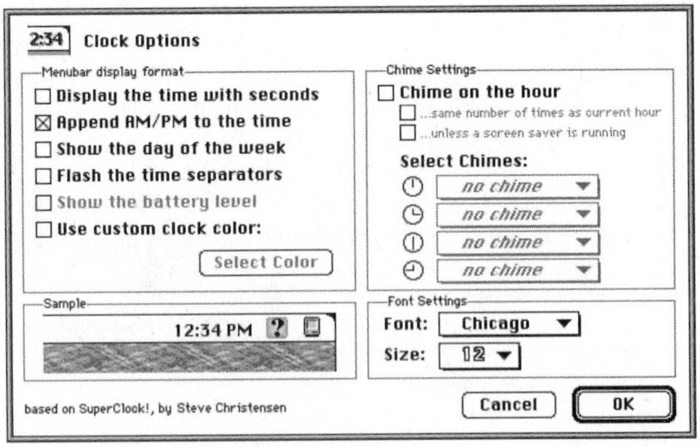

Fig. 11.11
Use this screen to control the function and appearance of the Menubar Clock.

Use this screen to choose the font and size for the clock information, whether the seconds will be visible, whether hourly chimes will sound, and so on.

> **Note**
>
> The Menubar Clock options in System 7.5 are based on the shareware utility SuperClock! If you're using an operating system prior to 7.5, SuperClock! provides the same functionality.

Numbers

Use the Numbers Control Panel to modify the appearance of numbers in Finder windows. Changes made in the Numbers window will also impact many Macintosh software applications.

Double-click the Numbers icon in the Control Panels folder to access the window shown in figure 11.12.

Pop-up list of pre-defined number formats ⟶

Sample of selected number formatting options ⟶

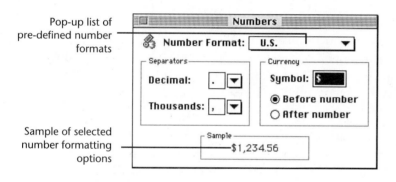

Fig. 11.12
Use the Numbers Control Panel to customize the appearance of numbers in Finder windows.

To customize your number format, follow these steps:

1. The pop-up list of predefined number formats works in the same manner as the lists for date and time formats described in the preceding section.

2. Choose the desired symbols for use as decimal points and commas from the pop-up lists in the Separators section of the Number window.

3. Type the character you want to use for the currency symbol in your number format. You can also indicate whether the currency symbol is to be placed before or after the number by selecting the appropriate radio button.

Any changes made for number formatting options will be reflected in the sample box at the bottom of the Number window.

Tip
Use the Key Caps Apple Menu Item to see available currency symbols from different countries.

III

Customizing Your Mac

Apple Menu Options

The Apple Menu Options Control Panel allows you to control the functionality of the Apple Menu. A window as shown in figure 11.13 opens.

Fig. 11.13
Use The Apple
Menu Options
window to set up
submenus on the
Apple Menu.

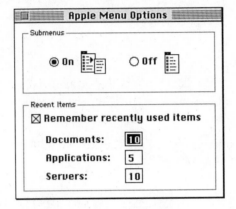

■ If the submenu option is turned on, Apple Menu items such as Control Panels and Chooser produce submenus when highlighted. This allows you to choose a specific option without opening a new window or dialog box.

■ The Apple Menu also displays recently used applications, documents, and file servers. Use the Apple Menu Options controls to set the number of applications, documents, and servers to be displayed.

Shareware

Up to this point, this chapter presented desktop controls that are standard parts of the Macintosh operating system. Because the Macintosh possesses an open architecture in its operating system design, almost unlimited additional desktop controls are possible. Many individuals and companies have taken advantage of this open system architecture to create applications and Control Panels which extend your control over the desktop.

This section provides information on some of the popular shareware programs available for desktop control. Shareware programs are available at low or even no cost from many sources, including user groups and electronic bulletin boards. (See Chapter 28, "Shareware and Other Cool Stuff," for a detailed discussion of shareware.)

Greg's Buttons

Greg's Buttons is a Shareware Control Panel that allows you to change the appearance of buttons, check boxes, and radio buttons in all of your applications. The Control Panel also allows modification of the background color of menus and dialog boxes, and enables you to change the system font for your Macintosh.

To install Greg's Buttons, drag the Control Panel file to the closed System Folder icon and restart your Macintosh. Upon restart, you will immediately notice the changes made by Greg's Buttons. Figures 11.14 and 11.15 illustrate the differences in dialog box, font, and button appearance created by this Control Panel.

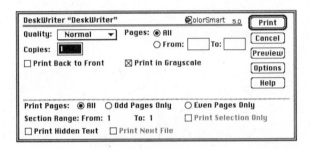

Fig. 11.14
Standard print dialog box from Microsoft Word 5.1.

Fig. 11.15
Print dialog box from Microsoft Word 5.1 with Greg's Buttons in effect.

Double-click the Greg's Buttons icon in the Control Panels folder to control the programs modifications to your system.

General Preferences

When the Greg's Buttons Control Panel is launched, the window shown in figure 11.16 opens.

III

Customizing Your Mac

Fig. 11.16
This is the first of four Greg's Buttons control screens.

Activate or deactivate the appropriate check boxes to turn Greg's Buttons on and off, to show or suppress the Greg's Buttons startup icon, and to show or suppress the shareware message.

Other Greg's Buttons control screens are accessed by clicking the boxes to the right of the Greg's Buttons window.

Button Preferences
Click the button preferences box to open the screen shown in figure 11.17.

Fig. 11.17
Use this screen to control button appearance.

To modify button formatting options, follow these steps:

1. Select from 3 check box styles, 3 radio button styles, and 2 push button styles by clicking the desired options.

2. Activate the Embossed Push Button Titles check box to create a more 3-D look for button text.

3. The check box labeled System 7 Color Buttons allows you to activate or deactivate the button controls in Greg's Buttons.

Color Preferences
Click the color preferences box to display the screen shown in figure 11.18.

Fig. 11.18
Use this screen
to control menu,
window, alert, and
dialog background
color.

To change the color settings for your windows and dialog boxes,
follow these steps:

1. Use the check boxes to activate or deactivate the control options for
   Finder window, menu, and dialog and alert boxes.

2. Click the color box to the right of each option to open the color dialog
   box, as described earlier in this chapter. Select the color you want for
   each option.

3. Alert and dialog box color settings may cause problems in some applications. Click the Exclude Applications button to access and modify a
   list of applications in which alert and dialog box colors will not be
   changed.

System Font Preferences

The system font is used for menu headings, menu text, alert box text, and
dialog box text throughout the Macintosh system. (See Chapter 8, "All about
Fonts," for information about fonts.)

Click the system font preferences box in Greg's Buttons to activate a screen
like the one shown in figure 11.19.

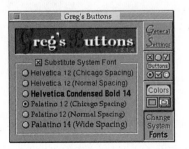

Fig. 11.19
Use this screen to
control system
font appearance.

III

Customizing Your Mac

Follow these steps to change your system font:

1. Select from the six available system font choices.

2. The check box labeled Substitute System Font allows you to activate or deactivate the system font controls in Greg's Buttons.

> **Caution**
>
> All the options in Greg's Buttons require alteration of the System file resources to work. These alterations may cause unpredictable problems with some software applications. Be sure to read all the documentation supplied with Greg's Buttons carefully to avoid unnecessary problems.

Desktop Textures

The Desktop Textures application allows you to choose from a variety of interesting desktop background patterns. These patterns provide alternatives to those available in the Desktop Patterns Control Panel described earlier.

Unlike most of the other programs described in this chapter, Desktop Textures is not a Control Panel. It is a standard application whose function it is to place a complex graphic image into the System file as the desktop pattern resource. The advantage to this approach is that the software need not launch at system startup time, and therefore requires no memory.

Installing a Texture

Double-click the Texture Installer icon to launch the application. A window similar to the one shown in figure 11.20 appears.

Fig. 11.20

The Texture Installer window enables you to view and install textures.

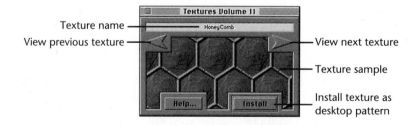

To choose and install a texture, follow these steps:

1. Choose the File menu option Open to select a particular texture file with which to work. A standard Open dialog box appears. Desktop Textures comes with four textures files from which to choose.

2. Use the next and previous arrow buttons to view the various textures contained in the texture file. Each textures file contains 10 to 25 different textures from which to choose.

3. Click the Install button to install the displayed texture.

4. Choose the File menu option Deinstall Texture to remove the texture currently in use from the desktop pattern, and return to using the pattern defined in the General Controls Control Panel.

Note

Installing a Desktop Texture does not prevent you from later using the General Controls Control Panel to choose a desktop pattern. You may find that all color options are removed from the General Controls window if a Desktop Texture file is in use, however. If this is the case, launch Texture Installer and choose the File menu option Deinstall Texture. Color options should now appear in the General Controls window.

Randomizing Textures

Desktop Textures comes with a second application called Texture Randomizer. This application will automatically install a different texture each time the Macintosh is restarted, or at any other time you choose.

Double-click the Texture Randomizer icon to access the screen shown in figure 11.21.

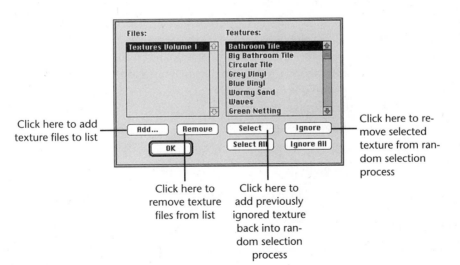

Click here to add texture files to list

Click here to remove texture files from list

Click here to add previously ignored texture back into random selection process

Click here to remove selected texture from random selection process

Fig. 11.21
Use the Texture Randomizer screen to add textures into a list of available choices for random selection.

III

Customizing Your Mac

To set up random textures for installation, follow these steps:

1. Click the Add button to access texture files. A standard Open dialog box appears.

2. All textures in the selected texture file will initially be included in the random selection process. To remove a particular texture from consideration in the random selection process, select the texture and click the Ignore button.

3. To reinstate a texture that has been ignored into consideration in the random selection process, select the texture and click the Select button.

4. When you finish, click OK.

From this point onward, any time you launch the Texture Randomizer application, a random texture from the list will be installed as the desktop pattern.

To access the textures list screen, hold down the Command and Option keys while launching Texture Randomizer.

Tip

Place the Texture Randomizer icon in the Startup Items folder inside the System folder if you want a random texture to be installed each time the Macintosh starts up.

Commercial Software

Several commercial software companies produce applications which can enhance your Macintosh desktop. The following sections look closely at the most popular of these packages, After Dark from Berkeley Systems. Other packages are briefly described, as well.

After Dark

▶ See "Screen Savers," p. 728

After Dark is a screen saver utility. The purpose of a screen saver is to reduce the chance that an image will be "burned into" your monitor screen if your Macintosh is left running unattended for extended periods. Screen saver utilities achieve this purpose by placing moving images on-screen, which prevents a static image from burning in.

The newset versions of After Dark include an Installer that places the various resources for the program in their correct locations

 Once AfterDark has been loaded, double-click the After Dark icon in the Control Panels folder or in System 7.5 select After Dark from the Control Panel sub-menu to open the window shown in figure 11.22.

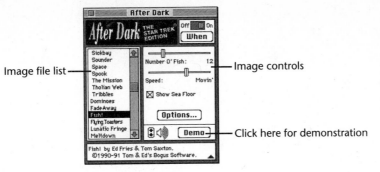

Image file list —

Image controls

Click here for demonstration

Fig. 11.22
Use the After Dark
Control Panel to
select the image
for use as a screen
saver.

To choose a screen saver image, follow these steps:

1. Choose the image you want from the list on the left side of the window. Any After Dark image file contained in the After Dark Files folder
   appears in this list.

2. Varying controls may appear in the box to the right of the image list,
   depending on the image file selected. Use the controls that appear to
   modify the way in which the screen saver image behaves. In figure
   11.22, for example, the number of fish that appear on the screen, their
   speed of movement, and the volume of the screen saver sounds can all
   be varied.

3. Click the Demo button to see a demonstration of the screen saver in
   action.

Click the Off/On button at the top of the window to activate and deactivate
the screen saver.

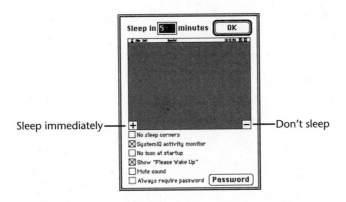

Sleep immediately —

Don't sleep

Fig. 11.23
Use this screen to
configure After
Dark to your
preferences.

III

Customizing Your Mac

Click the When button to access a second screen which provides additional screen saver controls, as shown in figure 11.23.

Options on this configuration screen allow you to do the following:

- Enter the number of minutes your system must remain idle in order for the screen saver to activate.

- Set the sleep corners. Moving the mouse pointer into the + sleep corner immediately activates the screen saver. Moving the mouse pointer into the–sleep corner prevents the screen saver from activating, regardless of the length of system inactivity. Drag the sleep corner indicators into the desired positions to set the sleep corner locations.

- Activate or deactivate the check boxes for various screen saver settings.

- Set a password. If you set a password, an activated screen saver image will not clear until the correct password is entered. This is an easy method of adding security to your Macintosh system.

Caution

The password option in After Dark is not a completely effective security device. If a user restarts the Macintosh with Extensions off or restarts from a floppy disk, the After Dark system will not load and the password will not be in force.

▶ See "Now Utilities," p. 719

Now Utilities

Now Utilities is a collection of several applications, Control Panels, and Extensions that enhance the functionality of the Macintosh operating system. Two of the components of Now Utilities are designed to modify the appearance of your desktop: Now Menus and WYSIWYG Menus.

Now Menus

The Now Menus Extension creates submenu functionality in the Finder similar to that provided by system 7.5.

In addition to providing submenus, however, Now Menus also allows you to change the order of appearance of your Apple Menu items.

Super Boomerang

This utility helps locate recently used files and folders by making a list, which it places on the Apple menu. Super Boomerang can find file and folder names and search files by content even if the files have been compressed.

WYSIWYG Menus

WYSIWYG Menus is an Extension which causes individual fonts in all font lists in all applications to display with their actual appearance. Instead of just seeing a list of font names, you will see each font name displayed in the actual typestyle for that font. The second major feature of the program is that it groups fonts into families accessible via sub-menus. This feature helps shorten font menus considerably and makes the process of selecting a font much easier.

ClickChange

For the ultimate in desktop control, take a look at ClickChange from DublClick Software. This package allows radical modification of nearly every aspect of your operating environment, including the following:

▶ See "System Enhance-ments," p. 711

- ■ *Cursor Appearance.* You can change the appearance of the mouse pointer and insertion point, and even design animated mouse pointers.

- ■ *Buttons.* Provides controls similar to the button options in Greg's Buttons described earlier in this chapter.

- ■ *Sounds.* Allows you to assign different sounds for each of many defined events. For example, one sound can be played at startup, another at shut down, another on insertion of a floppy disk, and so on.

- ■ *Scroll Bars.* Provides control over the appearance and functionality of window scroll bars.

- ■ *Colors.* Enables you to change the colors of almost all operating system components, including menus, check boxes, window borders, and so on.

- ■ *Windows.* Provides several options for window and dialog box appearance.

From Here...

This chapter explored some of the ways you can control the appearance of your desktop. You have used the standard Apple Control Panels, and have looked at some shareware and commercial programs which provide additional controls.

III

Customizing Your Mac

■ For additional information on shareware programs, see Chapter 28, "Shareware and Other Cool Stuff."

■ See Chapter 25, "Utilities," for more information on commercial software packages that can enhance your desktop work environment.

■ Read the next chapter, "Creating and Modifying Icons," for information on changing the icons your Macintosh displays.

Chapter 12

Creating and Modifying Icons

by Carman Minarik

The Macintosh operating system uses icons to represent files, folders, tools, controls, and many other items. The reasoning behind icon use is that people recognize better than they remember. It makes sense, therefore, for you to operate in an environment in which the icons being used are meaningful and easily recognizable for you.

Several methods are available for your use as you modify the icons used in your system. In this chapter, you learn the following:

- How to easily replace the icon for any disk, file or folder

- How to create and use your own icons with a drawing package

- The way your Macintosh keeps track of Finder icons

- How to use ResEdit to modify application icons

Copying and Pasting Icons

The fastest way to change the icon for a disk, file, or folder is to choose a picture you like, and insert this picture as the disk, file, or folder icon.

Choosing the Picture

The first step in replacing an item's icon is to choose the picture you want to use and copy it to the clipboard. This picture can come from a number of sources, including other disk, folder, or file icons, clip art, and original art created by you.

Icons from Other Disks, Folders, or Files

To select the icon of an existing disk, folder, or file for use as the icon of a different item, follow these steps:

1. Select the disk, folder, or file whose icon you want to use.

2. From the File menu, choose Get Info. A window similar to the one shown in figure 12.1 appears.

Fig. 12.1
The Get Info window displays the selected item's icon along with information about the item's size, location, version, and so on.

3. Click the icon in the upper left area of the window. A box outline appears around the icon.

4. From the Edit menu, choose Copy. The icon is now stored on the Clipboard.

Clip Art

◀ See "The Familiar Features of Macintosh," p. 44

Nearly any type of clip art can be used as an icon for a disk, folder, or file. Keep in mind, however, that the icon size is quite small. Each Macintosh icon is 32 pixels square. A pixel is the smallest unit that can be drawn on the Macintosh, and is equivalent to one dot on-screen. Any art selected for use as an icon will automatically be sized to 32 pixels square. If you choose a large, complex drawing for use as an icon, it may be reduced to the point that its detail is lost.

To select clip art for use as an icon, follow these steps:

1. Open the document that contains a drawing in a painting or drawing program in which you are comfortable working.

2. Use the method provided in the painting or drawing package to select the picture you want to use.

> **Note**
>
> In most drawing programs, such as MacDraw or Canvas, you select an object
> by pointing at it with the mouse and clicking. In most painting programs,
> such as MacPaint or HyperCard, you find a Selection tool, often in the shape
> of a dotted box, which you must use to drag around the desired picture.

   3. From the Edit menu, choose Copy. The selected picture is now stored
   on the Clipboard.

Original Art

You can also create your own original artwork for use as a disk, folder, or file
icon. Use any drawing or painting program you are comfortable with to create the artwork. Remember that the finished icon will be 32 pixels square. For
best results, try to keep the art you are creating close to that size.

When the picture is completed, select it, and from the Edit menu choose
Copy. The picture is now stored on the Clipboard.

Inserting the Picture as an Icon

Whether the source of the icon you want to use is an existing disk, folder or
file icon, a picture from clip art, or an original drawing you created, you must
copy the desired picture to the Clipboard. When that is done, follow these
steps to insert the picture as an icon:

   1. Select the disk, folder, or file whose icon you want to change.

   2. From the File menu, choose Get Info. A window like the one in figure
   12.1 opens.

   3. Click over the icon in the upper left area of the window. A box outline
   appears around the icon.

   4. From the Edit menu, choose Paste. The previously copied picture will
   now be used as the icon for the selected disk, folder, or file.

To return a disk, folder, or file icon to its original state at any time after its
icon has been altered, follow these steps:

   1. Select the disk, folder, or file to be changed.

   2. From the File menu, choose Get Info.

III

Customizing Your Mac

3. Click the icon in the upper left area of the window. A box outline appears around the icon.

4. From the Edit menu, choose Clear. The customized icon is removed, and the original item icon is restored.

Using ResEdit to Modify Icons

The process outlined to this point provides a fast, easy way to change the icons used to display disks, folders, and files. You may want to go beyond that, however, to take even more control over icons. An application called ResEdit, created by Apple, provides you with the tools to do more complex work with icons.

Using ResEdit, you can perform operations such as the following:

- Directly modify most disk, folder, or file icons

- Change the icons used in alert and dialog boxes

- Change the appearance of the icons assigned to new files as they are created from each software application

ResEdit Basics

ResEdit is an application program whose name stands for Resource Editor. This name very accurately describes the function of ResEdit—it is designed to edit the resources used in your applications.

◀ See "The Finder and its Contents," p. 72

All Macintosh files are made up of two components, known as the data fork and the resource fork. For any given file, both forks may contain information, or one of the forks might be empty. Application files, for example, may contain no information in the data fork.

The resource fork of a file is used to store elements of computer code called resources. A resource can be used for all types of purposes, such as creating a menu heading or drawing an icon. Because resources are stored in the resource fork of the file, they are readily available whenever needed by the application using the file.

ResEdit is designed to provide usable access to the resources in the resource fork of a file. The resources themselves are actually strings of programming code which have no meaning to most Macintosh users, but ResEdit provides editors which allow you to work with many of the resources on terms with which you are more comfortable.

ResEdit provides access to many types of resources, including fonts, menus, dialogs, and icons. This section is devoted to using ResEdit to manipulate icons.

> **Note**
>
> There is no requirement that a file contain anything, including icon information, in its resource fork. Even application files can contain no resources, and instead store all icon information in the data fork. If the file does not contain icon information in the resource fork, ResEdit will not be able to provide access to the icons.

To launch ResEdit, double-click the application icon. Click once to access a standard open file dialog box. From the File menu, choose Open to access a standard Open dialog box. Select the file whose resources you want to edit, and the screen shown in figure 12.2 opens. If the file you select has no resource fork, you are asked if you want to add one.

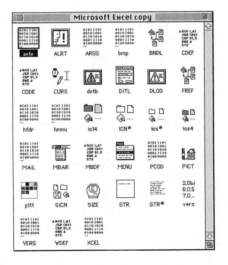

Fig. 12.2
The Type Picker screen shows the types of resources contained in a file.

III

Customizing Your Mac

This opening screen, called the Type Picker, shows all the types of resources contained in the file. The example shown in figure 12.2 shows several types of icon resources, such as ics4, ICN#, and ics#. Table 12.1 summarizes the different types of icon resources a file may contain.

Table 12.1 Icon Resource Types

Type	Description
ICON	32 by 32 icon used in dialog and alert boxes
SICN	16 by 16 small icon lists used in menus
ICN#	32 by 32 Finder icon - black and white
cicn	Color icon
icl4	32 by 32 icon - 16 colors
icl8	32 by 32 icon - 256 colors
ics#	16 by 16 icon - small icon used in By Small Icon view in Finder
ics4	16 by 16 icon - 16 colors
ics8	16 by 16 icon - 256 colors

To work with a particular type of resource, point at the desired resource type on the Type Picker screen and double-click. A screen like the one in figure 12.3 will appear. This screen is called a Resource Picker.

Fig. 12.3
The Resource Picker screen shows the specific resources contained in a file.

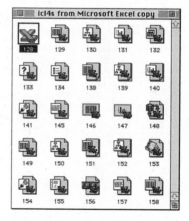

This screen shows all the specific resources of the type selected on the Type Picker screen that are contained in the file.

Note

Each resource in a file is identified with a resource type code, such as icn#, and a specific resource number. Resources can also have names, but many do not. The application using the resources will normally look for the code and the number when a specific resource is needed.

To select a specific resource to edit, point at the desired resource on the Resource Picker screen and double-click. A Resource Editor for the selected resource type will appear. The Color Icon Editor is shown in figure 12.4.

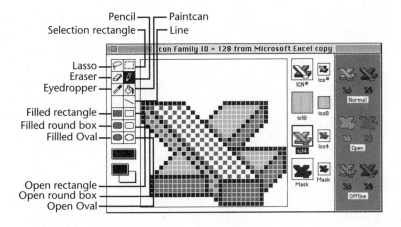

Fig. 12.4
The Resource Editor provides the tools to modify the selected resource.

This screen provides the tools to change the selected resources. The following sections will provide specific details on using the icon editors.

Caution

ResEdit makes direct changes to the resources of a file. Resources in many files are used in complex interconnections, and changing a single resource may have wide-ranging, unpredictable results. Always make changes on a copy of the file, not the original.

Using the Icon Editors

The Icon Editor screen is divided into four regions: tools, expanded icon area, icon types, and normal size icons.

Tools

The icon editor screen provides several tools you can use while modifying icons. Table 12.2 provides a description of each tool's use.

Table 12.2	Editor Tools
Tool	**Use**
	Select irregular areas
	Select rectangular shapes
	Erase parts of picture
	Draw pixel by pixel
	Pick up a color from a drawing area
	Fill an enclosed area with a color
	Draw a straight line
	Draw a filled box
	Draw a transparent box
	Draw a filled round-cornered box
	Draw a transparent round-cornered box
	Draw a filled oval
	Draw a transparent oval

If you are familiar with a painting package such as MacPaint, these tools work in much the same way. To use any of the tools, follow these steps:

1. Select the tool you want by clicking it.

2. Move the mouse pointer to the expanded icon area and position it where you want to draw.

3. Hold down the mouse button and drag to create the shape you want.

The three boxes beneath the tool palette are pop-up lists of colors and patterns. Use these lists to select the colors you want to use.

> **Note**
>
> The Eraser tool does not actually erase anything; it applies the currently selected background color to the pixels you drag it across.

Expanded Icon Area

You make the actual changes to the icon in the expanded icon area. This area allows pixel by pixel modifications to the image.

Because the largest icon size is 64 by 64 pixels, that is the size of the expanded icon area.

Icon Types

The icon types area allows you to move quickly from one icon type to another in the same icon family. An icon family is a group of different types of icons which share the same basic appearance characteristics.

The icon types area can save you the trouble of returning to the Type Picker screen between each edit of related icons. Click the icon type you want to edit, and it will be loaded into the expanded icon area.

Normal Size Icons

This area of the icon editor shows the icons in their normal size, as they will appear in use.

The left column of icons in this area shows how the icon will look when the file is not selected. The right column shows how the icon will look when it is selected. Icons are shown for open and off-line files, as well as the normal icon.

Changes made in the expanded icon area are reflected here.

Menus

Several of ResEdit's menu options are useful when editing an icon. The Transform menu, for example, provides the following options:

- Flip Horizontal
- Flip Vertical
- Rotate
- Nudge (In any direction)

Tip

You can paste any image from any painting or drawing program into the expanded icon area.

III

Customizing Your Mac

Tip
If you make changes to several icons in an icon family and then change your mind, use the Resource menu option Revert Icon Family. All changes to icons in the current icon family will be reversed.

◀ See "Organizing Your Hard Disk," p. 112

Each of these options will operate on any selected area of the drawing.

The Icon menu provides options for icon background color, and the Color menu allows you to select the color palette you want to work with.

Modifying Finder Icons

All icons are modified in much the same way. You may need to address some additional issues when modifying Finder icons, however.

The Finder keeps track of files and their associated icons in an invisible file called the Desktop File. To avoid needless rechecking of this file each time a Finder window is opened, the Macintosh is designed to reuse the Desktop File information whenever possible. This means that once the Finder records icon information for a particular application and its documents in the Desktop File, it will simply reuse that information for all future instances of that application and its documents.

This system is reasonably efficient and works quite well most of the time. It creates a problem when you modify your Finder icons, however, because you may not see any changes in the Finder windows after you complete your changes.

To ensure that the Finder is aware of the icon changes you have made using ResEdit, you must rebuild your Desktop File. To rebuild the Desktop File, follow these steps:

1. Close all open applications.

2. From the Special menu, choose Restart.

3. Hold both the ⌘ and Option keys while the Macintosh restarts.

4. A dialog box appears asking if you want to rebuild the Desktop File. Click OK.

5. The Macintosh will now rebuild the Desktop File and update any icons for which you have made changes.

> **Caution**
>
> Rebuilding the Desktop File will cause any comments entered into the Get Info window of any of your files to be deleted.

From Here...

In this chapter, you learned how to copy and paste icon information, and how to use ResEdit to modify existing icons.

- See Chapter 5, "Understanding the Desktop and Finder," for more information on copying and pasting.

- Chapter 11, "Changing the Look of Your Desktop," covers other changes you can make to your desktop appearance.

- Chapter 22, "Drawing and Painting," provides information on drawing and painting applications.

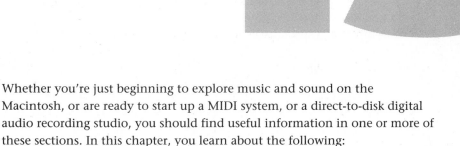

Chapter 13

Music and Sound

by Steve Birchall

Whether you're just beginning to explore music and sound on the Macintosh, or are ready to start up a MIDI system, or a direct-to-disk digital audio recording studio, you should find useful information in one or more of these sections. In this chapter, you learn about the following:

- Sound on the Macintosh

- Mysteries of MIDI

- Digital Audio and MIDI Hardware

Sound on the Macintosh

From the beginning, the hardware and software architecture of the Macintosh has included sound as a basic part of the computer. Its intended uses are mostly for System beeps, game sounds, and an elementary but effective form of speech synthesis called *MacInTalk*. In fact, when Steve Jobs first demonstrated the early 128K Macintosh in public, he carried it on stage and plugged it in, and it not only displayed `hello` on-screen, but also *spoke* it. In 1984, that simple example captured people's attention powerfully and dramatically. Except for some entertainment software, speech synthesis has been ignored until recently, with the advent of the AV versions of the Quadras and PowerMacs. To do it even acceptably well requires massive amounts of computational power.

The synthesizer chip in the early Macs was monophonic, but Apple began using a stereo chip in the Mac II series. You can make music with the built-in synthesizer chip, but you can't do much else with it. For System beeps and game sounds, however, the chip serves the purpose. Conceptually, it contains an oscillator with selectable wave forms, plus a spectrum-shaping filter and an envelope generator (for attack and decay characteristics). With it, software developers can create distinctive sounds to alert users to various problems or simply reinforce the fact that you have invoked a command. This audio feedback remains one of the Mac's most subtle but powerful features.

Game developers, on the other hand, find the synthesizer chip limiting. Unique and attention-getting sounds can mean the difference between a successful game or a failure in the market. With the competition from the latest 16-bit video game hardware, computer games need striking sound effects. One of the solutions is to use a library of sampled sounds. The concept is similar to the way wave table synthesizers use sampled sounds. Press a key, and the sampled sound plays back for you (but without any of the pitch changing and other alterations).

You can create your sampled sounds in any way. Record natural sounds. Develop new sounds on a large synthesizer. Alter and manipulate them electronically in various ways, and even play them backwards. When you're finished, simply digitize them and store them as Mac sound files.

Basic Digitizer: The MacRecorder

The most widely accepted tool for this kind of digitizing has been the Farallon *MacRecorder* (now sold by Macromedia). You can think of it as a low-end, inexpensive digital recorder. Its sound quality seems more like a table radio than a high fidelity system, but the storage space requirements are reasonable compared to full CD quality sound (CDs contain over 600MB of data). The hardware is contained in a small box that connects to one of the serial ports on your Mac. It accepts line level inputs from mixers, pre-amps, and synthesizers, and also has a microphone input. The digitizer circuit converts the analog signals into digital data and sends them into your Mac. It can record about 10 seconds for each data file. The software allows you to start and stop the recording, edit the sampled sound, adjust levels, and set the sampling rate.

Because the digitizer works at 8 bits, it has a signal-to-noise ratio of about 54 dB. Also, its maximum sampling rate of 24 kHz means that it can record frequencies only up to about 12 kHz. The trick in using devices such as the MacRecorder is to select a sound that has a narrow dynamic range and record it at the highest level possible without distortion. On playback, it will rise above the background noise and sound quite acceptable, either on the internal speaker, or on small external speakers. If you record at too low a level, it will sound noisy on playback. Just try again at a higher level. Also, select sounds that don't depend on high frequencies for their essential character, since MacRecorder won't digitize any frequencies above 12 kHz.

Newer Macs with Mikes

In the Mac IIsi and most succeeding models, including the PowerBooks, Apple began including a microphone and System software for digitizing sounds. The more powerful 68030 and 68040 processor chips in these models eliminated the need for an external digitizer. Some business-oriented applications (word processors, spreadsheets, e-mail, and so on) allow you to attach *audio notes* to your documents. For example, your boss could click a spreadsheet cell in your expense report and hear a verbal explanation as to why you are claiming a certain amount. Or you could attach a note to a word processing document to remind yourself to rewrite that section. On a PowerBook, the built-in mike enables you to record random thoughts while you're working on something else. It becomes a dictation machine (with a ten second limit).

QuickTime movies also have audio tracks, so don't overlook the possibilities of using sound in them. You can attach them to documents in much the same way as audio notes, providing the application accepts them. Particularly when your QuickTime movie is a Mac-generated animated clip, you want to use sound effects and voice-over narration to get your point across. Many collections of *clip sounds,* the audio equivalent of clip art, are available for this purpose, both commercially and as shareware.

Customizing Your Mac with Sounds

The standard System from Apple provides a choice of a handful of standard Alert Sounds—the familiar Boing, Clink-clank, Quack, and other sounds available on the Sound Control Panel. They can become boring after awhile but, fortunately, you can change them and also add new sounds.

Changing the Alert Sound

To change the Alert sound, follow these steps:

1. Open the Apple menu and choose Control Panels, and from the submenu choose Sound.

2. Click the sounds in the Sound list box. You will hear the sound through the Mac's speaker.

3. When you have selected the sound you want to use as the Alert sound, click it before closing the Sound control panel.

III

Customizing Your Mac

Adding Sounds

To access the sound recording capability, first open the Apple menu and select Control Panels; then select Sound from the sub-menu. You see the Sound control panel open (see fig. 13.1).

Fig. 13.1
The Sound control panel.

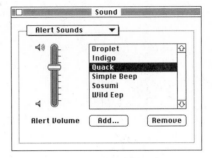

If your Macintosh can record new sounds, click the Sound In selection from the pop-up menu. If your Macintosh is equipped with recording equipment, you see sound sources displayed in the window. Choose one by clicking its icon.

Note that the Options button allows selection of a sound source. Other sound recording equipment may provide options that you can set (see the equipment manual).

The Sound Out selection on the drop-down list allows the user to select a playback device for sounds. The user may choose between mono and stereo, and select either 8-bit or 16-bit playback. The Rate drop-down list allows selection of playback frequency rate.

The volumes selection on the drop-down list allows playback levels to be set. Mute check boxes allow muting of playback devices without disturbing preset levels.

To add sounds to the Alert Sounds list box, follow these steps:

1. Click the Add button.

2. Place the microphone close to the source of the sound.

> **Note**
>
> If you are using a sound source other than the built-in microphone, step 2 may not apply.

3. Click the Record button.

You see the seconds timer "thermometer" begin to fill as the sound length indicator counts upward. This indicates that sound is being recorded. At the bottom of the timer, a number of seconds indicates the amount of time you have for the sound.

4. Click the Stop button.

To hear the sound and verify whether it was recorded correctly, click the Play button. If the sound is not to your liking, you can record another by repeating steps 3 and 4.

5. Click the Save button.

You are prompted to name the sound.

6. Type a name, and then click the Save button.

The sound is added to the Alert Sounds list box. You can select it by clicking it.

As you may have noticed, the buttons of the dialog act like those on a typical tape recorder. You may already understand that clicking the Pause button stops the recording temporarily. Click the Record or Pause button to proceed with the recording.

Click the Stop button to stop the recording. Unlike the Pause button, however, when you next click the Record button, the sound is lost and a new one recorded.

Removing Sounds

Removing a sound from the Alert Sounds list box is quite simple. Follow these steps:

1. Open the Sounds control panel.

2. Click the sound to delete.

3. Click the Remove button.

A dialog appears, asking you to confirm the deletion.

4. Click the OK button or press Return.

Sound Shareware

Apple's Sound control panel is useful, yet limited. To add more interesting sounds to your system try some of the shareware programs, such as the following:

- SoundStudio Lite allows recording and playback of sounds in many formats. Features include Drag and Drop playback and the ability to store a sound as a suitcase inside a HyperCard stack. The shareware registration fee is $10.

- SoundMaster enables the user to assign sounds to events, key strokes, and menu choices. Both playback frequency and sound level may be preset. SoundMaster may be registered for $15.

Kaboom!

An intriguing audio application is Kaboom! by Nova Development. It allows you to add sound effects to every Finder command and change your System beeps. It comes with a large library of digitized sound effects (see fig. 13.2), and you can record your own. For example, it will play the sound of trash cans rattling, flies buzzing, or a toilet flushing every time you empty the Trash.

Fig. 13.2
Add interesting sound effects to your Finder commands with Kaboom!.

Its sound recording and editing capabilities are similar to those on the old standby, MacRecorder. It also saves sound files in nearly every currently used format. That allows you to add recorded sounds to multimedia presentations, QuickTime movies, and custom applications.

Table 9.1 Typical Mac Sound File Formats	
Format	**Description**
FSSD	A standard sound file format recognized by most Mac sound editing applications.
System 7	The sound equivalent of fonts, these 8-bit samples are used for System beeps and similar functions.
AIFF	Audio Interchange File Format, another format recognized by most sound editors.
Movie	The sound track portion of a QuickTime movie can store digitized sounds.

The AV Macs

The Quadra AV Macs opened a new door for using both audio and video on the Mac. With an AT&T 3210 Digital Signal Processing (DSP) chip, some modifications in the hardware, and appropriate System software, these Macs essentially became hard disk-based digital recorders with performance equal to CDs (16-bit quantization, 44.1 kHz sampling rate).

Can you make your own CDs on the Mac? Well—yes and no. First of all, the typical optical disk drives do not use the CD format. Most of them use Write Once Read Many (WORM) technology, and a data format optimized for storing and retrieving database, word processor, and spreadsheet files quickly. A CD drive must read the data at exactly the right rate to re-create the sound. That's why CD-ROM drives have notoriously slow data access rates. In addition, the file format is optimized for the continuous stream of data that is in a digital audio file. Recently, some optical disc drives that record in the CD format have been introduced, but they are relatively expensive.

Storing CD-quality digital audio on a hard disk requires a high-capacity drive. If you want to edit or back up digital audio, you need more drives. You also need a Fast and Wide SCSI-2 interface to handle the vast amounts of data. To record 60 minutes of stereo, for example, you need a one gigabyte drive.

Suddenly that monster 500MB internal drive on your new Mac becomes rather puny. At least it will store your System Folder and a few applications. Editing means you must have someplace to store the results, namely another high capacity hard disk. If you have a great deal of material to edit, you will need more high capacity hard disks to make it instantly available.

III

Customizing Your Mac

The high-end disk-based editing systems in recording studios generally have a bank of high-capacity, high-speed disk drives connected to them. But if you are working with relatively short projects (such as radio spots and jingles, individual songs, and audio for short slide shows, training tapes, or store demos), you can work on a 250 or 500MB drive comfortably.

Other capabilities of the AV Macs include integration of phone, answering machine, voice mail, and fax so that you can use all of these capabilities without leaving your Mac. Speech recognition (*PlainTalk*) joins speech synthesis on the AV machines. With PlainTalk, you can implement voice control by means of third-party software. Also, Jabra has developed a PlainTalk-based application that will transcribe your verbal thoughts into word processor text. Don't get too excited. Right now, speech recognition works about as well as the early OCR software, so your spelling checker will get a healthy workout. For circumstances in which only short segments with a limited vocabulary are needed, however, current PlainTalk applications offer a solution.

Sound Assistance for the Handicapped

In addition to the audio feedback portion of the Mac Operating System, the game sounds, and all the musical capabilities, the Mac's sound can be greatly helpful to people with various types of physical disabilities. Clearly, voice control has applications for those who are not able to operate the keyboard. Speech synthesis can help those with impaired vision by reading aloud text that appears on-screen.

Voyager has published many books in Mac form for people who want to read them on-screen (such as during a plane flight), or analyze the text with word processing tools. With speech synthesis, the Mac can read them aloud. A library of such books is available from Voyager.

Speech synthesis also increases the effectiveness of educational software, especially for pre-schoolers. For speech impaired people, voice synthesis can help with the process of communicating with other people. Stephen Hawking, the astronomer and theoretical physicist, uses such a device to overcome his speech impairment. On the AV Macs, speech recognition helps many people who are unable to type at the keyboard to enter data.

What's appropriate varies with the individual you are helping. Remember that these sound assistance capabilities are an integral part of every Mac ever made. With some imagination and a little custom programming, you can implement them. Developments in this field often find their way back to the main portion of the market because non-handicapped people find them useful, too.

Mysteries of MIDI

As computer-controlled synthesizers began to gain popularity, the need to standardize the methods of controlling them became evident. Each manufacturer had its own system, none of them compatible with any others. No brand of synthesizer could exchange signals with any other brand. The lack of an industry-wide standard was slowing the growth of the industry and creating nightmares for both manufacturers and musicians. That was in the heyday of the Apple II—before the Mac existed.

According to legend, three engineers met during the June, 1981 NAMM (National Association of Musical Merchants) Show and tried to find common ground. Dave Smith of Sequential Circuits, I. Kakehashi of Roland, and Tom Oberheim of Oberheim Electronics developed the basic concepts. After the meeting, Smith actually wrote out the framework for the standard and presented it at the AES (Audio Engineering Society) Convention in November. At the January, 1982 NAMM Show, the ball was rolling. Seeing the convenience of a cross-brand interface, many other manufacturers joined in. They extended and modified the system, seeking to accommodate the needs of all manufacturers without making it overly complex. At the June, 1982 NAMM Show, the manufacturers met and approved the standard, giving it the name *Musical Instrument Digital Interface* (MIDI). During the following NAMM Show in January, 1983, several companies demonstrated MIDI-equipped synthesizers, and the rest is history. In 1984, the industry established an organization called the MIDI Manufacturers Association to oversee the standard and approve changes.

Over the years, the MIDI standard has been improved and tightened in various ways—and it has become the only standard in the industry. Nothing else has been proposed to compete with it. Nonetheless, MIDI is not perfect, and better systems will replace it in the future (a MIDI-2 version is still under discussion).

How MIDI Works

In the simplest, most basic terms, MIDI represents a musical performance with a sequence of numbers (computer data). MIDI records data about the setting of nearly every button, knob, foot pedal, and control wheel on any synthesizer. MIDI does not carry digital audio data, but deals with the control data needed to re-create that sound. A digital recorder, on the other hand, samples the actual sound, stores the data, and reproduces the original sound. The distinction is important.

With MIDI, you can replay a fresh performance each time, rather than a recorded representation of it. That means you can alter that performance in many significant ways on every playback. You can request faster or slower tempos, transposition to other keys, or changes in the instrumentation. You can think of MIDI as an electronic version of a player piano. It uses the ones and zeros of computer language instead of the punched holes in a piano roll to represent information about which notes to play, when to play them, and how long to play them. MIDI, like the reproducing piano, goes further and stores information about expression (tempo variations and dynamic changes, for example) to provide an accurate re-creation of a performance.

Another way to look at MIDI is as a digital extension of the old principle of voltage control in analog synthesizers. To play a series of notes (change the frequency of an oscillator), MIDI sends a digital signal that tunes the oscillator to frequency number 86, 187, and 255. To reduce the volume, it sends a signal that changes the output amplifier from volume level 139 to volume level 64. Just repeat this process for every control on your synthesizer, and you will have a flexible, expandable system. Since MIDI is an 8-bit system, it has 256 steps available for each control (numbered, in computer fashion, from 0 to 255). If you keep sending out the signals often enough, the system will be able to keep up with the flow of the music. The original MIDI specifications called for four MIDI clock pulses per quarter note. Many of the high-end sequencer applications now offer much greater resolution.

MIDI Hardware

To send the signals, MIDI uses serial communications protocols. The wiring used in MIDI systems consists of common off-the-shelf (inexpensive) parts. The connector is a five-pin DIN connector. They're widely used in Europe for hi-fi system connections. In the US, we use them for various special purpose equipment, such as MIDI, because the connectors prevent us from connecting MIDI outputs to analog audio inputs with RCA connectors, causing equipment damage. In a typical MIDI system, with audio, computer, power, and MIDI cables running all over the place, making this distinction about signal types by means of connector types simplifies things. At present, MIDI uses only pins 4 and 5 for signal, and pin 2 for ground. The other two pins are available for expanding the MIDI format in the future.

The MIDI cable is ordinary, twisted-pair shielded cable, commonly available and relatively inexpensive. In fact, LocalTalk cable for your Mac is also twisted-pair shielded cable. A MIDI cable always has a male DIN connector on each end. The female connectors reside on the equipment. The shielding (wire mesh wrapped around the twisted pair) reduces the possibility of picking up extraneous signals, or Radio Frequency Interference (RFI).

To some degree, every wire acts as a radio antenna and can pick up interference from nearby radio transmitters (usually CBs, taxis, police cars). Your cables also can pick up hum from light dimmers, power transformers, and similar sources. Look for MIDI cables with "industrial strength" construction and strain relief on the connectors.

Don't hesitate to replace faulty cables. Always handle them with care, especially during set-up and dismantling. Yanking the plugs out pulls the shielding loose from the ground pin on the connector, leaving the cable wide open to RFI. Also, winding cables tightly into a neat package and tucking the ends in can stress the shielding not only in the middle of the cable, but also at the connectors.

MIDI-to-Mac Interface

Every Macintosh needs a MIDI adapter to connect it to a synthesizer. This device connects to one of your serial ports (Printer or Modem) and provides the electrical interface between the computer and the MIDI system. It has three connectors, labeled In, Out, and Thru. A MIDI interface box serves the same function as a LocalTalk adapter but operates at a different voltage. Simple, basic MIDI adapters usually cost under $100, and you can get them from Apple and many other vendors. A slightly more elaborate version, called a *MIDI Thru Box*, has several Thru ports.

If you have a large and complex MIDI system, you might want to consider an intelligent MIDI interface. The difference is that it contains its own microprocessor. A smart MIDI interface can generate its own clock signals and keep the entire system synchronized more effectively than a basic MIDI adapter can. In addition, microprocessor-equipped MIDI interfaces usually offer SMPTE (Society of Motion Picture and Television Engineers) Time Code, the industry-standard format for synchronizing multiple audio, video, and film devices. Apple does not make an intelligent MIDI interface, but such interfaces are available from Opcode, Mark of the Unicorn, and other companies.

MIDI Connections

Connecting your Mac to a single MIDI instrument is simple. Plug the MIDI interface into the Modem or Printer port. Take a MIDI cable, plug one end into the Out connector on the interface and the other end into the In connector on your instrument. That permits MIDI data to travel from the Mac to the instrument. So far, so good. If you need to send data back to the Mac, you need to connect the Out port on the synthesizer to the In port on the interface. Some MIDI instruments don't have an Out port. The reason for sending data back to the Mac is to record what you've played on your instrument

III

Customizing Your Mac

with sequencer software. That's the quickest way to enter musical information into your computer.

If you have more than two MIDI devices (the Mac with its adapter counts as one of them), you have more choices to make. In most cases, you will want a daisy chain connection, using the Thru ports, instead of the Out ports. Because the MIDI Out port only sends output data from that unit's microprocessor, you won't be able to control the other synthesizers in the chain from the first one (the Mac). The Thru port copies the control signals the unit is receiving from the Mac, adds the output data from that instrument, and passes them on so the next unit can use them. That's generally what you want to be able to do.

You can daisy chain as many instruments as you want, subject to some practical limitations. Some instruments route the signal through the microprocessor before copying it and passing it on to the Thru port. This delays the signal slightly. The more times this happens, the longer the delay. After passing through about four or five such Thru ports, the signal is so late arriving at the next synthesizer that you can hear the delay. It sounds like everyone's playing off the beat, and it's quite objectionable. Some instruments have a non-delaying Thru port, enabling you to build long daisy chains. Check the owner's manual to find out.

Still another configuration is the star network, which requires a smart interface, or *Thru Box*. The Thru Box provides many Thru ports and sends identical copies of the signal, all synchronized in time, to each of its Thru ports to ensure that all instruments are playing at exactly the same time.

MIDI Data Structure

To understand how to use your MIDI chain, you need to know some things about the data packages being sent around the network and their structure. MIDI is an 8-bit system, which means that it can express 2^8 or 256 values for each aspect of the music it is describing. It transmits those numbers serially (one at a time, in rapid succession).

MIDI uses two types of bytes: Status Bytes and Data Bytes. Every MIDI message begins with the Status Byte and is followed by one or two data bytes (depending on what is needed). The Status Byte tells the receiving unit what control the following data will affect. It could be a Note On message, or the setting of a foot pedal, or a change in a patch. The microprocessor in the synthesizer sorts it all out and sends each signal to the proper device. Because it all takes place at a rapid rate, everything fits together and the synthesizer plays music.

MIDI Channels versus Sequencer Tracks

If you have more than one MIDI instrument, you need a way to send messages to specific devices. For example, certain messages might go to your main synthesizer to play melody and harmony. Others might go to a drum machine. Still others might go to another synthesizer to play the accompaniment and bass line.

How do you make sure that the right data gets to the right unit at the right time? MIDI Channels are the answer. MIDI divides data into two types: *System Messages* (for every device) and *Channel Messages* (for a device tuned to that channel). You can tune each device to receive a different channel, and each one in the chain will respond only to data being sent on that channel. MIDI provides 16 channels, and certain bits carry the channel information.

To route the data from each track on your sequencer to the right place, set each track for the MIDI channel of the instrument that should receive it. Polyphonic synthesizers can receive data from several sequencer tracks.

Of course, you must set each instrument to receive its particular channel(s). MIDI Channel Reception Modes confuse many people, and can cause inexplicable problems when configuring a system for a particular use if you forget this detail. You have a choice of four modes, as described in the following table.

Mode	Channel Reception	Synthesizer Operation
Mode 1	Omni On	Polyphonic
Mode 2	Omni On	Monophonic
Mode 3	Omni Off	Polyphonic
Mode 4	Omni Off	Monophonic

Omni On means that the device responds to messages on all channels. In the Omni Off modes, it responds only to its channel. Both are useful.

Mode 1 (Omni on, polyphonic) works well in most situations and usually is the default setting when you turn on the unit. Because it plays messages sent on any channel, you don't have to worry about what channel to use. In the polyphonic setting, it plays chords and different patches simultaneously, which is the typical way of playing on a synthesizer. If you have a MIDI instrument that refuses to play, set it to Mode 1 and see whether it responds.

Mode 2 restricts the synthesizer to playing one note at a time, on any channel. You probably won't use Mode 2 except on rare occasions.

Mode 3 (Omni off, polyphonic) is the setting you want when you are using sequencer software. It allows you to play chords and multiple patches but receives only on a designated channel. Sequencer software usually provides 16 tracks, imitating on-screen the multi-channel tape recorders used in studios. Thus, you can "record" a saxophone on track/channel 1, a trombone on track/channel 2, and so on. If you have a polytimbral synthesizer, you can set each patch to respond to a different channel. In this case, one synthesizer could handle both the saxophone and trombone parts simultaneously.

Mode 4 works with polytimbral synthesizers, turning them into a group of monophonic instruments. In the preceding example, the instrument could play the saxophone and trombone parts but not at the same time. That can be useful when you have many polytimbral synthesizers in the chain and want to use complex patches for each sound.

MIDI assigns Messages to two main categories: Channel Messages, which apply only to that channel, and System Messages, which apply to all devices, without regard to channel. A special case, the System Exclusive Message (SYSEX), applies to a particular brand and model of MIDI instrument (i. e. Yamaha DX-7, or Casio CZ-101). It operates effects unique to that device (the features that induced you to choose it over other brands). The End Of Exclusive (EOX) Message signals the end of a SYSEX. The following table shows the various types of MIDI Messages.

Sound and Music Software

Two major classes of software are available. One of them allows you to record and edit digital audio. This software deals with actual sound samples. At the high end, this software turns your Mac into a multi-track recording studio. At the low end, it behaves more like an ordinary stereo tape recorder with some digital editing capabilities thrown in. The other class of software allows you to work with MIDI data, but not actual sound. These MIDI sequencer applications operate MIDI synthesizers to produce sound. Most sequencer software uses the on-screen metaphor of a multi-track tape deck, but they only record and play back MIDI data, rather than sound.

The distinction between the two classes of software is becoming blurred because many sequencers now allow you to add digital audio tracks to your MIDI tracks. For example, you can record a vocal on top of a complex MIDI arrangement so that the synthesizers accompany the voice in perfect synchronization. Obviously, you can record acoustical instruments as well as voices and add narration to the musical background of a radio or TV ad. In fact, the distinction becomes even more hazy when you start to look at multimedia software which blends video, MIDI, and digital audio.

Some other types of musical software don't quite fit into these categories. One valuable addition to any Mac-based musical system is a *patch editor/ librarian.* With one of these devices, you can create and edit the patches (instrument definitions) on your synthesizer. With these devices, you can work on a larger, more legible screen and have a dedicated database manager to store and retrieve patches.

Automatic composition and accompaniment programs appeal to many users. Some, such as *Band-in-a-Box* and *Jam,* play chords and bass lines with the stereotypical accompaniment figures of a waltz, march, blues, and so on (see fig. 13.3). Others, such as M and Max, will create complex musical structures similar to the visual process of a kaleidoscope (see fig. 13.4). Finally, some applications can teach you to play an instrument and tutor you on music theory.

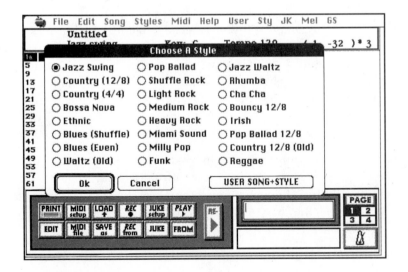

Fig. 13.3
Choosing a Style in Band-in-a-Box.

Fig. 13.4

M creates complex musical structures.

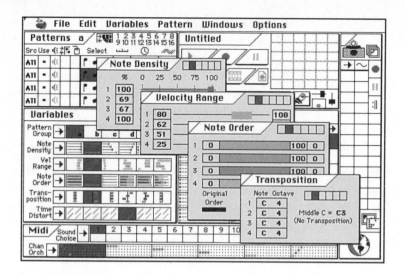

Evaluating MIDI Sequencers and Notation Applications

Musicians fight a constant battle against computer programmers. Music and programming are both complicated fields, filled with technical terms and unique methods of doing things that are difficult for outsiders to penetrate. As a result, the early music applications for personal computers generally did not work well for musicians.

If you wanted to use music software, you had to put up with its shortcomings. Often, programmers would ignore the niceties of musical notation, and musicians would turn away in disgust. Separate eighth or sixteenth notes with individual flags might be the easy solution for the programmer's problems, but they don't convey the same meaning that groups of eighth or sixteenth notes with beams instead of flags convey to a musician. A two-staff piano score is not the same as a 20-staff big band chart or orchestral score.

Programmers made similar mistakes in desktop publishing by using the term *font* for *typeface,* because they didn't take the time to learn enough about the typesetting industry. Although music software developers were slow to recognize this problem, they have learned and changed over the years.

The major applications now at least don't offend musicians. Nonetheless, music software as a category remains difficult to use. The distinction between computer software for music and a musical application running on a computer is extremely significant. The best single piece of advice is to try several brands before you buy one. Their human interfaces are different, and what works for you might not work for someone else.

Putting Music into the Mac

Entering musical data poses many problems. No one has found an easy way to do it. One solution has been to place a piano-like keyboard across the bottom of the screen. To enter notes, you simply click them, and they appear on the staff. That works for selecting pitches. Now what do you do about durations and rhythms? Dotted notes? Triplets? Usually, a palette of note values takes care of that. The downside is that you must constantly move back and forth between selecting a pitch value and a rhythmic value. It's slow. And if you're in the white heat of inspiration, it can kill the creative impulse. This approach works best when you're transcribing existing music into computer format.

The other popular method of inputting music is to record MIDI data into a sequencer application. Just play on your synthesizer, let the computer record all the MIDI data it produces, and you're done. You've captured all the notes, all the rhythms, and most of the nuances of expression.

This method seems like the ideal solution, but it has its own set of disadvantages. First of all, it will record what you play with too much rhythmic precision. When you try to translate the MIDI data into musical notation, you find that none of the notes you played fell exactly on the beat. As a result, the notation looks crazy—slightly syncopated 16th and 32nd notes tied across beats and bar lines in an overly precise attempt to capture the notes precisely as you played them. Four equal quarter notes will all have slightly different durations, because you played them that way. The notated music is nearly unreadable and unplayable in that form.

The old generation of minicomputer-based synthesizers (such as the Synclavier, and Fairlight) were plagued by this problem. Most sequencer software now includes an algorithm to average out the duration values and put them squarely on the beat and its subdivisions, with some latitude for expression. The term for this is *quantization,* but it is not the same as the quantization process that a digital sampler uses. It's the same word, but with completely different meanings.

People who have traditional musical training become frustrated with the avoidance of musical notation that results from this method of entry. Passport, in *Master Tracks,* used a workaround kind of bar chart notation. It shows pitch levels on the vertical axis, and durations as horizontal bars. For many people, this is more than sufficient. For others, it's not especially helpful.

The problem comes when you're trying to correct wrong notes or otherwise improve your MIDI sequence. Just where on this chart is that E flat 16th note in the third beat that should have been an E natural? You can find it, but not as easily as on a musical staff. Over time, learning this alternative notation scheme is not too difficult, but initially you must put forth some effort to learn it.

Coda addressed this problem with *Finale*. It allows you to enter notes on-screen in musical notation and hear them played back through MIDI synthesizers. Or you can play it on a keyboard, quantize it, and edit the resulting notation, which is about the best compromise available so far. Some sequencer applications are now more like integrated office applications. Instead of combining word processing, spreadsheet, and database applications, they combine sequencing, notation, and patch editing applications under one roof. Others offer separate applications that can talk to each other. Separate applications can be less expensive than integrated types, and require less RAM and processor speed. Integrated applications typically cost more and require more computing power. Opcode extended the integration process with its *Studio Vision* sequencer. It allows you to record digital audio tracks along with the tracks containing MIDI data. Others have followed suit, but it remains a rather specialized capability, and requires a sound card with a DSP chip.

Two new solutions to the note entry problem are on the horizon. The *Nightingale* notation application works with an optional scanner to input music. It's something like OCR (Optical Character Recognition) for music, which means that you could write it out on paper and scan it into the computer, where the software converts it to notation and MIDI data. The other possibility, though no company has discussed introducing such an application, would be to use something like the handwriting recognition on the Newton to convert notation into MIDI data.

Evaluating Notation Software

Printing music requires complex software. Entry-level software simply makes a screen dump of the graphics. More advanced applications use PostScript symbols and offer page layout capabilities comparable to *PageMaker* and *XPress*. In fact, because of the intricacies of musical notation, music printing applications become even more complex than ordinary layout applications.

The first solution was to use screen dumps, but bitmapped printouts for music look dreadful. Developers saw the need for a PostScript music typeface, and the Sonata font was introduced. Since then, many developers have created their own music fonts, both in PostScript and TrueType formats. The ability to change the size of the characters without losing resolution makes them ideal for musical notation.

Obviously, you need a PostScript or TrueType compatible laser printer—even the least expensive models—for printing music with the clarity needed. Inkjet and dot matrix printers are totally unsuitable.

Some music printing software can extract parts from a full score, which is a wonderful time-saving convenience. Look for the capability to transpose from scores in C (all instruments written in concert pitch) to the correct key for each instrument (Trumpet in B flat, Clarinet in A, Horn in F, and so on).

If you are writing for instruments with unusual notation requirements (lute and guitar, harp, and most percussion instruments), be sure that the software will accommodate them. Also, if you're writing vocal music, you must be able to type in the words in precisely the right locations under the notes. Complete flexibility with fonts, point sizes, and typestyles, along with hyphenation and positioning, are crucial. Some applications generate the *lead sheets* used in popular music. These have the melody and words only, but all the chords are indicated both in shorthand chord notation (C dim 7, A min) and in guitar tablature. Trying to print lead sheets with software lacking this specific capability can be frustrating.

For those who are working with non-traditional notation (mostly classical and jazz composers), the only answer is to create scores with graphics applications (CAD software, with your own custom library of symbols, would be a good approach).

Copy Protection

Copy protection can become a problem for many musicians, particularly if you are frequently performing outside your studio. Regrettably, the music software industry has been one of the more stubborn holdouts, and copy protected software is still common. In their defense, they do get ripped off by musicians who give copies to others. Music is a niche market, and the universe of potential purchasers is not as large as for word processing software. That leads to higher prices to recover development costs, which leads to more people stealing software. Look at it this way. If you write music, sell copies, and someone starts giving it away, you're not getting paid for your work. In that respect, software development and musical composition are quite similar.

What's aggravating to musicians about copy protection is that it frequently conflicts with System extensions to cause system crashes. No one wants to reboot in the middle of a performance!

The best solution is to use a specially tailored version of the System for music, especially for live performances. Strip out all but the most essential Extensions, virus protection, and other utilities and you can avoid most of the problems. Another aspect of copy protection is portability from one Mac to another. Even though you are using only one copy, you might want to transfer it from the Quadra 840 AV in your studio to a PowerBook, LC, Performa, or some other more portable Mac for use in a live performance. Or you might need to take it with you to do some sweetening at a recording studio. Shop carefully, and at least know the practical limitations imposed by any given copy protection scheme before you buy the software.

Shopping for Musical Software

First, you must decide whether you are a low-end or high-end user, because that affects what stores you are going to visit. The best known low-end sequencer is *Deluxe Music Construction Set* from Electronic Arts. Almost any software boutique, computer store, or mail order catalog that sells computer games and other educational and entertainment software carries it, or something similar. Many people find this kind of software truly liberating and don't need or want anything more sophisticated.

It's like the difference between an entry level paint program and an advanced PostScript illustration application. Without the knowledge and training in art, the latter becomes too difficult to learn and use. On the other hand, a Picasso or a Rembrandt could create a masterpiece with a basic paint program. Typically, low-end sequencers will play music on the Mac's built-in synthesizer chip, and will drive a MIDI synthesizer (although they might not operate all its functions).

For serious MIDI work, you will want something like *Master Tracks, Performer, Vision,* or *Cubase.* Many computer stores don't sell them (the market is too small), so you will have to visit a musical instrument store that carries both MIDI hardware and software or buy it through a catalog. Also, the professional audio dealers that sell studio-grade digital audio equipment often sell MIDI software. If you have difficulty locating musical applications, call the publishers, and they should be able to recommend dealers in your area or sell to you directly.

Generally speaking, you can get the lowest price on computer gear through a mail order or discount dealer. Because of the specialized nature of musical applications, however, this can become dangerous to your sanity—as well as expensive. You might pay more through a retail dealer than mail order, but you will also get the benefit of some advice on what's best for your needs and will be able to see it in actual operation. Spending $100 more to get the right software can be less expensive than throwing $500 away on something that you don't like or can't use, and having to spend still more to get what you want.

Some other ways to find friendly advice—join one of the user groups in music, or sign up for on-line services with music bulletin boards and conferences. For the really high-end products (Sonic Solutions and Digidesign), you will need to talk with a dealer in professional audio equipment who specializes in computer music. Call the manufacturers and ask for the names of dealers near you.

A new wrinkle in software marketing is the try-it-before-you-buy-it CD-ROM. The disc comes loaded with demo versions of all the software the company sells. You can try it out and determine whether it's the right software. When you're ready to buy a full working version, you call an 800 number, pay for the software, and receive an access code that unlocks the full working version. For several years, this technique has worked well for CD-ROMs stuffed with fonts (Adobe Type on Call), and now is beginning to enter the larger market (Instant Access and Software Access). The prices often are slightly lower than traditional catalog mail order prices.

Survey: Music Software

This brief survey of the most widely known musical applications will introduce you to the range and variety of products available. The following list is not complete but covers most of the popular products. In sequencer software with digital audio, the primary category, the major products are Cubase, Digital Performer, and Studio Vision. Computer music is a niche market, but it is also a fast-moving market. As with trends and fads in popular musical styles, some computer music products change quickly (they must in order to make the latest, hottest sounds), but others don't change much at all. Read the magazines aimed at the computer music market; the major Mac magazines focus their attention on business products, and most music and sound manufacturers don't even advertise in them. Program prices are provided when available.

Band-in-a-Box
$59 SRP Standard Edition (24 Styles)
$88 SRP Pro Version (75 Styles)

III

Customizing Your Mac

PG Music, Inc.
266 Elmwood Avenue, Suite 111
Buffalo, NY 14222
905-528-2368 Voice
905-628-2541 Fax

If you remember the accompaniment boxes that piano and organ players used to use to accompany themselves, you know what *Band-in-a-Box* can do. It automatically generates the other members of a small combo (bass, drums, piano, guitar, and strings), using any of the various styles (Jazz Swing, Bossa, Country, Blues Shuffle, and so on). Just enter the chords for a particular song into the lead sheet-style screen, set the key and tempo, and play along. It's also great for practicing alone when the rest of the band can't make it.

ConcertWare Pro
$339.95 SRP

Great Wave Software
5353 Scotts Valley Drive
Scotts Valley, CA 95066
408-438-1990 Voice
408-438-7171 Fax

ConcertWare started life as a simple music program for kids, but now has evolved into a full-fledged notation application. If you have a MIDI instrument, it will transcribe your playing into musical notation (and of course play it back for you). Notation and printing capabilities include guitar and percussion notation, automatic beaming, text insertion, and up to 32 staves.

Cubase Audio 2.0
$995.00 SRP

Steinberg
17700 Raymer Street, Suite 101
Northridge, CA 91325
818-993-4091 Voice
818-701-7452 Fax

Cubase Audio integrates a MIDI sequencer, score printing, and digital audio recording into a powerful high-end package. It features a flexible quantization algorithm with six different methods. You can edit on a bar chart or in musical notation, and a list edit window lets you assemble pieces of the music in the right order. Cubase also provides a drum editor, MIDI mixer, score printing, wave form editor, and the ability to add digital audio tracks to the MIDI tracks. For digital audio, it supports the Digidesign Audiomedia sound cards.

Cubase Lite
$149.00 SRP

Steinberg
17700 Raymer Street, Suite 101
Northridge, CA 91325

Cubase Lite, the low-end version of Cubase Audio, offers sequencing and notation but lacks the digital audio capabilities of its big brother. Cubase Lite works with MIDI instruments but not with the Audiomedia cards. Simpler to learn and to use, Cubase Lite is intended for musicians who don't want or need all the professional level functions.

Deluxe Music Construction Set
$129 SRP

Electronic Arts
1450 Fashion Island Boulevard
San Mateo, CA 94404
415-571-7171 Voice

One of the earliest music applications for the Mac, *Deluxe Music Construction Set* uses the built-in synthesizer chip to create sound. It even runs on a 512 K Mac. You can enter notes by selecting them from a note palette and dragging them onto the staff or by selecting them from an on-screen keyboard. It offers 26 pre-defined instrument sounds and an editor for creating your own sounds. It's fun and a great introduction to music on the Mac.

Digital Performer 1.4
$895 SRP

Mark of the Unicorn
1280 Massachusetts Avenue
Cambridge, MA 02138
617-576-2760 Voice
617-576-3609 Fax

Performer was one of the first serious sequencers and has gone through many changes to keep it up to date. It is part of a family of related products (notation, printing, and so on) that talk to each other, although it is not formally an integrated application. Digital Performer adds digital audio capability (with the Audiomedia cards or Mark of the Unicorn Digital Waveboard) to

III

Customizing Your Mac

the MIDI sequencer. See the following description of Performer for other
features.

Edit One
$149.95 SRP per editor

Opcode Systems, Inc.
3950 Fabian Way, Suite 100
Palo Alto, CA 94303
415-856-3333 Voice
415-856-3332 Fax

The *Edit One* library allows you to buy the patch editor unique to your particular instrument(s). That saves the expense of buying patch editors for instruments you don't own. These are the same editors that are in the *Galaxy
Plus* collection.

Encore
$595 SRP

Passport Designs, Inc.
100 Stone Pine Road
Half Moon Bay, CA 94019
415-726-0280 Voice
415-726-2254 Fax

Encore complements Passport's *Master Tracks,* providing notation entry and
music printing and layout. For musicians who are accustomed to writing
music the old-fashioned way (with real notes on a staff), *Encore* provides all
the right tools and layout capabilities to make you feel at home composing
on the computer. When you're finished, you can play it back through a MIDI
instrument or sound card to hear how your music sounds. *Encore* accepts
entry from a MIDI keyboard either by recording a performance in real time or
by the step-entry method (one note at a time from the keyboard). Or you can
select notes from a palette. It includes guitar notation, text insertion, and part
extraction and transposition. *Encore* supports both PostScript and TrueType
music fonts, includes Anastasia and Frets fonts in both formats, and can export EPS files to use in other applications.

EZ Vision
$99.95 SRP

Opcode Systems, Inc.

This entry level sequencer, designed for those who are just getting their feet
wet, is a subset of Opcode's *Vision.* It offers a 16-track MIDI sequencer, mixer,
and graphic editing window (link sections by connecting them graphically).

EZ Vision opens and saves MIDI files, and can export data to notation programs for printing.

Finale 3
$749 SRP

Coda Music Technology
6210 Bury Drive
Eden Prairie, MN 55346
612-937-9511 Voice
612-937-9760 Fax

Finale takes the notation approach to entering musical data, making it comfortable for composers and arrangers with traditional training. You can use a MIDI keyboard or an on-screen note palette for entry and editing. Finale offers many notation flexibilities and user-definable symbols to satisfy the needs of experimental and avant-garde composers. It generates lead sheets, and will extract and print parts from full scores, breaking multi-bar rests at rehearsal marks automatically. Its page layout, text insertion, and music printing functions are second to none. Finale includes special music fonts in both PostScript and TrueType formats. Finale plays back notated music through MIDI instruments.

Finale Allegro
$349 SRP

Coda Music Technology

Finale Allegro is the entry-level version of Finale, with all the essential tools but not the most advanced features. Emphasis on ease of use shortens the learning curve. If you decide to upgrade to its big brother, Finale will convert Allegro files without loss of data.

Galaxy
$149.95 SRP

Opcode Systems, Inc.

Galaxy is a universal patch librarian and editor compatible with over 140 synthesizers. The PatchTalk programming language enables you to create new patches and add them to the library with your own names. You can search on keywords to find them quickly. It supports Publish and Subscribe to make patches available to Opcode's *Vision* sequencer.

Galaxy Plus Editors
$399.95 SRP

Opcode Systems, Inc.

III

Customizing Your Mac

Galaxy Plus Editors enables you to access and modify a patch by clicking its Edit button, regardless of the instrument. Each of the 55 full-featured customized editors supports a particular synthesizer. If you have several brands and models of synthesizers in your system, this simplifies operations. It also supports Publish and Subscribe.

M
$199 SRP

Dr. T's Music Software
124 Crescent Road, Suite 3
Needham, MA 02194
617-455-1454 Voice
617-455-1460 Fax

For the curious and the adventurous, *M* creates musical patterns based on ideas you give it. This interactive composing and performing tool enables you to shape and alter the output while it's working.

Master Tracks Pro 5
$295 SRP

Passport Designs, Inc.

Master Tracks Pro 5 provides the sequencer side of the Passport application suite *(Encore* is the notation side). As its name suggests, *Master Tracks Pro 5* has been around for a long time, so it has been refined and improved considerably over the years. The MIDI sequencer handles up to 64 tracks with automated punch-in and punch-out (for editing tracks on the fly), plus an on-screen mixer. An important function for multimedia is a link from MIDI Time Code to SMPTE Time Code, which allows you to synchronize your MIDI sequence with audio and video tape, or film. You can edit sequences with event lists or graphically. Graphic display for individual controllers and notes simplifies editing.

Max
$395 SRP

Opcode Systems, Inc.

This unique application gives you a high-level graphic programming environment. In other words, with *Max,* you can represent musical events as icons and link them together graphically on-screen. Think of the possibilities for composing and improvising when you can work with sound modules as building blocks for larger structures. Named after Max Matthews, one of the pioneers of digital audio and computer music at Bell Labs, it enables you to create a wide variety of applications. *Max* programs can control synthesizers and other equipment, and generate music based on ideas you give it. It's much more flexible than most of the accompaniment software and is not limited just to accompaniment figures in various styles. If you're skilled in C programming, you can create your own sound-objects and use them in *Max* programs. Custom application developers as well as musicians can benefit from *Max*. It can play tracks from CDs, laser discs, and so on, to create interactive applications.

MiBAC Jazz Improvisation 1.5.8
$125.00 SRP

P.O. Box 468
Northfield, MN 55057
507-645-5851 Voice
507-645-9291 Fax

Similar to *Band-in-a-Box,* this application creates backgrounds and accompaniments. True to its name, it concentrates specifically on jazz improvisation. If you want to learn to improvise in various jazz styles without annoying other players, this is a great way to gain experience. It also prints lead sheets.

Miracle Piano Teaching System
$499.95 SRP

The Software Toolworks
60 Leveroni Court
Novato, CA 94949
415-883-3000 Voice
415-883-3303 Fax

Miracle Piano Teaching System combines an electronic piano with instructional software. Actually, the piano functions as a MIDI synthesizer, with 100 different sounds and a 49-key velocity sensitive keyboard. The software teaches you how to play the piano, and unlike a human teacher, is infinitely patient with your mistakes. For people who want to learn to play a keyboard, this hardware/software bundle offers an inexpensive way of getting started.

Music Mouse
$79 SRP

Dr. T's Music Software

Music Mouse uses the mouse to control one set of parameters vertically, and another horizontally. You can choose different tonal palettes (diatonic, pentatonic, and so on), and different instrumental sounds. You then move the mouse around and listen to the semi-automated sounds it creates for you. It's incredibly easy to play, and a lot of fun—a great way to take a relaxing break from number-crunching or word processing. Music Mouse works with the Mac's internal synthesizer chip or with external MIDI instruments.

Musicshop
$149.95 SRP

Opcode Systems, Inc.

Musicshop adds notation and printing to the sequencer functions of the *EZ Vision* MIDI sequencer.

MusicTime
$249 SRP

Passport Designs, Inc.

MusicTime offers entry-level composing and notation tools. You can enter music on-screen with a note palette, and hear it played back instantly through a MIDI instrument or sound card. You also can record music from a MIDI instrument (real-time or step-time) and let *MusicTime* transcribe it into musical notation. It creates lead sheets and extracts parts from scores.

Nightingale 1.3
$495 SRP

Temporal Acuity Products
300 120th Avenue NE
Building 1, Suite 200
Bellevue, WA 98005
206-462-1007 Voice
206-462-1057 Fax

The *Nightingale* notation program offers many refinements in adjusting symbols. The notes palette contains 86 symbols for note entry. It also accepts entry through MIDI in real-time or step-time mode. For vocal music, it has a Flow In tool that simplifies the process. Nightingale extracts parts and saves them as separate files. The company is developing an intriguing OCR application that converts printed music into notation on-screen.

OvalTune
$79 SRP

Dr. T's Music Software

OvalTune combines automated composition with colorful, changing graphics. It's like a computerized kaleidoscope with sound, providing endless hours of fun. You can record its output and play it back or use it in other applications. *OvalTune* works with MIDI synthesizers or from an included library of sampled sounds.

Performer 4.2
$495 SRP

Mark of the Unicorn

Performer 4.2, the latest version of one of the first sequencers offers all the capabilities of *Digital Performer*, except for the digital audio tracks.

Practica Musica
$125.00 SRP

Ars Nova
206-889-0927 Voice
206-889-0359 Fax

Practica Musica teaches you the basics of music theory. It covers topics such as intervals, chords, scales, keys, and harmonic progressions. It also teaches you how to hear all of these elements of music, with an integrated ear training course. Just like a human instructor, it plays examples of chords and their inversions, so you can learn to recognize them by ear. As the lessons become more complex, you'll learn to identify chords in harmonic progressions. If music theory is a mystery to you, this is the way to learn it on your own.

Rock Rap 'N Roll
$59.95 SRP (Floppy Disc)
$79.95 SRP (CD-ROM)

Paramount Interactive
700 Hansen Way
Palo Alto, CA 94304
415-812-8200 Voice
415-813-8045 Fax

If you want to see what it's like to play in a band, *Rock Rap 'N Roll* will give you a taste of the excitement. Designed for people with absolutely no musical experience, it allows you to select from a large library of sounds, styles, and musical phrases. You'll have the thrill of sitting at the console of an

III

Customizing Your Mac

on-screen recording studio with a multi-track tape recorder as you lay down all the tracks for sax licks, guitar riffs, drum solos, and vocals, then mix them into a stereo format. Go for the CD-ROM version because it has more sounds.

Studio Vision
$995 SRP

Opcode Systems, Inc.

Studio Vision has all the tools of a high-end MIDI sequencer, including the capability to record up to four digital audio tracks. It supports the Digidesign Audiomedia sound card and includes SMPTE Time Code for synchronizing to audio and video tape and film. *Studio Vision* allows you to edit digital audio with Digidesign's editing software. If you're creating radio and TV ads, or multimedia productions, or simply need to add live sounds to your MIDI sequences, *Studio Vision* is widely regarded as one of the best applications available.

TimeBandit 1.5
$495 SRP

Steinberg

TimeBandit performs a variety of useful functions for high-end users. It provides time correction for fitting an audio track into the time length of a slightly longer or shorter video track without changing the pitch. Or, it can raise or lower the pitch of an instrument that was out of tune with the other tracks, but without changing the timing. Another capability is harmonization, or the process of thickening the sound by adding one or more parallel tracks just slightly out of tune (to simulate the effect of a chorus or string section). *TimeBandit* supports AIFF and Sound Designer file formats. It works off-line, because these bits of magic take time to calculate. If you need these utilities, this is one of the few such packages available for the Mac.

Trax
$99.00

Passport Designs, Inc.

Trax, the little brother of *Master Tracks,* uses the same interface, but is simplified for beginners. Trax lacks the advanced capabilities of Master Tracks, but it has enough power to satisfy most home users. This MIDI sequencer handles 64 tracks, with punch-in and punch-out, and an on-screen mixing panel. You can enter notes in real-time or step-time mode, and the editing tools are easy to use.

Unisyn
$395 SRP

Mark of the Unicorn

With *Unisyn,* you can create and edit your synthesizer patches on your Mac screen. The graphic editing tools make the process quick and easy. When used with *Performer,* it works in real-time as sequences play, so you can hear the results as you make changes. *Unisyn* is compatible with 150 synthesizers, both current and older models. The database stores and retrieves thousands of patches, using user-definable keywords.

UpBeat
$199 SRP

Dr. T's Music Software

UpBeat works specifically with drum machines. It simplifies the task of entering percussion patterns, and can record MIDI drum data in real time.

Vision
$495

Opcode Systems, Inc.

Vision offers all the same sequencing features as *Studio Vision,* but lacks the digital audio recording capability.

Survey: Sound Editing and Recording

The applications listed below allow you to work with sound samples, rather than with musical data. You can record sounds, alter various qualities of those sounds, edit and reassemble sounds in various combinations. To use these applications, you must have a Mac with a microphone and digitizing hardware or software, or use external equipment.

Audioshop
$89.95 SRP

Opcode Systems, Inc.

With *Audioshop,* you can record and edit Macintosh audio, using a familiar CD player-like interface. It allows you to edit a wave form with an on-screen window, where you can cut and paste different parts of the sound, just like editing text. It also plays tracks from CDs on a CD-ROM drive, using a playlist. It comes with two disks of sound samples.

Deck II 2.1

$399 SRP

OSC
480 Potrero Avenue
San Francisco, CA 94110
415-252-0460 Voice
415-252-0560 Fax

With *Deck II,* you can turn your Quadra 840 AV into an eight-track digital audio recorder. On the 660 AV, it provides up to six tracks. OSC developed the original software for Digidesign, and now markets its products independently. The original *Deck* recording software required Audiomedia, a NuBus card with a DSP chip to digitize the sound. This new version takes advantage of the DSP chip on the Quadra AV machines. It also works on other Macs with the Audiomedia card, the RasterOps MediaTime card, and the Spectral Innovations NuMedia card. *Deck* allows you to record each of the digital audio tracks independently, or in combination, so you can build up a complete musical structure by adding more sounds. Punch-in and punch-out let you start recording in the middle of a previously recorded track to fix fumbles and wrong notes. With track bouncing, you can mix several tracks down to one or two (all your vocals or all your drum tracks) and then use the newly freed tracks for more sounds. Instant access, non-destructive editing enables you to assemble all the sections of a piece, as well as edit out glitches and bad notes. The mixing panel controls volume and panning for all channels. It supports QuickTime movies, displays live video in a window, and imports MIDI Files.

Hyperprism

Arboretum Systems
P.O. Box 470580
San Francisco, CA 94147
415-931-7720 Voice
415-931-7725 Fax

Hyperprism enables you to design your own sound effects in real time. Start with an effect from its library, and make your own variations graphically on-screen. Hyperprism includes several filters, plus phaser, flanger, delay, ring modulator, and many other effects. It also offers a pitch follower and an envelope follow. It requires the Audiomedia sound card.

Kaboom!

Nova Development
23801 Calabasas Road, Suite 2005
Calabasas, CA 91302
818-591-9600 Voice

Kaboom! enables you to add new and more interesting sounds to your Finder commands. It comes with an extensive library of 8-bit samples. For example, you can have your Mac say "Lucy, I'm home!" instead of chiming at Startup. Or use the *Twilight Zone* theme for closing a file. It also has a nice 8-bit sound editor so that you can record your own samples and use them in QuickTime movies and multimedia presentations, or as Finder additives. You'll need a Mac with a built-in microphone to use the recording feature.

MacRecorder

Macromedia, Inc.
600 Townsend Street
San Fransisco, CA 94103
415-252-2118 Voice

MacRecorder combines an external 8-bit digitizer with sound editing software. Originally sold by Farallon, it is now marketed by Macromedia. It's especially useful with older Macs that lack a built-in microphone, but works with any Mac through a serial port. You'll need a microphone to plug into the digitizer box.

Digital Audio and MIDI Hardware

If you want to work at the CD quality level (16 bits, 44.1 kHz sampling rate), you need a high-end Mac. That includes not only a faster microprocessor chip but also an accelerated SCSI bus and mammoth high-speed hard disk storage capacity. For complex MIDI configurations, you need specialized controllers and may want to look at MIDI-operated special effects generators.

III

Customizing Your Mac

Where to Shop for MIDI Synthesizers and Sound Cards

Be prepared to shop outside the usual computer market. Music and digital audio are specialized markets. Most computer shops don't carry MIDI instruments. Large discount department stores may have acres of synthesizers on display, but none of them will have MIDI capability. To find these instruments, you must go to the musical instrument dealers. The manufacturers generally want dealers who specialize in music or audio equipment for musicians as the retail outlets for their MIDI equipment. The same is true of sound cards for digital audio. Some computer shops may carry sound cards, but you'll get better advice from the musical instrument and professional audio dealers. They'll also carry the software and peripherals that work in MIDI and digital audio systems.

Which Mac Do You Need?

All Macs have built-in sound capabilities, so even an old 512K Mac can run the entry-level software, especially the musical applications intended for preschoolers. Many of the low-end MIDI sequencers and 8-bit sound editors run on a Mac Plus, although you should have more than 1MB of RAM. If you haven't upgraded to System 7, you should do so because more and more software requires it.

The high-end sequencers and 16-bit recording and editing applications generally require at least the speed of a IIci and 8MB of RAM and assume that you are running System 7. Applications at this level generally are over 3MB, and you'll want to switch around from one to another, just as in desktop publishing, where you have large page layout application opens, but may need to have one or more word processors open, along with a few graphics applications.

MIDI Adapters

You'll need a MIDI interface to use a sequencer application. For most people, the simple, basic MIDI interface does enough to get started. As your system becomes more complex, you'll want to look at "smart" MIDI controllers. Also, MIDI Thru Boxes and MIDI Patch Bays provide greater flexibility in connecting MIDI equipment.

If you intend to do intricate multimedia work beyond the level of QuickTime, with several audio and tape decks on line, or transfer audio tracks to film, you need to consider the benefits of SMPTE Time Code. This format, developed by the Society of Motion Picture and Television Engineers puts timing signals on your tapes and film soundtracks, or embeds them in MIDI data.

Its purpose is to synchronize all of your equipment. A good example of the use of SMPTE Time Code is synchronizing dialog with images. Many of the "smart" MIDI interfaces include SMPTE synchronization.

SCSI Accelerators and Sound Cards

For digital audio recording, plan to get as much RAM as you can—massive amounts of data will be moving through your Mac. You will also need more hard disk capacity than you ever believed possible. One hour of stereo at a 44.1 kHz sampling rate with 16-bit quantization occupies 600MB. And you will want to back it up!

Beyond that, you must have drives with an access time of 18 ms or less, plus an accelerated SCSI bus. Some of the recent Macs come equipped with SCSI-2, but you can upgrade older Macs with a SCSI accelerator card, which is required for CD quality digital audio work. Without the Fast SCSI capability, your Mac can't transfer data from the hard disk fast enough to play it back.

In addition to the SCSI accelerator, you must have a digital audio card. Its function is to convert analog signals into digital audio data, and it's normally a NuBus card. It will have at least one DSP chip for this purpose. The Digidesign Audiomedia, Sonic Solutions SSP-3, RasterOps MediaTime, and the Spectral Innovations NuMedia are the common cards. Most of the available software supports one or more of them. A crucial difference between these cards and the DSP chips built into many Intel-based machines is the signal-to-noise ratio. Though a DSP chip may have 16-bit quantization and a 44.1 kHz sampling rate, and may be promoted as having "CD quality," its actual performance may not be good enough for digital audio recording, editing, and mixing. The less expensive models of these chips suffer from interior digital noise that may reduce their signal-to-noise ratio by as much as 10 dB. So, instead of the 90 dB you might expect from a 16-bit chip, you start at 80 dB.

Why is this important? As you bounce tracks in the overdubbing process, the noise starts to build up, just as it does on an analog multi-track recorder. Also, when you mix down 8 or 16 channels, the noise on each track gets added into the stereo mix, reducing the signal-to-noise ratio of your output well below even 80 dB. That's why the software developers require a sound card with a better quality DSP chip, such as the Motorola 56001. The Quadra AV machines use an on-board AT&T 3210 chip, which delivers similar performance.

Selecting Synthesizers

The choice is yours to make. Hundreds of brands and models are available, each one designed to appeal to a different kind of musician and a different set of needs. It's a very personal choice. If you are just beginning to explore the field, don't know what you're doing, and don't want to spend a lot of money on something you don't like—buy a used instrument. Go to your local musical instrument dealer and look for a low-end used MIDI synthesizer. You won't waste your money, because it always will be useful, no matter what other instruments you add to your system. The advantage is that you can learn what you need to know before you buy the synthesizer of your dreams. But don't get paralyzed by indecision. Buy cheap at first, until you know what you really want.

The current trend is away from the old style synthesizers and toward wave table (sampling) synthesizers. Soon the FM synthesizers (like the Yamaha DX-7 and its successors) will be antiques, as strange and out-of-date as a Moog synthesizer seems today. The popular music market pushes for instruments that are quick to adjust during live performances. Changing patches and fiddling with adjustments takes time. What a rock performer wants is a bank of buttons to push. Also, sampling techniques have improved, and the price of memory has dropped, making sampling synthesizers economically practical, and desirable. Today, a typical system would include one or more "black boxes" loaded with samples (many units provide space for user-downloaded samples also), plus a keyboard to control the sample boxes. Throw in some special effects processors, and you have a modern synthesizer system. Some sample boxes (such as Digidesign's Sample Cell) are actually NuBus cards.

Samples do not need to be recordings of actual instruments. They also can be real sounds which have been altered dramatically with special effects software. Samples can originate from true synthesizers, then further altered, shaped, and distorted beyond all recognition. In this way, you can have instant push button access to almost any kind of sound without having to figure out how to create it. The sampling synthesizer has made electronic instruments still easier to play and eliminated the need to learn difficult sound creation techniques. Most members of this new generation of synthesizers don't provide many sound modification possibilities because the samples themselves offer all the variations. You'll find a lot of action in the market in the area of outboard special effects processors, with unique, proprietary sound qualities. It's fast-moving and trendy, reflecting current pop music styles.

Libraries of samples, many on CD-ROMs, are on the shelves at the musical instrument dealers. In a sense, samples on a synthesizer now behave like fonts on a laser printer. Creating a sample has become a specialized skill, similar to creating a typeface. To do it well requires knowledge and skill, plus specialized hardware and software. On the other hand, the sound quality of synthesizers is improving considerably, and so is their ease of playing.

Keyboard, Wind, and String Controllers

The keyboard itself becomes an important aspect of the instrument, particularly for those who learned to play on an acoustic piano. The feedback of the size, weight, and mechanical resistance of the keys makes a great deal of difference to some people, and practically none at all to others. In addition, to achieve full use of the MIDI system's expressive capabilities, you may want a keyboard with advanced features. Velocity sensitive keys send MIDI data about how hard you pressed them (that is how loud you played that note). Aftertouch creates data about the way you released the key. Some even have pressure sensitivity for creating effects like vibrato. Thus, having a single master controller keyboard makes sense. Often, they have no sound generating capabilities, but simply control other instruments. Put all your money into one high-end keyboard, and play your other synthesizers with it through MIDI, instead of buying expensive keyboards on all of them.

Alternative controllers, designed for string and wind players also have their attractions. They are less common than they were a few years ago, but check the used equipment market. The IWI (Intelligent Wind Instrument), marketed by Akai was one of the first on the market. Yamaha followed with their WX-11 MIDI Wind Controller. Guitar synthesizers are available, and you can even find MIDI violins and cellos.

No matter what you choose as the ultimate instrument of your dreams, pay attention to the operating controls as well as the feel of the keyboard. Tiny LCD screens that deliver cryptic information don't make the synthesizer fun to play. Banks of buttons smaller than your fingertip and too close together with labels too small to read cause nothing but mistakes during performance. Be sure that the human interface makes your job as a player as easy as possible.

Hard Disk-Based Recording

Storing digital audio data on a hard disk instead of on tape has truly revolutionized the audio industry in many ways. It has all the advantages of digital audio in general (low noise and distortion, the ability to make an exact copy, and greater accuracy in editing). In addition, it has the inherent advantage of

III

Customizing Your Mac

disk over tape—nearly instant access to any point in the recording, which makes editing faster. Because all the operations are taking place on a desktop computer, software can perform all of the equalization, compression, mixing, and special effects generation that formerly required an elaborate collection of equipment in a recording studio. That implies one more benefit, which is truly remarkable. Editing digital audio becomes as easy as editing a word processing document. You can make changes without destroying the original, or any intermediate steps. You can listen to an edit before you commit to it, or even audition several edits before selecting the one that sounds best.

If you've ever edited analog tapes with a razor blade and splicing tape, you know all about the dangers of cutting into a master tape (in analog, you can't work with a copy because of the added noise). Finding the exact location isn't easy. Cut the wrong place and you can destroy the tape. If the performer doesn't like the exact way you carried out an edit, changing it is difficult, and sometimes impossible.

In digital editing, you can specify where the edit takes place, down to the sample (44,100 of them per second). You can tell the computer to connect Point A to Point D or Point Z without altering your original recording. Also, you can tell the computer to fade in the beginning of Segment 224 while it's fading out the end of Segment 86 (cross-fading), and specify how long the cross-fade should last. That's not possible with razor blade editing. In fact, you can assemble a finished production by making a list of all the segments you want to use, in the order you need them, and ask the computer to play it back for you as a continuous piece. Since all the data is on the hard disk, the software simply reads the appropriate sectors. That alone has changed the way film and video production are being done.

Survey of Hardware

For recording 16-bit digital audio on most Macs, you need a sound card to convert the analog signal from the microphone into a digital signal, and convert the digital signal back to analog form for playback. The AV Macs have this capability built into them. For advanced MIDI work, such as synchronizing with film, video, or other external equipment, you need special equipment described in this section.

Integrated Hardware and Software Systems
Session 8

Digidesign
1360 Willow Road

Menlo Park, CA 94025
415-688-0600 Voice
415-688-0777 Fax

Session 8 comes with a 16-bit digital audio card and a SCSI accelerator card, plus the software for direct to hard disk recording. It requires a IIci or faster. Features include digital mixing, track bouncing, random-access editing, special effects, SMPTE trigger, and MIDI Time Code. With its internal mix mode, all mixing, editing, and signal processing take place in the digital domain, providing clarity and freedom from noise build-up. An optional hardware mixer/controller provides the feel of a real recording console, and the ability to operate more than one fader at a time.

SonicStation II

Sonic Solutions
1891 East Francisco Boulevard
San Rafael, CA 94901
415-485-4800 Voice
415-485-4877 Fax

SonicStation II provides 12 tracks of disk playback, with two channel digital input and output. It includes two NuBus cards and software. The Sonic Solutions equipment is widely used in recording studios, and this is their entry-level package (others approach $100,000). Generally, it is available only from specialized pro audio dealers, but they'll be in a position to offer considerable advice in selecting and setting up a Mac-based professional studio. SonicStation II offers high performance suitable for those who plan to start a studio as a money-making business.

Sound Cards
Audiomedia II
$1295 SRP

Digidesign

Audiomedia II contains a Motorola 56001 DSP chip and the circuitry for digitizing analog audio into digital audio. Digidesign's Sound Designer II software lets you record, mix, edit, and play back digital audio. The Audiomedia II card offers high quality 16-bit sound at a 44.1 kHz sampling rate. It's available either as a NuBus card, or as a PDS card for the LC. (Note: Since the LC has only one slot, you can expand it with the LC MAX expansion chassis, available by mail order from DGR Technologies, 1219 West 6th St., Suite 250, Austin, TX 78703. Call 512-476-9855 or fax 512-476-6399 for information.

The Audiomedia card runs on the LC MAX, and you can have up to three other cards installed along with it.)

NuMedia
$1195 SRP

Spectral Innovations
1885 Lundy Avenue
San Jose, CA 95131
408-955-0366 Voice
408-955-0370 Fax

Oriented toward QuickTime users, *NuMedia* delivers 16-bit stereo performance for QuickTime soundtracks. This NuBus card uses the AT&T 3210 DSP chip, and also carries out compression and decompression for both audio and video.

Pro Tools
Digidesign

The *Pro Tools* digital audio card offers two 56001 DSP chips, and can handle four channels (up to 16 with expansion capabilities). Intended for exacting studio work, it delivers lower noise than the Audiomedia cards, and has balanced line outputs with XLR connectors.

Sample Cell II
$1995 SRP

Digidesign

Sample Cell II stores downloaded sampled sounds on a NuBus card. It handles 32 voices with eight polyphonic outputs, and you can install additional cards for more voices. A CD-ROM with an extensive library of sampled sounds, plus sample editing software comes with it.

Special Effects Processors

NuVerb
$1795 SRP

Lexicon
100 Beaver Street
Waltham, MA 02154
617-736-0300 Voice
617-891-0340 Fax

NuVerb brings the outstanding quality of Lexicon's famous reverb systems to a NuBus card. It has many other effects and interfaces with Digidesign.

Vortex

Lexicon

Vortex does for sound what morphing software does for images. This outboard effects processor transforms one sound into another over a specified period of time between 0.01 and 10 seconds. It's great for audio effects that accompany visuals. While an ear of corn becomes a box of cereal, for example, a synchronized sound effect can change along with the image. And that's only the beginning. Vortex has many more capabilities for creating subtle musical effects with various kinds of delay and modulation transformations.

MIDI Accessories

Apple MIDI Interface
$99.95 SRP

Apple Computer

The Apple MIDI Interface connects to one of your serial ports and provides one MIDI In and one Out.

MIDI Time Piece II
$595 SRP

Mark of the Unicorn
1280 Massachusetts Avenue
Cambridge, MA 02138
617-576-2760 Voice
617-576-3609 Fax

MIDI Time Piece II includes a 128-channel MIDI interface, with eight independent inputs and outputs, plus SMPTE interface and a MIDI patch bay.

MIDI Translator II
$59.95 SRP

Opcode Systems

An inexpensive, basic 16-channel MIDI interface, *MIDI Translator II* provides one MIDI In and three Out, plus LED activity indicators.

Studio 3

$319.95 SRP

Opcode Systems

Studio 3 offers 32 channels, with two MIDI In and six out, and SMPTE Interface Synchronizer.

Studio 4

$495.00 SRP

Opcode Systems

Studio 4 offers 128 channels, with 8 MIDI In and 10 out, and SMPTE Interface Synchronizer.

Studio 5 LX

$1195 SRP

Opcode Systems

Studio 5 permits you to expand your MIDI system in many ways. It has 240 channels, 15 MIDI Ins and Outs, activity LEDs, and SMPTE to MIDI Time Code conversion. You can chain up to six of them together.

From Here...

In this chapter, we've described how to add sounds to the Mac and how MIDI works, and also given you some information about the music software available for your Mac. If you are also interested in voice control or video you should read the following chapters:

■ Chapter 14, "Talking to Your Mac," which explains how to use speech recognition to give your computer speech commands, and how the computer can use text-to-speech technology to read text and numbers to you.

■ For more information on the video capabilities of the Macintosh, see Chapter 23, "Digital Photography and Desktop Video."

Chapter 14

Talking to Your Macintosh

by Carman Minarik

With the introduction of the Centris 660AV and the Quadra 840AV, Apple has created an entire suite of audio and video technologies for personal computers. The speech component of these technologies enables an AV Macintosh to recognize and respond to voice commands and to transform text into synthesized speech.

This chapter discusses the following topics:

- The technology known as PlainTalk

- The system requirements for use of PlainTalk technologies

- How to use speech recognition to control your Macintosh

- How to customize and add speech commands

- How to use the Text-to-Speech technology

What Is PlainTalk?

PlainTalk is a component of the audio/video technology included with the AV Macintosh computers. These technologies make use of the high-speed processing power combination of the 68040 CPU teamed with the AT&T DSP3210 Digital Signal Processor chip. The entire AV suite includes integrated video input and output, integrated audio input and output, and built-in tele-communication architecture, as well as PlainTalk speech technology.

The term PlainTalk is actually referring to two distinct capabilities: speech recognition and text-to-speech conversion.

Speech Recognition

The speech recognition component of PlainTalk is one of the most advanced implementations of speech technology available on a personal computer. The system is speaker-independent and accommodates continuous, natural speech patterns. Speech recognition is also easily customizable to your specific needs and preferences.

System Requirements

To implement speech recognition, you will need the following:

- An audio/video enabled Macintosh (Centris 660AV, Quadra 840AV, or Power Macintosh)

- A minimum of eight megabytes of RAM—16 megabytes is recommended

- The PlainTalk software

- A microphone

> **Note**
>
> The Centris 660AV and Quadra 840AV incorporate the AT&T Digital Signal Processor (DSP) chip, which allows the audio/video technology, including PlainTalk, to function. The Power Macintosh systems do not need this chip in order to function as AV systems. This can cause a problem for Power Mac users, however, since most of the software available for the audio/video Macintoshes is designed to look specifically for the DSP chip.

Activating Speech Control

Speech Setup

Speech recognition is activated through use of the Speech Setup Control Panel. Choose Speech Setup from the Control Panels submenu on the Apple Menu, or double-click the Speech Setup icon in the Control Panels folder in the System folder. A window similar to the one illustrated in figure 14.1 opens.

Click the On button to start speech recognition. The computer responds with the spoken phrase *Starting up*. Once speech recognition is activated, you will hear the phrase *Ready*.

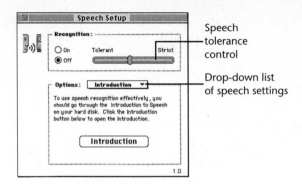

Fig. 14.1
Use the Speech
Setup window to
activate and
control speech
recognition.

Speech
tolerance
control

Drop-down list
of speech settings

As part of the speech startup process, the Status window shown in figure 14.2 appears. This window is always visible while speech recognition is activated and will automatically position itself in front of any Finder or application windows you open. As with any other Macintosh window, you reposition this window by dragging its title bar.

◀ See "The Finder and Its Contents," p. 72

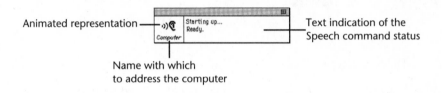

Animated representation

Name with which
to address the computer

Text indication of the
Speech command status

Fig. 14.2
The Status window
remains open in
front of all other
windows as long
as speech recogni-
tion is active.

The Status window has the following three sections:

- An animated picture representation of the speech recognition software's activities

- The name by which you should address the computer

- A text box showing the commands and responses of the speech recognition software

Using Speech Recognition

When speech recognition has been activated, you can give your Macintosh verbal commands. Keep these general points in mind when speaking to the computer:

- The PlainTalk microphone should be placed directly in front of you, from one to three feet away from your mouth.

III

Customizing Your Mac

■ You should speak in a continuous, normal speech pattern. Such things as long pauses and abnormal emphasis on words are not only unnecessary but will confuse the recognition process.

■ Excessive background noise will cause confusion in the speech recognition process.

■ Always address the computer with its designated name before giving the command; otherwise, you will not have the computer's attention and the command will be ignored.

■ Watch the Status window carefully. It will provide visual feedback on commands the recognition software has interpreted.

■ The speech recognition software is designed to recognize specific commands. If you add extra words or sounds to a command, the recognition process may become confused.

Speech Commands

The speech recognition is set up at the factory to recognize a particular set of commands, as detailed in the following paragraphs:

Hello. The computer will respond `Hello, welcome to Macintosh`.

What Day Is It? The computer will tell you the date according to its system clock.

What Time Is It? The computer will tell you the time according to its system clock.

Zoom Window. Produces the same effect as clicking the Zoom Box window control on the active window.

Close Window. Works as though you clicked the active window's Close Box, or used the File menu choice Close Window.

> **Note**
>
> The Close Window command will not work when the Alarm Clock is the active window.

Close All Windows. Equivalent to clicking the Close Box of the active window while holding down the Option key. All open Finder windows will be closed.

Note

The Close All Windows command works only in the Finder. It will not work when any other application is active.

Print...Copies. Prints the requested number of copies of the document in the active window.

Print From...To... Prints the requested page range of the document in the active window.

Print Page... Prints the indicated page number of the document in the active window.

Print Pages...To... Prints the requested page range of the document in the active window.

◀ See "Printing a Document—from A to Z," p. 206

Note

The Print Pages...To... command will not work if the Print choice is not located on the File menu for the application in use.

Is File Sharing On? The computer will open the Sharing Setup Control Panel and report the status of file sharing.

Start File Sharing. The computer will open the Sharing Setup Control Panel, activate File Sharing, and then close the Sharing Setup Control Panel.

Stop File Sharing. The computer will open the Sharing Setup Control Panel, deactivate File Sharing, and then close the Sharing Setup Control Panel.

Note

The File Sharing commands work only in the Finder; they will not work when any other application is active.

Open... Opens the requested Apple Menu item.

Switch To... Activates the requested application.

III

Customizing Your Mac

> **Note**
>
> The application must be open in RAM and listed on the Application menu in order for this command to work.

Menu Command. You can say any menu command in any application rather than choose the command with the mouse.

> **Note**
>
> This function may not work if the same command appears on more than one menu, if the menu command contains unpronounceable characters, or if the menu command is currently unavailable.

Dialog Box Button. You can say the name of any button in any dialog box rather than click the button with the mouse.

> **Note**
>
> This command will not work if the button name is unpronounceable. Some dialog boxes, for example, contain directional arrow buttons or buttons with icons that represent their action. Also, if the speech recognition Status window is covering the button, this command will not work.

Item In The Speakable Items Folder. You can say the name of any item placed in the Speakable Items folder (located in the Apple Menu Items folder in the System folder).

Restart. The computer will reply "Are you sure you want to restart?" If you answer "Computer, Yes" the computer will restart.

Shut Down. The computer will reply "Are you sure you want to shut down?" If you answer "Computer, Yes" the computer will shut down.

Setting Speech Options

Several options are available to you for controlling the way speech recognition works on your Macintosh. These options are accessed through the Speech Setup Control Panel.

Tolerance Setting

The Speech Setup window provides a Tolerance slider bar at the top of the window. This control is used to specify how precisely you must speak in order for the Macintosh to understand and respond to your commands. The further to the right the slider is positioned, the more precisely you must speak.

If the slider is positioned too far to the right, you may find that commands must often be repeated. If the slider is positioned too far to the left, inadvertent commands may be issued accidentally.

Choose Introduction from the drop-down list in the Speech Setup window to access the Introduction to Speech help system. Click the Introduction button to launch the system. The screen shown in figure 14.3 appears.

Tip
Move the slider only a short distance at a time, and test the results. The ideal setting for your environment may be very close to the initial setting.

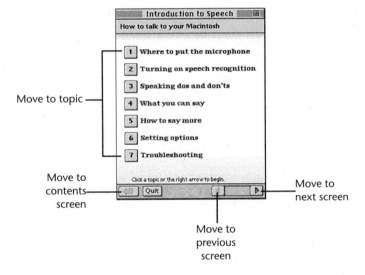

Fig. 14.3
The Introduction to Speech application provides help on using speech recognition technology.

Use the buttons on this screen to navigate through an on-line speech recognition tutorial.

Name Settings

Choose Name from the drop-down list in the Speech Setup window to access the name settings for speech recognition. The window options will change, as shown in figure 14.4.

III

Customizing Your Mac

Fig. 14.4
Use this screen to enter a name by which to address your computer.

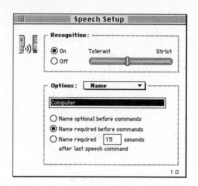

Enter the name by which you want to address the computer in the edit box. The name you enter will be used to get the computer's attention as you issue speech commands.

The radio buttons on this screen allow you to choose the following options for use of the computer name:

- If you do not want the computer name to be required before a command, select the Name Optional before Commands radio button.

- If you want the computer name to be required before a command, select the Name Required before Commands radio button.

- If you want to say the name after a command, choose the Name Required after Last Speech Commands radio button. Enter the number of seconds in which the name must be said after a command is issued.

Tip
When choosing a computer name, avoid one-syllable words and words that you use regularly. The computer can easily mistake similar sounds for its access name, and may respond to commands you did not intend to issue.

Tip
The second option, Name required before commands, is the safest and most reliable of these choices. The other options create more opportunity for erroneous commands to be processed.

Feedback Settings

Choose Feedback from the drop-down list in the Speech Setup window to access the feedback settings for speech recognition. The window options change as shown in figure 14.5.

Use this window to change these options:

- *Character.* Select the animation picture from the first drop-down list. Each option will place a different animated picture in left section of the speech recognition Status window.

- *Voice.* Select a voice from the second drop-down list. Both compressed and uncompressed voices are available. The compressed voices require significantly less memory space, but do not sound as natural as the uncompressed voices.

■ *Responding*. From the third drop-down list, choose a sound for the computer to play when it is responding to a voice command.

■ *Completed*. The fourth drop-down list allows selection of the sound the computer will play when a command is completed.

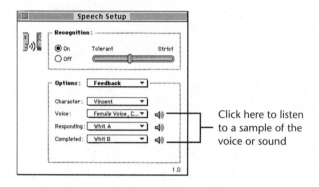

Click here to listen to a sample of the voice or sound

Fig. 14.5
The Feedback screen allows selection of animation, sounds, and voices.

Attention Key Setting

Choose Attention Key from the drop-down list in the Speech Setup window to access the attention key setting for speech recognition. The window options change, as shown in figure 14.6.

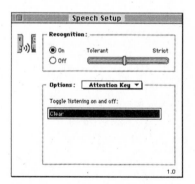

Fig. 14.6
The Attention Key screen has only one setting.

This window provides only one control. The key listed on this screen can be used to toggle the computer's attention to speech commands on or off. For example, figure 14.6 shows the Clear Key as the Attention Key. If you want to set the computer to ignore voice commands temporarily, just press the Clear Key once. When you want the computer to respond to voice commands, you just press the Clear Key again.

III

Customizing Your Mac

Set the attention key by pressing the desired key or key combination. The new attention key setting is shown in the setting box.

Customizing Speech Commands

The Macintosh comes to you from the factory able to respond to many speech commands, as listed earlier in this chapter. You will probably want to add your own commands to your computer's capabilities, as well.

Two methods can be used to add speech commands to your Macintosh: adding to the Speakable Items folder and creating speech macros.

Adding to the Speakable Items

The Speakable Items folder is located inside the Apple Menu Items folder inside the System folder. Saying the name of any item in the Speakable Items folder will cause that item to open. Since Macintosh file and folder names can be up to 31 characters in length, the name for these items can be quite descriptive.

Follow these steps to add a new item to the Speakable Items folder:

◀ See "Selecting and Moving a Group of Files," p. 118

1. Select the item you want to open with a speech command.

2. From the File menu, choose Make Alias. An alias of the selected file or folder will appear.

3. Click the name of the alias to select it.

4. Type the phrase you want to use to open this item. Use the same guidelines for choosing this phrase as you used for choosing the computer name earlier.

5. Drag the alias into the Speakable Items folder, which is in the Apple Menu Items folder inside the System folder.

The name of the alias will now be recognized as a speech command, and when the command is spoken, the associated item will be opened.

> **Note**
>
> You must turn Speech Recognition off and then on after adding new speakable items in order for the Mac to recognize the new items.

Using Speech Macros

Most current Macintosh computers, including the audio/video machines equipped with PlainTalk, allow automation of repetitive tasks with AppleScript. AppleScript is a basic programming tool which allows you to record a series of mouse or keyboard actions into a script. The script can then be played back later, re-creating the recorded steps.

The Speech Macro Editor application included as part of the PlainTalk system uses AppleScript tools to create or edit speech commands.

Launch the Speech Macro Editor by double-clicking its icon. The application is normally found in the Speech Technology folder inside the Apple Extras folder. A window similar to the one shown in figure 14.7 opens.

Speech Macro Editor

Fig. 14.7
The My Speech Macros window lists the speech macros currently in use.

This window lists the speech macros currently defined and in use. To edit an existing speech macro, point at the desired macro in the list and double-click. To create a new macro, use the Macro menu choice Create New Macro. In either case, a window as shown in figure 14.8 opens.

Script buttons

Script box

Fig. 14.8
Use this window to create or edit speech scripts.

III

Customizing Your Mac

To create a speech script, follow these steps:

1. Enter the name for the command. Use the guidelines described earlier for speech command names.

2. Select the context for the command from the drop-down list. The context indicates in which applications the command will be available.

3. Select the scripting tool to be used to create the script. AppleScript and the newest version of QuicKeys can both be used to create speech scripts.

4. Activate the Acknowledge check box if you want the speech recognition software to play the Responding and Completed sounds when the command is used.

5. Click the Record button.

6. Perform the steps you want included as part of this speech command. Any mouse or keyboard actions you make from the time you click the Record button will be recorded as part of the script.

7. When all the desired command steps have been completed, click the Stop button. You will see the script commands in the box to the right of the scripting buttons.

8. If desired, edit the script commands by changing the text in the script box.

9. Test the script by clicking the Run button.

10. From the File menu, choose Save. The script will be saved as part of the speech macro file.

For changes to speech macros to take effect, you may need to turn Speech Recognition off and then back on again. This will reload the speech macros into the system.

Note

The Speech Macro Editor can only record speech macros if the application you are using supports AppleScript recording. See the documentation for each application for information regarding its recordability.

Text to Speech

Text-to-Speech (TTS) technology allows the Macintosh to interpret textual data and read the information in a nearly natural voice.

You can choose from multiple voices and various sound quality levels for the synthesized voices.

System Requirements

To use TTS, you must have the following items:

- An audio/video capable Macintosh

- A minimum of 8MB of RAM (16MB is recommended)

- The PlainTalk software

- An application that supports TTS. The version of TeachText that ships with any AV Macintosh is one application that supports TTS.

Using Text to Speech

The TTS technology component of PlainTalk is only available in applications designed to use TTS. You cannot, for example, open a document in MacWrite and have your Macintosh read it to you. Using the following steps, however, you can have your Macintosh read nearly any document you want:

1. Open the document you want the Macintosh to read in the application you used to create it.

2. Select the part of the document you want the Macintosh to read.

3. Open the Edit menu and choose Copy.

4. Open a TTS-enabled application, such as the version of TeachText that ships with PlainTalk.

5. Open the Edit menu and choose Paste.

6. Open the File menu and choose Voices. From Voices submenu select the voice you want the computer to use as it reads your text.

7. Open the File menu and choose Speak All. The computer will now interpret the text and numbers on-screen and read the information in a synthesized voice.

If part of the document is selected, the File menu choice changes to Speak Selection.

8. To stop the reading process, open the File menu and choose Stop Speaking.

From Here...

In this chapter, you have learned about the PlainTalk speech technologies available on audio/video Macintoshes. You have seen how to use speech recognition to give your computer speech commands, and how the computer can use text-to-speech technology to read text and numbers.

- Chapter 7, "Organizing Your Files, Folders, and Disks," for additional information on managing files, folders, and disks.

- For more information on scripting, AppleScript, and QuicKeys, see Chapter 15, "Shortcuts."

- For more information on the video capabilities of the Macintosh, see Chapter 23, "Digital Photography and Desktop Video."

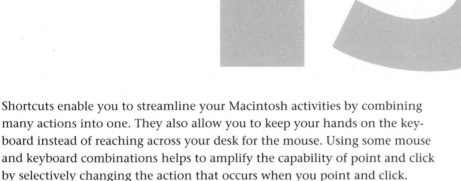

Chapter 15

Shortcuts

Shortcuts enable you to streamline your Macintosh activities by combining many actions into one. They also allow you to keep your hands on the keyboard instead of reaching across your desk for the mouse. Using some mouse and keyboard combinations helps to amplify the capability of point and click by selectively changing the action that occurs when you point and click.

Macros and scripting can also be powerful worksaving devices. When you have a routine that you repeat over and over again, a macro allows you to "record" and then "play back" the sequence of actions that you've taken. You do this record activity once, and then you give the sequence a name. You use this name to set the same sequence of events in motion the next time you're ready to perform your task.

Scripts are similar in many ways to macros. You combine many steps into a collection of commands that perform those steps when certain conditions are met. You might create a script that dials into your main office every day at the same time to deliver completed documents and to pick up the day's new assignments whether or not you're at your computer in the field office.

Or you might write a script that creates one type of form letter for 5th-grade parents, and a different form letter for 5th-grade teachers.

In this chapter, you learn about the following:

- Mouse shortcuts

- Keyboard shortcuts

- Finder shortcuts

- Using macros and FKeys

- Using System 7.5 Finder scripting

- Using AppleScript

Keyboard and Mouse Shortcuts

The Macintosh is known in the collective psyche as "the computer that you use with a mouse," but in reality, you still spend much of your time typing.

When you type, your hands stay over the keyboard (…bear with me, I know that's obvious), and when you use the mouse, you still have a free hand that could be put to good use (A-HA!, see? This could get interesting…).

With the amount of keyboarding and "mousing around" that we inevitably do every day, adding just a small amount of extra efficiency with keyboard and mouse shortcuts can really pay off.

Keyboard Shortcuts

You're blazing away, typing to your heart's content and rushing to meet an important deadline. The words just seem to be flowing from your thoughts directly to the keyboard. Even if you are a two fingered typist, you develop a certain rhythm and momentum that is easily interrupted if you have to grab at the mouse across the desk to make a quick menu choice to bold the next few words or to italicize the last few. Keyboard shortcuts enable you to work without this interruption.

Keyboard shortcuts are a combination of keystrokes (usually including one or more of the Shift, Option, ⌘, or the Control keys in combination with other keys) that allow you to perform an action that would otherwise require a menu selection. Figure 15.1 shows that the Command key (⌘), when pressed at the same time as the W key (indicated as ⌘-W), performs the Close Window Command. This action closes the Working with Windows window (which, conveniently, is showing a few other helpful keyboard combinations).

Next, figure 15.2 shows Microsoft Word being used, and the use of keyboard shortcuts in most Macintosh programs is similar. You choose bold from the menu, you type until you reach the end of the bold section, and you then turn bold off at the end of the phrase.

With a keyboard shortcut, you get to keep your hands on the keyboard, as follows:

You activate bold by typing ⌘-Shift-B, you type until you reach the end of the bold section, and then turn bold off at the end of the phrase by typing ⌘-Shift-B again.

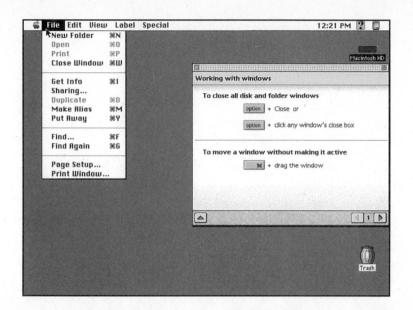

Fig. 15.1
Notice that ⌘-W in the File menu is a shortcut to Close File, and according to the Working with Windows window, Option-click in a window's close box will close all open windows.

Note

This kind of a command is called a *toggle*, after the toggle switch. When you flip a toggle switch, it has only two possible states—ON or OFF. The same is true of a toggle command in a software program. Typing ⌘-Shift-B in the previous example turns bold either off or on at the cursor point, or for the currently selected block of text.

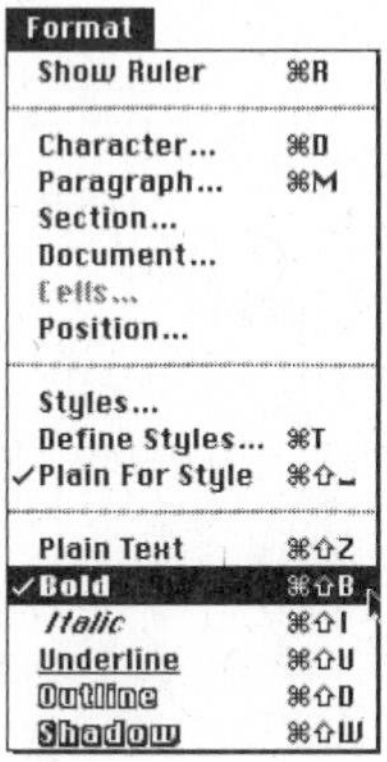

Fig. 15.2
This menu selection deselects the bold feature. You also can press ⌘-Shift-B to select it.

III

Customizing Your Mac

Explaining this next technique takes much longer than actually doing it. The power of using these shortcuts may seem minor until some of these commands start to become second nature.

If you're editing a document that already has a name, you press ⌘-S to save your work, and then you can return to typing—just like that. That smoothness alone beats using the mouse when you're entering text from the keyboard.

If you haven't saved the document previously, Word presents you with a dialog box. The text box for the document name is already highlighted (see fig. 15.3). Type the name. Notice that the Save button has a double black line around it—all you have to do to accept the name you typed is press Return.

The entire save operation, including entering characters into a dialog box and accepting the highlighted Save button, was accomplished without taking your fingers away from the keyboard.

Fig. 15.3
You could reach this Save dialog by selecting File and then Save with the mouse, but while you are typing it is easier and faster to type ⌘-S and accept the darkened ring around Save by pressing Return.

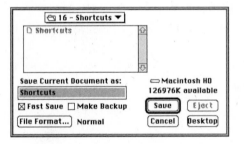

To print, you can press ⌘-P. Figure 15.4 shows the dialog box you get when you press ⌘-P. Notice that the number of copies is highlighted. The two options in this dialog box you will change most often are the number of copies and the page range (in a multiple page document).

If you want five copies, after you press ⌘-P, type **5** (see fig. 15.5).

If you also want to print pages 4 through 6 of a 12-page document, just type Tab-**4**-Tab-**6** (see figs. 15.6 and 15.7). In either case, the Print button is highlighted. When you're done modifying the print specs, press Return, and your document will be printed.

Again, this Command involved a dialog box that you had to navigate through to get your results—and you didn't need the mouse to do it!

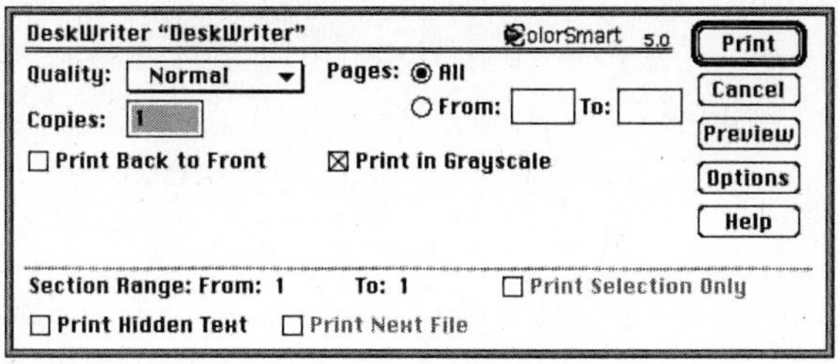

Fig. 15.4
One more example of how much easier it is to type a keyboard shortcut. Pressing ⌘-P brings you to this dialog.

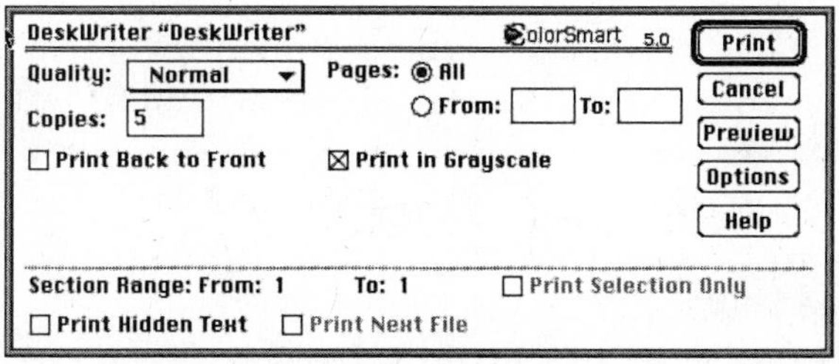

Fig. 15.5
Type **5** and you have your desired number of copies.

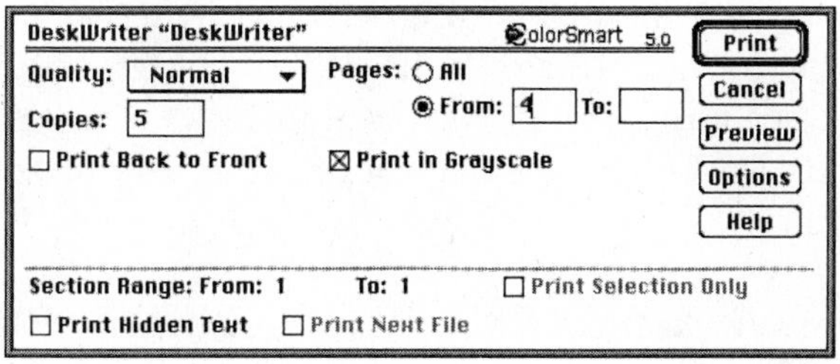

Fig. 15.6
Tab-**4** brings you across to enter the starting page 4,(notice that the selected radio button moved down from All in the last figure to From in this figure just because you typed the number 4 there).

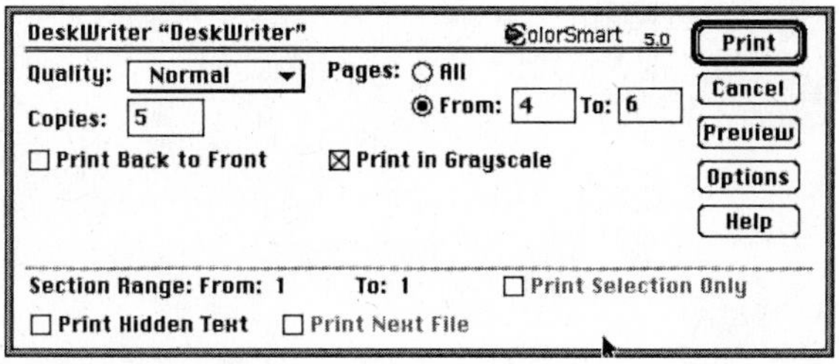

Fig. 15.7
At this point, you type Tab-**6**. The number 6 ends your print range at page 6. You selected the Print command and specified the number of copies and the page range without once taking your fingers off the keyboard.

Note

Although Microsoft Word was used for the preceding examples, most other programs use keyboard shortcuts in a similar way.

When you start using these keyboard shortcuts, first pick a few that you'll use consciously for a while. Remember how intimidating all the menu choices seemed at first, until you developed stable Mac habits?

Use ⌘-P to print and ⌘-S to save. Then move on to ⌘-X to Cut and ⌘-V to Paste. When you discover the power that using the Shift key with the navigation arrows on your keyboard gives you, there will be no turning back. Try it—you'll like it.

Mouse Shortcuts

You can use the mouse to select multiple objects (for example, documents on the desktop or graphic elements in MacDraw) by dragging a selection rectangle around them (see fig. 15.8). If you inadvertently select too many objects, you can click outside the area of the selected objects, which deselects all the objects, and then try again. Or you can Shift-click the unwanted object that was selected. The only object that will be deselected will be the object that you Shift-click.

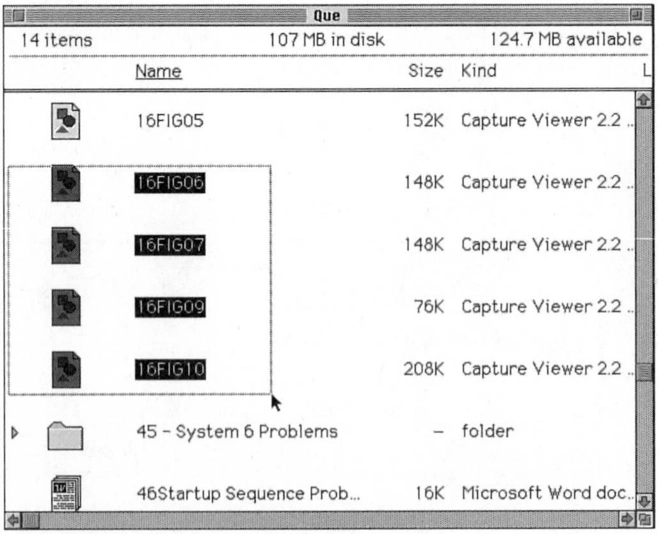

Fig. 15.8
When you click and drag across many icons, you select all the icons that fall within the selection rectangle.

Figure 15.9 just might look too familiar—all those folders open just because you had to find the folder that was in a folder that was in another folder.

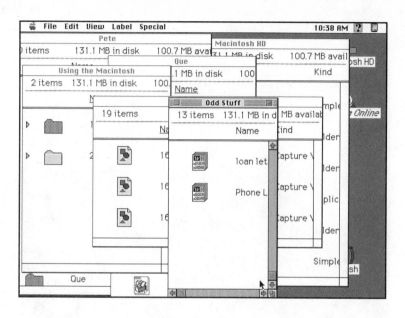

Fig. 15.9
Here is a perfect example of opening a folder to find the folder that has the folder within its folder.

When you're done, you can Option-click in the close box of the last folder you opened to make your screen look like figure 15.10.

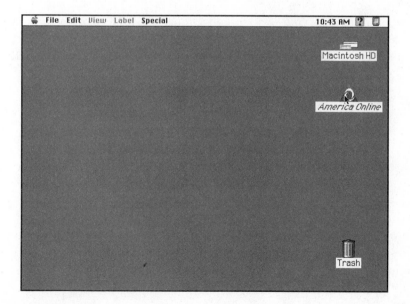

Fig. 15.10
All it took was one Option-click in the close box of the last window that was opened to turn the cluttered desktop in figure 15.9 into this!

Use Option-double-click on each icon starting from the Boot volume through each successive folder. When you get to the folder you're looking for, you will only have that last folder open on your desk (see fig. 15.11). When you Option-double-click in this manner, each previous window closes when you open the next one.

Fig. 15.11
This neat looking desktop is the result of using Option-double-click to access this folder.

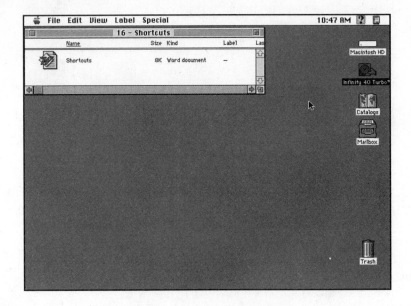

If you want to work your way back up through the folders, or if you want to jump directly to one a few levels back, press and hold ⌘ and click the active window's title—then just select the level you want to access (see fig. 15.12).

Fig. 15.12
With one ⌘-click on the folder name, you can go directly to any of the higher folders without opening any others.

More key combinations such as this one are explained in the Shortcuts window. To view these hints, just select Finder Shortcuts from the Balloon Help menu (see fig. 15.13).

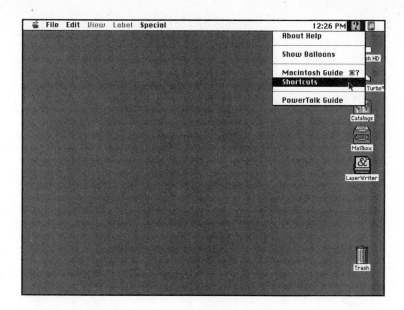

Fig. 15.13
More than just balloons are under the Balloon help icon.

Using Macros and FKeys

In the Mac realm, FKeys are defined two ways. The first way refers to the key combinations that start with ⌘-Shift and the third key held down at the same time is a number. ⌘-Shift-3 puts a screen image on your hard disk in PICT format, ⌘-Shift-4 sends a printout to the old Imagewriter printer, and ⌘-Shift-1 ejects a floppy disk.

The second way that FKeys are defined is a carryover from PCs that have function keys on their keyboards. These function keys can be pre-programmed to perform repetitive tasks at the touch of a key. The Apple Extended Keyboard has a row of similar keys, but they are generally ignored by both Apple and commercial program developers.

This setup allows these extra keys to be used by Macro programs, however.

Macro programs can be thought of as the ultimate in system customization. Macro programs allow you to automate just about any sequence of repetitive steps so that you can initiate them with one keystroke or with some other pre-determined trigger.

An example of a macro program is CE Software's QuicKeys program. QuicKeys enables you to assign an entire sequence of events to a single key combination. The sequence can be as simple as opening one folder directly from the Finder that is deeply nested many folders deep, yet is one that you access very often during the day.

III

Customizing Your Mac

Or the sequence can be as complicated as saving your current word processing work on your Great American Novel to your server file, opening PageMaker and exporting your word processing file into it for complex formatting tasks, and uploading the results to your editor halfway across wherever by modem.

Following is an example of a simple automation task, putting a header at the top of a ClarisWorks word processing document:

1. Start ClarisWorks and open a new word processing document.

2. Choose QuicKeys from the Apple Menu, as shown in figure 15.14. When QuicKeys appears, select ClarisWorks from the Sets menu to define this as a shortcut that will be available whenever you use ClarisWorks (see fig. 15.15).

Fig. 15.14

The first step in creating a QuicKeys Macro is to select QuicKeys from the Apple Menu.

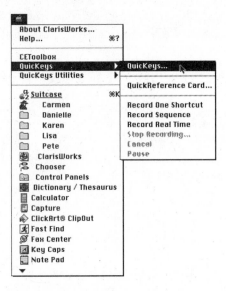

3. Choose text under the Define menu to show that this will be a text function (see fig. 15.16).

4. The next screen looks like figure 15.17. Under Text To Type:, type the text that will be called up every time the assigned keystroke is used.

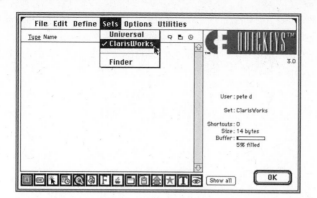

Fig. 15.15
Put this macro in the ClarisWorks set by selecting ClarisWorks from the Set menu.

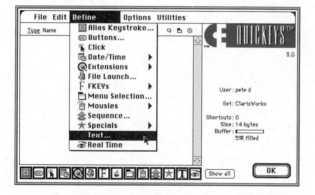

Fig. 15.16
The macro will contain text.

5. Still in figure 15.17, type a name for this sequence (in this example, the name is Header) and type the keystroke that will invoke it (in this example, Control-N). Click OK to leave this screen and again to leave the main QuicKeys screen.

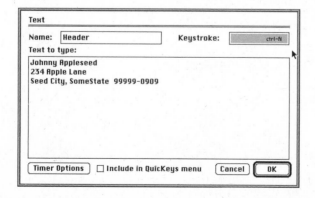

Fig. 15.17
Type the applicable text in the Text to Type fields. Give the macro a name and put the cursor in the Keystroke box. Then simultaneously type the two letter trigger for the macro there.

III

Customizing Your Mac

6. Go back to the ClarisWorks document. In order to be flexible about the placement of the header, excessive formatting was not recorded into this macro. In figure 15.18, the Insert Header option is selected from the Format menu, and centered text is selected.

Fig. 15.18

Select the place for the insertion of the name and address.

7. Figure 15.19 shows the result of pressing Control-N.

This header could have been automated way beyond the extent it was in this example simply by performing more actions. With QuicKeys, you can go between applications and folders and have all your actions played back quite accurately.

Fig. 15.19

From now on, no matter where you are in ClarisWorks, simply type the two key code (here it's Control-N) and the name and address appear at the Cursor.

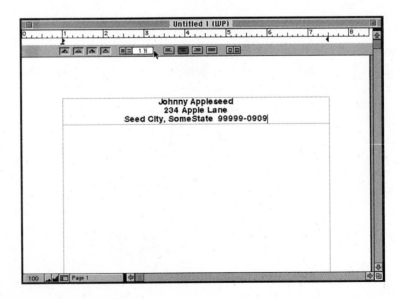

Recording and Writing AppleScripts

Like a macro, AppleScript is a way of saving repetitive steps into a simple move. In this case, the move is called a script. Think of a play and the actors—how do they know what to do? They follow a script, and so can your Macintosh.

The new System 7.5 discs contain everything you need to begin writing scripts, two of these are the applications Scriptable Text Editor and Script Editor. The function of each of these is exactly as the name implies. The Script Editor application is for recording, saving, running, and editing scripts—sort of a word processor dedicated to script writing.

The Scriptable Text Editor is a word processor—a very small one, but nonetheless a word processor. The Scriptable Text Editor is much like TeachText, another small word processor for writing ReadMe files and such on the Macintosh.

The major difference between the two is that Scriptable Text Editor is AppleScript-savvy—you can write scripts that it will follow. TeachText is not scriptable. That is the one criteria that any application must adhere to in order for it to understand an AppleScript that you write for it. It must be AppleScript-savvy.

Scriptable and Recordable Applications

Applications are not necessarily able to follow a script that you write; they must be AppleScript-savvy. Many of the newer versions of applications are ready for AppleScript. QuarkXPress, Adobe products, and others are already on the market with a version that is able to act out scripts.

There are two levels of AppleScript compliance. The first type is *scriptable*. This is an application for which you can write a script. The second type is *recordable*. This denotes an application for which you can record a script. Within these two different script types there are also levels.

Some applications allow scripting to nearly every feature contained within that application, others already have a scripting capability that is altered to accept AppleScript. With this type of application, you also have to know and understand the internal scripting of the application as well as AppleScripting. Scriptable Text Editor is an example of an application that is both scriptable and recordable and does not have an internal scripting process that differs from AppleScript.

III

Customizing Your Mac

Understanding the Language of AppleScript

If you've worked at all in the different applications of the Macintosh, you have some idea of how little the different manufacturers of applications agree about the way things should be done. Just the layout of the menus and the keyboard shortcuts are a good example. In QuarkXPress, the Style menu is for changing the attributes of text, and in Illustrator text is changed in the Text menu. In QuarkXPress, the keyboard shortcut for changing the view to Fit in Window is ⌘-0, in Illustrator it's ⌘-M.

So how do both of these applications interpret AppleScripts in the same way? They don't. That's where the Dictionary comes in. This is not the dictionary that runs a spelling check on your document, but rather a dictionary of terms that a particular application uses in its understanding of AppleScript. Which words and terms each application understands is completely up to the manufacturer, just as its level of AppleScript recordability or scriptability is.

You can view the terms available to you by using the Open Dictionary command in the File menu of Script Editor, which is covered in upcoming sections. For now, let's tour Script Editor and find out about writing and recording scripts.

Recording Simple Scripts

During the installation of System 7.5, you can choose to install the AppleScript supporting software and documentation (ReadMe files). If you choose this, you will be installing the applications discussed previously—Script Editor and Scriptable Text Editor—into a folder called AppleScript Utilities.

You don't need the word processor, Scriptable Text Editor, to write or record scripts. It just gives you a place to try out simple scripts while you're learning. The documentation has several examples for you to try that are done in this mini word processor.

Because Scriptable Text Editor is used in later examples, let's tour its window also. Along with these two applications, a folder called Useful Scripts is installed. This folder contains a few scripts already written that you can use.

Recording an AppleScript

Double-click the Script Editor icon, and the window shown in figure 15.20 appears. The upper portion of the window contains the names or description of your scripts as you save them. Below this scrollable list are four buttons: Record, Stop, Run, and Check Syntax. Record and Stop will begin and end a recording session. Just as with the buttons on a tape recorder, click Record to instruct Script Editor to begin a recording session for a script. After clicking this button, you perform the steps that you will want to repeat as part of a script. Click Stop when you finish the steps.

In the following example, you put that to work by creating a small script for the Scriptable Text Editor. (You'll need to launch this application for the example and then move both windows side by side to get the best view of your progress.)

Fig. 15.20
Use the application Script Editor along with its buttons to write and record scripts.

To record a script, follow these steps:

1. Click the upper portion of the Script Editor window and type a descriptive name.

2. Click the Scriptable Text Editor window to make it active and type a sentence.

3. Click Script Editor window to make it active, and click the Record button.

4. Return to the Scriptable Text Editor window and select the third word of your sentence. Choose Bold from the Style menu. Make any additional changes that you would like to include in the script.

5. Click the Stop button in the Script Editor window.

The commands that you recorded are now listed in correct syntax in the lower portion of the Script Editor window. Syntax is the structure with which a sentence is constructed. A script will only operate if it contains proper syntax. This is not a concern if you are recording because the Script Editor automatically interprets your moves and records them properly. If you are writing a script, however, you can use the Check Syntax button to ensure that you have written it correctly.

To apply the script that you have written, delete and type a new sentence in the Scriptable Text Editor window. Return to the Script Editor and click the Run button. The steps you recorded are applied to the new sentence. You've completed and applied your first script.

Editing Scripts

YourScript Editor and Scriptable Text Editor windows may look something like the windows shown in figure 15.21. In this figure, boldface formatting was added to the third word. If you read the script carefully, you can find where it states that this will happen. To edit this script, select the word **bold** and change it to the word *italic*. Click the Run button again and watch the results.

Scriptable Text Editor is a very small and simple-to-use application, but that doesn't mean you can't write or record scripts for more complex applications. The simple rules that you've learned here apply to any scriptable or record-able application.

Fig. 15.21
A close look at the recorded script will help you to understand how to write scripts of your own.

Formatting and Identifying the Parts of a Script

The formatting that Script Editor applies to the parts of a script is there to help you identify each of the component types. You can change the formatting by choosing AppleScript Formatting from the Edit menu. This prompts the window shown in figure 15.22, where you can edit the formatting by clicking a line to make a selection and using the Font and Style menus to choose new attributes. You cannot select single words of your script and change the formatting; you must make the changes here so that they are applied globally throughout the script.

There are eight components that are available to use when writing scripts. Each of these components has a different job. In table 15.1, these components and their functions are listed. Use this table to help you identify the parts of the script that you recorded. They'll help you even more as you begin writing scripts.

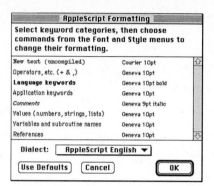

Fig. 15.22
The AppleScript Formatting window allows you to make global changes to the attributes of the text within a script.

Table 15.1   Scripting Terms and Their Functions

Term	Function
New Text	Text added to a script that has not yet been saved, run, or had its syntax checked. Also text that will not compile or run due to a syntax error.
Operators	Characters that perform an operation. A + symbols adds, a - symbol subtracts, and so on. Most operators produce a result, for instance, 1+1 (the operator being the plus symbol) produces the result 2. If you want to view the results of operators, choose Show Result from the Controls menu. (The Result window, shown in figure 15.23, also is used to display some error messages, so it's a good window to have open when writing and recording scripts.)
Language Keywords	Scripting terms available to all applications that are built into AppleScript.
Application Keyword	Scripting terms that are available specifically to the application.
Comments	Descriptive words, phrases, or sentences embedded into your script that are ignored by the computer and therefore are not considered when compiling the script.
Values	Characters of information that AppleScript uses.
Variables	Terms (numbers or words) that are used as containers for values.
References	Phrases used to identify specific objects so that the script can identify it. For example, word 3 of document 1 is a reference. References can be pasted into a script by selecting that object in the source application, copying it, and pasting it into the script. The reference for the object appears when you use the paste command (the object itself does not appear).

III

Customizing Your Mac

Fig. 15.23
The Results
window shows the
results of operators
but also displays
some error
messages.

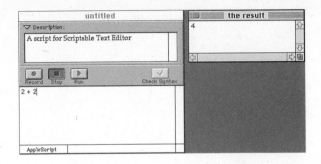

Other applications also have a list of terms that can be used by that particular
application. Each of these terms is available to you when you write scripts
that will be applied to that application only. To view these terms and their
definitions, you need to look at the Dictionary for that application. While in
Script Editor, choose Open Dictionary from the File menu. This action
prompts the familiar Macintosh dialog box in which you can select a
scriptable application. The dictionary window for that application opens and
from this you can click a term to view its definition. In figure 15.24, the dictionary for QuarkXPress has been opened.

Fig. 15.24
Each scriptable
application has a
dictionary of terms
that can be used
when writing
scripts for that
application.

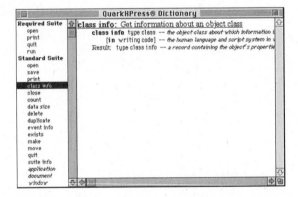

Writing Simple Scripts

Writing an AppleScript is more difficult than recording one. With writing
you're actually doing low-level programming, although some programmers
will have more difficulty writing scripts than will average users. What programmers know that you might not know (if you're not a programmer) is
how to formulate commands, in what order to place commands, and how to
nest commands.

The Check Syntax button is your closest ally in writing usable scripts, especially for those of you who are new to script writing. When you write a script,

you attempt to match the type of terminology you saw when you recorded a script. If you have done this correctly and clicked the Check Syntax button, the steps of the script are formatted and compiled, like those you see on the left side of figure 15.25.

An improper syntax will leave the text unformatted, like that on the right of the same figure. A script must be compiled in order to run, but the Run button performs a compile before it applies the script. The first word that does not follow proper syntax is selected when you press the Check Syntax button. Replace or delete the highlighted word and press Check Syntax until the script follows proper syntax and is formatted and compiled. This is your cue that the syntax is correct. A script containing improper syntax cannot be saved as a script, only as text.

Fig. 15.25
The example on the left is of a script with proper syntax. The example on the right is very similar, in fact, an attempt at the same script. Using the Check Syntax button, the first word in error is highlighted.

Saving Scripts

After you have a script, you need to save it. You save a script in the same way as you save any Macintosh document, but you have three formatting options. The Save dialog box is shown in figure 15.26. Following are the options: as a text file (this does not need to have proper syntax or to be compiled but you do need to hold down the Shift key as you select Save from the File menu), as a compiled script that can only be opened by Script Editor, or as an application that can be launched on its own like other Macintosh applications.

When you save a script as an application, you can also choose Stay Open (the script will remain open after it has been run), or Never Show Startup Screen (this is a description of the script displayed in a startup screen).

III

Customizing Your Mac

Fig. 15.26
Use the Save
dialog box to
save a recorded
or written
script. Choose the
type of save
method from
the pop-up
menu at the
bottom of the
window.

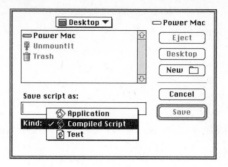

Another type of script is a Run-Only Script. These scripts can be run but not opened in Script Editor. Instead of Save, choose Save As Run-Only from the File menu.

Working with Scriptable Finder

Scriptable Finder is an AppleScript-savvy Finder. The first time this became available was in the AppleScript Developer's Toolkit CD-ROM, but it will be included in the System 7.5 discs. When you think about exactly what Finder operations are, you begin to see just a small portion of the possible power behind a scriptable Finder. Functions such as copying files to discs, mounting file servers, making aliases and sorting them, and so on, are all functions that you perform manually by using the Finder. Keeping in mind what Apple-Script can do, think about those steps that you can automate.

How about a script that watches a specific folder for changes and each time a file is added or updated within that folder, the Finder automatically logs on to a remote file server and backs up those files? On a grander scale, what about a script that on a specific day of the month searches for the latest version of a database, opens the document, prints labels, opens another document from another application, dumps the current database information into a mail merge, prints statements, and saves the current document with a new name? Or maybe instead of printing, it launches your internal fax software and faxes the statements to the list of clients. With this kind of power it's no wonder that Apple is encouraging even the passive user of Macintosh to become AppleScript aware.

A simple application script that you can write on your own is shown in the steps below. This script makes an alias of any file you select, then places that alias inside the Apple Menu items in the System folder. Once the alias has been placed there you can select it from the Apple Menu to launch the file.

This is an exceptionally handy way to launch applications without having to open several nested folders in search of the application's icon.

To write an application script for your Finder, follow these steps:

1. Double-click the Script Editor icon to launch the Script Editor application.

2. In the Script Editor window, type:

```
tell application "Finder"
try
Set thisFile to choose file with prompt "Pick a file to make an
alias of."
Make alias file with data alias (thisFile) at (folder "Apple Menu
Items" of folder "System Folder" of Startup Disc)
On error ErrText Number ErrNum
If ErrNum is not equal to -128 then
Beep
Display dialog ErrText buttons {"OK"} default button 1
end if
end try
end tell
```

3. Go to the File menu and choose Save As. Type a name for the script in the name field.

4. Choose Application from the Kind pop-up menu. This makes an application out of the script you just wrote.

5. Click the Never Show Startup Screen checkbox. This will keep the script from showing an icon when you start your computer.

6. Choose Desktop as a destination so that you are saving the script loose on your desktop. (Don't place it in a folder where you'll have to go searching for it.)

7. Click the Save button.

8. Choose Quit from the File menu.

Your script is now ready to run. If you double-click the script you will receive the message surrounded by quotation marks in line three of the script. This instructs you to click on a file which you want to make an alias of.

If there is an error, for any reason, and the Macintosh identifies that error as a -128 error, you will receive a warning dialog box along with a beep and an OK button to click.

 If you're serious about wanting to write scripts, the documentation on the System 7.5 disks can get you started. The more complex the task, the more complex the AppleScript will be. Use the documentation and try out the examples. They are designed to introduce you slowly to the concept of total automation, but AppleScripting for applications will take some time to master. Try creating simple scripts for printing series of pages or some other fairly easy task, and then you'll learn about the syntax through trial and error, and become a better programmer.

From Here...

In this chapter, we've covered a lot of ground! We've gone from maneuvering around complicated menus and dialog boxes without using the mouse, to simple macro automation and the QuicKeys application.

By the time we finished this chapter we used AppleScript for low level programming at the system level to take control of the Finder. The system customization possibilities are only bounded by your determination and imagination.

To supplement the preceding discussion of task automation in general, and the impact of System 7.5 and AppleScript with the Scriptable Finder in particular, refer to the following chapters:

- Chapter 3, "Mac Interface Philosophy."

- Chapter 9, "Sharing Data with Other Applications."

- Chapters 33–36, Part VI, "The Mac at Work."

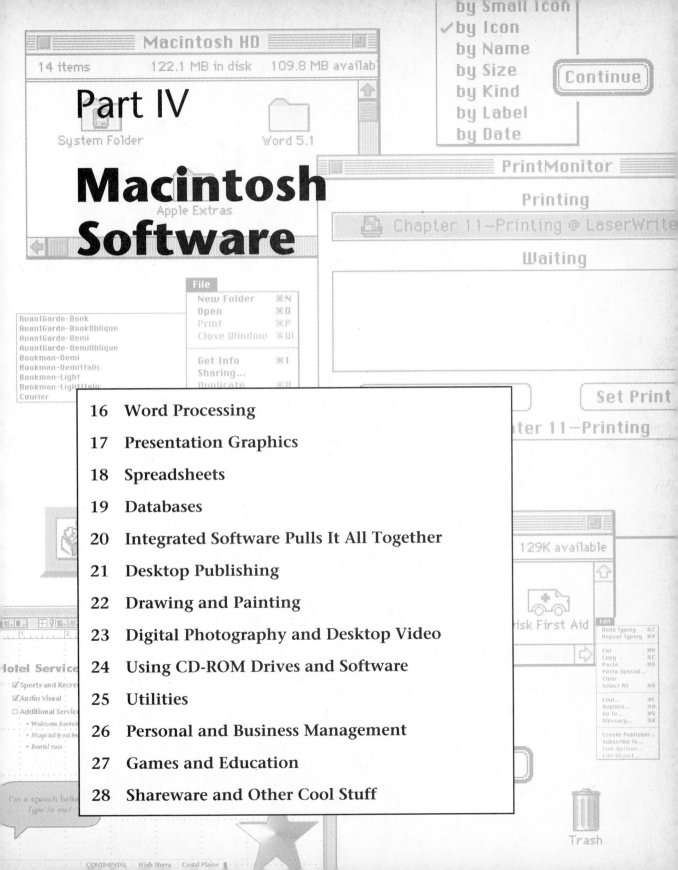

Part IV

Macintosh Software

by Small Icon
✓by Icon
by Name
by Size
by Kind
by Label
by Date

Continue

Macintosh HD

14 items   122.1 MB in disk   109.8 MB availab

System Folder   Word 5.1

Apple Extras

PrintMonitor

Printing

Chapter 11—Printing @ LaserWri

Waiting

Cancel Printing   Set Prin

Printing Status: Chapter 11—Printing

Pages To Print: 8
Status: preparing data

File

New Folder   ⌘N
Open   ⌘O
Print   ⌘P
Close Window   ⌘W

Get Info   ⌘I
Sharing...
Duplicate   ⌘D
Make Alias
Put Away   ⌘Y

Find...   ⌘F
Find Again   ⌘G

Page Setup...
Print Desktop...

AvantGarde-Book
AvantGarde-BookOblique
AvantGarde-Demi
AvantGarde-DemiOblique
Bookman-Demi
Bookman-DemiItalic
Bookman-Light
Bookman-LightItalic
Courier

Disk Tools

🔒 3 items   1.2 MB in disk   129K available

System Folder   Apple HD SC Setup   Disk First Aid

Edit

Undo Typing   ⌘Z
Repeat Typing   ⌘Y

Cut   ⌘X
Copy   ⌘C
Paste   ⌘U
Paste Special...
Clear
Select All   ⌘A

Find...   ⌘F
Replace...   ⌘R
Go To...   ⌘G
Glossary...   ⌘K

Create Publisher...
Subscribe To...
Link Options...
Edit Object...

Sample Obje

A abc

Hotel Services

☑ Sports and Recreation
☑ Audio Visual
☐ Additional Services
• Welcome baskets
• Hospitality suites
• Rental cars

Market

Business
Tourist
Group

Market Segments

Cancel   Previous   Next

I'm a speech balloon!
Type in me!

Trash

CONTINENTAL   High Sierra   Costal Plains
Hotel   Lodge   Inn

Chapter 16

Word Processing

by Gene Steinberg

First, there was a typewriter. To correct what you typed, you used an eraser or one of those messy cover-up liquids. To move text from one place or another and avoid the fuss and muss, you just started over again.

The arrival of personal computers brought something new to the process of preparing your documents: a word processor. In the beginning, you'd use a word processing program simply to edit text and maybe move it around to a different location in your document. As personal computers grew more sophisticated, word processing software also received more sophisticated document processing capabilities. You were offered a host of choices in areas of document formatting, text formatting, style tags, spell checking, and other features.

In addition to document handling chores, high-end word processing software can now also handle tasks such as mail merge and outlining with aplomb. There are macro capabilities, highly sophisticated search-and-replace capabilities, and elaborate equation and table creation tools. Some of the software discussed in this chapter adds support for Apple's PowerTalk, QuickTime, and other fancy system tools.

If you intend to do some desktop publishing work, you just might find that one of these programs we're about to discuss will be more than up to the task as well. Such features as kerning and hyphenation and justification settings, which were once confined to desktop publishing software, can now be found in word processing programs.

If you just want to write a few letters and other simply formatted documents, it's quite possible the programs' profiles in this chapter will provide more flexibility than you need. A program like WordStar's WriteNow, which has modest RAM and storage space needs, is apt to fill the bill. But if you want to have a wide range of document creation tools at your disposal, read on.

In this chapter you learn the following:

■ The important features of four major Mac word processing programs

■ The best word processing program for the kind of work you do

■ Exclusive, hands-on tips and tricks that you won't find in the typical software manual

Using Claris MacWrite Pro 1.5

MacWrite Pro, from Apple's Claris subsidiary, has a heritage that can be traced back to that free word processor that shipped with your first Macintosh in 1984. The program has undergone extensive revision since then, and, like the other word processors discussed in this chapter, it has become larger and more feature-laden. But it's remained true to its original purpose as a simple-to-use, no-nonsense product. Hardware, RAM, and storage requirements remain modest, and anything from a Mac Classic on should run MacWrite Pro without difficulty.

System Requirements

MacWrite Pro's software and hardware needs are modest. It will work on a Mac Classic or later, with 1MB of RAM under System 6 and 2.5MB RAM for System 7. The installation will take around 3.5MB of storage space on your Mac's hard drive.

MacWrite Pro Overview

MacWrite Pro is priced at about half what the other word processors we're describing in this chapter go for. It offers a simple, accessible interface, with three floating palettes offering tools for more sophisticated chores. Beneath its uncluttered work area, however, are such advanced capabilities as character-based style sheets, table of contents generation, and support for such features as AppleScript, PowerTalk, and QuickTime.

Using MacWrite Pro's Document Settings

When you first open MacWrite Pro, a blank document window appears on-screen (see fig. 16.1). Simple character formatting is available from the menu bar. You don't have to navigate through multiple dialog boxes.

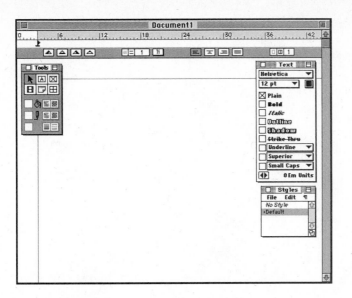

Fig. 16.1
Back to the basics:
MacWrite Pro's
simple work
environment.

Changing document margins is a matter of holding down the Option key
and selecting and dragging one of the four page guides. The pointer turns
into a double-sided arrow, and as you drag the margins back and forth, the
status display bar at the bottom of your document window registers the
changes. You can change the margin settings faster still by opening the Document dialog box from the Format menu, shown in figure 16.2.

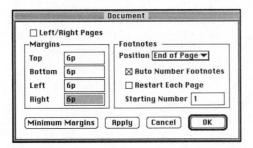

Fig. 16.2
Changing
document margins
can be done by
Option-clicking
and dragging page
guides, or through
this dialog box.

Setting up multiple-column documents can be done in two ways. The easiest
method is just to click the column button at the bottom right of the ruler bar,
as done in figure 16.3. You click the double-column icon to increase the
number of columns, and you click the single-column icon to decrease the
number of columns.

Fig. 16.3

A single click on the appropriate column icon can add to or decrease the number of columns in your document.

If equally sized columns don't suit your job, you can double-click the number displayed in the column button to display the dialog box shown in figure 16.4. You can use this dialog box to specify a separate width for each column.

Fig. 16.4

Setting up uneven column widths in your MacWrite Pro document.

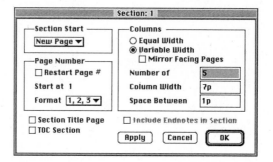

The setting at the left of the Columns window is a useful tool for creating long documents with multiple sections. You can begin a new section in the middle of a page or insert a page break to have the section start on another page. Custom page numbering can be set up with this dialog box as well.

> **Note**
>
> Each page in your MacWrite Pro document can have a different number of columns. This is useful when you're preparing complex reports and newsletters.

Using MacWrite Pro's Text Palette

Text formatting can be done in several ways in MacWrite Pro, but the easiest way is to use the Text palette, shown in figure 16.5. Typeface and size can be selected from pop-up menus. The twin arrows at the bottom of the palette enable you to increase or reduce space between selected text by em units. This is MacWrite Pro's method of establishing tracking (or range kerning) to improve letter spacing.

Fig. 16.5
MacWrite Pro's handy Text palette.

Using MacWrite Pro's Character and Paragraph Styles

Style sheets in MacWrite Pro can be set up on both the character and paragraph levels. This is useful if you want to apply local formatting to a paragraph, such as using italic or bold for emphasis. You can edit your paragraph styles using the handy Styles palette, shown in figure 16.6.

Fig. 16.6
Convenient pull-down menus allow you to edit style sheets right from the Styles palette.

To create a style based on your existing text, you click the File menu of the Styles palette and choose the New Paragraph Style option. You are asked to confirm your new style, which is then added to the palette. To modify the style, hold down the Option key and click the Style name, which displays the dialog box shown in figure 16.7.

A style can be specified as character- or paragraph-based. Each character or paragraph attribute can be customized to your requirements. To apply a style, click anywhere in the paragraph where you want to apply the style and then select the style name from the Styles palette. It takes effect immediately.

Fig. 16.7
Editing paragraph styles is easy in MacWrite Pro.

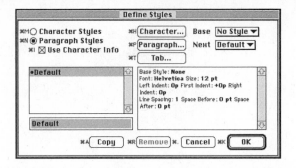

> **Note**
>
> Styles can be imported from another MacWrite Pro document by choosing Open Custom Styles from the File menu of the Styles palette. You then select the document from which you want to copy the styles, and they are added to your document.

Using MacWrite Pro's Tools Palette

Most of your basic document and paragraph formatting tasks can be done using the simple commands in MacWrite Pro's menu bar or from the Text and Styles palette. But you have additional choices available from the Tools palette, shown in figure 16.8.

Fig. 16.8
MacWrite Pro's Tools palette.

The following sections discuss the purpose of each tool, from left to right.

Selection Tool

This tool is the tool that's active when you do most of your work in MacWrite Pro.

Text Tool

This tool is used to create a custom text frame in your document. After you click the Text tool, you drag the frame across your page and use the status bar at the bottom left of the document window for accurate size information. This text frame is unanchored, so the text won't flow automatically from page to page (which is what normally happens with your standard page columns).

Picture Tool

This tool is used to create an unanchored picture frame (in the same manner as you create a text frame), which you use to import illustrations from other programs without actually inserting them into the text. MacWrite Pro imports pictures created in the standard formats, such as EPS, PICT, and TIFF.

Movie Tool

Use this tool to create an unanchored movie frame, which you can use to import QuickTime movies.

Note Tool

Create post-it notes in any portion of your document with this tool. You create a note by clicking this tool and dragging across your document page to the desired length and width of your post-it note. You can enter text inside the note frame in the same way that you enter text in any other part of your document.

Table Tool

This tool is used to create a table in your document. When this tool is selected, the Insert Table window appears and allows the user to specify the number of columns and rows for the new table.

Other Tools

The remaining tools in the Tools palette are used to create fills and lines and to select fill patterns.

Using MacWrite Pro's One-Step Tables

There are two ways to create tables in MacWrite Pro, depending whether you want to convert existing data to table form, or build one from scratch. In the first case, if you've got tab-delimited text (text with tabs that are used to separate fields), select the text you want to convert to table form and choose Insert Table from the Frame Menu, which opens the dialog box shown in figure 16.9. You can also build a table from scratch and enter the appropriate number of columns and rows in the Insert Table dialog box (or by using the Table Tool discussed below).

As you change the table formatting, the graphical display in the window changes to match your changes. You can also specify the column width, although this can be changed later on by selecting the table and dragging the handles.

Fig. 16.9
MacWrite Pro's
Insert Table
window.

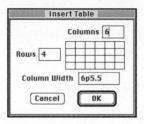

Tables can also be constructed by clicking the Table tool from the Tools palette and dragging across your document page. After you define the borders of your table and release the mouse, a dialog box appears asking you to define the number of columns and rows in your table.

Using MacWrite Pro's Spell Checker and Thesaurus

MacWrite Pro offers two ways to spell-check your documents. You can perform the usual batch spell-check of your document after you finish working on it. Or you can turn on interactive spell-checking, which flags possible spelling mistakes as you type, either by a beep or a flashing menu bar (you make the setting as part of the application's Preferences).

Note

Claris offers optional spell-checking dictionaries in French, Spanish, German, and British English, which can be selected separately for custom spell-checking after installation.

MacWrite Pro's Thesaurus helps you find an alternative for a selected word (see fig. 16.10).

Fig. 16.10
MacWrite Pro's
Thesaurus in
action.

You can select one of the choices made by the Thesaurus, and it replaces the selected word in your document.

Using MacWrite Pro's Find and Replace

MacWrite Pro's Find/Change dialog box, shown fully configured in figure 16.11, can be used simply to replace one text string with another. If you check the Use Attributes check box, as shown in the figure, you also can change character styles by checking the appropriate boxes.

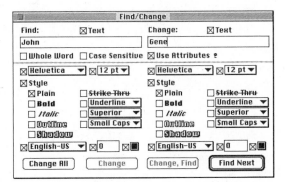

Fig. 16.11
MacWrite Pro's
Find/Change
dialog box.

In addition to searching for text and character-based styles, you can use wild cards to search for a character combination with unknown letters. You can also search for invisible characters, which commonly represent formatting commands such as tabs and paragraph returns. Although very flexible, MacWrite Pro doesn't go quite as far in its Find/Change capabilities as Nisus Writer, discussed later in this chapter.

MacWrite Pro's Advanced Features

MacWrite Pro may be modest in its RAM and disk storage requirements, and simple to use, but it doesn't prevent the program from offering some heavy-duty options to rival those found in the more expensive products discussed later in this chapter. Following are just a few of those features:

- *Automatic text wrap.* You can create sophisticated document layouts by having text wrap around a picture frame. The frame can contain simple shapes or even irregular objects, and you can control the spacing (offset) from the illustration to the text.

- *Zooming.* You can change your document view from 25% to 400%, and retain full document editing capabilities.

- *Notes.* We referred to MacWrite Pro's handy post-it notes earlier in this chapter in our discussion of the convenient Tools palette. If your Mac has a microphone, you can also record a message as part of your notes.

■ *PowerTalk.* If you have Apple's PowerTalk program, which is part of System 7 Pro or System 7.5, you can write and send e-mail directly through MacWrite Pro.

■ *Table of Contents Generation.* You can generate a Table of Contents list by defining paragraph styles as a TOC Style. Any text that has these styles applied to it can be used to generate your Table of Contents.

■ *Hyphenation/justification settings.* As with a desktop publishing program, you can adjust hyphenation and justification settings by using the program's Preferences (shown in fig. 16.12). You can specify the number of hyphens allowed in a row and define the number of letters before and after a hyphen.

Fig. 16.12
Hyphenation and justification settings in MacWrite Pro.

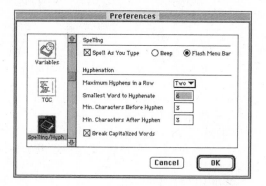

■ *Add-It.* MacWrite Pro's Add-It feature makes the program fully extensible, very much like some of the desktop publishing programs discussed in Chapter 21. Out of the box, MacWrite Pro includes Add-It modules to play QuickTime movies, add sound to your post-it notes, and provide table-creation capability.

Getting the Most out of MacWrite Pro: Hot Tips

■ *Increasing Screen Size.* To increase your screen real estate, you can collapse the floating palettes by clicking in the Close box. The palette is reduced to its title bar. A second click expands it to its normal size.

■ *Changing Application Defaults.* You can change your application settings by formatting a new document and saving it in MacWrite Pro Options format in the Save As dialog box (you store it in the Claris Folder, inside your System Folder). After this settings document is prepared, the formatting attributes in that document become a part of each new document you create in MacWrite Pro.

- *Keyboard Equivalents.* You can display keyboard equivalents in a dialog box by pressing and holding ⌘.

- *Merge Data Files.* If you have a Merge Data File (MDF) opened, you can't also open this file in the usual way, using the Open command from the File menu. You get a `This file already open` alert. To open this file, you must first close it (by using the Merge palette's Close button or by closing, rather than collapsing, the Merge Palette) before being able to reopen it as a standard file.

- *Overflow Symbol.* You may accidentally overflow a frame (for example, if you have a text or table frame, and then change the column dimensions, which produces an overflowed frame display). In some cases, the only way to get this "lost" data back is to increase the page size so that it's large enough to accommodate the overflowed frame. The easiest way to do this is to include the Scale value in the Page Setup dialog box (such as 25%).

- *Performance.* You can speed up MacWrite's screen display noticeably by selecting the Hide Pictures feature.

- *Low memory.* If a rectangle appears on-screen when you try to move an image, it may indicate that you're running out of application memory. You can assign additional memory to MacWrite Pro by quitting the program, highlighting the application icon, selecting Get Info from the Finder's File menu, and increasing its RAM allocation.

- *Show/Hide invisibles.* Using this option, as well as changing the view scale up or down, causes a screen refresh, and your document is reflowed correctly.

- *Text Wrap.* To flow text around graphics, you need to set your wrap frame to transparent. You can set transparency by using the Tools palette or the Modify Frames dialog box.

- *Styles.* There are four predefined paragraph styles that cannot be removed. These are Header, Footer, Footnote, and Default. There are two predefined character styles, Footnote Marker in the body of the text (Superior), and the Footnote Reference Marker (Helvetica, 10 pt, Superior).

Summary

The real charm of MacWrite has been ease of use and an uncluttered working environment. Without falling prey to the software glut that often occurs when you add new features, MacWrite Pro manages to offer most of the capabilities you'd want in a word processing program.

Using Microsoft Word 6

What do you do for an encore when you have the best-selling word processing program? In Word 6.0 for the Macintosh, Microsoft added features that help automate almost every element of the document formatting process. By letting the program figure out many of the steps for you, you're able to get up to speed quickly. In addition, they've taken existing features and added expanded capabilities. Feature for feature, it's hard to find a single program that does more than Word, but as they say, there's no free ride.

System Requirements

Word 6.0 is in many respects identical to its Windows counterpart, and it exacts a high price in terms of CPU horsepower, RAM, and storage requirements. Word 6.0 requires a 68020 Mac or faster, with 5 to 8MB of installed RAM, running System 7.0 or later. The program's Installer gives you several options for how well-equipped you want your copy of Word to be. If you choose to install everything, expect to use over 19MB of hard drive space.

Overview of Microsoft Word

If you're familiar with Word 6.0 for Windows, you'll be very much at home with the Macintosh version. The basic interface and features are nearly the same, but specific Mac features such as AppleScript, AOCE (PowerTalk), and Publish and Subscribe are added. If you've used previous Mac versions of Word, you'll find that many of your favorite features appear here in new settings, and the look and feel of the program is different as well. You'll probably want to spend a little time getting used to the program before producing any heavy-duty projects.

Using Wizards

When you create a new document, Word offers you a unique option, a Wizard. It's a feature that allows the program to guide you step by step through the process of formatting your document. You'll be presented with a list of available wizard templates when you select New from the File menu or press ⌘-N. If you choose a wizard template, you'll be taken through a procession of dialog boxes asking you the sort of document you want to create and guiding you through the basic formatting steps. You can opt to use an existing template, or just create a blank document, and format it to your taste.

Using AutoFormat

In keeping with its goal of letting the software figure things out for you as much as possible, Word 6.0 offers an AutoFormat feature, shown in figure 16.13. By selecting AutoFormat from the Format menu, you'll be able to apply a complete set of formats to your document.

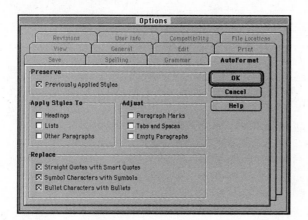

Fig. 16.13
Changing your preset formats with Microsoft Word is easy.

The formats themselves are actually defined in Word's Style Gallery, shown in figure 16.14. You can view a display of what a style looks like by choosing the name of the style.

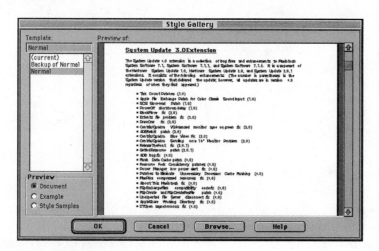

Fig. 16.14
Word's Style Gallery contains a set of standard and user-defined style sheets.

Using Word's Toolbars

You can activate most functions in Word by using the menu bar or keyboard command, or by using its wide selection of floating toolbars, each labeled by function. Word 6.0 offers a grand total of ten toolbars. You can move and reshape them individually or even add them to the top or bottom of your document window. Figure 16.15 shows all the toolbars, which, as you can see, might result in quite a crowded screen if you don't use them judiciously.

Fig. 16.15
All of Word's
standard toolbars
in action.

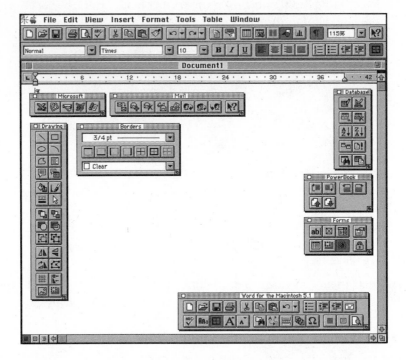

In addition to using the standard toolbar sets, you can customize the appearance of each toolbar by selecting whether to display color icons or large icons. If you hold down the ⌘ key and select a toolbar icon, you can drag it to another toolbar. You can also modify or create your own toolbars from a display of standard Word command icons. This allows you to gain easy access to your frequently used commands and features.

Formatting Documents

Before you enter text in your document, you'll want to use the Document Layout dialog box (from the File menu) to establish page margins, as shown in figure 16.16 below. You can set the positioning of headers and footers, and with the Layout sheet, set custom layouts for the first page of your document. (This dialog box may be slightly different under System 7.5.)

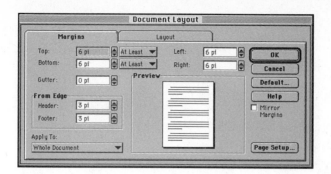

Fig. 16.16
Setting the layout of your Word document.

The Page Setup button at the lower right of the Document Layout dialog box is used for your standard Macintosh printer setup. Chapter 10, "The Printing Chapter," describes Macintosh printer settings in more detail.

Formatting Columns

Your Word 6.0 document can have a single column (which is standard), or you can create multiple columns, each with different widths depending on the needs of your project. Figure 16.17 shows the Columns dialog box.

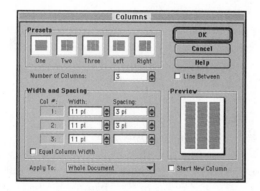

Fig. 16.17
Formatting a multiple column document made easy in Word 6.0.

By unchecking the Equal Column Width option, as done in the example, you can define each column separately, plus the amount of space between that column and the next one. The Preview area at the lower right of the Columns setup box gives you an idea of what your finished layout will look like before you click OK.

Using Word's Fonts Menu

One thing that will be missing at first glance is a conventional Mac Font menu. You can change fonts from the Format toolbar, or choose Font from the Format menu, which brings up the dialog box shown in figure 16.18.

Fig. 16.18
Word's Windows-
like Font dialog
box.

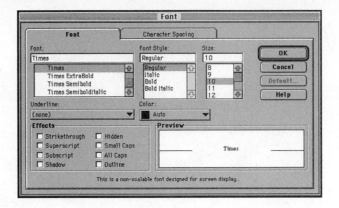

The Font dialog box in Word closely matches the one you get in the Windows version of the program. You use it to select basic character formatting
such as size, style, and color. That little file folder behind the Font file folder,
named Character Spacing, allows you to turn on automatic pair kerning,
which enhances the look of your documents.

Multiple Undos

Multiple Undos represents an idea that's been long in coming, which only a
few Mac software products support. You can undo a single action, or, if you
prefer, multiple actions, simply by repeatedly selecting the Undo command
from the File menu. In this chapter, the only other word processor discussed
that has a comparable capability is Nisus Writer.

Using AutoCorrect

Word's AutoCorrect utility is not an interactive spell checker like the one you
find in MacWrite Pro. Instead, it's a feature that stores your common misspellings, and corrects them on the fly. You can enter the mistakes you make
most frequently, such as *hte* for *the* in the example dialog box shown in figure
16.19.

As soon as you make a spelling error—or at least one you've already defined
in the AutoCorrect setup box—the program intercepts those keystrokes and
inserts the correct ones. It can also be used to insert frequently used text
simply by inserting a shortcut to the correct text string.

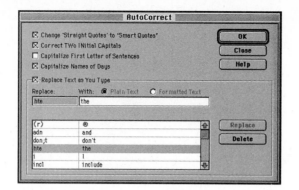

Fig. 16.19
Word 6.0's
AutoCorrect
feature fixes your
mistakes as you
type.

Using Word's Table Editor

Word has an advanced table editing tool that allows you to build your tables simply by spelling out the number of columns and rows. Or you can use the program's Table AutoFormat feature, which allows you to choose the kind of table you want from a selected group of templates. Figure 16.20 shows how the Table Editor works.

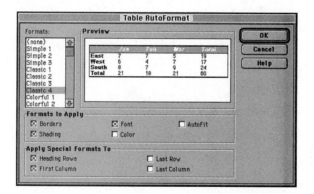

Fig. 16.20
Word's Table
AutoFormat dialog
box helps you
format a complex
table in seconds.

You can choose from a list of templates and preview the table format before you use it. Or you can take an existing table and modify it to your preferences. You can change such attributes as fonts, borders, shading, and color. When you select or deselect one or more of these formats, you'll see the preview area change to reflect your selection.

Using Word's Revisions Feature

Large documents are quite often a group effort. That means there are likely to be a number of versions to a single document before it's actually printed. Word has a Revision Marks feature that allows you to see who changed what and when so that changes can be easily tracked (see fig. 16.21).

Fig. 16.21
Using Word's
Revision Marks
feature enables
you to track the
change history of
your document.

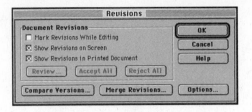

By turning on Revision Marks, you'll be able to review suggested changes in your document and then either accept or delete them separately, or accept or delete the entire set of changes as your needs require. You can also compare one version of a document with another to check for differences. The Options button at the lower right of the Revision Marks dialog box shown in figure 16.21 enables you to select another document for comparison.

Using Word's Drawing Tools

The rather weak drawing tools of Word 5 have been replaced with a Mac version of Microsoft Draw, the standard Windows drawing program. You can now put a drawing on any of three graphic layers—first, as part of the document so that text will run around it, second, as an overlay to your document, and third as a watermark (a backdrop that appears on your document pages). As shown in figure 16.22, you get a pretty decent selection of drawing tools.

Fig. 16.22
Word's drawing
tools.

Word won't replace a high-end drawing program, but it offers basic shapes, including polygons, tools to insert callouts, layering, grouping, rotating, reshaping freehand or polygon shapes, and a tool to align one object to another, or a selected object to a page. With a little effort, you can probably use these tools to create many pleasing illustrations without ever leaving the program.

Using Drop Caps

Adding drop caps to your document provides a fancy look, and Word 6.0 provides a quick, automatic tool to generate them. You just choose Drop Caps from the Format menu and enter the style information (see fig. 16.23).

Fig. 16.23
Word's Drop Cap
dialog box.

IV

Macintosh Software

To insert a drop cap in your paragraph, highlight the first letter in a paragraph, open the Drop Cap dialog box and select the kind of drop cap you want from the display in the Drop Cap dialog box. Then specify the typeface, the number of lines it occupies, and the space from the body text. The drop cap takes effect as soon as you choose OK.

Word's Advanced Features

Word 6.0 is a major upgrade to the program and adds many new features, and changes or improves on other features. Following are some of its more advanced capabilities:

- A Mail Merge Helper offers you a series of dialog boxes to guide you through the process of merging your address list into form letters, envelopes, or labels.

- You can add an item in your document to an index simply by highlighting the text and identifying or marking it for inclusion in the completed table of contents. You make the selection from the Mark Index Entry dialog box, shown in figure 16.24, which is available from the Insert menu when you select Index and Tables. A table of contents can be generated based on custom entries, or by using your existing styles for headlines and subheads.

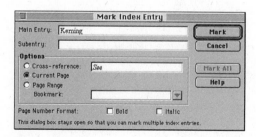

Fig. 16.24
Word's index
generation tools
offer you exceptional flexibility.

■ The movable Microsoft toolbar allows you to quickly launch another installed Microsoft program, such as Excel, simply by clicking the appropriate icon. When you quit that program, you're returned automatically to Word.

■ Word 6.0 allows you to create professional quality forms for invoices and reports.

■ Word 6.0's Macro creation feature allows you to record the actions you perform over and over again, and have the program repeat those steps via simple keyboard commands. You can use a macro to format a document, enter predefined information in a form, or build an index or table of contents—just to name a few of the possibilities you'll want to explore.

■ Choose Objects from the Insert menu to open Word's advanced Equation editor to build equations from scratch, or Microsoft Graph, a handy charting tool. The Object dialog box is shown in figure 16.25. You can also import QuickTime movies into your Word document and play them as part of a presentation. (You have to have Apple's QuickTime installed on your computer, however.)

Fig. 16.25
The Object dialog box introduces you to other handy Word features.

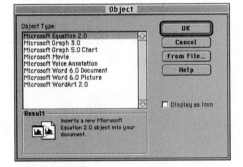

Getting the Most out of Microsoft Word: Hot Tips

■ To search and replace fonts (without altering text), use the Replace command in the Edit menu, or type ⌘-H.

■ If you've removed the formatting toolbar to save screen space, you can still change fonts by typing ⌘-Shift-D, which opens the Font dialog box.

■ You can activate automatic pair kerning in Word 6.0 by selecting the Kerning for Fonts option in the Font dialog box, under Character Spacing.

- If you decide to create a shaded background for a paragraph, be sure to test whether the text is readable or not. You might want to print a sample page just to be certain before proceeding with similar shading on a large document.

- Use templates if you plan to use the same styles over and over again for regular projects, such as books or newsletters.

- Use the Replace command in the Edit menu to delete text that has been formatted with a particular style. When you bring up the Replace window, pick from the list shown in the Format menu under Style the name of the style of the text you want to remove. The Replace box should be left blank. Click the Find Next button. If the text you want to remove appears, choose Replace and it's gone!

- To quickly bring up the Document Layout dialog box, double-click the gray area between your document page and the vertical ruler.

- You can use the Bullets and Numbering dialog box (in the Format menu) to create formats for bulleted or numbered lists in your document. Word's handy Sort feature allows you to fix the order of numbered items if you move them out of sequence.

Summary

With Word 6, Microsoft fulfilled almost anyone's wish list for what should be in a word processing program. It's not surprising that Word has been the number one Mac word processor year after year. And if you work in a mixed-platform environment, with Windows PCs working next to Macs, you'll be happy to know that the Mac and Windows versions of Word are nearly identical in most respects, and you can switch from one to the other with little or no training at all.

Using Nisus Writer 4

Nisus owes its origins to a text editing utility called QUED, which was first introduced in 1987. The program provided text editing tools primarily for programmers. In 1989, the text engine was incorporated with a graphics layer and other features were added to create a new all-purpose word processor known as Nisus Writer. Beginning with version 2.0, Nisus was localized (configured) for international markets and was also sold in such countries as Germany, France, Japan, and Korea. By version 3.0, the program shipped to such diverse locales as Bulgaria, Hungary, Poland, Romania, Russia, and Saudi Arabia.

System Requirements

Nisus Writer works on any Mac running System 6.0.7 or later, with 2MB or more of installed RAM. The full package uses approximately 6.5MB of hard disk storage space.

Nisus Writer Overview

Nisus Writer 4 is the latest update of a program with one of the most full-featured text editing engines you can find among word processing software products. Not only is there extensive support for multiple language editions, but the program offers highly sophisticated search/replace tools, drag-and-drop text, macros, multiple clipboards, unlimited undos, and noncontiguous selection. The following sections discuss some of these features and more.

Using Nisus Writer's Paragraph Rulers

Basic formatting in your Nisus Writer document is done by changing the settings on the paragraph ruler (see fig. 16.26). Copying the ruler settings to another part of your document where different formatting is being used will transfer the formatting of that ruler. The ruler's basic setup is similar to other Mac word processing programs: if you drag the arrows representing your page margins to the right or left, the margins on your page will change accordingly. If you drag just the bottom part of the left margin arrow to the left or right, you can set the indent for the first line of a paragraph.

Fig. 16.26
Nisus Writer uses a paragraph ruler for basic document formatting.

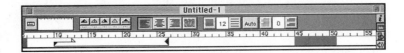

The other settings in the Nisus Writer ruler control tab stops, justification, line spacing, and paragraph spacing. The new version of Nisus Writer also adds the option of naming your ruler, as shown in figure 16.27. After the ruler is named, it appears in a pop-up menu at the left of the ruler bar, and you can use this feature to quickly change paragraph formatting.

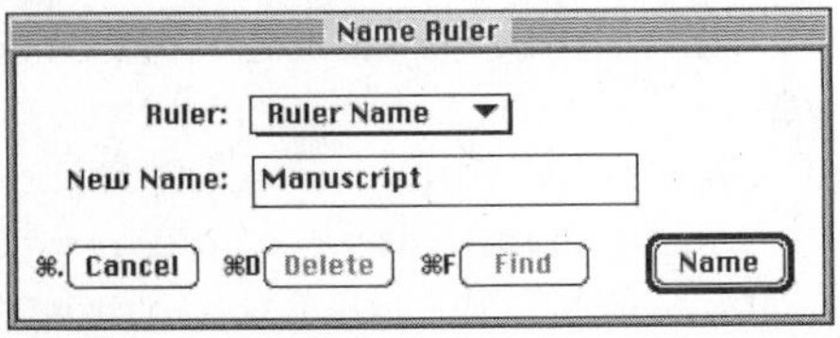

Fig. 16.27
Name your ruler, which, in effect, makes it the equivalent of a paragraph style sheet.

Changing Document Layout

Document layout settings are adjusted in the Layout window, shown in figure 16.28. The page icons to the left of the window are used to choose between a normal page and facing pages. The latter setting allows you to view your document as a *spread,* with both the lefthand and righthand pages onscreen.

Fig. 16.28
Changing your document layout with Nisus Writer's Layout window.

The numerical settings to the right of the page icons are used to set paper size and the margins for your text area. The icon at the right of these margin settings allows you to automatically center your text margins within a page (or you can choose Center Page from the Layout menu, which only appears when the Layout window is open). The icon with arrows pointing outward allows you to automatically expand page margins to the maximum area that your printer allows.

A convenient way to set up multiple columns is to use the Set Margins and Columns dialog box, shown in figure 16.29. You can activate this window by double-clicking anywhere inside the Layout bar or by choosing Set Margins from the Layout menu.

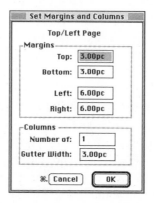

Fig. 16.29
Nisus Writer's Set Margins and Columns window allows you to quickly customize your document setup.

You can also set your page margins visually by clicking and dragging along the dotted lines that define the margins. Up to eight margins of equal width can be created in your document.

Using Nisus Writer's Graphics Palette

As I said previously in this chapter, don't expect a word processor's drawing tools to replace those of a high-end illustration program. Even within their limits, however, I've seen some well-constructed artwork. You bring up the graphics window simply by clicking the Show Graphics Palette icon (a stylized drawing) at the right side of your document window. Nisus Writer's Graphics palette, shown in figure 16.30, can also be used to edit PICT files imported into your document.

Fig. 16.30

A basic set of drawing tools for Nisus Writer.

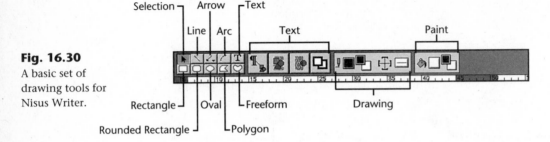

The tools used to create shapes and rules are at the left of the palette, and they're similar to what you'd find in most Mac drawing and word processing programs. The next three icons are called Object Attribute Menus. They are used to select how your graphic is to be used. The paragraph icon allows the graphic to be inserted at the cursor point in your document, essentially as another character in your text stream. The second icon toggles (click on and click off) to select whether your drawing will be in a layer above your text or below it. The latter setting is useful for creating a watermark effect in your document. The third icon toggles text wrapping on and off. When the icon shows text flowing around the graphic, you'll achieve the corresponding effect in your document.

Using Nisus Writer's Find/Replace Tools

One of Nisus Writer's unique features is its powerful search and replace capability, which allows you to establish complex, multilayered search strings and set up a replace string equally complex and multilayered. Nisus Writer calls this search capability *PowerSearch*, or GREP (short for Global Regular Expression Parser). The Find/Replace window, shown in figure 16.31, provides three levels of sophistication, depending on what sort of editing you want to do.

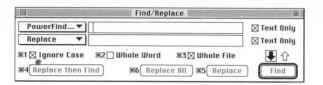

Fig. 16.31
Nisus Writer's powerful Find/ Replace capability lets you search for almost any attribute you can imagine in your document.

> ### Note
>
> Holding ⌘, as I did when creating screen shots of Nisus Writer windows for this book, displays a set of handy keyboard shortcuts, as well.

I'll give you just a brief example of the sort of stuff you can search for. Basic search/replace functions are done in the same way as many other Mac programs, but you'll want to read the program's detailed manual before you try any of the more sophisticated search routines, because a great deal of specialized syntax is involved.

Figure 16.32 shows PowerSearch+ in action. In the example, I look up the phrase *Page numbers (#) follow those items discussed in the manual*. This phrase will be changed so that the word *page* appears with the number in parentheses. Note that the page numbers in parentheses are changing each time this phrase is used, which serves to complicate the process.

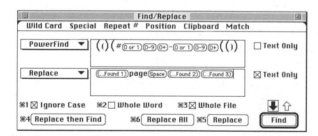

Fig. 16.32
An example of Nisus Writer's PowerSearch+ in action.

Each of the expressions shown above is selected from the various items in the Find/Replace window's menu bar. In addition to being able to search through an open document, you can search and replace text strings in closed documents. Be warned that this feature requires a bit of reading and some practice before you get the hang of it.

Using Nisus Writer's Multiple Clipboards

As you can see from what has been covered so far, Nisus Writer has several unique slants to text editing that you don't often find in other Macintosh programs (more such slants are described in the following sections).

One of the program's most useful features is its multiple clipboard capability. The Macintosh operating system gives you but one. When you cut or copy an item to the clipboard, it replaces what is already there. Some utilities, such as Olduvai's MultiClip Pro, get around this with a System Extension of one sort or another. Nisus Writer supports ten clipboards in the program, and you can select which one you want to choose from a submenu in the Edit menu, as shown in figure 16.33.

Fig. 16.33
When one clipboard isn't enough, Nisus Writer gives you ten.

The pull-down menu enables you to choose which of the ten clipboards you want to use for temporary storage of text or graphic elements. If one clipboard is full, you can select another. By using the Show Clipboard option in the Edit menu, you can quickly view the contents of your selected clipboard before deciding whether to replace them.

Noncontiguous Selection

This sounds like quite a tongue twister, but it's a feature seldom seen on Macintosh programs (we saw it once on Taste, a word processing program from DeltaPoint that's no longer being produced), and it's surely a feature that can be quite useful when editing complex streams of text. It refers to the capability of selecting separate, unconnected areas of text in your document simply by holding down the ⌘ and Option keys when you select text. See figure 16.34 for an idea of how noncontiguous selection looks on-screen.

Multiple Undos

This feature should be added to more Macintosh programs. In Nisus Writer, the changes you make to your document are stored in an Undo List, one by one, in the order in which they were made. Depending on the preferences you set for the application, you can have literally thousands of undos.

This multiple undo scheme has only one limitation. If you have more than a single document open, the changes are still stored in one list. You have to be careful to be sure you're not undoing a change in a different document.

Using Nisus Writer's Thesaurus

Nisus Writer's Thesaurus not only helps you locate the correct word when it's just at the tip of the tongue, but it gives you the definition for the word you selected as well, as shown in figure 16.35.

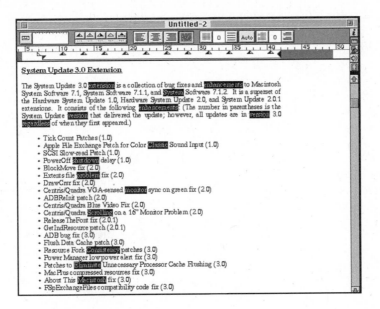

Fig. 16.34
Using Nisus Writer's noncontiguous selection feature.

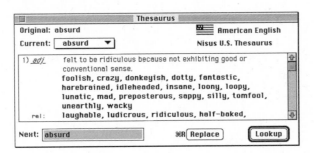

Fig. 16.35
Nisus Writer's Thesaurus in action.

The Thesaurus also retains a list of the words you have looked up in your document, in a pull-down menu, in case you want to choose another word instead of the one you originally selected.

Nisus Writer's Advanced Features

Nisus Writer combines sophisticated text processing tools with a wide range of features that make it the word processor of choice for many users. The following list describes just a few of these additional capabilities:

■ *Multimedia Features.* Nisus Writer includes a number of sound and video-related features, such as the capability to import and play QuickTime movies, add sound annotation to your documents, and provide text to speech capability in multiple languages.

■ *Macros.* Nisus Writer has a sophisticated macro editor that allows you to record repetitive actions and play them back through a simple keyboard command. Macros can be recorded in a catalog and then used in any open document.

■ *Graphic and text rotation.* Like many desktop publishing programs, you can rotate both graphics and text in your Nisus Writer document, though the capability is limited to 90° angles.

■ *Indexing and Table of Contents.* You can generate an index or table of contents by marking the entries in your text. When your document is finished, you can quickly generate your index or table of contents in a new document window, based on the entries you've marked.

■ *Drag-and-drop text.* Like Microsoft Word and WordPerfect (which are discussed next), you can select and drag text to a different position in your document. Holding the Option key while you drag selected text makes a duplicate copy of the text rather than moving the original.

■ *Character spacing.* Although automatic pair kerning isn't supported, you can use Nisus Writer's Set Tracking feature to reduce space between two characters or a range of selected text.

■ *PowerBook support.* If you are using a portable Macintosh, Nisus Writer puts up a display of remaining battery life in the status bar of your document window.

■ *WorldScript support.* Nisus Writer supports System 7.1's use of two-byte scripts for multi-language support. You can easily switch from left-to-right to right-to-left text entry by choosing a different language script.

■ *File merging.* You can generate form letters by merging the contents of two or more documents in your open document window.

■ *XTend support.* Nisus Writer supports Claris XTend translators, which allows you to open or insert text and pictures in a variety of formats, including EPSF graphics.

Getting the Most out of Nisus Writer: Hot Tips

■ If you're using a PowerBook, set the option to load Nisus Writer in RAM (in the Preferences settings). That will reduce disk access, giving you more useful battery life.

■ If you ⌘-click on a window title bar, the Windows menu opens, allowing you to select another document window, or stack or tile your open windows.

■ A quick way around handling Nisus Writer's often complex PowerSearch+ syntax is to first create your search and replace fields in PowerSearch. When you switch to PowerSearch+, the statements in the search and replace fields will be automatically translated to the more sophisticated search language.

■ You can save time, when spell checking the same document multiple times, by only spell checking changes. Immediately after a spell checking session, follow these directions:

> 1) In the document, choose Select All.

> 2) In the Spell Checking window, choose Ignore.

After that, any new changes you make will be checked, but the text that has already been checked and ignored will not be checked again, saving you time.

■ If you have used the spell checker and you start running low on application memory, go to the Catalog and double-click the Nisus Dictionary file. Nisus will reload the dictionary and remove your Skip All choices from memory, thus freeing up more to work with your document. This is an alternative to quitting and reassigning more RAM to Nisus in the Finder.

■ If you have a very large document on which you want to perform several Find/Replace actions, first give Nisus as much memory as possible in the Finder's Get Info box. Then go into Nisus and in the Editing preferences, set the number of undos to one. Open a copy of your file (not the original, because you can only undo one mistake) and perform the Find/Replace. That way Nisus will only store the last Find/Replace in the undo list, saving memory and speeding up the process.

■ To print page numbers on each page of your document, create a header or footer containing the page number variable. Click your insertion point near the top of the page on which you would like page numbering to start. Select Insert Header (or Footer) from the Format menu.

Choose Insert Page Number from the Format menu. The page number will now print correctly on that and each page that follows in your document.

- An easy way to copy the format of one section of text to another is to copy and paste rulers from the ruler margin. First click the ruler icon in the upper-left corner of the master ruler to show the ruler icons. Click the ruler that appears next to the section of text whose format you want to copy, and then choose Copy from the Edit menu. Move the insertion point to the first line of the section of text where you want to copy the format, and choose Paste.

- In Nisus, you control the placement of the header by choosing the page on which to insert the header. To place a header on each page except the first page, scroll to the second page, click the insertion point in the first paragraph, then choose Insert Header from the Format menu.

- To adjust text flow around a graphic, choose Text Wrap On from the Graphics palette, then choose Set Wrap Border from the Graphics menu. This dialog box allows you to set the margin (offset) between a graphic and the wrapped text. Enter 10 in this dialog box for a 10-point wrap border.

Summary

Some folks think Nisus is a bit eclectic as word processors go. And it's a sure thing that Nisus Software has done its best not to follow the pack in developing this program. But Nisus Writer has a selection of unique text processing features that you won't find in any other program. While deciding which program to buy, you should give this one a careful look.

Using WordPerfect

Although WordPerfect has been hugely successful in the DOS/Windows marketplace, the first attempt to produce a Macintosh program did not exactly set the world afire. WordPerfect 1.0 for the Macintosh, released in 1988, consisted largely of a direct port of their DOS software to the Macintosh environment, with a ruler added across the top of the document window. It took several years and several updates for the Macintosh version of WordPerfect to get a true Mac interface and develop a style of its own. WordPerfect became the first high-end word processor to support Apple's QuickTime, PowerTalk, and AppleScript and to produce a native Power Macintosh version.

System Requirements

WordPerfect works on a Mac Plus or better, using System 6.0.7 or later, with 2MB or more of installed RAM. The Power Macintosh version of WordPerfect requires 4.5MB or more of installed RAM. If you install the entire package (which includes a selection of fonts from Bitstream), expect to use between 10MB and 11MB of storage space (depending on whether you're using the regular Mac version or the native Power Macintosh edition).

WordPerfect Overview

WordPerfect has at last come into its own as a viable alternative to Microsoft Word on the Macintosh. The latest version is a uniquely Macintosh product that's fully System 7 savvy, with all that entails. WordPerfect has all the capabilities a high-end word processing program should offer, such as drag-and-drop text, grammar checking, an equation editor, a table editor, and the capability to generate a table of contents.

Using WordPerfect's Ruler Bars

Much of the formatting of your WordPerfect documents can be done directly from its ruler bars. WordPerfect has taken a different approach with these ruler bars, and has made them easier to understand than the comparable features of other programs. You can display or collapse them simply by clicking on the appropriate button on the first ruler bar at the top of your document, as shown in figure 16.36.

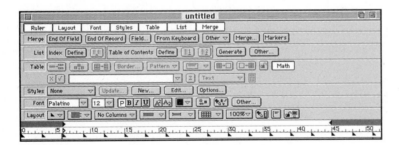

Fig. 16.36
WordPerfect's ruler bars, using labels as well as icons for clarity.

When you click the button, as done in figure 16.36, the display turns from gray to white, and the selected ruler bar appears at the top of your document. Clicking the button a second time causes the corresponding ruler bar to collapse. To ease the task of learning the functions of the various buttons, many are labeled by name rather than by icon. The following sections describe the functions of the various ruler bars in this figure, from top to bottom, beneath the first ruler bar.

The Merge Bar

This ruler bar is used to activate WordPerfect's document merging feature, which allows you to combine portions of separate documents, such as when you create a form letter.

The List Bar

This ruler bar is used to format an index or table of contents, and to create a list of document cross-reference information.

The Table Bar

This ruler bar is used to edit the tables you've created. The table creation process begins with the Layout Bar, described below.

The Extended Table Bar

This ruler bar is used to add numbers to your tables. It appears when you click on the Math button on the Table Bar.

The Styles Bar

This ruler bar is used to apply style sheets to text in your documents, to edit an existing style, or to create a new one.

The Font Bar

This ruler bar is used to change fonts and apply character formatting changes.

The Layout Bar

This ruler bar is used for your basic document and paragraph formatting. You can create columns, change line spacing, and change spacing between paragraphs. You can also use it to create a basic table template.

The Ruler

This ruler bar resembles the ones found in most word processing programs. You can use it to change left and right margins, column margins, and tab settings.

WordPerfect's Status Bar

This ruler bar appears at the bottom of your document (see fig. 16.37). It can be configured using the pop-up menu accessible from the down arrow at the left of the display. You can display such information as the date and time, what page and line number your cursor is positioned at, along with its exact position in inches (or picas or whatever measurement unit you've selected). If you're typing text in a table, it can display the number of the cell you're in.

If you're using a PowerBook, it will also display an icon showing estimated battery life.

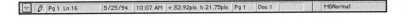

Fig. 16.37
Some of the
information
reported in
WordPerfect's
Status Bar.

WordPerfect's Button Bar

The Button Bar is a little closer to the sort of toolbar you find in programs such as Microsoft Word. Figure 16.38 shows the default Button Bar. It displays common formatting commands. The arrow at the left produces a pop-up menu that allows you to select alternate bars, one for Graphics and the other for Equations. You can position the bar at the right, left, top, or bottom.

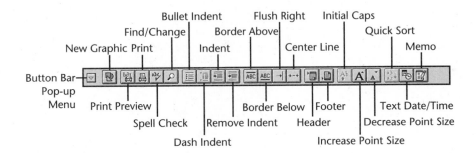

Fig. 16.38
WordPerfect's
infinitely adjust-
able Button Bar.

If you decide that the Button Bar could use a few changes, you can configure it to your own taste from a large palette of common WordPerfect command icons, or create a new one using the particular icons you want. You can also create custom Button Bars to store within a single document so that the Button Bar will only be available when that document is opened.

Using WordPerfect's Drawing Tools

WordPerfect is not intended as a replacement for your favorite drawing program, but it offers a decent selection of drawing tools. The Graphic Tool palette shown in figure 16.39 provides most of the basic tools you need to create simple drawings. WordPerfect even has a bézier curve tool to create curve segments.

A graphic can be produced as an overlay on your document, atop the text, inserted within the text at your cursor, or placed behind the text for use as a watermark. WordPerfect can also import graphic objects created in other programs in the common formats, such as EPS, PICT, or TIFF.

Fig. 16.39
For simple illustrations, WordPerfect's drawing tools will surely fit your needs.

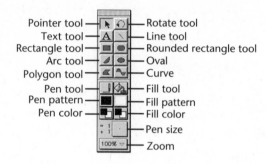

Using WordPerfect's Paragraph Styles

WordPerfect's Styles ruler bar offers an easy way to create or edit style sheets. The easiest way to create a paragraph style is to format a paragraph, then select New from the Styles ruler bar, which will display the dialog box shown in figure 16.40.

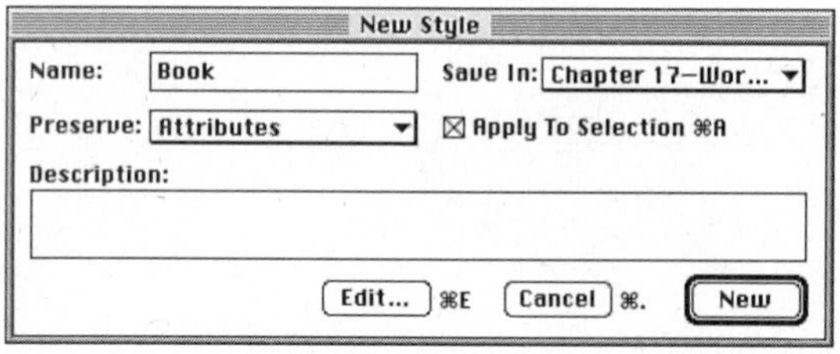

Fig. 16.40
Creating a new paragraph style in WordPerfect.

To modify your style, click the Edit button, which will bring up a small text window at the bottom of your screen, complete with its own ruler bars. You can change the formatting to your taste in the text window. When you click the window's close box, the format is added or modified. The name of your new style is added to the list displayed in the pop-up menu at the left of your Styles ruler bar.

> **Note**
>
> A WordPerfect style can be added to a *library* so that it will be made available to all the documents you create, or it can be saved with your existing document. You choose this option when you are creating or editing a style.

Using WordPerfect's Table Editor

WordPerfect offers a very flexible, easy-to-use table editor. You can insert a table directly into your document, or create a separate text box so that the table can be resized or moved without affecting the regular text. Before I touch on the highlights of WordPerfect's table creation tools, I'll describe briefly how a text box is created. First, you choose Text Box from the Tools menu, which displays the submenu shown in figure 16.41.

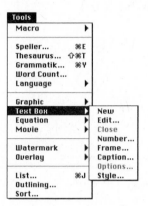

Fig. 16.41
Create a text box to build a floating table in your WordPerfect Document.

If you select New, an empty text box appears at the insertion point in your manuscript. You can click and drag on the handles of the text box to resize it (you'll see a status display of its size at the bottom of your document window).

Once your text box has been created, you can get down to the business of creating your table. A really quick way to build a table is to click the Table icon on the Layout Bar and then select the number of rows and columns you want in your table by dragging your mouse across the illustration shown in figure 16.42. The number of rows and columns are displayed at the top of the small graphical window.

Fig. 16.42
Drag your mouse across this template to create a table of the desired size.

If the preselected graphic doesn't display the table format you want, you can choose the Other option and enter the number of columns and rows for your table in a dialog box. You can also build a table by selecting New from the Table menu.

A WordPerfect table can also use selected text in paragraph form, or tab or comma-delimited form (used to separate fields), and create a table based on that text. (If you decide to convert your table back to text, WordPerfect can do that, too.)

WordPerfect provides a variety of tools to adjust the width and height of table cells, and to add borders and fills to your table. The Math bar is used to insert figures and formulas in a table, and the program is able to calculate totals based on the figures you enter.

Using WordPerfect's Spell Checker

WordPerfect's spell checker feature, shown in action in figure 16.43, provides enormous flexibility in a small display. The menu bar atop the spell check window allows you to choose whether to check the entire document, the remainder of the document, or just the text you have selected.

Fig. 16.43
WordPerfect's spell checker examines the manuscript for this chapter.

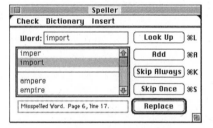

If you are using WordPerfect's multilingual tools, you can choose different dictionaries from the Dictionary menu. You even can create a user dictionary to add words that are not part of WordPerfect's regular dictionary.

Using WordPerfect's Thesaurus

When you cannot find the exact word for a particular setting, WordPerfect's Thesaurus, shown in figure 16.44, will help you choose it.

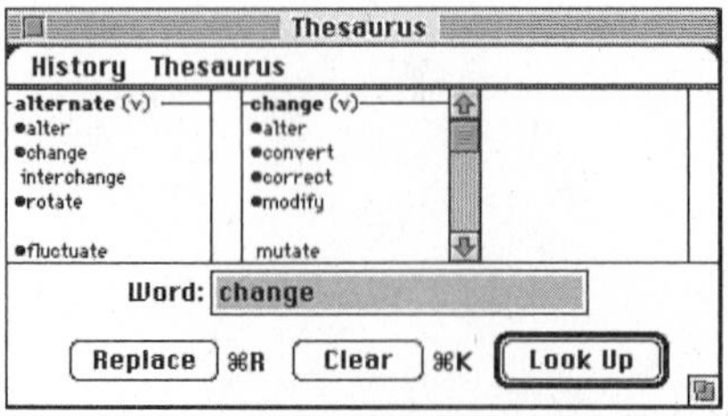

Fig. 16.44
WordPerfect's Thesaurus in action.

You can select one of the choices presented by the program, and have it re-place the selected word in your document. WordPerfect's Thesaurus window has another neat option. It can display synonyms and antonyms in separate windows.

Using WordPerfect's Bullet Indent Feature

WordPerfect makes easy work of creating a bulleted list. Simply select the text, and click the Bullet Indent button on the Button Bar. A bullet will be inserted ahead of the selected paragraphs, and the paragraphs will be in-dented to the right of the bullet.

Using WordPerfect's Find/Change Feature

WordPerfect provides a simple Find/Change window, shown in figure 16.45, but offers menu bar selections that add an enormous amount of flexibility to this feature. You can do a routine search and replacement of text, but you can also search by font or style, and add wild cards to the search routine to cover a range of possible character combinations.

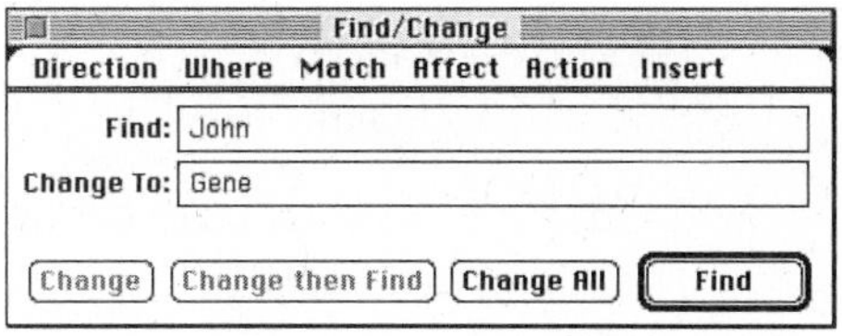

Fig. 16.45
WordPerfect's
Find/Change
dialog box.

The program's search capability extends to non-printing format characters as well, which include tabs, returns, indents, and page and column breaks. You can search from your insertion point to the end of your document, back to the beginning of your document, or restrict the search to selected text.

WordPerfect's Advanced Features

In terms of application size and system and hardware needs, WordPerfect occupies the middle of the range among the programs described in this chapter. But the feature list is very long. In addition to the ones described in detail previously, the following list describes some more of what WordPerfect can do:

■ *Macros.* This has been a mainstay of WordPerfect for several years. A small number of pre-built macros ships with the program. You can create your own simply by having the program record your actions, and then play them back with a convenient keyboard command.

- *Zooming.* You can change your document view from 25% to 800%, and retain full document editing capabilities.

- *Multi-Language.* WordPerfect supports WorldScript and the publisher will sell you special language modules that allow you to include text in several languages in your documents.

- *E-Mail.* If you have Apple's PowerTalk program, which is part of System 7 Pro or System 7.5, you can write and send e-mail directly through WordPerfect. (This feature is not yet supported in the first release of WordPerfect for Power Macintosh.)

- *Index or Table of Contents Generation.* You can generate a Table of Contents or Index list by defining text or paragraph styles in your document. An Index or Table of Contents can be generated easily when your document is finished.

- *Quicktime.* You can insert QuickTime movie clips directly into your document, in the same way you import a graphic file. A built-in movie controller allows you to click on the QuickTime movie and play it.

- *Redline & Strikeout.* Text slated for addition or deletion can be marked while editing your document and be removed with a single keystroke.

- *Equation Editor.* WordPerfect's handy Equation Editor, shown in figure 16.46, enables you to create and edit equations. You can also easily display equations created in the DOS, Windows, and UNIX versions of WordPerfect.

Fig. 16.46
WordPerfect's convenient Equation Editor appears as a floating palette above your document.

Getting the Most out of WordPerfect: Hot Tips

- You can use WordPerfect's Thesaurus even when the program isn't active. First open the Language folder (located inside your WordPerfect application folder). Double-click the Thesaurus icon, which will open the ST Utility. Enter the word you want to look up, and click the Look Up button. A list of suggested words appears.

IV

■ To change the default font in WordPerfect, select Preferences from the Edit menu. Click the Font icon. You can use the popup menu to select your default font. When you click on the OK button in the Preferences window, all new documents you create will use that default font. Any existing font that relies on the default font will also be changed.

■ To change default document settings, follow these steps:

1. Click the Styles button to bring down the Styles ruler bar.

2. Click the Edit button.

3. Highlight Document style and click Edit.

4. A small document window opens (see fig. 16.47). You change your default settings by using the ruler bars inside of this window, which are identical to the ones that display in a regular document window. For example, you can change the document margin settings, typeface size, tabs, columns, and so on.

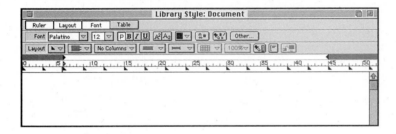

Fig. 16.47
Changing your default styles in WordPerfect.

5. Click the Close box of the window.

The changes you make will apply to all documents that rely on the default document style.

■ To select text by using the numerical keypad, do the following: Press Shift-8 to select upwards one line at a time, Shift-2 to select downwards a line at a time. Option-Shift-4 selects one word at a time to the left; Option-Shift-6 selects one word at a time to the right. Command Shift-4 or Command Shift-6 selects from the insertion point to either end of the line. Command Shift-8 or Command-Shift-2 selects from the insertion point to the top or bottom of the screen. You can substitute the directional arrows for the keypad, if you prefer.

■ When your cursor is in a table and you are displaying the Table ruler, you can see what look like capital letter T's above each column line. Dragging the main vertical part of the T moves that column line, and all columns to the right. Dragging the left or right serif, or small vertical line forming the tip at either end of the top of the T, moves the margins of the columns. You can drag and drop text and numbers from one cell to another just as you would move text outside of a table (or Option-drag to make a duplicate copy).

■ Here's how to add a row to an existing table: when you're in the last cell of the last existing row, just press Tab. To move the cursor to a tab set within a table cell, use Option-Tab. (Option-Tab indents, outside of a table.)

■ While you'll do most of the formatting of cell contents using the Table Number Format menu on the Math bar, one useful format for numbers is to align them flush right. Just use the Alignment menu on the Layout bar.

■ You may want to run a macro each time you open a new document to create, for example, a customized letterhead or form where the macro pauses for user input. Here's how: title the macro **OnOpenDocument** and save it in a blank document as stationery (in the Save As dialog box). The macro will run any time you create a new file using that stationery as a template. To run the macro with every new file you create, place the macro in the stationery document titled New Document Stationery and save it in the Stationery folder (located in the WordPerfect application folder). You can also title a Library macro "OnStartUp" and it will run every time you open WordPerfect. If OnOpenDocument is put in the Library, it will run when you open any existing document.

Summary

WordPerfect has not just cloned its PC and Windows products and put a Mac menu bar on them. WordPerfect has created a feature-filled, uniquely Macintosh program that has developed a strong following. WordPerfect also has been first on the block with a native Power Macintosh word processor, and has been very aggressive in offering regular upgrades with new features and performance enhancements. A comprehensive Help menu and the ability to print out your help text also makes it easy to get up to speed on this program.

Conclusions and Recommendations

There is no doubt that any of the programs discussed in this chapter will meet most of your document processing needs smoothly and efficiently. Each program has specific strengths that may be better suited to your purposes. Following are some thoughts to consider:

- MacWrite Pro has most of the features of the high-priced competition, with a simple, accessible interface and a very low purchase price. It adds to the mix some tools generally the province of desktop publishing software, such as automatic kerning and the ability to set hyphenation and justification parameters. If some of the specialized features offered by the competition don't appeal to you, MacWrite Pro may be all the word processing power you need.

- What can I say? Microsoft Word became number one in the marketplace not just with fancy advertising, but because the publisher has tried to understand the needs of users and respond to them. Word 6.0 is big and fat and requires large reserves of RAM and storage space. But it answers just about anyone's wish list for the ideal word processor. If you're an experienced Word user, and you have the right Mac hardware, you'll have little reason to change.

- Nisus Writer is fast, slick, and innovative. It has features that should be a natural part of word processing software, such as its multiple clipboards, multiple undos, and almost limitless find/search capabilities, but they remain exclusive to this program. It's a little different from the pack, and an acquired taste to some, but once you get used to it, there's no turning back.

- WordPerfect stumbled badly when it first came to the Macintosh, but the publisher learned its lessons well. This program is designed to meet the competition from Microsoft Word head-on, and offers its own unique package of features. It is a big program, though not quite as big as Word, with less stringent hardware requirements. It has a familiar, friendly interface, and it's relatively easy to use. It's surely worth consideration.

From Here...

This chapter discussed the most popular Macintosh word processing software products available and offered a few ideas for which one to choose for your document processing chores. Although these programs all have sophisticated document creation capabilities, you might find you need a true desktop publishing program instead (or you might want to use both, depending on the demands of the project).

■ Chapter 8, "All about Fonts," offers helpful hints on getting around in the Mac's confusing world of multiple font formats, and suggests ways to help you manage a font library.

■ Chapter 21, "Desktop Publishing," contrasts the capabilities of a true publishing program to word processing software, and gives you some suggestions as to which to choose.

■ If you encounter any difficulties along the way, read Chapters 37 and 38. These chapters describe how to troubleshoot common problems with your Mac and how you can solve those problems before they become serious.

Chapter 17

Presentation Graphics

by Dave Plotkin

Graphics are an important part of doing business today. Graphics help communicate ideas—from charts and graphs to timelines, flow charts, calendars, and general illustrations. Graphics play an important part in presentations designed to convince an audience to follow a new project plan, create and market a new product, or pursue a new course of action.

Creating business graphics presents a dilemma to the average person. On the one hand, business graphics are often created in a hurry, usually for some tight deadline. Further, they are most often created by people who have little artistic talent—or lack the time to exercise that talent even if they do have it. And yet, ideas and projects, even careers, can be markedly influenced by the quality of these graphics. Business graphics are often used in presentations to managers, potential customers, and other people who can have an important impact on the rest of your life. If a presentation is inadequate, it can accentuate the natural "stage fright" that many people feel when they are called on to present information to a group.

This chapter provides some background information about computer graphics and then discusses the features and capabilities of the following widely used graphics packages:

- Claris Impact
- DeltaPoint DeltaGraph
- Microsoft PowerPoint
- Gold Disk Astound
- Aldus Persuasion

The Evolution of Computer Graphic Packages

Computer-based graphics and presentation packages help busy business people put together presentations quickly. By providing a combination of text tools, drawing tools, a collection of clip art, and ways to arrange and rearrange the order of slides, these packages ease the creation of graphics and presentations. Presentation graphics packages make it possible to do more than simply lay out text in a word processor and print the results.

Business graphics and presentation packages have evolved over the years. An older, less friendly package could cause some head scratching if you hadn't used the package in a while. Graphic objects (such as the aforementioned flow charts) had to be built laboriously by hand, using rudimentary graphic tools. While it was not especially hard to construct, say, a calendar, from rectangles and the text tool, it was very time-consuming. Still, the increase in productivity over using less specialized tools, or even drawing the graphics and slides by hand, was so marked that people wholeheartedly adopted the new packages. The market grew, and as it did so, more graphics and presentation packages entered this profitable market. As with so many other things, competition drove the packages to improve.

Many of the newer graphics and presentation packages are easier to use, even when returning to them after an extended absence. Many of these packages use status-line messages and balloon help to remind you what to do next. This constant "hand-holding," coupled with tips on how to more effectively build graphics and presentations, increases your productivity and decreases your frustration in the process. In addition to the extra help, the tools have gotten more powerful. With some packages, it is possible to build a common business object (for example, an organization chart) with just a few mouse clicks. This enables you to focus more on the content and less on the mechanics of producing the presentation.

The new tools also make it easier to build more professional-looking presentations. Most packages come with carefully matched sets of templates. These sets of templates provide a common background for all your slides, as well as matched sets of font sizes. The templates are designed by graphic artists, and you may select from a wide variety—depending on the message you are trying to send. You can use a template that includes bright colors and bold fonts for a young, dynamic audience. Or, you can use muted colors and more traditional fonts for a more conservative audience. Either way, gone are the days when a mismatched set of colors and fonts could ruin an otherwise good presentation.

Many of the newer presentation packages also include some fancy features to dress up your presentation with very little additional work. These features include eye-catching transitions between slides, QuickTime animations, and sound. These more advanced features generally require more capable hardware. Of course, fancy effects and animations only work when you intend to use your Mac to make the presentation. Most presentations today (about 80%) are still delivered using printed media: either paper handouts or overhead projector slides. Most printed presentations are still in black and white, although this is slowly changing as the cost of color printers comes down.

Tip
For a more effective presentation, use a simple font: preferably a sans- serif font. Fancy fonts tend to distract your audience from the message.

IV

Macintosh Software

What Is Out There

The Macintosh business graphics/presentation package market was once dominated by only two packages: Aldus' Persuasion and Microsoft's PowerPoint. These two old-timers are still around, and they have been much improved. They have been joined by some very able competitors, however: Gold Disk's Astound, Delta Point's DeltaGraph, and Claris' Impact. All these programs include special features that set them apart from one another. They all try to combine ease-of-use with lots of power, and some are more successful than others at this most difficult of balancing acts. In the following pages, we will look at the features of each of these packages, and provide you with enough information to decide what package you want to invest your time and money in.

Claris Impact

Claris Impact combines considerable power with some unique features that make the creation of business graphics very straightforward. A Windows version of Impact is due late in 1994, the files will be interchangeable between the Macintosh and Windows versions of the product. Impact is one of the newer business graphics packages around, but it shows Claris' long heritage of building Mac programs. For example, the word processing portion of the package is highly reminiscent of Claris' word processing package MacWrite. While this package is light on the fancies such as slide show transition effects, it is easy to learn and use and a great deal of fun as well.

System Requirements

Impact comes packaged on five disks. The exact amount of hard drive space required depends on which options you install, but a full installation (all fonts and templates) requires 13.2 megabytes. Impact will run with either

System 6 (6.0.7 or later) or 7, although you must have at least 2MB for System 6, and 4MB for System 7. System 7 is needed to use features such as Publish, Subscribe, QuickTime movies, and Balloon Help.

The Drawing Document

Claris Impact is based around three document types. The first document type is simply called a "drawing" (see fig. 17.1). A "drawing" is just that—a blank sheet that you use to create diagrams using Impact's powerful drawing tools and "models" (more on these in a moment).

Fig. 17.1
The Drawing
Document.

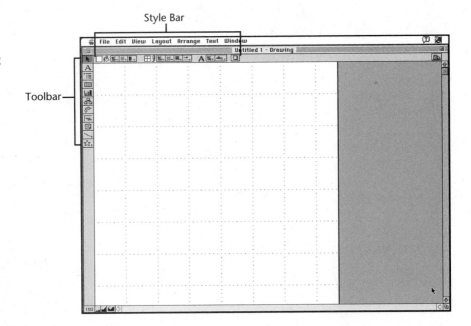

Using the Style Bar

Across the top of the screen is the style bar. The style bar includes buttons for specifying the fill pattern and color, as well as a variety of gradient shading options (including a user-defined gradient). The style bar also includes controls for setting the color, line style, and arrowhead style for the pen tool. The last set of buttons enables you to set the color, font, style, and size for freeform text.

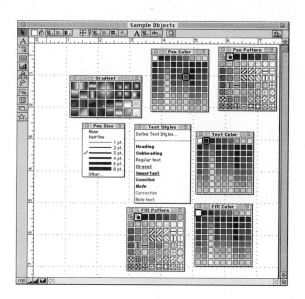

> **Note**
>
> Most of the menus that Impact makes available from the style bar can be torn off the style bar so that they remain open in the workspace. This capability to tear off a menu makes it easier to access the menu if you have to repeat the same operation multiple times (see fig. 17.2).

IV

Macintosh Software

Fig. 17.2
Tear-off menus make it easier to repeat functions on a drawing.

Using the Toolbar

The left side of the screen includes the toolbar—a set of buttons that make a variety of powerful drawing tools available. As with the style bar, you may tear off any palette to create a free-floating window that makes it easier to reuse the objects in the palette. The Shapes tool makes a palette of shapes available. These shapes include arrows, rectangles, cubes, stars, and other selections. You may select one of these shapes and use click and drag to locate and size the shape on the screen. The shapes may be filled with a pattern, color, or gradient. You may also change the color and weight of the border lines, and add a drop shadow. You may use the Reshape menu option to reshape the items in the shape palette. When you choose to reshape an object, Impact places additional highlighted points around the boundaries of the shape. Reshaping is easy—just click and drag the highlighted points on the shape to create your own shape.

Tip
If Impact's Shape palette doesn't include the shape you need, you can use reshaping to create your own shapes from the supplied shapes.

The Draw tool palette includes lines and curves, rectangles, ovals, bézier curves, and free-form shapes. As with the items in the Shape palette, you can add fills (including gradient fills), color, and a shadow. Draw objects may not be reshaped, however. Also included in the Draw tool palette are two connection tools (lines with small square dots on the ends). The connection tools may be used to join any two Shape palette objects with a line. Establishing this connection is a little tricky because you must drag the connector from the edge of one shape to the edge of the other. After you have done so, the connection remains attached to the shapes when you drag them around on-screen (see fig. 17.3). The two connectors either connect the shapes using lines with 90-degree angles or straight lines.

> **Note**
>
> You cannot use the connector tools to join objects from the Draw palette. You may draw the line using the join tools, but the connection is not preserved if you move one of the draw shapes.

Fig. 17.3
Connectors join Shape palette objects—even when you move the objects.

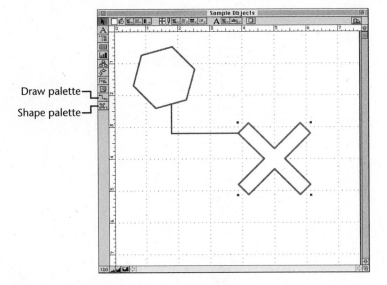

Using the Rest of the Tools

After you have placed Shapes and Draw objects on the page, you may use Impact's menu-based tools to arrange and align the objects. Objects on-screen are arranged in layers, with more recently placed objects hiding objects of which they are on top. You may change the order of these layers to display an object that is entirely or partially hidden. You may also align the centers, left, right, top, or bottom edges of multiple objects. You can rotate objects by any amount, flip them horizontally or vertically, and scale them any percentage. This scaling can be done independently in the horizontal and vertical direction.

You can customize most of the tools in Impact. For example, you can create your own fill pattern by modifying any of the supplied patterns. However, you cannot add more patterns to the pattern palette. You can create your own color gradients, defining not only the shading pattern and direction but also the colors used in the gradient. The pattern and gradient editors are easily available from the Layout menu.

Using Models

One of the features that really sets Impact apart from other business graphics tools is its *models*. Models are essentially templates for common business graphics, such as organization charts, flow charts, timelines, calendars, tables, numeric charts, and text outlines. To start creating one of these models, you select it from the toolbar at the edge of the screen. Click and drag on-screen to define the extent of the model (see fig. 17.4), and you are ready to start customizing. And can you ever customize!

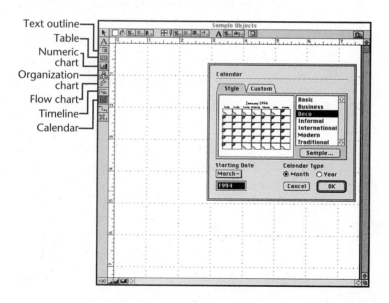

Fig. 17.4
Producing a complex business object is as easy as click and drag.

The first thing you can do is select a style for a model. Styles set background colors, fonts, line styles, and other attributes. The pre-built styles are available from a list, and in general are eye-catching. If none of the pre-built styles suit you, however, you can customize just about everything about a model. For example, even for a simple table, you may set the column width and row height, default text font and size, the grid display and color, and the number of rows and columns. You can also modify individual elements of the model while you are working on it.

> **Note**
>
> As you work with each model (you can have multiple models on a page), the toolbar changes to provide the tools appropriate for that model.

Claris has really done a nice job on the models. For example, the organization chart enables you to add coworkers, assistants, managers, and subordinates (see fig. 17.5). You may select from a variety of styles for displaying trees in the org chart and individually select box background, border color and weight, font size and style, and the types of information to be displayed in each box. Rearranging an organization is as simple as dragging a box to a new location. Depending on where you drop the box in relation to an existing box, the person will be a subordinate, coworker, or other. You can adjust the size of boxes, and decide whether all boxes on the same row will adjust to have the same width and height. You can even specify that all boxes that are higher on the organization chart also adjust their width and height as well.

> **Note**
>
> Positions on the organization chart can include only the name and title—you may not add more fields.

The timeline is simple to use but works well. You may add timeline tasks, and instruct Impact to automatically create the time increments across the top of the timeline. This model understands early and late finish and linked tasks. If you reschedule tasks, Impact will automatically reschedule tasks that depend on the rescheduled task. You may customize the line styles, specifying your own choices for the duration, slack, and percent-done lines (see fig. 17.6). You can also specify the colors, patterns, and shapes to use for the start and finish symbols. If you are more comfortable working with a table of numbers, you can modify the timeline using a table. You can click and drag task rows to reschedule, but this swaps the two rows—there is no way to grab a row from one place and drop it into the table.

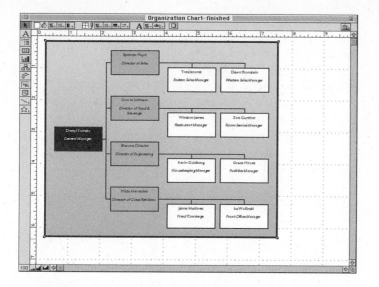

Fig. 17.5
The Organization
Chart can represent
a complex
organization.

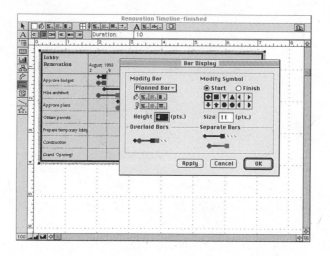

Fig. 17.6
You may custom-
ize all the markers
for a timeline.

Claris Impact doesn't forget about charts built from numbers. It can import
spreadsheet data, or you can type information into a table. This table enables
you to easily customize the chart title, axis labels, and the legend labels.
Impact can build 12 different types of charts—including such staples as bar
charts, stacked bar charts, pie charts, pictogram, line, and scatter charts.
As with other models, you pick from the provided styles or customize your
own. After you have built a chart, you can customize its look with the mouse.
For example, you can select sections of a pie chart and pull them out. You
can also change all chart colors, fill patterns, the 3-D angle, and other

attributes of the chart. You can customize the legend , its placement, and axis labels, use pictograms instead of staid bars, and add multiple number series.

The calendar model is really impressive. You may select a style for the whole calendar, as well as special styles to be applied to days (even separate styles for weekdays and weekends). In fact, you can select individual styles for a specific day of the week. For example, you can apply a somber style to everyone's favorite workday: Monday. You can select any individual day of the month and change the background, border style, font, style and size of the date number. You can add messages and attach clip art to a day as well. You can even schedule events on a day or set up events that stretch across multiple days (such as vacation) (see fig. 17.7).

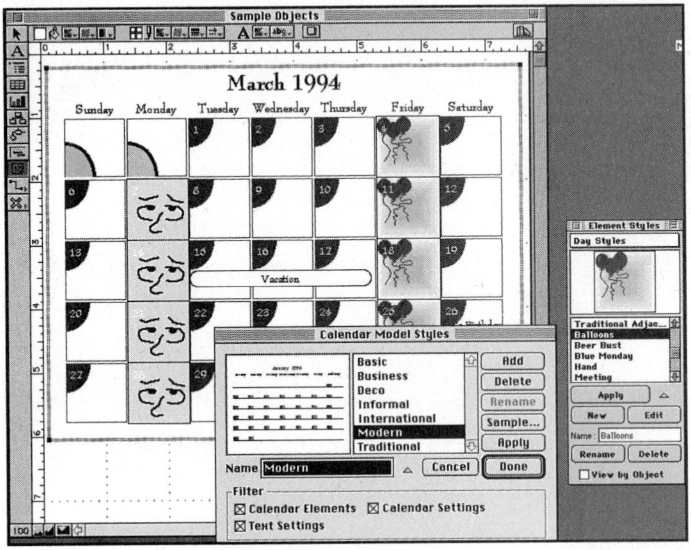

Fig. 17.7
You can customize a calendar just about any way you want.

Tip
Impact can translate one type of model into another. For example, you can turn a number table into a chart instantly, or convert a multi-level outline into an organization chart. Impact builds the levels of the chart based on the outline levels.

Even a simple table has considerable functionality. In addition to adding text and numbers in any "cell" of the table, you may highlight a range of cells that includes a blank cell at the end and click the "sum" tool. This places the sum of the highlighted cells in the formerly-empty cell. If you change any of the numbers in the range, the sum is updated to match.

The Report Document

The second type of document is called a "report." A report includes a decent word processor, reminiscent of Claris' MacWrite (I wonder why). You may create word-processed documents and include graphics and models. Of course, you can use text blocks in a Drawing, but the Report provides far more structure and text editing tools. A report works much better than a drawing if your creation is primarily text. If you add shapes, models, or draw objects to a report, Impact flows the text around these obstructions automatically (see fig. 17.8). The text automatically reflows if you drag the graphics to a new location. However, adding graphics objects to the text slows down the keyboard response considerably—most people will be able to out-type Impact when it is attempting to flow the text. Ideally, you should import or type your text and then add in the graphics.

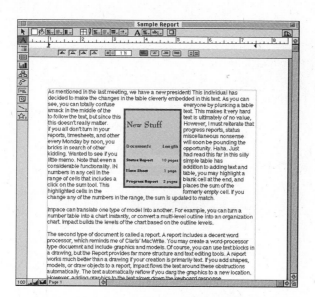

Fig. 17.8
A Report flows text around graphics automatically.

You have considerable control over text in the report, although not as much as you would with a dedicated word processor. A graphic ruler across the top of the screen enables you to easily set margins and tabs (left, right, center, and decimal). You may adjust the text alignment using a set of buttons. Still another set of buttons enable you to vary the spacing between lines in increments of .5 lines. You can even double-click the alignment indicators to specify paragraph formatting such as left indent, first line indent, right indent, line spacing, and spacing before and after the paragraph. Spacing can be set in lines, inches, picas, or centimeters. You can even split the document into a user-defined number of columns, specifying the width of each column and the distance between columns. Page breaks, date, time, headers, and footers are all available to customize your document. Of course, you can change the font, size, style, color, and effects for any text.

The Presentation Document

The third document type is Presentation. This is essentially a slide show. You may choose a style from the color or black-and-white styles. There aren't as many styles available in Impact as in presentation packages such as PowerPoint, but there are enough for most purposes. You choose a style from a dialog box that shows you a preview of the master slide (see fig. 17.9). At any time, you may change the master style and even filter out various parts of the master slide, such as the title, body, and background. Each style includes only a master slide. As with drawings and reports, you may add models, shapes, text, and draw objects to any slide and customize them in the same way. You may also modify an individual slide by clicking and dragging the text box (which contains any bulleted text items) to a new position. Adding a new slide is as easy as clicking a button, and you can access any slide in the presentation from a convenient pop-up list.

Fig. 17.9
The Preview dialog box makes it easy to pick a Presentation style.

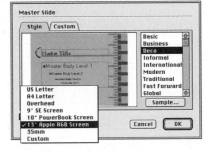

Tip
Impact does not have a variety of template slides such as those included in DeltaGraph Pro 3. Thus, you will have to construct those templates yourself, instead of choosing from a list of template slides.

You can change the look of every slide in the presentation by modifying the master slide. If you relocate the text box on the master slide, for example, Impact reformats all slides in the presentation to match the new location. Any objects that you add directly to the master slide will appear on every slide in the presentation. All of Impact's tools are available for modifying the master slide, but you can't save the modified slide style as a new master slide.

The Slide Manager

Impact's tools for arranging slides is not very sophisticated, one of the few places where this program doesn't quite measure up. The Slide Manager is a textual listing of the slides in your presentation. You may drag these text descriptions around to rearrange the slides and hide a slide so it doesn't show up in the presentation. There is no miniature graphical representation of the slides in the presentation, however.

Putting It All Together

When you have created a graphic or model that you want to use elsewhere, you can include it in a library. A *library* is a palette of saved objects. For example, the excellent tutorial has you create five different models using the drawing document. As you create each model, you add it to the library, and a miniature version of the model appears in the library palette. Later, you click and drag the miniature from the library palette to paste a copy of the model into a presentation. After you paste the object into a document, you can customize it as usual. Libraries are very handy for objects that you reuse frequently.

Presenting Your Work

Impact includes a spell checker for cleaning up your presentation. You may add unrecognized words to a personal dictionary. The spell checker makes suggestions for any words it doesn't understand.

After you have built a slide show, you may display it on-screen. Impact has a very limited number of options for customizing the actual presentation of the slide show. For example, it lacks the fancy slide transitions (wipes, rain, blinds, and so on) that dedicated presentation graphic packages include. You can choose the pointer to display during the show, select the slide and border color, use a fade between slides, and control the time between slides (or advance to the next slide manually). You can also set the slide show to loop continuously. You can instruct Impact to use *Progressive Builds* on text slides. This option instructs Impact to display one item of bulleted text at a time. This effect can dramatize your points, and you don't have to build the slides individually. However, Impact does not dim the old bulleted text when it displays the new item, as do some other packages.

> **Note**
>
> One big advantage of the Impact's simple slide show is that it is very fast—the next slide in the sequence is available almost immediately.

Impact does not include a slide viewer, so you can run a slide show only on a Mac on which Impact is installed.

You may print out your presentation for your audience. You can print the full-size slides or handouts. The handouts can fit between two and six slides per page but do not make allowances for areas on the handouts for note-taking.

Getting the Most Out of Impact: Hot Tips

- To quickly add a drop shadow to a shape, click the shape, and then click the Shadow tool near the right end of the toolbar. To easily modify the properties of the shadow, ⌘-click the Shadow tool. This action opens a dialog box from which you can set the shadow offset and color.

- It can get very tedious to add new workers to an organization chart one at a time. If you need to attach multiple workers to one individual, click that individual. ⌘-click one of the indicators (subordinate, coworker, or other). Type in the number of workers to add, and click OK.

- Impact comes with a great deal of clip art, arranged into libraries. You can use the Libraries tool on the toolbar to open a clip-art library on-screen and then click and drag clip art from the Library window. You can use Impact's tools to modify the clip art on-screen or to create a new piece of art. To add this clip art to a library, expand the Library window by clicking the expand arrow. Highlight the clip art in your drawing and click the Add button. You can also rename clip art by using the Rename button.

- Impact includes many flow chart symbols, but if the one you need isn't there, you can create your own. Select the Flow Chart tool and click the document to place a single symbol and open the flow chart library. Expand the library window by clicking the expand arrow. Click a supplied symbol (try to choose one whose design is similar to the symbol you need), and then click the New button (or click the Edit button to edit that shape). The selected symbol is opened in an editor window. You may use all of Impact's drawing, fill, alignment, group, text, and shape tools to customize the shape any way you want. Click OK to save the new or edited shape back into the Flow Chart library.

Summary

Claris Impact is an excellent product. A tremendous amount of effort has gone into making it easy to use. It doesn't have all the bells and whistles that the specialized presentation packages have, but the models are extremely useful. If you need an integrated graphics and presentation package for the Macintosh, this one is definitely worth looking at.

DeltaGraph Pro 3

DeltaPoint's DeltaGraph started out as the foremost charting package for the Macintosh. Its strong suit has always been a huge ensemble of chart types, including some esoteric styles that only a scientist or statistician could love. However, most people who purchase and use the product use just a few of the many chart types available.

As presentation packages such as PowerPoint have matured, their publishers have added a variety of charts to these products. In late 1993, DeltaPoint responded to this by adding presentation package features to DeltaGraph. The result was DeltaGraph Pro 3. This product combines power-charting features with a good selection of tools designed to make it easier to present those charts. Unfortunately, some of the features are not as easy to use as they could be, resulting in a steeper learning curve than with other products reviewed here.

Caution

DeltaGraph Pro 3 contains some annoying bugs that can cause the product to terminate unexpectedly or lock up your Macintosh. If that happens, all work since the last save is lost.

System Requirements

Like Claris Impact, DeltaGraph Pro 3 is a big program. It comes packaged on five high density disks, and a full install requires 13MB of hard drive space. Using charts in the product requires a Macintosh with a minimum of a 68020, but a 68030 and a math coprocessor are recommended for anything but the simplest applications. DeltaGraph Pro 3 requires at least system 6.0.2 with a minimum of three megabytes of free memory. System 7 is needed to use features such as Publish, Subscribe, QuickTime movies, Applescript, and Balloon Help.

Making Charts

With DeltaGraph's heritage, you would expect that it enables you to construct powerful charts, and that is one of its strongest features. You use two of four available *views* in DeltaGraph Pro 3 to construct charts.

Getting the Data Together

The first step in creating a chart is to lay out the data. Using the Data View, shown in figure 17.10, you may type data that will be converted to a chart, or you may import data from a variety of sources, such as an Excel or Lotus-format spreadsheet, delimited text files (tab, space, or comma-delimited), and Cricket Graph. The Data View looks much like a standard spreadsheet, with the data arranged in rows and columns. You use the first row and first column for the axis labels. You may widen the columns in the Data View by clicking and dragging the column divider lines. You may change the text formatting of data in the Data View, adjusting the font, size, and style, but the formatting is applied to all text in all cells—you cannot adjust just the contents of a single cell or a highlighted range. You may insert a blank row or column in the Data View; however, you cannot insert a single blank cell and force other cells to either move down or shift right to make room. You can transpose the positions of the rows and columns.

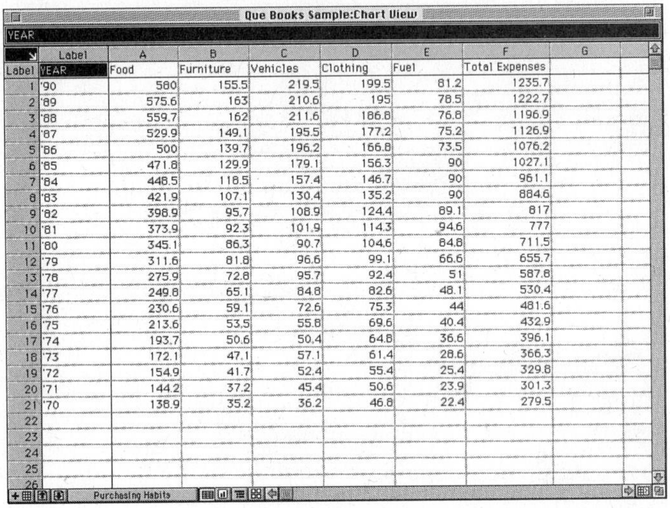

Fig. 17.10

You use the Data View to collect data for a chart.

	Label	A	B	C	D	E	F	G
Label	YEAR	Food	Furniture	Vehicles	Clothing	Fuel	Total Expenses	
1	'90	580	155.5	219.5	199.5	81.2	1235.7	
2	'89	575.6	163	210.6	195	78.5	1222.7	
3	'88	559.7	162	211.6	186.8	76.8	1196.9	
4	'87	529.9	149.1	195.5	177.2	75.2	1126.9	
5	'86	500	139.7	196.2	166.8	73.5	1076.2	
6	'85	471.8	129.9	179.1	156.3	90	1027.1	
7	'84	448.5	118.5	157.4	146.7	90	961.1	
8	'83	421.9	107.1	130.4	135.2	90	884.6	
9	'82	398.9	95.7	108.9	124.4	89.1	817	
10	'81	373.9	92.3	101.9	1143	94.6	777	
11	'80	345.1	86.3	90.7	104.6	84.8	711.5	
12	'79	311.6	81.8	96.6	99.1	66.6	655.7	
13	'78	275.9	72.8	95.7	92.4	51	587.8	
14	'77	249.8	65.1	84.8	82.6	48.1	530.4	
15	'76	230.6	59.1	72.6	75.3	44	481.6	
16	'75	213.6	53.5	55.8	69.6	40.4	432.9	
17	'74	193.7	50.6	50.4	648	36.6	396.1	
18	'73	172.1	47.1	57.1	61.4	28.6	366.3	
19	'72	154.9	41.7	52.4	55.4	25.4	329.8	
20	'71	144.2	37.2	45.4	50.6	23.9	301.3	
21	'70	138.9	35.2	36.2	46.8	22.4	279.5	

The Data View provides a certain amount of formatting control. You may format numbers with a fixed number of decimal places, as currency, percent, or in scientific notation (for example, 1.02E+03 is the equivalent of 1020). Date formats include MM/DD/YY, weekdays, year and month, and many others. You may sort columns of data into ascending or descending order.

The Data View contains an expression builder that enables you to apply functions to columns of data. For example, you may compute a running total of the contents in a column. The results of the calculations are stored in an empty, unused column. After the calculation has been performed, the results can be used when constructing a chart.

> **Caution**
>
> Results in a calculated column are not updated if you change the numbers in the column upon which the calculation is based. You must manually request a recalculation in order to update the results.

The expression builder includes a large number of powerful functions, such as square root, sum, average, standard deviation, transcendental (sine, cosine, arc tangent, and so on), logarithmic, exponential, differential, fill, and filter.

Building Charts from the Data

After you have all the data, the next step is to select and build the actual chart. To turn the data in the Data View into a chart, you must select the chart gallery. The chart gallery displays small samples of all the charts available (see fig. 17.11).

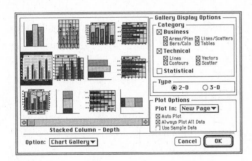

Fig. 17.11
The Chart Gallery enables you to pick the chart type you want.

To build a chart, select the chart type you want, set the options, and click OK. Alternatively, you can ask the Chart Advisor to suggest the type of chart that goes best with the format of data you have. Either way, DeltaGraph Pro 3 constructs the chart in a new chart view (see fig. 17.12).

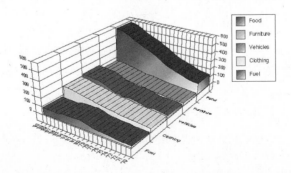

Fig. 17.12
A chart created from a Data View page.

> **Note**
>
> You can construct multiple charts from a single Data View page. For example, you may want to plot all the data in one chart, but only plot certain columns in another chart. You can highlight just those columns prior to constructing the chart and then create the chart as described above. The chart then includes only the selected columns.

DeltaGraph Pro 3 is capable of constructing 57 different kinds of charts, and can do sophisticated scientific analysis on your data, such as curve fitting. Charts are grouped into three categories: Business, Technical, and Statistical. In the Business category, you may view all the charts, or select from just areas/pies, lines/scatters, bars/columns, and table charts. The Technical category is split into Lines, Contours, Vectors, and Scatter charts. You may look at either 2-D or 3-D charts. Available charts include pie, bar, stacked bar, surface, spider, timeline, table, high-low, line, scatter, polar, area, range, step, and dozens of other types.

One of the more confusing things about DeltaGraph Pro 3 is that charts are not automatically updated when you change the data on the matching data page. You can update the data in the Data View and then click a button to update all charts based on that Data View page. Alternatively, you can use a button to jump from a chart to the matching Data View, make changes, and click a button to update the chart attached to the Data View. If the change you are making includes changing exactly which columns are plotted in the chart, you must make the revision in this second manner. This manner of updating charts is quite confusing because changing the datasheet doesn't necessarily change the chart.

Customizing the Chart

After you have built the chart, you can customize it directly in the Chart View. You can customize the chart in the following ways:

- Add a Heading and Axis Titles.

- Change the text size and formatting of any text. You can change all the axis text in one step or customize each individual label.

- Change the color and style of any line, including grid lines. You can also change the grid line spacing.

- Change the color, gradient fill, and fill pattern of any portion of the plotted graph. For example, an area curve has three colored areas: the side, end, and top. You can individually change any of these areas.

- Change a wide variety of options, depending on the chart type. For example, you can change the shape of the bars used in a bar chart, which planes are displayed in a 3-D chart, the width and height of bars in a bar chart, and the location of the ticks and labels on the chart.

- Show a legend, setting the symbol width and height, as well as the location in relation to the chart.

- For 3-D charts, you have complete control over the orientation of the chart. From a dialog box (see fig. 17.13), you can set the orientation (elevation and rotation), front-to-back perspective, and the vanishing point (vertical, horizontal, and depth effect). As you make adjustments to the settings, a 3-D rendering of a cube adjusts to show you the effect of your changes.

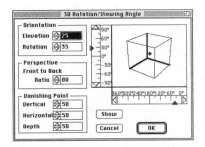

Fig. 17.13
You have complete control over the representation of a 3-D chart.

Building a Presentation with the Chart View

The Chart View is where you do most of your work to create a presentation. As discussed above, pages in the Chart View display any charts you have made, but there is far more you can do to create an eye-catching presentation. As with most other presentation packages, DeltaGraph Pro 3 makes matched sets of backgrounds and template layouts available. These sets are called *Layout Sets*.

Using Layout Sets

A Layout Set consists of a background and a set of about 12 different slide templates. These templates include Basic Layout, Title, Chart and Title, Two Charts and Title, Bullet Text and Title, and so on. Each time you create a new slide in the presentation, you can select one of these templates to set the layout of the slide. If you choose the Chart and Bullet Text template, for example, the resulting slide consists of a rectangle for the chart and a rectangle for the bulleted text. At any time, you can change the template associated with a slide to change the slide's layout.

You can load a Layout Set when you first start creating a presentation or load it later—modifying all slides in the presentation to give them the new background and adjusting the layout of the slides to match the new slide templates. The dialog box used for loading Layout Sets gives you a miniature preview of the Layout Set (see fig. 17.14).

Fig. 17.14
Preview of the Layout Sets makes it easy to pick one.

After you select a template to use, you can start filling in the information in the template. For templates that include a chart block, you can double-click the chart block, and DeltaGraph Pro 3 automatically opens the chart gallery so that you can select a chart type. After you select a chart from the gallery, the last-used Data View is opened so that you can pick the data to associate with the chart. You can either select data from that Data View page, switch to another Data View page, or create a new Data View page. Alternatively, you can instruct DeltaGraph Pro 3 to use a set of sample data instead. You can then revise the sample data for your own use.

For text blocks on slides, you can start typing in the Bulleted Text block to create a *text chart* of bullet points. The text chart consists of levels (much like an outline). The Layout Set sets the attributes of bulleted text blocks—including font, style, size, bullet style, and color for each level of text.

Modifying the Slide Layout

You can modify the layout of a slide in two ways. To modify just an individual slide, you can click and drag various components of the slide around. For example, you can click and drag a bulleted text block lower on the page. You can also add and resize objects, including charts, and directly change the font, size, style, and color of text—both freeform and text located in text blocks.

You can also directly modify a template in the Layout Set. If you modify a template, all slides that use that template are automatically modified. Changing a template works exactly like changing any other type of slide. You can modify a template or create a new template using a special toolbar that includes tools such as Bulleted Text block, chart, organization chart, text, graphic, and background tools.

Caution

Be careful about modifying templates. If you have changed the layout of an individual slide, changing the template for that slide will cause the slide to change to match the modified template.

For text blocks, you can modify the font, size, style, and color, as well as the bullet style and color. There is a special template in each Layout Set called the "Master Background." Any changes you make to the Master Background are reflected on all slides, regardless of the template they use. This is very useful for adding graphics (such as your company logo) that you want to appear on every slide. To save your changes, you need to save the Layout Set. You can either save over the original or create a new layout set. Any new templates you create are only available in that one Layout Set.

Using Graphic and Text Tools

DeltaGraph Pro 3 has a floating palette (see fig. 17.15) that contains a variety of tools for customizing slides. These tools are available both for customizing individual slides, and modifying templates and backgrounds.

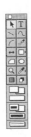

Fig. 17.15 The floating palette contains a variety of graphic and text tools.

There are tools for text, lines, curves, bezier curves, polygons, arrows, circles, a variety of rectangles (included rounded rectangles), and freehand drawing. Most shapes can be filled with color and pattern, and you can modify line color, style, and weight. You can also apply a drop shadow to a shape, fill it with a color blend, and use the eyedropper tool to transfer the style of one object to another object.

Note

If you select the text tool, DeltaGraph Pro 3 displays a graphical ruler. The ruler includes tools for setting tabs, text alignment, paragraph and line spacing, and margins.

The three buttons at the bottom of the palette provide drop-down palettes when you click them. These palettes enable you to directly set fill color and pattern for the foreground and background of drawn objects and lines. You can use another drop-down palette to make a line very wide.

Aligning, Grouping, and Layering Graphic Objects

DeltaGraph Pro 3 has a full complement of tools for aligning, grouping, and layering objects. The Align dialog box enables you to align objects by their edges (top, bottom, left, and right) or their centers (up/down or left/right). You can also align objects to the grid and set the fineness of the grid. You can group objects together. Once you have grouped a set of objects, you can move and size them as a single object. You can ungroup objects if you need to modify the component objects. When objects overlap each other, you can move an object in front of or in back of another object You can also rotate objects in 90-degree increments.

Using Libraries

Libraries are especially helpful in Chart View. A library is a collection of objects that are available in a window. You can use a library object by clicking it and dragging it to the active Chart View window. DeltaGraph Pro 3 comes with libraries of clip art and pictures, and you can create your own libraries of specially formatted charts.

> **Note**
>
> Clip art can be used for the shapes in pictogram charts, and the clip art provided is fully scalable without loss of resolution.

Using the Outline View

DeltaGraph Pro 3's Outline View presents the slides in your presentation in the form of an outline (see fig. 17.16). Slides that just contain graphics or charts simply display their titles, but slides that contain bulleted text display that bulleted text.

You can edit the titles of slides, as well as the bulleted text. Any content changes you make to the text in the Outline View show up in the slide text. The levels of bulleted text are displayed as outline levels, and you can change the levels of the text using the tools in the Outline View. You can also convert sublevels into bullets, and bullets into sublevels. Oddly, there is no direct way to create a new slide in the Outline View, although you can convert a bullet or sublevel into a Page title— effectively creating a new slide. You can collapse the levels of the outline and add speaker notes to any slide. These speaker notes may be hidden or displayed in the Outline View. You can click and drag a small icon alongside each slide number to rearrange the slides in the presentation. You can modify the font, size, and style of all text in the Outline View, but this change does not affect the actual slides. Any text style changes you make in the Outline View affects all the text in the Outline View—there is no way to adjust only a portion of the text.

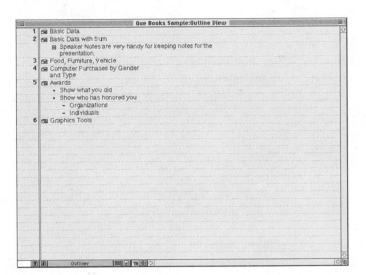

Fig. 17.16
The Outline View displays just slide text.

Using the Slide Sorter View

DeltaGraph Pro 3 also contains a Sorter View. The Sorter View is capable of displaying all the slides in your presentation in two ways: a textual list (see fig. 17.17) and a set of thumbnails (see fig. 17.18). In the textual list, you can rearrange the slides by dragging them within the list, remove them from displaying in the presentation, and pick a slide transition from a pop-up list. The thumbnail view displays miniature views of the slides. You can rearrange them or add/remove them from displaying in the slide show.

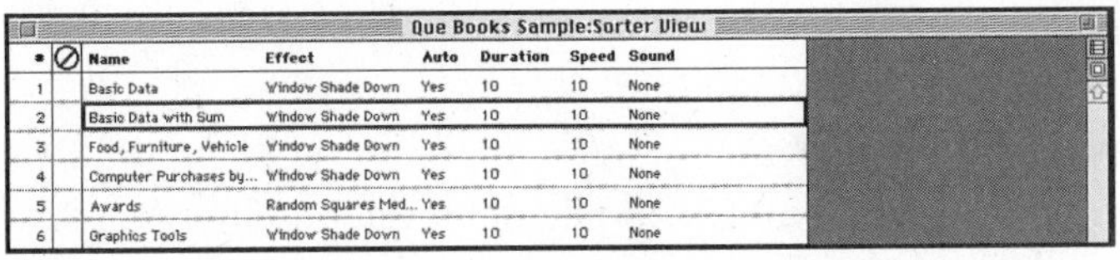

Fig. 17.17
The Sorter View as a textual list.

Fig. 17.18
The Sorter View
has thumbnails.

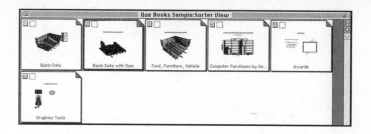

You can set the transition effects between slides only from the Sorter View. In addition to picking the transition from a pop-up list as mentioned above, you can select the transitions and other display effects from a dialog box. There are nine basic effects, such as wipe, window shade, iris, corner, and rain. Many of these effects have suboptions. For example, when you use the corner effect, you can select which corner the slide appears from. You can select a main effect and a suboption, and save this combination in a "Named Transition" list for easy reuse. When you choose a transition, you can preview that effect in the dialog box.

The Transition Effect dialog box also enables you to choose the duration for the slide on the screen or change slides manually. You can also attach or record sounds that play when the slide appears.

Presenting the Material

DeltaGraph Pro 3 has a spell checker for cleaning up your text. You can selectively check any of the views and add unrecognized words to a personal dictionary. The spell checker will make suggestions for replacements for words.

You can display your presentation on any Macintosh on which the program is installed, but there is no runtime version of the product for displaying the presentation on Macs that do not have the product. You can control your slide show either by setting the automatic options for the slides (including automatic loop-back) or by using a small on-screen control panel to move between slides. You can print the presentation out in full size or in 10 different formats of handout, including one that fits 15 miniature slides on a page. Some formats include areas for taking notes right on the handout, which is very handy for your audience.

Bugs and Problems

There are, unfortunately, quite a number of small bugs in this program, as well as things that are difficult to use. Bugs include:

- When you change the slide transition, the preview of the transition effect continues to show the old effect.

- When you display the combination Chart View/Data View, the Data View displayed does not always match the Chart View.

- The Command Bar in the Data View is not redrawn properly after using the Expression Builder.

- If you cut rows or columns of data from a Data Page, a crash can result, closing DeltaGraph Pro 3, and losing all work since the last save.

In addition to bugs, there are some things that make the product hard to learn and use. These include:

- The Chart Advisor often suggests a chart for which there isn't enough data in the Data View page. If that happens, you are on your own for picking a chart.

- Even if there is just a single chart on a page, you must select the chart before you can make any chart modifications.

- The whole connection between a chart in the Chart View and the Data View page is difficult to learn and tedious to use.

Getting the Most Out of DeltaGraph Pro 3: Hot Tips

- Prepare DeltaGraph Charts for Color Separation: you can prepare charts to use in color separations. To do so, create the chart, then select Colors from the Edit menu. In the Colors dialog box, select CMYK (Cyan, Magenta, Yellow, Black) in the Color Model menu and Custom Colors in the Color Set menu. You can then edit each of the colors to the exact percentage specifications of your process color system guide, such as Pantone's guide. Once you enter the exact percentages, click the "Save" button to save the palette. The color will then show up in the toolbox color palette when you exit the Colors dialog. Apply the custom colors to your chart.

- Link DeltaGraph Charts to DTP and Word Processor Documents: DeltaGraph supports EGO (Edit Graphic Object), which provides a dynamic link to DTP and word processor documents (System 7 is required for this). Hold down the Option key while copying or exporting a graph. This tells DeltaGraph to embed additional information it needs in order to edit PICT when it is passed back from the word processor or other client application. Once the EGO PICT has been created, paste or import it into any client that supports EGO, such as WordPerfect. Double-clicking the graphic in the client will launch and pass the chart to DeltaGraph (the server) for editing. When the editing is complete and the DeltaGraph window is closed, the modified graphic is automatically passed back to the client.

■ Avoid Repetitive Chart Formatting with Templates: Templates can save you a lot of time if you tend to do the same charts over and over, formatting them to the same specifications for text font, size, and style, title placement, and data series colors and patterns, label styles, or the settings on grids, ticks, and axes. Templates are stored in Custom Libraries, which you can open or create by clicking and holding the Library icon in the Command bar or choosing Libraries from the File menu. To add a chart to a library, simply select and drag it into the library window, where it will appear as a thumbnail icon. The chart can be saved as a template or with its data.

■ Display Chart Templates: DeltaGraph will automatically open your libraries and display your chart templates in the Chart Gallery if you place your libraries in the "AutoLibrary Folder," which is located in the application folder.

■ Interrupt Drawing: You can interrupt drawing to save time. This feature allows you to suppress redraw of graphics and charts until you have made all the desired changes. In the Preferences dialog box, select Drawing Preferences from the Option menu and make this selection from the Drawing Options. During redraw, simply hold down the mouse button to interrupt and make other changes before redraw continues.

■ Reusing a Tool from the Toolbox: If you double-click a tool in the toolbox, it will stay active rather than reverting back to the pointer after the first use.

■ Fix Data Gaps in Line Charts: If you have blanks in your data and try to plot a line chart, the lines will stop at the blanks. You can select Span Gaps in the Options dialog box and the points will be connected across the blanks.

■ Quicker Access To Formatting: Control-click any draw, text, or chart object in the chart view to display a dialog box changing a variety of attributes. Only the appropriate attributes for the object show up in the dialog box.

Summary

DeltaGraph Pro 3 has the strongest charting of any of the packages looked at here. However, there is a price for all this power: DeltaGraph Pro 3 also has the steepest learning curve. There are a lot of confusing things about this product as well, including the multitude of hard-to-interpret icons on the command bar and the imposing array of options in the icons and the menu options. I suspect that users coming back to this product after not using it for awhile (many people produce presentation infrequently) will take some time to get back up to speed.

Microsoft PowerPoint

Microsoft's PowerPoint first appeared about five years ago, making it one of the oldest presentation packages around. It is one of the easiest to learn to use, primarily because of its simplicity. It does not include many of the special features that provide both power and complexity to other packages. However, for a package you can pick up quickly and relearn after an extended absence, PowerPoint is superb. Unlike most of the competition, PowerPoint presentations can be played back on Macintoshes that do not have PowerPoint installed.

System Requirements

PowerPoint comes on four disks, plus a two-disk set of true-type fonts, and a disk containing the PowerPoint Viewer. A full installation of PowerPoint uses 8.4MB of hard drive space, including the Viewer. How much additional hard drive space is taken by the true-type fonts depends on how many of the fonts you have already. PowerPoint requires System 7.0 and 4MB of memory.

Using the Slide View

You use PowerPoint's Slide View to build individual slides. The Slide View provides a variety of tools, including text tools, graphic tools, and a tool for constructing graphs (see fig. 17.19).

Using Templates

PowerPoint supports "templates"—color schemes for the background of the slides in a presentation. PowerPoint provides 160 different templates, arranged into groups based on the type of medium you will be using for the presentation. Template groups include B&W overheads, Color overheads, video screen, and 35mm slides. As with other products that provide templates, PowerPoint's templates provide a consistent color scheme, font set,

Tip
PowerPoint cannot run on a Mac with System 6, unlike many of the other packages included here.

Tip
PowerPoint does not have the option of choosing from the variety of layouts that are available in DeltaGraph Pro 3.

bullet style, and background throughout a presentation. However, PowerPoint templates include only a single master slide.

Fig. 17.19
PowerPoint's Slide Viewer provides the tools to build Slides.

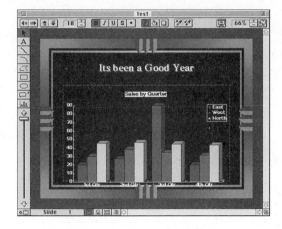

You can load a new template at any time; however, only a single template can be used in a presentation. The dialog box for loading templates provides a miniature preview of the templates.

Modifying the Slide Layout

You can change the layout of a slide in two ways. First of all, you can modify each individual slide by clicking and dragging items on the slide to resize or reposition them. You can also individually adjust the text font, size, and style of any highlighted text. You cannot adjust bullet attributes from the slide view.

The second way to adjust the layout of a slide is to change the master slide. Each template includes a Master Title block and a Master Body block (see fig. 17.20).

Tip
PowerPoint enables you to decide whether to apply a change in the Master slide to slides on which you have modified the formats.

The Master Body block sets the location and text attributes of bulleted text on the slide. You can change the size and location of both blocks, the color and style of bullets, and the font, size, and style of the text. Once you make changes to the master slide, most slides are adjusted to match the new template. However, PowerPoint does not override changes you have made directly on a slide. If you want the master slide changes to apply to a slide you adjusted yourself, you can use the menu option to reapply the master to a slide. You can save changed master slides as a new template.

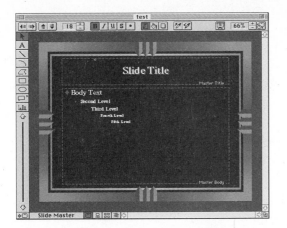

Fig. 17.20
The Master Slide.

Adding Text to a Slide

To add text to a PowerPoint slide, you simply click in the title block or body block and start typing. The Tab and Shift-Tab keys adjust the level of text and bullets. You can click and drag bullets to rearrange text on the slide. If you move a bullet, all text levels below that bullet move as well. This makes it quick and easy to rearrange text on a slide.

Adding Graphics to a Slide

PowerPoint has a good selection of graphics tools for customizing a slide. These include rectangles, circle/ovals, curves, lines, and a free-form shape tool. You also have a palette of special shapes, such as stars, arrows, triangles, text balloons, and others. To add a shape to a slide, simply click the shape and then click and drag the pointer on the slide.

> **Note**
>
> Once the shape is on the slide, it is difficult to move. You must click the shape's edge—clicking inside the shape doesn't work.

You can add text to all shapes except lines simply by double-clicking the border of the shape and typing in the text. This is handy for labeling shapes, as the text moves when you move the shape.

You can apply a variety of fills to all shapes except lines. Thirty-six fill patterns are available, and you can independently choose the foreground and background colors for the fill. However, you cannot create your own fill. You can also fill a shape with a shaded background. PowerPoint builds a shaded background from a single fill color. One "end" of the fill is set by the fill color, the other end is set according to the intensity of the color that you select. For example, you can choose a shade from a medium maroon to a very dark maroon. The shading dialog box enables you to pick the fill color, the shade of the fill color to fill to, seven shading directions (vertical, horizontal, diagonal right, etc.) and one of four variations on this fill (see fig. 17.21).

Fig. 17.21
The Shade Dialog box.

You can set the weight and color of lines for both lines and other graphic objects. Any line attributes you set for non-line objects apply to the object's borders. For lines, you can also set a style for any arrowheads you want to use.

You can apply a drop shadow to graphic objects, setting the color and offset of the shadow. Interestingly, if you have added text to an object, PowerPoint applies a shadow to the text as well.

You can align the edges or centers of multiple graphic objects. You can also group objects together in order to move and size them as a single object. PowerPoint enables you to layer objects by sending objects to the front or back. By using this tool, you can select which overlapping objects are visible on top of other objects.

A series of toolbar buttons across the top of the screen enable you to set exactly what attributes of a graphic shape you want PowerPoint to display. The fill button determines whether a shape (and its shadow, if it has one) are filled with color or transparent. The line button determines whether the line border of a graphic shape is visible, and the shadow button determines whether a shape's shadow is visible.

Building Graphs

PowerPoint's graphs are very simple, although they will serve the purpose for most people. To create a graph, you must select the graphing tool from the toolbar on the left side of the screen. When you click and drag an area on the slide, PowerPoint opens the graphing tool. All graph actions must be made in this separate program, which is somewhat more clumsy than making changes directly on the graph in the slide.

> **Note**
>
> If PowerPoint is not properly installed, the OLE resources necessary to run the Graphing Program may not be available—preventing the graphing tool from working.

The graphing tool consists of two separate windows (see fig. 17.22). The first window is a datasheet. Much like a spreadsheet, the PowerPoint datasheet is a grid of rows and columns. The first row and column are used for labels, and sample labels and data are always presented in a datasheet to get you started. You can change the number in a cell (intersection of a row and column) by simply typing over the sample data. You can also widen the columns by clicking and dragging the column dividers.

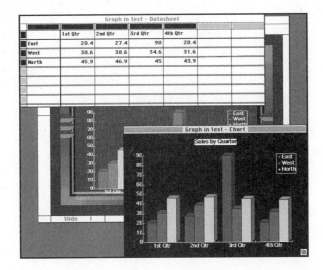

Fig. 17.22
PowerPoint uses a separate graphing tool.

The second window in the graphing tool displays a sample graph. This window is where you make modifications to the display characteristics of the graph. You can size the graph window to make it easier to work with.

PowerPoint has a small gallery of graphs. These include area, bar, column, line, pie, scatter, and combo. You can also choose 3-D versions of the area, bar, column, line, and pie graphs. Each category of graph has several options (up to 10). For example, if you choose a line graph, you can select from options that display the plotted points, connecting lines, a logarithmic scale, and others.

You can add titles to the graph or to the axes. Once you add text, you can modify the font, size, color, and style. You can set how the data labels display and even add a line with an arrow to highlight certain points.

> **Note**
>
> You cannot add text to the chart to use with the arrow!

Charts can have a legend, and you can set the line weight and style of the legend border, as well as the fill color and pattern for the legend background. You can also set the font for the labels in the legend. You can specify the location of the legend either by clicking and dragging or by specifying the location in a dialog box.

You can customize the graph by setting major and minor grid lines, and specifying how the tick marks are displayed. You can also set the line weight and style for any axis. You can customize the data series by setting the line weight and style, as well as the fill color and pattern.

Much as with DeltaGraph, you have quite a bit of control over 3-D graphs. You can set the elevation and rotation from a dialog box that uses a wire frame model to display how the changes affect the graph.

When you are finished working on a graph, you must exit the graphing tool and return to PowerPoint. When you exit the graph program, you must choose whether to update the PowerPoint presentation with the changes you made in the graph tool.

Tip

Unlike most other packages, you have full control of the text in the Outline View, and changes you make to the text style in the Outline View do affect the text on the slide.

Using the Outline View

PowerPoint's Outline View displays the text of the slides (see fig. 17.23). Each slide in the presentation is represented by at least a title line in the Outline View. Slides that contain bullets display all their text, with the bullet text arranged in levels in the outline. The text in the Outline View shows the font, size, and style of the text on the slide.

You can click and drag bullets to rearrange the text. All levels below the selected bullet move with the bullet. You can also use tools in the toolbar to adjust the text characteristics. You can promote or demote a selected bullet one level. If you promote a first-level bullet, PowerPoint automatically creates a new slide. You can also create a new slide by clicking the new slide button.

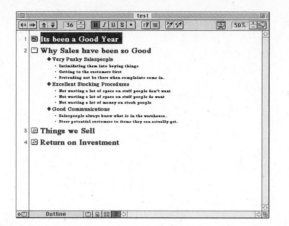

Fig. 17.23
The Outline View
displays the text
on your slides.

Note

Double-clicking the small slide icon alongside each slide title returns you to the slide
view to edit that slide.

Using the Slide Sorter View

The Slide Sorter View displays the slides in your presentation in miniature
(see fig. 17.24).

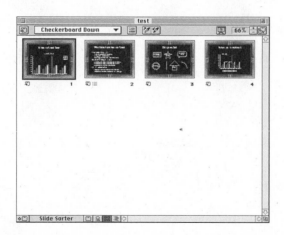

Fig. 17.24
The Slide Sorter
View.

You can rearrange the slides in the Slide Sorter View by clicking and dragging
them. You can also create new (blank) slides. For each slide, you can set a
transition effect that displays when PowerPoint moves the slide onto the

screen during a slide show. There are a wide variety of effects, and you can preview the effect from a dialog box. PowerPoint is very fast, and the effects add pizzazz to the screen show without getting in the way.

You can also set up PowerPoint to do "Builds" in the Slide Sorter View. A Build displays first-level bulleted text (and all bullets in lower levels below the displayed bullet) one bullet point at a time. You can set PowerPoint to "dim" earlier displayed bullets when it displays a new bullet, and even display the new bullet using any of the transition effects available for slide transitions. However, you can use only a single transition for all the bullets on a slide.

Using the Notes View

The Notes View is unusual and very useful. This view presents a miniature of the slide at the top of the page and an area to type notes below the slide (see fig. 17.25). You can add explanatory notes and hand these pages out to your audience, or you can type your speaker notes in the Note View for your own use.

Tip

You can leave the notes area blank and distribute the handouts, giving your audience a place to keep their own notes.

Fig. 17.25
The Notes View.

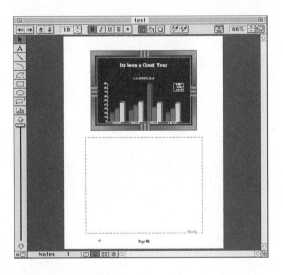

Modifying the Masters

All of the special views in PowerPoint (Slide, Notes, Handout, and Outline) have a master slide that sets the format of the view. Much as with Master Slide View (discussed earlier), you can modify the masters for these other views to customize the layouts. For the Note View, you can size the slide miniature and adjust the note area and text font, as well as add text and graphics. In the Outline View and Handout View, you can only add graphics and text to the Master—you cannot change the actual layout or fonts.

Presenting the Material

PowerPoint enables you to print out slides on a single page or use the Note View. You can also print out handouts with two, three, or six slides to a page. You can clean up your presentation using a capable spell checker.

PowerPoint is one of the only presentation packages that does not require that PowerPoint be installed on the Macintosh used for the presentation. Instead, the PowerPoint Viewer can be freely installed on other machines. This is an important consideration for people who need to make presentations on a large number of machines (perhaps at different sites).

Hints and Tricks

- Create Slides Quickly: PowerPoint includes a few keyboard shortcuts for people who want to get their thoughts down quickly. First, when you create a new slide, you can add a title by just typing—anything you type will automatically flow into the title box. After you've typed a title, press option-return to automatically switch the focus to the body. As you type now, your text is entered into the body of the slide. Press option-return again, and you automatically get a new slide, with the focus on the title. You can use option-return to create title/body/title/body in either slide or outline view.

- Create presentations from existing reports: If you have a report created in MS Word, and you'd like to consolidate it into a presentation, simply open the document in PowerPoint. PowerPoint will automatically distill the outline levels used in the document into a presentation.

- Instant duplicates: To duplicate any object instantly, hold down the Option key, then select the object you wish to duplicate and drag off a "duplicate" of the object. Position the duplicate version where you want it. If you want another copy made using the same relative position offsets, select Duplicate Again from the Edit menu or use Option-D.

- Changing Drawing Defaults easily: Draw an object like a rectangle, and give it the line, fill, line style, shadow, etc., properties that you want for your defaults. With this object selected, click the Pick Up Styles (eyedropper) button on the toolbar. Now unselect all objects on the slide and click the Apply Styles (eyedropper) button on the toolbar. When you use apply styles with no object selected, it applies the attributes to the presentation defaults.

- Select the object you want: If you're having trouble selecting exactly the object you want in a complex drawing, use the Tab key to sequentially select each object on the slide.

- Repair freehand drawings: At any time when you are drawing with the Freeform tool, you can hold down the Delete key to back up any drawing you did and "erase" part of your work. Erase back to the point where you were satisfied with the drawing and then continue drawing again.

- Quick-Draw in Slide Sorter: If you don't want to see each slide drawn in miniature in the slide sorter, press the Esc key while PowerPoint is drawing the miniatures. Any miniatures drawn after the Esc key is held down will be quickly drawn as slides with a large X across them.

- Position Objects Precisely: PowerPoint has a "magnetic grid" which is usually on. This grid helps you align objects quickly and easily. There are times, however, when you want to temporarily ignore the grid. This can be accomplished by holding down ⌘. While you hold down ⌘, the grid is temporarily turned off.

- Adding text to a graph: It would be handy to add text to a graph, especially for labeling arrows. However, the graph tool doesn't let you do this. Instead, you can use the text tool to add text blocks on top of the graph. Once you have typed in your text block, select the text block and the graph and use Group from the Arrange menu to group them together.

Summary

Microsoft's PowerPoint is one of the simplest presentation graphic tools around, but that doesn't mean it won't do the job for many people. This product is so easy to learn that most people won't need the excellently written manual, and the fact that it offers a Viewer module makes it attractive to people who must do presentations at multiple sites.

Astound

Another new challenger in the business graphics field is Gold Disk's Astound. Available in both Windows and Mac versions, Astound files are not only compatible between the products but even include players for creating a stand-alone presentation for both versions. Astound's charting module is not very strong, but this package excels in the special effects department, enabling you to easily incorporate more transitions than any other package reviewed here. Astound also makes it easy to incorporate sound and QuickTime movies and includes some of the friendliest documentation available for computer software products.

System Requirements

Perhaps because of all the sounds, clip art, and QuickTime movies included with this package, Astound is BIG. The package comes on nine disks, and a full install consumes nearly 21MB of disk space. The package requires System 6.0.8 or later, and 2MB (4MB recommended) of memory. You should also have a 68020 or faster microprocessor. System 7 support includes Publish and Subscribe, Balloon help, and QuickTime 1.5 compatibility.

Building Slides

When you first create a presentation, you have the option to choose a template for the slides. Astound is packaged with matched sets of templates that control the color scheme as well as the font styles used for text levels on the slides. The dialog box provided for selecting the templates displays a thumbnail preview of the slide styles included in the template (see fig. 17.26). You can apply a new template at any time, but the new template applies to all the slides in the presentation. Each template has about a dozen slide styles. These styles contain various placeholders for charts, title text, graphics, and bullet text. Each time you create a new slide, you can select from one of the available slide styles in the template or create the slide with no master (e.g., a blank background).

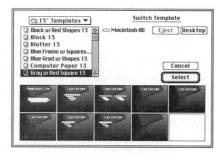

Fig. 17.26
You can see thumbnails of the slides when you select a template.

Modifying the Slide Structure

You can change the layout of a slide in two ways. The first way is to directly modify the slide. You can click and drag the placeholders to new positions on the slide, as well as add new placeholders to the slide. The placeholders can include a title, bulleted text block, charts, etc. You can apply new background schemes (solid colors, color gradients, picture, etc.) and change the font, size, and style for any text on the slide. There are two ways to change the style of text on a slide. First of all, you can select the text and make selections from the Text menu. You can also double-click the text level indicators in a bulleted text block.

Tip
If you modify
the properties of
a text level by
double-clicking
the text level
indicators in
the text block,
you can modify
the symbol that
Astound uses
for a bullet, the
bullet color, and
the paragraph,
line, and char-
acter spacing.

The second way to modify the structure of a slide is to directly modify one of the slide masters. You can use any of the slide modification techniques mentioned above.

If you modify a master, any slide that uses that master will be changed to match the new arrangement. You should make any changes to master slides prior to building slides that use that master, since changes you make to a master override any changes you have made to the slide itself. Astound is less versatile in this respect than PowerPoint, which preserves any changes you have made to a slide unless you specifically reapply the master.

> **Note**
>
> Astound lacks a slide on which you can make changes that are applied to all masters. Thus, to add a graphic to the background that will appear on all slides, you must add the graphic to all the master slide types.

Adding Graphics and Text to a Slide

You can add graphics and text to any slide in your presentation. Astound includes tools to easily customize text and graphics as well.

Tip
Astound in-
cludes more
pattern fills
than any other
package.

Astound's Text tool enables you to add text to a slide. When you click the slide with the text tool, Astound provides an instant text block that you can type in (see fig. 17.27). The text block includes tools for selecting the text level, alignment, tabs, indents, and margins. You can also set the text level by pressing the Tab key to increase one level, and the Delete key to decrease one level. Once you have added text to the block, you can change the font, size, and effect for either the entire block or just for any text you highlight. You can apply a pattern fill (selecting from 60 patterns) or a color gradient to the text in a text block. However, you cannot apply the pattern fill or color gradient to the text block background.

Astound provides a palette of graphic shapes you can use. These shapes include the standards (rectangles, rounded-corner rectangles, circle/oval, triangle) as well as some unusual shapes, such as stars, text balloons, arrows, free-form shapes, and free-form curves. You can add a shadow to any shape, and set the shadow offset from a well-designed dialog box that enables you to simply click and drag the shadow. You can set the shadow color, inside fill color, and border color, as well as the weight of the border line.

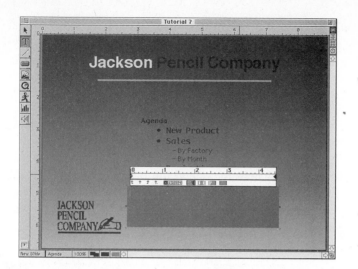

Fig. 17.27
Astound's text block includes many text formatting tools.

IV

Macintosh Software

Adding Charts to a Slide

Astound's charting tool is simple but should meet the needs of most people (see fig. 17.28).

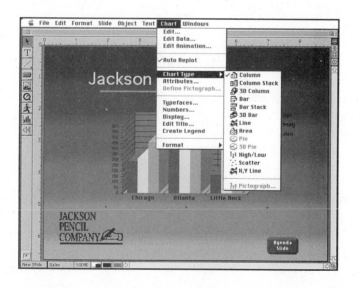

Fig. 17.28
Astound has a simple charting tool.

As with other business graphics packages, you can enter data in a spreadsheet-like datasheet or import data from Excel, Lotus, or Delimited text files. You use the first row and column of the datasheet for the axis labels. You can resize the column widths by clicking and dragging.

Tip
Unlike DeltaGraph Pro 3, Astound does not include any functions for summing data.

Once you have created a datasheet, you can highlight the data you want to include in a chart and create the chart. Astound includes 13 chart types, including bar, 3-D bar, pie, 3-D pie, line, area, high/low, and stacked bar. You can also create pictograph charts using clip art.

You can customize a chart in many ways. You can adjust the color, spacing, depth, and width of data series, set the number format, and the typeface used (font, size, and style) for each axis, as well as the legend and title. You can set the type of legend, as well as its location. You can also determine whether to show the floor panel, labels, major and minor grid, inside or outside tick marks, and the maximum and minimum for each axis. You can set the properties of grid lines (weight and color) individually, as well as any text labels. Once you have everything set up the way you want, you can even save a chart format for reuse later.

Caution

You should set the text label formatting options *before* making changes to the individual text labels using the text format tools because the text label formatting will override your individual changes.

Astound can also display a table containing the selected results from your datasheet. For this table, you can customize grid-line size and color, the border size, the typeface used for row and column titles, as well as the typeface used for the chart title and chart values. You can also set the number format and the table's interior color.

Adding Clip Art to a Slide

Astound comes with over 500 pieces of "clipmedia," arranged into libraries. To add a piece of clipmedia to a slide, you must open the library. The library window displays the images included in the library. Once the library is open, you simply click and drag the image onto the slide. You can change the size of clipmedia without affecting the quality of the image, but you cannot change the color or other properties. Unlike some other products, you cannot ungroup the parts of a piece of clipmedia so that you can modify the individual parts.

Adding Actors to a Slide

Another unique feature of Astound is its use of *Actors*. Actors are small animations that play when the slide that contains them is displayed during a slide show (see fig. 17.29). You can choose whether the Actor will play through its animation sequence just once or animate continuously while the slide is on the screen. Astound includes about 20 Actors.

> **Note**
>
> To create your own Actors, you must purchase a copy of Gold Disk's "Animation Works."

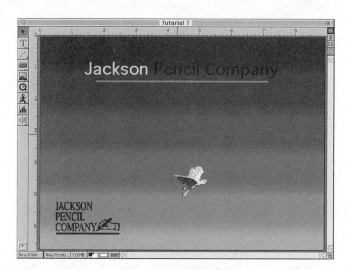

Fig.17.29
Actors are small animated characters that move during your slideshow.

You can establish a path for the Actor to follow. If you do, the Actor will move across the slide, following the path as it animates. The path is a simple straight line; however, you can create both an entrance and exit path for the Actor using an interactive dialog box.

Adding QuickTime Movies to a Slide

Astound comes with a variety of QuickTime movies. You can add a movie, and the movie will play when the slide it is on is displayed during a slide show. Astound even includes a QuickTime editor, which you can access by double-clicking a QuickTime movie. The editor enables you to choose whether the movie plays just once or loops continuously, set the loop direction (only forward, or play forward, then backward), set the sound volume, and set the animation speed. Using the editor, you can also view any frame of the animation and decide which static frame to display on the slide when the slide show is not playing.

Adding Sound to a Slide

Astound handles sounds as easily as it handles movies. The Sound tool enables you to load a sound, edit or play a loaded sound, record a new sound (provided you have at least a microphone), and attach the sound to a slide. Once a sound is attached to the slide, you can set its volume, determine whether it should play just once or loop continuously, and decide exactly when the sound should play (e.g., the sound should play during the last three seconds that the slide is on-screen). Astound comes with a collection of sound effects and music.

The sound editor displays the sound waveform in a window. You can display the waveform in various ways and change the waveform magnification to make it easier to work with. The sound editor enables you to cut, copy, and paste portions of the sound waveform.

Astound also enables you to add narration to either the current slide or to the entire slide show using the sound tool. When you add narration, Astound plays either just the current slide or the entire presentation. You can speak or input a music soundtrack while the slideshow is playing. Astound then automatically synchronizes the slideshow to the "narration." This is very handy for a self-running presentation. You can even select the sampling rate, whether the sound is mono or stereo, the amount of compression, and the number of bits (8, 16, or 32) used for sampling.

> **Note**
>
> Adjusting these settings enables you to trade sound file size for recording quality. For example, you can easily use a 5 kHz sample rate, 8-bit sampling, mono, and 3:1 compression for voice with little loss in quality. However, a music sound track would require at least a 22 kHz sampling rate and a 16-bit sample size in order to reproduce accurately.

Using the Color Gradient Tool

Tip
Astound's color gradient tool is more powerful than any of the others because it can use multiple colors.

Astound's color gradient tool is especially versatile (see fig. 17.30). You can create a gradient from a single color or select multiple colors that the gradient moves through. For example, you could select a gradient that starts with red, moves through blue, and ends up at green. You can select from six pattern directions for the gradient, such as up/down, upper left corner to lower right corner, from center, and so on. You can even cause the gradient to "burst" from a selected object on the slide. Once you have created a gradient, it is available for reuse from a pop-up box on the slide. You can also recall a gradient and make changes to it from the gradient editor.

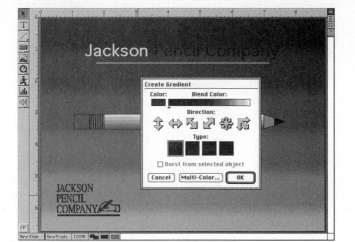

Fig. 17.30
Astound's color
gradient tool
enables you to
create a multitude
of gradient effects.

Using Fill Patterns

Astound's fill tool provides 60 different fill patterns but does not provide any
way to create your own pattern. However, you can set the foreground and
background colors independently from a pop-up "color-picker," available
from small buttons at the bottom of the screen.

Using Libraries

As mentioned earlier, clipmedia is packaged in libraries. Opening a library
displays a window containing the contents of that library. In addition to
clipmedia, you can open libraries of QuickTime movies, sounds, and Actors.
You can also create your own libraries of reusable objects. To add an object to
a new or existing library, you click and drag it to the library windows. Oddly,
although prepackaged objects have a name that appears below the object in
the library window, there doesn't seem to be any way for you to add a name
to your own objects or rename the objects in a prepackaged library. You can
open any presentation you have created as a library, enabling you to reuse
slides from that presentation easily.

Using Buttons and Interaction

Another powerful feature of Astound involves *Interaction*. You can set any
object on the screen to perform a prespecified action when you click the
object. These actions include moving to a predetermined slide, moving to the
first or last slide, restarting the slide show, going back or forward one slide,
or stopping the slideshow (see fig. 17.31).

Fig. 17.31
Astound's
interactive features
enable you to
closely control
your slides.

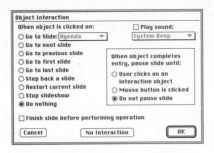

Tip
You can label
buttons with
text using the
text tool.

To help you use Interaction, Astound provides a Button tool. You can attach interaction to a button just like any other object, but since you expect to be able to click a button, it is more natural to attach interactions to buttons.

Making Transitions

Of all the packages reviewed here, Astound easily does the most outstanding job on *Transitions*. There are 22 slide transitions, including wipes, dissolves, tiling, snaking, and roll-ins. For most transitions, you can specify an edge or corner for the transition to start from. When you select a transition, Astound displays a preview using a miniature of the slide.

Slide transitions are just the smallest part of what Astound is capable of. You can apply transitions to text blocks, graphics, titles, QuickTime movies, Actors, charts, data series in charts, and sounds. Except for sounds (where the transitions are limited to fade in and fade out), you can apply about 20 different transitions to an object, and use separate transitions for entry and exit. These transitions include wipes, dissolves, fades, pixelates, zooms, and many others. The Select Object Transition dialog box enables you to see a preview of the transition you choose (see fig. 17.32).

Fig. 17.32
Astound's
transitions are
one of its most
remarkable
features.

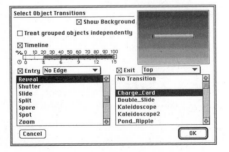

In addition to the normal transitions, you can apply special text transitions to blocks of text, including title blocks. Using these text transitions, you can cause blocks of text to move onto or off the screen one letter at a time, one line at a time, or one paragraph at time. You can set the entry point (top, lower left corner, etc.) and an additional special effect, such as whether the text bounces slightly when it reaches its destination. You can also force Astound to wait for a mouse click between text transitions.

> **Note**
>
> By combining the wait for mouse click with single line transitions, you can build the text block on a slide one line at a time. This gives you the ability to discuss each bullet point before moving on to the next one. Unfortunately, Astound cannot automatically dim previous bullet points.

Using the Timeline

With all the transitions, movies, and sounds you can apply to a slide, you need a way to coordinate the effects. For example, if you attach two sounds to a slide, how do you ensure that they don't play at the same time? Using Astound's Timeline tool, you can determine exactly when each action should happen and synchronize items (such as a text bullet and a sound) (see fig. 17.33).

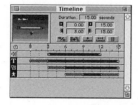

Fig. 17.33
The Astound
Timeline Window.

What Is a Timeline?

Each time you add an item to a slide, you can adjust the timeline for that item. The overall timeline indicates the user-defined length of time that the slide will be on the screen during a slideshow. The length of time that the object is displayed on the slide is represented by a solid blue bar. If the blue bar is of shorter duration than the overall slide, you can click the blue bar and drag it—positioning the appearance of the object at a different place in the time sequence. For example, if you place a 5 second sound on a 15 second slide, you can drag the sound's bar so that it plays when the slide is first displayed, at the end, or anywhere in between.

Transitions and the Timeline

In addition to the "normal display" blue bar, an object's timeline has two other parts: the entry transition and the exit transition. These transitions are displayed as striped blue bars, and you can click and drag special indicators to set the amount of time used for the entry and exit transitions.

> **Note**
>
> If you allow no time for the transitions, then the set transitions will not play.

The speed of the transitions depends on how much time you allow for them. If you allow a lot of time, the transition plays slowly. If you allow only a short time, the transition must occur very fast and may appear jerky as a result. You can ask Astound to set the best transition time, based on the complexity of the transition.

Synchronizing Items on the Timeline

Astound's Timeline tool displays a small window containing timelines for all the objects on the slide. At the left end of each timeline is a small icon that indicates what type of object each timeline is for. If you click the icon, a small preview of the item appears in the upper left corner of the dialog box. You can individually adjust each timeline, including the entry and exit transition times. The Timeline tool enables you to synchronize the effects and ensure that they work well together. For example, it is easy to ensure that two sounds don't play at the same time.

Using the Outline View

The Outline View presents each slide in your presentation in the form of a textual outline (see fig. 17.34).

Astound displays the title of the slide in bold, and any text on the slide is displayed just below the title. Different types of text (e.g., bulleted text blocks and the title) are separated by a line. Bulleted text is shown as an outline, with the various bullet levels represented as outline levels. You can collapse the text under a slide title so that just the title is displayed, and you can click and drag a small arrow indicator to move a line of text. Unfortunately, you can move only a single line of text at a time—text sublevels do not move automatically when you move the level that the text sublevels belong to.

You can add text at any level in the outline, and that new text is reflected on the slide. Although the Outline View does not display text formatting (e.g., style, size, etc.), you can determine the text formatting by highlighting the text you are interested in and using the Text menu to check the typeface. You can change the typeface using the Text menu, and the slide will reflect the change even though you can't see the change in the Outline View.

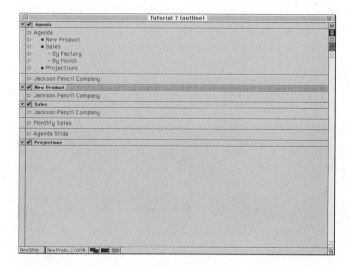

Fig. 17.34
Astound's Outline View.

Using the Slide Sorter View

As with most other business graphics products, Astound enables you to view your slides in a miniature Slide Sorter view. You can click and drag the slide miniatures to rearrange them, view the slide's timeline, and double-click any slide to return to the slide view with that selected slide on the screen.

Presenting the Material

You can check the spelling of words in your presentation with Astound's spell checker. You have the option to spell check just a single slide, or the entire presentation. The spell checker presents suggestions for words it doesn't recognize. Unfortunately, common abbreviations are not in the main dictionary, so you will have to add them.

Astound makes it very easy to test your presentation. The slide view contains a button that plays back just the current slide—this feature is very handy for testing transitions. You can use the built-in slideshow to play back the entire presentation, just the current slide, or the presentation from the current slide forward. You can set the slide duration to the normal slide duration (you can set this quantity from the slide view) or an override duration (e.g., three seconds per slide). This is also handy for moving quickly through the presentation. You can set the presentation to wait for a mouse-click before advancing to the next slide, advance whenever the mouse is clicked (overriding all time durations), loop back to the start when the presentation is done, and show the cursor.

Astound also supports 4 "notation pens," each with a different color. During a slide show, you can use the mouse to draw on a slide by pressing a number key to set the color and then clicking and dragging to draw on the slide (see fig. 17.35). Since one of the presentation settings tells Astound to advance to the next slide when you click the mouse, you can use the space bar to pause the presentation, allowing you to click and draw on the slide at any time.

Fig. 17.35
You can draw on a slide using the notation tools.

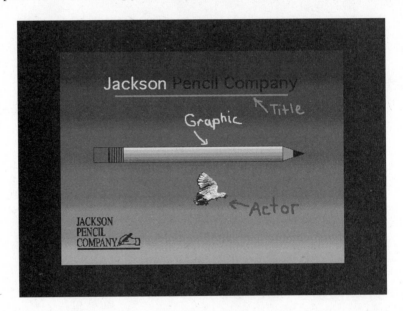

Astound can print slides, notes, the outline, and handouts. You can add notes to each slide in the special note view. You can select from six handout formats—ranging from one to six slides per page. Astound provides a lined area adjacent to each slide for taking notes.

Getting the Most from Astound: Hints and Tips

■ A powerful and easy-to-use function that many users don't take advantage of is the Distribution button in the Timeline window. Use this button to create an even distribution of selected object entrance and exit transitions. Simply select the objects you want to distribute over time, click the Distribution button, set the total time for transitioning all of the selected objects, and select the icon that represents how much overlap you would like between the object transitions. Astound then automatically calculates the proper timeline for each object.

■ By default, Astound assigns the same entry transition to each element of a chart, but it's easy to override the default transition. Double-click the chart element you would like to edit, and then open the Object Transition dialog to select a new entrance transition. Using this method, it's easy to have each bar in a bar chart appear in a different manner.

■ Normally, grouped objects are displayed in a timeline window as a single object. If you double-click a grouped object's icon in the timeline window, you can display the individual timelines for all of the objects in that group. This allows you to adjust the transition, timing, and other aspects of any object without disturbing the entire group.

■ The button tool is great for creating interactive buttons with a 3-D look, but many people like to use the button tool for creating interesting graphic backgrounds. By adjusting the beveled edges on the button, you can create an object that looks like a raised plaque or a carved inset on your background.

■ Because Astound allows you to set an entrance time as well as an exit time for each object on a slide, you can find that it is sometimes useful to combine what would be several slides into a single slide in which text, charts, and graphics appear and disappear at different times. This can sometimes result in a presentation with more continuity, and it also allows you to have fewer breaks in your sound effects. If you end up with object on top of each other, you can easily select the object underneath using the Timeline window.

■ To cause an object to fade into the background, draw a box on top of the object you want to fade out. Use a shade of gray for the box color. Select an Ink mode of Whiter or Blend from the Object menu. These modes can make objects appear more faint, but still be visible. Using the Timeline window, make this box appear on the slide at the time that you want the graphic underneath to fade.

■ Some complex objects can appear jerky when you apply transitions to them. Objects with gradient fills are especially hard to animate. A simple solution is to use the Convert to Bitmap command in the Object menu. Once the object has been converted to a bitmap, it will display much faster. You should also use Convert to Bitmap on existing bitmaps that you have resized in Astound. If a bitmap is not displayed on the slide at its original size, then Astound needs to scale it each time it gets displayed, hampering performance. Applying the Convert to Bitmap command creates a copy of the original bitmap at the new size, resulting in much faster playback.

Summary

Astound combines excellent multimedia support (movies and sound) with a remarkable range of transition effects. The Timeline support is unique among the packages reviewed here. The charting support is a little weak, and there is no support for the types of business objects ("models") that make Claris Impact such a strong contender.

Persuasion

Aldus Persuasion was one of the original presentation packages available for the Macintosh. It is still one of the most powerful, although the charting module is a little weak, and there are some usability problems—quite a few of the operations in Persuasion are not very intuitive. There are also some items that simply don't work, such as the Organization Chart module, which absolutely refuses to appear on a slide. Thus, if you need organization charts, you'll have to choose something else. However, the slide transitions, while not as strong as those in Astound, are more powerful than most of the other packages.

System Requirements

Persuasion comes on nine disks, and takes up 34.8 megabytes of disk space. This makes it the biggest package looked at in this chapter. Strangely, except for some clip art, Persuasion does not come with a lot of extra material, so there isn't really any way to cut down on the disk space used. The install procedure requires rebuilding the desktop—so if you use Persuasion, you will lose any desktop notes. Persuasion requires at least System 6.0.4 and 5MB, but many features are not supported with this minimal configuration. To make full use of Persuasion, you need at least System 7 and 8MB of memory. Even with this configuration, some operations may fail because of a lack of memory. System 7 support includes Publish and Subscribe, Balloon help, and QuickTime 1.5 compatibility.

Building Slides

Prs supports "Autotemplates"—standard slide configurations that you can use to give a common look to your presentation. Each autotemplate consists of at least five "masters" and a background. Masters are commonly used layouts, such as a title block and body text, title and chart, and so on. When you first install Persuasion, you can choose a default autotemplate. This default template is opened automatically whenever you create a new presentation. While it is not hard to choose a new autotemplate in place of the default template, it is an extra step you must take every time you create presentations. Unlike other packages, Persuasion does not prompt you automatically for an autotemplate. Changing the default autotemplate is quite an involved process. This is just one example of where Persuasion could benefit from improved usability. If you do choose to change the autotemplate, you can preview the available autotemplates from a dialog box.

Modifying the Slide Structure

You can directly modify the structure of a slide by clicking and dragging text blocks, graphics, charts, and other objects on the slide. Oddly, you can't click and drag a text placeholder until you have actually entered text into the placeholder—every time you click the text placeholder, Persuasion switches to the text tool so that you can enter text. This is another usability problem. You cannot apply a new background scheme directly to a slide, although the manual gives the impression that you can. You can modify the font, style, color, and effects for any text using a variety of palettes (see fig. 17.36). You can reapply the master to a slide to return to the default formatting for that master.

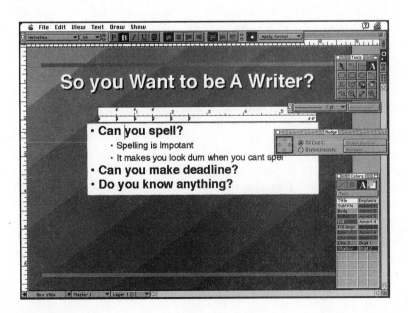

Fig. 17.36
You can use Persuasion's palettes to modify a slide.

You can also modify the slide structure by directly modifying a master. You can add placeholders to the master and rearrange the position of items on the master. If you modify the text properties, Persuasion uses the specified properties for bulleted text on the slide. You can create new masters and name them or import masters from other Autotemplates.

Persuasion does a better job of enabling you to modify backgrounds for slides than just about any other package. You can modify the standard background for an autotemplate; that change is reflected on all slides. You can add graphics and page numbers to a background, but you cannot add placeholders, so if you want a text block placeholder on every slide, you must modify each master. You can import a color scheme from another autotemplate, and either replace the current background or add the new background to a list of available backgrounds. You can also create a new background using the fill and drawing tools available in Persuasion. Once you have created new backgrounds, you can apply any available background to a master.

Adding Graphics and Text to a Slide

Persuasion has a whole palette of text and graphics tools for customizing a slide. You can use the text tool to add text blocks, and set the font, size, color, and effects for the text. You can also add a shadow to the characters in a text block, making for an excellent 3-D effect.

Graphics tools include rectangles, lines, ovals, freeform shapes, and freeform curves. You can fill the interior of a shape with a color, or a gradient fill. Oddly, patterned fills don't seem to be available. A line tool enables you to easily pick line thickness and type, as well as the arrowhead style for the line.

You can choose multiple objects and align them vertically or horizontally. You may also distribute them evenly along a line. You can group multiple objects into a single object and flip or rotate any object.

Persuasion's color palette tool is not very intuitive. The colors are labeled with object names (for example, Title or Body), but you can pick any color for any object. The buttons across the top of the palette enable you to pick colors for lines, background, text, and shadow, but they are poorly labeled and hard to figure out. You can also double-click any color to open a color-definition tool (see fig. 17.37). After opening the color-definition tool, you can copy and paste a color from the palette of available colors to replace a color in the color palette. It would have been easier to allow the user to simply click a replacement color.

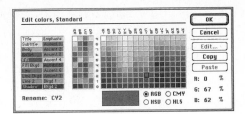

Fig. 17.37
Persuasion's Color
Definition Tool.

You can import QuickTime movies into a slide. Unlike Astound, you have very little control over when movies play—they play automatically when the slide is displayed during the slideshow.

Adding Charts to a Slide

Persuasion includes a simple chart builder that should meet the needs of most people (see fig. 17.38). Unfortunately, the charting application is a separate OLE (object linking and embedding) application, and it takes a long time to open. You must reopen the application each time you want to modify the chart.

Tip
For complete control of QuickTime movies, Astound does a better job than Persuasion.

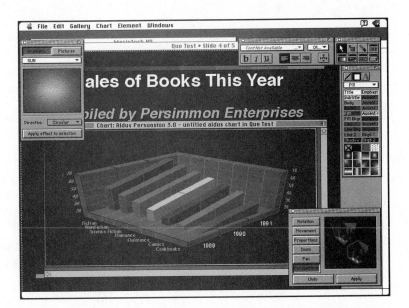

Fig. 17.38
Persuasion's Chart
Application is
simple but
effective.

Persuasion's chart gallery includes basic types of charts, including bar, pie, histogram, high/low, line, area, scatter, polar, radar, and spectral. Many of the basic types have additional options, and Persuasion presents a thumbnail preview of the chart type as you move the mouse pointer over each type of chart.

After you choose a chart from the gallery, Persuasion draws a sample on the screen, using sample data. You can edit the data in a spreadsheet-like table. You can also import data from Microsoft Excel and several standard formats, such as CSV files. You enter the title, subtitle, and axis titles in the first few rows of the datasheet, but once again, the controls for the datasheet are not very intuitive. In fact, despite the fact that the datasheet visually displays where axis titles are going to be placed, no combination of the many poorly explained controls could convince Persuasion to actually place the axis titles in the right place! As a result, the charting module gave disappointing results. I finally had to resort to manually clicking and dragging the axis labels where I wanted them.

You can modify text attributes, but only for all text of a particular type. That is, you can select any piece of text (e.g., one of the x-axis labels) and change the attributes, but the attributes change for all the text of that type (e.g., all the x-axis labels change). You can change the color of all grid lines and any of the data series, as well as the color and gradient fill pattern for any "walls" that appear in back of the data series. You can even apply gradient fills and picture fills to any object.

Persuasion has very complete 3-D chart controls. You can rotate the chart around any of the axes, move the chart in any direction, zoom in and out, pan, and adjust the perspective. The 3-D control dialog box previews the changes as you make them, and it's actually a lot of fun to play with these controls.

Adding Clip Art to a Slide

Persuasion comes with about 500 pieces of clip art, arranged into groups such as arrows, buildings, communications, computers, and people. You must import the clip art from a dialog box that does not actually show you a pre-view of the clip art unless you click a button to build a thumbnail preview. Depending on the complexity of the diagram, building a preview can take up to 15 seconds. However, once you have built a preview, it is available whenever you look at that piece of clip art. You can ungroup the clip art shapes and edit them using Persuasion's drawing tools.

Using Jump

Tip
Astound lets you attach a Jump action to a button, in addition to other screen objects.

Persuasion enables you to assign various *jump* actions to any object on the screen (see fig. 17.39). Clicking the object during a slide show causes Persuasion to take the specified actions. Actions can include jumping to the next slide, jumping to a specific slide, and opening an application or document. While not as powerful as Astound, the Jump feature is not as common in

Macintosh business graphics packages as it is in Windows, so this is a welcome feature.

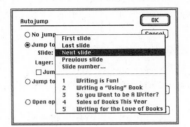

Fig. 17.39
You can assign a jump action to a screen object.

Making Transitions

Persuasion does an excellent job with special effects, including slide transitions. You can assign each object on a slide to a *layer*, and add one of 15 transitions to each layer. The layers are animated in layer number order. Thus, you can cause various objects on the slide to appear using different effects. Transitions include Fade, Glitter, Wipes, and Dissolves. You can attach a sound to each layer transition. Oddly, you can assign only the first layer transition and sound from the slide. To assign transitions and sounds for other layers of a slide, you must use the Transitions dialog box (see fig. 17.40).

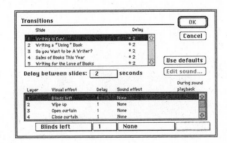

Fig. 17.40
The Transitions dialog box enables you to set transitions for each layer of a slide.

Autolayer is a very handy feature of Persuasion. When you click a text block and select Autolayer, Persuasion breaks up the block of text by paragraph or topic (e.g., major bullets). Each layer or topic is placed into a separate layer automatically. Since Persuasion places each layer on the screen one at a time, the effect of autolayering is to bring each point you want to make onto the screen individually. You can choose a "dimming" color so that earlier layers are dehighlighted when Persuasion places new layers on the screen. You can also assign a transition to each layer. The combined effect of a new paragraph or topic, coupled with the transition, is sure to catch your audience's attention.

Tip
Unlike Astound, you cannot specify an exit autoanimation.

Another attention-getting feature is *autoanimate*. Autoanimate enables you to select any object and have it move onto the screen. The effect is very simple—you can only choose the edge from which you want the object to appear. The object moves across the screen to its destination.

Using the Outline View

The Outline View presents each slide in your presentation in the form of a textual outline, with bulleted text levels displayed as levels in the outline. You can promote and demote levels and move levels (with all their sublevels) around in the outline. You can also collapse the text under an outline so that only the major headings are shown. You can change the text attributes in the outline, but those changes are not reflected on the slide. You can add text at any level in the outline, and the new text is displayed on the slide.

Using the Slide Sorter View

As with most other business graphics products, Persuasion enables you to view your slides in a miniature Slide Sorter View. You can click and drag the slide miniatures to rearrange them and double-click any slide to return to the slide view with that selected slide on the screen.

One unique feature of Persuasion's Slide Sorter is that you can create a new slide and demote other slides under it (see fig. 17.41). If you do, the headings of all those other slides appear on the new slide automatically. This is great for an opening agenda slide. If you modify the other slide titles, Persuasion automatically makes the changes on the agenda slide.

Fig. 17.41
The slides in this presentation are "demoted" below the first slide. As a result, the titles of all slides appear as bullet text on the first slide.

Presenting the Material

You can check the spelling of words in your presentation with Persuasion's spell checker. You have the option to spell check just a single slide or the entire presentation. The spell checker presents suggestions for words it doesn't recognize.

Persuasion's slide viewer is very useful. You can preview just the current slide or play the entire presentation. You can set the delay between slides, but you must set a time—you cannot leave a slide on the screen until you click the mouse or press a key. You can set the entire presentation so that all slides wait for a manual advance, but you must do this every time you run the slideshow.

Persuasion contains a note master that you can modify. The note master displays a miniature of a slide and provides space to type notes below the slide. You can modify the note master by changing the position of the slide and the text attributes of the note space. You can also add objects (such as a page number) to the background. Persuasion also has a handout master for printing audience handouts (see fig. 17.42). The handout master contains only a basic layout with three slides and lines for taking notes adjacent to each slide. You can add more slide placeholders, but this is tedious because you must manually edit everything on the handout master (each line in the note area is a separate object) to make room for the new slide.

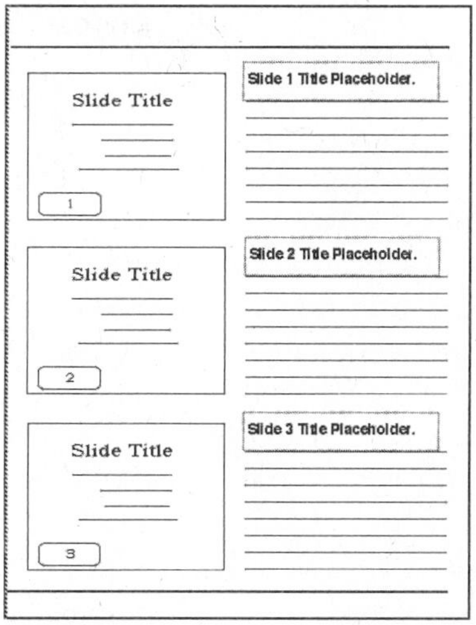

Fig. 17.42
Persuasion's
Handout Master is
hard to modify.

Persuasion comes with players for both the Macintosh and Windows, so you can play your presentation on any machine, even if Persuasion is not installed on it.

Getting the Most from Persuasion: Hints and Tips

■ To change the default settings for font, point size, style, alignment, or character and line space settings, choose Text Format from the Edit menu, and make your changes. Then, in the Text Format dialog box, click the Set Default button.

- If your presentation has a dark color scheme, change the color system to Inverse Grayscale or Black and White before printing proofs on a laser printer.

- To change the background of a slide, first switch to that slide's master using Slide Master from the View menu. You can only adjust the background of slide masters.

- Use the arrows or the edit boxes on the nudge palette to move objects, text, and shadows incrementally.

- To easily line up objects on separate slides in the same position, drag guides onto a new background you create. If the guides aren't visible, choose Guides from the Show menu, and then check Show Guides on the submenu.

- To change any colored Autotemplate to black and white, choose Color System from the Show menu, and then choose Black and White from the submenu.

Summary

Using Persuasion can be a constant battle to make it do what you want. Many actions appear to be simple, but you are often blocked from performing common actions for no apparent reason. A good example is the fact that you can't change the background of a slide without first entering the slide's master. The manual doesn't help: it is difficult to read because it is broken up into chunks that are hard for the eye to follow. The manual organization is also very poor—the manual covers the complexities of creating new masters and backgrounds before it tells you how to perform simple actions such as creating new slides and working with text and graphics. Finally, the failure of this product to produce organization charts, despite having slide masters that display them, is perplexing.

Conclusions and Recommendations

The business graphics packages available today for the Macintosh span a wide range of power and complexity. Which one should you use? That depends on your goals:

- If you need a package that has dynamite special effects, easy support for sound and graphics, animated Actors, and the ability to run on a PC, Astound is an excellent choice. Persuasion is also a good package but is hampered by bugs.

- If you need a package that packs full word processing with powerful and easy-to-use business objects (calendars, timelines, and so on), Claris Impact is the one you want. The Reporting document is unique in its text controls.

- If you want a fast, very simple package that you can pick up and use with virtually no training at all, you can't go wrong with Microsoft's PowerPoint.

- If you need the ultimate in charting power, DeltaPoint's DeltaGraph Pro 3 is the one for you.

IV

Macintosh Software

Chapter 18

Spreadsheets

by Mark Bilbo and Shelley O'Hara

The handwritten ledger has been used in business for literally hundreds of years. Double-entry accounting alone has a history of about three centuries.

The *spreadsheet*, for all its high-tech newness, is a very old idea; essentially, it's a sheet of rows and columns that contain tabular data.

Spreadsheets made their appearance on the personal computer scene in the early 1980s when the program VisiCalc was introduced. By today's standards, the program was simple and had few features. But, VisiCalc was wildly successful and became, in many cases, the reason for a business to purchase a personal computer.

While computers had been "number crunching" (performing mathematical calculations) for many years, VisiCalc enabled users to enter numbers on a screen in tabular form for the first time, add a few formulas, and have the computer do the math automatically—even when the numbers in the tables were changed.

In the years that have passed, the power of personal computers has grown and, along with them, the power and capabilities of spreadsheet programs.

This chapter provides an overview of the two most popular spreadsheet programs for the Mac:

- Microsoft Excel
- Lotus 1-2-3

Evolution of Spreadsheets for the Mac

Lotus 1-2-3 became the dominant spreadsheet program on IBM PC and PC clones, thus becoming as much of a standard in the business world as the pencil. Over the years, 1-2-3 brought powerful options to spreadsheets including macros for automating tasks, three-dimensional spreadsheets, "add-ins," and other features.

While 1-2-3 was almost monopolizing the DOS world, Microsoft introduced Excel on the Macintosh shortly after the computer's introduction in the mid-80s. While less powerful than 1-2-3 in relative terms, Excel took advantage of the Macintosh's graphic interface to take the spreadsheet another step forward due to its ease of use.

Lotus did not ignore the Macintosh, but seemed unable to bring their juggernaut of success into the graphical Macintosh world. The program Jazz fizzled and users continued to ask when 1-2-3 would come to the Macintosh.

Because it was the first to bring a spreadsheet program to the Macintosh, Microsoft became almost unstoppable. Excel continued to grow in power, adding analysis tools, extensive charting capabilities, macros, add-ins, formatting tools, and other features.

Ironically, with the growth of Windows on the PC, Excel began to invade Lotus 1-2-3's territory, even before 1-2-3 finally came to the Macintosh in 1992.

Microsoft Excel

Excel remains the leader in Macintosh spreadsheet programs. Excel has become one of the standard programs that almost every Macintosh user has and uses. At the same time, Excel is a very large and complex program; sometimes it's difficult to use.

System Requirements

Excel 5.0 comes on 800K disks. You can choose to do a typical installation, a minimum installation, or a custom installation. If you know which modules you need, you can do a custom installation and choose which parts of the program to install.

Excel runs on any Macintosh from the Plus on up and requires System 6.0.2 or higher. You need at least 2MB of memory to run the program and 4MB or more with MultiFinder or System 7. Keep in mind, however, that Excel's preferred memory size is 4MB and System 7 is around 2MB itself. So, a 4MB or more memory configuration is probably your best bet.

Excel takes advantage of, but does not require, a Floating Point Unit.

The Worksheet

Excel, like any spreadsheet program, uses a *worksheet* made of rows and columns. Customarily, spreadsheets use letters to indicate columns and numbers to indicate rows. Excel follows this convention (see fig. 18.1). Excel enables you to have several worksheets, all stored together in a *workbook*. *Worksheet tabs* appear at the bottom of the worksheet to indicate the current sheet.

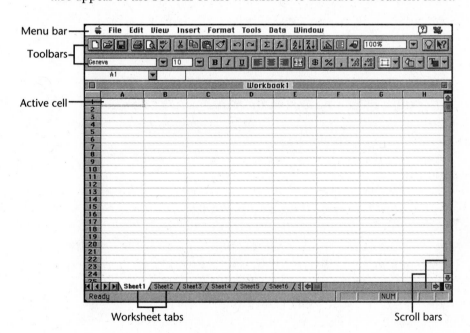

Fig. 18.1
The Excel worksheet.

The intersection of a column and row (the rectangles in fig. 18.1) are called *cells*. Data and formulas are entered into cells. Formatting and other commands are applied to individual cells or groups of cells.

Entering Data

Data is entered into a cell by clicking on the cell with the mouse and then typing. The data typed appears in both the cell and the Formula bar. When data is entered, the Enter and Cancel boxes appear in the Formula bar (see fig. 18.2).

Fig. 18.2
Entering data
in a cell.

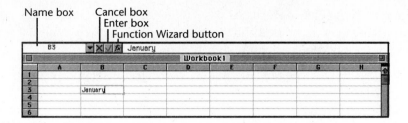

You also may confirm an entry of data and move to another cell by pressing the Enter key, the Return key, the Tab key, an arrow key, or clicking another cell. The difference with each of these lies in which cell is selected next. Enter leaves the current cell selected, Return selects the next cell down, Tab selects the next cell right, and clicking—as you may expect—selects the cell clicked on.

To cancel an entry from the keyboard, press Escape.

Two additional buttons are available. You can click the Function Wizard button to use the Function Wizard (see the "Entering Functions" section later in this chapter for information on this feature). Or you can click the Name box to insert a name in the formula or cell.

Using AutoFill

One feature unique to Excel that is enormously handy is the AutoFill feature. To use AutoFill, you type the first few entries in a series (January, February, March, for example). Select the entries by dragging the mouse pointer across the cells. Then drag the *fill handle*, the lower-right-hand corner of the selection rectangle, to automatically extend the series (see fig. 18.3).

Tip
As you drag the fill handle, watch the Name box in the Formula bar that displays the current value of the series. This is how you know when to stop and release the mouse button.

Excel shows a great deal of intelligence in AutoFill. You can enter entries such as "Month 1," and "Month 2," and Excel's AutoFill will extend the series as "Month 3," "Month 4," and so on.

Dragging down or to the right creates increasing series (1, 2, 3, and so on, for example). Dragging to the left or up will create decreasing series (5, 4, 3, and so on, for example).

The fill handle is best for quick entries of linear series. You can quickly enter sequential series of months, days, and numbers using the tool.

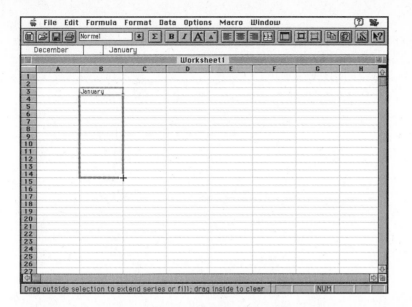

Fig. 18.3
Creating a column
of month names
by using the fill
handle.

Note

AutoFill doesn't need much in the way of "example" entries to do obvious series. If you need to enter the days of the week, for example, you can type "Monday," press Enter to confirm, then drag the AutoFill tool. AutoFill knows to enter "Tuesday," "Wednesday," and so forth.

AutoFill is a great time-saver and one of Excel's commendable features; it's simple, straightforward, and handy.

Using Fills and Series

Entering data can be repetitious. One test of a spreadsheet program's worth is the available tools that enable you to reduce the amount of data entry when using the worksheet.

Excel provides two fill commands Fill Down and Fill Right, in the Edit menu for entering repeated data. You also can use the Fill, Series command, also in the Edit menu, for more complex data entries.

To repeat the same text or data in a column, for example, you enter the value to be repeated. Then drag to select the cells in the column, making sure to select the first entry. From the Edit menu, choose Fill Down (or press ⌘-D) to copy the first cell's entry to the other selected cells (see fig. 18.4).

Tip
If you go too far, say dragging until reaching July when you wanted the series to be only to June, don't release the mouse button. Move the mouse back up until the Formula bar indicates that June is the current value.

For more complex fills, Excel has the Fill Series command in the Edit menu. After choosing the Series command, the Series dialog box appears with several options. The Series dialog box can be used to create linear, growth, and date series (see fig. 18.5).

Fig. 18.4

Filling a column using the Fill Down command.

Fig. 18.5

Creating a series using the Series dialog box.

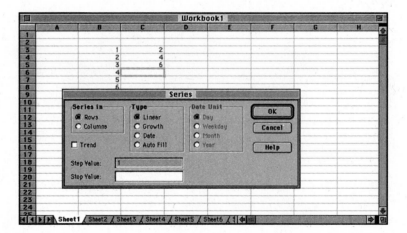

Series can be entered into rows or columns. You may choose the Linear option, in the Type area, to add the Step Value repeatedly to create the series (a step of 2 could create a series of 1, 3, 5, 7, and so on). Use the Growth option in the Type area to create a series in which the Step Value is multiplied repeatedly (a step of 2 could create a series of 1, 2, 4, 8, and so on). Use the Date option in the Type area, and the options in the Date Unit area to create a series of days, weekdays, months, or years. Choosing the AutoFill option, in the Type area, creates a linear series based on an example that's similar to dragging the AutoFill tool.

The Trend option check box enables you to create a linear or exponential growth series based on the example entries in your selection. The Trend option overrides the Step Value and calculates the step from the example values in the selection. You can use the Growth option in the Type area with the Trend option to create exponential series such as repeated doubling (2, 4, 8, 16, and so on, for example).

Creating Custom Fills

In addition to the Fill commands, you also can create a custom fill by using the Options command in the Tools menu, then clicking the Custom Lists tab. For example, you can create a list of parts or a list of customer names. Once the list is created, you can enter the first value and then drag the fill handle to fill in the remaining values.

Editing Data

You can edit data in the Formula bar or directly in the cell. To edit the contents of any cell, click that cell. You then use the standard Macintosh editing techniques to edit the data.

Using Cut, Copy, Paste, and Clear

The Edit menu's Cut, Copy, Paste, and Clear commands in Excel are slightly different from those of the Macintosh and there are more options available than you might expect.

You use Cut and Copy by starting out in the usual manner: select the material you wish to cut or copy. As you may expect, you drag through those cells you wish to select just as you normally make selections with the mouse.

After making the selection, you open the Edit menu and choose Cut or Copy, or use the standard keyboard equivalents. You can also use the Cut and Copy buttons on the Standard toolbar.

At this point, Excel acts differently than other Macintosh programs. The selection is highlighted with a moving, dashed box. The Status bar informs you that you may choose the destination, then press Enter or choose Paste to paste the selection (see fig. 18.6).

To complete a standard Macintosh cut-and-paste or copy-and-paste sequence, you click where you want the selection to be pasted and press Enter, or open the Edit menu and choose Paste.

Tip

To duplicate a selection in different locations of your worksheet, use the Paste command rather than the Enter key. Enter clears the Clipboard of the selection, but Paste leaves the copied selection on the Clipboard.

Fig. 18.6
Ready to paste a
cut selection.

	A	B	C	D	E	F	G	H
1								
2								
3								
4		January	February	March	April	May	June	
5	Electricity	75						
6	Water	25						
7	Gas	30						
8	Phone	65						
9	Waste disposal	15						
10								
11								
12								
13								

Excel offers, in the Edit menu, a Paste Special command that enables you to
paste various parts of the selection, perform mathematical operations on the
pasted data, and even eliminate blanks or transpose columns and rows (see
fig. 18.7).

Fig. 18.7
Paste Special offers
several useful
options.

The default All option, in the Paste area of the Paste Special dialog box, performs a regular paste, pasting the entire selection. Use the Formulas option in
the Paste area to paste the data and formulas from the selection, but not the
formatting (such as Bold, Italics, and the like). The Values option in the Paste
area will paste the text and numerical data, but will not paste the formulas in
the selection.

Tip
To copy format-
ting, you can
also use the
FormatPainter
button on the
Standard toolbar.

The Formats option in the Paste area is useful when you have performed a
complex formatting of a table or other arrangement in your worksheet and
wish to format another table in a similar manner. You use the Copy command, then the Paste Special, Formats command to copy just the formatting
from one selection to the other.

The Notes option in the Paste area pastes only the cell notes from the selection. Excel offers the option to annotate cells with text or even sound. This
Paste Special option enables you to copy notes to other locations in your
worksheet.

The Operation area enables you to do simple matrix types of operations by
adding two tables together, subtracting one from another, multiplying, or
dividing their values. You use these options by selecting the data, choosing
Copy from the Edit menu, then selecting the table of data with which you

want to perform the operation. Then choose the Paste Special command from the Edit menu. The Paste Special dialog box appears. Choose the option you wish to perform from the Operation area.

The Skip Blanks check box, when selected, enables you to paste a table, eliminating the blanks within it. Selecting the Transpose check box switches the rows and columns, "flipping" the table.

Excel also offers several options that apply to the Edit menu's Clear command. To access the Clear options, choose the Clear command from the menu. From the submenu, you can then choose to clear All (a standard Clear command), clear the formatting of the selection (eliminating such effects as bold, italics, and the like), clear the contents (which also will clear the values), or clear the cell notes.

Using Drag and Drop

One very useful editing technique Excel offers is Drag and Drop. An entire selection of data can be moved quickly from one location to the other just by dragging an edge of the selection box. You may have to practice using this option a bit with the mouse pointer; you need to be careful not to inadvertantly drag the fill handle. Overall, however, this option is very useful; you can "grab" a selection, then drag the selection wherever you need it, avoiding the several steps of Cut and Paste (see fig. 18.8).

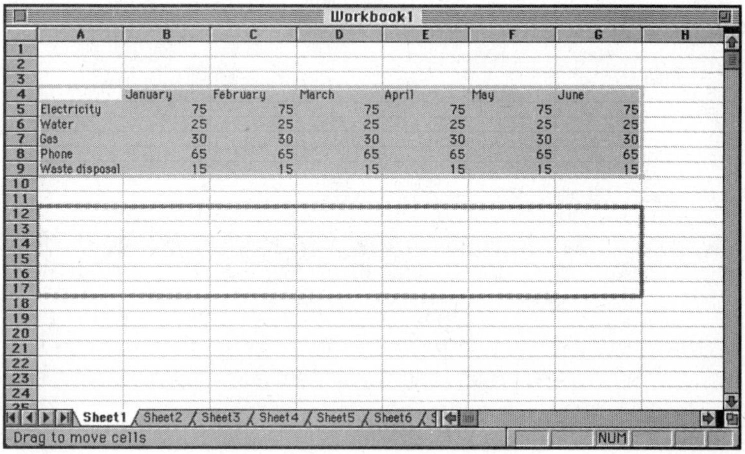

Tip
When doing complex formatting, the Clear, Formats command is extremely useful for clearing all formatting from cells while leaving the formulas, values, text, and other data intact; this enables you to redo your formatting.

Fig. 18.8
Moving a table with Drag and Drop.

Using Select Special

Excel offers a powerful selection command that gives you a number of options in making selections. Select the Go To command from the Edit menu and then click on the Special button. You see a dialog box containing several selection options (see fig. 18.9).

Fig. 18.9
The Go To Special
dialog box offers
numerous
selection options.

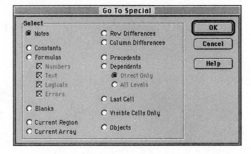

The Go To Special dialog box has so many different options that all of them cannot be fully discussed in a short chapter section. However, a few of the more interesting options are worth noting.

For example, the Formulas option in the Select area enables you to select erroneous formulas in a worksheet for correction. Because formulas are only displayed when the cell in which they are located is selected, you may find it difficult to track down erroneous formulas in a complex worksheet. This selection option can aid you.

Blanks is an interesting option in the Select area that is useful in formatting a table. You can select the table, then open the Edit menu and choose the Go To, Special command to select just the blanks in that table and apply formatting to the selected blanks.

The Row Differences and Column Differences options in the Select area enable you to select values in a row or column that differ from the one value you select before choosing the command.

> **Note**
>
> Excel also provides auditing commands and an Auditing toolbar for tracing precedents, dependents, and errors. *Precedents* are cells that are referred to by the formula in the active cell. *Dependents* are cells that contain formulas that refer to the active cell.

The Visible Cells Only option in the Select area is very useful in copying parts of tables. You can hide cells by using the column width or row height options, then use the Select Special command to select only the visible cells. Then use the Copy command from the Edit menu to put only the selection on the Clipboard for later pasting, leaving the hidden cells behind.

Select Special is rather complex. Fortunately, a Help button is available to aid you in learning how to use the many options.

Entering Formulas

Formulas are the mathematical or logical equations you enter into cells to calculate various values from your data. In Excel, you enter a formula by selecting a cell and typing an equal sign (=) to indicate that a formula is being entered (otherwise, your typing will be interpreted as data).

A *cell address* is entered into a formula by typing the letter and number that indicate the column and row of that cell. For example, to enter a formula that adds the values in the cells in column B, rows 2 and 3, you would type

=B2+B3

and then press the Enter (or Return) key to confirm the formula entry. The formula is automatically calculated and the resulting value appears. Figure 18.10 shows a column of numbers with an addition formula.

Addition formula

The basic mathematical operations, such as addition (+), subtraction (-), multiplication (*), and division (/), are offered. Many functions also are offered that can perform many complex calculations.

You do not have to actually type the addition operator in many cases. To enter a simple addition formula, you can press the equal sign (=), then click in sequence the cells you want to add. Excel automatically assumes the cells are to be added.

Tip
To enter a cell address without having to type, click the cell while entering a formula. The cell's address is automatically entered.

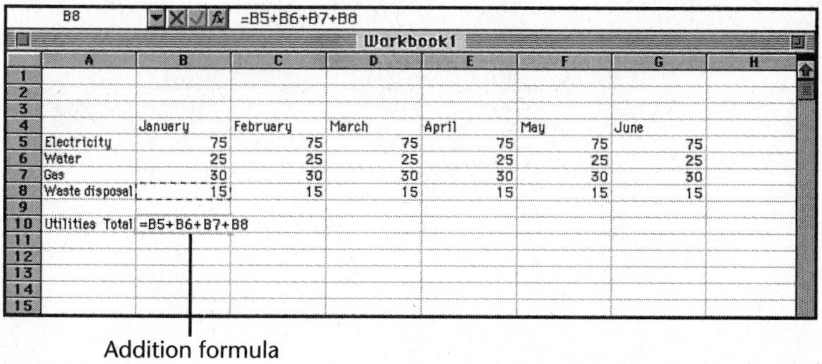

Fig. 18.10
Entering a simple formula to add a column of numbers.

> **Note**
>
> Remember that once you have entered a formula into a cell, you then can use the fill handle to duplicate that function into other cells. This is very handy in tables that sum columns or rows of numbers, because you can enter a summation formula and then drag the fill handle to duplicate that formula across the row or column.

Entering Functions

Excel offers a number of functions that perform many useful and powerful calculations and operations. A *function*, essentially, takes the *arguments* (values, cell addresses, text, and other data), performs an operation, then produces a resulting value. Excel has so many functions available that a separate reference manual is devoted to listing and detailing the functions.

You may enter a function in one of two ways: by typing the function name into an equation, or by using the Function Wizard. The Function Wizard enables you to select the function that you want. Then the wizard leads you step-by-step through the process of creating the function (see fig. 18.11).

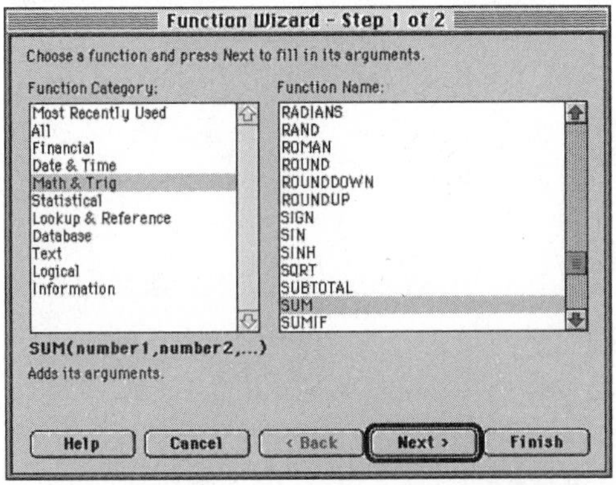

Fig. 18.11
Selecting the function to use.

> **Note**
>
> To quickly enter a formula that adds a row or column of numbers, click the cell that will receive the formula, then click the AutoSum button in the Standard toolbar (the button with the sigma symbol). Excel will even select the column or row for you, so you only need to press the Enter key to finish the formula.

To use the Function Wizard, click the Function Wizard button. A Function Wizard dialog box appears that groups the functions by category. Click the category (Math & Trig, for example) to view the functions of that type in the right-hand scroll box.

After you have selected the function you need, click the Next button. A second dialog box appears and Excel prompts you to enter the arguments for the function (see fig. 18.12). You can type the arguments directly in the dialog box or click the cells in the worksheet. After you enter all the arguments, click the Finish button.

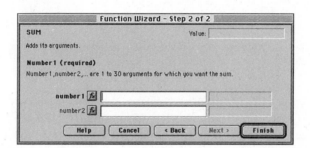

Fig. 18.12
Entering the arguments for a function.

Editing the Worksheet

You can edit the worksheet itself. You can adjust column widths and row heights, as well as insert and delete cells. You can hide columns and rows so that they do not display in the worksheet (but they still retain their values and formulas).

You can insert a column or row by selecting the entire column or row. (To select an entire column, click the column letter. To select an entire row, click the row number.) Then open the Insert menu and select the Columns command to insert a column, or the Rows command to insert a row.

To delete a column or row, select it. Then open the Edit menu and choose the Delete command.

You can insert cells by selecting the number of cells you want to insert. Then choose the Insert Cells command.

You can adjust the width of any column or row by dragging the border between the column letters or row numbers (see fig. 18.13).

Fig. 18.13
Adjusting column
width by dragging.

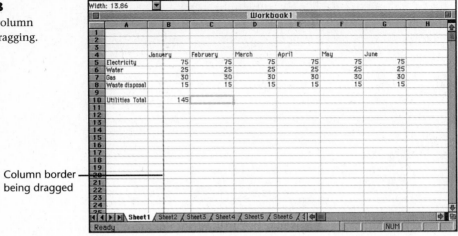

Column border —
being dragged

For more precise adjustment, open the Format menu and choose the Row
Height or Column Width commands. Each command has a submenu. To
change the column width, for example, select the Column Width command
from the Format menu. Enter the value in the Column Width dialog box (see
fig. 18.14).

Fig. 18.14
Adjusting column
width by typing a
value.

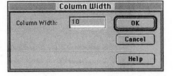

Tip
A shortcut for
setting a column
width or row
height to its
"best fit" is to
double-click the
divider to the
right of the
column or below
the row.

Both submenus also include Hide and Unhide commands which enable you
to hide the selected rows or columns. You can unhide the column or row and
see that the data in the column or row remained intact.

Using the Toolbar

Above the worksheet, and just below the menu bar, you see two toolbars.
Toolbars contain buttons and menus which enable you to perform many
functions by clicking the mouse. You can customize the toolbars, and you
can create your own. By default, you see two toolbars, the Standard toolbar
and the Formatting toolbar (see fig. 18.15). Tables 18.1 and 18.2 list the buttons with a short description.

Standard toolbar

Formatting toolbar

Fig. 18.15
The Standard and
Formatting
toolbars in Excel
contain shortcuts.

Table 18.1	Standard Toolbar Buttons
Button	**Description**
	Creates a new workbook
	Displays the Open dialog box so that you can open a workbook
	Saves the workbook
	Prints the workbook
	Displays a print preview of the worksheet
	Starts the Speller
	Cuts the selection
	Copies the selection
	Pastes the cut or copied selection
	Copies formatting
	Undoes the last command
	Repeats the last command
	Creates a SUM function
	Starts the Function Wizard
	Sorts the selection in ascending order
	Sorts the selection in descending order
	Starts the ChartWizard

(continues)

Table 18.1 Continued

Button	Description
	Draws a text box on the worksheet
	Displays the Drawing toolbar
100%	Enables you to zoom the worksheet display
	Displays tip information
	Enables you to get context-sensitve help

Table 18.2 Formatting Toolbar

Button	Description
Geneva	Displays a drop-down list of font selections
10	Displays a drop-down list of font sizes
B	Makes the selection bold
I	Makes the selection italic
U	Underlines the selection
	Aligns the selection with the left edge of the cell
	Centers the selection
	Aligns the selection with the right edge of the cell
	Centers the selection across multiple columns
$	Formats the selection as currency style
%	Formats the selection as percent style
,	Formats the selection as comma style

Button	Description
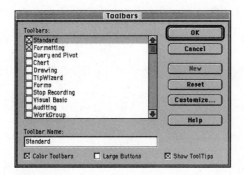	Increases the number of decimal places displayed
	Decreases the number of decimal places displayed
	Displays a palette of border selections
	Displays a palette of colors. You can use this palette to change the cell color.
	Displays a palette of colors. You can use this palette to change the color of the text in the cell.

IV

Macintosh Software

Tip
To see the name of a button, put the mouse pointer on the button. The tool name, called a *ToolTip*, pops up.

You can display other toolbars by using the Toolbars command from the View menu. To display a toolbar, select the check box next to its name (see fig. 18.16).

Fig. 18.16
Choosing to display another toolbar.

Understanding the Status Bar
The Status bar, below the worksheet, aids you by giving you one-line help information, displaying the program's current action, and displaying the keyboard mode (see fig. 18.17).

Hide a toolbar by deselecting the box.

Toolbars can be customized and you can add toolbars of your own. Excel's customization options are discussed later in this chapter in the "Customizing Excel" section.

Fig. 18.17
The Status bar
displaying help.

Help displayed—
for Format

In the left side of the Status bar, you normally see the word Ready, indicating that Excel is otherwise unoccupied and awaits your instruction. A one-line description of commands and buttons is also displayed here.

> **Note**
>
> To obtain one-line help for a menu command or button, place the mouse pointer on the command or button, then press and hold the mouse button. If you wish to execute the command, release the mouse button. If you do not want to execute the command, move the mouse pointer off the button or command.

Five mode indicators are used in Excel for the Macintosh. (A sixth is present on the screen, but only used in the Windows version of the program.) These indicate such things as when the caps lock is on, when the scroll lock is active, whether the fixed decimal size option is active, and other keyboard related modes.

Using Formatting

There are a great number of formatting options available in Excel to improve the appearance of your worksheet. Number formatting enables you to set the number of decimal places for numerical data, add dollar signs (or other currency symbols), and set date and time formats, fraction formatting, scientific notation, and the like.

For text, you have available all of the usual Macintosh formatting such as bold, italics, various fonts and font sizes, and the like. You can combine this formatting into Styles which enable you to apply combinations of formatting with a single menu choice.

You also can add borders to cells, you can shade cells, and you can apply patterns and colors.

Using and Defining Number Formatting

Applying number formatting requires a couple of steps in Excel. First you select the cells containing the numbers you wish to format; then choose the Cells command from the Format menu. The Format Cells dialog box appears. Click on the Number tab. In the Number tab, you see a list of the formatting categories to the left and the list of formatting codes available for the selected category to the right (see fig. 18.18).

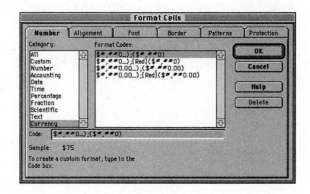

Fig. 18.18
Choosing a currency format.

Excel uses format codes with pound signs (#) to indicate digits, commas to indicate comma separators that will be used, parentheses to indicate that negative numbers are placed within parentheses, and other similar notations.

While it is not strictly necessary to understand the formatting codes in order to format numbers, it is useful to learn them so that you can create custom formats.

When you choose a format, the codes for that format appear in the Code box (you may, at this point, edit the formatting to customize it). You also see a sample of the formatting below the Code box.

If you want more help on number formatting, click the Help button in the dialog box.

Tip
A quick way to apply common formatting is to use one of the style buttons on the Formatting toolbar.

> **Note**
>
> Some foreign currency symbols are available in standard Macintosh fonts and can be inserted into custom number formats. Usually, you press the Option key to access these symbols. Choose the Key Caps desk accessory from the Apple menu to find the symbols you need.

Applying Text Formatting

The standard Macintosh text formatting options, with additional options useful for spreadsheets, are available through the Format menu. Text alignment options are accessed by opening the Format menu and choosing the Cells command. Then click the Alignment tab of the Format Cells dialog box that appears (see fig. 18.19).

Fig. 18.19
Setting text alignment.

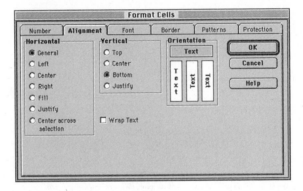

One particularly useful alignment option is the Wrap text option. You can use this option to wrap a paragraph of text within a cell. Press ⌘-1 to select the Cells command from the Format menu. Click on the Font tab. The fonts installed in your System file, their available point sizes, and the usual Macintosh style options (bold, italics, and so on) are available on the Font tab in the Format Cells dialog box (see fig. 18.20).

Tip

If you wish to use a particular font, font point size, and style as the default (or "normal") font for the worksheet, click the Normal Font check box before clicking OK.

Applying Cell Formatting

Excel offers many formats that can be applied to cells to add borders, patterns, shading, colors, and the like to improve the appearance of your worksheet.

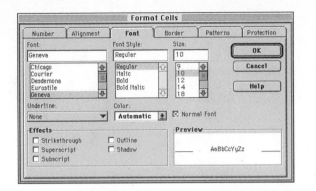

Fig. 18.20
Choosing a font
for the selected
text.

You can select the Cells command from the Format menu and then use two
of the tabs for applying borders or patterns: Border and Patterns. You can
apply borders to cells by selecting the cells, selecting the Cells command
from the Format menu, and clicking the Border tab of the dialog box that
appears. The Border tab enables you to choose the thickness of the border,
whether to use dashed lines, the sides of the selected cells that the border will
be applied to, color for the border, and shading for the cells (see fig. 18.21).

Tip
Click the Borders
button to display
a palette of com-
monly used bor-
ders. Click the
style you want.

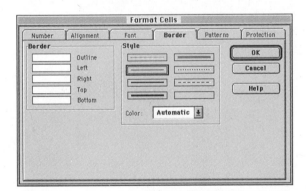

Fig. 18.21
Adding a border to
selected cells.

You can apply patterns by selecting the Format menu's Cells command. Then
click the Patterns tab of the Format Cells dialog box. From the Patterns tab,
you can choose a pattern, a foreground color—which is applied to the pattern
itself, and a background color—which fills the cell behind the pattern (see
fig. 18.22).

Tip
You can apply a
pattern by clicking
the Color button
on the Formatting
toolbar. From the
palette that ap-
pears, click the
color or pattern
that you want to
use.

Fig. 18.22
Choosing a
pattern and colors
to apply to the
selected cells.

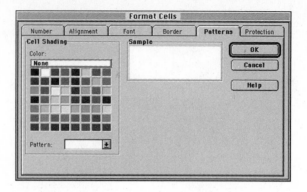

Using and Defining Styles

A *style* is a collection of formatting such as font, font point size, font styles,
borders, patterns, colors, and the other formatting discussed so far. The formatting is collected under a single style name and can be applied by opening
the Format menu and choosing the Style command.

After you have formatted a table or other section of your worksheet, you can
create a style "from example" by selecting the formatted cells, opening the
Format menu, and choosing the Style command. The Style dialog box
appears. Type a name for the style in the Style Name drop-down list box
(see fig. 18.23).

Fig. 18.23
Creating a
Table style.

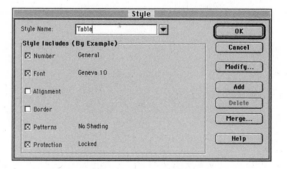

You will want to choose certain check boxes, in the Style Includes (By
Example) area, to determine which types of formatting the style includes. For
example, if you wish to create a style that only adds the borders and patterns
you created, you will want only the Border and Patterns check boxes to be
marked.

To modify the style, click the Modify button. You see the Format Cells dialog box. You can select which tab you want (Number, Alignment, Font, Border, Patterns, or Protection) and then make the appropriate change.

Once you have defined a style, you can apply that style to other selections by opening the Format menu and choosing the Style command. Select the style you want from the Style Name drop-down list box in the Style dialog box (see fig. 18.24).

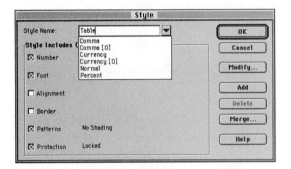

Fig. 18.24
Applying a defined style to a selection.

Using AutoFormat

One feature that Excel provides which is extremely helpful in formatting tables is AutoFormat. You can apply predefined styling to a selection by using the AutoFormat command in the Format menu. An AutoFormat dialog box appears listing format options and showing samples of the options (see fig. 18.25).

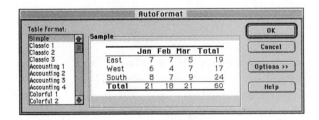

Fig. 18.25
The selection of AutoFormats that are available.

Charting Data

Excel offers the ChartWizard to simplify creating a chart. You use ChartWizard by first clicking the ChartWizard button on the Standard toolbar. You then draw a frame in the worksheet to hold the chart. ChartWizard then leads you through a series of five dialog boxes in which you set various charting options (see fig. 18.26).

Fig. 18.26
ChartWizard
takes over.

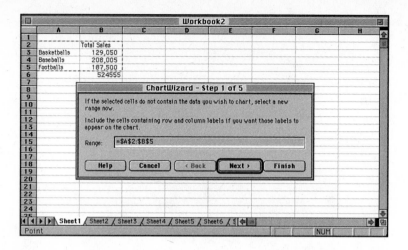

You go through the dialog boxes, indicating your charting preferences, then Excel draws the chart in your worksheet (see fig. 18.27).

Fig. 18.27
A completed chart
created with
ChartWizard.

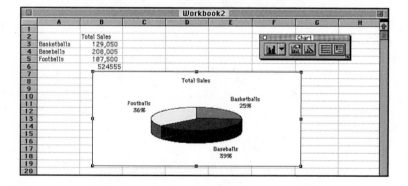

Tip
Heavily format-
ted tables do not
go well with
ChartWizard.
If you will be
charting your
table, keep the
formatting to a
minimum to
avoid heavy
editing.

Once a chart is created, you can edit the chart by double-clicking on the chart. Excel opens the chart in a separate window. The Chart toolbar is displayed (see fig. 18.28). Some different commands are also available on the Insert and Format menus. A dialog box is displayed listing format options and showing samples of the options.

You can use the Chart toolbar to change from one type of chart to another. You also can use the Chart toolbar to return to the default chart type.

You can change many other items by double-clicking the item in the chart. For example, to change the chart plot area, double-click the plot area. To change the pattern used for a particular series, double-click the series you want to change.

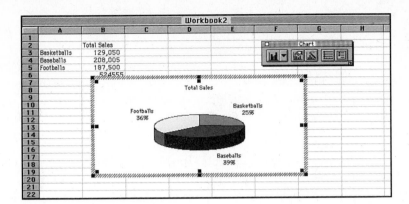

Fig. 18.28
A chart and the
Chart toolbar.

You can add a series to the chart by dragging it from the worksheet to the chart. Because the chart and the worksheet are linked, the chart is automatically updated whenever you make a change to the worksheet data. Likewise, you can drag a data point on the chart, and the corresponding worksheet value will be updated.

The chart is an object on the worksheet. As such, you can move it by dragging the border and resize it by dragging a selection handle.

Using Databases

Excel offers extensive database capabilities that enable you to manage lists of information. The Data menu contains several database commands, including the ability to create a data form for entering and editing records in a database, searching for records by using criteria, or just browsing through the database (see fig. 18.29).

Tip
Try creating a simple chart and experiment with making changes. Though editing charts can be difficult, you can learn how to format charts with some experimentation.

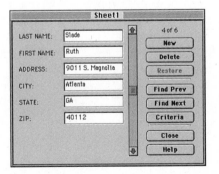

Fig. 18.29
Browsing a database of clients using the Form command.

The Data menu also includes commands for filtering records from a database using criteria which must be satisified. Over a dozen database functions are available for use in worksheets. These enable you to extract and use information from a database in your formulas, as well as perform various statistical analyses of data in the database.

Setting up a database in Excel is one of the easier procedures in the program. You enter the data in a tabular form. The first row contains the field names. Subsequent rows contain individual records. Each column is a certain field. For example, you can have fields for FIRST NAME, LAST NAME, ADDRESS, CITY, STATE, and so on.

Excel may not be able to completely take the place of a database program if you have large amounts of data to manage. However, for many users, Excel is sufficient for managing contact lists, small employee databases, mailing lists, and the like.

Sorting, Filtering, and Subtotaling Data

You can use the Data menu's Sort command to sort your database. In the Sort dialog box, you can sort a client database by last name or by Zip code, for example (see fig. 18.30).

Fig. 18.30
Sorting a
worksheet.

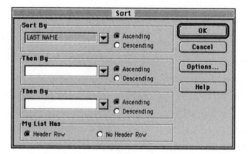

In addition to sorting, you can filter the database so that only certain records are displayed. For example, you can filter the data so that only clients in a particular state are displayed. Excel hides all the other rows that do not match the criteria you select (see fig. 18.31).

Fig. 18.31
Filtering a
worksheet.

	A	B	C	D	E	F	G	H
1	Client Database							
2								
3	LAST NAME	FIRST NAME	ADDRESS	CITY	STATE	ZIP		
5	Bluestein	Karen	102 Main	Indianapolis	IN	46256		
8	Beheler	Stacey	9055 S. 100 St.	Indianapolis	IN	46220		
10								

Open the Data menu and choose the Subtotal command. The Subtotal dialog box appears. Here, you can automatically create subtotals for a report (see fig. 18.32).

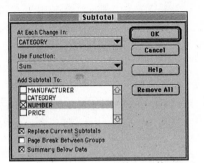

Fig. 18.32
Creating subtotals.

Using Outlining

Excel enables you to use *outlining* in your worksheets. Outlining is the ability to hierarchically nest data and display the data of the desired depth. This enables you to have great detail in your worksheets, while still being able to "collapse" the detail to summary levels to get an overall view.

When you have created a worksheet, Excel displays buttons along the top- and left-hand sides of the worksheet. You can click these buttons to set the level of detail you want displayed.

In addition to outlines, you can create pivot tables to summarize and analyze data.

Using Macros

Excel can record and execute a series of commands in a *macro*. This ability to automate tasks can be extremely useful in reducing repetitive work.

Excel's macro language is actually a programming language and is very sophisticated; you even can create new functions for use in your worksheets, and an application is included that enables you to create and design your own dialog boxes.

You do not have to spend hours of study, however, before using the macro feature. Excel has a Record command that enables you to record and store your steps as a macro as you take them (see fig. 18.33).

Fig. 18.33
Preparing to
record a new
macro in Record
New Macro dialog
box.

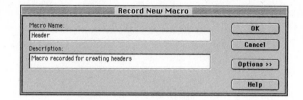

Excel keeps macros on a separate worksheet in the workbook (see fig. 18.34).

Fig. 18.34
An Excel macro in
the macro sheet.

```
' Header Macro
' Macro recorded for creating headers
'
Sub Header()
    With ActiveSheet.PageSetup
        .PrintTitleRows = ""
        .PrintTitleColumns = ""
    End With
    ActiveSheet.PageSetup.PrintArea = ""
    With ActiveSheet.PageSetup
        .LeftHeader = ""
        .CenterHeader = "&F"
        .RightHeader = ""
        .LeftFooter = ""
        .CenterFooter = "Page &P"
        .RightFooter = ""
        .LeftMargin = Application.InchesToPoints(0.75)
        .RightMargin = Application.InchesToPoints(0.75)
        .TopMargin = Application.InchesToPoints(1)
        .BottomMargin = Application.InchesToPoints(1)
        .HeaderMargin = Application.InchesToPoints(0.5)
        .FooterMargin = Application.InchesToPoints(0.5)
        .PrintHeadings = False
        .PrintGridlines = True
        .PrintNotes = False
```

Tip
As you become
more sophisti-
cated in your use
of Excel, you
may want to
learn the macro
language. One
way you can start
is by recording
simple macros,
then reviewing
the steps in the
macro sheet.

The steps of the macro language that Excel uses to execute the macro are
listed in the macro sheet columns and you can edit these steps to correct
errors or make changes to the macro.

Macros can be assigned to objects to create interactive worksheets and presentations. You also can assign macros to buttons in a custom toolbar for easy
access.

Using Drawing

Drawing can add to your worksheets, improving their appearance and em-
phasizing information. Excel offers several Drawing tools that enable you to
add, style, and edit graphical objects to your worksheets. You access the
Drawing tools by clicking the Drawing button. Doing so displays the Drawing
toolbar (see fig. 18.35).

Fig. 18.35
The Drawing
toolbar.

Excel's Drawing tools are object oriented. That is, you create objects: rectangles, ovals, lines, arrows, and the like. Tools and commands are provided that enable you to group objects, arrange their stacking order, and change their properties. You can add shading, patterns, and color to many of the objects.

While Excel is not a full-featured graphics program, you can use the Drawing tools to enhance your worksheets quickly and easily (see fig. 18.36).

Tip
To quickly access the Properties dialog box for any object, double-click that object in the worksheet.

IV

Macintosh Software

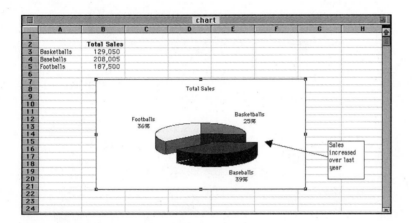

Fig. 18.36
A simple worksheet improved in appearance with the Drawing tools.

Customizing Excel

The main method of customizing Excel is to alter existing toolbars or create new ones. Because you can even create macros to assign to toolbar buttons, you can customize almost any feature in Excel to suit your needs.

The basics of customizing a toolbar are quite simple. From the View menu, you choose the Toolbars command. A dialog box listing the toolbars is displayed. You first display the toolbar you want to customize, and click the Customize button. You see the Customize dialog box with various buttons (see fig. 18.37).

Simply drag buttons on or off the toolbar to add or remove a function in the toolbar. You can even customize the Standard and Formatting toolbars, which are the initial toolbars displayed.

In the Toolbars dialog box, you also can create a new toolbar by typing the toolbar name, rather than by choosing a toolbar to edit and clicking the New button.

Tip
To obtain a small separation between toolbar buttons, drag a button on the toolbar just slightly to the right or left. Excel places a space between the button and its neighbor.

Fig. 18.37
Customizing
toolbars in Excel.

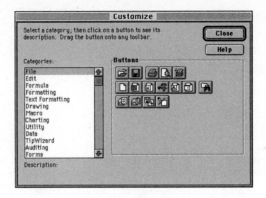

Note that some toolbars other than the Standard and Formatting toolbars are displayed as floating palettes (see fig. 18.38).

Fig. 18.38
A toolbar as a
floating palette.

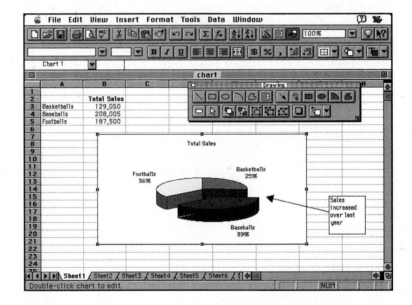

Tip
You can switch a toolbar to or from a floating palette by double-clicking the toolbar (but not the buttons on the toolbar). Even the Standard toolbar can be changed to and from a floating palette by double-clicking it.

Toolbars that are floating palettes remain in front of your worksheet. You can drag these toolbars around and resize them. Note that if you drag the toolbar above the title bar of the worksheet, the toolbar will move up to below the menu bar, along with the Standard and Formatting toolbars.

IV

Getting the Most Out of Excel: Hot Tips

- *Make use of the toolbars.* Even though Excel can be a complex and difficult program to run, toolbars are easily customized and can give you one-click access to Excel commands and features.

- *Make macros of the tasks you repeat often and spend some time learning the basics of the macro language.* You do not have to know the entire macro language to do some creative editing of macros that will enhance their usefulness.

- *Do formatting as the last step in creating worksheets.* Formatting often has to be redone after you edit data and cells, adding extra work. Also, if you are planning on charting your data, keep the arrangement and formatting simple and use the ChartWizard—ChartWizard can save a number of steps, but it is often confused by heavy formatting. You can add formatting after the chart has been created to enhance the table's appearance.

- *Resist the temptation to use tons of colors, patterns, borders, fonts, and other formatting.* Impressive looking tables and presentations can be created with a few judiciously applied formatting choices. Check out the AutoFormat command in the Format menu; often the formatting done by this command is sufficient.

- *Use the fill handle.* Not only can the fill handle create a number of useful and frequently used series, it also can duplicate formulas, thereby saving you a considerable amount of time.

- *Display a shortcut menu of commands, by pointing to the item you want to work with.* For example, to display a shortcut menu of toolbar commands, point to the toolbar. Hold down the Ctrl key and click and hold down the mouse button. You see a shortcut menu.

  Excel includes many keyboard shortcuts. If you like to use keyboard shortcuts, you can use on-line help to display a list of keyboard shortcuts. Select Reference Information from the Help Contents window and click Keyboard Guide. Select the topic for which you want to see shortcuts.

- *Store similar worksheets together in a workbook.* You can add or delete worksheets as needed. To name a worksheet, double-click the worksheet tab and then type the worksheet name.

■ *Create range names to make formulas easier to understand and easier to create.* For example, you may have ranges named SALES and EXPENSES. You can create a formula that subtracts EXPENSES from SALES. You can create a range name by selecting the range and by typing the name in the Name box next to the formula bar.

■ *Run the Speller so that you are sure your worksheet does not contain any spelling errors.* You can do so by clicking the Spelling button in the Standard toolbar. Excel compares all the words in your worksheet to words in its dictionary and then flags any words it cannot match. You can choose to replace the word with a suggested spelling, edit the word, or ignore the word.

■ *Use Excel's Find File command to help you manage files.* This file management feature shows you a preview of your worksheets. You can choose to delete, print, or copy worksheets using Find File.

Summary

Excel is an excellent choice in spreadsheet programs, especially if you are working with other Macintosh users and need to share spreadsheets with them. However, you will want to consider Excel's strengths before deciding on your spreadsheet purchase.

Lotus 1-2-3

The dominant spreadsheet program in the DOS word for a long time, Lotus 1-2-3 finally came to the Macintosh in 1992. While Lotus had faltered with the now defunct Jazz spreadsheet program, users were pleased when 1-2-3 came to the Macintosh. 1-2-3 for the Macintosh not only delivered the well respected power of 1-2-3, it also conformed well to the Macintosh user interface.

System Requirements

Lotus 1-2-3 comes on three 800KB disks and requires about 4.5MB to install. The Guided Tour, which comes with the program and introduces you to the spreadsheet, comes on two 800K disks and requires about 3MB of space to install.

1-2-3 requires 1.8MB of memory to run and will run on any Macintosh from the Mac Plus up. Note that with System 7, a 4MB minimum memory configuration is probably your best bet.

Using the Worksheet

Like other spreadsheet programs, 1-2-3 follows the convention of naming rows with numbers and columns with letters (see fig. 18.39).

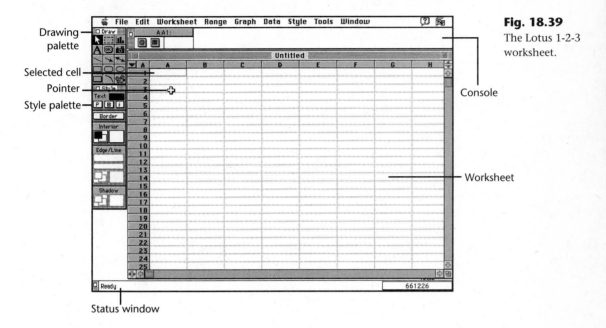

Drawing palette

Selected cell

Pointer

Style palette

Console

Worksheet

Status window

Fig. 18.39
The Lotus 1-2-3 worksheet.

As with Excel and other spreadsheet programs, the intersection of columns and rows are cells which are referred to by their addresses (column letter and row number).

Entering Data

1-2-3 follows the same basic procedure as other spreadsheets in that you enter data into a cell by clicking the cell to select it, then typing. The data appears both in the cell and in the Console (see fig. 18.40).

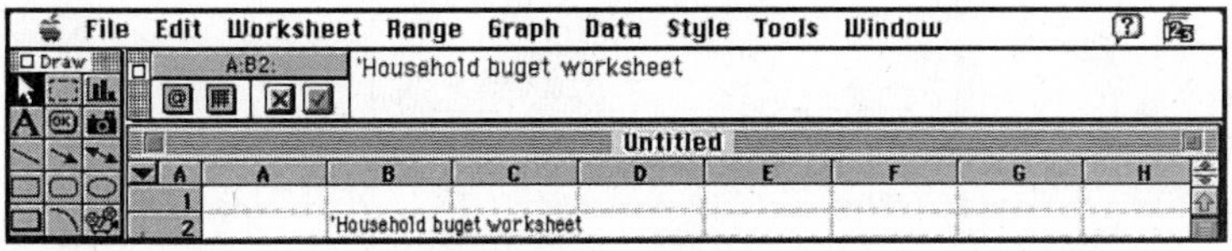

Fig. 18.40
Confirm and Cancel buttons appear.

Confirm and Cancel buttons appear in the Console, enabling you to click to enter or delete the data you type. You also can press Enter to enter the data and leave the same cell selected; Return to enter the data and move to the next cell down; or Tab to enter the data and move to the next cell right. Escape and ⌘-period (.) work for canceling your data entry.

Using Fills and Series

1-2-3 provides four copy commands that can be used for fills and one fill command used for creating series of data.

The Edit menu contains Copy, Right and Copy, Down which enable you to quickly duplicate a cell's contents. You can duplicate to the right in a row or down in a column simply by selecting the cells, starting with the cell containing the data (or formula) to be duplicated, and then by choosing the appropriate command.

1-2-3 offers an Edit Quick Copy dialog box that is a truly useful feature. Simply select the cell containing the data or formula to be duplicated, choose from the Edit menu the Quick Copy command, select any cell or any range of cells for the destination and press Return (see fig. 18.41).

Fig. 18.41
Quick Copy
duplicates the
selected data.

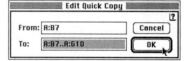

The Data menu's Fill command can be used to create linear series, date series, and time series (see fig. 18.42.).

Fig. 18.42
Creating a series
of months.

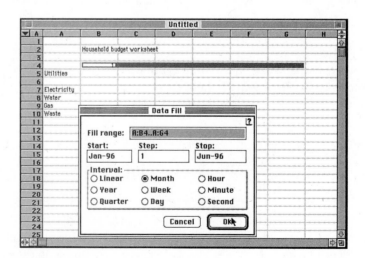

The 1-2-3 Fill command is not nearly as sophisticated as Excel's, and the lack of AutoFill or a similar feature is unfortunate. Still, basic series can be done quickly and easily. More sophisticated series also can be accomplished by creating macros.

Editing Data

1-2-3 has available the basic spreadsheet convention of editing data in a Console. Click to select the cell to be edited and the data or formula in the cell appears in the Console; you can use the standard Macintosh editing techniques.

One standout feature of 1-2-3 is in cell editing. You do not have to use the Console for editing cell contents (though in cases of long formulas or busy spreadsheets you may want to do so). Following the Macintosh interface, 1-2-3 enables you to double-click a cell to open the cell for editing so that you can make changes right in the cell using standard Macintosh editing procedures (see fig. 18.43).

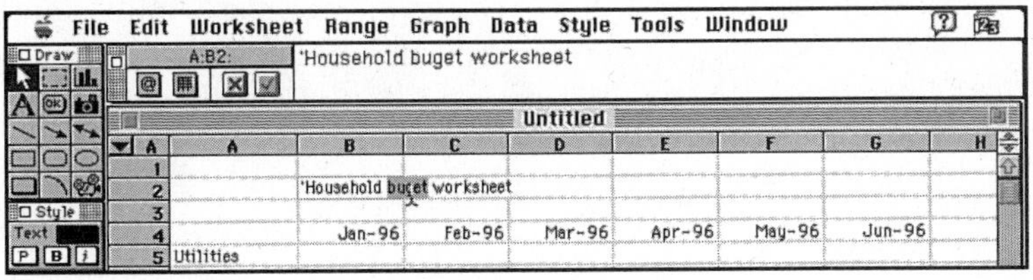

Fig. 18.43
Correcting text within cell editing.

Using Cut, Copy, Paste, and Clear

1-2-3 follows Macintosh conventions with the Edit menu's Cut, Copy, Paste, and Clear commands. Unlike with Excel, these commands behave exactly as you would expect based on your experience with other Macintosh programs.

Special move, copy, paste, and clear features are performed by choosing separate commands in the Edit menu. Paste Special and Clear Special have nested menus that enable you to choose whether to paste or clear the contents, formats, or styles of a cell.

Even though Quick Copy has been discussed, one more mention of the feature is justified. Lotus has designed the Quick Copy (and Move Cells) commands to be independent of the Clipboard. You can use the Quick Copy and Move Cells commands from the Edit menu without affecting the contents of the Clipboard.

Tip
Quick Copy and Move Cells are very handy when you need to copy or move cells across large worksheets. You can scroll the worksheet while the dialog boxes are on-screen or type a cell range directly into the dialog boxes.

Move Cells enables you to do a "cut and paste" operation quickly and without affecting the Clipboard's contents. Select the cells you wish to move, choose the Move Cells command from the Edit menu, click to indicate a destination, then press Return. The cells are moved.

Using Drag and Drop

I first saw the drag and drop feature in Microsoft Word, though I'm uncertain that this was the feature's first appearance. In any case, in my personal opinion, the creator(s) of the feature deserve a hats off for this logical extension of the Macintosh interface.

1-2-3 implements drag and drop with an interesting pointer effect. When you place the pointer at the edge of the selected cells to be moved, the pointer becomes a hand indicating that you can now "grab" the selection. Press the mouse button and the hand "clenches," indicating the selection has been "grabbed" and is ready to be moved to a new location in the worksheet.

This feedback is helpful in that drag and drop in other programs can be confusing at times when the program merely uses the standard pointer. A clear indication of the feature's functioning helps the user avoid errors in trying to move a selection. Give Lotus a gold star for making a great feature even easier to use.

Entering Formulas

1-2-3 begins formula entry with an addition sign (+). However, you also can use the equal sign (=) and the program will automatically convert. Like Excel, you can click a cell to enter the address of that cell into your formula. Unlike Excel, clicking another cell without entering an operator will *not* enter an addition sign, but rather will change the cell address to the last clicked.

This "lack of feature" is a feature in my mind in that I've run into too many cases in which I've clicked a cell, changed my mind, and clicked another only to find Excel thinking I mean to add everything together. 1-2-3 doesn't make the addition assumption, but rather waits for the user to choose the operator.

Entering Functions

1-2-3 begins functions with an at sign (@). To enter a Sum function, you type **@Sum** followed by the cell range to be summed. In the Console, 1-2-3 offers a pop-up Function menu that enables you to choose and paste the function into the cell, rather than having to type the function name.

The SmartSum command is much like the Excel Sum tool. You click to the right of a row or below a column. Then choose SmartSum from the Function menu. The sum formula is automatically entered and the cells are totalled.

Note

A truly great time-saver when you are building tables is that the SmartSum enables you to select a range of cells and enter sum formulas in the entire range. For example, if you have several columns of figures, you can create a totals line by selecting a row of cells below the columns and then by choosing SmartSum.

Editing the Worksheet

The worksheet itself can be edited: rows and columns can be adjusted in size, inserted and deleted, hidden or shown, and the basic worksheet colors can be changed.

1-2-3 combines the worksheet-related commands into a single Worksheet menu for convenient access. You can set global defaults for all your worksheets by choosing the Global Settings command from this menu and selecting options in the Worksheet Global Settings dialog box (see fig. 18.44).

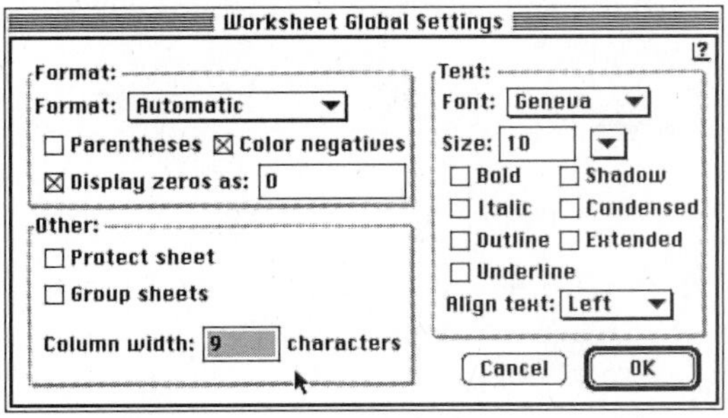

Fig. 18.44
Setting the defaults for all 1-2-3 worksheets.

Like Excel, 1-2-3 enables you to adjust column width or row height by dragging in the column or row labels.

For more precise adjustment, the Worksheet menu's Column Width and Row Height commands invoke dialog boxes that enable you to set the size of the selected columns or rows. The Hide/Show command enables you to hide or display selected columns or rows.

The Worksheet menu's Insert and Delete commands enable you to insert or delete columns, rows, selections, numbered amounts of cells, or whole worksheets (for three-dimensional spreadsheets).

You select one or more cells in the area to be inserted or deleted, then choose the appropriate command. A dialog box appears enabling you to indicate how you want the insertion or deletion to be handled (see fig. 18.45).

Tip
To automatically set a column or row to the best fit for the contents of the cells, double-click the divider between column or row labels.

Fig. 18.45
Inserting new
columns in the
worksheet.

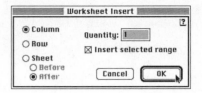

Tip
To quickly
insert or delete
a row or col-
umn, first click
in the row
number label
or the column
letter label and
then choose
the appropriate
command.

You also can adjust the colors used in the worksheet for displaying gridlines, negative numbers, the background, and other aspects of the worksheet itself by using the Adjust Colors command. Because staring at a monitor screen all day can be tiring, this is a nice feature to have. Being able to set the worksheet color combination to something you find easier on the eye is a welcome feature.

Understanding the Status Window

The 1-2-3 Status window is not as informative as the Excel version, but it does inform you what the program is doing at the moment:

Ready appears in the Status window to indicate that 1-2-3 is ready to accept a command.

Calc appears when 1-2-3 is doing a calculation.

Label appears when you are entering a text label.

Value appears when you are entering data or formulas.

A pop-up menu in the Status window enables you to also display the date, time, or available memory in the window (see fig. 18.46).

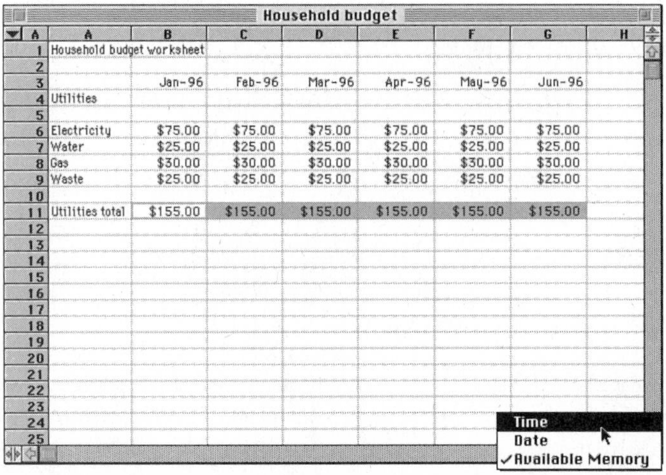

Fig. 18.46
Choosing to
display the current
time in the Status
window.

	A	B	C	D	E	F	G	H
1	Household budget worksheet							
2								
3		Jan-96	Feb-96	Mar-96	Apr-96	May-96	Jun-96	
4	Utilities							
5								
6	Electricity	$75.00	$75.00	$75.00	$75.00	$75.00	$75.00	
7	Water	$25.00	$25.00	$25.00	$25.00	$25.00	$25.00	
8	Gas	$30.00	$30.00	$30.00	$30.00	$30.00	$30.00	
9	Waste	$25.00	$25.00	$25.00	$25.00	$25.00	$25.00	
10								
11	Utilities total	$155.00	$155.00	$155.00	$155.00	$155.00	$155.00	
12								

Household budget

Time
Date
✓ Available Memory

Using Formatting

There are many 1-2-3 formatting features. You can format numerical values, align text, add colors, draw borders around cells, and perform a great many other enhancement operations on your worksheets.

Using and Defining Number Formatting

To apply a format to cell contents, you select the cells to be formatted. Then, from the Range menu, choose the Format command. The Range Format dialog box appears, enabling you to select the format to be used and set options for that format (see fig. 18.47).

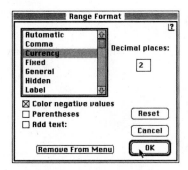

Fig. 18.47
Formatting cell contents.

1-2-3's formatting can be customized to some extent. You may set the number of decimal places, whether negative values are colored, and whether to add a text prefix or suffix.

Applying Text Formatting

The standard Macintosh text formating—fonts, font sizes, and font styles— are accessed through the Style menu's Font command. The command invokes the Style Font dialog box through which you make your selections (see fig. 18.48).

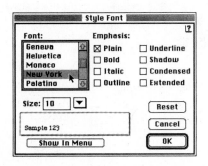

Tip

You can add commonly used formats to the Range menu by clicking the Show in Menu button. This enables you to choose the formats directly from the Range menu.

Fig. 18.48
Choosing to use the New York font.

Tip
Add commonly
used font formats
to the Style
menu by clicking
the Show in
Menu button.

Quick access to the Plain, Bold, and Italics font styles is provided by buttons on the Style palette at the left of the screen. Select the cells whose contents you wish to format, then click the button.

Colors can be applied to the contents of cells through the Style palette. Select the cells, then choose a color from the Text color pop-up menu (see fig. 18.49).

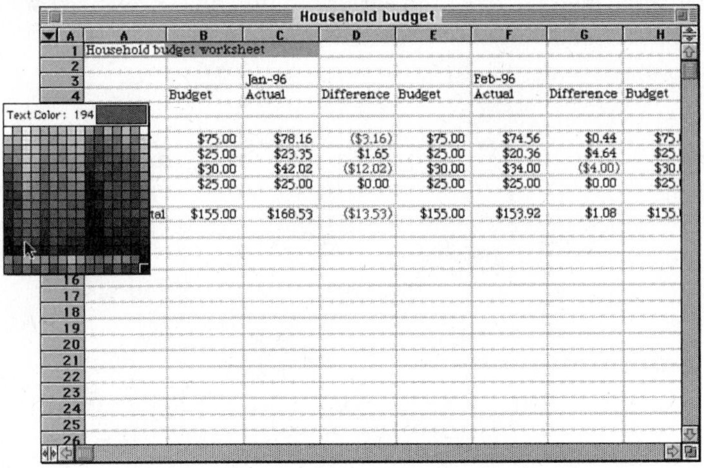

Fig. 18.49
Colorizing the
contents of a
selection of cells.

Note that the color pop-up menus will be different depending on the color capabilities and settings of your monitor. In the area of color, 1-2-3 gives much easier and more direct access to color than Excel using pop-up menus with up to 256 colors. Note that these pop-ups will look different if you have less than a 256-color capability.

> **Note**
>
> Avoid getting too adventurous with text coloring; few colors are actually that useful for text and some even make the text harder to read. Take background color into account also; for example, a blue background with red text causes a disturbing "jitter" effect when viewed.

Alignment of cell contents is available through the Style menu's Alignment nested menu. You have four choices: left, center, right, and general. General is the default alignment which right-aligns numbers and left-aligns text.

IV

Applying Cell Formatting

You can add borders and colors to cells. 1-2-3 offers seven border options (eight if you count None) and up to 256 colors each for the foreground and background colors.

You can quickly access borders through the Border pop-up menu in the Style palette. You also can use the Style menu's Border command (see fig. 18.50).

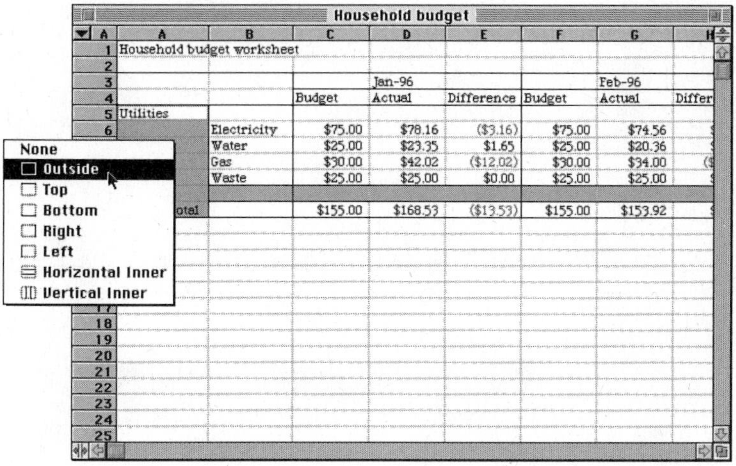

Fig. 18.50
Adding a border to selected cells.

Interestingly enough, apparently the only way to add color is through the color pop-up menu in the palette; there is no menu command equivalent.

Graphing Data

1-2-3 truly shines in the graph department. If you work with graphs a great deal, the ease of use of 1-2-3's Graphing feature makes the program a top choice.

Against Excel's rather clunky way of doing graphs (or in Excel terms, charts), 1-2-3's graphing feature feels like magic. Simply select the data, then choose the graph type you want (see fig. 18.51).

The graph appears almost instantly, ready for titling, and needing very little editing (see fig. 18.52).

Editing a 1-2-3 graph is a snap. You can drag the graph where you want it to be in the worksheet, resize it by dragging (just as you would expect to resize an object in a Macintosh program), and edit *any* element in the graph by double-clicking the element (see fig. 18.53).

Tip

While the pop-up Border menu is useful for quickly adding a border to cells, editing the borders is easier with the Style menu's Border command.

Fig. 18.51
Graphing data is
easy as 1-2-3.

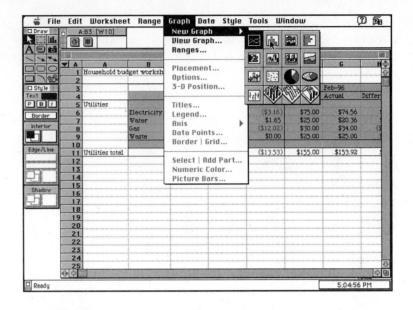

Fig. 18.52
A column graph of
budget figures.

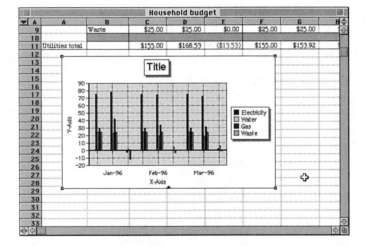

Fig. 18.53
Double-clicking
the graph's grid
opens the Graph
Border/Grid dialog
box.

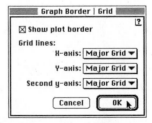

As you would expect in a Macintosh program, you can do such things as make font, font size, and font style changes to text in a graph by clicking the text to select it, and then by making font choices from the menus. Colors of the graph's bars, lines, boxes, and the like are easily changed by clicking the element to select it, and then by using the Style palette.

Changing ranges is about the only thing in 1-2-3 that gets to be annoying. This has to do with a rather strange side effect of 1-2-3's attempts to be as user friendly as possible and to redraw as you work. Often, when you are working with the Graph Ranges dialog box invoked through the Graph menu's Ranges command, the worksheet and dialog box are flipping madly about and selections are popping up and changing around crazily. It's enough to make you dizzy when all you wanted to do was change a cell range for a bar graph. But, if things get too confusing, sit back and wait. 1-2-3 will calm down presently.

Tip

A very nice effect is achieved by clicking the graph, and then by choosing to add a thin shadow frame (by choosing from the Style palette's Frame pop-up menu). Also, using a light shade of gray for the graph's enclosing box sets the graph off well.

> **Note**
>
> You can "tear off" the nested New Graph menu to make a Graph palette. Changing graphs from one type to another then is only a matter of clicking to select the existing graph, and then clicking the new type in the Graph palette. You also can display the Graph palette by choosing the Show Graph command from the Hide/Show submenu. (The Hide/Show submenu is located in the Window menu.)

All graph-related commands are also grouped in the Graph menu.

Using the Drawing Layer

1-2-3 has an invisible "layer" above the worksheet that you can draw on to enhance your worksheet's appearance. You can draw arrows, rectangles, rounded rectangles, ovals, arcs, and shadowed boxes on your worksheet. Pictures from the Clipboard, copied from graphics programs (or elsewhere) can be pasted in, as can QuickTime movies. Text boxes can be placed to add explanatory text (see fig. 18.54). The Draw palette contains the various tools you need to draw on your worksheet.

You also can choose whether to include drawn objects when you print your document. The File menu's Print Options command enables you to select which items will be printed.

Fig. 18.54
Arrows and text
boxes can be
added to a
worksheet.

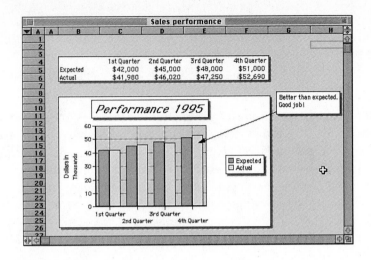

Using Databases

1-2-3 enables you to create and manage databases in ways similar to Excel,
but 1-2-3 also can connect to and work with external databases created in
such programs as FoxBase.

Creating a basic database in a worksheet is simple. You enter the data in
columns, select the cells containing the information (column headings
included), then choose the New Form command from Data menu.
Immediately, you are able to browse, enter, and edit records in your database
(see fig. 18.55).

Fig. 18.55
Using a form to
browse a database.

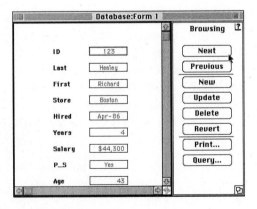

You can access your database from other parts of your worksheet by using the
Database functions in the pop-up Function menu's Database submenu.

IV

1-2-3 enables you to connect your worksheet to external databases with the Data menu's Connect to External command (see fig. 18.56).

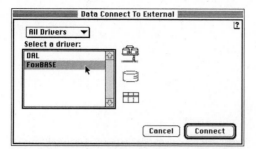

Fig. 18.56
Connecting to a
FoxBase database.

This ability to connect to external databases should appeal greatly to business users who have large employee databases or other information databases, especially those on network systems. 1-2-3 can connect worksheets to remote databases, send commands to them, periodically update the worksheet (refreshing the data), and even do the translation from IBM to Macintosh character sets.

Once connected to the external database, 1-2-3 treats the database as if it were part of the worksheet. All the commands used for working with a worksheet database apply to working with the external database.

Analyzing Data

Excel has, by far, a great deal more analysis tools available. But, 1-2-3 is not without features in this area. Unless you need the heavy-duty statistical analysis features of Excel, 1-2-3 may be sufficient for your needs.

The Data menu contains the Distribution and Regression commands. Both commands invoke dialog boxes that enable you to select cell ranges for the input and output data (see fig. 18.57).

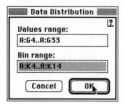

Fig. 18.57
Preparing to do
a distribution
analysis.

Using the statics functions in the Function menu of the Console, you can also obtain averages, sums, sumproducts, variances, maximums, minimums, counts, and standard deviations.

Using Macros

1-2-3 uses a unique approach to macros. The program continuously records your actions in the Macro Transcript dialog box which you can access through the Tools menu's Macro submenu. The Show Transcript command displays the listing of the commands that correspond to the actions you have taken (see fig. 18.58).

Fig. 18.58

Viewing the Macro Transcript.

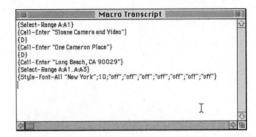

You use the standard Macintosh cut and paste techniques to incorporate command lines into your macro; then paste the Macro into a worksheet you intend to use for storing your macros.

You then select the cells containing the macro. Open the Range menu's Name submenu and choose the Create command. Name the cell range with the name you wish to use for the macro.

The macro can be added to your Tools menu or invoked through the Macro submenu's Run Macro command.

Working with 3-D Spreadsheets

You can have more than one worksheet within the worksheet window. This enables you to have three-dimensional spreadsheets. You can visualize this by imagining the worksheets as being "stacked" on top of one another (see fig. 18.59).

The view shown in figure 18.59 is a perspective split view, which is available by using the Split command in the Window menu. While good for viewing three-dimensional worksheets, this view is not easy to work with. Normally, the three-dimensional worksheet looks pretty much like any other. You can access the other layers of the worksheet by using the pop-up menu (click the triangle) in the upper-left-hand corner of the window (see fig. 18.60).

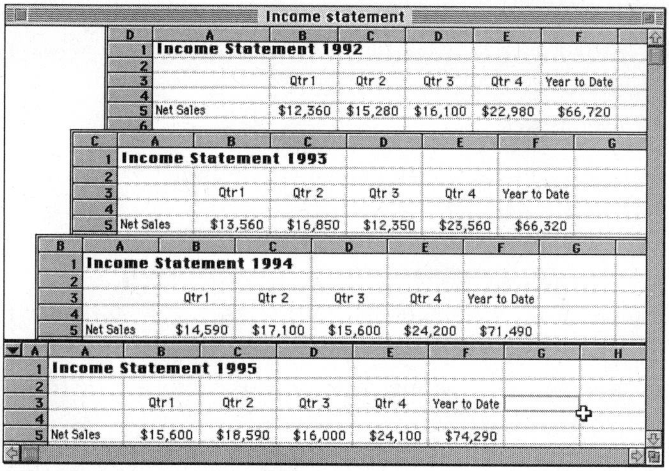

Fig. 18.59
Four worksheets
in the same
worksheet
window.

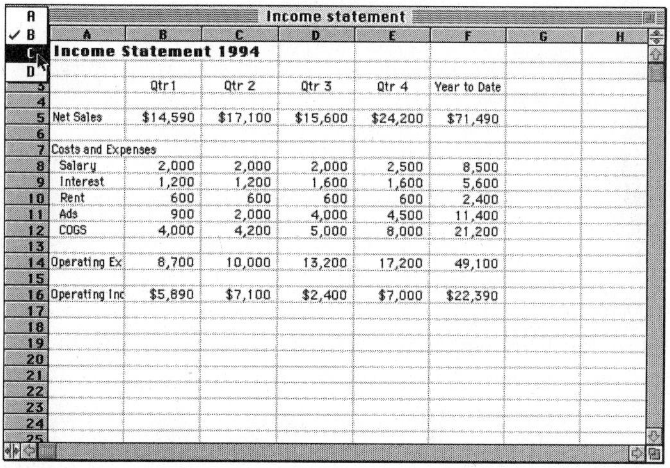

Fig. 18.60
Accessing
worksheet C.

Three-dimensional spreadsheets are created by using the Worksheet menu's Insert command. You have the option of inserting a number of other sheets either before or after the current one.

The true power of three-dimensional spreadsheets is that your formulas can refer to other sheets. By preceding a cell reference with the sheet letter, you reference the cell within that sheet. In the figure, for example, cell F5 on all the sheets contain the Year to Date sales. To total the year's sales for all the years, you would enter a formula such as:

+@SUM(A:F5, B:F5, C:F5, D:F5)

Three-dimensional spreadsheets are part of the reason 1-2-3 has been a long-standing favorite in the DOS world. And the ability to create complex, three-dimensional spreadsheets is an attractive feature for the Macintosh spreadsheet user as well.

Excel provides for a linkage between worksheets, but 1-2-3 is much easier to use in this respect.

Getting the Most Out of 1-2-3: Hot Tips

- DOS users of 1-2-3 who are new to the Macintosh world will be happy to find that they may press the slash key (/) and 1-2-3 Macintosh will perform in a similar manner as DOS. This can help ease the transition between platforms.

- Remember that 1-2-3 keeps a running transcript of your actions and you can turn almost anything you have done into a macro by copying the macro commands in the transcript.

- Viewing the macro transcript also can aid you in learning the 1-2-3 macro command language.

- If you work with 1-2-3 DOS users, keep your formatting fairly simple. Though 1-2-3 Macintosh can translate between the two versions, some formatting can be lost.

Summary

Lotus 1-2-3 remains my personal favorite in the spreadsheet category because of the program's ease of use. Unfortunately, due to the length of time Lotus took to bring the program to the Macintosh world, Excel remains the dominant and most popular spreadsheet among Macintosh users. Therefore, the 1-2-3 user is at somewhat of a disadvantage when it comes to compatibility within the Macintosh world. At the same time, 1-2-3 is so widespread in the DOS world that Macintosh users who deal with DOS 1-2-3 users will likely prefer the program due to the compatibility with DOS 1-2-3.

Conclusions and Recommendations

The past couple of years, the Macintosh spreadsheet world has been something of a "battle of the titans." Other spreadsheet programs have come and gone. A few have hung on, but there is no question that Excel and 1-2-3 are currently the dominant spreadsheet programs.

Both are excellent choices for business and personal use in terms of features and performance. However, as Lotus recently announced, it will not continue to revise 1-2-3 for the Mac; Excel has become the only option.

From Here...

Consider these chapters for more information:

- Chapter 17, "Presentation Graphics." Spreadsheets and graphics often go hand-in-hand in business. This chapter can show you available software for creating business presentations.

- Chapter 19, "Databases." 1-2-3 interfaces with database software enabling you to access large amounts of information. The programs that create and maintain these large pools of data are discussed in this chapter.

- Chapter 26, "Personal and Business Management." While a spreadsheet program can be used to manage finances, schedules, and contact lists, you may need software specifically geared in these directions.

Chapter 19

Databases

by Dave Plotkin

If you stop to think about it, the most valuable thing you have on your computer is your data. Whole industries are built on the gathering, exchange, and manipulation of data. In order to manage your data properly, you need a database. A *database* is an organized collection of related information. Two of the primary ways of storing database information are on paper or in a computer. An example of a database stored on paper is an address book. Of course, an address-book type of database can also be kept in a computer.

This chapter introduces you to the two most popular databases used on the Mac:

- Claris Filemaker Pro
- Microsoft FoxPro Mac

What is a Database?

The information in a computerized database is usually stored in the form of tables, with rows and columns in each table. Figure 19.1 illustrates the rows and columns in an address-book type database. Each row in table 1 contains a set of columns: Name, Address, City, State, Zip Code, and Phone Number. Rows in such a table are called *records*. The columns represent categories of related information that are present in each record (row). Each of these categories is called a *field*.

The information that pertains to one person is one record. The address-book database thus contains many records—one for each person you've noted.

Each record contains many fields, such as the person's name, address, phone number, and so on.

In addition to the address book mentioned in the preceding section, you can create all kinds of useful databases at home or in your business. These databases can include a list of your record collection, household inventory, a list of customers, invoices, orders, and inventory. Thousands of computer applications have been built that track and manipulate lists of information.

Computerized databases provide far more functionality than just storing information in tables, however. They can be used to design fancy forms for inputting and validating data, sophisticated reports for printing out the data, and queries that return only the data that matches specified criteria. Some databases have their own programming language so that a developer can create a complete application.

Two general kinds of databases exist: Flat-file and relational databases. *Flat-file databases* are simple lists. Your address book is a good example of a flat-file database. *Relational databases* are much more powerful. They are used to link information stored in more than one table or file. For example, you can have one table that contains a list of your customers and another table that contains a list of orders that those customers have placed. By linking these tables, you can include the customer names and addresses on a form that also shows the order information.

While it is certainly possible to keep databases on paper, large databases quickly become unwieldy when you try to maintain them on paper—and you can never find the data you are looking for.

Keeping your database on a computer has some significant advantages over the manual method:

- You can store a huge amount of information in a relatively small amount of space.

- You can instruct the computer search for that information quickly and efficiently.

- You can instruct the computer to print reports, mailing labels, and form letters from the results of such a search.

- You can create forms for data input.

- You can reorganize the database based on a different piece of information (field).

A computer-based database frees you from having to keep all your records on paper and lets you do more creative things with your time.

What is Out There

The Macintosh database market is largely ruled by two products: Claris' Filemaker Pro and Microsoft's FoxPro Mac. These are very different products, appealing to a very different set of audiences. Filemaker Pro is a simple, flat-file database that is easy to learn and use but lacks certain features. FoxPro Mac is a monolith with a programming language and a fairly steep learning curve. As such, it will probably appeal more to programmers and developers than to end users, but those that need the power of FoxPro Mac should check it out.

Filemaker Pro

Filemaker Pro is a simple database that gives up true relational capabilities for simplicity. However, Filemaker Pro does manage to provide the most-often used traits of relational databases successfully, making it an excellent choice for many database users. Filemaker Pro is available for Windows as well, making it also a good choice for developers who need an application that runs on multiple types of computers.

System Requirements

As database applications go, Filemaker Pro is not very large. It is packaged on four disks and takes up only about 4 MB of disk space for a complete installation. You only need 1.2 MB to install the application itself, without any examples or the help files. Your Macintosh must also be at least a Mac Plus with System 6.0 and 1 megabyte of memory (2 MB with System 7).

Setting Up a Database

The first step in setting up a database in Filemaker Pro is to select New from the File menu and name the database. Next you define the fields using the Define Fields dialog box. You define each field by typing the name into the Name text box, and selecting a field type from the Type radio buttons. Types of fields include text, number, date, time, picture or sound, calculation, and summary fields. As you add fields, they appear in the Define field dialog box (see fig. 19.1). You can sort the fields by order of creation, field name, field type, or in a custom order. If you choose to view the fields in a custom order, you can click and drag on the small arrow to the left of each field to rearrange the fields. You can also click an existing field and change any of its specifications.

Fig. 19.1
The Define Fields dialog box is where you define the fields for a database.

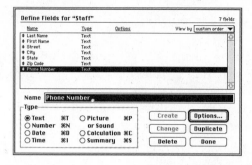

Tip
You can create a new field that is similar to an existing field by changing the specifications of an existing field and clicking the Create button.

Filemaker Pro enables you to enter auto-entry and validation options for each field in the Entry options dialog box (see fig. 19.2). Auto entry options include Creation date or time, Modification Date or time, or the creator or modifier name. You can enter a serial number and specify the starting number and increment for the data. You can also enter a data constant. Validations include checking that the field is not empty, ensuring that the value entered is unique across the database, ensuring that the value already exists in this field in the database, making sure that the data entered is of a certain data type, or that the entered data falls in a range between two values. You can combine some of these options. For example, you can specify that a value is unique and falls within a range.

Filemaker Pro has some other powerful field-specification tools available from the Entry Options dialog box. If a field contains frequently-used values, you can define those values as a list to be displayed as a pop-up menu, pop-up list, check boxes, or radio buttons. You can also look up information in another Filemaker Pro file and copy it into the current field as you add or edit records. To look up a field in another file, you must tell Filemaker Pro what field in your current file must match the contents of a specified field in another file. When Filemaker Pro finds a match, it copies the contents of the lookup field you specify in the other file into the current field. You can even specify what happens if Filemaker doesn't find an exact match: you can copy the next higher or lower value, leave the field blank, or use a constant value that you specify. Lookups are very powerful, but they do have some limits. If you change the value in the *trigger field* (the field used to match a value in the other database), Filemaker Pro will look for a new match. Filemaker Pro does not automatically look for a new match if you change the value in the lookup field of the other database, however.

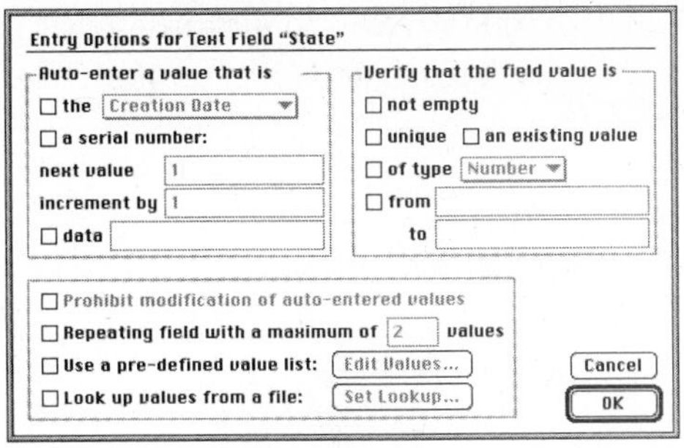

Fig. 19.2
The Entry Options
dialog box.

IV

Macintosh Software

Filemaker Pro incorporates a very powerful type of field called a *repeating field*. A repeating field enables you to attach multiple occurrences of fields to a single record. If you have a database that contains invoices, for example, you can create repeating fields that represent the line items on the invoices. These fields might be the item number, description, and the unit price. To set up a repeating field, you need to specify the field as repeating in the Entry Options dialog box and determine the number of repeats allowed. Although Filemaker Pro enables you to use up to 1000 repeats, you must leave room on your form for all the repeats—you can't display a smaller number and scroll through the repeating fields. This is an unfortunate limitation.

Tip
Use Edit Relookup to resynchronize the lookups if you suspect that the value in the lookup field has been changed in the other database.

Fields can be calculated or summary fields. If you select a calculated field, Filemaker Pro opens a dialog box for defining the calculation formula. You can type the formula into a text box, or select field names, arithmetic operators, and functions from scrolling lists to build the formula interactively. The operators include common functions such as plus, minus, multiplication, and so on. They also include Boolean operators such as AND and OR. You can choose from about 80 functions, including statistical, trigonometric, logarithmic, and *data type conversion* (convert data to text).

Summary fields enable you to perform operations across the records in your database. For example, you can determine the total, average, or count of a field in your records. You can also create a *running field* (a running total or a running count) that performs the select operation on all records from the first record through the currently viewed record.

Building a Layout

When you are done defining the fields in a database, Filemaker Pro builds a default layout for data entry (see fig. 19.3). Unlike many other database products, Filemaker Pro makes no distinction between forms and reports. This can be handy—you can enter data right on multiple-record report layout. There are various styles of layouts, including single record (form), columnar (tabular), multiple-record (report), mailing label, and an envelope template.

The mailing label layout enables you to pick from Avery label numbers or specify the margins, labels across, and label dimensions for custom labels. You may pick a new layout style at any time by selecting New Layout from the Edit menu.

Fig. 19.3
Filemaker Pro creates a default form when you define a database.

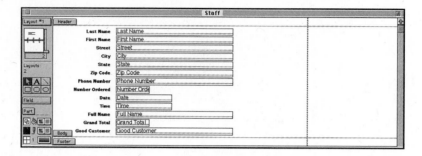

You can use the default layout that Filemaker Pro provides or create a new layout. You can rename the layout at any time. If the data you are displaying is narrow (doesn't take up the full width of the layout), you can specify multiple columns on the layout.

Defining the Parts of a Layout

Each layout is a collection of bands, or *parts*. These part include headers, footers, the body section, and summary parts. Summary-type parts include leading and trailing grand summaries, as well as summaries within the layout. To use a summary within a layout, you must specify a field to summarize on. Filemaker Pro sorts the records on the selected field. You can add summaries within summaries.

To add a part to a layout, click and drag the Part tool onto the layout. Filemaker Pro opens the Part Definition dialog box (see fig. 19.4). In addition to picking the type of summary and the field(s) to summarize on, you can choose when to provide page breaks and whether to allow summarized sections to go across page breaks.

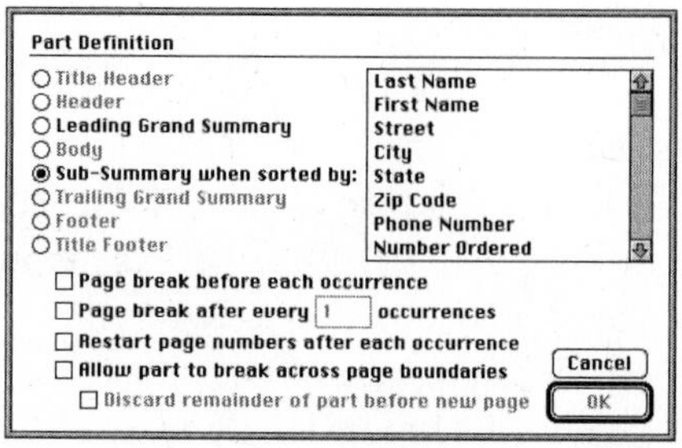

Fig. 19.4
The Part Definition dialog box.

Working with Fields in a Layout

You can add fields to a layout by clicking the Field tool and dragging it onto the layout. If you drag a field onto the form, Filemaker Pro pops up a New Field dialog box so that you can choose the field you want. You can have Filemaker Pro also create the field label at the same time, or create it yourself by using the Text tool.

All the fields in the database are displayed as text boxes by default, but you can customize the way fields are displayed and the data format of the fields.

For example, you can customize the database in the following ways:

- Increase the number of displayed lines in a text field. Text fields can hold up to 64,000 characters, so you may want to display more than the default single line. To increase the size of field, click the field to show the sizing handles, and then click and drag the handles to adjust the field size.

- Display a field with a valid list as a pop-up menu or pop-up list. A pop-up list displays the field's values in a window that appears when you click the field. A pop-up menu displays the valid values in a drop-down list with a scroll bar when you click the field. Either of these two options works well when there are a fairly large number of valid values (more than about five values). You can add an "other" option to a pop-up list. If you click the "other" option in browse mode, you can type the alternate value into the dialog box that appears.

- For a small number of valid values, you may want to display the values as check boxes or radio buttons. If you display check boxes, Filemaker Pro creates a check box for each valid value in the list. When you are entering data, you can click any check box to select the value. One difficulty with check boxes is that you can click multiple check boxes on the form, but only a single value is stored in the database. If you display radio buttons, Filemaker Pro creates a radio button for each valid value in the list. If you click a radio button, Filemaker Pro deselects any other radio button. You can add an "other" option to either radio buttons or check boxes as well.

- For repeating fields, you can choose how many repeating occurrences you want to display on this form. You can include any number of repeats up to the maximum number defined when you created the database. However, any occurrences you don't display can't be entered on the form.

Tip

If you plan to use multiple repeating fields to simulate a one-to-many relationship, align the fields next to each other to form a table of repeating values.

Formatting the Objects on a Layout

Filemaker Pro has a powerful set of formatting tools to customize a layout. You can add text blocks, lines, rectangles, rounded rectangles, and ovals to a form from a drawing toolbar (see fig. 19.5). To add a graphic shape, click the shape you want, and then click and drag on the layout to define the position and size of the object. You can choose the fill color and pattern, line color and pattern, and the line thickness of the graphic object from a set of dialog boxes that appears when you click the formatting buttons. You can add a page number, time, or date to a text block.

Fig 19.5

The Filemaker Pro toolbar.

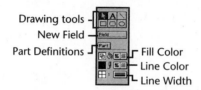

You can independently format the text that will appear in a field and the text format of the field's label. You can choose the font, size, style and effect, alignment (left, center, or right), and text color. Styles include shadow, hollow, bold, underline, italic, and several styles of underline. You can combine the styles to get some striking effects. You can also format the line thickness, style, and color of the field borders.

Filemaker Pro provides a large number of formatting gadgets to help you lay out your form. You can display rulers, use a snap-to grid with adjustable dimensions, align objects horizontally or vertically to each other, group multiple objects together so that you can work with them as a single object, and set the exact location and size for an object using the Dimensions dialog box. Another handy tool is the *t-square*. Looking much like the drafting tool of the same name, the t-square shows a set of crossing lines, making it very easy to align objects to a certain point on-screen. You can also use Filemaker Pro's Slide tool to close up "holes" left by unused fields (unused second address lines, for example) or by fields whose contents don't entirely fill the space available on the layout. Finally, you can adjust the order in which the cursor moves between fields when you press the Tab key (see fig. 19.6). Adjusting the order is sometimes necessary when you rearrange the fields on the layout. Filemaker originally orders the fields from left to right within a row, and from top to bottom. If you rearrange the fields, however, you can find the field focus jumping around on the screen. By rearranging the tab order, you can have the field focus move in a more orderly manner.

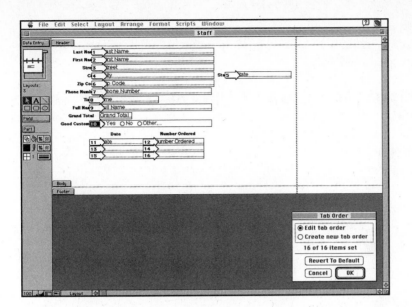

Fig. 19.6
Adjusting the tab
order of the fields
on a form.

IV

Macintosh Software

Formatting Field Display Values

Filemaker Pro offers many options for formatting field values. For example,
you can format a time field value as 12 or 24 hour, specify the exactness of
the time displayed, and choose the separator character. Field displays don't
change how the data is stored in the database. When you edit a field, it
shows you the exact data you are entering. However, when you move the
focus away from the field, Filemaker Pro redisplays the field in the specified
format. When you set the field format, you can set the format of the text for
the field. You can also set the text format from the Format menu.

You can set the format for numeric fields. You can choose the number of
decimal places, use percentage or currency, and use a thousands separator (for
example, a comma). For decimal numbers, you can specify the currency symbol, the thousands separator symbol, and the decimal point symbol. You can
format negative numbers with a negative sign, parenthesis, or a "CR" symbol.
You can also print negative numbers in a different color.

You can format a number as a Boolean value. If you format the number as a
Boolean value, you can specify zeroes as one value (either Yes or No) and
non-zeroes as the other value.

Date field formatting is very versatile. You can format the date in a variety of
different orders, and with different abbreviations for the month, day, and
year. If none of the predefined formats suit you, you can define date format
completely from scratch, defining the day, month, date, and year formats

Tip
To keep the
field and its label
together as you
rearrange items on
the layout, group
them together.

independently. You can choose to show the month and day number with a leading zero if the number is only a single digit. You can also choose the separator character.

Navigating Through Your Layouts and Records

Moving through your layouts and records is straightforward, if somewhat different from other Mac applications. To switch layouts, you can click the layout selector in the upper left corner of the screen (see fig. 19.7). Filemaker Pro presents you with a list of layouts to pick from (see fig. 19.8).

Fig. 19.7
The Layout selector allows you to switch layouts.

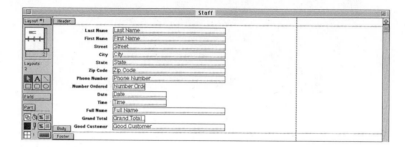

Fig. 19.8
The rolodex makes it easy to move through records and layouts.

The rolodex symbol just below the layout selector enables you to switch between records. To move through your records one at a time, just click the top (to move forward) or bottom (to move back) rolodex page. You can use the small tab sticking out to the right of the rolodex symbol to move through records as well. To move through the records, click and drag the tab to the record you want. Filemaker Pro displays the number of the currently selected record below the rolodex. You can click this number and type the number of the record you want.

Finding and Sorting Your Data

You can sort the records in your database using the Sort records dialog box (see fig. 19.9). You can select the fields to sort on from the Field List on the left side of the dialog box, and move the fields into the Sort Order list on the right side. You can sort on multiple fields at a time. For example, you can sort on last name, and for people with the same last name, sort on first name. You can reorder the fields in the Sort Order dialog box by clicking and dragging the small arrow at the left side of the field. You can sort any field in ascending or descending order. If you choose to sort on a field with a value list, you can even sort the records in the same order as the values in the value list.

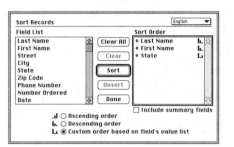

Fig. 19.9
The Sort Records dialog box.

Filemaker Pro makes it simple to locate records that meet search criteria. In Find mode, you simply type the information you are looking for into the fields on a layout. When you type a find criteria into a field, Filemaker Pro finds all the records where the fields start with the text string you typed. You can also specify an exact match, where the field contents must exactly match what you typed. You can use special symbols to search for records where the field contents are greater than, less than, or between the values you typed. For example, you can type A...M into the Last Name field and Filemaker Pro retrieves all the records with last names that start with the letters A through M.

You can use wild cards to substitute for either a single letter or a string of letters. If you type find criteria into multiple fields, Filemaker Pro does an "and" find: it only brings back records where all fields match the criteria you typed. Doing an "or" search is more difficult. In order to have Filemaker Pro bring all records that match any of the find criteria, you must use multiple requests. This can get quite tedious if you are looking for a lot of criteria. You have the option to bring back only those records that do NOT meet your find criteria.

Once you have executed a Find, you can switch back to Browse mode and use just the "found set" (results of the find). You can delete the found set, edit the values, and switch to another layout (such as a mailing labels layout). To return to working with all the records, select Find All from the Select menu.

Tip
To search for blank fields, use the exact match character (=) all by itself. To search for nonblank fields, use the exact match character and select the "omit" option for the find.

Writing Scripts and Using Buttons

Filemaker Pro supports *buttons*. A button is any graphic object you place on the screen. When you click a button in Browse mode, it executes a command that you select from the Define Button dialog box (see fig. 19.10). To define a button action, you must be in Layout mode. Select the object you want to use as a button, and then choose Define Button from the Scripts menu. Available commands include re-executing the Find or Sort that was active when the button was created, paging up and down, moving through fields, running the Spell checker, changing to Browse, Find, or Preview mode, duplicating a record, adding or deleting a record, printing the record or found set, deleting the found set, and virtually any of the menu commands available in Filemaker Pro. A button can also be configured to run a script.

Fig. 19.10

The Define Button dialog box.

One of Filemaker Pro's more powerful features is the Scriptmaker. Scripts enable you to automate tasks that you or your users perform on a regular basis. These scripts might, for example, do a Find, switch to a mailing label template, and print the results. You can attach display scripts in the menu bar, or attach them to buttons (see previous paragraph). To create a script, you must first name the script in the Define Script dialog box. This dialog box also enables you to delete script, duplicate scripts, edit scripts, and rename scripts.

A script is a series of commands that Filemaker Pro executes whenever the script is run. A script can run all the commands mentioned above for a button (including finds and sort), as well as additional commands, such as doing a relookup, sending an Apple event, importing and exporting records, and doing page setup. A script can also run another script. To create a script, you select the commands you want to use from the Available Steps list in the Script Definition dialog box (see fig. 19.11). You can double-click the step or click it and then click the Move button to move the step to script command list. You can click and drag the steps in the script command list to rearrange them at any time.

Some script commands need additional information in order to work properly. For example, if you select the Go to Layout script command, you must specify the layout to go to. When you select a command that requires additional information, Filemaker Pro modifies the Options section of the Script Definition dialog box to request the specific needed information.

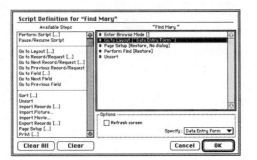

Fig. 19.11
The Script Definition dialog box.

Using Filemaker Pro's Security

Filemaker Pro can be installed on a network, and you can define security for multiple users. Security access is defined in terms of a group, to which you attach specific users. You can define the layouts accessible to a group. You can also define field properties: which fields are accessible, which fields are hidden, and which fields are available as *read-only*. A set of passwords can be placed in a group so that different users (with different passwords) can share the same security access. As with everything else, the security dialog box is straightforward and easy to understand (see fig. 19.12).

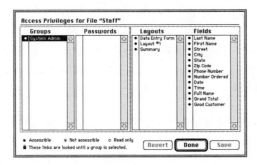

Fig. 19.12
The Access Privileges dialog box.

Getting the Most Out of Filemaker Pro: Hot Tips

■ To calculate a person's age from a field containing their birth date (Birthdate), use the following formula:

> Year(Today) - Year(Birthdate)-If(Today < Date(Month(Birthdate), Day(Birthdate), Year(Today)),1,0)

■ You can use Filemaker Pro's calculations and string-handling functions to format phone numbers. This formula uses the If function to format a 7 digit phone number differently from a longer phone number that contains an area code. Finally, if the phone number is longer than 10 digits (for example, an international phone number), the phone number is left as entered: If (Length(Abs(TextToNum(PhoneNum))) = 7, Left(Abs(TextToNum (PhoneNum)),3)& "-" & Middle (Abs (TextToNum (PhoneNum)), 4, 4), If (Length (Abs (TextToNum (PhoneNum))) = 10, "(" & Left (Abs (TextToNum (PhoneNum)),3) & ")" & Middle (Abs ITextToNum (PhoneNum)), 4, 3) & "-" & Middle (Abs (TextToNum (PhoneNum)), 7, 4), PhoneNum)).

■ To change a field on a Layout to a different field, press the Option and ⌘ keys, and then double-click the field. This brings up the new field dialog box. Select the field you want to replace the selected field with. This action replaces the field, but retains the field formatting.

■ You can separate check boxes and radio buttons in a set with a blank line by placing a blank line in the value list. You can also separate scripts in the script menu with a separator by creating a script with the name "-".

■ If your database contains duplicate records, but you want to generate only a single form letter for each set of duplicate records, use a subsummary. For example, if you have a database in which you record donors of artwork, you might have a person in the database multiple times if they have donated multiple pieces of art. Set up the form letter with the name and address fields at the top of the letter along with any initial portion of the letter. Any references to fields with different values (such as the references to the artwork donated) are located in a leading subsummary by donor name part. Any additional remarks and the closing of the letter should be in a trailing subsummary by donor name part.

■ To add serial numbers to an existing database, add a field to the database that uses the serial number option for field formatting. The serial number field will be blank in all records. Use the export function to export the database in Filemaker Pro format. Import the database back into Filemaker Pro. During the import process, Filemaker Pro will number the records and assign sequential serial numbers.

Summary

Filemaker Pro is a powerful flat-file database that gets around some of its limitations by using repeating fields and lookups. The long text data fields and the easy creation of layouts contributes to its ease-of-use. However, Filemaker Pro is not a relational database, and if you need more than just a few repeating fields, or the ability to do true relational joins, you will need to look elsewhere.

FoxPro for Mac

Microsoft's FoxPro for Mac is at the other end of the spectrum from Filemaker Pro. Where Filemaker Pro is a flat-file database, FoxPro Mac is truly relational. FoxPro for Mac also includes a full programming language/development environment in the form of the venerable xBase programming language. Many things that are fairly simple to do in Filemaker Pro require writing a program in FoxPro Mac. On the other hand, you can achieve many things with FoxPro Mac you would never be able to do with Filemaker Pro. Just be prepared to spend time learning to use this product effectively.

FoxPro Mac evolved from the Windows product, which itself was an offshoot of its DOS-based predecessor. Files can be easily be exchanged between the PC and Mac versions of the product, and FoxPro Mac adheres to most of the Mac user interface correctly. FoxPro Mac includes a powerful report writer, screen-building tool, query builder, and expression builder.

System Requirements

FoxPro Mac is big, shipping on 8 disks and installing 725 items on your hard drive for a total of 17 M. FoxPro Mac also requires at least 4 MB of memory (8 is recommended) and System 7.

Building a Table

The first step in defining a database application in FoxPro Mac is to define the structure of the tables you will be using. The New dialog box enables you to build new tables, programs, files, indexes, reports, labels, screens, menus, queries, and projects. If you choose to build a new table, FoxPro Mac opens the Table structure dialog box (see fig. 19.13). You use the Table Structure dialog box to enter the field definitions for the database. You can select the field name, type, width (size), and number of decimal places. You can rearrange the fields in the dialog box by clicking and dragging the button to the right of each field.

Fig. 19.13
Defining a Table
Structure.

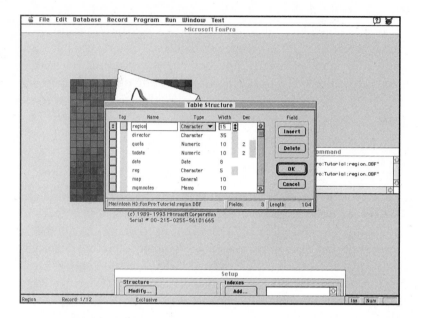

FoxPro Mac supports a wide variety of field types, including character, floating point, numeric, date, logical, memo, and general. You can store almost anything in a general field, including graphics. Character fields can be up to 255 characters. If you need more room than that, you must use a memo field, which can hold large amounts of text.

You can use the Setup menu option in the Database menu to define indexes for the database. An index is a way to establish the order of the records in the database. If you don't establish an index, the records are displayed in the order in which you entered them. The index presents the records in order of the fields you select. For example, you could define a customer database that is indexed on Lastname and Firstname. You can define multiple indexes for a database and select between them, instantly modifying the order in which records are displayed. An index can be ascending or descending, and you can require that the values in the index fields be unique. You can also filter records on the index fields. FoxPro Mac's excellent expression builder makes defining index filters very straightforward. You can choose from over 100 string, logical, math, and date functions. You can also use system variables.

IV

After you define your table, you have the option of immediately entering records. FoxPro provides a very simple form that displays all your fields in a stacked format.

Working with Your Data

FoxPro Mac enables you to work with your data using either a custom-built screen or Browse mode. Browse mode presents the data in a spreadsheet-like format, with records in rows and fields in columns. You can adjust the width of a column by clicking and dragging the border between columns. You can also rearrange the columns by clicking and dragging the column headings and set the font for the entire grid. Unfortunately, there is no way to save this layout. You can edit the information in Browse mode by typing in the new or modified information into the fields. You can also split the Browse mode window into two parts which can either scroll together (synchronized) or separately (unsynchronized). You can activate Change mode, which displays the records in the database in a simple, vertically stacked arrangement of fields (see fig. 19.14).

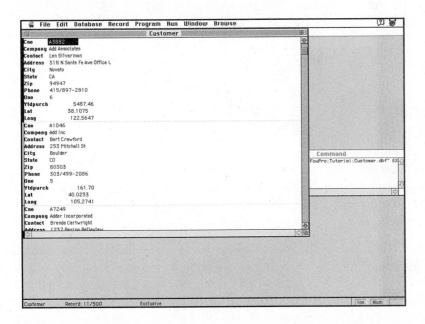

Fig. 19.14
The Change window of Browse mode.

FoxPro Mac is a relational database, and it is very straightforward to join tables so that you can use the fields from multiple joined tables on a single screen. FoxPro Mac will even suggest the join condition if the join fields in the two tables are named the same (though they don't have to be). However, although it is possible to create a one-to-many join between tables, FoxPro Mac lacks a repeating panel (or Filemaker's repeating fields) to show the results of that join on a screen. It is possible to include a browse window (see the Hot Tips section) to display the many side of the join on the screen, but it takes quite a bit of code-writing to accomplish this.

Building a Custom Screen

FoxPro Mac's custom screen builder makes designing data input screens fun. It includes a wide variety of tools for customizing the screen and making it attractive to the user. The first step in creating a new screen is establishing the general layout. The Screen Layout dialog box (see fig. 19.15) enables you to establish the size and location of the screen on the desktop. You can click and drag an image of the screen, or adjust the position and size using spinner controls. You can set the title and name of the screen, and change the color of the screen background. You can even specify a graphic file to use as a background for effect.

Fig. 19.15
The Screen Layout dialog box.

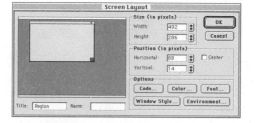

You can set many options for a custom screen design. The Window style button enables you to set various window attributes. These include which objects appear in the window (close box and whether the window is moveable), border style (none, single, double, panel, or system), and the overall window type (system, dialog, alert, or user).

Tip
To present your user with a message, use an alert-style window that pops up under program control.

The Code option in the Screen Layout dialog box enables you to attach snippets of program code to the screen. You use the Screen Code dialog box to write the code that executes when the screen opens, closes, and when you click the window. The code must be written in xBase, FoxPro Mac's built-in programming language (see "Programming FoxPro Mac," later in this chapter).

When you have the basic screen size, color, code, and so on, it is time to add objects to the screen. You can quickly prototype a screen by using the quick screen feature on the Screen menu. You have the option to choose a horizontal or vertical layout, and a maximum field width. From the quick screen, you can choose which fields to place on the screen, although the default of all fields in the database often works well (see fig. 19.16).

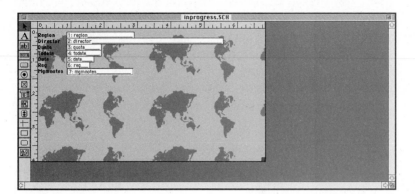

Fig. 19.16
Building a screen layout in FoxPro Mac.

Adding Fields to a Screen

You can also add fields to the screen by using the tools in the toolbox along the left side of the screen (see fig 19.17).

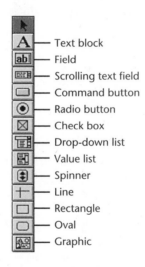

Fig. 19.17
Add fields to the screen by using the tools in the toolbox.

The field tool lets you click and drag a rectangle on the screen to define a field. When you release the mouse, FoxPro Mac pops up the Field dialog box. You can select whether the field is an input field (field or variable from the database) or an output field. An output field is an expression that you can build to display a result based on a formula that can use fields, variables, and all the FoxPro Mac functions. From the Field dialog box, you can also set the field style, including 3-D style, whether the field is selected or disabled when you enter the form, a valid range of values, and the field format. You establish the range of values by entering a procedure (written in xBase) or an expression to set the low end of the range and the high end of the range. Expressions are built using the Expression editor. The field format lets you specify a variety of formatting options, depending on the type of field. For text fields, you can specify alpha only, all uppercase, the text alignment, and removing the extra spaces (trim). For numeric fields, you can left justify, suppress leading zeroes, use currency or scientific format, set the format when the number is negative, and suppress the number if it is zero.

The Clause section of the Field dialog box enables you to enter snippets of code for the field. There are four clauses available: When, Valid, Message, and Error. The When clause controls what happens when a field is selected. If the code in the When clause doesn't return a .T. (true), you can't access the field. The Valid clause controls the code that is executed when you attempt to exit a field. If the code doesn't return a .T. (true), you can't exit the field. This code snippet can thus be used to ensure that a valid value is entered into the field. The Message clause enables you to write a message that FoxPro Mac displays on the status line when you enter the field. Finally, the Error clause lets you code custom error messages to be displayed if the code you add returns a .F. (false). Although these clauses give you more flexibility and power than Filemaker Pro's automatic entry and field validation options, they also require considerably more effort to use.

In addition to fields in a text format, you can add fields to the form as drop-down list, check box, radio button, spinner, pop-up list, or pop-up list with text box. For a check box, you can specify the check box prompt, whether the check box is initially checked, and whether to disable it. You can use When and Valid clauses to modify the check box behavior if you like. Check boxes are only available for Boolean (true or false) fields or numeric fields.

Radio buttons are groups of circles with labels. When you select one of the radio buttons in a set, any other selected radio button is deselected. You can attach a radio button to character or numeric database fields. You specify the prompts (text next to each radio button), as well as whether the radio buttons are laid out horizontally or vertically, and the space between radio buttons. Once again, you can use the When and Valid clauses to modify the radio button behavior.

Pop-ups are used for setting values or choosing from a list of related items. You can type prompts into the Popup dialog box, and attach the pop-up to a character or numeric field. You can also draw the prompts from an array, a field in another file, or from a database structure.

You can define spinners for a numeric or text database field. For a spinner, you can define the minimum and maximum values and the increment values. You can also use formulas to define the upper and lower ends of the spinner range. Using formulas is handy—you can change the spinner range based on values in other fields.

Adding Graphics to a Screen

You can add lines, rectangles, rounded rectangles, pictures, and buttons to a screen. For lines, you can specify the line thickness, style, and color. For rectangles and rounded rectangles, you can specify the border thickness, style, and color, as well as the fill color and pattern. For a rounded rectangle, you can also set the amount of rounding at the corners. For a picture, you can load a graphics file or display the contents of another field. If the picture is not the right size for the area you allot to it, you can clip the picture (if it is too big) or scale the picture to fill the frame or retain its shape (if it is too small).

You can attach code to a button. Buttons can be text, graphics, or even invisible. When you click the button with the mouse, the attached When clause code executes.

Using Other Screen Design Tools

The screen builder in FoxPro Mac has many other tools to help you with your layout efforts. You can display rulers across the top and down the side of the screen. A line on the ruler shows the current mouse pointer position. You can also turn on a snap-to grid to help you align objects. Unfortunately, you can't align objects to each other. You can group objects together so that you work with them as a single object. You can also change the stacking order of objects to determine which objects are on top when objects overlap. You can use the Object Order dialog box to set the order in which objects are accessed on-screen when using the keyboard. The Object Order dialog box contains a list of all objects except graphic and text objects. These objects are listed in the order they will be accessed on the screen. To change the order, click and drag the objects in the list. You can also arrange objects by column or by row.

Tip

To place a circle or oval on a form, select the rounded rectangle and choose the circular shape from the palette of shapes available.

Testing a Screen

One of the difficulties with FoxPro Mac is that you can't just switch from Design mode to Test mode to check out how a screen is going to work. Instead, you must instruct FoxPro Mac to generate the screen so you can then run it. On a simple screen, this process takes about 15 seconds as the application generates the necessary code. As screens get more complex, the compile time goes up. This compile/test/fix cycle must be repeated every time you make a screen change.

Tip

To use a large area of the screen as a button, create an invisible button and place it over the area of the screen you want.

Running Queries

FoxPro Mac has a robust query builder that enables you to set selection criteria for retrieving your data. The query builder is called RQBE (relational query by example). RQBE is based on the concept that you should be able to retrieve data in a query by giving an example of the type of data you want.

The RQBE window provides a multitude of options (see fig. 19.18). The tables list enables you to pick the tables you want for the query. Once you select a table from the list, you can click the Fields check box to bring up a list of fields in that table. You can select the fields you want to include from the list. You can also build functions that include the fields in the table, and add these to the list as well. For example, you can specify a summary function to appear in the query result. If you click the Add button, you can add more tables to the query. All tables after the first table must be related to one of the existing tables in the query. When you add a table, FoxPro Mac requests the join condition in a dialog box. This join condition is then added to the Selection Criteria area near the bottom of the window.

Fig. 19.18
The RQBE
Window.

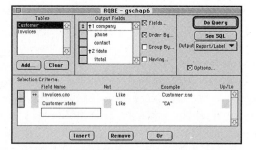

Clicking the Order By check box enables you to use some of the output fields to set the order of the records in the query result. You can sort the output on these fields in either descending or ascending order. You can also rearrange the order of the Order By fields by clicking and dragging them in the list. Clicking the Group By check box enables you to designate the fields you want to group the output by. For example, you might order records by Last Name, but you might group the records by State. The results of the query would show groups of records for each state, and within each state, ordered by Last Name. You can even specify the conditions under which a particular group will be included in the query result. For example, you might want only certain states included. Setting the group criteria is done by clicking the Having check box. The criteria you set for Having can include formulas and summary functions.

The Selection Criteria area near the bottom of the RQBE window is where you set the actual criteria for including records in the query. As mentioned earlier, any join conditions between related tables appear here as well. The selection criteria can include fields, constants, comparison operators (Like, Greater than, and so on), and expressions.

The Options check box enables you to set options for the query. You can select the form name, create a quick report, suppress the report details and just see any summary expressions you have defined, suppress column headings, and output the query results to a file or the printer. The quick report is very handy—it displays the query output in simple list or columnar report format.

You can output the query in a number of different formats. As mentioned in the last paragraph, you can output a report (see fig. 19.19). You can also output the results in a Browse window, graph, and even a new table. Unfortunately, the results of a query are read-only: even in Browse mode, you cannot edit the query's output. This puts FoxPro Mac at a disadvantage to Filemaker Pro in this regard.

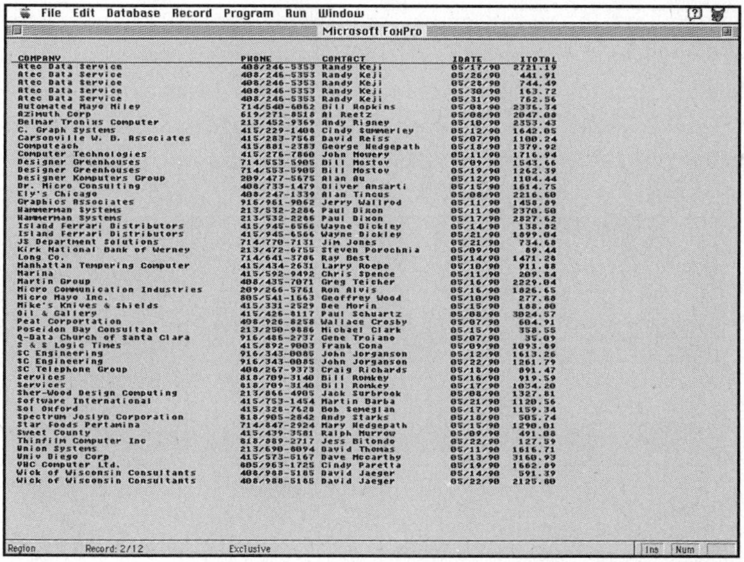

Tip

To order by a field you don't want to show in the query, add the field to the Output Fields, select the field to be ordered by, and then remove it from the list of Output Fields.

Fig. 19.19
Outputting the results of a query as a report.

When you build a query, FoxPro Mac creates an SQL (structured query language) statement in the background. Although you can't edit this SQL, you can copy it into your own programs, thus enabling you to produce the same results as the query in your own program.

Building Reports

FoxPro Mac includes a powerful report writer. You can create a report from scratch, or modify a report created through the use of a query (this is much easier). You can also open a new report and instruct FoxPro Mac to create a quick report that you can then use or modify. However, if you must join the results of more than one table together, you must start from a query or use the table join function so that you can establish the join conditions.

The Report builder includes most of the tools available in the screen builder, including the Field tool, Text tool, Graphic tools (rectangle, line, rounded rectangle), and Picture tool. You cannot place check boxes, spinners, lists, and so on, on a report. You also cannot edit data on a report, unlike Filemaker Pro.

The primary difference between a report and the screen builder (other than that you can't enter data in a report) are objects called bands. *Bands* break up a report into clearly defined areas. Examples of bands include page headers and footers, group headers and footers, and the detail band. A default report includes all the bands except the group band. To create a group band, you must specify the field(s) to group by. FoxPro Mac automatically adds the necessary group band to the report. For example, the report layout shown in figure 19.20 groups records by Company. You probably will want to create a calculated or summary field to total any numeric fields that appear in group bands (see fig. 19.21). You can force a report to move to a new page when a group changes, and even reprint the group band on subsequent pages.

Fig. 19.20
A report definition that includes a group band (grouped by Company).

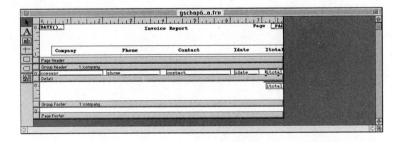

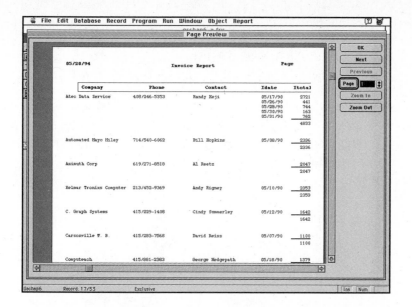

Fig. 19.21
A report grouped
by company, with
a summary field for
the invoice totals.

You can specify a summary header and footer for the report as a whole, and use multiple columns in a report if the data you need to show is not very wide. You can use the Print When dialog box for any field to suppress repeating values. You can also print the field when the group changes, and only print the field when an expression is true. Unfortunately, you must set the Print When properties field by field.

> **Note**
>
> FoxPro Mac supports the creation of mailing labels. When you open a new mailing label file, you are given the chance to select from various sizing of Avery labels. FoxPro Mac then places you in the report writer with an appropriately sized template available for you to customize.

Creating Your Own Menus

You can create your own custom menus in FoxPro Mac. The menu dialog box (see fig. 19.22) enables you to construct your own menu from scratch or just add items to FoxPro Mac's standard menus. For each menu bar item, you can add menu items. For each item, you can add additional items, thus constructing a cascading menu. At the end, you must attach a snippet of code to a menu option. FoxPro Mac executes this snippet of code whenever the user selects the menu item. You can use the expression builder to set up a condition that grays out (disables) a menu item when a formula is true. This enables your application to determine when it is appropriate for a menu option to be selectable. You can set a keyboard shortcut for a menu option, set up a message to be displayed in the status bar when the user selects the menu option, and give the bar its own number (overriding the strange coding scheme that FoxPro Mac uses). You can add separator bars in the menu as well. A Try It button shows you how your menu will look, complete with cascading items. However, the menu is not functional—you can't select an item to see if it works.

Fig. 19.22
The Menu dialog box.

Building a Project

FoxPro Mac provides a tool called a *Project* to bind all the pieces of your application together. These pieces include queries, screens, databases, reports, and menus. You can either create all the pieces beforehand and add them to a Project, or create the Project first and create all the pieces from within the Project dialog box (see fig. 19.23).

Fig. 19.23
The Project dialog box.

Editing items from the Project dialog box is very simple—highlight the item you want and click the Edit button. FoxPro Mac opens the appropriate editor so that you can work on that item. You can add items to the Project in the same way. Oddly, you must be careful to exclude certain files from a Project. This rather strange process involves adding the file (for example, a table) to the Project, and then excluding it. An excluded file still shows up in the Project, but it has special properties. For example, unlike included files, you can modify the contents of an excluded file after you build the Project into an Application (see below). This is usually necessary for database tables, because most database applications involve entering new data into tables. Thus, most tables must be excluded from a Project.

Once you have gathered all the tables you need (both included and excluded) into a Project, you can have FoxPro Mac generate an application. The contents of the Project are used to create an application file that you can run from the Program menu. The process of generating an application doesn't take very long, but if you make any changes to component files in the Project (for example, change a report), you must regenerate the application. This delay in your ability to test your application will probably increase the number of errors in your final application.

Programming FoxPro Mac

FoxPro Mac uses one of the most popular programming languages of all time: xBase. As mentioned, you can attach xBase code snippets to fields, graphics, and buttons. Microsoft has extended xBase considerably to handle graphic objects. It has a huge number of commands available. Even so, xBase is starting to show its age. It doesn't handle event-driven control very well, and the editor, while adequate, doesn't provide any hint that you can have made an error until you actually try to run the code. Another problem is that almost everything requires that you write code. For example, even a simple set of buttons to navigate through records requires that you write a program! Almost any other database provides simple functions such as record navigation without having to program.

Getting the Most Out of FoxPro Mac: Hot Tips

■ If you want to use a complex SQL statement in a program to retrieve data, you can have FoxPro Mac write the SQL statement for you. Open the RQBE window and set up the query, setting all the options and table joins that you need. Click the See SQL button to open the SQL window. Use the mouse to highlight all the text in the SQL box. Use Edit Copy to place the SQL statement on the clipboard. Return to the program editor and paste the SQL text into your program.

■ You can attach a set of radio buttons or a list to either a character or numeric database field. However, what gets stored in the database varies depending on the field type. If the database field is a character field, the actual text of the radio button prompt or the list item is stored in the database. If the database field is numeric, FoxPro Mac stores the number of the radio button prompt or the list item in the database.

■ FoxPro Mac does not include a repeating panel to display the many records that correspond to the one record for tables that joined in a one-to-many relationship. To add a Browse window to a screen, you must use the following steps:

1. Create a parent screen that will encompass the GET screen (one table) and the Browse window.

2. In the setup code for the parent screen, define a window with the attributes you want the Browse window to have, but don't ACTI-VATE the window. For example:

    DEFINE Window browse;
    FROM 13.85, 3.00;
    TO 22.85, 90.00;
    FONT "MS Sans Serif", 8;
    NO FLOAT;
    NUCLEASE;
    NONE;
    IN WINDOW main

    Main is the name of the parent window as specified in the Screen Layout dialog box for the parent screen. To obtain the FROM and TO coordinates, draw a rectangle in the parent window where you want the Browse window to be and note the dimensions as displayed in the status bar.

3. Include a BROWSE command in the setup code. For example:

    BROWSE WINDOW wbrowse in WINDOW wmain NOWAIT SAVE

4. Create a separate screen for the GET (one table) fields.

5. In the setup code for the GET screen, include the following command:

    #WCLAUSES in WINDOW wmain

6. Generate a screen set that includes both the parent screen and the GET screen.

Summary

FoxPro Mac has a lot going for it: a robust screen builder and report writer, and an excellent query engine. On the other hand, you must compile screens before you can test them, and build Projects to compile into Applications before you can try your efforts. You must also plan on writing code for many operations, including some simple ones. Still, if you need a relational database application that is fast, well-documented, and has the ability to run virtually unmodified in Windows and DOS, FoxPro Mac is a good choice.

Conclusions and Recommendations

The two databases looked at here probably couldn't be more different. For people needing a quick and easy solution that doesn't require complex relationships between table, Filemaker Pro is an excellent choice. You can do application development with Filemaker Pro, but you are limited by the lack of any kind of a programming language. However, the macro facility is quite powerful.

FoxPro is a good choice if you need the full power of an application-development environment. You do pay the price in complexity (programming is necessary for most tasks) and in compiling screens, reports, and so on into an application.

Chapter 20

Integrated Software Pulls It All Together

by Peter Durso

Integrated software packages are bundles of software that combine word processing and spreadsheet modules with any combination of graphics, communications, and database modules into a single purchase.

Early integrated software packages were not very integrated. In fact, for quite some time, integrated software packages more closely resembled the current crop of Office offerings from Microsoft and WordPerfect in that they were separate packages. You wanted to put a graphic into a report and then incorporate spreadsheet results? More often than not, you had to get out the tape and scissors and head for the copying machine to get your "integrated" report.

Integrated software has come a long way, but the integration is more complete in some cases than in others. Not all integrated software is created equal, as you will see.

This chapter examines three integrated packages, and how they compare to each other regarding ease of integration of their multiple functions:

- ClarisWorks (Claris)

- WordPerfect Works (WordPerfect)

- MS-Works (Microsoft)

Using ClarisWorks

With ClarisWorks you can work with text, graphics, and spreadsheet information in a truly seamless environment.

Claris, an Apple company, is the publisher of the MacDraw II and MacDraw Pro products. It is also the publisher of MacPaint and MacWrite. Both the MacPaint and MacWrite programs were originally standard issue with the purchase of a Macintosh. The word processing, painting, and drawing tools that are provided in ClarisWorks will look very familiar to anyone that has used these packages. The tools generally are very powerful and well-integrated.

System Requirements

ClarisWorks will work on any Macintosh from a Mac Plus on up with system software version 6.0.5 or later. System 6 requires 1MB of system RAM. If you are using System 7, you need 2MB of system RAM. System 7.0 or System 7.0.1 requires System 7 Tune-Up, Version 1.1.1. System Tune-Up is available from Apple Computer, Inc.

ClarisWorks only requires 600K of hard disk space, and you can vary system RAM requirements depending on your Macintosh configuration.

If you are using System 6.0.5 or higher with MultiFinder, or if you are using System 7, and you have enough RAM, you can increase the allocated memory for ClarisWorks to as much as 2,048K.

ClarisWorks will benefit from this extra allocation if you expect to work with multiple documents simultaneously, with documents that contain many graphics objects, in the paint environment, or on very large compound documents.

If you are using System 7 and you have only 2MB of memory, or if you are using a PowerBook, you may reduce your ClarisWorks memory allocation to as low as 768K.

Features and Capabilities

Any system that tries to do everything at once will have some deficiencies. The most glaring ones here are that you cannot apply paragraph styles in the word processor, and you cannot include graphics in the database.

With these deficiencies noted, ClarisWorks provides power and accessibility when used in home or educational settings. You can easily run a small business with this package.

When you first open ClarisWorks, MS-Works, and WordPerfect Works, you are presented with a screen that lets you open a particular segment (sometimes called a "module") of the program (see fig. 20.1). ClarisWorks gives you the choice of either Word Processing, Drawing, Painting, Spreadsheet, Database, or Communications.

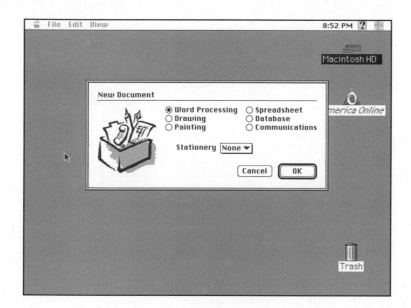

Fig. 20.1
When you open ClarisWorks, a screen, similar to those that open the other packages discussed in this chapter, appears.

When you open ClarisWorks in Word Processing, Spreadsheet, Draw, or Paint modes, you have access to the tools from the other three modules, as shown in figure 20.2.

Figure 20.3 shows that the Communications and Database modules are separate, with their own set of tools, and without access to the tools of the other modules.

Compound Documents

Compound documents, such as the one shown in figure 20.4, are an example of an advantage that a fully integrated environment gives you over conventional Publish and Subscribe or Copy and Paste methods. That advantage is simplicity.

Fig. 20.2
When you open ClarisWorks in Word Processing, Spreadsheet, Draw, or Paint modes, you have access to the tools from the other three modules.

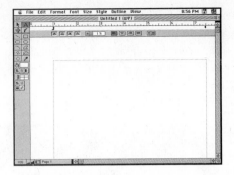

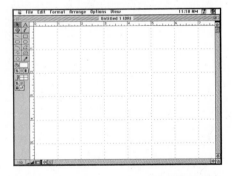

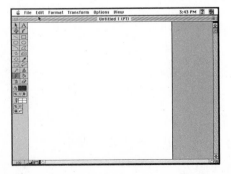

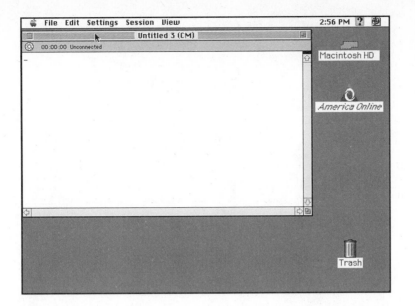

Fig. 20.3
The Communications and Database modules are separate, with their own set of tools, and without access to the tools of the other modules.

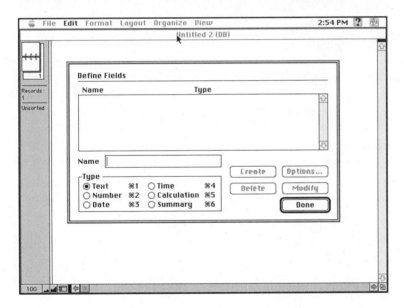

Fig. 20.4
ClarisWorks makes compound documents a snap! All the elements of this document were created within *one* ClarisWorks document.

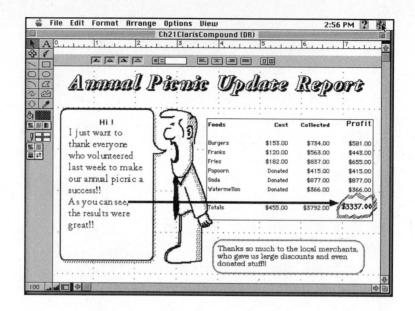

The document shown in figure 20.4 was created by ClarisWorks and saved in only one document. When a similar document is created in WordPerfect Works, it takes a minimum of two documents and the process creates some "editions" in a special folder reserved for this purpose in the system folder. This is a result of WordPerfect using Publish and Subscribe for its integration. In MS-Works, it took two documents and some copy-and-paste actions.

Spreadsheets with Charts

The Spreadsheet and Chart functions of ClarisWorks are smooth. You can customize the look of the charts, text, headings, and number formats just like in a freestanding spreadsheet program (see fig. 20.5).

The chart displaying the success of the fictitious annual picnic in figure 20.4 is a spreadsheet that was created by selecting the Spreadsheet tool, dragging a box to create a spreadsheet area, and then entering the data to crunch the numbers. It was also very easy to manipulate the position of the chart in relation to the hands of the cartoon figure so that the chart looks as if it's being carried by him, and to paint the ragged circle around the final total.

Database Capabilities

Figure 20.6 displays the kind of results you can achieve with the ClarisWorks Database module.

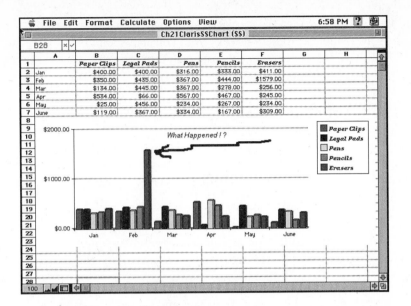

Fig. 20.5
Spreadsheets can be customized and enhanced easily in ClarisWorks.

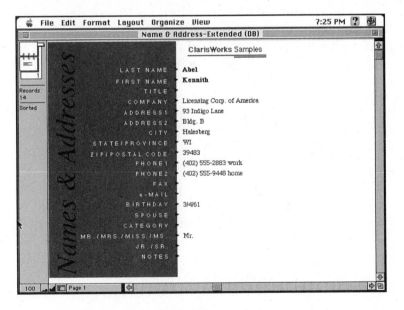

Fig. 20.6
A nice touch that is unique to a ClarisWorks database is its capability to define multiple choice fields.

Unfortunately, because there are no picture fields, you cannot create, say, a real estate database with the home that is for sale shown with each address record.

Avery label templates are provided, which can be very convenient. You can even use DBF-format files. The ability to use DBF-format files allows you to use an industry standard file format for sharing database files with others. As long as the database program used by your colleagues supports the DBF-files, you can use ClarisWorks to create output files that their programs can use, or you can use ClarisWorks to read files that they have created on their system.

Communications

If you need a full-fledged communications program, you should probably look elsewhere. The biggest shortcoming of ClarisWorks in this area is that you have to set those pesky items in the line settings each time you dial out. The baud rate, stop bits, and so on should be saved for each entry in the phone book. They are not.

None of the packages discussed in this chapter substitute for a complete communications program. Because on-line services such as America Online and Prodigy supply their own communications front-end programs, this aspect of the integrated package will probably be used the least anyway.

You can automate your required responses and cause the program to wait for specified responses from the host system by using ClarisWorks Macros.

Getting the Most from ClarisWorks: Hot Tips

- ClarisWorks has a simple and Super Undo command. It is in the File menu and is called Revert.

    You can experiment with a document. Change the text format, stretch a graphic, change colors and if you don't like the results, select File Revert and your document goes back to the last saved version.

- If you've visually aligned two objects and they aren't perfectly aligned when you print your document, don't yell at the laser printer. Open your document. Turn off Autogrid under Options. Then click on the larger of the two mountain range pictures next to the number 100 at the bottom left of the ClarisWorks screen. They are called the zoom controls. Click until you change that 100 to 1,600 or 3,200. Your drawing is now huge. With some practice, you will find the offending misaligned two edges of your drawing. Select one of the objects and use the arrow keys to nudge the edges into perfect alignment.

- If you receive a document from someone that you cannot open successfully in another application, try opening it with ClarisWorks. ClarisWorks has a significant number of translation modules that can open or save to and from many non-ClarisWorks formats.

- In the ClarisWorks Spreadsheet, if you Show Shortcuts, the palette presents you with an array of different chart types to choose from as soon as you create your spreadsheet. With one click on the chart type you desire, you eliminate the need to go through the menus to define each aspect of your chart before you even see it.

- When you are using ClarisWorks Shortcuts, palettes can be put out of the way and still be handy if you collapse them instead of closing them. This way, you only need to click on the collapsed window to regain the full view of the palette, without poking through the Edit menu.

Here are some items in the Preferences menu:

- *Smart Quotes (Text Preferences)* Gives you a chance to have curly quotation marks and apostrophes. They can really dress up invitations, formal product announcements, resumes, just about anything. This will get rid of those annoying straight quotes and apostrophes that look very machine-like and unprofessional.

- *Show Invisibles (Text Preferences)* Shows you all the usually invisible special characters in your document. These codes do not print even if you choose Show Invisibles. Seeing the invisible character codes embedded in your documents can help you understand why some of the formatting habits you bring over from typewriters (such as spacing between columns instead of using tabs) simply are not reliable in a word processor.

- *Date Format (Text Preferences)* When you use the Insert Date feature under the Edit menu, the format is determined from one of the five formats represented here.

- *Mouse Preferences (Graphics Preferences)* Here you tell ClarisWorks that lines you draw will be constrained to exact multiples of n degrees, where n is the number that you type in the Shift Constraint box.

- *Show Names (Palettes Preferences)* This puts the names from the description field of the Edit Shortcuts box on the Shortcuts palette instead of the buttons.

Summary

The level of integration for ClarisWorks has always been high. In its current incarnation (Version 2.1), an individual might never have to go beyond the features provided by this package. The most expensive package described here, ClarisWorks ($299 list) is widely available at steep discounts and is bundled with some Mac configurations.

Using WordPerfect Works

WordPerfect Works accomplishes its integration by implementing Publish and Subscribe. For example this can put a spreadsheet applet into a WP document, complete with its own set of tools.

This works but it is not as seamless as it could be. It simply takes too long, for example, to open a spreadsheet embedded in a word processing document when you have to double-click the spreadsheet and wait for a spreadsheet applet to activate so that you can work on it.

System Requirements

WordPerfect Works works on any Macintosh from a Mac Plus on up with system software version 6.0.5 or later. System 6 requires 1MB of system RAM. 2MB of system RAM is required if System 7 is in use. RAM usage can be brought down to 900K if you are tight on memory.

Features and Capabilities

When you first open WordPerfect Works, you have the choice of either Word Processing, Drawing, Painting, Spreadsheet, Database, or Communications. Figure 20.7 shows the WordPerfect Works opening screen.

Fig. 20.7
When you first open WordPerfect Works, you are presented a screen similar to those that open the other packages discussed in this chapter.

When you open WordPerfect Works in Word Processing, Spreadsheet, Draw, or Paint modules, you use Publish and Subscribe to share portions of one document with any of the others. Figure 20.8 shows the opening screens of the various modules.

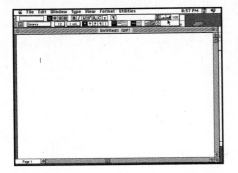

IV

Macintosh Software

Fig. 20.8
These are the opening screens of the various WordPerfect modules. To share data between documents, you must use Publish and Subscribe.

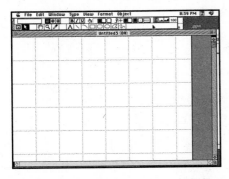
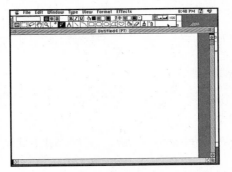

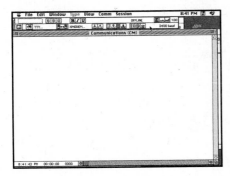
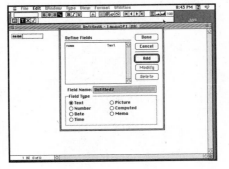

Compound Documents

Using Publish and Subscribe, you can achieve the results shown in figure 20.9.

The main advantage of using Publish and Subscribe is that the person that creates the spreadsheet can subscribe to a graphic that is published by a graphic artist and on a server to which both users have access. Any changes made to the graphic are available to the spreadsheet according to the update schedule specified by each party.

Fig. 20.9
A document similar to the one in figures 20.4 and 20.14. This document was created in WordPerfect Works with Publish and Subscribe.

Spreadsheets with Charts

Figure 20.10 shows the same concept when applied to a spreadsheet and its chart. The chart is created in a Draw document. Again, any updates made to the numbers or changes made to the chart can be made readily available to those that subscribe across a network.

Fig. 20.10
Publish and Subscribe at work again, this time with a chart of the spreadsheet.

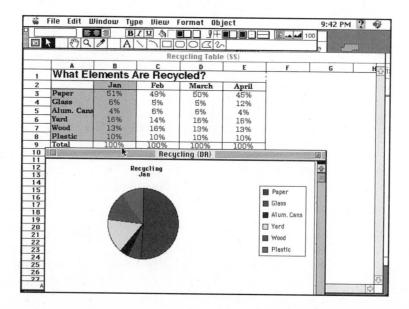

Database Capabilities

Figure 20.11 shows what can be accomplished with the database module. As with ClarisWorks, there is no provision for picture fields for this database.

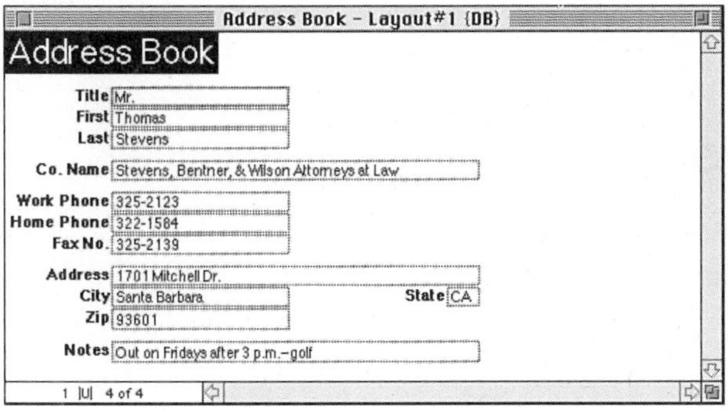

Address Book – Layout#1 (DB)	
Address Book	

Title	Mr.
First	Thomas
Last	Stevens
Co. Name	Stevens, Bentner, & Wilson Attorneys at Law
Work Phone	325-2123
Home Phone	322-1584
Fax No.	325-2139
Address	1701 Mitchell Dr.
City	Santa Barbara
State	CA
Zip	93601
Notes	Out on Fridays after 3 p.m.–golf

1 |U| 4 of 4

Fig. 20.11
The database layout of WordPerfect Works is functional.

Communications

This phone book stores the connection settings along with each telephone number—a real help if you dial onto your favorite service very often. The interface is quite good, too.

Buttons on the toolbar allow easy access to the common commands, and the status line shows you the date and time. WordPerfect Works also shows you the terminal emulation, file transfer protocol, and dial-up speed.

You can automate procedures that allow you to log onto remote systems, complete with specified wait times before sending text strings, expected responses from the host, and your password.

Getting the Most from WordPerfect Works: Hot Tips

■ When you type a date into a spreadsheet cell, WordPerfect Works recognizes it as a date, converts it into a serial number, and formats it as a date.

■ If you type @ into a WordPerfect Works database field or spreadsheet field, you will get the current date. If you type # into a database or spreadsheet time field you will get the current time.

■ Be very aware of the extra Editions files that you produce as you use Publish and Subscribe to integrate documents. In producing the examples for this chapter and experimenting along the way I managed to put nine documents in a folder called WPWorks-Editions, in my system folder. If you personally produce many documents you will also be experimenting, failing, and stopping in midstream for any of a dozen good reasons. This will propagate duplicate and stillborn Editions. Now multiply this potential for accumulating extra Editions files times the dozens or hundreds of people that can group author documents over a network.

Summary

The telecommunications package of WordPerfect Works is the most full-featured of the three products investigated in this chapter. This package is also the only one discussed that allows you to apply useful paragraph styles as do full-blown word processors.

Using Microsoft Works

Microsoft Works is a loosely integrated collection of functional software programs. To share information between the word processor and the spreadsheet module, for example, you have to use cut and paste to do it.

System Requirements

Microsoft Works will work on any Macintosh from a Mac Plus on up with system software version 6.0.5 or later. System 6 requires 1MB of system RAM. 2MB of system RAM is required if System 7 is in use.

Features and Capabilities

When you first open Microsoft Works as seen in figure 20.12, you are presented a screen similar to those that open the other packages discussed in this chapter.

Fig. 20.12
When you first open WordPerfect Works, you have the choice of either Word Processing, Drawing, Spreadsheet, Database, or Communications. There is no Paint module in Microsoft Works.

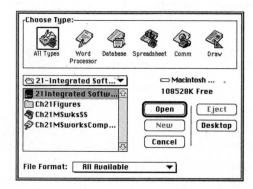

When you open Microsoft Works in Word processing, Spreadsheet, or Draw modes you use copy and paste to share portions of one document with any of the others. Charts appear in their associated spreadsheet documents, rather than in a separate draw document, as in WordPerfect Works. Figure 20.13 shows the opening screens of the various modules.

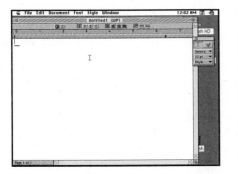

Fig. 20.13
These are the opening screens of the various WordPerfect modules. To share data between documents, you must use Publish and Subscribe.

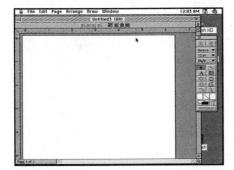

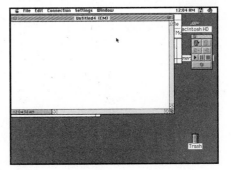

Following are some of the features added to Microsoft Works 3.0:

- Headers and Footers with automatic date, time, and page numbers

- Business, education, personal, and communications stationery documents to help you get started

- An improved mail merge feature to make it easier to create form letters

- Charts that appear with their spreadsheets and can be manipulated there

Compound Documents

Using cut and paste, you can achieve the results shown in figure 20.14.

Fig. 20.14
Microsoft Works will let you produce this document, similar to Figures 20.4 and 20.9.

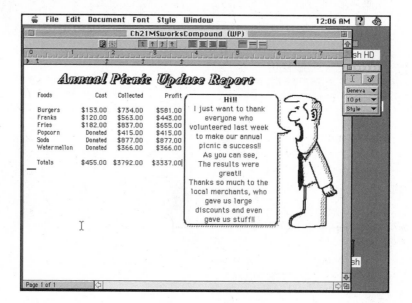

Spreadsheets with Charts

Fig 20.15 shows the results of creating a chart from within the spreadsheet program. You can easily add graphic elements and comments. In this example, it's the arrow with the What Happened Here ? ! printed above it.

Database Capabilities

Figure 20.16 shows what can be accomplished with the database module. As with ClarisWorks and WordPerfect Works, there is no provision for picture fields for this database.

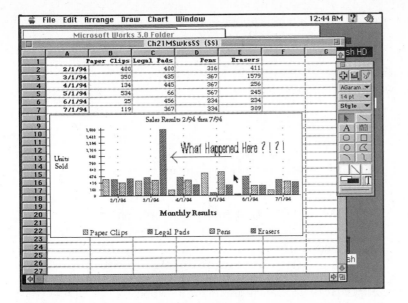

Fig. 20.15
You can add emphasis to your graphs made from Spreadsheets, as in the "What Happened Here?!" shown here.

IV

Macintosh Software

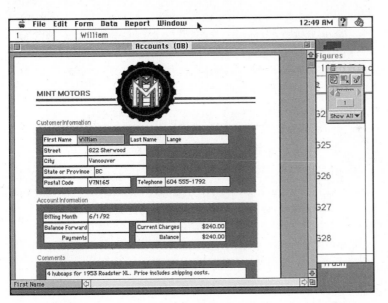

Fig. 20.16
Microsoft Works lets you dress up a database file with cut and paste.

Communications

This module is user-friendly and easy to use. The tools to designate a capture to folder and to open a connection are right on the tool palette, but there is no phone book feature.

As with the other communication packages described in this chapter, you can automate your logon sequences.

Getting the Most from Microsoft Works: Hot Tips

- Use Print One from the File menu to quickly print the current document with the current printer settings.

- You can change the color of the text in one cell without affecting the rest of the spreadsheet. Highlight the cell you want to change, select Format character from the Format menu, then choose the color you want under Style, and click OK.

- Use the Microsoft Works status bar at the bottom of the communications window to track the time and cost of a communications session. You get a detailed picture of your current connection and previous connection costs in the Show Info dialog box of the Connection menu.

- Each Database Document in Microsoft Works can have up to 16 reports.

- When you choose the Show Stationery box from New Spreadsheet, only Microsoft Works 3.0 stationery will be previewed. Other stationery documents, such as those created under the Finder with Macintosh System 7 or from earlier versions of Microsoft Works, will not be previewed.

- Instead of using a filter to display part of a database, use the Match Records command from the Data menu to have Microsoft Works display a part of the database that you specify.

- If you have a color monitor and you want to see how a Microsoft Works Chart will look when printed in black and white, change the color setting to Black and White in the Monitors dialog box from the Macintosh's Control Panel. Microsoft Works will display the chart with the various patterns that will be printed out on a black-and-white printer.

- When you are setting print margins for a document, you don't have to type "in" for inches or "cm" for centimeters because Microsoft Works handles such details. However, if you do type "cm" and the unit of measure is inches, Works will do the conversion.

- You may want to print a database report directly from the Finder; that is, print the document by selecting its icon and then select print from the Finder's File menu without starting Microsoft Works first.

In this case, make sure that report view is displayed when you save the Database document for the last time before printing.

- To check spelling in only a part of a Microsoft Works document, highlight the part of the document that you want to check (even a single word). When Microsoft Works finishes checking the selection, you can choose to continue to check the entire document by clicking the Continue Check button.

Summary

The method of integration provided by Microsoft Works is barely more than the minimum kind of integration provided by the operating system. However, it is less confusing than the proliferation of editions caused by the Publish and Subscribe functions in WordPerfect Works.

Conclusions and Recommendations

The separate packages that are sold today in "Office" suites are more completely integrated than the earliest integrated packages ever were. This is largely due to the standard data handling methodology imposed by Windows and the Macintosh interfaces, both of which have raised user expectations in this regard.

ClarisWorks is the most advanced package discussed in this chapter regarding seamless interplay between modules.

WordPerfect has some level of interplay because it integrates System 7 Publish and Subscribe. WordPerfect Works was originally published by Beagle Works, a company that is no longer with us. Beagle Works had been around since the days of the Apple IIe computer. (WordPerfect Works still saves its documents with the document type of Beagle Works.)

MS-Works is the least integrated of this trio, not even supporting Publish and Subscribe. It also has the weakest word processing module.

Separate full-fledged word processing, spreadsheet, flat file management, draw, paint, and communications software could easily cost $1,000 or more, so you need to balance integration against your other needs.

Admittedly, all of these packages offer a big bang for your software buck. The main selling point for the integrated package these days is that it gives you a lot of functionality for a very reasonable price (read cheap).

Chapter 21

Desktop Publishing

by Gene Steinberg

The word processing software discussed in Chapter 17 has taken on many of the features of desktop publishing software. They offer page layout, basic drawing tools, the ability to flow text around an irregular shape and the capability of importing text and pictures in a variety of file formats. One of the programs described, MacWrite Pro, even has settings for automatic kerning and hyphenation and justification, quite similar to the programs that we're going to describe in this chapter. Microsoft has also added support for kerning pairs in their latest version of Word.

In addition to basic publishing capabilities, high-end word processing software can handle such chores as mail merge and outlining with aplomb. There are macro capabilities, highly sophisticated search and replace capabilities, and elaborate table creation tools that have few equals in the publishing software arena.

For many basic desktop publishing chores, you might just find that one of these programs will be more than up to the task. But when it comes to handling sophisticated page layouts, color separations and trapping, and support of sophisticated typographic features, you'll want to consider the programs we're going to describe in this chapter.

In this chapter, you learn the following:

- The real differences between word processing and publishing software.

- The major features of the four major desktop publishing programs.

- Exclusive, hands-on tips and tricks that you won't find in your desktop publishing software manuals.

What Is Out There?

Before 1985, typesetting required expensive computers and hardware and was the province of a printer or specialty pre-press establishment. You could pay anywhere from ten thousand to well over a million dollars for these tools of the trade. Typographers required special skills far beyond those associated with normal typing.

Desktop publishing had its beginnings in 1985, with two very important developments. One was the introduction of the original Apple LaserWriter, a printer that used the PostScript page description language to provide sharp reproduction of printed pages. The other event was the arrival of programs like Aldus PageMaker and Ready,Set,Go, both of which are profiled later in this chapter. Together they created a revolution in publishing that has affected every nook and cranny of the industry.

Mac publishing software is a highly competitive market, with programs competing on the basis of features and the best performance. The software we're about to describe here have suggested retail prices from $395 up to $995, but all offer a mixture of high-end publishing features such as color separations and sophisticated kerning and hyphenation and justification settings. We'll be discussing not only Aldus PageMaker, but its arch rival in publishing software, QuarkXPress. We'll also be profiling another pioneer in the publishing software sweepstakes, Ready,Set,Go, and a very specialized product, FrameMaker, which was originally created to produce technical documentation on workstations.

Using Aldus PageMaker 5.0

Aldus Corporation literally began in Paul Brainerd's garage workshop in 1984, and the new company's first software product, PageMaker 1.0 for Macintosh, shipped in July 1985. Over the years, the program grew in size and flexibility, and the latest version is a sophisticated publishing tool used by design studios and magazines alike. PageMaker uses the metaphor of a mechanical board, very much reminiscent of the way mechanical artists used to assemble pages in the days of traditional typesetting. You use your mouse and keyboard to move elements around a virtual pasteboard that appears on your Mac's screen.

System Requirements

Aldus PageMaker 5.0 shares code with its Windows counterpart, and the addition of new features has taken its toll. Installed, the program can take up to

15MB on your hard drive. It requires a Macintosh II or better, running System 6.0.7 or later, with 5MB to 8MB RAM, minimum. Large documents, filled with graphics, require even more RAM to run efficiently. Expect to need another 24MB of RAM and additional couple of megabytes of disk storage to install the native Power Macintosh version.

Using Page Setup

To begin constructing your PageMaker publication, you select New from the File menu, or press ⌘-N, which displays the Page setup window shown in figure 21.1.

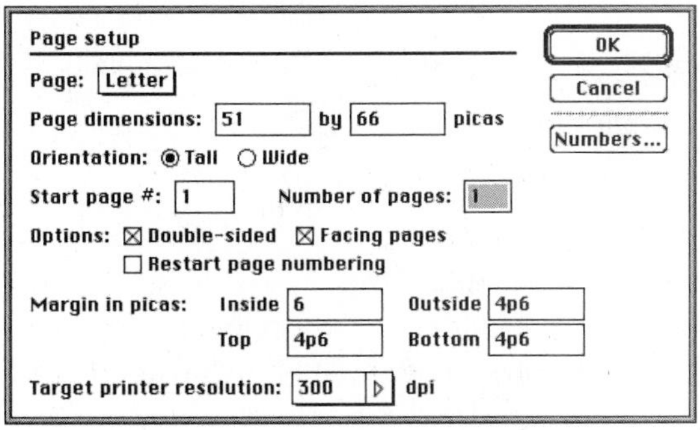

Fig. 21.1
The basic setup of your document is established in PageMaker's Page setup box.

There are default settings for common page sizes, such as Letter or Legal, but you can enter a custom page dimension in the box, in inches, picas, or whatever measurement system you've established in the program's preferences settings (available from the Preferences command in the File menu). If you're using automatic page numbering, you can select the starting page number, and the number of pages in your document. You'll want to specify your page margins now, but these can be changed later on, should you decide to modify your document formatting.

A Tour of PageMaker's Pasteboard

Once you've opened up your default document, you'll see a virtual page on your Mac's screen that, if viewed at 100%, matches in dimension the size you've specified, as shown in figure 21.2. If you don't have a large monitor, the page will be scaled to fit the size of your screen, plus the borders of your pasteboard. If you select Facing Pages in your Page setup box, all pages beyond page 1 will appear on your screen as a two-page spread. (The Styles palette and Control palette that are shown are not displayed unless you select them from the Windows menu.)

Fig. 21.2
A blank page, like
a blackboard,
ready for you to
create your
publication.

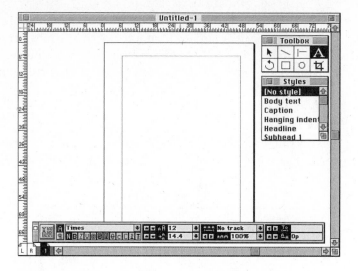

The pasteboard, to the right and left of your document pages, can be used as a holding area, just as mechanical artists used to do in the days of traditional typesetting. You can place text and picture elements there, and move them on to your page as you continue to modify the layout of your publication. Basic formatting can be done through menus, dialog boxes, and keyboard shortcuts, but you can do it more quickly with PageMaker's selection of floating palettes, which we'll discuss next.

Using PageMaker's Toolbox

The basic functions of creating your PageMaker publication are controlled with the toolbox. The features are similar to other Mac programs, and at least some of the tools are probably familiar to you. But let's examine the toolbox palette, listed in table 21.1, from left to right.

Table 21.1 PageMaker's Toolbox	
Tool	**Use**
	The Pointer Tool. You can use this tool to select picture and text objects, and to resize or move them.
	The Line Tool. You can use this tool to draw a straight line. Holding down Shift while the line is being drawn will constrain the line to an exact 45 degree angle.
	The Constrained Line Tool. You can use this tool to create lines at exact angles. It doesn't do any more than the regular Line Tool, but you don't have to bother holding Shift as your line is drawn.

Tool	Use
A	*The Text Tool.* You can use this tool to create text.
↺	*The Rotating Tool.* You can use this tool to rotate text and pictures. The process is a bit imprecise, though, and you will fare better if you use the Control Palette instead. We'll get to that shortly.
▭	*The Rectangle Tool.* You can use this tool to create a rectangular box. Once it's selected, you click the page and drag to the dimensions of your box. If you hold Shift, you get a square.
○	*The Ellipse Tool.* You can use this tool to create an ellipse. You select the tool, click the page, and drag. The Shift key will constrain the ellipse to a circle.
✄	*The Cropping Tool.* You can use this tool to crop your graphic, so only a part of it appears in your publication.

Using PageMaker's Style Sheets

To speed formatting of your document, you'll want to take advantage of PageMaker's flexible style sheets. Styles can be selected from a floating palette, shown in figure 21.4, which is displayed (or hidden) by selecting Style Palette from the Window menu or by pressing ⌘-Y (see fig. 21.3). A selection of standard styles are provided with the program, which you can alter or add to as you prefer.

Fig. 21.3
PageMaker's Styles palette.

To modify a style, simply hold ⌘ and click the style name listed in the palette. This action will bring up the window in which you can edit the selected style. To create a new style, press ⌘-3. You can define a new style or edit an existing style in a window like the one shown in figure 21.4.

Fig. 21.4
Modifying or
adding paragraph
styles in
Pagemaker is easy.

You can modify all paragraph formatting attributes of an existing style, or create new ones, through a simple procession of dialog boxes. To edit a style sheet, click the style's name, then the Edit button. Otherwise, click the New button which lets you create a style based on an existing one, or to format a new one from scratch. Once a style is changed, all paragraphs in your publication that carry that style tag will be changed, too. Local formatting, though, such as words set in italic or bold for emphasis, will be left untouched.

Using PageMaker's Control Palette

The programmers at Aldus and Quark are in hot competition with their software on a feature-for-feature basis. When QuarkXPress introduced a floating measurement palette to control basic text and picture formatting, PageMaker's programmers tried to do them one better with their own Control Palette, shown in figure 21.5. At first glance, it looks similar to Quark's, but if you look closer, you'll find some new wrinkles, especially when it comes to paragraph formatting.

Fig. 21.5
PageMaker's
Control Palette in
its text formatting
guise.

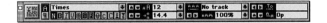

Through a selection of icons and pop-up menus, you can control most of your basic text formatting. The white boxes on the palette represent formats you can change simply by clicking in the box and typing the name of your new typeface, size, leading or character scaling. Clicking on the down arrow to the right of the white boxes will produce a pop-up menu of options, such as the font selections shown in figure 21.6.

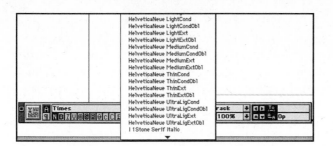

Fig. 21.6
You can select fonts from a convenient pop-up menu on PageMaker's Control Palette.

Beneath your type selections are a set of icons for type styles, such as bold, italic, underline and so forth. To the right of these styles, you can select line spacing, type size and horizontal scaling, tracking and kerning, and whether the type will fall above or below the baseline. We've saved the little paragraph label, at the bottom left, for last. Click it, and PageMaker's Control Palette dons a new identity, as shown in figure 21.7.

Style sheet list box

Fig. 21.7
Another way to select style sheets in PageMaker.

The Paragraph view of the Control palette enables you to change the paragraph attributes of your text. At the right of the paragraph style sheet list box is a series of boxes showing paragraph spacing and indents. Below the list of style sheets are icons to set text flush left, flush right, centered, and justified. If you click the paragraph icon, now highlighted (or the character view icon, which is dimmed), the standard Control Palette will return.

The Control Palette lives one more life, and the metamorphosis is accomplished simply by selecting a graphic or text object. This action brings up a display that allows you to move and scale your graphic or text object (see fig. 21.8). The Apply button in the palette changes appearance depending on the object selected.

Move buttons

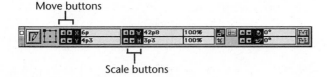

Scale buttons

Fig. 21.8
The Control Palette is also used to adjust the pictures in your PageMaker publication.

Setting Columns in PageMaker

If your document has a single column, you're ready now to add text and pictures to your document. But if you want to create a publication with two or more columns, there's one additional step to take and that is to choose Column guides from the Layout menu, which opens the window shown in figure 21.9. Enter the number of columns you want to create in this window, along with the space between columns.

Fig. 21.9
Dividing your text into multiple columns.

```
┌─────────────────────────────────────────────┐
│ Column guides _____    ┌───OK───┐ │
│                                   ├────────┤ │
│                                   │ Cancel │ │
│ Number of columns:      [2  ]     └────────┘ │
│ Space between columns:  [1  ]   picas        │
└─────────────────────────────────────────────┘
```

You can establish a separate format for your left and right hand pages, for a more decorative layout. Once you bring text into your document, it will fall within the guides you've just created.

Using Master Pages in PageMaker

If you have recurring elements from page to page, such as headers, footers or page numbers, or a special logo, you'll want to place them on a master page, so they'll automatically appear in all the pages you create for your publication. Setting up a master page involves selecting the icons labeled L-R at the lower left of your PageMaker document window.

The master pages look identical to a regular blank page on your screen. Whatever items you place there will show up on the corresponding right or left hand page. You can also create automatic page numbers, by clicking on the location of the page where the numbers are to appear, and typing ⌘-Option-P. The code LM or RM will appear on the Master Page at the point where the page numbers will be displayed.When you return to your regular document page, you'll see the correct page numbers. Your document will begin with whatever page number you entered in the Page setup box which was discussed earlier, but you can change that setting at any time.

> **Note**
>
> Master page items that appear on your regular document pages cannot be edited, but you can cover individual items up with a box containing a white fill to prevent them from being printed. If you want to prevent all master items from printing, make sure Display Master Items in the Layout menu is unchecked.

Creating Text

Most PageMaker users create text in a word processing program and import the text into PageMaker. It's not that you cannot enter text directly on your layout page, but if your typing speed ever exceeds 30 words a minute, you'll find that direct text entry isn't this program's forte. You are better off using your word processor. PageMaker will even import style tags from Microsoft Word (described in Chapter 17), which is useful if that's your word processor of choice.

Another option is to use PageMaker's own built-in word processing tool, the Story Editor, which is shown in figure 21.10. The Story Editor will display your text in a generic typeface, but you get full spell checking and search capabilities. And text entry is quite speedy; it'll keep up with the fastest typist. The text you create here will appear at your insertion point in your PageMaker publication.

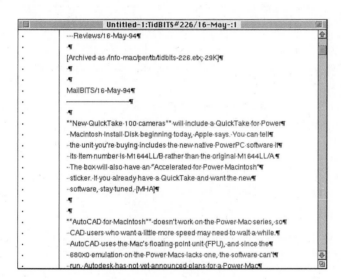

Fig. 21.10
Use PageMaker's Story Editor to enter text in your document.

PageMaker's Advanced Features

Creating simple documents is easy in PageMaker, and its more sophisticated features are readily accessible. We'll describe some of them here:

- *Table of Contents.* When you establish your style sheets, you can also indicate whether the style is to be included in the Table of Contents. When you generate your table of contents after your document has been completed, you'll be able to have it automatically incorporate the correct material. The contents can reflect your current document, or you can generate a table of contents for an entire book, consisting of a number of documents.

■ *Index.* You can select portions of your text and have them included in an index. Once the index is complete, it can be generated for a single document or a series of documents that would comprise a book.

■ *Color Separations.* You can generate both process and spot color separations in PageMaker. You can select colors from libraries such as Dainippon, Focoltone, Pantone, Toyo, and TrueMatch.

■ *Aldus Additions.* Out of the box, PageMaker comes with over 20 Additions, which are advanced scripting routines that provide additional capabilities to the program, such as creating drop caps, or reordering the pages in printer's spreads form, to ease your printer's page assembly burden. New additions are available as an option, including one that will add automatic trapping capability to the program.

Getting The Most Out Of Aldus PageMaker: Hints and Tips

■ Combine multiple stories into a single story. If you have multiple stories (separate text blocks) that you'd like to combine into a single threaded story, move all the text blocks to a common area (a single page or the pasteboard), select them all with the Pointer tool, cut (or copy), then select the Text tool, create an insertion point and paste. The copied text blocks will be pasted in a single story, in order from bottom to top.

■ Use templates to specify default settings. Create a blank PageMaker publication, save as a Template, and check "Save preview." When you want to create a new file, simply open this template. If you use QuicKeys or another macro utility, you can even redefine "New" to actually open this template, and even open page setup as if it were a new publication.

■ Templates are a great way in general to save even simple settings, not just for a full blown document template.

■ PageMaker doesn't give an option to not underline spaces, but it's easy enough to use the Story Editor's "Find and Change" to remove underlines from any space. Simply type a space and in the "Find" field, choose Underline from the attributes options, and type a space band in

"Change" with no underline option (or the text set to Normal). You can even create a special style if you have some instances where you may want some spaces underlined but others not-just use the appropriate style where desired and include the style in the search criteria (but don't change the style when you find and change.)

■ Occasionally a user will need to freeze page numbers, or have a publication with two sets of page numbers on each page (for technical documents, or periodicals that reference both the current issue and the yearly volume). This can be done relatively easily using the "Build booklet" Addition. This addition has an option to "Preserve page numbering." Simply run this addition with one set of page numbers set on the master page (for example, you set the starting page number to "1000"), choose a layout of "None." When the addition is finished, it will have copied the master page number markers to the local pages, and frozen the existing page numbers. Then change the numbering sequence in Page setup to the second set of numbers (such as "1"), and add a new page number marker on the master pages.

■ A quick and easy way to export just a few elements on a page without using the entire page as a bounding box is to use the "PSGroupIt" Addition. This Addition works by exporting the selected elements as an EPS, then placing it back in, thus creating a group. The EPS file that this Addition creates can be placed into any other application that imports EPS files, and has a bounding box limited to the selected elements. The EPS file should be saved in the directory that the original publication is in.

■ Aldus FreeHand users are used to deselecting elements by pressing Tab rather than clicking on an empty area of the page. You can accomplish a similar action in PageMaker by using the pointer tool toggle (⌘-space bar). This command allows you to switch back and forth between the tool you've selected and the Pointer tool.

Using FrameMaker 4

Frame Technologies FrameMaker had its origins in 1986 as a technical document creation program for Sun workstations running Unix. It migrated to personal computers in 1989, when the first 68030 Macintosh models afforded enough power to handle FrameMaker's sophisticated publishing features. That same year the program also became the one and only desktop publishing program to support the NeXt computer.

The latest versions of FrameMaker feature four-color separations, and free rotation of text and graphic objects. They also incorporate sophisticated cross-referencing tools, flexible table formatting, and the ability to create side heads, to the left or right of your text margins. A QuickAccess bar offers easy access to many of its sophisticated features. If you're used to a highend word processing program, such as Microsoft Word or WordPerfect, getting up to speed with FrameMaker is not a difficult task, but the more sophisticated features are apt to take a while to master.

System Requirements

Like its UNIX and Windows counterparts, FrameMaker exacts a high toll in hard drive and RAM space. It requires a 68020 Mac or faster, with 58MB of installed RAM, running System 6.0.7 or later, but System 7 is recommended. Expect to fill roughly 15MB of hard disk space fully loaded. The Power Macintosh version of FrameMaker requires 16MB of RAM, and at least 18MB of hard disk space.

Creating a New Document

FrameMaker comes with a selection of templates that you can use in building your own document. They cover the basic categories of document creation, from a simple business card to a long technical publication. When you type the standard keystroke for creating a new document, ⌘-N, you have four choices, shown at the bottom of the window in figure 21.11.

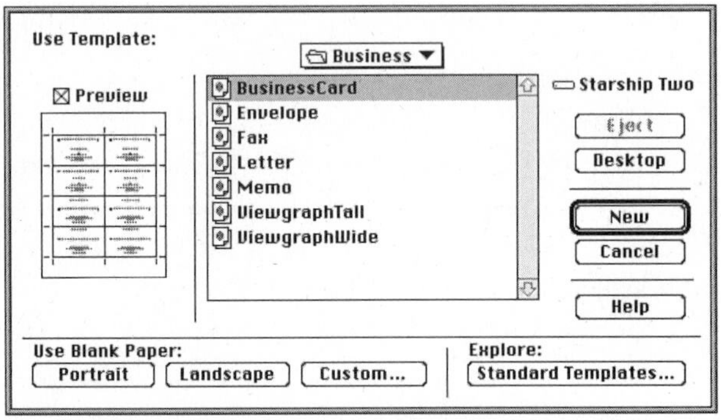

Fig. 21.11
You can build a new document from scratch, or adapt one of the existing templates to your needs.

When you click the Explore Standard Templates button, you'll bring up a graphical display of the templates that are supplied with the program. Just click the name of the template to learn more about it. The Show Sample option, shown at the bottom of the window in figure 21.12, will actually open a document window showing the template full size on your screen. If you want to examine a hard copy before modifying your template, you can print it the same as any other document.

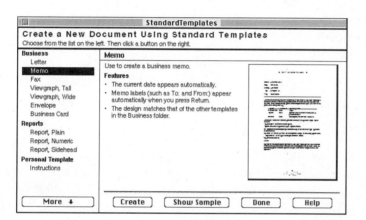

Fig. 21.12
FrameMaker allows you to preview a template before you decide whether to use it or not.

The Create button, at the bottom of the window shown in figure 21.12 above, will open a new document window containing the very same formatting attributes of your template. You can then create your text and illustrations, and they'll match the characteristics of the original. Or you can modify the template or create a new one.

Using FrameMaker's QuickAccess Bar

Your new document page in FrameMaker follows after the ones you create in your favorite word processor, at least visually. We'll explore the tremendous power of this program in a moment, and you'll begin to see some of the differences. But for writing a simple document, a letter or a memo, you can use the QuickAccess Bar, shown in figure 21.13, to handle basic character and page formatting.

Like most features in FrameMaker, you will find immense power beneath the surface when you begin to explore. An example is that QuickAccess bar. At the very least, clicking on an icon activates the pictured function, such as a text attribute, or saving and printing a document.

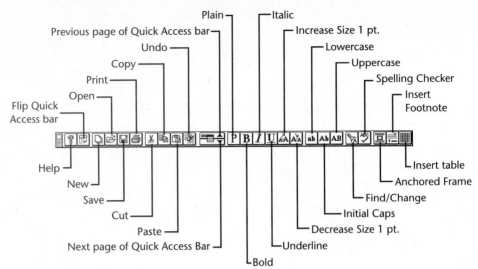

Fig. 21.13
FrameMaker's QuickAccess bar looks on the surface much like what you'd find in a program like Microsoft Word.

But if you click one of those small up and down arrows at the center of the QuickAccess bar, it undergoes a decided metamorphosis. There are four separate bars, each providing functions for a specific FrameMaker feature. The one we've shown so far handles your word processing chores. If you click the down arrow once, as shown in figure 21.14, you'll see a number of icons that reflect the creation of graphics, such as you're likely to find in an illustration program.

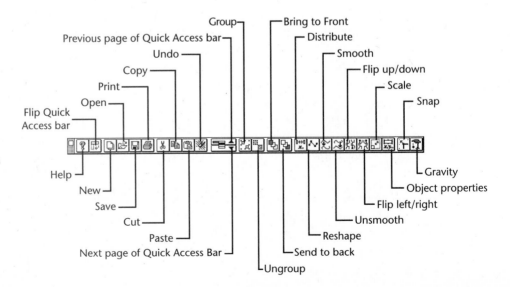

Fig. 21.14
The QuickAccess bar in one of its four identities.

The third position, when you click the down arrow, displays another set of graphics tools, which you use to edit your graphics. The final QuickAccess bar format provides tools for table creation. FrameMaker's highly sophisticated table editor is discussed shortly.

Using FrameMaker's Paragraph Designer

FrameMaker excels at creating long, complex documents. In this way, it's a modern-day equivalent of the very expensive book typesetting computers of years ago. After you've decided the size page you wish to use, whether it's portrait or landscape, and the page dimensions, you'll want to create paragraph and character styles to speed document creation. Every formatting element of your document can be established in advance, saved as a template, and even exported to other documents to ensure a consistent look and feel to your publications.

FrameMaker's unique Paragraph Designer is shown in figure 21.15. You can access the Paragraph Designer by choosing Paragraphs from the Format menu and Designer from the sub-menu. Since FrameMaker excels in its repository of keyboard shortcuts, you can get there just by typing ⌘-M.

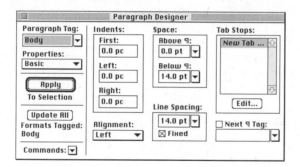

Fig. 21.15
Just the first part of FrameMaker's Paragraph Designer window.

The Paragraph Designer lets you adjust six basic properties of your paragraph text, simply by selecting the item on the pull-down menu. These include:

- *Basic.* This window is used to establish paragraph spacing, indents, and line spacing.

- *Default font.* This window sets your character attributes, such as size, style, color and whether to turn on automatic kerning. The Character Designer, covered in the following section, can be used to change the style for individual characters.

> **Note**
>
> FrameMaker's regular font menu shows only the name of the font family, not the individual styles. This is unlike most other Mac programs and is sometimes confusing till you get used to it. Individual styles in a font family are selected by choosing Style from the Format menu, or as part of the Default font properties in the Paragraph Designer.

■ *Pagination.* This window establishes whether a paragraph will have a normal style, whether it should begin where it falls or at a specific location on the page, and whether the paragraph will be used as a running head or a side-head. The side head is FrameMaker's unique contribution to desktop publishing. It allows a headline of text to extend beyond the left or right margin of a column of text. Figure 21.16 shows a side head.

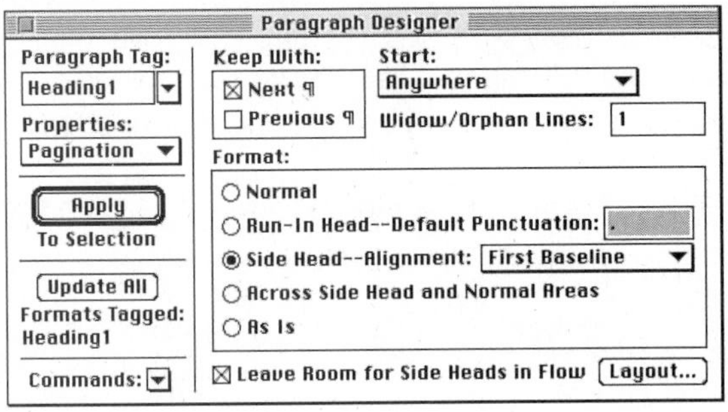

Fig. 21.16
Side heads can
be formatted
automatically in
FrameMaker's
Paragraph
Designer.

■ *Numbering.* This window allows you to set an automatic numbering format for paragraphs. If a paragraph is moved out of sequence, the numbers will be changed to reflect the new location.

■ *Advanced.* This is your tool for setting special typographic formatting. There are adjustments for hyphenation and word spacing, and an adjustment for rules above or below the paragraph.

■ *Table cell.* When used together with FrameMaker's sophisticated table editor, you can format each cell separately. You can set the amount of space between the border of the cell and the text and whether it will be top, center, or bottom aligned within the cell.

The Paragraph Designer can be used to change the format of a single selected area of text, or all text having the same style name. Once you've created your paragraph formats, you can export them to other documents.

Your completed paragraph styles are saved in what is called a *Catalog*, and
you can click the paragraph icon at the top right of your application window
to bring up a floating palette of styles, as shown in figure 21.17. To change
the style of a selected paragraph, just click the style's name in the catalog
palette.

Fig. 21.17
FrameMaker's
Paragraph Catalog
Palette.

Using FrameMaker's Character Designer

When you apply a new style to a paragraph, normally all the text in that
paragraph will take on the characteristics of the format. But you can also
create a separate set of styles for individual characters, so you can easily select
italic or bold for emphasis, once you've created the right format.

The Character Designer, shown in figure 21.18, consists of a single window
that you use to make your basic paragraph settings. Once you've set your
character settings, you can apply them from a palette that's accessed by clicking the icon at the upper right of your document window.

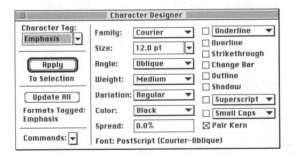

Fig. 21.18
FrameMaker's
Character Designer
changes the format
of individual
characters without
affecting para-
graph formatting.

Using FrameMaker's Spelling Checker and Thesaurus

Once your text has been written, you'll find the program has a capable spelling checker and thesaurus to check your text. If you're just looking for the
correct word to apply to a particular situation, you highlight the word you
want to change, and bring up the Thesaurus from the Edit menu, or press
⌘-Shift-T, as was done in figure 21.19.

Fig. 21.19
Finding the
right word in
FrameMaker.

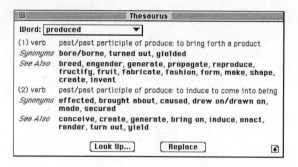

The next step is to spell check your document, by selecting Spelling Checker in the File menu or just typing ⌘-L. While spell checking is in progress, as shown in figure 21.20, you'll have the option to correct misspellings, ignore flagged words, or add new words to the program's custom dictionary.

Fig. 21.20
FrameMaker tries
to catch your
spelling errors.

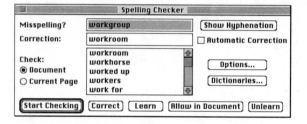

Using Illustrations in FrameMaker

When you want to add an illustration to your FrameMaker document, you can import or place a picture from your favorite illustration software, or create one from scratch.

Before I try my own hand at drawing a picture, I'll import one from one of my favorite illustration programs. First select Import File from the File menu, and choose File from the sub-menu. You have two options when you place a picture in your FrameMaker document, as shown in figure 21.21.

Normally you'd import by reference, as you do in other publishing software. The document carries a low-resolution PICT representation of your picture, and a link is established to the original graphic. When you print your document, the information contained in that graphic is downloaded to your printer, too.

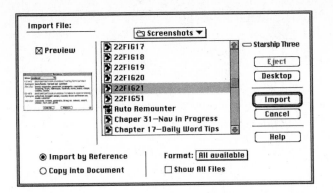

Fig. 21.21
FrameMaker's Import File dialog box.

The second option, Copy into Document, actually incorporates your graphic file into your FrameMaker document. This has the advantage of freeing you from worrying about the original graphic, and you don't have to bring that file with you if you take your file to a service bureau for high resolution output. But you still have to keep the original on hand to reimport in case you want to change it. And the side-effect is to make your FrameMaker file much, much larger.

Most popular graphic formats, such as EPS, PICT and TIFF, are supported by FrameMaker. You'll see a small preview of your picture before it's imported. Just select the file you want to bring in and click the Import button. If the picture is a PICT or TIFF file, you'll bring up a Scaling window, as shown in figure 21.22, which allows you to scale the picture before it finally shows up in your document.

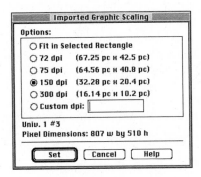

Fig. 21.22
FrameMaker's Graphic Scaling window.

FrameMaker is not intended to replace such sophisticated PostScript drawing tools as Adobe Illustrator or Aldus FreeHand, which is discussed in Chapter 23, "Drawing and Painting." But for simple drawings, FrameMaker is sufficient. To create an illustration in your document, choose Tools from the Graphics menu or press ⌘-3, or select the triangle icon from the upper right of your document window. Either way, you'll bring up a familiar set of drawing tools, as shown in figure 21.23.

Fig. 21.23
FrameMaker's set of drawing tools.

After you design the basic shape of your drawing, you can use the pen and fill patterns offered by the program to enhance your drawing. You can choose from a selection of black and white or color patterns.

Using FrameMaker's Table Tools

Just about any table you can imagine can be created quickly with FrameMaker's table creation tools. It's an area in which this program excels over all other publishing software, and most word processing programs as well. You can control every element of your table, from the basic shape, to the formatting of text and graphics and the positioning of that text inside the table.

Tables can also be copied from one place to another inside a document or from one document to another. For now, we'll just create a simple table and give you an idea of how easily it's done. To begin, choose Insert Table from the Table menu, which opens the window shown in figure 21.24.

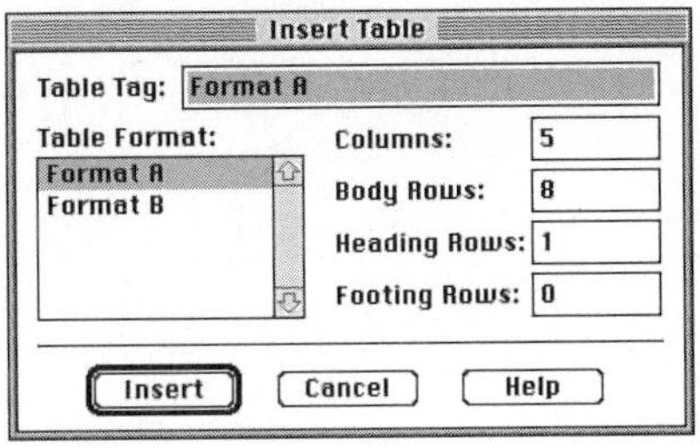

Fig. 21.24
Building a table
from scratch is
quick work in
FrameMaker.

Your table consists of columns and rows, and a single column of a single row
in the table is considered a cell. Once you've specified how many columns
and rows your table will have, you click the Insert button, which will place
the new table at your cursor's insertion point in your document, as shown in
figure 21.25.

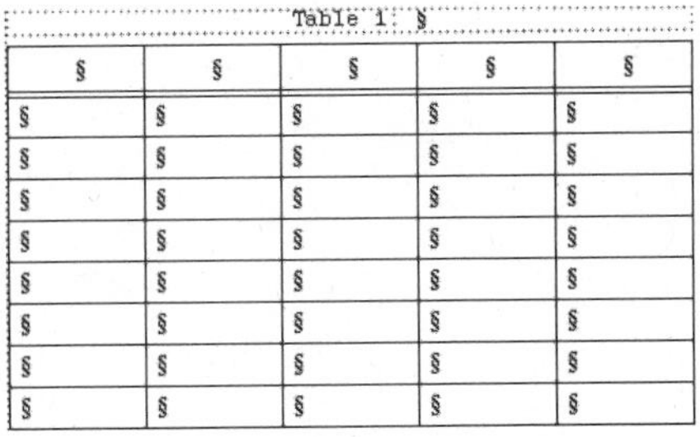

Fig. 21.25
Building the
outlines of your
new table.

Before you begin to enter your text, you can resize and modify your table to
your heart's content, till it meets your expectations. When you click the
table, you can drag the selection handles at the right or left of the table to
increase its width. You can use both the Paragraph and Character Designer
windows, described above, to modify formatting. Text and graphics can be
separately aligned in each cell. Your topmost row, for example, can have
centered headlines, and your body copy in the rows below can be set flush
left or rotated. We've created a sample table, shown in figure 21.26, to give
you a general idea of how it shapes up.

There is one more FrameMaker Designer to discuss—the Table Designer. You
will find it in the Table Menu, and it allows you to customize your tables still
further. The first pull-down menu, showing Basic cell properties, as shown in
figure 21.27, allows you to set cell spacing, margins, and the positioning of
the table.

Fig. 21.26

Each cell in a table can receive its own special formatting.

Table 1§				
Sales§	**1991**§	**1992**§	**1993**§	**1994**§
Gene§	$22,000§	$23,000§	$24,000§	$25,000§
John§	$27,020§	$28,930§	$29,300§	$30,200§
Peter§	$35,000§	$36,000§	$37,240§	$38,093§
Chip§	$31,000§	$35,000§	$41,200§	$45,300§
Tom§	$54,111§	$35,000§	$24,000§	$36,000§
Nancy§	$24,00§	N/A§	$32,000§	$24,000§
Ruth§	$19,200§	$31,000§	$34,000§	$35,000§
Barbara§	$21,000§	N/A§	$48,000§	$54.000§

Fig. 21.27

Using FrameMaker's handy Table Designer to customize spacing and table positioning.

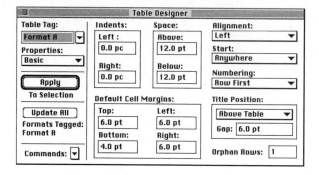

To give your table a fancy look, you'll want to choose the third selection in the Properties pull-down menu in the Table Designer. It controls shading. You can add a fill to the headlines, for example, and leave the body copy alone, as shown in figure 21.28, or apply a fill to the entire table.

Fig. 21.28

Shading headlines to give your table a bit of sparkle.

Table 1§				
Sales§	**1991**§	**1992**§	**1993**§	**1994**§
Gene§	$22,000§	$23,000§	$24,000§	$25,000§
John§	$27,020§	$28,930§	$29,300§	$30,200§
Peter§	$35,000§	$36,000§	$37,240§	$38,093§
Chip§	$31,000§	$35,000§	$41,200§	$45,300§
Tom§	$54,111§	$35,000§	$24,000§	$36,000§
Nancy§	$24,00§	N/A§	$32,000§	$24,000§
Ruth§	$19,200§	$31,000§	$34,000§	$35,000§
Barbara§	$21,000§	N/A§	$48,000§	$54.000§

As with the Paragraph and Character Designer, you can apply your changes to a single table or all tables in your document that have the same format name.

FrameMaker's Advanced Features

Just describing FrameMaker's features can take a book in itself. The steps we've described are relatively easy to master, and they allow you to create a wide variety of documents, from a basic form letter to a school textbook or technical manual. Here are some of FrameMaker's power user features that, despite their sophistication, are not all that difficult to learn once you've mastered the basics.

- You can automatically generate an index and/or table of contents, by applying styles or tags to portions of text. Once your document is completed, you can use FrameMaker's Generate/Book feature, found in the File menu, to build the index and table of contents from a single document or a group of documents.

- FrameMaker's Equation palette allows you to easily build all manner of equations. The program will check your equation syntax as you type your equation, and display a question mark where an additional figure or argument needs to be inserted. Each symbol of your equation can be selected from the palette, shown in figure 21.29. Just click the kind of element you want, and it will appear at the insertion point in your document.

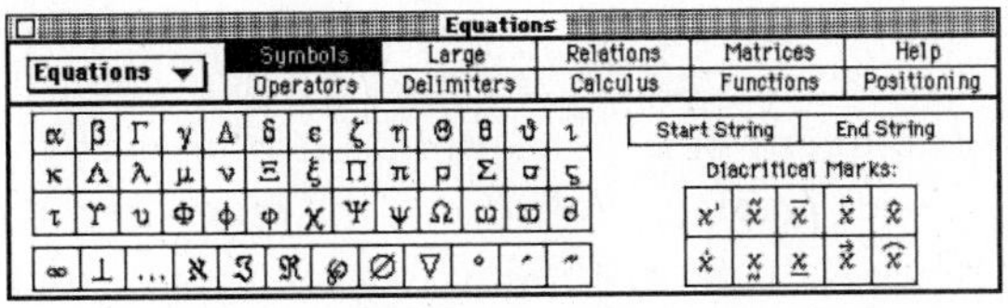

Fig. 21.29
A choice palette of ready-to-use symbols to help you easily create the most complex equations for your document.

- FrameMaker uses hypertext cross-references that allow you to click a portion of your document, and immediately be taken to another part of the document that contains related material. Formatting the cross-references are done with styles or tags, same as a table of contents or index.

- FrameMaker provides document comparison tools that allow different versions of a single document to be examined for updates. This feature is useful when creating a publication in a workgroup environment, where separate copies of the same document may be revised on different computers, even in an office that uses Macs, Windows computers, and Unix workstations.

Getting the Most Out of FrameMaker: Hot Tips

- Use FrameMaker's powerful search feature to locate text in every element of your document, including style tags and headers and footers.

- When you need a quick answer to a problem while creating a FrameMaker document, press ⌘-/, which will change the cursor into a question mark, and click the command you want to know more about to bring up an informative Help window.

- By clicking on a head and then applying a new format with the Paragraph Designer, you can apply the new format, say a side head or a running head, to just that headline or all headlines in that document that have the same attributes.

- You can import and export formats, including master page setups, between documents.

- You can click the toolbar to select any of four different QuickAccess views, which include text formatting, graphic creation, graphic editing, and table editing.

- If your FrameMaker document needs to be exported to the Windows or UNIX environments, your documents are binary compatible, so they can be opened in any of these platforms. If you select Windows compatibility in your program preferences, the program will warn you if the file name exceeds the DOS/Windows naming convention.

- Character and paragraph formats, document setup, tables, color definitions and other document characteristics can be stored in a master template, which can be used as a format library. Any of these attributes can be separately and seamlessly imported into a new document,

- You can use FrameMaker's conditional text feature to offer several variations of a single document. To use this feature, you go to Special menu, select Conditional Text, and use the Edit option. Then you highlight the material that will be considered conditional, then apply that condition to a specific portion of the document, whether text, tables or graphics.

- Use FrameMaker's status line display at the bottom of your document window to check formatting and other characteristics of your document.

■ Almost every major feature in FrameMaker has a keyboard shortcut, and sometimes several shortcuts. They're all spelled out in the Quick Reference guide that ships with the program.

■ In the Power Macintosh version of FrameMaker, you have a special command that allows you to take a FrameMaker equation and have it run on Apple's Graphing Calculator. The resulting graphic image can then be copied into your FrameMaker document.

Using QuarkXPress 3.5

Quark, Inc. was founded in 1981 as a developer of software for the Apple II and the Apple III platforms. Typeface, an Apple III typesetting program released in 1982, is considered a forerunner of QuarkXPress, which debuted in 1987. QuarkXPress offers high end document creation features such as color separations, trapping, multiple color models, and advanced hyphenation and kerning tools. Despite its sophistication, the learning curve is nowhere near as steep as it used to be. Anyone reasonably skilled on a Macintosh should be able to pick up this program in short order.

System Requirements

QuarkXPress will work on any Mac running System 6.0.5 or later, with 4MB or more of installed RAM. Fully configured, the program uses around 6MB of disk space. The Power Macintosh version adds about 1MB to application size, and an additional 2MB to system memory requirements.

Getting Started in QuarkXPress

Before covering some of the features of QuarkXPress, I want to give you an idea of how the program operates. Once you get the hang of it, you'll find QuarkXPress is as easy to learn as any of the other publishing programs covered in this chapter. QuarkXPress uses a frame metaphor. All of your text is contained in text boxes, which you define before creating or importing text. All of your pictures are in picture boxes. These are the building blocks for your documents.

Aldus PageMaker uses a single pasteboard for the entire document. QuarkXPress establishes a separate pasteboard area for each page or spread. This has the advantage of giving you more room to stuff text and picture elements, but it sometimes means that unused elements aren't seen once you switch to another page, and may be forgotten or ignored (and besides they increase the size of your document).

To create a blank QuarkXPress document, select New from the File menu (and choose Document from the sub-menu), or press ⌘-N, which displays the Page setup window shown in figure 21.30. (The Page Sets box shown at the upper right of the window only appears if you are using a QuarkXTension called Kitchen Sink, described later in this chapter.) The measurements shown may differ depending on the size of the last document you created.

Fig. 21.30
Create the basic layout of your QuarkXPress document.

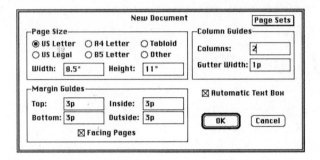

You can establish settings for page size, page margins, the number of columns and the space between columns. That little item at the upper right corner of the window, Page Sets, is part of a neat little add-on to QuarkXPress, Kitchen Sink, which we'll discuss in more detail a bit later on.

A Tour of QuarkXPress's Pasteboard

Your blank QuarkXPress document contains a text box, with the margins and columns you've just established, as shown in figure 21.31. If you don't have a large monitor, the page will be scaled to fit the size of your screen, aligned to the left. If you chose Facing Pages in your document setup box, all pages past page 1 will appear on your screen as a two-up spread.

Fig. 21.31
Your new QuarkXPress document, ready for you to add text and graphics.

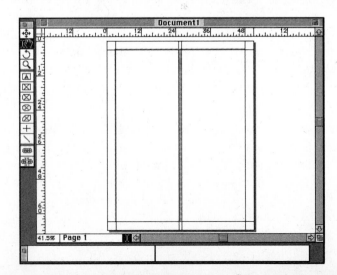

At this point, you can continue to format your document and create style sheets, or you can click the textbox, and begin typing away. QuarkXPress has a default text style, called Normal, that is in effect on every new text box you create. As we'll explain later on, you can change this default style whenever you wish.

Using QuarkXPress's Tool Palette

QuarkXPress has several floating palettes, and like other Macintosh software, basic functions are activated with a click of the Tool Palette. Some of these Tool icons are a little different from other programs and deserve further explanation.

Table 21.2   QuarkXPress's Tool Palette

Tool	Use
✛	*The Item Tool.* This tool is used to move, group, ungroup, and cut, copy, and paste text and picture boxes and rules.
🖐	*The Content Tool.* This is your default tool, when you click a text or picture box. You can enter and edit text, and modify and scale pictures.
↺	*The Rotation Tool.* This tool is used to freely rotate text and picture boxes. This tool is about as precise as the one in PageMaker, so you are better off specifying rotation manually, using the famous *QuarkXPress Measurement Palette*, which we'll discuss shortly.
🔍	*The Zoom Tool.* This tool is used to enlarge or reduce the view scale in your document window.
Ⓐ	*The Text Box Tool.* This tool is used to create your text box.
⊠	*Rectangular Picture Box Tool.* This tool is used to create your picture box. Holding down Shift constrains the rectangle to a square.
⊗	*Rounded-corner Rectangle Picture Box Tool.* This tool is used to create a rectangular picture box with rounded corners. Holding down Shift constrains the rectangle to a square.
⊗	*Oval Picture Box Tool.* This tool is used to create an oval picture box. Holding down Shift constrains the oval to a circle.
⊘	*Polygon Picture Box Tool.* You use this tool to create a variably shaped polygon picture box.

(continues)

Table 21.2 Continued	
Tool	**Use**
⊞	*Orthogonal Line Tool.* Not as obscure as it sounds. This tool is used to create a vertical or horizontal rule.
◹	*Line Tool.* This tool is used to create rules at an angle. Holding Shift constrains the line to 45-degree angles, producing results that can be the same as the tool above (so long as lines are constrained to horizontal or vertical positions).
▦	*Linking Tool.* This tool is used to flow text from one text box to another by linking them. The default setting in QuarkXPress generally allows text to flow automatically from one text box to another.
▦	*Unlinking Tool.* This tool is used to break the text flow between text boxes.

Using QuarkXPress' Style Sheets

Formatting style sheets in QuarkXPress is similar to PageMaker. You can create and edit paragraph styles by selecting Style Sheets menu in the Edit menu. After a style is created, it appears in the floating Style Sheets Palette, shown in figure 21.32. This palette can be displayed or hidden through the View menu. As explained in the preceding section, the Normal style is your default document text setting, which you are free to change to your taste.

Fig. 21.32
QuarkXPress' Style
Sheets Palette.

If you want to change a style, simply hold ⌘ and click the style's name shown in the palette, which will bring up the window we've illustrated in figure 21.33.

Every element of your paragraph, including whether to include rules above and below it, can be established as a style sheet. Like Microsoft Word, you have a Next Style pop-up menu, which allows you to automatically activate another style, when you press the Return key. This is useful for setting subheads, as the Return key will switch you to the next style, most often for the body text. Local text changes, such as using italic or bold for emphasis, don't change when you switch styles, unless you hold the Option key. That choice removes all local changes to the style sheets.

Edit Style Sheet

Name:

Text

Keyboard Equivalent:

keypad 1

Based on: *No Style*

Next Style: Text

Character
Formats
Rules
Tabs

TimesNewRomanPS; 10 pt; Plain; Black; Shade: 100%; Track Amount: 0;
Horiz Scale: 100%; Alignment: Justified; Left Indent: 0p; First Line: p10;
Right Indent: 0p; Leading: 12 pt; Space Before: 0p; Space After: 0p; Next
Style: Text;

OK   Cancel

Fig. 21.33
QuarkXPress's
easy-to-use style
sheet editor.

Using QuarkXPress' Measurement Palette

The programmers at Quark had the right idea here. It has proven popular
with users of the program, and has been imitated elsewhere, such as in Aldus
PageMaker. QuarkXPress' Measurement Palette, shown in figure 21.34, is a
simple tool that you can use to easily modify the attributes of a text or picture box.

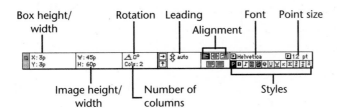

Fig. 21.34
QuarkXPress'
Measurement
Palette allows you
to easily change
settings in text and
picture boxes.

The Measurement Palette consists of two parts, and the look changes depending on the sort of element you've selected. If you've selected a text box, for
example, the displays on the left half of the palette are used to control the
location of a textbox, whether it's rotated or not, and how many columns it
has. The display at the right applies to the content of the box. It allows you
to change typeface, size, line spacing, styles, such as bold, italic, or underlined, or whether the text is set flush left, right, centered, or justified. A right
arrow indicates a pop-up menu. So if you click the area to the left of the
name of the typeface you're using, you'll see a reduced-sized font menu, as
shown in figure 21.35.

Fig. 21.35
Choose your fonts
from a convenient
pop-up menu on
QuarkXPress'
Measurement
Palette.

If you've selected a picture box, the Measurement Palette will take on a different identity, as shown in figure 21.36. The selections at the left are similar to
the ones shown when a text box is selected, and can be used for adjusting the
position and rotation of your picture box.

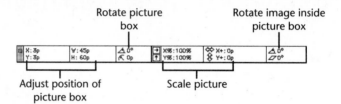

Fig. 21.36
The Measurement
Palette changes its
look when a
picture box is
selected.

At the right of the Measurement Palette are settings for adjusting and scaling
your graphic inside the picture box. You can rotate this picture separate from
the picture box itself, which provides additional control over the look of your
document.

Document Layout Palette

The Document Layout Palette in QuarkXPress is a convenient way to navigate
from page to page, as shown in figure 21.37. You can hide/display this palette
by selecting the Hide (Show) Document Layout command in the View menu.
Once the palette is displayed, just double-click the icon bearing the number
of the page you want to switch to. You can also reorder the positioning of the
page by selecting its icon and dragging it to another position in the layout.
The vertical rule separates left and right hand pages.

Fig. 21.37
Page navigation
and order
switching made
simple with
QuarkXPress'
Document Layout
Palette.

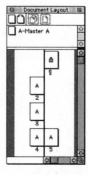

In addition to going to another page or moving them about in your layout, you can delete a page (which will bring up a confirming dialog) or apply a master page to it.

Using Master Pages in QuarkXPress

QuarkXPress's master pages are enormously flexible. You can create up to 127 master pages for each document, and unlike FrameMaker or PageMaker, you can edit the elements from your master page in your regular document pages. Using the Document Layout Palette described in the preceding section, you can apply any master page to any selected page in your document. This is a useful tool if you decide you want to change the master pages that apply to individual pages.

With so many master pages available, you can customize each one with a different set of recurring text, numbers, or illustrations. To create or modify a master page you can double click it in the Document Layout Palette, or choose Display Master-from the Page menu. Except for a few wrinkles, the master page, shown in figure 21.38, looks very much like your regular document page.

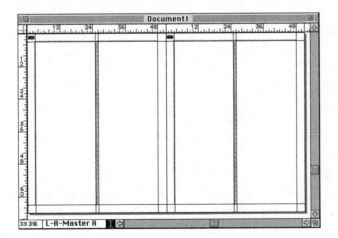

Fig. 21.38
A QuarkXPress master page.

That little wrinkle I referred to is that little "link" icon at the upper left of your document window. Normally, automatic linking between the text boxes on adjacent pages is automatic. But you can use this feature to unlink your master page, in case you don't want your text to automatically flow to another page.

IV

Macintosh Software

Creating Text in QuarkXPress

QuarkXPress has a decent word processing engine, so you can easily enter text in your document without the need to import it from a word processing document. You can spell check your document, and find and change text and formatting.

But if your layout is complex, with type snaking around graphics, and consists of a number of columns, you might find that the going gets a bit slow, especially if your Mac offers less than Quadra level performance. So don't be prepared to toss that word processor just yet. Like PageMaker, QuarkXPress will import style sheets generated in Microsoft Word.

Advanced QuarkXPress Features

QuarkXPress has been the program of choice for a number of newspaper and magazine publishers, so it goes without saying that there are a wealth of sophisticated tools to create and format your document. Following are a few of QuarkXPress's high-end features:

- *Automatic Trapping.* When you are printing color separations, you need to deal with such issues as trapping. Trapping is a means of compensating for misalignment of colors that occurs when you are printing a multi-color document. QuarkXPress allows you to customize trap information in your document, for better printing results.

- *Color Separations.* QuarkXPress can create spot and process color separations. Such color libraries as DIC, Focoltone, PANTONE, Toyo, and Trumatch are supported with on-screen representations.

- *Vertical Justification.* Both line spacing in a paragraph and between paragraphs can be adjusted automatically, so your text fills an entire text block.

- *Reshaping Picture or Text Boxes.* Not only can your text box be a rectangle or a square, but you can also reshape your text box (or a picture box), with the options shown in figure 21.39.

Fig. 21.39
You can reshape your text box to provide special graphic effects in QuarkXPress.

QuarkXTensions

A QuarkXPress XTension is, in its own way, very much like the Extensions you use to enhance the functions of the Mac operating system. Only in this case, the enhancements are provided to QuarkXPress, and give it capabilities that aren't included in the core program. We'll cover two popular XTensions here. There are dozens, and they're all available through a mail order dealer, XChange, whom you can call at 800-788-7557.

Vision Contents

This XTension, from Visions Edge, as shown in figure 21.40, allows you to automatically generate a table of contents in your QuarkXPress document.

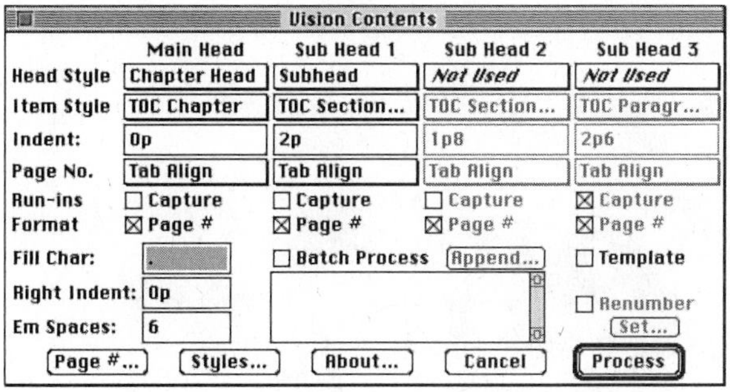

Fig. 21.40
One of the many QuarkXPress XTensions to enhance the program's feature-set.

Vision Contents will automatically recognize heads and subheads in a document, or among a group of documents, and allow you to quickly build an accurate table of contents, fully formatted and ready to print.

Kitchen Sink

A few words cannot do justice to this XTension, from programmer Paul Schmitt's *a lowly apprentice productions* (or alap for short). You can customize your document settings in a number of ways, such as automatically opening your file on the last page you were working on when the document was closed, or building a library of default document page setups. The Co-Pilot feature, shown in figure 21.41, allows you to click an iconic representation of your document or spread, and immediately go to that position in the actual document itself.

Fig. 21.41
You can do just about everything with alap's Kitchen Sink XTension for QuarkXPress.

Another feature, Command Pad, opens a floating palette with icons representing commonly-used functions when a specific XPress tool is selected. You can change views up to 1200% of the original size, and add flash and flourish to your document windows with the XTension's customizing options.

Getting The Most Out Of QuarkXPress: Hints and Tips

> **Note**
>
> Some of the tips below, which are the favorites of some of Quark's own technical support people, require version 3.3 or later.

- To automatically indent copy at a given point in a paragraph, say after a bullet or a number, press ⌘-\, which is the QuarkXPress Indent Here command. All copy in a paragraph will now be aligned at the point where the indent is established.

- If you have a crash when opening a specific page in an XPress document that contains pictures, hold ⌘ when opening the QuarkXPress document (in version 3.3) to automatically reimport all graphics. This will help in situations where bad screen PICTs are causing crashes.

- The free Thing-a-ma-Bob XTension from Quark contains a feature that will create true typographic piece fractions from a selected set of numbers.

- To quickly change an automatic page number, select a page in the Document Layout palette and press the page window in the lower left-hand corner to bring up the section window.

- Click once on the number below the page icon in the Document Layout Palette to view that page. This is cool, because you don't have to double-click a page to go to it and you can navigate between pages while keeping a separate page or page range selected.

- If you're encountering a Postscript error when printing, try printing in Rough mode, in the Print dialog box. This will suppress all the graphic images in the document and print only QuarkXPress elements and text. If the document prints, you know the error is related to an imported graphic.

- The Get Text dialog now has sticky buttons. Once Include Style Sheets is pressed, it stays pressed.

- QuarkXPress 3.3 allows you to shade a grayscale TIFF through the Shade item in the Style Menu. In previous versions of the program, you were able to do this only under Other Contrast functions.

- In traditional typesetting, dot leaders, such as those used on an order form, are generally done with wordspace between the leader character. QuarkXPress allows you to establish two character leaders, using any two characters, in the Tab setup box.

- To scale a picture to automatically fill a picture box, press ⌘-Option-Shift-F. This command will retain the picture's proportions; as a result, the graphic may not precisely fill the picture box, if the proportions are different. ⌘-Shift-F will change the proportions of the graphic object, as needed, to fill the picture box.

Using Ready,Set,Go 6

Manhattan Graphics was a traditional typesetting and printing company that was established in New York City in the early 1970s. Work on Ready,Set,Go started in 1984, when the first Macs shipped, and version 1.0 of Ready,Set,Go first appeared in January 1985, months ahead of Aldus PageMaker, thus making it one of the first desktop publishing programs to be introduced for the Macintosh, but it's had a long and somewhat checkered history, as we'll explain. Version 3.0, which appeared in November 1986, was the first publishing program to include automatic hyphenation, something that's taken for granted in publishing and word processing software today.

Manhattan Graphics transferred marketing rights to Letraset in 1987, but continued to develop the program. A high-end version, DesignStudio, appeared early in 1990. The new version featured an extensible architecture that supported modules known as Annexes, which are similar to a QuarkXPress XTension, automatic vertical justification, four-color separations and other publishing tools that later showed up in other desktop publishing software.

The original release of DesignStudio was less than a success in the marketplace, in part because of the name change and price increase, according to its publisher. Finally, the rights to the program reverted to its developer, Manhattan Graphics, who lowered the price to $395 and restored the original name. They have continued to develop Ready,Set,Go and improve its range of highend publishing features.

System Requirements

In addition to its slim price tag, Ready,Set,Go has modest RAM and storage requirements. It will work on any Macintosh computer with 2MB of RAM running System 6 or later, and requires 4MB RAM for System 7.0 or later. The installed program consumes less than 4MB space on your hard drive, including the full stock of Claris XTend translators.

Getting Started in Ready,Set,Go

If you are familiar with QuarkXPress, you will find some of the features of Ready,Set,Go are not dissimilar. Like XPress, Ready,Set,Go places text in a text box, and pictures in a picture box. These elements form the cornerstone of your document.

You'll probably find familiar aspects in other areas of Ready,Set,Go. The Tool Bar seems to have elements of both XPress and PageMaker in it, but it has its own individual feel. Ready,Set,Go's pasteboard, like PageMaker's, consists of a single workspace that applies to all pages in your document.

A Tour of Ready,Set,Go's Pasteboard

When you first launch Ready,Set,Go, it creates a default, untitled document, with a series of floating palettes surrounding it, as shown in figure 21.42.

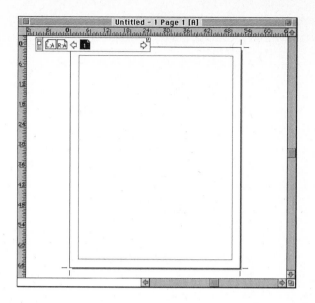

Fig. 21.42
An untitled
Ready,Set,Go
document.

IV

Macintosh Software

The number icons on the floating palette at the top of your screen represent page numbers and, at the left, master pages. All of these palettes may be moved around your screen, in whatever location you choose.

Your Ready,Set,Go document page is blank. In order for you to enter text or graphics, you first have to create a frame, using one of the tools that are provided. We'll review those tools next.

Using Ready,Set,Go's Tool Bar

Ready,Set,Go's Tool Bar has its own unique touches, though everything is marked reasonably clearly as to function, as listed in Table 21.3. The tools are covered as they appear, from left to right, row by row.

Table 21.3 Ready,Set,Go's Tool Bar	
Tool	**Use**
▶	*Object Pointer Tool.* This tool is used to select objects and to move objects around your document page.
↺	*Rotation Tool.* This tool is used to freely rotate selected text and picture objects. As you rotate the object, you'll see the angle of rotation displayed at the bottom left of your document window. If you want exact precision, you might make these settings numerically in the text and picture block setup windows.

(continues)

Table 21.3 Continued

Tool	Use
	Hand Tool. When you click this tool, the pointer changes to a hand and you can move your document page dynamically across your Mac's screen.
	Zoom Tool. This tool is used to enlarge or reduce the view scale in your document window.
	Text Block Tool. This tool is used to create text blocks.
	I-beam Pointer Tool. After your text block has been created, you click this tool and then on your text block to enter or edit text.
	Linking Tool. This tool is used to direct text flow by linking one text block to another. Text flow can be also established automatically for newly created pages.
	Rectangular Tool. This drawing tool is used to create a rectangular box. You can constrain it to a square by holding Shift.
	Picture Block Tool. This tool is used to create a picture block to hold your document's graphics.
	Cropping Tool. This tool is used to crop graphics.
	Line Tool. This tool is used to create lines constrained to 90 degree angles.
	Diagonal Line Tool. This tool is used to create lines at an angle. If you hold Shift, the lines will be constrained to 45 degree angles.
	Rounded Box Tool. This tool is used to create a box with rounded corners. Holding down Shift constrains it to a square with rounded corners.
	Oval Tool. This tool is used to create an ellipse, or, when you hold Shift, a circle.
	Polygon Tool. This tool is used to create a polygon, an object containing more than three angles.
	Polygon Editing Tool. This tool is used to add or delete points, in order to customize the shape of the polygon.

Using Ready,Set,Go's Style Sheets

Ready,Set,Go has a sophisticated style sheet editor that works on both the paragraph and character level. To create a style sheet, choose Styles from the

Document menu, or type ⌘-H. Then select New from the window, which opens a dialog box like the one shown in figure 21.43. You can establish all the major formatting of your paragraph, from typeface, style, leading and alignment, to kerning, tracking and whether or not to hyphenate, in the Style Specifications Box.

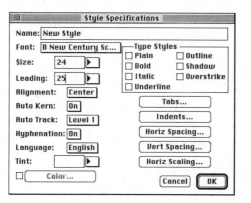

Fig. 21.43
Ready,Set,Go's
Style Specifications
box.

As with other publishing software, you can highlight a block of text, and have the format appear in your Style Specifications box. If you want to use the style sheets from another document, you can easily import those styles to your new document. Your finished styles appear in a Style palette, as shown in figure 21.44, which actually doesn't show up on your screen (except for its title bar) until a style has been created. You can display this palette by selecting the Document menu, choosing Palettes, and highlighting Show Styles.

Fig. 21.44
Ready,Set,Go's
Style palette.

Using Ready,Set,Go's Floating Palettes

Ready,Set,Go doesn't have a Measurement Palette or a Control Palette quite like those found in its two higher-cost competitors. Instead, it offers two separate palettes that provide many of the same functions. The palette shown in figure 21.45 shows text attributes.

The Typography Palette displays your basic text formatting, such as typeface, size, style, leading and alignment (such as flush left, flush right, centered or justified). Other text formatting is done from the Format menu or from the Style palette.

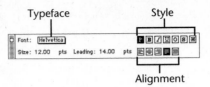

Fig. 21.45

Ready,Set,Go's
Typography
palette.

The Specifications palette, shown in figure 21.46, is used to change the size and position of a text or picture block.

To change the size and position, just click the appropriate specification in the palette, and enter the changes you want to make.

Fig. 21.46

Adjusting the size
and position of a
text or picture
block.

Using Ready,Set,Go's Text Blocks

Ready,Set,Go's text blocks offer an extraordinary degree of flexibility in addition to basic size and position settings. You can bring up the Text Block Specifications box by double-clicking on a text block with the Object Pointer tool selected, or press ⌘-M, as we've done in figure 21.47.

Fig. 21.47

Just a glimmer of
what lies beneath
the surface in
Ready,Set,Go.

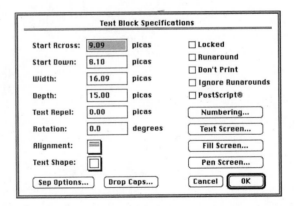

In addition to setting size and position, you can set the degree of rotation and where the text will align on the page. The graphical pull-down menu labeled Alignment lets you have text align automatically at the top of the page, at the center, or at the bottom. Additional settings allow for two varieties of vertical justification, to spread either individual lines or the space between paragraphs, to fill a text block. The Text Shape option changes the shape of the text block from a rectangle to a variety of shapes, from ellipses to polygons.

Sep Options controls Ready,Set,Go's sophisticated automatic color trapping tools. Drop Caps creates automatic drop caps at the top of your text block, and offers you the choice of typeface, color, and separate trapping options. There are additional settings for ruled borders (Pen Screen) and fills (Fill Screen).

Ready,Set,Go's picture box offers an equally flexible range of settings, along with the ability to have overlapping text run around a graphic.

Using Master Pages in Ready,Set,Go

Your Ready,Set,Go document can be formatted with up to 54 separate master pages, 27 left, 27 right. Each master page can contain text and picture blocks that will appear automatically on the page to which they apply. Like FrameMaker and PageMaker, the items you place on a master page cannot be edited on a document page.

Creating Text in Ready,Set,Go

Ready,Set,Go uses Claris XTend translators to import text in many popular word processing formats. These same translators can be shared with other programs that support XTend technology, offering you a lot of flexibility. But you don't have to go to another program for your text. Ready,Set,Go has its own word processing tools that are good enough for many users. You can find and replace text, using format and style. And there's a decent spell checker at hand as well, as shown in figure 21.48.

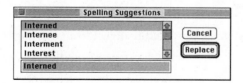

Fig. 21.48
Ready,Set,Go finds your spelling errors before your readers do.

The only disconcerting aspect of Ready,Set,Go's word processing capabilities is its means of handling justified text. As you type characters, they seem to fly across the page, which sometimes becomes distracting. Experienced users of the program will set text in flush left mode, than switch to justified mode when they're finishing typing.

Advanced Ready,Set,Go Features

As you've seen so far, Ready,Set,Go offers much of the power and sophisticated document creating abilities of programs costing twice as much. Here's some additional features that make this program attractive for many users.

- Ready,Set,Go can create spot and process color separations, and supports RGB, TIFF, RIFF, and EPSF files. The Pantone color library is supported.

- You can import QuickTime movies and include them as part of your document. Just double-click the movie icon and use the player controls to view your movie.

- Like Aldus PageMaker, and QuarkXPress, Ready,Set,Go has an extensible architecture. The software ships with several Annexes, as shown in figure 21.49. The format is open for third-party programmers to provide additional modules.

Fig. 21.49
Ready,Set,Go's Annexes provide room for additional features for this publishing program.

```
Auto Kern Specs...
Auto Track Specs...
Character/Word Count...
Fonts Used...
Open Script...
Pictures Used...
Save Page/Spread As EPS...
Slide Show...
Strip Fonts...
```

Getting The Most Out Of Ready,Set,Go: Hints and Tips

- When copying a text or picture object from one page to another, the object will appear in the exact same position as on the original page.

- If you hold the Option-Shift-C key, the selected text and picture objects will automatically center in the middle of the page.

- If you have a text of a certain size and press the ⌘-\ keys, the text will automatically be scaled to fit within the text box. This feature works in graphics as well. You can also select the Scale to Fit function from the Text menu for text, and the Scale Graphic to Block command from the Graphics menu for graphics.

■ If you press ⌘-/ while a text block is selected, it will scale the textbox to the size of the text. The same results occur with a picture box.

■ If you highlight some text, and hold the ⌘-[, the formatting for that text, such as fonts, size, leading and kerning, will be copied. You can transfer the text styling to another text area by selecting that text and typing ⌘-].

■ In Ready,Set,Go, you can establish text glossaries, similar to the feature used in Microsoft Word. You highlight text, select Glossaries, then Text from the Document menu, click Define and name the Glossary. From now on, whenever you press ⌘-G, click the Glossary name and click, the text in the selected Glossary will be inserted at the cursor. You can also use the Edit Paste Glossary command if you don't want to bring up the Glossary dialog box. A similar feature is available for graphics. Graphic objects stored in the Glossary will be placed in the same location as they were when they were originally stored.

■ To assign a master or default page to a particular page, click and hold the page icon in the page palette at the top of your document window, and you will bring up a Grid menu showing your available master pages. Simply highlight the master page you want, and it will be applied automatically to that page. You will see the name of the current page and its associated master page in the title bar of the document window.

■ For foreign language composition, you can set hyphenation and language on a style sheet. You can also apply hyphenation and spelling dictionaries to single paragraphs. (Foreign language dictionaries are an optional extra.)

Summary

Choosing a publishing software package is a matter of personal taste. We've covered the highlights of the major programs here, and I hope you'll use it as a guide in deciding which program to buy. If you are already a user of an existing publishing software product, I hope my capsule descriptions will help you explore other options that might be available. Having more than one program at hand is very common among desktop publishing professionals these days.

Conclusions and Recommendations

If your document creation aspirations are modest, the word processing software described in Chapter 17 may provide all the power you need. But if your needs demand more sophistication, here are some things for you to consider.

- Aldus PageMaker is a full-featured, flexible publishing tool that has been a top seller in both its Mac and Windows versions. Graphic artists who have a background in traditional layout and design take easily to this program. The addition of sophisticated typographic tools and color separation capability make it more than capable of handling any job you have.

- Frame Technology's FrameMaker is a very specialized program, part word processor, part desktop publishing, part drawing program. Its elaborate equation editor, indexing, table of contents tools and cross-referencing capability make it ideal for large, structured documents, such as manuals and textbooks. Its basic features are readily accessible, but when you want to do some of its fancier tricks, you might find it takes a little while to become adept at them. But the program is no more difficult to learn than any of the word processing software discussed in Chapter 17.

- QuarkXPress is a highly sophisticated publishing tool that has found a home in many advertising agencies, magazines, and newspapers. It takes a back seat to no other program in offering fast performance, precision color and typographic features, and the growing library of XTension add-ons provide a way for you to customize the program to your taste.

- Ready,Set,Go from Manhattan Graphics is the senior member of the desktop publishing software lineup. It was there ahead of all of the other programs we've discussed. It offers some unique document creation features, color separation capability, and fast, slick performance that belies its low price. It is the only program among this group that promises to provide direct support for Apple's QuickDraw GX technology in a future version. Where cost is a factor, this may be just the program for you.

From Here...

This chapter described four of the most popular Macintosh desktop publishing programs, each offering a different twist to the task of creating your documents.

- Chapter 8, "All about Fonts," provides valuable information about fonts and how to use them in your documents.

- If you're deciding whether to buy a desktop publishing program, read Chapter 16, "Word Processing."

- Chapters 37 and 38 discuss the steps you need to take to troubleshoot common problems with your Mac and how you can solve them before they become serious.

Chapter 22

Drawing and Painting

by Cyndie Klopfenstein

In the world of electronic art, you can render art on the computer screen in two basic ways. *Vector-based* is used to refer to a drawing program such as Adobe Illustrator, Aldus Freehand, or Deneba Canvas. It is a type of drawing made up of contiguous lines. Usually, vector-based programs have tools such as Bézier curves, scissors, and blend, as well as object-drawing tools such as circles, squares, and so on. Selected objects have handles, or nodes, for editing their size, shape, and content. Objects can have a fill and a stroke (outline), and you can choose options such as overprinting for trapping purposes.

Pixel-based applications create art from dots. A pixel is either on or off. If you zoom in very tightly to art created in a pixel-based program, you would see that it is made up of millions of square pixels—sort of a close-up view of the screen door, with some of the holes of the screen filled in. Those pixels that are turned on create a solid area. Color pixel-based art is made up of different colored pixels, but still either on or off. Examples of pixel-based programs are Claris BrushStrokes and Fractal Design Painter. Adobe Photoshop is another very popular example.

In this chapter, you learn the major differences between vector- and pixel-based applications, and you also learn about the following:

- Tracing scans in illustration programs

- The drawing tools and how they work

- Bézier curves and the types of tools that create them

- Color creation and selection

- Lassoing objects in pixel-based programs

- Plug-Ins and what they add to a program

■ What kinds of applications work best for photo editing

■ Adding and deleting text in pixel-based documents

This chapter tours these programs in a logical progression. It starts with the three most popular vector-based programs on the market—Adobe Illustrator, Aldus Freehand, and Deneba Canvas. From there you explore the pixel-based programs, where you work primarily with photos and bitmap images. The chapter starts with the simpler of the two, BrushStrokes from Claris, and then tours Fractal Design's Painter.

Adobe Illustrator

This high-end, versatile member of the vector-based programs has super text-handling features, works great on little Macs on up to the Power Macs, and handles color creation, blends, and separations like no other. It has a following easily divided into two groups: those artists that use it primarily for illustrating scanned logos and those who use it for custom-design creation. You'll find that the tools are easy and intuitive, and you'll soon be able to make your way around the menus and toolbox without help, using the documentation only for the occasional challenge.

Using the Drawing Tools

The five drawing tools (Pen, Brush, Freehand, Oval, and Rectangle) are the most frequently used tools in Illustrator. Of these, the Bézier curve tool is the one you'll find yourself turning to with a certain degree of regularity. With the Bézier pen tool you can draw perfectly straight lines, any degree of angled line, and all sorts of curves (see fig. 22.1). By closing the path (that's what a line is called—a *path*), you end up with a shape that can be filled with color. The outline of the shape, called the stroke, can also contain color. Open paths and closed paths (paths that have joined ends) can have fills, but open paths often fill in an unexpected manner.

To draw a straight path, click, hold down the Shift key, and click again. You can continue the path, either curved or straight (add the Shift key), around to form a shape and end it by choosing another tool, ⌘-clicking in an open area of the document page, clicking the beginning handle of the path, or by clicking the end of another path (thereby joining the two paths). Paths, or portions of paths, drawn with the Shift key pressed are constrained to the nearest 15-degree angle.

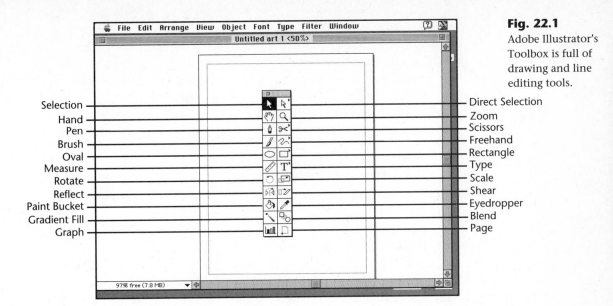

Fig. 22.1
Adobe Illustrator's
Toolbox is full of
drawing and line
editing tools.

To draw a curved path, click, choose a new position, click and drag. Drag in the direction opposite of where you want to go with the curve. The illustrations in figure 22.2 show how the Bézier curves work. Each time you click with this tool, a handle is created. Handles can be deleted and added with the pop-up menu attached to the Scissors tool.

Fig. 22.2
Drawing curves
takes some getting
used to if this is
your first experi-
ence with the
Bézier pen tool.

The next two tools, the Brush and Freehand tool, are used similarly. Using either of these is more like drawing with a pencil. To draw, click the tool and click in the document area. Hold the mouse button down while you move the mouse and the line appears. Both of these line types are very sensitive to each little bump you make with the mouse, but by setting the tolerance in the Preferences dialog box to a higher number, you will make the line somewhat more forgiving. The difference between these two tools is that the Brush tool emulates a paintbrush, while the Freehand pen emulates a pencil or pen. With the Brush, you can dictate a stroke width (double-click the tool), and calligraphic pen style, or a brush tip. To color the Brush line, choose a Fill color in the Paint Style dialog box. The Freehand tool draws lines more like those created with the Bézier pen tool. They are single lines that are colored by choosing a Stroke color in the Paint palette.

Tip

If you choose the Oval or Rectangle tool and then Option-Click on the document area, you can type specific height and width values in the fields of the resulting dialog box.

The Oval and Rectangle tools in the Toolbox enable you to draw squares, rectangles, circles, and ovals very quickly and easily. Just as you did with the Bézier pen tool, you constrain a shape with the shift key. Hold the shift key down while drawing a rectangle and it is constrained to a perfect square—an oval to a perfect circle.

Tracing a Scan

With the Bézier pen tool, you can easily trace a scanned image. Scans that are to be traced must be saved as a PICT image. PICT is a file format for graphics—a language, if you will. Adobe Illustrator can open a PICT image as a template for tracing or it can be placed in the document. For tracing, use the Open command in the File menu. When you choose Open, a dialog box appears, allowing you to choose the Template or Illustration you want to open (see fig. 22.3).

Fig. 22.3

Using the Open dialog box, you can access an illustration or a template.

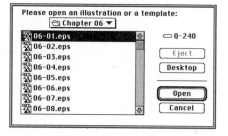

Locate the PICT image you want to trace and click Open. The scanned image appears in the exact center of the page as a gray, bitmap image. Use the Bézier or Freehand pen tools to draw the image just as you would trace an image under a piece of paper. The higher resolution your scan is, the larger, and more full of detail the template is. A scan resolution of 300 to 500 is quite sufficient. You can hide the Template (the scan) by choosing Hide Template from the View menu. You may want to do this if you have parts of the image traced and want to get a good look at it without the template confusing the view.

Choosing a View

Views besides Hide/Show Template are also available. Each view has its benefits. In the Artwork view, the illustration is shown much like a wireframe representation. No color appears and all objects on all layers can be seen. In the Preview mode, colors show and opaque objects hide objects that are below them. In either view, the Hide and Show commands of the view menu can temporarily remove objects from view. This is especially helpful if you need to edit an object that lies below or very close to another object. Simply select the object and choose Hide from the View menu, the selected object is removed from view, and you gain full access to the object below. Use the Show command of the View menu to make all hidden objects visible.

Filling and Stroking Objects and Paths

As you complete paths and objects with the drawing tools, they can be filled or stroked using the Paint Style dialog box shown in figure 22.4 (⌘-I). A fill is the color that resides inside a path or object, the stroke is the color of the outline. If you draw an open path (one that does not have the end and beginning meet), the fill may be unexpected. Figure 22.4 shows some examples of the way Illustrator fills open paths. Closed paths are more predictable. The inside of the path is filled with the Fill color and the outlines of the Path are colored by your selection in the Stroke field of the Paint Style dialog box (see fig. 22.5).

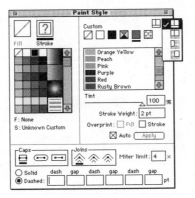

Tip

Use the Arrange menu's Lock command to Lock an object so that it is not inadvertently selected but remains in View.

Fig. 22.4

In the Paint Style dialog box, you can choose a fill color, pattern, or gradient, and a stroke color, pattern, and width.

Fig. 22.5
Open and closed paths fill differently. Closed paths fill the entire area of the enclosure.

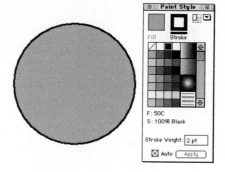

To apply a color, follow these steps:

1. Select an object or objects, and click the Fill or Stroke icon in the upper left corner of the Paint Style dialog box. An underline appears below the active swatch.

2. Pick a color from the color swatches directly below the Fill and Stroke icons, create a process color (click the process color swatch in the row of swatches to the right), or choose a Pantone color (click the custom color swatch, also at the right).

3. The next swatch is for selecting a pattern (or so that you can create patterns of your own). Apply these to the fill or stroke of an object. If you have the Fill swatch selected, you can also choose from a preset list of gradient fills or create a custom gradient fill by clicking the Gradient swatch and double-clicking one of the gradient names to prompt the Gradient palette (see fig. 22.6).

Fig. 22.6
Create custom Gradients and Patterns in the appropriate palettes.

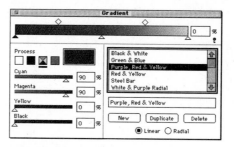

In the Stroke Weight field, type a value for the width of the outline. The values are measured in points, and you can use numbers to the tenth of a point. If you have the Stroke swatch selected, you can choose a dashed or solid line style. At the bottom of the Paint Style dialog box, in the fields to the right of the Solid and Dashed buttons, type values (measured in points) for the length of the dash and the gap. For an even dashed line, numbers should repeat themselves. Figure 22.7 shows examples of values that create the dashed line below it. You can also control the end caps of lines. You have three options: Butt cap, Round cap, and Projecting cap. Figure 22.6 shows examples of the three types of caps.

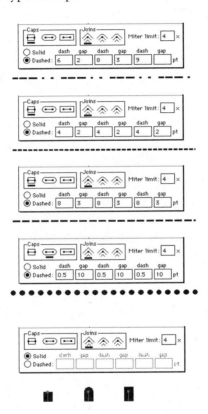

Fig. 22.7
Use the dashed line fields to enter a value for gaps and dashes.

Fig. 22.8
Choose one of the three end cap options to dictate how you want the ends of lines to appear.

In the Joins section of the Paint Styles dialog box, you dictate the type of corner you want to make. Your options are Sharp, Round, or Bevel. Each of these options is further affected by the Miter limit amount. The larger the number you enter in the Miter field, the more drawn out the corners are. Figure 22.9 shows examples of joins and miter amounts.

Fig. 22.9
In the Paint Style dialog box, you can also change the joins and miters of a line.

Tip
If you click the down arrow in the upper right corner of the Paint Style dialog box, you can expand or collapse the size of the dialog box for access to only those areas of the dialog box with which you currently are working.

Fig. 22.10
The three type tools each are used for different kinds of text. Text on a page, Area Type, and Path Type.

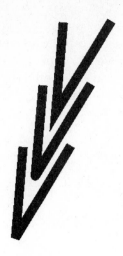

Adding Type to Your Document

Use the Type tool in the toolbox for adding text characters into the document. Text can be floating on the page, constrained inside a shape (Area Type), or free-form along a path or object (Path Type). To access each of these tools, click and hold down the mouse button on the Type tool to make a selection (see fig. 22.10).

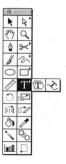

In order to create Area Type, draw an object first (for instance, an oval or a rectangle) and then click the object with the Area Type tool. When you begin typing, the text will fill the shape. To type along a path, draw a line with the Bézier or Freehand Pen tool, choose the Path tool, and click the path. Begin typing, and the text will follow the path. Use one of the selection tools (the top two arrows of the toolbox) to select the I-beam cursor of the type, and you can move the starting point to another position on the path. You can see these results in figure 22.11.

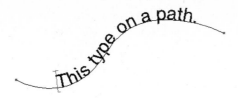

Fig. 22.11
Position the I-beam
along a path to
choose the
placement of
the characters.

Path Type can also be applied to a shape. Use this method when you want to
place type in a curve, like in figure 22.12. Use the Selection tool to move the
I-beam of the starting point.

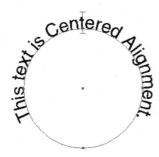

Fig. 22.12
In the Artwork
view, you can see
the type applied to
a circle using the
Path Type tool. The
circle has no stroke
or fill and will not
print.

Using the Character Palette

After the characters are typed, select them by dragging through them with
the Type tool, and choose the Character palette from the Type menu (⌘-T),
shown in figure 22.13. This palette, like Paint Style, can be expanded and
collapsed using the switch icon in the bottom right corner (middle, if the
dialog box is already expanded). Use the arrows beside the fields to scroll to
a font, size, or leading choice, or type the desired selection in the field. For
Baseline Shift, Leading, and Tracking, you cannot scroll. You must type the
value. Press the Return or Enter key, or click the document area to accept the
choices applied to the selected text.

Tip
Choose centered
alignment, and
click the top cen-
ter of the circle to
make the text flow
evenly down both
sides of the circle.
The I-beam is
placed at the
point where you
click (refer to
fig. 22.12).

Fig. 22.13
The Character
palette allows you
to make text
attribute changes.

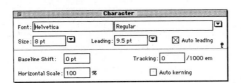

Making Text into Graphic Objects

Because Illustrator is a drawing program, one of the best features is its capability to edit the shape of individual text characters. To do this, you must first
select with the Selection tool the text and choose Create Outlines from the

Type menu. This makes each letter a graphic object with handles that can be edited like all other object handles in Illustrator. The drawback is that the text is no longer text. The font cannot be changed, and it cannot be hyphenated automatically. Other attributes, such as leading, are no longer options. In figure 22.14, you see text characters that have not been converted to curves on top, and those below after Create Outlines. This view is the Artwork view.

Fig. 22.14
Use the Create Outlines option to change text characters into editable objects.

The Transformation Tools

The next four tools on the Toolbox are the transformation tools: Rotate, Scale, Reflect, and Shear. These tools are used on objects (or text) and apply the attribute for which they're named. Each of these options can be applied to the original or applied to a copy. For example, if you select an object and Option-click with the Reflect tool (where you click the document is the point from which the transformation takes place), you prompt a dialog box where then you choose Vertical or Horizontal and click the Copy button (see fig. 22.15). This action makes a duplicate of the object and flips it horizontally or vertically, whichever you choose in the dialog box.

Fig. 22.15
Use the Copy button in the dialog box to apply the effect to a duplicate of the selected object.

Plug-in Filters

New to Illustrator is the use of *filters,* or add-on features. Illustrator is shipped with several sample filters such as Objects, Pathfinder, and Select. Each of these filters compliments the capabilities of Illustrator. The Select filter allows you to select all of the objects in your document that have the same fill color or same stroke color. You can also select all stray points which are handles left behind when an object was not entirely deleted. Other applications call these filters Plug-Ins, XTensions, Extensions, and Add-Ons.

> **Note**
>
> To make a global color change, click an object that has the fill or outline color you want. Choose Select from the Filters menu, and then choose Same Fill Color or Stroke Color. All objects matching that Fill or Stroke color are selected, and you can choose a new color in the Paint Style dialog box.

Making Graphs

Illustrator has a fairly comprehensive graph feature. With this feature, you can quickly create graphs of all sorts. The indicators on the graph can be custom-drawn objects. Use the Graph tool in the Toolbox to begin the graph. When you click the document, the Graph Data dialog box appears. Type the values for the graph in the dialog box. Use the Graph menu to choose the type of graph (pie, bar, and so on), columns, axis, and more.

Getting the Most from Illustrator: Hot Tips

- *Reducing PostScript Banding.* Postscript banding often occurs in large areas of tints or gradated screens. To reduce the occurrence of banding, use a Step number divisible evenly into the resolution. For instance, if you're outputting to film at 2540 dpi, try an lpi or screen ruling of 254 or 127 rather than the traditional 133, 150, 200, or 300.

- *Drawing parallel angled lines.* By using the Constrain Angle Preferences setting in Illustrator, you can set the angle to which all objects are drawn. For instance, if you are drawing several 30° lines, set the Constrain Angle to 30° and draw straight lines with the Pen tool while holding down the Shift key. All lines are then constrained to the 30°. To return to regular drawing mode, reset the Constrain angle to 0°.

- *Applying line weights.* To set a mini-default for fill and stroke colors and patterns without resetting the choices in the Paint dialog box, click on the object containing the fill and stroke that you want to duplicate. Use the keyboard equivalent to invoke the Paint dialog box (I collapse the palette and move it as far to the right of the active work area as possible); then press Return or Enter. Now, still using the pen tool, draw the new object. The fill and stroke attributes of the first object are applied to new objects until you change the settings in the Paint dialog box or until you repeat the steps above for choosing mini-defaults.

- *Printing difficult PostScript.* When creating art for importation to another program, such as a logo imported into a QuarkXPress document, always create the logo in a new Illustrator document by itself. A very common mistake is to create many different versions of the logo on the same document page and then import the graphic, moving it around in the page layout program until only the desired logo shows. With PostScript, the entire page is rasterized, even though only a small image shows— this creates longer imaging times that you might be charged by the minute for.

- *Printing separations.* Illustrator does not print separations in its native format. Images must be imported into a page layout program that supports separations or into Adobe Separator which ships with Illustrator. When using a page layout program to generate separations, be sure that each of the colors that you want is listed in the color palette of the page layout program or the separation plate for that color will not print. Separator is particularly adept, especially when you want to print only specific plates of the document, specify registration marks, and need to choose an lpi amount that reduces the occurrence of banding.

- *Eliminating Stray Points.* When deleting guidelines, remember to always press the Delete key twice. Pressing it once removes the line, but leaves the anchor points in place. These anchor points are positioned at the opposite far reaches of the document edge and are considered part of your image. When importing the image, the stray anchor points are used to determine the image size. The preview of the page layout program may warn you of this. Be wary of any preview that looks exceedingly small. The Plug-In Select, Stray Points also allows you to delete any anchor points missed. Choose this option and then press Delete to remove all stray points inadvertently left behind.

- *Repeating Objects to Form Circles.* To form circular borders with a selected object, draw a circle in the size of the desired border. Draw, copy, or type an object at a point along the circle. If you want to repeat the object around the circle 20 times, divide 360° by 20. Select the object and choose the rotation tool. Option-Click on the center point of the circle, and use the resulting number (18 in our example) in the Degree field of the Rotate dialog box.

- *Joining paths.* To join two separate open paths and meld the anchor points, try moving one of the anchor points completely away from the other path, releasing the line and then moving the anchor point back. Because of the resolution of the monitor, it sometimes seems impossible to perfectly align two lines, especially in Preview mode. By dragging one line away and then back, you allow the line you're moving to snap to the first line. After you've placed the two lines together, choose Join (⌘-J) from the Arrange menu.

Summary

Adobe Illustrator is one of the most widely used illustration programs for the Macintosh or Windows environments. It's easy to see why. It has superior text-, line-, and color-handling capabilities and the new filter technology adds extra kick to some of the hardest parts about illustrating. You'll find that whether you are a designer making marker comps or a production person drawing corporate logos, Illustrator has the tools you need to get the job done quickly and easily.

Aldus Freehand

FreeHand 4.0 has made great strides in intuitiveness and a comfortable, easy user interface. The newest version relies much more heavily on palette than did its predecessors. The palette, a floating window, can be accessed and left in the document area for repeated use. A central palette, called the Inspector, allows you to view many different objects and their applied attributes from a single, handy location. Like Illustrator, this vector-based program is for contiguous line drawings. Although you can place halftone TIFF, PICT, and EPS images, you cannot edit them from within FreeHand. That's a job for a pixel-based painting program (see the following section). The Place feature is primarily for the tracing of scans or to view photos when you wish to design around them.

The biggest change yet just might be the manuals. Both the Macintosh and the Windows version of FreeHand are shipped with exactly the same documentation, sort of a unisex handbook. But this documentation is unlike any other. A great deal of planning went into the layout and design of this manual, and you'll find information extremely easy to find and the steps a breeze to follow. The only shortcomings of the manuals are in the depth of the information. If you're new to FreeHand you'll have no trouble working through the process, but if you're an old pro, the manual won't help you to stretch your creative drive in uncharted territories. This is not a drawback unique to FreeHand—most manuals don't help you with the advanced techniques.

Using the Drawing Tools

As with most illustration programs—and most programs in general, for that matter—the Toolbox is the focal point. In FreeHand, the Toolbox and the Inspector palette are both focal points. The tools of the Toolbox are somewhat common. You have the Selection tool, the Text tool, several drawing tools (Rectangle, Polygon, Ellipse, Line, Freehand, Pen, and Bezigon), a Cutting tool, and a few different types of transformation tools. In figure 22.16, the tools are titled.

Fig. 22.16

The Toolbox of FreeHand offers several different drawing tools, a text tool, a selection tool, and a number of transformation tools.

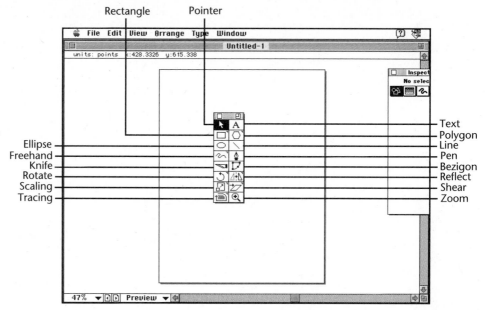

Paths are closed or open and are drawn with one or more of the drawing tools mentioned previously. Figure 22.17 shows examples of both a closed and open path. Paths have handles for editing the line. The more handles you have, the more complex the line is. Handles translate directly into print time. The more handles a document has, the longer it takes to print. Handles are not the only cause of extended print time, however.

Fig. 22.17
On the left is an example of an open path. It can contain a fill, but the fill cannot be seen and will not print until the path is closed.

To draw lines or shapes in FreeHand, you have only two options: draw by dragging or draw by placing points. For example, to draw a rectangle, select the Rectangle tool, click a starting point, hold the mouse button down and drag. The object is shown by a temporary bounding box so that you can see the size and shape before you release the mouse button to accept the object you've drawn. If you release the mouse button, and don't like the shape, Delete the move, Undo (⌘-Z) the move, or click, hold the mouse button down, and drag on one of the handles with the selection tool to edit the shape. The Pen tool and Bezigon tool both make lines by clicking to place points (handles). If you click a point, hold the mouse button down, and then drag the line will become curved, just like the Bézier curves of Illustrator.

All handles are editable. Some objects, such as ellipses and rectangles, must be ungrouped before they can be edited. Handles that are part of a curve segment also have handles for editing the curve. You can click the handles at the intersection of the curve to display them. If you click a corner handle, you can make it a curve by clicking and dragging the handle. A curve appears on-screen following the handle in the direction you are dragging. If you click it again and drag in the opposite direction, the line preceding the handle becomes curved.

Working with Views

Viewing artwork in FreeHand offers you two options: Keyline mode and Preview mode. As you can see in figure 22.18, each view has its advantages. The primary advantage for the Keyline mode is the speed with which the screen redraws. In Keyline, you are viewing the illustration as though it were a wireframe representation of your work. Colors are not displayed, and all parts of objects are visible—even those covered by other objects in Preview mode are visible. Viewing with the Preview mode enables you to see all colors and objects that are not covered by other objects. Layers affect both of these views.

Fig. 22.18
In the Keyline mode, the artwork appears as a wireframe.

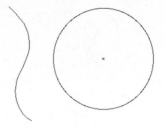

Working with Layers

Using Layers, you can choose to make some items visible (in either view), and other items hidden. To do this, you simply place items you want to hide on a layer by themselves and click the check mark next to the layer name in the Layers palette (see fig. 22.19). All items on a hidden layer are removed from view. To display them, click in the area of the vacated check mark and a new check mark appears. All items on that layer are again visible.

Fig. 22.19
In the Layers palette, you can duplicate layers, remove layers, move objects between layers, and select layers as nonprinting or nonviewing.

Layers can also be used to make drawing easier in complex illustrations. If you are creating an illustration that is very busy and made up of several components, you might find it easier to work with the components if you divide them into like groups and put all of those items on a single layer. For example, you could have a text layer, a scanned image layer, a tracing layer, a grid layer, and maybe a placed art layer. By shuffling the layers and hiding some, you can then easily work on tracing the scan, correcting typing errors, or repositioning placed art without the cluttered view of all layers at once.

Adding Color

You add color to drawn objects by using the Color list, Color mixer, and Tints palettes shown in figure 22.20. Each of these palettes interacts with the other two palettes and enables you to create custom colors, define Pantone or other standard colors, and create tints of the colors you add to the document. After a color is created (in the Color mixer palette), or a tint defined (Tints palette), you can drag and drop it on the Color list palette. The Color list is where you select a color to add to an object. The two icons in the upper left of the palette are for selecting either the Fill or a Line. The line might also be the outline color of an object. Click the object to which you want to apply color, choose the correct icon (Fill or Line), and click the color name in the list at the bottom of the Color list palette. This applies color to all selected objects or lines.

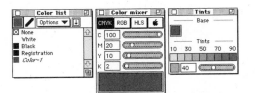

Fig. 22.20
FreeHand has three major palettes for choosing, mixing, and applying colors.

Using Text

Even though FreeHand is an illustration package, its text-handling and page layout features are better than some of the desktop publishing software. Text is added to a document in a box called a text block. This text block can be made up of one column or several columns, can contain tabular text or paragraph text, and can be linked to other text blocks.

All type is added to the document by using the Text tool from the toolbox. Click the document area to add text and a tab ruler along with a box for inserting the text appear (see fig. 22.21). Type characters as you normally would and use the tab ruler for defining tab stops and indents. Like other handles in FreeHand, the handles of a text block are editable. Just click and drag to change the size of the text block. The small box at the bottom right corner of the text block is to indicate an overflow of text or whether the block is linked to another block.

Text can also be bound to a path or to fill a shape. Type the text, and with the Selection, tool select both the text and the path and choose Bind to Path from the Type menu. For text in a shape, use the Flow inside Path command, also in the Type menu.

Fig. 22.21
Click the docu-
ment area to
activate a text
block.

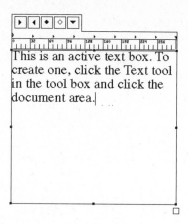

This is an active text box. To create one, click the Text tool in the tool box and click the document area.

Tracing a Scan

Although FreeHand certainly has the tools for custom art, it also has strengths in tracing art. You may use custom art for several reasons. You may want to re-create a customer logo, incorporate existing drawings into your electronic file, or to use the scan as a guideline for some other part of your illustration. In any case, placed images in FreeHand are not limited to just a view for tracing without printing as they are in Illustrator. You can move the scanned image to a layer that doesn't print, you can change the color so that it is light enough to see lines drawn over the top of it, and you can view the image in Keyline mode. Placed images also reside outside the actual FreeHand file so that they don't increase your file size substantially.

Summary

FreeHand 4.0 has made great strides in merging the desktop publishing and illustrating worlds. It has also become one of the friendliest programs to new users. By understanding the palette interface, even the most inexperienced of users can make their way around the options of FreeHand. In addition, the manuals are superb. Text handling, page layout, and illustration have all come together in FreeHand. This product would be a much less expensive start than purchasing a word processing, desktop publishing, and illustration package separately.

Getting the Most from Freehand: Hot Tips

■ *Simplifying PostScript Graphics*. Always keep your drawn art that is imported into other page layout programs as simple as possible, never more than a single graphic per page. A PostScript imagesetter rasterizes the entire document area, not just the area you've cropped to.

■ *Smoothing Traced Images*. Tracing a scanned image is a great way to add difficult pieces to your art without all the time it would take to draw from scratch. Use the Simplify command in the Arrange menu to re-move dots. This also works great on pieces that you've drawn and that are too complex for an imagesetter to output.

■ *Reducing PostScript Banding*. To create a graduated fill with a dark or light point in the center that fades to the outside, draw one side and gradu-ate the fill in the direction you want. Then, using the clone tool, make a clone that joins at the center. Use the Artwork view so you can accu-rately align the object and its clone if the seam between the two objects shows.

■ *Choosing a Resolution*. Select your printer resolution before you begin working on the document. This number is used to calculate the number of steps to a blend. A chosen resolution lower or higher than the actual output will result in PostScript banding in tints and graduated screens.

■ *Delete, don't hide objects*. Though it is often recommended, do not use white boxes to cover up unwanted portions of your artwork. Another object adds to the complexity of your document and will show if you place your artwork on a colored or tinted background. Use the knife tool to cut away the part or create a mask. When using a mask, make sure that you use an object with only the necessary items. Don't mask out items that won't show, delete them.

■ *Faster Preview*. The more complex your illustration is, the longer it will take to draw, this applies to all computer graphics. Keep your illustra-tions simple, and, whenever possible, work in Artwork view, which draws faster because it doesn't render the fills and patterns.

■ *Proof Printing*. Put all like objects on a single layer, especially text, so that you can print only that layer for proofreading.

Deneba Canvas

Another of the vector-based programs, Canvas, has been around for some time. Its market share is not nearly that of Adobe Illustrator or FreeHand, but it is a very similar program. The tools for working in Canvas resemble those discussed in the first two sections of this chapter. In fact, other than a few minor name discrepancies, they are duplicates in function and form. Canvas is in the same general price range as Illustrator and FreeHand but is less common, which may mean some difficulty outputting files to a service bureau, should you need to.

Canvas's focus—and therefore strength—lies in technical illustrations. Many of the tools and options are geared toward home planning, illustrations requiring callouts, and dimension labeling. Figure 22.22 shows an example of this type of illustration. This particular example was created in Canvas, and most of the items you see were automatic functions or options of the toolbox or menus.

Fig. 22.22
The strengths of Canvas lie in technical illustrations such as this one.

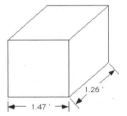

Using the Primary Tools

The Tool Box is where you find the power of illustration programs, and Canvas is no different. The Canvas Tool Box contains tools for selecting, erasing, typing, lines, objects, and transformations—all tools discussed in previous sections (see fig. 22.23). Painting tools such as Lasso, Spray Can, and Paint Bucket are also included, and this is the first time we've discussed these in this chapter. This is the type of tool that's typical to a pixel-based program, but rarely found in a vector-based program.

Drawing with the basic tools is basically the same universally. Click the tool icon (Line tool, Oval tool, Arc tool, and so on) in the Tool Box, click in the document area, hold the mouse button down, and drag. If you're drawing Bézier curves, you click, move the mouse, click and drag in the direction opposite where you want the curve to go. In figure 22.24, some of the different drawing tools and their methods are illustrated.

Paint tools
Arrow   palette   Freehand   Polygon

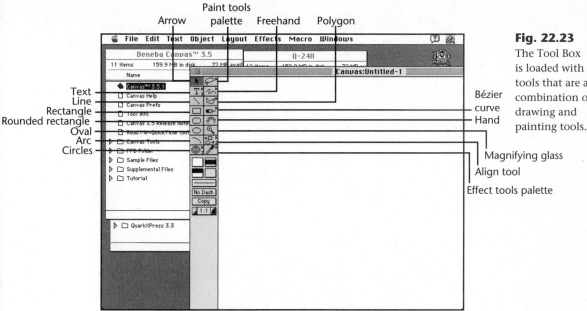

Text
Line
Rectangle
Rounded rectangle
Oval
Arc
Circles

Bézier
curve
Hand

Magnifying glass
Align tool
Effect tools palette

Fig. 22.23
The Tool Box is loaded with tools that are a combination of drawing and painting tools.

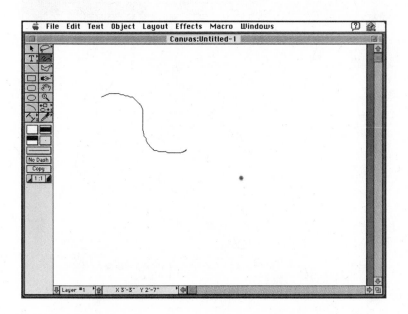

Fig. 22.24
Drawing tools in most illustration programs work pretty much the same.

Fig. 22.24
Continued

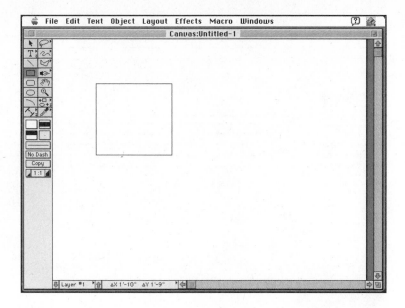

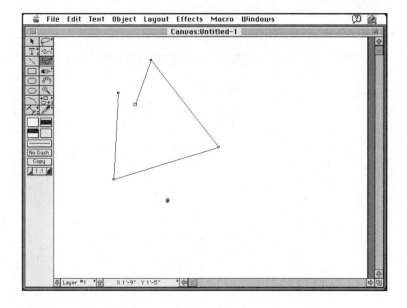

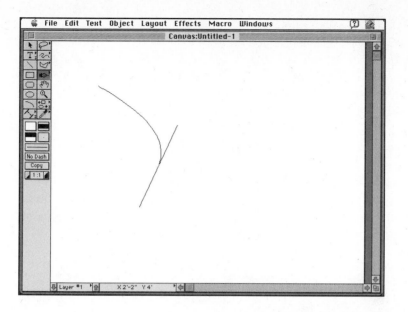

Fig. 22.24
Continued

Objects that you have drawn in Canvas are editable, but they must be entered into the Edit mode. Adding an object to the Edit mode is as simple as double-clicking it with the Arrow tool (selection tool). The Polygon and Bézier Curve tools can be set to automatically enter the Edit mode in the Preferences of Canvas. Another way to automatically enter the Edit mode is to select the Arrow tool immediately after placing the last handle (anchor point) of an object you have drawn. While you are in the Edit mode, the Arrow tool changes to a gray arrow to remind you of its status. When the Arrow is positioned over an edit point (handle) it changes to a cross hair. Click and drag handles to edit their position. After you finish editing your object, exit the Edit mode by double-clicking outside the object, by pressing Return, or by pressing Enter. You can select several handles to edit at one time by holding the Shift key to select the consecutive points.

In the lower half of the Tool Box, you'll find the patterns, background, foreground, and other attributes buttons. Again, this is a combination of drawing and painting tools. But they work the same way: click the tool with the mouse, click the document area, and hold down the mouse button to disperse paint (such as with the Spray Can), click inside an object to fill (Paint Bucket), or click a color to change the line color.

Tool Manager is an external application that allows you to choose the tools that you want available to you during a drawing session in Canvas. The best part of this feature, and surely the reason for its inception, is the capability to free up as much memory for more complex files by not running every feature under the sun—sort of like a Plug-In, Filter, or XTension, but with definable interface. Tools in the Tool Box use a down-facing arrow indicator in the bottom right corner to let you know that the tool has Tool Manager options. Figure 22.25 shows this indicator. You have seen the right-facing indicator before, in Illustrator. It prompts a familiar drop-down or pop-up list (whichever terminology you prefer) from which you can make other tool choices. After you develop a list of tools in the Tool Manager with which you're comfortable, you can choose to save it as a Tool Set for instant recall into other illustrations you begin.

Fig. 22.25
These double down-facing arrows in the bottom right corner tell you that other tools are available if you have chosen them in the Tool Manager.

Double down-facing arrows

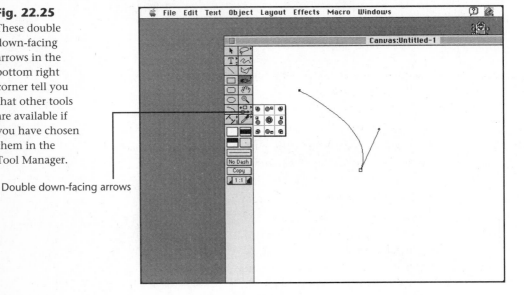

Another feature that Canvas shares with some paint programs is tear-off menus (see fig. 22.26). You will find that the differences between a tear-off menu and a palette are minimal. Palettes are generally accessed through a menu and remain floating above your artwork where ever you place it. Some can be collapsed and expanded to further hide them but leave them accessible. Tear-off menus usually cannot be collapsed, but they can be moved or closed. Both are used in the same manner: select an object and click the selection in the palette to apply.

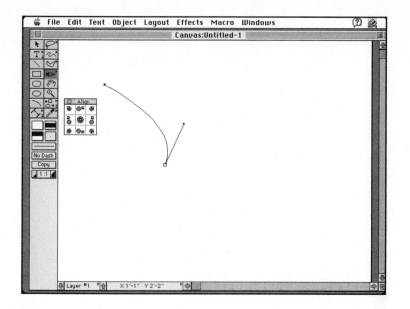

Fig. 22.26
Tear-off menus give you immediate access to hidden options, and they stay in the document area until you close them.

Changing Views

Aside from scrolling around in your document, Canvas provides a few ways to change the view size but not ways to view in wireframe or artwork mode. You are always in the Preview mode in Canvas, and you always see the colors and patterns applied. This can be a major drain on memory because objects must be rendered fully. To change view size, the simplest way is to use the Zoom In/Zoom Out palette icon located at the very bottom of the Tool Box (see fig. 22.27). Just slide the Arrow tool over to the enlargement or reduction size you need and release the mouse button; the view size changes.

Adding Color to Objects

Color is added to Canvas objects using the RGB Color dialog box found in the Edit menu under Managers. (Managers are tools controlled by the Tool Manager and are only available if you have chosen them to be in the Tool Manager.) RGB colors are great for displaying your work on the monitor but aren't very useful if you intend to have your artwork printed. For that, you have the Color Info Manager which allows you to choose between RGB, HSV, CMY, CMYK, and Pantone color options. If you click the Pantone button, you will not see a palette of colors from which to choose—only a dialog box for entering the Pantone number of choice. In figure 22.28, both the RGB

Color and Color Info Manager dialog boxes are shown. Also under Managers (located in the Edit menu) is the Gradient Fill manager. As with Illustrator and FreeHand, you can create a blend of one color to another and apply it to objects.

Fig. 22.27
Use the Zoom In/ Zoom Out palette for changing view size.

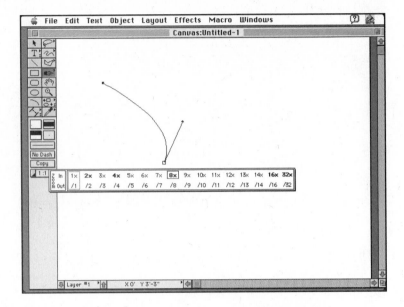

Fig. 22.28
Color is accessed using one of these dialog boxes: RGB Color or Color Info Manager.

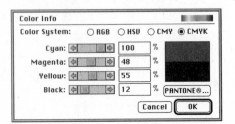

You can only have one color palette open in the document at a time. In the RGB Color Manager, you open a palette by clicking the Get Colors button and choosing from the list of Color Tables in the Color Tables folder. The color palette that you have chosen appears in all of the color options in Canvas.

To apply color to an object, select it and choose Color Info Manager. Mix your color by typing in values or using the sliders. Click Pantone to define a color of this module. Click OK and the object's color is changed.

The Pantone Color Window (Windows menu) allows you to view the list of colors and pick a color from it. You can create custom color sets from which to choose colors and add, delete, edit, cut, copy, paste, duplicate, and remove colors from these sets.

Working with Type in the Document

In the Text menu you can select a size, font, justification method, leading, kerning, and style for your text. If you choose the Text tool from the Tool Box and hold the mouse button down, you will get the options. Make your choice from either the menu or the Tool Box and click in the document area to begin typing. Also in the Text menu is the Type Specifications dialog box. You can choose Type from the Text menu to see the dialog box shown in figure 22.29. This dialog box provides the simplest way to make multiple attribute changes to Text. It also sets up the default for all text that is typed into the document. The Type Specifications dialog box is an external tool that is accessed by choosing it in the ToolPicker dialog box.

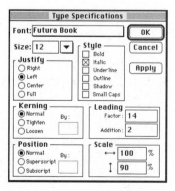

Fig. 22.29
Choices in the Type Specifications dialog box become the default for type in that document. Change the defaults by coming back here, or override them using the Text menu.

You can type paragraph text or caption text in a Canvas document. The two are differentiated by whether or not you need margins. Paragraph text allows you to set margins such as when you're using Canvas for page layout and want to define columns. To do this, click and drag the Text tool (from the Tool Box) to define the size of the column. Other text tools are available only if you have enabled Text Utilities in the Canvas Tools Folder by using the ToolPicker.

Getting the Most from Canvas: Hot Tips

- *Using the Callouts.* Use Canvas to open Illustrator 88 or 1.1 documents so that you can utilize the features of the automatic measured callouts. Save any Illustrator file (up to 5.0) in a 1.1 or 88 format so that Canvas can import it.

- *Using Tear-Off palettes.* When using the same type of arrowhead, for example, use the tear-off palettes to keep access handy.

- *Switching from RGB.* Canvas defaults to RGB colors. Make sure that you are working in the correct color system before you begin choosing colors. Remember that it is unlikely that your monitor is displaying the color accurately, so choose from either a CMYK color swatch book or Pantone fan, and compile your colors accordingly.

- *Printing Layers.* Place like objects on the same layer so that you can print specific layers quickly for proofing. This is especially true of text. Being able to proofread only the text without waiting for a complex document to print is a considerable timesaver.

- *Text from Word Processors.* Rather than typing extensive text in Canvas, type it in a word processor that doesn't take extra time to draw the objects you've created. Once complete, use Publish and Subscribe to update and track the text. For company disclaimers that must appear on all marketing material but that are updated yearly, this can be a priceless tip.

- *Choosing Points for a Blend.* When blending objects, use the Point-to-Point option. This will give you added control over how the objects rotate when blended. Without Point-to-Point the objects will align points—upper-left anchor to upper-left anchor, and so on.

- *Speeding the Preview.* Since Canvas does not have a wireframe or artwork view, illustrations can take a long time to draw. To speed things up, complete the illustration before adding patterns, colors, and so on.

Summary

Many of the tools of Canvas are from the drawing-type programs and some from the painting programs—this makes Canvas a good investment if you find yourself stuck between these two worlds of electronic file creation. Its price is comparable to Illustrator or FreeHand, but neither of these programs offers the painting tools as Canvas does.

On the other hand, because Canvas has such a small user base, many of the service bureaus are not accustomed to outputting this kind of file. This can be bad news if you've spent a great deal of time only to learn that the job can't be printed.

The documentation on Canvas is very glitzy but organized in a manner that may require that you look in several areas to discern how to perform a certain function. Canvas's tools are geared particulary well toward creating technical illustrations, and therein lies the strength.

Claris BrushStrokes

This program is a scaled-down version of the big boys, such as Adobe Photoshop or Aldus Photo Styler. But its size is probably the most becoming feature. Not everyone needs the power (or the expense) of a program like Photoshop.

BrushStrokes is also a great program to have in addition to one of the more complex programs. Even if you have the budget to own a more expensive program, with expense generally comes size, and with size comes memory requirements. (See table 22.1, later in this chapter.)

Many painting-type projects are simple and don't require the use of a full-blown program. This is the niche for BrushStrokes. Pixel editing scanned images is an ideal use for BrushStrokes. You certainly don't need a $450 program to do this.

None of this is to say that BrushStrokes is limiting. It's not. It has features that enable you to create the look of fine art paintings, bitmap images, and full-color, pixel-based drawings.

The Tool Palette and Tear-Off Menus

Still focusing on the tool palette, BrushStrokes introduces tools such as Spraycan, Eyedropper, and Paintbucket, which are fairly common to paint

programs. Even though you can find these tools in some illustration packages, they seem to fit best here in pixel-based programs. The Tool palette is
displayed in figure 22.30.

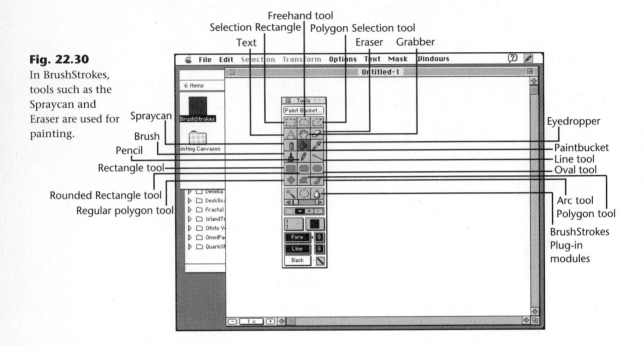

Fig. 22.30
In BrushStrokes,
tools such as the
Spraycan and
Eraser are used for
painting.

Text and Object tools are found here as they would be in an illustration
program, but they work differently. After an object or text is added to the
drawing, it becomes a grouping of pixels. In fact, all objects in this type of
program are made up of pixels. You cannot click objects to delete them or
edit their handles as you can in the vector-based programs.

In BrushStrokes, parts of a painting are selected with a different kind of
selection tool: the *lasso*. The Rectangle, Freehand, and Polygon are all lasso
selection tools. The Oval lasso is one of the Plug-Ins that shipped with
BrushStrokes. To use any of these selection tools, just choose the tool from
the Tool palette, click and drag to encompass the part of your painting that
you want to edit, as shown in figure 22.31.

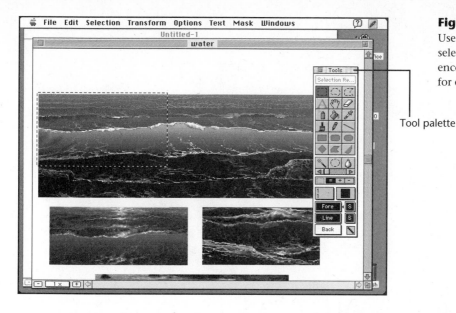

Fig. 22.31
Use one of the
selection tools to
encompass an area
for editing.

Tool palette

The Magic Wand Plug-In is also a selection tool, but it is not a lasso tool. To select all objects of the same color, choose the Magic Wand and click on the color you want to choose. All pixels in your document that are the same color as the color you clicked are selected and ready for editing.

Each of the painting, object, and eraser tools works with basic Macintosh mouse skills. You click and drag to stretch out an object, click and hold down to disperse paint, or click and drag to erase part of a painting. When you erase, you're actually painting over the top with whatever color is chosen as the background color. (More about colors later in this section.)

The lower portion of the Tool palette is for selecting colors (see fig. 22.32). A foreground color is the color you paint with. It is the color that is dispersed when you use any of the painting tools. A background color is the color you erase with. It is the color that is used to cover selected parts of your painting when you use the Eraser tool. The Line color is the color that the Line tool puts down. You can use the color drop-down, tear-off menus by clicking the button and choosing a new color from the pop-up color palette. If you continue to hold the mouse button down and drag away, the palette will tear off and remain wherever you release the mouse button. Toggle between the color wheel and color palette by clicking the Mode button at the top of the tear-off menu. Whatever color you choose will be displayed as the color of the button on the Tool palette—be it a Foreground, Line, or Background color.

Fig. 22.32
Use the Color pop-up palette to select a Background, Foreground, or Line color.

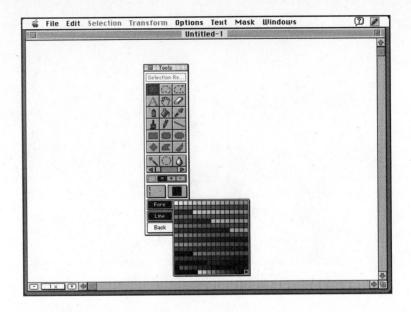

Another method for choosing a color is to use the Eyedropper tool. If you already have a painting in your document area, you can copy a color used in that painting to the foreground color for use by other painting tools. Click the Eyedropper tool in the Tool palette and then click the color you want to copy. It is placed in the Foreground color button.

Working with Views

To zoom in or out on a portion of your drawing, select it with one of the selection tools and then use the field in the lower left corner of the document window to type in a value for enlargement or reduction. You can also use the Minus button to reduce the view or the Plus button to enlarge the view. Unlike Illustrator or Freehand, BrushStrokes does not have a wireframe or artwork view.

Typing Text into a Graphic

Using the Text tool from the Tool palette, you can add type to your painting. You can add text in two ways, but once you release the box that contains the text, the characters become part of the image, called a *bitmap*. Click the Text tool, click the document area where you want the text to be, and drag out a box the approximate size that you want the text to occupy. In the second method, you only click in the document area and BrushStrokes draws a box of a predefined size. From the Text menu, you select a size, font, style, and the type of alignment. Choose a Foreground color (the color that the letters are painted with) and then type the text. When you are finished typing, if you don't like the position or your box isn't big enough, you can use the handles to edit the box or click inside the box and drag it to a different position. If you click outside the box, the text is added to the graphic, as was done in figure 22.33. To remove text, you must paint over it with one of the painting tools, choosing a Foreground color to match the surrounding area.

Fig. 22.33
Text placed in the image area becomes a bitmap. It is no longer editable as text.

Working with Non-Native Graphics

In BrushStrokes, you can open graphics that were scanned or created in other environments or programs. They can be a TIFF, PICT, MacPaint, or PixelPaint format. After they have been opened into BrushStrokes they can be saved as a PICT, TIFF, or Startup Screen. You might want to scan an image to use a part of your painting, or open an existing graphic and edit it by adding text or colored objects.

Adding and Using Plug-In Modules

Plug-In modules are mini-applications that you can add on to BrushStrokes. Some Plug-Ins are very small and only perform one function as with the oval selection tool discussed earlier. Other Plug-Ins are more complex and some even work with other paint programs. Plug-Ins need to be stored in the

BrushStrokes folder or in a folder just inside BrushStrokes, in the System folder, or in the Preferences folder inside the System 7 folder. After they're installed properly, they become a part of the program and work seamlessly.

Getting the Most from BrushStrokes: Hot Tips

- *Adding color.* Instead of trying to create a color to match a specific color, pick up a sampling of the color with the eyedropper and then edit the positioning of the marker on the color wheel slightly. This will give you a color very close to the original color.

- *Making Selections.* Although the polygon tool allow you to make an irregularly shaped selection, selecting objects that contain a single color or similar colors are easier to define by using the Magic Wand Plug-In. Set the tolerance to pick up the colors you need.

- *Hiding Mistakes.* Unlike illustration programs, a paint program does not layer or accumulate objects. Therefore, using the paint brush loaded with the foreground color is an effective way to delete objects.

- *Working with Text Characters.* Because text becomes part of the painted image as soon as you release the selection, type the text into a new document, color it, move the letters, and edit until you are satisfied with the results. Then select the text and choose copy, and paste the text into your image, making sure to postion it before you release the selection.

- *Choosing a resolution.* For optimum printing quality, the resolution you create your image at should follow the same rules as resolutions for halftones. A formula for determining the correct amount is simple:

  Screen frequency (lpi) X 1.5 = Image Resolution (dpi).

  If you intend to reduce or enlarge the painting as you output the file, factor that number in also. For instance, if you have painted a $4 \times 5"$ image and you intend to enlarge it 200% (you will use an $8 \times 10"$), the formula looks like this.

  Screen frequency (lpi) $\times$ 1.5 = x
  $x \times 8"$ 4 = Image Resolution (dpi).

  Enter the resolution amount in the Resolution field of the Document Setup dialog box. Your image may not display properly at resolutions other than 72 dpi.

Summary

BrushStrokes is a smaller paint program, but it still can turn out professional pixel-based art and edit TIFF, Paint, and PICT format files. The text-handling capabilities are limited but sufficient. Its low cost makes it a good backup system or stand-alone product if you're only occasionally doing this kind of work.

Fractal Design Painter

Painter is a fairly new contender in the paint program ring. But this new-comer is by no means a minor player. It has extreme ideas about how an electronic file should be created by a fine artist and follows through with those ideas by putting action into their claims. This program not only has superior photo-editing capabilities and color separation handling, but also has superior custom art creation tools. The palettes of Painter are many and extensive. Most have tear-off menus so that whatever you're working on is handy. For those fine artists who say that their style can't be duplicated by a computer, they haven't tried Painter.

You know Painter is different as soon as it arrives. Its authentic paint-can packaging and the small-sized manuals are maybe just a little too cute. But getting past the fluff and into the meat of the program, you're not surprised that the company uses such gimmicks to promote this highly advanced and finely tuned product. The best part of the manuals is the Companion. It picks up right where the regular documentation leaves off. All software manuals can be expected to teach you the basics about running the program, but the Companion teaches you about piloting the rocket after you learn to fly the glider. In short, Painter is a unique and adept program, especially for fine artists, photo editors, and illustrators; it is easy to use with great documentation support.

Using the Primary Tools

The tools of Painter are almost all found in palettes. You have Brushes, Friskets, Paper, Color, and Expression palettes to work from in addition to the Tool Box and menus. To understand Painter, imagine yourself as an artist—say, Van Gogh. Look around your work area, and what do you see? Pens, pencils, charcoal, chalk, oil paints, water colors, and mediums of all sorts—canvas, paper, glass, and so on. These are the tools of Painter, but this is the twentieth century and you do own a Macintosh. So now what do you have? All of the tools of Van Gogh placed in easy-to-use palettes and the seemingly limitless options that are a part of the electronic world.

The primary tools of Painter are the brushes and color palettes. With these two palettes you can select from a wide range of painting tools and shades of color with which to paint. Painter palettes are similar to palettes in other Macintosh programs (see fig. 22.34). Open the palette from the menu, use the scroll bar to find the tool of choice, and click the tool. Most of the palettes can be zoomed open to show more options by clicking the zoom box in the upper right corner of the palette window. After you have clicked on a tool in the palette, that tool (or its function) is ready to be applied to the open document. The document might be an imported scanned photo, art from a Photo-CD, art created in Fractal Design's Sketcher, or perhaps a piece that you have created entirely in Painter. Regardless of the origination, the tools work the same. Apply the tool by pressing and holding the mouse button, or with a stylus from a digitizing pen and pad.

Fig. 22.34
Palettes are the primary tools of Painter. Use the zoom box to show more options. Click the zoom box again to collapse the palette to the original size.

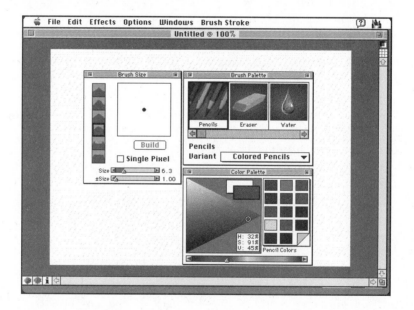

As you choose a tool from the Brush Palette, the dialog box area below the scrollable tool list changes. The variants of the selected tool are found in the Variant pop-up menu. Variants are the options for that tool and are selected by clicking and dragging the mouse to the desired variant. Other options besides Variants might also be available depending on the brush type you have chosen.

The Brush Size Palette, shown in figure 22.35, works in conjunction with the Brush Palette by enabling you to edit the size of the brush, the numbers of bristles, and the angle with which the brush paints.

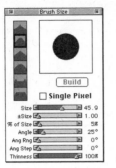

Fig. 22.35
Use the Brush Size Palette to edit the brush size, angle, bristles, and so on.

The Paper Palette is for selecting a background texture. In figure 22.36, you can see a sampling of the paper types available as they appear in the Paper Palette. Only some of the brushes are affected by the type of paper to which they are applied. You can combine brush types and paper types to add more *feel* to your paintings. To determine if your brush type is affected by the paper type, check to see whether the word *Grainy* appears in the Method pop-up menu. If so, that tool will be affected by the paper it is used on.

Fig. 22.36
Use the scroll bar to find a paper type that suits your painting. Not all brush types are affected by the type of paper to which they are applied.

In the Color Palette (see fig. 22.37), you can choose the color of the applied paint. You can use any color of the spectrum with any of the brushes, but the preset color palette is a sampling of colors that are normally associated with the brush that you have chosen in the Brush Palette.

Fig. 22.37

The Color Palette enables you to define the color that the brush applies. You can use any color with any brush, not just those in the predefined swatches.

Besides being able to edit the brush size, you can also define the intensity (or *buildup*) with which the color is applied. Options for buildup include the following: Soft, Grainy Soft, Grainy Hard, Grainy Edge Flat, Soft Paper, and more. With the Brush Behavior Palette, you can define the Saturation, Spacing, and Wet Fringe from sliders that control that type of setting and other attributes.

Working with the Toolbox Contents

The Toolbox of Painter plays a minor role next to the Brush and Colors palette (see fig. 22.38). It does not hold the same importance that the Toolbox of each of the applications we have already discussed. It has a zoom box like the other palettes of Painter, and clicking it shows and hides the Frisket tools. It also includes the Zoom tool (for enlarging and reducing your artwork on screen), the Grabber tool (for positioning the artwork in the active window), the Brush tool (for selecting a Brush from the Brush palette), the Eyedropper tool (for picking up a color selection from inside your painting), and so on. The Frisket tools that only show when you have zoomed the palette are for masking parts of your painting.

Using the Editing, Retouching, and Special Effects

There are quite a few other attributes that you can add to a painting. These include the following: Add Lighting, Color Overlay, Adjust Dye Concentration, Apply Surface Texture, and Apply Screen. Each of these options can be applied to art that you have created or to a scan that you have opened inside Painter. A number of typical transformation tools are also available, such as Rotate, Distort, Scale, and Flip Vertical/Horizontal. Photo editing tools are also numerous: you'll find tools such as Soften, Sharpen, Focus, Brightness/Contrast, Equalize, and Posterize. All of these combined—or individually—make for an extremely adept photo editing and retouching program.

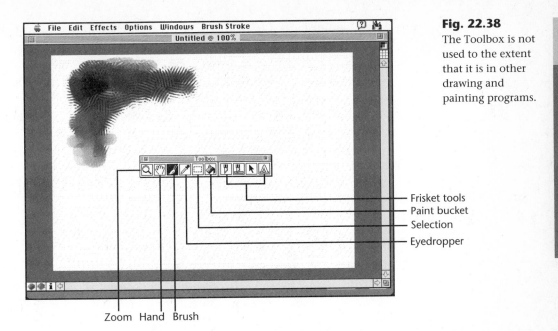

Fig. 22.38
The Toolbox is not
used to the extent
that it is in other
drawing and
painting programs.

Special effects are also possible here. You are given the tools for Highpass,
Motion Blur, Blob, Marbling, and Glass Distortion. These options are easy
to use and most come with their own window or dialog box (as do the
transformation and attribute tools) for applying or adjusting that feature
of the painting.

Like other pixel-based and vector-based programs discussed in this chapter,
Plus-Ins can be used with Painter. After they are installed, you access them
from the Effects menu.

Cloning

The Cloning feature of Painter enables you to perform photo retouching
without affecting the original scan or graphic. It also enables you to trace
over originals and transform photos into pencil sketches, oil paintings, Van
Goghs, or Seurats. After you make a clone of your artwork by using the File
menu, you're ready to begin editing the painting, tracing, or painting or
drawing on top of the image.

Working with Friskets

In the world of traditional fine art, a frisket is used to cover up portions of a
painting to keep from getting paint on that part that is covered. It might also

be used by an airbrush artist to define an area for editing. Either way, friskets are used similarly in Painter. Use them for defining areas that you want to add color to or to cover areas where you don't want to accidentally add color. The Toolbox has four additional tools for creating friskets that are available only when you use the zoom button to expand the Toolbox to its full size. There is also a Frisket Palette that turns Friskets on and off, smoothes them, and controls the feathering amount, among other options. Friskets can contain a color and can be transparent or opaque. Use the Magic Wand (a selection tool from the Toolbox) to select all pixels of a like color and then make them a frisket. This would allow you to change the color of all the pixels inside or all the pixels outside the frisket selection.

Getting the Most from Painter: Hot Tips

- *Choosing a resolution.* (This tip also appeared in Claris BrushStrokes, but is important here, as well.) For optimum printing quality, the resolution you create your image at should follow the same rules as resolutions for halftones. A formula for determining the correct amount is simple:

  Screen frequency (lpi) $\times$ 1.5 = Image Resolution (dpi).

  If you intend to reduce or enlarge the painting as you output the file, factor that number in also. For instance, if you have painted a 4 $\times$ 5" image and you intend to enlarge it 200% (you will use an 8 $\times$ 10"), the formula looks like this.

  Screen frequency (lpi) $\times$ 1.5 = x
  $x \times 8" \div 4$ = Image Resolution (dpi).

  Enter the resolution amount in the Resolution field of the New Picture Size dialog box. The total document size, based on this resolution and the width and height you have chosen, is displayed below this field.

- *Extending Painter.* When working with several objects, use Fractal Design's Painter X2. This extension allows you to create a scrolling portfolio of thumbnail views of painted objects. These objects are dragged to the image area and placed floating above the layer below. Each item is a frisket that can be feathered to any degree.

- *Adding Brushes.* In addition to the palette of brushes already available in Painter, other libraries of brush styles can be added as a Plug-In. High-end users will find the expanded collection can be customized to fit their artistic style.

■ *Straightening your Lines.* Though you generally don't paint perfectly straight lines with a brush, it is an option in Painter. Choose Brush Stroke, Draw Straight Lines. If you'd like to draw lines and make them into guide lines or grids, choose Options, Grid Overlay.

Summary

Painter is probably one of the most unique programs to hit the market in some time. It is specifically geared toward the fine artist making the transition to electronic art, a switch that can be nearly seamless but will open up a whole new world of possibilities. For the first time, traditional fine artists can have multiple medias and paper textures in the same creation. It stands separate from the other products in this chapter because of its very specific purpose and unique features.

Conclusions and Recommendations

The five programs discussed in this chapter are all produced with the artist in mind. The type of artist you are, or what your style is for a particular job, will help you to decide which of the products are best for you. Illustrations that do not require a great number of technical callouts are handled equally well by Illustrator or FreeHand. For those of you who draw objects to scale and need the ability to very quickly add measured callouts or add dimension to objects, you'll find Canvas quite adept at this type of art.

Brush Strokes and Painter are vastly different, though both are pixel-based and both are for editing or creating painting-type art. A beginner might be very at home with a small, easy-to-use application like BrushStrokes, but an experienced artist will feel limited. Painter, on the other hand, offers the fine artist many texture, paper, and brush options that feel more like working traditionally.

Other factors, such as price, hard disk space, and so on, may also have a bearing on the program you choose. In table 22.1, further comparisons between the programs are shown.

Table 22.1   Application Comparisons

Application	Vector/ Pixel Based	Approximate Retail (Street) Price	Hard Disk	RAM Requirements
Illustrator	Vector	$389.95	4.5 MB	5 MB rec.
FreeHand	Vector	$389.95	3.5 MB	8 MB rec.
Canvas	Vector	$251.90	6.2 MB	2 MB
BrushStrokes	Pixel	$45.95	2 MB	4 MB
Painter	Pixel	$264.95	5.3 MB	2.5 MB

Chapter 23

Digital Photography and Desktop Video

by Rob Sonner

The Digital revolution is here and won't be leaving anytime soon. This chapter deals with Digital Photography and Desktop Video. This field was largely made possible by the folks at Apple Computer and would not have existed in the same way without Adobe Systems, Inc.

Digital Photography and Desktop Video are perhaps two of the most underestimated and powerful capabilities and the best-kept secret about the Apple Macintosh computer. Every day, people scan photographs, digitize their movies, and touch up and print their works of art without ever having to leave their desk—*desktop*, that is.

Working on the desktop means never having to look or move away from your Macintosh. All your work efforts and the tools necessary to complete these efforts are self-contained in your computer.

This chapter takes a brief look into five programs:

- Adobe Photoshop 2.5.1

- Adobe Audition 1.0/Adobe Premiere 2.1 LE

- QuickTime 1.6.1 and 1.6.2

Adobe Photoshop

Adobe Photoshop has stormed the marketplace since its inception in 1989 and has literally spawned thousands of digital photography labs in people's homes and offices. Professional photographers and artists using Adobe

Photoshop for just a few months wonder how they ever managed without it. They can hardly see themselves returning to the traditional darkroom mixing chemicals. Newcomers are immersed in a new world with the power of millions in their hands for only a few hundred dollars.

Adobe Photoshop allows you as the computer user to create, edit, manipulate and take charge of working with all forms of color images. You can create Photo composites with ease and retouch images that have been tarnished over time. Adobe Photoshop has something to offer for every individual, whether that person is an artist, photographer, or casual user.

Finding your way around the program is easy in version 2.5.1, where many complicated tasks have been streamlined down to one or two steps and are available in floating palettes. In Photoshop, mixing chemicals and preparing separations for the print house are never more than a mouse click away.

Along with Photoshop's extensive bag of tools, revolutionary third-party plug-ins for Photoshop such as Kai's Power Tools (designed by Photoshop wizard Kai Krause and published by HSC Software, Inc.) and Paint Alchemy (published by Xaos Tools, Inc.) have made designing an easy task in Photoshop, giving you the power and glory to illustrate creations beyond your wildest dreams with simplicity and ease.

It's preferable to have a color Macintosh system and 24-bit color, although you'll be okay with an 8-bit configuration. Photoshop runs on all black-and-white Macintoshes, provided adequate memory is available. Also, there is an Indexed Color feature that will optimize any 24-bit color document for optimal viewing of 24-bit images on an 8-bit system.

What Is the Difference between 24-Bit Color and 8-Bit Color?

On a Macintosh, 24-bit color is represented on-screen by 16.7 million different colors referred to as three-channel or RGB images. The channels are Red, Green, and Blue, which account for all the colors in the spectrum. Although the eye cannot see all these shades and hues, the colors can be simulated on-screen in a way the human eye can understand. To achieve 24-bit color on your Macintosh, you must have a 24-bit video card such as ones made by Super Mac (Thunder 24) and Radius (Precision Color) or enough Video RAM (VRAM) installed on the motherboard.

When referring to 8-bit color, you're dealing with 256 colors optimized for your screen viewing. An 8-bit color image is a single channel image containing a maximum of 256 colors and uses a reference lookup table to preview your image on screen dithering the 16.7 million colors down to the most common 256 in a matter of seconds.

Memory/System Requirements

Photoshop is an easy-to-learn program that is fun for the beginner and has the power to take seasoned professionals to new places and quality levels of work output. After all, in this business, time and work are money.

You must know what you need to effectively run Photoshop. A standard Macintosh with 8MB of RAM is the bare minimum required. The more RAM your system has, the better off you will be. Don't worry—you don't have to drive down to your local computer store and buy all the memory you can squeeze into your Macintosh. Sit down and see what your options are.

Sometimes, not as much RAM is needed as you might expect. Photoshop has its own built-in Virtual Memory that utilizes your hard disk as extra RAM. The latest version, 2.5.1, can use up to two hard drives as scratch disks, whereas version 2.0 and 2.01 were limited to just one. These scratch disks temporarily hold the essential data needed for the active documents in Photoshop by storing the information in free space on the designated drive when RAM is insufficient.

One caution about using Virtual Memory: as Photoshop physically has to write the information to disk, speed and performance slow dramatically. If you find yourself waiting long periods between operations in Photoshop, this may be the time to upgrade your RAM.

The RAM allocated to Photoshop may be changed while the program is not running by selecting the Photoshop icon in the Finder and pressing ⌘-I to display the Get Info dialog box. In the next example, you can see that I have increased memory to 20000K. Based on your system's configuration, this actual number will change slightly.

When at all possible, give Photoshop as much memory as allowed by your system configuration (see fig. 23.1). I always leave a small buffer equivalent to approximately 2MB of RAM to allow for system heap expansion. Also, this is very helpful for switching to another program, such as the Chooser, to select a printer or a file server or to browse through folders in the network without having to quit Photoshop.

Fig. 23.1

Adjusting
Photoshop's
memory
allocation.

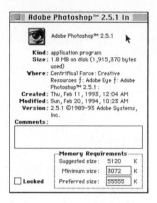

Photoshop stores three copies of every document you are working on in memory, be it virtual or real memory (RAM). Naturally, the more RAM you have, the better off you will be performance-wise and speed-wise. The first copy of your document in memory is the actual working copy you see on-screen. The second copy is an exact clone for reference purposes only to expedite some of the more time-consuming procedures such as channel and composite operations as well as screen refreshes, or what I refer to as a *cache copy*.

The third and most important copy of your document in memory is your Undo copy. With this copy, you can use the Undo command (⌘-Z) to restore your document to its previous state before your last move. Photoshop currently cannot do multiple Undos because of the mass of memory required to accomplish the task. The File menu, however, contains a Revert option that will take you back to the previously saved version of your document should something go horribly wrong necessitating such an action.

When you launch Photoshop for the first time, you will be running with the program's default settings. At this point, I highly recommend a visit to the Preferences, where you'll find the necessary settings to ensure the program's smooth operation. The Preferences settings are found in the File menu of Photoshop and have a further submenu. Consult your manual for specifics on these settings. The main preference that interests us at this time is the Scratch Disks preference, which is necessary only if you utilize a second drive as a scratch disk (see fig. 23.2).

In the Units preferences, in the File menu > Preferences submenu, you can set the default unit of measure. My default unit of measure is usually the pixel, but based on your personal preference, you can set this however you want. Other options include inches, centimeters, picas, and points in the Units Preferences dialog box (see fig. 23.3).

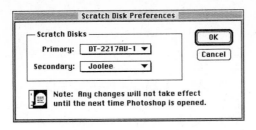

Fig. 23.2
Defining Scratch Disks for Photoshop's virtual memory.

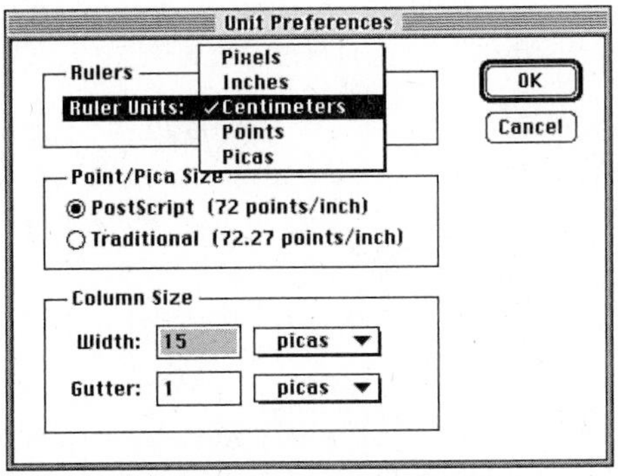

Fig. 23.3
The Unit Preferences dialog box.

Adobe recommends that your System settings for Memory Cache (in the Memory Control Panel) are set to 32K and that the System's Virtual Memory is turned off (see fig. 23.4). Photoshop greatly appreciates having this domain reserved for its internal memory manager. The maladies that can arise when using System virtual memory with Photoshop's virtual memory can prove destructive.

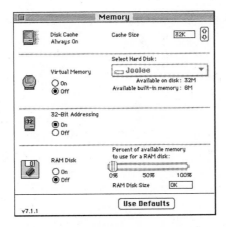

Fig. 23.4
The Memory Control panel.

Using a Scanner

Many scanners are compatible with Photoshop, ranging from low-priced flatbed scanners all the way to high-resolution Leaf scanners for slides and transparencies. The one thing they have in common is the standard Acquire plug-in configuration for Photoshop, and they usually ship with a stand-alone scanning program proprietary to the particular scanner you choose. A considerable amount of documentation is written about different scanners—from magazine article reviews to university journal documentation. A visit to your local library can open this information to you. Before buying your scanner, make sure that the one you get is truly the right one for you.

If you own Photoshop and want to take Digital Photography seriously, you shouldn't be without the services of a scanner. You don't need to own a scanner because many service bureaus sell scanning services and most large cities have several outfits that lease on-site scanning services. In the long run, however, you'll find that owning your own scanner will be much more cost-effective.

When scanning directly into Photoshop, you can set your document size, resolution, and Image mode (including line art) before you scan. This allevi-ates the time-consuming task of repeated file conversions. As soon as you scan, you can immediately manipulate your image. Photoshop allows you to save images in more than 15 file formats, which provides compatibility with a host of other programs and platforms like IBM-compatible PCs and Scitex. The native Photoshop 2.5 format saves files more quickly than other file formats and clears the memory buffer for prolonged and better Photoshop performance.

Getting Started with Photoshop

Like all Macintosh programs, Photoshop has standard pull-down menus with all the normal, recognizable features, as well as some that will not be as famil-iar. This chapter covers some of the essential ones to get you started and on your way in Photoshop in no time at all.

The New command at the top of the File menu opens a dialog box in which you can define your initial document size. In the diagram, the document size is 512 pixels by 512 pixels with a resolution of 72 dots per inch (dpi) in the RGB Mode (see fig. 23.5).

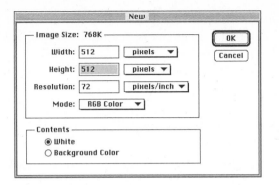

Fig. 23.5
Creating a new
document in
Photoshop.

Now that you have a clean white canvas, there are many places you can go.
You can place an image into your new document from your hard drive by
using the Place command, acquire a document by scanning an image by
using the Acquire command, open an existing image from your hard drive, or
create a new image using Photoshop's tools and filters. The Acquire submenu
is where scanner Acquire plug-in modules show up in your Photoshop. You'll
know whether you have these because many—if not all—popular scanners,
such as the ones manufactured by Microtek and UMAX, ship with an Adobe
Photoshop Acquire plug-in module, as well as with a stand-alone application
program for scanning (see fig. 23.6).

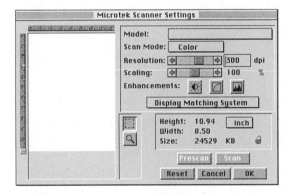

Fig. 23.6
Example of an
Acquire plug-in for
the Microtek
scanner.

Changing Image Size

When you import an image into Photoshop, you can customize its physical
size and resolution freely and at will. Downsizing your image can be done to
maintain proportion so as not to lose touch with the aspect ratios. This is
frequently used when finalizing a project in Photoshop, but should always
be taken into consideration ahead of time before you even begin working.
Ask yourself what you want or your customer wants.

More often than not, consulting with your printer or service bureau gives you the most insight as to what you need to determine when making such decisions. The key is to consult and finalize the details before you start the project. This way you'll always have an understanding with your client and between you and the printer—which is *very* important.

You should know a few things about resizing your image. You can downsize an image with no trouble and no degradation. In the General Photoshop preferences, make sure that Bicubic Interpolation is selected in General Preferences. Each new pixel that Photoshop creates in the upscaled result is averaged from the values of the immediate surrounding pixels. Upsizing your bitmap image is more difficult because in theory you cannot create what is not already there. This is your best bet if you do need to increase the overall size and resolution of your image.

Tip
Anytime you upsize an image in Photoshop, be sure to run the Unsharp Mask Plug-In filter located in the Filter > Sharpen menu.

The other option is to use Nearest Neighbor, which takes the nearest corresponding pixels and assigns these values to the newly created pixels in the upscaled image. The result of using the Nearest Neighbor is a faster, although less precise, alternative. The look of your image will be rather choppy and will have a noticeably exaggerated pixelated effect as well. If your original source image is intentionally pixelated or is aliased text (such as Macintosh screen shots and fonts) and you want to keep these qualities, Nearest Neighbor is an excellent choice. Otherwise, it's best to stay with Bicubic Interpolation.

Remember, just as when you create a new document, when you resize a document, you can make your changes based on the different Units settings available in Photoshop. You can even resize based on image size percentage (see fig. 25.7).

Fig. 23.7
The Image Size Dialog Box from the Image menu.

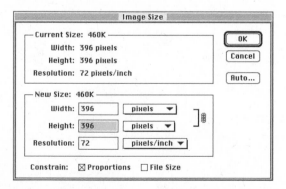

Changing Canvas Size

The Canvas size command in the Image menu refers to the overall big picture of the image you are working with in Photoshop. If you were to downsize the Canvas, you'd cut off parts of your image. Photoshop warns you before this happens. The chief purpose of Canvas size is to increase your workspace around an image.

This is not without its loophole consequences—the larger your Canvas is, the more memory your image requires to manipulate and store. Never work with a larger Canvas than necessary. This becomes very apparent the more you work in Photoshop, because image size is geometrically progressive and expansive.

Exporting Files from Photoshop

Below Acquire in the File menu is the Export menu (see fig. 23.8). There you will find a series of export modules for custom file definitions such as for Adobe Illustrator, Amiga, ImageWriter Color, and Film Strips. Consult your Adobe Photoshop manual for more information on these and other Export file types.

Fig. 23.8
Photoshop's
Export submenu.

Using Photoshop's Toolbox

In Photoshop's vast array of powers, you can use selection tools to define specific areas to edit. This gives you the ability to paste an entire image (or portion thereof) inside or behind an isolated portion of an image. To create selections, Photoshop's Toolbox contains four tools specifically reserved for making selections. The Toolbox can usually be found in the upper left corner of your screen.

IV

Macintosh Software

At the top of the Toolbox are the Rectangle and Ellipse Marquee selection tools, represented by dashed lines (see fig. 23.9). When you're using one of these tools, your selection will be represented on-screen by what appear to be marching ants—dashed blinking dotted lines that march around your selection. You can constrain the movement of these tools to perfect circles and squares by double-clicking the Marquee tool and selecting the Constrained Aspect Ratio option in the dialog box that appears.

The Lasso tool is where you truly have control to make freeform arbitrary selections. You can also make multiple selections with any of the tools by holding down the Shift key during the selection process. Holding down the ⌘ key enables you to subtract areas from your selection. Also, to lock certain preferences into a particular tool, double-click the tool's icon in the toolbox. This action displays a dialog box with the tool's preferences, such as feathering and constraining proportions, as well as a fixed pixel ratio size.

The last remaining selection tool is the Magic Wand. Magically, this tool's icon looks like a miniature wand, and when you click the mouse around or on a particular color value in your document, the Magic Wand searches the immediate area for similar colors and outlines them with the now familiar marching ants.

Fig. 23.9
Double-clicking any of the selection tools displays a dialog box, enabling you to set preferences for that individual tool.

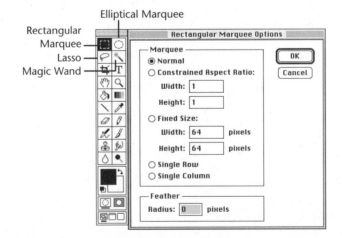

Tip
Double-clicking any of the tools in the Toolbox opens a custom preference dialog box for that particular tool.

> **Note**
>
> Anytime marching ants appear on-screen, hide them temporarily and maintain your selection with Hide Edges under the selection menu. The opposite Show Edges takes effect and shows in its place if the selection's edges are invisible. Toggle back and forth quickly with the keyboard shortcut ⌘-H.

The Cropping tool is one of the most helpful tools in Photoshop. You can crop images in a couple of short steps with total control. Select the tool from the Toolbox and drag the marquee over the area you want to crop in on. At this point, you can adjust the crop area by grabbing the handles at any of the four corners and making your necessary adjustments. When you double-click the Cropping tool icon in the Toolbox, you get a dialog box that allows you to set the specific dimensions of your crop and even the resolution you want after the crop. Also, setting dimensions allows you to maintain a certain aspect ratio. Figure 23.10 shows the Toolbar.

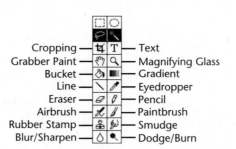

Cropping — Text
Grabber Paint — Magnifying Glass
Bucket — Gradient
Line — Eyedropper
Eraser — Pencil
Airbrush — Paintbrush
Rubber Stamp — Smudge
Blur/Sharpen — Dodge/Burn

Fig. 23.10
The Toolbar.

When performing this operation, you need to take your interpolation setting into consideration; once again, Bicubic is your best choice. If for some reason you're cropping in and scaling up to the resolution you desire for the cropped area—this is a must—make sure that you are in the Bicubic Interpolation mode for the same reason discussed a few pages back: you need to use sample image data from a broader range of pixels for more accurate image detail.

When you have marked the area to crop, move the mouse into the center of the selected crop image. The mouse icon turns into scissors. Click the mouse, and your crop is complete. Clicking outside the selected area cancels the crop, leaving your image untouched.

You can insert text into your Photoshop image by selecting the Text tool. With the Text tool selected, click the mouse. A dialog box where you can enter your text appears on-screen. Enter the text you want to insert, set your Font, and click OK.

As long as the text remains highlighted with the marquee, you can reposition the text. Once the selection is dropped, you can no longer move the text by itself.

The Grabber tool allows you to move around your document by literally *grabbing* the document. This allows you to move through your image area without having to use the scroll bars. This is especially helpful in the Full Screen modes, when the menu bars are hidden.

Tip

Make sure that the Anti-Aliased box is checked in the Text Edit dialog box for best results with PostScript fonts. This ensures that your type is smooth instead of the aliased "stair-stepped" effects of bitmap fonts.

Tip

You can access the Grabber tool on the fly as you're using any other tool by pressing and holding the space bar; to return to the selected tool, release the space bar.

The Magnifying Glass tool is most handy for zooming in and out on your image. The keyboard shortcut when using any other tool is ⌘-space bar. Pressing ⌘-Option-space bar activates the De-magnifying Glass for zooming out on your image.

The Paint Bucket tool enables you to fill areas with the foreground color.

The Blend/Gradient tool allows you to make gradients by blending the selected Foreground and Background colors in your image. Double-clicking the Toolbox icon opens a dialog box where you can set particular preferences of your gradient (see fig. 23.11). Options enable you to create Linear or Radial gradients with control of the midpoint skew on the color blend. You can also do a full spectrum in a Clockwise or a Counterclockwise direction.

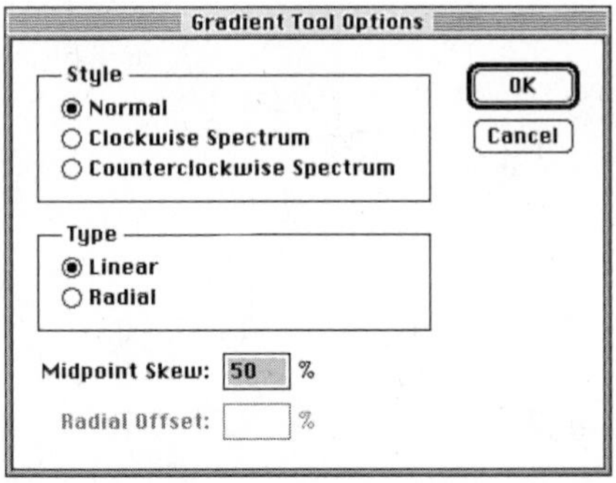

Fig. 23.11
The Gradient tool preferences.

The Line tool enables you to paint straight lines on your image in the selected Foreground color. Holding down the Shift key constrains the lines to 45-degree-angle multiples.

Tip
In either the Paint Brush or Pencil tool, holding down the Option key changes the tool to the Eyedropper so you can select a Foreground color.

The Eyedropper tool enables you to select your Foreground and Background colors from an image without having to call up the Color Picker. Normal selection of the tool enables you to choose the Foreground color; holding down the Option key assigns a new Background color. The Eyedropper Options dialog box is shown in figure 23.12.

The Eraser tool erases areas of your image to the selected background color based 1:1 on the icon to image ratio. What you see is what you get. Double-clicking the Eraser tool in the Toolbox erases your entire image. By holding down the Option key while erasing, your image loads your last saved version, enabling you, magically, to selectively revert parts of your image.

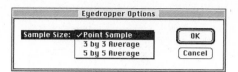

Fig. 23.12
The Eyedropper
tool allows you to
pick a single color
or an average over
several pixels.

Note

Feathering a selection is a task you'll become very familiar with quickly. A feathered selection allows for the selected area, when modified, to have a smooth, meticulous look as well as a consistent smooth edge. In the real world, a feathered edge equates into a smooth, soft, tapered look. If you fail to use feathered selections when necessary, the result is very apparent with sometimes jagged and raw blotchy edges, Any selection can be feathered by selecting "Feather" from the Select pull-down menu and entering a pixel radius number.

Also, by double-clicking the selection tools in the Toolbox, you can enter a feather radius value as well.

Tip
Try using the
magic eraser with
feathered Lasso
tool selections.
This Eraser tool
erases to your
selected back-
ground color
(as chosen in the
Color Picker),
leaving you with a
soft tapered look
rather than a hard
pixelated edge.

The Pencil tool enables you to draw straight or freeform lines. Holding the Shift key while you apply the Pencil constrains the movement horizontally or vertically. Figure 23.13 shows the Pencil Options dialog box.

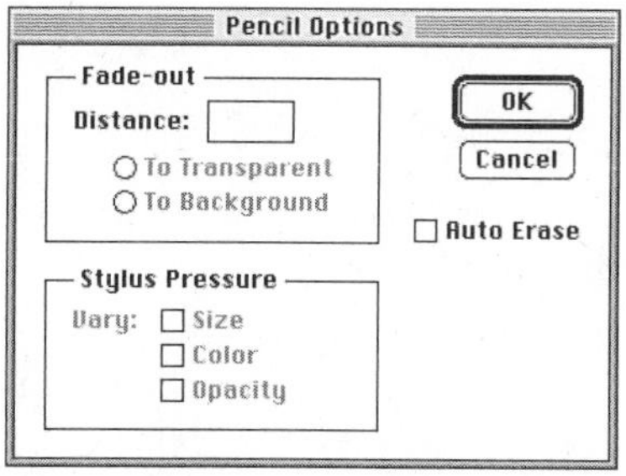

Fig. 23.13
Pencil tool
preferences.

The Airbrush tool works in much the same was as the traditional airbrush. It spreads a light layer of the selected Foreground color on your image. If you have a pressure-sensitive tablet attached to your Macintosh, you can vary the pressure of the Airbrush tool. Figure 23.14 shows the Airbrush Options dialog box.

Fig. 23.14
Preference dialog
box for the
Airbrush tool.

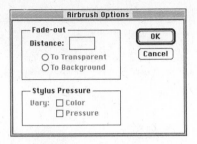

The Paintbrush tool enables you to paint your image by using any of the brushes in the Brush Palette. You can create your own custom brushes and the apply mode in which you will do your painting. The apply modes are found in the Brush Palette. The most common apply mode is the Normal apply, which is just what you would see if you applied opaque paint to a canvas. Other apply modes allow you to only paint areas that are darker than your paintbrush color (Lighten mode) or paint areas that are lighter than your paintbrush color (Darken only). Try each of the apply modes to get a feel for what they can do. The brushes work in the same way as many of the tools. Consult the *Photoshop User Guide* for specific and detailed information pertaining to brush selection, manipulation, and creation. Figure 23.15 shows the Paintbrush Options dialog box.

Fig. 23.15
Paintbrush tool
preferences.

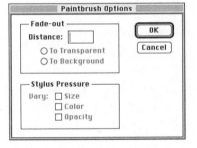

The Rubber Stamp tool allows you to sample and clone different portions of your image from one location to another while preserving the nature of the orientation point. When selecting the tool, hold down the Option key and select the originating point of the area from which you want to clone. Upon releasing the Option key, move the cursor to the destination area. You can clone across different images, and you can set your Brush size from the Brush Palette as well as its characteristics. The Impressionistic effects of the Rubber Stamp are amazing, and the From Saved option will allow you to Rubber Stamp back in portions of your image from the previously saved version. Figure 23.16 shows the Rubber Stamp Options dialog box.

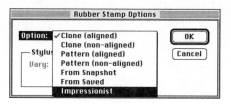

Fig. 23.16
The many options
available in the
Rubber Stamp tool.

The Smudge tool enables you to smudge precise areas of your image, like digital finger painting. The Smudge tool is pressure-sensitive when used with a tablet such as a Wacom tablet. Figure 23.17 shows the Smudge Tool Options dialog box.

Fig. 23.17
Options of the
Smudge tool allow
you to digitally
finger paint.

When selected, the Blur/Sharpen tool sharpens or blurs the areas of the image over which the tool passes. To toggle between Blur/Sharpen, you just Option-click the tool in the Toolbox. This also works while in the document; the icon reflects which tool is currently active. This tool is also pressure-sensitive when a drawing tablet is attached to the Macintosh. Double-clicking the tool displays a dialog box with all these options at the end of the paragraph (see fig. 23.18).

Fig. 23.18
Toggling the Blur
and Sharpen tool.

The newest tool to come to Photoshop is the Dodge and Burn tool. While this is a practical technique in the darkroom, Photoshop brings this tool out into the light for you to use right from your desktop (see fig. 23.19). Option-clicking on the icon toggles between the two. While working in the document, the Option key has the same tool-toggling effect.

Fig. 23.19
The Dodge and
Burn tools.

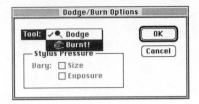

Choosing Your Foreground and Background Colors

At the bottom of the Toolbox is the Photoshop Color Picker. The two large squares each show the currently selected Foreground and Background colors. The left square represents the Foreground, and the right represents Background color. On-screen, the left square appears to be sitting slightly in front of the one on the right.

If you click either the Foreground or the Background square, the Photoshop Color Picker appears on-screen, allowing you to choose your color visually with a complex full spectrum palette (see fig. 23.20). You can precisely dial in your desired color by using any of the numeral entry charts for RGB, CMYK, HSB, or LAB.

Fig. 23.20
Photoshop's Color
Picker.

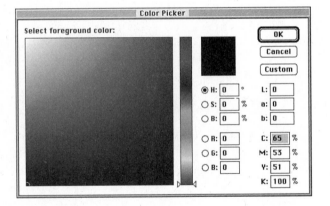

Clicking the Custom button opens the Custom Pantone color picker (see fig. 23.21). You can either scroll for the entire list, or if you know the name of the equivalent Pantone Matching number, you can enter it in the Find #: box and scroll right to it. It's as simple as can be. Choosing the exact Pantone color in a CMYK Photoshop image is highly reliable for color accuracy.

You will also notice in the bottom of the Toolbox above and below Color Picker squares that there are little arrows and little Black/White squares. Clicking the squares resets the color picker to Black and White, and the double arrow toggles and switches the Foreground and Background Colors.

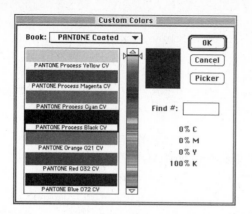

Fig. 23.21
Photoshop's
Pantone Color
Picker.

Working with Selections in Photoshop

After defining a selection in your document, you can save the selection to be recalled at any time. It's as simple as choosing Save Selection from the Select menu. When you save additional selections, the Save selection becomes a hierarchical menu, at which time you can choose to either save a selection over one that is already in existence or to create a new Alpha Channel. Saving selections does not come without its toll in memory usage. Every time a selection is saved adding an Alpha Channel, an additional Channel is added to your document, increasing your file size, but it does not affect finished look.

Alpha Channels can be edited or deleted by using the Show Channels palette found in the Windows pull-down menu and then selecting Delete with the desired channel highlighted. Alpha Channels are very common in video for superimposing text or objects into a defined area leaving the underlying image area untouched.

The way this applies to Photoshop is by storing selection data in an Alpha Channel you can access what is otherwise transparent to you and the actual working image. The amount of Alpha Channel use varies from one user to another; typically, expert Photoshoppers will use 10-12 Alpha Channels to store their transparent selection data.

To merge an image into another image, you can copy and paste. Initially, when you paste one image on top of another, it becomes a floating selection. This means you can grab it, move it, and otherwise tweak it in any way, shape, or form that you want—even delete it. After the selection is dropped, however, you can no longer edit it as a floating selection. Images can be pasted over another image or into complex selections. The possibilities are endless.

One exercise you should try once you feel comfortable in Photoshop is to copy and paste images onto one another and head straight into the Composite Controls command on the Edit menu. The art of compositing in Photoshop is truly magical and effortless. I recommend consulting your *Photoshop User Guide* for details on what comprises the Composite Controls, as these will truly give you some spectacular and unbeatable results on your finished images.

Using Third-Party Plug-In Packages

Along with the spectacular composite and pasting controls of Photoshop, you should immediately become familiar with the image calculation features of Photoshop. German-born artist and Photoshop commando Kai Krause has made himself a devout following with insider tips he authored about Photoshop's calculation modes. Originally these tips were written in Microsoft Word format and uploaded to the computer network America Online where he gained international recognition. Now they are available virtually anywhere a computer and modem exist via the Internet. You can obtain the tips not only on America Online and CompuServe, but also through Anonymous FTP by accessing the host ftp.netcom.com and going to the pub/hsc/Kais_Power_Tips/mac_tips directory.

Kai's Power Tools

These tips not only garnered Kai much respect worldwide but inspired him to publish software to complement Photoshop. In order to get the most out of Photoshop with a minimum amount of effort, every Photoshop user should own a copy of Kai's Power Tools (see fig. 23.22). KPT 2.0 is a set of 33 plug-in filters for Photoshop where you, the Photoshop user, can explore an endless combination of seamless tiled textures and multiple gradients, as well as a Fractal Explorer that infinitely loops and makes looking for the perfect iteration easy and intuitive.

Other third-party plug-in packages worth checking out include Paint Alchemy and Terrazo from Xaos Tools, Inc., Andromeda Series filters, and the three volumes of Aldus Gallery Effects.

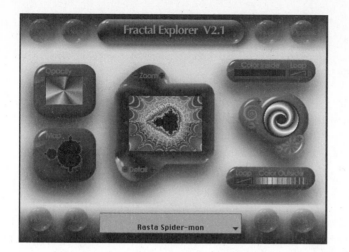

Fig. 23.22
Kai's Power Tools
Fractal Explorer
User Interface.

Shareware Plug-In Packages

Photoshop is a unique program in that it can virtually be expanded in many different ways with the addition of third-party plug-ins, whether it is a new file format that will be supported or more filters. An excellent source of third party Shareware Photoshop filters is America Online, offering a small package of filters called Chris' Filters (written by a college student by the name of Chris Cox) and another by a group who call themselves Alien Skin and their new Black Box Filters, which include effects like the Drop Shadow plug-in. Demonstrations of Andromeda filters are also available.

You have just had a quick overview of Photoshop, giving you the needed insight to get yourself started. What you have here is the nuts and bolts approach to Photoshop; there is more to tell which is more than can ever be written in any book, and more than has ever been written in any book. Photoshop is very much a self-learning program which only you can control based on the need to learn and the desire to learn. Experiment. Work. Play. Photoshop.

Getting the Most from Photoshop: Hot Tips

- If you're using a Power Macintosh with Photoshop 2.5.1, make sure that you obtain a copy of the Power Macintosh Photoshop Plug-In. It is available free from Adobe Systems and available on many online services such as America Online and CompuServe as well as the Internet.

- When viewing a selection in Photoshop characterized by the marching ants on your screen, hide the selection's edges for the best possible preview with the keyboard shortcut ⌘-H.

- You can quickly snap to the Magnifying Glass tool from any other tool in Photoshop by holding down the ⌘ and the space bar together; the cursor will turn into a magnifying glass with a + on it. With the magnifying tool selected, clicking the mouse to enlarge the image or dragging a marquee rectangle selection tool to define an area you want to zoom into are quick ways to isolate an area of an image you want to view. When you press the Option key on the keyboard in addition to ⌘ and the space bar, the magnifying glass turns into a de-magnifying glass and will have a distinguishable minus sign (–) as the cursor and has the exact opposite of the magnifying glass. Pressing ⌘-Option – zooms your Photoshop document to the smallest possible size 1:16 of the 1:1 size, and pressing ⌘-Option + quick zooms to the 1:1 size ratio. In Photoshop 2.5.1 LE, ⌘- reduces the view to the next lowest ratio (that is, 2:1 becomes 1:1), and ⌘+ magnifies the view to the next highest ratio (1:1 becomes 2:1, 2:1 becomes 3:1, and so on).

- The Hand tool can be activated at any time from anywhere by holding down the space bar on the keyboard and click-dragging your image rather than using the scroll bars.

- In a Photoshop document in normal view, a number in the format of a 1:1 ratio appears in the window's title bar. This number represents the ratio of pixels to the screen based on 72 pixels to the inch. When the ratio is 1:1, it means you are viewing your image at a 1:1 ratio at 72 DPI and not necessarily at the true resolution of your document. If you're working in a 300DPI document, the 1:1 screen ratio will undoubtedly appear to be zoomed in and cropped up. There is no need to worry. Just work the logistics of the algorithm into the picture and the numbers will pan out.

- Engaging the Caps Lock key changes most of the cursors for Photoshop's tools into a cross hair. This is extremely helpful when you need to see exactly where you are trying to crop or which pixel you want to select for the Rubber Stamp tool.

- A copy of the Shareware CDEV Window Shade is one of the most valuable additions that is not directly a part of Photoshop that you can add to your list of accessories. Available from America Online, this Control

Panel acts as a roll-up Window Shade for all windows on your Macintosh, including those in Photoshop.

■ The Show Info floating palette located in the Window menu in Photoshop is a very small and indiscreet tool (when shown). It constantly displays all the pixel information of your image as the cursor passes over it. It does not use any additional memory and works all by its lonesome. It provides the location of your cursor with X/Y coordinates as well as the RGB and CMYK values in your image.

■ The New Window also found in the Window menu will create an active clone of your working image giving you a second view of your document at a different magnification. Any changes made in one window always reflect themselves in the actual image window. Each window can be set to different magnifications so you can work with two distinct views simultaneously

■ The Variations feature is very handy for color correcting scanned images quickly. You access this feature under Image > Adjust > Variations. Photoshop displays several images that allow you to change the color in the shadows, midtones, highlights, and saturation. By comparing your original image to the variations on-screen, getting accurate color is as easy as point and click.

Summary

Adobe Photoshop is considered by many to be perhaps the most useful software tool designed for the Macintosh for both the editing of color scanned images and photographs alike. It was, and still is, one of a kind in terms of similar applications.

One of the main useful features built into Photoshop is its ability to accept and use plug-ins designed by third-party developers such as HSC Software (Kai's Power Tools) and Xaos Tools (Paint Alchemy). In fact, many paint and drawing programs have followed suit and reconfigured their overall structure to follow suit and also allow the use of third-party plug-ins.

Naturally, there are many paint programs developed and sold for the Macintosh over the years. Perhaps the closest match is Painter from Fractal Designs and more recently Pixel Paint Pro from Pixel Resources, Inc.; but still, nothing is quite like Photoshop.

Adobe Audition

The Adobe Audition 1.0 software package brings together two of the hottest digital imaging programs in a special fully functional Limited Edition: Photoshop 2.5.1 and Premiere 2.1.

The Limited Edition version of Photoshop and the unabridged full shipping version of Photoshop are nearly the same in many ways. The top end of Photoshop LE is restricted by its high-end output limitations and cannot work in four color CMYK mode-making output of color separations nil. Photoshop LE is intended for those who are not planning to do color separations and high-end imaging.

All in all, Audition is an excellent beginning kit if one is unsure whether the full feature versions of the software (Photoshop and Premiere) are the right choices. Whether Audition is initially purchased for a trial run or received as part of a software/hardware bundle, the new user can get a fairly good feel for what each program can and cannot do. Upgrading from the Audition package to the full-blown retail versions is very affordable direct from Adobe Systems and many third-party resellers.

System Requirements

Adobe Audition can be operated on any QuickTime compatible Macintosh with a 68020 microprocessor or greater, although Adobe recommends a 68030 processor for smoothest operation. It is also recommended you have a CD-ROM drive, a color monitor, and video card with at least an 8-bit color depth (256 colors or gray scale). Your work will look much better for color accuracy because the image color will not break up if you have a 24-bit Video Display Card installed in your system.

Effectively, this means you must have a Macintosh II or newer model in order to run Premiere and Photoshop and a minimum of 4 megabytes of RAM installed in your machine. The more memory you have to run the program, the better off you will be in the long and short run of operations.

The Adobe Audition programs are primarily System 7 applications, which means for optimum program performance your System should be loaded with System 7. Both programs will run on System 6.0.7 or newer versions, but need 32-bit QuickDraw (version 1.2 or newer) installed on the older Macintosh models in order for the programs to run. Newer Macintoshes have 32-bit QuickDraw built into the System, and QuickDraw is available on the CD-ROM that is shipped with the software.

Adobe Premiere 2.1 LE

In Adobe Premiere, you can make your debut as the Director and the Producer as well as the Editor of your own movie. The funny thing is, when all is said and done, your budget need not be millions of dollars and you won't have piles of film strips littering the floor.

Adobe Premiere LE allows you to put your ideas from your desktop into motion without having to leave your seat. Creating high-quality, full-color QuickTime MooVs with stereo sound has never been so easy. As you may expect, Premiere 2.1 LE does require version 1.5 of the QuickTime extension to be installed in your system to run.

Adobe Premiere is the award-winning QuickTime movie creation and editing application for the Macintosh. Released initially immediately following the advent of QuickTime in 1991, the program has grown by leaps and bounds along with the QuickTime movie-making movement, meeting the advanced needs of the desktop Videographer as well as addressing the wants of the casual QuickTime movie maker.

Getting Started with Premiere

Inside Premiere is a very elegant and easy-to-use interface. Everything is on the desktop and easily within reach of your mouse. Premiere's design has remained consistent since its beginning. With the current release, version 4.0, the nuts and bolts essentials are still there along with the addition of increased performance, power, and flexibility. It is safe to say that Adobe Premiere is the industry standard for commercial QuickTime Movie making.

In Premiere, your desktop can be configured any way you want with the Construction Window (the physical big picture of your project) along with the Project Window. It is very easy to be up and running in little or no time at all (see fig. 23.23).

When setting up your movie, you can pull images from many places and different programs. Some 3-D animation packages, such as Infini-D, will save animation in what is called PICS format (different from PICT). PICS are a string of PICT files that are stored in a similar fashion to the Scrapbook format. Frequently I make my movies from individual PICT files and store all the images in a common folder to avoid confusion later in the production process. Generally you want to work with smaller image files in the 300 x 200 pixel size range. Sometimes there will be several different scenes which will have their own set of characteristics and thus maybe several working folders.

Fig. 23.23
The Premiere
Interface.

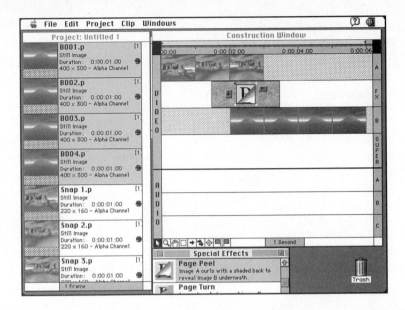

> **Note**
>
> Label your folders with appropriate names, such as Premiere Project Scene 1, Premiere Project Scene 2, and so on, to keep track of scenes and their images. Remember that you're the Director and the Producer; if you're disorganized in the way you manage your files, your production could also be disorganized.

When inserting images into your movie, they first go into the project window where you can complete much of your outline work in the movie towards the final project. The default duration of an imported frame is one second when it is imported into Premiere. Very often, you will find yourself reducing this number to a couple of frames per image or even one frame per image. It depends on your sequence of images that you will be assembling into an animation/QuickTime movie. Experiment with what's right for your particular project. Of course, a different set of logistics takes precedence if you are actually capturing video. In order to capture video directly to your Desktop, you will need to purchase the complete Adobe Premiere package.

In the Import window, which is accessed via the File menu, you can either Import an individual file (be it PICTs or Sounds) on an individual basis or Import a whole folder with the click of your mouse or a series of individual images. This will depend upon your particular situation of course. If you select Multiple it will allow you to strategically select some files and not others by either double-clicking on the files you want (or highlighting and selecting the Open button).

Clicking Folder enables you to select a Folder of Images containing both images and sound data files. This feature is particularly helpful when you are working with a large number of images. You don't have to sit by your computer and attend your mouse as you click and navigate through every single image. This is a timesaving feature unlike no other—it has saved me many hours of production time.

The Project versus the Movie

When you're working on a project in Premiere, your saved work in Premiere is called a Project and your final project a Movie. The Project window where the thumbnails of your working images appear is your content manager (see fig. 23.24). This vertically oriented window can be rather large. The scroll bars can become long based on the number of actual images in your movie project. This is limited to your monitor size and will not extend beyond its limits. Naming your images before importing them in an alpha-numeric format will make for easier work and understanding once you get going on your movie project. An example of this would be B001, B002, B003, and so on.

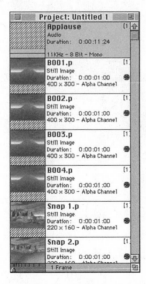

Fig. 23.24
Premiere's Project
Window.

While traversing through Premiere and setting up your project, you should note that before you get to your layout phase, it may be necessary to edit your film clip's frame duration. The default setting is 00:00:01:00, which translates into one second. If each and every frame of your movie is one second, it will run very slowly (longer than you'd probably care), and undoubtedly it will have a very choppy feel.

Special Effects and Superimposing

As seen in figure 23.25, the Project Window contains two boxes: a white box with two buttons and a mid-level gray box labeled Duration (which is also accessible for the selected image by selecting "Duration" from the Clip menu). The white box with labels RGB and Alpha contains the types of images being used in your project. For most movies you will want the RGB button selected because that is what you will be working with. As with standard video editing, Alpha Channels in Premiere are for superimposing text over an image. An example might be film credits rolling at the beginning or end of the film or the addition of clouds to a scene. More specifics on this feature can be found in the *Adobe Premiere User Guide* on using Alpha Channels and other related special effects.

Fig. 23.25
The closeup view of a still in Premiere.

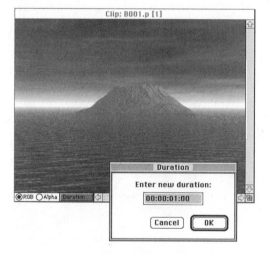

Early versions of QuickTime would only play back on the Macintosh 15 frames per second at a 160 x 120 pixel frame size. However, this has increased over the past three years with each succeeding version. The current QuickTime 2.0 effectively allows for full-speed, full-frame, full-screen 640 x 480, 30 frame-per-second (fps) playback, which is equivalent to that of a motion picture.

Of course, you can easily run one image for ten seconds in your project/ movie by dialing in the duration to ten seconds.

The fun only begins by moving your images into the Construction Window. This is a drag-and-drop operation that may take some practice before you get the hang of it. Try it a few times. This way you can see what happens. You will soon assume complete control over your video editing bay.

You can drag a whole series of film clips from the Project Window to the Construction Window by Shift-clicking the frames you want to select, which may be several hundred or a thousand, or maybe just one or two. It depends on what size or type of project you're working on (see fig. 23.26).

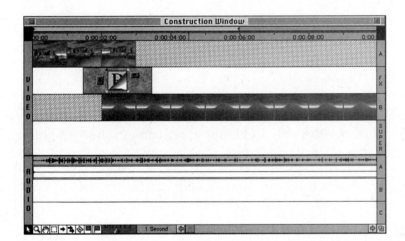

Fig. 23.26
Premiere's
Construction
Window.

You can have two different film tracks in any given movie at any given time. This is particularly useful for editing between several different clips in a given project. This is also useful for setting up transitions (Special Effects) between different clips. Putting these Special Effects into your movie is as easy as a click and drag of the mouse.

The scenario that works best is a series of snapshots—like your family vacation to the desert Sand Dunes. You define those as series A. You also have another part of your family vacation that you want to include in your project; you define this trip to the red sunset with the beautiful sunset over the island as series B. You can run a Special Effect to smooth out the transition between Series A and Series B, and also depict where the first film clip drops off and the second clip comes into the movie. Figure 23.27 shows the Special Effects palette.

Fig. 23.27
Special Effects
palette.

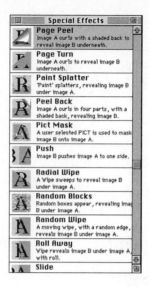

Nothing is worse than an abrupt change between scenes. This is where the transition comes into play. You drag any of the 42 effects from the Special Effects floating palette into the FX strip as the transition between film strip A and film strip B. You can include up to three separate sound tracks in your movie project. The individual sound clips need to be imported and moved into your Construction Window in the same fashion that the images are imported and assembled into place.

To add Special Effects to your movie production is made very easy in Premiere. It is a drag-and-drop procedure. In the "F/X" channel in the Construction Window, you simply drag your desired effect into place and move it into its designated location. The length of the transition/Special Effect can be adjusted by dragging the width, and some of the Special Effects can be customized as to direction and A/B video clip effect entrance and exit.

Assembling Film Clips in the Construction Window

At any time, you can move the starting points and ending points of your different project segments, which is determined by you—the director/editor of the movie project. The beginning and ending scenes in the Construction Window are very easy to visually sync up as far as starting and ending points of video and sound clips alike. The first clip will start at the left of the Construction Window in track A and move right X number of frames. Where that first clip ends, the second begins in track B. Be sure and read in depth about the sound file formats supported in Premiere 2.1 LE; most are supported. The accompanying filters and special effects fit into *the big picture*.

This section provides only a quick overview, but consulting the user guide is never a bad idea; infinite wisdom can be gained from doing this.

Note that the yellow band at the top of the Construction Window is your effective work area. The red arrow at either side of the band is for adjusting the width (length) of your work area. Drag the arrows to adjust your workspace.

Putting the Finishing Touches on Your Project

When you finish setting up your project, the next step is to actually create your movie. All you need to do is compile your movie for viewing. In the Project menu, select Make > Movie (⌘-K) (see fig. 23.28). In the present dialog box, you need to give your movie a file name and, before saving, click the Options button, which will allow you to depict your final file size, compression format, and Frames Per Second (FPS) (see fig. 23.29). Many restrictions here depend on the capabilities of which QuickTime version you're running in your System. The new QuickTime 2.0 will support larger video image sizes as well as faster and smoother playback, generally supporting full screen 640 x 480 QuickTime movies at 15 FPS on virtually all Macintosh models. QuickTime 1.6.1 can only handle, at best, 320 x 240 images at 12 FPS tops.

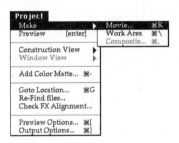

Fig. 23.28
Making your movie.

You are presented with a standard dialog box as to where you want to save your movie.

Fig. 23.29
Saving your movie to your hard disk.

Be sure to click the Options button before you proceed to OK (see fig. 23.30).

Fig. 23.30
Premiere's Project
Output Options.

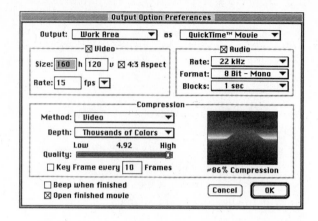

The Project Output Options dialog box is where you can set up the specifications of your final movie. You can tell Premiere to compile the images only for your work area or for the entire project, create a QuickTime movie, or create a QuickTime composite. (See the *Premiere User Guide* for more information.)

In Premier 2.1 LE, you can only save your movies with thousands of colors, whereas in the full release version, you can save your movies in true heroic fashion with 24-bit color.

The Quality slider bar located in the Options dialog box gives you the option of how much compression versus image quality you want in the final product. As with all QuickTime prior to 2.0, there are several different types of QuickTime compression, including Photo JPEG, Cinepak, and Video (as well as an option of none) from which you can choose. Also, be sure to select your movie output size. The output size greatly affects the viewing size of the movie. What you set here is what you'll see when you play it back.

When your movie is finished compiling, a window with the finished product appears on-screen so that you can see the results of your work (see fig. 23.31). Now that we've discussed the making of a QuickTime movie in Premiere 2.1 LE, it is up to you whether you want to jump on the bandwagon and create one yourself. The information provided in this chapter on both Photoshop and Premiere should be more than enough to get you started.

Also, if you decide to upgrade to the full version of Premiere, you will gain even more added flexibility and ability by being able to perform image grabs from videotapes played on your VCR or other similar media. While this requires a little more time and experience with Premiere, it is something that is very easy—and loads of fun—once you get the hang of it.

Fig. 23.31
The final movie in Premiere.

- A film clip in the Construction Window and in the Project Window is only a reference to the original file on your hard drive. It is important NOT to delete any of the original clips until you are positive you are done working with the movie's construction and have finished making your movie.

- When making a movie, you may find it helpful to first make your movie once in a smaller size as sort of a means to go by. This takes less time and less disk space and is an excellent way to see what you're working with. This is often the next step after using Premiere's built-in Preview option before the final completed project. Using Preview often leaves out complex transitions and effects in your movie and will not display accurately.

- When applying a filter (⌘-F bring up the filter list) to a clip, it will affect the whole clip. You can use the razor tool to split the clip. If you are importing individual clips into your Project, applying a filter will once again apply only to one clip at a time.

- Making your own 3-D movies in Premiere is easy. Simply apply the Color Offset filter. Offsetting the red channel to the left causes the image to drop back while offsetting the red channel to the right creates the 3-D effect that your image is moving towards you. In order to view this 3-D effect, you will need a pair of 3-D glasses.

- Premiere uses many filters that are Photoshop plug-in compatible. If there are any third-party Photoshop filters that you would like to use in Premiere, you may want to check with the software developer to ensure proper compatibility; all you need to do is place them in your Premiere Plug-Ins folder.

■ The adjustable double-sided yellow arrow is what defines your work area. The yellow arrow at either end also acts as a handle. You can adjust the size of your work area accordingly by adjusting the placement of these arrows. While in Make Movie, you can specify whether you want to make a movie out of the Entire Project or simply the Work Area you have defined.

Summary

Working in Adobe Premiere, you, as an ordinary Macintosh computer user, can easily seat yourself in the Director's chair at little expense. Although you cannot create huge full-scale productions, you are well on your way to making your own Hollywood.

If you have a scanner, I suggest that a good starting point is to take some scans of family photos and assemble them into a movie for playback on your computer. Apply different effects, use your Macintosh's built-in sound recording board (if equipped), and record your voice narrating your movie scenes. The full version of Premiere has the capability to output to videotape for home viewing in your VCR or similar viewing device.

There are so many uses for Premiere, and I know this is just one example. This is how I started. To this day, I'm very proud with my first QuickTime MooV, as it was a very satisfying experience after all the work and effort. I will leave it up to you to decide where you want to go from here. There are so many possibilities.

Apple QuickTime is a software extension that gives your Macintosh the capability to play and create desktop video and sound. Without QuickTime, your Macintosh is only a noisy, idle machine. This is okay for people who don't expect more, but I'm absolutely positive you will want as much as QuickTime can offer.

QuickTime has revolutionized Macintosh and desktop video in the '90s. Without it, the Macintosh would not be the Macintosh as it's known. QuickTime resides in your computer as an Extension (INIT) in your System Folder's Extensions Folder and will load itself at startup. QuickTime is recognized by its distinctive look: the icon with the big Q.

QuickTime is an inconspicuous piece of software created by Apple. Most of the time, it just sits transparently in your System. Many tasks taken for granted cannot be accomplished without the aid and presence of QuickTime. The QuickTime Extension ships with every Apple Macintosh and Power Macintosh. QuickTime is a staple of the Apple way of computing and is no longer the unknown entity that it was the first year or so if its existence.

Apple has been steadily expanding and building upon the power of QuickTime, and it has been adopted as an industry standard. Even many Microsoft Windows programs for IBM and compatible PCs can recognize and use QuickTime/JPEG compression.

QuickTime is rather small in physical file size (Version 1.6.1 is 837 kilobytes) and uses only about 20K of memory when not in use. It is a very smart extension memory-wise, as opposed to other system Extensions and Control Panels that sometimes use large chunks of RAM continuously.

Using QuickTime for Compression

The most common form of QuickTime compression is JPEG (pronounced "jay-peg") compression. JPEG stands for Joint Photographic Experts Group (named after the group that wrote the standard), and is a proprietary graphic file compression format exclusive to raw JPEG/JFIF and JPEG Pict files. It is especially effective at compressing and archiving large color graphic files. JPEG compression is very fast. With the speed of today's Macintosh computers, you can barely ascertain the elapsed time difference saving/exporting a JPEG compressed image vs. saving an image without compression. Compression ratios 1/15th to 1/20th of the original file size can be achieved.

JPEG compression is not altogether foolproof—it is what is called *lossy compression*. The amount of loss/degradation of your image is adjustable and can be controlled. In addition, several compression formats are available: Video, Photo - JPEG, Cinepak, and Animation as of version 1.6.1.

The way QuickTime works is based on algorithms and mathematical permutations of your images. The graphic's pixel information in the graphic is analyzed by the QuickTime extension. For example, each RGB (Red, Green, and Blue) image is referred to as a multi-channeled image, as interpreted by your computer and your graphics programs. It is displayed to your monitor in the exact same way color images are viewed from a television screen: one color and pixel at a time in rapid succession.

What QuickTime/JPEG compression does is look for each of the Red, Green, and Blue layers. In the case where there is a large area of solid color, it takes the solid color values of each color and applies an algorithmic code value for each of the three color layers. The more solid an area, the more compression can be achieved. JPEG compression gets tough when an image has a particularly large amount of detail, where it takes more code to break down the image into formulas representing the pixels rather than storing all the color information. The more detail there is in an image, less overall compression will be achieved.

When decompressing or opening a JPEG compressed image, QuickTime goes on a search and interpolates the code it originally created. For example, the areas with more detail are compressed less. Image areas with less detail are largely ignored by QuickTime because the human eye will not see the apparent loss in detail. Where QuickTime sees more detail, it pays more careful attention to its work and takes greater care when compressing.

Using QuickTime MooVs

QuickTime is very useful in production environments, but the program is also a fun source of entertainment. Many CD-ROM games for the Macintosh require QuickTime to play back animation movies (spelled MooV). A wide variety of QuickTime MooVs is available from many sources—CD-ROMS, such as those shipped with Adobe Premiere and Adobe Audition. There are also full-length titles available in QuickTime format such as Ludwig Van Beethoven: Symphony #9, The Voyager Company, and the Beatles' "A Hard Days Night."

QuickTime serves a number of useful purposes beyond digital entertainment. For example, many manufacturing industries use QuickTime MooVs as an interactive learning device for employees as well as for staging on-screen product demonstrations. NASA uses QuickTime/JPEG compression technology for beaming satellite photographs from faraway locations like Jupiter back to Earth for viewing by conventional means.

Included on all Macintosh computers when shipped is the QuickTime MoviePlayer (and sometimes Simple Player). Both are QuickTime Movie applications and can also be found on all the QuickTime installer disks Apple ships. This disk also ships with PictCompressor, which specifically deals with still JPEG/QuickTime compressed PICT files.

On the Power Macintosh, the MoviePlayer and the Simple Player have been made obsolete in lieu of the new and improved SimpleText. Much the same as TeachText, SimpleText not only can read text files and open PICT files, but also play sounds and run QuickTime Movies.

Getting the Most from QuickTime

The following hints and tips will help you get the most out of QuickTime:

- QuickTime is not just for movies! You can use QuickTime compression in applications like Adobe Photoshop to compress PICT format images up to 1/20th of their original size. When saving an image in Photoshop as a PICT, Photoshop will prompt you with an additional choice of QuickTime compression (only if QuickTime is installed), complete with a slider control to set the amount of compression.

- If you are making movies for the first time, you may be surprised to discover the amount of hard disk space required to make and store them. If you have an interest in making more extensive projects than just a couple minutes, it is advisable to check out large hard drive and external storage systems such as Digital Audio Tape (DAT).

- When choosing hard drives to use for QuickTime and AV purposes, notice the drives on the market labeled specifically for AV use. These drives have faster access times and are designed for high performance.

- Sometimes a QuickTime movie will appear to look more like an animated flip-book (or rapid slide show) than a movie. This can be caused if a movie is run on a slower machine, or if there are a lot of frames-per-second in the movie. With quicker and better algorithms for compression/decompression, QuickTime 2.0 relegates this problem as a thing of the past. Full-screen video is now possible at 15 frames-per-second on the Macintosh LC475.

- Although QuickTime 2.0 will allow lower-end machines to create and use video, keep in mind that you get what you pay for when purchasing machines. Bigger is better in the case of creating movies—especially if 3-D rendering is involved, where a coprocessor is a must in the 68000 series of Macintosh.

- QuickTime 2.0 is music for Macintosh users' ears. QuickTime now supports MIDI and 16-bit audio with compression rates that can reduce a 300MB CD-quality digital recording of Beethoven's 5th Symphony to fit on an 800K floppy disk.

- QuickTime 2.0 supports MIDI, 4-to-1 compression of 16-bit audio tracks, and text tracks, as well as the enhanced speed performance gains.

Other features of QuickTime 2.0 we can all rejoice about are improved cross-platform compatibility with Windows and DOS-compatible PC machines. QuickTime 2.0 for Windows is expected to ship later this year.

Summary

What you can look forward to with QuickTime 2.0 is larger smoother play-back of QuickTime movies. In version 1.6.1 a 320 x 240 pixel movie played back at 12 fps was considered amazing and high tech. With QuickTime 2.0 you can now do the same thing with full-screen 640 x 480 pixel movies at up to 15 fps. The smaller format 320 x 240 movies can now play back at 30 fps with no evident System slowdown and include support for time-code-based professional-level video editing capabilities at up to 60 fps with high-end data throughout at up to 3MB per second, as well as MPEG recognition and support.

Conclusions and Recommendations

While QuickTime is typically Freeware from Apple Computer, Inc. and is shipped with all current versions of System software, it has also been made readily available in the past from online services such as America Online and CompuServe as well as the Internet. Version 2.0 will not be made available electronically, however. Nothing other than your ordinary Macintosh computer is required to run QuickTime. It is possible with current versions of QuickTime (version 1.5 or newer) that it can be run under System 6 with limited advantages. It is preferable that if you are in fact using an older Macintosh (such as a Mac IIci or older), you upgrade to System 7 when using QuickTime.

Chapter 24

Using CD-ROM Drives and Software

by David Busch

When the Macintosh was first introduced, the idea of more than 600M of software on a single disc that costs less than a dollar to produce and which could be sold for $5.00 to $50.00 was only an impossible dream. After all, the first Macs could access only 400K of programs or data before it was necessary to spit out a disc and insert a new one.

Today, multimedia discs that combine sound, high-resolution images, QuickTime video clips, or even full-motion movies are within the reach of any Macintosh owner. You can add CD-ROM technology to the long list of innovations that received their first strong support from Apple Computer and the Macintosh community.

While the "new" CD-ROM explosion is shaking the foundations of both the Macintosh and PC worlds, the detonation's fuse extends back to the late 1980s. Apple primed the cannon by offering some of the first affordable CD-ROM drives, the AppleCD SC, along with pioneering discs like Apple Developer Group's Developer Helper (also known as "Phil and Dave's Excellent CD"). This early entry was no speed demon: data access times were in the 500-600 ms range in an age when a fast hard disc could find any sector in 28 ms or less.

Thanks to the easy expandability offered by the Mac's built-in SCSI interface, since 1988 it's been easy for any Macintosh owner to buy and connect up a CD-ROM drive. The growing installed base of drives has in turn sparked the development of multimedia CD-ROM discs that use the features of the Macintosh. Of course, as in many "Which comes first, the chicken or the egg?" situations, even after chickens were plentiful, the market was remarkably barren of eggs. That's changing now with the daily introduction of new and exciting CD-ROM software offerings.

This chapter provides the following:

- A quick introduction to CD-ROM technology

- An explanation of the hardware requirements

- An overview of the best software on the market

CD-ROM Technology

You probably don't care to know the technology behind the CD-ROM, so I'll boil it all down to a single sentence: CD-ROMs are circular, 4.75-inch write-once, read-many times (WORM) discs in which digital information is represented very compactly by tiny holes that can be read with lasers attached to high-resolution sensors. That's enough techno-babble.

Where Did CD-ROM Technology Come From?

CD-ROMs have been around in one form or another for nearly a decade, and other formats of optical disc (which is what a CD-ROM actually is) have been sold since the first laser discs became available in 1974.

Capable of storing up to 680M of information on a single disc, CD-ROMs were at first almost exclusively devoted to distributing large databases of information. Telephone directories, massive computer reports, census data, huge operations manuals, scientific bibliographies, and other text-oriented material were efficiently stored on these laser discs.

The advantage of using CD-ROMs for data distribution was obvious—the discs could be mass-duplicated with the same manufacturing techniques used for the higher-volume CD audio disc, and read by anyone equipped with a CD-ROM player, which was a modified version of consumer audio CD players. Information providers could distribute massive amounts of information, which could be read by anyone with a $500-$800 CD player. The cost to the originator of the disc could be a few dollars per disc, or more, depending on the quantity ordered and, if necessary, could be recouped by charging those who used the information $150 to $2000 for the privilege of accessing the data.

Still, the market for CD-ROMs was limited. Discs filled with scientific or business data were of interest only to scientists or business people. An $800 CD-ROM player could be easily justified by a business or educational institution, even in quantities, and the value of the information made $150 discs a bargain. However, consumers were not interested in buying $200 dictionaries, $99 full-text reproductions of books they could purchase for $19.95 in hard cover form, or other similar software, even when the price of drives dropped to the $400 level and below.

Why CD-ROMs Will Become Standard Equipment

Shrewd industry analysts predict that CD-ROM drives will become a non-optional, standard part of every Macintosh sold sometime in 1995. Only the need for a few low-cost entries in Apple's war for market share with the PC world have kept this change from happening sooner. The following sections cover the key reasons why we're now seeing a growth of CD-ROM drives.

Stunning Simplicity

Most of all, the CD-ROM makes an overpoweringly attractive add-on by virtue of its simplicity. Once you've successfully installed a CD-ROM drive in your computer (and many Mac systems, including all AV Macintosh and Power Macintosh configurations, now come with these drives already installed), all you need to do to enjoy a CD is pop the disc in the drive and follow the included installation instructions.

There's no need to swap multiple floppy discs in and out. Frequently, CD-ROM software runs directly off the CD-ROM, with only a few files stored permanently on your computer to speed operations a little. And, often, the exact same CD-ROM can be used with both Macintosh as well as IBM PC and compatible systems, so you may not even need to know what kind of computer you own to buy the right disc!

Enhanced Applications with Sound and Motion

Applications provided on CD-ROM can be enhanced with sound, graphics, and multimedia features that are difficult to integrate into floppy-disk-based offerings without commandeering massive chunks of precious hard disk space. Computer multimedia—sound plus graphics—equals computers that can do everything that videotape players or sound/slide or filmstrip projectors could do—and much more, thanks to computer interactivity. There is now a vast new market for software that takes advantage of the sound capabilities of Macintoshes and the storage facilities of the CD-ROM.

CD-ROM Technology Makes a Lot of Sense for Vendors

Software has traditionally been delivered on floppy disk. Large applications may require four to ten disks, or more, depending on whether the vendor uses the older 800K format for compatibility with earlier Macs, or takes a chance and releases a product on 1.44M diskettes. The disks are easily damaged, can be accidentally erased, and must be duplicated by the end-user to provide back-up copies as a safety measure.

One compact disc can replace hundreds of floppies (at much lower cost), they're difficult to damage, and expensive to pirate. Vendors can load up the disk with tons of free extras, such as clip art or fonts, which cost them virtually nothing but have a high perceived value in the customer's eyes. You get more and the vendor pays less. Everybody wins.

Lower-Cost CD-ROM Drives and Interfaces

CD-ROMs could have become a success even if drives remained at the $400-$500 price point we saw before 1994. Given the advantages of CD-ROM software, a $500 player was a bargain. But prices didn't stop their plunge at $400. The drop has been as dramatic as the rise in disk sales.

At the beginning of 1994, I purchased a state-of-the-art external CD-ROM drive for my Quadra 650 for $289.00. Today, you can see advertisements in mail order catalogs for equivalent units for $199, including one listed at $139 (or $79 if you purchase it with a $99 Grolier Multimedia Encyclopedia). CD-ROM drives today cost what floppy disk drives cost last year. I could predict that prices will stabilize at the $125-$199 level, and still be proved perilously pessimistic before the next update of this book is due.

Lower-Cost CD-ROM Discs

The plummeting cost of the discs themselves also is driving the CD-ROM revolution. The price-performance ratio is becoming more attractive in two ways: you're getting much, much better discs at a much, much lower cost.

CD-ROM encyclopedias were originally developed as a lower-cost alternative to a hardbound encyclopedia, with some fancy retrieval options thrown in. You might pay $500 or more for a set of encyclopedia books that strain your bookshelf, and force you to page through several volumes and a dozen articles to find all the information you need on a topic (The phrase *"See also:"* was the original version of hypertext!).

Today, if you want that text encyclopedia on CD-ROM, you can probably pick one up for $25 or so. They have been largely supplanted by $395 multimedia encyclopedias (which never really sold for much more than $149 and which now have $89-$99 street prices—or less) with the same text you got before, supplemented by hours of video clips, tons of sound bites, thousands of still photographs, animation, and other things. The product you get today is hundreds of times better than the one you purchased a year or two ago, and costs much less.

CD-ROM Standards

We must delve back into CD-ROM technology for a moment to explain the different standards you should understand when purchasing a disc. But don't worry, we're only going to get one toe wet. I'm going to tell you what the standards are, but nothing at all of how they work.

All CD-ROMs are not alike. The digital data on them can be written using one of several different standards. These have names like Red Book, Yellow Book, Green Book, and Orange Book, after the color-coded covers of the manuals overseen by the Dutch manufacturer, Philips N.V., which developed the technology and serves as a guardian and clearinghouse for many of the standards applied to these discs. I'll refer to the common names of each of these standards, because odds are slim that you'll ever have the need or desire to actually peruse a Red, Yellow, Green, or Orange book itself.

- *CD-Audio.* This standard defines the familiar audio CDs that you've probably been enjoying on your home CD player for years. Digital audio data is stored in bits and bytes just like computer programs, and then read and converted to music through a device called a digital-to-analog converter (DAC) in your audio system.

  Computer CD-ROM drives can also read audio CDs. You may need a special driver program to start the audio CD playing and to change from track to track. To hear the sound, you can plug a set of headphones into the headphone jack on your CD-ROM drive, and connect its output to your amplifier or speakers.

- *ISO-9660/High Sierra.* This International Standards Organization (ISO) standard defines a type of data structure that can be read by DOS/Windows, Macintosh, or Commodore Amiga computers, when those platforms are equipped with appropriate driver software. Many CD-ROMs are furnished in this format and include both Mac and PC access software, which can, in turn, read the same data files, or a special set created for each type of computer, on a so-called *hybrid* disc. Since CD-ROMs have so much storage space, it's often possible to develop ISO-9660 discs that provide virtually the same functions and features on both types of computers.

- *CD-ROM Interactive.* This CD-ROM format, often called CD-I, is most often used in stand-alone players that are connected to a television set and keyboard/keypad. You won't use CD-I discs in your computer CD-ROM drive.

■ *CD-ROM XA*. This CD-ROM format is an extension of the ISO-9660 standard, adding support for discs that are erasable and updatable. All other types of discs have their data written to them at one time, in a so-called single session. Most of the discs you use in your CD-ROM drive were actually pressed, like waffles coming out of a waffle iron, exactly as audio CDs are produced.

However, we now have a new kind of disc that can be written to by a laser/magnetic device (generally costing $3000 and up, and used only by companies rather than individuals). Since these discs can be written to more than once (and some types can be erased and rewritten), they are called multi-session discs. Kodak Photo CDs, which incorporate photographs scanned by your photofinisher, are a type of multi-session disc. Others are written as part of a database updating process.

Nearly all CD-ROM drives now sold are XA compatible. The only XA-format discs you are likely to encounter will be Photo CDs you create from your own photos with the help of your finisher, or Photo CDs compiled by others for sale as high-resolution clip art.

The CD-ROM formats discussed in the previous section are all well-established, and you probably don't have to worry about any new ones being introduced for the next few years (although Kodak continues to enhance its Photo CD format).

What you can expect are CD-ROMs that take advantage of new software and hardware technologies built into your computer system. These include:

■ *Video*. QuickTime for the Macintosh and other video technologies will see extensive application in CD-ROMS during 1995 and beyond. Each technology makes it possible to display small video images on your screen, bringing CDs to vivid life. Since none of these technologies are pervasive as yet, the CD-ROMs which require them will include run-time versions and install them on your hard disk as required. Additional video technologies have been announced that will bring full-screen, more realistic video to CD-ROMs during the coming years.

■ *New Operating Systems*. In the Macintosh world, System 7.5 and QuickDraw GX (which has yet to draw broad support from vendors) will offer software developers some new tools for bringing you faster, more realistic on-screen graphics.

- *Faster Hardware.* The Power Macintosh 6100, 7100, and 8100 models have all proved to be from four to ten times faster than equivalent Quadra models when running native software, and 1995 will be the year when all major applications—including those that depend on CD-ROM—convert to that mode. Apple's "fat binary" format lets a single application run in an optimized mode on either Power Macs or 680x0-based Macintoshes, so those who choose to remain with our older systems will still be able to run the same applications (albeit at lower speeds!).

These faster Mac systems, coupled with triple- and quadruple-speed CD-ROM drives should make CD-ROM software even more practical and popular in the coming years. We may be in the middle of a revolution, but the changes are only beginning.

CD-ROM and Multimedia

Most CD-ROM software are multimedia discs, which, in the broadest terms, means they contain something more than just text. To qualify as "multi" media, a CD-ROM may have pictures, video, sound, animation, plain text, linked text (hypertext), and other features in various combinations. Any Macintosh equipped with the cheapest CD-ROM drive can view text; to access multimedia features, you'll need something more in the way of hardware.

The term *multimedia* predates desktop computer technology by many years. Educational tools using filmstrip or slide projectors linked to synchronized cassette recorder sound tracks have been classroom workhorses for decades. Business conferences and seminars are spiced up by motion picture or slide-show/sound extravaganzas that often feature dozens of projectors, massive screens, and thundering speakers. You'll even find this brand of multimedia at amusement parks.

Desktop multimedia was initially a way to harness the power of the personal computer to manage all the sound and visual elements of these presentations in a new way. However, the sheer size of image and sound files used restricted desktop presentations to relatively simple productions, such as those generated by Microsoft PowerPoint or Aldus Persuasion.

CD-ROMs, which can easily store 70 minutes or more of music, or up to 680M of image files, freed developers from most storage constraints. For the first time it became possible to produce multimedia programs that could be stored on *and run from* a single, compact disc.

The Macintosh and CD-ROM Technology

Part of the reason the Macintosh has had a head start in CD technology is the Mac, manufactured and marketed by a single company, has always been fairly well-standardized. Until the last few years, when the Macintosh line grew into separate Performa, LC, Quadra, PowerBook, DuoDock, and PowerMacintosh lines (have I forgotten a couple?), there wasn't the bewildering variety of Mac models we have today to confuse the issue. A Mac was basically a Mac.

For example, every Macintosh sold in the last six or seven years has a built-in SCSI (small computer systems interface) port, so anyone who wants to use a CD-ROM drive could buy a SCSI model and plug it in, and then drag a few extensions to the System folder so the Mac could recognize the new drive. Then, restart the Mac, and you are in business.

All Macs since the very first one introduced in 1984 have had a graphical interface and quality sound built in, too. Basic Mac sound is much superior to the tinny speaker most IBM PC users find in their stock machines. The 256-color displays required to view multimedia CD-ROMs are the only feature needed for multimedia that is actually optional. So, a "standard" color Macintosh is pretty much CD-ROM-ready, and many of these machines are being sold with a CD-ROM drive built in.

Macintosh Multimedia Hardware Requirements

As you can see, external drives are very easy to add to a Macintosh system (CD-ROM drives are even available as battery-powered units for PowerBooks) but they may also be mounted internally in some models. Your drive supplier can sell you a replacement face plate, if required, to accommodate the internal drive. Some Macs with a built-in CD-ROM drive can even start up from a CD, if it's one made especially for that Mac (that is, it has compatible system software and appropriate enabler). That's a slow option, of course, but a valuable one if you someday find your start-up hard disk has died.

You'll need to add a few extensions to your System folder to make your Mac recognize your CD-ROM drive, provide audio CD capabilities, and use all your software. The High Sierra Access, ISO-9660 Access, and Audio CD Access extensions should be furnished with your drive. You'll also need Foreign File Access to be able to recognize files on PC-oriented CD-ROMs. Other multimedia-oriented extensions will be installed by software requiring them: you may need to update your QuickTime or Sound Manager extensions to use the latest CD-ROMs, for example.

CD-ROM drives come with a Control Panel that could be used to enable or disable the supplied caching software with any drive on your system—not just with the CD-ROM drive. You may also want accessories like Voyager's CD Audio Toolkit, which lets you access audio CDs from within HyperCard stacks.

Sound Considerations

CD-ROM software often has sound, and all Macs have good-quality sound built in, which can be made better by plugging external speakers into the jack on the back of the unit. That may be all you need for multimedia use. You can, however, purchase add-on sound cards for NuBus-equipped Macs if you need more sophisticated sound capabilities. Most of us don't need that much quality unless we're doing high-end audio production.

Later Macs also have sound recording capabilities built in, and some are even furnished with a microphone. I purchased a cheap microphone for my Quadra, and get good enough quality. Some models, such as the lamented AV Macs and the new PowerMacintoshes in AV dress, record CD-quality sound with no additional hardware, using the Sound control panel.

Do I Need an Internal or External CD-ROM drive?

As noted above, Macintosh owners can purchase CD-ROM drives as internal units mounted in the same case as their CPU, video card, and disk drives, or as an external unit that is connected to the main computer with a cable. Which is best for you? There are advantages to each type of drive:

- Internal drives are less expensive. You're not paying for a case or power supply with an internal drive—just the bare drive itself and an inexpensive ribbon cable to connect it to the interface. An external drive will cost $60-$100 more.

- Internal drives are "cleaner." That is, you don't have extra power, data, and audio cables trailing around. Everything is inside your computer.

- Internal drives don't take up any additional desktop space.

■ Internal drives move with your computer—and don't move without it. Having an internal drive means you have one less thing to unplug and move when you relocate your system, which can be quite often for those who cart their computers around to perform demos. It also means it's more difficult for an unethical person to run off with your CD-ROM drive without taking the whole computer. A compact drive may fit inside a briefcase, but an entire system won't.

■ External drives are easier to install. Just plug and play.

■ External drives don't use up a precious drive bay in your computer, which may be important if you have a Mac with limited internal space.

■ External drives can be used with more than one computer, if each has its own interface. Just unplug the drive, plug into the new system, and then restart or reboot. A single CD-ROM drive can be used with multiple computers in a pinch—or regularly if you must save money.

Double-, Triple-, Quad-Speed Drives, Changers, and Towers

Your choices of CD-ROM drives has grown significantly in the past year. Nobody should really consider a single-speed drive. But can you safely purchase a double-speed unit with the triple- and quad-speed drives coming on the market? And what about these multi-CD units you see advertised?

For most people, a double-speed drive will be the prudent choice through 1995, unless the prices on the faster units drop sharply. I paid $169 for the last double-speed drive I purchased: would it have been worthwhile to spend twice as much for a triple-speed unit?

No. In fact, it might have made more sense to buy two double-speed drives for the price of one triple-speed unit, and thereby have twice as many discs online at one time. If I used both discs equally, I could probably make up for the slower transfer rate by the time I'd save not swapping CD-ROM discs constantly.

If you really want to use more than one disc frequently, investigate the six-disc changers from Pioneer and others. These units still have only one CD-ROM reader inside, but can switch internally from one disc to another very quickly. Each phantom drive is addressed by a different drive letter, so you can access multiple discs quickly and easily. Since the $1000 changers are often quad-speed units, once the disc you want is mounted, access is that much faster.

There are also CD-ROM "towers" containing four to eight or more CD-ROM drives. Each drive is accessed by a different drive letter, so you can quickly run out of alphabet if you have several connected to your computer. They are most often required by network users and electronic bulletin board systems (BBSs) that must make different CD-ROMs available to multiple users, simultaneously.

CD-ROM drives mounted in individual computers can also be shared over a network. If each Mac on the net has its own CD-ROM drive, it's like having three or four CD-ROM drives in one computer.

Caddies or No Caddies?

The first CD-ROM drive for the Macintosh used caddies. Today, you can purchase drives that don't use them. Are they inconvenient? Not necessarily: they may provide *more* convenience. If your CD-ROM drive uses caddies, you'll want to buy a separate caddy for each CD you use frequently, or perhaps all the CDs you own if you don't have a large collection. Then, you'll find it more convenient to use these CDs; instead of opening the jewel box, sliding open a drawer, dropping in the disc, closing the door (and using the reverse process to unmount the disc), you just grab the caddy you want, and slip it in the drive. I love caddies. People with children or clumsy coworkers love caddies; they protect the disc from fumble-fingers. In truth, CD-ROM caddies are only inconvenient for those who have zillions of CD-ROMs and not enough caddies; people who pay $9.95 each for caddies instead of $3.50 or less (some stores sell them for full price, while others sell the exact same caddies at a heavy discount), or those who must share CD-ROMs among different types of drives.

An Overview of CD-ROM Software

If you looked at the software best-seller lists, you'd think that the only CD-ROMs available for purchase are games and encyclopedias. However, those two categories are only the tip of the iceberg. There's a large market for games because Macintosh users are constantly looking for new thrills, and an old game must be replaced with a new one at frequent intervals. CD-ROM games for the Mac sell by the truckloads.

At the opposite end of the turnover spectrum are multimedia encyclopedias and reference works. Each Mac owner probably needs only one of these per type, but vendors are still able to sell these for $75 and up—much more than the average price of most CD-ROMs. Moreover, every home and business user can benefit from an encyclopedia, so the market is vast.

In reality, there are nine other major categories of discs available for the Mac, each important in its own way. The following sections will look at each of them in turn, with a description of a few of the key CDs available. But first, let me list the key types of discs for your review:

- Business

- Reference

- Education

- Children's Movies/Multimedia

- Games

- Music

- General Interest

- Graphics

- Shareware

- Applications

There is a 12th category of CD-ROM software, the so-called "adult" CD-ROM (although I imagine it is purchased almost exclusively by men). While these sell extremely well, I won't bother to describe the leading entries in the category. In one sense, they don't really qualify as computer software, since the fact that the material is available on CD-ROM is only an incidental factor in its appeal.

Instead, we'll look at the true computer-oriented offerings in more detail.

Business

Business CD-ROMs are those you can use in your work, apart from those containing specific applications. These are often business reference works, packed with data that can be used for marketing. Others can improve your business skills, or help you operate your computer more efficiently.

Some typical entries in this category include:

- **Wilson Learning Interactive Series.** These discs use exercises, simulations, videos, and self tests to help you meet business challenges.

Titles in the series include Connect for Success, Decide for Sure, Relate with Ease, and Keep Your Cool. More than just self-improvement discs, the Wilson series helps you move up the ladder more efficiently.

■ **Great Business Jokes.** Here's a quirky entry, but one worth looking at. This disc presents more than 175 business jokes in QuickTime movies that use professional stand-up comics. You've never heard of any of these comedians, but, better yet, you haven't heard all the jokes either! We found some clever new nuggets sprinkled in among a few golden oldies. Business people can spice up their speeches with gems like, "Our CFO is so cheap, he sends his voice-mail postage due!" Or, "Oh, the product isn't delayed..it just doesn't match the description on the packaging yet." Figure 24.1 shows the product in action.

Fig. 24.1
The comics aren't nationally-known, but neither are the gags on Great Business Jokes.

■ **PhoneDisc USA.** Why let your fingers do the walking when your computer does the job much better? The Residential, Business, and Reverse directories aren't cheap, but is that Information operator so helpful when you're looking for Fred Q. Schwartzmiller, Inc.—somewhere on the West Coast? Or if all you need are some addresses, and don't even *care* about the phone numbers? PhoneDisc USA is *fast*. It doesn't wait for you to finish typing in a name; as you key in the first few letters, the program races ahead to list the first name meeting the parameters entered so far. The disc is updated quarterly, and you'll want to keep current to avoid too many wrong numbers, but PhoneDisc is a valuable addition to any business library.

Reference

Reference works are what CD-ROMs are all about; one compact disc containing everything you need to know, with all the facts, figures, maps, and other data, for a specific area of knowledge. Encyclopedias are very popular, especially since Microsoft raised the ante by porting its popular Encarta offering over to the Macintosh.

Amidst all the multimedia offerings, you'll still find a few text-heavy works. The reference category is a little more forgiving of multimedia weakness than others, because all we really need are the facts. Some top discs to look for in this category include:

- **Microsoft Bookshelf.** If you can only find room for one reference CD-ROM among your collection of games or personal interest discs, this is the one you should have. The seven printed volumes converted to CD-ROM format for this disc include: The American Heritage Dictionary, Second College Edition, Bartlett's Familiar Quotations, Fifteenth Edition, The Concise Columbia Dictionary of Quotations has 6,000 additional quotes of more recent derivation; The Concise Columbia Encyclopedia, Second Edition, covers 15,000 topics with text, images, and animation; the Hammond Atlas has low-detail, but still useful maps of continents, countries, and US. States, accompanied by flag images, audio clips of national anthems, and pronunciations of key geographic names; Roget's II Electronic Thesaurus contains brief synonyms and antonym lists for a collection of key terms; The World Almanac and Book of Facts includes statistics, facts, zip codes, and trivia.

- **Microsoft Encarta.** If Microsoft Encarta is any indicator of the by-products we can expect from Bill Gates' quest for Total World Domination, Chairman Bill can dominate my world anytime. Simply put, Encarta is nothing like any encyclopedia you've ever worked with—electronic or otherwise—starting with its name. Everything about Encarta seems specifically included to dazzle you, from the moment you open the slick packaging and view the lush full-color manuals to that first moment when the impressive splash explodes on your screen. Sure, it's manipulative, but Encarta makes you love being toyed with. Encarta includes eight hours of audio (itself pretty impressive on a CD-ROM that could hold only 75 minutes of digital audio). In addition to the pervasive narration, there's 200 natural animal and bird sounds, words and phrases in 60 foreign languages, and 1500 pronunciations of geographic place names alone.

- **Grolier's Multimedia Encyclopedia.** This disc contains the complete text of Grolier's 21-volume Academic American Encyclopedia, comprising nearly 33,000 articles. You'll also find 8000 new or updated articles which reflect the latest developments in the world of politics, entertainment, and other areas. The program has eleven key sections, which each let you access the available database of information in different ways. You'll find a title list if you care to search through article titles in alphabetical order (much like a conventional encyclopedia). There's a word search function, too, which rapidly scans through the built-in index to locate all articles that meet criteria you type in. Because of the thoroughness of its articles, this encyclopedia is a top choice for older students.

Education

I've lumped into the Education category a vast range of discs that cover every subject taught in primary and secondary school, as well as college. These range from language study courses like Applied Optical's Language Discovery to Queue's Origins of the Constitution. Nearly every discipline is well-represented on the Macintosh, because of the popularity of this platform in schools.

- **Let's Visit France.** On the surface, Let's Visit France (and companion CDs that cover Mexico, South America, and Spain) bears a striking resemblance to one of those film strips you sat through in French II while your teacher sneaked off to the lounge for a quick break. A pleasant voice provides interesting commentary as a parade of postcard-perfect still color photos marches across the screen. Dig a little deeper, and you'll find that this disc has significant advantages over either videotapes or film strips. Let's Visit France can be used by a single student or a group, without the need for a teacher to supervise operation of a VCR or film-strip projector. The student can select English or French narration, add helpful on-screen subtitles, and stop the show at any time to review a scene, jump to another part of the presentation, or get additional information from the index. (See fig. 24.2.)

- **San Diego Zoo Presents: The Animals.** What a great disc! San Diego Zoo's The Animals is still as fresh and interesting as the latest multimedia extravaganza on the market. A live-action tour through the exhibits of one of the world's premier zoos, this disc has everything you'd expect from a first-rate CD-ROM: stunning video clips on an amazing range of topics, thousands of photographs and pages of information on animals and their habitats, and hours of audio narration. The core of this disc centers around the animal "exhibits," which can be accessed from a graphical main menu that resembles a three-dimensional map of the zoo itself. Your mouse can wander up and down paths leading to habitat types (tropical rain forest, savanna, grasslands, mountains, etc.) or other zoo centers of interest (research center, library, nursery, tours, stories, or kid's area). Click on that portion of the main map, and you're instantly transported to a new area to explore.

Fig. 24.2
Let's Visit France offers a tour of the country in both French and English.

- **Shakespeare on Disc.** If you think of Shakespeare as some dead guy they *tried* to force you to read in 11th grade literature class, you'll probably want to skip this review. We're not passing judgment here; the old Bard is tough going for some, and reading things you like (instead of Shakespeare) is infinitely better than not reading at all. But, if you love great literature, drama, or history, you'll be interested in Shakespeare: The Complete Works of William Shakespeare, whether or not you happen to be a serious student of Stratford-On-Avon's most famous dramatist. You can get all this in paperback at about the same price, of course. What makes the CD-ROM version of Shakespeare so valuable is the remarkable access you have to his words, using the DiscPassage character-based interface. You can search by phrase, subject, or title to find a specific passage you're interested in. Or, you can browse through all the works at leisure using the same parameters, looking for something interesting that you might not have known was there.

- **Sleeping Beauty.** One of a series of discs from Ebook, Inc., Sleeping Beauty is a combination of text, imagery, a little animation, and sound that carries the fairy tale genre into a new realm. That feeling of listening to a familiar story, told by a pleasant-voiced narrator, never quite loses its appeal. There's a little childhood left in the oldest person and this CD catches and holds the attention. The Sleeping Beauty disc lets you page through the text with mouse clicks. Icons on the pages invoke sound files, or audibly read the whole page. Pastel illustrations, some animated to a small degree, by Judith K. Jones, who also retold and narrated the text, appear on certain pages, greatly enhancing the experience. The table of contents permits viewing the pictures or hearing the sound files independent of reading the text.

■ **Scary Poems for Rotten Kids.** This disc is a compilation of 14 poems sure to be appreciated by subteenagers who are engrossed with gross things; always macabre, sometimes funny, spiced with a good dose of ick, but never downbeat enough to induce nightmares. Kids can have the book read to them, or they can use the mouse to click on individual words, phrases, and objects in the illustrations. The poems are engaging enough that children don't seem to miss the eye-catching animation and underlying effects interactive books provide. Our test children rolled on the floor throughout "Acid Rain," in which the narrator describes a rain "that came down in heavy drops; it washed away my shoes and socks; it washed the hair off from my head, it took my ears, and then I turned red." Children under seven probably won't understand the "fake" horror in these poems, and while the excellent illustrations aren't grisly, they are comic-book explicit, so you'll want to steer preschoolers away from this disc.

Movies/Multimedia

Television didn't really kill off motion pictures, as everyone predicted in the early 50s. And phonograph records (or, audio CDs today) didn't kill off radio programming. Instead, TV created vast new markets for movie productions, while giving us something to escape from when we did venture back to theaters. And radio and the recording industry complement each other nicely, encouraging consumers to enjoy both.

Today, many kinds of media happily co-exist. *Jurassic Park* raked in $900 million in revenues at the box office worldwide is on its way to becoming the most profitable movie ever. Yet, it's expected to reap another $1 billion after its October 4, 1994 release on home video. Can you imagine what a CD-ROM based on this hit would collect?

Movies are as much a part of our lives today as music has been for centuries. Obviously, we love to watch films and videos, and welcomed the change from small home screens with their fuzzy pictures in the 50s, to the large "home theater" television sets of today. So, would you really be interested in taking a step back to watch a film like *It's a Wonderful Life* on your computer monitor? Or, could you watch the Beatles' classic *A Hard Day's Night* in a tiny window taking up only a couple inches of a Macintosh's screen? The answer is, yes—if something more were provided.

That's what CD-ROM technology gives you movie buffs: the capability to combine full-motion video with immediate access to scripts, biographies, cast lists, and other goodies. You get that with Voyager's version of *A Hard Day's Night.* You get a great deal more with other movie-oriented discs, like *Microsoft Cinemania '94* or *Movie Select.* These discs combine video clips with music, movie reviews, trivia, and other bonuses that tell you everything you want to know about a particular movie, star, director, or studio.

- **Microsoft Cinemania '94.** This disc is a movie buff's dream! It combines reviews, biographies, filmographies, and summaries covering thousands of movies, actors, directors, and producers with priceless film clips. Included are Leonard Maltin's capsule reviews (a sentence or two) of more than 19,000 movies from his Movie and Video Guide 1994; more than 1200 insightful and detailed reviews from the always-superb Roger Ebert, excerpted from his Video Companion 1994; brief reviews of 2500 films from Pauline Kael's 5001 Nights at the Movies; and Baseline's detailed reviews of classic and recent films from The Motion Picture Guide. There are also 4000 cast lists and biographies extracted from Baseline's Encyclopedia of Film and Ephraim Katz's Film Encyclopedia.

- **The Honeymooners' Funniest Moments.** Jackie Gleason's Honeymooners skits (eventually expanded to half-hour "telefilms") are most fondly remembered of all early television. Some 48 classic scenes from 70 "lost" episodes are brought to life on this great CD-ROM, available in a combined PC/Macintosh format. Also packed into the 400+ megabyte disk are text articles on The Honeymooners' series that include a comprehensive history of the show and helpful comments about the scenes, along with the title and original air date of each clip. The CD-ROM format gives you the power to review favorite clips over and over again, for pure enjoyment or study (watch Gleason's eyes bug out when he notices the burglar in his apartment—it's a classic "take"). The format also makes it possible to group like-scenes together so you can compare and contrast comedy techniques without spending hours rewinding and advancing videotapes. This disc is shown in figure 24.3

Fig. 24.3
These are some of
The Honeymoon-
ers' funniest
moments.

Games

Games are the biggest moneymakers in the CD-ROM industry, so you'll find a
lot of effort put into developing flashy products that make the best use of the
Macintosh's sound and graphics capabilities. The list of top-sellers changes
almost weekly, but some leading contenders at the time this book was written
include:

- **Battle Chess.** Battle Chess is one of many chess programs on the market for Macintoshes. Why is it unique? The main distinction that Battle
  Chess has over its competitors is its graphic depiction of animated com-
  bat when one piece captures another. Why is this important? For the
  most part, it isn't. Battle Chess has very slick animation, and by virtue
  of the large amount of space on the CD-ROM, a large amount of digitized audio. At one time, such displays of animation virtuosity were of
  themselves a reason to select a product. But animation for its own sake
  isn't enough anymore. The game of chess has been played for hundreds
  of years without animation, or computers for that matter. Where animation might be used effectively is in interactive tutorials. Battle Chess
  does have a tutorial, but the use of animation here too is less effective
  then it might have been.

- **Who Killed Sam Rupert?** Who killed Sam Rupert? With eight suspects, but only six (compressed) hours to find the culprit, using only a
  collection of interviews, an enterprising assistant, and some fairly

nebulous clues, you will probably exhaust the majority of the allotted time figuring out the answer to that question. *Who Killed Sam Rupert* is an interactive, multimedia murder mystery in which you have the opportunity to act as detective in solving the murder of Sam Rupert, a restaurant owner known for his famous wines. This game gives you the opportunity to collect clues, observe live-action video questioning of suspects by your assistant (Lucy Fairwell), evaluate forensics results, perform follow-up questioning of suspects, even check alibis, and eventually request a warrant for the arrest of your prime suspect.

- **Lunicus.** You've repaired an ancient alien device, and find it contains videotapes of the Jurassic Era. Unfortunately, the device's owners have been alerted and are coming back to reclaim their property. The United Nations' Moonbase Lunicus is the only hope for Earth's salvation...and you're in charge of the rescue!

Music

Music CDs were once fairly rare, but are now becoming more numerous. You'll find a mixture of discs ranging from classical music (with in-depth discussions of various pieces) to more pop-oriented CDs. The best on the market include:

- **Xplora 1. Peter Gabriel's Secret World.** The noted pop star is your host as he takes you backstage at a concert, behind the scenes at the Grammy Awards, and into the studio with him to mix a Top 10 single. You get 140 minutes of video and audio and 100 full-color photographic images.

- **A Hard Day's Night.** Is this a music CD, a long-form music video, or just a movie? The Beatles' first film has been brought to the Macintosh on CD as all three, in a disc that was voted by MacUser magazine as the #1 CD-ROM of all time! You can view the entire film in interactive form, and see the original script and two other short films by the director, Richard Lester. Also included is the movie's original trailer.

- **The Residents Freak Show.** This disc by the San Francisco art music group has spectacular animation, encompassing both music, interactive story-telling, and digital art in one stunning package.

General Interest

The General Interest category includes everything and anything, from looks at our national parks, to discs devoted to U.S. and foreign travel. You'll find

CDs on parenting, and others that collect information on Yoga or wines of the world. Among the best:

- **Mayo Clinic Family Health Book.** Now you can take advantage of Mayo Clinic wisdom in your own home through the comprehensive family health guide on this CD-ROM. Within its hundreds of pages of hypertext-linked information you'll find clues that alert you to medical emergencies that should be attended to by a professional, comforting descriptions of treatments and their follow-up, and a rich vein of basic medical and health lore. Navigating the easy-to-use Macintosh interface, you'll find more than 50 video clips and animations that shed light on complex health topics with well-narrated mini-presentations. The 400-plus full-color still illustrations can be accessed almost instantly by clicking on icons embedded in the text. Over an hour of audio narration adds extended verbal captions to the photos, charts, and drawings.

- **Total Baseball.** If your home (or mind) is full of baseball memorabilia, this package will be a welcome addition to the clutter. Supplemented by more than 600 photographs and 20 sound clips, Total Baseball contains enough articles and statistics, (some 2300 pages worth) to satisfy even the most die-hard baseball fanatic, and may help bring order to your interest in this all-American pastime. The drop-down menus and search methods, although a bit cumbersome, open the door to articles which are exceptionally well-written, detailed, and fluid. While perusing Total Baseball, the reader finds topical information sorted under a host of categories such as *The History, The 100 Greatest Players, Streaks and Feats, Tragedies and Shortened Careers, Scandals and Controversies*, and many more. Those looking to take advantage of a CD-ROM for its sound features will enjoy the sound clips, twenty in all, which include bites from Goose Goslin's 1935 World Series winning hit, Don Larson's 1956 World Series perfect game, and Hank Aaron's 1974 715th home run.

- **Kathy Smith's Fat Burning System.** This is a health and fitness CD-ROM that lets you create your own tailored workout and diet plan, with information on nutrition and exercise. It's billed as a "10-Week Fat-Burning System."

Graphics

Graphics CDs for the Macintosh are heavily concentrated in clip art for desktop publishing. You'll find EPS, PICT, and TIFF files available from a number of sources at reasonable prices. Don't forget to check out shareware discs, which may have public domain images scanned from government publications, old books, or other sources. Some top-selling discs in this category include:

- **Pixar 128.** This disc includes 128 different photographic quality textures in 512 x 512 pixel format, and can be used by Pixar Typestry, Adobe Photoshop, or other graphics applications.

- **Click Art from T/Maker Click Art.** This clip-art pioneer offers a wide variety of disks for the Macintosh, including Animals and Nature (150 images), Artistry and Borders (375 varieties), and Sports and Games (180 action-packed pictures).

- **Metro Imagebase.** You'll find 2000 high-quality images, covering everything from business to borders on this disc, equally divided between 1000 EPS and 1000 TIFF images.

- **Architectural Photofile.** Available from Loggia, this disc has bridges, churches, housing, industry, transit, and more.

Shareware

Shareware discs have to be among the best bargains of any CD-ROMs you can buy. Most have from hundreds to thousands of ready-to-run applications, fonts, utilities, clip art, and other files. Many are public domain or freeware, while others are shareware you can try out for a specified period of time. If you continue using the product after you've evaluated it, you should send a small registration fee to the author, usually $5.00 to $30.00. Among the standout discs we've seen:

- **Shareware Breakthrough.** Quantum Axcess produces some of the best shareware discs on the market. They don't just throw shareware at you and leave you hanging. The disc is furnished with a snazzy shell that lets you browse through the offerings, read about the files in the categories that most interest you, and then launch and run programs for a test drive. This disc is shown in figure 24.4

- **Wayzata's Best of Macintosh Shareware.** This disc has a huge number of fonts, graphics applications, games, personal productivity programs, business software, and other programs that you can try before you buy.

- **PowerTools for the Macintosh.** This disc has Desk Accessories, Education programs, graphics programs, INITs, CDEVs, sounds, and a variety of utilities.

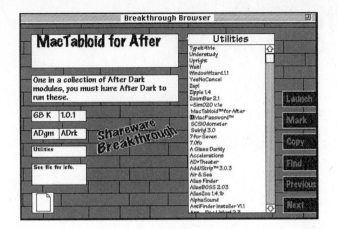

Fig. 24.4
Shareware
Breakthrough has
a great assortment
of try-before-you-
buy software.

Applications

If I wanted to bet money on a growth market for the future, I'd sock everything I had into the prospects for CD-ROMs containing enhanced versions of
applications that had only been available on floppy disk before. Only a few
key products are available on CD-ROM at this time, but by early 1995 you
can expect the market leaders in virtually every category to go this route.
Adobe Photoshop and other Adobe products have led the way. It doesn't
make a lot of sense to review the applications you can get now on CD-ROM,
since they should be evaluated on the basis of how well they perform as applications, not how good they are as CD-ROMs. Look for Microsoft Office,
Quicken, Adobe's entire product line, and other key programs to go to CD-
ROM soon. Other highlights:

- **Strata Studio Pro.** This high-end ($1500) 3D modeling and anima-
  tion program is already furnished with a great CD-ROM that includes a
  library of shapes you can use in your own projects.

- **Adobe Photoshop.** The CD-ROM edition of this leading image-editing software includes 5 Kai's Power Tools filters, 50 high-resolution
  stock photos, a Type on Call CD-ROM, Adobe Technical Notes, Expert
  Tips, 150 digital images from Digital Art & Photography Show, and try-
  out versions of Adobe Dimensions, Adobe Illustrator, and Adobe Premiere software.

Hot Tips for Getting the Most from Your CD-ROM

- Make sure you've installed all the appropriate extensions to get the most from your CD-ROM drive: the Foreign File Access, High Sierra File Access, ISO 9660 Access, and Audio CD Access extensions that came with your CD-ROM drive probably were installed with the drive. If not, find a copy and drag them to your System Folder.

- Desktop publishers can save precious hard disk space by using clip art CD-ROMs. More than 600M of image files can be stored on a single disc.

- Look for "hybrid" CD-ROM discs that can be used on both Macintosh and IBM PC platforms. If your organization has both types of systems, you can often get double-duty by using the same disc with Macs and PCs both.

- Macintoshes are quite a bit more multimedia- and CD-ROM-friendly than PCs. The drives can cost less and are easier to install, since you don't need a separate interface card.

- If you're installing an external drive, you don't even need to open the Macintosh up. Indeed, all you may do is plug in the power cable, un-plug a daisy-chain cable going from an external hard disk to any other external devices in that particular SCSI chain, and plug it into the new CD-ROM drive instead. Then connect the CD-ROM drive to the other external device (hard disk, scanner, etc.) with a second daisy-chain cable, and make sure each has a different SCSI ID from the other de-vices. (All can be set externally.) Then power up the Mac, drag a few files from the supplied installation disk to your System file, and restart. Presto! There is your CD-ROM drive.

- CD-ROMs are difficult to damage, but you should still treat them with caution. Handle only by the edges, and avoid getting fingerprints on the shiny surface (opposite the label or printed side). If you do need to clean a CD-ROM, always wipe with a soft cloth in a radial direction (center to outside, for example), rather than in the same direction as the disc's rotation: you'll reduce the chances of creating scratches along one of the data "tracks."

- A PC equipped with a SCSI interface card that has an external port can easily share an external CD-ROM drive with a Macintosh. Simply unplug the drive from the Mac's daisy chain of devices, and connect to the SCSI port of the PC. The PC must have the necessary software required to recognize the CD-ROM drive, of course.

- If you have a small collection of CD-ROMs, you may want to purchase a protective caddy for each. However, many users just buy one caddy for each of their frequently used discs, and purchase a few extras that are shared by all their other discs.

- Don't forget that caddies make a great way to "baby-proof" your Mac. I keep all the discs that my four- and six-year-old children use frequently in caddies. They've learned which end to insert in the drive first, so I don't have to worry that they'll damage an expensive disc with rough handling—the disc never leaves the caddy.

- If you have a CD-ROM drive, you also have a potential gateway to low-cost permanent storage of large quantities of information: it's now relatively inexpensive to have custom CD-ROMs made especially for you. If your business generates a large database of information that doesn't change, but which you'd like to have available (such as old accounting records), many CD-ROM service bureaus can create a "custom" single-copy CD-ROM for $100-$200. If you'd like to distribute copies of the same data to multiple users in your organization, you can get 100 duplicates for as little as $1500.

Conclusions and Recommendations

CD-ROM technology will bring you more powerful software, better graphics, entertainment, vital information, and improved education, as costs for both the drives and discs come down to a ridiculously low price. CD-ROMs will not only become standard in the near future, they will become *the* standard, by which every other Macintosh peripheral and program will be judged. The key points to keep in mind from this chapter are:

CD-ROM drives are likely to become standard equipment on the Macintosh in the near future because of their simplicity, the enhanced applications they make possible, and the lower cost of distributing large volumes of software and data files.

Macs now can be fitted with external or internal CD-ROM drives. External units are easy to install—you just plug them into the SCSI port of your Mac, or, if you already have an external SCSI device, fit the CD-ROM drive into the "daisy-chain" of devices. Internal drives are often furnished preinstalled in new computers, but can be added later. It's often best to have your computer store handle the installation. Internal drives are less expensive and take up less desk space, but are otherwise identical to the external versions.

A variety of CD-ROM formats are on the market. Some are intended only for use with IBM-PCs, but there are also "hybrid" discs that can be used equally well with a Macintosh or a PC. Some special formats, like Kodak PhotoCD, have other features. PhotoCDs, for example, can store roughly 100 of your own snapshots on a special disc provided by your photofinisher. Virtually all CD-ROM drives sold today are "XA" compatible—meaning they can handle PhotoCD discs and some other newer formats.

One of the most exciting aspects of CD-ROM technology are the new multimedia applications, which combine still photos, video, sophisticated sound, and other computerized features to give you a rich, involving, and interactive experience. You'll find entire movies on CD-ROM, as well as encyclopedias that show you moving images, music, and sound effects along with their text articles.

The key software categories available for Macintosh CD-ROMs include Business, Reference, Education, Children's Movies/Multimedia, Games, Music, General Interest, Graphics, Shareware, and Applications. These can help you in your work, schooling, hobbies—or just when you want to have a good time.

Chapter 25

Utilities

by Carman Minarik

Utility software is a general term used to describe software packages which do not fit neatly into a software category such as word processing or spreadsheets.

Various types of utility software are used for such functions as protecting your Macintosh from viruses, recovering lost or damaged files, preventing images from burning into the monitor screen, and compressing files to conserve disk space.

In this chapter, you learn about the following:

- Utilities that enhance your operating system

- File management utilities

- Utilities for graphic files

- File compression utilities

- Utility collections

System Enhancements

Many utilities are used to enhance or extend the functionality of the Macintosh operating system. This type of utility is used to extend your Macintosh's control over fonts, provide information regarding your hardware and its operation, and so on.

The following sections provide information on several system enhancement utilities.

Suitcase

Suitcase, from Fifth Generation Systems, is a font management utility. It allows you to group fonts into sets, and open or close font sets at any time. Suitcase also allows you to use more fonts than the Macintosh operating system normally allows. For more information about fonts, see Chapter 8, "All About Fonts."

Under System 7.1, fonts are stored in the Fonts folder in the System folder. Any fonts stored in this folder are automatically loaded at startup time. Up to 128 fonts or suitcases (groups of fonts), can be present in the Fonts folder. This system works fine for relatively small numbers of fonts or font suitcases. Two problems become evident, however, as the number of installed fonts increases.

> **Note**
>
> Under operating system versions prior to System 7.1, fonts are stored in the system file.

First, all the fonts and font suitcases present in the Fonts folder will automatically load at startup time. If the number of fonts is very large, this process can take a considerable amount of time.

A second problem manifests itself when you are working with software. All the fonts in the Fonts folder are displayed on every font list or font menu in every software application you use. This can be unwieldy, especially if you are using many fonts. Even though you may use particular fonts only rarely, they will appear on all the font lists all the time.

The Suitcase utility program addresses these problems by allowing you to group fonts and font suitcases into sets. You then decide which sets are to be opened at startup time. You can also open font sets at any time during use of your Macintosh, and close them again when you are finished with them. In this way, fonts are available on the font lists and menus any time you need them, but are not in the way when you don't.

Suitcase is an Extension, and as such must be located in the Extensions folder inside the System folder to operate. When Suitcase is installed and functioning, you will notice the Suitcase choice available on the Apple menu.

When you select the Apple menu option Suitcase, the screen shown in figure 25.1 appears.

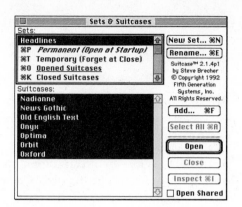

Fig. 25.1
This screen is used to create font sets, add fonts to sets, and open sets for use.

This screen allows you to complete the following tasks:

- Create, delete, or rename font sets

- Add fonts or font suitcases to sets

- Remove fonts or font suitcases from sets

- Open font sets for use

- Close font sets to remove fonts from use

> **Note**
>
> Fonts can be opened by the Macintosh operating system or by Suitcase, but they should not be opened by both. That is, a font present in the Fonts folder inside the System folder should not be included in a Suitcase font set.

Suitcase provides additional utilities for working with desk accessories, FKey and sound files, managing font conflicts, and compressing font and sound files that are seldom used.

Adobe Type Manager

Adobe Type Manager (ATM) is a font utility that performs two basic functions. First, ATM allows non-Postscript printers to print Type 1 Postscript fonts. Second, ATM allows the Macintosh to display accurate Postscript fonts on the monitor screen. For more information about fonts, see Chapter 8, "All About Fonts."

Adobe Type Manager in effect makes the advantages of TrueType font technology available for Postscript fonts. Because a huge library of high quality Type 1 Postscript fonts exists, this can be a tremendous advantage to you as a Macintosh user.

ATM is made up of two parts: a Control Panel and a hardware driver. The Control Panel is named ~ATM, and must reside in the Control Panels folder inside the System folder.

One specific hardware driver exists for Macintosh computers using the Motorola 68000 processing chip, and another hardware driver exists for all other Macintosh computers. Table 25.1 describes the use of these drivers.

Table 25.1 ATM Hardware Drivers	
Macintosh	**Driver**
Plus, SE, Classic	~ATM 68000
All others	~ATM 68020/030/040

The appropriate driver for your Macintosh should be located in the System folder.

Once ATM is properly installed, it can be accessed like any other Control Panel. Follow these steps:

1. Open the Apple menu and choose Control Panels.

2. Choose ~ATM from the resulting window, and the screen shown in figure 25.2 opens.

Fig. 25.2
The Adobe Type Manager screen allows activation or deactivation of ATM.

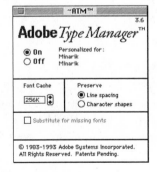

In addition to turning ATM on and off, this screen can be used to set the size of the font cache. The larger the font cache, the faster ATM will be able to image fonts on-screen.

Toner Tuner

Toner Tuner, from Working Software, Inc., is a print utility which allows you to set the darkness level of printing on any inkjet or laser printer. This can create substantial savings in ink or toner cartridge expenses over time. This is especially true if you print many rough drafts of your documents, where the print quality is not critical. For more information on printing, see Chapter 10, "The Printing Chapter."

The Toner Tuner extension adds new controls in the print dialog box for all software applications. Figure 25.3 shows the print dialog from Canvas with Toner Tuner installed.

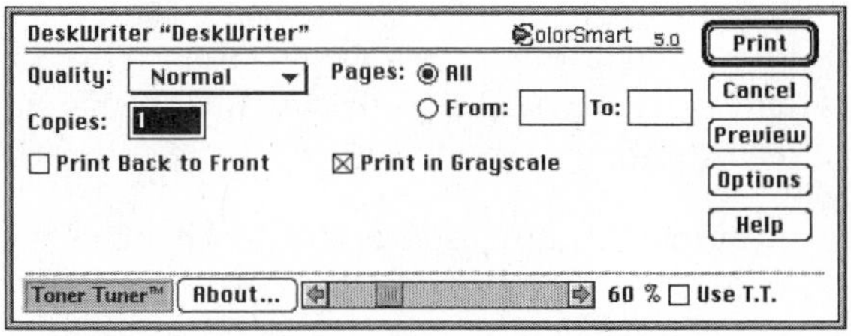

Fig. 25.3
Toner Tuner adds an option bar to the Print dialog in all software applications.

The controls added by Toner Tuner allow you to choose the percentage of normal darkness to use when printing. The lower the percentage, the lighter the print will be, and the less ink or toner will be used.

PopChar

PopChar, available free through most shareware distribution channels, is a Control Panel utility which can display the entire character set for any selected font. Most Macintosh fonts contain many characters beyond the standard letters and numbers. These characters are normally accessed by pressing a key combination. For example, to place a registered trademark symbol into your document, you would press Option-R (in most fonts). PopChar eliminates the need to remember the key combinations by producing a table of available characters from which to choose.

When PopChar is installed, a small icon is added on the menu bar. This icon will be available from within any software application. Point at the PopChar icon and hold the mouse button to open the screen shown in figure 25.4.

Fig. 25.4
Use this pop-up
screen to choose
the characters you
want to use in
your document.

Select the desired character from this screen, and it will be placed in your document at the insertion point location.

SCSIProbe

SCSIProbe, available through shareware channels, allows you to view information about and activate any SCSI devices installed on your Macintosh.

SCSI stands for Small Computer System Interface, and is pronounced *scuzzy*. It is a high-speed data transfer connection available on all Macintosh computers. Up to seven devices can be attached in a SCSI chain. That is, one SCSI device can be attached to the Macintosh, a second SCSI device can be attached to the first, and so on. Typical SCSI devices include hard disk drives, CD-ROM drives, tape backup drives, and scanners.

Part of a Macintosh computer's initial startup sequence includes checking the SCSI port for any attached SCSI devices. If a device is not attached or is not powered on at startup time, the Macintosh will not be aware of the device's existence. Normally, the Macintosh does not check the SCSI port again until the next system startup.

The SCSIProbe utility is a Control Panel, and can be launched from the Control Panels folder. SCSIProbe will recheck the SCSI port for attached devices, and display a screen similar to the one illustrated in figure 25.5.

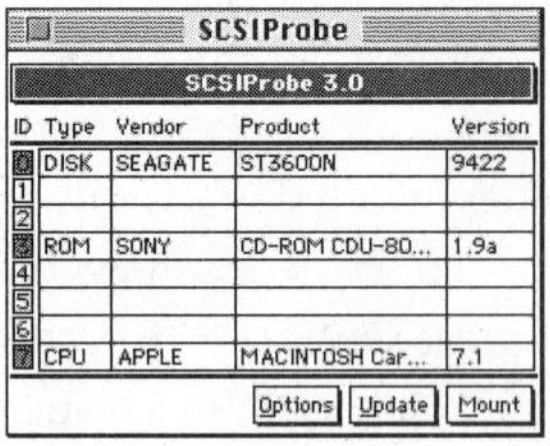

Fig. 25.5
Use SCSIProbe to
identify and
mount SCSI
devices.

This screen shows the device type, manufacturer, model number, and version number for each installed SCSI device.

If a device appears in the SCSIProbe list that is not currently available on your Macintosh desktop, click the Mount button. SCSIProbe will mount the device.

SuperClock!

SuperClock! is a shareware Control Panel utility that places the current time on the Menu Bar in all applications. SuperClock! also provides extensive user control over the appearance and functionality of the clock.

Once installed, SuperClock! is accessed from the Control Panels folder. A window will appear providing options for clock, timer, and alarm controls. When you click the Clock option, a screen like the one in figure 25.6 appears.

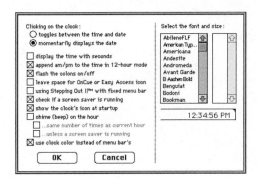

Fig. 25.6
Use this screen to control the function and appearance of SuperClock!.

Use this screen to choose the font and size for the clock information, whether the seconds will be visible, and so on.

Figure 25.7 illustrates the function of SuperClock!, showing the Microsoft Word Menu Bar with SuperClock! installed.

SuperClock! is included with System 7.5.

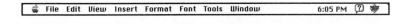

Fig. 25.7
SuperClock! places the current time in the Menu Bar.

TechTool

TechTool, from MicroMat Computer Systems, is a utility application which performs the following three basic functions:

- TechTool provides in-depth system information, including your Macintosh's date of manufacture and total hours of operation.

- TechTool resets the Parameter RAM of your Macintosh. The Parameter RAM contains information such as the alert sound settings, desktop patterns and colors, Macintosh name and network number, and so on. Corrupted Parameter RAM settings can cause many problems which can be corrected by resetting the Parameter RAM. This process is often referred to as *zapping the PRAM*.

- TechTool thoroughly rebuilds the Desktop file on your Macintosh. The Desktop file is an invisible file which contains icon and location information for the files on a disk. Damaged Desktop files can cause serious problems, so the Desktop file should be rebuilt occasionally.

> **Note**
>
> Rebuilding the Desktop file and zapping the PRAM can both be accomplished through key combinations built into the Macintosh operating system. TechTool, however, will do a more thorough job than the operating system.

When TechTool is launched, the screen shown in figure 25.8 opens.

The system information is immediately available. Click the appropriate buttons to zap the PRAM or rebuild the Desktop file.

Fig. 25.8
The TechTool window displays system information.

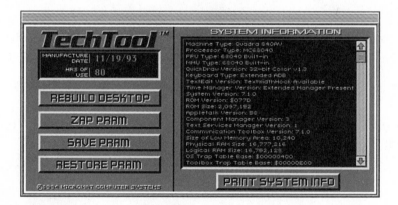

MacErrors

MacErrors, available free through shareware channels, is a database of common Macintosh error numbers. Whenever the Macintosh operating system cannot complete a requested task, an error message is displayed in an alert box. This error message often contains an error number. MacErrors will provide a corresponding description for each error number.

Launch MacErrors, and the window shown in figure 25.9 opens.

Enter an error number in the Error box, and the corresponding error code and description is displayed.

Fig. 25.9
Use the MacErrors window to see descriptions of Macintosh errors.

Now Utilities

Now Utilities, from Now Software, Inc., is a collection of seven utilities designed to enhance the operation of your Macintosh. Now Utilities contains the following components:

- *Startup Manager* allows you to control the loading of Extensions, Control Panels, and startup items. It automatically disables Extensions that crash, and helps keep conflicting Extensions separate. Startup Manager allows you to choose which Extensions and Control Panels will load at startup time.

- *Super Boomerang* is an enhancement added to the directory dialog box in all applications. It keeps track of the most recently used files and folders and makes them available as a list within the Open dialogs, and also on the Apple menu.

- *NowMenus* allows the Apple menu to cascade for up to five levels of submenus. NowMenus also allows you to change the order of appearance of Apple menu items, and allows you to change the menu font.

- *WYSIWYG Menus* causes fonts on a font menu in any application to be displayed in their own typefaces.

- *NowSave* automatically saves your work in any application at specified intervals. You can set it up to save based on elapsed time, number of keystrokes, or number of mouse clicks.

- *Now Scrapbook* allows you to create catalogs of graphics, text, sounds, and QuickTime movies. Items in these catalogs can be easily retrieved into your documents.

- *Now Profile* provides a detailed report on your Macintosh system configuration. This can be extremely helpful when you are trying to isolate a problem with your system performance.

NowMenus is built into System 7.5.

File Management

The Macintosh Finder provides an easy-to-use, intuitive interface for managing your files. It may not provide every capability you might wish for however, and some processes may not work exactly the way you want them to. That's where file management utilities come in. For more information about file management, see Chapter 7, "Organizing Your Files, Folders, and Disks."

File management utilities allow you to do things such as recover lost or damaged files, optimize your disk performance, open files more easily, and copy files more quickly. The following sections describe some of the commonly used file management utilities.

Norton Utilities

Norton Utilities, from Symantec Corporation, is perhaps the most well-known file and disk recovery software available. With Norton Utilities, you will be able to repair floppy disks and hard disks, and retrieve data which otherwise would be lost.

When you launch Norton Utilities, the screen shown in figure 25.10 appears.

Fig. 25.10

The main Norton Utilities screen provides access to the major Norton Utilities functions.

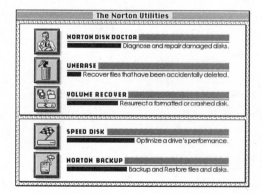

This screen provides access to the major Norton Utilities functions:

- ■ *Norton Disk Doctor.* This function diagnoses and repairs most disk problems. Descriptive screens appear, providing information on the nature of each identified problem and advice on how to proceed.

- ■ *Unerase.* This feature allows you to recover files that have been moved to the Trash, even after the trash has been emptied.

- *Volume Recover.* This option allows recovery of files from disks that cannot be repaired with Norton Disk Doctor.

- *Speed Disk.* This is a disk optimization program which will speed disk access by defragmenting files on the disk.

- *Norton Backup.* This option allows you to backup the contents of your hard disk to floppy disks.

Norton Utilities also provides additional capabilities, such as the following:

- Password protection for your files

- The ability to divide large hard disks into separate partitions

- File deletion which cannot be recovered (for confidential information)

- A disk access indicator for your monitor

- Fast floppy disk duplication

MacTools

MacTools, from Central Point Software, provides file and disk recovery, as well as other utility functions. Like Norton Utilities, the central purpose of MacTools is recovery of lost data. Figure 25.11 illustrates the MacTools screen as the software analyzes and repairs a disk.

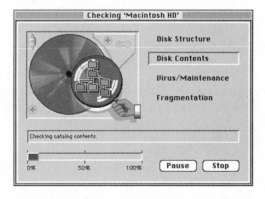

Fig. 25.11
The MacTools screen displays information regarding the disk being checked.

In addition to disk repair, MacTools provides the following utility functions:

- Recovery of deleted files

- Virus protection

- Hard disk backup to floppy disks

■ Fast floppy disk duplication

■ Disk access indicator for your monitor

■ File defragmentation

■ File repair capability for Microsoft Word and Microsoft Excel documents

Disk First Aid

Disk First Aid is a disk repair utility included with the Macintosh operating system. It lacks the sophistication of Norton Utilities or MacTools but can be very effective for repairing damaged disks.

Macintosh users who are experienced in disk and file recovery recommend that for maximum protection against lost data you should have all three of these utilities (Disk First Aid, MacTools, and Norton Utilities) available. Each of these applications has strengths and weaknesses, and problems that one package cannot begin to diagnose may be easily repaired by one of the other two.

Disk First Aid is included with System 7.5.

Mr. File

Mr. File, from Softways, is a file management utility which provides the capability to copy, move, find, rename, and delete files in the background. This allows you to use your Macintosh for other functions without waiting for these file management tasks to be completed.

Mr. File takes the form of a Desk Accessory under System 6, and an Apple Menu Item under System 7. The utility is therefore always available on the Apple menu. Choose the Apple menu option Mr. File, and the window shown in figure 25.12 opens.

This window displays many of Mr. File's central capabilities, such as the following:

■ Copy files and folders

■ Find files and folders

■ Move files and folders

■ Erase files and folders

Fig. 25.12
The Mr. File folder window allows you to view, copy, rename, move, and erase files in the background.

These tasks are all completed in the background. That is, you will retain control of your Macintosh and can work on other jobs while these tasks are being completed.

Mr. File allows you to have as many task windows open at one time as you need. You can, for example, copy three folders, rename two others, and erase five files all at the same time, using separate windows.

Mr. File also provides the following additional capabilities:

■ Create lists of items, even from different folders, to view or launch

■ Launch applications from folder or list windows

■ Format or erase disks more quickly than the Finder

■ View file details such as file type and creator

DART

DART (Data Archive/Retrieval Tool) is available from Apple Computer. Its purpose is to archive floppy disk images. Archiving of floppy disk images with DART has the following two primary benefits:

■ The disk image is compressed so that the disk information can be stored in less space.

■ The disk can be duplicated more quickly and more accurately than by using the Finder's disk copy routine.

When the DART application is launched, the screen shown in figure 25.13 opens.

If you are creating a disk archive, the source will be a floppy disk and the destination will be a DART file. The floppy disk will be copied to the DART file and compressed, significantly reducing the disk space required.

Fig. 25.13
Use the DART
screen to choose
a source and a
destination for the
copy procedure.

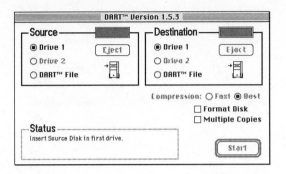

If you are creating a floppy disk copy, the source will be a DART file and the destination will be a floppy disk. The file will be decompressed and copied to the floppy disk. The information will also be verified as it is copied, using a more stringent verification process than that employed by the Finder. You also have options to format the floppy disks as they are being copied onto, and to make multiple floppy disk copies from the DART file.

Graphics

Graphics utilities allow you to manipulate picture and video files on your Macintosh. Such utilities might be used to play QuickTime movies, capture screen images as graphic files, or set a complex pattern or picture as your desktop background.

VisualClips

VisualClips, from Sound Source Unlimited, is a QuickTime playback utility packaged with a collection of high quality QuickTime movies. The utility is called VideoBeep and takes the form of a Control Panel.

VideoBeep allows you to assign QuickTime movies for playback when specified system events occur. For example, you can assign one movie to play when the Trash is emptied, and a different movie to play when a disk is inserted.

Choosing the VideoBeep Control Panel will open the window shown in figure 25.14.

In addition to assigning the movie for each system event, this screen provides controls for the location of the video window and the sound volume setting.

Fig. 25.14
Use the VideoBeep
screen to assign
QuickTime movies
to system events.

When VideoBeep is set up, you will be treated to entertaining video clips as you work with your Macintosh. Whenever a particular system event occurs, the associated QuickTime movie will play automatically.

Capture

Capture is a screen-capture utility manufactured by Mainstay. It allows you to save parts of the currently visible screen or the entire screen as a graphic file. This graphic file can then be printed, or opened and manipulated in a program such as Canvas or Illustrator.

Capture is a Control Panel, and as such must be located in the Control Panels folder in the System folder. Opening the Capture Control Panel will produce a window as shown in figure 25.15.

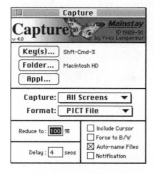

Fig. 25.15
The Capture
window allows
you to choose
what will be
captured, the file
format it will be
captured in, and so
on.

This screen allows you to do the following:

■ Select a key combination to perform a screen capture

■ Select a folder to store the graphic files in

■ Choose to capture all screens, the main screen, or a part of the screen you select

- Choose to save the resulting graphic file to the clipboard, as a PICT file, as a TIFF file, or as a MacPaint file

- Automatically reduce the screen image

- Delay the capture for a specified period of time

With Capture installed, you need only press the designated key combination to capture the screen image to the clipboard or a file.

If you choose to capture a selection, your mouse pointer changes shape when the key combination is pressed. You can then drag around the portion of the screen you want to capture.

Desktop Textures

The Desktop Textures utility, available as shareware, allows you to choose from a variety of interesting desktop background patterns. These patterns will be much more complex than those which can be created through use of the General Controls Control Panel. For more information, see Chapter 12, "Creating and Modifying Icons."

When the Texture Installer application is launched, the window shown in figure 25.16 appears.

Fig 25.16
Use the Texture Installer window to view and install textures.

This window is used to select the desired desktop pattern from the collection of textures.

The Desktop Textures package also comes with an application called Texture Randomizer which can be placed in the Startup Items folder. This program will automatically choose a random texture each time the Macintosh is started up.

Compression

File compression utilities reduce the amount of disk space required to store files. This is possible because most computer files contain significant amounts of repeated information. That is, in order to be usable, many computer files are actually larger than they need to be. Compression utilities remove the repeated information in a file, and store the file much more efficiently.

> **Note**
>
> Compressed files are not usable in their compressed form. They must be decompressed before use. Therefore, if you plan to use compression utilities as a means to move large files from one Macintosh to another, be sure that the compression utility is available on both computers.

DiskDoubler

DiskDoubler is a file compression utility from Fifth Generation Systems. It will compress files or folders, reducing their size to as little as 50% of original.

The DiskDoubler application can compress and expand items using the screen shown in figure 25.17.

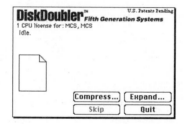

Fig. 25.17
Use this screen
to select files
or folders
to compress
or expand.

As items are being compressed or expanded, compression statistics are displayed on this screen.

DiskDoubler is also available as a desk accessory or Apple Menu item, so it can be accessed at any time regardless of the software currently in use.

DiskDoubler will automatically expand any compressed file which is opened, either from the Finder or from within an application. When the file is closed, DiskDoubler will automatically compress the file again.

AutoDoubler

AutoDoubler is also from Fifth Generation Systems and uses the same type of file compression system as DiskDoubler. AutoDoubler, however, does not compress individually selected files or folders. Instead, AutoDoubler automatically compresses all the files on your disk.

The file compression takes place in the background, so any time your Macintosh is not processing information, AutoDoubler automatically begins compressing files. Any file that is opened, either from the Finder or within any application, will automatically be decompressed.

AutoDoubler is a Control Panel, and must be located in the Control Panels folder inside the System folder. You can select files and folders to exclude from automatic compression so that items such as your system files and frequently used applications will always remain uncompressed.

TimesTwo

TimesTwo, from Golden Triangle Computers, is not technically a file compression utility. It is actually a disk driver that replaces the driver supplied by Apple. The TimesTwo driver is designed to arrange information on the disk in such a way that repeated information within a file is automatically compressed.

Because TimesTwo is a device-level driver, the chances of incompatibilities with software and system extensions, an occasional problem with compression utilities, is greatly reduced.

TimesTwo will roughly double the usable size of your hard disk. The disk will actually report larger amounts of remaining disk space in the Finder windows. Files on the disk will show their actual sizes in the Finder.

As with all file compression techniques, increased disk storage capacity is achieved at the expense of speed. Disks using TimesTwo will provide slower access times than identical disks not set up with TimesTwo.

Screen Savers

The purpose of a screen saver utility is to reduce the chance that an image will be "burned into" your monitor screen if your Macintosh is left running unattended for extended periods. Screen saver utilities achieve this purpose by placing moving images on the screen, thus preventing a static image from burning in. For more information, see Chapter 12, "Creating and Modifying Icons."

After Dark

After Dark from Berkeley Systems is probably the best known of the screen saver utilities. The After Dark package consists of two parts: the After Dark Control Panel and the After Dark Files folder. The Control Panel is installed in the Control Panels folder inside the System folder, and the After Dark Files folder is installed in the System folder.

When the After Dark Control Panel is opened, the window shown in figure 25.18 appears.

Fig. 25.18
Use the After Dark Control Panel to select the image for use as a screen saver.

This screen is used to choose the desired image for the screen saver, and to set such options as the volume for any associated sound files which will be played as part of the screen saver.

Once After Dark is installed, the screen saver image will be activated automatically when the system has been idle for the specified period of time.

After Dark provides controls for length of idle time, starting the screen saver immediately, and preventing the screen saver from starting. You can even add password protection for your Macintosh as part of After Dark's functionality.

Many screen saver images are available for use with After Dark, including Star Trek, Marvel Comics, and Walt Disney collections.

Virus Protection

Computer software code created for the sole purpose of disrupting the functionality of your Macintosh is called a virus. Viruses range from relatively harmless amusements to incredibly destructive programs which cause permanent data loss.

Viruses are created by individuals and hidden in the programming code of other software. As the legitimate files are copied from one computer to another, the virus is spread as well. Most viruses are designed to automatically copy themselves onto any computer they come in contact with.

Virus protection software is designed to identify virus programs, and protect your Macintosh from them.

Symantec AntiVirus

Symantec AntiVirus for Macintosh (SAM) is manufactured by Symantec Corporation. It is one of the most comprehensive virus prevention, detection, and removal utilities available for your Macintosh.

SAM is made up of two components: SAM Intercept and SAM Virus Clinic. SAM Intercept is a Control Panel, and works in the background to prevent a virus from infecting your Macintosh. It scans automatically for known viruses, and monitors your system for suspicious activity that might indicate the presence of a virus. SAM Virus Clinic is an application which thoroughly inspects your files and disks for evidence of virus activity, and provides the capability to remove many viruses once they are discovered.

SAM provides an extraordinary level of control over the virus protection process. The screen illustrated in figure 25.19 shows some of SAM's options.

Fig. 25.19
The SAM Intercept scan controls provide many options relating to the virus scan process.

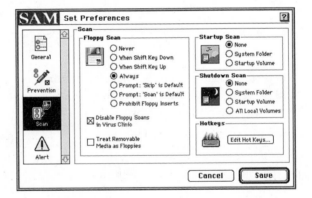

SAM Intercept provides options for automatically scanning floppy disks for viruses when they are inserted, scanning the system and desktop files automatically when the Macintosh is started or shut down, and automatically scanning system activity for any suspicious actions.

SAM Virus Clinic provides extensive capabilities for identifying files or disks infected with any of the known viruses. When a virus is identified, SAM is usually able to remove the virus and its effects from the infected file or disk.

Disinfectant

Disinfectant is a virus prevention utility distributed free of change by North-western University. This utility is available through most shareware channels. Disinfectant operates as an application for scanning and repairing disks and files, and also as an extension for automatically monitoring your system for virus activity.

Disinfectant differs from most commercial virus protection packages in that it does not scan for viruses at specific times such as when a floppy disk is inserted. Instead, it monitors disk and file activity for the indications of a virus attack. When such indications occur, Disinfectant operates to prevent the virus from becoming active. As a result of this approach, Disinfectant rarely causes any problems such as conflicts with software or system extensions.

From Here...

In this chapter, you explored some of the many utility packages available for your Macintosh. You reviewed both commercial software and free programs that can add functionality and enjoyment to your Macintosh experience.

- For more information on Extensions and Control Panels, see Chapter 5, "Understanding the Desktop and Finder."

- See Chapter 8, "All About Fonts," for more information on fonts and font use.

- For more information on printing with your Macintosh, see Chapter 10, "The Printing Chapter."

- See Chapter 11, "Changing the Look of Your Desktop," for additional information on customizing the look of your desktop.

Chapter 26

Personal and Business Management

by Mark Bilbo

Computers and business have gone hand in hand for many years now. One of the first applications of the computer was in managing company finances. Before the invention of the personal computer, however, only large corporations could afford to purchase, use, and maintain computers. Today, even the smallest one-person business not only can afford but needs a computer.

At first, the Macintosh was not widely accepted as a business machine. Today, however, an enormous variety of powerful business software is available for the Macintosh—from home finance applications to full business accounting and management software.

Along with the standard, more familiar categories of personal finance, business finance, income tax, and project planning, a new category has arisen and "heated up" in recent times. This new category is called *Personal Information Management.* Software included in this category ranges from programs that enable you to create calendars and schedules with reminders (by using *Time and Schedule Managers*) to high powered, computerized versions of the old Rolodex (by using *Contact Managers*).

Many packages are on the market that can help you manage your personal or business affairs. This chapter highlights some of the more popular software in the following categories:

- Personal Finance Management
- Business Management

■ Income Tax Planning and Filing

■ Project Planning

■ Personal Information Management

Personal Finance

One of the early successes of the Macintosh was personal finance management software. Although not the first such package, the Dollars and Sense program by Monogram software was one of the early attempts to bring double-entry accounting down to a personal level and enable average Macintosh owners to keep track of their finances.

Although Dollars and Sense faded in the late '80s (more because of poor management by the owner rather than the quality of the software), the vacuum was quickly filled by Quicken, which has now become the dominant personal finance program not only on the Macintosh but in the DOS and Windows world as well.

Quicken is not without competition. Andrew Tobias's Managing Your Money is also a popular personal finance program.

Other more specialized programs also exist that can help you plan your investments, manage your mortgage, and handle your estate.

Quicken

Quicken first appeared as a small check-writing program. The program's biggest asset was its ease of use and simplicity. Over the years, Quicken's steadily increasing power lead to its current dominance in the personal and small business finance category. Intuit, Quicken's publisher, has consistently brought more power to the program while maintaining the ease of use that has characterized Quicken.

At Quicken's heart is the orginal check-writing function. This function is one of the features that makes Quicken familiar and easy to use. Figure 26.1 shows a check written with Quicken.

Checks written in Quicken look pretty much just like the checks in your checkbook—you don't have to learn a whole new way of doing things.

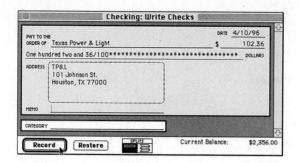

Fig. 26.1
Writing a check
with Quicken.

What is different between handwritten checks and using Quicken to record
checks is the use of categories. In Quicken, *categories* are the dividing up of
your expenses and income sources in ways that enable you to track where
your money is going.

For example, a check to the light company belongs in the category
Utilities:Gas & Electric. The amount of each check you write to the light company is added up so that at any time you can see how much money you are
spending on the electricity in your home (see fig. 26.2).

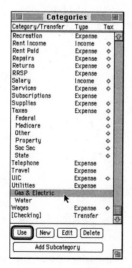

Fig. 26.2
Categorizing a
utility payment.

Not only does Quicken provide predefined sets of categories, but you can
modify these sets and even create your own categories to suit your personal
needs.

Quicken also enables you to set up classes to further subdivide your payments in useful ways. Small business users, for example, might have classes to track employee sales or project specific expenses.

Quicken goes beyond simply managing your checking account. You can also track credit card, cash, liability, portfolio, and money market accounts (see fig. 26.3).

Fig. 26.3
Creating an
account to
track your Visa
card.

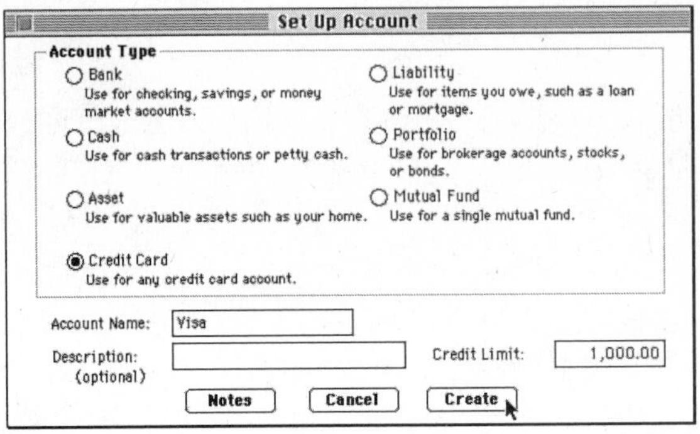

Fig. 26.4
A charge for
gasoline is entered
in the Visa
register.

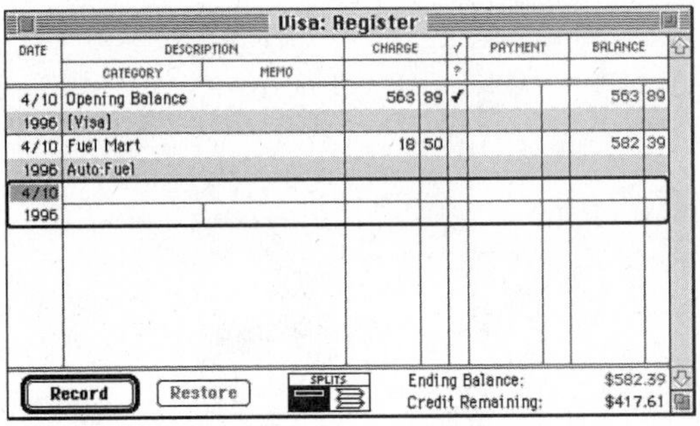

Tip
When you set
up your
Quicken cat-
egories, have
last year's tax
return handy
so that you can
set up catego-
ries that will
match your
usual deduc-
tions.

Each account—including your checking account—has a register into which you enter transactions that reflect your purchases and payments (see fig. 26.4).

Quicken tracks each account's balance, recording your transactions and its effect on your finances. In the case of credit card accounts, you even see the remaining balance on the card to help you avoid charging over your limit.

Quicken enables you to enter budgets for each income and expense account (see fig. 26.5).

Category	Jan	Feb	Mar	Apr	May	Jun
Inflows						
Bonus	0.00	0.00	0.00	0.00	0.00	0.00
CPP	0.00	0.00	0.00	0.00	0.00	0.00
Gift Received	0.00	0.00	0.00	0.00	0.00	0.00
Gross Sales	0.00	0.00	0.00	0.00	0.00	0.00
Interest Earned	0.00	0.00	0.00	0.00	0.00	0.00
Old Age Pension	0.00	0.00	0.00	0.00	0.00	0.00
Rent Income	0.00	0.00	0.00	0.00	0.00	0.00
Salary	2,200.00	2,200.00	2,200.00	2,200.00	2,200.00	2,200.00
From Checking	0.00	0.00	0.00	0.00	0.00	0.00
From FB&T Mortgage	0.00	0.00	0.00	0.00	0.00	0.00
From FBT Savings	0.00	0.00	0.00	0.00	0.00	0.00
From Home	0.00	0.00	0.00	0.00	0.00	0.00
From Visa	0.00	0.00	0.00	0.00	0.00	0.00
Total Inflows	**2,200.00**	**2,200.00**	**2,200.00**	**2,200.00**	**2,200.00**	**2,200.00**
Outflows						
Ads	0.00	0.00	0.00	0.00	0.00	0.00
Auto:						
Fuel	50.00	50.00	50.00	50.00	50.00	50.00
Service	0.00	0.00	0.00	0.00	0.00	0.00
Total Auto	**50.00**	**50.00**	**50.00**	**50.00**	**50.00**	**50.00**
Bad Debt	0.00	0.00	0.00	0.00	0.00	0.00
Bank Charges	0.00	0.00	0.00	0.00	0.00	0.00
Benefits	0.00	0.00	0.00	0.00	0.00	0.00
Total Budget Inflows	2,200.00	2,200.00	2,200.00	2,200.00	2,200.00	2,200.00
Total Budget Outflows	50.00	50.00	50.00	50.00	50.00	50.00
Difference	2,150.00	2,150.00	2,150.00	2,150.00	2,150.00	2,150.00

QuickBudget   Fill Row   View by: Month ▼

Fig. 26.5
Creating a
Quicken budget.

Tip
Quicken has an
Autofill feature
that enables
you to type
only the first
few, unique
letters of a
category to
invoke the
category name.

One of the powerful features of a personal finance program in general and
Quicken in specific is budgeting. Quicken enables you to track your finances
against the budget you enter with graphs and reports to watch your budget
progress (see fig. 26.6).

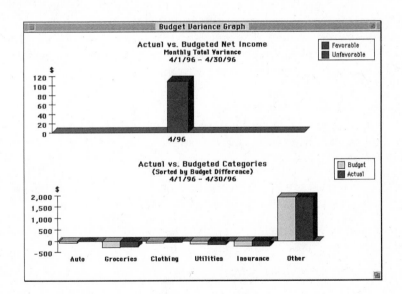

Fig. 26.6
Checking the
monthly budget.

Tip
Quicken has a
zoom feature in
all reports and
graphs. To see
more detail,
double-click
the category or
item in which
you are inter-
ested.

Tip
For faster trans-
action entry,
take advantage
of Quicken's
Memorize fea-
ture.

Quicken offers a wide variety of reports and graphs. Business reports such as payroll, accounts receivable and payable, balance sheet, and others are of-fered in addition to the personal finance reports such as net worth, budget, tax schedule, and so on.

Quicken works with programs such as MacInTax for tax reporting and plan-ning. Use the Tax Schedule Personal Finance report to export tax information in a format that can be read by tax reporting software. Using Quicken to-gether with a tax reporting program saves you a great deal of time when April 15th comes around. For more information on tax software, see "Income Tax Planning and Filing" later in this chapter.

Quicken also interfaces with CheckFree, the electronic bill payment service. CheckFree is an independent company that handles payment requests, trans-mits Electronic Funds Transfers (EFTs), or mails laser printed checks to your payees. With this service (which costs about $10 per month plus transaction charges), you can almost eliminate printed and handwritten checks.

Intuit also offers the Quicken Visa card with electronic statements down-loaded over modem or sent to you on disk. Reconciling your Quicken Visa can then be done quickly through the program.

At about $49, Quicken is a bargain. And if you shop around, you can many times find Quicken bundled with other software packages, such as MacInTax, and save even more money. The program's ease of use combined with the power it offers has made Quicken the leading personal and small business finance manager. You can't go wrong with this one.

Managing Your Money

Andrew Tobias' Managing Your Money (MYM), published by Meca, is also a popular personal finance manager, although the program is often more diffi-cult to use than Quicken.

Tip
After you set up
graphs and
reports in a
manner that is
useful to you,
you can use the
Memorize
feature to store
the customized
report for later
access.

Like Quicken, MYM imitates the checkbook in appearance and in the meth-ods you employ to enter transactions (see fig. 26.7).

Like Quicken, MYM tracks the amounts of transactions. Instead of using cat-egories, however, MYM records everything in accounts.

Although MYM offers registers for accounts, you cannot directly enter trans-actions into the registers. You also cannot edit transactions while in the regis-ter, which you can do with Quicken. When you double-click a transaction in the register, however, the Write Checks screen appears in edit mode (refer to fig. 26.7).

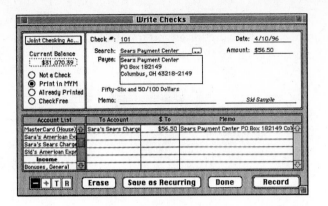

Fig. 26.7
Entering a check
with Mananging
Your Money.

MYM simplifies some tasks by enabling you to set up a transaction as recurring. You can even add a reminder to alert you when a transaction is due to
occur (see fig. 26.8).

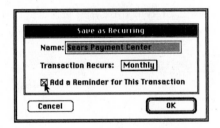

Fig. 26.8
Adding a recurring
transaction.

You can record a transaction as recurring in the Write Checks screen by clicking the Save As Recurring button. Later, you can invoke recurring transactions singly or in groups (see fig. 26.9).

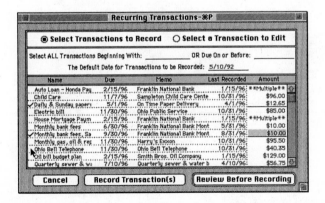

Fig. 26.9
Selecting a group
of transactions to
enter at once.

MYM enables you to set budgets for each account. Instead of displaying all the accounts at once, MYM requires you to set a budget in a separate window for each account (see fig. 26.10).

Fig. 26.10
Setting a Clothing account budget.

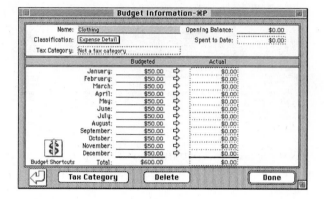

Your budgets can be compared against your actual spending through the Analyze Budgets vs. Actuals report provided by MYM (see fig. 26.11).

Screen Reports-⌘P

Analyze Budgets vs. Actuals

5/10/94

	Budgeted	Actual	Difference	Over/Under Budget	Budget as % of Total
Net Income					
Income					
Sid's Semi-Monthly Pay	$16,200.00	$9,625.00	($6,575.00)	(40.6%)	43.7%
Sara's Monthly Pay	$18,150.00	$21,000.00	$2,850.00	15.7%	49.0%
IRA's Dividend & Interest	$100.02		($100.02)	(100.0%)	0.3%
College Savings Interest	$1,110.00	$1,421.21	$311.21	28.0%	3.0%
Bonuses, General	$1,500.00		($1,500.00)	(100.0%)	4.0%
Total Income	$37,060.02	$32,046.21	($5,013.81)	(13.5%)	100.0%
Expense					
Automobile Expenses					
Auto Maintenance & Repai	$450.00	$95.50	($354.50)	(78.8%)	1.5%
Honda Loan Interest	$90.00	$173.08	$83.08	92.3%	0.3%
Total Automobile Expenses	$540.00	$268.58	($271.42)	(50.3%)	1.8%
Bank Fees & Charges	$90.00	$80.00	($10.00)	(11.1%)	0.3%
Clothing	$300.00	$50.00	($250.00)	(83.3%)	1.0%
Child Care	$2,250.00	$672.00	($1,578.00)	(70.1%)	7.4%
Entertainment	$900.00		($900.00)	(100.0%)	2.9%
House Furn, Fix & Repair	$600.00		($600.00)	(100.0%)	2.0%
Gifts, Weddings, etc...	$250.02		($250.02)	(100.0%)	0.8%
House, Food & Living	$5,400.00	$3,500.00	($1,900.00)	(35.2%)	17.7%
Insurance	$600.00	$206.76	($393.24)	(65.5%)	2.0%
Medical & Dental					

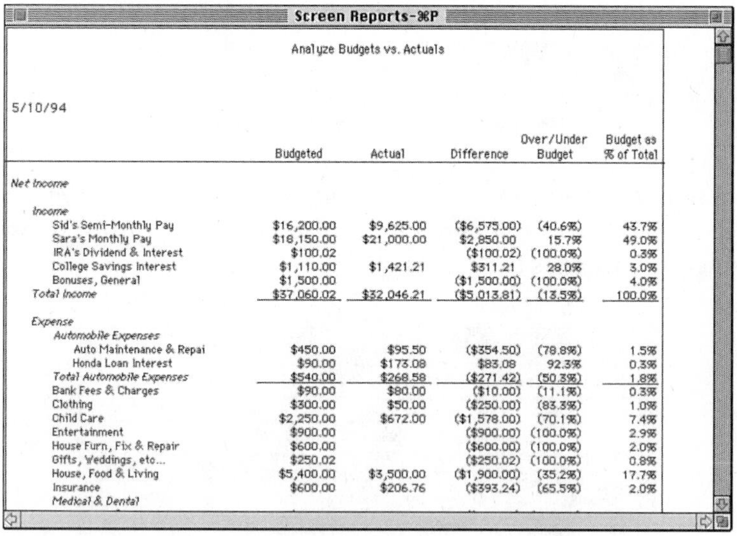

Fig. 26.11
Comparing actual expenditures versus a budget.

MYM provides a large number of reports, including tax forms filled out based on your MYM accounts, transaction reports, and planning reports (such as amortization schedules, budget reports, and so on). Many of the reports also can be graphed (see fig. 26.12).

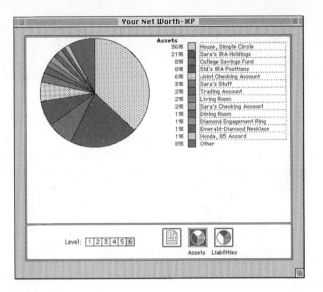

Fig. 26.12
Graphing the
assets that
contribute to your
net worth.

A feature of MYM worth noting is the tax planning provided in the program. When you create your accounts, you can link the accounts to the appropriate lines in the tax forms. When you enter transactions throughout the year, you can check on your progress (see fig. 26.13).

Fig. 26.13
The 1040 form in
MYM can help you
plan your income
taxes.

MYM can display the 1040 form, schedules A through F, and SE complete with the amounts from your transactions.

Overall, Managing Your Money can be a difficult program to use. Before Quicken's recent upgrade, MYM had some features that gave the program something of an edge in power and might have made putting up with the program's obstinate behavior and dozens of cluttered screens worth putting up with.

MYM also seems to attempt to do too much in one program. For example, reminders are provided to alert you to appointments you need to keep. There doesn't seem to be much reason to include such a feature in a finance management program. A number of schedule-keeping programs are available, as described later in this chapter.

Quicken is by far the easier program to use and has as much power as MYM, especially now that Quicken 4.0 has added portfolio management. Your best bet now would be to go with the winner.

WillMaker

Creating a will used to mean a trip to the lawyer's office and attendant fees. In recent years, however, more people have begun to create their own wills, often using paralegal assistance or books.

Now your Macintosh can help and save you a great deal of time and money. WillMaker 5 by Nolo Press uses an interview format, asking you the necessary questions and stepping you through the process of creating a will. State specific laws are addressed, and you can update your will at any time.

Included in the latest release are living will and final arrangements modules. For about $40, WillMaker 5 is far less expensive than a trip to the attorney's office.

Related to will-making and home finance, Nolo's Living Trust program, which sells for about $45, can help you set up a living trust that avoids probate costs and delays (good in every state except Louisiana).

Nolo Press also has Personal RecordKeeper that can help you organize your finances and your estate by tracking important legal, personal, and financial records. The $30 program tracks your credit card numbers, household inventory, securities, and other important information. Exporting to Quicken is supported to help you track your net worth.

Wealth Builder

For more serious investment planning, the investment and planning modules of Quicken and Managing Your Money may not be sufficient. WealthBuilder, a program devoted solely to applying a widely accepted investment plan to your personal finances, can help in this area.

This $60 program can even connect by modem to obtain quotes on securities, obtain market briefs, price history information, and more, although this service requires an additional monthly fee.

WealthBuilder does more than simply track your investments; it also helps you to strategize and plan. If your investments are significant enough to require that you spend time overseeing them and making plans, you may want to consider bringing in your Macintosh to help.

Market Analyzer Plus

If you play the stock market, you may want to consider software direct from Dow Jones. Market Analyzer Plus interfaces on-line with the Dow Jones News/Retrieval service to access up to fifteen years of price and volume history. You are able to chart the information and apply several statistical analyses.

The program is not cheap, costing about $225 but the serious investor will want to consider this product carefully.

Business Finance and Management

The Macintosh had an uphill climb being accepted in the business world. For some years, the Mac was considered a novelty or a "niche" machine—useful in a limited way in only certain areas. In time, however, solid business software began to appear. Combined with the ease of use of the Macintosh user interface, the Mac is now often regarded as an ideal business computer. The expenses of training are far less on the Mac than in the DOS and Windows world. And labor is far more expensive than any computer or software.

So many business oriented packages are available today that the Mac user has almost an embarrassment of riches. Accounting packages, business forms programs, sales forecasting software, asset management, and a great many other business related packages are available. This section surveys the available software.

Accounting

Accounting is a task well-suited for turning over to a computer. Keeping track of a company's finances is an important task and computers are less prone to math errors than human beings.

Additionally, the quick reporting of an accounting package can reduce headaches greatly by providing fast, up-to-date information on a company's financial position.

MYOB

Mind Your Own Business is a name that initially might be difficult to take seriously, but MYOB has become the top Macintosh accounting program—primarily due to its ease of use. At the same time, MYOB has full general ledger, checkbook management, A/R and A/P, and a wealth of reports.

Recent upgrades have added CD-ROM on-line help (obviously you will need a CD-ROM drive to take advantage of this feature), an easier startup procedure, recurring transactions for frequently produced invoices, and other features to help the small business user take full advantage of the program.

Best! Ware sells the package for about $100 list, but you can find MYOB for about $60 if you shop around. A version that includes a payroll module sells for about $50 more.

Home and small business users will want to consider this package to manage their business finances.

Peachtree Accounting

Small business users may be interested in the Peachtree offerings. Peachtree Accounting has won awards and been praised for being easy to learn and easy to use.

The program offers unlimited (actually limited only by your available hard disk space) numbers of accounts, customers, transactions, employees, and so on instead of setting limits that could cause trouble when your business grows.

The standard accounting modules are offered, including general ledger, A/R and A/P, job costing, inventory, purchase orders, budgeting, and more. You can also create custom business forms.

The around $120 package is compatible with System 7 features such as Publish and Subscribe, core Apple events, and Balloon help.

Peachtree also offers Insight Accounting, which formerly was a series of separate programs sold as the Insight Expert Accounting System. Peachtree integrates the programs into a single package and enables the user to install them separately or as an integrated system.

Insight offers reports that are meant to aid you with more expert advice to interpret and analyze your data and to spot problems and trends in advance. The program sells for about $300.

MacP&L

Start Accounting offers a full, serious accounting package for larger businesses. MacP&L, which sells for around $190, has over 100 standard reports and has more accounting modules than just about any other package. Check writing, A/R and A/P, inventory, payroll, project revenue, general ledger, expense tracking, invoicing, and more are fully integrated. MacP&L is fully System 7 savvy and works with AppleScript.

A multiuser version is offered that works over AppleTalk. The $380 package allows three users with more user optional capacity available by upgrade.

MultiLedger and CheckMark Payroll

CheckMark offers an accounting system for larger businesses. MultiLedger handles A/R, A/P, G/L, inventory, and other necessary accounting functions. The single user version sells for about $230 and a five user multi-user version is about $400.

MultiLedger also has payroll capabilities with CheckMark Payroll, which can handle accrued vacation, sick leave, retirement savings plans, government forms, and other important payroll issues. Tax tables can be changed within the program or updates can be ordered. The $170 program can be used alone or in conjunction with MultiLedger or MYOB.

Timeslips III

Freelance professionals need a way to track their time and process billing for clients. Timeslips III offers a TS Timer desk accessory that accumulates the information as you work. Then TS Report will generate invoices and reports to aid you in your billing and record keeping. The $200 program is offered by Timeslips Corp.

Timeslips II can be extended with TAL Timeslips Accounting link to generate customized income reports and link to accounting software. Accounting Link sells for about $60.

ShopKeeper Plus

For the retail store owner, ShopKeeper offers the ShopKeeper Plus package geared towards the management of a retail store. This package is something a video store owner or convenience store owner might consider.

The $320 package handles five different types of customer records and the same number of different inventory models. Bar code, order entry, cash drawer control, customer billing and vendor ordering (including automatic ordering), trade-ins, refunds, discounts (by item or customer), promotionals, and other retail features are provided.

ShopKeeper Plus also interfaces with different Macintosh general ledger accounting packages to make managing your store's finances easier.

The Palo Alto Software Business Tools

Palo Alto offers some unique tools that the business owner may want to consider. The Toolkits use interview techniques and organized methodologies to aid you in creating business and marketing plans, make sales and marketing forecasts, business budgets, and employee handbooks. All of the packages sell for about $75 with the exception of the Employee Handbook Toolkit which runs about $10 less.

- *Business Plan Toolkit* uses the interview technique to guide you through financial and business charts, cash flow, profit and loss, and other important business considerations. The software can help teach business planning. It would be worthwhile to home or small business users who are just entering the business world.

- *Marketing Plan Toolkit* helps you plan marketing strategy, including gathering information, focusing on your market, developing tactics, projecting forecasts, and creating budgets. The program then helps you analyze results.

- *Business Budgeting Toolkit* is geared for the manager who needs to create and plan budgets, including accounting for tactics, strategies, tracking, follow through, and other approaches to keep your department or business on track financially.

- *Employee Handbook Toolkit* is meant to help those who need to create comprehensive employee handbooks. Rather than start from scratch and re-invent the wheel, you can use this document on disk to create a full employee handbook quickly.

Informed Foundation

If your business is large enough to need forms, you will appreciate having a form system such as Informed Foundation by Shana Corporation. This $245 package is aimed at large companies with networks who can benefit from transferring their paper forms to the Macintosh.

The package enables users to fill out, sign, distribute, route, create, edit, and format forms. Time taken to fill out forms can be reduced by automatic calculations and error checking. Links can be established to databases and accounting packages. Digital signatures can be attached with PowerTalk.

GraceLAN Asset Manager

A business with computer assets to manage and a network with many Macintoshes may consider TechWorks' GraceLAN Asset Manager program (about $500). The asset tracking database is aimed primarily at the individual responsible for maintaining and tracking computer hardware, software, and controling maintenance schedules.

Full information about hardware and software can be stored, including user, location, serial numbers, purchase and warranty information, and so on. The program will perform software version audits over a network to enable the network manager to keep users current. One interesting feature is Asset Manager's capability to import electronic versions of vendor catalogs to update information on available products.

Income Tax Planning and Filing

April 15th is a date few people find pleasant. However, there are some steps you can take to at least make tax day less stressful. The first step is to maintain financial records with a personal finance package such as Quicken (see Personal Finance Mangement earlier in this chapter). With a personal finance manager, you can accumulate tax information throughout the year leaving you with only the task of reporting the information when tax time comes around.

With income tax software, you can further simplify the process by having the software link your financial information to the appropriate forms and even laser print the forms ready to sign. The home business user—having to fill out a number of complicated IRS forms—will certainly want to consider automating this process.

MacInTax 1040 and MacInTax State

The leading tax software package is MacInTax by ChipSoft. MacInTax 1040 is updated each year to reflect changes in the tax code. MacInTax 1040 imports information from personal finance programs such as Quicken and fills the tax forms out for you. If you plan ahead and create your Quicken categories with tax day in mind, you will have to do very little editing.

MacInTax 1040 performs those complex IRS calculations for you. It helps you avoid math errors (which are easy to make with those convoluted tax form instructions) and can flag errors and potential problems. The $40 package can save you much more than the price by helping you avoid hiring someone to do your taxes.

ChipSoft also offers the $25 MacInTax state, supporting 20 states with income taxes. The program takes information from your federal tax forms and fills out your state forms for you.

To save even more money, watch for MacInTax/Quicken bundles. At the time of this writing, the two programs together were being offered for about $50 from various sources.

MacInTax Tax Planner and Tax Savings Guide

ChipSoft offers two helpful packages to aid you in preparing for tax time. The Tax Savings Guide offers tips and suggestions on how you can lower your tax bill. The MacInTax Planner is a software package that enables you to create "what if" scenarios to check on the effectiveness of different strategies to lower your tax bill. The Savings Guide sells for about $15 and the Planner for about $20.

Project Planning

Businesses of all sizes need to plan their projects carefully, creating schedules, maintaining goals, and tracking progress. Software is available for the Macintosh to aid you in your planning endeavors.

The available software ranges from the large Microsoft Project, which can manage large projects even over networks, to unique tools such as Inspiration and IdeaFisher, which help you "brainstorm."

Microsoft Project*

The $450 Microsoft Project is aimed at the medium to larger businesses. With this program, you accumulate all of a project's information and then present it in formats such as PERT, GANTT, or spreadsheet. You can employ an outliner to simplify (or *collapse*) an outlined form so that you see the overall picture.

Microsoft Project offers useful features common to Microsoft programs such as a customizable toolbar to give you one-click access to frequently used commands. The program is networkable and can even share files with the Windows version of the program.

MacProject Pro

Claris Corporation is known for creating useful but easy-to-use software. MacProject Pro, which sells for about $400, continues this tradition. Schedules, budgets, personnel, resources, and other project-related information can be entered and managed easily. The program spots schedule and resource conflicts. MacProject Pro includes scripting to automate common tasks and one click access to frequently used commands through a floating palette.

Data can be shared with the Windows version, and you can create links to programs such as the Filemaker Pro database and the Claris Resolve spreadsheet program. (Claris is also known for doing an excellent job in integrating its application software.)

ManagePro

For the manager, Avantos offers ManagePro. The $250 package is aimed at aiding the manager organize, set goals, work with people, delegate, and track progress. Three tool sets are offered: Goal, People, and Action.

Information is entered through a spreadsheet like interface, ManagePro creates to do lists, goal lists, status boards, time lines, calendars, and reports.

The program has been well-received—the Windows version has even won awards.

Inspiration*

Inspiration is an interesting offering from Inspiration Software. The $170 program helps you brainstorm by enabling you to create flow charts, write outlines, develop the flow of a process, lay out a project, and much more. Inspiration displays your work in both graphical and outline form.

With Inspiration, you can brainstorm to develop your project and then use the presentation tools to create a presentation to present your work.

IdeaFisher*

IdeaFisher is one of the more unique offerings in the planning software arena. The $100 tool features a large database with associative connections and problem solving questions. The program is rather large, taking up some 7MB of disk space.

IdeaFisher is meant to help you speculate and consider ideas by making suggestions and associations. IdeaFisher can be used to generate ideas for articles, proposals, advertising, marketing, products, even names. Of course, you do the thinking, but IdeaFisher makes suggestions and associations you might not have come up with on your own or ones that might suggest new lines of creativity.

You can also create your own idea library and add questions to the database.

IdeaFisher Systems also offers the Business and Grant Proposals Module. This $70 module is an add-on that works with IdeaFisher to help you deal with proposals both for business and grants. Questions are presented to help you think of angles you may not have considered, assist critical thinking about the proposal, even help you avoid cliché terms and choose more effective wording.

TopDown Flowchart

Flowcharting is a common need in business to plan and layout a process. TopDown Flowchart by Kaetron Software Corporation is intended to help you create flowcharts quickly and easily. It includes 110 predefined symbols. You can also create your own symbols. Connecting lines are automatically made as you add symbols and intelligently reroute when you rearrange or resize symbols. Symbols automatically resize to fit the text you enter in them. You can also double-click to create nested levels in the flowchart. The package sells for about $200, and a multi-user pack is available.

FlowChart and OrgChart Express

Kaetron offers a small, simpler flowcharting program called FlowChart Express for about $100. This package is intended for the user who needs to create basic flowcharts quickly.

For the person in charge of a company's organization charts, OrgChart Express for $120 can help by enabling the creation of orgcharts in a matter of minutes. The program enables quick and easy shuffling around of people and positions and offers automatic aligning. Database information can be imported to create orgcharts automatically and many formatting and styling features are offered to enhance the orgchart's appearance.

Personal Information Management

The Personal Information Management (PIM) category has arisen only recently. Essentially, the category is a collection of personal management tools and could be considered the electronic version of the well-known Day Timer.

Two broad subcategories within the PIM category are time and schedule managers—calendars and appointment reminders, and contact managers. These programs maintain your mailing and phone lists, replacing the old Rolodex.

Time and Schedule Managers

Having the Macintosh keep your schedule is a perfect job for a computer. Computers rarely "forget" (they usually "forget" only when the hard drive goes belly up) and if you work at your Mac everyday, having the computer pop up and remind you of appointments automatically is an ideal computer function.

Now Up-To-Date

My personal favorite in the time-management area is Now Software's Now Up-To-Date. The $70 program centers on a calendar that has features consistent with the Macintosh interface—double-click on a day in the calendar, and that day's schedule window appears (see fig. 26.14).

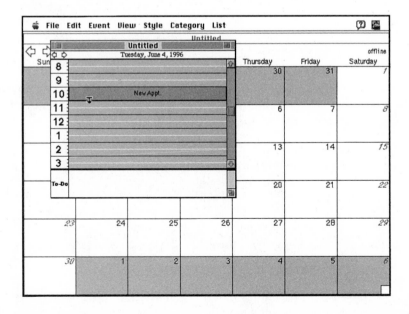

Fig. 26.14
Adding an appointment in Up-To-Date.

Now Up-To-Date supports seven event types, including appointment, to-do, holiday, and banner. Events can be categorized. You can also customize the categories and create category sets. Priorities can be set and customized. Schedule recurring events easily with daily, monthly, weekly, and other combinations of occurrences, including a customizable recurrance.

Four different calendar views are offered, including year, month, week, and multiday (see fig. 26.15).

Fig. 26.15
Viewing the
week's schedule.

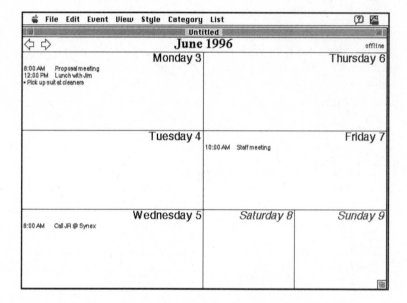

Now Up-To-Date is very much a Macintosh program. It allows you to double-click days, drag events around the calendar, and change meeting times by dragging. You use the Mac actions you expect to encounter.

The Reminder extension is included to interface with your calendar and provide a menu clock and reminders in the menu bar or in dialogs.

Up-To-Date works over networks for businesses that need to share schedules. You can set Up-To-Date to automatically access servers and update to and from the server to keep everybody posted about your schedule, view their schedules, and set meetings with times broadcasted to other users.

First Things First Proactive

I've always liked the First Things First (FTF) approach of the floating calendar icon that hovers over your desktop and puts your schedule only a double-click away.

IV

This $100 Visionary Software package has been upgraded to do more than just act as a calendar program. It includes outlining capabilities, multiple calendar views, and reminders. Networking is supported for offices that need everyone to be aware of each other's schedules.

With FTF, you can create plans by outlining and then drag them to the calendar to quickly set your schedule. Documents and applications can be launched from the calendar or through the pop-up reminders.

In Control

In Control by Attain is an $85 package that takes the outline approach to organizing your schedule. You respond to questions about when and what needs to be done to outline your tasks. You can then prioritize, sort, and categorize project tasks. Then the integrated calendar helps you keep track of when tasks need to be done.

Reminders are offered to alert you to approaching appointments and deadlines, and scripting is included for automating In Control functions. You can also link to other software or print to popular paper organizers.

DateBook Pro

Aldus offers DateBook Pro, a time-management program for about $50 that combines a calendar, schedule, to-do listing, and alarms. You can view your schedule in various ways, including the standard year, month, week, day formats, but also in text, time bar, and Gantt chart formats.

With DateBook Pro, you can customize calendars by using icons and banners. You can print wall charts and schedules. Printing in Daytimer as well as other popular organizer formats is supported.

InfoDepot

InfoDepot by Chena Software is a unique product in the PIM arena. Information is collected in a custom table. You then can view the information in various ways. You add scheduling with the built-in calendar or time line, and use date- and time-calculation formulas to compute schedule dates. Searching and sorting are provided to help you sift through information, and custom layouts enable you to focus on specific information. Connections to other documents can be created, and AppleScript is supported for automating tasks.

The $200 package is more powerful than the average scheduling/organizing PIM but incorporates similar features. Overall, the program is more a powerful database-like package that also aids you in creating your schedule as you organize your project information.

Contact Managers

"It's not what you know but who you know" is an oft repeated cliché which is not strictly true. However, who you know is a critical issue in business. Managing your contacts, keeping mailing lists, and maintaining address books has become more difficult in a rapidly changing business world. Recently, the category of Contact Managers has arisen as more programs are produced to aid you in this area of business life.

Contact managers can come to your aid by maintaining databases of contacts (names, phone numbers, addresses, and similar information), enabling you to quickly find the right person to call.

Now Contact

Now Software recently entered the contact manager category with Now Contact. The $70 package offers Now's ease of use applied to contact management. Names, numbers, and addresses can be easily entered and then accessed quickly in a variety of customizable formats.

Now Contact offers a built-in word processor to enable you to quickly create form letters, labels, and envelopes. QuickContact enables you to access your contacts while in other programs.

Touchbase Pro

Aldus offers Touchbase Pro for about $50. The Touchbase Pro database enables you to maintain lists of contacts with multiple notes, alternate phone numbers, custom text, and check boxes. Pop-up menus speed data entry. Searching and sorting helps you locate specific contacts quickly. You can use the built-in letter processor to create form letters and envelopes or export to your word processor.

ACT!

The bestselling contact manager is from Symantec for about $170. ACT! not only enables you to create a database of contacts but to manage schedules, do mail merge for form letters and envelopes, and create custom reports. ACT! has fully customizeable fields and a history log.

Although ACT! is powerful, the program's price is steep. Admittedly, the combined power of managing schedules and contacts makes this program a worthy contender for the executive (or executive secretary). The average user may want to consider a less expensive package, however.

Conclusions and Recommendations

A great number of packages are available in these categories, and it seems that everyday new ones are released. Recommendations are not easily made. Personal experience suggests that you consider the following programs, however.

In the Personal Finance category, Quicken is the most widely used package and for good reason. The program is easy to set up and use, and will quickly have you managing your personal or even small business finances with greater ease. Quicken is rapidly becoming one of those *can't-live-without* packages.

In business accounting, MYOB has a similar ease of use reputation. And ease of use is a top priority to my mind when choosing a program that will be used to manage your finances. A program that is difficult to use can create headaches as errors are introduced and corrected with difficulty.

MacInTax has been around the longest in the tax software category. You would do well with this one. Combined with a good personal finance program (such as Quicken), MacInTax can help alleviate many headaches at tax time.

Claris Corporation is one of my favorite Macintosh software companies. They have a reputation of creating easy to use, *Mac-like* software. MacProject Pro is a good choice in the project planning category.

In the area of Personal Information Management, I prefer Now Software's programs. Now Up-To-Date and Now Contact are well-written programs that have many helpful features. You won't go wrong with Now Software.

From Here...

From here, consider the following chapters for information regarding other business-related software:

- Chapter 16 discusses word processing packages. Many contact managers enable you to export names and addresses to create mailing lists. The mail merge feature of word processors can help you create and print the form letters.

- Chapter 17 discusses presentation graphics. If you are going to be doing scheduling, planning, and financial management, you are probably also going to be presenting your work to others. This chapter shows you software geared towards creating presentations.

■ Chapter 18 covers spreadsheets. A business user will also want a good spreadsheet program to create custom formulas and layouts to work with the information accumulated by finance management programs. This chapter shows you what is available.

Chapter 27

Games and Education

by Dave Busch

Among its many distinctions, the Macintosh was the first computer sold with a game built into its system software. Puzzle, the simple sliding-numbers game installed as a Desk Accessory on the early 1984-edition Macintoshes, is still present in System 7.1 in modified form (see fig. 27.1). That's your first clue that games, education, and Macs were *made* for each other.

Indeed, the first Mac manual's inviting full-color photos of bicycle-riding college students toting Macs around campus in overgrown camera bags set a tone for the platform that Apple has ironically been fighting to overcome ever since. Today, the Macintosh may *mean* business, but it's been at home with games and educational software (the distinction is often a fine line) for more than a decade.

Fig. 27.1
Puzzle is a Desk Accessory game that has been furnished with every Macintosh sold since 1984.

It's easy to see why the Mac was especially friendly to games and education software—many of its innovations are essential for these kinds of programs. The key types of business applications—word processors, spreadsheets, and databases—can function perfectly well (although on a rudimentary level) without graphics, sound, or color (and actually *did* for a decade in the PC world!). A mouse, buttons, and dialog boxes are useful luxuries when you're developing a spreadsheet but hardly a necessity. But try to imagine a game or educational program without these features!

Without the Macintosh and later systems that copied its features, we'd still be playing boring old text-based Adventure games or learning Spanish from screen after screen of multiple choice quizzes. For many people, the programs in this category are just as important as word processors are in the business community.

After all, games and education software perform key roles in our lives. Everyone likes to take a break from the tedium of work now and then, and a well-written game can be more relaxing, and challenging, than the best television show or a potboiler novel. As long as you mix computer games with other types of entertainment (sports, movies, hobbies, and so on), a session with The 7th Guest can be fun, healthful, and an excellent way to stretch your mind a bit.

Educational programs, on the other hand, are *designed* to exercise your mental muscles. Many, such as Hyperglot's *Learn To Speak Spanish* (shown in fig. 27.2) are pure teaching/training programs. The student runs through drills, memorization exercises, practice sessions, and a series of tests until the material is mastered. Other educational software combines game elements, such as *Where in the World Is Carmen Sandiego?* This kind of software may be designed for children as young as three, who can learn colors and shapes, to adults who want to master a foreign language.

Fig. 27.2
Learn To Speak Spanish is a pure teaching/training program.

This chapter looks at some of the leading games and educational software, and explains how well it fulfills your need for fun, entertainment, and learning. There are quite a few programs worthy of mention, so the discussions are a little less detailed in terms of "how to" than in some of the other chapters in this book. I'll still describe system requirements where appropriate and give you a feeling for how the program works. Software packages reviewed in this chapter include the following:

- *Just Grandma and Me* and *Putt-Putt Goes To The Moon*

- *KidPix, Four Footed Friends,* and *Busytown*

- *Learn to Speak Spanish*

- *Black American History: Slavery to Civil Rights*

- *Where in the World is Carmen Sandiego?*

- *Oregon Trail* and *Treasure MathStorm*

- *SimCity 2000* and *The 7th Guest*

- *Lemmings, Railroad Tycoon,* and *Populous*

What Is Out There

There is a great deal of overlap among the programs profiled in this chapter, but in general, Macintosh game and educational software fall into one of three categories:

- *Children's Software.* I've listed this as a separate category, because these programs, aimed at the very young, often have very low-key educational goals. Some programs, such as *KidPix*, provide young Mac users with a fun time and, perhaps, a little practice using the mouse and menus. Others, such as *Just Grandma and Me*, can be used on two levels. Smaller children can have an entertaining story read to them and then "play" on each page by clicking various objects. Older kids can use the interactive features to learn to read and expand their vocabularies.

  A typical program in this category, *Just Grandma and Me*, is shown in figure 27.3.

Fig. 27.3

Just Grandma and Me is a typical children's software program, with lots of fun and a little learning mixed in.

- *Education.* Educational programs vary greatly in format, depending on whether they are aimed at older or younger students. Primary and middle school students also soak up knowledge like a sponge, but they spend more time learning if the lessons are cloaked in arcade-style clothing. So educational software aimed at younger audiences has a high game content.

  On the other hand, Programs such as *Learn To Speak Spanish*, or *Barron's Complete Book Notes* are clearly designed for older students, with nary a game in sight. Instead, these programs mimic secondary or college classroom texts in format, with computerized or multimedia enhancements that take advantage of the Macintosh's power.

- *Games.* Many excellent programs have no pretensions of teaching you anything useful, although a few (simulations such as *SimCity 2000* or *SimEarth*) may satisfy your curiosity about how things work. Others, such as *The 7th Guest* or *HellCab*, exercise your ability to solve problems. Still other pure games purport to be nothing more than arcade-style shoot-em-ups, in the manner of *Stellar 7*. These programs are aimed at Mac owners of all ages, from about six through adult. We'll look at an interesting clutch of games in this category shortly.

Many of the programs mentioned in this chapter are available in two versions: one is sold in floppy disk form and installed on your hard disk. A second, enhanced version is available on CD-ROM, with added features such as video or sound. The CD-ROM version, which is often only a few dollars more than the disk-based edition, may be installed to your hard disk or run directly from the CD. *Busytown, SimCity 2000* and *Oregon Trail* are examples of children's, game, and educational programs available on both disk and CD-ROM.

Children's Software

Five of the most popular programs in this category are *KidPix*, available in floppy disk format; *Just Grandma and Me, Putt-Putt Goes To The Moon,* and *Four Footed Friends,* which are sold in CD-ROM packages, and *Busytown,* which is available both on disk and CD-ROM. We'll look at *Just Grandma and Me,* and *Putt-Putt* in some detail, and then take brief looks at the other three programs.

Just Grandma and Me

This entry in Broderbund's Living Book series is a perfect example of what a child's CD-ROM should contain. Children can have the book read to them, or they can "play" inside the pages, activating a series of fanciful scenarios just by clicking various objects they see. There's enough fun and whimsy to please any kid from age 3 to 8, a liberal sprinkling of options designed to keep interest high after repeated sessions and solid educational content that encourages young students to think of learning as a treat rather than a chore.

The same is true of other Living Books from Broderbund, which include best-sellers such as *Arthur's Teacher Trouble* (filled with spelling-bee fun), *The Tortoise and the Hare,* and *New Kid on the Block.* Most of the material in this section apply to the other programs in the line.

System Requirements

Just Grandma and Me is furnished on a single compact disc, so you'll need a CD-ROM drive connected to your Mac to use it. It requires 2.5MB of RAM and a 256-color video display. For best performance, turn off virtual memory, disable any screen savers you've installed, and close any other open programs you may have running. Apple's Launcher or At Ease interfaces can cause problems with this program's sound routines, so they should be disabled. Drag them out of your Startup Items folder and then restart your Mac. If you have a Macintosh LC and are still using System 6.0x, you may notice occasional sound dropouts.

Overview of Just Grandma and Me

Just Grandma and Me is a lively adaptation of Mercer Mayer's popular line of books about "Little Critter," a cute young mammal of indeterminate species (we vote for groundhog). Young Critter takes a bus to the beach for a day of fun with Grandma and the other animals on holiday. Sand-filled hot dogs, going snorkeling (but not too deep!), and uncooperative beach umbrellas are all part of the low-key adventures the two enjoy.

Youngsters can choose to have the book read to them. *Just Grandma and Me* comes to life as Critter reads the story. The characters actually move around the page through life-like animation and react to the story with giggles or short responses. The effect is more like watching a cartoon than reading a book. All the while, a pert background tune sets the light-hearted mood for the story. Mercer Mayer's stories and illustrations have already become children's classics, so on this level alone, *Just Grandma and Me* is an excellent disc.

Choosing a Mode

While Read to Me mode may be the best introduction to the disc, most kids will soon be chomping at the bit to review the book in its interactive mode. The child turns pages manually and clicks a special icon with the mouse to have the text on that page read aloud. Beginning readers can click individual words to have them read individually.

You can select the mode you want by clicking the appropriate button in the main screen, shown in figure 27.4. Notice that you can also choose from English, Japanese, or Spanish narration. Those studying one of those languages can use *Just Grandma and Me* as a tool to practice foreign language conversation, too. Once you've heard the story a few times in English, the Spanish version, for example, almost translates itself in your mind.

A special options menu offers a scrolling preview of each page; the child can choose a page and jump directly to it. One tip: don't neglect to read the credits, hidden inside this option menu. You'll be treated to a five-minute mini-cartoon featuring an inept witch and a hot five-piece jazz combo.

Fig. 27.4
The main screen lets you choose reading or playing mode and an appropriate language for the narration.

Playing inside Pages

No child will be able to resist exploring the individual objects on each of the 12 pages in this book-disc. Delightful animated sequences are triggered by clicking almost any person or item on the page. In the opening scene, shown in figure 27.5, Grandma and Critter walk to the curb and wait for their bus. If you click the front door of the home they just left, a doorbell chimes. Click one of the windows and the phone rings, Grandma's answering machine picks up and reports that she is not home. If you "open" the mailbox by the street, a mysterious hand reaches out of it and slams the door shut.

Fig. 27.5
Delightful animated sequences, such as the arrival of this bus, are triggered by clicking objects shown on each page.

There are lots of surprises on each page. For example, something different happens each time you go back to that mailbox. One time you may find a cat sleeping inside, or you may be pelted by a cascade of tumbling golf balls.

The silliness includes some visual and audio puns aimed at more astute kids. Click an ordinary rock by the roadside, and you're treated to a few bars of string-bending "rock" music. Children can easily spend hours "playing" inside the story.

In interactive mode, you may take as long as you like on each page, clicking a right-arrow icon to advance to the next or a left-arrow icon to go back to the previous page. The child may click the page number button at the bottom of each page to return to the main menu at any time.

Summary

Just Grandma and Me is another of those discs that set the standard for all the other "talking storybook" CD-ROMs that follow. The story is charming, the length just right for short attention spans, and the animation of Mayer's artwork first-rate. Even the background music is catchy and varied enough to soothe parents annoyed by purple dinosaur sing-alongs.

Just Grandma and Me is recommended for households with preschoolers who like to "play" with computers, even though they can't yet read. This disc might be their head start toward early reading. Beginning readers will also enjoy the book, exploring the simple words and phrases by reading for themselves, repeating the words after Critter says them aloud, or by clicking words they are unsure of to hear the correct pronunciation.

Finally, older students will find the book an enjoyable way to practice their conversational and comprehension skills in English, Spanish, or Japanese.

Putt-Putt Goes To The Moon

Children aged three and up are entranced by Putt-Putt, the little purple convertible with a real child's voice but the appetites and inclinations of a humanized automobile. The adventures of Putt-Putt, who likes motor oil on his Tire-O's cereal, form the basis of this easy—but involving—preschoolers' game.

The story unfolds one bright morning as Putt-Putt visits a Fireworks Factory owned by his friend Mr. Firebird, shown in figure 27.6. The child can use the mouse to click various items in the factory with a puffy, over-sized arrow cursor. Clicking the window pane opens the window, allowing a butterfly to flutter in. Soon, Putt-Putt's puppy (which he adopted in his previous adventure, *Putt-Putt Joins the Parade*) leaps at the butterfly but instead, presses a forbidden lever that launches Putt-Putt on a skyrocket to the Moon. To return home, Putt-Putt has to find missing rocket parts and 10 Moon Crystals, through various adventures on Luna.

Fig. 27.6
Putt-Putt's adventure starts out in Mr. Firebird's fireworks factory.

System Requirements

Putt-Putt Goes To The Moon is available in both floppy disk and CD-ROM versions. Both require a Macintosh LC III or later system with 256-color video display and 2M of RAM. The version that comes on floppy disks requires 13M of free hard disk space for program files. The CD-ROM version can run directly from the CD, saving hard disk space.

Running Putt-Putt Goes To The Moon

Putt-Putt can run using one of several different screen sizes on your Mac, depending on the speed of your system. "Small" and "medium" are best for slow systems, those with small monitors, or with only 256K of video memory. The "large" and "smoothing" modes use as much of your screen as possible, but can reduce the speed at which the program runs if you don't have a fast Quadra, LC III, Performa, or Power Macintosh model. Sometimes, turning off INITs and Extensions can speed up the animation of the program a little.

On the Moon, Putt-Putt soon lands in trouble, as a bridge collapses, throwing him into a puddle of moon goo (see fig. 27.7). When the child clicks on the horn button on Putt-Putt's dashboard, Rover, a lonely lunar terrain vehicle, comes to the rescue. Abandoned by one of the Apollo moon missions, Rover, like Putt-Putt, just wants to go home. Together, they perform good deeds for the Moon People while assembling the pieces of the rocket needed to return to Earth.

Fig. 27.7
Putt-Putt lands in hot water soon after he arrives on the Moon.

Even the youngest child will be able to complete the story-adventure by randomly moving Putt-Putt from scene to scene and clicking various objects found in each. As he moves around the Moon, Putt-Putt encounters a host of other characters, who help him along with advice, refreshments, and the odd jobs he needs to earn his rocket pieces.

Putt-Putt's "user interface" was obviously designed for curious preschoolers who have mastered the mouse or a joystick. No keyboard commands at all are required (except ⌘-Q to exit). Parents can access the remaining keyboard commands to turn sound on/off (⌘-M and ⌘-D for music and dialog, respectively), pause or restart the game (space bar or ⌘-P), or change the sound volume (square bracket keys). Games in progress can be saved to disk and resumed later.

Although a child can perform the various deeds required to assemble the rocket in a different order each time, the game doesn't vary much from play to play. Those with young children will know that this is a definite plus! The same preschoolers who want to hear a story repeated over and over love to work their way through Putt-Putt's universe again and again, seeking out familiar situations they find entertaining.

Adults may find the repetitive music and sound effects in *Putt-Putt Goes To The Moon* annoying, but kids are oblivious as they play along.

Summary

It's tough finding programs that young children can enjoy, and *Putt-Putt Goes To The Moon* is one of the best available. The graphics are more cartoon-like than photorealistic, but that's exactly what kids want and expect. The educational content is minor but sufficient, considering the 3- to 7-year-old audience for this program.

Brief Looks: KidPix, Four Footed Friends, and Busytown

One classic and two new entries show the direction children's software is taking. *KidPix* provides drawing tools that even the youngest child can enjoy, while *Four Footed Friends* and *Busytown* demonstrate the lively animation possible from CD-ROM-based programs. Here's a brief look at each of these three offerings:

KidPix

KidPix, shown in figure 27.8, is a classic children's painting program that takes the pioneering MacPaint toolbox to new—and if you can imagine it— easier-to-use levels. The chief enhancements—beyond full color, of course— are whimsical tools that perform fun functions on the child's drawing with minimal effort.

Fig. 27.8
KidPix provides many new and whimsical tools for young artists.

For example, there's a rubber stamp tool that stamps little pictures (there are more than 100 to choose from) such as dogs, palm trees, dinosaurs, clowns, and major household appliances. A Mixer tool adds special effects, such as spots, stripes, or flower patterns, to the drawing. To move parts of a drawing, the kid just clicks a moving van icon and selects the portion to relocate with the mouse. The skidding noise sound effects during the move are priceless.

Indeed, all the sounds in this program have been selected to add appeal. Pouring paint from the paint bucket evokes distinct gurgling sounds. Clicking the Undo icon summons a hilarious "Oh no!" Tool sounds can be turned off, or the child can record his or her own sounds on Macs equipped with a microphone.

KidPix will run on nearly any Mac, but you'll get the most benefit from it with systems equipped with a color monitor. Even very young children who are not ready for even simple games can learn to use the Mac with Broderbund's *KidPix*. If your kid can hold and click the mouse button, the youngster will enjoy this program.

Four-Footed Friends

The animation alone is worth the price for this T/Maker entry for children. The 3-D modeling is incredibly realistic, with more in common with Roger Rabbit than Bugs Bunny. One look at the interface, an animated Interactivator, will show you what I'm talking about (see fig. 27.9). The Next Page arrow button doesn't sit there idly waiting for you to click it—it jumps, twirls, and twists to catch the child's attention! This program makes the best use of QuickTime we've seen in a children's program.

As with other animated storybooks, you can listen to the story (told with a delightful English accent), click phrases to hear them repeated, or select individual objects in the illustration to bring them to life. Mrs. Cow's blouse changes from red to a flowered pattern, and an ever-growing pile of hay is produced on her dinner plate when you click it a few times. Other four-footed friends include General Rhinoceros, Kangaroo, Nanny Goat, and Madame Elephant. Each is accompanied by a silly poem that will make kids grin (see fig. 27.10).

Your guides include Pablo, who lets you color your own pictures, Wendy the bookworm, who helps kids learn to read and spell, and Albert, the number worm, who provides facts and figures. You can access a Storybook Library, complete with Card Catalog previews to choose a page.

IV

Macintosh Software

Fig. 27.9
The Interactivator's lively interface features four bookworm friends and some rather lively buttons.

Fig. 27.10
Clicking Mrs. Cow's plate adds the hay she is requesting.

Richard Scarry's Busytown

Busytown is certainly an apt name for this program! *Busytown* will keep children from 3 to 7 occupied for hours on end through 12 different energetic activities that let kids experiment with objects, manipulate real machines, and even practice working behind the counter of a fast food restaurant. Our four-year-old tester cried when we told her it was time to stop playing *Busytown*.

This Paramount program is available in both floppy disk and CD-ROM formats. If you have a CD-ROM drive, the disc version is worth the extra money. It is spiced with lively songs and includes an extra playground, Busy Tunes, that lets the child choose from a selection of songs. CD-ROM users can run the program from the disc, but those with the floppy version will need about 12M of free hard disk space to hold the program files.

We received this Paramount disc shortly before author Scarry died, so the loss was even more acute when we looked at what his imagination had wrought. *Busytown* is populated by creatures such as Bananas Gorilla, who needs to wind his way through a maze to a bunch of bananas without losing any fruit to a horde of photographers. At Bruno's Deli, the child can help Huckle the Cat piece together complex food orders using an animated machine, choosing from cheese, hot chocolate, soda, and other delicacies.

Other playgrounds ask kids to help build a house, deliver items from a warehouse to various locations in Busytown, serve as an aide to Dr. Diane as she bandages hapless Norbert the Elephant, build and furnish Captain Salty's ship before it sets sail, or put out fires. Many of the activities have overt educational goals, such as the seesaw that can be balanced only by putting equal number totals on either side. Others, such as the Busy Tunes Jukebox, are just fun.

The program is furnished with a study guide that helps parents choose activities for developing kids: language/prereading, math, problem solving, social, emotional, physical, motor development, art, or music skills. But, don't get too high minded when you turn your kids loose with this program: they're likely to insist on playing in Busytown at their own pace.

Other Winners

You'll find a wealth of other great children's programs available for the Macintosh that I couldn't describe in any detail. These include:

- All the Broderbund "Living Books," from *Arthur's Teacher Trouble* to *New Kid on the Block*.

- Discis "Kids Can Read" series, especially *Scary Poems For Rotten Kids*.

- Humongous' Fatty Bear series (e.g., *Fatty Bear's Birthday Surprise*), which are interactive stories in the Putt-Putt vein.

- Stickybear's Early Learning series.

- Sierra Online's wonderful *Alphabet Blocks*, with the adorable Bananas and Jack.

- Any of The Learning Company's excellent Reader Rabbit programs (*Ready for Letters*, and others).

Education

Ever since Minnesota Educational Classroom Consortium (MECC) and others began distributing programs such as Speedway Math for the pre-Mac Apple II line ages ago, teaching games have been popular in schools and homes. These programs have certain things in common: visual and auditory "rewards" for successfully completing a level or lesson, ways to keep score (measure progress), and a strong game element. Competition (against the computer or other students) may or may not be a major component.

Today, you'll still find MECC programs among the best sellers—the venerable *Oregon Trail* has gained new life with a CD-ROM edition that features video and sound. But other companies have developed innovative teaching tools that use the power of the Mac to educate in new ways. In this section, we'll look at *Learn To Speak Spanish*, *Black American History*, and *Where in the World is Carmen Sandiego?* in detail, and then review several other important Mac educational programs, including *Oregon Trail* itself.

Learn To Speak Spanish

Hyperglot's *Learn To Speak Spanish* provides almost everything you need to learn this language except a stern teacher to rap your knuckles when you get something wrong. In that sense, it makes a perfect complement to a formal language program, rather than a complete stand-alone system. Hyperglot offers other CD-ROMs for French, German, Italian, Chinese, Japanese, Russian, and English.

System Requirements

You'll need a 256-color Macintosh such as the Mac LC III or Performa 450 or higher (a 68030/25 MHz machine or faster), 4M of RAM, and System 7. This is a CD-ROM-only product, so you must have a CD drive installed in your Mac. An external microphone or MacRecorder is required if you want to record your own voice to compare with the native speakers in the program.

Using Learn To Speak Spanish

Learning a foreign language thoroughly involves equal parts of studying vocabulary, memorizing grammar rules, and practicing conversation. Hyperglot's *Learn To Speak Spanish* provides a smattering of all three. There's a fun-to-use vocabulary module that will help you build an impressive Spanish vocabulary in no time.

The conversational portion of the program lets you listen and learn from self-paced sessions with native (Latin American) Spanish speakers. You can even practice pronunciation by recording your own voice through your Mac, and comparing the results with the correct pronunciation.

Your study begins from the main screen (shown earlier in this chapter in fig. 27.2), which shows the first 15 of the 30 available lessons/chapters. These all center around the conversational situations that occur during the typical business or pleasure trip to a Spanish-speaking country. You can choose from Arrival, Changing Money, Getting a Taxi, Arriving at the Hotel, and other traditional scenes.

Each chapter starts with an introduction screen and a short video clip, actually shot in Mexico City. You can move from scene to scene by clicking navigational arrows at the top of the screen, or you can click the title bar to bring up a toolbar of buttons that lead to chapter sections such as vocabulary drill, communications skills, or a word jumble game.

The Vocabulary screen, shown in figure 27.11, lets you listen and learn new vocabulary words, and practice recording them in your own voice. You learn words by selecting one of the chapter's new words from a scrolling list. A definition of the word appears in a window, and vocabulary notes about the word appear in another. For example, if you select tiene (he/she has), you'll see that it is a form of the word tener and that you'll learn to conjugate that verb in Chapter 6.

If you click the Hear in Context window, a short video clip taken from that chapter's movie will play with a native speaker using the word in context. You may repeat the clip as many times as you want, which will probably be necessary: unlike Spanish students and, sometimes, their teachers, actual speakers of the language tend to slide words together and otherwise make them sound different in full sentences than when you pronounce them alone.

Fig. 27.11
The Vocabulary screen shows you a word, its definition, and a conversation that uses it in context.

At the bottom of the vocabulary window is a recorder pane. If your Mac or PC has a microphone attached, you can click the Record button. The word will be pronounced and then recording starts. You can record the word yourself. Click Play, and both your version and the actual pronunciation will be played back, as many times as you wish.

Other Modules

The Vocabulary Drill module lets you practice your new vocabulary, either in Spanish-to-English or English-to-Spanish mode. You can record your own pronunciation here, too.

The Story Screen lets you see and hear the native speaker using everyday Spanish at normal speeds. You can practice saying longer Spanish sentences, and deciphering it as it's actually spoken. You may watch the chapter's full movie clip or work through it sentence by sentence.

There's also an Action Screen that provides a continuation of the story, with several native speakers engaging in a dialogue. This more advanced mode will really give your comprehension a workout.

The Listening Skills screen repeats sections of the chapter's movie but with blanks which you must fill in with the correct word. This tests how well you've mastered the vocabulary of the chapter. The Communications Skills screen, shown in figure 27.12, requires you to type in lengthy responses.

Fig. 27.12
If you've mastered
Spanish, you can
type your re-
sponses in this
dialog box.

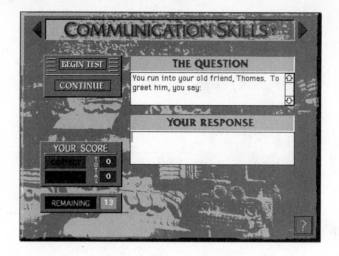

Exercise screens test your grammar skills, asking you to change articles from singular to plural or provide the correct verb tense. If you get stumped, you can click the Show Answers or Show Grammar buttons for help.

Other games and exercises are available. Drag and Match asks you to do things such as drag an indefinite article to the noun it agrees with, while Word Jumble gives you five jumbled sentences to unscramble. The Help screen appears when you click the Question Mark icon (see fig. 27.13).

Fig. 27.13
Help is available
with the Question
Mark icon.

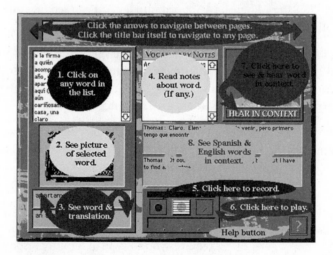

The text and workbook are good and oriented, like the CD-ROM, to conversational Spanish as it is used in travel settings. It can give you all the grammar you need to get by if you work through its exercises religiously.

Summary
Learn To Speak Spanish is aimed at an older audience—high school to adult beginners. It has everything you need to learn simple Spanish conversations except a stern teacher. You can practice conversation, build your vocabulary, sharpen knowledge of grammar rules, and learn while listening to native speakers discussing travel topics in everyday situations.

Black American History: Slavery to Civil Rights

This program provides a taste of another type of educational program that is increasingly common: audiovisual presentations that might have been given in classrooms using VCRs five years ago or with filmstrip projectors and audiotaped narration 15 years ago. Today, the same type of material can be presented much more effectively on CD-ROM, using the power of the Macintosh to add cross-indexing and a measure of interactivity.

Black American History is available from Queue, which also offers similar programs on other topics, such as *Let's Visit France*.

System Requirements
Any Macintosh with a color monitor and CD-ROM drive will be fine for this program. You'll need System 6.0.7 or higher, or any version of System 7, and 2M of free random access memory (RAM).

Exploring Black American History
Black American History is more than a CD-ROM presentation on the history of African-Americans: it's a complete course of study that can be used in middle schools, junior high, and high schools. In addition to a variety of illustrated, narrated programs covering everything from the Colonial Period to Protest Movements, there are tests that measure student comprehension, a teacher's guide, answer key, and historical documents for further study.

Actual voices of leading figures involved in the events, including the Reverend Dr. Martin Luther King, Jr., bring this aspect of our history to vivid life. Dramatic presentations representing more than 75 African-American personalities, from Sojourner Truth and Harriet Tubman to Thurgood Marshall and Ralph Bunche add strength and reality to the program.

Your course starts from a main menu screen, shown in figure 27.14, with nine choices, such as The Abolitionists, Reconstruction, The Harlem Renaissance, and The Depression. Clicking one of these sections leads to a 15-minute narrated presentation, illustrated with historical photos, drawings, and charts.

Fig. 27.14
Black American History's Main Menu offers nine topic choices.

While viewing a section, the student can access an index at the click of a magnifying glass icon to view related topics or page through faster than the normal display by clicking left and right arrow buttons. Text display can accompany the spoken narration, or sound can be turned off if a silent mode is desired in the classroom.

At the end of each section, the student can be quizzed with multiple choice questions to see how well the material was understood (see fig. 27.15). Scores can be printed or stored to your hard disk. The program is clever enough to store scores in a miscellaneous section if the student enters an invalid name or ID number by mistake. Most teachers will prefer to sort out stray scores later rather than have the student denied the opportunity to take the test through an error.

A password-protected Class Manager program provided on the disc helps the teacher view scores, edit names, and delete records. Up to 100 names can be included in each class file.

The narrated texts include important written materials accompanied by speech and sound effects on topics such as The Quest for Freedom, Supreme Court Cases, and Black Voices.

Under the latter section, for example, you can hear speeches by James Baldwin, Martin Luther King, Langston Hughes, and others. The Quest for Freedom has narrations on African-American business leaders, achievers in literature, arts, and sports, and pieces on their roles as patriots, soldiers, scientists, and inventors.

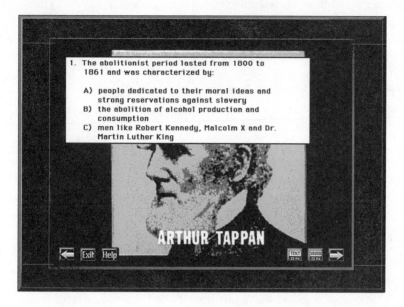

Fig. 27.15
Multiple choice questions test student retention of the material.

Supreme Court Cases cover four key court decisions that have had profound effects on our history, including *Brown vs. the Topeka Board of Education*, and the historic Dred Scott decision. An image from one of the presentations is shown in figure 27.16.

Fig. 27.16
Historic photos accompany the narration in *Black American History*.

Summary

Although the programs on this disc are basic slide-show audiovisual material, enhanced by additional spoken word segments, it's convenient to have all this information on a single CD instead of a dozen audiotapes, film strips, videotapes, or other media. *Black American History* is a CD-ROM that belongs in every classroom where history is studied, examined, and cherished.

Where in the World Is Carmen Sandiego?

Today, *Where in the World Is Carmen Sandiego?* is perhaps the classic edutainment program for the Mac. It's not enough that students must answer challenging geography-based questions, they must use their knowledge to find the evil criminal mastermind, Carmen Sandiego. Aimed at ages 6 to 12, there are also versions of this program that deal with USA geography and historical events.

System Requirements

Carmen Sandiego is available on floppy disk in a black-and-white format and will run on just about any Macintosh from an ancient Mac 512E or Mac Plus up through Mac SE, SE/30, or Mac II systems. The new Deluxe Editions on CD-ROM require a color Macintosh and CD-ROM drive and have new sound-effects, movie-like music tracks, and more vivid animations.

Running with Carmen Sandiego

You can explore 30 of the world's great cities in tracking down Carmen and nine cohorts, all members of Villains International League of Evil (VILE). Using a portable videophone that provides direct personal communications and news flashes, the player picks up clues by flying around the world to interview witnesses and suspects. You can review evidence, dossiers on suspects, and information about particular countries. A World Almanac is packaged with the game to let you look up more key facts on your own.

Once you've signed in, you'll be issued a videophone and Dataminder, shown in figure 27.17, and receive a briefing on your next case. You can review the case file and then click the Travel button to fly to your first destination.

Once there, a yellow note pad displays your options for seeking clues. Some clues help you find the culprit's next destination, while others can be used to identify the gang member.

Each stop includes snapshots of the country and city being visited, with various tidbits of information cleverly worked into the plot. For example, a tour guide may recall that the suspect asked about Spanish exploration and produce a snapshot of a Cerro Silver Mine. With those clues in hand, you're off to investigate New World mining activities in Lima, Peru (see fig. 27.18). All during the game, a digital clock ticks off the remaining seconds allowed for your quest.

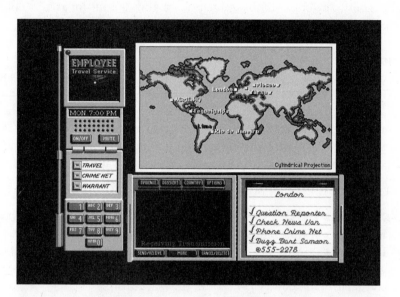

Fig. 27.17
The videophone and Dataminder are your key tools for finding Carmen Sandiego and cohorts.

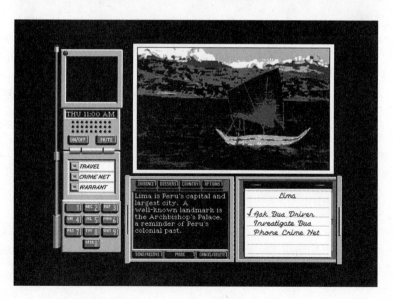

Fig. 27.18
It's off to Lima, Peru, for another round of interviews in the quest for Carmen Sandiego.

Once enough evidence has been collected, the gumshoe can issue a warrant for the arrest of a suspect. To get a valid warrant, you must gather all the evidence identifying that particular crook. Once Carmen's gang has been rounded up, you may snare Carmen herself if you're lucky, and gain a conviction in court. The object of this game is to obtain warrants for as many of the crooks as possible or track them to their hideouts before time runs out.

Summary

This educational game pits a student's knowledge of world geography against fleeing master criminals as the youngster attempts to track down Carmen Sandiego and her gang. The video and animation in Carmen Sandiego are first-rate, and the problems challenging. It's no wonder that this game has spawned a top-rated television show and other spin-offs. The books supplied with the various versions of the game are themselves valuable study aids. This classic deserves its ranking on the best-seller lists.

Brief Looks at Oregon Trail and Treasure MathStorm

Two more types of educational programs are represented by *Oregon Trail*, a simulation, and *Treasure MathStorm*, a game which includes many well-thought-out math lessons. Both are typical of a large group of teaching software available on disk and CD-ROM for the Macintosh.

Oregon Trail

Now you can face the same perils as the pioneers, including disease, snakebites, and starvation! Your party sets out from Independence, Missouri in its quest for Oregon's Willamette valley. Choose your supplies wisely, plan the most efficient routes, and be prepared to buy or barter what you may need along the way.

This MECC program, shown in figure 27.19, runs on a Mac Plus or later in its floppy disk version, requiring only 1M of RAM (4M with System 7). The new CD-ROM version has enhanced video and sound.

As you start the game, you can choose an occupation (see fig. 27.20) and then select your supplies from Matt's General store (see fig. 27.21). You'll want to buy enough oxen, clothing, bullets, spare wheels and axles, and food to last for your journey. Only $1,600 is available for purchases, but luckily, money went a lot farther in those days!

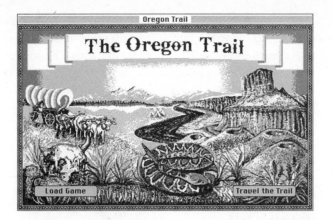

Fig. 27.19
Setting out on the
Oregon Trail.

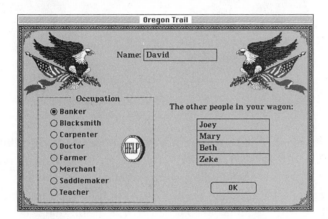

Fig. 27.20
Choose your
occupation from
among those
listed.

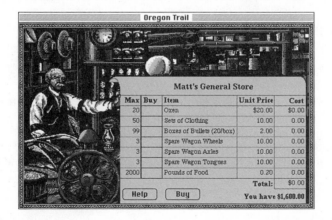

Fig. 27.21
Matt's General
store is your last
stop before
departing on the
trail.

You can also select the month you start in (planning for good weather), choosing other options along the way from a menu of activities (see fig. 27.22). A map is available to check progress, along with a helpful guidebook of tips and lore. You may check your health status or rations, and choose to trade, talk, rest, or hunt. The pace of your journey can be set from steady to grueling (if you're up to it).

Fig. 27.22
This screen helps you track your progress along the Oregon Trail.

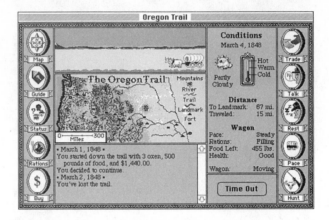

Oregon Trail has remained popular for a decade because of its thrilling simulation of the conditions of pioneer days. Though greatly enhanced with graphics and sound, its text and simple graphics heritage show through. Most students will enjoy learning about the Oregon Trail from the game, but it can get repetitious with frequent playing. This is one lesson that is best learned and then left behind. The journey is well worth the effort, however.

Treasure MathStorm

Treasure MathStorm, from The Learning Company (those Reader Rabbit folks), is an alpine adventure game that helps kids 5–9 learn math, money changing skills, while honing problem-solving capabilities. It's typical of the learning intensive programs that take a more serious approach to educational games. Kids find these programs a lot of fun, but they'll have to sharpen their math skills to a fine edge to get through the challenging exercises.

This program requires a color-equipped Macintosh with 2M of RAM, and System 6.0.7 or later, or System 7 and 3M of RAM. A hard disk is also required to store the program files.

Each of the activities independently adjust to the abilities of the child, presenting more difficult problems as the youngster masters concepts, so the game always remains challenging and fun. Along the way, they'll pursue elves, solve problems, set the clock in the Time Igloo (shown in fig. 27.23), balance the scale in the Gold Room, and count the crystals in the Crystal Cave.

Fig. 27.23
Children learn how to tell time in the Time Igloo.

The child takes the role of SuperSeeker, trying to rescue Treasure Mountain from the icy clutches of the Master of Mischief, who has cast an evil spell. To find him and release the mountain, the child must capture his elf-henchmen by solving their math problems.

Various modules of the program drill the student in a selection of math skills. For example, the child can enter the Store to purchase nets for snaring elves (see fig. 27.24). There, a friendly shopkeeper teaches the child how to make change.

Fig. 27.24
Learning to make change is only one of the activities children can spend time on in the Store.

The youngster can earn more tools in the Time Igloo, where an elf shows the child how to set a clock and tell time. Other adventures teach the child to recognize number patterns, understand inequalities, and solve problems in his or her head.

You are probably familiar with *Reader Rabbit*, but may not be familiar with this program, or others from The Learning Company, such as *Treasure Cove*. All feature sprightly music, exciting animation, and challenging problems for kids to solve as they learn.

Other Winners

Additional educational programs that you'll want to know about include:

- *Word Munchers*, from MECC, a dressed-up version of an Apple II classic that lives on in classrooms all over the country.

- *Mario Teaches Typing*, from MacPlay, in which your Donkey Kong hero (does anybody remember Donkey Kong?) introduces you to the computer and typewriter keyboard (does anybody remember typewriters?).

Games

Pure games for the Macintosh fall into several neat categories. There are simulations that model real-world situations and give you the opportunity to fool around in them. *SimCity 2000*, *Railroad Tycoon*, and *Populous* are among the best-known of these games. Another group of best-sellers are the "virtual reality" best-sellers, typified by *The 7th Guest* (and its sequel, *The XIth Hour*), *HellCab*, and *Myst*. These games all provide realistic 3-D settings that you can wander around in, hopefully solving the puzzles or challenges built into the mini-universes.

A third type of game attempts to duplicate various popular arcade style-games, ranging from martial arts fighting games to jet-fighter/spaceship shoot-em-ups and "gentler" games such as *Lemmings*.

The final main category consists of games that duplicate common board or card games, but with computerized enhancements. Here, you'll find *Battle Chess*, poker and casino games, and role-playing games such as *Lord of the Rings*.

SimCity 2000

Interested in being your own city planner, with the power to subdivide land, create residential, commercial, or industrial areas, and then supply police or fire protection? Welcome to *SimCity 2000* (see fig. 27.25)!

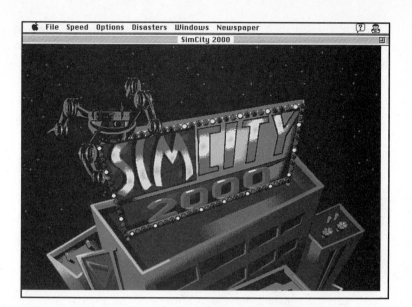

Fig. 27.25
Welcome to SimCity 2000's enhanced 3-D graphics!

The original Maxis *SimCity* was one of the most addicting Macintosh games ever, and launched a whole genre of simulation games, ranging from *Civilization* to Maxis' own *SimAnt*, *SimFarm*, and *SimEarth*. There are even several third-party books written on how to play the game. Now, the game has been taken into the third dimension with *SimCity 2000*. We're happy to report that this new CD version from Interplay is more fun and entertaining than the floppy-disk-based original.

System Requirements
SimCity 2000 is intended for the Macintosh Color Classic, or any member of the Mac II, LC, Centris, Performa, Quadra, or PowerBook families with an internal or external color display capable of showing 256 colors. You'll need 2.5M of free RAM, and 3M of hard disk space. System 7 or above is required. It's a CD-ROM game and requires a CD-ROM drive.

Playing SimCity 2000
Build your own city from scratch, or work with one of the supplied scenarios to meddle in the affairs of a real-life city such as Buenos Aires or Tokyo. Your town will be populated to capacity with simulated citizens—Sims—who build houses, churches, stores, and factories, pay taxes, and can die off or move away if you muck things up too badly. But do a good job and your city will grow and prosper.

Your tool kit is the floating palette at the left side of the screen, shown in figure 27.26. Just click an icon to turn the cursor into a lean, mean building machine that can run electric lines, bulldoze trees or burnt-out tracts, create new residential, commercial, or industrial districts, or perhaps build an airport or nuclear power plant. As the city develops, it is shown in the main window.

Fig. 27.26
Your tool palette and city are shown in this window.

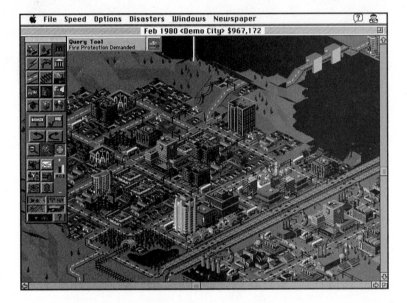

You'll need to create residential zones, which will grow and prosper based on the amount of pollution (don't put them too near industrial zones!), traffic density, population density, access to roads, and available parks and utilities.

Commercial zones should be nearby, too, providing your Sims with places to work and shop. Industrial zones are for heavy manufacturing. You'll need police and fire departments, stadiums, seaports, powerplants, and airports to keep your city thriving. But these amenities are expensive. Your city must grow large enough to support them.

Various pull-down menus let you control the speed of the game, activate or deactivate disasters, open or close informational windows, and view the scuttlebutt in the daily newspapers. A selection of windows provides graphs that track important growth and economic factors over time or show the distribution of resources.

Managing a city is tougher than it looks. If you raise taxes too high, building will be stifled. Fail to allocate sufficient funds to police or fire protection, and crime, arson, and even unchecked grassfires can wreak havoc. Creating a successful SimCity requires a delicate balance of planned growth, attractive amenities, and shrewd taxation to cash in on voter pleasure with their working and living environment. It also helps to have a lot of time to waste making haste slowly. (I once let a SimCity scenario run 24 hours a day for three months on an old Mac Plus, fine-tuning my way to the multi-zillion dollar megamegalopolis level.)

Once a year, you'll receive a budget report, similar to the one shown in figure 27.27, detailing how you did. You can make corrections then or let your current plan run a little longer to see if things improve (if trends are bad, they usually don't, without deliberate effort).

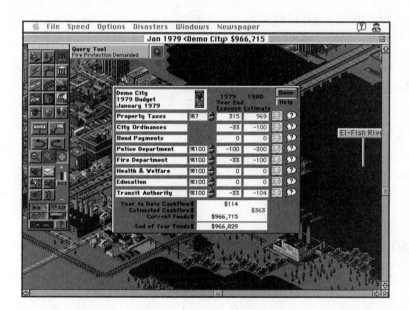

Fig. 27.27
Your yearly budget report gives the good news—and bad—for your Sim city.

As you work with the program, you'll find a few ways to cheat or at least reduce your overhead to acceptable levels. For example, any property abutted by at least one section of road or railway may be considered "connected" to the transit system, even though the road or track doesn't go anywhere. Or you may discover that not building an airport is an admirable way to keep your fire department costs in check since plane crashes are the most frequent cause of fires in SimCity.

The 3-D graphics in this new version are welcome enough, but the animations and music, along with many of the voice-over effects, get old real fast. Luckily, you can disable any and all of these from the Options menu. You can set the program to take you automatically to the site of any disaster or major event (saving you the trouble of hunting for it) and choose to try out your readiness by unleashing a disaster of your choice from a tempting list that includes fire, flood, air crash, tornado, earthquake, monster (your typical Tokyo-eating Godzilla clone), and nuclear meltdown. These can be disabled entirely through another option if you'd rather have a few years of peace and quiet.

Summary

The original city simulator has grown up, giving you an attractive 3-D view on things that was lacking from the old aerial-view, floppy-disk-based version. You can use your political and economic acumen to create and manage a thriving city or end up getting ridden out of town on a rail. Everything is under your control in *SimCity 2000.*

The 7th Guest

Before there was *Myst*, we had *The 7th Guest*, which broke new ground in the interactive virtual reality game field for its vivid, realistic 3-D graphics, great sound, tough puzzles, and slick interface. It was one of the first CD-ROM games to spawn a spin-off book of hints and tips. Once you've played this game, you'll find its imitators pale more quickly than the ghosts that haunt the center stage.

System Requirements

You'll need a CD-ROM drive and a color-capable Macintosh with a 256-color display to play *The 7th Guest*. At least a 68030-based machine (or a faster 68040 or Power Macintosh) is recommended to view the animations smoothly. The game runs in 4M of RAM or more.

You and that extra guest

You play the game in the role of the mysterious Ego, whose viewpoint is used to view the three-dimensional, virtual-reality setting of the eerie Stauf mansion. Use the mouse to move through the various rooms, following cues from a floating skeleton hand that wafts about the screen to guide you.

Many of the rooms and settings contain puzzles to be solved. Each is preceded by a playlet acted out by the ghostly apparitions of six of the last guests to stay at the mansion. Then, you'll be faced with the puzzle itself and a clue—or two. For example, in one room you'll find a cake decorated with miniature gravestones and skulls and sliced up into cubes. You're asked to remove the cubes of cake so that each piece is the same shape and contains exactly two of each type of decoration—plus one adorned with nothing but icing.

You can easily spend an hour or more working with the puzzle. Many are fairly simple maze-type challenges (once you've figured them out!): jump two squares forward, one back, three forward, one back, and so forth to spell out a word or phrase using the characters found on the spaces you land on. Since the clues are sparse (sometimes, you don't even know the goal of the puzzle), it takes some real thinking to figure out what to do. Ego and the owner of the mansion, Stauf, provide comments that can help—or lead you astray.

If you get stumped, you can visit a book of clues in the Library, at the cost of some points. After the third visit to the book for the same puzzle, the puzzle is solved for you automatically so you can proceed to the next. Solving each puzzle unlocks one or more rooms in the mansion. When you finally complete the game, you'll find that all the rooms are unlocked the next time you play, and you can then work the puzzles in any order you choose.

All the elements of *The 7th Guest* work together to evoke the proper mood. You might want to play this game alone, with the lights down low. The Fat Man's haunting music provides the appropriate backdrop as you roam through dimly lit halls and rooms. The disembodied voices add a discomforting presence. If that weren't enough, the tableaux acted out by the ghostly guests are chilling all by themselves.

Warning: the environment ranges from bawdy to grotesque, so this game is not recommended for those under 15. Puzzles are represented by a grisly throbbing brain, the game "cursor" is a floating human eyeball, and supernatural effects are preceded by macabre chattering teeth.

The game's main menu is actually a Ouija board/oracle called the Sphinx, which handles major game functions, such as loading and saving games, quitting, and so forth. You can save up to 10 versions of the scenario, using a name of your choice with up to 13 characters (clever number, eh?).

The chief weakness of this game is one that's common to all games of this genre: essentially, it's a puzzle you play through once, like a crossword. Once you've solved it, there's not much point in playing it again, except to revisit the gorgeous graphics. In addition, the puzzles are, by definition, inflexible. There's only one way to solve each puzzle, and if you can't figure that out, you're stuck (or must visit the book of clues).

The puzzles have been structured to challenge experienced players and new-comers alike and do vary in difficulty. But there are many players who will find most of the puzzles too hard, while others will find them too easy. All these "defects" are known to come with the territory. For your money, you'll get many hours of playing fun from *The 7th Guest*.

Summary

The 7th Guest is a spectacular virtual reality puzzle best played alone in a dark room. The stunning effects and feeling you get of complete immersion and involvement in the game's environment make this game a novel, haunting experience in more than one sense of each of those words. Even after you've solved all the puzzles, you may still want to play the game a few times to recapture the eerie feelings.

Brief Looks at Lemmings, Railroad Tycoon, and Populous

These three games represent leading-edge contenders in important game categories, and are well worth a brief look in this chapter.

Lemmings

Lemmings isn't a game, it's an industry. Lemmings are everywhere. You'll find a crippled but fully playable version on your local computer bulletin board as a teaser to get you buy the full 120-level game. If you have a Sega Game Gear, you may have a tiny plug-in edition you can take with you as long as your batteries hold out. There's the original program, *Lemmings*, of course, as well as *More Lemmings*, and *Oh No! More Lemmings!* We're expecting them to turn up to rip Jason to shreds in Friday The 13th, Part 13 any day now. What's with Lemmings, anyway? See figure 27.28 for your first clue.

Simply put, Psygnosis' *Lemmings* is one of the most alluring arcade-style games you're likely to play. The object is simple enough: find a way for the cute but stupid Lemmings to find their way to the exit of each level's ob-stacle-strewn screen. That's not as easy as it sounds, since each lemming has only one skill, ranging from digging and chopping to floating or simply get-ting in the way (more or less as a foreman, so to speak). Some Lemmings are able to explode when you tell them to.

Usually, though, you can convince them to work in the combinations neces-sary to move the required number of them out the exit so you can graduate to the next level. Lose too many, though, and you'll be forced to repeat the screen until you get it right.

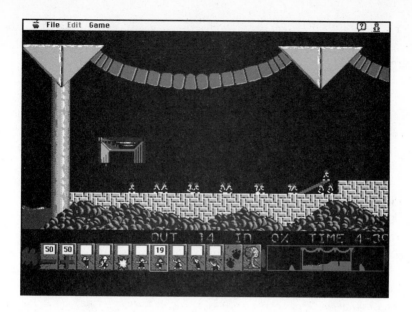

Fig. 27.28
You must figure out how to best assign skills to your crew of Lemmings in order to lead as many of the cute but stupid creatures to safety as possible.

Lemmings requires a 256-color Macintosh with at least 4M of RAM, running System 7 for the most enjoyment. A special black-and-white only version is available in the package for older Macs, however. In that edition, animation is reduced to improve game speed to acceptable levels.

Successfully getting through a level requires you to assign appropriate skills to Lemmings at the right time, so they'll build bridges, dig holes, float down steep chasms, block other Lemmings from falling off the edge of the screen, as necessary. Each screen presents you with a new puzzle, so there are 120 different puzzles to solve in the original game and more with each new edition. *Lemmings* has levels that are simple enough for younger players and tougher ones to stump teenagers and adults.

Railroad Tycoon

Attribute *Railroad Tycoon*'s longevity to its addictive qualities and the dreams of players to amass a fortune to equal their wildest dreams. A combination of *SimCity* and *Monopoly*, *Railroad Tycoon* lets you ride the Reading Railroad, or another of your choosing, as you build a steel-railed empire in England, Europe, or the United States.

Play is simple but grows more complex as the scenario builds. You start out by laying a few miles of track and connecting two cities with a rail system. Each city supplies goods and passengers, and streams of money into the railroad's coffers. As financing permits, expand into new territories, add more trains, larger engines, and haul different types of freight.

Most of the *Railroad Tycoon* games we've played bog down quickly once the rail system grows beyond a certain point. It becomes increasingly difficult to figure out how to route trains to take best advantage of supply and demand among the cities, while managing an unwieldy arsenal of rolling stock. The game has various complexity levels, which allow for takeovers, stock purchases, active competition among overlapping rail systems, and other subtleties. *Byte* Magazine's Jerry Pournelle once reported this game as his favorite of the month—for months on end. That's how engaging this game is—and a tribute to its capacity for endless variations.

Populous

Play God as you build cities, recruit armies, and slay your enemies with earthquakes and other disasters in this SimCity-on-steroids simulation. Where SimCity gives you a relatively small map with a single city to manage, *Populous* places entire continents at your disposal. You have the power to raise land out of the sea or sink islands into the depths at your whim. Is that power, or what?

Populous gives you a few scenarios to run, with grassland, desert, and ice planet worlds all available for manipulation. You have the ability to create towns and villages populated by peaceful farmers or belligerent warriors, at your pleasure. The computer acts as your nemesis, creating hostile communities that will eventually invade your lands and devastate your populations—unless you are well prepared (or, maybe, attack first!).

This game has a lot more action in it than *SimCity* and pioneered the 3-D terrain graphics we see today in many other games. It's an excellent choice for those who want to try their hand at world-building.

Other Great Games

There are a host of other great games for the Macintosh that you'll want to look for, including these best-sellers that span all the categories discussed in this chapter:

- *The Journeyman Project*. This CD-ROM game features 400M of 3-D images and 30 minutes of video using professional actors. Your job as a member of the Temporal Protectorate is to discover and correct disturbances in the flow of time!

- *Myst*. The object of this surrealistic CD-ROM adventure may be to discover what in the heck the game is about! Explore the Isle of Myst through vivid QuickTime movies as you attempt to solve the game's unspoken puzzle.

- *HellCab.* Wander around New York City from the Empire State Building to the hidden Roman Coliseum as you try to save your soul from your cabdriver, Ramon's, mysterious boss. This is another CD-based virtual reality game with a gritty Big Apple edge.

- *Battle Chess.* Watch an entire medieval world at war on your chess-board!

- *SimAnt, SimEarth, SimFarm.* Maxis just can't stop simulating things, and has created a unique set of sequels to *SimCity* that don't really resemble each other after you get past the name. Each will appeal to a different sort of game player.

- *Jump Raven.* This latest arcade shoot-em-up puts you in charge of a so-phisticated space craft against insidious enemies. A CD-ROM-only extravaganza.

Conclusions and Recommendations

Macintosh owners have never had a richer field of games and educational software to choose from. Color displays are almost a prerequisite for most of the best and brightest software in these categories, and an increasing number of titles are available either in enhanced CD-ROM versions or only on CD. Sound plays an important part, too, so those of you with external speakers and amplifiers plugged into your systems will enjoy most games just that much more.

The software profiled in this chapter are by no means all the good programs available. However, you've gotten enough of a taste of some major programs to know whether you want to explore that genre further. Unlike business software, games must be judged using more subjective criteria. While not everyone wants to use Microsoft Word, for example, it's fairly universally admired, even if grudgingly. However, some people hate a particular top-selling game, while loving another that doesn't sell nearly as well. Your best bet is to listen to the opinions of friends and colleagues with game tastes similar to your own, and if at all possible, try out the game before you buy it.

Chapter 28

Shareware and Other Cool Stuff

by Gene Steinberg

Some of your favorite Macintosh programs didn't first appear on a dealer's shelves or in a mail order catalog. They were posted in the software libraries of an online service or a local BBS. Or they were included in the disks that some Mac user groups provide.

For every commercial Macintosh program, you can choose from literally dozens of others that will not cost you a cent, or are priced much lower than anything you can buy at your software dealer. This software ranges from a simple "hack" that will enhance the functionality of the Mac Finder or a printer driver, to full-blown arcade games that rival and often exceed the quality of many commercial products.

Some of this software may be created by a young, budding programmer looking toward a future career as a software engineer. (Some of these programmers do ultimately end up in the computing industry writing commercial products.) Some of the software is written by programmers who work full-time for Apple and other manufacturers but have managed to find a little spare time to indulge their personal fantasies. Others just write this sort of stuff for the sheer pleasure of it.

In this chapter, you learn the following:

- What freeware and shareware are all about

- Some of the most popular freeware and shareware products you'll want to try

Before describing some of my favorite programs, this chapter acquaints you with a few of the ground rules about the types of software about to be discussed.

Shareware

Shareware is offered on a try-before-you-buy basis. The publisher or author of the software offers it to you for a free trial period, usually ranging from a week to a month. During that time, you can use it to your heart's content and decide whether you like it.

If you like the software and want to continue using it, you are asked to pay a fee to the author or publisher. Sometimes gentle—and not-so-gentle—reminders ask you to register the software each time you launch it (or open a Control Panel). You should observe these messages—just as you are paid for your work, a programmer deserves payment, too. Sometimes the payment of your fee will unlock additional features of the program, which is an added inducement to register (in addition to getting rid of those reminders, of course).

If you do not like the software, you are expected to discontinue using it and remove it from your computer's disk.

Freeware

As the name implies, freeware costs you nothing. You can use it as much as you want, although some authors ask for a postcard or some e-mail if you like using their product. The author retains copyright to the program, however, and may impose restrictions on your right to give it away or post it on an online service or local BBS.

Public Domain

With public domain software, the author or publisher is giving up all rights to the program, and you may use and distribute it as you see fit, without restriction.

Caution

Although shareware is usually written by highly skilled programmers and may be comparable or superior to many commercial products, the authors or publishers usually do not have the resources to test this software as thoroughly as the software you buy from your software dealer. Pay particular attention to the ReadMe files that come with any shareware you use. If you have problems using any of this software, discontinue using it right away and let the author know about the problems you're having, in case a newer version is available. As of the time this book is written, the software discussed in this chapter works on my computers (including a Power Macintosh). The prices we list for shareware were current when this book went to press, but they are subject to change without notice.

System Utilities

It's probably best to think of Apple's system software as a blackboard, ready to be filled-in with a little chalk and some creativity. Parts of this book explain some of the cool things you can do with Apple's system software. Now you see some of the cool things you can do with handy add-ons you are apt to find indispensable when you are given chance to try them out.

AppliWindows
Type: Freeware

If your Mac's desktop is as cluttered as mine, you'll appreciate AppliWindows. One of its key features is its capability to hide other open application windows when you switch to a different program. Such programs as Now Menus offer this feature, and Performa users get a similar capability with the software that Apple provides, but AppliWindows adds some additional features to the mix.

First is the capability to display a submenu of your open application windows. You can bring up this submenu from System 7's application menu, or have it pop up on your desktop by using a keyboard command, or automatically when you click your mouse on a predefined "hot spot" on-screen. (I prefer the right and left edges for hot spots.) You can also designate a keyboard shortcut to automatically cycle through open applications. AppliWindows is the brainchild of Hiro Yamamoto, a physicist who also wrote SuperBoomerang (currently part of Now Utilities from Now Software).

Open-Wide
Type: Freeware (just send a postcard if you like it)

When Apple wrote the standard Open and Save dialog box, they didn't leave enough room to fit a file name containing all 31 characters. Programmer James W. Walker's answer is Open-Wide, a Control Panel that enables you to customize the size of the Open Dialog box to contain a complete long file name.

You can also make the dialog box longer so that it includes a bigger portion of a disk or folder's directory. Open-Wide also has an Exclude feature so that you can prevent Open-Wide from activating in the very few Mac programs that don't support such manipulation.

PowerBar
Type: Shareware ($25.00)

Here's another idea Apple ought to have included with System software but didn't, leaving lots of opportunities for programmers to fill. PowerBar creates a window of colorful icons that represent applications, control panels, files, folders—anything that creates an icon. You can customize the icon palette to your heart's content, but a single click activates the program or document you select. I configured my own personal PowerBar window to give you just a taste of what you can do (see fig. 28.1).

You also get some Finder enhancements. One is the capability to hide windows when you switch programs (such as AppliWindows), the capability to restart, shut down, and even empty the trash. PowerBar also creates a floating status bar providing information in free RAM, disk space, and battery life (if you're using a PowerBook).

Fig. 28.1
PowerBar displays a colorful palette of document and program icons.

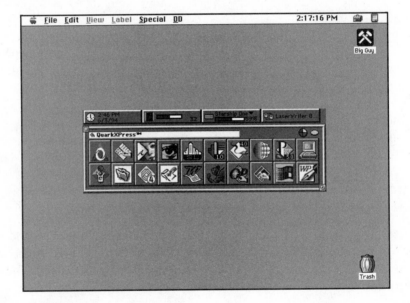

PowerStrip
Type: Shareware ($10.00)

The word *power* has a nice ring to it, as Apple realized when it was added to the words Macintosh and Book. This particular power utility puts up a status bar (at the top or bottom of your Mac's screen) containing neat rectangular boxes that you can configure to display things such as the amount of free RAM, available hard disk space, and time and date.

If you are using the Power product with the word *Book* after it, you also get a display of CPU speed, modem status, and available battery life. Author Michael Caputo has a little competition in this area now—from that neat Control Strip that ships with the newest PowerBooks—but this utility is worth a try anyway.

ScreenPlay
Type: Freeware

ScreenPlay is an Extension that does to startup screens what some screen savers do to their rotating processions of artwork. After ScreenPlay is installed (it's a System Extension), you create a folder called Screens and place it in your System Folder.

To use the program, simply copy your startup screen files into that folder. You cannot name them *StartupScreen*, as you normally do with a custom image, but the files must be saved in your draw or paint program in the regular startup screen format. Each time your Mac starts, a different image is selected. The images appear alphabetically and change each time you boot your Mac.

System 7 Pack
Type: Shareware ($29.95)

When System 7 first came out, the then teenaged programmer, Adam Stein, wrote a utility that enabled you to easily add menu commands to the Finder. What began as a simple single-purpose program has expanded into a handy utility that can change all sorts of Finder functions.

In addition to adding new keyboard shortcuts, you can use System 7 Pack to speed up file copying by up to 300 percent, add custom links between documents and applications (so you don't get the dreaded application is missing message), rid yourself of those ZoomRects that appear when you launch an application, and add loads of other Finder improvements. Each time Apple updates the Finder, however, Adam has to update System 7 Pack to deal with the changes. But this program is surely worth a trial. It's become one of the most popular shareware programs around.

Control Panels and Extensions

Where do I begin? In addition to the utilities that enhance areas of system performance described in the previous sections, a great deal of programs extend into new realms as well. The following sections describe a few possibilities for you to consider.

DepthMaster
Type: Shareware ($20.00)

If you frequently work with 16-bit or 24-bit color, and then you want to relax and play your favorite game, you can sometimes be stopped cold. Most Mac games prefer the 8-bit (256-color) setting—few are uncomfortable with more than 16 colors. High color depths also can slow screen redraw (unless you're using a very fast Mac or a very expensive accelerated video card).

Victor Tan's DepthMaster is a Control Panel that enables you to set a custom monitor depth and sound level for each program you launch. When you switch programs, the settings change. There is also a user-configurable hot menu that allows you to make on-the-fly color depth changes through a pop-up menu. It's activated via keyboard command.

Eclipse
Type: Shareware ($10.00)

In every list of shareware, the name Andrew Welch comes up. Andrew is a young, prolific programmer who has also worked on commercial software. He has a long history of interesting, innovative products. (One of his popular shareware games is discussed shortly.) Andrew has made shareware a full-time job. His company, Ambrosia, even has a technical support representative— and they accept credit cards in payment for their software.

Eclipse is a plain and simple screen saver that does nothing more than dim your Mac's screen after a preset time and display a single picture (the one supplied or a picture you want to include instead) or a clock. Eclipse doesn't make spaceships, fish, or elaborate shapes flutter about your screen, nor elaborate synthesizer-born sounds. It uses very little memory (less than 15K in fact) and seems to have little potential for conflict with anything else. If simply protecting your Mac's screen from potential burn-in is all you want, this program may be the one to try.

Flash-It
Type: Shareware ($15.00)

Computer books such as this one have zillions and zillions of *screen shots* (images taken from a Mac's screen) to demonstrate how a program works or looks. Apple gives you a very limited ability to make screen shots by typing ⌘-Shift-3. You cannot select the size of your screen capture (and it can get mighty large when you have a big monitor) or scale it to your preference unless you later edit it in a draw or paint program.

With Nobu Toge's Flash-It, you can capture a screen image in black and white or color, save it as a file, print the captured image, or just copy it to the clipboard to paste into another program. You can also configure the program to record the foremost window, even if it's a pull-down menu of some sort. You may even find that some of your favorite Mac books and articles contain screen images captured with Flash-It.

PopChar
Type: Freeware

Let's face it, Apple's Key Caps desk accessory is awkward to use. When you want to find the keyboard combination for a special symbol or accent, you have this constant switching back and forth and cutting-and-pasting routine to deal with. PopChar simply puts up a little P icon at the corner of your menu bar (you decide where in the handy Control Panel). When you click the P icon, the window shown in figure 28.2 opens. PopChar displays the full character complement of your selected font. You just drag the cursor across the window and select the character for which you are looking. The character appears at the cursor on your document. (For a complete list of the special characters accessible on your Mac's keyboard, see Appendix B, "Special Characters.")

If you click the upper right corner of the window, a More button appears. This second window includes space for you to enter an entire series of characters and then have them appear in your document at the cursor.

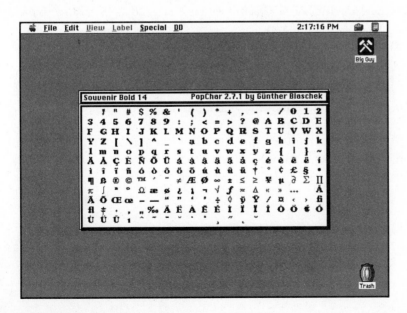

Fig. 28.2
PopChar's handy alphabet list.

SmartKeys
Type: Freeware

SmartKeys has become a favorite for desktop publishers. It provides six forms of automatic conversion that help speed up your keyboard entry and has many configurable options.

The most popular feature is SmartKeys' capability to automatically convert stick-up quotes to curly quotes. You can also prevent typing more than one space between letters or sentences (an old typewriter habit that is sometimes difficult to avoid), convert such letter combinations as *fi* or *ffl* to their ligature equivalents, kill doubled caps (a common spelling mistake), convert two hyphens to long (*em*) dashes, and convert the lesser than (<) and greater than (>) keys to commas and periods (the lowercase version of those keys).

All these features can be separately turned on or off on a program by program basis. If you're using telecommunications software that won't support curly quotes, long dashes, or ligatures, for example, you can deactivate those features while you use that program.

Symbionts
Type: Shareware ($20.00)

The name of this program doesn't really describe what it does, which is manage your startup programs on your Macintosh. You can activate or deactivate the programs in your Extensions and Control Panels, just like other init managers, by using the handy Control Panel (see fig. 28.3). You can also control the fonts you stored in System 7.1's Fonts folder and startup programs in the Startup Items folder.

In addition to turning your Extensions and other stuff on and off, Symbionts provides a display of how much RAM your favorite Extensions are using. As with commercial startup management programs, you can also use Symbionts to create sets. This feature is useful if certain Extensions you use regularly don't get along with other Extensions. You can quickly alter what Extensions load at each startup by switching sets.

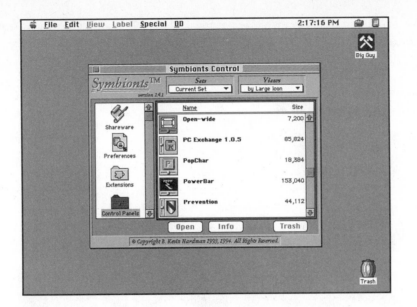

Fig. 28.3
Symbionts manages your System Extensions, Startup items, and fonts.

Games

Glider

Type: Freeware

Glider is an arcade game that takes you on a fun-filled journey on a paper airplane through 15 rooms. You are blown skyward by floor vents and forced to dodge obstacles such as light bulbs and wall sockets. Figure 28.4 shows Glider in action.

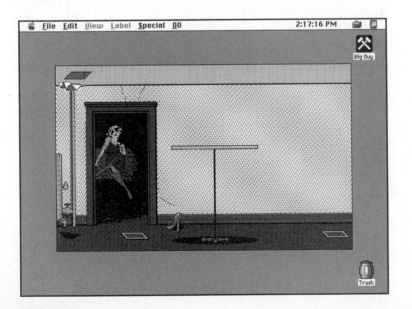

Fig. 28.4
Dodging household hazards with Glider.

The game is in black and white. That means you can get full enjoyment from this game on an all-in-one black-and-white Mac, such as a Mac Plus or Classic, and still get good performance.

Jewelbox
Type: Shareware ($10.00)

Like Tetris (which we're going to discuss shortly), Jewelbox is a puzzle game that involves assembling three or more objects in a row. The objects in this case are jewels, which appear at the top of the window and then fall to the bottom. The rows can be horizontal, vertical, or diagonal. You receive points based on the number of rows you can create. Figure 28.5 shows the game in progress. The game includes superior 256-color graphics and a truly haunting soundtrack.

Fig. 28.5

Catch the jewels as they fall to build a row of matching designs.

Despite the elaborate screen display and high-quality soundtrack, system requirements for Jewelbox are modest. You need a color Macintosh with 2MB or more RAM, running System 6.0.5 or later (6.0.7 or later to hear the soundtrack).

Klondike
Type: Shareware ($10.00)

If you enjoy a good game of cards, you'll get a kick out of Klondike, Shown in figure 28.6. Klondike is a full-color game of solitare, complete with sound effects. According to the program's author Mike Casteel, one registered owner boasts of having played more than 15,500 games of Klondike. (We're just wondering how much work was involved in keeping score.)

The game is quite unpretentious. There are no spaceships to destroy and no villians to slay. Just a nice, relaxing card game to while your leisure time away, between book chapters or whatever projects you happen to be working on at the moment.

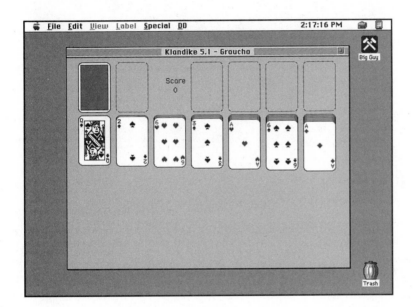

Fig. 28.6
Time to relax and play a game of solitaire with Klondike.

Maelstrom
Type: Shareware ($15.00)

If you're into high-tech, shoot-em-up arcade games, Andrew Welch's Maelstrom is your cup of tea. In this game, you travel across outer space, protecting yourself against evil ships and entities. It's full-color with elaborate four-channel-based sounds. And it's easy to learn and fun to play.

Figure 28.7 shows a random Maelstrom screen, which will give you an idea of the level of high-quality artwork that was used in creating this program.

Maelstrom has been highly acclaimed by magazine reviewers and is considered very much a match to some of the best commercial products out there. Because it is shareware, you'll have a chance to see whether you can become proficient in it, too, before you decide whether to keep it or not.

Fig. 28.7
Enter the Mael-
strom to fight evil-
doers of all shapes
and sizes.

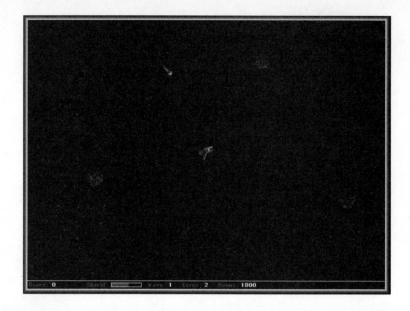

RapMaster
Type: Freeware

I put RapMaster in the games category even though it's not a game in the
traditional sense. It's more a form of recreation—or *creation*. RapMaster, written by Adobe programmer Brian K. "Beaker" Ressler (one of the authors of
Illustrator and Premiere), puts up a single window that represents your virtual
drum machine (see fig. 28.8).

You can choose from a small set of canned rhythm tracks, adjust tempo, add
some special effects, and even record voice-over commentaries, if your Mac is
equipped with a microphone. There is nothing to win except hours of enjoyment when work time gets a little dull. Just make sure the boss isn't watching—can you imagine a whole office full of would-be DJ's?

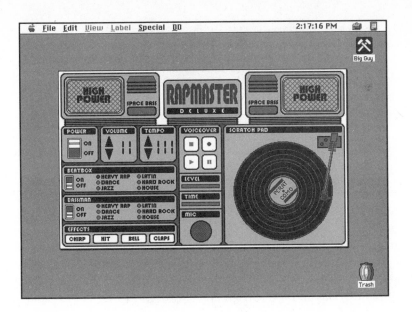

Fig. 28.8
Want to become a
DJ on your Mac?
RapMaster shows
you how.

Tetris Max
Type: Shareware ($10.00)

Tetris Max is a fun-filled, colorful game without aliens or spaceships to destroy. It has high-quality music and sound effects, and professionally rendered art. Figure 28.9 shows Tetris Max in action. The rules of the game are simple. At the top of the window, you will see a procession of oddly shaped blocks appear and drop toward the bottom. As the blocks are dropping, you can position the blocks as to where they land.

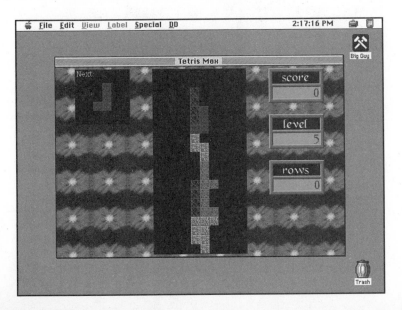

Fig. 28.9
The author's
caught playing
Tetris Max rather
than writing this
chapter.

When a row is completely filled with blocks, it disappears, and the rows above move down to take its place. You must orient the blocks as they fall to fill the pit's horizontal rows. The game ends when the pit becomes filled with blocks. Your game score is based on the number of rows you eliminate. The game has multiple levels of increasing complexity.

Fonts

Chapter 8, "All About Fonts," gives some pointers on how to use fonts on your Macintosh. This section covers a rich resource for new fonts and new font designers—shareware. Some of the fonts you'll find are simple knock-offs of commercial fonts, but others are very original, or provide a scalable font alternative to some of the classic Mac bitmap fonts. I have to admit to being a little arbitrary in selecting fonts for this chapter. I selected faces that are either especially well-done or especially unique, such as the ones based on the *Star Trek* programs and the Tolkien fantasy novels.

Beatnik
Type: Shareware ($5.00)

Available in: TrueType

If you grew up in the 1950s and remember such programs as *Howdy Doody, The Honeymooners, Your Show of Shows,* or *Captain Video,* you'll want to give this font a try. Take a look at Figure 28.10 and see for yourself.

Fig. 28.10
Remember the 1950s? Here's Marty Bee's Beatnik font.

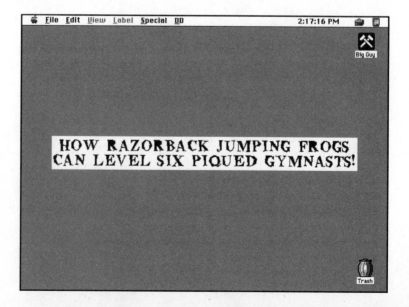

Devora
Type: Shareware ($10.00)

Available in: PostScript and TrueType

Devora, from Joe Devine, is a bold condensed sans serif font that's appropriate for display use above 187 points. According to the author, it was strongly influenced by Aurora Condensed. The font contains the full character set, and kerning pairs are carefully tuned by hand. Figure 28.11 shows a sample of Joe Devine's Devora.

Fig. 28.11
A sample of Joe Devine's Devora.

Epic Gothic
Type: Shareware ($10.00)

Available in: PostScript and TrueType

Epic Gothic is another carefully rendered font from designer Joe Devine. It's a straightforward sans serif font, suitable for text or display use. According to the author, it was inspired by Novel Gothic and is also reminiscent of Futura Bold and Kabel. The font contains the full character set, and kerning pairs are carefully tuned by hand. Figure 28.12 shows a sample of Epic Gothic.

Fig. 28.12
A sample of Joe
Devine's Epic
Gothic.

St. Francis

Type: Freeware (for non-commercial use only)

Available in: PostScript and TrueType

This font is nothing more nor less than a scalable font rendering of San Francisco, that classic bitmap font that ships with every Mac. And best of all, it's free—as long as you don't use it for commercial purposes. Otherwise, the author, Hank Gillette, asks that you contribute what you think the font is worth. Figure 28.13 shows a sample of the St. Francis font.

Fig. 28.13
The classic bitmap
font reborn as St.
Francis.

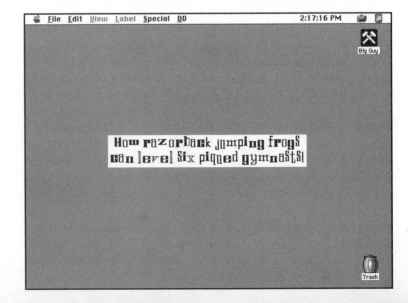

Tengwar-Gandalf
Type: Freeware

Available in: PostScript and TrueType

This cleverly designed font is based on the letter forms depicted in Tolkien's *Lord of the Rings* fantasy novels. Tengwar-Gandalf is not meant for writing business letters to your new client, as you can see in figure 28.14. The documentation that comes with this font goes to great length to describe the character sets included and how they relate to the mythical universe created in these books.

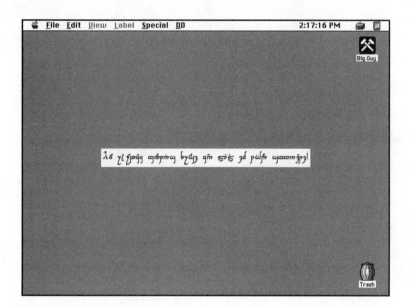

Fig. 28.14
Tengwar-Gandalf's intricate letter forms.

TNG Monitors (Star Trek)
Type: Shareware ($5.00)

Available in: Postscript and TrueType

If you're a fan of *Star Trek: The Next Generation,* which recently stopped production on syndicated television, you'll recognize the typeface shown in figure 28.15. Even if you're not a *Trekker,* you'll appreciate the high-quality workmanship that went into drawing this font, and you'll probably also find it useful for display typesetting.

Fig. 28.15
A font patterned after the one used on Star Trek TV shows.

Business and Productivity

The next few sections deal with programs that can help you organize your time, record the time you've spent on a project, bill your clients, or even allow you to do your work more efficiently.

Address Book
Type: Shareware ($30.00)

Address Book is one of the neatest all-in-one Rolodex-type programs I've used. You can store the names, phone numbers, and addresses of your friends and business contacts, print envelopes and address lists in a variety of formats, and dial their phone numbers. Figure 28.16 shows Address Book.

The program also has a variety of sort options, which are useful if you're generating a mailing list. If I have any criticism to voice of this product, it's the envelope addressing feature, which requires you to manually enter the address or cut and paste from the address book. It doesn't automatically transfer. But in most other respects, the program does most of what you want in terms of keeping an address listing.

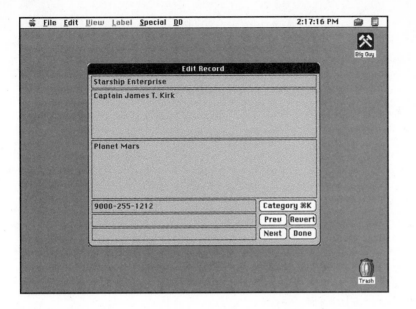

Fig. 28.16
Address Book
helps you keep
track of your
friends and
business associates
all in one simple
program.

MacInterest

Type: Freeware

Suppose that you're buying a new car. It costs $15,000 and the dealer is
charging you 9.5% interest for a 60-month loan. What's your monthly payment? No need to reach for your calculator. Just enter the figures in the
simple MacInterest window, and the information will be displayed almost
immediately (see fig. 28.17).

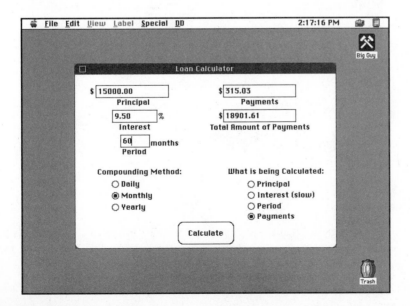

Fig. 28.17
How much should
you be paying
each month for
that new car?
MacInterest tells
you.

Or say you know only the price and the payments, but not the interest. MacInterest can tell you that, too. It also has two additional calculation windows designed to show returns for a single investment or for periodic investments.

Notify
Type: Shareware ($10.00)

It's 3:00 p.m., and what's next on your schedule? Oh yes, that staff meeting that you've been dreading. Wouldn't it be nice if you had a convenient way to be reminded of such events? Notify is a Control Panel you can program to remind you of information you choose. You even indicate when you want to receive the reminder. (see fig. 28.18).

You can schedule up to three advance notification warnings, so you'll be prepared for the main event, whatever that is. Notify is simple, straightforward, without a great deal of bells and whistles. It just gets to the point and then gets out of your way.

Fig. 28.18
Just enter what you want Notify to tell you about and when the reminder is to display.

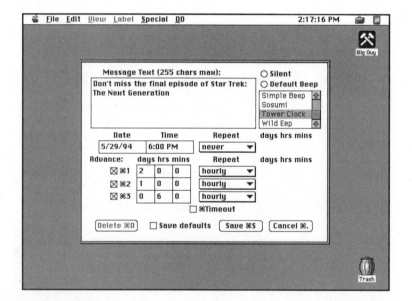

Personal Log
Type: Shareware ($15.00)

You no longer need to enter longhand comments into a notebook to keep a diary. With Personal Log, you can fill in your entries directly from your Mac's keyboard. And it goes much, much farther than one of those regular note pad programs.

With Personal Log, you can password-protect your files so that only *you* can retrieve them. It also has a search feature that enables you to quickly retrieve a specific entry. This program can be used, for example, to record information about that just-concluded business meeting (without fear that someone else will read your notes) while it's still fresh in your mind. If you have Apple's Speech Manager installed, you can even record voice annotations.

Service Invoice
Type: Freeware

Service Invoice is a simple point-and-click invoicing and accounts receivable program designed for the small businessperson. You don't deal with complex ledger entries or inventory control. Just enter the information you need, and the program does the rest, as shown in figure 28.19.

In addition to handling the invoicing and accounts receivable chores, Service Invoice comes with a companion program, called MailingsTI, that generates mailing labels based on your invoice files. You can also use a custom logo for your invoices, but the program only supports PICT images.

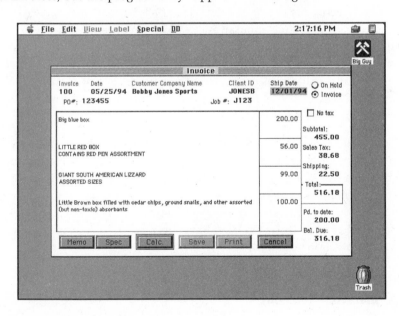

Fig. 28.19
Service Invoice figures your customer's bill for you.

TimeTracker
Type: Shareware ($5.00)

How often do you wish you could keep better track of the time you spend on various projects? You could go through the usual process of entering your start and stop times in a log, remembering to check your watch when you begin your work, or you can let TimeTracker figure it out for you.

TimeTracker lets you configure multiple windows with separate notes describing your work project. When you start, simply open your project window, click Start, and the program takes over from there. When you're done, click the same button, which now says Stop. Resume your time log of the project at a later time if you intend to continue working on it. The log windows can be saved for later review when billing time rolls around.

Other Stuff

Consider this category a hodge-podge, consisting of programs that do not neatly fit into the other categories described in the chapter but are nonetheless useful in their own way. Some are general-purpose applications. The first to be discussed is almost an essential tool for every Mac user.

Disinfectant
Type: Freeware

The Macintosh world has been lucky in terms of computer viruses. There are only a few dozen virus strains out there to inflict damage and aggravation. In contrast, the PC world has thousands of viruses to contend with. Even though the chances that you might be affected by a computer virus are not terribly great, you need protection. In addition to some very fine commercial programs that provide virus protection of various degrees of sophistication, one program is available that will do much of what you want. And to top it all off, it's free.

John Norstad's Disinfectant provides what I'll call basic virus protection. It includes an application and Extension that seeks out known virus strains and reports when one is trying to infect your Mac. As new virus strains are discovered, Disinfectant is updated within days and posted on the major on-line services and local BBS boards. The only real limitation is its inability to seek out so-called "Trojan Horse" viruses. But otherwise, this program may be all the virus protection you need.

DiskDup+
Type: Shareware ($25.00)

Whatever sort of floppy disk copying you can imagine, DiskDup+ from Roger D. Bates can do. You can make exact, track-for-track copies of 400K, 720K, 800K, or 1400K floppy disks. In addition, you can generate labels, read Apple disk image files, and mount disk images on your desktop, just as if they were regular floppy disks. This feature is especially useful if you're trying to install software that comes on a high-density floppy disk, and you only have an 800K disk drive (and it's done without an Extension). You do it all from a single application window (see fig. 28.20).

It would take half a chapter to list all of the additional features offered in DiskDup+, so here are just a few more. The program works on almost any Mac, with as little as 1MB of RAM installed. If the Mac does not have enough memory available to contain the contents of a floppy disk, the program uses a two-pass process. You can also make multiple copies by entering the number of copies you want to make in the window shown in figure 28.20. If you have a defective floppy with bad sectors, DiskDup+ can recover all readable files.

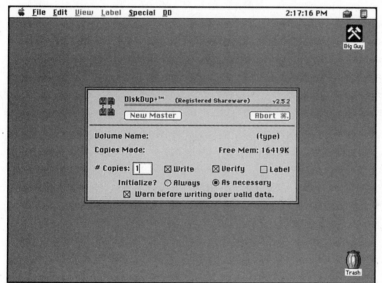

Fig. 28.20
DiskDup+ in action.

Drag.n Back
Type: Shareware ($30.00)

One axiom exists that is of crucial importance when you work on your Mac. *Backup, backup, backup.* Even the most reliable Mac system will crash on occasion. Hard drives may develop directory damage or may fail. A regular backup routine is very important so that your valuable data is protected in case something goes wrong.

Drag.n Back, from programmer Tzeshan Chen, is a System 7 Extension that puts up an icon on your desktop. When you want to backup your work, simply drag the file icons to the Drag.n Back icon. The program prompts you to select a disk on which to store the files. The routine usually takes about a minute to complete. Because the backup files are stored on the backup disk in standard Finder format (not in a proprietary archive), you can restore your data quickly and easily.

SoundStudio Lite
Type: Shareware ($10.00)

SoundStudio comes in several forms. This is the basic version, which allows you to record and play back sounds in a variety of formats. After you record a sound, you can save it in the standard System 7 format or as a separate suit-case inside a HyperCard stack.

You can also use System 7's Drag and Drop feature to automatically play and sound the file. The only limitation in the length of the sounds you record is the amount of RAM you have installed on your Mac and the amount of free storage space available on your hard drive.

Speedometer
Type: Shareware ($40.00)

Just how fast is your Mac? Speedometer, the popular shareware benchmarking program, tests a number of aspects of your Mac's performance, such as raw CPU speed, number crunching capability, disk performance, and how fast your Mac's internal video or video card rates. You can do a quick test, as shown in figure 28.21, or you can run your Mac through a more thorough set of performance ratings.

Fig. 28.21
Speedometer checking math speed on a Power Macintosh.

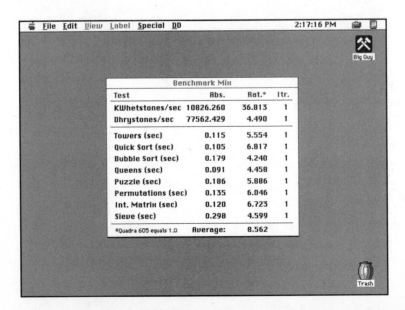

Benchmark Mix			
Test	Abs.	Rat.*	Itr.
KWhetstones/sec	10826.260	36.813	1
Dhrystones/sec	77562.429	4.490	1
Towers (sec)	0.115	5.554	1
Quick Sort (sec)	0.105	6.817	1
Bubble Sort (sec)	0.179	4.240	1
Queens (sec)	0.091	4.458	1
Puzzle (sec)	0.186	5.886	1
Permutations (sec)	0.135	6.046	1
Int. Matrix (sec)	0.120	6.723	1
Sieve (sec)	0.298	4.599	1
*Quadra 605 equals 1.0	Average:	8.562	

Speedometer includes a special machine file that contains ratings of most popular Mac models, so you can see just how your computer scores in comparison to others. It's also a useful diagnostic tool for seeking out possible software or system conflicts. A sudden drop in performance, for example, could be an indication of trouble ahead.

ZTerm
Type: Shareware ($30.00)

Chapter 29, "Getting Online," describes many of the popular programs you can use for telecommunications. One of these programs is shareware, ZTerm, from Dave Alverson. Like the higher-priced programs, it supports the super-fast zmodem protocol (explained in Chapter 29).

You can customize terminal settings like the higher-priced programs, choose from several file transfer protocols, and build a Phone List file to hold a list of the online haunts you visit most often. There's also a limited macro creation capability to help you automate your session log-ons. And unlike most programs we've discussed, ZTerm will actually run on a Mac 512K (129K ROM or later) and is compatible with operating systems as far back as System 4.1.

From Here...

There are literally thousands of little software gems available on the on-line services and local BBS. This chapter has only scratched the surface, and I frankly admit that some of the programs described here are included for no reason other than the fact that they represent my personal preferences. For every program described, dozens of others are available that are as good or better. That's what makes the search for cool shareware fun. Enjoy your exploration of the online software libraries, and remember, if you do decide to keep a shareware program, send the author a check so that the author is encouraged to update the software—and maybe write more stuff, too.

If you encounter any problems in using any of the software described in this chapter, read Chapters 37 and 38. These chapters discuss the steps you need to take to troubleshoot common problems with your Mac and how you can solve problems before they become serious.

Part V

Reaching Out

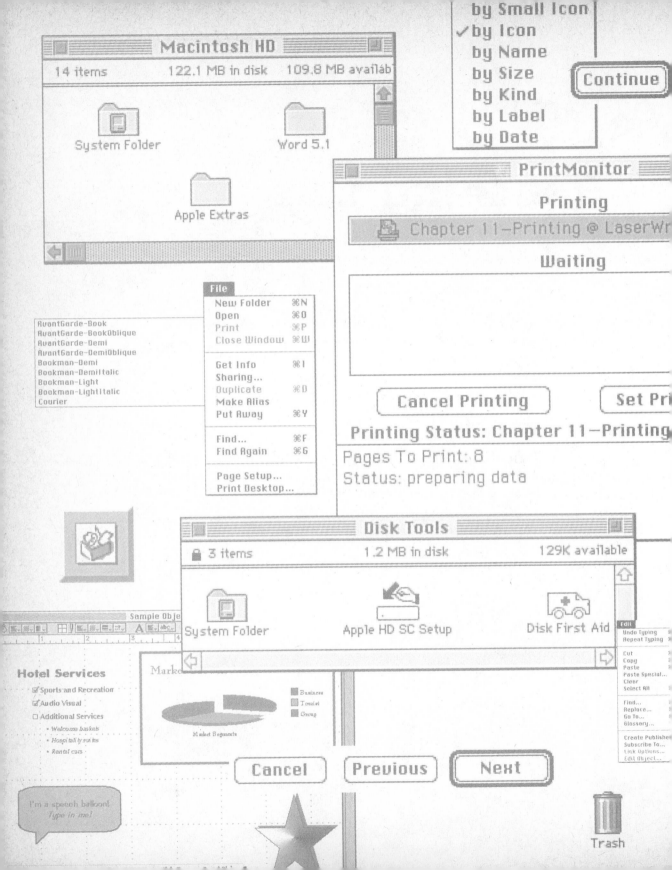

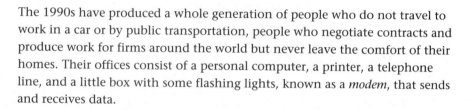

Chapter 29

Getting Online

by Gene Steinberg

The 1990s have produced a whole generation of people who do not travel to work in a car or by public transportation, people who negotiate contracts and produce work for firms around the world but never leave the comfort of their homes. Their offices consist of a personal computer, a printer, a telephone line, and a little box with some flashing lights, known as a *modem*, that sends and receives data.

Other work situations involve folks who work in separate offices, often in different parts of the country. But rather than travel to and from these disparate locations, they use modems to stay in touch.

The little box that squawks and squeaks when you connect to another telephone line is a gateway to a vast world that begins with other modems and extends to such locales as bulletin board services, online services, and a huge, seemingly intangible body known as the Internet.

In this chapter you learn about the following:

- How a modem works

- Choosing a modem

- Selecting telecommunications software

- Using your modem for faxing

- How to network with another computer by telephone line

- How to log onto a BBS—and even how to create your own BBS

Telecommunications Hardware

The word *modem* stands for *"modulate/demodulate."* Remember that your Macintosh is a digital device that speaks in little ones and zeros, but your telephone is an analog device that transmits and receives sounds. A modem converts computer data to sounds that are transmitted across a telephone line and reassembled at the other end into files that can be read by the receiving computer.

The first modems used an acoustic coupler to connect to your telephone line. You physically took your telephone handset and placed it on top of the modem, or attached a little plastic or rubber fitting directly to the handset. The unit cost hundreds of dollars and managed to transfer data at the rate of a mere 300 bits per second (bps). When you consider that there are eight bits to a byte (or character of data, in computer lingo), you can well imagine that files consisting of several hundred kilobytes of data would take many hours to transfer to another computer.

Later models plugged right into your telephone line. Like all computer-related products, modem performance has increased in quantum jumps, and the prices have gone down. High speed modems are now available, costing as little as $100, and a broad range of products selling for under $300 are available at most dealers.

External or Internal

Internal modems for desktop Macs, with a few exceptions, haven't really caught on. One big reason is that not all Macs have NuBus expansion slots (or any expansion slot, for that matter). Few, if any, of the current crop of high speed modems are available for installation inside your desktop Mac. One recent exception is a version of the Apple Express modem that installs inside the communications slot of the Macintosh LC-575 (also known as the Performa 575, 576, and 578).

▶ See "Power-books and Duos," p. 995

But the notebook market paints a different picture. For convenience in traveling with your PowerBook or Duo, you will prefer having an internal modem installed. You don't have to deal with ungainly cables and a separate unit and power supply when you sit in your hotel room trying to dial up an online service or a remote computer. You just plug in a standard telephone cable to the jack at the rear of your computer, launch your communications software, and you're in business.

How Fast?

The 300 bps modems are largely history, as are most of the 1,200 bps models that followed it. And it wasn't so long ago that a 2,400 bps modem cost over $200 and anything faster was out of the question for most Macintosh users, not only because of the price of admission, but also because very few users, and certainly none of the online services, supported 9,600 bps connections and above.

The online services have jumped on the high speed bandwagon. Just as you can purchase a new Macintosh with workstation performance for less than $2,000, there has been a concomitant performance boost and price drop in high speed modems. You can buy an external V.32bis modem, which supports up to 14,400 bps data and fax connections, at prices beginning at $100. And you can purchase internal PowerBook modems with similar speed capability for less than $200. With such a wide range of options available to you, it is not a bad idea to purchase the fastest modem you can afford.

Data Speed versus Fax Speed

Some entry level products still advertise 2,400 bps data performance and 9,600 bps fax. Other models employ V.42, a hardware compression technique, to gain faster throughput of uncompressed files. The following list examines some of these strange V-style names and discusses what the names mean in terms of modem performance:

- **V.22bis.** This designation is just your ordinary 2,400 bps modem.

- **V.32.** This designation is the standard for sending data at up to 9,600 bps.

- **V.32bis.** This designation means the modem is capable of data transmission at speeds of up to 14,000.

- **V.42.** This standard involves Microcom Networking Protocol (known as MNP) and relates strictly to various error correction schemes.

- **V.42bis.** This standard covers hardware compression, in which data is compressed on-the-fly as it is sent by your modem, and decompressed at the other end of the line by the receiving modem. In theory, you are supposed to be able to get 4:1 compression, up to 57,600 bps with a 14,400 bps modem; in practice, figure on something closer to 2:1. The net effect is that file transfers take less time, reducing your connection time—and perhaps your phone bill.

V

Reaching Out

> **Note**
>
> Files that are already compressed do not benefit from V.42bis hardware compression.

And V.Fast?

By the time this book is published, another new high speed standard, V.34, will be available. V.34 will support data connections of 28,800 bps, with a potential throughput of data with hardware compression (see the previous discussion of V.42bis) of over 115,200 bps—assuming that your Macintosh hardware can support anything that fast. (Most likely it won't.)

Before the release of the final V.34 standard by the ITU-TSS (an organization that makes these decisions on a worldwide basis), a number of modems came out featuring something called V.Fast, or VFC for short. This product line uses a *data pump* (data processing engine) from Rockwell based on the preliminary V.34 standard. The final approval of the standard means that V.Fast modems will require new data pump installations to be fully compatible (which will be offered by the manufacturers at extra cost).

Wireless Modems

Tip

When transferring data by cellular telephone, try not to move your car. Also use the ZMODEM file transfer protocol so that you can quickly resume an interrupted session where you left off.

If you are among the growing fraternity of cellular telephone users, you may be interested in the new generation of wireless modems designed to cope with the unique conditions presented by this growing technology. One common situation is when transmission quality decreases as you move from one cell to another, or when passing through an area with tall buildings or tunnels that might inhibit good quality connections.

A standard modem can work, but you'd want to purchase a model offering Microcom's MNP Level 10, a special error correction technique that you need for fast, error-free transfers. A quick check of the modem specification sheets will provide this sort of information.

If you are using a conventional modem, you will also need a special interface kit that will allow your modem to be attached to the special jacks that are found on some cellular phones. The other alternative is a dedicated cellular modem, costing more than a regular modem, but not so expensive when you factor in the cost of that interface. Higher-cost products incorporate a cellular telephone and a modem in one convenient unit. One such product, from Air Communications Inc., is priced at around $1,500. Motorola, Inc., which makes a line of popular cellular telephones, is also intent on introducing one of these all-in-one products.

Installing Your New Modem

Setting up your new desktop modem is usually quite easy. Configuring your software to the modem is more difficult, as described in detail in the next part of this chapter. Because a PowerBook's internal modems present a different level of installation issues, this section doesn't cover them. The section concentrates instead on how to set up a standard desktop modem. Following are some basic steps you should follow after you unpack your modem:

Caution

Even though installing an internal modem into the PowerBook 100180c series is often easy, dealer setup is usually recommended. The PowerBook's delicate circuitry is sensitive to static discharge (the kind of current buildup that happens when you walk across a new carpet) and can be damaged easily. Most dealers charge between $25 and $50 for installation. When it comes to a PowerBook Duo or the new PowerBook 500 series, installation is much more complex, and you definitely should have your dealer perform the installation for you.

---

1. Attach a modular telephone cable, with one end connected to your telephone line, and the other connected to the jack at the rear of your modem, which is usually labeled *line*.

2. If you intend to have your regular telephone use the same line, attach its plug to the second jack on the modem, which is usually labeled *phone*.

3. Attach the matching connector of the modem cable to the rear of your modem and plug the other one into the modem port on your Macintosh. This is best done with both products off.

Note

If you intend to attach multiple devices to your Mac's modem port, look into a switch box or a utility that can automatically switch port connections. You can find these devices at your computer store.

---

4. Plug your modem into the wall socket. If it uses an external power supply, as many do, make sure that the other end is attached to the appropriate slot on your modem.

5. Turn on your modem. Check the owner's manual for instructions as to whether certain display lights should be lit when the product is

V

Reaching Out

working. Many Supra models, for example, will show an OK light in the LED display.

6. If your modem fails to light, make sure everything is hooked up correctly. If you cannot get it to work, contact your dealer or the manufacturer's technical support people.

7. If everything works okay, turn on your Mac and get ready to telecommunicate.

Caution

Every time you install a new modem, you will probably have to reconfigure your telecommunications software to support the new product. So before jumping in and trying to log onto your favorite services, make sure your software is set up to support your new hardware, as described in the next section of this chapter.

Telecommunications Software

After your new modem is installed, you need to have a means by which your Mac can convert data to a form that can be processed by your modem, and to receive data that comes from a remote modem or BBS. Many new modems ship with software for both faxing and telecommunications, so the decision of what to use is more or less made for you. Other modems come a la carte— you have to purchase a software package. And there are times when the software that ships with your new modem may not have the features and power to do the kind of work you need done.

That's when you will want to purchase dedicated telecommunications software.

What's Available

Although most Macintosh software provides point-and-click simplicity, complexities are embedded into your telecommunications software that often seem alien to the Macintosh's concept of plug-and-play. You often have to deal with arcane issues related to modem connection strings, handshaking, port speeds, local echo, and other terminology that frequently crops up as

Telecommunications Software

you simply try to connect from one point to another. This section first discusses some of the popular software products that are available. The section then outlines how to set up a couple of these programs and acquaints you with the terminology you need to know to avoid problems.

> **Note**
>
> You can often get away with not reading the manual for many Macintosh products, but the same doesn't necessarily hold true with a modem. Before setting up your new modem for the first time, read the manual carefully. Modems come in all sizes and flavors, with different setup routines. To avoid problems later on, at least read the following sections covering how to get up and running.

MicroPhone (Software Ventures)

MicroPhone comes in three flavors, depending on just how sophisticated you want to make your communications sessions. The basic MicroPhone LT package is offered at no extra cost with many modems and costs less than fifty bucks at software retailers. It supports all the common connection schemes, including ZMODEM (described later in this chapter), and comes with connection scripts for some of the major online services, such as CompuServe and GEnie. It also reads scripts created in the more sophisticated versions of the program. The biggest limitation of the program is the inability to create your own scripts, but if you just do simple log-on/log-off sessions, this probably won't present a problem. Modem profiles are also supplied for all the popular makes and models, making it easy for you to get up and running.

The high-end versions are MicroPhone II and MicroPhone Pro. The core applications are the same, but the options differ. The Pro version gives you TCP/IP tools for Internet connections and a fax modem software package. The best part of the program is its Watch Me feature, which allows the software to record all the steps you take in connecting to a BBS or online service. You can then play back that script with a single set of keyboard commands or by clicking on an icon, as shown in figure 29.1.

You can even build your own scripts from the ground up. The large, illustrated manuals give you hints and tips on creating your own custom telecommunications sessions. You can use the supplied connection profiles as a guide. After your script has been created, the software can analyze it for you and point out syntax errors.

Fig. 29.1
Click the icon representing your favorite service, and MicroPhone automatically connects you to that service.

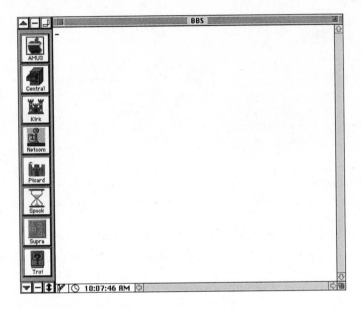

SITcomm (Aladdin Systems)

SITcomm is the new kid on the block as telecommunications software goes, but one of its principal authors, Leonard Rosenthal, was one of the software engineers behind the original MicroPhone, and the program's sophistication belies its simplicity. A particularly useful feature of SITcomm is its capability to enable you to perform most of your day-to-day telecommunications by clicking a few buttons on its simple interface, as shown in figure 29.2.

Although the program doesn't create its own scripts, the publisher provides some canned connection routines for popular online services and many BBS front-ends. In addition, you can use AppleScript to create your own more complicated telecommunications processes. Aladdin also includes a compression/decompression tool using its StuffIt technology to compress your files before you send them, and to expand files, (automatically, if you want) after they are downloaded to your computer from another service.

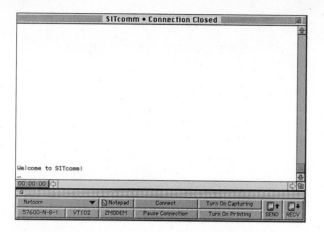

Fig. 29.2
SITcomm's simple
point-and-click
interface makes
the often
difficult job of
telecommunicating
simple.

A rather personal touch provided with the software is a female voice that intones, "Connection Established," when you successfully log onto a service and, "Connection Closed," when you disconnect. When you quit the program, the voice exclaims, "Good-bye." In case you prefer to do your work in quieter surroundings, the software allows you to disable the voice.

Smartcom II

The folks who brought you the Hayes command set are also the publishers of a popular telecommunications software product. Smartcom II offers a reasonably sophisticated set of telecommunications tools, along with online help and a neat set of icons, known as SmartButtons, to display common commands.

Smartcom II also has a scripting routine, known as Autopilot, that helps automate your standard telecommunications routines so that you can recall them with simple commands. It also supports Apple's new PowerTalk technology and AppleEvents.

Smartcom II provides direct support for all the products from Hayes Microcomputer, but also works with just about any other Hayes compatible modem on the market with little or no setup difficulties, as shown in figure 29.3. Smartcom II is positioned at a price between the lowest and highest cost products, and makes a very suitable compromise for users who don't need advanced scripting.

Fig. 29.3
Hayes Smartcom II
can be configured
automatically for
most popular
modem products.

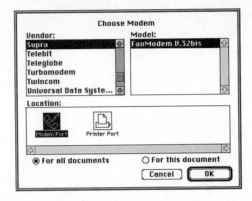

White Knight

Years ago there was a full-featured telecommunications program, Red Ryder, that was offered as a shareware program. As it grew in sophistication, it eventually blossomed into a commercial package. Over the years it has had numerous upgrades to fix bugs and add new features. The publisher, FreeSoft, even gave it a name transplant to White Knight because of some licensing issue over the original name. The software also had a positively huge number of versions. Where most software barely makes it into the revision 5.0 class, White Knight is currently at version 12.00, as author Scott Watson continues to tweak its interface and improve its performance.

White Knight offers an extraordinary amount of power coupled with a huge array of menus and submenus that can sometimes seem daunting to many users, as shown in figure 29.4. But when you get over the somewhat involved nature of its interface (which has improved in the newest versions of the program), you'll find just about all of the features you need in a communications package, with support for all the necessary file transfer protocols, terminal emulation setups, and a very sophisticated scripting scheme. A handy 270-page manual helps take you over the rough spots.

You can create a script, called a *procedure* in White Knight parlance, from the ground up, step by step, and let the program debug it for you, or let the program create one for you, very much in the manner of MicroPhone IIs "Watch Me" capability, described in the preceding section.

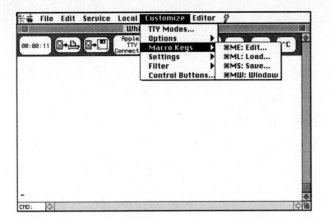

Fig. 29.4
If you take a little time to learn the ins and outs of White Knight, you'll find that White Knight is a program that offers extraordinary power to handle your telecommunications chores.

Zterm

Zterm has one strong argument in its favor: it's shareware. You can try Zterm for yourself and see whether you like it. If you don't like it, you can discard it and try one of the commercial products instead. If you like the program, send the author a check for $30.

Zterm supports most of the sophisticated file transfer protocols you need, such as ZMODEM (which is discussed in more detail later in this chapter). It also handles ANSI graphics, which are useful when you connect to PC-based bulletin boards. It does what it does without fuss or muss in a single application, without a disk full of support files except for some sample macros to help you log onto popular services. Figure 29.5 shows the program's straightforward interface.

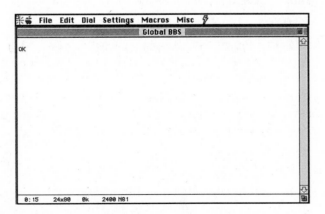

Fig. 29.5
Zterm, a shareware favorite, is strong competition for many of the commercial communications programs.

V

Reaching Out

You can download a copy of Zterm from your favorite BBS or online service. Some prepackaged shareware disks also include Zterm, but you still have to remember to pay the shareware fee if you decide to continue using the program. A licensed version (meaning the shareware fee is already paid) is offered with many Global Village modems.

Installation and Setup

Although the telecommunications software described so far varies widely in interface and features, some basics in setting up the program to your modem and your needs are very much the same. This section describes how to configure these programs. Illustrations from different software packages demonstrate the basic steps you need to follow to configure any of these programs.

> **Note**
>
> Before setting up your telecommunications software for your new modem, check the modem's instruction manual about special strings and other settings that are necessary to get the best performance.

Tip

When setting up your telecommunications software for a new service, check the instructions on that BBS welcoming screen or in any printed instructions you have about special modem settings.

When you begin the process of setting up your software, you will encounter settings that may seem confusing at first glance if you haven't worked with a modem before. Each setting describes a different way that your modem will communicate with another modem or BBS, or the data transmission scheme used to move data back and forth. After you make your settings, they will apply for most connections you make, though there are apt to be differences.

Before launching your new software, turn on your modem and double-click the software's icon.

Before changing any modem settings, first see whether your modem has a built-in profile. This profile will adapt the software to work properly with your modem. If your modem has such a profile (or modem module), select that option. Many of the other adjustments will be established automatically. Figure 29.6 shows a profile using Aladdin's SITcomm. The following pages list common modem setup commands and our suggestions for most configurations:

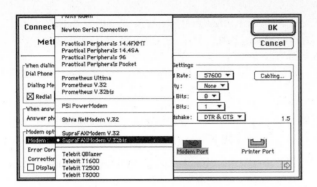

Fig. 29.6
Choose a profile that matches the make and model of your modem, or whatever alternate setting that's recommended by the manufacturer.

■ *Baud rate.* This setting can be confusing. It refers to the maximum speed supported by your Mac's modem port, but it does not necessarily refer to the maximum speed your modem supports. Normally, you set the baud rate to equal your modem's highest connection speed or the next highest figure offered by the software. Not all software offers a 14,400 bps baud rate, even though many modems support that speed. If your modem supports V.42 hardware compression, set the port speed to at least double the modem's speed.

> **Note**
>
> Most telecommunications software supports a maximum baud rate of 57,600 bps. But a slower Macintosh, or even a PowerBook, may work more efficiently (with fewer transmission errors) with a lower speed setting (38,400 bps or less, for example).

■ *Flow control.* You have a choice of two basic methods. One is X-On/X-Off, in which a signal, X-Off, is sent by the receiving modem whenever the computer to which it's attached overruns with data, to give the modem time to process the information; X-On is sent for the data flow to resume. The second method is known as *hardware handshake*, which requires a special cable that's normally provided with modems capable of 9,600 bps speed or faster. In the latter case, the cable does the flow control. This setting is the one most modern modems require.

V

Reaching Out

- *Data bits*. As mentioned previously, computer data is made up of 1s and 0s. Data is sent in little pieces, called *packets*, either 7-bit or 8-bit in size. Unless the connection service instructs you otherwise, stick to the default setting provided in your software.

- *Parity*. This setting is a basic error-checking scheme supported for the older, low-speed modems. Unless your modem manual says otherwise, leave it off or set it to *none*.

- *Stop bits*. This setting refers to the number of bits added to the end of each character of information. The usual setting is 1, although MicroPhone also offers an auto option (which is the default setting).

- *Initialization string*. This setting is the set of commands, usually preceded by the command AT (for *attention*) that is sent by your telecommunications software before a connection has begun. The string turns special features, such as hardware compression, error correction, and flow control, on or off. If the software has a built-in profile for your modem, you won't have to fiddle with this setting unless the place to which you are connecting requires a special setting.

After you configure the software to your modem, you must consider additional issues. The first issue is the terminal settings. The services you're connecting with may use a Mac, a PC, a workstation, or even a mainframe computer. They do not necessarily support all 256 characters available on a typical Macintosh font; usually only the basic 128 ASCII keystrokes are accepted. So characters such as curly quotes, em-dashes, and even foreign accents produce nothing but blank boxes or no response when you type them.

The most common setting is TTY in the terminal setup window for MicroPhone Pro (see fig. 29.7). Another option is VT100 or VT102. Usually the BBS or online service to which you're connecting will specify a terminal option, which you should follow. Following are some of the common terminal commands you'll see in the program's setup window

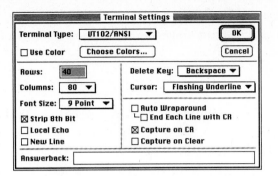

Fig. 29.7
Terminal setup
window for
Software Ventures'
MicroPhone Pro.

- *Local Echo.* When you select this choice, each character you type is echoed or displayed on your computer's screen. Because most of the places to which you'll be connecting already *echo,* or return, the characters you type to your computer, you should leave this option off.

- *Half/full duplex.* This setting more or less works in concert with Local Echo. With the standard full-duplex setting, data can flow between both connection points at the same time, including the characters you're typing. Half-duplex allows data to be sent in one direction at a time.

Tip

If everything you type while connected to another modem produces double characters, such as *AA, BB,* and so on, turn off Local Echo in your software's terminal settings.

Sending and Receiving Faxes

In years past, if you wanted to receive a fax, you bought a separate fax machine. But this became a little involved if you only had one telephone line and had to share it with your modem. Faxing is much simpler now; with the proper software, most new modems incorporate fax capability.

Using your Macintosh and a modem as a fax machine has its advantages and disadvantages. The following sections describe some pros and cons to consider before you decide which route to take.

V

Reaching Out

Fax Modem Advantages

The main advantage is convenience. You can send and receive faxes on the same telephone line you use send and receive data, and you only have to purchase one product that usually costs much less than a traditional fax machine.

Most fax software offers an address book feature of some kind. You can keep a database of those to whom you normally send faxes and even broadcast a fax to a number of recipients with a single Fax command (see fig. 29.8).

Fig. 29.8
Using FaxSTF from STF Technologies, a fax is sent to an entire mailing list.

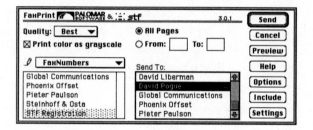

If you intend to use the faxed material as part of a document of some sort, some faxing software includes an optical character recognition (OCR) tool to convert the contents of your fax into editable text (see fig. 29.9).

Fig. 29.9
Delrina's FaxPRO for Macintosh is one of the packages that includes OCR capability.

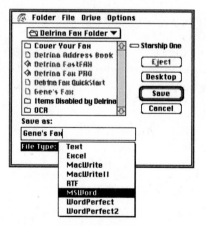

Another advantage is to the environment. All the faxes you send and receive are stored as image files on your computer. You don't have to print anything; you can just read the documents on-screen after you receive them.

Fax Modem Disadvantages

Fax software is generally QuickDraw-based, meaning that if the document you want to fax contains EPS graphics, they'll only show up as a low-resolution PICT image. The latest generation of fax software from such software publishers as Delrina, Global Village, and STF do support scalable fonts in both PostScript (with Adobe Type Manager) and TrueType formats, for sharp reproduction. Several PostScript printers also have fax options, too.

Tip
You can use a PostScript emulator program such as Freedom of Press to fax PostScript graphics. The downside is slow performance compared to a true PostScript output device.

Another disadvantage comes into play when you want to receive faxes when you are not using your Macintosh. You normally have to leave the Mac on 24 hours a day anyway (unless you're using a PowerBook that's been put to sleep with the Wake On Ring option selected in the PowerBook Control Panel), if you expect to be receiving faxes at hours when you're not at work.

If you want a paper copy of your fax, you must open your received fax with your fax modem application and print it, as shown in figure 29.10. (Some programs print faxes automatically, however.) The process of receiving and then printing is apt to be less convenient and take much longer than a dedicated fax machine could handle the process.

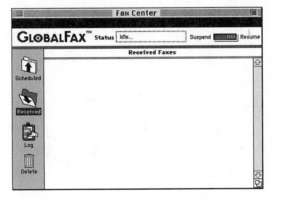

Fig. 29.10
Global Village's fax software uses a single DA to handle your faxing chores, including opening and printing your fax documents.

The final limitation comes into play when you want to fax a document that's not stored on your Macintosh and for which you only have a printed copy. You have to use a scanner to read the image file before you can fax it. Again, the stand-alone fax machine knows no such limitation.

► See "Sending Faxes," p. 1005

If you use a portable Macintosh and travel frequently, however, and need to send and receive documents from remote locations, a fax modem can be quite a timesaver, despite its limitations. Chapter 35, "On The Road," discusses fax software in more detail, and briefly describes some of the popular fax software packages that are available.

V

Reaching Out

Using Apple Remote Access

Chapter 34 discusses techniques for networking your Macintosh. In this section, I describe a method you can use to log onto your own Macintosh or to your network from anywhere in the world. All you need is a Macintosh, a modem, and a software package from Apple called Apple Remote Access.

Apple Remote Access first made its appearance on Apple's PowerBook line, but it works on any Macintosh. With a little help from System 7's File Sharing on the receiving end, you can telephone a Macintosh that is also equipped with this program from any remote location, log onto that Mac, and bring up its shared files right on your desktop. Transferring files is a simple matter of dragging them to your own Mac's mounted volumes.

Apple Remote Access enables you to create an individual document for each remote location you intend to contact, as shown in figure 29.11. You just enter the telephone number of the connecting modem, your name and your password (if it applies), and then click the Connect button.

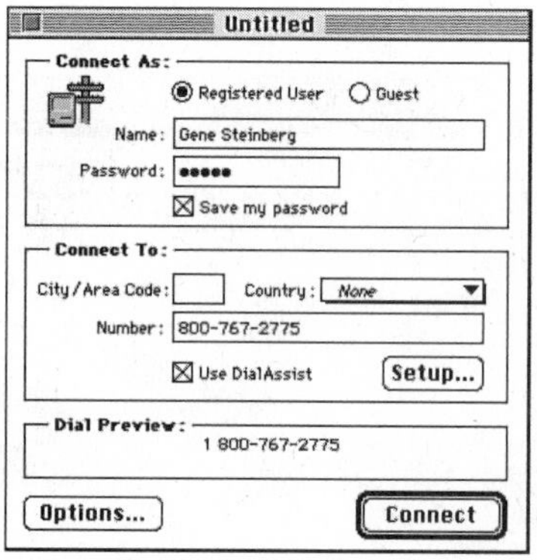

Fig. 29.11

Simple setup for Apple Remote Access. Note that the number we've used here reaches Apple Customer Assistance lines.

Apple Remote Access is supplied in two versions. The first version is a low-cost client version, which is used strictly for logging onto another computer. In order to send files, you need to have the server edition installed. After you log onto the remote Macintosh, a message confirming connection with the remote Macintosh network appears (see fig. 29.12).

Fig. 29.12
Connection with
your remote
Macintosh
network is
confirmed.

After you hook up to your network, open the Chooser and select AppleShare. The name of the Macintosh to which you are connected should show up on the list. After you log onto the network, you can mount any shared volume on your Mac's desktop. For specifics on networking your Mac, see Chapter 33, "Networking."

▶ See "Setting Up
Your Computer
for Remote
Access," p. 960

> **Note**
>
> Even with a high speed modem, your file transfer speeds with Apple Remote Access are a fraction of what they would be when one Mac is directly networked with another with a LocalTalk or Ethernet connection. Large files can take many long minutes (even several hours) to reach your computer by telephone lines. When telephone bills are taken into consideration, sometimes sending the disks with an overnight carrier might be a better method if you don't have a pressing deadline.

Connecting to an Electronic Bulletin Board System

A *Bulletin Board System* (or *BBS*) is a computer dedicated to handling both software and messages, most often concerning a specific topic (such as computing or audio, for example). You connect with that service by using a modem. You generally need to register your name and a password so that the people who run the BBS, known as system operators (or *sysops* for short) can keep track of the folks who are using the service. The difference is mostly in size and in the range of features available.

A BBS may be run by a single individual with a single telephone line and a single computer, or it may use several telephone lines and a bank of several computers. Some hardware and software manufacturers set up a BBS to provide technical support and update files. Computer user groups will set up a BBS to share files and information. Services are available for those who have a special interest, such as audio or science fiction.

Depending on the service you contact, access may be free or restricted to certain users (members of a group or owners of a specific product, for example). In some cases, you may have to pay a fee for access.

Making the BBS Connection

This section explains how to log onto the Arizona Mac User's Group BBS, and takes you through a quick tour of the service.

The first step is to log onto the service by using telecommunications software (see fig. 29.13). Your software will do the connection chores for you, so you usually don't have to mess with any of those AT commands (but you'll learn more about them shortly).

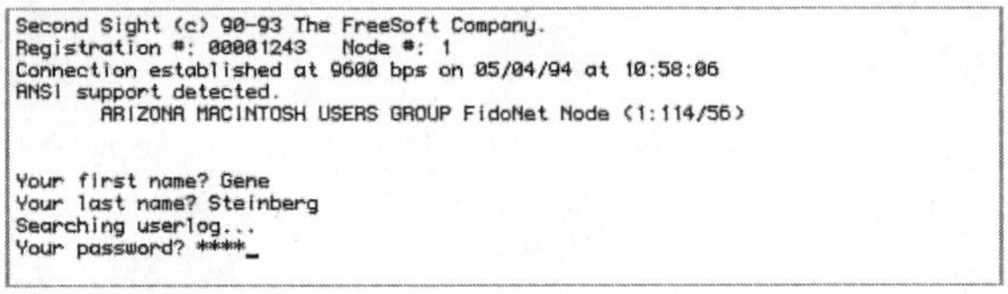

Fig. 29.13

Logging onto your favorite BBS.

```
Second Sight (c) 90-93 The FreeSoft Company.
Registration #: 00001243   Node #: 1
Connection established at 9600 bps on 05/04/94 at 10:58:06
ANSI support detected.
        ARIZONA MACINTOSH USERS GROUP FidoNet Node (1:114/55)


Your first name? Gene
Your last name? Steinberg
Searching userlog...
Your password? ****_
```

> **Note**
>
> In BBS parlance, the act of sending a file to another modem or service is called *up-loading*. The process of receiving a file on your Mac's drive is known as *downloading*.

Some software packages offer scripting routines that will log onto a BBS with just a click or two. In the example in this section, all this information is entered manually. In most cases, the password is echoed (displayed) with an asterisk or left invisible so that people looking over your shoulder cannot see what you type.

Upon entering the correct name and password, the software checks your status on the BBS and then admits you to the service, as shown in figure 29.14.

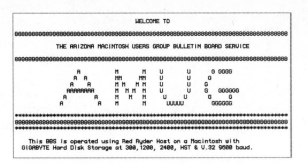

Fig. 29.14
You are welcomed
to the BBS.

After entering the BBS, you are given a set of options in navigating through the service, which can usually be selected by typing a single letter or number (such as the letter N for New Files). This example goes right to the software libraries, which are almost always a very popular feature.

Many local BBSs have large libraries of freeware and shareware. Figure 29.15 shows the listing of newest uploads.

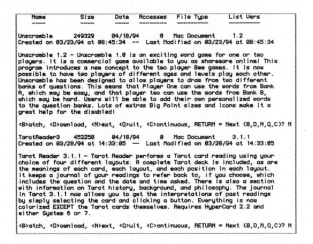

Fig. 29.15
A listing of the
newest files
available on a
typical user
group BBS.

Selecting a File Transfer Protocol

After you select a file to download to your computer, you must make still another decision—the way you want it transferred. The BBS software will often give you a choice of file transfer protocols (see fig. 29.16).

Fig. 29.16
Before you can
download a file,
you must pick one
from column A.

```
Download using what protocol:

1) XMODEM-CRC
2) XMODEM-Checksum
3) XMODEM-1K blocks
Z) ZMODEM
Q) Quit

Which one (1, 2, 3, Z or Q)?
```

Each modem transfer scheme gives you different sets of features and options. Following is a brief explanation of the transfer protocols supported by most telecommunications software:

■ *XMODEM.* This file transfer technique is available in all the telecommunications software products discussed in this chapter. XMODEM sends out your data in little pieces, ranging in size from 128 bytes to a kilobyte, and uses error checking to make sure that the data is transferred properly.

■ *YMODEM.* This method is essentially the same as XMODEM, but you are also able to send files as a *batch*, or a group, by using a single set of instructions. The files are then transferred in sequence.

■ *YMODEM-G.* This technique is a subset of YMODEM, with one twist. If an error in transmission is found, the file transfer stops. You get faster data throughput. If your connections are less than optimal, however, you end up having to start the transmission over and over again.

■ *ZMODEM.* Where available, ZMODEM offers the fastest throughput and is the one I use and recommend. It uses a technique similar to YMODEM in sending data, but doesn't abort a transmission if an error occurs. Instead, the data is re-sent. The biggest advantage of ZMODEM occurs when your transmission is interrupted for any reason (such as when your phone disconnects). You can resume downloading where you left off without losing data, although sometimes you have to alter the settings in your communications software to allow it to pick up where it left off.

After you review new files, or download a few, you can review other features that might be offered on a BBS, such as news and views on the topics to which the board is devoted, or even exchange messages with other users.

Ending the Session

When you finish your session, you end the session, or *log off*, as shown in figure 29.17.

```
** Are you sure you want to leave the AMUG BBS **
Did you post a message or Upload a file this session?
      Please, don't leave without a word!
*******************************************************

<Y>es, disconnect now
<S>end Mail to the SYSOP before leaving.
<N>o! Return me to the Main Menu

(20 minutes left) Command <Y,S,N> ? Y


Thank you for visiting the AMUG BBS!

Please limit your access to once every 12 hours.
Hope we see you soon!



Elapsed time this call: 2 minutes.
Thank you for calling!

Please disconnect now.


Second Sight, Copyright 1990-1993 The FreeSoft Company,
105 McKinley Rd., Beaver Falls, PA, U.S.A. 15010. All rights reserved.
Voice: (412)846-2700. Originally Written by Scott Watson.
Version 3.0 by Jeff Dripps.
```

Fig. 29.17
A single keystroke
is all that's
necessary to tell
the BBS it's time to
leave.

If you watch your communications software in action, quite often you'll see little commands displayed that represent the information used by your modem to begin and end a connection. Literally pages of modem commands can be found in your modem manual. The following list describes a few that apply to a typical Hayes-compatible modem. You will probably use them from time to time during your telecommunicating activities. In order to activate these commands, you must end your instruction with a return.

> **Caution**
>
> Not every modem supports the exact set of commands described in this chapter. The commands described represent typical models. Check your owner's manual to determine which commands apply to the modem you have.

- *ATA*. Answers telephone line.

- *AT&F*. Reverts your modem to factory settings.

- *AT&F1*. On some high speed modem designs, this setting turns on such features as error correction, flow control, and hardware compression.

- *ATLX*. This command adjusts the volume of your modem's speaker. If X is 0, the speaker is at its lowest setting, 1 the next lowest, 2 the default or medium level, and 3 the highest volume level.

- *ATMX*. This command turns your modem's speaker on or off. If X is 0, the speaker is off, if X is 1, the speaker is on.

- *ATDT [phone number].* This command tells your modem to connect using the phone number you type. The T at the end of the command represents a typical touch-tone telephone. A pulse phone gets a P instead.

- *ATZ.* Resets the modem to its default settings.

Setting Up Your Mac as a Host

Just as you can log onto other bulletin board and online services with your Mac and your modem, you can almost as easily set up your Macintosh to create your own BBS. You may want to establish your own service to share information and files with those with similar interests. If you are running your own business, say a service bureau, you can use a BBS to send and receive work from your clients.

Setting up a BBS has some downsides. For best performance, you need to dedicate a single Mac and a separate telephone line to the task. You could, in theory, do work on the Mac while other users are logged on, but you'll exact a severe performance penalty and maybe risk a lost connection during a CPU-intensive operation, such as printing or processing data. If your BBS is set to run day and night, you must keep your Macintosh running as well. If your Mac uses a separate monitor, you can turn off the screen at night when you're not working on the computer.

A number of programs that allow you to turn your Mac into a small online service are available. The one we used in the preceding example was Second Sight, published by FreeSoft, which developed White Knight. A number of other commercial and shareware products are available, but the one discussed next has one advantage over them all, even though it may be lacking in terms of features: it's free.

The program used to set up a BBS in this example is called Mini BBS, a settings module that ships with MicroPhone II and MicroPhone Pro from Software Ventures. Setting up the BBS is relatively simple. First you launch the program, and then click the User's icon on the bottom of the main program window. You'll have the choice of creating a New User, or deleting or changing existing user settings. Because this example uses the program for the first time, you choose the New User setting, which brings up the window shown in figure 29.18.

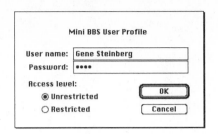

Fig. 29.18
In this example, I entered my name and password, and granted myself Unrestricted access.

After you've established a core set of users of your BBS, the next step is to click the Run BBS icon, which brings up the window shown in figure 29.19.

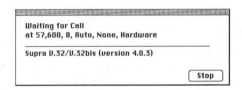

Fig. 29.19
Waiting for your first call.

This BBS has its limitations. You have to grant a user a name and password in advance. He or she cannot log onto your service as a new user and enter the information. Also, BBS activity is largely limited to sending and receiving files. You cannot send and receive e-mail with it. But for many of you, the simple ability to transfer files may be all the power you need. If not, you'll want to consider one of the dedicated host (or BBS) software packages.

From Here...

This chapter showed you the basics of how to purchase a new modem and software, how to send and receive faxes, how to network with another Mac with a modem, and how to get in touch with a BBS or even set up one of your own. A huge world of telecommunications opportunities is open for you to explore. The following chapters describe this world:

- Chapter 30, "Using America Online and CompuServe," discusses two of the most popular online services.

- Chapter 31, "Using eWorld," describes Apple's new consumer-oriented online service.

V

Reaching Out

Chapter 30

Using America Online and CompuServe

by Gene Steinberg

Once you are comfortable using your modem and telecommunications software, you will be ready to find sources for information and files, as well as exchange electronic mail with other users. An ideal source of these resources is an online service.

Picture an online service as something akin to many bulletin board services all rolled into one service. You have meeting places to share information and files, known as *forums*. You have places where you can read the latest news, check stock prices, and go shopping. There are special events, such as online conferences, where you can meet fellow users, and even industry experts and celebrities (we "met" the star of TV's "Brisco County" at a recent conference on America Online, for example).

On the surface, the two online services described in this chapter are as different as day and night. CompuServe in its raw form presents a command-line-based interface not dissimilar from the user group BBS pictured in Chapter 29. You navigate through the service by giving keyboard commands. America Online's user interface is graphic, offering point-and-click simplicity for its members, whether they are using a Mac or a PC. Two programs are available that provide a graphical front-end to CompuServe, however. This chapter discusses both of these programs.

In this chapter, you learn the following:

- How to join America Online and CompuServe
- How to gain the most from your online visits

■ Some neat and sometimes exclusive sources for information and software

■ A number of shortcuts and tips to make your online travels easier and more fun

How to Install America Online Software and Sign Up

America Online has not only become a Wall Street phenomenon with its popular stock offering but has experienced a huge membership growth. To join America Online, you can't just open your telecommunications software and sign on. America Online has its own proprietary software you use to log onto the service. Before joining, you must get a copy of the software disks. America Online's software is often bundled with a newsstand magazine, or even with new modems or telecommunications software. You can also order a copy directly from America Online by calling 800-827-6364.

America Online's system and hardware requirements are simple. You need a Macintosh with 4MB or more of RAM, running System 6.0.5 or later, and a modem. When you sign onto America Online for the first time, have the credit card you'll be using for the billing of your online charges handy (or you can have your monthly charges deducted from your checking account)—you have to enter that information in the text entry fields during the America Online software installation process. Your America Online installation kit includes a certificate that contains a special registration number and a password that you need to enter when you sign up for the service. At this point, make sure that your modem is properly connected to your Macintosh and a telephone line, and that it's switched on.

Installing America Online Software

America Online ships on a single double-density (800KB) disk. When you are ready to join America Online's online community, restart your Mac with Extensions off (hold the Shift key at startup under System 7), and then insert your first America Online disk. Double-click the Installer icon. The welcome screen shown in figure 30.1 appears.

Fig. 30.1
Preparing to install
America Online's
software.

Click the Continue button. You are asked to specify the location on your hard drive for installation of your new software. The entire installation process should take no more than a couple of minutes.

After your new software is installed, go to the location on your hard drive where America Online's software is located, and double-click the application icon. The opening screen appears (see fig. 30.2).

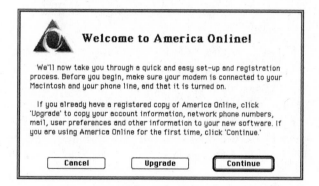

Fig. 30.2
Getting ready
to sign up as a
member of
America
Online.

V

Reaching Out

America Online's software probes your Mac's serial ports to see where your modem is connected, as shown in figure 30.3.

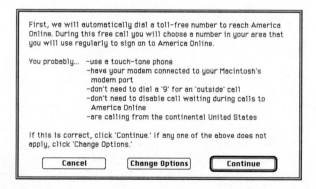

Fig. 30.3
Making sure that
your modem is
hooked up
correctly.

During the next minute or two, America Online tests your modem to determine what type of modem it is and the speeds that it supports. A high-speed
modem is generally specified as Hayes Extended, but you can choose a profile
from a list of popular models that may perform better with the one you're
using, as I've done in figure 30.4.

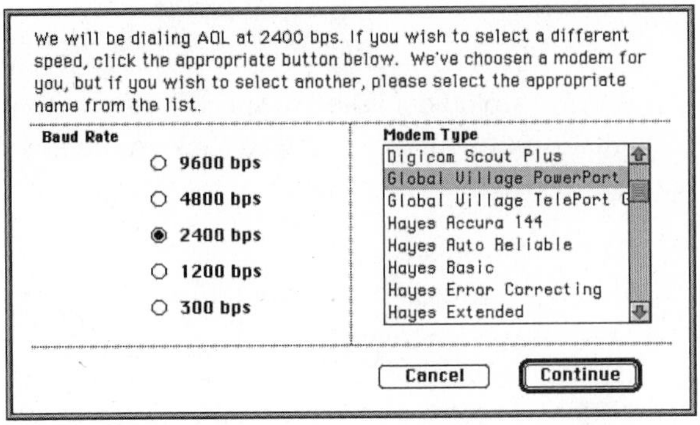

Fig. 30.4
Choosing the
correct modem
configuration
profile.

We will be dialing AOL at 2400 bps. If you wish to select a different
speed, click the appropriate button below. We've chosen a modem for
you, but if you wish to select another, please select the appropriate
name from the list.

Baud Rate

- ○ 9600 bps
- ○ 4800 bps
- ● 2400 bps
- ○ 1200 bps
- ○ 300 bps

Modem Type

Digicom Scout Plus
Global Village PowerPort
Global Village TelePort C
Hayes Accura 144
Hayes Auto Reliable
Hayes Basic
Hayes Error Correcting
Hayes Extended

[Cancel]   [Continue]

At this point, you can Connect to America Online's host computer by clicking the Connect button, or you can recheck your settings by clicking the
Cancel button and then the Setup button on the program's main window.
When you log onto the service for the first time, a procession of information
screens asks for your certificate number and password, your name, address,
and telephone number, and then your billing information (see fig. 30.5).
This procedure is explained further later in the chapter.

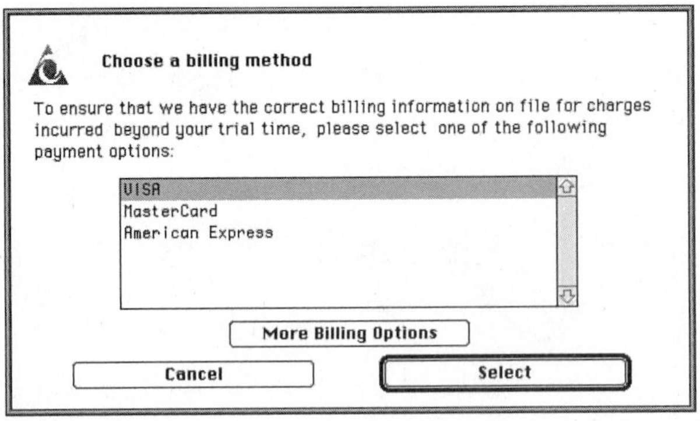

Fig. 30.5
Your America
Online charges
can be billed to
most popular
credit cards.

Choose a billing method

To ensure that we have the correct billing information on file for charges
incurred beyond your trial time, please select one of the following
payment options:

VISA
MasterCard
American Express

[More Billing Options]

[Cancel]   [Select]

As a final step before you log onto AOL for the first time, you are asked to
select your *mailing address*—your screen name. America Online's host computer suggests a screen name for you based on your first name and possibly
an initial for your last name, followed by numbers (if someone else already

has this screen name). At this point, you can accept the name offered by the software or select one that you consider more appropriate, at which point the host computer will check it against the membership roster to make sure that it's not already taken. Members typically choose a screen name that is an abbreviation of their real name or use a word that reflects some personality trait.

Then it's time to enter America Online (see fig. 30.6).

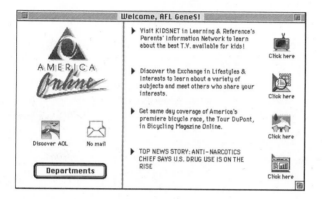

Fig. 30.6
After the sign-up process is over, it's time to be welcomed to the friendly world of America Online.

Overview of America Online Services

When you are signed up for America Online, it's time to log onto the service for the first time. Your first visit should consist of a guided tour, during which time you become acquainted with the service and look over features you may want to check out later on. If you have America Online's sounds turned on, as soon as your welcome screen appears, a voice announces that "You've got mail." Sure enough, you'll see a You've Got Mail icon on your America Online Welcome screen (see fig. 30.7). If you look closely at the upper right of your Mac's menu bar, you'll also see a flashing Mailbox icon.

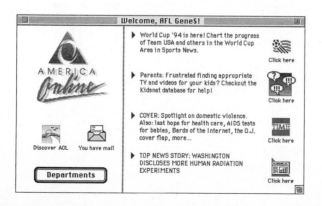

Fig. 30.7
Your first e-mail on America Online.

Double-click the Mail icon to view and read your new mail. Your first letter is signed by AOL president Steve Case. It introduces you to the service and offers a brief description of some of the special services you might like to check on your online visit. America Online's electronic mail features are discussed later in this chapter.

Look at the Welcome window, which contains a list of major online events. The top news of the day is displayed at the bottom right of the listing. The listing changes from time to time. Double-clicking the appropriate icon takes you to the source of the special announcement.

America Online divides its service into distinct departments so that you can easily locate the areas you want to visit. This sample visit takes you on a guided tour.

> **Note**
>
> The fastest way to get around America Online is to use a Keyword. You can type a shortcut by entering the keystrokes ⌘-K, which opens the Keyword window, and then enter the name of the place you want to visit.

A Brief Tour of America Online

The Discover AOL button, located at the left side of your Welcome window, is a handy gateway to previewing the service, learning more about America Online (as a company), and finding out about the new services being offered.

Fig. 30.8
Discover AOL, the quickest way to learn about the hottest features on America Online.

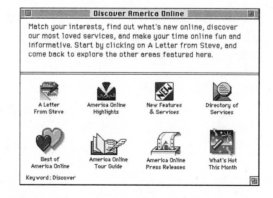

To begin your guided tour, click the Discover AOL button, which opens the window shown in figure 30.9.

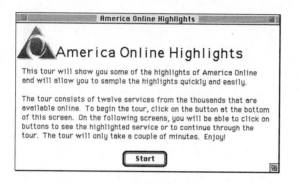

Fig. 30.9
America Online
Highlights, a brief,
guided tour of the
service.

When you click the Start button, you are taken through a procession of windows, each describing a popular feature on America Online (see fig. 30.10). To learn more about the displayed feature, you can click the Show button (at the lower right corner of the window), or click the left arrow to continue the tour.

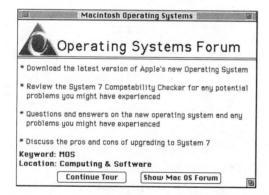

Fig. 30.10
One of the popular
computing and
software forums
on America
Online.

After you complete the tour, click the next icon on the list, the New Features & Services icon (see fig. 30.11). A list of the latest additions to the service appears. If any of the items on the list interest you, double-click the name. Within seconds, AOL's host computer will transport you to that area of the service.

Fig. 30.11
New features are
being added all
the time to
America Online.
Here's just a few
of the recent
additions.

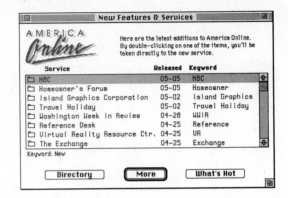

If you're in search of information about a topic or want to see whether a
particular interest is addressed by a support area on America Online, search
the Directory of Services (see fig. 30.12).

Fig. 30.12
America Online's
Directory of
Services allows
you to search for a
particular online
area.

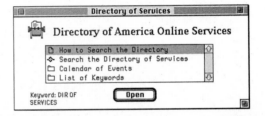

If you want to examine resources offered by America Online about the rapidly burgeoning multimedia area, for example, enter that topic in the search
field. The information shown in figure 30.13 appears on-screen.

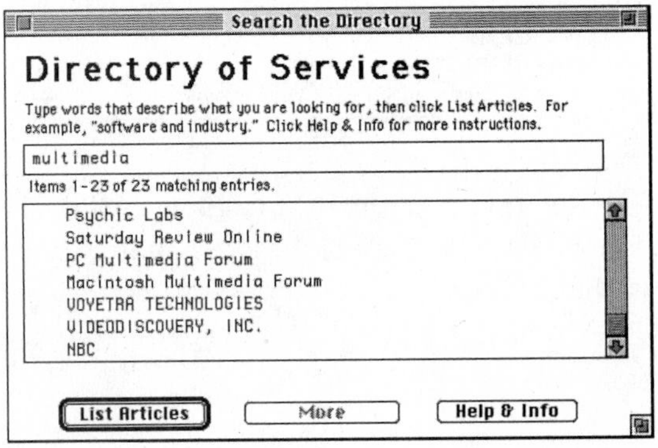

Fig. 30.13
Looking for
information on a
particular subject
is a snap with
AOL's Directory of
Services feature.

The next item, at the lower left of the Discover America Online window, is the Best of America Online area (see fig. 30.14). To find out more about a particular area, double-click the listed item. In some cases, you receive additional information about a new service, and in other cases you are taken directly to that support area.

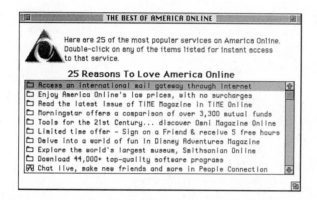

Fig. 30.14
The Best of America Online highlights the most popular features on the network.

America Online Departments

Now that you've had a brief tour of America Online's services, take a peek beneath the Departments button that appears on your Welcome screen and see what lies beneath it. This setup will change as new services are added, but the most recent setup is shown in figure 30.15.

Fig. 30.15
America Online, divided into nine separate departments.

Each department is clearly labeled as to its purpose. The following sections explore them one-by-one—you can probe beneath the surface later on. Each area has a directory of services listing at the right of the window. Double-clicking on a directory entry will take you to the service that's listed. On the

V

Reaching Out

right are icons representing the most popular visiting areas. The sections list the areas from left to right, exactly as the icons are displayed.

News & Finance
Keyword: News

The first area is News & Finance (see fig. 30.16). Each area of news coverage has its own folder, and inside that folder is a listing of the top headlines, along with detailed stories prepared by the major news services, such as Reuters.

Fig. 30.16
For the latest information from the front pages of your daily newspaper and the financial section.

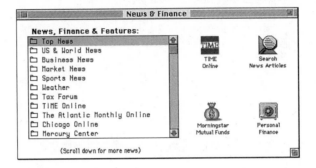

While you're online, you can also open the pages of the latest issue of publications such as *Time* magazine and read indepth features about the major events of the day, as shown in figure 30.17.

Fig. 30.17
Before it hits the newsstand, the contents of Time magazine appear on America Online.

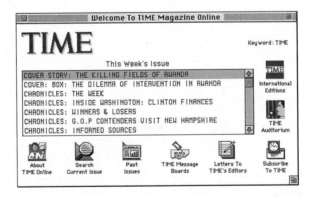

After you've explored *Time*'s features, or caught up with the day's events from on the national and international front, you may want to examine your stock portfolio. Just type the AOL keyword Stocks, which will open the Quotes and

Portfolios window. To start with, let's track one of our favorite stocks—America Online's, of course—as shown in figure 30.18.

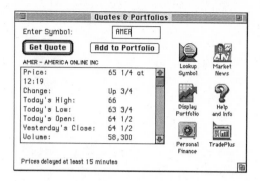

All the major stock markets are listed in Stock Market Quotes. During the daily trading session, quotes are usually provided with at least a 15-minute delay. Each company has its own symbol on the exchange to which it's a member, so you'll want to use the Lookup Stock Symbol feature (located at the top right of the Quotes and Portfolios window) to find the one that applies to your stock. The Add to Portfolio button (adjacent to the Get Quote button) is for information purposes only. You can use it to keep track of your favorite stocks. You do not have to purchase the stocks for which you want regular pricing information.

Entertainment
Keyword: Entertainment

The next stop on your online journey takes you to AOL's Entertainment area (shown in fig. 30.19), where you can read the latest news from the wonderful, wacky world of show business, find out what critics think of that new movie or video you wanted to see, or even take a few moments out of your busy day to review your daily horoscope.

Each feature shown in the directory window at the left of the Entertainment area's screen takes you to a different area on America Online. And after you check out those areas, you are given a whole set of additional options. This type of exploration is informative and fun. For now, let's review Book Bestsellers, as shown in figure 30.20, just to catch a peek at how our favorite books are faring on the sales charts.

Fig. 30.19
Information about
entertainment gets
top billing on
America Online.

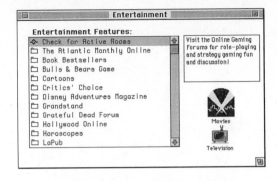

Fig. 30.20
Book Bestsellers on
America Online
lists the nation's
most popular
literary works.

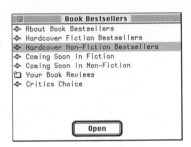

America Online's Entertainment area also includes special areas devoted to children, such as Cartoons and Disney Adventures Magazine. Children will be both entertained and educated when they visit these online locales.

Travel & Shopping
Keyword: Travel

Whether you have a business trip or a vacation in the planning stages, or you want to buy a new car or a new computer, America Online's Travel & Shopping department, shown in fig. 30.21, is a place you'll consult often for information and buying tips.

Fig. 30.21
Travel & Shopping
are featured in
one of America
Online's popular
departments.

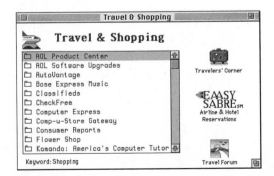

One of the most popular features among AOL's travel resources is American Airline's Eaasy Sabre, your own personal online travel agency. You can book airline reservations, car rentals, and hotel reservations from the comfort of your own home or office, without leaving your Mac's screen.

If you need help planning your travel itinerary, you'll find a wealth of information from which to choose. One resource is Travelers' Corner, shown in figure 30.22. Sponsored by the editors of Weissman Travel Reports, this forum offers profiles about your favorite U.S. and worldwide travel destinations in concise, easy-to-read form. And as with other areas on America Online, you can easily save or print the contents of a text window from this department.

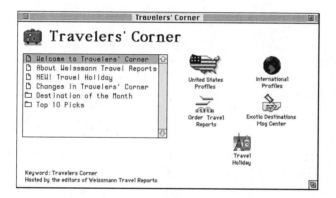

Fig. 30.22
America One's Travelers' Corner provides comprehensive reports about travel spots worldwide.

Since travel and shopping go hand in hand, you can also use AOL's vast information resources for updated information on new products before you plunk down those hard-earned dollars to make a purchase. One such resource is *Consumer Reports* magazine (see fig. 30.23). Many of the major test reports published in the magazine are provided in easy-to-read online form, including the annual auto issue.

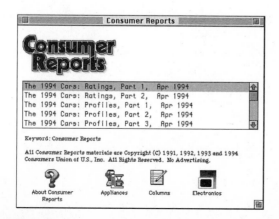

Fig. 30.23
Consumer Reports online, for updated information on new products before you make your purchase.

V

Reaching Out

Computing & Software
Keyword: Computing

Over the years, I've found many of the tips and tricks I've learned about my Macintosh in America Online's computing forums. Every aspect of Macintosh computing is represented in these forums, as shown in figure 30.24. And dozens of the major hardware and software manufacturers are represented in the service's popular Industry Connection area.

Fig. 30.24

America Online's Computing & Software center for both novice and experienced Mac users.

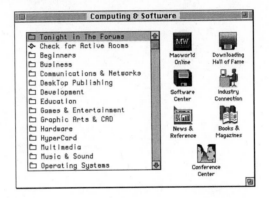

America Online provides a separate forum for each area of your Mac pursuits, from the Beginners Forum to a forum devoted to Mac Utilities. Each forum contains an active message area, huge software libraries, and regular conferences on all areas of Mac computing. The computing area even has its own special virtual auditorium, called the *Rotunda,* where noted Macintosh experts are often found holding special conferences.

One of the most popular America Online forums is the Macintosh Multimedia Forum, which covers everything from CD-ROMs to creating your own presentations and QuickTime movies (see fig. 30.25).

Fig. 30.25

The center of America Online's multimedia universe, the Mac Multimedia Forum.

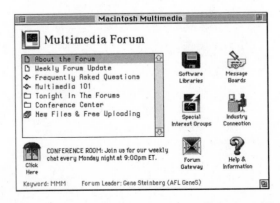

People Connection

America Online is not just a warm and friendly place to visit and receive information and files. You'll find a community spirit throughout the network, best exemplified by its People Connection area, a place where you can meet AOL members with similar interests or just hang out to spend the time of day.

The favorite hangout is The Lobby which is a public chat area where you can shoot the breeze with your online friends or just hang out, have a soft drink, and spent a little time (see fig. 30.26).

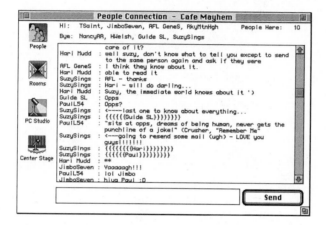

Fig. 30.26
The Lobby is your gateway to America Online's People Connection area.

With America Online, you can create a private chat room to have a private meeting with your online friends. Regular events are staged in the Center Stage auditorium, where recent conferences have featured show business personalities from stage, screen, and television as well as noted authors.

You can even have a private conversation with another America Online member whenever they're online by using an Instant Message, which is an interactive e-mail system (see fig. 30.27).

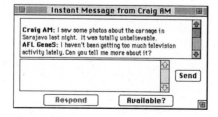

Fig. 30.27
It's easy to exchange an interactive message with an online friend using AOL's Instant Message feature.

The Newsstand
Keyword: Newsstand

You can make a trip to your corner newsstand on America Online by simply clicking an icon or typing a keyword. The Newsstand, shown in figure 30.28, is not unlike one you would find in your own home town. You'll find a selection of magazines and newspapers available. In addition, you can read daily commentaries from many of your favorite columnists.

Fig. 30.28

A quick trip to the corner newsstand on America Online.

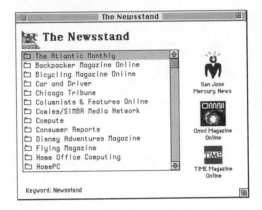

Many of your favorite magazines are located on AOL's virtual newsstand. And more are being added all the time. You'll find magazines on such diverse topics as audio, computing, current events, and science fiction. Major newspapers, such as the *Chicago Tribune*, *New York Times* and *San Jose Mercury News*, offer each daily edition and special lifestyle areas so that you can learn more about the cities they cover.

Lifestyles & Interests
Keyword: Lifestyles

The Lifestyles & Interests area is basically a combination of parts of AOL's newsstand joined with special areas devoted to wide-ranging subjects such as baby boomers, genealogy, ham radio, photography, and wining and dining (see fig. 30.29).

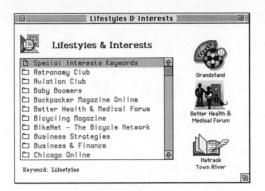

Fig. 30.29
Join a club or hang
out at in AOL's
Lifestyles &
Interests area.

Among the more popular areas are those devoted to the interests of senior
citizens and fans of Star Trek. If you have a gift for gab, you might consider
checking out the Express Yourself center. In this center, you can read about
active debates on a host of subjects, or, if you're so inclined, you can participate in a debate in the Issues & Debate Forum.

Learning & Reference
Keyword: Learning

If you have young children—or a young, active mind—you'll want to visit
AOL's Learning and Reference area, shown in figure 30.30.

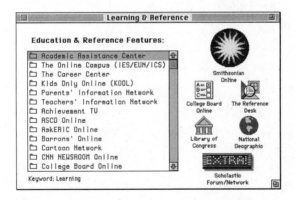

Fig. 30.30
AOL's popular
Learning and
Reference area.

The range of services offered in this area seems astounding. You can enroll in
college-level courses online, search the content of *Compton's Encyclopedia*, or
even seek interactive help from a professional educator to solve your
children's homework problems. That last feature is called *Teacher Pager*, by
the way.

Members Online Support
Keyword: Help

America Online is a service with a simple-to-learn interface—it's friendly and it's inviting. But sometimes you may run into difficulties logging on. Maybe the software is not working as it should, or you may be seeking information about your monthly bill. Whatever the reason, America Online has a free support area that offers the help you need. And if you need to converse with someone about your problem, you can meet with a customer representative online in a special live chat room and get immediate assistance.

Using America Online's E-mail Feature

The byword on America Online is *communication*. Millions of pieces of e-mail are sent throughout the service—and across the world—every month through AOL's popular Internet connection. Chapter 33 covers the Internet in detail.

Composing E-Mail

Composing e-mail on America Online is a simple process. First, you bring up the e-mail window, shown in figure 30.31, by selecting Compose Mail from the Mail window or by typing ⌘-M.

Fig. 30.31
America Online's e-mail form, for sending electronic mail across the globe.

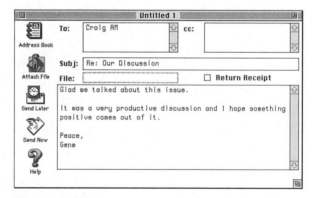

You first enter the screen name of the recipient of your letter. If you don't know the member's screen name, you can consult your custom Address Book, or search America Online's member directory by the member's real name. One or the other will usually bring you the screen name you want, as long as that person has an online address.

You can use any typeface that's installed in your Mac in the body of your e-mail messages, but if the recipient doesn't have the same typeface installed, the letter will appear only on the default typeface your recipient has chosen.

For more information related to fonts, see Chapter 8, "All About Fonts."

Attaching a File

To attach a file to your e-mail, simply click the Attach File button. America Online provides compression tools from StuffIt (published by Aladdin Systems) to create archives that reduce the size of your file, reducing the time it takes to send them.

Sending E-Mail

Before you send your e-mail, give it a subject. The subject is then followed by the contents of your letter.

Choose Send Now to speed your letter on its way, or choose Send Later to add the letter to the queue for dispatch when you log off through a FlashMail session. (The following section discusses FlasMail in detail.) To get confirmation when the letter has been received, click the Return Receipt button.

If the recipient of your letter is not a member of America Online, you can send it through the network's Internet Connection. Chapter 32, "Connecting to the Internet," discusses the special addressing requirements of Internet e-mail.

America Online Shortcuts and Hot Tips

America Online is a warm, friendly place, and the software is easy to use. If you want a complete how-to manual for the service, I suggest Que's *Using America Online,* 1994. I collected the following handy tips and tricks from that book that I think you may find very useful in your online visits:

- When you have a problem, check out the America Online's free Online Support area (Keyword: Help). Interactive online help is available in case you need to solve a problem right away.

- To get a quick reading of the amount of time you've spent online, type the keyword **Clock.**

- Traveling from one place to another on America Online is easy with a keyword. Just select Keyword from the Go To menu, or type ⌘-K followed by the name of the place you want to visit.

Tip

America Online's Address Book feature is a valuable tool—it enables you to build your own custom Rolodex of friends, acquaintances, and business associates. And this feature is extremely flexible. For example, you can send e-mail to a number of recipients at the same time, which is convenient when you want to notify business associates about a special online meeting.

V

Reaching Out

■ You can save and print any text window you open during your online visit by selecting Save or Print from the File menu.

■ You can use the Address Memo feature in your America Online software's Mail menu to convert a note you're typing to an e-mail window. Just add the recipient's name and the subject of your message, and you can send it on its way.

■ If you're on the road with a notebook Mac, you can quickly back up your data by sending e-mail to yourself on America Online and attaching the file you want backed up to the message. Chapter 36, "On the Road," discusses more tips and tricks of staying in touch while traveling.

■ America Online's FlashMail feature enables you to automatically log onto America Online at regular intervals, check mail, and receive files attached to your mail. You can schedule a FlashSession by selecting FlashSessions from the Go To menu, which will open the window shown in figure 30.32.

Fig. 30.32
FlashMail is a way to automate your America Online sessions.

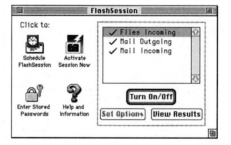

■ Using an Instant Message (⌘-I) enables you to have an interactive chat with another AOL member.

■ When you have problems logging onto America Online, check your modem. Make sure that it's hooked up properly to your Macintosh, and make sure that it's turned on. Recheck your modem connection profile in the Setup box (select the Setup box from the main America Online application window).

■ America Online has instituted a Parental Controls feature, which allows a parent to exclude access to certain online areas to their children. You can activate this feature in the free Online Support area.

Using CompuServe

CompuServe, a division of the large tax preparation organization, H&R Block, is the senior member of the online service team. CompuServe is huge, sprawling, and sometimes daunting for newcomers, but even its basic text interface is simple to learn and use. If you want to attach a graphical look to your CompuServe sessions, there are two programs—CompuServe Information Manager and CompuServe Navigator—that you'll want to check out further. This chpater discusses both of these programs.

How to Join CompuServe

You can join CompuServe in several ways. Special Introductory Membership booklets are packaged in a number of hardware and software packages. You can use your existing modem and software to sign up, and the membership booklet will give you step-by-step directions on joining the service, along with an offer of free connection time. A copy of the sign-up booklet can also be requested from: CompuServe Information Service, P.O. Box 21212, Columbus, OH 43220.

As an alternative, you can purchase a copy of the graphical frontend programs, CompuServe Information Manager, or CompuServe Navigator from your favorite software reseller. Both packages include information on joining the service, along with a temporary user identification number and password, which you need to enroll as a member.

Before logging onto the service for the first time, it's a good idea to have your temporary member information and your billing information at hand. You can use a major credit card,have the charges deducted from your checking account, or have your online charges billed to your business. Before attempting to sign on, make sure that your modem is properly connected to your Macintosh and a telephone line, and that your modem is switched on.

Using CompuServe's Standard Interface

After you join CompuServe, you can use your regular telecommunications software for your regular visits. You travel through the service or activate a specific function by entering a keyboard command at the prompt. When you run into trouble, there's an extensive range of member support services you can visit for assistance when the going gets a little difficult. Just type GO HELP at the prompt in your communications software, and you are taken to the network's customer assistance area.

Tip:
Navigation
on CompuServe
is easy, as long
as you know
the correct GO
word. To get the
current list, type
GOINDEX at the
prompt symbol.

CompuServe is divided into a number of departments, covering well over 1,000 different areas of interest. This chpater covers some of those areas, but the network is huge and it would take a large book to explain it all. If you want to learn more about CompuServe, I recommend Que's *Using CompuServe*. This chapter just touches on the highlights.

The first time you log on, you'll need to get used to CompuServe's text-based interface, which involves typing commands on your Mac's screen rather than clicking icons (although you can do that, too, by using the special software described later in this chapter). Most of the command prompts are simple to navigate. First you dial up your local CompuServe phone number, and then you enter your user identification number and password (see fig. 30.33).

Fig. 30.33
You navigate
through the
CompuServe
network by using
keyboard com-
mands.

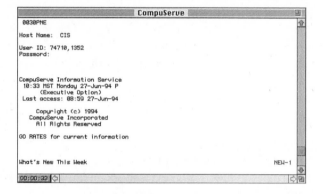

Once the welcoming text appears on-screen, you simply type your command at the Enter choice! prompt. The numbers at the left of the screen will take you to the listed areas. If you want to travel to a particular spot, simply type the correct Go word (which you can find by checking CompuServe's Master Index, explained previously).

> **Note:**
>
> CompuServe offers several service options at different rates. Some of the services shown in this chapter may require ordering an optional service. Contact CompuServe directly for the latest information.

CompuServe Departments

In order to simplify your travels through CompuServe, the areas are divided into a broad list of categories. Depending on your interests, you can confirm your visit to a single area or go from place to place as you prefer. As explained later in this chapter, you can even automate your online session by creating your own script consisting of your travel itinerary and review it offline with a program known as CompuServe Manager.

For now, this chapter concentrates on brief descriptions of some of CompuServe's most popular areas.

Macintosh Forums
Go Word: Macintosh

Macintosh users can choose from a number of forums, depending on which aspect of Macintosh computing interests you. Each forum consists of a message area where members, both novices and experts, can discuss problems, solutions, or even that fancy new piece of Macintosh hardware that's just come out. The second part of the forum is its software libraries. These libraries consist of new programs, both shareware and freeware, demonstrations of commercial software, and product updates.

When you enter the Macintosh area, you have a choice of which forum to enter (see fig. 30.34). As with a restaurant menu, you make your choice by typing the number displayed on the left side of your screen.

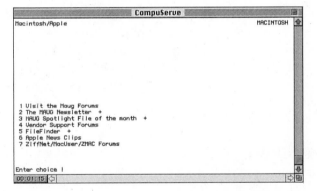

Fig. 30.34
CompuServe's
Macintosh
computing area.

If you want to discuss your favorite Macintosh programs, visit the Macintosh Applications Forum. You'll find the latest updates to Apple system software in the Macintosh Developers Forum. If you're new to the world of Mac computing, you may want to spend time in the Macintosh New Users and Help Forums.

Reference Library
Go Word: Reference

This CompuServe area allows you to literally have an encyclopedia at your fingertips and scores of text material from popular journals. The principle online reference is *Grolier's Academic America Encyclopedia,* which consists of 21 volumes. You can search articles on whatever topic interests you—for a research project, a homework assignment, or just to learn about something you didn't know before.

Shopping
Go Word: Shopping

Online shopping is an increasingly popular activity. You can find the merchandise you want at CompuServe's The Electronic Mall or by joining the Shoppers Advantage Club. You get discount prices, and you don't have to contend with traffic jams. If you need additional assistance before you make your purchase, you can read a copy of the latest issue of *Consumer Reports* magazine during your online visits.

Financial Information
Go Word: Financial

Whether you invest in the stock market, or just want to hear how your favorite company is faring in the marketplace, you can track their progress with an online stock quotation. You can also find a wealth of information on managing your money and getting the most out of your investments. As one example, Money magazine maintains a FundWatch Online area that reports on mutual funds.

Travel & Leisure
Go Word: Travel

Your travel plans are made easier with a visit to American Airline's Easy Sabre or Worldspan Travelshopper. You'll be able to make airline and hotel reservations and reserve a rental car right in front of your computer. The Zagat

Restaurant Survey will help you look for the best restaurants in the city you're going to visit—or even in your home town.

Entertainment & Games
Go Word: Entertainment

The latest entertainment news is available in CompuServe's Showbiz Forum. You'll be able to read reviews of the latest movies, videos and TV programs, and hear the latest juicy stories on your favorite stars, or catch up on what's been happening on a soap opera that you missed. The Gamers' Forum features discussions about your favorite games, helpful advice you'll want to use the next time you play, demo software, and even a number of online games.

News, Sports and Weather
Go Word: News

It's like having a newspaper at your fingertips, but you turn the pages simply by selecting the items that interest you. The major news services provide regular summaries and full features on the top news of the day. You can read about the exploits of your favorite teams, or check the latest weather in any city around the world.

We've barely scratched the surface here. The last directory of CompuServe services we read had over 100 pages describing the categories supported on the network, along with a listing of current Go words, to make your visits easy and fun.

CompuServe Messages

Before describing the software that will put a new look on your CompuServe sessions, I want to discuss one more very popular feature offered by this service—forum messages.

Messages on CompuServe are grouped by topics. You can post a new message or a reply to an existing message. Your reply becomes part of a *thread,* in which an original message and all of the responses are grouped together for easy browsing. Figure 30.35 shows a typical message thread.

Fig. 30.35
Messages are
grouped by thread
on CompuServe.

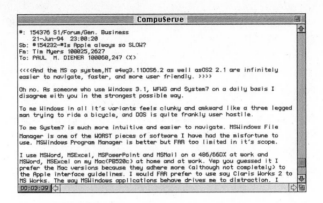

After reading this message, you have the option of replying directly to it or posting an additional message of your own. To follow the progress of an online conversation, you type **rr** to read the responses. If you want to skip that thread and read another topic, just press Return.

Using CompuServe Information Manager

CompuServe Information Manager (known to experienced users as MacCIM) allows you to put a pretty face on your CompuServe sessions, with a palette full of neat icons and status displays that greatly simplify your travels through the network. MacCIM frees you, in part, from the text-based interface and is apt to reduce your online charges, as well. You can purchase MacCIM at many software resellers, or download a copy directly from CompuServe. If you choose to download a copy, the charges will be billed to your account. The offer also usually includes an online usage credit.

Installing CompuServe Information Manager

CompuServe Information Manager will work on a Mac Plus or later, with 2MB or more installed RAM, running System 6.0.4 or later. The installer comes on two double-density (800K) disks and uses the familiar Apple installer for a simple one-click installation, as shown in figure 30.36.

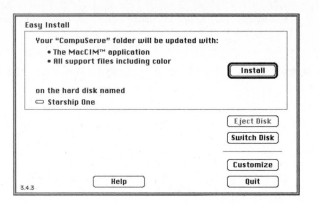

Fig. 30.36
Installing CompuServe Information Manager is a oneclick process, with a couple of disk swaps needed.

While the installation is progressing, Disk 1 is ejected and you are prompted to insert Disk 2. The installation process concludes with a request for Disk 1 to be reinserted. Your new software will be located in a folder that will be created by the installer on the drive you designate.

If you are not already a CompuServe member, launch the Signup application (located inside the application folder). This application opens the window shown in figure 30.37.

Fig. 30.37
The handy Signup application quickly sets up your CompuServe membership.

You are taken through a series of dialog boxes and asked to supply your billing information. You are also offered several membership options, so you'll want to proceed carefully to choose which type of membership you want. The decision you make now isn't etched in stone. You can always decide to add or eliminate an optional service at a later time, even change your billing method.

V

Reaching Out

Now it's time to launch your MacCIM application by double-clicking the application icon.

CompuServe Information Manager's Connection Settings

Whether you're a new member or an experienced CIS traveler, you'll need to adjust your connection settings for the best performance from your modem and to choose alternate connection numbers in case the first access number is busy. To configure these settings to your requirements, select Settings from the Special menu, and choose Connection from the sub-menu, which opens the window shown in figure 30.38.

Fig. 30.38
Setting up your automatic log on options with CIM's Connection Settings.

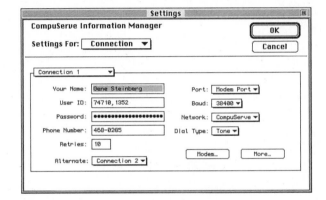

After you enter your name, User ID, password, and connection number, you can customize the program to your make and model modem. That setting is found by clicking the Modem button at the lower right of the Settings window. By default, a standard Hayes-compatible model is selected, but there are built-in profiles for a number of popular modems. If your model isn't shown, refer to the modem's manual for suggested adjustments or just use the default setting for now. CompuServe's support areas can suggest a different set of options for you, if it's necessary to improve connection performance.

Getting Around CompuServe with MacCIM

After you establish your connection settings, browse through the network and get used to your new software. Clicking the icons displays many of the major CompuServe areas you may want to visit. In addition, there's a Favorite Places to Go window that you can customize to your taste (see fig. 30.39).

Fig. 30.39
MacCIM's Favorite Places to Go window can be customized to show your favorite CIS stopping points.

The icons across the top of the window allow you to go directly to your selected area, or you can customize the window deleting one of the areas the program selects for you and adding some of your own. The major CompuServe services are displayed in icon form in the Browse window (see fig. 30.40).

Fig. 30.40
MacCIM's Browse window is divided into the major areas available on CompuServe.

Not all CompuServe areas can be displayed by icon; some require the standard command-line terminal interface. If you decide to visit such an area, MacCIM will automatically switch to Terminal mode (see fig. 30.41). You can then use keyboard commands to take you around that area. When you choose to switch to a department that supports an icon display, the regular MacCIM graphical interface returns.

V

Reaching Out

Fig. 30.41
Some
CompuServe areas
only support
terminal mode,
and MacCIM
switches over
automatically
when it's
necessary.

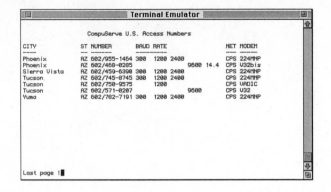

Where icons are supported, such as in CompuServe's popular computing forums, the display is simple and informative. Whenever new information is available for a particular forum, the Newsflash icon is highlighted, and you'll see a text display window offering information about features and upcoming events in that forum (see fig. 30.42).

Fig. 30.42
NewsFlash
window gives you
the latest news
about upcoming
events in a
CompuServe
forum.

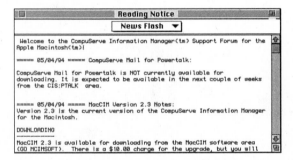

During your forum visits, you just click the appropriate icon to activate a function. If you want to examine a library, click the Browse Libraries icon. Icons also represent forum messages and allow you to enter a chat room.

Participating in CompuServe's message areas is a relaxing, informative and often entertaining process. You have the chance to share your views with fellow members, and with one of the visiting experts who are often found in a particular forum. Before deciding whether to post a message in a forum, browse one of the existing messages by selecting the Browse Messages icon, shown in figure 30.43, or select Browse from the Messages menu.

Fig. 30.43
Forum Status
window allows
you to visit a
particular area of a
forum by clicking
on aicon.

You'll probably want to read the messages one by one to begin with, but you
can also mark messages for automatic retrieval before you leave a forum. This
feature allows you to read all of the messages while you're offline, and even
compose responses, which can be posted automatically when you revisit the
forum. This is a time- and money-saving step. When you browse through
software libraries, you can also mark individual files for retrieval, as shown in
figure 30.44. When you leave an area, you receive a prompt asking whether
you want to transfer (or download) the files you've marked (or selected) to
your Mac before you go.

Fig. 30.44
Marking files for
automatic retrieval
involves simply
checking a
directory listing.

	Filename	Title	Submitted	Size	Accesses
	BLDSKR.SIT	Bloodsuckers 1.1- swat bugs before ...	5/8/94	461.5K	27
	POLYRI.SEA	Polyris 1.0.1 (sequel to Quadris)	5/7/94	54.5K	59
	QUADRI.SEA	Quadris 1.1.0	5/2/94	58.5K	217
	SHOOT3.SIT	Shooting Stack 3.0	4/29/94	195.5K	96
⊠	TETLIT.SIT	Tetris Light 1.0- small & quick Tetris	4/25/94	35.5K	88
	SNKBYT.SIT	Snake Byte- remake of classic Apple ...	4/25/94	453K	80
	POING.SIT	Poing 1.0- guide a ball over tagets w...	4/25/94	200K	63
	OPDIVA.SIT	Operation Diva1.0- Shoot-em-up m...	4/25/94	402.5K	169
	JETPAK.SIT	Jetpack 1.0- jet your player throug...	4/25/94	857K	95
	TETMAX.SIT	Tetris Max 2.3- 256 colors, great s...	4/24/94	825K	691
	MAELUP.SEA	Maelstrom 1.3.x -> 1.4.0 Updater	4/22/94	84K	242
	MAELST.SEA	Maelstrom 1.4.0 Installer	4/22/94	757K	196
	MAELPR.SEA	Maelstrom 1.4.0 Press Release	4/22/94	42K	62
	CHIRPR.SEA	Chiral 1.0.0 Press Release	4/22/94	79.5K	40
	FRKTET.SIT	Frank's Tetris V1.0.1- small on disk...	4/21/94	15.5K	77
	DM201U.SIT	Digital Messiah 2.0.1 updater and se...	4/21/94	36K	80
	CHIRAL.SEA	Chiral 1.0.0 Installer	4/20/94	1M	226
	SUPSLT.SEA	SuperSlithers 1.0.0	4/17/94	154K	149
	CLRFAL.SIT	ColorFall 1.01.sit - UPDATE!	4/17/94	88K	53
	PHETA2.SEA	Spacestation Pheta 2.5	4/15/94	157K	1121
	PHE2UP.SIT	Spacestation Pheta 2.x to 2.5 Updater	4/15/94	35.5K	57

Library Files — Info · Abstract · Mark · View · Retrieve · Delete
Browsing "Arcade/Action Games [2] "

Like America Online, CompuServe provides direct support for files compressed in StuffIt (.sit) format. If the files you retrieve are compressed in this
format, you have the option of automatically expanding them immediately
after you log off.

Using CompuServe Navigator

Compared to the other methods of interacting with CompuServe, CompuServe Navigator is like an automatic pilot system. You create a script, known as a *Session File,* and the program proceeds to execute the script by logging onto CompuServe and performing the actions you specify. You can use this technique to do things such as check the latest news, retrieve messages, and check for new files in a computing forum, and send and receive e-mail—all in the same session with no active intervention on your part.

Installing CompuServe Navigator

CompuServe Navigator will work on a Macintosh 512KE or later (running System 4.1 or higher). The program comes on a single double-density (800KB) disk and uses a one-button installation technique. You insert the application disk in your Mac's floppy drive and double-click the application archive (see fig. 30.45). You then are prompted as to where you want to install your new software.

Fig. 30.45
Double-clicking the icon begins the process of installing CompuServe Navigator.

Creating Your Own Session Script

After the application is installed, open the application folder and double-click the Program icon. A selection window similar to the one shown in figure 30.46 appears.

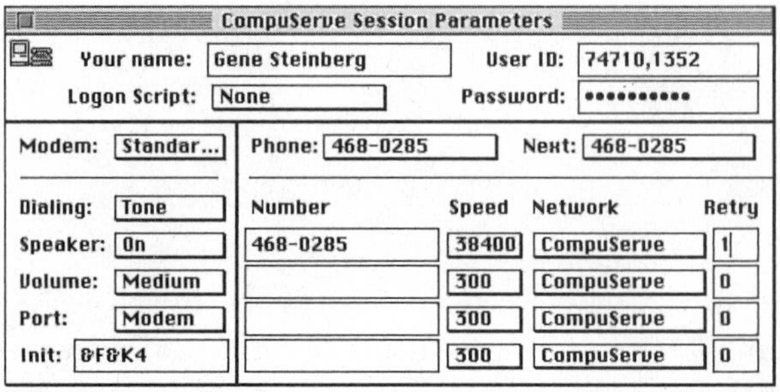

Fig. 30.46
CompuServe Navigator's selection window.

CompuServe Session Parameters

| Your name: | Gene Steinberg | User ID: | 74710,1352 |
| Logon Script: | None | Password: | •••••••••• |

| Modem: | Standar... | Phone: | 468-0285 | Next: | 468-0285 |

Dialing:	Tone	Number	Speed	Network	Retry
Speaker:	On	468-0285	38400	CompuServe	1
Volume:	Medium		300	CompuServe	0
Port:	Modem		300	CompuServe	0
Init:	&F&K4		300	CompuServe	0

Think of the selection window as your building block for your online sessions. It consists of tiles, each of which represents an special topic or interest on CompuServe. By double-clicking each tile, you can build your custom script for your visits to CompuServe.

But first you need to set up your session parameters, which is the information the program needs to work with your modem, dial your local access number, and log onto the CompuServe network. To set up your session, first double-click the CompuServe Session Parameters tile, shown in figure 30.47.

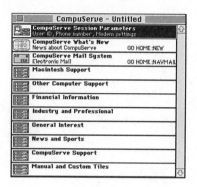

Fig. 30.47
Configuring CompuServe Navigator to your session profile.

First enter your name, user identification number and then your password. The password appears on-screen as round dots so that someone looking over your shoulder won't know what it is. Because anyone who has access to your computer can use the script, you might be better off in some work situations not entering your password so that the program requests it each time you begin your sessions.

At the left of the session parameter window is a list of modem setup options. Chapter 29 discussed some of these choices. If you dislike the squawks and squeaks your modem makes when it connects to a service, you may choose to turn the speaker off. The modem pull-down menu gives you the option of some standard modem setup strings, depending on whether you're using standard 2400 bps service or logging on at 9600 bps or 14,400 bps.

◀ See "Telecommunications Hardware," p.824

> **Note**
>
> CompuServe Navigator doesn't include a selection of special modem strings for popular models. If you have any connection problems, check your modem's instruction manual for information about special settings for use with this program.

V

Reaching Out

When your session parameters are established, close the window and begin to build your script.

After you establish your session parameters, the foundation for running your online session is built. Now you have to give the program something to do once you're logged onto the service.

Double-clicking each tile, as done in figure 30.48, gives you a range of options that become part of the script routine that's run when you log on.

Fig. 30.48
Pull-down menu sets up your CompuServe e-mail options.

Tip
As soon as you have finished entering your session information in the Navigator program, be sure to save your file so that it can be used again as often as you want.

In the preceding example, I am configuring the e-mail options. Each choice you select from this menu becomes a part of your connection script. The items with ellipses open an additional menu, enabling you to write a message or send a file.

After you make your e-mail choices, you can decide which forums you want to visit during your session. I selected CompuServe's popular Macintosh support areas, which include a number of computing forums, plus support areas run by major hardware and software manufacturers.

Each forum offers a window with three pull-down menus (see fig. 30.49). You click the menu to decide what to do during your forum visit, whether to visit the forum, post and receive new messages, or download specific files.

Fig. 30.49
CompuServe Navigator lets you automate your forum visits.

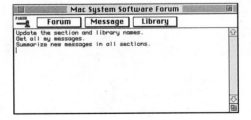

After you build your session script, examine it to see whether you need to make any changes before you run your session. Select the Preview command in the Session menu, as shown in figure 30.50. The script in the figure includes visits to many of the Macintosh forums, a check for e-mail, and a look at some of CompuServe's new online features.

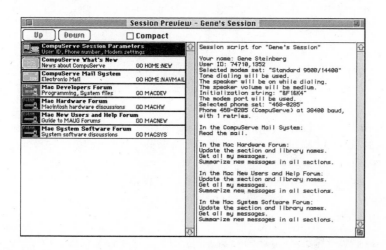

Fig. 30.50
Before you run your session script, it's a good idea to give it a once over.

You can double-click a tile to modify its routine. If you want to change the order in which your session is carried out, just click once in a tile to highlight it and click the Up or Down buttons at the top left of the Session Preview window to reorganize your session. Because your Session Parameters must be used at the start of your online visit, you can't change the order of that tile.

Last Step—Running Your Session

You have two options in running your session. You can do it right away by selecting the Run command from the Session menu. Or you can conduct your session at a predetermined time by using the Run at Time command, which brings up another window, allowing you to choose when you want your session to take place.

When the session begins, you can monitor its progress in a terminal window, as shown in figure 30.51. Each step of your session appears in that window, and you can then playback the session after you log off to review its progress.

V

Reaching Out

Fig. 30.51
Your first scripted online session is now in progress.

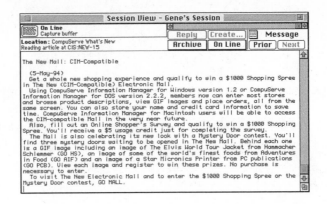

The script created in the preceding example is just a sample and uses just a small set of the scripting possibilities available to you when you format your session script. When you become more experienced navigating the CompuServe network, you'll find many options not touched upon in this section.

CompuServe Shortcuts and Hot Tips

Tip
When you have to do interactive work in your CompuServe Navigator session, you can activate the Terminal mode, which allows you to run your entire session manually.

After you spend a couple of hours traveling among the huge CompuServe network, you should be able to find the places you want to visit without difficulty. But here are a few tips on how to make your online excursions more productive:

■ When you have a problem, type **GO HELP** at the prompt to visit CompuServe's customer support areas. You'll find separate categories covering basic assistance with navigating through the network, retrieving billing information, and changing your password.

■ You can receive assistance on using your MacCIM software by typing the go word **MCIMSUP**.

■ You can receive assistance on using your CompuServe Navigator software by typing the go word **NAVSUP**.

■ You can save and print any text window you open in your MacCIM software just by selecting Save or Print in the File menu.

■ You can download any of thousands of high resolution graphics saved in CompuServe's GIF format and view them in MacCIM or many popular image editing programs, such as Adobe PhotoStop.

- Before you travel, you can obtain a list of your local access numbers for the CompuServe network with the GO word **PHONES**.

- As you develop a list of online friends, you can use MacCIM's Address Book feature to store their names and online account numbers.

- In order to make your online visits more productive, you can create separate session scripts with CompuServe Navigator, say one for business, one for Mac computing, and one for shopping.

- To quickly reach your favorite CompuServe area, enter **Go** [*name of area*] at any message prompt. If you're using CompuServe Information Manager, type ⌘-G followed by the name of the place you want to visit.

- MacCIM offers an easy way to return to the places you visit most often. When you're using a service, select Favorite Places from the Services menu to add that place to your Favorite Places to Go menu.

Conclusions: AOL versus CIS

Both America Online and CompuServe offer a broad range of information resources. You could probably choose just one of these services and be content. America Online's friendly graphical interface provides a sense of small-town community. Its popular People Connection area enhances this personal touch. Its price of admission is apt to be more pleasing as well. CompuServe seems huge and sprawling and sometimes expensive, but programs such as CompuServe Information Manager and CompuServe Navigator help bring the service down to manageable proportions and help you save money besides.

Many users maintain memberships in both services and log onto the one that best supports the features they are seeking at a particular moment. You may consider getting a trial membership for both to see which one best fulfills your expectations.

From Here...

This chapter offered a brief overview of America Online and CompuServe. It provided information on how to sign up and how to navigate through these services quickly and efficiently.

■ If you're a newcomer to the often complex world of modems and tele-communications software, see Chapter 29, "Getting Online."

■ Chapter 31, "Using eWorld," gives you an introduction and a few pointers about Apple's new online service.

■ Chapter 32, "Connecting to the Internet," tells you how to easily join millions of online travellers along the information superhighway and seek out discussion groups, information, and a bunch of Macintosh software.

■ If your online encounters cause you any problems with your Mac, check out Chapters 37, "Troubleshooting," and Chapter 38, "Preventive Maintenance."

Chapter 31

Using eWorld

by Gene Steinberg

In America Online's formative years, it was actually intended as an adjunct to Apple Computer's existing online service, AppleLink, and was to be called AppleLink Personal Edition. Instead, America Online went out on its own to become a major player in the online universe.

Now Apple has gone back to the basics, establishing its own consumer-oriented online service, eWorld, with software and a point-and-click graphical interface that is quite reminiscent of America Online. In fact, the eWorld software is licensed from America Online providing more than a few similarities, as shown in this chapter.

eWorld was first announced in late 1993 and became available during the spring of 1994. Apple's new service is distinguished from America Online with a more business-oriented approach. The service includes Apple's own support services (which were formerly only available on AppleLink), plus a number of magazine publishers, hardware and software publishers, and business information services.

eWorld has another unique feature that separates it from other online services: it can be accessed world-wide. And depending on where you log onto the service, you can interact with eWorld in French, German, or Kanji.

The metaphor of an "online community" is very apparent during your travels through eWorld. The artwork and interface appear very much like a small city, with buildings and shopping areas centered around a "town square," and a number of places to just relax and hang out. Apple calls this a *real world metaphor*.

In this chapter, you learn the following:

- How to order and install eWorld software

- How to gain the most from your visits to eWorld

- Some neat and sometimes exclusive sources for information and software

- A number of shortcuts and tips to make your online travels easier and more fun

How to Install eWorld Software and Sign-Up

Like America Online, eWorld uses its own proprietary software to log onto the service. So before signing on, you must get a copy of the software disks. A coupon for the software or a set of disks is packed with new Macintosh computers. Copies will also be available from resellers and mail order catalogs. In addition, you can request a copy of eWorld software directly from Apple Online Services at 800-775-4556.

eWorld's system and hardware requirements are simple. You need a Macintosh with 4MB or more of RAM running System 6.0.7 or later and a modem. Before signing onto eWorld for the first time, it's a good idea to have the credit card you'll be using for billing of your online charges handy because you have to enter that information in the text entry fields during the eWorld software installation process. Your eWorld installation kit includes a certificate or envelope containing a special registration number and a password that you'll need to enter when you initially sign up for the service. At this point, you should make sure your modem is properly connected to your Macintosh and a telephone line, and that it's switched on.

> **Note**
>
> Online services typically charge a basic monthly fee that may or may not include a period of time spent online. You may pay extra for additional hours spent using the service or for accessing optional services that are offered. Please contact the online service directly for current billing information before signing up.

Installing eWorld Software

eWorld usually ships on two high-density disks, but Apple will provide the 800K variety (double-density) if you request it. Now that you're ready to join eWorld's online community, restart your Mac with Extensions off (hold down the Shift key at startup under System 7) and then insert your first eWorld disk. Double-click the Installer icon. The welcome screen appears (see fig. 31.1).

Fig. 31.1
Preparing to install eWorld's software.

Press the Continue button. You are asked to specify the location on your hard drive for installation of your new software. During the installation process, you will receive some requests to insert or reinsert a disk, but the entire process will take from five to ten minutes to complete.

> **Note**
>
> If you use the Easy Install option, you will be presented with a dialog box asking to restart the computer at the completion of the installation process. If you choose a custom installation, you should still restart your computer before using eWorld software for the first time.

When your new software is installed, go to the location on your hard drive where eWorld's software is located, and double-click the application icon. The opening screen appears (see fig. 31.2).

eWorld's software will probe your Mac's serial ports to see where your modem is connected, as shown in figure 31.3.

V

Reaching Out

Fig. 31.2
Getting ready to
sign up as a
member of
eWorld.

Fig. 31.3
Making sure that
your modem is
hooked up
correctly.

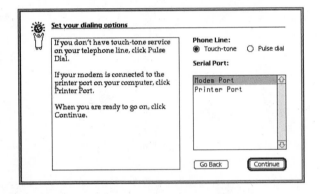

During the next couple of minutes, your modem will receive test signals to
determine what type of modem it is and the speeds that it will support. A
high-speed modem is generally specified as Hayes Extended, but you can
choose a profile from a list entitled Modem Type that is closer to your modem, as shown in figure 31.4.

Fig. 31.4
Choosing the
correct modem
configuration
profile.

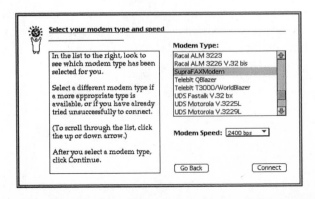

Signing Up

At this point you can Connect to eWorld's host computer or click the Go Back button to recheck your settings. After you log onto the service for the first time, a procession of information screens appears. You must provide your certificate number and password, your name, address, and telephone number, and your billing information, as shown in figure 31.5.

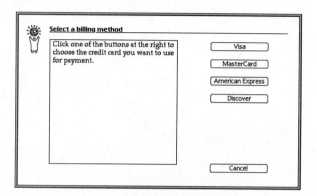

Fig. 31.5
Your eWorld charges can be billed to most popular credit cards.

The final information request from eWorld allows you to exercise your own creativity. You are offered a proposed screen name (your online address) based on your first name and the initials of your last name, followed by numbers (if someone else has this screen name already). At this point, you can accept the name offered by the software, or select one that you consider more appropriate, at which point the host computer will check it against the membership roster to make sure that it's not already taken. As with America Online, you might like to choose a screen name that closely matches your real name or one that reflects some aspect of your personality.

Then it's time to enter eWorld (see fig. 31.6).

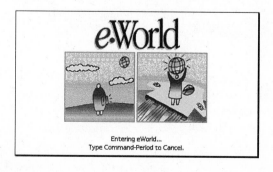

Fig. 31.6
After the sign-up process is over, time to pay your visit to eWorld's town square.

V

Reaching Out

Overview of eWorld Services

After you establish your eWorld account, the next step is to get online for the first time. Your initial visit is apt to be one of getting acquainted, to become familiar with the new interface and surroundings. As soon as your welcome screen appears, if you have eWorld's sounds turned on, a voice announces that "You Have Mail," and, sure enough, a little mail truck (it's red on a color monitor) appears at the bottom of eWorld's town square (see fig. 31.7). If you look closely at the upper right of your Mac's menu bar, you'll also see the flashing icon of a small mail truck.

Fig. 31.7
Your first E-mail on eWorld.

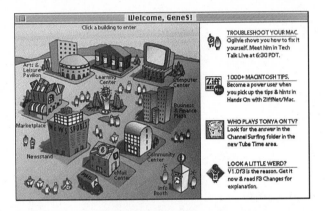

> **Note**
>
> When you log onto eWorld for the first time after you've established your account, there may be a short delay in entering the service to allow custom artwork for eWorld to be downloaded to your computer. It's stored in a special database file in your eWorld software folder. As artwork is updated to reflect new or improved services, there will be additional artwork transmissions, but most shouldn't take more than a minute or two to complete. The initial artwork transfer will take much longer than that, however.

Double-click the mail icon to view and read your new mail. Your first letter is simply a welcome from the staff at Apple Online Services, including a brief description of some of the special services you may want to check out on your online visit. Some of eWorld's electronic mail features are described later in this chapter.

At the left of your welcome window is a list of major online events, or even the top news of the day, as important events occur. The listing will change from time to time. Double-clicking the appropriate icon takes you to the source of the special announcement.

eWorld's town square is surrounded by nine buildings, each of which takes you to a specific area on the service. We'll visit each of these places during our brief online tour, but the names of these locales basically sums up their content. They include the following, from left to right on the screen:

- Arts & Leisure Pavilion
- Learning Center
- Computer Center
- Marketplace
- Business & Finance Plaza
- Newsstand
- Community Center
- eMail Center
- Info Booth

Whenever E-mail is in your mailbox, the little red truck pulls up just below the eMail Center.

> **Note**
>
> The quickest way around eWorld is a Shortcut. You can type a shortcut by entering the keystrokes ⌘-G, which bring up the Shortcut window, and then enter the name of the place you want to visit.

A Brief Tour of eWorld

Because eWorld is owned and operated by Apple Computer, you'll probably be eager to visit the service's Computer Center first. Double-click the building's icon (or just type the Shortcut **Computer**), which takes you to the area pictured in figure 31.8.

Fig. 31.8
eWorld's Computer Center, your gateway to Apple's online support services.

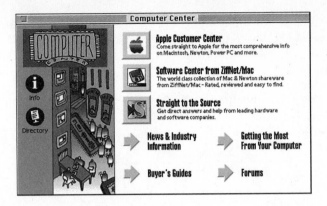

The Computer Center is a big resource for computer-related information and direct support from a number of hardware and software companies. This example goes straight to Apple's own forum. Double-click the big Apple icon, which will bring you to the area shown in figure 31.9.

Fig. 31.9
Apple's Customer Center serves both end-users and developers from around the world.

This section spends just a short time combing Apple's support resources. You can get the latest news about Apple products here, along with answers to your pressing problems. There is even a regular schedule of interactive conferences sponsored by Apple to talk about new products and provide advice on how you can get the most from your computer.

Probe a bit deeper now, into that gray arrow labeled Apple Products & Technologies, which takes you to the window shown in figure 31.10.

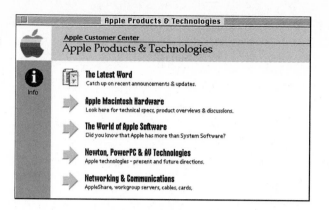

Fig. 31.10
Here's your
resource for the
latest news about
Apple's complete
product line.

Like most Mac users, you will probably want to explore the first category, The Latest Word, a little more deeply. It contains the latest information about the newest Apple products and hardware and software updates. This should be quite a popular spot, considering how often Apple is releasing new products nowadays!

Each of the remaining areas in this section is devoted to a specific type of Apple product. You'll be able to examine product specifications, get upgrade information, and learn more about Apple's strategies for the future. For now, return to the main window of the Apple Customer Center and click Quick Answers (see fig. 31.11).

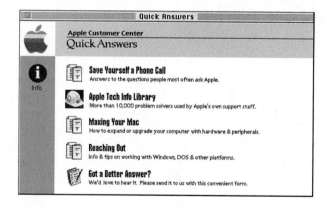

Fig. 31.11
Before calling
Apple Customer
Assistance, you
may actually find
the answers you
seek right here.

Apple's customer support people use a library of more than 10,000 Tech Info articles to find answers to vexing questions. That very same library is available to you on eWorld, in the Quick Answers section. You'll find information

V

Reaching Out

on a host of subjects ranging from (to cite just a couple of obscure examples) the use of composite SIMMs to what *sync on green* means and why it is not supported on newer Macintosh models.

Following are some more of the services that Apple is offering in this area of eWorld:

■ The *Save Yourself a Phone Call* forum provides a ready library of frequently asked questions and answers. As with other text items on eWorld, you can Save the text window for later review or Print the text, as you prefer.

■ If you want to get more mileage out of your computer, try *Maxing Your Mac*. This section provides information on the upgrade possibilities, such as adding more RAM, an additional hard drive, or attaching a scanner or CD-ROM.

■ *Reaching Out* is a section on connectivity, how to deal with the multiplatform working environment that contains Macs and computers running DOS, Windows, and other operating systems.

■ If you feel you have some valuable advice to offer Apple on the information you've received in this area, the *Got a Better Answer?* department is for your feedback.

■ The place that will probably be one of the most popular in Apple's Assistance Center is the *Apple Software Updates* library. According to eWorld management, eWorld is the only online service to offer the full available library of Apple software updates for their products. Clicking the Apple Software Updates icon in the Apple Customer Center window takes you to Apple's software library. You have a choice of software for the Apple II and Newton lines. Figure 31.12 shows the Macintosh software update library.

Fig. 31.12
Apple's Macintosh software update library.

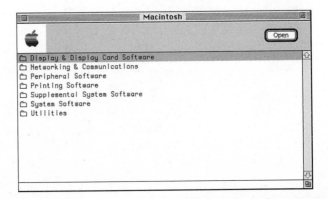

The software library is divided into several major product categories. The System Software contains system versions 6.0.8 through 7.0.1 (the last system version that Apple offered for free distribution). The Utilities library contains such items as Apple's Disk Copy program and other useful utilities. Networking & Communications offers the latest version of Apple's Network Software Installer and other product enhancements. Supplemental System Software contains a range of enhancement programs and maintenance updates that are released from time to time.

A number of other hardware and software manufacturers are represented in eWorld's Computer Center. They offer online support, product information, and software updates.

Arts and Leisure Pavilion

Shortcut: Arts

In the Arts and Leisure Pavilion, you can explore the world of entertainment, receive information on fine dining (including recipes), and learn about your favorite computer and video games. There's even a special Travel area that features Wish You Were Here. This forum, sponsored by Tribune Media Services of Chicago, offers travel news, tips, advice and other information you'll want to know before you pack your bags on your next trip. Figure 31.13 shows the Arts and Leisure Pavilion.

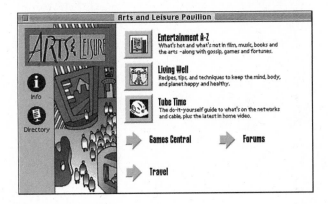

Fig. 31.13
eWorld's Arts and Leisure Pavilion.

In Pavilion's Entertainment AZ area, in addition to news and views on everything from books to television programs, you can find reviews of all the new movies. Figure 31.14 shows a review of a recent flick.

Fig. 31.14
eWorld provides refreshingly honest reviews you'll want to read before you visit your local movie theaters.

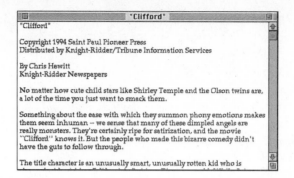

Gossip about favorite entertainers is often a hot subject. The Entertainment AZ area features the latest gossip, too. I checked out a recent selection of news items from The Hollywood Report, which reported on possible future projects from director Steve Spielberg and a possible film project for Michael Jackson.

eWorld's Tube Time! features the latest news about broadcast and cable TV, information about upcoming video releases and a very active discussion board for you to express your views about your favorite shows and videos (see fig. 31.15).

Fig. 31.15
Learn what's coming on TV and video in eWorld's Tube Time!

If you've been missing out on your favorite soap operas, or happen to like two that are on at the same time, you can catch up on all the steamy action you may have missed in Tube Time!'s Soap Opera Summaries.

Learning Center

Shortcut: Learning

The eWorld Learning Center contains a vast repository of information that you can easily search for most any topic under the sun, and maybe even subjects that extend beyond the sun (see fig. 31.16).

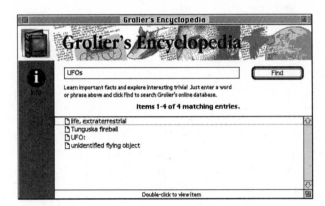

Fig. 31.16
A search of Grolier's Encyclo-pedia on the ever fascinating topic of UFOs.

Grolier's Encyclopedia, which you can reach in the Learning Center's main window, is just like having an encyclopedia on your computer's screen. You simply enter the information you want to search in the field at the top of the search window, and a list of articles on that topic appear in the list of matching entries. Now all you have to do is double-click the article title to view the article about that subject. As with all text windows on eWorld, you can Save or Print the contents of that window for later review.

Marketplace

Shortcut: Market

You've learned a little about your Macintosh, caught up on news and gossip on favorite entertainment topics, and even conducted a little research into eWorld's online encyclopedia. Now you're ready to go shopping with eWorld's Marketplace (see fig. 31.17).

Many of you have received Apple's Software Dispatch CD-ROMs. But even if you've not received a copy, or you don't have a CD player to view it on, you can examine the entire catalog on eWorld. You'll be able to learn about all the software products available through Software Dispatch, download demos of many products or place your order from the convenience of your own computer.

Fig. 31.17
The Marketplace
is a center of
shopping news
and information,
and an online mall
combined.

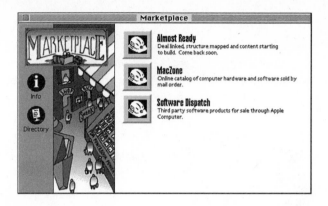

Another online store is run by the folks at MacZone, the same popular mail
order dealer who advertises regularly in many Macintosh magazines and
ships millions of catalogs through the mail. You'll be able to explore the
entire product line on eWorld, receive information about the products you
want to buy, and place your order, direct.

Business & Finance Plaza
Shortcut: Business

The Business & Finance Plaza provides information about how to handle
personal and business finances. eWorld's Business & Finance Plaza is a major
information center on the service (see fig. 31.18).

Fig. 31.18
eWorld's Business
& Finance Plaza,
where you can
learn how to save
and invest money
and examine your
stock portfolio.

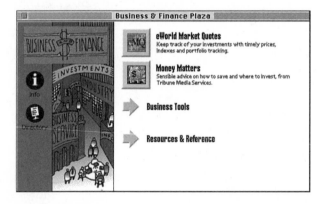

With eWorld's Market Quote service, you can keep up-to-date on current
stock prices. Figure 31.19 shows the status of Apple's stock as of the time this
chapter was written.

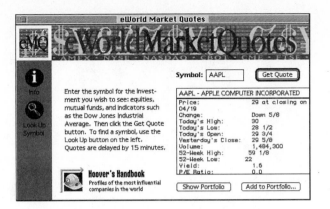

Fig. 31.19
During the trading day, here's where you can keep up-to-date on current stock prices.

Market Quotes covers the major stock exchanges. Prices are up-to-date within 15 minutes so that you can keep close tabs on your entire portfolio. Because each company has its own symbol on the exchange to which it's a member, you should use the Look Up Symbol feature, located at the right in the Market Quote window to find the one that applies to your stock. The Add to Portfolio button at the bottom of the Market Quotes window is for information purposes only, so you can keep track of your favorite stocks. You do not actually have to purchase the stocks for which you want regular pricing information.

If you want to learn more about a company before deciding whether to make an investment or just for general information, click the Hoover's Handbook icon (located at the lower left of the window) and enter the name of the company you want to know more about.

Money Matters is an online financial advice center (see fig. 31.20). You can explore tips on saving money, or look up information for savings or next year's taxes. You can see how to choose the best investment opportunities, and how to seek out the investment information you need as you build your portfolio.

Money Talks is a place where you can do the talking, a message board where you can share your experiences, learn tips from visiting experts, and hear what other eWorld members have to say. The Vault is the Money Matters auditorium, where regular interactive events are held featuring fellow members and financial experts.

Fig. 31.20
eWorld's Money
Matters forum, for
advice on counsel
from the world of
finance.

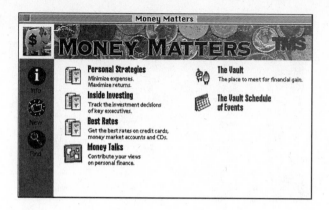

Newsstand

Shortcut: Newsstand

Another information resource is eWorld's online newsstand, shown in figure
31.21. Here you can catch up with the latest news from Reuters and other
sources, complete scores, schedules, news from the world of sports, and capsule summaries from USA Today.

Fig. 31.21
A trip to the corner
newsstand on
eWorld involves
the act of clicking
the Newsstand
building icon.

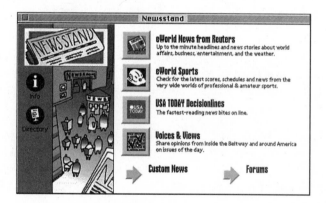

Voices & Views is a collection of articles from your favorite columnists on all
sides of the political spectrum. Because editorial cartoons are part of most any
newspaper's Op-Ed page, this area is no different. You can download GIF files
featuring cartoons by your favorite political cartoonists.

The Voices & Views area contains two more spots of interest. The first area is
The Soap Box, a message area where you can share your views about local,
national, and world events with fellow members (and sometimes a visiting

journalist). The second is The Press Gallery, an interactive online auditorium where regular events featuring fellow members and guest experts are held.

> **Note**
>
> A GIF file is a special image file that you can download and view on your Macintosh. eWorld's software libraries contain special GIF viewing applications that will allow you to open, view, and print these picture files. Some image editing software, such as Adobe PhotoShop, can also be used to view a GIF file.

Community Center

Shortcut: Community

When the time comes for you to just sit back and hang out after a long work-day, or just for a brief period to recharge your batteries, you'll want to visit eWorld's Community Center, shown in figure 31.22.

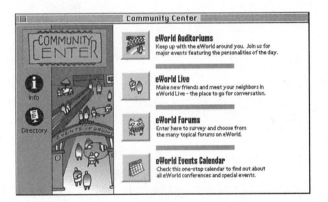

Fig. 31.22
eWorld's Community Center allows you to spend some leisure time with other members, join special events and learn about new eWorld features.

The Community Center has regular interactive activities in several online auditoriums. You can chat with other members and eWorld personnel. While here, you can check the Calendar for upcoming events, and Community Connection is an active, lively message board that you'll want to explore at your leisure.

The last item we'll mention here is Community Forums, which houses some special areas, including a special Disabilities Forum, which is designed to represent the interests of the disabled. The forum, shown in figure 31.23, is an important resource that you may decide to consult often.

Fig. 31.23
eWorld's Disabilities forum, part of the Community Center.

In addition to learning about new medical developments that will be important for those with special needs, there are regular live interactive conferences, message areas where you can share your views with others, and a vast library of useful information. We'll draw particular attention to The Trace Center Cooperative Library, where you can do special research to learn about over 18,000 products specially designed for disabled people, and consult medically related reports and other important documents.

eMail Center

Shortcut: eMail
Exchanging electronic mail is the focal point of any online service (see fig. 31.24).

Fig. 31.24
eWorld's eMail Center, a single repository of all your E-mail related efforts.

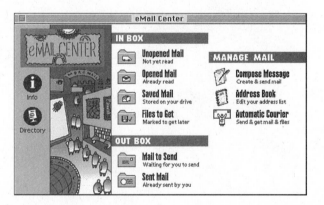

In the In Box, you can view all your mail, whether unopened or recently opened. You'll be able to retrieve files attached to your E-mail from here. You'll want to consult the Out Box for information about mail you've just sent, and recheck mail before it goes to its recipient. If the letter you've sent has not yet been read, you have the chance here to Unsend or delete it now.

eWorld's E-mail capability has some especially interesting slants to it, so we'll devote some attention to that, as shown in figure 31.25. First let's click on the Compose Message icon (or simply type Command-N).

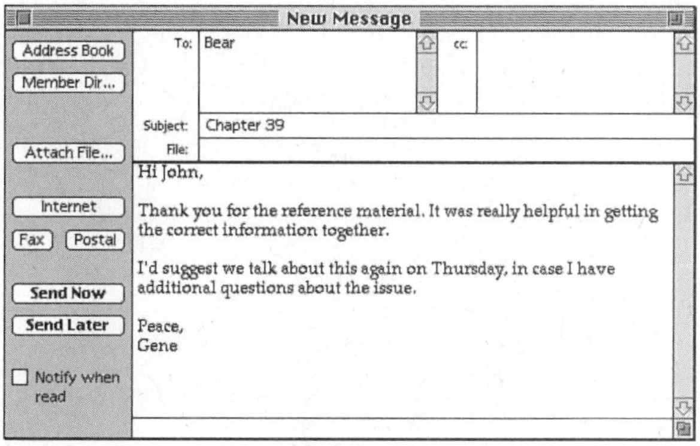

Fig. 31.25
With eWorld, creating new E-mail is a snap.

To send E-mail messages, you first must enter the screen name of the recipient of your letter. If you don't know the member's screen name, consult your custom Address Book or search eWorld's member directory by the member's real name. If that person has an online address, one method or the other will usually bring you the screen name you want.

> **Note**
>
> You can use eWorld's Address Book feature to build your own custom Rolodex of friends, acquaintances and business associates. You can send E-mail to a number of recipients at the same time, which is useful when you want to notify business associates about a special online meeting, for example.

Each message has a subject followed by the contents of your letter. You can use any typeface installed in your computer in your E-Mail messages, but take into consideration whether the recipient has the same typefaces. Otherwise, the letters will show up in the default typeface the recipient of your E-mail has selected.

If you want to attach a file to your E-mail, simply click the Attach File... button. eWorld provides compression tools from StuffIt (published by Aladdin Systems) to create archives that reduce the size of your file, and thus reduce the time it takes to send them.

V

Reaching Out

You can use the Send Now command, which will dispatch your letter on its way, or the Send Later command, which adds the letter to the queue for dispatch when you log off from an Automatic Courier session. (This procedure is discussed in more detail later in this section.) If you want confirmation that the letter has been received, click the Notify when read button.

If the person you want to write to doesn't have an online address (on eWorld or any other service), you can have your letter sent by Fax or Postal mail (which is an extra cost option). Your final address option is one that is discussed in more detail in Chapter 33, "Connecting to the Internet." For now, just click the Internet button to bring up the set of instructions shown in figure 31.26.

Fig. 31.26
Sending your eWorld mail through the Internet.

You have to follow a special format for sending Internet E-mail, which is described in more detail in the following chapter. You cannot attach files to Internet mail, nor do you have the option to remove, or *Unsend*, mail before it has been read.

Finding Your Way Around

In addition to clicking building icons and checking out the available services, you can create your own custom Shortcuts for eWorld places you visit often. The Places menu has a selection where you can Edit Your Shortcuts (see fig. 31.27).

The first field gives you the name of the eWorld area, and the second names its Shortcut. If you are unsure of a shortcut for a particular place, simply bring up the Shortcuts window by selecting Go To Shortcut from the Places menu, or typing Command-G. If you're unsure of which Shortcut to use, select from the list at the left of the text entry field, as shown in figure 31.28.

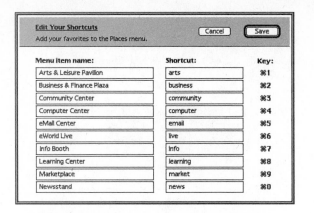

Fig. 31.27
Once you get used
to eWorld, you'll
find places you
want to check out
regularly.

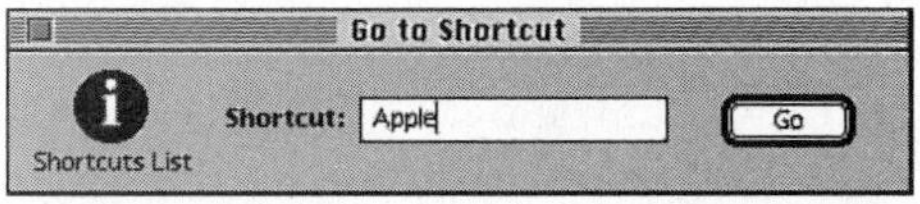

Fig. 31.28
eWorld's Shortcut
menu gets you
where you want to
go as quickly as
possible.

You can add up to ten Shortcuts, all accessed by the Command key, plus a number from 1 through 0. You can stick with the choices that have been selected for you or pick your own.

When your visit to eWorld is over, simply select Quit from the File menu or press ⌘-Q. You'll see a confirmation window asking if you really want to disconnect from eWorld. You have the option of logging off and leaving the application open for connecting again at a later time, or just quitting the program.

eWorld Shortcuts and Hot Tips

After you've spent a couple of hours traveling among the eWorld community, you should be able to find the places you want to visit without difficulty. Following are a few tips on how to make your online excursions more productive:

- When you have a problem, check out the eWorld Info Booth (Shortcut: Info), as shown in figure 31.29. You can get quick assistance with your questions, ready solutions to your problems, and examine your current bill.

V

Reaching Out

Fig. 31.29
eWorld's Info Booth provides the help you need when you have questions about your bill or navigating the service.

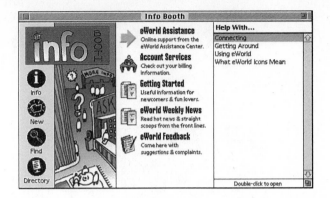

■ For a quick refresher course on what eWorld's unique information icons mean, drop by the Info Booth and click the What eWorld Icons Mean listing in the Help With at the right of the Info window, as shown in figure 31.30. For a ready explanation on what a specific icon signifies, simply click that icon.

Fig. 31.30
eWorld's icons explained.

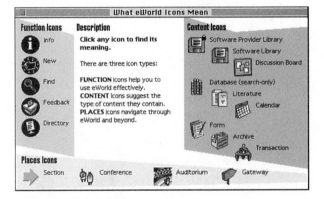

■ You can save and print any text window you open in your eWorld software, just by selecting Save or Print in the File menu;

■ If you have eWorld and you have Newton Mail, you can share the very same mailboxes on both services.

■ As you travel from place to place, you can change the modem profile, using the service's Locality feature in the File menu.

■ You can automatically log onto eWorld at regular intervals, check mail and receive files attached to your mail through the service's Automatic Courier feature. Setup is done by selecting Automatic Courier from the eMail menu, which will bring up the window we've shown in Figure 31.31 below.

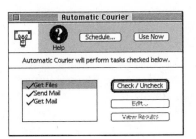

Fig. 31.31
Setting up your regular E-mail sessions on eWorld is easy with Automatic Courier.

■ eWorld allows you to not only attend online conferences, but through its One on One feature, have an interactive conversation with a fellow eWorld member. You can open a One on One window right from the Membership menu, or by typing ⌘-E.

■ For a complete calendar of upcoming eWorld events you'll want to attend, visit the Community Center.

■ If you cannot get connected to eWorld, check your modem, make sure that it's hooked up properly to your Macintosh, and make sure that it's turned on. Recheck your modem connection profile in the Setup box that's reached from the main eWorld application window.

■ If you need help getting connected, call eWorld customer service at 800-775-4556. Telephone lines are staffed Mondays through Fridays from 6:00 a.m. to 6:00 p.m. Pacific Time.

How Does eWorld Compare to Other Online Services?

If you're a member of America Online, you will find many similarities in eWorld's software. These similarities will make the process of getting used to eWorld easy. Past the surface resemblances, however, Apple has many changes in artwork and the way the user interacts with the online service.

The initial iteration of eWorld has more of a business orientation than America Online. Although eWorld offers games, entertainment, and travel information, it does not offer a true equivalent of America Online's popular People's Connection at this stage in the new service's development.

eWorld exploits its Apple connection to great advantage, which is one of its major advantages over other online services. Apple's Customer Assistance Center is designed to provide all of the services previously offered through AppleLink, and AppleLink memberships are gradually being folded into eWorld. In addition to the technical information that has been offered to dealers and developers over the years, Apple is providing a full slate of consumer information services as well, so you'll have full time access to information about your computer should you need additional information or run into some sort of difficulty. You'll also be able to easily locate the official Apple software updates and utilities that are often difficult to come by elsewhere.

Even if you already have a membership with the other online services, you'll want to consider adding eWorld, not just because of the availability of Apple information, but because of its own unique interface and range of services.

From Here...

This chapter introduced you to Apple's new online service, eWorld. You learned how to sign on for the first time, as well as information about some of its major features. The chapter even gave you a few hints to make your eWorld visits more worthwhile.

- Chapter 30, "Using America Online and CompuServe," provided a few pointers about two of the USA's largest online services.

- Chapter 32, "Connecting to the Internet," tells how you can easily join millions of online travelers along the information superhighway and seek out discussion groups, information, and a great deal of Macintosh software.

- If your online encounters cause you any problems with your Mac, check out Chapter 37, "Troubleshooting," and Chapter 38, "Preventive Maintenance."

Connecting to the Internet

by Gene Steinberg

In the preceding three chapters, you learned how to telecommunicate on your Mac, how to set up your own BBS, and how to join and use three of the major national online services. And that's only the beginning.

Imagine joining a worldwide bulletin board or online service with more than 15 million members, with a software library consisting of hundreds of thousands of files, an information repository consisting of millions of messages, and daily global transfers of electronic mail numbering in the millions of transactions.

Imagine being able to reach that worldwide repository of information, discussion groups, and software libraries right from the desktop of your Mac, no matter which model you have, no matter which system software version you are using, and no matter where in the world you might be at any given moment. All you need is software, a modem and a telephone line (or other network connection), and you can join the true center of our information superhighway universe, the Internet.

In this chapter, you learn the following:

- ■ The history of the Internet

- ■ Simple ways that you can access and use the Internet

- ■ What services are available on the Internet and how to use them

- ■ What those strange Internet commands mean

The History of the Internet

At the very minimum, the word Internet describes the interconnection between two networks. But when we look back to the origins of what we call the Internet, we see the very beginnings of computer networking in general. Even your local user group BBS or one of the commercial online services owes much in the way it's run to the shape and form that the Internet has taken.

At first, like so many endeavors that ended up in the hands of civilians, the Internet began in the late 1960s as a government project, under the aegis of the U.S. Advanced Research Projects Agency. It was known then as ARPANET, and it was an experiment to learn the best methods to exchange data among remote computers. At first, the new computer network was installed on four educational institutions located in California and Utah.

The next step in the growth of the Internet occurred in the 1970s, as networking methods or *protocol* were developed to enable computers of all shapes, sizes, and operating systems to communicate with each other seamlessly. The outgrowth of this work resulted in a technique known as *packet switching,* in which computer data is reduced to small pieces, or *packets*, and sent out across the network. Each packet contains information about its origin and ultimate destination. When this data reaches its destination, the address information is removed from all of the little pieces and they are then put back together into their original form.

The local telephone number you use to dial up your favorite online service is known as a *packet switching node* that is able to send the data between your computer and the services host computer. All of this complex magic is done behind the scenes. All you need is your Macintosh, some communications software, and a modem.

Step Two

Because it began as a government-supported project, network traffic in the early stages of the Internet consisted of civilian and military information. The burgeoning network became popular with scientists and other researchers who used it to engage in correspondence, known as electronic mail, or e-mail for short, with their colleagues, and to send information files. Central computers or sites were established in which to store files, using the File Transfer Protocol (or ftp), which we'll discuss in more detail later in this chapter.

Individual e-mail exchanges also blossomed into mailing lists, in which information was sent to a large number of users, in the form of collections of correspondence, articles and reports. Internet users with special interests created

Usenet (*users network*) discussion groups in which messages were posted about their favorite topics and responded to by other users.

Preparing for the Future

By 1983, the burgeoning network was split into two parts—one was dedicated to military use and and the other was dedicated to civilian use. The method used to transfer data along the network is called *Transmission Control Protocol/Internet Protocol* (or TCP/IP for short).

Today, the Internet stretches beyond the borders of any single country. It has no central authority or governing body. It knows no limitations in terms of the type of computer or the operating system it uses. So the user of a Macintosh Running System 7.5 can easily communicate with another user who has a mainframe computer or even an IBM clone running OS/2, to name just a few examples. Ancient boundaries of gender and race are also less relevant on the Internet, which has become truly a global community.

Accessing the Internet

At one time, getting Internet access was difficult. You had to work at a place where access was available, or be able to log onto a network at a local educational institution, or even set your own computer up as an Internet server. It wasn't always a terribly cost effective proposition either. But times have changed. Many low-cost options are available now to most anyone who wants to explore the Internet. The major online services, such as America Online and CompuServe, are rapidly rolling in greater access to Internet services. They have also set aside special forums or meeting places to offer advice to newcomers to get over the rough spots.

This chapter is designed to introduce you to the Internet and to help you get started with your Internet access. It would take a large book to cover the length and breadth of the information and services the Internet offers. At the end of this chapter, a few books about the Internet are recommended.

For now, get ready to travel across the Internet from the comfort of your own home or work area and your own Macintosh.

Your Internet Mailing Address

If you are already a member of an online service with Internet access, you already have a screen name or number, and it's very easy to adapt that address for Internet use. An Internet mailing address contains your screen address followed by the location of the service you are using to access the Internet, which is referred to as the *domain*. The address is generally specified in lowercase letters and numbers.

A typical Internet mailing address, for example, may be typed as follows: **aflgenes@aol.com**, which refers to someone with an America Online address, or **74710.1352@compuserve.com**, which refers to someone who is a member of CompuServe.

The information at the left of the @ character is your account name or number, and the information to the right of the @ is the domain. Notice that the domain identifies not just the name of the service but contains a suffix that identifies the kind of service it is. Following are some examples:

- *gov* refers to government-affiliated.

- *edu* identifies a university or other educational institution.

- *com* refers to a commercial or industrial entity.

- *mil* refers to the military.

- *org* refers to a organization such as a user group.

- *net* refers to a network or service center.

Note

Sometimes a geographic domain is used rather than an organizational domain. This often applies to Internet addresses originating outside the U.S.A. In these situations, you will find a two-character country code added at the end of the address, such as .US for the United States and .CA for Canada.

If you are unsure how to address your electronic mail, check with your service provider for the information. Sending Internet e-mail through one of the major online services is similar to sending it to another member of that service, except for the way that the address is entered. The content of the letter will have a subject and then the content, just like the letters you normally send through your electronic mail service.

What is Netiquette?

No doubt upon gaining Internet access, you'll want to jump into one of the ongoing discussions, in one of the Newsgroups or IRCs (Internet Relay Chat). The IRC is described later in this chapter. Over the years, the Internet, though largely unregulated and unsupervised, has developed some forms and conventions you should know about before jumping into an online discussion.

Following are a few tips based on hard-won experience on the "net":

- ■ You will be tempted to jump in on a discussion that interests you. Our advice is don't. Spend a little time reading messages or following discussions. Quite often there will be a set of FAQs (Frequently Asked Questions), text files that will provide a list of ground rules for a specific discussion group, and responses to typical user questions. After you develop a feel for the flavor of a particular group, then it's time to consider posting a message of your own.

- ■ There are literally thousands of Newsgroups and many IRC groups (referred to as *channels*). The number of messages you are likely to encounter is in the hundreds of thousands. You can quickly become overwhelmed by the sheer volume of information if you don't pick and choose carefully. To begin with, you should restrict yourself to only a small number of discussion groups, take time to digest the messages, and only add more when you feel you can devote the time necessary to follow up all of the information you'll receive.

- ■ When you respond to a message, consider that you are not just posting a response to a single person, but to an audience that could number in the millions. If you decide you want to restrict your audience to a single person, send that person e-mail instead.

- ■ Before writing your message, carefully choose the appropriate forum. It wouldn't necessarily be a good idea to promote the use of a Macintosh in a discussion group oriented towards users of Microsoft Windows, for example, unless you want to risk generating a lot of ill-will.

- ■ Show respect and be polite when you post a message. If you disagree with someone's statement, try to stick to the issues, and refrain from personal attack. Such attacks are regarded as "flaming," and while they may be entertaining on some television talk shows, they are not considered good taste on the Internet.

- ■ When responding to someone else's message, quote the relevant portions of that message at the beginning of your response, or before each part of your message that refers to that message. The usual convention is to place a *forward* sign, or to signify a quote mark, at the beginning of each line, as follows:

V

Reaching Out

```
>I've access to a Mac Centris 610.
>When I try to run Norton Speed Disk,
>I get "System files not supported in System 7"
>Where can I get an update of Norton, or
>is this software now obsolete/upgraded/replaced??????
```

■ If you are accessing the Internet from one of the commercial online services, your Internet address (which was described earlier in this chapter) can be used as your personal signature, but your name and affiliations may be placed there as well, as shown in figure 32.1. Some users also include their address and phone number, but before you do this, consider whether you feel that you want to give this information out to millions of strangers. Others add a statement or "motto" that reflects some aspect of their personality. Before preparing your own signature, you might want to see how others do it first.

Fig. 32.1

Typical Usenet newsgroup signature. The information below the signature is the long and twisted path taken by the message before it reached its destination.

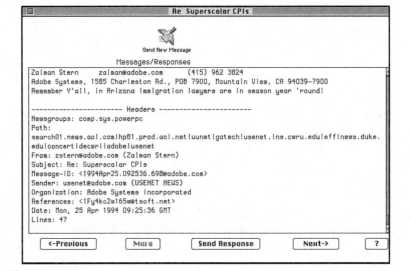

■ Keep your messages short and to the point. You are reaching an audience of millions of people, and you don't want to waste anyone's time, since many users pay high charges for Internet access. Also try not to cross-post, and send your message to more than one newsgroup at a time (unless you feel it's really necessary).

■ Choose a subject title that really describes the topic of your message. It is better to use "Type 1 Crash in System 7.1" than "System Crash" if you are seeking advice on solving a problem in a Macintosh newsgroup.

■ Express emotions and humor with care. When you speak with someone in person, very often body language and the inflection of your voice would reveal whether you are serious or not, or whether you are angry or happy about something. On the Internet, your words alone must be the mirror of your feelings. Experienced online users express emotions with *smileys* (:)). If you look at these symbols sideways, they look like a smiling face. Variations on the basic smiley include ;-) and :-(and many more.

■ Before you respond to a message, take the time to see whether someone else has already answered it. Time on the busy Internet is at a premium, and reading the same sort of message over and over again wastes everyone's time, including your own.

Internet Access Through Netcom

The simplest way to access the Internet is through a service provider, a facility much like a bulletin board service that specializes in Internet connection. A number of local and national firms offer this sort of access. Each provider offers its own suite of services, with charges ranging from fixed monthly rates to hourly fees, depending on the level of access you want. Usually all you need to connect is a modem and telecommunications software, such as the kinds we discussed in Chapter 30, "Getting Online." This chapter uses Netcom On-Line Communication Services as an example of how you can reach the Internet.

Basically, the server provider is setting up the Internet connection using its own facilities. You simply use your Macintosh, your modem, and your communications software to log onto that service in the same way you would log onto any other online service. But you're apt to find differences, because a service such as Netcom is command-line based and does not provide the familiar graphical interface that is familiar to a Mac user.

◀ See "Getting Online," p. 823

Following is a typical Netcom online session in which you explore some of its features and even download (ftp) a file from Apple's own ftp server. For more information about signing up for Netcom access, call (800) 501-8649.

You begin your session by launching your telecommunications software, and having the program dial up the service providers local access number. After you connect, the prompt shown in figure 32.2 appears.

Fig. 32.2

The front door of
your Internet
service.

```
┌──────────────────────────── BBS ────────────────────────────┐
│ OK                                                           │
│ ATDT222-3900                                                 │
│ CONNECT 14400/ARQ                                            │
│                                                              │
│ netcom11 login: genes                                        │
│ Password:                                                    │
│ Last login: Thu Apr 28 14:02:42 from NETCOM-phx1.netc        │
│ SunOS Release 4.1.3 (NETCOM) #1: Wed Sep 23 05:06:55 PDT 1992 │
│ NETCOM On-line Communication Services, Inc.                  │
│    >>>>                                                       │
│    >>>>  4-04-94:  RESEARCH TRIANGLE PARK (Raleigh-Durham, NC) POP │
│    >>>>            is now on-line!  (919) 558-8900            │
│    >>>>                                                       │
│    >>>>  4-09-94:  /u2/ftp has been moved to /ftp.            │
│    >>>>                                                       │
│    >>>>  4-29-94:  Alameda POP will be undergoing maintenance today. │
│    >>>>            Users there may experience unreliable connections because │
│    >>>>            of this. Alameda users please save your work often. │
│    >>>>                                                       │
│                                                              │
│ This disk usage summary is for the last 2 days.              │
│ Your average usage to date is:     1.22 meg                  │
│ At this rate your disk charge will be: $   0.00              │
│ Your account balance is:        0.00                         │
└──────────────────────────────────────────────────────────────┘
```

As with other online services or even a local BBS, you must first type your
user name at the *netcom login:* prompt, and then press Return. Then you enter
your password on the next line. This password is not echoed on your
computer's screen, so type it very carefully. If you make a mistake, you'll have
a chance to enter it again.

> **Caution**
>
> Some telecommunications software allows you to make a script of your log in rou-
> tine, which can be played back whenever you log onto a particular service. Just be
> aware that if your password is recorded by the program, it is available to any other
> user who has access to your computer.

The next step is to identify the type of terminal you're using. Most telecommunications programs support VT 100, so type that selection and then press
Return. To get the friendliest Netcom interface, type **menu** at the next
prompt, which produces the display shown in figure 32.3.

Fig. 32.3

Netcom's menu-
driven interface.

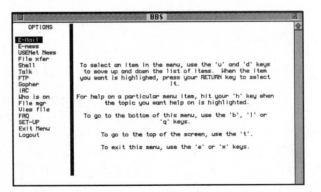

Use the up- and down-arrow keys or the letters *u* and *d* to select a particular item on the menu, then press Return (or Enter) to activate that selection.

In this example, you first check out some newsgroups. Activate one of Netcom's newsgroup readers by selecting the Exit menu and then pressing Return. Enter **tin** at the prompt, as shown in figure 32.4.

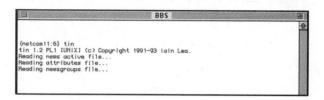

Fig. 32.4
Selecting a newsgroup through tin.

This particular news reader is simple to use, because it's menu driven. You can use the letter *g* as a go to command, which allows you to enter the name of a specific newsgroup you want to visit. We've selected *comp.sys.mac.hardware*, a very popular newsgroup if you want tips, tricks, and information on using your Macintosh. The messages in a newsgroup are threaded; that is, the messages that relate to a single topic are kept together, which makes reading those messages easier.

Tip
If you hit the wrong command or enter the wrong area, press ⌘-Z to return to the Netcom prompt. Then type *menu* and press Return to return to the regular menu.

If you want to respond to a particular message, press F (for followup) and then enter the text of your message in a small text editing window that appears at the top of your terminal screen. The letter *q* typed by itself will generally allow you to exit a specific area and return to the previous screen. When you return to the main Netcom prompt, enter the command **menu** to restore the menu-driven directory.

Next you visit an ftp server and look for some Macintosh software (ftp is explained in more detail later in this chapter). An obvious choice is Apple's software library. To get there, move the selection to *FTP*, and at the information prompt, type **ftp.apple.com**, and press Return. If Apple's ftp server isn't busy, you see the prompt shown in figure 32.5.

The UNIX commands you need to navigate through Apple's server are discussed in more detail later in this chapter. For now, log in as *anonymous*, and enter your Internet mailing address at the *password* prompt. Remember that the characters you type won't be echoed on your computer's screen, so type carefully. If you make a mistake, you will probably have to exit and log onto the ftp server a second time (type **bye**, press Return, and then type **menu** to return to the main Netcom directory of services).

Fig. 32.5

Apple's ftp server.

```
                              BBS
 Current working directory is /u2/genes.

 Enter name of machine to connect with: ftp.apple.com
 Type 'bye' at the ftp> prompt to return to menu

 Connected to bric-a-brac.apple.com.
 220 bric-a-brac.apple.com FTP server (IG Version 5.93 (from BU, from UUNET 5.51)
  Sun Nov 21 14:24:29 PST 1993) ready.
 Name (ftp.apple.com:genes): anonymous
 331 Guest login ok, send ident as password.
 Password:
 230 Guest login ok, access restrictions apply.
 ftp> ls
 200 PORT command successful.
 150 Opening ASCII mode data connection for file list.
 apda
 README
 dts
 alug
 pie
 echt90
 shlib
 bin
 etc
 dev
 boot
 cdrom
 pub
 apple
 .login
 public
 .logout
 .cshrc
 software
 226 Transfer complete.
 109 bytes received in 0.0077 seconds (14 Kbytes/s)
 ftp>
```
```
 ⌚ 4:55:01 PM
```

If your log in is successful—and it usually is—you can view the contents of the server by typing **ls** and then pressing Return, which will produce a display of the main file directory. To view the contents of one of the subdirectories you see, type **cd** followed by the name of the directory you want to visit; choosing **mac** takes you to Apple's Macintosh software libraries. Each successive **cd** command will take you one level deeper through the directory hierarchy, and the *ls* command will list the contents of that directory.

Or type **ls -R**, which will produce a listing of all files in your current directory and in all the directories below that one (and it can get mighty long). It's probably better when starting out to navigate through an ftp server one directory at a time.

We've selected some system software updates to download, as shown in figure 32.6.

Although the available software is updated from time to time, software files usually have an .hqx extension at the end of their name. This extension indicates the files are in bin/hex format, which is a format that converts Macintosh binary files to text consisting of letters and numbers. A number of shareware bin/hex converters that will reassemble these files to their original form are available. Compression programs, such as Bill Goodman's Compact Pro or Aladdin System's StuffIt products, also have built-in bin/hex converters.

Fig. 32.6
A listing of
software available
from Apple's ftp
server.

In contrast, the extension .txt is simply a text file you can retrieve without need of additional conversion software.

To retrieve a file, type **bin** or **binary** to enter the downloading mode (remember to press Return after you enter the command), and then type **get** plus the full name of your file (including the extension). The file will then be transferred to Netcom's own computer, which stores the file until you are ready to receive it.

After you retrieve the file you want, type **bye** to exit the ftp server, and then **menu** at the Netcom prompt to bring up the regular menu display. You use the *file xfer* section to select and then download the files directly to your Mac.

When you're finished with your session, the *logout* keystroke, followed by a return, or the same selection on Netcom's menu will end your session and disconnect your modem from the service. If you run into trouble at any time, type **help** or **?** to display a list of helpful information that will answer many of your questions.

America Online's Internet Center

Beginning in 1993, America Online began to offer Internet access through the comfort of its friendly graphical interface. This is a boon to the Mac user who has grown accustomed to pointing and clicking. America Online's Internet Center provides not only direct access to a number of Internet features, but helpful advice on the ins and outs of the net (see fig. 32.7).

V

Reaching Out

Fig. 32.7
The Internet
Center on America
Online has
introduced
thousands of
members to the
vast resources of
the Internet.

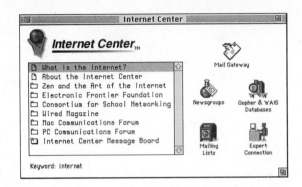

The first mission of America Online's Internet Center is to educate users of
the vast network. A variety of topics are listed on the main directory on the
left side of the window that contain informative text files. One of these
items, "Zen and the Art of the Internet," is an online book, with chapters and
subheads, offering well-written sets of introductory text. There is also a message board where newcomers (often referred to on the Internet as *newbies*)
can discuss issues related to access to the network.

America Online's Newsgroups area has become one of its most popular
Internet features. To go to that area, choose the Newsgroups icon (or just type
the AOL keyword **Newsgroups**), which will open the window shown in
figure 32.8.

Fig. 32.8
America Online's
Newsgroups center
is a repository for
thousands of
discussion areas.

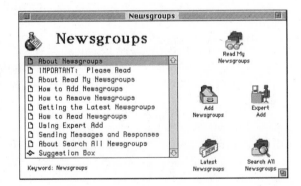

You can choose from a representative portion of popular newsgroups, and
the list is updated daily. If you know the exact name of a particular discussion group, you can click on the Expert Add icon and enter the name of the
group you want to join, as shown in figure 32.9.

The newsgroup selected in figure 32.9 contains some interesting discussions about the PowerPC, both the Macintosh and IBM versions, along with helpful hints and tips about using Apple's new Power Macintosh.

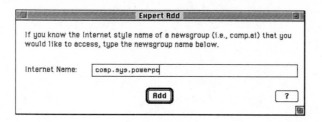

Fig. 32.9
If you enter the exact name of a newsgroup in the Expert Add box, you can add that group to your list (known as *subscribing*).

America Online's Internet Center also includes Mailing Lists and Gopher/ WAIS database search capability (which is described in more detail later in this chapter). Using the same, familiar graphical interface, you can search for a mailing list that contains information about the topics that interest you. Click the Mailing Lists icon at the main Internet Center window (refer to fig. 32.7), and then click the Search icon. Enter the topics that interest you, as done in figure 32.10.

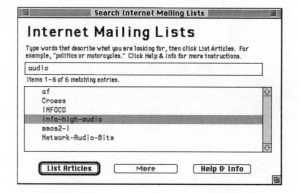

Fig. 32.10
Whatever your interests, you are likely to find a mailing list that provides the information you want.

V

Reaching Out

In order to subscribe to a mailing list, simply send e-mail to the address listed in the description. You'll probably have a response within just a few days.

Internet Features

A few Internet features, such as Usenet and ftp, have already been mentioned in this chapter. The following sections describe some of the most popular Internet features in more detail, along with some advice on how to use them.

ftp

These letters stand for *file transfer protocol*. They describe the technique you use to store, send, and receive files on the Internet. Literally hundreds of thousands of files across the world are available to you by ftp. You can select from the latest Apple system software updates on Apple's own *ftp.apple.com* server and other locations. You can also locate commercial demos, updates, freeware, and shareware at various sites. Some of the major software publishers have also established ftp servers so users of their products can easily get information files, updates, and other files.

You can gain access to an ftp site in many ways. You can access an ftp as a registered user, in which you have to give a user name and password, just like you do when you log onto any bulletin board or online service. That way access to certain files can be restricted. You also have the option of logging onto some of these sites by *anonymous ftp*, which means you give a user name of "anonymous," and usually, enter your Internet e-mail address as your password. By using that technique, you can access the files that are publicly available.

> **Note**
>
> Some ftp sites may require that you use the password "guest" instead. If your regular e-mail address won't work, try this method.

In addition to Apple's ftp server, you may want to log onto the server named *sumex-aim.stanford.edu*. The selection there only begins with Apple's software updates. A vast repository of commercial updates are available, as well as demos and shareware and freeware. When the going gets crowded, you may want to search out a *mirror* site, which offers the same file selection as the original server.

To start a session, type **ftp *hostname*** and press Return. An alternate way to begin a session is to type **ftp** and press Return. Then type **Open *hostname*** to establish a connection.

Archie

With all those thousands upon thousands of files available throughout the global Internet network, some sort of search mechanisms are necessary to locate the files in which you're interested. One such tool is Archie (which has nothing in common with the comic book character, but is derived from the word *archive*). The Archie systems contain information about the files you can transfer to your computer through anonymous ftp and they're updated monthly.

Searching an Archie database isn't quite Mac-like, but it isn't terribly difficult either. In order to take the mystery out of the process, we've logged onto AT&T's Archie server, *archie.internic.net,* in order to give you an idea of how the process is done. Since the very same data is accessed by any Archie site, it doesn't really matter which one you access.

First, access the Archie server, by typing the commands *telnet archie.internic.net.* If the server isn't offline or backed up processing information requests, a message screen appears, similar to the one shown in figure 32.11.

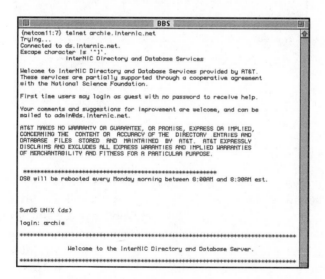

Fig. 32.11
Looking for files on the Internet with a little help from Archie.

At the archie> prompt, enter **show search** followed by a return in order to define your search criteria. For the sake of simplicity, enter **set search sub** at the next archie> prompt. What this means is that your search string can form all or part of a name. This gives you many more possibilities to explore when you don't know the exact UNIX name of the file you want (and sometimes those names are quite predictable in advance).

The example shown in figure 32.12 uses the word *macintosh,* which produced a lengthy list of ftp sites that contain Macintosh-related software and other information. The actual search filled many screens of text, so we've just included a sample of what we've found. The next step would be to visit the sites that seem interesting to view their software libraries.

You can limit your search to a specific file. You'll get a list restricted to the ftp sites that carry that file.

Figure 32.12

A sample of the results of Archie's database search.

Gopher

Gopher is another useful Internet search tool—one that can be used not only to locate the source of a file or text information but will actually transfer that file to your computer. This capability gives Gopher an advantage over Internet search mechanisms. It's also menu-driven, so you don't have to get involved with arcane command lines in order to retrieve the information you want. If you run into a problem using Gopher, just type **help** at the command prompt.

Following is a sample of a Gopher search using Netcom's terminal interface. Even in its raw form, using Gopher to locate the Internet files you want is simple.

The first step in the process is to log onto your Internet service provider and then connect to the Gopher server by entering **Gopher** at the prompt, which displays an information screen similar to the one shown in figure 32.13.

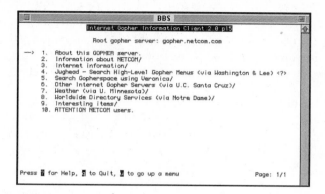

Fig. 32.13
Using Gopher to locate files and information on the Internet.

To navigate through Gopher's menu, press the down-arrow key enough times to take it to the search mechanism you want, and then press Return. Depending on the information you want, you may have to travel through several menus, using the same procedure. If you run into trouble at any point, press **?** for assistance.

For this search process, select information about Apple's new Power Macintosh line. You need to navigate a couple of menus, all clearly labeled, to retrieve the information. Sometimes the servers are busy, and the process may seem to bog down for a few minutes at a time for every request you make. But within a few minutes, you can get the results shown in figure 32.14.

Tip
When you cannot remember the commands for a specific Internet function, pressing **?** or typing **help** displays the information you need.

V

Reaching Out

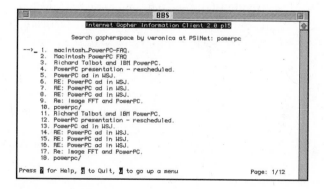

Fig. 32.14
Gopher searches Internet servers for Power Macintosh information.

Usenet

Usenet Newsgroups are the closest equivalents of the discussion forums you'll find on your local BBS, or one of the commercial online services. But like the rest of the Internet, Usenet has its own built-in traditions and structure. If you're used to posting messages, you'll find the surroundings somewhat familiar; but many discussion groups are not moderated, meaning there is no *sysop* (system operator) to control the flow of discussion and redirect or remove messages that aren't germane to the topics with which the group deals.

Other discussion groups have a moderator who reviews messages before they are posted and omits messages that are in bad taste, unduly inflammatory, or not relevant to the topics being discussed. Because these moderators are largely hobbyists working on their own time, however, do not expect a much greater degree of regulation than in an unmoderated newsgroup.

Thousands of newsgroups exist, with discussions ranging from cooking to rock music, and from computers to flying saucers. Whatever topics interest you, you'll find a vast, often overwhelming list of newsgroups to add to your roster for regular reading and participation.

Before deciding whether to participate in an ongoing discussion, take a few moments to read the section about Netiquette earlier in this chapter. Read the messages and learn the flavor of the discussion. When you're ready to jump in, you'll be welcomed as an equal in the discussions at hand.

WAIS

The definition of this acronym says it all: *Wide Area Information Service*. WAIS is an Internet search mechanism that helps you look for text documents across the net. The only limitation is that the documents need to be specially indexed for WAIS. In contrast, Archie is used to help you locate a file, based on the file's name—it doesn't search the contents of the files themselves.

Telnet

Telnet is a remote control system. It enables you to log onto another computer at a remote location as if it were your own computer. Your own Mac will behave as if it's a terminal attached to that far-off computer. It doesn't even matter what sort of computer it might be or what operating system it runs.

Internet Relay Chat (IRC)

Previous sections in this chapter described the process of communicating on the Internet in terms of joining Usenet discussion groups, sending e-mail, or transferring files to and from your computer by using ftp. This section discusses a different form of communicating on the net.

The Internet Relay Chat is essentially something that resembles talking to others on your CB Radio or even the interactive conferences you can have on online services such as America Online and eWorld. Participants assemble in groups called *channels* and have long discussions about various subjects.

IRCs have gained worldwide attention in the news media in recent years. During 1991 Persian Gulf War, information about the status of the war was available to users gathered in a single *channel*. Then again in 1993, when a coup was attempted against Russian President Boris Yeltsin, ITS participants in Moscow gave live reports about the situation.

How to Interact with an IRC

First, you need Internet access with a service provider who offers an IRC connection. This example uses the Netcom service to simulate a search of available IRC discussions (see fig. 32.15).

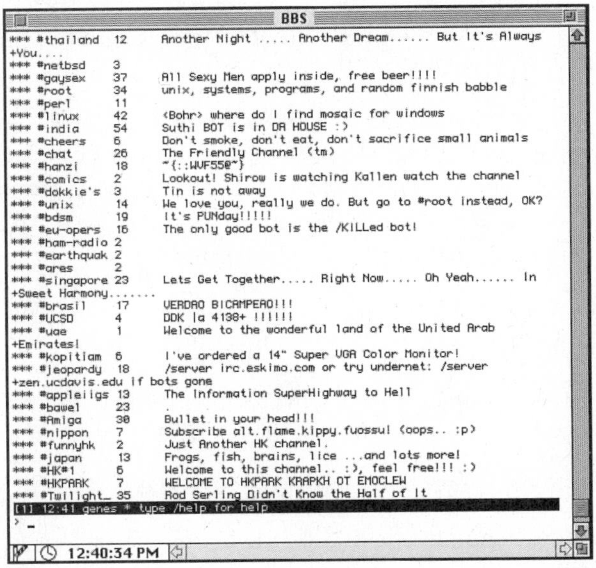

Fig. 32.15
Getting started in an Internet Relay Chat.

Because you are dealing with a command line interface, you must learn a few simple commands to get started. First, you must remember to type a slash (/) in front of each command, and then enter the command followed by pressing Return. The command you'll use most often to begin with is /help.

A second command you'll want to read before exploring the world of IRCs is /etiquettel; you'll want to know the channels ground rules before jumping in. To bring up a list of available discussion channels, type the command **/list -public** and then press Return.

When you locate a channel you want to join, type the command **/join #[channel name]**. A display of the nicknames of the participants appears, along with those who have just entered and left the chat. You can send a message to an individual user by typing the command **/msg [user name]** and then typing the the text of your message.

Making Sense of Those Arcane Unix-style Commands

Tip
As with all Internet groups, before you jump into an IRC chat, take a little time to get your feet wet and learn what's being discussed and the flavor of the conversation.

For most of you, the Internet will present an unMac-like appearance, at least until the graphical interfaces offered by the major online services cover more Internet services, or unless you use a special front end program that puts a nicer face upon your transactions with the Internet. But many of you cannot access the Internet by pointing and clicking; you have to type the names of the commands you want to activate.

Following are a few basic UNIX commands that will help you navigate easily through many Internet services. If the command you need to know isn't shown here—and were just covering the basics—a simple **help** or **?** entered at the prompt will usually display the information you need. To activate the following commands, always type a return at the end of a text line:

- *passwd* is used to change your password. When you enter a new password, what you type won't be visible (so do it carefully).

- *ls* requests a directory or list of file names. The *ls* function has a few options you can add to bring you additional information in the file list.

  ls -A lists all files, except those having . or .. names.

  ls -l provides a long listing of files, including size and when they were last modified.

  ls -R allows you to see a list of files in the current directory and in all of the directories below the current one.

■ *cd* is the command to change the directory you've accessed, equivalent to moving up and down through directory folders on your Macintosh. You can move down one directory level by entering the *cd* command all by itself. Typing *cd ..* will take you up one directory level. The command *cd $HOME* will take you to the main or root level of a directory.

■ *mkdir* is the command you use to create a new directory, the equivalent of the New Folder command on your Macintosh.

■ *rmdir* is the command used to remove a directory that you've created, as long as you have write privileges for it.

■ *chmod* is reminiscent of what you can do with System 7's file sharing. It allows you to change the level of protection for a file (its *mode*) so that you can modify or delete the file.

■ *rm* followed by the name of a file allows you to delete a file, so long as the *mode* of the file (described above) allows you to remove it. This is the equivalent of the Empty Trash command on your Macintosh. There's no way back once the file is gone.

■ *cp* is the command to copy files.

■ *finger* allows you to get a list of other users on your system, along with their name, if they are logged on, or the last time they logged onto the system.

■ *binary* places you in the mode to receive files on your Macintosh from an ftp site. You may also use the abbreviation *bin*.

■ *get* followed by the name of the file allows you to retrieve that file and transfer it to your Internet service providers computer or directly to your Macintosh.

■ *write* is a command used to send messages directly to another user's computer. You have to use *write* on each line of text you send in your message. To close a message, it's traditional to use either *o* or *-o-* to signify the message's conclusion.

■ *talk* sets up your Mac to engage in a one-on-one or interactive conversation with another user. What you type will be visible to the other user, provided that user has also engaged the *talk* command.

■ *logout* is the command you use to end your session and your modem will disconnect from the other line. If you see the message Not login shell, you may be logged onto another service by way of your service

V

Reaching Out

provider. If you see this message, before you can engage *logout* you must first use *exit*.

> **Note**
>
> If you log onto a remote system that doesn't recognize the standard logout command, try commands such as exit, quit, or bye. The characters ^] enable you to log off from a telnet connection.

In the coming years, the major online services will add more and more Internet services, so the issue of dealing with a command-line interface will probably be short-lived. Because most of the commands are simple and straightforward, you may find you actually like to use them at times.

Shortcuts and Hot Tips

Even if you are an experienced traveler across the online services, you will find the Internet to be a strange place at first (I did), with a list of unstated rules and conventions you will likely not be familiar with. You may also sometimes find yourself sailing across uncharted waters seemingly without a rowboat or paddle. Before becoming discouraged, take a little time to explore your new surroundings carefully. Here's a few suggestions that will help make your Internet visits more pleasant:

- Don't be discouraged by flamers (people who resort to personal attack in an effort to get across a point). Just respond to such messages calmly and with good taste—or ignore them altogether, even if you are the subject of attack.

- Rather than remember complex UNIX-based commands for different functions, try using your telecommunication software's built-in scripting (if such a feature is available), a macro program, or even AppleScript to automate your sessions.

- When accessing files from an ftp server, be patient when the performance seems to bog down. Many other users may be trying to access files at the same time you are.

- When you cannot log onto an ftp server because it's busy, search for a mirror site, which may have exactly the same files available.

■ Some Internet service providers may charge extra for storing large files. When you transfer a file from an ftp server, be sure you download that file to your computer as soon as possible to avoid paying extra charges.

■ One of the most popular sources for Macintosh software is *sumex-aim.stanford.edu*. It's also a very popular ftp site, and sometimes you may have to wait a while to get access to it.

■ If you cannot locate a file, let an Archie server do the finding for you. Archie's search capability was discussed earlier in this chapter.

■ Internet newsgroups often have sets of text files containing frequently asked questions (FAQs) that provide background information about the newsgroup, and answer common questions. Be sure to review these text files before posting your first message.

■ When you first visit a newsgroup, take a look-but-don't-touch approach until you get the feel of the group. Many newsgroups are populated by veterans who are sometimes sensitive to the arrival of *newbies,* newcomers whom they sometimes consider inexperienced and uninformed. If your approach to the discussion group is planned carefully, and you've taken the time to inform yourself of its history and conventions, you will soon be welcomed as a regular participant.

■ Don't oversubscribe to mailing lists or newsgroups. There is such a volume of information to be had, you are apt to find your e-mail flooded with mail you simply don't have time to read.

From Here...

This chapter introduced you to the largest online service on Earth, but it only scratched the surface of the extraordinary range of services and capabilities of the Internet. The discussion has simply tried to whet your appetite for more information. I hope you'll spend time cruising the net in search of information, conversation, or just plain fun.

If you want to learn more about the inner workings of the Internet and its fascinating early history, add *Using The Internet* (Que Books 1994) to your library. The book is friendly, well-written, and will answer many—probably most—of your questions about this global computer network. Another helpful book is *Internet Starter Kit* from Adam C. Engst (Hayden Books 1993), which includes a selection of software strictly for Macintosh users.

- Chapter 29, "Getting Online," tells you the ins and outs of buying and setting up your modem and getting connected.

- Chapter 30, "Using America Online and CompuServe," discusses two of the most popular online services.

- Chapter 31, "Using eWorld," describes Apple's new consumer-oriented online service.

- Chapters 37 and 38 describe the steps you need to take to troubleshoot common problems with your Mac and explain how you can solve them before they become serious.

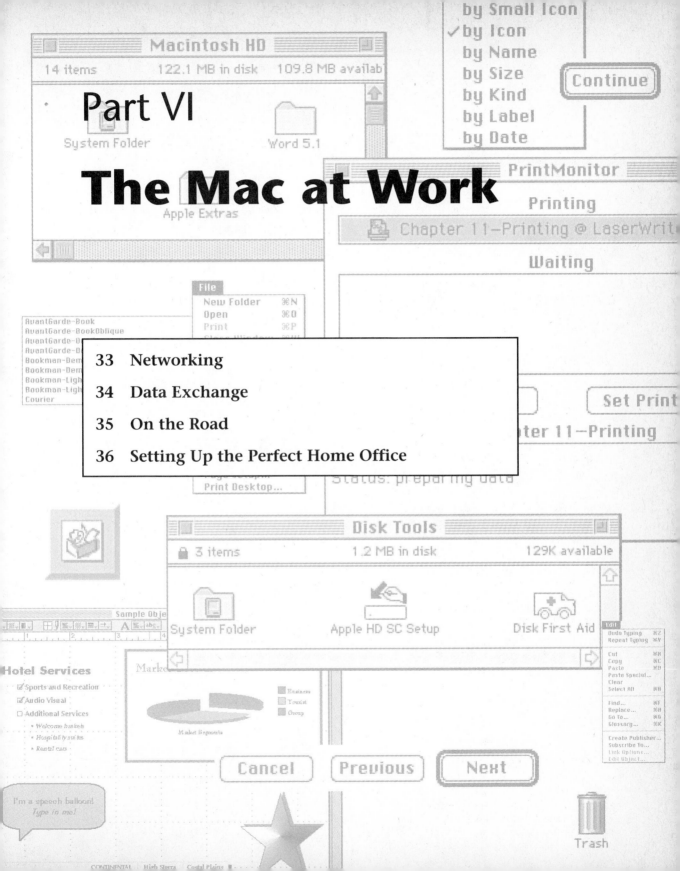

Part VI

The Mac at Work

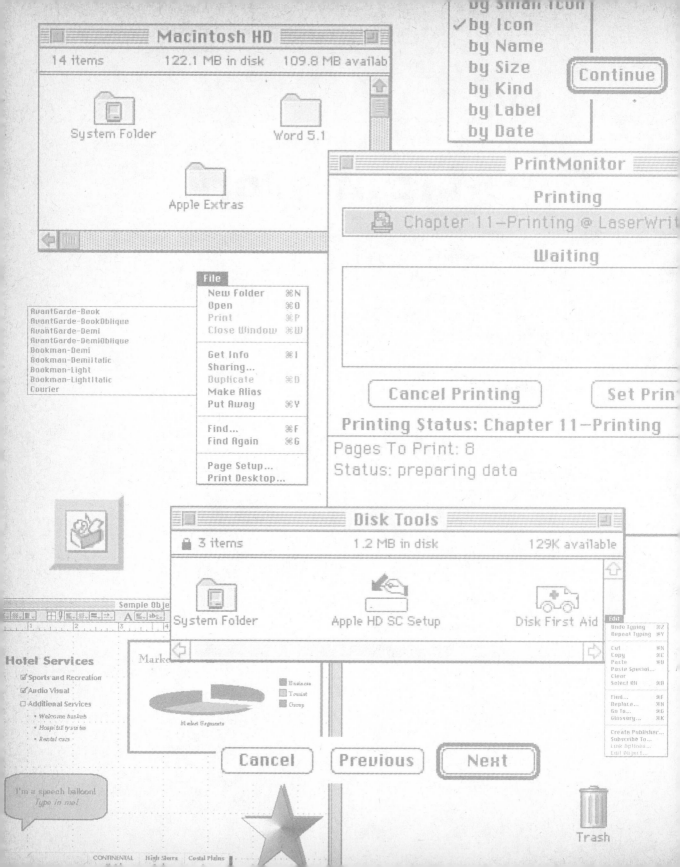

Chapter 33

Networking

by Ian Stokell

Networking is an increasingly important aspect of computing. Connecting computers together makes maximum use of valuable resources and allows users to enhance their productivity through direct, and indirect, interaction with others. It also allows for the immediate sharing of files and computing devices.

In this chapter, you learn the following:

- Hardware and software requirements, and the benefits of networking

- How to connect a Macintosh to a network

- Sharing your files with other users, and accessing other Macintoshes on the network

- Security, monitoring and management issues, including passwords and access privileges

- How to hook up a printer

- How to connect to a larger network.

Networking Overview

For the single user using a stand-alone Macintosh computer, networking is of little concern. But whenever two or more computers are in the same office or location, the benefits of connecting them together can be great.

Benefits of Networking

If the 1980s was the decade of the personal computer (PC), then the 1990s will be the decade of the networked PC.

For home users, the significant networking capabilities of the Macintosh are of little concern, unless they have more than one system to connect together. Usually, a printer is the most that they would attach to their Macintosh, through the printer port built into all systems. Stand-alone Macs in an office or workgroup environment have very limited appeal, however.

Connecting two or more Macintoshes together greatly enhances computing efficiency and makes maximum use of the valuable resources (hard drives, printers, CD-ROMs, and so on) of an office or workgroup.

Connecting together all the Macintoshes in one geographic area, such as an office, (called a *local area network*), allows for users of different machines to access other Macintoshes and, in turn, allow them to access their systems.

Why would they do that? There may be just one or two printers in a single office to be shared by multiple users. Or there may be a single CD-ROM for everyone to use. Also, one Macintosh's hard drive may be hardly used, and the others may be used almost to capacity on a daily basis. Instead of buying a larger hard disk for everyone, why not just access, through the network, an unused hard disk on another machine?

In this day of tight budgets, optimizing the performance and accessibility of relatively expensive computing resources is a necessity.

Peer-to-Peer or Dedicated File Server

A peer-to-peer network allows all users on the network to access all other computers (providing the individual computer owners allow it). In this way users can access resources attached to other computers, such as printers and CD-ROMs, as well as folders and files on other hard drives. Users can access files on someone else's computer, and even store files and folders there. As already mentioned, this is especially useful if one computer on a network is hardly used, and the others are regularly used to capacity.

There are other benefits, too. Peer-to-peer networks allow users to have complete control over their stored data. They choose who has access to it themselves without a third party, such as a network administrator, having to be involved.

However, there lies some of the problems. To access another user's computer, that computer has to be turned on. If it is off and you need some vital piece of information in a hurry, you may be out of luck.

Additionally, backing up corporate data on a regular basis is vital. This is often done on a daily basis to ensure no valuable information is lost in the event of system failure. On a peer-to-peer network, you either have to make sure that all users back up files on a daily basis, which is virtually impossible, even on a small network, or you have a single administrator accomplish the task. But that can be extremely difficult for the administrator if the files are dispersed around multiple hard drives on the network. The larger the network, the more difficult the task.

Also, security is another problem for peer-to-peers. Preventing unauthorized access to important corporate, and personal, data can be problematic if the data is stored on different computers. It can also be a troublesome task for the owner of the computer on which it resides, as they have to allow a number of Registered Users access to the data, allocating access privileges to individual users or groups as needed.

While peer-to-peer is often the best way to go for many smaller networks, when a lot of users are involved, or security and backup is vital, a dedicated file server may be best.

Simply put, a dedicated file server is a computer that is used to store all the important company information that needs to be kept safe and secure. Having a file server has many benefits.

For a start, with all the important information kept in one place, backing up by a network administrator, or someone allocated the task, can be pretty straightforward. Often it can be automated using special software.

Another benefit is that users on the network know where to find important corporate information and files. As they are used and updated, so they can be regularly backed up.

However, vital information should be backed up onto another computer, or at least a second hard drive, or tape drive, connected to the file server. You should make sure that if a second file server setup is not available for use in the event of the main file server going down, one can be quickly configured to do the job. If there is a single file server for a network, and that server goes down, so does the network. Precautions have to be taken in the event of a file server crash.

Security is another important benefit of a dedicated file server. With all the important files and information in one place, the network administrator can easily control and monitor access.

VI

The Mac at Work

Smaller networks may not need to allocate a computer to be used as a dedicated server, however. Also, companies requiring just a small network may not have the financial resources to tie up a computer just as a server. In a small office, if a computer is not switched on and it contains information that someone wants, all you have to do is walk over and turn it on. That is not so easy if a smallish network is dispersed throughout a number of rooms or floors of an office building.

In addition to third party software programs that do the same thing, Apple has a couple of programs designed to help out with the administration and management of a file server. One is called AppleShare File Server, and lets you set up a Macintosh as a file server with special features designed to allow for extensive organization, access, and management of files, disks, and devices on a network. There is also another program called AppleShare Print Server that is designed to increase printing efficiency by making a computer a print server responsible for printing requests from network users. The computer takes network printing requests and, if the printer is busy, stores them for execution when it is free again.

Hardware/Software Requirements

The alternative to a stand-alone Macintosh is a networked Macintosh. Networking can be as simple—or as complicated—as the user wants. The degree of complexity of a network depends upon the job it is designed to do. In its simplest form, two desktop systems are connected together with a single cable.

Although that may sound simple, the computing platform dictates just how difficult a task that is. For users of most IBM PCs and compatibles, that can be a highly complicated task, involving such elements as the selection of a networking protocol (Ethernet or Token Ring, for example), the purchasing and installing of the relevant network interface cards (NICs), the configuring of the boards, the selection of the correct cabling, and the installation and setting up of the necessary networking software.

With the Macintosh, however, much of the decision-making and installation procedures are unnecessary or already taken care of. This is because the Macintosh comes with networking capability already built-in, in the form of Apple's LocalTalk hardware and AppleTalk software.

Networking two desktop PCs involves the installation of hardware (the NIC and the corresponding cable, for example) and the networking software.

The network interface card (NIC) is a card containing the necessary electronic circuitry to connect a computer to the network. It fits into an available expansion slot in the computer and operates in conjunction with the networking software to send messages across the network.

For IBM PCs and compatibles, networking usually requires opening up the computer case to install the NIC, to which the cable is then connected. For the Macintosh, that is not necessary, however, because it already has a LocalTalk or Ethernet interface built-in. All that is required from a hardware standpoint is to attach a LocalTalk or LocalTalk-compatible cable to the printer port of the Macintosh.

That is fine for connecting two Macintoshes together in order to share files. But if you want to attach an Apple LaserWriter printer, for example, that can be used by both computers, you need to take another step.

Even if you are just connecting two Macintoshes together and you want to share a LaserWriter printer, you will need to plug a LocalTalk connector into the printer port—and not just a LocalTalk cable.

A LocalTalk connector has a single piece of cable at one end that plugs straight into the printer port, and then two sockets at the other end of the main box. These two sockets allow for two LocalTalk cables to be plugged in—one of which goes to another Mac, the other directly to the printer. You can plug a LocalTalk connector into the printer as well, so that it can also connect to two Macs, and actually just acts as another link in the chain. You need something in all of the available sockets in the LocalTalk connectors however, so the Macs at either end of the network need to have a terminator in the free socket of their connectors (see fig. 33.1).

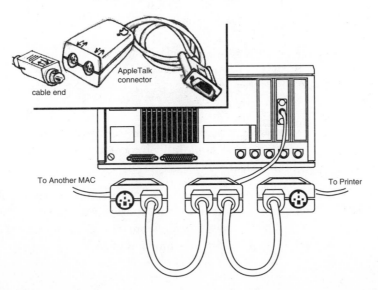

Fig. 33.1
LocalTalk connector used to connect Macs and printer in bus network.

This bus, or daisy-chain connection, is the simplest form of network. In it, the computers and printers on the network are joined together one after the other. The cable goes from one computer or printer to the next. In a bus, the number of connectors corresponds to the number of Macintoshes or other network devices to be connected. This is the most common form of network. There are limitations to this, however. For a more detailed look at the limitations, refer to the last section in this chapter, "Connecting to a Larger Network."

A word here about LocalTalk, Ethernet, and Token Ring. The major attraction of using Ethernet or Token Ring rather than LocalTalk is bandwidth—that is, you can send more data faster with Ethernet and Token Ring. With LocalTalk, bandwidth can reach 0.23 megabits per second (Mbps). However, that is considerably less than Ethernet's 10 Mbps, and Token Ring's high-end 16 Mbps. But you pay a price for that added bandwidth. With LocalTalk, the interface is built-in, and the cabling is cheap, shielded, twisted pair. With Ethernet and Token Ring, you need to purchase a separate NIC to slot into your Macintosh, and the cabling is more expensive.

Hooking together Macintoshes in a small network is relatively easy if you are using the AppleTalk protocol over LocalTalk cabling. Plugging in LocalTalk connectors and cabling is only one step in the task, however. You still have to configure your software.

> ### Note
>
> NICs will be required if the network is to be either EtherTalk-based, which is the name for AppleTalk over Ethernet cabling, or TokenTalk-based, which is the name for AppleTalk over Token Ring cabling.
>
> Not all Macintoshes have an available expansion slot for accommodating the required NIC. However, the new Power Macintoshes and some 680X0-based Macs, do have an Ethernet interface built-in.

Installing network software is next. However, for Macintoshes running System 7, it is not necessary because AppleTalk protocol software is already built-in to the operating system.

But what is a protocol? For data to travel on a network, it needs to adhere to certain rules and regulations in order to avoid confusion and chaos. That's where the network protocol comes in. Simply put, the protocol dictates the rules and regulations controlling the transmission of data.

Hooking together two Macintoshes could not be easier if you want to use AppleTalk with LocalTalk cabling. With everything built-in, all the users need to do is connect a cable to LocalTalk connectors, which in turn connects to their printer ports, and then configure the software.

Here is where the uninitiated user will need step-by-step help. Unlike much of the Macintosh interface, which is relatively intuitive, configuring the networking software so that the two machines can share files and resources requires instruction.

Connecting the Macintosh to the Network

Having plugged the cable into the printer port of both machines, the next step is to sort out the built-in AppleTalk software so the two systems can talk to each other and share resources and files.

Turning AppleTalk On

First you must make sure that AppleTalk is on. If it isn't, you have to turn it on. Follow these steps:

1. Open the Apple menu at the top left of the menu bar, and select Chooser (see fig. 33.2).

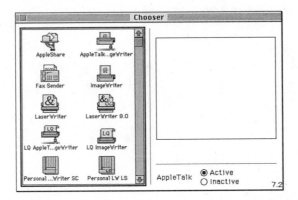

Fig. 33.2
There is both an Active and Inactive AppleTalk button at the bottom right of the screen.

2. Select the Active button. Now, when you shut down the Macintosh AppleTalk will automatically restart when turned on again.

> **Note**
>
> If you are connected to a file server, for example, and you turn AppleTalk off, a message appears informing you that services will be disconnected.

If your network has zones, they will be listed in the bottom left corner. You can choose to which zone to belong. More about that in a moment.

3. Close the Chooser.

Choosing a Network Connection

For users with just a TokenTalk connection, you do not have to select a connection; the LocalTalk Built-In icon will already be selected in the Network icon in the Control Panel menu. EtherTalk or TokenTalk users, however, will need to select a network connection.

To choose a network connection, follow these steps:

1. Open the Apple menu and choose Control Panels.

2. Double-click the Network control panel.

3. Choose the networking connection icon required.

> **Note**
>
> By changing a network connection, you may lose network services already in use. What is then required is to reconnect to the network services on the network being joined.

4. Click OK.

5. Close the Network control panel.

Selecting a Zone

The network administrator assigns zones to break up the network and make it easier to manage. When you make AppleTalk active, you can also select the zone to which you want to belong. Other users seeking to share your files will need to know where to find you. Selecting a zone helps them locate your Macintosh. For more information about zones, see the last section of this chapter, "Connecting to a Larger Network."

1. Open the Apple menu and select Control Panels (see fig. 33.3).

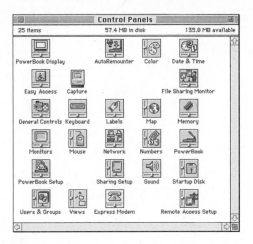

Fig. 33.3
Control Panels
opened.

2. Double-click the Network control panel (see fig. 33.4).

Fig. 33.4
The Network icon.

3. Networking option icons will be displayed. Click the desired network connection. A zone list will be displayed when the icon is clicked again. The zone selected by the network administrator as the default zone will be displayed. Select a different one if that is not the one required. A dialog box will warn you that any active services will be disconnected.

4. Click OK.

5. Close the Network control panel.

Name Your Macintosh

Before your computer will appear in the Chooser of the computers of other network users, you have to give it a name. You also have to name yourself if you are sharing your own folders with other users. Follow these steps:

VI

The Mac at Work

1. Open the Apple Menu and choose Control Panels.

2. Open the Sharing Setup control panel, shown in figure 33.5.

Fig. 33.5
The opened
Sharing Setup
control panel.

3. In the Owner Name text box type in the primary user of the Macintosh—probably you.

4. In the Owner Password text box, type in your password, which can be up to eight characters long. This is a security measure designed to prevent unauthorized access to your private files.

5. In the Macintosh Name text box, type in a name. This name appears in others users' Choosers when they want to access your computer.

The File Sharing and Program Linking sections of the Sharing Setup control panel will be used a little later.

Having connected to the network, chosen the network connection, and named your Macintosh, it is now time to both designate which files on your own hard disk you want others to see and use, and to access other computers in order to use their files and to store information.

Sharing Your Files with Others

In order for others to share designated files from your hard drive, you have to make them available as shared files. If you allocate a folder as one that can be shared, users connecting over the network can access all those files within that folder. This next section shows you how.

As a security precaution, you can designate which files can be accessed by others, and to what degree. You can also stipulate who gets to access what. There are different levels of access for other users, from just the ability to read the file, to the ability to change it.

Before setting up files and folders for sharing, you must have named your Macintosh as detailed earlier.

Establishing Shared Files

To establish shared files, follow these steps:

1. Open the Apple menu and choose Control Panels.

2. Double-click the Sharing Setup control panel (see fig. 33.6).

   We've been here before, when you had to establish the name of your Macintosh and its owner—probably you.

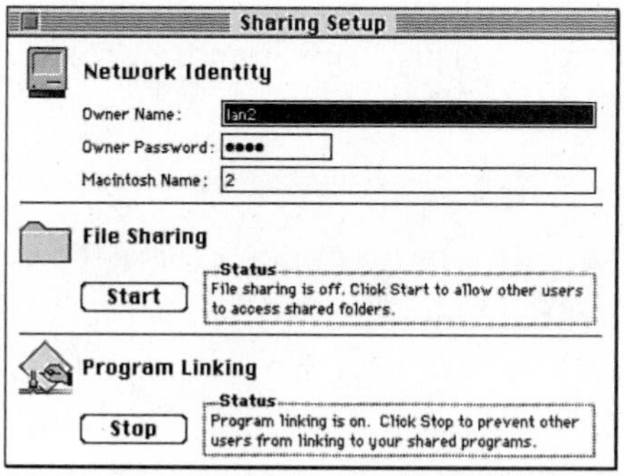

Fig. 33.6
The Sharing Setup control panel.

   About midway down the box there is a section called File Sharing.

3. Click the Start button in the File Sharing box. The label changes at the outset telling you that file sharing is starting up. It then says that file sharing is on. The button will then change from Start to Stop. To turn off file sharing on your Macintosh, click the Stop button.

4. Close the Sharing Setup control panel.

5. Close Control Panels.

Establishing a Shared Disk/Folder

With the exception of floppy disks, which cannot be shared, any disk or folder can be shared. CD-ROMs can also be shared. To share a disk or folder, file sharing must be switched on. If it isn't, go to the previous section and switch it on.

To share a disk or folder, take the following steps:

1. Select the disk or folder to be shared.

2. Open the File menu and choose Sharing to open the Sharing dialog box (see fig. 33.7).

Fig. 33.7
The Sharing dialog
box.

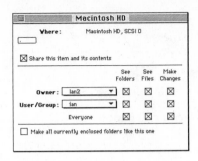

3. In the top section is a box with the title Share This Item and Its Contents. Click this box.

   You also appoint access privileges from the second section. We'll return to access privileges later.

4. Close the dialog box by clicking the Close box in the top left.

   A dialog box appears with the option to Save the changes to access privileges you have just made.

5. Click Save.

Now everyone on the network can access that folder or disk.

Specifying Individuals to Access Your Files

You may not want everyone to have access to that information. In fact, you may only want a couple of specified people to have access to it. To do that you have to name them; in doing so you make them a registered user.

Follow these steps:

1. Open the Apple menu and select Control Panels.

2. Double-click the Users & Groups control panel (see fig. 33.8).

Fig. 33.8
Users & Groups
control panel.

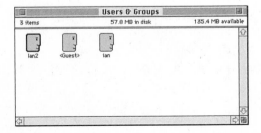

When you open it for the first time, there will be a quest icon in it, along with your own icon. If the latter is missing, you need to name your Macintosh.

3. Open the File menu and choose New User.

Another icon appears in the box titled New User.

4. Type in the name of the new user you are adding.

> **Note**
>
> When that new user tries to access your computer, he or she will have to type in the exact name you give the file. Remember to take a note of the exact user name.

At this point you can either exit the Users & Groups window or choose to assign a password to the new user. Passwords are always a good idea, unless you don't care who has access to your computer.

Here's what you do if you want to assign a password:

5. Open the user icon that you just named. A new dialog box opens containing various options. The first text box at the top is titled User Password (see fig. 33.9).

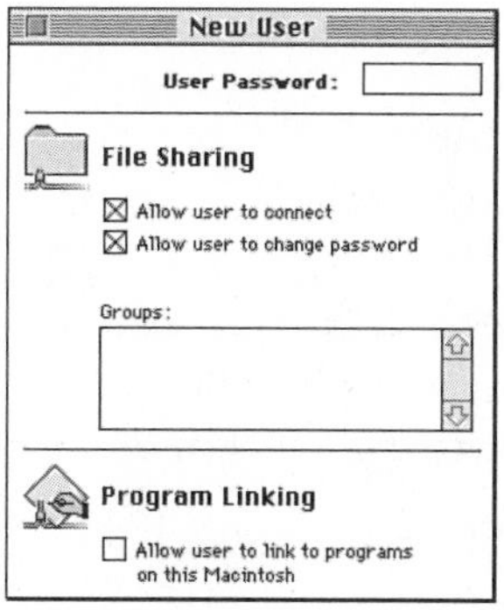

Fig. 33.9
User Password text box.

6. Type in the password to be used by the user.

There are also File Sharing and Program Linking options that you can assign at this point.

7. Close the dialog box.

VI

The Mac at Work

At this point, another dialog box appears asking you to Save, Don't Save, or Cancel the changes.

8. Select Save.

9. Close the Users & Groups dialog box.

You can remove a registered user or group at any time by simply dragging the relevant icon to the trash. However, you cannot get rid of either the owner's icon or the guest icon.

In order to save time if there are groups of people that you want to access your computer, you can create a new group instead of a new user by selecting New Group from the File menu when the Users & Groups control panel has been opened.

The procedure is the same as for a new user, except that the new icon will be initially titled New Group, instead of New User. Once complete, just drag the user icons you want included in the new group and drop them onto the new group's icon. The user icons remain in the Users & Groups window, as well as moving inside the new group's icon.

Your own Macintosh owner's icon and the Guest icon do not have to be included in any group.

All the members of a group can be identified by clicking open the group's icon.

When you click the icon of an individual user, the password box appears again (refer to fig. 33.9). Halfway down is a section called Groups, listing all the groups to which the user belongs.

Letting Users Access a Specified Disk

To allow registered users to access specific folders and disks on your computer, you have to set up the folder or disk for sharing.

Before doing so, you must ensure that file sharing is on, by following these steps:

1. Select the folder or disk (not a floppy) that is to be shared.

2. Open the File menu and choose Sharing (see fig. 33.10).

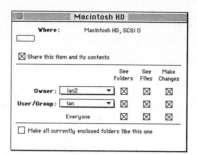

Fig. 33.10
The Sharing dialog
box.

The Sharing dialog box appears. In the top section there is a box titled Share this item and its contents.

3. Select this box if not already selected.

Midway down the window is a pop-up menu called User/Group.

4. Click the menu and choose who you want to access the specified folder/disk. Only one name/group can be chosen.

In the middle section of the windows, three boxes correspond to the Owner (probably you), the User/Group you just selected, and Everyone. The three boxes, once selected allow them to See Folders, See Files, and Make Changes to the specified folder/disk.

If you do not want everyone to have access to the specified folder/disk, you must make sure that the three boxes along the bottom of the mid-section that corresponds to Everyone are not selected. When they are deselected, only the Owner and the User/Group you just selected have access privileges.

5. Close the Sharing dialog box.

A dialog box appears.

6. Select Save.

Accessing Other Computers on the Network

Having allowed other users to access your files, you will now want to connect to other computers on the network.

VI

The Mac at Work

Connecting to Another Computer's Shared Disk

Whether accessing a network file server or a hard drive on another Macintosh on the network, the way you connect is the same.

However, there is some information you will need before you can take the required steps to access the other computer. In the first place, you will need both the name of the other computer and the zone it is in, if your network has zones. In addition, you will need to find out if it allows guests to log on, or whether you are already listed as a registered user. If the latter is true, you will need both your user name and password that applies to that other machine, whether a file server or a personal Macintosh.

> **Note**
>
> A generic guest account allows anyone on the network to access the disk. When file sharing is first initiated, guest access is automatically allowed. You need to remove this if you do not want everyone to be allowed access to your computer. I highly recommend that you do not have this feature on if you have private files on the disk. If you want everyone to have unlimited access to your disk, however, leave it activated. More on this later in this chapter.

The owner of a networked Macintosh can list those users who are *registered* to access the computer. Those users are then assigned *access privileges* that allow them to use and change certain resources and files. More about access privileges later.

To connect to a shared disk on someone else's Macintosh, follow these steps:

1. Open the Apple menu and select Chooser. (AppleTalk should be active at this point in order to allow you to access the other computer as shown in figure 33.11.)

Fig. 33.11
The opened
Chooser.

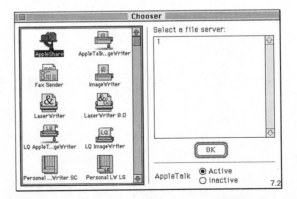

In the top left you will see a box containing some icons, including those for printers and AppleShare.

2. Select the AppleShare icon.

If the network you are on has zones, you will need to select the zone where the computer you are seeking is located. This is why you need to know the information beforehand.

3. Select the name of the computer you want to access.

4. Click OK.

At this point, a dialog box appears. You must now either choose the Guest option (if that Macintosh allows quests), or the Registered User option. If you choose the Registered User option, do the following:

5. Type your correct user name in the Name box.

6. Type your password in the Password box.

7. Click OK.

At this point another dialog box appears listing the available shared disks (see fig. 33.12).

Fig. 33.12
Available shared disks dialog box.

8. Select the shared disk you are interested in.

9. Click OK.

10. Close the Chooser.

Using an Alias To Connect Automatically

You can use *aliases* to connect to a shared disk automatically.

VI

The Mac at Work

You need to be connected to a shared disk first. Follow the steps in the previous section, "Connecting to Another Computer's Shared Disk," and then follow these steps:

1. Select the shared disk in which you are interested.

2. Open the File menu and choose Make Alias.

    An icon appears with the name of the shared disk and the word *alias* attached to it.

3. Type in a new name if so desired. You can also keep the original name.

4. Drag the new alias icon to anywhere on the desktop for easy access.

You can then disconnect from the aliased disk by simply dragging the original icon into the trash.

The next time you want to access that shared disk, double-click the aliased icon you left on the desktop. A password dialog box will appear if you originally connected to the shared disk as a registered user. At this point, you need to type in your password to access the disk.

Connecting Automatically at Startup

You can also set up your computer so that it automatically connects to a shared disk when you start it up. Follow these steps:

1. Open the Apple menu and select Chooser (see fig. 33.13).

Fig. 33.13
The opened
Chooser.

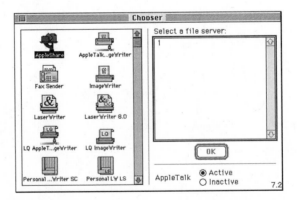

In the top left you will see a box containing some icons, including those for printers and AppleShare.

2. Select the AppleShare icon.

3. Select the name of the computer you want to access.

4. Click OK.

At this point a dialog box appears. You must now either choose the Guest option (if that Macintosh allows guests), or the Registered User option. If you choose the latter:

5. Type your correct user name in the Name box.

6. Type your password in the Password box.

7. Click OK.

At this point another dialog box appears listing the available shared disks (see fig. 33.14).

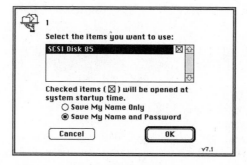

Fig. 33.14
Available shared disks dialog box.

There are small check boxes next to all the shared disks listed in the dialog box. You check the boxes of the shared disks you want to connect to automatically at startup.

8. Check the boxes.

When a check box of a shared disk is selected by a registered user, two additional buttons appear.

The Save My Name Only option will require the registered user to enter a password when he or she connects at startup. The Save My Name and Password option will save both and connect automatically at startup with no input from the user. This is not the recommended option as anyone using your computer will therefore be able to access the shared disk without having to know the password. By selecting the Save My Name Only option, the user of your computer will have to know your password to access.

9. Click OK.

10. Close the Chooser.

Security, Monitoring & Management

Physically setting up a network is only part of the operation. You then have to implement security procedures, such as passwords and access privileges, in order to safeguard the privacy of your files. There are also a number of monitoring and management activities that might be required, such as setting up the computer for accessing remotely or transferring ownership of a disk or folder.

Passwords

A suitable password will generally stop unauthorized access to a folder or disk. This section deals with changing your own password, and changing a user's password.

> **Note**
>
> A password is important if you want to prevent access to your files. It must be complex enough so someone cannot guess it easily, and yet not so complex that you need to write it down because you can't remember it. If you write it down, it can be compromised by someone accidentally finding it—or you losing the piece of paper it is written on. Don't use anything obvious, like your first name, or your initials, or your spouse's/children's names. Preferably use a combination of letters and numbers.

To change your own password, follow these steps:

1. Open the Apple menu and choose Control Panels.

2. Open the Sharing Setup control panel (see fig. 33.15).

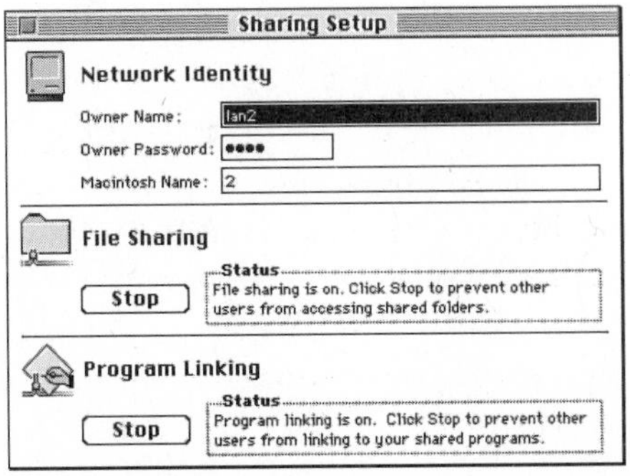

Fig. 33.15
Sharing Setup
control panel.

In the top section of the Sharing Setup control panel window is a text box called Owner Password.

3. Type a new password in the box, up to eight characters.

> **Note**
>
> The password is case-sensitive—if you are using a combination of upper- and lowercase letters, don't forget which is which!

4. Press the Tab key so that the letters in your new password are replaced by a *bullet*. This is an added measure to help maintain the privacy of your password.

5. Close the Sharing Setup control panel.

As the owner of the Macintosh, you can change the passwords of the users you have listed that have access to your computer. Follow these steps:

1. Open the Apple menu and choose Control Panels.

2. Open the Users & groups control panel.

The Users & groups window displays all the icons of the users and groups that have access to your Macintosh.

3. Select and open the user icon you want to change the password of, by double-clicking it.

A window opens displaying the user's password in the top right. There are just bullets in the box, corresponding to the user's password.

4. Click the User Password box.

5. Type in a new password, up to eight characters. (See previous note concerning password selection)

6. Close the password window.

A dialog box appears asking if you want to save the changes.

7. Select Save.

Registered users can also change the password they use to access a shared disk on someone else's computer, unless the owner of the computer they want to access (or the network administrator) has chosen to limit that option.

VI

The Mac at Work

To change your password if you are a registered user, follow these steps:

1. Open the Apple menu and select Chooser. (AppleTalk should be active at this point in order to allow you to access the other computer.)

   In the top left you will see a box containing some icons, including those for printers and AppleShare.

2. Select the AppleShare icon.

   If the network you are on has zones, you will need to select the zone where the computer you are seeking is located.

3. Select the name of the computer you want to access.

4. Click OK.

   At this point a dialog box appears, asking to connect as a Guest or a Registered User. The Registered User button is already selected. At the bottom of the box is a button called Set Password.

5. Click the Set Password button.

   A dialog box appears listing spaces for old and new passwords (see fig. 33.16).

Fig. 33.16
Password dialog box.

6. Type your old password.

7. Press Tab.

8. Type your new password.

9. Click OK.

   At this point, another dialog box appears requiring you to type in your password again.

10. Type in your password again.

11. Click OK.

Access Privileges

You can change access privileges to folders and disks that you own. The next section covers establishing a folder that you own on a remote computer.

There are a number of options and reasons for varying the level of accessibility and the degree to which users can change a file that you own.

Obviously, not everyone in an organization will need to be able to access and change all files. Additionally, you may not want everyone to be able to read all files. Maybe just a specific group or department needs access to certain files. Or you may want users to be able to read and print a file, but not change it. That's where Access Privileges come in. You can customize users' access to the files you own.

To allocate privileges, or review existing ones, on folders and disks that you own, follow these steps:

1. Select the folder or disk concerned.

2. Open the File menu and choose Sharing (see fig. 33.17).

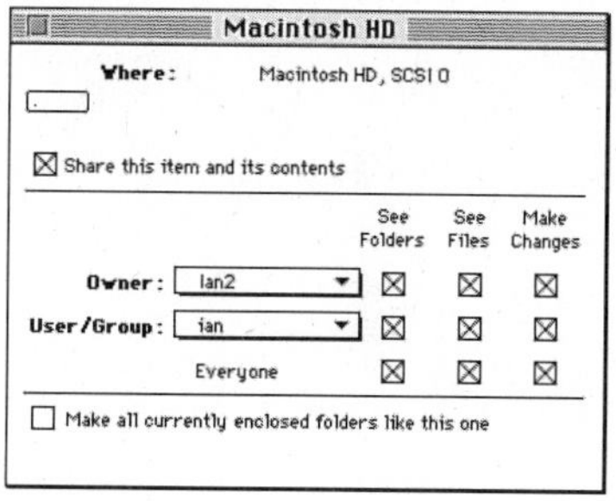

Fig. 33.17
The Sharing dialog box.

In the top section of the Sharing dialog box, you'll see a box called Share this item and its contents. However, this box does not appear if the folder is inside a shared folder.

In the middle section are the names of the Owner, the specified User/Group, and Everyone. When you first create a folder, you automatically become the owner, and are therefore capable of granting access privileges to that folder. The User/Group must be named on the computer on which the folder resides.

Next to them are three boxes: See Folders, which allows users to read folders within shared folders; See Files, which allows the user to access files within folders; and Make Changes, which allows the user to change a folder or disk, for example, by editing it or deleting it.

VI

The Mac at Work

The Sharing dialog box will change slightly depending on whether your shared disk in question is on your own computer or someone else's.

If you create a folder on someone else's computer, the Sharing dialog box will list both your name that you used to connect to the computer, and your access privileges, on the top section of the window.

Additionally, when the folder in question is on a computer other than your own, the Owner and User/Group options will need to be typed in manually. However, when the folder is on your own computer, those categories will be displayed via a pop-up menu, listing all the options available.

In the bottom section of the Sharing dialog box are an additional two boxes: Make all currently enclosed folders like this one, which will give all the folders inside this one the same privileges; and Can't be moved, renamed or deleted, which will prevent any of those actions occurring to the folder. The latter option is especially useful if you want to make sure that a folder stays in the same place. With the former option, it is worth noting that each new folder added to the newly created folder will automatically have the same access privileges as the one in which it is contained.

> **Note**
>
> When you use your own computer locally, you automatically have access to all the files residing on it. Also, when connecting to your own computer over the network, you also have access to all of the files that reside on it. See the next section, "Connecting to Your Own Computer Remotely."

Setting Up Your Computer for Remote Access

You can access your own computer from another computer on the network. You may not be able to get to your own computer for some reason, but you can still access all the files on it across the network.

The first steps in setting up your computer to allow you to access from across the network, are to make sure it is turned on, and that the file sharing feature is also on.

Following these steps:

1. Open the Apple menu and choose Control Panels.

2. Open the Users & Groups control panel.

3. Open the icon with the bold outline. This is the Owner icon (see fig. 33.18).

Fig. 33.18
Owner File Sharing screen.

In the top section there are three check boxes.

4. Select the Allow user to connect and Allow user to see entire disk boxes. If they are already selected, don't touch them.

5. Close the File Sharing dialog box.

6. Close the Users & Groups control panel.

You can now access your computer from across the network. You will need to enter your password to do so. The owner password to use can be found in the Sharing Setup control panel. See the note in the Passwords section with regards to the importance of choosing a suitable password.

> **Note**
>
> To deny yourself access to your own computer from across the network, merely deselect the Allow user to connect and Allow user to see entire disk boxes. If no X is in those boxes, you will be denied access to your computer from the network.

Changing User Access to Your Computer

So you've been benevolent in your allocation of access privileges to users who are connecting to your Macintosh, only to find out that they're changing things they are not meant to be changing. Even worse, there is one user that is really messing things up, and you want to deny him access to your computer completely. Well, both problems can be dealt with easily.

◀ See "Using Apple Remote Access," p. 840

To reduce the access privileges of users, follow these steps:

1. Select the shared folder in question.

2. Open the File menu and choose Sharing (see fig. 33.19).

Fig. 33.19
The Sharing dialog
box.

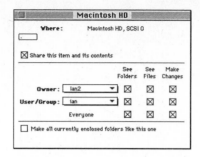

In the top section there is a check box labeled "Share this item and its contents." The box will be checked.

3. Check on the box. There should now be no X in the box.

4. Close the window.

A dialog box appears asking whether you want to Save, Don't Save, or Cancel the action.

5. Select Save.

The folder is no longer a shared folder. No one from the network can now access that folder.

Now comes the real troublemaker that you don't want accessing your computer at all. Here's how you get rid of him or her:

1. Open the Apple menu and choose Control Panels.

2. Open the Users & Groups control panel.

3. Open the user icon of the person to which you want to deny access (see fig. 33.20).

Fig. 33.20
User Password
window.

The first box in the File Sharing section, just below the User Password, is labeled "Allow user to connect."

4. Remove the X in the box. Removing the X will deny this user access the next time he or she attempts to log on.

5. Close the window.

A dialog box appears, asking if you want to save the changes.

6. Select Save.

If the user is connected, he or she will be disconnected straight away.

Guest users can also be denied access. When you deny access to Guests, only Registered Users (people you specify) have access to your computer.

To deny access to guests, follow these steps:

1. Open the Apple menu and choose Control Panels.

2. Open the Users & Groups control panel.

3. Open the Guest icon (see fig. 33.21).

Fig. 33.21
The Guest window.

A window appears. The top section of the box is titled File Sharing. A check box is labeled "Allow guests to connect."

4. Select the box. There should be no X in the box.

5. Close the window.

A dialog box appears giving you the chance to save the changes.

6. Select Save.

Now guests cannot access your computer. Only Registered Users can access.

Monitoring Activities

File sharing is on, and you have users connected to your computer. But you want to know who it is, and what they're doing. There is a control panel designed specifically for that.

VI

The Mac at Work

To find out who is connected, follow these steps:

1. Open the Apple menu and choose Control Panels.

2. Open the File Sharing Monitor control panel.

The File Sharing Monitor control panel window opens (see fig. 33.22).

Fig. 33.22

The File Sharing
Monitor window.

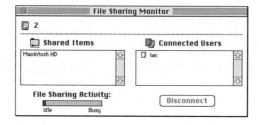

The window is divided into a left and right scrolling list window, with Shared Items on the left and Connected Users on the right. At the bottom of the window is a sliding level labeled File Sharing Activity. There is also a Disconnect button.

The Shared Items list displays all disks and folders. Any files or folders contained within those folders displayed are also accessible to users.

The Connected Users list shows all users connected to your computer.

You can disconnect any user displayed in the Connected User list by following these steps:

1. Select the user that you want to disconnect from your computer in the Connected User list.

   To select more than one user at a time, hold down the Shift key while choosing the users to be disconnected.

2. Click the Disconnect button.

   A Disconnect dialog box appears (see fig. 33.23).

Fig. 33.23

The Disconnect
dialog box.

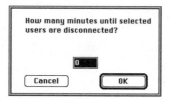

The box offers you the chance to type in the number of minutes before the designated user is disconnected. Typing a **0** disconnects him or her immediately. Unless it is an emergency, give the user enough time to save whatever changes he or she has made to the file that he or she is working on.

3. Click the OK button.

4. Close the File Sharing Monitor window.

The user will now be disconnected in the number of minutes you specified.

The user will receive a message informing him or her that he or she will be disconnected.

Transferring Ownership of a Disk/Folder

You do not have to "own" all the folders or disks on your computer. The folder or disk can be owned by any registered user or group on the network. Ownership can also be given to everyone on the network. Make sure that you transfer your private files out of the folder first, though.

Why would you want ownership of a folder? The owner of the folder can change the access privileges.

However, even if you give up ownership of the folder, if it is residing on your computer, you can still open and use it, and even change ownership of the folder again any time you like.

To transfer ownership of a shared folder or disk, follow these steps:

1. Select the folder or disk to be transferred.

2. Open the File menu and choose Sharing.

In the middle section is the Owner pop-up menu. Pull down the list of possible owners.

3. Select the new owner from that list.

4. Close the Sharing dialog box.

A dialog box appears giving you the chance to save the changes.

5. Click the Save button.

Another dialog box appears, asking you to confirm the changes.

6. Click OK.

VI

The Mac at Work

The ownership of that folder or disk has now been transferred to the specified party. You can still access it though, because it is on your computer.

Linking Programs

If the same material is to be used in different documents, you can save time by *linking* the information between the two. Then, when you update the material in the original document, it will automatically update in the other. You can usually choose not to have this happen automatically if you don't want it to; in which case, you can have it set so the information must be updated manually. But the fact that it can be set up to happen automatically can be extremely beneficial.

Documents can be linked from your Macintosh to another on the network or between two documents on your own computer. Other network users can also link their documents to documents and files on your computer.

The information in the original document is usually referred to as the *source*, while the place where it is to be inserted is usually called the *destination*.

You have control over who can link to your documents, what documents they can link to, and whether you will allow linking at all.

However, before the linking of programs and documents can begin, the programs must be set up to allow for linking. It is worth remembering though, that all Macintosh programs do not necessarily allow for linking.

How linking is implemented varies between programs. However, they all follow the same general pattern. Here's what you have to do:

1. Select the information that is to be linked. For example, highlight the text and choose Copy from the Edit menu.

2. Open the destination document where the information is to be inserted, and position the text at the correct place.

3. Using whatever is the special linking option from that application, paste the information into the destination document.

Now, when the information is updated in the source document, the destination document will update at the same time.

If you want everyone on the network to be allowed to link his or her programs with programs on your computer, you can specify guest access for program linking.

Follow these steps:

1. Open the Apple menu and choose Control Panels.

2. Open the Users & Groups control panel.

3. Open the Guest icon (see fig. 33.24).

Fig. 33.24
The open Guest
window.

In the lower section of the screen, there is a check box labeled "Allow guests to link to programs on this Macintosh."

4. Select this box. There should now be an X in the box.

5. Close the Guest window.

If you are worried about allowing for unlimited access to your programs over the network, you can also name specific users to link to your programs.

Follow these steps:

1. Open the Apple menu and choose Control Panels.

2. Open the Users & Groups control panel.

3. Select New User from the File menu, if you are naming the user for the first time. Type the name of the user.

4. If the user already has been named for file sharing, open his or her icon.

The user icon opens. The bottom section of the window is titled Program Linking. Notice the Allow User To Link to Programs on this Macintosh check box (see fig. 33.25).

5. Select this check box. It should now have an X in the box.

6. Close the window.

A dialog box appears asking whether you want to save the changes.

7. Click Save.

VI

The Mac at Work

Fig. 33.25

The user window.

The next step is to set up your program to allow other network users to link to it.

To do this, AppleTalk must be active and you have to have named your Macintosh.

Follow these steps:

1. Open the Apple menu and choose Control Panels.

2. Open the Sharing Setup control panel (see fig. 33.26).

Fig. 33.26

The Sharing Setup control panel.

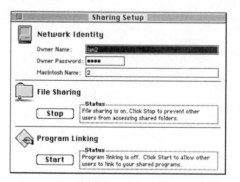

At the bottom of the window is a section called Program Linking.

3. Select the Start button in that section.

The text in the Status box will change after program linking is initiated. The Start button will turn into a Stop button.

4. Close the Sharing Setup control panel.

Troubleshooting

You need to do a couple of things if you have problems. Make sure the networking system software has been installed properly. Then make sure that all necessary cables (and expansion boards, if you have them) are connected properly.

Switching on System 7's Balloon Help may help you figure out the problem if it involves menus or commands.

Make sure that any files that were installed in the Preferences folder or the Extensions folder are still there.

Following are some common problems and some suggestions on how they may be solved:

■ If no device icons are showing in the upper left section of Chooser, you have to ensure that the AppleTalk Active button is selected at the lower right of the window. Also, if the Apple Share icon is missing, you need to check that the AppleShare file is in the Extensions folder, which is in the System Folder on your hard disk.

■ If no device is listed in the upper right window of Chooser, and you have zones on your network, you need to check and make sure that the zone which contains the device you want to connect to is selected in the AppleTalk zones list in the bottom left window. If you cannot connect to a shared folder on a remote computer you need to check with the owner of that computer to ensure file sharing is on. Also, ensure that the device you want to connect to is selected in the upper left window of Chooser.

■ If you can't find a file or folder, or you can't make the changes you want, you may not have been allocated the necessary access privileges. You need to check with the owner of the file or folder.

■ If your name or password is not accepted, you need to first check with the owner of the other Macintosh, or the network administrator, and confirm your exact password spelling, and whether you are in fact listed as a Registered User.

■ If the Sharing Setup icon will not open, the file sharing capability has not been installed correctly. The same reason applies if the file sharing section of the control panel is missing, or the Sharing Setup control panel is absent. To remedy these problems, ensure that the Extensions

VI

The Mac at Work

folder contains both the Network Extensions file and the File Sharing Extension file and that they are in the Extensions folder in the System Folder. Also make sure that the Control Panels folder contains the Sharing Setup control panel. If you add any of them, restart your computer.

Hooking Up a Printer

Connecting a printer is a simple matter of plugging the printer cable into the printer port at the back of your Macintosh. But there are other things to consider if the printer is connected to a Macintosh that is part of a network. You will need to use an AppleTalk connector with two sockets to plug into the printer port of the Macintosh. The use of the connector for linking Macintoshes to a printer is explained in the "Hardware/Software Requirements" section of this chapter.

After you connect a printer to your Macintosh, you need to set up the software so that the computer can print to it.

The first thing that you do is move the printer driver that corresponds to the printer you just connected into your Extensions folder. The printer driver is software that allows a specific type of printer to communicate with a Macintosh.

If you used the Easy Install option when you installed your Macintosh System software onto your hard drive, you don't have to worry because all the System printer drivers as well as Print Monitor software have been automatically placed into the appropriate places.

The Installer program on the System software Printing disk can also be used to install the relevant driver, if it is not already installed.

An alternative for installing the required printer driver, is to drag its icon onto the System Folder on your hard disk. The Print Monitor must be included to use a LaserWriter.

Now you need to choose the printer you want to use on the network. Follow these steps:

1. Open the Apple menu and select Chooser (see fig. 33.27).

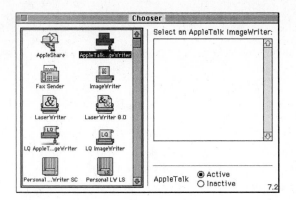

Fig. 33.27
The Chooser
window.

On the top left of the screen will be a window containing icons of types of printers you have available, along with the AppleShare icon. If you don't have zones on your network, this window will take up the whole left side of the window.

If you have zones, another window will be on the bottom left side showing zones available.

On the upper right side will be a window containing a list of available printers.

Below that will be a section labeled Background Printing. This allows you to choose if you want to be able to continue working on the Macintosh while it is printing. If you do, you need to select the On button.

The final section at the bottom of the right side lets you choose to have AppleTalk Active or Inactive. To use a network device, or print to a LaserWriter that is connected to the printer port, the Active button needs to be selected.

2. Select the type of printer you want to connect to in the upper left window.

3. You need to select the zone in which the printer is located only if you have zones on your network. This window will not appear if there are no zones.

4. Select the printer you want to use in the upper right hand window.

5. Close Chooser.

VI

The Mac at Work

> **Note**
>
> You also use Chooser to connect to a printer directly attached to your Macintosh. However, instead of selecting the name of the printer, you have to choose which port your printer is connected to, the printer port or the modem port.

 QuickDraw GX in System 7.5 lets the user display and control printers using printer icons on the desktop. A user drags the document to be printed over to the icon. Multiple printers can be displayed on the desktop, allowing for the user to choose which printer to print from.

By double-clicking a printer icon, a print queue status window is revealed, allowing for the user to control printing of the print job. Document icons can be dragged to other printers in order to shift printing to another printer identified by an icon on the desktop.

Connecting to a Larger Network

The difficulty involved in integrating or expanding a small AppleTalk Macintosh local area network into a larger corporate network depends on a number of factors. Initially, whether LocalTalk, Ethernet, or Token Ring was used for the initial LAN, and whether the rest of the larger network uses the same technology, will be a major contributing factor.

A full explanation of expanding such a LAN into an enterprise-wide network is beyond the scope of this chapter. However, an overview of some of the technology involved will give an idea of the task.

In the first place, as already stated, whether LocalTalk, Ethernet, or Token Ring was used for the initial LAN will have an effect on how you proceed.

For simplicity's sake, suppose that the entire network is running AppleTalk over LocalTalk cabling. Don't forget, however, that LocalTalk bandwidth is considerably less than both Ethernet and Token Ring. As a result, while LocalTalk may be useful and convenient for small LANs and departmental networking, the bandwidth factor alone may mean one of the higher bandwidth technologies will be used to connect the individual LocalTalk LANs. The cable used to connect all the different LANs, or subnets, is called the *backbone*.

For a start though, suppose that everyone connected to the network is using AppleTalk over LocalTalk cabling. There's no problem here until you start add many users. As with other cabling systems, there is a limit to the number of devices that can be attached to a network, and the distance it can cover. While this may vary depending on new products from various companies, generally, the recommended maximum number of nodes (computers and printers, for example) that can be supported in a single LocalTalk network bus is 32. The recommended maximum distance, in terms of cabling, is typically 1,000 feet. As mentioned, these figures vary depending on the product used.

Through the use of a bridge, the number of nodes can be increased to a LocalTalk maximum of 254. A bridge is a device that connects two buses in order to expand the number of nodes that can be supported on the network. It also extends the recommended distance, in terms of feet. A single LocalTalk bridge, for example, will connect two 32 node buses into a 64 node network. A bridge will also amplify the incoming signal before sending it onto the next bus. You can keep adding bridges until you reach 254 nodes.

A bridge will see the connected buses as a single network, however. To improve management of a network with a lot of nodes, you can use a router, instead of a bridge. Unlike a bridge, which sees just a single network, a router, or rather, the routing software contained in the computing device, will divide the expanding network up into separate networks. The router software can then allocate zones to the network, for example, zone A on one side of the router, with zone B on the other. This can cut down on network traffic and therefore improve network performance. Unlike a bridge, a router can keep traffic being sent to the same zone in which it originates from going to the next bus unnecessarily.

Routing software can also be installed in a computer, such as a Macintosh. The computer would need to have two NICs installed, if necessary, corresponding to the cabling systems used in the two networks it is connecting. So routers can also be used to join two different network cabling systems together. In this way, a smaller LocalTalk LAN can be incorporated into a larger company-wide network. You cannot just join two different network cabling systems together. You need a device that can support both cabling systems, and software that can be configured to reformat the packets of data moving between one type of cable and the other.

Cost is a deciding factor between using a bridge or a router for many users. Bridges are usually less expensive than routers. As with all computing technology, however, cost eventually declines. And along with cost, the distinction between the two devices is also blurring, with many bridges now being

VI

The Mac at Work

sold with some routing capabilities. The current distinction between the two is also outside of the scope of this chapter, and could probably constitute a book in itself. This overview is just designed to give an idea of the technology.

In large LocalTalk networks, you can use both bridges and routers together. The bridges can be used to connect LocalTalk busses, while a router or two can be used to divide the expanded network into two or three separate networks in order to improve network performance and make management easier.

Users should be grouped in the same zone as those they need to communicate with the most. Keeping most of their traffic within the same zone cuts down on network traffic. You can still access computers outside of the zone by using the Chooser.

As mentioned previously, you can use a router to connect a LocalTalk subnet to a higher speed Ethernet backbone. When the data packets reach the destination LocalTalk subnet, another router would be used to reformat the packets for transferring on to the LocalTalk subnet, and eventually to the target Macintosh.

If you want a higher performance network, you can start off with Ethernet for all the LANs. AppleTalk over Ethernet cabling is called EtherTalk. The extra bandwidth will cost you, however; you need to install Ethernet NICs for each Macintosh, unless, like some Macintosh models, they have an Ethernet interface built-in.

The cabling is a more expensive coaxial type. It can be either Thin Ethernet or the more shielded Thick Ethernet. Also, it can be 10BaseT, which is a form of Ethernet that runs over twisted pair cabling. While the NICs can be used to connect the Macintoshes to the Ethernet network, an external adapter may be needed for an Apple LaserWriter printer, as it only has LocalTalk built-in.

As mentioned earlier, all network cabling systems have their limitations. In the case of EtherTalk the maximum distance for the network bus is generally 1,640 feet, and the most nodes it will support is 100. However, the most nodes that can be connected in a single AppleTalk network is still 254. You then need to add a router to extend the number of nodes.

When using AppleTalk Phase 2 protocols on Ethernet cabling (as opposed to the older and less flexible Phase 1), the physical zone limitations of LocalTalk do not apply. Instead of having one zone on one side of the router, and a second on the other side, zones can be assigned according to a logical instead of a physical layout. That is to say, you can have some of zone A's computers on one side of the router, and some of zone A's computers on the other side.

A quick word about Token Ring, originally an IBM proprietary cabling system used to connect many of its computing products. AppleTalk over Token Ring cabling is called TokenTalk. While Token Ring can be even faster than Ethernet, it is also more expensive. You connect a Macintosh to a Token Ring network in much the same way as you do for Ethernet. You either install a Token Ring NIC into your computer for direct access to the Token Ring network, or you connect your LocalTalk LAN to the Token Ring network using a router, or routing software on a file server.

As a final note on this short overview of expanded networking, AppleTalk networks do not have to be confined to connecting to other networks in the local geographic area. They can also be connected to networks located far away, over the public telephone networks, for example. They do this using bridges and routers designed for wide area networks (WANs), in much the same way as ordinary bridges and routers are used to connect LANs together, or a LAN to a backbone.

A Brief Note on System 7 Pro

At the end of 1993, Apple released an enhanced version of System 7, called System 7 Pro, designed for business-oriented users, to mixed reviews. While the operating system is essentially the same as the standard version that ships with all Macintoshes, it contains some added extras designed to make networking a little easier.

System 7 Pro's three main enhancements center around the new PowerTalk, which offers communications capabilities; AppleScript, which allows for the customization of applications; and QuickTime, which allows the user to add multimedia movies to their documents. Both QuickTime and AppleScript were already available, and still are, as extensions to System 7. System 7 Pro is priced considerably higher than System 7.

Using PowerTalk, users can consolidate electronic communications features, such as electronic mail, faxing, and on-line database searching into a single interface. PowerTalk is the new AOCE (Apple Open Collaboration Environment) client, and offers such desktop accessories as: AppleMail, which gives users one access point for communications, and Key Chains, which allows for the use of a single log-in capability to on-line accounts.

System 7 Pro's PowerTalk is a client package, which supports peer-to-peer messaging from within applications. The separate server package is called PowerShare.

From Here...

This chapter covers the basics of networking Macs together. But connecting computers together is not confined to in-house networks. You can also connect to other users via electronic mail, on-line services, and bulletin board systems (BBSs) among other options. In addition, mobile users also have a number of options, including wireless communication and Apple Remote Access.

■ Chapter 34, "Data Exchange," exchanging files with PCs is discussed along with cross-platform applications.

■ Chapter 35, "On the Road," a number of subjects are covered, including electronic mail and wireless communications.

■ Chapters 29–32 cover a variety of subjects related to connecting with other users. These include BBSs, online services, Apple Remote Access, and the Internet.

Data Exchange

by Carman Minarik

In many organizations, Macintoshes and IBM-compatible PC's must coexist and exchange information. Home Macintosh users also may need to exchange data with PC users. In this chapter you explore the various methods of transferring files between the Macintosh and PC computing platforms.

In this chapter, you learn the following:

- The difference between file transfer and file translation

- How to transfer files using floppy disks, networks, or other cabling

- How to use Apple File Exchange to transfer files

- How software utilities can make the file transfer process easier

- How to use cross-platform compatible applications

- How to translate files using MacLink Plus

- Differences between Macintosh and PC file types

- How PC emulation can allow you to run PC software on your Macintosh

General Concepts

The two questions that you must ask yourself when transferring files between your Macintosh and a PC are *How do I move the file from one computer to the other?* and *How do I use the file on the other computer?* While each of these questions raises unique issues, they are rarely addressed independently.

The first step toward exchanging information between a Macintosh and a PC is to physically transfer the file from one machine to the other. While both Macintosh computers and PCs use similar media (hard disks, floppy disks, CD-ROM, and so on) to store information, the manner in which data is arranged on the media is drastically different on each platform.

After the file has been moved to the computer where it is needed, the issue becomes how the file can be made usable. Picture an American tourist in Germany. The American is physically in Germany, but unless he can speak German, he may not be able to communicate. The same problem exists for files moving from one platform to another. Just because a file is physically located on a particular computer does not mean that any software on that computer can open the file.

File Transfer

File transfer is the process of moving a file from one machine to the other. You can transfer a file using floppy disks, network systems, or direct cable connections between computers.

Disk Transfer

The most common method of transferring files from one platform to another is to use a floppy disk. Both PCs and Macintosh computers can use a 3.5-inch floppy disk, but the formats are different. If you place a Macintosh formatted floppy disk in PC, it can't be read. Similarly, a Macintosh without special software will want to format any PC-formatted disk placed in its drive.

To alleviate this problem, Macintosh computers with *high-density* drives can read and write PC-formatted diskettes. High-density drives are able to use 1.44MB disks, and have been standard on all Macintosh models since the SE/30 was introduced. In order for the Macintosh operating system to recognize a PC-formatted disk, however, software such as Apple File Exchange or Macintosh PC Exchange must be loaded.

Apple File Exchange

Even though the Macintosh high-density drive is physically able to read PC disks, special software is needed to actually transfer files. The Macintosh comes with an application called Apple File Exchange, which is a software program designed to transfer files between the Macintosh and a PC-formatted floppy disk. Some Macintosh models also ship with Macintosh PC Exchange, which will be discussed in detail later in this chapter.

> **Caution**
>
> Apple File Exchange must be launched *before* the PC floppy disk is inserted in the floppy drive. Otherwise, the Macintosh will treat the disk like any other non-Macintosh formatted disk, and prompt you to initialize it. This situation is alleviated if PC Exchange is loaded.

> **Caution**
>
> Launch Apple File Exchange by double-clicking its icon. Apple File Exchange can often be found in the Utilities folder on the hard disk.

Tip
Apple File Exchange is not copied to the hard disk automatically as part of the system installation process. You may need to manually copy the application from the Tidbits system installation disk to the hard disk.

When launched, Apple File Exchange shows a transfer window similar to that shown in figure 34.1.

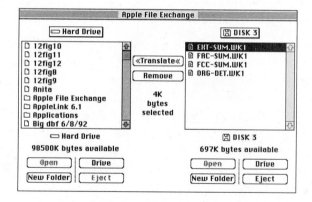

Fig. 34.1
The Apple File Exchange window allows you to transfer Macintosh, PC, and Apple II files.

Initially, the left side of this window displays the contents of the Macintosh's hard drive. When a PC disk is placed in the floppy drive, the contents of that disk are displayed in the right side of the window.

Use the following guidelines while working with Apple File Exchange:

- A file can be selected in either window by clicking the desired file.

- Hold down the Shift key while clicking files to select a continuous range of files.

- Hold ⌘ while clicking files to select discontinuous files.

- The arrows on the Translate button confirm the direction of the transfer.

VI

The Mac at Work

■ Click the Translate button to transfer the files.

You can use the standard Macintosh file dialog controls in the Apple File Exchange window to choose other disks, folders, and so on. Be sure you have selected the appropriate folder in which to transfer files.

Commercial Utilities

Apple File Exchange can be used effectively to transfer files from one platform to another. The software is somewhat cumbersome, however, in that you must remember to run the application before you place a PC-formatted disk in the floppy drive. Commercial utility programs exist which allow PC disks to be mounted on the Macintosh desktop in the same way that Macintosh disks are mounted.

The most popular of these utilities are DOS Mounter from Dayna Corporation, Access PC, and Macintosh PC Exchange from Apple. All of these packages allow the Macintosh to mount, format, and copy information to and from PC disks as well as Macintosh disks.

Each of these utilities operate in much the same manner. The software is in the form of a Control Panel which automatically launches at system startup time. The Control Panel extends your operating system's ability to recognize and use floppy disks to include PC-formatted disks as well as Macintosh disks. In addition, the Special menu option Erase Disk allows you to choose whether to format the disk as a Macintosh disk or as a PC disk. Both high density and low density disks are supported. Figure 34.2 shows a PC-formatted disk as it would appear on a Macintosh with Apple's Macintosh PC Exchange software installed.

Fig. 34.2
PC Exchange allows the PC disk to be used exactly like a Macintosh disk.

> ### Caution
>
> When using floppy disks to transfer files between PCs and Macintosh computers, be sure the disks are formatted properly. High-density (those with an HD stamped on them, and two square corner holes rather than one) PC disks must be formatted 1.44MB and standard PC disks must be formatted 720K. If a standard disk is formatted 1.44MB, the Macintosh will not be able to read the disk.

Network Transfer

Files can also be transferred from one platform to another using network wiring. If the Macintosh computers and PCs are connected to a compatible network (AppleTalk, Novell, Tops, and so on) files can usually be transferred either peer-to-peer or via a file server. For more information on networking, see Chapter 33, "Networking."

Commercial software such as Farallon's PhoneNET PC allows PC users to connect to Macintosh file servers and transfer files much in the same manner as a Macintosh user would. Products such as Novell's NetWare for Macintosh allow Macintosh users to connect with Novell file servers.

Cable/Modem Transfer

Other common methods of transferring files include direct cable connection or connection over phone lines using modems. For more information on transferring files, see Chapter 29, "Getting Online."

Utilities such as MacLinkPlus/PC allow direct connection of Macintosh computers and PCs via a special cable and software. Modems can be connected to both Macintosh and IBM-compatible computers allowing files to be transmitted over standard telephone lines. Software communicating via modem varies greatly, but nearly every communication software package includes standard file transfer options.

File Translation

In order for a file that has been transferred from one platform to another to be displayed or modified, the file must be in a format compatible with software on the destination computer. The file format determines how an application stores information. Each application uses its own method of encoding the information it creates. File translation is the method used to get a file into a format another application can use. If no file translation is available, files created on other platforms may be unusable.

Two basic methods exist for translating files. The first involves use of software applications with file translators built-in. Microsoft Excel, for example, contains file translation capabilities for 18 different file types.

The second method involves use of translation software such as MacLink Plus from DataViz. This type of software provides translation where no application-based translators exist.

Application-Based Translators

Many current applications automatically translate files created in different applications or applications on different platforms. For example, Microsoft Excel for Macintosh can automatically read files created in earlier versions of Excel, files created in Excel for Windows, files created with Lotus 1-2-3 for DOS, and many others.

Microsoft Excel also automatically creates files which are compatible across platforms. For example, a file created in Microsoft Excel for Windows can be read by Microsoft Excel for the Macintosh without any translation. A file created with Microsoft Excel 4.0 for the Macintosh can be used by Lotus 1-2-3 for MS-DOS just by saving the file in the proper format using Excel's built-in Save Options as shown in figure 34.3.

Fig. 34.3

The application-based translators supplied with Microsoft Excel are listed here. Many software packages provide similar capabilities.

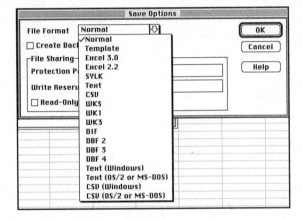

As another example, opening a WordPerfect 5.1 for MS-DOS file in Microsoft Word 5.0 for the Macintosh can be accomplished using Word's built-in translators.

Many software packages allow translation of different file types. Some packages go one step further, and actually use the same file formats for their Macintosh and PC versions. This is the ideal situation, since no translation of any kind is needed to use files created with these packages across platforms. The following list shows some of the major software that uses identical file formats for both Macintosh and PC:

- Microsoft Excel 4.0

- FileMaker Pro 2.0

- PowerPoint 3.0

- PageMaker 5.0

- FoxPro 2.5 (Mac) and 2.6 (PC)

- Microsoft Project 3.0

- QuarkXPress

Translator Utility Software

In addition to the translation capabilities built-in to software such as Microsoft Word and Excel, commercial software is available to handle more complex or less common translations. The most popular of these packages is MacLinkPlus from DataViz. MacLink Plus can translate word processing, spreadsheet, and graphics files between dozens of applications.

Launch MacLink Plus by double-clicking its icon, and the screen shown in figure 34.4 opens.

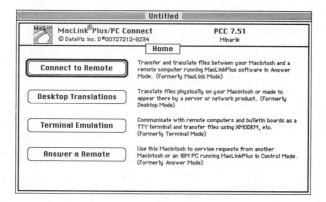

Fig. 34.4
Use this screen to choose a basic operating mode. For standard file translation, choose Desktop Translations.

This screen allows you to choose among MacLink Plus's modes of operation. Each operating mode is described on the screen. Choose Desktop Translations to open the screen illustrated in figure 34.5.

This screen is used to select the files you want to translate. When selecting files, keep the following points in mind:

- You can use the standard Macintosh file dialog controls on this screen to choose other disks, folders, and so on.

- A file can be selected in either window by clicking the desired file.

- Hold down the Shift key while clicking files to select multiple files.

Fig. 34.5
Use this screen to select the files to translate.

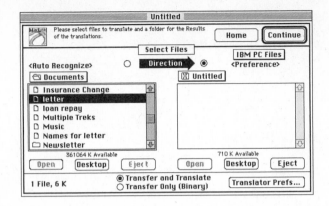

From this screen, follow these steps to automatically translate files:

1. Select the files to be translated.

2. When you have selected the files you want to translate, click the Continue button. A new screen appears, showing the progress of the translation.

By default, MacLink Plus provides automatic translator selection based on the type of file being translated. Automatic translator selection works well for many files, but in some cases you may need to set the translators manually. From the Preferences menu, select Manual Operation, and activate the check box in the resulting dialog box.

When Manual Operation is activated, a new screen, as illustrated in figure 34.6, appears after the file selection screen in the translation process.

Fig. 34.6
Use this screen to set the desired translator for use.

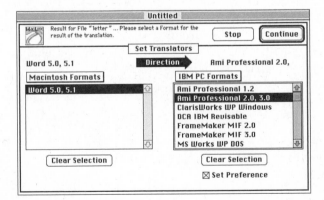

This screen indicates the file type of the selected files, and allows you to select the translator you want from the displayed list. Select the desired translator and click the Continue button. The screen shown in figure 34.7 opens.

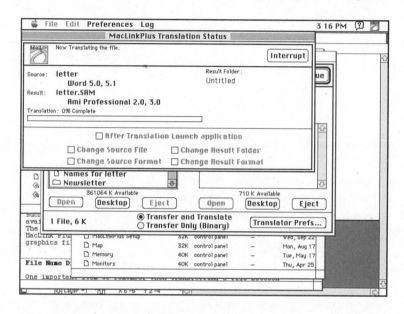

Fig. 34.7
This status screen displays the progress of the translation, and shows any errors that may occur.

When the translation is completed, a new file in the selected format will be created in the chosen destination.

File Name Differences between Platforms

When transferring a file between Macintosh and PC platforms, you should keep in mind how to name the file. The Macintosh allows long file names and use of most characters, while PCs have more stringent naming rules. Table 34.1 lists the naming differences on Macintosh and PC systems.

Table 34.1	File Name Conventions	
File System	**Number of Characters**	**Illegal Characters**
MS-DOS (PC)	8 maximum with an optional 3-character extension	angle brackets <> asterisk * comma , colon : equal sign =

(continues)

VI

The Mac at Work

Table 34.1 Continued		
File System	**Number of Characters**	**Illegal Characters**
		pipe |
		null
		plus sign +
		quotation marks ""
		question mark ?
		slashes /\
		square brackets [ ]
		space
Macintosh	31 maximum	colon :
		null

Not only do PCs and Macintoshes require different naming conventions, they also recognize files in different ways. PCs rely on the three-character extension in a file name to determine which application was used to create the file. Macintosh applications check the file's type and creator information, which is stored within the file itself. Table 34.2 shows commonly used file type equivalents between Macintosh and PC platforms.

Table 34.2 File Types		
File Type	**PC Extension**	**Macintosh Type/Creator**
ASCII Text File	.TXT	TEXT/ttxt or
		TEXT/MSWD
Canvas	.CVS	drw2/DAD2
FileMaker Pro	.FM	FMPR/FMPR
Lotus 1-2-3 Worksheet	.WKS	LWKS/L123
Microsoft Excel Worksheet	.XLS	XLS4/XCEL
Microsoft Excel Chart	.XLC	XLC3/XCEL
Microsoft Excel Workbook	.XLW	XLW4/XCEL
Microsoft Excel Macro Sheet	.XLM	XLM3/XCEL
Microsoft Word	.DOC	WDBN/MSWD
PageMaker	.PM4	ALT4/ALD4

File Type	PC Extension	Macintosh Type/Creator
QuarkXPress	.QXD	XDOC/XPRS
GIF Graphic File	.GIF	GIFf/Bozo
TIFF File	.TIF	TIFF/8BIM

Text File Differences between Platforms

Even if no translation software is available, some files can be used on a different platform if they are converted or saved in some generic format first. Most word processing, spreadsheet, and database applications allow files to be saved in a text-only format. In this format only the base character information is saved and all formatting such as font, size, bold, italic, and so on, will be lost.

ASCII Files

ASCII (American Standard Code for Information Interchange) is the name given to a set of codes that defines the base set of text and numbers that can be used on a computer system. Most computer systems adhere to the standard set of ASCII codes as shown in table 34.3.

Table 34.3	ASCII Codes		
Code	**Character**	**Code**	**Character**
9	(Tab)	10	(Line Feed)
12	(Form Feed)	13	(Carriage Return)
27	(Escape)	32	(Space)
33	!	34	"
35	#	36	$
37	%	38	&
39	'	40	(
41	)	42	*

(continues)

VI

The Mac at Work

Table 34.3   Continued

Code	Character	Code	Character
43	+	44	,
45	-	46	.
47	/	48	0
49	1	50	2
51	3	52	4
53	5	54	6
55	7	56	8
57	9	58	:
59	;	60	<
61	=	62	>
63	?	64	@
65	A	66	B
67	C	68	D
69	E	70	F
71	G	72	H
73	I	74	J
75	K	76	L
77	M	78	N
79	O	80	P
81	Q	82	R
83	S	84	T
85	U	86	V
87	W	88	X
89	Y	90	Z
91	[	92	\
93	]	94	^

Code	Character	Code	Character
95	_	96	'
97	a	98	b
99	c	100	d
101	e	102	f
103	g	104	h
105	i	106	j
107	k	108	l
109	m	110	n
111	o	112	p
113	q	114	r
115	s	116	t
117	u	118	v
119	w	120	x
121	y	122	z
123	{	124		
125	}	126	~
127	(Delete)		

Note

The standard ASCII character set includes only codes 0-127. Some computers, including most PCs, also use an extended ASCII character set (codes 128-255) that includes other machine-specific characters.

Text Files

Files that contain only characters and numbers conforming to standard ASCII codes are usually referred to as text files. Almost every application allows saving or exporting of data in text file format. However, not all text files are exactly the same.

When a Macintosh application creates a text file, the end of each line is marked with a single carriage return character. When a text file is created by a PC application, the end of each line is marked with a carriage return character and a line-feed character. When text files are transferred from a Macintosh to a PC, they're missing this line-feed character. When text files are transferred from a PC to a Macintosh, they contain extra line-feed characters.

Transfer utilities such as Apple File Exchange provide options to change the line-feed characters as shown in figure 34.8.

Fig. 34.8
This screen allows you to select options to enhance text file translation.

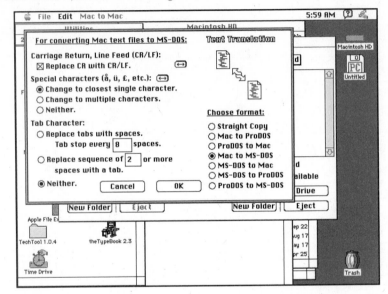

From the translation menu (Mac to DOS, Mac to Mac, etc), choose Text Translation to access this screen. Other Apple File Exchange options available on this screen include replacing special characters and replacing tab characters with spaces.

Format Differences between Platforms

Some file format differences exist that cannot be resolved easily, even with translation software. Certain types of files may not have exact counterparts on other platforms, and some features or capabilities of a particular application may have no equivalent in another application.

Text and basic formatting will nearly always translate properly. The next sections discuss some limitations on the translation process which may prevent perfect translation of information beyond the basics.

Fonts

Font formatting controls the appearance of text. The term font comes from the printing industry, and refers to a specific typeface with a specific size and type style. Helvetica 12 Point Bold is a description of a font. For more information about fonts, see Chapter 8, "All about Fonts."

If you create a file using a certain font on one platform and then transfer that file to another platform, the document will look different unless an equivalent font is available.

> **Note**
>
> Fonts on a Macintosh are stored as part of the operating system so that they are available to any Macintosh application. Fonts on a PC are stored as part of the individual applications. The Microsoft Windows operating environment allows font handling on a PC similar to that on a Macintosh. Windows also supports TrueType font technology, like a Macintosh. It is therefore much more likely that you will find equivalent fonts for your transferred documents if you are moving files between Macintosh and Windows applications than if you are moving files between Macintosh and MS-DOS applications.

Graphics

Graphic files are difficult to translate from one platform to another. Some graphic file formats, such as EPS (Encapsulated PostScript) and TIFF (Tagged Image File Format), do exist on both the Macintosh and PC platforms. Even when using these file formats, however, the image will usually not translate perfectly. For example, Macintosh EPS files contain both the printer information for the graphic image and a screen representation of the image. EPS files on a PC do not contain a screen component. An EPS file transferred from a PC to a Macintosh might print properly, but may not be visible on the screen.

A related problem occurs when graphic images are contained within other documents. An example is a logo contained in a word processing document. When you convert documents from one platform to the other, any graphic images in the file are usually lost.

Sounds

There is no common format for sound files on Macintosh and PC systems, so sound information is usually lost when translating a file which contains sound.

Emulation

You may find that your needs go beyond file translation, and that you must actually run PC software on your Macintosh. Emulation is the name given to the process of running software from one platform on another platform. Your Macintosh can be made to emulate a PC.

The most popular emulation solution is a software application called SoftPC from Insignia Solutions. When the SoftPC application is launched, MS-DOS opens in a window on the Macintosh where you can run PC software.

Another approach to PC emulation on a Macintosh involves use of hardware. A company called Orange Micro offers the OrangePC card, which contains an Intel 486 processor and plugs into any Macintosh with a NuBus slot. Apple's Macintosh Quadra 610 computer took a similar approach, including the Intel 486 processor as part of the package. Unfortunately, the Quadra 610 has been discontinued.

When comparing hardware and software solutions, keep the following points in mind:

- SoftPC is less costly than a hardware solution.

- SoftPC is not as fast as a hardware solution. This is particularly important if Windows-based software must be used.

- Hardware solutions do not support Macintosh CD-ROM drives or Macintosh printers. Soft-PC allows you to use your Mac printer and CD-ROM for PC applications.

From Here...

In this chapter, you learned the basics for transferring and translating files between the Macintosh and PC platforms. You have seen several methods of transferring files, and have looked at many issues impacting the translation of files between platforms.

- For more information on opening and saving files, see chapters 5 and 7.

- To learn more about networking, see Chapter 33.

- See the software descriptions in Chapters 16 through 28 for more information on individual software applications.

- See Chapter 8 for a detailed discussion of fonts.

VI

The Mac at Work

Chapter 35

On The Road

by Gene Steinberg

Chapters 29 through 32 discussed the ways you can get in touch with the entire world by using your Macintosh and your modem. When you take your work on the road, you can remain in touch by using these same tools.

Most desktop Macs, except perhaps the original compact models (such as the Plus and Classic), are not really suited for work on the road. Apple therefore created the PowerBook line. It all started back in 1989 with an ungainly product known as the Mac Portable, which, despite its girth (it weighed 16 pounds), had some unique features for a portable computer, some of which have become mainstays of Apple's PowerBook line, such as an ultra sharp (and expensive) active matrix screen. The original PowerBook 100, in fact, is considered in many ways a miniature version of the original Portable.

In this chapter you learn the following:

- The latest portable computers available from Apple

- The accessories you need when you take your Mac on the road

- How to send e-mail and fax and print documents while you're on the road

- How to hook up your notebook Mac to a monitor or projector for giving presentations

PowerBooks and Duos

Gone are the days when a Macintosh of any sort was priced higher than its PC-based counterparts and you had to resort to that other platform when you needed portability. Apple learned its lessons well after its first foray into the production of notebook computers, best exemplified when the PowerBook made its debut in 1991. Now you'll find a wide array of portable options in the Apple line from which to choose. The following sections cover the basics of this product line. Because Apple is always adding new products to its arsenal, you can expect continuing changes in the months to come.

PowerBook 1xx Series

The PowerBook 1xx Series notebook models are based on the original PowerBook design first introduced in October of 1991. They sport common features, such as an integrated trackball and palm rest. They contain slots for RAM expansion and the installation of an internal modem. Like desktop Macs, they have AppleTalk and modem ports. They also include a special 30-pin SCSI jack that requires a specially designed plug.

PowerBook 145B

This model forms the bottom of Apple's PowerBook line. It has a 25Mhz 68030 CPU, which puts it on nearly equal footing with such desktop Macs as the IIci in terms of performance, except for math related work. This model lacks an FPU, but you can look to third-party suppliers such as Digital Eclipse to provide this sort of upgrade path. The 145B has a 10-inch passive matrix screen with a 640x400 pixel black-and-white display (smaller than your standard 13/14-inch desktop monitor). It weighs in at approximately 6.8 pounds and can accept up to 8MB RAM.

PowerBook 165

The PowerBook 165 is quite similar to the 145B, but offers upgraded performance in several areas. It uses a 33Mhz 68030 CPU, again without an FPU. Unless you are doing math-intensive work, such as spreadsheet calculations and 3-D rendering, you probably won't notice the difference. The 10-inch 600x400 pixel passive matrix screen supports 16 levels of gray. This model is especially suited for presentations or as a substitute for a desktop Mac—you can connect a regular monitor (up to 16-inch) to its external monitor port. A dual display mode gives you the option of showing one image on the internal screen and another on your external monitor. You can install an internal modem or expand RAM up to a total (with motherboard RAM) of 14MB. The 165 also weighs in at 6.8 pounds.

PowerBook 500 Series

This model line represents the first major change in Apple's popular all-in-one PowerBook design. On the surface, the PowerBook 500 series are comparable to the older models in terms of size and weight. At a cursory glance, they may even look similar. But every aspect of these new models has been improved. They all sport 68LC040 CPUs and have promised upgrade paths to PowerPC. You get 16-bit CD-quality audio, same as the Power Macintosh line, and twin speakers are provided.

Gone is Apple's trackball, and in its place is the Apple Trackpad, a new solid-state pointing device, sometimes known as Midas (see fig. 35.1). Instead of moving a trackball, your finger does the walking instead, literally. When your finger moves across the trackpad, twin layers of electrodes beneath the surface of the pad sense the movement of your fingers and move the cursor accordingly. A special Control Panel adjusts the speed of cursor movement. In Apple's original announcement on the new products, they boasted that users learned how to navigate on-screen with the new trackpad in five minutes flat!

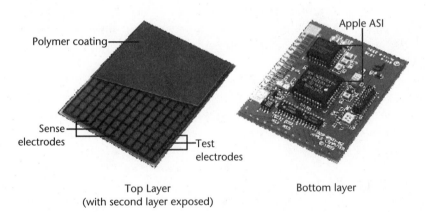

Polymer coating

Apple ASI

Sense electrodes

Test electrodes

Top Layer
(with second layer exposed)

Bottom layer

Fig. 35.1
This diagram shows the complex checkerboard assembly of electrodes that senses finger movement across the Apple trackpad.

Many standard features from desktop models are included in these models. Networking is improved with a built-in Ethernet port. Instead of pushing a button at the back of the unit to turn it on, you can power up the 500 Series PowerBooks with the keyboard. The keyboard also adds function keys to the mix, something that used to require the addition of an auxiliary keyboard or an Extension that remapped function keys. CD-like 16-bit sound is supported, and twin speakers provide stereo reproduction.

Like PC notebooks, PCMCIA expansion is offered using an optional module. There's also a PDS slot for third-party expansion possibilities. The batteries use an onboard processor to provide an accurate status report on battery life.

VI

The Mac at Work

The new models also include a package of handy utilities known as the PowerBook Mobility Bundle that are designed to help with your on-the-road computing tasks. They also monitor the computer's day-to-day status. These utilities are described in more detail later in this chapter.

> **Note**
>
> Because the 68040 CPU has an internal dual-clock architecture, similar in some respects to a 486DX2, Apple revised its speed designation. The PowerBook 540cs CPU, for example, is described as having a 680LC040 running at 66/33 Mhz.

PowerBook 520

The entry level product in the new PowerBook line is faster than any of the original PowerBook products. The 520 sports a 50/25Mhz 68LC040 CPU, and a passive matrix screen offering 16 shades of gray. It includes a 160MB hard drive, 4MB of RAM, standard, and a single battery with an advertised lifespan of 1.5 to 3 hours under normal use between charges. The unit tips the scales at 6.3 lbs.

PowerBook 520c

This model is virtually identical in configuration to the 520. The main difference is a dual-scan passive matrix color screen offering 256 colors. This unit weighs in at 6.4 lbs.

PowerBook 540

This model adds to the mix a 68LC040 CPU running at 66/33Mhz, equivalent in performance to high-end Macintosh Quadra models, except for the lack of integrated floating point unit. It offers an active matrix screen sporting 64 shades of gray. This model ships with two batteries and offers 4MB RAM and a 240MB hard drive in its base configuration. It weighs 7.1 lbs. Most of the increased weight can be accounted for by the fact that it has two batteries.

PowerBook 540c

The top of the new all-in-one PowerBook line offers an active matrix dual resolution color screen. Standard display is 256 colors, with the option of thousands of colors in 640×400 mode. Resolution switching can be done on the fly without having to reboot. Other specs are pretty much the same as the 540. This unit weighs 7.3 pounds.

PowerBook Duos

Apple's Duo line is designed to offer the best of both worlds—desktop and portable computing. The basic unit is smaller than the regular PowerBooks, less than an inch and a half thick, and weighs in at less than 5 pounds. It is designed to mate with a docking device, known as the *Duo Dock*, which adds built-in Ethernet and NuBus card expansion, essentially converting the computer into a desktop model. Like the original PowerBooks, all Duo models include a built-in trackball and palm rest. You need the Duo Dock for floppy drive support.

PowerBook Duo 230

This model is a carryover from the original line. It comes with a 9-inch 16 color grayscale passive matrix screen and a 33Mhz 68030 CPU, and weighs a little over 4 pounds. Battery life is advertised as 2 to 4.5 hours. It comes standard with 4MB RAM and an 80MB hard drive, with an option for 120MB, and you can expand RAM up to 24MB.

PowerBook Duo 280

The newest PowerBook Duos are based on the older 270 and 270c. They sport a 68LC040 CPU running at 66/33 Mhz (to quote Apple's new dual-speed scheme once again). This model and the top-of-the line 280c will have PowerPC upgrade paths. The 280 weighs in at just 4.2 lbs, and has a 9-inch active matrix 16 color grayscale screen, with a resolution of 640×400 pixels. The lone disk storage option is a 240MB hard drive. The supplied NiMH battery has an advertised life of two to four hours.

PowerBook Duo 280c

This model is essentially identical to the Duo 280, but it offers an 8.4-inch active matrix color screen, with 256 color resolution at 640×480 pixels, and an option of 16-bit color (thousands of colors) at 640×400 resolution. Onboard hard drive capacity expands to 320MB. This model weighs 4.8 lbs.

PowerBook Duo Dock II

This device provides the desktop capability for the Duos. You mate the Duo into this unit, essentially sliding it on, and you get a floppy drive, built-in Ethernet and space for NuBus expansion.

VI

The Mac at Work

Useful Accessories

Tip
Always travel with a set of system backup disks, hard disk diagnostic disks, and floppy backups for your most important software packages so that you can quickly get up and running in the event of a disk crash.

Before leaving on a trip, you'll probably want to get some useful accessories that are bound to make your PowerBook work more effectively on the road. The following sections concentrate strictly on items that you can easily pack in an overnight bag. A visit to your favorite dealer will reveal many more treasures from which to choose.

Portable Fixed Hard Drive

PowerBook drives usually have limited capacity and are expensive to replace. If you're doing a large presentation or heavy-duty graphic work requiring lots of storage space, youll want to consider products such as the APS Technologies Companion II or the Liberty portable drives, both of which offer the extra storage capacity you may need in small, convenient cases. The APS product includes their DaTerm digital active termination circuit, which helps reduce fiddling around with SCSI connections during a trip.

Portable Removable Hard Drive

If you need to transfer files to different locations, a removable drive is a plus. The new 3-1/2 SyQuest cartridges, available in both 105MB and 270MB varieties, weigh just three ounces and are especially suitable for travel. APS Technologies offers removable mechanisms in its Companion II line. The PLI Infinity Turbo models also offer a good mixture of portability and convenience.

Powerbook Carrying Cases

So many shapes and sizes are now available that you are bound to find one that meets your needs. Some products combine an overnight bag with a compartment for your PowerBook and some accessories. Other cases are hardly larger than the computer. Our suggestion is that you get one with straps to hold your Mac securely, with a sufficient amount of cushioning to protect it. There should be a pouch or two that are large enough to contain phone and SCSI cables, disks, and whatever accessories you need on your trip.

SCSI Disk Adapter

This cable allows PowerBooks and Duos (with the exception of the 140, 145, 145b, or 170) to be used as a hard drive on your desktop Mac.

SCSI System Cable

The PowerBook doesn't accept a standard SCSI cable, but this special cable enables you to attach an external hard drive or another SCSI device to your PowerBook.

Caution

The PowerBook SCSI Disk Adapter cable and the SCSI System Cable are frequently confused with one another, even by some dealers. The Apple version of the former, the product that turns your PowerBook into a SCSI disk, is dark gray and about 9-1/2 inches in length. The cable used to connect another hard drive to your PowerBook is a lighter gray and about 18 inches in length. The difference is in the 30-pin connection jack that hooks to your Powerbook. The SCSI system cable has one pin missing, which you can see at the upper left when the plug is facing you.

SCSI Terminator

You can buy a standard SCSI terminator for anywhere from $10 to $20, but you might want to consider the $99 APS Technologies SCSI Sentry, an active terminator that uses digital circuitry to maintain proper current and impedance across the SCSI chain, and reduce problems that sometimes affect a SCSI setup.

Extra Battery and Recharger

If you need to do a long work session on the road, or if you're using one of the original all-in-one PowerBooks with a short battery life, a second battery and a separate recharger will keep you running when power is low.

Modular Telephone Cord

You can buy a modular telephone cord at your supermarket, if your modem wasn't shipped with one (although they usually are). Just get a simple cable with the standard RJ-11 modular jacks at each end.

Digital Phone Switch

One of the manufacturers of PowerBook modems, Global Village, offers such a product, which provides an interface between a PBX digital phone system and your PowerBook's modem.

PowerBook Management Software

Programs such as CPU from Connectix, PB Tools from Inline Software, and Power To Go from Claris provide tools to monitor power use and to allow you to quickly change settings to maximize battery life. The PowerBook Mobility Bundle shipped with the new 500 Series models also provides a set of useful utilities to get the maximum amount of working time between charges.

Tip

To get the maximum battery life from your PowerBook, turn off AppleTalk, File Sharing, and, if you have enough RAM, set up a RAM disk in your Memory Control panel.

VI

The Mac at Work

> **Note**
>
> Although Apple suggests caution when running your PowerBook through the x-ray devices at an airport security check-in, the chances are slight that you would be at risk of damage to your data. If in doubt, insist on a manual inspection, and have your PowerBook left in the Sleep mode, rather than shut off, so that its startup routine can be quickly observed by the airport security personnel.

Portable Printer

While your traveling bag is apt to get crowded with all the accessories you can buy, if you intend to create many documents, you might want to bring along a portable printer, too. Apple, GCC, Hewlett-Packard, and other manufacturers offer lines of small printers that you can use to process your mission-critical documents during a trip. Don't expect any of these models to be speed demons compared to your desktop printer, but they more than make up for their slower performance in terms of convenience.

TV/VCR Interface

If you expect to use your PowerBook to generate a slide show or other presentation, you'll want to bring an interface unit, such as the Lapis LoTV Portable at hand. These products allow you to hook up many PowerBook models directly to a TV or VCR.

PowerBook Mobility Bundle

Apple's new PowerBook and Duo line is bundled with a set of software designed to make it easier to stay in touch while on the road and to work with the data you create when you return to your home or office. Following is a brief summary of what it includes:

- *Apple Remote Access*. Chapter 29, "Getting Online," discussed this program in detail. The most attractive feature to the traveler, aside from the easy connectivity to your Mac's desktop, is its DialAssist utility. This program, shown in figure 35.2, enables you to customize telephone settings to make it easier to dial out from wherever you happen to be traveling.

  Settings for your area code and country make dialing those complex international country codes less of a chore. You can establish a prefix to get an outside dialing line or to reach your preferred long distance carrier. There's even a special suffix setting where you can enter your credit card or calling card number (the numbers themselves appear only as bullets on the Mac's screen).

> **Caution**
>
> Be careful when storing passwords or calling card numbers in your communi-
> cations software. Someone who gets access to your computer may also be
> able to place calls with your phone credit card, even though the number
> can't be read.

- *PowerTalk* (bundled with top-of-the-line PowerBook models). Apple's system-level electronic mail system, PowerTalk, enables you to create an in box and an out box on your desktop, where you can send and re-ceive communications. You can establish special settings, depending on where you are located, so that when you log onto your network after returning to the office, you can automatically send your communica-tions.

- *eWorld.* You get a special sign-up offer for Apple's eWorld online service and a software disk. Apple's new online service is described in Chapter 31, "Using eWorld."

- *PC Exchange.* This utility, which is also included with many desktop Macs, allows you to mount MS-DOS disks on your Mac's desktop, and to perform simple data conversions.

- *Easy Open Translators.* The ability to transfer files from one format to another, or from one computer platform to another is detailed in Chap-ter 34, "Data Exchange."

- *Apple File Assistant.* When you return to your home or office, you can use this handy utility to synchronize the files you've created on the road with the ones on your desktop Mac.

VI

The Mac at Work

■ *Power Management.* Apple's unique Control Strip, shown in figure 35.3, provides a comprehensive look at the status of various systems on your PowerBook, ranging from the remaining battery life to whether AppleTalk and File Sharing is on or off.

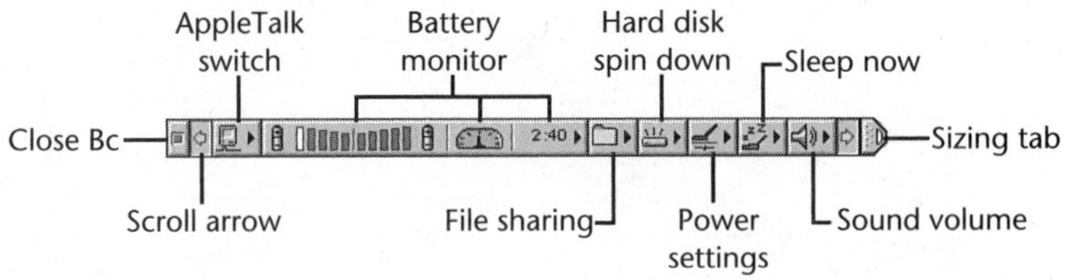

Fig. 35.3
Apples Control Strip provides an on-screen display and control panel for various system functions.

In addition to monitoring these functions, you can use the Control Strip to change settings, or even customize it to show only the status information you select.

Using On The Road

Even though you may be traveling, there are times when you need to fax or print a document, but you have neither a telephone nor a printer handy. Through a nifty program from Connectix, called On The Road, you can continue printing and faxing, just as if you actually had a modem or printer attached to your computer.

When you are back at your office or home, as soon as you reattach your Macintosh to your network or phone line, On The Road automatically configures the Mac to your location (somewhat in the way PowerTalk does). The program displays an icon indicating your location, as shown in figure 35.4.

Fig. 35.4
Connectix On The Road is accessible by a Finder level pull-down menu.

The settings On The Road uses to determine your location are set in the program's preferences, as shown in figure 35.5. In situations where you may

the software, upgrade to this new version because it offers 9600 bps access (with a connection number that supports that speed).

Before you create a new locality profile, get a list of local phone numbers. To do that, simply log onto America Online and type the keyword **Access**. That keyword will take you to the free area shown in figure 35.6. This department allows you to search America Online's huge database of connection numbers throughout the U.S. and Canada.

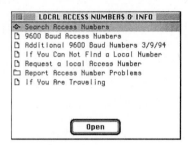

Fig. 35.6
Local access numbers are found easily on America Online.

The quickest way to find the numbers you want is to click on the Search Access Number's listing in the directory, shown in figure 35.6. You'll see a search screen like the one shown in figure 35.7. Enter the area code of the city you're visiting in the field. If you want to concentrate on 9600 bps numbers alone, just enter the words **and 9600** after the area code.

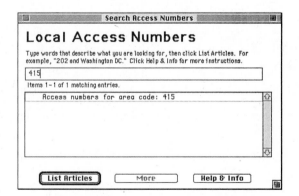

Fig. 35.7
America Online's speedy search mechanism tries to find the local connection numbers you want.

To see the list of numbers, just double-click the listing in the directory window. If suitable numbers aren't found, try a neighboring area code and see what it produces for you. Save the entire list, in case you have difficulty connecting with the first number you select.

After you obtain a list of numbers, create a new Locality profile for the cities you intend to visit. Simply select New from the File menu of your AOL software and choose Locality from the sub menu. You'll see a window like the one shown in figure 35.8.

Fig. 35.8
AOLs Connection Settings window, ready for you to enter access numbers for the cities you intend to visit.

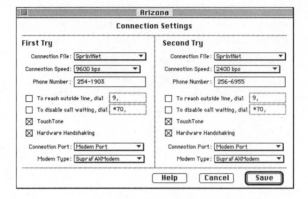

If you are uncertain how to select a profile for your modem, simply review your Setup box, which is reached from the main window of your AOL software. Copy the settings from Connection Port, Modem Type, and other options from there. If your portable Mac has a different make and model modem, you'll want to see whether a profile is available for that model or be guided by the manufacturer's instructions. If suitable instructions aren't available, try Hayes Basic or Hayes Error Correcting, which are offered in the pull-down menu under Modem Type.

> **Note**
>
> America Online has a free support library for modem profiles. Just enter the Online Support area (Keyword: Help), and click the Modem Help icon, which is at the right of the Online Support forum window.

At the top of the Locality window is the space to enter the number for your first connection attempt. I suggest you choose an alternate number (even if it's in a different city) for your second connection attempt to ensure that you can log on in case the local number is busy.

> **Note**
>
> There is actually a second way to get a local access number from America Online, using the methods described in the section on eWorld later in this chapter. The descriptions provided in that section apply in almost identical fashion to AOL.

Using CompuServe On The Road

Because CompuServe's access number search mechanism doesn't sport a fancy icon for CompuServe Information Manager, I just used my regular telecommunications software to get a list of connection numbers. Log onto the service in the normal way, as described in Chapter 30, "Using America Online and CompuServe." Type the Go words **GO PHONES** to display the directory shown in figure 35.9.

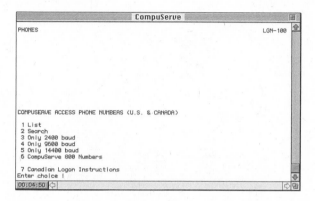

Fig. 35.9
CompuServe's convenient phone number search mechanism.

After you enter the area code of the city for which you seek a telephone number, a list of the available phone numbers appears. You'll have the option of choosing a standard 2400 bps connection number or one supporting the newer 9600 bps and 14,400 bps offered by CompuServe, as shown in figure 35.10.

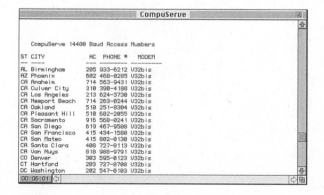

Fig. 35.10
High-speed connection numbers merit a special listing on CompuServe.

VI

The Mac at Work

Whether you're using a regular telecommunications program or CompuServe Information Manager or CompuServe Navigator, you can save the terminal window showing the phone numbers for which you searched. That way you can review them later when you are on the road.

Using eWorld On The Road

Apple's new online service uses more of an automated phone number search process than CompuServe. In order to change your access number, you launch the eWorld program and then click the Local Setup pop-up menu, which produces a Get Local # choice, shown in figure 35.11. (The method I'm about to describe can actually be employed in essentially the same way to locate a new access number on America Online using, of course, your AOL software.)

Fig. 35.11
The first step in using eWorld's phone number search routine.

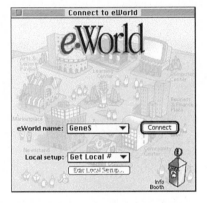

Click the Connect button to access eWorld's 800 telephone search service, and when the opening screen appears (see fig. 35.12), enter the area code for which you seek telephone numbers.

Fig. 35.12
Finding local connection numbers eWorld style.

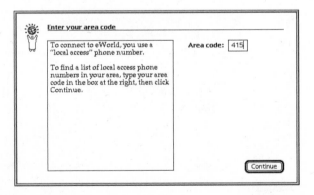

If local access numbers are available, they'll appear in the next screen, shown in figure 35.13. You just click the ones you want to add. If a local number is not available, you can choose an alternate area code to try.

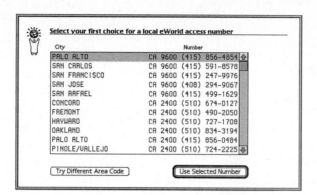

Fig. 35.13
eWorld suggested connection numbers in the city you selected.

After the numbers are added, you are logged off and the standard Locality window appears, with your selected numbers already entered for you. The next step is simple. Click the Save Setup window, which opens a Save As dialog box. Enter the name of your new Locality profile. To make it easier to find later on, you can name the connection settings after the city to which you're traveling. Once saved, the name of the new Locality settings shows up as on the Local Setup pop-up menu.

Using MCI Mail

Unlike the regular online services, MCI Mail concentrates on one specific function: serving as your electronic post office. You can send and receive e-mail, or have your letters delivered by the post office or sent as a fax. You pay an annual fee and receive an 800 telephone access number. Receiving mail doesn't cost you extra, but you have to pay for each message you send. The pricing schedule depends on the size of the message and whether a copy is being sent by snail mail or fax. You can get additional information on MCI Mail by calling (800)444-6245.

Going Wireless

You sometimes may travel to places where no telephone line is handy, but you still need to be able to stay in touch. Cellular telephones are a ubiquitous site on the American landscape these days, but as described in Chapter 29, "Getting Online," they present unique problems in maintaining stable connections.

Wireless Modems

One solution to this dilemma is the arrival of devices that incorporate a cellular telephone and a modem. Manufacturers such as Motorola are introducing

Tip
If your travel plans change, use such services as America Online and CompuServe and their Easy Sabre feature to make car rental, hotel, and plane reservations.

VI

The Mac at Work

these units that, although presenting the utmost in convenience while traveling, are apt to exact a higher price than a separate phone and modem.

Connecting to a Cellular Telephone

As explained in Chapter 29, cellular telephone connections aren't nearly as stable as your regular home telephone. As you travel from place to place, the signal from your telephone is passed off from one cellular center to another. The quality of the signal can vary as you pass around buildings and hilltops. To cope with this occurrence, Microcom has an MNP-10 error correction protocol that's supported by some modems. The manual for your modem should indicate whether this scheme is supported.

A modem that doesn't have MNP-10 will most likely work, but it will work at reduced efficiency. You also need an interface to hook up directly with many cellular telephones. Global Village has a variation, a product called *PowerPort Coupler*, a base to which you can attach the headset of your cellular phone (or even a pay phone). The other end hooks into your PowerBook. This acoustic coupler promises reliable transmissions at up to 9600 bps.

Giving Presentations

◀ See "What is Out There," p. 403

◀ See "Adobe Photoshop," p. 649

Giving a presentation used to mean lugging around a slide projector and tray or a VCR from place to place. Armed with a PowerBook, the right presentation software, and some video projection devices, you can now give highly professional slide shows and other demonstrations wherever you travel.

Chapter 17, "Presentation Graphics," reviewed several of the most popular software packages for generating charts and slides. These include Claris Impact, DeltaGraph Professional, Microsoft PowerPoint, and Gold Disk Astound.

◀ See "Adobe Audition," p. 670

◀ See "QuickTime," p. 670

In addition, you can generate attractive charts with Adobe Illustrator. A growing number of Mac programs support Apple's QuickTime technology, which allows you to easily create audio and video multimedia presentations. Chapter 23, "Digital Photography and Desktop Video," describes the magic you can produce with programs such as Adobe PhotoShop, Apple's PhotoFlash, and Video Director.

> **Note**
>
> Since complex digital video presentations may consume a great deal of disk space, you may find it convenient to carry a portable hard drive in your travels.

Using a Large Screen TV

One convenient way to play your presentations from your notebook Macintosh is with a large screen TV. Although it's not something you want to carry around on a trip, some large auditoriums are equipped with a monitor of this sort. Models such as Mitsubishi's line of 37-inch monitors cost many thousands of dollars, but provide extraordinarily clear images, more crisp than most normal TVs with comparably sized screens.

This sort of installation isn't quite plug and play, however. Your Mac deals with RGB signals, and a TV speaks NTSC (or PAL and SEC for international setups). This setup therefore will generally require an adapter interface of some sort.

Using an Overhead Projector

A less costly alternative to a monitor—and one more suited to a larger auditorium—is an LCD projection panel. These devices are designed to fit on top of an overhead projector, just like a slide. The panel acts as an external monitor, and you can project exactly what you see on your Mac's screen. Projection panels that are small enough to fit conveniently into a briefcase or a shoulder bag are available.

Although far less expensive than a large screen TV, LCD projection panels aren't necessarily cheap, especially the ones that offer full color output. An LCD projection panel can cost more than a top-line PowerBook, so if you only need this sort of accessory occasionally, you might find a dealer who will rent a unit for you.

Some products actually combine the projection panel and a projector into a single unit, complete with a carrying case for travel. If you plan on giving presentations at locations where local projection equipment isn't available, this may be an alternative to consider.

Presentations On The Cheap

You can use one more method to show a Mac-created presentation. Just visit a local service bureau that has a film recorder. They'll be able to take your document files and transfer them to slides. This back-to-basics approach also shows that the old fashioned slide projector is not quite obsolete yet.

Amplifying The Sound Portion of Your Presentation

Your Mac's internal speakers may be suitable for a small gathering in a small room, but they don't provide nearly enough volume for a larger setup. But your Macintosh is capable of offering very high quality sound, especially the newest PowerBooks with 16-bit audio output, which is equivalent to a audio compact disk.

A number of powered loudspeakers are now available for audio and video use, such as the popular AppleDesign Speakers, which will fit neatly into an overnight bag. You can mount them beside a large screen monitor. For a larger auditorium, you may want to acquire a standard public address amplifier and speaker system.

> **Note**
>
> When you buy a set of powered speakers for your Macintosh, spend a little time listening to them before you take them home. As with the loudspeakers you buy for your stereo system, the sound varies tremendously from model to model, and they may sound different when moved from one environment to another. Listen carefully for clear, undistorted reproduction of both music and speech, especially at room-filling volume levels.

From Here...

This chapter provided helpful hints and explained how to use your Mac most effectively to stay in touch on the road. It also provided a list of the accessories you might want to buy before you take your trip.

- Chapter 29, "Getting Online," tells you the ins and outs of buying and setting up your modem and getting connected.

- Chapter 30, "Using America Online and CompuServe," talks about two of the most popular online services.

- Chapter 31, "Using eWorld," describes Apple's new consumer-oriented online service.

- Chapters 37 and 38 describe the steps you need to take to troubleshoot common problems with your Mac and explain how you can solve them before they become serious.

Chapter 36

Setting Up the Perfect Home Office

by Mark Bilbo

The office used to be a place in a city center to which people drove each day. The home and the office were usually separate places, sometimes distant from one another. Today, increasing numbers of people are finding it convenient not just to bring work home from the office but to bring the office home. Many people have moved their offices completely home.

As desktop computer power has grown and information "highways" have become more common, many options for home businesses have opened up. Many people set up businesses for telecommuting, contracting their services, or working freelance.

This chapter helps you efficiently set up your home office by covering the following considerations:

- Creating a safe and comfortable work environment

- Protecting your Macintosh from damage by power surges, dust, and theft

- Purchasing helpful accessories for the home office

- Examining hardware choices that are both affordable and well-suited to the home office

- Examining software choices to increase productivity and enable you to work more easily with your main office

Products mentioned in this chapter are widely available through your dealer, computer superstore, or favorite mail-order company unless otherwise specified as "direct" (meaning available only directly from the manufacturer). Competing products are also available through the same sources. You may want to use the recommendations in this chapter as basic guidelines to enable you to do comparison shopping.

Creating a Work Environment

Setting up a home office involves more than putting your Macintosh on a desk in the den. Whether you are planning to work only a few hours a week or full-time, you will need to create a work environment that is both safe and comfortable.

This section talks about concerns often overlooked when a home office is set up: choosing a safe location to place the Macintosh, protecting your investment by safeguarding the computer, choosing and adjusting furniture to avoid back and neck pains, and other considerations.

Choosing a Safe Location

After spending a few thousand dollars on a computer, you don't want to endanger your investment. You also should think carefully about issues such as lighting, noise, and space when locating your Macintosh.

Although computer equipment is more durable than you might suspect, computers are senstive to some elements. When choosing a location for your home office, think about the following potential problems:

- *Direct sunlight.* Just as long-term exposure to direct sunlight can heat up your car, your Macintosh can reach damaging temperatures if sunlight falls on the case for extended periods of time. Locate the Macintosh away from windows, or be sure to close curtains or blinds to avoid this problem.

- *Temperature extremes.* Both high heat and extreme cold are damaging, but extreme heat is more likely to damage your computer. Normal room temperature (or slightly cooler) is best for computer equipment. As a rule of thumb, if you are comfortable, your Mac will be comfortable.

> **Caution**
>
> Don't forget to think about what happens when you leave your home office or even your home on long trips. The room may be perfectly comfortable during the hours you work, but what about when you are gone? Temperatures below 50 degrees or above about 120 degrees can damage the Macintosh as well as your floppy disks.

- *Moisture.* You certainly would avoid placing your Macintosh in water, but you should also consider humidity. Condensation can be destructive to your Macintosh. Avoid damp rooms.

> **Caution**
>
> Keep food and drink away from the computer. One coffee or soft drink spill can cause expensive damage. Avoid placing the Macintosh in areas of the house where the family commonly carries food and drink.

Tip
One way to avoid dangerous spills is to use travel mugs with lids. Also, avoid placing the mug on the same desk with your Macintosh.

- *Dust and smoke.* Dust is an enemy of computers. Dust can get into hard and floppy drive mechanisms and block the exhaust vents of the Macintosh. Dust can also coat the electronics inside the Macintosh and cause the components to overheat. Avoid dusty rooms. Smokers should be aware of the risk they take exposing the Macintosh to tobacco smoke. Avoiding smoking in the home office is the best solution. The second best solution is to locate the Macintosh in a well-ventilated room.

- Believe it or not, you should vaccuum your computer. Suncom Technologies offers a cleaning kit that includes a vacuum suitable for removing dust from your Macintosh, as well as other useful cleaning items for your floppy disk drive, monitor screen, and mouse, for only about $30.

- For the truly cheap (such as myself), you can get away with using an ordinary home vacuum to clean your Mac. With the Macintosh off, I use the attachments meant for upholstery to clear the exhaust vents and clean the Macintosh of dust. Don't laugh—it works. Just be gentle, and don't jam anything into the Macintosh's insides.

VI

The Mac at Work

- *Vibration.* Excessive vibration can cause hard drive failure. Washing machine spin cycles can shake floors and walls, especially in older homes. You may need to avoid placing the Macintosh too close to utility rooms.

- *Poor grounding.* The Macintosh, as with all computer equipment, needs to be plugged into a three-pronged outlet with a good ground. Avoid the use of two- to three-prong adapters. In older homes, you may want to have the wiring checked even if you have three-prong outlets because sometimes the ground is not actually connected.

You may have other considerations depending on where you live and the particular conditions of your home. Users on the West Coast, for example, must consider earthquakes and avoid placing the Macintosh beneath shelves because the items on the shelves (or the shelves themselves) may fall. Carefully consider the location for your home office. Anticipating hazardous conditions is better than having to correct the problem later.

Choosing a Comfortable Location

You will most certainly avoid areas that are obviously uncomfortable when locating your Macintosh, but a few considerations may not be immediately obvious, such as lighting, noise, and space.

- *Lighting.* Indirect lighting is best and should fully illuminate the work area. Avoid placing your desk in a location where your monitor screen will reflect sunlight or lamplight. A glare can cause eyestrain that leads to headaches and tension.

- *Noise.* Choose a quiet location, especially if you will be working in your home office full-time. Using a room right next to the den or family room, for example, could limit your ability to work without distractions.

- *Space.* Ample space is often a problem for setting up a home office. Ideally, your home office should be in a separate room for several reasons. One important reason is home office tax deductions, which are easier to make when you have a clearly defined home office area (check with your tax professional on home office deductions; IRS rules are known for changing frequently).

An important consideration is whether the room has a door that locks. If you have children, you are already aware of the reasons to have a door that locks.

Tip

Floor lamps that illuminate the ceiling and indirectly light the room are available. Halogen lamps of this type are often inexpensive and come with dimmers.

Tip

Glare screens or filters over your Macintosh monitor screen reduce the problem of reflected light. These items range from about $30 to $75.

Finding your eight-month-old niece chewing on a disk might be cute, but the disk rarely survives. Also, closing doors reduces noise.

You should try to have sufficient space to enable you to gather all the items you need to work in a single, easily accessible location. If your Macintosh is upstairs and your reference books are downstairs, for example, you may spend much of your work time running up and down stairs trying to find an article.

People may have once thought that comfort had no place in the office, but today the understanding that comfortable people are more productive people is growing. Good, indirect lighting, a low noise level, and perhaps a nice view out a window can contribute to a productive environment for your home office—more than you may think.

Protecting Your Macintosh

Four threats to your Macintosh exist, but you can take inexpensive action to prevent or reduce them. These threats are dust, power surges, static electricity, and theft.

Dust

You may have located your Macintosh in a room that has little dust, but dust is always in the air. Dust covers are inexpensive—running from $10 to $20—and can protect your Macintosh from harmful dust buildup. You can purchase dust covers at your local Apple dealer or through mail order.

Tip

Air filtration devices can reduce the amount of smoke in a room. They cost around $60 to $100, which is much cheaper than a Macintosh repair.

> **Caution**
>
> Dust covers are meant to protect your computer while the computer is turned off. Leaving dust covers on a computer while it is running can cause heat buildup by blocking the ventilation of the computer's casing. If you use your computer for long periods, you might also want to let it cool before placing the dust cover on.

Two notable products in the dust cover category are the ThinSkin and the HardTop keyboard covers by Basic Needs. The ThinSkin keyboard cover remains on your keyboard at all times and prevents dust, liquids, and food particles from falling into your keyboard. (Yes, I know I said don't eat and drink around the computer, but the author is a hypocrite and knows others are going to have the cookie-crumbs-in-the-keyboard problem, too.) The ThinSkin's worth the $16 or so—that's one tenth the price of a new keyboard.

The HardTop keyboard cover is more durable—made of the same material as football helmets—and is impact resistant. The HardTop costs from about $15 to $17.

Power surges

The greatest enemy of the Macintosh or any electronic equipment is the power surge. Normal voltage levels in the U.S. are around 110-120 volts, but infrequent, short surges (or *spikes*) of as much as ten times the normal voltage level can occur for various reasons.

Power-surge protectors block these sudden, brief increases of voltage, which can literally burn holes in the computer's internal board. While 1,000 volt spikes are rare, smaller but still damaging surges are not uncommon.

No Macintosh owner should be without a power-surge protector. Power-surge damage to computer equipment is painfully expensive and much more costly than a good protector.

When you choose a power-surge protector, consider these qualities:

- *EMI/RFI filters.* Avoiding technical discussions, EMI and RFI are "noise" in power lines that can degrade the electronic components in your Macintosh. A good power-surge protector includes these filters.

- *Rapid response time.* Response time represents how quickly the power-surge protector acts and is expressed in nanoseconds (billionths of a second). The lower the number is, the faster the protector acts to prevent damage to your Macintosh.

- *Failure indication.* Audible alarms are now included in many protectors to indicate that the protection circuitry has ceased to function.

- *Modem/fax protection.* If you have a modem or fax modem, you will want to have protection from power surges on the phone lines, too. Modem/fax protection is included with many models of surge protectors.

Caution

Be aware that there are power *strips* that provide extra outlets but offer no protection for your Macintosh. Make certain to purchase a power-surge protector.

Nothing can protect your Macintosh from direct lightning strikes on power lines. Do not assume that a power-surge protector will guard you and your Macintosh during thunderstorms. Your only safe course of action during a thunderstorm is to shut

---

down and unplug the Macintosh. If you have a modem, you should disconnect the modem from the phone line.

A case in point: My stepfather left his computer plugged in, though turned off, during a thunderstorm. A lightning strike on the power line fused the power-surge protector, and then proceeded to burn a one-inch hole in his computer's main board.

Many people have home offices to avoid living in the city. Some even move to more rural areas. Unfortunately, rural areas are more prone to another power problem: brownouts. *Brownouts* are when the power level falls. You will notice that the lights in the house go dim either briefly or for noticeable periods of time.

These kinds of power fluctuations can damage your Macintosh and can cause you to lose data. You may want to consider an Uninterruptable Power Supply (UPS). These devices use batteries to deliver emergency electricity during brownouts and power failures long enough to enable you to safely save your data and shut down your Macintosh.

A UPS is an expensive piece of equipment and, so, should be considered only if you experience frequent power problems that the power company cannot (or will not) address, and if data loss would be severely damaging to your home business work. Kensington offers four UPS "Power Backer" models ranging from $280 to as much as $660. The more expensive models can deliver more power over longer periods.

Static electricity

Static electricity is merely an annoyance to a human being, but those sharp little jolts can be death to disks and computer components. If you live in a dry climate or find yourself being popped when you touch doorknobs, your data and even your Macintosh could be in jeopardy.

Inexpensive antistatic sprays are available through dealers, mail order, and even many ordinary office supply stores. Use the sprays liberally and frequently on carpeting around your computer, the area in which you walk when working, and even the upholstery of your desk chair.

If you live in an area where static electricity buildup is a frequent occurrence, you may also want to consider purchasing an antistatic pad to place beneath your desk chair, especially if you have a rolling chair.

Tip

Ask your power company about lightning arrestors on your power lines if you live in an area of frequent thunderstorms.

VI

The Mac at Work

Theft

Your Macintosh is an investment that you should protect the best you can. You should consider protecting your Macintosh from theft.

You may consider insuring your Macintosh. Because homeowner policies often do not cover equipment used in business pursuits, you may need additional insurance. Some companies specialize in insuring computers even against occurrences such as power surges. You can find several advertisements for computer insurance in the back of major computer publications such as *MacUser* magazine. Be certain to consult with your insurance agent about such policies.

Another option is to secure your Macintosh. Kensington offers an Apple Security System for about $35 that enables you to chain the Macintosh to your desk. (Of course, you need a sturdy desk.)

Selecting Furniture

Furniture issues relate to *ergonomics*, which essentially means having a work environment that is healthy. Many have become aware of problems caused by poorly designed office environments, but few are aware of some simple steps that can be taken to reduce or avoid the problems.

Desk and Chair Considerations

Your office desk and chair should, if at all possible, be chosen together. Desks are generally constructed to have uniform heights, so the chair should be adjustable; you should be able to raise and lower the office chair so that you can work comfortably and sit with a straight back.

The desk should have ample space to enable you to arrange your Macintosh and work tools, and still have a decent workspace. You should be able to arrange your work items so that you avoid excess bending and stretching.

Look for a chair that offers good back support. Sitting for long periods with poor posture can result in painful back problems. The ideal chair height places your elbows at about a ninety degree angle when you are typing. Having a chair with an adjustable height enables you to achieve this position.

Monitor Considerations

The ideal monitor position places the monitor about 18 inches from your eyes, which is normal focusing distance. Your eyes then do not have to constantly work to focus on the monitor screen.

The monitor height should place the screen so that you are looking straight ahead. Stands for monitors and for Macintoshes with built-in monitors are available at many Apple dealers and office supply stores. Be certain to purchase a sturdy one. Avoid the temptation of the cheap plastic stands.

Keyboard Considerations

Keyboards have been at the center of a storm of controversy because of the appearance of repetitive stress disorders such as carpal tunnel syndrome. The problem lies with the stresses of repetitive motions of the fingers, hands, and wrists.

While no absolute agreement exists on how to avoid the problem entirely, you can take some steps to reduce the threat of this expensive (and painful) problem.

Many companies now offer *wrist savers*, which are padded rests used with keyboards and mice. These devices enable your wrists to be at rest rather than strained to maintain proper typing or mouse-maneuvering positions.

LB Innovators offers several of these items with price ranges from about $15 to $25. The WristSaver supports your wrists and reduces strain during typing. The WristSaver MousePad is a mouse pad that includes a wrist rest. A combination package including both wrist rests is available.

Some of the most innovative products aimed at reducing the problem of carpal tunnel syndrome come from Apple Computer. The new Apple Adjustable Keyboard looks odd with its split design, but this keyboard enables you to adjust the angle of the two halves of the keyboard so that your wrists are at natural angles instead of bent to fit a straight keyboard. The keyboard currently sells for about $150 through mail order and includes wrist rests.

One possibility for avoiding strain is one I have used. The old QWERTY design of the keyboard came out of an odd solution to the problem of keys jamming on the original typewriters. Frequently used keys were deliberately spaced widely. The result is that your hands and fingers do more "traveling" as you type. While my evidence is anecdotal (that is, pure personal experience as opposed to some scientific study), I can say that I come away from long typing sessions feeling much less "strained" when using the Dvorak arrangement than when I used QWERTY.

The Dvorak keyboard has been around for decades but has never gained wide acceptance because of the huge number of typewriters that would have to be replaced (being mechanical, they would have to be replaced with Dvorak typewriters rather than simply reconfigured, as computer keyboards can).

VI

The Mac at Work

Fortunately, computers can easily be switched to a Dvorak keyboard configuration and back again.

The Dvorak keyboard arrangement places the most frequently used letters on the home keys. This arrangement enables you to spend approximately 70 percent of your typing on the home keys as opposed to about 50 to 55 percent, reducing the amount of movement your hands have to do. I switched four years ago and found that the Dvorak arrangement reduced the amount of "reaching" necessary when typing.

If you are interested in switching to the Dvorak arrangement, be aware that a period of adjustment and retraining is needed. Also, you need a Dvorak keyboard layout to install in your System file.

Nisus Software at (619) 481-1477 sells MacQWERTY for $45 direct. The product contains two Dvorak keyboard layouts, a customization program, and keytop stickers. For retraining yourself, consider Mavis Beacon Teaches Typing from Software Toolworks at about $50, available through dealers and mail order.

After MacQWERTY is installed on the Macintosh, you switch between the standard QWERTY arrangement and the Dvorak arrangement through the Keyboard control panel (see fig. 36.1).

Fig. 36.1
Choosing a
Dvorak keyboard
arrangement.

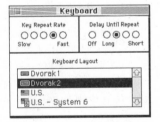

I am sold on the Dvorak keyboard arrangement, but you should keep in mind the following considerations that will affect your decision about switching:

- *Dvorak is not widespread.* If you move between offices or companies, you may need to do as I do and carry the Dvorak keyboard software around with you. (Dvorak keyboard software for the IBM exists, and shareware versions are available on many online services.)

- *Retraining takes some time and effort.* So don't make the switch during a busy time or you'll be down to hunting and pecking.

■ *Typewriters can't be converted.* If you have to use a typewriter (although nobody should have to by now), you'll be hunting and pecking when you make the changeover.

Overall, if you spend the bulk of your time working at your own computer (home, office, or both), or if you work almost exclusively with computers (Macintosh or IBM PC), the barriers to switching are far fewer than ever. And the Dvorak keyboard is far easier to type on once you make the switch.

Mouse Considerations

Heavy users of the mouse often find their wrists and hands bothering them. You wouldn't think moving a small device around in a small space could have such an effect, but over time, even small motions can cause pain.

One of the LB Innovator's WristSaver MousePads might give just the support you need, but you should also be aware that other possible solutions exist.

Apple offers an ergonomically designed mouse for about $80. The Apple Desktop Bus Mouse II is more comfortable to use. Mouse Systems offers one of my personal favorites in the mouse category: the optical mouse. Optical mice use a special mouse pad and have no moving parts, using instead reflected light to detect motion. I find that optical mice are easier to move; they glide more smoothly than the standard roller ball type mouse. They're also easier to keep clean. The Mouse Systems Little Mouse is ergonomically designed to be easier on the hand and wrist, and costs in the neighborhood of $70.

Some find that the solution to a mouse problem is not to have a mouse at all. Some people prefer the trackball, which looks something like an upside-down mouse. The ball is on top, and you move it by using your fingers. Trackballs take a bit of adjusting to at first, but many people find that trackballs reduce the amount of movement the wrist must make and prefer them to mice.

Mouse Systems offers the A3 Trackball for about $70. This device has built-in wrist support and is designed to fit the hand.

One of the most popular trackballs is the Kensington Turbo Mouse, which is so widespread now that you can even obtain optional, decorative balls to replace the supplied ones. The Turbo Mouse costs around $110 and comes with software to enable you not only to adjust the sensitivity of the trackball but to customize the buttons and create *hot spots* (areas that have special meaning and invoke specific actions) on-screen by using special functions.

VI

The Mac at Work

The TrackMan by Logitech is a relatively new entry. The TrackMan reminds me of a seashell, but the design makes sense. Your palm rests on the case, and you move the ball with your thumb. The buttons are right at your fingertips. The TrackMan costs about $139 list, but you should be able to find lower prices by mail order. The only drawback to the TrackMan is that no left-hand version is available.

Which mouse is best and whether a mouse or trackball is best are highly subjective. If you have a dealer nearby, you might want to go for a test drive before making up your mind.

Odds and Ends

You should consider some issues that don't fall into any particular category. Obviously, you'll need supplies such as diskettes, printer ribbons or toner, paper, and the like.

A good disk storage box provides a helpful way to protect your floppies from dust. Attractive, oak storage boxes are available, as well as stackable "lazy susan" storage systems. An ordinary, inexpensive plastic disk storage box does the job just fine, however.

If you need to carry disks around, consider purchasing a disk wallette. Soft-side wallettes are available from ABCOM for price ranges of about $10 to $16. One interesting portable carrier from MediaMate sells for only $10. The Flex-Pack holds 10 disks, expanding and collapsing accordian style to sit on a desk or to be carried.

CD holders, such as the Sony CD Holder for about $15, can protect your CD-ROMs. Of course, your local department stores also carry CD cases that work fine. (Audio and computer CDs are physically identical.)

MediaMate also offers the WorkPac which, for about $30, gives you a compact mouse pad, a five-disk carrier, a disk/CD storage box, a copy clip to hold documents to the side of your monitor while you work with them, and a three-pronged outlet surge protector in one package.

PowerBook users who have to plug in at remote sites should also check out MediaMate's Power Tamer—a small, inexpensive surge protector.

Just for the heck of it, PowerBook users can purchase MagnaStone balls for the built-in trackball. Stone Age Technologies offers an assortment of interesting looking replacement balls for around $20 each. They are available for all PowerBook and PowerBook Duo models.

A good PowerBook carrying case is a must for the home office user who transports his or her PowerBook between home and office or remote sites. There are simply too many carrying-case options around to even begin discussing them in detail, but a few companies are worth mentioning by name.

Targus has long been known for making carrying cases for laptop computers and provides a wide array of cases with various options. You can find a quality carrying case to fit almost any budget. Many types are available, ranging from inexpensive cases for your PowerBook to leather carry-on luggage with room for your PowerBook, cellular phone, and a change of clothes. Targus case prices run from as low as $35 to as high as $250.

Kensington has been a Macintosh standard for some years now. You won't go wrong with one of the NoteBook Traveler cases, which runs from about $50 up to $115. The I/O Design Ultimate brand is also worth considering, especially if you want style. The prices run from the low $50s to $150 and are very attractive; especially the PowerBook Attache at the high end of the price range.

Choosing Hardware

Setting up a home office may require some hardware purchases. First, of course, you need a Macintosh. But these days, so many models are available that choosing a Macintosh can be a confusing task. Also, many Macintosh models have separate monitors, so you need to choose one to go with the computer.

A printer is a necessity, but you probably don't want to spend an arm and a leg. Printer prices have become much more reasonable in recent years. You can find many good printers—even laser printers—for reasonable prices.

Some other hardware choices are worth exploring. One you should definitely consider is a fast fax modem. No home office can really survive without one today.

Getting the Best Deals

Times were that mail order had the best deals. This can often be true today, and you will want to compare prices. However, recent Apple pricing structures have closed the gap between dealer, computer store, and mail-order prices on Macintosh computers. Even Apple's direct prices are reasonable now.

Pick up a copy of *MacUser*, *MacWorld*, or *Mac Home Journal* to locate mail-order houses. Many mail-order ads list prices to enable you to compare with your local hardware source. Do some shopping around not only on price but some other considerations.

Mail order is many times less expensive, but having a local dealer to take your Macintosh back should a problem arise is often worth the price difference. You should spend some time finding out just how helpful the dealer is before spending extra money, however. Take some time, ask questions, sit down with the Macintosh or other equipment, and try it out.

Before spending any extra money, make sure that the dealer will be there after the sale. Check to see how warranty repairs are handled. Does the dealer have a technician on site, or does the dealer send the Macintosh off for repairs? If the machine has to be shipped, doing it yourself will take about the same amount of time.

Does the dealer offer technical support, or will the dealer be calling Apple with your questions? Now that Apple offers technical support (as do many mail-order companies), buying from a dealer doesn't offer much of an advantage unless the dealer has knowledgeable people available to you on location.

If you are in need of training, ask whether the dealer offers training or knows of training in your area. Be aware that many home training courses are available through mail-order sources, however, and that the bookstores are filled with books on using the Macintosh.

Overall, if you are paying extra to go through a dealer, make certain that you are purchasing more than just the equipment. Mail order is still a viable alternative because many companies now offer technical support by phone and have fast turnaround on repairs. You should ask about these issues when considering a mail-order company as well.

Keep in mind that rock-bottom prices come most often from sources (mail order or otherwise) that offer little after-sale support. If you know exactly what you want and need, you can get the best prices. If you need some help, however, your best value is to spend some extra money for after-sale support.

One suggestion about hardware: subscribe to *MacUser* and the *Mac Home Journal*. *MacUser* is well-known for its thorough evaluations of hardware, and *Mac Home Journal* is oriented toward home and home-office users.

Ideal Home Macintoshes

The ideal home-office Macintoshes in the "if you can at all afford it, do it" category are the Power Macintoshes using the PowerPC. This new line of Macintoshes will rapidly make everything else pretty much obsolete. If you are just starting out, your best bet is to buy the most advanced technology possible in order to avoid being left behind in the years to come.

The only drawback to the PowerPC models is that most current Macintosh software runs only in an emulation mode that does not take full advantage of the new processor's speed and power. Software upgrades are following quickly, however. You should check for PowerPC "native" labels on your software purchases or verify that a PowerPC upgrade is coming.

The Power Macintosh comes in three models. Which you choose depends on your budget and need for power. The 6100/60 is the least expensive, running about $1,800 in the 8MB memory, 160MB hard drive configuration. For about $500, you can obtain a built-in CD-ROM and a 250MB hard drive. A version with SoftWindows—the software that enables your Power Macintosh to do a decent emulation of a 486SX and run DOS software—is available.

The two faster, more expensive models—the 7100/66 and 8100/80—offer more speed, more expandability, and larger hard drive options (the 8100/80 has a 1,000MB hard disk configuration available).

The 6100/60 strikes me as a good, solid home-office computer at a reasonable price. The Power Macintosh is definitely the future of the Macintosh and again, when you are first starting out, your best option is to purchase the most current technology possible.

This is not to say that the other Macintosh models are in danger of disappearing overnight. Far too many non-Power Macintoshes are out there, and companies will find it profitable to support them for years to come.

For the budget conscious, the Performa series of Macintoshes makes excellent home office/home computer choices. Which Performa you choose will depend mainly on the options you want, such as a built-in CD-ROM, hard drive size, memory size, and so on. Performas are widely available now in electronics stores such as Circuit City and can even be found at Sears. Performas have the advantages of being all-in-one packages that include a monitor, a keyboard, and software. Several models even come with modems. Apple offers support and service for the Performas.

Home office users who travel will want to take a look at the PowerBook Duos. The 230 and 255 are reasonably priced at about $1,530 and $2,260. The biggest difference between them is hard drive size, which is 120MB and 200MB respectively. The advantage of the Duos is the Duo Dock docking station, which sells in the area of $1,000 or so depending on options. With the Duo Dock, the PowerBook Duos double as desktop computers as well as laptops. You can also obtain less expensive docks with fewer options from Apple and other companies.

Monitors

Because so many monitors are on the market today and new models are being introduced almost every other day, it seems, giving specific recommendations is almost a lost cause. Some general suggestions can be made to give you some guidelines, however.

Unless you know exactly which monitor you want, you should probably avoid mail order. The best way to determine which monitor is for you is to see the monitor—perhaps even sit and work in front of the monitor for a while.

A 13- or 14-inch diagonal monitor is best for general use. When you start moving into larger monitors, you start needing more video memory in your Macintosh. Unless you work with full-page ads or two-page illustrations, don't be talked into a large monitor.

Printers

A printer is an essential these days. In recent years, printers have come down in price and improved in quality. You have a wide selection from which to choose, but a few stand out.

For inexpensive printing, the Apple StyleWriter II can hardly be beat. The price is about $350. The printer is slow, but the print quality is good. You won't want to try to print a novel on the StyleWriter II, but for light printing, the printer is a good choice. Consumables run about $22 to $25 per 500 pages.

That said, you should be aware that GCC offers a laser printer that doesn't cost much more than the StyleWriter II. The PLP II lists at $660 but can be found at just below $500. The printer is slow in laser printer terms (about four pages per minute maximum) but runs about twice as fast as the StyleWriter II. Consumables run about $35 per 2,500 pages for toner and about $300 per 15,000 pages for the drum. For more information on printers, see Chapter 10, "The Printing Chapter."

Stepping up in quality and speed, the Apple LaserWriter Select 360 offers twice the resolution, a 10-page-per minute engine, and high-quality images for about $1,500. Toner cartridges run about $90 per 4,000 pages.

Overall, Apple and GCC printers remain my top picks. Both companies offer a wide variety of laser printers beyond the two mentioned here, and you cannot go wrong with a printer choice from one of them.

CD-ROM Drives

No question here—if you want CD-ROM capability, get a NEC. NEC has long produced some of the best CD-ROM drives around; the 3X models are some of the fastest yet. Speed is critical in using CD-ROMs, and the triple speed 3Xs are a jump ahead of the current double-speed standard. Not every CD takes advantage of the triple speed, but new titles that utilize the speed are becoming available. The 3Xs will play current CDs. These drives cost around $430 to $560. You can find less expensive CD-ROM players, but few things are worse than a slow CD-ROM.

One player to avoid is the Apple PowerCD. Although this player is inexpensive and has features that sound good (such as the capability to connect to the TV to show Kodak PhotoCDs and play audio CDs), the drive is a single speed drive, and you'll find yourself going for coffee (maybe running errands) waiting for images to appear. All CD-ROM drives play audio CDs, but this capability is rather a non-feature because none (including the PowerCD) are as portable as a Sony Discman.

Modems and Fax Modems

Modem terminology is too confusing to even bother with these days. You are assaulted with MNPs and V dots this and thats and something called a *bis*.

The bottom line for a home office user is get the following:

■ 14,400 bps. Faster modems are available, but the faster speeds are not widely supported. The 14,400 speed is becoming more widespread and should become more or less the standard fairly soon. The 14,400 modems can also operate at 2,400 and 9,600, which are common speeds. Avoid modems advertised with higher speeds. The standards for higher speeds—at the time of this writing—have not even become fully official, despite the fact that modems using the speeds are already available. Unless you are certain you can connect to another modem with the same higher speed standard, you will spend the extra money but not get the faster speed.

VI

The Mac at Work

■ Look for MNP2-5 data compression features and V.42 error correction. (V.32 exists and costs less, but you cannot have enough error correction.) V.42bis data compression is nice, too.

You don't have to understand all of these techie labels. V.32 and V.42 are basically just error correction features that help overcome the noise on phone lines, and V.42 is more recent than the V.32. The *bis* on the end of either specifies a data compression scheme that can speed up your modem transmission—provided the modem to which you are connected has the same data compression capability. If both 14,400 modems have V.42/V.42bis, for example, they can communicate at effective speeds of 57,600 bps which, in technical terms, means they can blaze.

■ Look for Group III fax in fax modems and check to see whether the modem is send-only or send-and-receive. Group III is pretty much the only standard you'll find in fax modems, but it never hurts to check. Be aware that some models of fax modems send faxes but do not receive them.

■ Beware of speed claims in fax modems. It's not uncommon for the fax bps rate to be higher than the data bps rate. A fax modem may send and receive faxes at 9,600 bps but only send and receive data at 2,400 bps. Ads will often still refer to the modem as a 9,600 bps modem, however, so you have to read the smaller print.

With all this information in mind, one suggestion is the Zoom Fax Modem PKT 14.4, which sells for about $200. Zoom modems are usually among the least expensive in their class, and I've found their products to be reliable.

Hayes has been the premier modem company for years and set the standard for modems. Hayes was also known for being the most costly. However, the Accura line is actually reasonably priced. The Accura 144+Fax144 sells for about $240.

Choosing Software

Much of this book is devoted to Macintosh software and evaluations of the same. Instead of duplicating that effort here, this chapter is concerned with some recommendations for home-office users. It also mentions some software that sometimes falls between the cracks, not fitting well into any category other than useful.

Purchasing Software

In the past, software was sold "as is" with no warranty. This absurd state of affairs has changed considerably as competition has heated up, and money-back guarantees are now widespread.

When you are considering a software purchase, check the warranty. Can you return the software if you find it to be defective or incompatible with your system? What if it simply does not live up to its promises? Even if the manufacturer does not offer a return policy, many times the dealer or mail-order company will.

Mail order is an excellent source for software for the home office. Two companies I have dealt with come immediately to mind: MacWarehouse and MacConnection. Both companies stock virtually every Macintosh software product on the market, and both have been consistently helpful, friendly, and quick. Overnight delivery is even available for a nominal charge.

MacWarehouse is found at the following address:

> MacWarehouse
> PO Box 3013
> 1720 Oak St.
> Lakewood, NJ 08701-3013
> Orders: 1-800-255-6227
> Fax orders: 1-908-905-9279
> Customer Service: 1-800-925-6227
> Orders taken 24 hrs, 7 days a week.

MacConnection can be contacted at the following address:

> MacConnection
> 14 Mill St.
> Marlow, NH 03456
> Orders: 1-800-800-2222
> Fax: 1-603-446-7791
> Demo Downloads: 1-603-446-0100
> Orders taken from 8 a.m. Monday to 5 p.m. Sunday Eastern.

Both companies offer upgrades to many products, simplifying your upgrade ordering. And MacWarehouse recently became an Apple authorized printer and scanner reseller.

Worthwhile Words

Chapter 16, "Word Processing," covers word processors in greater depth than in this chapter, but you should consider a couple of points when choosing a home-office word processing program. One of the biggest issues is compatibility with the office or offices with which you deal.

If you are bringing home work from an office that uses WordPerfect (Mac or DOS), for example, it would make sense to have WordPerfect on your home-office Macintosh.

What if you do not deal with a specific office, however? The question then becomes how to deal with many different formats. Translation software is available to help you in this case (see "Working with Other Formats" later in this chapter).

Once you get past the issue of dealing with different formats and other word processors and computers, choosing a word processor for your home office becomes a matter of which is best suited for your kind of work. Chapter 17 can help you with this decision.

If you work with text more than anything, however, one of the best word processors to have is Nisus. Nisus is by far the most text-oriented of the Macintosh word processors and has at least one feature I've not found anywhere else: GREP (Global Regular Expression Parser).

GREP came out of the UNIX operating system and is an extremely powerful (although potentially arcane) text manipulation system. GREP works with something called *regular expressions* (which is where the *RE* in the GREP comes from). Regular expressions are patterns using special symbols to stand for types of characters. For example, :d stands for any digit from 0 to 9. You could search for ZIP codes starting with 7 by typing 7:d:d:d:d. Or, if you do something like what I often do and transpose letters in certain words like *from* and *form*, you can use a search pattern something like this: f\(\[or]\)\(\[ro]\)m to find *form* and *from* but nothing else. You can even set up the search and replace to transpose the letters when you click the Replace button (see fig. 36.2).

Looks complicated doesn't it? Well, that's because GREP is complicated. Fortunately, Nisus has the PowerSearch option that simplifies things considerably (see fig. 36.3).

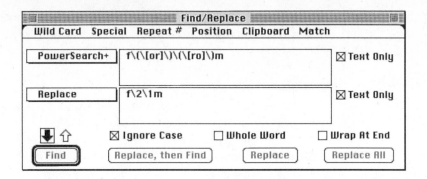

Fig. 36.2
Finding and
transposing *form*
and *from*.

Fig. 36.3
PowerSearch
makes GREP
easier to use.

PowerSearch enables you to choose GREP elements from menus in the Find/Replace dialog box. The full GREP is available as PowerSearch+.

I'm not going to try to tell you that learning GREP is easy, but GREP is outrageously powerful for text work. Even if you have to sit with a manual for a while and knock a regular expression around until it works, you can still create a powerful find and replace that can save you immense amounts of time later. Combined with macros (which Nisus has), you can perform amazing text formatting and editing procedures.

Nisus also works with the DataViz translators, so even if you have to deal with other word processors on other computers (even PCs), you can perform translations back and forth.

The more well-known word processors, such as Microsoft Word and WordPerfect, are large, powerful packages but have become more oriented toward desktop publishing. If you're like me and work mostly with words, Nisus is a worthy choice because it is more text oriented.

VI

The Mac at Work

If you need to combine text with layout and design (say, to create and format manuals), you'll probably need Microsoft Word. But if you just want to write, give Nisus a look.

Quick Financials

◀ See "Personal
Finance,"
p.734

If your home office is going to be your place of employment, you'll need a financial management package. The top program—and for good reason—is Quicken. Quicken is just perfect for use in a home-office setting. Quicken combines both personal financial management and planning with basic business-related features such as a decent collection of business reports (see fig. 36.4).

Fig. 36.4
Quicken's set of business reports.

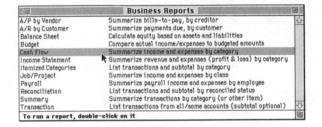

Quicken is not a full accounting package, but is just the right size for home-office use. The program can do basic accounts payable and receivable, print your checks, and even handle basic payroll. Quicken also easily interfaces with ChipSoft tax programs such as MacInTax to help you with the insane self-employed-tax-filing headache.

Working with Other Formats

Home-office users often have to deal with computers other than the Macintosh as well as file formats other than the ones used by the software they have. The main suggestion I have here is to run—do not walk—to get MacLink Plus/Translators Pro by DataViz.

Included with this extremely useful translation software is Apple's PC Exchange, which enables your Macintosh SuperDrive to work with DOS-formatted disks, and even format the disks in DOS format (see fig. 36.5).

Version 7.5 of the software has over 1,000 translation combinations, but you don't have to spend time choosing your way through all of these. MacLink does the work for you, recognizing file formats and popping up with only a couple of choices if there is a question.

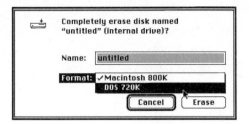

Fig. 36.5
Formatting a disk
for DOS.

The best part is that DataViz's translators also work with many other vendor products. I regularly use them to save word processing files in DOS formats (see fig. 36.6).

Fig. 36.6
Nisus recognizes
DataViz translators.

The convenience is worth the approximate $100 price of the package when you can format a disk for DOS, and then use the Save as command to save your files onto the disk, and hand the disk to DOS users or calmly pop their disks into your Mac's drive and open their files.

Even if your word processor or other software program doesn't interface with the DataViz translators, MacLink Plus translation software can do the processing for you.

If you deal with really oddball formats, get CanOpener 2 by Abbot Systems for about $60. With this program, you can crack open just about any file any time.

VI

The Mac at Work

File compression can make dealing with the DOS world a pain. Here's an inexpensive suggestion: ZipIt. ZipIt is sold by Tommy Brown—the author of the program—and is only $10. You can order ZipIt at the following address (ZipIt is not available through dealers or mail order):

> Tommy Brown
> 110-45 Queens Blvd. Apt. 716
> Forest Hills, NY 11375

A more advanced (and more pricey) option is Stuffit Deluxe for about $70. Stuffit Deluxe can handle both zip and arc compressions (see fig. 36.7).

Fig. 36.7
Preparing to decompress an IBM PC arc file.

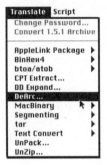

Stuffit Deluxe is also a must-have program for the program's compression and archiving capabilities (see "Handling Crowded Hard Drives" later in this chapter).

Enhancing Your System

Several system enhancement packages are available, but only one falls into my can't-live-without category. Now Utilities by Now Software contains seven items, two of which are absolute necessities.

Super Boomerang used to be shareware but migrated into the commerial sphere with the Now Utilities package. Super Boomerang enhances your Open and Save dialogs in extremely useful ways. For starters, folders and files are automatically added to menus in your dialogs for easy access (see fig. 36.8).

Your most recently opened folders and files are added to the menus as you work. You may add a folder or file to the menus as *permanent* (meaning they stay until you remove them) by pressing the space bar while the mouse pointer is on the folder or file name in the menu. Key commands can be added to the folder and file choices. Super Boomerang keeps track of where you were last. When you open a dialog later, you find the same files you last saw. You even have a Find command in the Open and Save dialogs.

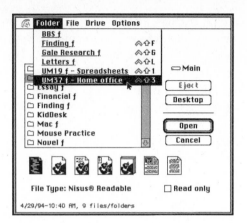

Fig. 36.8
The Folder menu in the Open dialog gives quick access to folders on your hard disk.

Included in Now Utilities is Now Menus, which works with Super Boomerang. File menu Open commands become hierarchical menus with the last files you opened in the current application listed for quick access to files. Your Apple menu (in System 7) becomes a fully customizable menu with heirarchical submenus and optional key command shortcuts (see fig. 36.9).

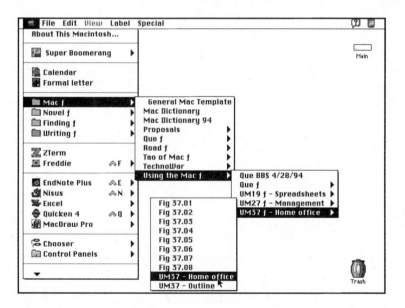

Fig. 36.9
The Apple menu with Now Menus installed.

Now Menus also enables you to have other menus, one in each corner of your monitor, and pop-up menus keyed to key combinations. If you have a large monitor, you can set up a key combination that causes the Mac menu bar to appear as a pop-up menu anywhere you click the mouse button while holding down the keys.

Now Utilities also has an enhanced scrapbook; a control panel that will automatically save your work after a specified amount of time, number of keystrokes, or number of mouse clicks; a control panel to change your font menus to display the font names in their own font so that you can see how the font actually looks before choosing it; and a Startup Manager that enables you to control system extensions, control panels, and even create sets of applications and documents that you can start when you switch on your Macintosh. Or you can create *worksets* to open groups of applications and documents when you double-click on the workset.

Now Utilities sells for about $85 and is well worth the price.

Keeping on Schedule

Now Software also sells a calendar program that is worth considering. Now Up-To-Date can keep your schedule and pop up to remind you of approaching appointments (see fig. 36.10).

Fig. 36.10

Entering a meeting appointment.

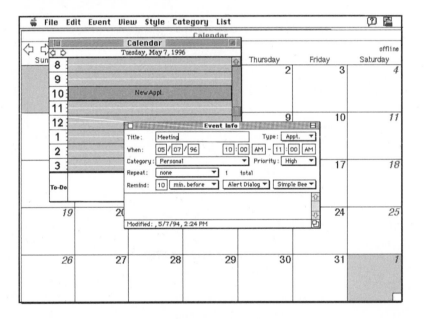

Now Up-To-Date enables you to schedule appointments, enter "to dos," put banners on your calendar, set reminders of upcoming events to display in the menu bar or appear in a dialog, and more. The Reminder control panel included with Now Up-To-Date will put the time and date in your menu bar and flash reminders at you so that you don't miss your appointments.

Protecting Your Data

If you are working at home, you want to do the best you can to protect your hard drive's data. You need to consider three things: viruses, backups, and what to do after things go wrong.

Warding Off Viruses

I've used Symantic Anti-Virus for some time now and, even with constantly exchanging disks, communicating with bulletin boards, and logging on to on-line services, I haven't had a problem with a virus. SAM automatically scans your drives or System Folder at startup or shut down, scans floppy disks when you insert them (an option you'll want to use), or do full scans when requested (see fig. 36.11).

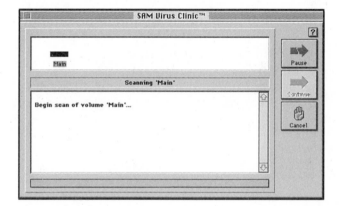

Fig. 36.11
SAM searching for virus infections.

One of the things I like best about SAM is that Symantec provides a bulletin board you can log onto to obtain updates for the virus definitions—free. Registered users also receive notification of new viruses and how to configure SAM to detect them. The program is about $65 but well worth the price.

Keeping Backups

You definitely need backups of your data. The only question that remains for the home-office user is how to accomplish the backup.

I never use backup software; I rely on making my own floppy backups of documents with which I work. This system requires the user to track which files have been backed up, but I find it easier to use and less time-consuming.

Mainly, I find this approach less time-consuming because in day-to-day work, only a few files on your hard disk actually change. Popping a floppy in and copying the changed files is quick and painless. You also do not have to purchase any software. Of course, if you forget to back up a critical file, you may end up kicking yourself. Backup software takes more time, but will keep track of which files have or have not been backed up.

To simplify things, get DiskFit Pro from Dantz Development for about $75. The program is easy to use, creates Finder readable backups (that is, you can pop any backup disk into your floppy drive and read the contents without using the backup software), and even has a reminder control panel (see fig. 36.12).

Fig. 36.12

The easy-to-use DiskFit Pro backup program.

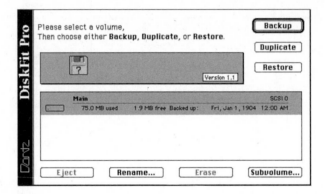

Damage Repair

You've guarded against viruses and kept backups, but no matter how much safer you are now, something is bound to go wrong some time. You should consider two products that can help when your hard drive goes south.

Norton Utilities for the Macintosh by Symantec has pulled me out of problems more than once. The $95 program can repair problems on your hard disk before they develop into major disasters, or can help you recover trashed or damaged files or disks after disaster strikes (see fig. 36.13).

The Norton Utilities package also includes a disk optimizer, an encryption program (to scramble files and hide the contents from prying eyes), a backup program, and some other interesting software items. I've only found the encryption program and the disk doctor useful, however (the optimizer is nice but doesn't work with compressed hard disks).

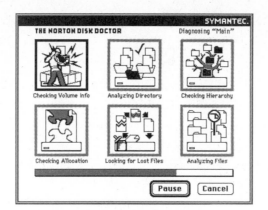

Fig. 36.13
Norton Utilities
checking a hard
disk.

I'm also coming to rely more on the competing product MacTools. Norton Utilities has not been upgraded in a long time and may end up being left behind. MacTools provides quick recovery of files accidentally trashed (a life saver when you empty the Trash and get this "uh oh" feeling in the pit of your stomach), saves the formatting information of your hard disk and other important data in case of a crash, and includes other useful items such as disk optimization, backup, background disk checking, and more. MacTools 3.0 is selling for about $85.

Handling Crowded Hard Drives

A rule of thumb with computers is that data expands to fill all available hard disk space. It never fails that when you first bring your Macintosh home, you are quite sure you'll never fill up all that nice, clean disk space.

It isn't much later, however, that you start wondering just how small one of these "byte" things must be when you fill up 80 or 120 million of them like a crowded closet.

You can take two steps to deal with bulging and overloaded hard disks: archiving and data compression.

Archiving Data

No question here—the top archival program is Stuffit Deluxe by Aladdin Systems for about $85. No Mac user should be without this one. Stuffit can compress your files into "sit" archive files, achieving an average compression of about 50% (see fig. 36.14).

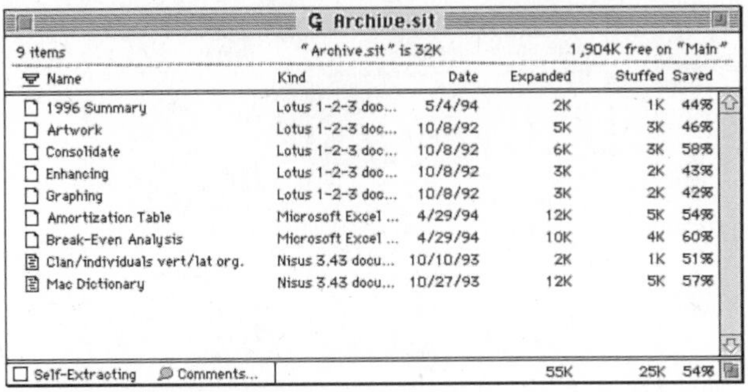

Fig. 36.14
A Stuffit archive averaging 54% reduction in space required.

9 items	"Archive.sit" is 32K			1,904K free on "Main"	
▽ Name	Kind	Date	Expanded	Stuffed	Saved
1996 Summary	Lotus 1-2-3 doo...	5/4/94	2K	1K	44%
Artwork	Lotus 1-2-3 doo...	10/8/92	5K	3K	46%
Consolidate	Lotus 1-2-3 doo...	10/8/92	6K	3K	58%
Enhancing	Lotus 1-2-3 doo...	10/8/92	3K	2K	43%
Graphing	Lotus 1-2-3 doo...	10/8/92	3K	2K	42%
Amortization Table	Microsoft Excel ...	4/29/94	12K	5K	54%
Break-Even Analysis	Microsoft Excel ...	4/29/94	10K	4K	60%
Clan/individuals vert/lat org.	Nisus 3.43 docu...	10/10/93	2K	1K	51%
Mac Dictionary	Nisus 3.43 docu...	10/27/93	12K	5K	57%
☐ Self-Extracting ☐ Comments...			55K	25K	54%

Stuffit can also unpack zip and arc files from the DOS world as well as several of the other Macintosh compression formats.

Not only will Stuffit help you reduce the space needed to store infrequently used data files, but the program is invaluable if you need to transmit files over modem, reducing the transmission time by as much as one half on average.

Compressing Data

Stuffit Deluxe also comes with Stuffit SpaceSaver, which will automatically compress and decompress data on your hard disk. Special folders that will compress files dropped into them can be set up. You can create Stuffit archives by merely changing the name of a folder. Options can be set to automatically compress files that have not been worked with a certain amount of time and a great number of compression options can be set.

Stuffit SpaceSaver is a file level compression system meaning that the software compresses files on your hard disk as opposed to the driver level compression systems that compress the entire disk. SpaceSaver is one of the best file compression systems on the market, but it does have one drawback: the software can slow your Macintosh noticeably. On newer, faster machines (mine's a bit old now), this is not going to happen as much, but if you have an older Mac, you may end up pulling your hair out as SpaceSaver decides to start compressing files (at times I would have killed for a Cancel button).

Because you should get Stuffit Deluxe and SpaceSaver is included, try it out. You may find SpaceSaver to be the perfect answer to a crowded hard disk. And SpaceSaver has and is receiving excellent reviews.

Driver level compression is a bit more risky, but I still prefer it. And only one real choice exists in this category: Stacker for Macintosh. Stacker has been around in the DOS world for ages, and I was glad to see the product come to the Macintosh world.

Driver level compression does techie voodoo to your hard drive's driver software. That can be risky. But I have to point out that I've been using the very first release of Stacker for over a year now without a problem (pretty amazing for a first release).

Installing Stacker is a bit more complicated than, say, Stuffit SpaceSaver. You need to back up your hard disk and then run an installer program that converts your data into the new format. The installation is a bit time-consuming, but you only have to do it once. After installation, your hard disk comes up about twice as big. My old 40MB internal, for example, now thinks it's an 80MB drive.

Now you don't get exactly twice as much space, and tests show that Stacker does slow your Macintosh some. But I still have over 70MB of data stored on a 40MB drive (with some room to spare) and haven't noticed much of a difference in speed. Applications do seem to take a tad longer to start up, but nothing to complain about.

Home-office users are almost always strapped for cash and hard drives aren't cheap. To almost double your hard disk space, $65 is a bargain.

Preventing Screen Burn

I'll tell you a secret. Screen burn hasn't been a problem with personal computers for years. But it's gotten to be too much fun to prevent it, so why stop now?

Screen burn happens when the same high-contrast images stay on your monitor screen for hours—like those ghostly letters you see on older ATM machines. The monitor's *phosphor* (in English: the stuff that makes the screen glow) becomes weaker over time, and if one image stays on-screen for long periods of time, that image can become imprinted on-screen.

Thing is, it's been years since computers sat around with text-only displays burning their phosphor with Log on: prompts. And anybody that can remember screen-burned computer screens is dating themselves as an old-timer.

To save some bucks, turn the brightness control on your monitor down if you leave your computer for any length of time. Of course, that's not nearly as fun as the following, um, safety necessities:

- *Opus 'n Bill.* Bloom County fans will surely find a definite need to protect their Macintosh screen with images of Opus, Bill the Cat, Rosebud the Basselope, and others. After seeing this one, I've decided screen burn is a horrifically urgent problem that needs immediate attention for $30. I'm sure Delrina, the manufacturer, will agree.

VI

The Mac at Work

■ *UnderWare.* Just remember when your spouse asks about folders walking off your desktop, dragons melting your Trash icon, flying saucers, and more, to look very serious and talk about the great lengths you've undergone to prevent phosphor damage to your monitor. Hopefully the rubber chicken won't be on-screen during the discussion. UnderWare is $30 from BitJugglers.

■ *Star Trek: The Screen Saver.* Since when do Star Trek fans need an excuse? $34 from Berkeley Systems, which also has the now-famous After Dark for about $30. You have not *lived* until toasters have flown across your screen.

Kid Proofing

I love this one. If you have kids, you'll like it as well. You know the kids are going to want to use the computer, but you don't want them getting into your office files, right?

KidDesk, $25 from EdMark, hides your data and applications from young mousers but enables them to have one-click access to games and educational software (see fig. 36.15).

Fig. 36.15
One desktop setup
in KidDesk.

You can use Apple's At Ease software to accomplish basically the same thing, but it's not nearly as nice for kids. KidDesk also enables you to set up different application and document sets for kids. And they have their own appointment calendar (junior Day Timer trainees, I guess), calculator, and other desk accessory-like options.

School teachers will want to take a look at this one because of the feature of setting time limits on computer use.

From Here...

From here you may want to consider part IV of the book and the chapters on software. Chapters 16 through 28 cover different categories of software and discuss the leading products in each to help you make purchase decisions.

- Chapter 29, "Getting Online," explains how to connect to bulletin boards and on-line services as well as remote office sites. If you are going to be telecommuting, consider this chapter as well as Chapter 30, "Using America Online and CompuServe," because you can communicate remotely through these services (especially CompuServe).

- Chapters 33, 34, and 35 in this part of the book can also help. Networking, data exchange, and being on the road are all issues related to the home office when the home office must connect with other sites remotely (even while on the road).

VI

The Mac at Work

Part VII

Troubleshooting and Preventive Maintenance

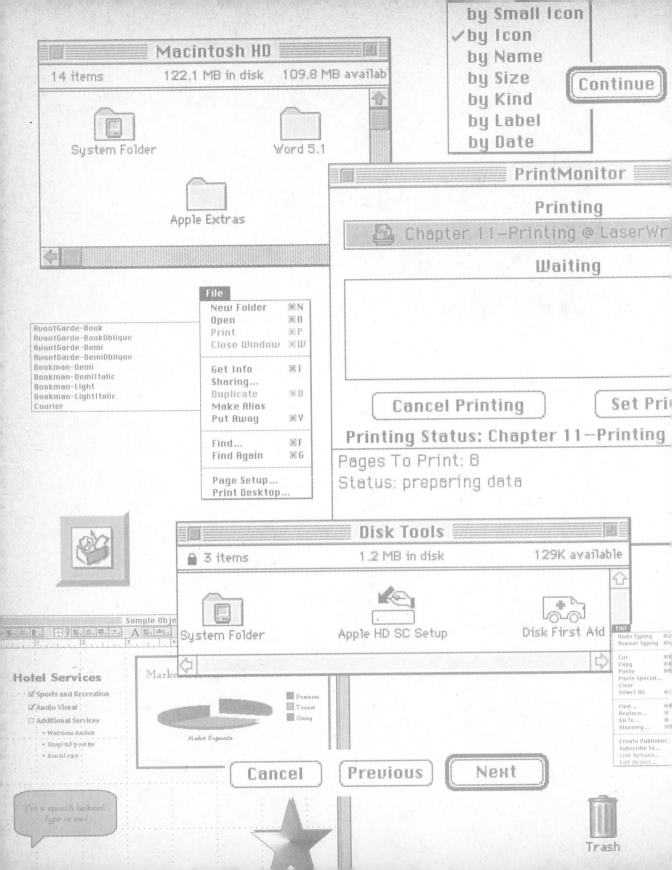

Chapter 37

Troubleshooting

by Gene Steinberg

Like any personal computer, your Macintosh will crash on occasion—sometimes when you're involved in finishing a mission-critical document. If you follow a few simple steps, however, you'll be able to get your computer up and running again. And if you take a few simple precautions, you'll even be able to prevent many of these problems from occurring in the future.

In this chapter, you learn the following:

■ How to solve common Macintosh problems

■ How to find the causes of Init (Extension) conflicts

■ The best way to reinstall your system software

■ How to diagnose problems with floppy disks and your hard drive

■ How to solve printing problems

Why Is My Computer Crashing?

A computer always decides to crash when least expected. You may be working late on a special project that needs to be on the boss's desk (or on your desk, if you're the boss) first thing in the morning. In just a few minutes, you are ready to print your document, and then your computer locks up.

Or you've arrived at work late again, and you need to turn out an annual report by lunch time. You start your Mac, and it freezes at the Welcome to Macintosh screen.

Your Mac can crash for many reasons. Hardware-related problems sometimes occur, but a Mac is a pretty reliable piece of equipment, and most Macintosh peripherals are designed and manufactured to give years of trouble-free service. You'll find that hardware problems are seldom responsible for a crash. Later in this chapter, you get some hints on looking for hardware-related troubles.

By far the biggest factor causing erratic Mac behavior is a software conflict of some sort. Every time Apple revises its system software—and despite thousands of hours of testing—some programs will require revision. This is especially true of programs that change Finder capabilities, such as adding fast copy capabilities, providing the ability to compress a file by pulling down a menu from the Finder's menu bar, or opening and closing font resources on-the-fly.

Older software versions may not be compatible with System 7 features such as file sharing or 32-bit addressing, or may not work with one of the newer 68040 or PowerPC models. The best advice is to contact the publisher (or the program's author if it's shareware or freeware) about getting an update. Where the cost of an update may be too daunting for you, sometimes the publisher can give you a workaround so that you can continue to use the software.

Inits or System Extensions are especially prone to conflicts. Each of these utilities will patch a specific resource in your system software to provide some enhanced capability, such as interactive spell checking, or screen saving capability. Two Extensions that do the same thing (such as Norton's Directory Assistance II and Now's SuperBoomerang, or Alsoft's MasterJuggler or Symantec's Suitcase) often collide and cause a crash or other erratic behavior. Your choice in this case is decide which of the programs to use.

Tip

Before you install new software, check the publisher's ReadMe file or special inserts in the software package for information about compatibility with other software and possible special installation requirements.

Installing these utilities on a Macintosh is simple—usually you just drag them to your System Folder and restart. But it's a good idea to treat the Mac's System Folder with respect. Too many system enhancements will not provide entertainment; they'll provide untold hours of aggravation. The process of configuring your Mac should be fun, but you should also choose the software you use carefully.

The following sections describe the steps you need to take to diagnose common Macintosh problems, and to reinstall your system software, should the need arise. You'll want to keep this chapter on hand, maybe with a bookmark, in case you need to refer to it later on.

But first you need to make sure you have an emergency startup disk ready. You'll need this on hand for the day your Mac fails to start properly.

Apple's Emergency First Aid Disk

If you are a user of System 7, you're lucky. Apple has made an emergency disk for you. It's called Disk Tools (the disk is labeled "Utilities" on Macintosh Performa models), and it comes with your System 7 installation disks (see fig. 37.1). Disk Tools contains a copy of Apple's Disk First Aid and HD SC Setup. In case your Mac won't start, you can use this disk to boot your Mac and test for routine disk directory or SCSI driver problems.

Fig. 37.1
Apple's Disk Tools floppy disk contains the basic tools you need to check and update your Mac's hard drive.

Throughout this chapter, I'm going to refer to the term SCSI, which is short for Small Computer System Interface. It's a specification that defines how a computer and its peripherals, such as CD-ROM drives, hard drives, tape drives, or scanners, communicate with each other. All Macs from the Plus on support SCSI, which allows you to easily hook up seven devices to your Mac. One of these devices is usually your Mac's hard drive. Some high-end Macs even allow you to install several drives inside the computer.

If you're using one of the commercial hard disk repair programs, such as MacTools or Norton Utilities, you will receive a set of emergency disks that you can use to start your Mac in the event of trouble. Or you'll receive instructions on how to make such a disk.

If you are using System 6, your System Startup or System Tools disks contain minimal System Folders that will boot your Mac. You should make a backup of these disks and maybe remove some of the extra utilities you don't need (aside from System and Finder, of course) and install copies of Apple's disk repair and formatting program.

> **Note**
>
> When you back up a boot floppy, use Apple's Disk Copy, shown in figure 37.2, or a commercial program that can make a track-by-track copy of a floppy, such as MacTools FastCopy or Norton's Flopper utility. These programs will correctly copy boot blocks to the new floppy so that these floppies will boot your Mac properly. A straight Finder copy is not always successful in transferring all this data. Apple's Disk Copy is available from online services such as America Online or CompuServe, or from a local Mac user's group.

Fig. 37.2
Apple's handy and free disk copying program.

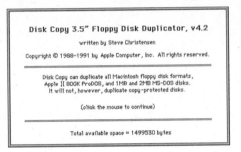

Startup Conflicts

The following sections describe typical Macintosh problems and their solutions. You'll find a common thread in all of these descriptions. The cause is generally related to an Extension conflict, a problem with your System software, or a problem with a SCSI device attached to your Mac (such as a hard drive or scanner). Even if your specific problem isn't discussed in these sections, the solutions described may apply in your situation.

Disk Icon with a Blinking "?"

When you boot your Macintosh, it looks for a disk that has a working System Folder, with a System and Finder in it. If all you see on your Mac's screen is a disk icon with a blinking question mark in it, as shown in figure 37.3, it may mean any of the following:

- You don't have a System Folder installed on any of your drives.

- Your System and/or Finder is damaged.

- Your boot drive (or any drives that have a System Folder) are not being recognized for some reason (see the section, "Hard Disk Problems," later in this chapter).

- You have a SCSI-related conflict.

Fig. 37.3
A blinking
question mark
inside a floppy
disk icon at
startup often
indicates damaged
or missing System
software.

Try the following steps to get your Mac running again:

1. Restart and place your System 7 Disk Tools disk in your floppy drive. If you are using System 6, try the System Tools or System Startup disk.

2. If your Mac boots normally, check your hard drives for the presence of a System Folder, and make sure that a System and a Finder is inside that folder.

3. Even if you have a System Folder that looks okay, reinstall your System software. Follow the instructions in the section, "Why a Clean System Installation?" later in this chapter.

Tip

If a visual search doesn't reveal a System Folder, use the Finder's Search function (⌘-F or select Find from the File menu).

4. If your hard drive(s) won't mount, run Disk First Aid or one of the commercial hard drive repair/diagnostic programs, such as MacTools or Norton Utilities.

5. If you have any external SCSI devices attached to your Mac (such as a hard drive or scanner), power down, disconnect the SCSI cable at the rear of your Mac, and turn it on again.

Disk Icon with a Stationary (Nonblinking) "?"

When you boot your Macintosh, SCSI device drivers are loaded into memory. If there's a SCSI-related conflict of some sort, your Mac may not start properly. The quickest way to diagnose this problem is to power down, disconnect the SCSI cable from your Mac's SCSI port, and restart.

If your computer still won't work properly, please follow the steps described in the preceding section.

Disk Icon with an "X"

This problem has a fairly simple solution. The display usually follows an attempt to start with a floppy disk that cannot boot your Mac. Normally, the disk is ejected, and after several seconds, your Mac will boot from whatever startup disk has been selected. If you then see a blinking or solid question mark inside that disk icon, please read the two preceding sections for further suggestions.

Sad Mac Icon

When your Mac boots, for the first time, or during a restart, it does a brief set of self-diagnostic tests to make sure all components are working properly. Then the SCSI device drivers are loaded into memory. If something should go wrong during this testing process, you may see a Sad Mac icon on your screen, as shown in figure 37.4.

Fig. 37.4
A Sad Mac often indicates SCSI or system-related troubles.

On early Macs, models released before the SE, one row of numbers and letters is displayed below the Sad Mac. On the SE and later models, two letters are displayed. These codes may change from model to model and may mean different things in different installations. Following are the most common causes and solutions for a Sad Mac:

- Your new RAM was installed incorrectly. Power down and make sure the SIMMs are firmly seated in their slots (but *do not* force them into position), and oriented in the proper direction.

- A RAM SIMM has gone bad. If your Mac has more than a single bank of RAM, remove the RAM in one bank as a test. If it still doesn't work, reinstall and try the other bank.

- Your keyboard or mouse has a problem. Power down, remove and reseat the devices' cables, and try again. Or try another mouse or keyboard.

- A NuBus or PDS expansion card has gone bad. To check for this, power down, remove the expansion card, and power up again.

- You have a SCSI-related conflict, or one of your drives has a bad or corrupted driver on it. To check for this problem, follow these steps:

  1. Power down your Mac and its peripherals, disconnect the SCSI cable, and try to boot your Mac.

2. If the problem is still present, try restarting with your System 7 Disk Tools disk or the corresponding System 6 startup floppy.

3. If you still cannot start your computer, restart with a floppy disk, but hold down the ⌘-Option-Shift-Delete keys (all at the same time), to prevent use of your internal drive as a startup device.

4. If the Sad Mac icon remains sad, turn off power, open the Mac's case and carefully disconnect the power and SCSI cables attached to the internal drive. (If your Mac is under warranty, contact your dealer or Apple for help.)

5. Restart the Mac with a floppy startup disk. If it runs okay with the internal drive disconnected, contact your dealer about repair or re-placement of the drive.

   If all else fails, call your dealer or contact Apple Customer Assistance at (800) SOS-APPL. Be sure to write down the full set of numbers displayed beneath the Sad Mac icon—these numbers may help the service technician to diagnose your problem.

Mac Intones a Series of Chimes Rather Than the Normal Startup Sound

As mentioned earlier in this chapter, when you start your Mac, it undergoes a series of self-tests to make sure all systems are "go" for a startup. These tests begin at the point you power up. If the sound you hear is something other than the normal startup chord (what some Mac users call the *chimes of doom*) it may mean:

■ Your new memory upgrade was not installed correctly.

■ A RAM SIMM has gone bad.

■ A NuBus or PDS expansion slot is not working correctly.

■ There has been a hardware failure.

To check for these problems, follow these steps:

1. Power down and remove and carefully reseat your RAM upgrade. If the update was performed by a dealer or private consultant, contact that party immediately for assistance.

> **Caution**
>
> According to Apple's latest service policy, they won't void your warranty if you install an upgrade card, DRAM, VRAM, or internal modem inside your Mac, as long as you don't damage the computer. If the computer is damaged as a result of an upgrade performed by someone other than an Apple service provider, they won't fix it under your product warranty. This new service policy does not cover compact Macintosh models, such as the Plus, SE, or Classic, because of the high voltage risk posed by the presence of your computer's picture tube when you open the case. Therefore, opening the compact Mac's case could void your product warranty (although most all of these products are long out of warranty by now).

2. Power down and remove any newly-installed RAM or NuBus expansion cards. Power up again and see whether everything works okay.

3. If the expansion card is needed for video, just reseat the card for now, and try again.

4. If your monitor will work with your Mac's internal video circuitry (if available), try using your Mac without its video card as a test.

5. Power down and remove the SCSI cable from your Mac's SCSI port.

6. If none of these steps work, call Apple Customer Assistance at (800) SOS-APPL or your dealer.

Mac Freezes or Bombs After the Happy Mac Icon

At this step in the startup process, your Mac is loading system software into RAM. If you crash at this point, it may mean one of the following:

■ Your System and/or Finder is damaged.

■ You have a SCSI conflict.

■ You have a hard drive directory problem, preventing System software from loading.

To get your Mac running again, try the following steps:

1. Under System 7, restart with the Shift key held down. You will see the Welcome to Macintosh startup screen with the words Extensions off beneath it (if you aren't using a custom startup screen), as shown in figure 37.5.

Fig. 37.5
If you don't have a custom startup screen, you'll see a visual indication that you've disabled System Extensions under System 7.

2. If your Mac starts normally, follow the instructions in "Diagnosing Extension Conflicts," later in this chapter.

3. If your Mac still fails to boot normally, restart and place your System 7 Disk Tools disk in your floppy drive. If you are using System 6, try the System Tools or System Startup disk.

4. If the Mac starts up without any problem, reinstall your System software, following the instructions in the section, "Why a Clean System Installation?," later in this chapter.

5. If your Mac still fails to boot, power down your Mac and all attached peripherals and disconnect the SCSI cable from your Mac's SCSI port.

6. If disconnecting SCSI devices restores your Mac's normal operation, power down, and reinstall each SCSI device, one at a time, until the problem returns. Be sure you check for proper cable, termination, and SCSI address settings.

Note

A *terminator* is a device that contains a resistor that, in effect, completes an electrical circuit. An improperly terminated SCSI chain may fail to boot, not read or write data properly, or even crash a hard drive.

Caution

Never attach or remove SCSI cables, or change SCSI address numbers or the position of termination blocks or adjustments while the power on your Mac and attached devices is turned on. Doing so could damage your Mac's SCSI chip, as well as your SCSI peripherals.

Mac Freezes or Bombs after One of Your Extensions Loads

As your Mac continues to boot, each of your startup programs, called System Extensions (or Inits under System 6), will load, one at a time. If your Mac freezes or produces a bomb message while Extensions are loading into memory, it may mean one of the following:

- The Extension whose icon just appeared on-screen or the one following that icon is conflicting with other software.

- The Extension whose icon just appeared on-screen or the one following that icon is damaged.

- Your System and/or Finder is damaged.

- You have a SCSI conflict.

To get your Mac running again, try the following steps:

1. Remove or disable the Extension that loaded just before your Mac crashed—and the one that was to load next.

2. If now your Mac starts okay, remove or disable all Extensions but these two and try again.

3. If your Mac crashes again, consult the directions provided by the publisher or author of the conflicting programs about possible conflicts or workarounds—or call the publisher for assistance.

4. If you still cannot get your Mac to start properly (under System 7), restart with the Shift key held down. You will see the `Welcome to Macintosh` startup screen with the words `Extensions off` beneath it (if you aren't using a custom startup screen).

5. If your Mac starts normally, follow the instructions in "Diagnosing Extension Conflicts," later in this chapter.

6. If your Mac still fails to boot normally, restart and place your System 7 Disk Tools disk in your floppy drive. If you are using System 6, try the System Tools or System Startup disk.

7. If the Mac starts up without any problem, reinstall your System software, following the instructions in "Why a Clean System Installation?" later in this chapter.

8. If your Mac still fails to boot, power down your Mac and all attached peripherals and disconnect the SCSI cable from your Mac's SCSI port.

9. If disconnecting SCSI devices restores your Mac's normal operation, power down, and reinstall each SCSI device, one at a time, until the problem returns. Be sure you check for proper cable, termination, and SCSI address settings.

Mac Freezes or Bombs at the Desktop

After all of your Extensions load, the first startup program, the Finder, is launched. If your Mac crashes at this stage, it may mean one of the following:

- You have an Extension conflict.

- Your System and/or Finder is damaged.

- The desktop files used to maintain file icons and application/document links are damaged.

- You have a SCSI conflict.

- You have a hard drive directory problem, preventing System software from loading.

To get your Mac running again, try the following steps:

1. Under System 7, restart while holding the Shift key. You will see the Welcome to Macintosh startup screen with the words Extensions off beneath it (if you aren't using a custom startup screen).

2. If your Mac starts normally, follow the instructions in "Diagnosing Extension Conflicts," later in this chapter.

3. If your Mac still fails to boot normally, restart and place your System 7 Disk Tools disk in your floppy drive. If you are using System 6, try the System Tools or System Startup disk.

   If the Mac starts up without any problem from the floppy disk, reinstall your System software. Follow the instructions in "Why a Clean System Installation?" later in this chapter.

4. If your Mac still fails to get past the Desktop, rebuild the desktop by following these steps:

   - Restart with Extensions off and hold down the ⌘-Option keys after startup, and before the Desktop pattern appears.

   - When a window appears asking whether you want to rebuild the Desktop, press OK.

   - You will see that message appear for each hard disk volume you have.

> **Note**
>
> If you have a large number of fonts installed, it will take much longer for the desktop to rebuild because the icon for each font file has to be read and loaded into the Finder's desktop files.
>
> If your desktop won't rebuild successfully, check with your local Mac user's group or an online service such as America Online, CompuServe, or eWorld for a copy of DeskTop Reset from Symantec or TechTool from MicroMat. Either of these programs will delete the desktop files, forcing a more thorough desktop rebuild. Finder enhancement programs such as PrairieSoft's DiskTop can also delete your Mac's desktop files.

5. If your Mac still fails to boot, power down your Mac and all attached peripherals and disconnect the SCSI cable from your Mac's SCSI port.

6. If disconnecting SCSI devices restores your Mac's normal operation, power down, and reinstall each SCSI device, one at a time, while carefully watching cable, termination, and SCSI address settings.

System Problems

There is probably nothing more disturbing than to have an application suddenly quit during a work session on your Mac, or to see a bomb message of some sort. Although it's relatively easy to use, your Mac works by a complex relationship of many systems, ranging from your screen, to your keyboard, mouse, and CPU. Data is funneled back and forth in a constant stream, and if some of the messages do not get through, your Mac will fail to work correctly.

Many of the problems that generate a startup crash can also cause your Mac to fail while you're actually doing work on it. The following sections discuss many of the problems and common solutions.

The Application Has Unexpectedly Quit

This sort of message can happen right after you first launch an application or at some point during the work session. Often you'll see an error message of some sort, such as a `"Type 1"` (bus) error, `"Type 2"` (address) error, or Type `3 (illegal instruction)` error. Sometimes the messages don't really describe the problem. When you experience this sort of problem, it may mean:

- The application you're using is not compatible with your Macintosh or operating system. This may be especially true when you use very old software under System 7, or on a Centris, Quadra, or Power Macintosh model.

- Because applications load information about your installed font library when they launch, when an application unexpectedly quits shortly after it's launched, it may indicate that you have a damaged font suitcase.

- The application doesn't have enough memory to run.

- The application is in conflict with one of your System Extensions.

- The application may be damaged and should be reinstalled.

- The System and/or Finder is damaged.

Caution

If an application quits, be sure to restart your Mac right away. If you continue to work with another program or relaunch the application that quit, you will most likely experience a system crash in short order because your Mac is now running in an unstable state.

The following steps will help you get your Mac running again:

1. Make sure the program is compatible with your computer and operating system. If in doubt, contact the author or publisher.

   If an upgrade isn't available, you may be able to get the program to run within some limitations, say, with System 7's 32-bit addressing feature turned off, an 040 Mac's Cache Switch, or the Power Macintosh's Modern Memory Manager feature, in the Memory Control Panel, disabled.

2. Strip your library of installed fonts to only the basic system fonts, such as Chicago, Geneva, Monaco, or New York, and see if the program launches correctly.

3. If you use a program like MasterJuggler or Suitcase to run your font library, close all fonts opened through these programs.

Tip
A quick way to isolate a bad font suitcase is to double-click on the suitcase file (under System 7). A bad font suitcase will be reported as damaged.

> **Note**
>
> If you are using the Font and Sound Valet utility from the Suitcase package (from Symantec) to compress your fonts, try expanding them before use. System 7.1 and later may be incompatible with older versions of this utility.

4. Give the application more memory to run. Highlight the application icon and select Get Info from the Finder desktop. Then increase the memory allocated to the program by 500K or more, and try again (see fig. 37.6).

Fig. 37.6
If you have enough free RAM, giving a little more memory to an application is easy.

5. Restart with Extensions off (Shift key held down at startup for System 7 users). If the problem is due to an Extension conflict, it will quickly go away.

6. Reinstall the application.

> **Caution**
>
> Be sure new software installations are done with Extensions off. Application installers are especially sensitive to the presence of virus software and other startup programs.

7. Reinstall your System software. Follow the instructions in "Why a Clean System Installation?" later in this chapter.

You Get a System Bomb

Sometimes the application doesn't quit at all or you aren't using any particular program, but a bomb message appears on-screen. Regardless of whether the bomb message describes the error, it indicates some breakdown in the complex chain of communication in which your Mac is engaged every moment that it's on.

The steps described in the preceding section apply equally to a System bomb message, but I would like to add a few more pieces of advice:

1. If the bomb message has a Restart button at the lower right side (see fig. 37.7), click the Restart button. Sometimes (but not often) your Mac will restart.

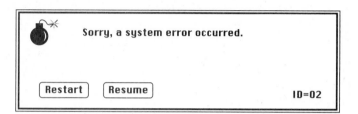

Fig. 37.7
When the complex chain of actions and reactions of your Mac breaks down, it may crash.

2. If you can successfully restart your Mac this way, hold down the Shift key upon restart to disable Extensions. Then follow the instructions presented in the preceding section.

The Mac Freezes without a Bomb Message

Regardless of whether you see a system bomb message, the causes of a freeze are usually the same. Somewhere along the line, the delicate chain of communication among your Mac's systems has broken down. Follow the steps outlined in the preceding section to diagnose and fix the problem.

> **Note**
>
> A force quit, ⌘-Option-Esc, will sometimes get your Mac running again. Because your Mac will be running in an unstable state, however, restart immediately after saving your work.

Cannot Change the Name of a Folder or Disk

The process of changing an icon's name should be simple. You click the icon's text, and, after waiting a second or two (for System 7 users), the icon is highlighted and surrounded by a black rectangle. Under the following circumstances, you can't rename the icon:

- The disk or file is being shared through File Sharing, or another network software setup. To change the icon's name, turn off sharing.

- The file is locked. You can unlock the file by highlighting the file icon, selecting Get Info from Finder's File menu, and unchecking the "Locked" checkbox at the lower left of the Get Info window.

- There is disk directory damage. To diagnose or repair this problem, run Apple's Disk First Aid or one of the commercial hard drive repair/diagnostic programs, such as MacTools or Norton Utilities.

- A shared disk has been used on a System 6 Mac. If this is the case, Apple's Disk First Aid version 7.2 or later, or a free Apple utility, Rename Rescue (available from the major online services) can restore the renaming capability.

Cannot Delete a File

This is an all-too-common problem. You are finished using a file, or you never needed it in the first place, and you toss it into the trash can. Then you try to delete the file, and you get a message that it's locked or busy. The following list examines the possible causes for both these symptoms:

- The file is itself an application that's opened. Quit the application to delete it.

- The file is an Extension that's presently in use (some can be deleted, others cannot). You need to restart with Extensions off to delete the file.

- The program used to create the file is still open, even though the document window is closed. You must also quit the application. (This will happen with Microsoft Word and other programs.)

- The file is really locked. To unlock the file, select the file icon, choose Get Info from the Finder's File menu, and uncheck the Locked box at the bottom left of the Get Info window, as shown in figure 37.8.

- The file is damaged. Run Disk First Aid or one of the commercial hard disk diagnosis/repair programs, such as MacTools or Norton, and determine whether the damage can be fixed.

Tip
To delete a locked file, hold down the Option key while selecting Empty Trash from the Finder's Special menu.

Tip
One fast way to remove a damaged file that won't delete is to create a new folder with the same name as the damaged file—and delete that one too. That should allow you to remove both files.

Fig. 37.8
Here's how to
unlock a file so
you can remove it.

Cannot Delete a Font

This is an error that first reared its head under System 7.1. You try to delete a
font suitcase from your Fonts folder (inside the System Folder), and when you
drag the font to the trash, you get a –39 error.

If this happens, follow these steps:

1. Drag the Fonts folder outside of the System Folder and leave it on the
   Desktop.

2. Restart your Mac while holding down the Shift key (to disable Extensions). A new empty Fonts folder will be created inside your System
   Folder, but don't worry about that for now.

3. Drag the font suitcase you want to delete to the trash. You should be
   able to empty the trash now.

4. Just in case the original Fonts folder was subject to directory damage of
   some sort, open it, drag all of the fonts inside it to the closed System
   Folder icon.

5. All the fonts will be moved to the new Fonts folder.

6. Delete the old Fonts folder, and restart normally.

Files Have Lost Their Icons

The information about your file icons is stored in two invisible database files
under System 7, called the *desktop files*. System 6 users have all this information in one file. A system crash, software conflict, or the process of restoring a

hard drive after reformatting may result in a damaged or incomplete desktop file. Your icons become generic document icons, and your document files lose their relationship with the creator programs. If this happens, follow these steps:

1. Rebuild the desktop file. Hold down the ⌘-Option keys after you restart your Mac, before the desktop pattern appears.

2. Shortly after your Mac's desktop pattern appears, a message appears asking whether you want to rebuild the desktop. Press OK for each hard drive volume you want to update (see fig. 37.9).

Fig. 37.9
The first step to rebuilding the desktop.

Caution

If you're using an idle-time file compression program such as AutoDoubler, More Disk Space, Now Compress, or StuffIt SpaceSaver, make sure that the compression Extension is running when you rebuild the desktop. Otherwise, files won't have the correct icons.

3. If the file icons don't change to their normal status, try rebuilding a second time, even a third time.

4. If the process still won't work, try Symantec's Desktop Reset or MicroMat's TechTool. These programs are free, available from local user groups or the major online services. These programs allow you to delete the old desktop files, which results in the desktop being re-created rather than updated (as is done normally).

The Application Cannot Be Found

Your document files have a special relationship with the application that was used to create those documents. If the application is installed on your Mac (on any hard drive that's mounted), just double-clicking on the document will launch the program and then open the document. As described in the preceding section, the Finder maintains this information.

At one time or another, all of us casually double-click on a document only to receive a message similar to the one pictured in figure. 37.10.

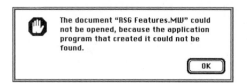

Fig. 37.10
If your desktop needs to be rebuilt, or you don't have the right program, you'll see this message when you double-click on a document.

If this happens, it may mean any of the following:

■ You do not have the program that created the document.

> **Note**
>
> If the file you cannot open was created in a popular word processor format, such as MacWrite or Microsoft Word, you may be able to open it by using the Open dialog box from another word processor (or even just by dragging the document icon to the application icon of your word processor under System 7). Sometimes you can open a file in a program that reads straight text, but formatting information, such as type styles, tables, and complex layouts, may be lost.

■ The desktop file is damaged. Follow the directions in the previous section for rebuilding the desktop.

Settings Made in the Views Control Panel Won't Stick

Under System 7, the Views Control Panel is used to set your default font for directory listings (the standard is 9-point Geneva); settings in this control panel also determine whether small-, medium-, or large-sized icons appear on your desktop, and whether to show hard drive capacity, and other adjustments (see fig. 37.11). Sometimes the settings you make revert to default every time you restart. If this happens to you, follow these steps:

Fig. 37.11
The Views Control
Panel helps you
customize the way
your Mac's desktop
will look.

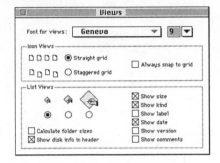

1. Go to the Preferences Folder inside your System 7 System Folder.

2. Select the Finder Preferences file, and drag it to the Trash (you cannot delete it until the next restart, because the file is always open).

3. Restart your Mac. Open the Views Control Panel and change the settings to your preference.

4. Trash your old Finder Preferences file, which clearly has become corrupted somehow.

Mac Freezes After Installing System 7

Apple offers System 7 upgrade kits with a one-button installation capability. Most times it works, but sometimes it doesn't, and crashes occur when you boot under your new operating system or frequently while you are at work on your Mac. If this happens to you, consider the following possibilities:

■ You're using a hardware expansion card, such as a video display adapter, that needs a ROM upgrade to work with System 7.

■ You need to update your hard drive to support System 7's new file system. This step replaces the SCSI driver with a new one.

■ You are running Extensions that aren't compatible with System 7.

■ You don't have enough RAM installed to run System 7. Apple recommends 2MB, minimum, but you should consider 4MB at the very least to allow you to use at least some of your favorite Extensions and to run any of the popular Macintosh applications.

■ You need to do a "clean" system software installation. For full details on how to do this, follow the instructions in "Why a Clean System Installation?" later in this chapter.

The Date on Your Mac Reverts to 1904 or 1956

Default system settings, such as the date and time, mouse tracking speed, network settings, screen depth, sound level, startup disk, and other adjustments are stored in a small memory bank called *PRAM* (parameter RAM). This little chunk of memory is powered by a small lithium battery inside your Mac. Sometimes the settings you make just don't stick, or you restart your Mac and it reverts to system defaults. When this happens, you should follow these steps:

1. Zap the PRAM. This clears the PRAM of corrupted data and often fixes the problem.

2. To zap the PRAM under System 7, hold down the ⌘-Option-P-R keys at startup, wait until two or three startup tones sound and then release the keys.

3. To zap the PRAM under System 6, hold down the ⌘-Option-Shift keys and select Control Panels from the Apple menu. When you are asked whether you want to zap the PRAM, okay the dialog box.

4. Before getting back to work, recheck all of your standard Control Panel settings. You will find that sound levels may be too low, mouse tracking speeds too slow, and that your selected monitor settings (such as black and white or color) have changed.

5. If zapping the PRAM doesn't cure your problem, contact your dealer about testing your Mac's internal battery for possible replacement.

> **Note**
>
> The process of installing a memory or modem upgrade on a PowerBook or a new expansion board on a modular Mac may automatically zap the PRAM. Don't be alarmed if this happens; it's usually quite normal.
>
> Sometimes you can cure a corrupted PRAM problem by actually removing the Mac's battery for approximately 10 minutes and then reinstalling it. The battery is generally on the main logic board. If your Mac is still under warranty, let your dealer do it for you.

Hard Disk Problems

Like system software, a hard drive is used and abused every moment you are running your Mac—with the possible exception of a PowerBook (if your drive is in the Sleep mode). The hard drive is also the one arena of Macintosh use that is not always quite plug and play.

Many hard disk problems may manifest themselves as possible Extension conflicts or corrupted system software, which makes them a little harder to diagnose.

Here are a few typical problems that you're likely to encounter at one time or another with your Mac and its complex SCSI chain.

Tip

If your Mac won't boot after adding a new SCSI peripheral, power down all of your equipment, and disconnect the SCSI cable. Then restart—the problem could be due to a SCSI conflict, bad cables, or termination.

Hard Disk Icon Does Not Show Up On the Desktop

When you first boot your Mac, a hard drive's SCSI driver is loaded into RAM. When your desktop pattern appears, all your hard disk icons should be displayed shortly thereafter. If a hard disk icon is missing, it may mean any of the following:

> **Note**
>
> Although you cannot see your SCSI driver, it is, like a printer driver, a communications tool. It allows your Macintosh to send commands to your hard drive about reading and writing data. If it becomes corrupted for some reason, you will experience system crashes, the failure of your hard drive icon to mount, or possible disk directory damage.

- The hard drive is not properly connected to the SCSI chain.

- SCSI device is not properly terminated.

- The hard drive is damaged.

- The hard drive wasn't turned on until *after* you booted your Mac.

- You have a SCSI-related conflict.

- If it's a removable hard drive, you need to install a special mounting Extension for its icon to appear on your Mac's desktop.

- The disk is not properly formatted.

Here are a few steps to help you get your hard drive to work properly again:

1. Use Apple's Disk First Aid or one of the commercial hard drive diagnostic/repair utilities, and see whether they can store or fix your drive.

2. Update (*not* reformat) the drive using Apple's HD SC Setup from your System 7 Disk Tools disk (for Apple's own drives) or the disk formatting utility you prefer.

3. Power down your Macintosh, then turn on your SCSI devices first, and wait for 10–20 seconds for them to spin up. Then restart your Mac.

4. If that doesn't work, power down your Mac once again, and any attached SCSI accessories, and check cables, termination, and SCSI ID settings.

Caution

External drives generally have push buttons, knobs, or dip switches to change SCSI ID numbers, and the numbers themselves are usually displayed clearly (if not, check the manual that came with the drive). It's also very easy to accidentally push an ID selector button while moving a drive, so examine the drive carefully before powering it on. With internal drives, ID numbers are set with jumpers inserted at the bottom of the drive on its controller board. You may want a dealer to assist you in changing this setting. A convenient way to examine SCSI ID numbers that are not readily visible is to use the freeware SCSI Probe utility which is available on all the major online services and from many user group BBS. Some hard drive formatters also come with utilities that allow you to check for SCSI ID numbers. None of these programs, however, will show when two drives occupy the same ID number.

---

5. Reinstall your SCSI devices, one at a time, adjusting SCSI setups as needed.

6. If the problem is isolated to a single device, try using that device with a new set of cables, with and without termination.

7. Check the manufacturer's instructions or look over the rear panel of your drive case for such things as switchable termination, or whether or not the device is designed to be installed in a particular spot on your SCSI chain (some devices work best when installed last).

8. If you are using a removable device, check the manufacturer's manuals for instructions about the installation of special mounting Inits or using a special formatting program.

9. Don't be afraid to experiment a little on your SCSI chain. As long as you make sure everything is properly connected when you power on, and that no two devices occupy the same address number, you can remove termination or even add a second termination block (on a long SCSI chain) if necessary to get it to work.

> **Note**
>
> The Macintosh IIfx requires a special black-colored terminator block to handle its ultra-fast SCSI chain. Although this terminator might also function on Macintosh Quadra models, it doesn't work reliably on a Power Macintosh.

There Are Duplicate Hard Disk Icons on the Desktop

This is one ailment we've not encountered, but it's possible to happen under some rare circumstances. Following are some possibilities:

- Two of your hard drive volumes have the same icon and disk name. As long as the drives occupy different ID numbers, or are on different partitions of the same drive, they'll both show up on your desktop. Just rename one of the drives to ensure less confusion.

- The SCSI device driver is damaged. Just update the drive or reformat the drive to fix this problem.

The Disk Cannot Be Opened

This is another infrequent situation. Your disk icons show up on the desktop, but you are unable to open the disk directory without a crash or an error message of some sort. Should this happen to you, it may mean one of the following:

- The hard drive is damaged.

- The hard drive SCSI driver is corrupted.

To diagnose or repair these problems, follow the steps outlined in the previous section.

Drive Freezes While Reading or Writing Data

Your Mac starts normally, all the disk drives are mounting on the desktop, but as soon as you copy a large file to a disk, the drive freezes. If the drive has an activity light, the light remains lit. If this should happen to you, it may indicate one of the following:

- Your SCSI chain is not properly terminated.

- You are using worn or low-grade SCSI cables.

- The SCSI driver is corrupted.

- There is an Extension conflict.

- System and/or Finder are corrupted.

Although the last three issues are worth exploring if all else fails, your most likely solution to the problem is one of the first two. Sometimes the usual SCSI setups, terminating the first and last device on the chain, don't work. On a long SCSI chain, you may need a second terminator in the middle of the chain or at the very end. Using poor quality cables, especially on a Centris, Quadra or Power Macintosh model, can result in poor current transfer, which would produce a problem of this sort.

Apple's HD SC Setup Cannot Find Your Hard Drive

There are two really nice things about Apple's home-brewed disk formatting utility—it's free, and it comes with the System disks that ship with every new Macintosh. If your Mac has an Apple hard drive, it was formatted with this program right from the factory. HD SC Setup does have some major limitations:

- It won't format a drive that doesn't have Apple's custom controller chip.

- You cannot create more than a single Macintosh partition with it.

So if you try to format or update a drive, and HD SC Setup cannot locate the drive on your Mac's SCSI chain, consider these possibilities:

- You're using a non-Apple drive. Your only solution is to use a non-Apple formatting program. You can get one from the drive's manufacturer, your dealer, or one of the mail-order houses that sells Mac software.

- The drive isn't hooked up properly. Check the standard SCSI issues, cables, termination, and SCSI address number.

- The drive is damaged. Check the drive with Disk First Aid or hard disk repair/recovery programs such as MacTools or Norton Utilities.

If the above suggestions don't help, contact your dealer or Apple Customer Assistance at (800) SOS-APPL for advice.

Recovering Damaged Files

There are three words that you should always keep in mind when working on an important document on your Mac—*backup, backup, backup.* High-end publishing and word processing software can often be configured to make an automatic backup copy as a hedge in case something goes wrong with the original file. If your software doesn't have this capability, use your program's Save As feature to make another copy with a different name, and have that additional copy written to a different drive (a floppy disk if necessary) for additional protection.

Following are situations where you may have a file go bad:

- Your Mac crashes while a file is being saved.

- There is directory damage on your hard drive, preventing files from being written properly to disk.

- There are bad blocks on the drive, sectors that will not accept data properly.

- You have an Extension conflict.

- You have a SCSI-related conflict.

Here are some steps to take to protect your files:

1. Backup all of your mission-critical data regularly, once a day at the very minimum.

2. Important files should receive backups several times during a work session.

3. Check your hard drive at least once a week with Disk First Aid or MacTools or Norton Utilities.

4. Use your hard disk formatting program to "verify" the drive every three months. Some disk formatters will automatically map out or "hide" bad blocks during such a test.

5. Backup and reformat your drive at least once a year.

6. When adding new SCSI peripherals to your Mac's SCSI chain, check the new device all by itself for proper operation.

7. For a hard drive or removable device, check its capability to read and write large files without error messages. Recheck the drive after all of your SCSI devices are running in their normal order.

If you have a file come up damaged despite taking the right precautions, there are no guarantees, but sometimes you can recover all or part of a file. Follow these steps:

1. Restart with Extensions off (Shift key held down at startup under System 7) and try opening the file again.

2. Use a text editor or a word processor that can read text, such as Microsoft Word or WordPerfect, to extract the text from your document, as shown in figure 37.12.

Tip
Can Opener from Abbott Systems (available at many software resellers) is another program that can often recover parts of a corrupted file.

VII

Troubleshooting

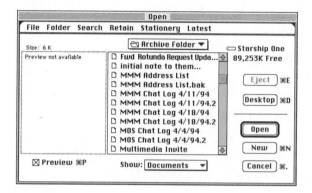

Fig. 37.12
The standard Open dialog box for WordPerfect can be used to select and open files created in many formats other than the program's own.

3. Try MacTools CP FileFix, which is designed to repair damaged Microsoft Excel or Word files, but will sometimes repair other damaged files as well (see fig. 37.13).

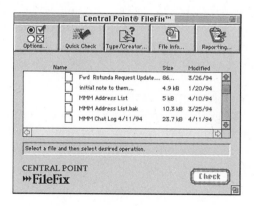

Fig. 37.13
CP FileFix, part of the MacTools package from Central Point Software, is able to recover some damaged files.

Recovering Deleted Files from the Hard Disk

This is the error everyone dreads. You are in a rush to complete a job, and you trash (then delete) the wrong file. System 7 has made it more difficult to accidentally remove a file, because you have to manually select the Empty Trash button (though some programs will do this automatically for you).

Here are the steps to help you recover your files:

1. As soon as you realize the file was mistakenly deleted, do not write any more files to that drive.

2. Run a program like MacTools' CP Undelete or Norton Disk Doctor to recover the files.

3. Check the file immediately after recovery for damaged or missing data.

4. If the recovered file will not open in the program in which it was created, use a word processor or text editing program to try to retrieve the text portion of the file.

Floppy Disk Problems

Second only to a hard drive, floppy disk mechanisms on a Mac get really heavy workouts. We pop our disks in and out with abandon, and depend on the disks to always work properly.

Floppy disks are kept in shirt pockets, back pockets, in purses, car trunks, glove compartments, shoe boxes, file cabinets, anywhere with a few extra inches to spare (we haven't looked inside the refrigerators of any of our computer-using friends yet). They get little respect, but if something goes wrong, the words of aggravation and annoyance know no bounds.

Cannot Eject a Floppy Disk

You are finished using a floppy disk, and you dismount the icon, by trashing it or hitting the ⌘-Y (Put Away) keys under System 7. The floppy icon disappears, but the disk remains inserted in the drive. Or you pop in a disk, and it doesn't show up on a desktop.

If this happens to you, follow these steps:

1. Restart your Mac, and hold down the mouse button as your Mac boots. When you hold down the mouse button, it will signal the drive to eject the floppy disk.

2. If the disk doesn't eject, take a paper clip, bend one end of the clip's wire into a straight line and push that wire into the small hole below and to the right of the floppy disk drive opening. That will usually result in the disk being ejected.

After the floppy disk is removed, inspect the disk for surface damage. If the disk appears undamaged, try it again in the drive, or try another disk. If the drive refuses to eject the disk, try the following:

1. Clean the floppy drive with 3-M floppy disk cleaner.

2. If the drive still won't eject the disk without our brute force technique, reinstall your system software, using the instructions provided in "Why a Clean System Installation?" later in this chapter.

3. If a new system installation won't fix your problem, contact your dealer to have the floppy drive inspected.

Cannot Initialize a Floppy Disk

You insert a new, unformatted floppy disk into the drive, and nothing happens. Or you have a disk mounted that you want to reformat, and after selecting Erase from the Finder's Special Menu, you get a message that the disk is locked (see fig. 37.14).

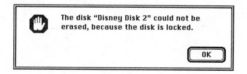

> **Tip**
> It's normal practice for Apple dealers to replace a bad drive. But some repair shops, many of which advertise in the Macintosh magazines, may offer to rebuild the drive and save you money.

> **Fig. 37.14**
> Sometimes the message that the floppy disk is locked just isn't so.

Look at these problems separately. If the disk is inserted correctly in the drive and won't mount an icon on the desktop, follow these steps:

1. Restart, but hold down the mouse button. The disk should eject automatically during the restart process.

2. If the disk is not ejected, straighten the end of a paper clip and push it into the small hold below and to the right of the floppy drive's opening.

3. If the disk cannot be ejected by these techniques, contact your dealer for assistance.

> **Note**
>
> The newest Macintosh models, produced since the summer of 1993 (and all PowerBooks), use a floppy drive that lacks the automatic inject feature, in which the disk is pulled into the drive mechanism after being inserted most of the way. With the newer mechanism, you need to gently but firmly place the disk into the drive.

For the floppy disk that can't be formatted, try following these steps:

1. Eject the disk and examine the write/no-write tab from the rear of the disk (it's at the upper left).

2. Make sure that the little tab is moved all the way down into the write position. Sometimes you have to move the tab up and down a couple of times for it to work.

3. Reinsert the disk.

4. If the floppy still shows up as locked, discard the disk (unless you need the files on it).

> **Note**
>
> Some software is shipped on disks that lack the little write/no-write tabs; they can only be erased if you place tape over the little opening. Because the tape may get caught in the drive mechanism, if you no longer need the disk, you should probably just discard it.

Reverifying a Floppy Disk

Here's the problem: You reformat a floppy disk, and somewhere during the verifying disk stage under System 7, the message changes to reverifying, and the process continues for additional minutes. What's going on here?

System 7 has added a feature to preserve floppy disks with damaged blocks (sections of the disk that cannot be read from or written to reliably). The Finder will mark these bad portions of the disk so that data won't be written to them, very much as a hard disk formatter will lock out bad blocks on a hard drive.

Caution

If you get a reverifying message when you format a floppy, unless you absolutely need the disk, you are better off discarding it. After part of the disk is damaged, the rest of the disk is apt to go bad too.

Floppy Disk Is Unreadable

You put in a floppy disk you know has files on it, and your Mac puts up a message asking if you want to initialize the disk. Here are some of the reasons why this might happen:

- The floppy drive is dirty.

- The floppy disk is damaged.

- You are trying to read a 1.4MB (high-density) disk on an 800K floppy drive.

- You are using a super drive (FDHD drive) to read a high-density disk formatted as an 800K disk.

Following are some things you might try to salvage the disk:

1. Use 3-M floppy drive cleaner to clean your floppy drive.

2. Examine the disk itself for possible signs of damage.

3. Check to make sure the metal shutter at the bottom of the disk slides back and forth smoothly. Sometimes moving it back and forth will free a stuck shutter.

4. If your high-density drive is trying to read a 1.4MB disk formatted on an 800K drive, take a small piece of tape and cover the small hole on the disk at the upper left, when observed from the front of the disk (*not* the one with the write/no-write tab on it).

Note

This little hole opposite the write/no-write tab is used by the high density floppy mechanism to identify the disk as a 1.4MB floppy. Covering the hole will fool the drive into accepting it as an 800K floppy.

> **Note**
>
> Some of the older modular Macintosh models, such as the cx/ci/Quadra 700, are veritable dust magnets. Over time, more and more dust is drawn into the drive by the cooling fan on the power supply, which is located behind the drive. The usual solution is to have a dealer or your friendly Mac guru clean out the interior of the computer with a miniature vacuum cleaner or with a can of compressed air.

Floppy Disk Is Damaged

As explained at the start of this section, floppy disks get no respect from most of us. So when you insert a disk that you know has data on it, and you get a message asking if you want to initialize the disk, it may come as a shock, but it happens more often than it should.

Following are some of the reasons why this might happen:

- The floppy disk media is damaged.

- The floppy drive is dirty or needs repair.

- You are trying to read a high-density (1.4MB) disk on an 800K floppy drive.

- You are trying to read a high-density disk in a Mac's super drive that was formatted on an 800K drive.

Tip
Even if you get the high-density disk formatted in 800K format to work on your Mac's super drive, it's best to copy the data to a correctly formatted floppy disk as soon as possible.

There's little hope to recover your data if the disk is seriously damaged, but following are some things you might want to try:

1. Examine the floppy disk and make sure that the write/no-write tab is firmly at the top or bottom position.

2. Examine the metal shutter at the bottom of the disk and make sure it moves freely and snaps back in position when you let go of it.

3. Use a drive diagnostic/recovery tool like MacTools or Norton Utilities to try to repair the disk or recover your files.

If all or most of the disks you insert in your Mac's floppy drive cannot be read, try this:

1. Clean the drive with 3-M floppy drive cleaner.

2. If you have an older Mac, clean the inside with a portable vacuum cleaner, or a can of compressed air (but be careful not to blow the dirt back into the drive mechanism).

3. If all else fails, contact your dealer to repair or replace the drive.

Printing Problems

The following sections detail common printing-related ailments and describe a few ways to solve the problems should you encounter them.

Most times, selecting Print from the File menu or pressing the ⌘-P keyboard combination and okaying the Print dialog box is enough to get your document printed in a satisfactory manner. But sometimes, no matter how hard you try, you just cannot get your document printed.

◄ See "How the Printing Process Works," p. 203

◄ See "QuickDraw GX," p. 230

Jagged Printing

As you saw in Chapter 8, "All about Fonts," the Mac's font handling can be confusing. You have PostScript fonts, both Type 1 and Type 3, TrueType fonts and bitmap fonts. Both PostScript and TrueType fonts are scalable, meaning they should print in any size you select at the maximum resolution of your printer.

But jagged printing is an all too common problem. Following are a few techniques to help you find a solution:

- If you're using PostScript fonts, make sure that both screen and printer fonts are installed correctly by following these steps:

    1. Under System 7, you should copy the fonts to the closed System Folder icon, and the Finder will figure out where they go; just as shown in figure 37.15.

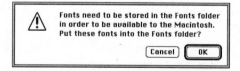

Fig. 37.15
System 7's Finder knows just where your fonts belong.

    2. Under System 6, you need to install screen fonts with Font/DA Mover and copy printer fonts directly to the System Folder.

> **Note**
>
> Font resource managers such as MasterJuggler, from Alsoft, and Suitcase, from Symantec, enable you to install your fonts in locations other than the System Folder and still have them work normally. The manuals that come with these two products provide the information you need on setting up your font library this way. Review Chapter 8 for further tips and tricks on organizing your font library.

> **Caution**
>
> If you are using TrueType fonts, under System 6, you must install the TrueType Init, which rasterizes or processes the fonts for printing. This Init is only supported for System 6.0.7 and 6.0.8, but users of 6.0.5 have also been able to get it to work.

> **Note**
>
> If you are using PostScript fonts with a QuickDraw printer, such as Apple's StyleWriter or Hewlett-Packard's DeskWriter, you need Adobe Type Manager to process the fonts correctly for printing.

PostScript Errors

Here's the problem: You've just tried to print a document, but you are confronted with a screen message that a PostScript error has been generated. You try printing again, and you get the same message. These messages may signify any of the following:

- Your printer doesn't have enough memory to process the document.
- You are using the wrong printing software.
- Your printing software is damaged and needs to be replaced.
- You have an Extension conflict.
- Your System software has been damaged and needs to be replaced.

By far the most common problem is that the document is too big or too complex to be processed. If you're using a PostScript printer, turn it off then turn it back on again. This will flush data from the printer's memory bank, and sometimes allow it to process a document more effectively.

If that doesn't work, try to find out the specific printer error by following these steps:

1. If you're using background printing and Apple's PrintMonitor program, pull down System 7's application menu (at the upper right of the menu bar) after printing begins and select PrintMonitor.

2. Keep PrintMonitor on your screen and watch the status messages describing the printing process. (If there is an error, the cause of the error will flash on the screen briefly.)

3. If the error uses the words VMerror, it means the printer doesn't have enough memory to process the document.

4. Try opening the Chooser from the Apple menu and turning off background printing.

5. If the VMerror message persists, try simplifying the document by using fewer fonts.

6. If your document still won't print, select Unlimited Downloadable Fonts in the Options section of your Page Setup box.

> **Caution**
>
> Using the Unlimited Downloadable Fonts option slows down printing because fonts are first downloaded and then flushed from RAM to make way for additional fonts. If you select this option, be sure that the Wider Print Area option is not selected.

7. Consider getting a memory upgrade for your printer—if one is available.

> **Note**
>
> Some laser printers cannot handle the full width of a legal-sized page without a memory upgrade. Check your printer's manual for details.

If the error contains the word limitcheck, it means the document contains graphic images that contain too many paths to process. In this case, follow these steps:

1. Go to the drawing program in which the document was produced and look for a feature called *split paths* or *split complex paths*.

Tip
Some programs,
such as Adobe
Illustrator, will
make a permanent
change to your
document if you
choose split paths
as an option. Make
this setting only
on a copy of your
illustration.

2. Remove objects or elements from your illustration file that are not being reproduced in your final document.

If you still cannot print your document:

1. Try running with Extensions off (Shift key held down at startup under System 7).

2. If your document prints okay with Extensions off, check the section on "Diagnosing Extension Conflicts" later in this chapter.

3. If disabling Extensions fails to resolve your problem, reinstall first your printing software, then your System software. See the section, "Why a Clean System Installation?" later in this chapter.

PrintMonitor Quits or Crashes

Apple's print spooling application has but one advantage over every other software solution on the market—it's free. But it has its share of problems. Sometimes, for no apparent reason, the PrintMonitor application will quit while printing is in progress. Following are some of the reasons why it happens:

■ You are the victim of a bug in System 7.0 and System 7.0.1.

■ PrintMonitor doesn't have enough memory to process your documents.

■ You have an Extension conflict.

■ Your printing software is corrupted and needs to be reinstalled.

■ Your System software is corrupted and needs to be reinstalled.

Let's describe that first problem, involving System 7.0 and 7.0.1. It involves a bug that will cause PrintMonitor to fail if you quit the application from which you're printing while the printing process is still underway.

Here are the usual solutions to your problem:

1. Leave the application open until printing is complete.

2. Get a copy of the System 7 Tune-Up from your Apple dealer, Apple Customer Assistance, or one of the online services. It fixes the PrintMonitor bug. (This problem does not exist in System 7.1 or later.)

3. Reinstall your printing software.

If the previous solutions fail to resolve your problem try the following:

1. Restart with Extensions off (Shift key held down at startup) and try to print your document again.

2. If printing proceeds normally with Extensions off, read the section, "Diagnosing Extension Conflicts" later in this chapter.

3. If printing problems persist, reinstall your printing software and then, if necessary, your System software. See "Why a Clean System Installation?" later in this chapter.

Not Enough Memory to Print

Actually, two problems are involved here. The first occurs when you truly do not have enough memory to print your document, and you get a message asking whether you want to turn off background printing, or that printing will resume when sufficient memory is available (see fig. 37.16).

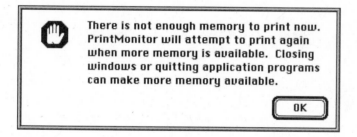

There is not enough memory to print now. PrintMonitor will attempt to print again when more memory is available. Closing windows or quitting application programs can make more memory available.

OK

Fig. 37.16
When there's not enough memory to print your document, PrintMonitor will remain idle until more memory is available.

The second problem happens when you see a window asking you to bring PrintMonitor to the front. You see a dialog box with two buttons, one of which allows you to adjust PrintMonitor memory size. Some programs generate print files that require more memory to print than others. This is true of QuarkXPress, for example.

If you get this type of message, follow these steps:

1. Press OK.

2. If the message repeats itself, okay the memory adjustment again.

3. If the memory adjustment request won't go away, cancel printing and locate your PrintMonitor application. It's in the Extensions folder under System 7 (loose in the System Folder under System 6).

4. Highlight the PrintMonitor icon and select Get Info from the Finder's File menu.

5. Increase the RAM allocation for PrintMonitor by approximately 100K (see fig. 37.17).

Fig. 37.17
Increasing PrintMonitor's RAM allocation will often fix annoying printing problems.

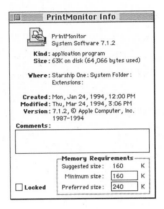

Diagnosing Extension Conflicts

The most frequent cause of a system crash, an application quitting, or the failure of your Mac to boot properly is a conflicting System Extension (or an Init for System 6 users). It can happen to most anyone, especially if you've added a number of startup programs to your Mac's System Folder.

You can simply remove Extensions from the System Folder on a trial-and-error basis until things begin to work correctly again, but an Init manager program can simplify the process. There is even an Init manager that will help to automate the conflict solving process.

How Does an Init Manager Work?

▶ See "Hard Disk Repair and Optimization," p. 1117

An Extension Manager is an Extension that controls which programs load when you boot your computer and which do not. Some of these utilities will also flag an Extension that crashes your Mac upon startup and offer to disable the offending program before continuing with the startup process.

These programs allow you to systematically disable your startup programs and change Init loading order. Some will even enable you to create startup sets so that you can run two Extensions that may normally conflict with each other in separate sessions, especially if both are needed to perform a needed function—such as an Extension that controls your scanner, or mounts a removable disk.

The No-Frills Method of Checking Init Conflicts

Whether or not you have an Init manager, and I recommend that you get one, such as the freeware Extensions Manager from Apple (shown in fig. 37.18), the following is a way to determine whether an Init conflict is causing crashes and startup problems:

Fig. 37.18
Apple's free Extensions Manager program allows you to turn Extensions on and off simply by clicking on their name in the list window.

1. If your Mac produces a bomb message or crashes before or after a certain Init loads (you can determine this by which icon has appeared on your screen when the crash happens), remove or disable that Init.

2. Restart your Mac.

3. If the problem goes away, try running it in a different loading order. This can be done by changing the startup order in your Init manager program, or just by renaming the Init.

4. If you add a hard word space to the Init's name (Option-Space), it'll load toward the beginning of the lineup.

5. If you add the letter z or a tilde (~) to the name of the Init, it'll load towards the end. See figure 37.19 for an example.

> **Note**
>
> Under System 7, you can place a Control Panel program in the Extensions folder to move it ahead of the pack. To make an Extension load later, put it in the Control Panels folder, or leave it loose in the System Folder. Any startup program (other than files like System Enablers, which load when your Mac boots) placed loose in the System Folder gets last priority in loading.

Fig. 37.19
Renaming an Extension is as simple as selecting the icon, and adding a character such as a tilde to the name.

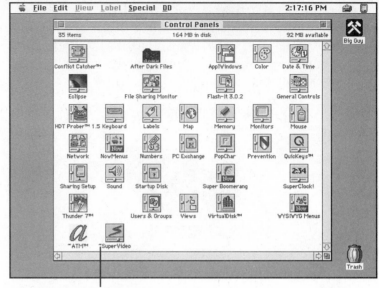

Tilde added to the beginning of the file name

Tip
To quickly diagnose an Init conflict, disable all your Inits, or, under System 7, restart with Extensions off, by holding down the Shift key.

6. If you can't isolate the offending Init this way, disable everything, or restart with Extensions off and remove all Inits from the System Folder.

7. Add three or four Extensions to your System Folder at a time, restarting each time. Try to duplicate the steps necessary to trigger the crash if a simple restart won't do it.

Following these steps, you should be able to isolate the source of your conflict quickly. After you've decided that a specific Extension is causing a crash, contact the software publisher or author (if it's shareware or freeware) and see whether they are aware of your problem. Tell them the steps you took to duplicate the crash or odd system performance. Quite often an update is already available that will address the problem.

Reinstalling System Software

Your Mac's system software is the single most used and abused software you use. Every minute your computer is running, resources from your System Folder are in use by the various programs you run. And don't forget that the Finder itself is an application.

All it takes is a single crash to corrupt a system resource, and this can come back to haunt you later on when your Mac hangs at the Welcome to Macintosh startup screen, or crashes for unexplained reasons, even if all of your Inits are disabled.

Even if your Mac behaves in a flaky manner occasionally, it is a good idea to reinstall system software on occasion, as a precaution against troubles showing up later.

Why a Clean System Installation?

The most effective way to reinstall system software is a clean installation. The standard system installation will replace your system support files, such as the Finder, Extensions, and Control Panels, but the system file itself is merely updated. In most cases, it may not make much of a difference, but if the system gets really corrupted due to a crash or software conflict, the net result is that the problems you might be having will just continue without letup.

But the simple technique outlined here builds a brand new System Folder for you. You won't lose any of your treasured startup programs, or even any of the special settings you've made, but you will be taking an important step toward removing the source of many of the problems you might be having with your Mac.

Preparing for a System Installation

Your System 7 kit or any Macintosh manufactured since the middle of 1991 includes a disk labeled Disk Tools (or "Utilities" on Performa models), described previously in this chapter. This disk contains a basic startup System Folder plus two useful tools. One of these tools is Disk First Aid the other is Apple's HD SC Setup, a no-frills hard disk formatting program. If you are still using System 6, you'll probably find these two programs on one of your Utilities disks.

Follow these steps:

1. Start or restart your Macintosh and immediately insert the Disk Tools disk into the floppy drive.

2. After the startup process is complete, the icon for the Disk Tools floppy drive should appear at the upper right corner of your screen. The icons for your installed hard drives should appear below it.

3. If your computer ejects the Disk Tools disk—and you have a newer Macintosh—make sure the disk comes direct from your computer's installation kit.

Caution

The latest Macs use a System Enabler, an Extension that allows the system software to recognize the new hardware. These models will absolutely not boot unless the correct System Enabler is installed.

---

4. If the startup process is successful, look for the Disk First Aid icon, and double-click the program (see fig. 37.20).

Fig. 37.20
Disk First Aid can seek out and repair minor disk directory problems.

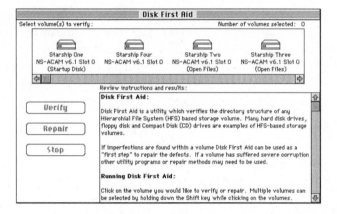

Note

A system software installation involves moving a number of files, rewriting boot blocks to your startup disk, and installing new files. If there is even slight directory damage, the installation process may be unsuccessful. Disk First Aid will take a few minutes to analyze your hard drive and make minor repairs.

---

5. If Disk First Aid reports that the drive has damage that cannot be repaired, you have two choices. The first is to backup your data and reformat the drive. The second choice is to run one of the commercial hard drive utilities, such as MacTools or Norton Utilities, and see if they fare better in fixing the hard drive.

Caution

Do not install system software before checking your hard drive for possible directory damage. If the hard drive repair utilities cannot fix the problem, back up your data and reformat. Even if your drive works okay now, a system software installation may not be successful, or your drive may crash at some time in the future, resulting in the loss of your valuable data.

---

6. If you have an Apple hard drive, you should update the SCSI driver using HD SC Setup, shown in figure 37.21. Updating simply replaces the SCSI driver, it doesn't involve initializing or reformatting the drive, and it should not affect your data in any way.

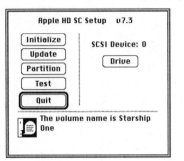

Fig. 37.21
HD SC Setup can be used to update, initialize, or verify your Apple hard drive.

7. To update the drive, simply click in the Update button. The process takes just a few seconds to complete.

8. If HD SC Setup cannot locate a drive to update, it means the hard drives you're using are not Apple's. You will want to update the drive using the formatting program supplied with the drive instead.

9. After the preliminaries are out of the way, go to the System Folder on your startup disk, open the folder, and locate the Finder icon.

10. Create a new folder labeled Old Finder, and place the Finder icon in that new folder (see fig. 37.22).

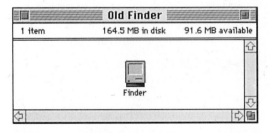

Fig. 37.22
Burying your Finder in a new folder keeps the system installer from recognizing your old System Folder.

11. Rename your System Folder. You can call it anything you want, but for the sake of this discussion, I'll call it Storage.

Installing Your New System Software

With the preliminaries out of the way, it's time to get to the main course. You now want to check your hard drive for the presence of a second System Folder.

1. Restart your Macintosh. Within a few seconds, the Disk Tools disk should be ejected from the floppy drive.

   > **Note**
   >
   > You will see a picture of a disk with a flashing question mark on-screen—don't be alarmed.

2. If your Macintosh starts up normally from your hard drive, it means there is indeed a second System Folder there, and that could truly be the source of your troubles.

3. If there is a second System Folder, follow the steps described previously to disable it—removing the Finder and renaming the folder. Or trash it entirely (after making sure that you don't want to keep anything inside it).

   > **Caution**
   >
   > Having more than one System Folder on a single drive is an invitation to weird startup problems, crashes, and other unexplained behavior.

4. Select your first installation disk. On the newest Macintosh and Power Macintosh models, it is labeled InstallMeFirst. On older Macs, it is called Install, Install 1, System Tools, or System Startup.

   > **Note**
   >
   > New Macintosh and Power Macintosh computers with internal CD-ROMs usually are supplied with all system software on a CD. Before removing your old Finder, be sure your Mac will successfully boot with the CD-ROM. After starting your Mac with the CD, you will see an icon labeled Install System Software (see fig. 37.23). Double-click that icon to begin the installation process.

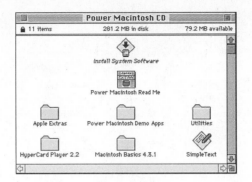

Fig. 37.23
System software
and other
programs on a
CD-ROM.

5. Restart and place the first system installation disk in the floppy drive.

6. The Welcome to Macintosh message should appear on-screen in a few seconds.

7. If you are installing System 7, the Installer application is opened automatically. If you are installing System 6, you must select the Installer icon from the floppy disk directory and double-click it. You will see a window much like the one shown in figure 37.24.

Fig. 37.24
Apple's system
installer program,
ready to do its
stuff.

8. For most purposes, choosing the Easy Install option will allow the installer to build a System Folder with the resources necessary to run your Macintosh.

> ### Note
>
> A list of what will be installed will appear in the installer program's main window. The Customize option will allow you to select special features, such as networking software, QuickTime, CD-ROM Setup or other special features that may be needed by your Mac (see fig. 37.25). If in doubt, check your computer's manual, or go for the Easy Install. You can always install additional features, by themselves, later on without having to replace the system again.

Fig. 37.25
You can use the Easy Install or opt to Customize your system installation, as you prefer.

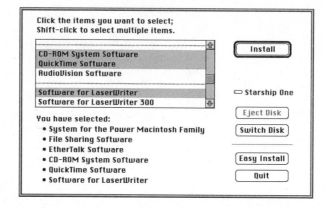

> ### System 7.5 Note
>
> Apple's new system software version will provide many new ways to customize your system installation. You'll even be able to choose which utilities are placed in the Apple Menu Items, Extensions and Control Panels folder (see fig. 37.26).

Fig. 37.26
Apple's System 7.5 installer brings new features to a custom system installation.

9. If you're doing a floppy system installation, assemble the disks you need. The Installer will ask for them as necessary.

10. When the installation is complete, quit the Installer application.

> **Note**
>
> On a System 7 floppy disk installation, you will see a darkened screen, and a small window in its center giving you the option to Restart or Shut Down.

11. Choose the Restart option. Your Mac will restart, and the disk inside the floppy drive will be ejected.

What Do I Do Next?

If the system installation is successful, your Mac will start normally, and you'll be at the Finder desktop in just a short time. Before restoring anything from the Storage folder, your original System Folder, take some time to work with your Mac to make sure everything is running correctly.

> **Note**
>
> If you receive a message that your system installation has been interrupted for any reason, you may have a bad set of system disks or a SCSI-related conflict. To be sure, power down your Mac and its accessories, remove the SCSI cable from the rear of your Mac (if one is plugged in there), and then power up your Mac and attempt the system installation again.

> **Note**
>
> If you have just upgraded from System 6 to System 7, the desktop files of all of your mounted hard drives will be rebuilt automatically. This is a normal process. The files used to manage the desktop under System 7 are different from earlier system versions.

If your Mac now runs normally, follow these steps:

1. Return to your Storage folder, and drag special application folder icons, such as the Aldus or Claris folders, to the new System Folder (see fig. 37.27).

Fig. 37.27
Application-
related files in
your Storage
folder should be
moved to your
new System
Folder.

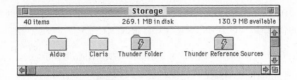

> **Note**
>
> You may also find a plethora of loose files in the System Folder that are labeled data, preferences, or settings. These are likely application configuration files that you will need to retain special settings in certain programs.

2. If you are using System 7—any version—most of your non-Apple startup programs will be in the Extensions and Control Panels folder. Don't restore files that are already duplicated in your new System Folder.

3. Select just a few of your original Extensions and drag the files to your new System Folder icon, as shown in figure 37.28.

Fig. 37.28
Select just a few
Extensions at a
time to move to
your new System
Folder.

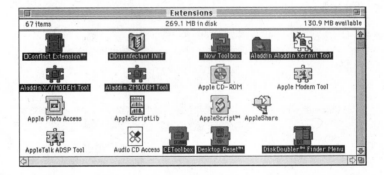

4. Restart your computer and run a few programs, copy some files to and from a floppy disk or another hard drive, and make sure that everything is working okay.

5. If your Mac performs in a satisfactory manner, continue to add your Extensions to your new System Folder, a few at a time, followed by a restart.

6. If a problem returns, you may have isolated a potential software conflict.

7. If your Mac runs normally, continue the install/restart process until all Extensions and Control Panels are restored.

8. Go to the Preferences folder inside your Storage folder, and move all preference files and application-specific folders, except those that are duplicated, to your new System Folder. That will restore all application and Extension settings.

9. If the problems return after reinstalling all of your old files to the new System Folder, reread the preceding section on locating Init conflicts.

SCSI Voodoo

Even though each manufacturer of a SCSI product may be following Apple's specifications, the combination of a number of devices from different manufacturers may produce unexpected results. The newest Macintosh models, especially the Quadras and Power Macintosh lines, have very fast SCSI controllers and can transfer data at extremely rapid rates. These models are also sensitive to the presence of poor cables and termination. It is worth spending extra money to buy the highest quality cables; don't buy thin, bargain-basement products, because you will only pay for it later in additional aggravation in getting your Mac to work correctly.

It is also a good idea to buy all of your cables from one manufacturer, to ensure they are all of uniform quality and meet the same specifications. A slight mismatch in electrical specifications among cables can be responsible for SCSI chain disorders. If you have a long SCSI chain with several devices, you might want to consider buying a digital active terminator, such as the APS SCSI Sentry, from APS Technologies. This device monitors the condition of the SCSI chain and helps maintain correct termination voltage.

Caution

The maximum allowable length of a SCSI chain is a little over 19 feet. When you figure the total length of all your SCSI cables, you should add several feet to cover the internal SCSI cables in the Mac, plus the internal cables inside each of your SCSI peripherals. Use the shortest cables you can buy. If cable length exceeds the maximum, some devices may not mount, you may experience erratic performance or unexplained system crashes. If you need to install additional SCSI devices, you might consider a SCSI accelerator, which supports many Macintosh models that have NuBus expansion slots. These accelerators will provide a second SCSI bus to your Mac, allowing you to hook up additional drives and other peripherals.

Never turn your Mac on or off with a loose SCSI cable. Do not remove or attach SCSI cables while your Mac or peripheral devices are powered on. At the very least, you run the risk of crashing a hard drive. At worst, you may also damage your Mac's SCSI controller chip, which will require logic board replacement or repair.

Hardware Problems

There are truly times when all the software conflict testing won't help, because the problem lies with your Mac hardware. Most often a hardware problem is clear. You try to boot your Mac, and it won't produce a startup sound. Or your start your Mac and you hear a procession of chimes—the *chimes of doom*. Testing for hardware troubles may require a dealer's service technician, but following are a few tips as to what you can do yourself before you bring your computer or its accessories in for repair:

1. If you've just installed a new hardware product inside your computer, such as a NuBus or PDS expansion card, remove it and then carefully reseat the card in the expansion slot.

   Before you roam around the inside of your Mac, make sure that you've followed the manufacturer's instructions about grounding yourself to the Mac's chassis while it's plugged in or using the static wrist pad that is sometimes included.

2. Start your Mac.

3. If you've installed a memory upgrade, either DRAM or VRAM, remove and reseat the memory module.

   > **Caution**
   >
   > Make sure that the memory module is seated firmly at both ends, but do not force it. There is the risk that you will break the module or the Mac's RAM bank.

4. Restart your Mac.

   If the added hardware is correctly installed and your Mac still won't boot without warning chimes, or with no startup sound at all, remove the hardware and try again.

5. If your Mac now works correctly, contact the dealer or the manufacturer's support people about your problem.

6. If you haven't installed any new hardware, and your Mac or accessories are under warranty, contact the dealer or the manufacturer for service.

> **Caution**
>
> Even if you are experienced at handling the inside of your computer, an attempt to repair the problem yourself may void the warranty.
>
> Never open your Mac's case or remove or reconnect SCSI cables while your Mac and SCSI peripherals are turned on. Either step can risk serious damage (or an electrical shock if you touch the wrong part inside your computer).

7. If the problems you experience are intermittent, it is still a good idea to have a service technician examine your computer equipment. An infrequent problem is apt to become more frequent over time, and a minor problem left untouched could blossom into a major and expensive affair later on.

In Chapter 38, "Preventive Maintenance," we describe software that is designed to diagnose potential software and hardware troubles. While such software products will sometimes only give you a series of benchmark tests, those test results may alert you to potential troubles.

From Here...

Now that you've learned a few tricks to get you out of trouble should problems arise, it's time to do some preventive maintenance.

- Chapter 38, "Preventive Maintenance," provides some helpful hints to help you reduce the likelihood of having problems with your Mac.

- You'll also want to read Part II, "System 7 Essentials," Chapters 4 through 10, for more valuable information on setting up and using your Macintosh.

Chapter 38

Preventive Maintenance

by Colin Bay

As you read in this chapter and the preceding chapter about all the things that could go wrong with your Macintosh, you may start to feel paranoid or lose confidence that the computer is going to keep working. It's important to keep these things in perspective. Possibly, you could skip this entire chapter, never do any preventive maintenance to your Macintosh, and have years of use with no problems, no broken components, no lost files, and no electrical failures.

But things do go wrong sometimes, even with a well-made computer. The main point is that by building a few good habits and being aware of potential problems, you can increase your chances of long, trouble-free use of your Macintosh. You don't have to spend all day on prevention to protect yourself from the most common hazards.

If you don't read any further, remember these two things—save often as you work and back up your data regularly. These are the two most important preventive measures you can take.

In this chapter, you learn the following:

- How to reduce workplace hazards

- How to develop good working habits for prevention

- How to keep the various components of the Macintosh system clean

- Become familiar with utility maintenance software

- How to set up a schedule of periodic maintenance tasks

Your Macintosh's Environment

Just as you need protection from the elements, your Macintosh needs to be protected from the environmental hazards around it. Liquids, temperature extremes, and irregularities in electrical power can all take their toll. But they're all preventable if you follow some basic guidelines.

Liquids

A little thirst can be a dangerous thing: keyboards don't often fail, but when they do, spilled liquid is the most common cause. To fill your floppy drive with water or to get coffee inside your monitor, you would have to do something unusual. But because the keyboard lies flat and is the part of the computer that's closest to you, it's vulnerable as you sit in your chair sipping a drink.

If you ever use your Macintosh outside—not an unusual occurrence, if you own a PowerBook—make sure that you keep it protected from rain, water fights, and lawn sprinklers. Liquid from any source can short-circuit your keyboard or other parts of you Macintosh. Sometimes drying out is all a keyboard needs to function again, but the damage can be worse.

Power Problems

Like a stereo, a Macintosh is a sensitive piece of electronic equipment, full of chips, transistors, resistors, and capacitors—all of which expect a normal range of electrical power. If they don't get the power, they can fail temporarily, or in severe cases, a component can burn out and need to be replaced.

Though people speak of "power surges" collectively as the main electrical danger to a computer, there are actually several kinds of electrical irregularities that, if not countered with basic preventive measures, can damage your Macintosh.

Spikes and Surges

A *spike* is a sudden, extreme rise in the intensity of your incoming power line, so fast that it is usually measured in nanoseconds. A *surge* is not as fast or extreme, more like a gradual wave of increased power, but can also cause damage. Because the electronic components of the Macintosh are guaranteed to work only within certain levels of power, a spike or surge can overheat a component such as a chip or "jump" between electrical channels in the same way the electricity in a spark plug jumps the gap. A lightning strike is an extreme example of a spike.

Your best protection against spikes and surges is a good surge protector. Some models are a single added connector between your power plug and the wall outlet; most, however, include a power strip with 46 added outlets, convenient for plugging in a monitor or external drive in addition to the Macintosh. Remember, however, that overloading the circuit by plugging in to many things at once defeats the purpose of the surge protector—keeping your Macintosh running.

Lightning

If lighting hits your house or a nearby power line, you'll wish you had a good surge protector. However, even then the power can be so strong that it can jump between electrically isolated components of the surge protector. If you want to truly protect your Macintosh during a lightning storm, the surest method is this: unplug it from the wall completely. That way, there's no conducting path from your house's electrical system to the Macintosh.

Power Failure

Even the best of public utilities sometimes has power outages, whether from lightning strikes, snowstorms, or collisions with utility poles. Very brief losses of power may not affect your Macintosh at all because it contains a residual amount of power for a fraction of a second. However, if the power goes off and stays off, you're out of luck if you haven't saved lately. Saving your work regularly is the best defense against power failures and many other problems.

If your business depends on your Macintosh never going down unexpectedly, it's worth investing several hundred dollars in a UPS (uninterruptible power supply). A UPS contains constantly charged batteries that can keep your Macintosh running for some length of time (often 30 minutes or more) in the event of a power failure. This can give you enough time to save data, quit applications, and shut down your Macintosh safely. UPS units generally also give power all the time, filtering out spikes, surges, and voltage drops.

Static Electricity

No matter how clean the power source that goes into the back of your Macintosh, you can always add to it with static. If you find yourself making sparks when you touch the doorknob, or shake hands, you may have a static prone combination of carpet and shoes. You can buy an anti-static pad to absorb the extra charge.

Static really comes into play when you open up your Macintosh to add memory, insert or remove a card, or just look around. The simplest way to discharge the static is to touch the metal shielded box containing the power supply before you touch anything else. You can easily tell where the power supply is because the power cord at the back of the Macintosh goes into the power supply.

Magnetic Fields

Hard disks are usually pretty well shielded from stray magnetism, but floppy disks are not. Because the surface of floppy disks (inside the hard plastic case) is a form of magnetic media, it can be erased or damaged by being too close to a magnetic field. Common sources of magnetic fields are electric motors and strong power supplies.

In fact, your Macintosh contains such a power supply, so it's best not to leave floppy disks laying against the back part of the computer. Wherever the power cord goes into the back of the Macintosh is where the power supply sits.

Holding a floppy disk to a refrigerator with a magnet is an obvious invitation to data loss, but other magnetic sources are less obvious. Some travelers have reported floppy disk problems from passing through airport X-ray machines. This is most likely caused by the electric motor moving the conveyer belt rather than by the X-rays. If you have valuable data on floppy disks, and the disks go through airport security more than a couple of times, it's worth passing them through by hand.

Dust and Smoke

Some parts of your Macintosh can deal with dust and smoke much better then others. None of them are in much danger of dust unless it's extreme. Smoke will deposit a film on your monitor and can have a cumulative effect on the read and write heads (analogous to the heads on a VCR or cassette player) of floppy and hard disk drives, so it's best not to use the Macintosh in a consistently smoky area over the long term.

Dust can cause two kinds of problems: mechanical and thermal. The mechanical problem is dust collecting on drive heads, decreasing their sensitivity and accuracy. The thermal problem can happen inside the CPU. If excessive amounts of dust collect on the chips and other parts inside the case, it can have an insulating effect and cause some components to heat up more than they should.

Once again, however, you don't need to be a fanatical duster or buy an expensive air filtration system for your office or den. Just keep the room relatively clean and check inside your Macintosh once or twice a year to see if dust has built up.

Temperature

Your Macintosh is comfortable in a wider temperature range than you are, but you should avoid extremes on the hot side. Acceptable temperature ranges, which are similar for most Macintoshes, are listed in the technical specifications in your Macintosh documentation.

For example, the Power Macintosh 6100 can be used at temperatures from 50° F to 104° F. Because storage is less demanding than use, this Macintosh can be safely stored at an even wider range of temperatures, from -40° to 116.6° F. Notice that you're more likely to reach the upper extreme than the lower one. Although you're unlikely to leave the computer outside in a blizzard, it could reach very high temperatures if you leave it in your car in direct sunlight on a hot day. To be on the safe side, don't leave your Macintosh in a place that would make you uncomfortably hot.

Regardless of the temperature in the room where you work, don't block the ventilation openings on the Macintosh. The circuitry and machinery, because so much power is running through it, can create a significant amount of heat, which needs to dissipate. If you block the vents, heat may build up more than it should and damage electrical components or gradually shorten the useful life of your Macintosh.

Good Work Habits

If people saved their work and backed up their disks religiously, most of the data loss in the personal computer world would be taken care of. If you only skim this chapter, remember these two things: *Save often! Back up regularly!* The other tips are helpful, too, but these first two are paramount.

Save Early and Often

Almost every long-term computer user, Macintosh or otherwise, has a story about working on an important project for three hours without saving, then losing it all in an accident: you nudge the power cord, the program crashes, the electricity fails, your son steps on the power strip and turns it off. If you save your work every five or 10 minutes, then that's the most work you're likely to lose if one of these mishaps happens to you.

The exception is when you've made a major change (say, deleting 80 rows of a spreadsheet), and you aren't sure you want the change to be final. In that case, you can save the changed work under a new name, letting you change your mind later without losing any data.

Back Up Your Files

Worse things than a power failure can happen: a destructive virus, accidental deletion of a file, a hard disk failure. The first question you'll get from technical support or your network administrator is, "Do you have a recent backup?" All computers and hard disks will fail eventually, if you use them long enough—years and years, in some cases. But when something does fail, you should have important data backed up. A common scheme, explained on most backup software documentation, is to back up all of your data once a week and then make daily backups of the files that changed that day.

If you don't have a tape drive (in the case of office network) or a shared file server, you can back up to floppy disks. Most backup software can compress data so that it doesn't need as many disks, but even so, you could end up with a lot of floppy disks.

If you have too much data for floppy disks, you can back up just your documents, which decreases the size of the backup. This requires, however, that you keep the original installation disks for your system software and application programs—but you should be doing that anyway. Because the installation disks can also fail, get in the habit of making a floppy backup set of the installation disks before you install a new software package. A one-time backup is enough for applications because those files rarely change.

Delete Unused Applications and Documents

Unused files can clutter up your hard disk unnecessarily. Copy old documents to floppy disks in case you need them later. In the case of application files, make sure that you have them on the original disks.

Especially good candidates for deletion are outdated application versions. For some applications, you may want to keep the old version around for a little while for compatibility, but this usually isn't necessary. For example, a new version of a word processor will usually save a file in the old format as well as let you open files created by the old version. If you leave old versions of applications on your hard disk after installing the new one, you could double-click a document and open the wrong version of the software.

Keep the System Folder Lean

There are hundreds of programs you can buy that modify the system to do neat things, but try to avoid the temptation of overdoing it. These system extensions and control panels, in excess, use up extra memory and increase the chances of a conflict with each other.

The same thing goes for fonts: each font you have installed in your system uses up a little memory. You can keep rarely-used fonts in another folder and install them only when you're actually going to use them.

Use the Shut Down Command

You can save yourself potential trouble and keep your Macintosh hard disk healthy by always choosing the Shut Down command from the Special menu when you're ready to power down. Why not just turn off the power? When you choose Shut Down, the system cleans itself up in preparation for turning off, gives you a chance to save any documents you forgot to save, quits any open applications, and saves any adjustments you may have made to the Finder desktop (moving a folder, for example). If you turn off your Macintosh in the middle of things, you lose all these safeguards.

Keep Only One System Folder

If you copy a large group of files from another disk, perhaps a network instal-lation folder or Apple system disks, you could end up with multiple copies of the system folder on your own hard disk. Look through your folders some-time to make certain there isn't an extra system folder buried somewhere on the disk. A system folder—even if it has a different name—contains at least the System and Finder files.

If you have more than one system folder on your disk, when the Macintosh starts up or applications try to access system files, there could be some confu-sion about which system folder is supposed to be the active one.

Don't Move Devices with the Power On

Once again, you might do this all the time with no problems, but you would be pushing your luck. If you move parts of your computer system with the power on, you risk pulling out a power cord, jarring a hard drive by dropping it, or damaging sensitive components of a printer. You should also avoid plugging or unplugging things such as the keyboard, monitor, mouse, or external drive while the Macintosh's power is turned on.

If you have a printer, external drive, monitor, keyboard, mouse, and perhaps another device attached to your Macintosh, you can get quite a collection of cables. Arrange them so that they're out of the way as much as possible. If a power cable is hanging by the side of your desk where someone might bump it and pull it out, you're tempting fate.

Turn SCSI Devices On and Off in Order

SCSI devices include external hard drives, CD-ROM drives, scanners, tape drives, and anything else that is connected to one of these devices. If the Macintosh is turned on before these devices, it may not recognize them when the system starts up.

The order is reversed when you shut down: choose the Shut Down command and turn off the Macintosh; then turn off the other SCSI devices. If the Macintosh is still on and you turn off a device such as an external hard drive containing your system software, it's the same as cutting the power before choosing the Shut Down command. Because the Macintosh itself is a SCSI device, and the most important one, it's best not to disrupt the SCSI chain while the Macintosh is on.

Give Your Monitor a Rest

Have you ever noticed how automated teller machines at banks often have the words burned into the screen from sitting there for so long? The same thing can happen to your Macintosh monitor if you leave it on for many hours with no change in the picture. If you leave your Macintosh on for weeks at a time without using it, a shadow of the image on the screen will gradually begin to become a permanent mark. That's why screen saver programs were developed.

The truth is, black-and-white monitors are more likely than color monitors to have burned-in images, but most screen savers are used on color Macintoshes. A cheaper method is to simply turn down the brightness dial on your monitor when it's going to be left on unused for a long time, but this method isn't nearly as entertaining as a screen saver. Besides, some screen savers offer extra features such as password protection. This gives you a convenient method of keeping unauthorized people from walking by your office and using your Macintosh or seeing your confidential files.

Keep Your Software Current

Keeping up with the latest versions of software can actually be a form of preventive maintenance. Due to the complexity of software and the variety of configurations it must run on, it's virtually impossible to write a program that does everything you want it to, in the right way, in every situation. Although the most severe bugs are found and taken care of before the software is commercially distributed, little glitches may remain. That's why updates can be helpful. If you have anti-virus software, as you should, it becomes particularly important to find out if new Macintosh viruses have been discovered.

Software companies periodically release updates to system software and applications. Usually, they add new features and capabilities, but sometimes they'll release a new version with only minor changes that improve compatibility with a certain Macintosh model, other software, or new devices such as CD-ROM drives. If you fall into the category of people who could be helped, it's good to know about software updates.

When to Buy Updates

This is not to say that you need to buy every new version that comes out for every software package you own. If the current version of an application fulfills all of your needs, there's no need to buy the new one. However, if the new version offers features that would make your life easier and allow you to produce better work, the update is probably worth the cost.

Where to Learn About Updates

How do you find out about updates? A first step is to mail in the registration card that comes with every Macintosh computer or application program. Most developers will send you information about upcoming changes so you'll know when a new version is available. Occasionally, they'll send a free update.

If you use your Macintosh a lot, it's also a good idea to subscribe to a monthly Macintosh magazine such as *MacUser* or *Macworld*. They will generally have news of the latest versions of software, potential problems, and reviews of new software. If subscribing seems like overkill, you can still pick up some useful information by buying one or two issues a year and seeing what's new.

Many manufacturers of anti-virus software maintain a bulletin board or a hotline number you can call to find out if there are new viruses. When a new virus is found, they generally issue an update or a small piece of extra code that allows your software to identify the new virus.

Keep Things Clean

You don't need to be a compulsive cleaner. Your computing will be more comfortable and reliable, though, if you give a few items a quick once-over from time to time.

Keyboard

Other than liquids, which you should keep away from the keyboard, the keyboard can collect lint, dust, and crumbs between the keys, as well as grime and other deposits on the surface of the keys. For example, if you've ever peeled an orange at your desk, you probably sprayed some juice or rind particles on your keyboard.

To clean the keyboard, follow these steps:

1. Shut down your Macintosh and turn the power off.

2. Use a barely damp cloth to clean the surface of the keys, avoiding strong or sideways pressure, which could pop off one of the key caps.

3. Gently turn the keyboard upside down to free crumbs or dust that has fallen between the keys.

Mouse

The mouse contains a roller ball that spends all day going back and forth along your desk or mouse pad. You might be surprised at how much dust, lint, and dirt it can pick up after a year or two of use in a dirty room. If you notice the mouse pointer jumping when you move it or failing to roll smoothly, it's probably because of dirt inside. Fortunately, it's easy to clean.

Follow these steps to clean your mouse:

1. Shut down your Macintosh and turn the power off.

2. Turn the mouse upside-down to expose the roller ball, and release the round, plastic piece surrounding the ball.

   For a new mouse, turn the ring counterclockwise to release the ball. For an older mouse, locate the grooved edges of the ring. Press down and toward the top of the ball to release it.

3. Roll the ball into one hand to prevent it from falling and getting dirtier.

4. Wipe the ball clean with a soft, dry cloth that doesn't shed lint.

5. Blow to remove dust or lint inside the mouse.

6. Moisten a cotton swab with some isopropyl or rubbing alcohol (not so much that it drips) and clean the rollers inside the mouse.

7. Replace the ball and reattach the back mouse cover.

If you own a trackball or another pointing device, it could probably use cleaning as well. Consult your documentation for details on cleaning these devices.

Monitor

Because you may be spending hours a day staring at your monitor, it's worth keeping it clean. Dust accumulates quickly because of the static of the monitor screen, and it's hard to keep from touching the screen sometimes when you point at it.

You can use a lint-free cloth and some standard window cleaner to wipe the screen clear. Be sure to use only a small amount of cleaner, so the excess liquid doesn't drip down inside the monitor case or into the Macintosh. Better yet, spray the cleaner on your cloth rather than directly on the screen. If you want to spend more money for the convenience, you can buy individually packaged lens-cleaning or monitor-cleaning cloths.

Floppy Disk Drives

In the early days of the Macintosh, everything ran from floppy disks and hard disks were seen as an expensive luxury. Now virtually every Macintosh has a hard disk, but you still need to keep your floppy disk drive in good working shape. Don't look down on it—you still need it for installing software, transferring information to other computers, and perhaps backing up your data.

Covering the Floppy Opening

Some of the newer Macintosh models have a built-in hinged cover that protects the floppy drive opening from dust particles. For the other floppy drives, you needn't worry too much about dust unless the room where you use your Macintosh is unusually dusty. If so, you can cover the floppy drive opening, when not in use, with a yellow sticky note.

Replacing Old Floppy Disks

One other important preventive measure for floppy drives can also protect your data: get rid of old floppy disks. If a floppy disk is several years old and has been used regularly, the media surface can get worn out. When this happens, the disk can have errors that leave a file unreadable. It can also have bits of magnetic material flake loose and stick to the read or write head in the floppy drive.

So if you're saving, opening, or copying a file on a floppy disk and a dialog box says there's been an error reading or writing a file, don't delay. Immediately copy the files to another disk and throw away the bad floppy disk. Just throw it away without a second thought—the 50¢ you might save by keeping an old disk isn't nearly worth the lost data you put in jeopardy by keeping the disk.

Logic Board

The logic board is the large board at the base of the Macintosh's insides. It contains the main processor, memory, and other key functions. Most of the time, the best thing to do to keep your Macintosh's logic board clean is to just leave it alone. If you break a connection by dusting it too vigorously, you'll wish you could have your dusty, functioning logic board back again. A small amount of dust won't hurt it.

If the logic board is thick with dust when you open up the Macintosh case, you can simply blow to clean off the dust. Just make sure you don't blow the dust into a sensitive part of the computer, such as the floppy disk drive.

For most Macintosh models, you can open the case by lifting the two tabs at the rear of the computer. See the documentation for your specific model to see how to open it. For compact Macintoshes such as the Plus, SE, or Classic models, it's best not to open the case at all. The built-in monitor, like all monitors, can harbor high-voltage charges for some time after the computer is turned off. For these models, leave the inside workings for a qualified technician. Besides, opening compact models can void your warranty.

CD-ROM Drives

CD-ROM drives are pretty durable, but they rely on the accurate alignment of the laser beam that reads information from the compact disc. The key preventive measure for a CD-ROM drive is thus to treat it gently when moving it.

Your CD-ROM may or may not use a disc caddy. If it does, the inside of the drive is relatively protected from dust and dirt, but you should keep the caddy clean. If your CD-ROM is caddyless—that is, you can place a disc directly on the tray without using a special case—don't leave the disc tray out, where it can collect dust.

You should also keep your discs clean by handling them only on the edges. Especially avoid dirt or fingerprints on the underside of the disc, which is where the drive reads the data.

Essential Utilities

◀ See "System Enhancements," p. 711

The prudent Macintosh user will own one each of at least four types of utility software. Some software packages include a collection of programs that cover most or all of these categories.

Backup

The first rule of backup is this: if you don't want to lose your data, back it up. It sounds obvious, but many computer users don't bother to back up even their most important files. If you back up daily, a day's work is the most you could lose in a disaster. If you back up only weekly or monthly, you could spend a long time catching up in case of a disk failure. A good backup strategy, used regularly, can give you peace of mind and save you if something goes wrong.

◀ See "Compression," p. 726

If you've done a lot of customizing to your system or no longer have original program disks, include the system folder or program files in your backup. This is usually impractical, however, if you use floppy disks for your backup.

The simplest and cheapest form of backup involves the mouse: you drag your essential files to a floppy disk to copy them. Then you repeat with other floppy disks until you have backup copies of all of your important data. This approach soon runs into limitations, though. What happens if you have a file bigger than a floppy disk's capacity of 1.44MB? What about if you have hundreds of files and can't spend all day figuring out which files can fit best on which disks? What if your data would fill up 200 floppy disks?

That's why you need a backup utility. A good backup application lets you select what folders and files you need to back up, compresses the data so it takes up less space, supports high-volume storage devices such as tape drives, and keeps track of all the details of which files were backed up when. Then if you mistakenly overwrite a file or your hard disk goes bad, you still have your data.

Backup Types

Backups of your data come in three types: full, differential, and incremental. The major backup applications support all three backup types, each has a specific use depending on your needs.

A *full* backup makes copies of every file. If you make a full backup every day, all you ever need to restore lost data is one set of backup disks (or tapes, if you have a tape drive). The disadvantage is that performing a full backup takes the longest time of the three backup types.

A *differential* backup makes copies of files that changed since the last full backup. A common scheme might be to do a full backup on Friday and differential backups on the other weekdays. To restore data, you need just two backup sets, the full backup and the differential backup from the day before the data was lost. The downside of this backup type is that each day's differential backup is at least as big or bigger than the previous day's, so you use more disks or tapes.

An *incremental* backup makes copies of files that changed since the last backup of any kind. A common scheme here is to do a full backup on Friday and incremental backups on the weekdays. This scheme uses fewer disks or tapes than differential backups or daily full backups because there is no duplication of files: if you already have a backup of a file in its current state, it doesn't get backed up in the incremental backup. The disadvantage is that you may have to assemble several sets of backups (one full set and as many as four incremental sets) to re-create your whole disk in case of disaster.

You can use a backup method that best fits your needs. For example, if you need to be ready to restore files fast and don't care how many backup disks or tapes you need, a differential strategy may be best. If you're willing to go through a few more steps in return for faster backup times and less money spent on backup media, the incremental route is probably best. Make sure the backup package you buy supports that method.

Backup Applications

Dantz Retrospect is one of the most popular backup applications available. It supports a wide variety of tape drives as well as backups to other media such as floppy disks and removable hard drive cartridges. Retrospect also allows you to back up only certain files based on criteria such as how old the file is, whether it's an application or document, and so on. You can store all of these specifications in a script and reuse them later, freeing you from setting up each backup from scratch (see fig. 38.1).

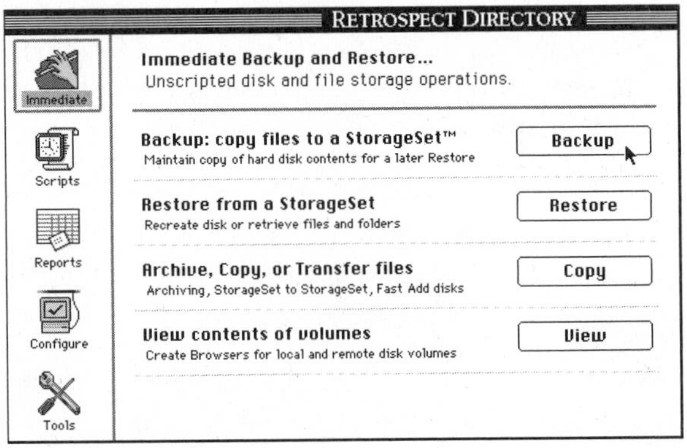

Fig. 38.1
The Retrospect backup application.

Dantz is also the developer of DiskFit, a backup application directed at the single user with less demanding backup needs. DiskFit specializes in

Finder-format backups. Rather than combine many files into one archive that can be opened only by the backup application, a Finder-format backup leaves each file in its original form so you don't need the backup application to copy the file back to the hard disk. The disadvantage of this backup format is that it doesn't support password protection or space-saving compression.

Fifth Generation Fastback was once a standard in Macintosh backup but has since been passed up in popularity by Retrospect. Because Fifth Generation has been acquired by Symantec Corp., the product's future is uncertain. Nonetheless, Symantec is sure to supports its users by offering an alternative if it is discontinued.

Redux, from Inline, is a typical Macintosh backup application. Like several competitors, Redux allows you to set up unattended backups. For example, you can leave work at 5:00 Friday afternoon and have your backup start at 6:00 after you're gone. Redux also allows automatic formatting of floppy disks to reduce the steps you have to go through for a manual backup.

Among the utility collections, Central Point MacTools and Norton Utilities for the Macintosh (now both owned by Symantec) include backup applications. MacTools Backup can make full, differential, or incremental backups with or without compression and in Finder format if you wish. It supports a small list of tape drives as well as network drives, can scan files for viruses before backing up, and allows scheduling for unattended backups. Norton Backup includes many of the features of Retrospect and other backup applications but on a smaller scale. Norton Backup is one of the faster products in performing backups to floppy disks.

Hard Disk Repair and Optimization

A Macintosh utility that repairs hard disks could save your data some day. If a hard disk fails mechanically—for example, if the motor simply dies or one of the rotating disks inside cracks—there is very little you can do. However, most hard disk problems happen at the software level, not the hardware level. Hard disk repair is listed as a preventive measure because many disk problems can be nipped in the bud by disk repair applications, before you notice that anything is wrong. And you can speed up your hard disk's performance by removing file fragmentation with a disk optimization application.

The Macintosh's File System

The *file system* is responsible for keeping track of where your files are on a disk, allocating them extra space when you add information to them by saving, reading them when applications need access to data, and deleting them when you put them in the Trash.

In the early days, the Macintosh used what is called MFS (Macintosh File System), a relatively simple file system that let you group files in folders in the Finder while internally storing them so that every file on a disk was in the same folder. This worked fine for 400K floppy disks, but as hard disks started getting more common, a file system that could offer higher performance and greater capacity became necessary.

The current Macintosh file system, called the Hierarchical File System (HFS), has an intricate structure. It involves a tree of index and leaf nodes that catalog up to many thousands of files and folders on a disk for the most efficient access. Occasionally things can go wrong in the record-keeping. Most often this can happen after a system error or power failure, when files aren't cleaned up and closed in the normal way. That's when a hard disk repair application can become important. Some hard disk repair applications can also find other problems, such as multiple copies of the system folder, invalid file dates, and corruption of the desktop database, which keeps track of which icons and documents are associated with a particular application.

Disk Fragmentation

Because files are created, changed, and deleted at different times and in no particular order, a disk necessarily contains fragmented files. For efficient use of space, a new or saved file may fill up a previously free chunk of space on a disk, use a little more space later, and perhaps put the rest of its contents near the end of a the disk's storage area. The blocks of space used are thus *discontiguous*, or fragmented.

Normally, fragmentation is no problem because the file system keeps track of the location of each fragment in a file. However, the more fragments a file has, the longer it takes the disk to read the file because the disk head must jump from place to place on the disk. High fragmentation also slightly decreases your chances of recovering lost data with a data recovery tool. That's where hard disk optimization applications are useful.

Hard disk optimization applications can copy parts of files to and from free areas on your disk so that every file is in one piece, unfragmented. They can organize the files on your disk so that all the unused space is together, which helps to decrease future fragmentation. Finally, most hard disk optimizers even let you decide which folders or types of files should be stored at the beginning of a disk. If the files that rarely change are together at the beginning, then they are less likely to cause fragmentation around them.

Hard Disk Repair and Optimization Applications

There are collections of utilities on the market that offer whole suites of data protection and data recovery applications, including hard disk repair and optimization. There are also stand-alone disk optimization applications and a free hard disk repair application that comes with your Macintosh. However, in the case of disk repair, you get what you pay for.

MacTools, from Central Point (now owned by Symantec), includes a repair utility, DiskFix, that fixes software problems on hard disks. In addition to problems in a disk's actual file system, DiskFix can find viruses, warn you when you have a certain number of files that haven't been backed up, fix problems in the desktop database, and assess the overall level of fragmentation on your disk. You can schedule DiskFix to run automatically at intervals you specify.

MacTools also includes Optimizer, a hard disk defragmentation application. Optimizer displays a color map of the contents of your disk, identifying which areas contain fragmented and unfragmented applications and documents. You can use the map to click any area of the disk and see the file it contains. Before you optimize your disk, you can see a list of fragmented files that shows how many pieces each file is split into on the disk.

The main competitor with MacTools is Norton Utilities for the Macintosh (NUM). Because they are now owned by the same company, Symantec, the technology from the two products may soon be pooled. NUM is the better known of the two utility collections, but it (as of this printing) hasn't been updated for a couple of years. The Disk Doctor application doesn't detect quite as many kinds of problems as DiskFix, but it generally works somewhat faster (see fig. 38.2).

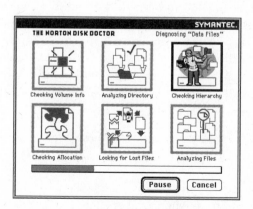

Fig. 38.2
The Norton Disk Doctor hard disk repair application.

Also in the NUM package is Speed Disk, a hard disk optimization application. Speed Disk provides the same basic disk defragmentation functions as its competitors (see fig. 38.3).

Fig. 38.3
The Norton
Speed Disk
defragmentation
application.

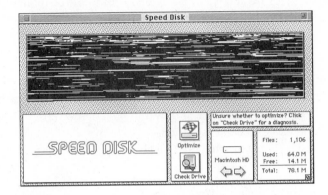

The granddaddy of Macintosh disk optimization applications is ALSoft's Disk Express, which has been available in some form since the mid-1980s. Disk Express has the advantage of long experience in disk defragmentation technology. However, this product is at a disadvantage in price because the utility collections offer several data recovery tools for a slightly greater price.

For hard disk repair, your minimum defense is Disk First Aid, a small utility included by Apple with the Macintosh system software. Disk First Aid fixes only a few of the problems that the other hard disk repair applications can deal with handily. However, if you don't have another utility, run Disk First Aid periodically. It can repair your disk in certain situations and is better than nothing.

One kind of disk repair you can easily do without using a program at all: rebuilding the desktop database. The desktop database is a pair of invisible files that keep track of which icons go with which files and which documents should launch which applications. Double-clicking a document and having its associated application open is made possible by the desktop database. This desktop database can become corrupted, resulting in generic blank page icons or documents that won't launch an application that you know is on your disk.

To rebuild the desktop by yourself, follow these steps:

1. Turn on your Macintosh.

2. Hold down the Option and Command (⌘) keys until a dialog box asks whether you want to rebuild the desktop.

3. Click OK.

One side effect of rebuilding the desktop is deleting any comments you have added to the Get Info window for a file. You can see or add comments by selecting the file and choosing Get Info from the File menu in the Finder. If you don't want to keep track of shortcut key combinations, a shareware program called Desktop Reset can rebuild the desktop. Desktop Reset is available from on-line services and from other distributors of public domain software.

Virus Protection

Happily, the community of Macintosh users has been neglected by writers of computer viruses, compared to the world of DOS-based PCs, where viruses and their variants number in the thousands. But that fact is small consolation if your data is lost or your system becomes unstable because of a virus. If you ever download a file from a BBS (bulletin board service), get a shareware floppy disk from a friend, or use your disks in an unprotected campus computer center, your system could get a virus. Any sharing of files with an infected disk can transfer a virus.

◀ See "Virus Protection," p. 729

Anti-virus software has three main functions: background checking, disk scanning, and repairing. Each is important for a complete line of defense against viruses.

Background Checking

Most Macintosh viruses take effect when you run an application or load a system extension or control panel. The virus may make changes to the system file, modify routines in memory, or attach itself to other files on your disk. Some viruses deliberately attack your data, trying to garble files or erase your disk.

When this happens, viruses leave telltale traces, usually a recognizable chunk of computer code in the file they attach themselves to. This code identifies them like a signature. When anti-virus software is loaded as a system extension, it can wait in the background, checking each program before you run it to see if it contains any known virus signatures. If so, the anti-virus software can stop the program from running.

Background checking can also stop even unknown viruses by watching for suspicious behavior, as well. For example, if a program goes around the standard file system's methods of deleting files, or if it tries to reformat a hard disk, the background checker can warn you before it happens. Background checking can also block a floppy disk from being made available to the system until it is scanned for viruses.

Disk Scanning

It's smart to periodically scan your disk for viruses even if your anti-virus program has background checking turned on. You could have viruses that are lying in wait but haven't been activated yet. The scanning portion of the software goes through the files on your disk looking for recognizable virus signatures.

Anti-virus software may also create a *checksum*, a mathematical encapsulation of the unique characteristics of a file. If an application has changed—because being infiltrated by a virus changes the application file—comparing the current checksum with a previously recorded one.

Repairing

Sometimes all you can do if a file is infected by a virus is to delete it. However, some viruses can be *cleaned*, or removed from the infected file, without permanent damage. In some cases, anti-virus applications can reconstruct the original state of the file or system component without the virus.

Anti-Virus Applications

The best-known Macintosh anti-virus product is SAM (Symantec Anti-Virus for Macintosh). SAM has been through several generations of revisions and is widely used in corporations where Macintoshes are a standard. It offers a variety of security features that can make sure, for example, that floppy disks are always scanned for viruses (see fig. 38.4).

Fig. 38.4
The Symantec
Anti-Virus for
Macintosh
application.

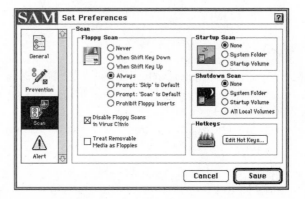

A runner-up in market share is Virex, which has also been in the Macintosh anti-virus business for years and offers many of the same features as SAM. One major selling point of Virex, besides general protection from viruses, is its speed in scanning your disks (see fig. 38.5).

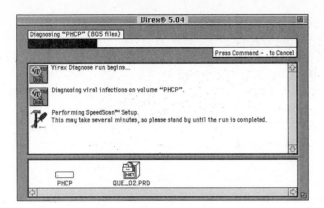

Fig. 38.5
The Virex anti-
virus application.

Central Point MacTools includes Central Point Anti-Virus, which also offers
the typical background checking, disk scanning, and repair capabilities. The
Anti-Virus module is sometimes sold on its own as well. Several other
MacTools modules, such as DiskFix and Backup, incorporate the same anti-
virus technology.

The best-priced anti-virus application is Disinfectant, written by John
Norstad. It's free. Disinfectant is available from on-line services and from
other distributors of public domain software.

Anti-virus researchers are very good about pooling their information for the
good of the Macintosh community when new viruses are found. Usually
updated virus signatures or new versions of anti-virus software are available
within just a few weeks of a new virus's initial discovery, even if the virus was
initially found as far away as Europe.

Diagnostics

Diagnostic software, though perhaps not strictly essential, can be a helpful
addition to your library of utility software. These packages are designed to
identify potential problems before they happen, like a periodic physical exam
for your Macintosh. Most diagnostic applications concentrate on Macintosh
hardware, either specific or general, and others offer limited software features
as well.

Micromat's MacEKG is a general hardware diagnostic tool that reports the
characteristics of the various components of your Macintosh: memory, video,
SCSI devices such as hard disks, and other areas. You can use MacEKG to do
benchmark testing of components to see how they compare with other
Macintoshes or peripheral devices.

The FWB Hard Disk Toolkit, a SCSI disk utility, can be purchased in one of two options, Professional or Personal. The Personal package contains a less technically-oriented subset of the Professional package. The Hard Disk Toolkit focuses on hard disks, though it can display limited information on other SCSI devices such as CD-ROM drives or scanners. You can use this utility to reformat hard disks with multiple partitions, protect a disk with a password, run benchmarks to check your disk's speed, and update your disk's drivers (the hidden software that lets the disk communicate with the Macintosh system) (see fig. 38.6).

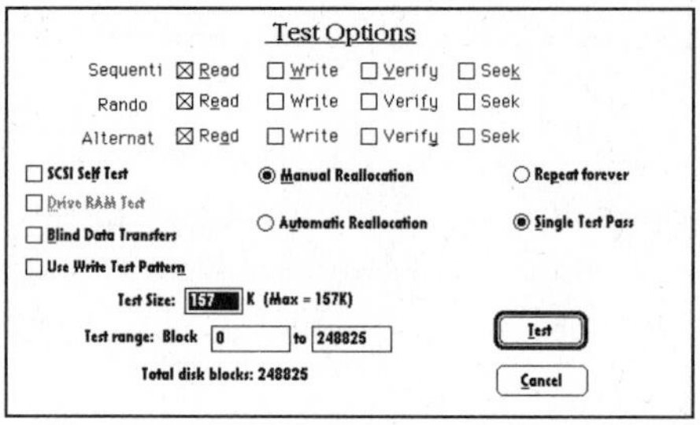

Fig. 38.6
The Hard Disk
Toolkit SCSI utility
application.

Help!, an application from Technosys, concentrates more on the software configuration side of diagnostics. You can use Help! to identify memory problems and scan your system folder to catch incompatibilities between system additions such as extensions and control panels. Help! also increases potential storage space by checking the contents of your disk for duplicate files.

Maintenance Schedule

If you took care of all of the preventive maintenance items in this chapter every time you turned on the Macintosh, you'd never find time to do any work or play any games. That's not the purpose of this chapter. Fortunately, most of these preventive tasks need to be done only occasionally. A small investment of time can bring a big dividend in reliability.

Following are maintenance items grouped by suggested frequency. For details on each item, see the corresponding paragraphs earlier in this chapter.

Many Times a Day

- Save the document you're working on. Save, save, save.

Daily

- Choose Shut Down from the Special menu in the Finder before turning off the power to the Macintosh.

- Back up important documents that have changed since you last backed them up.

- Perform a virus scan on any new software you get from an on-line service, BBS (bulletin board system), or a friend. Viruses don't develop by themselves; they have to come from someone else.

Weekly

- Do a full backup of your data.

- Clean your monitor screen. Fingerprints and dust can accumulate quickly.

- Scan your entire hard disk for viruses. It should take only a few minutes to scan.

Monthly

- Optimize your hard disk with a hard-disk defragmentation application.

- Run Disk First Aid or, if you have one, a hard disk analysis application.

- If you're short on disk space, weed out useless information. Copy unused applications, documents, or system extensions to floppy disks, in case you need them later, and then delete the files from your hard disk.

- Read a Macintosh magazine, if you subscribe, to watch for software updates and useful new products.

- Clean the inside of your mouse or trackball.

- Clean your keyboard if it's dirty.

- Check the time by opening the Date & Time control panel. If the clock loses time rapidly, you may need to have the computer's internal battery replaced by your dealer. Normally, the battery should last for years.

Yearly

- Open your Macintosh case and check for excessive dust.

■ Rebuild your desktop. You may want to do this more often if copying files begins to take longer, file icons turn to the generic blank page icon, or there's an increasingly long delay between when you double-click a document and its associated application starts up.

From Here...

For other information about solving problems that can happen while you use the Macintosh, you can refer to the following chapter:

■ Chapter 37, "Troubleshooting," goes through a list of symptoms and explains what causes each symptom and how you can fix the problem.

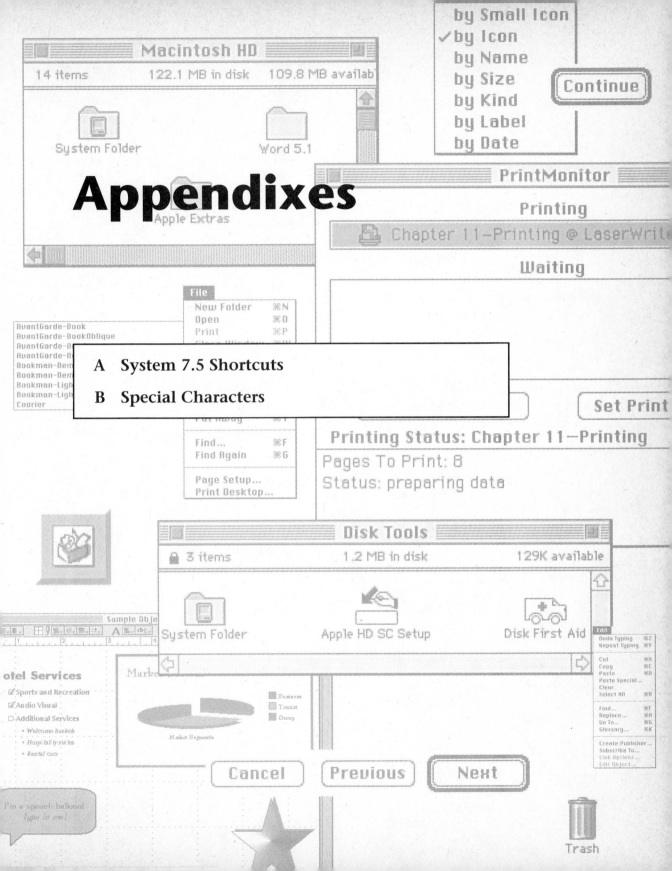

Appendixes

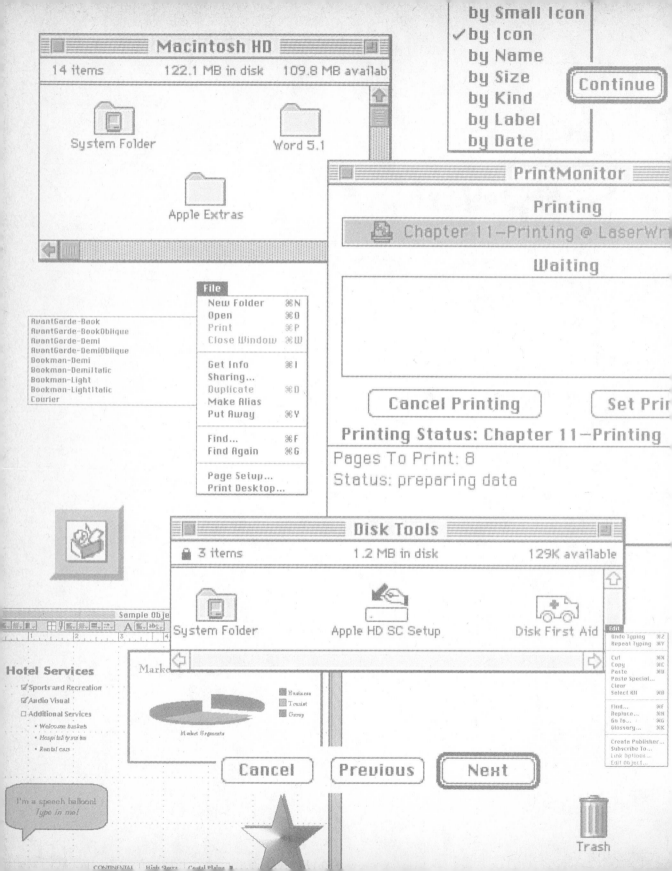

System 7.5 Shortcuts

You can use keyboard commands to work quickly in the Finder. Selected shortcuts are listed by category in this appendix. Other keyboard commands are listed in the menus.

Working with Icons

To open an icon	Double-click the icon
To copy an icon into another folder (instead of moving it)	Option-drag the icon
To clean up selected icons	Shift-Clean Up
To clean up and sort icons	Option-Clean Up
To edit the name of the selected icon	Return or Enter
To cancel moving or copying an icon as you're dragging it	Drag the icon to the menu bar
To select an icon by name	Begin typing the name
To select the next icon alphabetically	Tab
To select the previous icon alphabetically	Shift-Tab
To select an icon to the left or right (in icon views only)	Left arrow or right arrow
To select an icon above or below (in any view)	Up arrow or down arrow
To select more than one icon	Shift-click the icons or drag to enclose the icons
To select no icon (making the desktop active)	⌘-Shift-up arrow or click the desktop pattern

Working with Windows

To close all disk and folder windows	Option-Close or Option-click any window's close box
To move a window without making it active	⌘-drag the window
To open a pop-up menu of the folders and disk that contain this folder	⌘-press the window title
To close a window after opening one of its icons	Option-Open or Option-double-click the icon
To zoom a window to the full size of the screen it's on	Option-click the zoom box

Working with List Views

To change how items are listed	Click a column heading
To expand the contents of the selected folder	⌘-right arrow
To collapse the contents of the selected folder	⌘-left arrow
To move an item to the top level in the window	Drag the icon to top of window (below title bar)
To expand all the contents of the selected folder	⌘-Option-right arrow or Option-click the triangle
To collapse all the contents of the selected folder	⌘-Option-left arrow or Option-click the triangle
To expand or collapse the contents of every folder in the window	Choose Select All, then expand or collapse the contents

Using Directory Dialog Boxes

To cancel	⌘-period or Escape
To move up one level	⌘-up arrow or click the disk icon
To move to the desktop level	⌘-D
To select an item by name	Begin typing the name
To select the next or previous item	Up arrow or down arrow
To display, instead of open, the original of an alias	Option-open the alias
To open the selected item	Return or enter or ⌘-O or ⌘-down arrow
To eject the selected disk	⌘-E
To create a new folder (in Save dialog boxes only)	⌘-N
To make the directory or the name box active (in Save dialog boxes only)	Tab

Restarting the Computer

To rebuild the Desktop file	Hold down ⌘-Option while computer starts up
To turn off all system extensions when starting up	Hold down Shift while computer starts up
To eject floppy disk (to avoid using it as the startup disk)	Hold down mouse or trackball button while computer starts up
To bypass internal hard disk when starting up	Hold down ⌘-Shift-Option-Delete while computer starts up
To reset the Chooser and control panel settings (stored in parameter RAM)	Hold down ⌘-Option-P-R while computer starts up

Miscellaneous Options

To make the desktop active	⌘-Shift-up arrow or click the desktop pattern
To skip the warning message and to delete locked files in the Trash	Option-Empty Trash
To reverse the current setting of "Always snap to grid" (in the Views control panel) while moving an icon	⌘-drag the icon
To erase a disk automatically when you insert it	Hold down ⌘-Option-Tab while inserting the disk
To take a snapshot of the screen	⌘-Shift-3
To hide a program's windows when you switch to another program	Option-make another program active (by choosing it from the Application menu or by clicking one of its windows)
To select an item in a list in the Chooser	Begin typing the name
To make the next list active in the Chooser	Tab
To make the previous list active in the Chooser	Shift-Tab
To choose Guest when connecting to another computer	⌘-G
To choose Registered User when connecting to another computer	⌘-R
To set the language to English (if WordScript is installed)	⌘-left arrow
To set the language to the system script	⌘-right arrow
To set the language to the next script in the Keyboard menu	⌘-space bar
To set the language to the next language in the current script	⌘-Option-space bar

Special Characters

The following tables show examples of special characters that can be easily accessed on the Mac by pressing either Option or Option-Shift in combination with the keys listed across the top of the table. The fonts shown here represent just a few of the many fonts available for the Mac. The fonts you have to choose from depend on what software is installed on your system.

Option +	1	2	3	4	5	6	7	8	9	0	-	=	[	]	\	;	'	,	.	/
Apple Chancery	¡	™	£	¢	∞	§	¶	•	ª	º	–	≠	"	'	«	…	œ	≤	≥	÷
Arial	¡	™	£	¢	∞	§	¶	•	ª	º	–	≠	"	'	«	…	æ	≤	≥	÷
Arial Narrow	¡	™	£	¢	∞	§	¶	•	ª	º	–	≠	"	'	«	…	æ	≤	≥	÷
Book Antiqua	¡	™	£	¢	∞	§	¶	•	ª	º	–	≠	"	'	«	…	æ	≤	≥	÷
Bookman Old Style	¡	™	£	¢	∞	§	¶	•	ª	º	–	≠	"	'	«	…	æ	≤	≥	÷
Century Gothic	¡	™	£	¢	∞	§	¶	•	ª	º	–	≠	"	'	«	…	œ	≤	≥	÷
Century Schoolbook	¡	™	£	¢	∞	§	¶	•	ª	º	–	≠	"	'	«	…	æ	≤	≥	÷
Chicago	¡	™	£	¢	∞	§	¶	•	ª	º	–	≠	"	'	«	…	æ	≤	≥	÷
Courier	¡	™	£	¢	∞	§	¶	•	ª	º	–	≠	"	'	«	…	æ	≤	≥	÷
Courier New	¡	™	£	¢	∞	§	¶	•	ª	º	–	≠	"	'	«	…	æ	≤	≥	÷
Geneva	¡	™	£	¢	∞	§	¶	•	ª	º	–	≠	"	'	«	…	æ	≤	≥	÷
Helvetica	¡	™	£	¢	∞	§	¶	•	ª	º	–	≠	"	'	«	…	æ	≤	≥	÷
Hoefler Text	¡	™	£	¢	∞	§	¶	•	ª	º	–	≠	"	'	«	…	æ	≤	≥	÷
Monaco	¡	™	£	¢	∞	§	¶	•	ª	º	–	≠	"	'	«	…	œ	≤	≥	÷
Monotype Corsiva	¡	™	£	¢	∞	∫	¶	•	ª	º	–	≠	"	'	«	…	œ	≤	≥	÷
Monotype Sorts	②	♥	✌	✎	⑤	♥	❦	❧	❻	❼	❼	②	❾	→	⑧	⑩	❾	⑦	⑧	↔
New York	¡	™	£	¢		§	¶	•	ª	º	–		"	'	«	…	æ			
Palatino	¡	™	£	¢	∞	§	¶	•	ª	º	–	≠	"	'	«	…	æ	≤	≥	÷
Skia	¡	™	£	¢	∞	§	¶	•	ª	º	–	≠	"	'	«	…	æ	≤	≥	÷
Symbol	ℑ	♠	≤	´	°	/	ƒ	∞	≈	…	∠	↑	®	™	∩	⊃	—	"	≥	√
Tekton Plus Regular	¡	™	£	¢	∞	§	¶	•	ª	º	–	≠	"	'	«	…	æ	≤	≥	÷
Times	¡	™	£	¢	∞	§	¶	•	ª	º	–	≠	"	'	«	…	æ	≤	≥	÷
Times New Roman	¡	™	£	¢	∞	§	¶	•	ª	º	–	≠	"	'	«	…	æ	≤	≥	÷
Wingdings	☺	✚	●	○	✛	☉	○	◉	①	①	☽	✳	☙	☚	☜	☞	☟	✧	⌘	⌧

Option +

Option +	A	B	C	D	E	F	G	H	I	J	K	L	M	N	O	P	Q	R	S	T	U	V	W	X	Y	Z
Apple Chancery	å	∫	ç	∂	´	ƒ	©	˙	ˆ	Δ	˚	¬	µ	˜	ø	π	œ	®	ß	†	¨	√	∑	≈	¥	Ω
Arial	å	∫	ç	∂	´	ƒ	©	˙	ˆ	Δ	˚	¬	µ	˜	ø	π	œ	®	ß	†	¨	√	∑	≈	¥	Ω
Arial Narrow	å	∫	ç	∂	´	ƒ	©	˙	ˆ	Δ	˚	¬	µ	˜	ø	π	œ	®	ß	†	¨	√	∑	≈	¥	Ω
Book Antiqua	å	∫	ç	∂	´	ƒ	©	˙	ˆ	Δ	˚	¬	µ	˜	ø	π	œ	®	ß	†	¨	√	∑	≈	¥	Ω
Bookman Old Style	å	∫	ç	∂	´	ƒ	©	˙	ˆ	Δ	˚	¬	µ	˜	ø	π	œ	®	ß	†	¨	√	∑	≈	¥	Ω
Century Gothic	å	∫	ç	∂	´	ƒ	©	˙	ˆ	Δ	˚	¬	µ	˜	ø	π	œ	®	ß	†	¨	√	∑	≈	¥	Ω
Century Schoolbook	å	∫	ç	∂	´	ƒ	©	˙	ˆ	Δ	˚	¬	µ	˜	ø	π	œ	®	ß	†	¨	√	∑	≈	¥	Ω
Chicago	å	∫	ç	∂	´	ƒ	©	˙	ˆ	Δ	˚	¬	µ	˜	ø	π	œ	®	ß	†	¨	√	∑	≈	¥	Ω
Courier	å	∫	ç	∂	´	ƒ	©	˙	ˆ	Δ	˚	¬	µ	˜	ø	π	œ	®	ß	†	¨	√	∑	≈	¥	Ω
Courier New	å	∫	ç	∂	´	ƒ	©	˙	ˆ	Δ	˚	¬	µ	˜	ø	π	œ	®	ß	†	¨	√	∑	≈	¥	Ω
Geneva	å	∫	ç	∂	´	ƒ	©	˙	ˆ	Δ	˚	¬	µ	˜	ø	π	œ	®	ß	†	¨	√	∑	≈	¥	Ω
Helvetica	å	∫	ç	∂	´	ƒ	©	˙	ˆ	Δ	˚	¬	µ	˜	ø	π	œ	®	ß	†	¨	√	∑	≈	¥	Ω
Hoefler Text	å	∫	ç	∂	´	ƒ	©	˙	ˆ	Δ	˚	¬	µ	˜	ø	π	œ	®	ß	†	¨	√	∑	≈	¥	Ω
Monaco	å	∫	ç	∂	´	ƒ	©	˙	ˆ	Δ	˚	¬	µ	˜	ø	π	œ	®	ß	†	¨	√	∑	≈	¥	Ω
Monotype Corsiva	å	∫	ç	∂	´	ƒ	©	˙	ˆ	Δ	˚	¬	µ	˜	ø	π	œ	®	ß	†	¨	√	∑	≈	¥	Ω
Monotype Sorts																										
New York	å		ç		´		©								ø		œ	®	ß	†	¨				¥	
Palatino	å	∫	ç	∂	´	ƒ	©	˙	ˆ	Δ	˚	¬	µ	˜	ø	π	œ	®	ß	†	¨	√	∑	≈	¥	Ω
Skia	å	∫	ç	∂	´	ƒ	©	˙	ˆ	Δ	˚	¬	µ	˜	ø	π	œ	®	ß	†	¨	√	∑	≈	¥	Ω
Symbol	≡			∂	↔	⊗	♥			◡		≠	∈		∘		ℜ	∝		⌡	≠	∉	♣		←	℘	⊕	×
Tekton Plus Regular	å	∫	ç	∂	´	ƒ	©	˙	ˆ	Δ	˚	¬	µ	˜	ø	π	œ	®	ß	†	¨	√	∑	≈	¥	Ω
Times	å	∫	ç	∂	´	ƒ	©	˙	ˆ	Δ	˚	¬	µ	˜	ø	π	œ	®	ß	†	¨	√	∑	≈	¥	Ω
Times New Roman	å	∫	ç	∂	´	ƒ	©	˙	ˆ	Δ	˚	¬	µ	˜	ø	π	œ	®	ß	†	¨	√	∑	≈	¥	Ω
Wingdings																										

Shift + Option +

Shift + Option +	1	2	3	4	5	6	7	8	9	0	-	=	[	]	\	;	'	,	.	/
Apple Chancery	⁄	¤	‹	›	ﬁ	ﬂ	‡	°	·	,	—	±	"	'	»	Ú	Æ	˘	ˇ	¿
Arial	⁄	¤	‹	›	ﬁ	ﬂ	‡	°	·	,	—	±	"	'	»	Ú	Æ	˘	ˇ	¿
Arial Narrow	⁄	¤	‹	›	ﬁ	ﬂ	‡	°	·	,	—	±	"	'	»	Ú	Æ	˘	ˇ	¿
Book Antiqua	⁄	¤	‹	›	ﬁ	ﬂ	‡	°	·	,	—	±	"	'	»	Ú	Æ	˘	ˇ	¿
Bookman Old Style	⁄	¤	‹	›	ﬁ	ﬂ	‡	°	·	,	—	±	"	'	»	Ú	Æ	˘	ˇ	¿
Century Gothic	⁄	¤	‹	›	ﬁ	ﬂ	‡	°	·	,	—	±	"	'	»	Ú	Æ	˘	ˇ	¿
Century Schoolbook	⁄	¤	‹	›	ﬁ	ﬂ	‡	°	·	,	—	±	"	'	»	Ú	Æ	˘	ˇ	¿
Chicago							‡	°			—	±	"	'	»		Æ			¿
Courier	⁄	¤	‹	›	ﬁ	ﬂ	‡	°	·	,	—	±	"	'	»	Ú	Æ	˘	ˇ	¿
Courier New	⁄	¤	‹	›	ﬁ	ﬂ	‡	°	·	,	—	±	"	'	»	Ú	Æ	˘	ˇ	¿
Geneva								°			—	±	"	'	»		Æ			
Helvetica	⁄	¤	‹	›	ﬁ	ﬂ	‡	°	·	,	—	±	"	'	»	Ú	Æ	˘	ˇ	¿
Hoefler Text	⁄	¤	‹	›	ﬁ	ﬂ	‡	°	·	,	—	±	"	'	»	Ú	Æ	˘	ˇ	¿
Monaco								°			—	±	"	'	»		Æ			¿
Monotype Corsiva	⁄	¤	‹	›	ﬁ	ﬂ	‡	°	·	,	—	±	"	'	»	Ú	Æ	˘	ˇ	¿
Monotype Sorts																				
New York								°					"	'	»		Æ			¿
Palatino	⁄	¤	‹	›	ﬁ	ﬂ	‡	°	·	,	—	±	"	'	»	Ú	Æ	˘	ˇ	¿
Skia	⁄	¤	‹	›	ﬁ	ﬂ	‡	°	·	,	—	±	"	'	»	Ú	Æ	˘	ˇ	¿
Symbol	∨	⇔	⇐	⇑	⇒	⇓	◊	ϒ	⟨	®	∇	±	©	Π	∪	∫	→	⌡	⌉	ℵ
Tekton Plus Regular	⁄	¤	‹	›	ﬁ	ﬂ	‡	°	·	,	—	±	"	'	»	Ú	Æ	˘	ˇ	¿
Times	⁄	¤	‹	›	ﬁ	ﬂ	‡	°	·	,	—	±	"	'	»	Ú	Æ	˘	ˇ	¿
Times New Roman	⁄	¤	‹	›	ﬁ	ﬂ	‡	°	·	,	—	±	"	'	»	Ú	Æ	˘	ˇ	¿
Wingdings																				

Shift + Option +	A	B	C	D	E	F	G	H	I	J	K	L	M	N	O	P	Q	R	S	T	U	V	W	X	Y	Z
Apple Chancery	Å	ı	Ç	Î	´	Ï	˝	Ó		Ô		Ò	Â	˜	Ø	∏	Œ	‰	ˆ		¨	◊	„		Á	¸
Arial	Å	ı	Ç	Î	´	Ï	˝	Ó	ˆ	Ô		Ò	Â	˜	Ø	∏	Œ	‰	ˆ		¨	◊	„		Á	¸
Arial Narrow	Å	ı	Ç	Î	´	Ï	˝	Ó	ˆ	Ô		Ò	Â	˜	Ø	∏	Œ	‰	ˆ		¨	◊	„		Á	¸
Book Antiqua	Å	ı	Ç	Î	´	Ï	˝	Ó	ˆ	Ô		Ò	Â	˜	Ø	∏	Œ	‰	ˆ		¨	◊	„		Á	¸
Bookman Old Style	Å	ı	Ç	Î	´	Ï	˝	Ó	ˆ	Ô		Ò	Â	˜	Ø	∏	Œ	‰	ˆ		¨	◊	„		Á	¸
Century Gothic	Å	ı	Ç	Î	´	Ï	˝	Ó	ˆ	Ô		Ò	Â	˜	Ø	∏	Œ	‰	ˆ		¨	◊	„		Á	¸
Century Schoolbook	Å	ı	Ç	Î	´	Ï	˝	Ó	ˆ	Ô		Ò	Â	˜	Ø	∏	Œ	‰	ˆ		¨	◊	„		Á	¸
Chicago	Å		Ç																							
Courier	Å	ı	Ç	Î		Ï		Ó		Ô		Ò	Â	˜	Ø		Œ	‰	ˆ		¨	◊	„		Á	¸
Courier New	Å	ı	Ç	Î	´	Ï	˝	Ó	ˆ	Ô		Ò	Â	˜	Ø	∏	Œ	‰	ˆ		¨	◊			Á	¸
Geneva	Å		Ç		´										Ø	∏	Œ					◊				
Helvetica	Å	ı	Ç	Î	´	Ï	˝	Ó	ˆ	Ô		Ò	Â	˜	Ø	∏	Œ	‰	ˆ		¨	◊	„		Á	¸
Hoefler Text	Å	ı	Ç	Î	´	Ï	˝	Ó	ˆ	Ô		Ò	Â	˜	Ø	∏	Œ	‰	ˆ		¨	◊	„		Á	¸
Monaco	Å		Ç		´										Ø	∏	Œ					◊				
Monotype Corsiva	Å	ı	Ç	Î	´	Ï	˝	Ó	ˆ	Ô		Ò	Å	˜	Ø	∏	Œ	‰	ˆ		¨	◊	„		Á	¸
Monotype Sorts	)	↣	(	↩	◆	↪	➡	↝	✓	⇨		⇨	↳	✎	①	➃	➅	➤	⇨		①	↕	➤	➔	◆	↦
New York	Å		Ç												Ø		Œ					◊				
Palatino	Å	ı	Ç	Î	´	Ï	˝	Ó	ˆ	Ô		Ò	Â	˜	Ø	∏	Œ	‰	ˆ		¨	◊	„		Á	¸
Skia	Å	ı	Ç	Î	´	Ï	˝	Ó	ˆ	Ô		Ò	Â	˜	Ø	∏	Œ	‰	ˆ		¨	◊	„		Á	¸
Symbol		J		↓	↔	⌠	〉	⌡	)	↓	◆	〉	Σ	✻	↓	+	∈	™	⏐		←	◊		©	J	⏐
Tekton Plus Regular	Å	ı	Ç	Î	´	Ï	˝	Ó	ˆ	Ô		Ò	Â	˜	Ø	∏	Œ	‰	ˆ		¨	◊	„		Á	¸
Times	Å	ı	Ç	Î	´	Ï	˝	Ó	ˆ	Ô		Ò	Â	˜	Ø	∏	Œ	‰	ˆ		¨	◊	„		Á	¸
Times New Roman	Å	ı	Ç	Î	´	Ï	˝	Ó	ˆ	Ô		Ò	Â	˜	Ø	∏	Œ	‰	ˆ		¨	◊	„		Á	¸
Wingdings	①	✎	②	←	★	➚	⌧	↘	✐	⇦	⇨	⇧	↖	↗	✻	⊙	⌚	➚	↓	▥	✳	◄	↖	☑	←	✓

Glossary

32-bit addressing. The method the Macintosh uses to access RAM above 8 megabytes.

A/UX. A form of UNIX available for the Macintosh. See also *UNIX*.

Accelerator board. An option card that, when installed in the Macintosh, enables the computer to operate and manipulate data at a faster rate.

Acoustic modem. A modem with two cups that fit around a telephone's handset; converts a computer's signals into sound and back again. See also *modem*.

Active window. The top or front window on the Desktop. It has a highlighted title bar.

ADB. See *Apple Desktop Bus*.

Adobe Type Manager (ATM). An outline font utility that allows postscript font scaling on the screen and on non-postscript printers.

Adobe Type Manager GX (ATM GX). Adobe Type Manager for QuickDraw GX. See also *QuickDraw GX*.

Alarm Clock. A desk accessory that displays the current date and time. The alarm can be set to alert you at a specified time.

Alert box. Contains a warning when you ask the Macintosh to do something that can cause loss of data or when other errors occur. See also *dialog box*.

Alias. An icon that represents an original file folder or disk.

Apple Desktop Bus (ADB). The connectors on the back of the Macintosh that allow connection of the keyboard, mouse, joysticks, graphics tablets, touch screens, track balls, and so on.

Apple HD SC Setup. A system utility file packaged with the Macintosh that initializes and sets up an Apple hard disk.

Apple menu. The far left menu at the top of the Macintosh screen.

Apple menu items. Items available on the Apple menu of the Desktop for immediate use. In System 7, these applications, folders, and files are placed in the Apple Menu Items folder.

AppleScript. Apples scripting system that allows you to automate tasks.

AppleShare. An operating system designed to enable a Macintosh to become a server to other Macs on the same network.

AppleTalk. A communications network used to connect Macs and share peripheral devices such as printers. AppleTalk is the communication protocol by which data is transferred. Also called LocalTalk.

Application. A program that enables the user to create, enter, and design information. Examples are word processors, spreadsheets, and paint programs.

Application menu. A menu on the right end of the menu bar that allows you to switch between active applications. It also allows you to hide applications, including the Finder.

Application template. A file developed to guide the creation or design of documents. See also *template*.

Arrow keys. The four keys that move the insertion point left, right, up, and down in a word processor file and that change the active cell in a spreadsheet.

ASCII (American Standard Code for Information Interchange). A standard computer text format in which each character is represented by seven bits. See also *text file*.

Assembler. A program that translates symbolic codes, or assembly language, to machine language. See also *compiler*.

Asynchronous communication. A means of transmitting data between computers. A special signal indicates when each character starts and stops.

ATM. See *Adobe Type Manager*.

Auto answer. The capability of a modem to answer an incoming call and to establish communications without human assistance.

Autocall. The capability of a computer-controlled modem to place a telephone call.

Autotrace. A feature in drawing and page layout applications that enables the user to trace around shapes and lines of an image.

Background execution. A program that can continue operating without user commands and without interrupting a procedure operating in the foreground. See also *MultiFinder* and *multitasking*.

Balloon Help. Context-sensitive help available through System 7 and many System 7 applications.

Baseline. The horizontal line that defines the bottom of each character, excluding the descenders, in a font family.

BASIC (Beginner's All-Purpose Symbolic Instruction Code). A common programming language that is easy to learn but relatively inflexible.

Baud rate. A measure of the speed at which a modem modulates signals. Bits per second is a more meaningful measure of modem speed. See *Bits per second*.

BBS. See *bulletin board system*.

Beta test. The first test of a new product outside the laboratory. This test is the final step before a full market release. Because many product bugs are found in the beta test release, producers do not consider the beta version to be a final version.

Bézier curves. Mathematically generated line that can display non-uniform curves; used to create PostScript fonts.

Binary. A numbering system based on a series of ones (1s) and zeros (0s) used to encode text and numerical information.

Bit (binary digit). The smallest unit of computer information. A 1 or a 0 code electronically represents on or off, respectively.

Bit-mapped font. A font composed of dots. Used primarily for screen representation of fonts.

Bit-mapped image. An image consisting of dots, in which one dot represents one or more bits of the image (depending on whether color or other attributes are used). A Mac Plus uses one bit per dot.

Bits per second (bps). A measure of the number of useful bits of data transferred over a communications line.

Bomb. An abnormal termination of a program. A bomb occurs when a program unexpectedly halts due to a bug or encounters data conditions it cannot handle. See also *bug*.

Boot. To start a computer by loading the operating system (System file and Finder) into memory. The operating system software tells the Macintosh how to load other programs.

Bridge. A device that enables you to connect networks so that members on one network can communicate with members on another network. See also *gateway*.

Buffer. A section of memory that temporarily holds information from I/O (input/output) communications, including data transfer through a modem or reading and writing to your disk. The buffer holds information when the computer is sending information faster than the device can receive it.

Bug. A problem in a software program. Initially named after a moth that caused the failure of an early computer (1945) at Harvard University. Today, a bug usually refers to an inappropriate or inaccurate line of programming code that causes the program to halt execution or respond incorrectly. See also *bomb*.

Bulletin board system (BBS). A telecommunications facility used to share information with others through the use of a modem and specialized communications software.

Bundled software. Software included with your Macintosh, such as the System Tools disk, Utilities disk, and HyperCard. Such a package deal includes hardware and software.

Bus. A path through which information is shared between one part of a computer and another.

Button. A location on the screen where the user can click to initiate a command for the Macintosh to take some predefined action.

Byte. A collection of eight bits. A byte can store a single character of information.

Cache. See *RAM cache*.

Calculator. A desk accessory that looks and acts like a four-function calculator.

Cancel button. A button in dialog boxes that the user can click to cancel a command.

Caps Lock key. A key located on the lower left corner of the Macintosh standard keyboard that, when pressed, causes alphabetic characters to be displayed in uppercase format but does not affect numeric keys or symbols.

Carrier detect. A modem function that detects whether another modem is sending a carrier signal. If the carrier signal is not detected, your modem generally disconnects itself and hangs up.

Cathode-ray tube (CRT). The screen used in computers in which light produced by a cathode strikes a phosphor coating on the screen.

CDEV. An acronym for Control panel DEVice. A program that adds functionality to a Mac and is controlled by a Control Panel.

CD-ROM (Compact Disc-Read-Only Memory). A disc that can store as much as 600 megabytes of data. A CD-ROM uses the same technology as audio CDs, but is used to provide a computer access to large quantities of information.

Central processing unit (CPU). The computer's main information processing unit. In a Macintosh, the CPU is a single silicon chip called the microprocessor. See also *microprocessor*.

Chip. A tiny piece of silicon with an integrated electronic circuit photoengraved on its surface.

Chooser. A desk accessory that enables the user to choose the printer on which the document is to be printed. For the Chooser to function, the printer resource files must be installed in the current System file. In a networking environment, the Chooser can be used to connect and disconnect the Macintosh from the network and choose from among devices connected to the network.

CISC. An acronym for Complex Instruction Set Computer. A microprocessor that includes a large number of instructions, many of which take several steps to perform. CISC processors are not as fast as the alternative design, called RISC. See also *RISC*.

Click. To place the mouse pointer (arrow) on an item on-screen, and quickly press and release the mouse button.

Clip art. Artwork, bought on disk, that can consist of bit-mapped graphics, object graphics, or encapsulated PostScript files.

Clipboard. A temporary storage location that holds cut and copied information.

Clock speed. The actual operating speed of the computer's microprocessor.

Close. A command that closes a window or document.

Close box. A small box located at the top left of some windows. Clicking the Close box causes the window to close.

CMYK. The four colors—cyan, magenta, yellow, and black—used in the color separation process that can be combined to form any other color.

Cold boot. Using the power switch to turn on your Macintosh.

Color separations. A process used in offset printing in which separate plates are used to print different colors of ink on a page producing multiple colors. As the name implies, each color has its own plate. When all color plates are placed atop each other, the final product is produced.

Command. A menu option that causes an action. A command tells the Macintosh what to do next.

Command key. A key that, when pressed in combination with other keys, performs a command or action. The command key has a picture of an Apple and a "cloverleaf" on it.

Commercial software. Software that is copyrighted and sold for profit. Commercial software cannot be copied and distributed to others without the approval of the software publisher.

Compiler. A program that translates source code to machine language. See also *assembler*.

Computer-aided design (CAD). Applications that take advantage of a computer's power to design architectural, mechanical, electrical, civil, schematic, IC, and various other types of drawings. Using the two- and three-dimensional capabilities of the application, the user can develop highly complex structures. Commonly referred to as computer-aided drafting and design (CADD).

Condensed type. A typeface in which the space between the characters is less than the normal spacing of the typeface. See also *font* and *kerning*.

Continuous tone image. An image that contains gradient tones from black to white. In a scanned image, the tones are converted from continuous to halftone images. See also *scanner* and *optical character recognition*.

Control (Ctrl) key. A key located on the left side of the standard keyboard, whose function varies depending upon the application being used.

Control panel. A desk accessory in System 6 that's used to personalize such features as the pattern on the Desktop, the speed of the mouse movement, and the volume of the warning beep.

Control Panels folder. A folder in System 7 that resides in the System Folder and contains control panels. Replaces the Control Panel desk accessory of System 6.

Coprocessor. See *Math Coprocessor.*

Copy. A command used to make an exact replica of text, an entire document, or a graphic. The Copy command is located in the Edit menu. Using Copy does not modify or delete the original.

Copy protection. A method of preventing unauthorized duplication of software. See also *write-protect tab.*

Current startup disk. The startup disk whose System files the Macintosh is using.

Cursor. The blinking vertical bar that indicates where keyed text will appear. Also called *insertion point.*

Cut. A command that removes selected information from a document and temporarily places it in the Clipboard.

Cylinder. The total number of disk tracks that can be written or read for a specific disk-head position. On a double-sided floppy disk, a cylinder is two tracks; on a hard disk, it consists of four or more tracks. See also *track.*

DA. See *desk accessory.*

Data. The information processed with a computer application or program. Also called *information.*

Database. A collection of related information that is organized for storage and retrieval. A database may contain names, addresses, and phone numbers, for example.

Data fork. The portion of a Macintosh disk file containing the user's data.

Default. The settings that hardware or software have when first installed.

Defragment. To increase the amount of usable space on a hard disk by rewriting files so that they are stored on contiguous sectors or parts of the hard disk.

Delete key. A key that you press to remove information from a document. Using this key is the same as using the Cut command except that the information is not placed on the Clipboard; it is deleted permanently. See also *cut*.

Delimiter. A special character used by applications and communications software to indicate the end of a line or to separate one field from another or one record from another.

Desk accessory (DA). A small application (located in the System file) that is accessible from the Apple menu. Examples are the Alarm Clock, Chooser, and Control Panel. Other more complex desk accessories are mini-spreadsheets, a thesaurus, and a bibliography maker.

Desktop. The work area of the Macintosh. The screen, disk icons, Trash can, and menu bar that you see when you start your Mac.

Desktop file. A file created on all Macintosh disks by the Finder. It is hidden from the user and contains information the Finder uses to locate files, folders, and icons.

Desktop publishing. An integrated package of certain applications that enables the user to design the layout of pages, determine the size and location of graphics, modify and locate text, and produce a document. Desktop publishing programs integrate page layout, text entry, graphics design, and printing into one overall application.

Dialog. A message from the Macintosh requesting further action or information from the user. In most instances, the user can respond by typing a response or clicking a button. When accompanied by a beep, the user is being warned that something may happen that the user has not anticipated. See also *alert box*.

Digitizer pad. A peripheral device that is similar to the mouse but enables the user to choose drawing tools, menu commands, and other functions, as well as to draw shapes without using the applications interface.

Dimmed command. A menu command that appears gray on-screen and cannot be used while dimmed. Usually another command must be completed or a selection made before the dimmed command can be accessed.

Dimmed icon. Represents a document, folder, or application on a disk that has been ejected. The image still resides on the Desktop, but the contents of the folder or disk cannot be opened.

Direct-connect modem. A modem that connects directly from the computer into the telephone line outlet and bypasses the telephone handset.

Directory window. The window that lists the contents of a disk. Using the View menu, the user can alter the appearance of the directory and have the contents displayed in small icons, large icons, and words.

Disk. A device that uses magnetic medium to store information. Disks can be floppy or hard. The Macintosh uses 3.5-inch, hard-case floppy disks.

Disk drive. Holds the disk and retrieves information stored on the disk. The user must insert a floppy disk into the floppy disk drive. A hard disk drive has a built-in disk permanently installed.

Disk drive port. A port on the Macintosh designed to be connected to an external floppy disk drive. See also *port*.

Disk server. A disk drive, generally on a network, that is available to all users.

Document. A generic term describing whatever the user creates, using an application on the Macintosh. A document can be a letter, article, picture, table, or spreadsheet, among others. A document contains the information the user has entered and saved.

DOS (Disk Operating System). A shortened name for PC-DOS and MS-DOS, which are the complete names of the operating system for IBM and IBM-compatible computers. DOS is a set of instructions. See also *operating system*.

Dot-matrix printer. A printer that forms characters and graphics from pins impacting the paper through an ink ribbon. The ImageWriter printers are dot-matrix printers.

Dots per inch (dpi). A measure of screen and printer resolution by the number of dots per linear inch. The higher the number of dots, the better the resolution. The ImageWriter II operates at 144 dpi, and the LaserWriter operates at 300 dpi. See also *resolution*.

Double-click. An action used to open applications, documents, or folders. Double-clicking is performed by clicking the mouse button twice in rapid succession.

Download. A procedure in which a user transfers data from a remote computer's database to the user's computer and stores the data on a hard disk or floppy.

Downloadable font. A font that is downloaded (sent from your Macintosh to your printer).

dpi. See *dots per inch*.

Drag. A mouse technique used to select text and move objects on the screen. To select text, place the pointer at the beginning of the text you want to select, hold down the mouse button, move the pointer to the end of the selection, and release the button. To move an object, point to the object, hold down the mouse button, move the pointer to the location you want the object to appear, and release the mouse button.

Drag and Drop. An editing technique that allows you to copy or move text by dragging a selection with the mouse. See also *drag*.

Driver. Software that tells the Macintosh how to operate an external device such as a printer. A driver is located in the System Folder or Extension Folder.

Duplex. A communications protocol that allows for two-way communication. A half-duplex communication transmission can go only one direction at a time. In full-duplex communication, transmission occurs in both directions simultaneously.

Edit menu. A menu that contains the copying and cutting features and the Undo command.

Electronic mail. See *e-mail*.

e-mail. A messaging system that enables the user to send and receive messages to people in and outside the user's computer network. Outside messages are generally sent using telephone lines. A message can be as simple as a quick note or as complex as multiple documents and files.

Em dash. A dash the width of the capital letter *M*.

Em space. A space that is the width of the letter *M* of a specified typeface and type size. See also *en space*, *font*, *kerning*, and *leading*.

Emulation. A feature that enables one device to imitate another.

Encryption. To substitute characters to hide the original meaning of a document from those people who do not have the enciphering program.

En dash. A dash the width of the capital letter *N*, usually half the width of an em space.

En space. A space that is the width of the letter *N* in a specified typeface and type size, usually half the width of an em space. See also *em space*.

Enter key. A key that confirms an entry. Similar to the Return key.

EPS (encapsulated PostScript). A file format that uses PostScript language to store an image.

Ethernet. A standard for local area network hardware.

Expansion card. An internal card that enables additional features to be added to the computer's processing capability, telecommunications capability, and so on.

Expansion slot. A location inside the Macintosh that allows the installation of an option card to perform additional functions. See also *option card.*

Extension. A system program that extends the capabilities of System 7's features. See also *INIT.*

Fax/modem. A modem with fax capabilities. See *modem.*

File. Information stored on disk. Documents and applications are examples of files.

File format. The set of instructions used to store information.

File server. A node on a network that has a disk drive, software, and processor that is available to all users. File-server software controls access to individual files, and multiuser software enables several users to access the same file simultaneously.

File synchronization. A method that enables people who work with the same file on two different systems to synchronize the files to ensure that they are working on the most recent version.

Fill. To paint an enclosed area with black, white, color, or shading.

Finder. A file and memory management utility that keeps the Desktop organized, thus enabling users to find and open files or folders. The Finder must always be in the System Folder for your Macintosh to operate properly (with the exception of HyperCard).

Fkey. A utility program similar to a desk accessory that runs when the user presses one of the number keys along the top of the keyboard in combination with ⌘ and Shift. Fkeys should not be confused with the Function keys at the top of extended keyboards.

Floppy disk. A removable secondary storage medium that uses a magnetically sensitive, flexible disk enclosed in a plastic envelope or case.

Folder. Holds related information in one location like the folders in an office file cabinet. A folder can contain files, other folders, graphics documents, or other information.

Font. A collection of letters, punctuation marks, numbers, and symbols that appear in the same typeface, style, and size. The Macintosh comes with a number of typefaces, such as Monaco, Chicago, and Geneva. See also *bitmapped image*, *outline font*, and *PostScript*.

Font/DA Mover. A System 6 utility that moves fonts and DAs from one System to another or from a floppy disk to a System.

Font substitution. A Macintosh activity that substitutes one font for another when the font required by a particular application is not available.

Footer. Text that is automatically printed at the bottom of each page. See also *header*.

Fragmentation. A situation in which various parts of a file are stored on more than one sector of a hard disk.

Freeware. Software shared without costs to the user, with the intention that the software be shared by others and distributed throughout a large network of users. See also *public domain software* and *shareware*.

ftp. An acronym for file transfer protocol. On the Internet, an ftp server provides files for transfer.

Function key. A key that can be programmed to perform a particular function.

Gateway. In a computer network, the hardware and software used to connect two different types of computer networks. See also *bridge*.

Get Info. A command on the File menu that provides the following information on the file: locked or unlocked, creation date, modification dates, size, and user-entered notes.

Gigabyte (G). Around one billion bytes (1,073,741,824 bytes) or 1,024 megabytes.

Gopher. An Internet service that allows you to locate files and information on the Internet.

Grayscale. A degree of screening ranging from white (0% screen) to black (100% screen) applied to images created with various graphics and drawing applications.

Grouping. A feature of drawing and page layout applications in which two or more objects are combined so that they are treated as one object.

GUI (graphical user interface). The way the Mac and the Mac user interact with each other. The GUI takes full advantage of graphics by using icons and the mouse.

Hard disk drive. A disk drive contained inside or residing outside the Macintosh. The drive contains permanently installed disks that hold much more information than a floppy disk does and retrieves information faster.

Hardware. The physical parts of the Macintosh: the screen, keyboard, mouse, disk drives, casing, cables, and all the electronic mechanisms and boards inside the Macintosh. Hardware also includes other pieces of computer equipment, such as printers and modems.

Hanging indent. A word processing format in which the first line of a paragraph is flush with the left margin and all subsequent lines in the paragraph are indented.

Hayes-compatible modem. A modem that sets modes and features with the AT command set that was developed by Hayes Microcomputer Products.

Header. Text that is automatically printed at the top of each page. See also *footer*.

Hierarchical database. A database that organizes information in tree-like structures.

Hierarchical File System (HFS). A system that enables the user to organize information with folders. The user can organize applications, documents, and other folders within folders to create levels in a hierarchy. See also *Macintosh File System*.

Highlight. Usually means to select something so that it appears different from the surrounding information. When a piece of information is highlighted, the user can initiate a command to modify that information, for example, you highlight a word when you are ready to make it bold.

High-profile SIMM. An in-line memory module that, when installed, is not flush with the motherboard.

HyperCard. An object-oriented application, developed by Bill Atkinson, that the user can modify. Using a scripting language called HyperTalk, you program HyperCard to create applications called stacks, which consist of cards that have buttons, icons, and fields that can perform other functions or can be linked to other stacks or cards. You can use HyperCard (which is ideal for sharing information in an approach that is visually appealing and understandable) to access many different types of information. See also *HyperTalk*.

HyperTalk. The programming language used to program HyperCard stacks and to create user-defined functions. HyperTalk is an "English-like" scripting language. HyperTalk uses scripts to reference information and to build the command structure within the stack. See also *HyperCard*.

Hypertext. The retrieval of text and ideas throughout various documents and files without regard to order.

I-beam. The shape the mouse pointer takes when the user is entering information or editing text. The pointer resembles the uppercase letter *I*.

Icon. A graphic representation of a file, folder, disk, or command. A file is generally represented as a sheet of paper, for example, and a folder looks like a manila folder.

ImageWriter. The first dot-matrix printer designed specifically for use with the Macintosh.

ImageWriter font. A bit-mapped font designed to be printed using the ImageWriter.

Impact printer. A printer that forms characters by striking an inked ribbon against paper. See also *dot-matrix printer*.

Incremental backup. One of two types of backups in which only those files changed since the last backup are backed up.

Information service. A service accessed through telecommunications software that enables users to access financial, news, and entertainment databases. See also *bulletin board system* and *on-line services*.

INIT. A utility file (called *extension* in System 7) located in the System Folder. After you place an INIT file in the System Folder and restart the Macintosh, the INIT file becomes active. See also *extension*.

Initialize. To prepare a disk to be used by the Macintosh. Generally, when you initialize a disk, the Macintosh structures the disk into sectors and tracks. After a disk has been initialized, the Macintosh can use it to save information to and retrieve information from. Also called formatting a disk.

Inkjet printer. A printer that forms characters by spraying tiny streams of ink onto paper.

Input device. A device (such as a mouse, keyboard, trackball, or graphics tablet) that inputs information into your Macintosh.

Insertion point. See *cursor*.

Installer. A separate application used to install software on your hard disk.

Integrated software. A software package containing spreadsheet, database, word processor, and telecommunications applications in which the component programs freely exchange data.

Interface. An electronic link between different computer devices, such as the computer and a mouse. The point where two elements meet. The connecting point between the Macintosh and the ImageWriter II, for example, is an interface. An interface may exist between two pieces of hardware, two pieces of software, or a piece of hardware and a piece of software.

Internal modem. A modem installed into a computer slot. A modem that is built directly into the computer.

Internet. A collection of computer networks that make up the information superhighway.

Invisible file. A file that does not appear on the Desktop and that cannot be copied, erased, or moved.

Kerning. In word processors, page layout software, and advanced drawing applications, the process of adjusting the spacing between letters. Typically used to reduce the space between pairs of letters. Kerning is an automatic feature with QuickDraw GX.

Kilobits per second (Kbps). A measure of data transfer speed, in thousands of bits per second.

Kilobyte (KB). 1,024 bytes. A common measure of file size. A typical double-spaced page is 1.5KB.

LAN. See *local area network*.

Landscape. A page orientation in which the printer prints the image horizontally. The page top is the longest side of the paper.

Laser font. An easily scaled font defined by mathematical formulas.

Laser printer. A printer that forms characters and graphics by moving a laser beam across a photoconductive drum. The printer then projects the image onto paper. Macintosh laser printers are called LaserWriters. See also *toner*.

LaserWriters. Apple's line of laser printers.

Launch. The act of double-clicking an application to start it.

Leading. The amount of vertical spacing, in points, between baselines of type.

Lisa. The first computer to use the Mac interface, including the mouse and icons. The Lisa was unsuccessful due to its high cost.

Local area network (LAN). Computers linked with cables and software. The computers can share files and external devices such as printers and disk drives. Many offices are linked together with LANs to improve communication and efficiency.

LocalTalk. The hardware portion of Apple's LAN system used to connect Macs to LaserWriters and other Macs.

Logic board. The board inside the Macintosh responsible for organizing and executing instructions.

Lookup field. A database field that the database management system uses to find information contained in a table.

Low-profile SIMM. An in-line memory module flush with the motherboard when installed.

MacBinary. A format that enables Macintosh files to be stored on non-Mac machines without any loss of data.

Macintosh File System (MFS). A method of organizing files and folders where folders cannot be nested within folders. Followed by the Hierarchical File System (HFS). See also *Hierarchical File System.*

Macintosh User Group. An association of Macintosh enthusiasts of various levels of proficiency who meet to discuss issues relating to the Mac. User groups are located throughout the country. Many have a newsletter, which provides members with updated information and tips.

Macro. A small program of stored commands that, when retrieved, replays the commands to perform a task. It can be activated to do repetitive tasks simply by typing a letter or number that represents the macro program. Usually created with a macro application, although macro creation is available within some applications.

MacTCP. Apples version of TCP/IP, which allows Macintoshes to communicate with other mainframe and other hosts. See also *TCP/IP.*

Mainframe. A large-capacity computer shared by many users. Its central processing unit (CPU) generally is housed in an air-conditioned room, and the terminals are located at various sites.

Marquee. The dotted line drawn around text or graphics by using the mouse pointer.

Math Coprocessor. A component that assists the main processor with floating-point math operations, such as those used in complex spreadsheets and graphics.

Megabyte (MB). A unit of measure representing 1,048,576 bytes (or 1,024KB) of storage capacity on a disk or in RAM. Hard disks are typically measured in terms of the amount of storage capacity. A 20MB hard disk indicates that the storage capacity of this disk drive is 20MB and holds approximately 20,480KB of information.

Memory. The primary internal location within the computer where internal instructions are stored. The location in the Macintosh's central processing unit that holds information. Some of this memory is used by applications as necessary to do complex calculations or sort data (RAM). Other memory is permanently used by the Macintosh and is not accessible to the user (ROM). See also *random-access memory (RAM)* and *read-only memory (ROM)*.

Menu. A list of commands available to the user. You can open a menu by clicking the menu's name at the top of the screen. The user holds down the mouse button, moves the mouse pointer down the list of menu commands, and then releases the mouse button on the command needed.

Menu bar. The top line on-screen. It horizontally lists the menus available to the Macintosh user. See also *menu*.

MFS (Macintosh File System). The original filing system used by the Macintosh in which files and folders remain at the same organizational level. See also *Macintosh File System*.

Microcomputer. A small, relatively inexpensive computer developed primarily for use by one person. Also referred to as a personal computer or home computer. A Macintosh is a microcomputer.

Microfloppy disk. A 3.5-inch flexible disk contained within a semi-rigid plastic casing. See also *floppy disk*.

Microprocessor. A small silicon chip containing a large number of electronic components. The microprocessor chip can operate on large amounts of information when used with other computer components.

Minifloppy disk. A 5.25-inch flexible disk contained in a flexible plastic casing, used in many microcomputers. See also *microfloppy disk*.

Modem (modulator/demodulator). A peripheral device that enables computers to communicate by telephone lines.

Monitor. The screen associated with a computer. The light-blue Macintosh Plus and SE monitors are located directly above the disk drives, all contained in one cabinet. The Macintosh II has a separate monitor, which is not enclosed with the CPU or disk drives. Monitors can be color or monochrome.

Motherboard. The main board (also called the *logic board*) in the Macintosh that contains the central processing chips, RAM, and expansion slots.

Mouse. A hand-held device used to navigate on the Macintosh screen. The mouse can be used to access the menus and select information. When you move the mouse, the pointer moves on-screen in the corresponding direction.

MultiFinder. A component of the Macintosh's System software that enables the user to load into memory multiple applications and switch among them. MultiFinder also allows for concurrent tasks to take place at seemingly the same time, which is known as *multitasking*.

Multimedia. Information presented in visual, auditory, and text formats.

Multitasking. A computer capability in which two or more programs are loaded into memory simultaneously. The CPU attends to all programs at once by switching back and forth between them—a process known as *time slicing*. See also *MultiFinder*.

Nanosecond. One billionth of a second.

Nesting. The placement of files within folders.

Network. A computer communication pathway using hardware and software that links multiple computers and peripheral devices so that each computer or device shares information. See *Node* and *Local area network*.

Node. A device on a network (such as a computer, a hard disk, or a printer) that can send and receive information. See also *network*.

NuBus. A high-speed information pathway for the Mac II family of computers.

Null modem. A cable connecting two computers. Used for communication purposes rather than a modem.

Object-oriented programming (OOP). A programming language in which program elements are conceptualized as objects that can pass messages to each other.

On-line help. A file contained within an application that can provide the user with help as the application continues.

On-line services. Various databases available to users who have a modem and telecommunications software. They offer access to business, education, travel, and entertainment databases (among others). Two popular on-line services are CompuServe and America Online, which are offered to members who pay a membership fee and a monthly access-time fee. In most instances, members can download information, files, and applications of interest. See also *bulletin board system.*

Open. The act of accessing a document for changing or viewing.

Open architecture. A computer design that enables third parties to design components and other improvements for use with the System.

Operating system. The System Software, which controls the functioning of the Macintosh and the direction of information flow among computer components. See also *System Software.*

Optical character recognition. A technology by which printed characters are optically scanned and translated into codes that the computer can process. The device that has this capability is known as an optical character reader (OCR) or scanner. See also *scanner.*

Optical disc. A disc on which music or data is recorded in the form of small pits. The data or music is retrieved with a laser beam.

Option card. Generally, a specialized piece of electronic circuits, installed by your Apple dealer, that enhances the performance of your Macintosh. An example is the installation of an accelerator card. See also *expansion slot.*

Option key. A Macintosh key used with other keys to perform particular operations.

Outline font. A PostScript font formed of outlines, which are then filled in. A printer font used to describe font characteristics for laser printers. Outline fonts generally have greater resolution than bit-mapped (screen) fonts. See also *bit-mapped image, font,* and *PostScript.*

Pack/unpack. To compress data for the purpose of storage or transmission. Unpacking is decompressing a file and returning it to its normal state.

Page description language (PDL). A language used to describe printer output.

Page preview. A feature of many Macintosh applications that gives the user a view of the printed page before actually printing the document.

Pantone Matching System. A standard system for choosing colors based upon ink mixes. A color wheel generally provides the necessary information for choosing colors for color applications and monitors.

Parallel port. A connection to a computer through which eight or more bits are transmitted simultaneously in one direction. See also *disk drive port*.

Parameter RAM. Memory devoted to certain System settings such as the time, date, and the alarm clock.

Parity bit. An extra bit appended to a character whose value is used to check for errors in the transmission of data.

Partition. A physically separate section on a hard disk that can be used with the same or a different operating system.

Paste. A command that retrieves from the Clipboard a copied or cut piece of data and places the data at the insertion point in a document.

Path. The hierarchical path to a folder, application, or document file that reflects the organization of a particular group of information.

PDD. See *Portable Digital Document*.

PDS. An acronym for Processor Direct Slot, an expansion slot found in some Macintosh models.

Peer-to-Peer. A network arrangement where computers on the network access each others disks and printers, rather than those of a dedicated network server.

Peripheral device. A unit of computer hardware such as a printer, modem, or external hard disk drive. Peripheral devices usually are connected to the Macintosh with cables.

Personal computer (PC). A generic term used to describe a computer designed for use at home or in a small-business setting. In general, a Macintosh is not referred to as a PC. The term has come to mean any IBM computer or IBM-compatible computer.

PhoneNET. A system that allows computers to be networked using standard phone plugs.

Phosphor. A chemical material used to coat the inside of cathode ray tubes (CRTs) on which electrons are targeted to produce images.

Pica. A unit of measure equal to 12 points, or approximately one-sixth of an inch.

PICT. An object-oriented graphic format used by many Macintosh graphics programs.

Pixel (picture element). A single dot or picture element on the Macintosh display.

Point. A unit of measure used to indicate size of line or type. An inch consists of 72 points.

Pointer. An icon, usually arrow-shaped, that reflects the movement of the mouse.

Pop-up menu. A menu located somewhere other than the menu bar.

Port. A connection socket on the back of the Macintosh that enables the user to connect a printer cable, hard disk drive, modem, keyboard, or mouse to the Macintosh.

Portable Digital Document. A technology in QuickDraw GX that allows a document to be printed to a file in a format that can later be printed on another computer, whether or not the computer has the software used to create the document. See also *QuickDraw GX*.

Portrait mode. A page orientation in which the top of the printed image is along the short side of the paper.

PostScript. A page description programming language written by Adobe, Inc. to prepare an image for printing on a laser printer. PostScript fonts are used with PostScript-compatible printers. These fonts are widely recognized as the standard in near-typeset quality printing.

PostScript interpreter. A program built into PostScript-compatible printers that converts PostScript commands into the print image. See also *PostScript*.

Power Macintosh. Apples new line of computers that use the PowerPC processor.

PowerBooks. Apple's line of notebook computers.

PowerPC. The RISC processor that is found in the Power Macintosh. The processor was developed jointly by Apple, IBM, and Motorola. See also *RISC* and *Power Macintosh*.

PowerTalk. A feature that allows communications, such as electronic mail, to take place from within an application.

Printer buffer. Additional memory storage that enables the computer to send data for printing at a faster rate than the printer can accept.

Printer driver. The software containing the instructions that enable the computer to communicate with the printer.

Printer font. A font designed for printing and not just for display.

Printer port. A serial port designed for the connection of a printer or modem to the computer. See also *serial port*.

Printer server. On a network, a printer available to all network users.

Printer spooling. The process by which documents to be printed are stored in a memory outside the computer's RAM, enabling computer processing to continue while the printer is working.

PrintMonitor. The program that allows printing to take place in the background.

Program. A set of instructions, usually in the form of a programming language, that tells a computer what to do.

Programmer's switch. A switch on the side of many Macintosh computers that enables you to reboot the computer and access the Macintosh's debugging utility.

Programming language. A language used to write programs for the Macintosh. Many languages are available, including Object Pascal, C++, BASIC, FORTRAN, and SmallTalk/V. The code, words, and symbols used to send commands and instructions to the computer.

Proportional spacing. In typesetting or printing, the characteristic in which wider letters take up more space than narrower letters.

Protocol. In computer telecommunications, the set of commands, rules, and procedures determining how information travels between computers. See also *handshake*.

Public domain software. Software that can be copied without copyright infringement. See also *shareware* and *freeware*.

Publish and Subscribe. A technology that allows Macintosh programs to share data.

Pull-down menu. A menu that appears only when accessed by the user. At all other times, only the menu titles are visible.

QuickDraw. Part of the Macintosh's ROM that facilitates the generation of images for the screen and for some printers.

QuickDraw GX. The next generation of Apples imaging technology. QuickDraw GX which makes many fancy font tricks available at the system level.

QuickTime. Apples animation and digital video technology.

Radio button. A round button, found in dialog boxes, that you click to choose a particular option.

RAM. See also *random-access memory*.

RAM cache. A portion of the RAM memory that can be designated to hold data that is used repeatedly by an application.

RAM disk. A program that sets aside part of the Macintosh's memory and programs the computer to recognize this memory as a disk drive.

Random-access memory (RAM). The part of the Macintosh's memory that allows temporary storage of data. Because RAM is only temporary, any information left in RAM is lost when the computer is turned off.

Readme file. A file often included on applications that updates the user as to any changes made in the accompanying documentation.

Read-only memory (ROM). The part of the Macintosh's memory that permanently stores System information and contains the information needed to start up. Also called *firmware*.

Reboot. The act of restarting the computer.

Record. A set of related fields in a database. A record contains information unique to an individual or object.

Relational database. A database in which any field or record of one file can be tied to any other field or record by using a common key field.

Removable media. Typically a cartridge containing magnetic media such as a disk or tape that can be removed from the computer's storage device.

ResEdit. A utility application capable of editing the resources of other applications. ResEdit enables you to customize such applications as the Finder, to change menu commands, or to modify the appearance of icons.

Resolution. The number of dots per inch (dpi) displayed on a screen or a printed document. See also *dots per inch*.

Restart. To reset a computer to its startup state without turning off the power. The Macintosh has two procedures for restart: a menu command and the programmer's switch. Also referred to as a *warm boot*.

Return key. The key, located to the right side of the main keyboard, that instructs the Macintosh to move the cursor to the next line. Similar to the Enter key.

RISC. An acronym for Reduced Instruction Set Computer. A microprocessor that has fewer instructions than a CISC processor. The instructions are simpler and as a result, the processor operates faster than a CISC processor. See also *CISC*.

ROM. See *read-only memory*.

Root directory. The first level of organization of the top level created when the disk is formatted.

Run. The act of executing a program or an application.

Sans Serif Font. A kind of typeface without the small cross strokes across the ends of the main strokes of each character. See also *serif font*.

Save. A command instructing the Macintosh to store information on disk.

Save As. A command instructing the Macintosh to save the current document using a different name or file format or on a different disk drive.

Scanner. A device used to capture graphics and text for use in Mac applications. See also *optical character recognition*.

Scrapbook. A desk accessory used to store pictures and text. The Scrapbook, located in the System Folder, can be accessed in the Apple menu. In contrast to the Clipboard, the Scrapbook permanently stores information.

Screen dump. A picture of the screen sent to a file or to a printer for printing.

Screen font. A font used for display and for printing on QuickDraw printers.

Screen saver. A utility, usually in the form of a desk accessory, FKey, extension, or control panel, that prevents image "burn in" by automatically filling the screen with a form of animation during a period of user inactivity.

Script. A series of commands written in the HyperTalk programming language for HyperCard.

Scroll. A method of moving within a document. Using the scroll bars located on the right and bottom of the screen, the user can move forward, backward, left, and right to see other portions of the document. Scroll arrows, located in the scroll bars, move the document one line or column at a time in the direction desired. The user can scroll continuously through a document by clicking the arrow and holding the mouse button.

SCSI. An acronym for Small Computer Systems Interface. SCSI (pronounced scuzzy) is a standard interface for connecting hardware peripherals.

SCSI port. A port located on the back of the Macintosh that enables the user to connect a SCSI cable from a peripheral device to the Macintosh.

SCSI terminator. A device placed at the end of a chain of SCSI devices that ensures proper operation of the SCSI interface.

Sector. On a disk, the smallest continuous physical space for saving data. Multiple sectors define a track. See also *track* and *cylinder*.

Security system. A password-protection software utility that enables the user to protect files or disks from unwanted intruders. Most security utilities enable the user to set a password and to encrypt files.

Select. An operation used to indicate where the next action should take place. To select an object, the user double-clicks the icon or word or drags the mouse across the object.

Serial interface. A form of data transmission in which the bits of each character are transmitted sequentially one by one over a single channel or wire. The most common serial interface is the RS-232 cable and connector.

Serial port. A connector on the back of the Macintosh that enables the user to connect serial devices using a serial interface. See also *printer port*.

Serif font. A kind of typeface that has small cross strokes across the ends of the main strokes of each character. See also *sans serif font*.

Server. On a network, any device or computer that all users can share.

Shareware. Copyrighted computer programs that users can try on a trial basis. If you like the software, you are expected to pay a fee to the program's author. See also *public domain software* and *freeware.*

Shutdown. The process of saving all work, closing all folders and files, ejecting all disks, and turning off the power of the computer.

Signal-to-noise ratio (S/N). The ratio of the level of a received electric signal to the level of the interfering noise.

SIMM. An in-line memory module that plugs into the motherboard or the logic board.

Size box. A box located in the lower right corner of the active window that contains two overlapping smaller boxes. Clicking and dragging in the smaller of the two boxes enables the user to decrease the size of the active window. Clicking and dragging in the larger box increases the size of the active window.

Slot. A location on an internal board where additional cards can fit.

Small Computer System Interface (SCSI). A standard interface that enables the user to connect a peripheral device to the Macintosh.

Software. A generic term for computer programs. Software tells the computer hardware how to perform its work. Software can be categorized into many areas, including systems software, utility software, and applications software.

Spooler. A printer software utility that enables the user to send multiple documents to the printer and continue working while the printer receives each spooled document for printing.

Spooling. The act of storing data in a buffer until it is needed.

Spreadsheet. A program using a rectangular grid of rows and columns. The intersection of a row and a column is a cell. The spreadsheet can manipulate values, and the user can specify interrelationships among the values. The program can calculate results using formulas and macros. Advanced spreadsheets integrate graphics, charts, buttons, macros, and functions.

Stack. A HyperCard document or application. A group of related cards. Each card is a record and each record (card) has a number of fields.

Startup disk. A disk that contains the System files the Macintosh needs to get started. A startup disk must contain the System file and Finder and generally contains printer resources and desk accessories. The start-up disk is the first disk inserted into a floppy disk system. In a hard disk system, the startup disk is contained on the hard disk and automatically boots when the power switch is turned on. See also *boot.*

Startup screen. The opening screen containing words and graphics that appears when booting the Macintosh. Many utilities enable the user to customize the startup screen.

String. A specified sequence of characters (a word, phrase, or number).

Style. A variation of a font that can be displayed in boldface, italic, shadow, outline, underline, and strikethrough styles, to name a few.

Style sheet. A set of predefined format and text commands that can easily and quickly be incorporated into a new document.

StyleWriter's. Apple's line of inexpensive inkjet printers.

Suitcase. The icon that represents a set of fonts or desk accessories.

SuperDrive. Apple's high-density floppy disk drive that can read 400K, 800K, and 1.44 megabyte Macintosh disks as well as 720K and 1.44 megabyte DOS formatted disks.

Surge suppressor. A device that filters the power going to your computer to protect your computer from surges and spikes in the power lines.

SYLK (Symbolic Link). A file format developed by Microsoft for spreadsheets and databases. Used for transferring data between incompatible applications.

System 6. A version of the Macintosh operating system that can run on older Macintosh systems with limited memory and older processors. Many of the features of System 7 are not available to computers using System 6.

System 7. Apple's latest version of the Macintosh operating system.

System file. A file that contains information the Macintosh uses to operate and start up. System files cannot be opened in the usual manner but can be modified. The Macintosh cannot operate without a System file.

System Folder. The folder that contains the important System and Finder files necessary to boot up and run the Macintosh.

System heap. The area of memory set aside for storing system information about files and resources.

System software. The files, extensions, control panels, utilities, desk accessories, fonts, and resources located in the System Folder as provided by Apple. This software is all the Macintosh needs to run properly. See also *operating system*.

System Tools disk. Software disks packaged with the Macintosh that provide the user with various tools to facilitate using the Macintosh.

Tab-delimited file. A data file in which tabs separate individual records or data elements. See also *delimiter*.

TCP/IP. An acronym for Transmission Control Protocol / Internet Protocol. A standard for communications between networked computers. See also *MacTCP*.

Tear-off menu. A feature of some Macintosh applications that enables the user to pull down a menu and to keep the menu visible while working. The menu also can be moved to a more convenient location within the active window.

Telecommunications. Sharing information over phone lines through the use of a modem and telecommunications.

Template. A document created for repeated use. By using the Save As command, the user can save each use of the template with a unique name and still maintain the original template for future use.

Terminal emulation. To make a computer act like a terminal for use with a modem and host computer such as a mainframe. Terminal emulation software enables the user to customize the Macintosh to recognize and use the control codes required to access the host's data.

Text file. A computer file that contains sequences of bits that represent characters. Also known as an ASCII file. See also *ASCII*.

TIFF (Tagged Image File Format). A scanned image-saving format. See also *optical character recognition*.

Title bar. The multilined bar at the top of the active window that displays the title of the document or window.

Token-ring network. A network in which information is passed from one node through another in a ring-like shape.

Toner. A black powder used in laser printers and photocopiers that serves as ink in the printing of characters and images. See also *Laser printer*.

Tool Box. A collection of drawing and painting tools found in many applications such as HyperCard, MacDraw, and MacPaint.

Track. A location on magnetic media that stores data. Tracks are concentric circles on the surface of a disk made up of sectors. One or more tracks make up a cylinder of disk space. See also *cylinder* and *sector*.

Trackball. A pointing device that essentially is an inverted mouse, in which the ball is located on top of the device. The user moves the ball rather than the device, which remains stationary. A pointed arrow on-screen reflects the ball's movement just as though a mouse is being used. See also *mouse*.

Tractor-feed printer. A printer that advances paper through the use of pins that fit into pre-formed holes on the edges of the computer paper.

Trash can. A storage location on the Desktop used to discard documents, folders, and applications.

Typeface. The basic font family design, such as Times or Monaco. See also *font*.

Type size. The height in points of the characters in a font. See also *font*.

UNIX. An operating system developed by Bell Laboratories for minicomputers. UNIX, regarded as a powerful, general-purpose operating system, enables several programs to run simultaneously. It can easily be transferred from one computer type to another.

Upload. A procedure in which a user transfers information from his or her computer to a remote computer.

Usenet. Newsgroups on the Internet that serve as forums for the discussion of thousands of topics.

User group. A group of people who have an interest in a particular computer or a particular type of application such as desktop publishing.

Utilities disk. A disk packaged with the Macintosh that contains utilities used to maintain your computer system. Examples of utility programs contained on this disk are the Font/DA Mover and the Installer.

Video card. A circuit board containing the video controller and related components that connects into a computer to control the video display. See also *video controller circuit*.

Video controller circuit. A circuit that modifies digital information to create the signal necessary for display on a computer screen. See also *cathode-ray tube (CRT)*.

Video RAM. A section of RAM devoted to screen information. In the Macintosh, the video RAM stores a bit-mapped image of the screen display. See also *random-access memory (RAM)*.

Virtual memory. The use of the available space on a hard disk to increase the RAM available for application use.

Virus. A series of computer program lines designed to alter the normal functioning of a computer by destroying data, corrupting system files, locking users out of the computer, or flashing messages on-screen at predetermined times. In many cases, the user may be unaware that a virus exists in the system until it is too late to protect the existing data. A virus is generally passed from disk to disk and from computer to computer through disk sharing or telecommunication file transfers.

Virus-protection software. A utility software program designed to check existing files and applications for the presence of a virus. Some protection software identifies the strain of virus and tries to eradicate it. Other software just informs the user that a virus exists.

Visual interface. The system of representing files, folders, and commands in symbols, such as icons, that easily can be recognized.

Volatile memory. Memory that loses its contents when the power is removed.

WAIS. An acronym for Wide Area Information Service. WAIS is an Internet search mechanism that helps you locate text documents on Internet that are indexed for WAIS.

Warm boot. The act of selecting the Restart command on the Special menu so that the computer boots without turning the power off and on.

Window. The area on the Desktop that displays information. To view a document, the user uses a window. Windows can be opened or closed, moved around on the Desktop, resized, and scrolled through.

Word processor. An application that enables the user to enter characters to create documents, including letters, newsletters, and graphics. Examples include MacWrite II, Microsoft Word, and WordPerfect. Word processors are becoming more advanced with features such as macro support, page layout capabilities, file import/export, mail-merge features, footnoting, and spell-checking features.

Word wrap. In word processing, a text-entry feature in which typed text automatically advances to the next line at the end of a line.

Wristwatch cursor. Appears on-screen when the Macintosh is busy performing some activity. During the time that the wristwatch is on the screen, the user cannot access additional commands. The wristwatch's hands turn, indicating that the Macintosh is working.

Write-protect tab. A small tab or box built into a 3.5-inch disk casing to prevent accidental erasure or overwriting of disk contents. See also *copy protection*.

WYSIWYG. An acronym for What You See Is What You Get. (Pronounced wizzy-wig.) The term refers to a program that shows documents on the screen the way they will look when printed. Typical Macintosh programs are WYSIWYG programs.

Zone. An AppleTalk network in a series of interconnected networks joined by bridges.

Zoom box. A box located on the right side of the title bar that the user clicks to expand the active window to its maximum size. By clicking the zoom box again, the user can return the window to its previous size.

Index